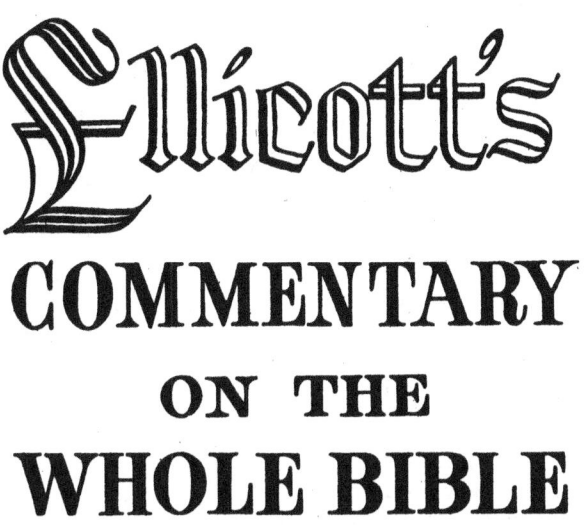

Ellicott's
COMMENTARY
ON THE
WHOLE BIBLE

A VERSE BY VERSE
EXPLANATION

EDITED BY
CHARLES JOHN ELLICOTT

VOLUME II

Deuteronomy — II Samuel

WIPF & STOCK · Eugene, Oregon

Wipf and Stock Publishers
199 W 8th Ave, Suite 3
Eugene, OR 97401

Ellicott's Commentary on the Whole Bible Volume II
Deuteronomy - II Samuel
By Ellicott, Charles J.
ISBN 13: 978-1-4982-0137-7
Publication date 3/20/2015
Previously published by Cassell, 1897

This is a reprint of the 1959 Zondervan edition. Originally published in 1897 by Cassell as A Bible Commentary for English Readers.

Deuteronomy
BY
THE REV. C. H. WALLER, M.A.

Joshua
BY
THE REV. C. H. WALLER, M.A.

Judges
BY
THE VERY REV. F. W. FARRAR, D.D., F.R.S.,
Late Dean of Canterbury.

Ruth
BY
THE REV. R. SINKER, M.A.

I. Samuel
BY
THE VERY REV. H. D. M. SPENCE, M.A.,
Dean of Gloucester.

II. Samuel
BY
THE REV. F. GARDINER, D.D.,
Professor of Divinity, Middletown, Connecticut, U.S.A.

CONTENTS

	PAGE
INTRODUCTION TO DEUTERONOMY	1
DEUTERONOMY	8
EXCURSUS TO DEUTERONOMY	98
INTRODUCTION TO JOSHUA	103
JOSHUA	107
EXCURSUS TO JOSHUA	161
INTRODUCTION TO JUDGES	165
JUDGES	170
EXCURSUS TO JUDGES	272
INTRODUCTION TO RUTH	277
RUTH	279
INTRODUCTION TO I. SAMUEL	289
I. SAMUEL	294
EXCURSUS TO I. SAMUEL	431
INTRODUCTION TO II. SAMUEL	443
II. SAMUEL	444
SUPPLEMENTARY NOTE ON THE TEXT OF II. SAMUEL	511

THE FIFTH BOOK OF MOSES, CALLED
DEUTERONOMY

INTRODUCTION
TO
THE FIFTH BOOK OF MOSES, CALLED
DEUTERONOMY

INTRODUCTION TO THE BOOK OF DEUTERONOMY.

I. Analysis of the book.—Before entering into any discussion as to style, authorship, or particular difficulties, it is absolutely indispensable to have clearly before us the structure of the book in its present shape.

The book of Deuteronomy consists of—

(*a*) A TITLE (chap. i. 1—5, inclusive). This title is twofold, and states (1) that these words were spoken to all Israel by Moses between Sinai and Kadesh-barnea, in view of their first attempt at the conquest of Canaan; (2) that all this Law was *declared* (*i.e.*, apparently re-delivered and *written*; see Note on chap. i. 5) in the eleventh month of the fortieth year, immediately before they actually entered the country, and after Sihon and Og had already been overcome.

(*b*) AN INTRODUCTORY DISCOURSE (chap. i. 6; iv. 40 inclusive), followed by the appointment of three cities of refuge on the eastern side of Jordan, in the territory conquered by Moses. In this discourse Moses reviews Israel's journey from Sinai to the banks of Jordan, for the purpose of exhortation, dwelling upon those points only which bear directly on the enterprise in prospect—the passage of Jordan, the conquest of the seven nations, and the position of the chosen people in the promised land.

(*c*) THE DEUTERONOMY PROPER, or repetition of the law (chap. iv. 44 to end of xxviii.).

This contains—
(1) *A title* (chap. iv. 44—49).
(2) *Repetition of the Decalogue* (chap. v.).
(3) *Its Exposition*, and this
  (α) generally, as creating a certain *relation between the people of Israel and their God*, who had given them this law (chaps. vi.—xi.).
  (β) particularly, *in relation to the land* which God was giving them. This land is considered
    (i.) As the seat of the *worship* of Jehovah (chap. xii. 1 to xvi. 17).
    (ii.) As the seat of His *kingdom* (chap. xvi. 18 to end of xviii.).
    (iii.) As the sphere of operation of certain particular rules of person, property, society, and behaviour (chap. xix. to end of xxvi.).
(4) *Its Enactment*, as the law of the land of promise, written on Mount Ebal, and enforced by blessings and cursings (chap. xxvii.).
(5) *Its Sanction* in Israel, for all time, by a most tremendous denunciation of rewards and penalties, in force even to this day (chap. xxviii.).

(*d*) THE SECOND COVENANT, which is to follow the Sinaitic covenant, and to redeem Israel from its curse, "*the covenant which the Lord commanded Moses to make with the children of Israel in the land of Moab, beside the covenant which* He made with them *in Horeb*" (chaps. xxix., xxx.)

(*e*) CONCLUSION. Moses's resignation of his charge to Joshua. Delivery of the *law* to the priests and elders, and of the *book* to the Levites (chap. xxxi.). Moses's last song (chap. xxxii.), blessing (chap. xxxiii.), and death (chap. xxxiv.)

Hebrew Divisions of Deuteronomy.

The Jews have divided Deuteronomy into eleven portions, for reading in the synagogue. Seven of these comprise chap. i. 1 to xxix. 8. The other four follow the chapters, viz., chap. xxix. 9 to end of xxx., chap. xxxi., chap. xxxii., and lastly, chaps. xxxiii. and xxxiv.

The first seven portions are of an average length of six columns in Bagster's Polyglot Bible. In no instance do they appear to mark any important logical division of the book, except in the case of that portion which begins with "judges and officers" (chap. xvi. 18). The companion lessons from the prophets are chiefly from Isaiah. Each division is named from its opening words in Hebrew. The complete list is given below.

1. *D'bārim*, "The words," chap. i. 1.
2. *Va-ethchannan*, "And I besought," chap. iii. 23.
3. *'Ekeb*, "Because" (if), chap vii. 12.
4. *R'êh*, "Behold," chap. xi. 26.
5. *Shôph'tim*, "Judges," chap. xvi. 18.
6. *Thêtzê*, "Thou goest forth," chap. xxi. 10.
7. *Thâbô*, "Thou comest in," chap. xxvi. 1.
8. *Ni-tzâbim*, "Standing," xxix. 8.
9. *Vay-yêlek*, "And went," xxxi. 1.
10. *Hâazinu*, "Hear," chap. xxxii. 1.
11. *V'zôth hab-berâkah*, "And this is the blessing," chap. xxxiii. 1.

The distinction between the covenants in chaps. xxviii. and xxix. has been obliterated by this division.

Further analysis of the specific enactments of Deuteronomy, chaps. xii. to xxvi.

As these chapters have been recently made the subject of special criticism with a view to show that they stand apart from the rest of Deuteronomy and belong to a much later period than the Exodus, a special analysis and examination of their contents is given below.

The *first* thing that appears in these enactments of Deuteronomy is that all alike are *laws of holiness*. The principle is, "Ye shall be holy for I am holy."

DEUTERONOMY.

Secondly, they are laws of holiness *for the land of Canaan regarded as the abode of Jehovah and His people.* And the land is considered

(1) *As the seat of the worship of Jehovah* (chaps. xii. 1—xvi. 17 inclusive). Here it is enacted that every monument of idolatry must be destroyed (chap. xii. 2—4). The place of sacrifice and national worship must be chosen by Jehovah (chap. xii. 5—14). What must be sacrificed and eaten there, and what may be slain and eaten elsewhere (chap. xii. 15—28). Abolition of all idolatrous rites (chap. xii. 29—32). Utter extermination of all prophets or promoters of idolatry (chap. xiii). Personal purity of Jehovah's worshippers, and especially from unclean animals in food (chap. xiv. 1—21). The second tithe, the *holy food* that either they or their poor must eat before Him (chap. xiv. 22—29). The poor law of His holy land (chap. xv. 1—18). Law of firstlings (arising out of the Exodus) (chap. xv. 19—23); and the three great feasts, beginning with the passover (chap. xvi. 1—17).

(2) *As the seat of the kingdom of Jehovah* (chap. xvi. 18 to end of xviii). Judges and officers in every city, to judge justly (chap. xvi. 18—20). No secret rites or images allowed therein (chap. xvi. 21, 22). No unclean victims to be offered (chap. xvii. 1). "Offer it now unto thy *governor*, will he be pleased with thee, or accept thy person?" (Mal. i. 8). No idolaters to live (chap. xvii. 2—7). The written law to be supreme, whether with priest or judge or king; and the requirements of the kingdom (chap. xvii. 8—20). The requirements of the priest (chap. xviii. 1—5); of the Levite (chap. xviii. 6—8). No consultation with familiar spirits and no hidden arts to be permitted, but *the Prophet* to be above all (chap. xviii. 15—22).

Obviously these two sections delineate the constitution of Israel in two aspects, as a church, and as a state. These were not separated under the theocracy. From these two aspects of the land of Israel arise the following *laws*, namely :—

(3) *Laws concerning the Person in the Land of Jehovah.*—Cities of refuge for the manslayer (chap. xix. 1—10); punishment of the murderer (chap. xix. 11—13); landmarks (chap. xix. 14); witnesses (chap. xix. 15—21); laws of warfare (chap. xx.); undiscovered homicide (chap. xxi. 1—9); captive women (chap. xxi. 10—14); the firstborn's birthright (chap. xxi. 15—17); the incorrigible son in Israel (chap. xxi. 18—21); the death penalty and the Divine image (chap. xxi. 22, 23).

N.B.—It is remarkable how the precept given to Noah, "Whoso sheddeth man's blood, by man shall his blood be shed, for *in the image of God made he man,*" embraces both the first and last laws of this section.

(4) *Laws concerning Property in the Land of Jehovah.*—Lost property (chap. xxii. 1—4); distinction of dress for the sexes (chap. xxii. 5); the bird's nest and its rights (chap. xxii. 6, 7); the house (chap. xxii. 8); the vineyard (chap. xxii. 9); the plough (chap. xxii. 10); the clothing (chap. xxii. 11); and, lastly, the memorial fringe, by which to remember all the commandments of Jehovah (chap. xxii. 12, and comp. Numb. xv. 37—41).

N.B.—The appropriateness of this precept, as closing a section, will be manifest on consideration.

(5) *Laws concerning the Conjugal Relations of God's People* (chap. xxii. 13—30).

N.B.—Again it should be observed how the last verse of this chapter recalls the *principle* of Lev. xviii. 6, &c.

(6) *Laws concerning the Purity of the Congregation of Israel* (chap. xxiii. 1—8). For the sequence of (5) and (6) comp. Matt. xix. 1—12, 13—15.

(7) *Laws concerning the Purity of the Camp in war* (chap. xxiii. 9—14).

(8) *Divers Laws of Holiness, to preserve the Land of Jehovah as a Land of Humanity, Purity, and Truth.*— Humanity to escaped slaves (chap. xxiii. 15, 16); purity from fornication and other deadly sin (chap. xxiii. 17); "Without are dogs and whoremongers" (chap. xxiii. 18); no usury (chap. xxiii. 19, 20); fidelity in vows (chap. xxiii. 21—23); the right of wayfarers (chap. xxiii. 24, 25); conjugal fidelity (chap. xxiv. 1—4); domestic felicity (chap. xxiv. 5); humanity to the poor and friendless and fatherless (chap. xxiv. 6—22), and to criminals (chap. xxv. 1—3), and to beasts (chap. xxv. 4), and to the childless dead, and to their widows (chap. xxv. 5—10), and in quarrels (chap. xxv. 11, 12); honesty in trade (chap. xxv. 13—16); the cruel race of Amalek—the embodiment of inhumanity in Scripture—to be exterminated (chap. xxv. 17, 18).

N.B.—With this section compare the miscellaneous precepts of Lev. xix.

The land and its inhabitants are hallowed, and we are told at last who "shall in no wise enter therein." The precepts in this section would supply a complete parallel to Rev. xxii. 15: "Without are *dogs*, and sorcerers, and *whoremongers*, and *murderers* . . . and whosoever loveth and *maketh a lie.*"

(9) *The Services of Thanksgiving for the Inheritance given to Israel,* which are prescribed in chap. xxvi. appropriately conclude this portion.

We are now in a position to discuss a further important question, namely—

II. **The Date of the Deuteronomy.**—The question, in its most recent aspect, especially concerns the portion we have just analysed—"the statutes and judgments" of chaps. xii.—xxv. The earlier and later portions of the book are admitted to be the work of Moses. But an attempt has been made to separate these specific enactments from the remainder of the book. It is maintained that these "statutes and judgments" are the product (*a*) of Israel's maturity in Palestine, or rather of that period of national decay which resulted in the Babylonish captivity, or (*b*) of the restoration. The age of Jeremiah, or Ezekiel, or Ezra, has been suggested as the source of these precepts. Their position in Deuteronomy is ascribed to the hand of a later editor, who is said to have incorporated them with the work of Moses, and completed the Pentateuch in its present shape.

It is true that this theory does not require us to contradict a series of sentences such as "The Lord spake unto Moses, saying," which we find prefixed to Mosaic enactments in the earlier books. The name of Moses does not occur in Deut. xii.—xxvi. But these statutes and judgments are incorporated in the book as part of Moses' exhortation; and he speaks in the first person in chap. xviii. 17: "The Lord *said unto me,* They have

DEUTERONOMY.

well said that which they have spoken." The portion opens with the words of Moses, in language that can bear no later date: "Ye are *not yet come unto the rest and to the inheritance*, which the Lord your God giveth you." There is as yet no selected seat of worship. And it closes with words spoken in the name of Jehovah while Israel is still in the wilderness (chap. xxvi. 1), and entering into covenant with Jehovah there (chap. xxvi. 16—19). Thus we have Moses in chaps. xii., xviii., and xxvi. The analysis already given shows the perfect unity and order of the whole portion. Where are the items that belong to a later date? By whose authority were they incorporated with the Mosaic code?

A code like this admits of being regarded in three different aspects. Two of them would belong to it more especially as the work of Moses; the third would have little importance in his hands, but would be essential in the view of those who ascribe these enactments to a later date. The law given here may be regarded (1) *As an Ideal Code or Standard of Behaviour*; (2) *As a Prophetical Code, a Picture of a State of Things yet to be*; (3) *As a Practical Code, an Outcome or Expression of the Aspirations of a People at a certain Period of History.*

Of these three, the (1) *ideal* and (2) *prophetical code* are almost neccessarily the work of an individual working under the inspiration of a Higher Power. The code, regarded as (3) an *expression of national taste and will*, adjusts itself to the theory and practice of a certain age, and will never be far in advance of the actual morality of the period which gives it birth. To which of these three views do the statutes and judgments of Deuteronomy most easily adjust themselves? If the two first are prominent, we shall have obtained a strong presumption in favour of the Mosaic authorship, other things being supposed consistent therewith. If, on the other hand, the Deuteronomic code seems rather to reflect the practice of the people in later times, the presumption will be, so far, in favour of the modern theory to which we have alluded above.

Let us test the code in Deuteronomy in each of these three aspects. And let us take the last of the three first.

CAN DEUTERONOMY BE REGARDED AS (3) A MERELY PRACTICAL CODE?

We have seen that the first section of the code (Deut. xii. 1 to xvi. 17) contemplates *the land of Israel as the seat of the worship of Jehovah*; the second section (chap. xvi. 18, to end of chap. xviii.) *contemplates it as the seat of His Kingdom*. The remainder of the code gives rules of behaviour in detail—the laws of person, property, and relation among His people. To what period of history will these rules adjust themselves?

In the first section, the *seat of worship is as yet not fixed*. There is to be a "place" which Jehovah shall choose, but it is not yet chosen. The distance of this place from the borders of Israel is matter of uncertainty. The extent of the conquest is undefined. The abominations of Canaanitish idolatry are still unexplored by Israel. They are not known hitherto. The strictness of the enactments against idolatrous prophets and teachers is beyond anything ever heard of in practice, and is still matter of prophecy in the return from the exile (see Zech. xiii. 2, 3). Nothing like it, if we except the consternation occasioned by the erection of the altar Ed (Josh. xxii.), is discernable in *the general feeling* of the nation of Israel—not only until after the exile, but even until after the close of the Old Testament. The law of release is named by Jeremiah only as being broken, and is by him expressly ascribed to the period of the Exodus (Jer. xxxiv. 13). The three great feasts are to be celebrated annually, in the place which the Lord shall choose; but *we are not told where*.

All this is perfectly consistent with the standpoint of Moses "in the plains of Moab, by Jordan near Jericho." But it is not easy to discover any other period which would suggest it, or even in which it would be intelligible. What writer of later date could so wholly ignore Shiloh, or Jerusalem, or Gerizim, or Samaria? Granting the possibility, with what purpose could he take such a view? Must not the alternative be between the Mosaic authorship and deliberate forgery?

I have never been able to realise the discrepancy regarding the place of sacrifice, which is alleged by some, between the rule of Exod. xx. on the one hand, and that of Deut. xii. on the other. The choice of Jehovah makes the seat of worship in either passage. The seat of national worship will be (it is intimated) "in one of thy tribes." But this does not preclude the acceptance by Jehovah of an occasional sacrifice in another place. The point is that *He*, and not the worshipper, *must in every instance select that place*. The nations worshipped where they would. Israel must "not do so unto the Lord their God." (See Notes on Deut xii. for more on this subject.) We may say that in point of fact there was an intimate connection between the religious and political unity of Israel. Before the seat of government and religion was firmly established at Jerusalem, and while the country was still unsettled and disturbed, we find that sacrifices were accepted by Jehovah in various places, as from Gideon at Ophrah, from Manoah at Zorah, from Samuel at Bethlehem and elsewhere. Again, after the disruption, Elijah offered on Carmel—Jerusalem, from the nature of the case, being inaccessible to *Israel*. But when the kingdom of Samaria was perishing in the reign of Hezekiah, and still more when it had passed away in the reign of Josiah, these kings rightly exerted their authority to centralise the national worship, to which political disunion was no longer any bar.

Or let us take the second section of the code, in which the land of Israel is regarded as the *seat of the government of Jehovah* (chap. xvi. 18, to end of xviii). The establishment of local courts of justice is ordered. We cannot conceive that Israel remained without them until the exile. In fact the "judges and officers" of Deut. xvi. 18 were already appointed in the time of Joshua, and were summoned by him to the assembly which he convened before his death (Josh. xxiii. 2). The presence of famous judges, kings, or prophets, may have occasionally fostered a tendency to overcentralize the administration of justice (see 1 Sam. viii. 1—3; 2 Sam. xv. 4), but we cannot conceive the establishment of local courts, or the promulgation of Jethro's admonitions against bribery (see Notes on Deut. xvi. 19) as having been deferred until the exile or the return. The enactment against groves and pillars (enforced by Joshua, chap. xxiii., upon these judges and officers) is not likely to have originated at a time when altars of Baal were as numerous as the very streets. The fact that Hezekiah and Josiah (almost alone in all history) were found to carry out the instructions of Deuteronomy will not prove that these instructions originated with them. That their work was done in the face of popular feeling is clear from the immediate restoration of idolatry by Manasseh, and by the successors of Josiah. The

DEUTERONOMY.

code against idolatry was certainly not the expression of popular feeling at that date.

It is noticeable that twice over in Deut. xiii. it is enacted that the teacher of idolatry shall be put to death "because he hath sought to thrust thee away from the Lord thy God which *brought thee out of the land of Egypt*" (Deut. xiii. 5, 10). No later deliverance is alluded to. But even Joshua's exhortation against idolatry records later experiences than this (Josh. xxiv. 8—13).

The *form of government* in Israel, as depicted in Deut. xvii. xviii., shows as little fixity as the seat of national worship. "The priests the Levites, and the judge that shall be in those days," are not expressions that we can assign to any given period of Israel's history in Canaan. Natural enough, as coming from the lips of Moses, they are almost ludicrous as an expression of the national desire for a particular rule. The position of the king is depicted even more vaguely. We have observed in the Notes on Deut. xvii., that no later writer could have ignored the throne of David thus. And if Jeremiah foretold the *cessation of the kingdom* (Jer. xxii. 30), how could the age of Jeremiah have given birth to the laws that concern the king? Again, the relation of the prophet to the government is left far too uncertain for later Jewish history. When we consider the important part played by the priests in Judah from Jehoiada onwards, and the evident struggle for religious supremacy between them and the kings, with the equally important action of the prophets in Israel, is it conceivable that any constitutional writer of the date of Jeremiah or the exile, would have left us the bare outline that we find in Deut xvii. xviii.? Not less important is the position given to the written law in chap. xvii. 8—13. It was absolutely essential to define this when Scripture first came into existence. If not settled then, when could it be? It agrees with what we find in the opening of Joshua (see notes on Joshua i. 1—8), and whenever allusion is made to Scripture in later times. But that Scripture should be solemnly delivered to God's people and be preserved among them, and its authority remain for seven centuries wholly undefined, is inconceivable. Yet the definition is entirely suited to the period when nothing but *the law* had been written down.

But if, on the other hand, it is asserted that these views of the church and state of Israel proceeded not from national feeling at the time of the Exile or the Return, but from the mind of some great reformer, some individual prophet, we may fairly demand an explicit answer to the question, who that prophet or reformer might be? If Jeremiah, or Ezekiel, or Ezra is to be taken as the author of the code in Deuteronomy, we are brought face to face with the question of style and language. The language of Deuteronomy is totally distinct from the extant writings of all these. And if the author of Deuteronomy is an anonymous writer, a new difficulty presents itself. By what authority did he promulgate these laws, and how did he contrive to get them accepted, not only as canonical Scripture, but as the work of the great national Lawgiver? For "there arose not a prophet since in Israel like unto Moses."

From these considerations it seems certain that the view of the *church* and *state* of Israel in Palestine, given in Deut. xii. to xviii. inclusive, is not that of any later period than the Exodus. *The laws of person, property, social relation, and behaviour*, given in chapters xix. to xxvi., remain to be examined. In these laws the standpoint of the wilderness is no less conspicuous than in the more general principles laid down before. The law of the manslayer comes first. Its date is fixed beyond dispute by the cities of refuge. Three are not noticed; for they are already determined on the east of Jordan (Deut. iv. 41—43). Three on the west of Jordan are still *to be separated*, in the territory conquered by Joshua. Three more are regarded as possibly necessary in the future. But *they have never been assigned yet* (see notes on Deut. xix. 8—10). With what period of history is this piece of legislation consistent, except the last days of Moses's life?

We come next to the *laws of warfare* (chap. xx.), and we find the nations of Canaan still mentioned as unconquered. The distinction given between "the cities that are very far off," and the cities of the doomed nations, is the very same upon which the Gibeonites traded as that *which Jehovah had given to His servant Moses* (Josh. ix. 24), and by which they contrived to save themselves from the sword of Joshua. Was the passage in Deuteronomy constructed from that in Joshua? If so, the plea of the Gibeonites still proves the antiquity of this distinction. Or was the passage in Joshua fashioned to suit an enactment which was the production of a later date? Take the law in Deuteronomy as the genuine work of Moses, and the narrative in Joshua as true, and the agreement is perfect. It is difficult to devise any other hypothesis which will account for either the history or the law.

The laws of chap. xxi. bear the stamp of antiquity on their very face. The last of them, which concerns hanging, again supplies a striking coincidence with the life of Joshua, who hanged the kings of Jericho, and Ai, and the five kings of the southern confederacy upon trees *until eventide*, and buried them at sunset. The agreement with Joshua's practice is perfect. There is little notice of the practice of hanging in Israel in later times. We know that the Assyrians constantly left the bodies of their enemies impaled on stakes and exposed to view between the earth and heaven, but there is no proof that any such practice ever obtained in Israel. "The kings of the house of Israel are merciful kings," was the consolation of the defeated Syrian monarch Ben-hadad (1 Kings xx. 31). Would he have trusted himself to the hands of a king of Assyria, as confidently as he surrendered himself to Ahab? The Gibeonites who hanged Saul's sons in Gibeah observed no such restriction as that which Moses commanded in Deut. xxi. 23 (see 2 Sam. xxi. 9, 10). The strict observance of this law by Joshua, and its neglect in the days of David, are entirely consistent with other examples of a similar kind.

The laws of *property* and *conjugal relation* in chap. xxii. are an expansion of the code in Exodus and Leviticus. There is no inconsistency. But some of the details are unmistakably primitive, and point to a time when the country was very thinly peopled. They are suitable to the time of the first conquest by Joshua —not so suitable to later days.

When we come to the laws concerning the admission of strangers or proselytes (chap. xxii.) we find unquestionable traces of the Lawgiver of the Exodus.

The Ammonites and Moabites "*met not Israel with bread and water.*" They "hired Balaam to curse" the people. The part taken by the Ammonites in this enterprise is not recorded in Numbers. The details cannot be obtained from the narrative as given there. The considerations urged in verse 7 are suitable to a time when the memory of Egypt was fresh. The words spoken by Isaiah concerning proselytes (chap. lvi. 6, 7) are wholly different in character. And these very

DEUTERONOMY.

clauses of Deuteronomy are cited in Nehemiah (xiv. 1, 2) as *written in the book of Moses.*

There remains only one more section to be considered—the *laws of humanity* in chaps. xxiv., xxv. Here once more the personal recollections of the Exodus, concerning Miriam and Amalek, are striking, and cannot be ascribed to any later date. The law that the children shall not die for the fathers (chap. xxiv. 16) is directly referred to in 2 Kings xiv. 6, as *written in the book of the Law of Moses.* Other details in this portion which point to a primitive state of society have been indicated in the notes.

The twenty-sixth chapter, with its services of thanksgiving on the entrance of Israel into Canaan, would lose all the peculiar charm of freshness that it possesses, if it were ascribed to a later date. From the lips of Moses it is singularly beautiful and appropriate, all the more when we remember his own eager desire to enter the land of promise—a desire which was not granted. The reference to Jacob as "a Syrian ready to perish" is thoroughly natural in the historian of Genesis, and the whole thanksgiving is itself a reflection of Jacob's words in Gen. xxxii. 10. But there is no reference to any experience later than the Exodus. And the mind that would place the origin of such a service in the time of Jeremiah, or after the exile, must be strangely constituted.

If, then, the laws of Deut. xii. to xxvi. in all these particulars evidently breathe the very air of the Exodus, and of that particular scene to which they are ascribed, what becomes of the view that they are the offspring of a later date? If we take away all that evidently bears the stamp of primitive authorship, is there anything in the remainder that necessarily bears a different stamp? The supposed disagreement in the edicts regarding tithes is refuted by Jewish practice. The second tithe is an institution peculiar to Deuteronomy. It does not contradict the law in Numbers, because it is a matter wholly distinct. It is the *second tithe*, not the first; *a holy thing*, and not a common rate. The Jewish commentator Rashi speaks almost with derision of those who would confuse the two. The supposed difficulty concerning the priesthood is sufficiently met by the undesigned but explicit allusion to the rebellion of Num. xvi., in Deut. xi. 6, not to mention the Thummim and Urim in chap. xxxiii. 8.

There is also a further reason why the author of Deuteronomy should be comparatively silent regarding the special duties and position of the priests, except in relation to that which was now for the first time delivered to Israel—the *book of the law of God.* The priests themselves were there to guard their rights. They were a family established by the highest sanction in a place of unapproachable dignity and authority in Israel. Moses could not touch the subject without reverting to the memory of his departed brother (only six months dead) at every moment. Eleazar and Phinehas were now the guardians of Aaron's post.

We now revert to (1) THE IDEAL CODE.

When we consider the Law of Deuteronomy as an *ideal* and *prophetical* code, our task becomes much easier. The commandments here given cannot be observed in the letter without the spirit of loving fidelity to Jehovah. The attempt to reduce them to a system, and guard them from disobedience in the smallest detail, resulted in the unbearable yoke of our Lord's time, of which we have the tradition in the Talmud. It cannot be said that the exhortations of Deuteronomy contain in themselves any such system. But no law can create in any people a higher *standard* of practice than is conformable to their nature. "What the Law could not do, in that it was weak through the flesh," was to make its ideal the practical standard of behaviour. Even if the outward enactments are not infringed, the motive so constantly inculcated could never become the law of the human heart, except spontaneously; and this requires the "new creation." "I will put my laws into their minds, and write them on their hearts." "Thou shalt surely give him" is a right which the Law may enforce. "Thine heart shall not be grieved when thou givest unto him" (Deut. xv. 10) is beyond the power of law to insure. "It shall not seem hard unto thee when thou sendest him away free from thee" is a similar sentence (chap. xv. 18). "If thou shalt keep all these commandments to do them, which I command thee this day, to *love the Lord thy God, and to walk ever in his ways*" (chap. xix. 9), proves that in the details of the Law no less than in its general exposition, "*the end of the commandment was love.*"

If this *ideal* aspect of Deuteronomy is recognised, we may at once set aside the notion that it was the mere expression of the national taste and will. Such ideals come, not from below, but from above. The heart of man, under the direct teaching of the Spirit of God, may receive them; they were never formed by any process of abstraction and generalization, from the common practice of any nation of mankind.

When it is proved that the view of man's destiny given in Gen. i. 26, and his primæval state in Paradise as described in Gen. ii., were the laboured attainment of ages of human progress, then we may admit the first great commandment to have been evolved in the same way. The *fall of Israel* is interwoven with the whole of sacred history as closely as the *fall of man.* Was this exalted standard of behaviour—the highest ever inculcated upon mankind—a Divine revelation in the beginning of their history, or did it arise in the dark days when Jehovah said, "Though Moses and Samuel stood before me, yet my mind could not be toward this people; *cast them out of my sight, and let them go forth?*" (Jer. xv. 1). To ask the question almost answers it. The whole analogy of sacred history requires the ideal code of Israel to stand at the beginning of their national life. The shadow of Sinai stretches over the whole length of the ages from the Exodus of Israel to the Exodus of Christ. But if it is urged that though the outlines of the code in Deuteronomy may be primitive, yet the details are modern, and were gradually developed during the course of Israelitish history, we may fairly demand to have these later details distinctly pointed out. After close examination, we have failed to discover them even in the alleged discrepancies between the Deuteronomy and other portions of the law. The Jewish Mishna supplies an abundance of details of the kind that arise in a long and laboured application of legal principles to particular cases. The language of Deuteronomy is singularly free from the kind of detail suggested by practical difficulties in the application of the law. It is singularly free from any trace of contact with the history of Israel in later times.

It remains to consider (2) THE PROPHETICAL CODE.

Closely connected with the *ideal* aspect of Deuteronomy is the *prophetical character of the code.* That the ideal has not been realised is as certain as anything in history. *Was it intended to be?* and, if so, *when?* The book of Deuteronomy itself supplies a somewhat

DEUTERONOMY.

remarkable answer to this question in two passages, which are given here at length, and side by side, for the purpose of comparison.

CHAPTER XXXI.	CHAPTER XXX.
(16) And the LORD said unto Moses, Behold, thou shalt sleep with thy fathers; and <u>this people will rise up, and go a whoring after the gods of the strangers of the land, whither they</u> go to be among them, and <u>will forsake me, and break my covenant which I have made with them.</u> (17) <u>Then my anger shall be kindled against them in that day, and I will forsake them, and I will hide my face from them, and they shall be devoured, and many evils and troubles shall befall them; so that they will say in that day, Are not these evils come upon us, because our God is not among us?</u> (18) <u>And I will surely hide my face in that day for all the evils which they shall have wrought, in that they are turned unto other gods.</u> (19) Now therefore write ye this song for you, and teach it the children of Israel: put it in their mouths, that this song may be a witness for me against the children of Israel. (20) For when I shall have brought them <u>into the land which I sware unto their fathers,</u> that floweth with milk and honey; and they shall have eaten and filled themselves, and waxen fat; then will they turn unto <u>other gods, and serve them, and provoke me, and break my covenant.</u> (21) <u>And it shall come to pass, when many evils and troubles are befallen them, that this song shall testify against them as a witness;</u> for it shall not be forgotten out of the mouths of their seed: for <u>I know their imagination which they go about, even now, before I have brought them into the land which I sware.</u>	(1) <u>And it shall come to pass, when all these things are come upon thee, the blessing and the curse, which I have set before thee, and thou shalt call</u> them <u>to mind among all the nations, whither the LORD thy God hath driven thee,</u> (2) <u>and shalt return unto the LORD thy God,</u> and shalt obey his voice according to all that I command thee this day, thou and thy children, with all thine heart, and with all thy soul; (3) that then <u>the LORD thy God will turn thy captivity,</u> and have compassion upon thee, and will return and gather thee from all the nations, whither the LORD thy God hath scattered thee. (4) If any of thine be driven out unto the outmost parts of heaven, from thence will the LORD thy God gather thee, and from thence will he fetch thee: (5) <u>and the LORD thy God will bring thee into the land which thy fathers possessed, and thou shalt possess it;</u> and he will do thee good, and multiply thee above thy fathers. (6) And the LORD thy God will circumcise <u>thine heart, and the heart of thy seed,</u> to love the <u>LORD thy God with all thine heart, and with all</u> thy soul, that thou mayest live. (7) And the LORD thy God will put all these curses upon thine enemies, and on them that hate thee, which persecuted thee. (8) <u>And thou shalt return and obey the voice of the LORD, and do all his commandments which I command thee this day.</u>

It appears from chap. xxxi. that the constitution given to Israel by Moses would be immediately violated, and that this fact was well known beforehand. From chap. xxx. it is no less manifest that the great Lawgiver foresaw a time when Israel would return and repent after great affliction, and that they would then be restored, and keep the law perfectly (see verses 6 and 8 above).

Under what circumstances this event will take place, and how far the precepts of the Deuteronomy may hereafter be literally observed, it is perhaps impossible to determine.

The full answer to this question is one of "the secret things that belong to the Lord." But we may obtain an approximation to the answer thus: The whole of the Deuteronomic code is presented as an expansion of the Decalogue. It is the application of a sermon, of which the "ten words" spoken on Sinai are the text. It is the application of these words to Israel, God's chosen people, in the promised land. *Every particular application of the Divine Law must be temporary in detail.* The more perfectly the code is suited to a given condition of affairs, the more transitory its application to the *minutiæ* of daily life must necessarily be. So long as the times are changeable, the permanent code must be somewhat general, from the very nature of the case.

The most curious instance of a prophetical code in Scripture is the code of Law given for Ezekiel's temple in the latter portion of his prophecy. I cannot find that this code was ever held by the Israelites to have the full force of law. It *could not be* fulfilled in all particulars, from the very nature of the case, except under certain conditions. That its promulgation *as law* was *contingent on the moral condition of the people,* seems clear from Ezek. xliii. 10, 11. "*If they be ashamed of all that they have done, show them the form* of the house, and . . . *all the laws thereof :* and *write it in their sight, that they may keep* the whole form thereof, and *all the ordinances thereof, and do them.*" No one can prove that the laws of Ezekiel's temple have ever been kept; nor is it possible to say how far they ever will be observed in the shape in which they were delivered, for the supposition of the sentence just quoted is, that these laws were suitable to the state of Israel at the time. If they were not minded to receive them, the fulfilment must be deferred. Supposing them not to be "ashamed of all that they had done" for more than twenty centuries after Ezekiel wrote, the fulfilment of Ezekiel's ideal must take place under wholly different circumstances; and many of its details must of necessity be modified to suit the change of times.

It is needless to add that the comparison between this portion of Ezekiel and the code in Deuteronomy cannot affect the question of the date of the Deuteronomy in any way.

The code in Deuteronomy is not so visibly prophetical as the ritual of Ezekiel's temple, because the foundation of the code in Deuteronomy is not an outward visible fact. But it is none the less true that the standard of morality in Deuteronomy is unattainable except under one condition, and that is "that the heart of Israel should be circumcised to love Jehovah their God with all their heart and with all their soul." As the ritual of Ezekiel's temple is impossible without the temple itself, so is the morality of Deuteronomy unattainable without this heart-circumcision. This is provided by the *second covenant,* the covenant made in the land of Moab, "besides the covenant in Horeb," which still holds Israel under its curse.

Manifestly the true fulfilment of the Deuteronomy in

DEUTERONOMY.

Israel requires a national and spiritual restoration of the Jews.

It is worth while to observe that the whole Decalogue is, literally and verbally, a prediction of its own fulfilment. The ten commandments, with the exception of the fifth, are all in the *future indicative*. The two great commandments are both future indicative. "Thou shalt love the Lord thy God ... and thy neighbour," contains "thou *wilt* love him," as the stronger contains the weaker form of speech. "Ye shall be therefore perfect," in Matt. v. 48, contains, *Ye will be*. If "one jot or one tittle shall in no wise pass from the law, until it is all done," all carried out in fact (Matt. v. 18), then clearly He who gave it signified in the same breath His intention that men should keep it; and, if His word shall not pass away, the Law will one day be kept, not merely in those literal details which must vary with every change of times and manners, but in spirit and in truth.

Actual predictions in the laws of Deuteronomy are not wanting. More especially we may refer to the prophecy of the prophet like unto Moses in chap. xviii., and the well-known prophecies in chaps. xxviii, xxxii., and xxxiii. I do not think the law concerning the king in chap. xvii. is necessarily a prediction. It seems to me that any thoughtful man who had watched the development of the nations descended from Terah, as Moab, Ammon, Edom, or Midian, must have foreseen that Israel would not remain long in Palestine without feeling the necessity for a form of government which other nations could recognise, and by which national intercourse could be maintained—a government embodied in some responsible and perpetual representative head. So far from feeling any difficulty in the mention of a king in Deuteronomy, I apprehend that no man who attempted to frame a constitution for the people in the country which God was about to give them, could possibly have avoided the question whether there should be a king or not. And if the king was mentioned, some sketch of his authority and its limitations could not be left out. What more do we actually find in Deuteronomy xvii.? That the relation of the Church to the written Word of God should be there delineated for all time (see Note on chap. xvii. 8—12) seems to me a very much more remarkable indication of prophetic insight, and of the mind of a "man of God."

III. **Unity of the Book of Deuteronomy.**—Upon the whole, the result of this examination and analysis of the several parts of Deuteronomy, is to produce a strong impression of the *unity* and *symmetry* of the whole. The middle portion is found to be quite as suitable to the date of the Exodus, in respect of its subject matter, as the earlier and later portions of the book. But when we come to consider the

IV. **Style** of the language in which it is written, and especially of the Hebrew original, the probability already established rises almost to the certainty of demonstration. The style of the Hebrew of Deuteronomy is unique. It is to all other Hebrew what the Latin of the Augustan age and the purest Attic Greek are to later stages and imitations of those two classic tongues. The poetry of David, the proverbs of Solomon, the visions of Isaiah, the lamentations of Jeremiah, and the polished Hebrew of Ezekiel, all have their separate beauties. The style of Deuteronomy bears no resemblance whatever to any of them—far less to the mixture of Hebrew and Chaldee which we find in Ezra, or the imitated Hebrew of the latest prophets. While there are undoubted archaisms in Deuteronomy (the words for "he" and "she" are not distinguished in the Pentateuch, and similarly the word for "damsel" of Deut. xxii. 15 to end, is not to be distinguished from the common word for a "boy," except by the pointing), yet the diction throughout is that of a highly-educated and cultivated mind. There is *no difference whatever* between *the Hebrew of the middle portion and that of the rest of the book*. And the occurrence of Deuteronomic phrases, in Jeremiah or elsewhere, does not touch the argument. Quotations from the Bible in a volume of sermons do not prove the Bible to have been made up from them. The *setting* of the phrases is a matter of quite as much importance, as the occurrence of the phrases themselves. Even when judged by the concordance, the Hebrew of Deuteronomy will be found distinct from that of the prophets. And it must be remembered that no concordance ever exhibits a writer's style. The most it can do is to analyse his vocabulary. It can tell us little or nothing of the structure of his thoughts. Further, the application of one uniform system of vowel-pointing, accentuation, and division, to the whole of the prose of the Old Testament, has tended greatly to obscure the characteristic differences of the Hebrew writers. No one who has not read passages from several Hebrew writers without vowel-points, could at all imagine what a difference the absence of these makes to the perceptibility of the style. It is to be feared that too much of the attention of modern commentators has been absorbed by the external dress and uniform of the Hebrew of the Old Testament to allow them to perceive what the *style* of a Hebrew writer really is. Unless some excuse of this kind may be made, I find myself wholly unable to conceive how the Hebrew of Deuteronomy can be attributed by scholars to any known writer among the later prophets. The style of Joshua alone bears any resemblance to it. The *ruggedness* of Samuel and David, notwithstanding all David's command of language, exhibits a most remarkable diversity.

The culture of the prophets is wholly different from that which we find in the Pentateuch. At the same time it is very possible that the Hebrew style of Moses was peculiarly his own. It may well be supposed to have been above the level of the common language of the nation. The early Egyptian education and varied experience of Moses would tend to produce a somewhat special mode of thought and expression.

V. **Commentaries on Deuteronomy.**—I regret that the time allotted to me for this work has not permitted me to make use of modern commentaries to any appreciable extent. Canon Espin's notes in the *Speaker's Commentary* I found useful. I thought it my duty to pay special attention to modern critical theories about later authorship, and in order to test them I found it necessary to ascertain somewhat precisely what the Jewish view of the various enactments in Deuteronomy was. I therefore read Rashi's commentary carefully throughout, and in all cases of difficulty, consulted other Jewish writers also. The references to the Talmud in Rashi are numerous; and these, in many instances, I verified. In particular the alleged discrepancy concerning the laws of tithe was entirely cleared up to my mind by this means. I am satisfied that no contradiction between Deuteronomy and the earlier books of the Pentateuch can be reasonably maintained.

THE FIFTH BOOK OF MOSES, CALLED
DEUTERONOMY

CHAPTER I.—⁽¹⁾ These *be* the words which Moses spake unto all Israel on this side Jordan in the wilderness, in the plain over against ² the Red *sea*, between Paran, and Tophel, and Laban, and Hazeroth, and Dizahab. ⁽²⁾ (*There are* eleven days' *journey* from Horeb by the way of mount Seir unto Kadesh-

<small>1 Or, *Zuph.*</small>

(5—1) INTRODUCTION.

(1) **These be the words which Moses spake unto all Israel.**—The first two verses and the three that follow form a kind of double introduction to the book, and perhaps more especially to the first portion of it, which ends with chap. iv. 40.

On this side Jordan.—Literally, *on the other side Jordan* from the writer's or reader's point of view.

In the wilderness.—These words define still further the expression which precedes: "on the wilderness side of Jordan," or "before they crossed the Jordan, while they were still in the wilderness." Strictly speaking, the words "in the wilderness" cannot be connected with what follows, for "the plain" described is on neither side of Jordan, but below the southern end of the Dead Sea.

In the plain—*i.e.,* the *'Arâbah.* Usually the plain of Jordan; here the valley that extends from the lower end of the Dead Sea to the head of the Gulf of Akabah.

Over against the Red Sea.—Heb., *opposite Sûph.* In all other places in the Old Testament, when we read of the Red Sea, it is *Yam Sûph.* Here we have *Sûph* only. On these grounds some take it as the name of a place. (Comp. Vaheb in Sûphah, Num. xxi. 14, margin.) But we do not know the place; and as the Jewish paraphrasts and commentators find no difficulty in accepting Sûph by itself as the sea, we may take it of the Gulf of Akabah. The plain between Paran and Tophel looks straight down to that gulf.

Between Paran, and Tophel . . .—Literally, *between Paran, and between Tophel and Laban, &c.:* that is, *between Paran on the one side, and Tophel and Laban and Hazeroth and Dizahab on the other.* This is the literal meaning, and it suits the geography so far as the places are yet identified. The small map at p. 239 of Conder's *Handbook to the Bible* shows the desert of Paran stretching northward from Sinai on the left, and on the right, Tophel and Hazeroth (the only other places identified among these five) at the two extremities of a line drawn from the southeast end of the Dead Sea in the direction of Sinai. Tophel is taken as Tufileh, and Hazeroth is 'Ain Hadra. Laban must be some "white" place lying between, probably named from the colour of the rocks in its neighbourhood. Dizahab should be nearer Sinai than Hazeroth. The Jewish commentators, from its meaning, "gold enough," connected it with the golden calf. And it is not inconceivable that the place where that object of idolatry was "burned with fire," and "stamped" and "ground very small," till it was as "small as dust," and "cast into the brook that descended out of the mount" (chap. ix. 21), was called "gold enough" from the apparent waste of the precious metal that took place there; possibly also because Moses made the children of Israel drink of the water. They had enough of that golden calf before they had done with it. If this view of the geography of this verse be correct, it defines with considerable clearness the line of march from Sinai to Kadesh-barnea. It lies between the mountains on the edge of the wilderness of Paran upon the west, and the Gulf of Akabah on the east, until that gulf is left behind by the traveller going northward. It then enters the desert of Zin, called here the plain, or 'Arâbah. This desert is bounded by ranges of mountains on both sides, and looks down to the Gulf of Akabah. Behind the western range we still have the wilderness of Paran. On the east are the mountains of Edom, which Israel first had on their right in the march to Kadesh-barnea, and then on their left in a later journey, in the last year of the exodus, when they compassed the land of Edom. Tophel lies on the east of this range, just before the route becomes level with the southern end of the Dead Sea.

But the whole of the route between Paran on the left and those other five places on the right belongs to Israel's first march from Sinai to Kadesh. It takes them up the desert of Zin, and, so far as these two verses are concerned, it keeps them there.

(2) **Eleven days' journey from Horeb . . .**—In our English Version this verse forms a separate sentence; but there seems nothing to prevent our taking it as completing the first verse. The route between Paran on the one side and the line from Tophel to Hazeroth on the other is still further defined as "a distance of eleven days' journey from Horeb in the direction of Mount Seir, reaching to Kadesh-barnea." The position of this last place is not yet determined with certainty. But the requirements of the text seem, upon the whole, to demand that it should be placed high up in the wilderness of Paran, not far from the border of the wilderness of Zin. It must be close to some passage out of the wilderness of Zin into the Negeb, or south of Judah.

Kadesh-barnea.—In the regular narrative of the exodus we read of the place to which the twelve

barnea.) ⁽³⁾ And it came to pass in the fortieth year, in the eleventh month, on the first day of the month, *that* Moses spake unto the children of Israel, according unto all that the LORD had given him in commandment unto them;

B.C. 1451.

a Num. 21. 24.

⁽⁴⁾ *a* after he had slain Sihon the king of the Amorites, which dwelt in Heshbon, and Og the king of Bashan, which dwelt at Astaroth in Edrei: ⁽⁵⁾ on this side Jordan, in the land of Moab, began Moses to declare this law, saying,

---

spies returned as *Kadesh* (Num. xiii. 26), and of the place at which the period of unrecorded wandering closed (Num. xx. 1), in the first month of the fortieth year, as *Kadesh*. The name Kadesh-*barnea* first appears in Moses' speech (Num. xxxii. 8), where he refers to the sending of the twelve spies. And with the exception of three places where the name is used in describing boundaries, Kadesh-*barnea* is always found in speeches. This first chapter of Deuteronomy is the only one which contains the name both with and without the appendage -*barnea*, which connects it with the wanderings of Israel (verse 32). Upon the whole, it seems most likely that only one place or district is intended by the name.

We have now obtained the following view of this first short introduction to the Book of Deuteronomy. It consists of words spoken (in the first instance) to all Israel on their march from Sinai to Kadesh-barnea. But the following verses show that the Law was further "declared" to Israel in the plains of Moab, at the close of the fortieth year of the exodus and of Moses' life. It does not seem possible for us to separate entirely what was spoken earlier from what was declared later. In several places we have the record of words spoken: for example, in this very chapter (verses 9, 16, 18, 20, 29, 43), and chap. v. 5, &c. And the very name Deuteronomy implies the repetition of a law previously given. Further, the exhortations contained in this book are all enforced by the immediate prospect of going over Jordan and entering the promised land. But when Israel marched from Sinai to Kadesh-barnea, it was with this very same prospect full in view. It does not appear, by what Moses "said" at that time (verse 20), that he had any thought of their turning away from the enterprise. But if so, what supposition is more natural than this—that he delivered the same kind of exhortations in the course of that earlier journey which he afterwards delivered in the plains of Moab? And although the distance is but eleven days' march, the Israelites spent something like three months on the way, and in waiting for the spies to return from Canaan.

We conclude, then, that the first two verses of Deuteronomy are an editorial introduction, stating that the substance of this book was first delivered to Israel by Moses between Sinai and Kadesh-barnea. The further introduction which follows (in verses 3—5) shows the words to have been re-delivered in the plains of Moab, and preserved in their later rather than their earlier form. But it is also possible that the two first verses of Deuteronomy are an introduction to the *first* discourse above. (See Note on chap. iv. 44.)

Is it possible to advance a step further, and conjecture with any degree of probability to what hand we owe the first two verses of the book? The expression "on the other side Jordan" (which some take to be a technical term) seems strictly to mean on the opposite side to the writer. The writer must also have been acquainted with the places mentioned (three of which are not named in the previous books); he could not have drawn his knowledge from the earlier part of the Pentateuch. And so entirely has the geography of Deut. i. 1 been lost by tradition, that all the Targums and Jewish commentators agree in spiritualising the passage, and say, "these are the words of reproof which Moses spake to all Israel in respect of their behaviour at these various places." Laban points to their murmuring at the *white* manna. Dizahab to the *golden* calf, and so on. Even Rashi, usually a most literal commentator, says, "Moses has enumerated the places where they wrought provocation before the PLACE"—a Rabbinical name for Jehovah: for "the whole world is His place, though His place is more than the whole world." This introduction to Deuteronomy seems the work of one who had known the wilderness, and yet wrote from Palestine. Joshua, the next writer to Moses, and possibly also his amanuensis, may have prefixed it to the book. If he did not, it is wholly impossible to say who did.

⁽³⁾ **And it came to pass in the fortieth year, in the eleventh month.**—The "and" is the real beginning of Deuteronomy, and connects it with the previous books. The moral of these words has been well pointed out by Jewish writers. It was but eleven days' journey from Sinai to Kadesh-barnea—the place from whence Israel should have begun the conquest of the promised land; but not only eleven days of the second year of the exodus, but eleven months of the fortieth year found them still in the wilderness. "We see that they could not enter in because of unbelief."

^(3, 4) **Moses spake unto the children of Israel . . . after he had slain Sihon . . . and Og.**—The conquest of these two kings and their territories was one of the exploits of the fortieth year. (See Num. xxi. 21—35.) Before the eleventh month of that year, not only Sihon and Og, but also the five princes of Midian, "who were dukes of Sihon, dwelling in the country" (Josh. xiii. 21), had also been slain (Num. xxxi.). This completed the conquest, and was the last exploit of Moses' life. In the period of repose that followed he found a suitable time to exhort the children of Israel, "according unto all that the Lord had given him in commandment unto them." From chap. xxxiv. 8, we learn that "the children of Israel wept for Moses thirty days." These days would seem to be the last month of the fortieth year, for "on the tenth day of the first month" (probably of the next year, Josh. iv. 19) they passed over Jordan. Thus the *last delivery* of the discourses recorded in Deuteronomy would seem to lie within a single month.

⁽⁵⁾ **On this side Jordan, in the land of Moab.**—This would be *on the other side of Jordan* from the stand-point of the writer, or of the readers for whom the book was intended, which is Palestine.

Began Moses.—"Began," *i.e.*, "determined" or "assayed."

The Promise of the   DEUTERONOMY, I.   *Lord to Israel.*

⁽⁶⁾ The LORD our God spake unto us in Horeb, saying, Ye have dwelt long enough in this mount: ⁽⁷⁾ turn you, and take your journey, and go to the mount of the Amorites, and unto ¹ all *the places* nigh thereunto, in the plain, in the hills, and in the vale, and in the south, and by the sea side, to the land of the Canaanites, and unto Lebanon, unto the great river, the river Euphrates. ⁽⁸⁾ Behold, I have ² set the land before you: go in and possess the land which the LORD sware unto your fathers, *a* Abraham, Isaac, and Jacob, to give unto them and to their seed after them.

⁽⁹⁾ And I spake unto you at that time, saying, I am not able to bear you myself alone: ⁽¹⁰⁾ the LORD your God hath multiplied you, and, behold, ye *are* this day as the stars of heaven for multitude. ⁽¹¹⁾ (The LORD God of your fathers make you a thousand times so

Marginal notes: 1 Heb., *all his neighbours*. 2 Heb., *given*. *a* Gen. 15. 18. & 17. 7, 8.

To declare.—The emphatic reiteration of what had been already received from God and delivered to Israel may be intended. But the Hebrew word here employed occurs in two other places only, and in both is connected with *writing*. (See chap. xvii. 8, "thou shalt write upon the stones all the words of this law *very plainly*" (*bâêr hêtêb*, in writing and in making good). Again, in Hab. ii. 2, "write the vision, and *make it plain* upon tables." The etymological affinities of the word also suggest the idea of writing. It would seem, then, that at this period Moses began to throw the discourses and laws that he had delivered into a permanent form, arranging and writing them with the same motive which influenced the Apostle Peter (2 Pet. i. 15), "Moreover, I will endeavour that ye may be able after my decease to have these things always in remembrance."

In this discourse the history of Israel, from the time of their departure from Sinai, is briefly recapitulated (chap. iii. 29), and with a short practical exhortation. This portion of history comprises three periods of the exodus: (1) *The march from Sinai to Kadesh-barnea*, with the sending of the twelve spies and its results, related more at length in Num. x. 11 —end of chap. xiv. The characteristic feature of this period is *failure* on the part of both leaders and people to rise to their high calling. Moses (Num. xi.), Aaron and Miriam (Num. xii.), Joshua (Num. xi. 28), the spies, who were also rulers (chaps. xiii., xiv.), and the people throughout, all in turn exhibit the defects of their character. In the end the enterprise is abandoned for the time. (2) *The thirty-seven and a half years that follow* are a period of disgrace, as appears by the absence of all note of time or place in the direct narrative between Num. xiv. and Num. xx. Certain places are mentioned in Num. xxxiii. which must belong to this period, but nothing is recorded of them beyond the names. A single verse (Deut. ii. 1), is all that is assignable to that period in this discourse of Moses. This long wandering was also a *period of training and discipline*. (3) *The fortieth year of the exodus*, in which the conquest of Sihon and Og was effected, and Israel reached the banks of Jordan. The sentence of death pronounced against their elder generation having been executed, a new life was now begun.

⁽⁶⁾ **The Lord our God spake unto us in Horeb.**—The "Lord our God," "Jehovah our Elohim," is the watchword of the whole book.

Ye have dwelt long enough in this mount. —From the beginning of the second month of the first year of the exodus (Exod. xix. 1) to the twentieth day of the second month of the second year (Num. x. 11). This was the *period of organisation*, in which the people received the Law and were organised as a church militant, an army encamped around the tabernacle of God. This year and its institutions fill up exactly *one-third* of the text of the Pentateuch.

⁽⁷⁾ **Enter the mount of the Amorites**—*i.e.*, the southern part of Judah, from which the five kings of the Amorites, the southern confederacy of Josh. x. (which see), arose to attack Gibeon. Israel would have marched into the heart of this territory had they entered from Kadesh, "by the way of the spies."

And unto all the places nigh thereunto.— The rest of the promised land is thus described: *In the plain*—of Jordan. *In the mountain*—the hill-country of Judah in the south, Mount Ephraim in the centre, and the mountainous district further north. *In the Shephêlah*—Philistia. *In the Negeb*—the land afterwards assigned to Simeon, in the far south of Judah. *And by the sea side* to the north of Carmel (see Josh. ix. 1; Judges v. 17), the coasts of the Great Sea over against Lebanon, and in the territory of Asher and Zebulun, as far as Phœnicia (Gen. xlix. 13).

The land of the Canaanites, and unto Lebanon.—The Canaanites held the plain of Esdraelon and the fortresses in the north. From Lebanon, the conquest would extend ultimately to the north-east, even to the great river, the river Euphrates.

⁽⁸⁾ **To give unto them.**—Note that the land is promised *to Abraham, and to Isaac, and to Jacob*, not only to their seed. The promise is not forgotten, though the three patriarchs are in another world. (Comp. Acts vii. 5, and Heb. xi. 16. See also Note on chap. xi. 21.)

^(9—18) In these words Moses appears to combine the recollection of two distinct things: (1) the advice of Jethro (Exod. xviii.), by following which he would be relieved from the ordinary pressure of litigation; (2) the still further relief afforded him by the appointment of the seventy elders. These last received the gift of prophecy, and were thus enabled to relieve Moses from some of the higher responsibilities of his office by representing his mind and reproducing his personal influence in many parts of the camp at once. Jethro's advice was given on their first arrival in Horeb: when it was carried into effect we are not told. The seventy elders were appointed (Num. xi.) between Sinai and Kadesh-barnea, shortly after they left Sinai. It is quite possible that both institutions came into existence at the same time. The seventy elders would have been of great service in the selection of the numerous judges and officers who were required.

⁽⁹⁾ **I am not able to bear you myself alone.**— Repeated almost exactly from Num. xi. 14.

⁽¹¹⁾ **The Lord God of your fathers . . . bless you.**—This appears to belong distinctly to the Book of

many more as ye *are*, and bless you, as he hath promised you!) (12) How can I myself alone bear your cumbrance, and your burden, and your strife? (13) ¹ Take you wise men, and understanding, and known among your tribes, and I will make them rulers over you. (14) And ye answered me, and said, The thing which thou hast spoken *is* good *for us* to do. (15) So I took the chief of your tribes, wise men, and known, and ² made them heads over you, captains over thousands, and captains over hundreds, and captains over fifties, and captains over tens, and officers among your tribes. (16) And I charged your judges at that time, saying, Hear *the causes* between your brethren, and *ᵃ* judge righteously between *every* man and his brother, and the stranger *that is* with him. (17) *ᵇ* Ye shall not ³ respect persons in judgment; *but* ye shall hear the small as well as the great; ye shall not be afraid of the face of man; for the judgment *is* God's: and the cause that is too hard for you, bring *it* unto me, and I will hear it. (18) And I commanded you at that time all the things which ye should do.

(19) And when we departed from Horeb, we went through all that great and terrible wilderness, which ye saw by the way of the mountain of the Amorites, as the LORD our God commanded us; and we came to Kadesh-barnea. (20) And I said unto you, Ye are come unto the mountain of the Amorites, which the LORD our God doth give unto us. (21) Behold, the LORD thy God hath set the land before thee: go up *and* possess *it*, as the LORD God of thy fathers hath said unto thee; fear not, neither be discouraged.

(22) And ye came near unto me every one of you, and said, We will send men before us, and they shall search us out the land, and bring us word again by what way we must go up, and into what cities we shall come. (23) And the saying pleased me well: and *ᶜ* I took twelve men of you, one of a tribe: (24) and *ᵈ* they turned and went up into the mountain, and came unto the valley of Eshcol, and searched it out. (25) And they took of the fruit of the land in their hands, and brought *it* down unto us, and brought us word again, and said, *It is* a good land which the LORD our God doth give us.

(26) Notwithstanding ye would not go

1 Heb., *give*.
2 Heb., *gave*.
ᵃ John 7. 24.
ᵇ Lev. 19. 15; ch. 16. 19; 1 Sam. 16. 7; Prov. 24. 23.
3 Heb., *acknowledge faces*.
ᶜ Num. 13. 3.
ᵈ Num. 13. 24.
B.C. 1490.

Deuteronomy. It can hardly be a record of what was spoken long before. It brings the living speaker before us in a way that precludes imitation.

(12) **Your cumbrance.**—The original word is found only here and in Isa. l. 14: "They are a *trouble* unto me, I am weary to bear them."

Verses 13—15 recall very exactly what is said in Exod. xviii.

(16) **And I charged your judges . . saying.**—These instructions given by Moses are an admirable expansion, but only an expansion, of those of Jethro (Exod. xviii. 21), that the judges must be "able men, such as fear God, *men of truth, hating covetousness*"—a sentence older than the Decalogue itself.

(17) **The judgment is God's.**—Comp. St. Paul in Rom. xiii. 1—4, which is, again, only an expansion of this sentence. For the latter part of this verse comp. Exod. xviii. 22—26.

(18) **And I commanded you at that time all the things which ye should do.**—"At that time," *i.e.*, after your departure from Horeb. This is as much as to say that the exhortations given in Deuteronomy had already been given on the way from Sinai to Kadesh-barnea. (Comp. what has been said above on the two first verses of this chapter.) This verse goes far to justify the view taken there.

(19) **By the way of the mountain of the Amorites.**—Rather, *in the direction of the mount*. They did not *pass* the Mount of the Amorites, but went through the "great and terrible wilderness" from Sinai to Kadesh-barnea. So Moses says in verse 20, "Ye *are come* unto the mount of the Amorites."

(21) **Fear not, neither be discouraged.**—The last clause of this verse reappears in St. John xiv. 27, "Let not your heart be troubled, *neither let it be afraid*."

(22) **And ye came near . . . and said, We will send.**—A new aspect is here given to the sending of the twelve spies. In Num. xiii. 1 the incident is introduced thus: "And the Lord spake unto Moses, saying, Send thou men." We learn here that the proposal in the first instance came from the people. Moses would naturally refer it to Jehovah, and, when approved, the scheme was carried out.

They shall search us out the land, and bring us word again by what way we must go up, and into what cities we shall come.—We read in verse 33 that the Lord "went in the way before them to search out a place" for them to encamp in. But here the spies and Israel proposed to take the guidance of their march into their own hands. It is noticeable that in the campaigns of Joshua, *not one step was taken without Divine direction*. Thus the sending of the twelve spies, in the light in which the people intended it, was an act of unbelief. "In this thing (verse 32) ye did not believe the Lord your God." (See also Note on Josh. ii. 1.)

(24) **The valley of Eshcol.**—See Num. xiii. 24.

(25) **It is a good land.**—In Num. xiii. 27 they all say, "Surely it floweth with milk and honey, and this is the fruit of it." In Num. xiv. 7 Joshua and Caleb describe it as an "exceeding good land."

up, but rebelled against the commandment of the LORD your God: ⁽²⁷⁾ and ye murmured in your tents, and said, Because the LORD hated us, he hath brought us forth out of the land of Egypt, to deliver us into the hand of the Amorites, to destroy us. ⁽²⁸⁾ Whither shall we go up? our brethren have ¹ discouraged our heart, saying, The people *is* greater and taller than we; the cities *are* great and walled up to heaven; and moreover we have seen the sons of the *^a* Anakims there.

⁽²⁹⁾ Then I said unto you, Dread not, neither be afraid of them. ⁽³⁰⁾ The LORD your God which goeth before you, he shall fight for you, according to all that he did for you in Egypt before your eyes; ⁽³¹⁾ and in the wilderness, where thou hast seen how that the LORD thy God bare thee, as a man doth bear his son, in all the way that ye went, until ye came into this place. ⁽³²⁾ Yet in this thing ye did not believe the LORD your God, ⁽³³⁾ *^b* who went in the way before you, to search you out a place to pitch your tents *in*, in fire by night, to shew you by what way ye should go, and in a cloud by day.

⁽³⁴⁾ And the LORD heard the voice of your words, and was wroth, and sware, saying, ⁽³⁵⁾ *^c* Surely there shall not one of these men of this evil generation see that good land, which I sware to give unto your fathers, ⁽³⁶⁾ save Caleb the son of Jephunneh; he shall see it, and to him will I give the land that he hath trodden upon, and to his children, because he hath ² wholly followed the LORD. ⁽³⁷⁾ *^d* Also the LORD was angry with me for your sakes, saying, *^e* Thou also shalt not go in thither. ⁽³⁸⁾ But Joshua the son of Nun, which standeth before thee, he shall go in thither: encourage him: for he shall cause Israel to inherit it. ⁽³⁹⁾ Moreover your little ones, which ye said should be a prey, and your children, which in that day had no knowledge between good and evil, they shall go in thither, and unto them will I give it, and they shall possess it. ⁽⁴⁰⁾ But *as for* you, turn you, and take your journey into the wilderness by the way of the Red sea.

⁽⁴¹⁾ Then ye answered and said unto me, *^f* we have sinned against the LORD, we will go up and fight, according to all that the LORD our God commanded us

---

¹ Heb., *melted.*

B.C. 1491.

a Num. 13. 29.

b Ex. 13. 21.

c Num. 14. 29.

² Heb., *fulfilled to go after.*

d Num. 20. 12, & 27. 14.

e ch. 3. 26. & 4. 21. & 34. 4.

f Num. 14. 40.

⁽²⁷⁾ **Because the Lord hated us.**—A most astounding commentary on the events of the exodus up to that date. It is a stronger expression than any recorded, even in Num. xiv. 3.

⁽²⁸⁾ **Whither shall we go up? our brethren have discouraged our heart.**—So Caleb says in Josh. xiv. 8, "My brethren made the heart of the people melt." For the rest of the verse see Num. xiii. 28.

⁽²⁹⁾ **Dread not, neither be afraid of them...**—The reminder that "Jehovah went before them" did not avail, for they had already chosen *men* to go before them.

⁽³¹⁾ **The Lord ... bare thee, as a man doth bear his son.**—From this comes the expression in Acts xiii. 18, "He bare them as a nursing father in the wilderness."—Rev. N. T., margin.

⁽³³⁾ **Who went in the way before you, to search you out a place.**—Comp. Num. x. 33, "The ark of the covenant of the Lord went before them ... to search out a resting place for them;" and St. John xiv. 2, "I go to prepare a place for you;" and Heb. vi. 20, "Whither the forerunner is for us entered, even Jesus." On the whole manner of this cloud-guidance, see Num. ix. 15—23.

⁽³⁴⁾ **Was wroth, and sware.**—See Ps. xcv. 11, "I sware in my wrath, that they should not enter into my rest."

⁽³⁵⁾ **Surely...** Comp. St. Luke xiv. 24, "None of those men which were bidden shall taste of my supper."

⁽³⁶⁾ **Save Caleb.**—Caleb is here placed by himself, as the one exception *among the people.* Joshua, as Moses' substitute, the exception among the recognised leaders, is named separately.

⁽³⁷⁾ **Also the Lord was angry with me for your sakes.**—Here, again, Moses combines his own rejection, an event of the fortieth year of the exodus, with the rejection of the people in the second year. The reason was the same—*unbelief.* "Because ye believed me not" was the reason given to Moses in Num. xx. 12. "Ye did not believe the Lord your God" is the reason for the rejection of the people, given above in verse 32. As the spies presumed to investigate the route and order of the conquest, a matter of Divine guidance, so Moses presumed to alter the prescribed order for the miracle in Kadesh. Like transgressions incurred like penalties. The fault for which the people had suffered could not be overlooked in the leader. (See also Notes on chaps. iii. 23—28; xxxii. 49.) This and verse 38 should be taken as a parenthesis.

⁽³⁹⁾ **Moreover your little ones.**—This continues the sentence of Jehovah from verse 36.

Which ye said should be a prey.—In Num. xiv. 3, "that our wives and children should be a prey." (See also verse 31.)

⁽⁴⁰⁾ **But as for you, turn you, and take your journey into the wilderness by the way** (in the direction) **of the Red Sea.**—In Num. xiv. 32 the parallel sentence is, "As for you, your carcases, they shall fall in this wilderness."

⁽⁴¹⁾ **We have sinned ... we will go up and fight.**—The emphatic *we* of this verse may be compared with the "we" of verse 28. In both instances it was *we*, without *Jehovah.* It was a change from cowardice to presumption, not from unbelief to faith.

And when ye had girded on every man his weapons of war, ye were ready to go up into the hill. ⁽⁴²⁾ And the LORD said unto me, Say unto them, Go not up, neither fight; for I *am* not among you; lest ye be smitten before your enemies. ⁽⁴³⁾ So I spake unto you; and ye would not hear, but rebelled against the commandment of the LORD, and ¹ went presumptuously up into the hill. ⁽⁴⁴⁾ And the Amorites, which dwelt in that mountain, came out against you, and chased you, as bees do, and destroyed you in Seir, *even* unto Hormah. ⁽⁴⁵⁾ And ye returned and wept before the LORD; but the LORD would not hearken to your voice, nor give ear unto you. ⁽⁴⁶⁾ So ye abode in Kadesh many days, according unto the days that ye abode there.

CHAPTER II.—⁽¹⁾ Then we turned, and took our journey into the wilderness by the way of the Red sea, as the LORD spake unto me: and we compassed mount Seir many days. ⁽²⁾ And the LORD spake unto me, saying, ⁽³⁾ Ye have compassed this mountain long enough: turn you northward. ⁽⁴⁾ And command thou the people, saying, Ye *are* to pass through the coast of your brethren the children of Esau, which dwell in Seir; and they shall be afraid of you: take ye good heed unto yourselves therefore: ⁽⁵⁾ meddle not with them; for I will not give you of their

1 Heb., *ye were presumptuous, and went up.*

Ye were ready to go up into the hill.—Some render, Ye *made light of* going up.

⁽⁴³⁾ The last clause comes from Num. xiv. 44.

⁽⁴⁴⁾ **As bees do.**—This should be observed as illustrating what is said of the hornet in Exod. xxiii. 28—30, and further on in Deut. vii. 20; Josh. xxiv. 12. The incidental mention of the bees in this place shows that the writer of Deuteronomy was familiar with the spectacle of a company of men pursued by bees.

In Seir, even unto Hormah.—Conder (*Bible Handbook*, p. 250) understands this Seir as the range of hills round Petra. There is another Seir in the territory of Judah (Josh. xv. 10). As to Hormah, the Jewish commentator Aben Ezra says, "the name of a place or the verb," *i.e.,* either unto Hormah, or unto utter destruction. But in our version the word Hormah is always taken as a proper name. The situation of Hormah is unknown.

⁽⁴⁵⁾ **And ye returned and wept before the Lord.**—This fact is not related in Num. xiv. It shows the personal knowledge of the writer, and that the narrative is not simply drawn from the earlier books.

⁽⁴⁶⁾ **So ye abode in Kadesh many days.**—Better, *and.* In Num. xiv. 25 the command was, "*To-morrow* turn you, and get you into the wilderness." This command was broken by the attack on the Canaanites, made on the morrow after the command. We cannot be certain that the many days spent in Kadesh were spent after the defeat. It may be merely a note of the fact that the time spent in Kadesh was considerable. The mission of the spies alone occupied forty days.

According unto the days that ye abode there.—The Jewish commentator Rashi, quoting from *Séder 'Olâm,* says they spent nineteen years in Kadesh, and nineteen in their wanderings.

II.

⁽¹⁾ **Then.**—In the original simply "And." There is no note of time.

By the way of the Red sea.—*i.e.,* in the direction of the Gulf of Akabah, *southwards.*

As the Lord spake unto me.—In Num. xiv. 25, as noted on chap. i. 40.

Many days.—Until near the close of the thirty-ninth year of the exodus.

⁽³⁾ **Ye have compassed this mountain long enough: turn you northward.**—Apparently this command must have been issued when they were in Kadesh the second time, at the commencement of the fortieth year (Num. xx. 1). It was from this encampment that Moses sent messengers to the king of Edom asking permission to pass through his territory. It would be interesting to know *when* it was decided that Israel should enter the land of promise by passing over Jordan, instead of going through the *Negeb.* Did Mount Seir, or the territory of Edom, lie wholly on the east, or partly on the west of Israel when they were encamped in Kadesh? If Edom had acquired any territorial rights to the westward during the thirty-eight years' wandering, it might have been necessary for Israel to ask his permission to go by the way of the spies, and in that case the decision to pass Jordan may have been taken in consequence of Edom's refusal. But if, as Conder (*Bible Handbook,* p. 250) appears to think, the permission asked was to go eastward between the mountains by the W. el Ghaweir to the north of Mount Hor, or the W. Ghurundel to the south of it (see Stanley's Map in *Sinai and Palestine* for these), then the decision to pass the Jordan must have been taken *before* this period. The reason for the step would then be similar to what we find in Exod. xiii. 17, that the people might not have to fight their way into the country through the land of the Amorites. The miraculous *eisodus* across Jordan would thus become still more analogous to the miraculous *exodus* from Egypt.

⁽⁴⁾ **Ye are to pass through the coast.**—Literally, *Ye are passing through the border.* This was apparently said before the permission was asked, and in view of the request made for it (Num. xx. 17). But Edom *refused to let Israel pass through his coast or border* (Num. xx. 21).

They shall be afraid of you.—According to the prophecy in the song of Moses (Exod. xv. 15), "Then the dukes of Edom shall be amazed."

⁽⁵⁾ **I have given mount Seir unto Esau.**—It is worthy of notice that the development of Ishmael preceded that of Isaac, and the inheritance of Esau was won earlier than that of Jacob. (Comp. Gen. xxv. 16 with chap. xxxv. 23—26, and Gen. xxxvi. 31 with chap. xxxvii. 1.) Isaac and Israel were still strangers

land, ¹ no, not so much as a foot breadth; ᵃ because I have given mount Seir unto Esau *for* a possession. ⁽⁶⁾ Ye shall buy meat of them for money, that ye may eat; and ye shall also buy water of them for money, that ye may drink. ⁽⁷⁾ For the LORD thy God hath blessed thee in all the works of thy hand: he knoweth thy walking through this great wilderness: these forty years the LORD thy God *hath been* with thee; thou hast lacked nothing.

⁽⁸⁾ And when we passed by from our brethren the children of Esau, which dwelt in Seir, through the way of the plain from Elath, and from Ezion-gaber, we turned and passed by the way of the wilderness of Moab. ⁽⁹⁾ And the LORD said unto me, ² Distress not the Moabites, neither contend with them in battle: for I will not give thee of their land *for* a possession; because I have given Ar unto the children of Lot *for* a possession. ⁽¹⁰⁾ The Emims dwelt therein in times past, a people great, and many, and tall, as the Anakims; ⁽¹¹⁾ which also were accounted giants, as the Anakims; but the Moabites call them Emims. ⁽¹²⁾ ᵇ The Horims also dwelt in Seir beforetime; but the children of Esau ³ succeeded them, when they had destroyed them from before them, and dwelt in their ⁴ stead; as Israel did unto the land of his possession, which the LORD gave unto them. ⁽¹³⁾ Now rise up, *said I*, and get you over ᶜ the ⁵ brook Zered. And we went over the brook Zered.

⁽¹⁴⁾ And the space in which we came from Kadesh-barnea, until we were come over the brook Zered, was thirty and eight years; until all the generation of the men of war were wasted out from among the host, as the LORD

1 Heb., *even to the treading of the sole of the foot.*
ᵃ Gen. 36. 8.
2 Or, *Use no hostility against Moab.*
ᵇ Gen. 36. 20.
3 Heb., *inherited them.*
4 Or, *room.*
ᶜ Num. 21. 12.
5 Or, *valley.*

---

and sojourners, while the Ishmaelites were princes, with towns and castles, and the Edomites dukes and kings.

⁽⁶⁾ **Ye shall buy meat . . . and . . . water.**—Comp. Gen. xiv. 23, "Lest thou shouldest say, I have made Abram rich," and chap. xv. 1, "I am thy shield, and thy exceeding great reward."

⁽⁷⁾ **The Lord thy God hath blessed thee.**—There is nothing unreasonable in the view suggested by these words, that the Israelites acquired wealth by trade or by ordinary occupations during their wilderness journey. They had skilled workmen among them.

⁽⁸⁾ **When we passed . . . from . . . Esau . . . through the way of the plain from Elath.**—The route from Seir, after Esau's refusal, was *southward* to Ezion-geber, at the head of the Gulf of Akabah, and Elath, a few miles south-east of Ezion-geber, on the same coast. They then *turned northward*, and going round the territory of Edom, reached the country of Moab.

⁽⁹⁾ **Distress not the Moabites . . . I have given Ar unto the children of Lot.**—The children of Lot, like those of Ishmael and Esau, had their earthly inheritance *before the children of Abraham.*

⁽¹⁰⁻¹²⁾ These three verses which follow should be read parenthetically.

The Emims.—See Gen. xiv. 5, 6, for the first mention of Rephaim, Zuzim, Emim, and Horim. (The termination *im* is plural in Hebrew, and, like cherubim, does not need the additional *s*.) These tribes were flourishing in the time of Abraham, but were conquered before the exodus.

The children of Esau succeeded them.—A partial mixture of the two races resulted in this case, and from their union sprang the Amalekites, Israel's inveterate foes (Gen. xxxvi. 12, 22).

As Israel did unto the land of his possession.—On the east of Jordan in Moses' lifetime, as well as on the west of Jordan under Joshua. It is not necessary, therefore, to make the parenthesis (verses 10—12) editorial, though it forms no essential part of Moses' speech.

⁽¹³⁾ **Now rise up, said I.**—A continuation of the order in verse 9. The words "said I" are not needed.

The brook Zered is not yet identified. (See Num. xxi. 12.) Several streams run into the Dead Sea on its eastern side south of Arnon; Zered is possibly one of these. Or it may be a tributary of Arnon, which has one large tributary running from south to north.

⁽¹⁴⁾ **Until we were come over the brook Zered.**—The root *zârad* in Chaldee means *to prune.* The name "Zered" signifies the luxuriant foliage and the young shoots, especially of the willow, which are cut off with the knife: so the Targum takes it (Num. xxi. 12). Probably the valley was so named from the "willows of the brook" which grew there. But it was the "valley of pruning" to the "vine" which God had "brought out of Egypt" in another sense. The last of the fruitless branches was here taken away, and the vine "purged, that it might bring forth more fruit."

Thirty and eight years; until all . . . men of war were wasted out from among the host.—The census did not take place until some months later. A plague intervened, which cut off twenty-four thousand. The observation that at the brook Zered all the men of the older generation were "wasted out of the host" indicates an intimate knowledge of the incidents of the exodus. But it is quite natural to suppose that, as the survivors of that generation became fewer, those who remained would become marked men. Every man of the twelve tribes (excluding Levi?) who passed the census at Sinai was doomed. The fortieth year of the exodus had more than half expired when they came to the brook Zered. All who remained alive in that year knew that they had a short time to live. Probably more notice was taken of the last few deaths than of all the rest of the six hundred thousand put together.

sware unto them. ⁽¹⁵⁾ For indeed the hand of the LORD was against them, to destroy them from among the host, until they were consumed.

⁽¹⁶⁾ So it came to pass, when all the men of war were consumed and dead from among the people, ⁽¹⁷⁾ that the LORD spake unto me, saying, ⁽¹⁸⁾ Thou art to pass over through Ar, the coast of Moab, this day: ⁽¹⁹⁾ and *when* thou comest nigh over against the children of Ammon, distress them not, nor meddle with them: for I will not give thee of the land of the children of Ammon *any* possession; because I have given it unto the children of Lot *for* a possession. ⁽²⁰⁾ (That also was accounted a land of giants: giants dwelt therein in old time; and the Ammonites call them Zamzummims; ⁽²¹⁾ a people great, and many, and tall, as the Anakims; but the LORD destroyed them before them; and they succeeded them, and dwelt in their stead: ⁽²²⁾ as he did to the children of Esau, which dwelt in Seir, when he destroyed the Horims from before them; and they succeeded them, and dwelt in their stead even unto this day: ⁽²³⁾ and the Avims which dwelt in Hazerim, *even* unto Azzah, the Caphtorims, which came forth out of Caphtor, destroyed them, and dwelt in their stead.) ⁽²⁴⁾ Rise ye up, take your journey, and pass over the river Arnon: behold, I have given into thine hand Sihon the Amorite, king of Heshbon, and his land: ¹ begin to possess *it*, and contend with him in battle. ⁽²⁵⁾ This day will I begin to put the dread of thee and the fear of thee upon the nations *that are* under the whole heaven, who shall hear report of thee, and shall tremble, and be in anguish because of thee.

⁽²⁶⁾ And I sent messengers out of the wilderness of Kedemoth unto Sihon king of Heshbon with words of peace, saying, ⁽²⁷⁾ ᵃ Let me pass through thy land: I will go along by the high way, I will neither turn unto the right hand nor to the left. ⁽²⁸⁾ Thou shalt sell me meat for money, that I may eat; and give me water for money, that I may drink: only I will pass through on my feet; ⁽²⁹⁾ (As the children of Esau which dwell in Seir, and the Moabites which dwell in Ar, did unto me;) until I shall pass over Jordan into the land which the LORD our God giveth us. ⁽³⁰⁾ But Sihon king of Heshbon would not let us pass by him: for the LORD thy God hardened his spirit, and made his heart

¹ Heb., *begin, possess.*

ᵃ Num. 21. 21, 22.

⁽¹⁵⁾ **The hand of the Lord was against them.**—The best comment on this discipline is to be found in Psalm xc. 8, 9, "Thou hast set our iniquities before thee, our secret sins in the light of thy countenance; for all our days are passed away in thy wrath."

⁽¹⁸⁾ **Ar.**—According to Conder, "Rabbath-Moab," the present ruin *Rabba*, north of Merah.

⁽¹⁹⁾ **And when thou comest nigh.**—Compare Note on verse 9.

⁽²⁰⁾ **In old time.**—See Gen. xiv.

Zamzummims = Zuzims (Gen. xiv. 5).

⁽²¹⁾ **The Lord destroyed them before them.**—It is noticeable that the conquest of Canaan is here brought into the domain of common history, by comparison with the conquests of gigantic races accomplished by Edom, Moab, and Ammon. The value of this analogy to Moses and Israel is plain. If the children of Lot, Ishmael, and Esau—who were but Gentiles, although they were Abraham's seed—were able to dispossess these gigantic races, how much more would Israel be able to dispossess the Canaanites under the personal guidance of Jehovah?

⁽²³⁾ **The Avims which dwelt in Hazerim, even unto Azzah, the Caphtorims . . . destroyed.**—"In Hazerim" should apparently be rendered "in villages." It does not occur elsewhere as a proper name; it is plural in form, and is found in this sense in some other places. "Azzah," *i.e.*, Gaza. The Caphtorim: comp. Amos ix. 7: "The Philistines from Caphtor." (See Gen. x. 14.) Some make the country of Caphtor to be Cyprus or Crete. But at least this statement makes Philistia the scene of a conquest, and the Philistines of the time of Joshua would thus appear to be a mixed race.

⁽²⁴⁾ **Pass over . . . Arnon.**—The territory from Arnon northward to Jabbok had been taken from Moab by the Amorites, and was to be possessed by Israel. (See on Num. xxi. 24.)

⁽²⁵⁾ **The fear of thee.**—Compare Exod. xv. 15, 16: "All the inhabitants of Canaan shall melt away, fear and dread shall fall upon them."

⁽²⁶⁾ **Kedemoth.**—Mentioned as a city in the plain of Jordan, belonging to Heshbon (Josh. xiii. 18).

Words of peace.—By this message Sihon was excepted from the catalogue of the doomed kings and nations, according to the distinction drawn in chap. xx. 10, 11, 15, 16. He therefore brought his fate upon himself. He was offered the privileges of the Moabites whom he had conquered, and refused to accept the position.

⁽²⁹⁾ **Until I shall pass over Jordan.**—This was already determined.

⁽³⁰⁾ **The Lord thy God hardened his spirit, and made his heart obstinate.**—Jehovah gave the strength to Sihon, as He had done to Pharaoh, and as He does to all. Sihon was responsible for using the strength which God gave him in opposition to the Divine purposes. To "harden" a man's spirit is not necessarily a moral process any more than the hardening of steel. "*Made obstinate*" is the same verb used

obstinate, that he might deliver him into thy hand, as *appeareth* this day. ⁽³¹⁾ And the LORD said unto me, Behold, I have begun to give Sihon and his land before thee: begin to possess, that thou mayest inherit his land. ⁽³²⁾ ᵃThen Sihon came out against us, he and all his people, to fight at Jahaz. ⁽³³⁾ And the LORD our God delivered him before us; and we smote him, and his sons, and all his people. ⁽³⁴⁾ And we took all his cities at that time, and utterly destroyed ¹the men, and the women, and the little ones, of every city, we left none to remain: ⁽³⁵⁾ only the cattle we took for a prey unto ourselves, and the spoil of the cities which we took. ⁽³⁶⁾ From Aroer, which *is* by the brink of the river of Arnon, and *from* the city that *is* by the river, even unto Gilead, there was not one city too strong for us: the LORD our God delivered all unto us: ⁽³⁷⁾ only unto the land of the children of Ammon thou camest not, *nor* unto any place of the river Jabbok, nor unto the cities in the mountains, nor unto whatsoever the LORD our God forbad us.

CHAPTER III.—⁽¹⁾ Then we turned, and went up the way to Bashan: and

a Num. 21. 23.

¹ Heb., *every city of men, and women, and little ones.*

b Num. 21. 33, &c.; ch. 29. 7.

c Num. 21. 24.

d Num. 21. 33.

ᵇOg the king of Bashan came out against us, he and all his people, to battle at Edrei. ⁽²⁾ And the LORD said unto me, Fear him not: for I will deliver him, and all his people, and his land, into thy hand; and thou shalt do unto him as thou didst unto ᶜSihon king of the Amorites, which dwelt at Heshbon. ⁽³⁾ So the LORD our God delivered into our hands ᵈOg also, the king of Bashan, and all his people: and we smote him until none was left to him remaining. ⁽⁴⁾ And we took all his cities at that time, there was not a city which we took not from them, threescore cities, all the region of Argob, the kingdom of Og in Bashan. ⁽⁵⁾ All these cities *were* fenced with high walls, gates, and bars; beside unwalled towns a great many. ⁽⁶⁾ And we utterly destroyed them, as we did unto Sihon king of Heshbon, utterly destroying the men, women, and children, of every city. ⁽⁷⁾ But all the cattle, and the spoil of the cities, we took for a prey to ourselves. ⁽⁸⁾ And we took at that time out of the hand of the two kings of the Amorites the land that *was* on this side Jordan, from the river of Arnon unto mount Hermon; ⁽⁹⁾ (Which Hermon

---

in Joshua i. 6, for "*Be of a good courage*." An unyielding spirit and a courageous heart are good or bad according to the use made of them. Sihon used them badly, Joshua used them well. God's gifts were the same to both. (See also Josh. xi. 20.)

(31) **Behold, I have begun to give Sihon.**—Notice that in all the conquests of Israel Jehovah gave the order to begin the attack. (See chap. vii. 2, and Note on Josh. xiii. 1.)

(33) **And his sons.**—As the Hebrew is *written*, it should be *his son* (possibly a person of distinction).

(34) **And utterly destroyed.**—*i.e.*, *devoted* to destruction. They made them *chêrem*, like the spoil of Jericho. This could only be by Divine direction. The word implies nothing less. It will be seen, therefore, that the narrative asserts in this case an extermination of Sihon's people by the express command of Jehovah.

(36) **Aroer.**—According to Conder, "the ruin 'Ar 'Air, on the north bank of Wâdy Môjib." (But he makes the Aroer of Num. xxxii. 34 a different place, and marks it as unknown. Why?)

The city that is by the river.—The description suggests Rabbath-ammon, but this cannot be referred to here.

III.

⁽¹⁾ **Then.**—In the Hebrew, a simple *And*. The history of this movement is given in Num. xxi. 32, 33. For *Edrei*, see Num. xxi. 33, from which this whole verse is repeated.

⁽²⁾ **And the Lord said unto me . . . .**—This verse repeats Num. xxi. 34.

For I will deliver him should be rather read thus, *for into thy hand have I delivered him*.

(4, 5) These details are not given in Numbers. Professor Porter, in the *Giant Cities of Bashan*, has well described the impression made upon him by verifying this description in detail. "The whole of Bashan," he says, "is not larger than an ordinary English county." That "sixty walled cities, 'besides unwalled towns a great many,' should exist in a small province, at such a remote age, far from the sea, with no rivers and little commerce, appeared to be inexplicable. Inexplicable, mysterious though it appeared, it was true. On the spot, with my own eyes, I had now verified it. A list of more than *one hundred* ruined cities and villages, situated in these mountains alone, I had in my hands; and on the spot I had tested it, and found it accurate, though not complete." Many of the cities in the mountains are not ruins. Rooms, doors, bars are entire to this day. The *region of Argob* is distinctly marked out by its natural boundaries, and well described by the same writer.

⁽⁶⁾ **We utterly destroyed them.**—Devoted them, made them *chêrem*, as above (chap. ii. 34).

⁽⁹⁾ **Sirion.**—(*Sion*, chap. iv. 48.) Sirion, or Shirion, and Shenir, are thought to have similar meanings. But the Targum intepretes Shenir as the "rock of snow." Shirion, according to Gesenius, means "glittering like a breastplate." It would not be safe to assert that the mention of the *Sidonian* name of Hermon makes this verse an addition after Israel was in Palestine, though it might be so. The Jewish commentator Rashi points out that, including the name Sion (chap. iv. 48), "this mountain has four names. Why mention them? To declare the

the Sidonians call Sirion; and the Amorites call it Shenir;) ⁽¹⁰⁾ All the cities of the plain, and all Gilead, and all Bashan, unto Salchah and Edrei, cities of the kingdom of Og in Bashan. ⁽¹¹⁾ For only Og king of Bashan remained of the remnant of giants; behold, his bedstead *was* a bedstead of iron; *is* it not in Rabbath of the children of Ammon? nine cubits *was* the length thereof, and four cubits the breadth of it, after the cubit of a man.

⁽¹²⁾ And this land, *which* we possessed at that time, from Aroer, which *is* by the river Arnon, and half mount Gilead, and ᵃ the cities thereof, gave I unto the Reubenites and to the Gadites. ⁽¹³⁾ And the rest of Gilead, and all Bashan, *being* the kingdom of Og, gave I unto the half tribe of Manasseh; all the region of Argob, with all Bashan, which was called the land of giants. ⁽¹⁴⁾ Jair the son of Manasseh took all the country of Argob unto the coasts of Geshuri and Maachathi; and called them after his own name, Bashan-ᵇhavoth-jair, unto this day. ⁽¹⁵⁾ And I gave Gilead unto Machir. ⁽¹⁶⁾ And unto the Reubenites and unto the Gadites I gave from Gilead even unto the river Arnon half the valley, and the border even unto the river Jabbok, *which is* the border of the children of Ammon; ⁽¹⁷⁾ The plain also, and Jordan, and the coast *thereof*, from Chinnereth even unto the sea of the plain, *even* the salt sea, ¹under Ashdoth-pisgah eastward.

⁽¹⁸⁾ And I commanded you at that time, saying, The LORD your God hath given you this land to possess it: ᶜ ye shall pass over armed before your brethren the children of Israel, all *that are* ²meet for the war. ⁽¹⁹⁾ But your wives, and your little ones, and your cattle, (*for* I know that ye have much cattle,) shall abide in your cities which I have given you; ⁽²⁰⁾ until the LORD have given rest unto your brethren, as well as unto you, and *until* they also possess the land which the LORD your God hath given them beyond Jordan: and *then* shall ye ᵈreturn every man unto his possession, which I have given you.

⁽²¹⁾ And ᵉI commanded Joshua at that time, saying, Thine eyes have seen all that the LORD your God hath done unto these two kings: so shall the LORD

---

a Num. 32. 33; Josh. 13. 8, &c.

b Num. 32. 41.

c Num. 32. 20.

¹ Or, *under the springs of Pisgah*, or, *the hill*.

² Heb., *sons of power.*

d Josh. 22. 4.

e Num. 27. 18.

---

praise of the land of Israel, which had four kingdoms glorifying themselves in it, and each of them saying, 'It is called after my name!'" But there are several notes of this kind in the Pentateuch. (See Gen. xxiii. 2, xxxi. 47; Num. xiii. 22; also Joshua xiv. 15.)

(10) **Salchah.**—"The present large town *Salkhád*, east of Bashan." (*Conder*). (See also *Giant Cities of Bashan*, p. 75.)

(11) **Of the remnant of giants**—*i.e.*, of the nation of Rephaim in these parts. (See Note on Gen. xiv. 5.)

His bedstead.—The word may mean either bedstead or coffin. Both the word for "bedstead" and the word for "iron" have given rise to some discussion and difficulty. An iron bedstead and an iron coffin are almost equally improbable. *Basalt* has been suggested as an alternative. But though there is basalt in Argob, there is none in Rabbath-Ammon. Conder, who has recently explored Rabbath, has discovered a remarkable throne of stone on the side of a hill there, and he suggests that the Hebrew word rendered "bedstead,", which properly signifies *a couch with a canopy*, may apply to this. The word for "iron" (*barzil*) in Talmudical language means also "*a prince*," and this meaning has been suggested for the name *Barzillai*, which we find in the same district in later times. "His canopied throne was a princely one, and yet remains in Rabbath of the Ammonites," would be the meaning of the passage, on this hypothesis. The dimensions of the throne recently discovered are said to be nearly those given in this verse.

After the cubit of a man.—*Ish* (not *adam*), the distinctive and emphatic word for a man. Some think that the cubit of *any man* is meant; others that the man himself for whom it was made, *viz.*, Og, is intended. (Comp. Rev. xxi. 17, "according to the measure of a man—*i.e.*, of an angel.")

(13–17) Comp. Num. xxxii. 33–42, and Notes thereon.

(13) **The land of giants**—*i.e.*, of Rephaim.

(14) **Jair took . . . unto this day.**—The last words of this chapter seem to point to a later hand, as of Joshua, describing the completion of the conquest. The expression "unto this day" is characteristically common in Joshua, or in the editorial notes inserted throughout that book. (See *Introduction* to Joshua. "On the Style of the Book.")

Geshuri and Maachathi—*i.e.*, the Geshurite and the Maachathite, the inhabitants of Geshur and Maachah. "The Maachathites, near the Jordan springs (comp. Abel-Beth-maachah, 2 Sam. xiv. 15), and the Geshurites, rather farther east" (Conder, *Bible Handbook*, p. 254). Talmai, king of Geshur, was the grandfather of Absalom (2 Sam. iii. 3), who took refuge with him after he killed Ammon (2 Sam. xiii. 37). "Argob, Trachonitis, or El-Lejja, has been an asylum for all malefactors and refugees ever since" (*Giant Cities of Bashan*, p. 92).

(16, 17) **And unto the Reubenites and unto the Gadites I gave.**—The circumstances are detailed in Num. xxxii. They desired the land for their cattle.

(18, 19) This is a summary of the agreement made and described in Num. xxxii. 20–32. (See also Note on Josh. i. 12.)

(21, 22) **I commanded Joshua at that time . . . . Thine eyes have seen.**—"Thine

do unto all the kingdoms whither thou passest. (22) Ye shall not fear them: for the LORD your God he shall fight for you. (23) And I besought the LORD at that time, saying, (24) O Lord God, thou hast begun to shew thy servant thy greatness, and thy mighty hand: for what God *is there* in heaven or in earth, that can do according to thy works, and according to thy might? (25) I pray thee, let me go over, and see the good land that *is* beyond Jordan, that goodly mountain, and Lebanon. (26) But the LORD *a* was wroth with me for your sakes, and would not hear me: and the LORD said unto me, Let it suffice thee; speak no more unto me of this matter. (27) Get thee up into the top of ¹Pisgah, and lift up thine eyes westward, and northward, and southward, and eastward, and behold *it* with thine eyes: for thou shalt not go over this Jordan. (28) But charge Joshua, and encourage him, and strengthen him: for he shall go over before this people, and he shall cause them to inherit the land which thou shalt see. (29) So we abode in the valley over against Beth-peor.

CHAPTER IV.—(1) Now therefore hearken, O Israel, unto the statutes and unto the judgments, which I teach you, for to do *them*, that ye may live, and go in and possess the land which the LORD God of your fathers giveth you. (2) *b* Ye shall not add unto the word which I command you, neither shall ye diminish *ought* from it, that ye may keep the commandments of the

a Num. 20. 12; ch. i. 37.

¹ Or, *the hill*.

b ch. 12. 32; Josh. 1. 7; Prov. 30. 6; Rev. 22. 18.

eyes are the witnesses of all," &c. The conquest of Sihon and Og, as well as that of Amalek, was to be impressed upon Joshua (comp. Exod. xvii. 14) as a precedent for his encouragement, and also for his instruction. It is remarkable that no details are given us of the battles against Sihon and Og, or of the capture of the cities, except in Josh. xii. 6, "Them did Moses the servant of the Lord smite." We see the reflection of Moses' campaign, which is unwritten, in the recorded campaigns of Joshua. The peculiar form of the sentence, "Thine eyes are they that see," may also serve to remind us of the fact, that though the Law was given by Moses, no eye saw its full breadth and grasp until it came into the hand of Jesus, the antitype of Joshua.

(23) Here begins the second section according to the Jewish division, called "And I besought" (*vaeth channân*).

(23—28) **And I besought the Lord at that time.**—Two things Moses is recorded to have asked *for himself* in the story of the exodus. The first is written in Exod. xxxiii. 18, "I beseech thee shew me thy glory;" the second is before us here. "O Lord GOD (Adonai Jehovah), thou hast begun to shew thy servant thy greatness and thy mighty hand . . . I pray thee let me go over and see the good land beyond Jordan." It would seem that Moses desired not so much to view the land (which, indeed, was granted him), but to see the greatness of Jehovah manifested in the conquest, as he had seen it in the victories over Og and Sihon. While we cannot allow for a moment that "the old fathers looked only for transitory promises" (see Notes on chaps. v. 16, xxii. 7), yet it is impossible not to feel in this prayer of Moses the pressure of the veil which hung over the unseen world before the coming of our Saviour, who "brought life and immortality to light through the Gospel." Moses evidently did not realise that he might see the works of Jehovah and His glory still more clearly in the other world.

(26) **For your sakes.**—Because "I will be sanctified in them that come nigh me, and before all the people I will be glorified" (Lev. x. 3; Num. xx. 12, 13); and also because the death of Moses and the succession of Joshua were "for a testimony of things to be spoken after," a figure of things to come. Moses, like Ezekiel (chap. xxiv. 15—24), was made a sign.

(26) **Let it suffice thee.**—Literally, *enough for thee*, or, as it is paraphrased by Rashi from older commentators, "Far more than this is reserved for thee; plentiful goodness is hidden for thee." And so indeed it proved. For on some "goodly mountain" (Hermon or "Lebanon,") Moses and Elias stood with the Saviour of the world, and spake of a far more glorious conquest than Joshua's, even "His exodus, which He should fulfil at Jerusalem" (St. Luke ix. 31).

(27) **Northward, and southward.**—Southward, literally, *Teman-ward*. The *negeb*, or "south" of Palestine, is not named here.

(28) **For he shall go over.**—Emphatic, *he it is that shall go over, and he it is that shall make them to inherit;* not Moses.

(29) **So we abode in the valley over against Beth-peor.**—Moses' burial-place, as appears by chap. xxxiv. 6. It is a significant finishing touch to the scene described above. This verse also concludes the recapitulation of Israel's journey from Horeb (chap. i. 6) to the banks of Jordan, with which this first discourse of Moses begins. The remainder, contained in chap. iv., is the practical part of the discourse, which now begins.

IV.

(1) **Now therefore hearken.**—The whole point of the exhortation in this chapter is the same which we find in Joshua's address to the people (Josh. xxiv.), that they should serve Jehovah. And the ground of the exhortation is His revelation of Himself in Horeb as their God.

The statutes . . . and the judgments.—Perhaps we should say "institutions and requirements" in modern language. For "judgments," see Exod. xxi.—xxiii.

That ye may live, and go in.—*Life* is put before *possession*. The penalty of the broken law is death.

(2) **Ye shall not add unto the word.**—*The word*, not "the words." The *word* is the substance of the Law. The *words* in which it is expressed may be more or less. The law of Moses contains in it the germ of all revelation to the very end.

LORD your God which I command you. ⁽³⁾ Your eyes have seen what the LORD did because of ᵃBaal-peor: for all the men that followed Baal-peor, the LORD thy God hath destroyed them from among you. ⁽⁴⁾ But ye that did cleave unto the LORD your God *are* alive every one of you this day.

⁽⁵⁾ Behold, I have taught you statutes and judgments, even as the LORD my God commanded me, that ye should do so in the land whither ye go to possess it. ⁽⁶⁾ Keep therefore and do *them;* for this *is* your wisdom and your understanding in the sight of the nations, which shall hear all these statutes, and say, Surely this great nation *is* a wise and understanding people. ⁽⁷⁾ For what nation *is there so* great, who *hath* God *so* nigh unto them, as the LORD our God *is* in all *things that* we call upon him for? ⁽⁸⁾ And what nation *is there so* great, that hath statutes and judgments so righteous as all this law, which I set before you this day?

⁽⁹⁾ Only take heed to thyself, and keep thy soul diligently, lest thou forget the things which thine eyes have seen, and lest they depart from thine heart all the days of thy life: but teach them thy sons, and thy sons' sons; ⁽¹⁰⁾ *specially* the day that thou stoodest before the LORD thy God in Horeb, when the LORD said unto me, Gather me the people together, and I will make them hear my words, that they may learn to fear me all the days that they shall live upon the earth, and *that* they may teach their children. ⁽¹¹⁾ And ye came near and stood under the mountain; and the ᵇmountain burned with fire unto the ¹midst of heaven, with darkness, clouds, and thick darkness. ⁽¹²⁾ And the LORD spake unto you out of the midst of the fire: ye heard the voice of the words, but saw no similitude; ²only *ye heard* a voice. ⁽¹³⁾ And he declared unto you his covenant, which he commanded you to perform, *even* ten commandments; and he wrote them upon two tables of stone. ⁽¹⁴⁾ And the LORD commanded me at that time to teach you statutes and

a Num. 25. 4, &c.

b Ex. 19. 18.

¹ Heb., *heart.*

² Heb., *save a voice.*

⁽³⁾ **Your eyes have seen.**—Literally, *your eyes are they that see*—i.e., you are witnesses of these things. The men who perished by the plague because of the iniquity of Beth-peor—to the number of 24,000—seem to have been all members of the younger generation; for they had already passed the brook Zered. (See on chap. ii. 13.)

⁽⁵⁾ **That ye should do so in the land.**—It should never be forgotten that there is a special connection between *the law of Moses and the land of Canaan.* It cannot be kept in many of its precepts, except by a chosen people in a protected land.

⁽⁶⁾ **This is your wisdom and your understanding in the sight of the nations.**—The laws of Jehovah in Israel, and the constant presence of Jehovah with Israel, would make an impression upon the world that it would not be easy to resist. For, he adds, "what nation is there so great, that hath God so nigh unto them?"

⁽⁸⁾ **What nation is there so great, that hath statutes and judgments so righteous?**—These words direct our attention to the law of Moses, as distinctly *in advance of the time* when it was given.

⁽⁹⁾ **Only take heed to thyself.**—The exhortation contained in the following verses lays special emphasis on one point—the worship of the invisible Jehovah without images. This more than anything else would tend to separate the religion of Israel from that of all other nations.

Teach them thy sons, and thy sons' sons.—A command which Israel evidently failed to obey. For a generation speedily rose up "which knew not Jehovah nor yet the works which he had done for Israel" (Judg. ii. 10). It is worth while to observe that we cannot find any trace of a system of national education in Israel until many years later. When education is purely parental, it is likely to be neglected in many instances. It is not every parent who finds himself able to "teach his sons, and his sons' sons."

⁽¹⁰⁾ **The day that thou stoodest before the Lord thy God in Horeb.**—The Church of Israel dated from Sinai, as the Church of Christ does from Pentecost. It is noticeable that the giving of the Law appears to have taken place about fifty days after the Passover in Egypt. Jewish writers associate the Feast of Pentecost with the memory of the event. A similar association, and a contrast between the first and last Pentecost, appears to have been present to St. Paul's mind in 2 Cor. iii. The law given at Sinai is the "ministration of death," and is contrasted with the "ministration of the Spirit"—the letter that killeth with the Spirit that giveth life. (Comp. also Gal. iv. 24—26, and Heb. xii. 18—24.) The word "specially" is not in the Hebrew of this verse.

The day . . . in Horeb is not only to be regarded as a *special* subject of instruction; it is the root of the whole matter.

Gather me the people together.—The Greek here is ἐκκλησίασον, which might be paraphrased according to New Testament language, "Form a Church of this people." The "day of the assembly" alluded to in this and other passages (as chap. x. 4) may be similarly paraphrased as "the day of the Church." It seems to be the source of the expression used by St. Stephen, "the Church in the wilderness" (Acts vii. 38). Thus the analogy between Israel's receiving the *letter* of the law at Sinai, and the gift of the Holy Spirit in Jerusalem is still further brought out.

⁽¹¹⁾ **Darkness, clouds, and thick darkness.**—The "blackness, and darkness, and tempest" of Heb. xii. 18.

⁽¹³⁾ **His covenant . . . ten commandments.**—See on chap. v.

judgments, that ye might do them in the land whither ye go over to possess it.

(15) Take ye therefore good heed unto yourselves; for ye saw no manner of similitude on the day *that* the LORD spake unto you in Horeb out of the midst of the fire: (16) lest ye corrupt *yourselves*, and make you a graven image, the similitude of any figure, the likeness of male or female, (17) the likeness of any beast that *is* on the earth, the likeness of any winged fowl that flieth in the air, (18) the likeness of any thing that creepeth on the ground, the likeness of any fish that *is* in the waters beneath the earth: (19) and lest thou lift up thine eyes unto heaven, and when thou seest the sun, and the moon, and the stars, *even* all the host of heaven, shouldest be driven to worship them, and serve them, which the LORD thy God hath ¹ divided unto all nations under the whole heaven. (20) But the LORD hath taken you, and brought you forth out of the iron furnace, *even* out of Egypt, to be unto him a people of inheritance, as *ye are* this day. (21) Furthermore the LORD was angry with me for your sakes, and sware that I should not go over Jordan, and that I should not go in unto that good land, which the LORD thy God giveth thee *for* an inheritance: (22) but I must die in this land, I must not go over Jordan: but ye shall go over, and possess that good land. (23) Take heed unto yourselves, lest ye forget the covenant of the LORD your God, which he made with you, and make you a graven image, *or* the likeness of any *thing*, which the LORD thy God hath forbidden thee. (24) For *a*the LORD thy God *is* a consuming fire, *even* a jealous God.

(25) When thou shalt beget children, and children's children, and ye shall have remained long in the land, and shall corrupt *yourselves*, and make a graven image, *or* the likeness of any *thing*, and shall do evil in the sight of the LORD thy God, to provoke him to anger: (26) I call heaven and earth to witness against you this day, that ye shall soon utterly perish from off the land whereunto ye go over Jordan to possess it; ye shall not prolong *your* days upon it, but shall utterly be destroyed. (27) And the LORD shall scatter you among the nations, and ye shall be left few in number among the heathen, whither the LORD shall lead you. (28) And there ye shall serve gods, the

1 Or, *imparted.*

a ch. 9. 3; Heb. 12. 29.

He wrote them.—See on chap. x. 2.

(15) **Ye saw no manner of similitude.**—The worship of the *invisible* Jehovah is here specially insisted on. The difficulty of learning to worship one whom we cannot see is, happily, one which our education does not enable us to realise in its relation to Israel of old. All nations had their visible symbols of deity. Centuries afterwards the world described the followers of Christ as *Atheists*, because they had no visible God. It is especially recorded in praise of Moses that "he, endured as seeing Him who is invisible" (Heb. xi. 27).

(16) **Lest ye corrupt . . . and make.**—The connection between idolatry and corruption is twofold. First, it changes "the glory of the *incorruptible God*" into an image of His corruptible creatures. Secondly, it always ends in corrupting the idolater. Man was made to have dominion over the works of God's hands. He cannot *worship* anything in creation, which he was not intended to *rule*. He can only fulfil his destiny when he strives after the Divine likeness, rising to that which is above him, instead of stooping to that which is below.

(17, 18) **Likeness of any beast . . . fowl . . .**—There may be an allusion to the animal idolatry of Egypt here.

(19) **The sun, and the moon, and the stars.**—The purest worship of antiquity—that which we find among the Persians—hardly escaped this snare.

Which the Lord thy God hath divided unto all nations.—The heavenly bodies could never be regarded as special protectors of any *one* nation. But Jehovah was pledged to be the God of Israel. This appears to be the argument of verses 19 and 20.

(21—23) **The Lord was angry with me for your sakes . . . I must die in this land . . . but ye shall go over . . . Take heed unto yourselves.**—The argument appears to be this: "I cannot go with you to warn you; therefore take the more heed when you are alone." The same line of thought appears in St. Paul's last appeal to Timothy: "Fulfil *thy ministry*; for *I am* now ready to be offered" (2 Tim. iv. 6).

(24) **The Lord thy God is a consuming fire.**—The writer of the Epistle to the Hebrews makes use of this in chap. xii. 29, to enforce the lessons not of Sinai, but of Pentecost, and of the voice of "Him that speaketh from heaven" by the Spirit whom He has sent.

(25) **Shall have remained long.**—Literally, *shall slumber*—a very suggestive expression. Prosperity often sends true religion to sleep, and brings conventional, or fashionable, religion in its stead.

(27) **And the Lord shall scatter you.**—Our familiarity with this fact in history must not blind us to its force when uttered as a *prophecy*. The fact that the Jews were taken captive for idolatry, and dispersed for the rejection of JESUS, is a remarkable proof that the real reason why they were brought into Canaan, and kept there, was to be witnesses for Jehovah.

(28) **And there ye shall serve gods, the work of men's hands.**—That is, "you shall be *in bondage* to them," being ruled by their worshippers. And so

work of men's hands, wood and stone, which neither see, nor hear, nor eat, nor smell. ⁽²⁹⁾ But if from thence thou shalt seek the LORD thy God, thou shalt find *him*, if thou seek him with all thy heart and with all thy soul. ⁽³⁰⁾ When thou art in tribulation, and all these things ¹are come upon thee, *even* in the latter days, if thou turn to the LORD thy God, and shalt be obedient unto his voice; ⁽³¹⁾ (for the LORD thy God *is* a merciful God;) he will not forsake thee, neither destroy thee, nor forget the covenant of thy fathers which he sware unto them.

⁽³²⁾ For ask now of the days that are past, which were before thee, since the day that God created man upon the earth, and *ask* from the one side of heaven unto the other, whether there hath been *any such thing* as this great thing *is*, or hath been heard like it? ⁽³³⁾ Did *ever* people hear the voice of God speaking out of the midst of the fire, as thou hast heard, and live? ⁽³⁴⁾ Or hath God assayed to go *and* take him a nation from the midst of *another* nation, by temptations, by signs, and by wonders, and by war, and by a mighty hand, and by a stretched out arm, and by great terrors, according to all that the LORD your God did for you in Egypt before your eyes? ⁽³⁵⁾ Unto thee it was shewed, that thou mightest know that the LORD he *is* God; *there is* none else beside him. ⁽³⁶⁾ Out of heaven he made thee to hear his voice, that he might instruct thee: and upon earth he shewed thee his great fire; and thou heardest his words out of the midst of the fire. ⁽³⁷⁾ And because he loved thy fathers, therefore he chose their seed after them, and brought thee out in his sight with his mighty power out of Egypt; ⁽³⁸⁾ to drive out nations from before thee greater and mightier than thou *art*, to bring thee in, to give thee their land *for* an inheritance, as *it is* this day.

⁽³⁹⁾ Know therefore this day, and consider *it* in thine heart, that the LORD he *is* God in heaven above, and upon the earth beneath: *there is* none else. ⁽⁴⁰⁾ Thou shalt keep therefore his statutes, and his commandments, which I command thee this day, that it may go well with thee, and with thy children after thee, and that thou mayest prolong *thy* days upon the earth, which the LORD thy God giveth thee, for ever.

⁽⁴¹⁾ Then Moses severed three cities on this side Jordan toward the sun rising;

¹ Heb., *have found thee*.

Rashi explains it. Captivity was the means of eradicating idolatry from Israel rather than encouraging it. But the cause of a people and its idols is so constantly identified in the Old Testament, that those who are in bondage to a nation may naturally be described as in bondage to its gods. The gods were even held to be sharers in the captivity of the nation. It is said of Bel and Nebo, in Isa. xlvi. 2, "They could not deliver . . . but *themselves are gone into captivity.*"

(29, 30, 31) Comp. chap. xxx. 1—5 for a more explicit promise and prophecy of the same thing, and see Note on that passage.

⁽³²⁾ **For ask now . . . whether there hath been any such thing.**—The same argument is afterwards employed by St. Paul (Rom. xi. 29) for the restoration of Israel: "for the gifts and calling of God are without repentance," *i.e., irrevocable.* He did not go and take Him a nation out of the midst of another nation in order to abandon them at last. He never did so much in the way of personal and visible interposition for any people; and He will not forsake the work of His own hands. Moses had proved the truth of what he says here in many scenes of sin and peril averted by his own intercession. (See especially Num. xiv. 11—21, and comp. 1 Sam: xii. 22.)

⁽³⁷⁾ **Because he loved thy fathers.**—The reasons for God's choice of Israel are frequently stated in this book; and they are always stated in such a way as to enforce the doctrine of God's sovereignty, and to show the Israelites that their own merit was in no way the ground of God's choice.

⁽³⁹⁾ **Know therefore . . . and consider.**—"Consider," *i.e.,* reckon (the word for "impute" and "account" in St. Paul's argument to the Romans). Do not indulge any polytheistic notions regarding the Deity. "To us there is but One God." If every nation has its separate deity, how is it that Jehovah controls them all? His various dealings with Egyptians, Moabites, Ammonites, Edomites, Amorites, as well as with Israelites and Canaanites, mark Him as Lord of all. "There is none else." There are *no more gods*; if you desire to leave Him behind, there is no one else to serve. Compare Isa. xliv. 8: "Is there a God beside me? yea, there is no Rock. *I know not any.*"

THE APPOINTMENT OF THREE CITIES OF REFUGE.

⁽⁴¹⁾ **Then Moses severed.**—The word "then" appears to be a note of time. It would seem that the appointment of the three cities of refuge on the eastern side of Jordan actually followed this discourse.

On this side Jordan.—Heb., *b' 'éber hay-yardên.* The expression is here defined by the words that follow, "toward the sun-rising," and it need not, therefore, be taken to fix the writer's point of view. By itself, the expression would naturally mean, on the *other* side of Jordan.

(42) that the slayer might flee thither, which should kill his neighbour unawares, and hated him not in times past; and that fleeing unto one of these cities he might live: (43) namely, ª Bezer in the wilderness, in the plain country, of the Reubenites; and Ramoth in Gilead, of the Gadites; and Golan in Bashan, of the Manassites.

(44) And this is the law which Moses set before the children of Israel: (45) these are the testimonies, and the statutes, and the judgments, which Moses spake unto the children of Israel, after they came forth out of Egypt, (46) on this side Jordan, in the valley over against Beth-peor, in the land of Sihon king of the Amorites, who dwelt at Heshbon, whom Moses and the children of Israel ᵇ smote, after they were come forth out of Egypt: (47) and they possessed his land, and the land ᶜ of Og king of Bashan, two kings of the Amorites, which were on this side Jordan toward the sun rising; (48) from Aroer,

a Josh. 20. 8.
b Num. 21. 24; ch. 1. 4.
c Num. 21. 33; ch. 3. 3.
d ch. 3. 17.
1 Heb., *keep to do them.*
e Ex. 19. 5.
f Ex. 20. 2, &c.; Lev. 26. 1; Ps. 81. 10.

which is by the bank of the river Arnon, even unto mount Sion, which is Hermon, (49) and all the plain on this side Jordan eastward, even unto the sea of the plain, under the ᵈ springs of Pisgah.

CHAPTER V.—(1) And Moses called all Israel, and said unto them, Hear, O Israel, the statutes and judgments which I speak in your ears this day, that ye may learn them, and ¹ keep, and do them. (2) ᵉ The LORD our God made a covenant with us in Horeb. (3) The LORD made not this covenant with our fathers, but with us, *even us*, who *are* all of us here alive this day. (4) The LORD talked with you face to face in the mount out of the midst of the fire, (5) (I stood between the LORD and you at that time, to shew you the word of the LORD: for ye were afraid by reason of the fire, and went not up into the mount;) saying,

(6) ᶠ I am the LORD thy God, which

---

(43) **Bezer** is as yet unidentified.
Ramoth in Gilead, though famous in the history of Israel as the scene of Ahab's death and of the anointing of Jehu (1 Kings xxi. and 2 Kings ix.), is also as yet unknown.
Golan has given a name to the district of Gaulonitis. But it is as yet also unknown. We may hope that when the survey of Eastern Palestine is concluded, these ancient sites will be recovered.

SECOND DISCOURSE.

(44—49) These words form an introduction to the second discourse, which occupies the larger portion of the book—from chap. v. 1 to the end of chap. xxvi. There is no real break between. The present introduction differs from what we find in chap. i. 1. There is no intimation that *this portion* of Deuteronomy was a repetition of what had been delivered between Sinai and Kadesh-barnea. What follows is said to have been *spoken* in the land of Sihon and Og, after the conquest by Israel.

(46) **On this side Jordan.**—Literally, *on the other side.* The same expression in verse 47 is defined by the addition, "toward the sun-rising."
The whole passage (verses 44—49) may be editorial, and added by Joshua in Canaan. But there is no *necessity* for this view.

(48) **Mount Sion.**—See Note on chap. iii. 9.

V.

This chapter contains a recapitulation of the Decalogue itself and of the circumstances of its delivery. The repetition of the Ten Commandments is the true beginning of the Deuteronomy, as their first delivery is the beginning of the Law itself.

(1) **And Moses called all Israel, and said.**—What follows is thus presented to us as an actual exhortation, not merely a portion of a book.

The statutes and judgments.—The religious *ordinances and institutions,* and the general *requirements.* The mention of these is prefixed to the Decalogue, of which they are only *the application*—to a special people under special circumstances. More precisely, the words apply rather to what follows the Decalogue than to the Ten Commandments themselves. (See chap. vi. 1.)

(2) **The Lord our God made a covenant with us in Horeb.**—It must never be forgotten that the Law *is a covenant* in its *very form.* (See Note on verse 6.)

(3) **Not . . . with our fathers, but with us.**—That is, according to the usage of the Hebrew language in drawing contrasts, not *only* with our fathers (who actually heard it), but *with us also,* who were in the loins of our fathers, and for whom the covenant was intended no less than for them; and, in fact, every man who was above forty-two at the time of this discourse might actually remember the day at Sinai.

(4) **The Lord talked with you face to face.** —Yet they saw no manner of similitude (chap. iv. 12), *i.e.,* no visible form; but the very words of God reached their ears. So in Exod. xx. 22, "Ye have seen that I have talked with you from heaven."

(5) In this verse a colon seems too large a stop after "the word of the Lord." Perhaps it should rather be read thus: "*I* stood between Jehovah and you at that time (for ye were afraid by reason of the fire), and ye went not up into the mount." The cause of their not going up into the mount was not their fear, but the express prohibition of Jehovah, as may be seen by Exod. xix.

. (6) **I am the Lord thy God.**—It should never be forgotten that this sentence is an integral part of the Decalogue, and also the *first part.* The declaration of Divine relationship, with all that it implies—the covenanted adoption of Israel by Jehovah—*precedes all the*

brought thee out of the land of Egypt, from the house of ¹bondage. ⁽⁷⁾ Thou shalt have none other gods before me.

⁽⁸⁾ Thou shalt not make thee *any graven image, or any likeness of any thing* that *is* in heaven above, or that *is* in the earth beneath, or that *is* in the waters beneath the earth: ⁽⁹⁾ thou shalt not bow down thyself unto them, nor serve them: for I the LORD thy God *am* a jealous God, ᵃ visiting the iniquity of the fathers upon the children unto the third and fourth *generation* of them that hate me, ⁽¹⁰⁾ ᵇ and shewing mercy unto thousands of them that love me and keep my commandments.

⁽¹¹⁾ Thou shalt not take the name of the LORD thy God in vain: for the LORD will not hold *him* guiltless that taketh his name in vain.

⁽¹²⁾ Keep the sabbath day to sanctify it, as the LORD thy God hath commanded thee. ⁽¹³⁾ Six days thou shalt labour, and do all thy work: ⁽¹⁴⁾ but the seventh day *is* the ᶜ sabbath of the LORD thy God: *in it* thou shalt not do any work, thou, nor thy son, nor thy daughter, nor thy manservant, nor thy maidservant, nor thine ox, nor thine ass, nor any of thy cattle, nor thy stranger that *is* within thy gates; that thy manservant and thy maidservant may rest as well as thou. ⁽¹⁵⁾ And remember that thou wast a servant in the land of Egypt, and *that* the LORD thy God brought thee out thence through a mighty hand and by a stretched out arm: therefore the LORD thy God commanded thee to keep the sabbath day.

⁽¹⁶⁾ Honour thy father and thy mother, as the LORD thy God hath commanded thee; that thy days may be prolonged, and that it may go well with thee, in the land which the LORD thy God giveth thee.

⁽¹⁷⁾ ᵈ Thou shalt not kill.

⁽¹⁸⁾ ᵉ Neither shalt thou commit adultery.

---

requirements of the Law. The Law is, therefore, primarily a covenant in the strictest sense.

⁽⁷⁾ **Thou shalt have none other gods before me.**—Literally, *upon my face, in addition to my presence*; or, as Rashi says, "in any place where I am, that is, in the whole world." "Whither shall I go from Thy Spirit, or whither *shall I flee from Thy face?*" Idols are, at the very best, only masks which man puts upon the face of God, insulting to His dignity, and tending to conceal Him from our view.

(8, 9) These two verses should be closely connected, according to the idiom of the original, "Thou shalt not make to thyself any of these things *for the purpose of* bowing down to them or worshipping them."

⁽⁹⁾ **Visiting the iniquity of the fathers upon the children.**—There are no sins which so surely entail penal consequences upon succeeding generations as the abominations of idolatry. All idolatry means the degradation of the Divine image in man. But it is not meant here that the soul of the son shall die for the father. The penalty extends only "to them that hate me."

⁽¹⁰⁾ **Them that love me.**—We have an echo of this commandment in the words of our Saviour: "If ye love me, keep my commandments" (John xiv. 15). The promise of His presence with us through the "other Comforter" compensates for the absence of any visible image. As *love* in this verse is practical, so is *hatred* in the previous verse. To hate God is to disobey His commandments.

⁽¹¹⁾ **Take . . . in vain.**—Literally, *Thou shalt not put the name of Jehovah thy God to vanity: i.e.,* to anything that is false, or hollow, or unreal. Primarily, it is false swearing that is forbidden here; but the extension of the principle to vain and rash swearing, or the light use of the Name without real cause, is sufficiently obvious.

(12—15) The language of this commandment is identical with the form it takes in Exodus only so far as the 13th and 14th verses are concerned; and even here the special mention of the ox and the ass is confined to Deuteronomy. The introduction and the close of the command, which gives the reason for it, are different here. The reason drawn from the creation is not mentioned; the reason drawn from the exodus is. This fact illustrates the observation that in Deuteronomy we find "the Gospel of the Pentateuch." If for the exodus of Israel we substitute here "the exodus of Christ, which He accomplished at Jerusalem," not so much by His *death as by His resurrection*, we have a reason for keeping *not the Sabbath, but the Lord's Day.*

It is worth while to observe that the Israelites had express authority given them to *enforce the observance of the Sabbath upon Gentiles*, when these could be regarded as "strangers within their gates." The words Isa. lvi. 6 seem to show that "strangers" who "took hold of the covenant" of Jehovah were expected to "keep His sabbath from polluting it." For an example of its enforcement, see Nehemiah xiii. 16, 20, 21.

If any difficulty is felt at the variation of the form of the commandment from that which we have in Exodus, it should be observed, first, that the *command itself is not altered*, as appears by verses 13, 14, compared with Exod. xx. 9, 10; and secondly, that in this exhortation Moses calls Israel to hear the statutes and judgments which he, as their mediator, commands them, and that he is free to enforce them by such reasons as may seem to him best.

⁽¹⁶⁾ **That it may go well with thee . . .**—In this form St. Paul cites the commandment in the Epistle to the Ephesians (chap. vi. 2, 3). As to what may be made of this promise, see a Note on chap. xxii. 7, and a quotation from the Talmud on the point.

(17—20) The wording of these four commandments is the same with that of Exod. xx.

(19) *Neither shalt thou steal. (20) Neither shalt thou bear false witness against thy neighbour.

(21) *Neither shalt thou desire thy neighbour's wife, neither shalt thou covet thy neighbour's house, his field, or his manservant, or his maidservant, his ox, or his ass, or any *thing* that *is* thy neighbour's.

(22) These words the LORD spake unto all your assembly in the mount out of the midst of the fire, of the cloud, and of the thick darkness, with a great voice: and he added no more. And he wrote them in two tables of stone, and delivered them unto me. (23) And it came to pass, when ye heard the voice out of the midst of the darkness, (for the mountain did burn with fire,) that ye came near unto me, *even* all the heads of your tribes, and your elders; (24) and ye said, Behold, the LORD our God hath shewed us his glory and his greatness, and *we have heard his voice out of the midst of the fire: we have seen this day that God doth talk with man, and he *liveth. (25) Now therefore why should we die? for this great fire will consume us: if we ¹ hear the voice of the LORD our God any more, then we shall die. (26) For who *is* there *of* all flesh, that hath heard the voice of the living God speaking out of the midst of the fire, as we *have*, and lived? (27) Go thou near, and hear all that the LORD our God shall say: and *speak thou unto us all that the LORD our God shall speak unto thee; and we will hear *it*, and do *it*.

(28) And the LORD heard the voice of your words, when ye spake unto me; and the LORD said unto me, I have heard the voice of the words of this people, which they have spoken unto thee: they have well said all that they have spoken. (29) O that there were such an heart in them, that they would fear me, and keep all my commandments always, that it might be well with them, and with their children for ever! (30) Go say to them, Get you into your tents again. (31) But as for thee, stand thou here by me, and I will speak unto thee all the commandments, and the statutes, and the judgments, which thou shalt teach them, that they may do *them* in the land which I give them to possess it. (32) Ye shall observe to do therefore as the LORD your God hath commanded you: ye shall not turn aside to the right hand or to the left. (33) Ye shall walk in all the ways which

a Rom. 13. 9.

b Rom. 7. 7.

c Ex. 19. 19.

d ch. 4. 33.

¹ Heb., *add to hear*.

e Ex. 20. 19.

---

(21) **His field.**—These words are not found in Exod. xx. The children of Israel had now become, or were just about to become, landowners; hence the addition is appropriate in this place. There is also another slight verbal alteration. One word only is used for "covet" in Exod. xx. 17; here two are employed. The idea of the one is to "delight in," and the other to "lust after."

(22) **He added no more**—*i.e.*, He spoke no more in this manner; or, there were only ten commandments. So verse 25: "If we add to hear"—*i.e.*, in this fashion.

(23—27) The speech of the elders to Moses is more fully and exactly described here than in Exod. xx., where it is briefly summarised as expressing the mind of the whole people.

(25) **Why should we die?**—The instinctive dread of death awakened by the Divine presence, and especially by the declaration of the Divine law, bears eloquent testimony to the truth that man was made to bear the Divine likeness, and to live a holy life.

(26) **For who is there of all flesh, that hath heard.**—A famous passage in the Talmud makes all nations hear the words of the Law, every people in its own language. The thought is remarkable as bringing out a further analogy between the revelation at Sinai and the revelation on the Day of Pentecost, when every man heard in his own language the wonderful works of God.

(28—31) **And the Lord heard the voice of your words . . .**—The Divine comment on the words of the people is recorded only in Deuteronomy; but in order to obtain a complete record of it, we must refer to chap. xviii. 18, 19. It will appear by comparison of the two passages that the promise of the prophet like unto Moses was given at this very time: "They have well said all that they have spoken. I will raise them up a prophet from among their brethren, like unto thee, and will put my words in His mouth." It is not a little remarkable that He who gave the Law from Sinai "in blackness and darkness and tempest" should, on that very day, acknowledge the need of a different form of teaching for His people, and should promise it then and there. But it must not be forgotten that He "whose voice then shook the earth" is the very same Person who "speaketh from heaven" now. He who pronounced the Law in the letter writes it on the heart by His Spirit. The Angel of the covenant and the Prophet like unto Moses are one. He who gave the Law on Sinai died under it on Calvary, and provided for its observance for ever.

(29) **O that there were such an heart in them.**—Literally, *Who will give that there shall be this heart in them, to fear me, and to keep all my commandments all the days?* He who asked the question has also supplied the answer: "*I will put* my laws in their hearts, and in their minds will I write them." Or, more exactly, in Heb. viii. 10, "*Giving* my laws into

the LORD your God hath commanded you, that ye may live, and *that it may be* well with you, and *that* ye may prolong *your* days in the land which ye shall possess.

CHAPTER VI.—⁽¹⁾ Now these *are* the commandments, the statutes, and the judgments, which the LORD your God commanded to teach you, that ye might do *them* in the land whither ye ¹go to possess it: ⁽²⁾ that thou mightest fear the LORD thy God, to keep all his statutes and his commandments, which I command thee, thou, and thy son, and thy son's son, all the days of thy life; and that thy days may be prolonged.

¹ Heb., *pass over*.

a ch. 10. 12; Matt. 22. 37; Mark 12. 30; Luke 10. 27.

b ch. 11. 18.

² Heb., *whet*, or, *sharpen*.

⁽³⁾ Hear therefore, O Israel, and observe to do *it*; that it may be well with thee, and that ye may increase mightily, as the LORD God of thy fathers hath promised thee, in the land that floweth with milk and honey.

⁽⁴⁾ Hear, O Israel: the LORD our God is one LORD: ⁽⁵⁾ and *a* thou shalt love the LORD thy God with all thine heart, and with all thy soul, and with all thy might. ⁽⁶⁾ And *b* these words, which I command thee this day, shall be in thine heart: ⁽⁷⁾ and thou shalt ² teach them diligently unto thy children, and shalt talk of them when thou sittest in thine house, and when thou walkest by the way, and when thou liest down, and

---

their understanding, *I will also write them* upon their hearts." The need of a Mediator like themselves was well stated by the people; it was also met by Him who said, "They have well said all that they have spoken."

VI.

FIRST PORTION OF THE COMMENTARY ON THE LAW (chaps. vi.—xi.).

⁽¹⁾ **These are the commandments, the statutes, and the judgments, which the Lord . . . commanded . . . that ye might do them in the land.**—After the Decalogue itself has been recapitulated, Moses proceeds to apply its principles to the conduct of Israel in the promised land. The first part of the application is more general, and concerns *the relation of Israel to Jehovah*, who has brought them from Egypt through the wilderness to the promised land. This portion concludes with chap. xi. The precepts that follow are particular, and concern the *land of Israel* viewed as the seat of (1) the *worship* and (2) the *kingdom* of Jehovah. But the whole discourse, from chap. iv. 44 to the end of chap. xxvi., is presented to us as one unbroken whole. (See Introduction for a complete analysis.)

The commandments.—Literally, *this is the commandment, the statutes, and the judgments.* The "commandment" is the *duty* imposed on Israel by the covenant of the ten words—its application to their daily lives. This application includes (1) statutes, religious ordinances, or institutions; and (2) judgments, requirements, actual rules of behaviour. The two words "statutes" and "judgments," in the original, may sometimes represent two aspects of the same thing. For example, the Passover is an ordinance, or "statute," or, as we should say, an "institution." The rules for its observance are "judgments," or requirements. The thing itself is permanent; the rules for its observance may vary. It was originally eaten standing, and in haste. But after Israel was at rest, it was eaten by them reclining, and in an attitude of repose. Again, the moral law as a whole was eternal; but its application to the life of Israel was very different from its application to ourselves. The word here rendered "commandments" is now commonly employed by the Jews to signify any religious duty or good work.

⁽³⁾ **That ye may increase mightily . . . in the land.**—The position of Israel in the land, and their continuance therein, depended entirely on their fulfilment of the purpose for which they were brought there—the observance of the Law of Jehovah, as it applied to their peculiar situation.

⁽⁴, ⁵⁾ **Hear, O Israel . . .**—These two verses are styled by our Lord "the first and great commandment" in the Law. The first words of the Talmud concern the hours when this form should be recited in daily morning or evening prayer—"Hear, O Israel: Jehovah our God is one Jehovah." The unity of Jehovah, as opposed to the belief in "gods many and lords many," is the key-note of the Jewish faith. "*We* worship one God in Trinity, and Trinity in Unity." But this truth, though visible in the Old Testament by the light of the New, was not explicitly revealed until it came forth in history, when the Father sent the Son to be the Saviour of the world, and both sent the Holy Spirit to represent Him in the Church.

⁽⁵⁾ **With all thine heart, and with all thy soul, and with all thy might.**—The word "heart" has been taken both as "thought" and "affection." Hence, perhaps, the *four* terms, "heart, mind, soul, and strength," which we find in St. Mark xii. 30. Rashi says upon the expression "all thy heart"—"with both natures" (the good and evil nature). "With all thy soul" he expounds thus: "Even though He take it (thy life) from thee." And "with all thy might" he paraphrases in a truly practical and characteristic fashion, "*With all thy money,* for you sometimes find a man whose money is dearer to him than his life (or body)." Or, as an alternative, "in every condition which He allots to thee, whether prosperity or chastisement. And so He says in David, 'I will *take the cup of salvation* (deliverances), and *I will call on the name of the Lord*' (Ps. cxvi. 13); and again. '*I shall find trouble and heaviness,* and *I will call on the name of the Lord*'" (verses 3, 4.) It is an interesting illustration of the passage, though the *verbal* connection on which it is based will not hold.

⁽⁷⁾ **And thou shalt teach them diligently.**—The same Jewish commentator remarks that there should be no hesitation in answering anything that a man might ask. Had this system of education been carried

when thou risest up. (8) And thou shalt bind them for a sign upon thine hand, and they shall be as frontlets between thine eyes. (9) And thou shalt write them upon the posts of thy house, and on thy gates.

(10) And it shall be, when the LORD thy God shall have brought thee into the land which he sware unto thy fathers, to Abraham, to Isaac, and to Jacob, to give thee great and goodly cities, which thou buildedst not, (11) and houses full of all good *things*, which thou filledst not, and wells digged, which thou diggedst not, vineyards and olive trees, which thou plantedst not; *when thou shalt have eaten and be full ; (12) *then* beware lest thou forget the LORD, which brought thee forth out of the land of Egypt, from the house of ¹bondage. (13) Thou shalt *b* fear the LORD thy God, and serve him, and shalt swear by his name. (14) Ye shall not go after other gods, of the gods of the people which *are* round about you; (15) (for the LORD thy God *is* a jealous God among you) lest the anger of the LORD thy God be kindled against thee, and destroy thee from off the face of the earth.

(16) *c* Ye shall not tempt the LORD your God, *d* as ye tempted *him* in Massah. (17) Ye shall diligently keep the commandments of the LORD your God, and his testimonies, and his statutes, which he hath commanded thee. (18) And thou shalt do *that which is* right and good in the sight of the LORD : that it may be well with thee, and that thou mayest go in and possess the good land which the LORD sware unto thy fathers, (19) to cast out all thine enemies from before thee, as the LORD hath spoken.

(20) And when thy son asketh thee ²in time to come, saying, What *mean* the testimonies, and the statutes, and the judgments, which the LORD our God hath commanded you? (21) then thou shalt say unto thy son, We were Pharaoh's bondmen in Egypt; and the LORD brought us out of Egypt with a mighty hand : (22) and the LORD shewed signs and wonders, great and ³sore,

a ch. 8. 9, 10, &c.

1 Heb., *bondmen*, or, *servants*.

b ch. 10. 12, 20 & 13. 4.

c Matt. 4. 7.

d Ex. 17. 2.

2 Heb., *to morrow*.

3 Heb., *evil*.

---

on from the first, the history of Israel would have been very different from what it is.

(8) **And thou shalt bind them** . . .—From this precept the Jews derive the use of the Tephillin, the portions of the Law which they bind upon the head or arm when about to pray.

(10—13) The song of Moses supplies a prophetic comment upon this in chap. xxxii. 15 : " Jeshurun waxed fat, and kicked . . . then he forsook God." " In all time *of our wealth*, good Lord, deliver us."

(13) **Thou shalt fear the Lord thy God, and serve him.**—Literally, *Jehovah thy God thou shalt fear, and him shalt thou serve : i.e.,* Him only, as translated by the LXX., and cited by our Lord in His temptation. It is remarkable that all His answers to the tempter were taken not only from Deuteronomy, *but from one and the same portion of Deuteronomy*—chaps. v.—x. inclusive—the portion which applies the principles of the Decalogue to Israel's life.

And shalt swear by his name.—Comp. Exod. xxiii. 13. " Make no mention of the name of other gods." The principle was not unknown to the patriarchs. Laban appealed to the "God of Nahor," but "Jacob sware by the fear of his father Isaac" (Gen. xxxi. 53). (Comp. Jer. v. 7 : " Thy children have forsaken me, and sworn by . . . no-gods.")

(15) **From off the face of the earth.**—Literally, *of the ground*. Absolute extermination is threatened by the fire of His jealousy.

(16) **Ye shall not tempt the Lord your God.** —In the LXX., " Thou shalt not tempt," and so where our Lord used it against the tempter (Matt. iv. and Luke iv.).

As ye tempted him in Massah.— How did they tempt Him in Massah? By raising the unbelieving question, " Is the Lord among us, or not ? " (Exod. xvii. 7). Even by the side of Satan upon the giddy pinnacle of the Temple, our Saviour refused to doubt the care of Jehovah. He would not throw Himself from thence into the arms of the angels to escape Satan, but "He endured as seeing Him who is invisible." To this standard of action Israel was called in face of the powers of evil. But it was not always realised.

(18) **And that thou mayest go in and possess.** —This should be taken with what follows, "Possess," so as " to cast out all thine enemies from before thee " (verse 19). There was no question now whether Israel should pass the Jordan ; but how far the conquest of Canaan would be completed, or within what period of time, depended upon their faithfulness to His decrees. That it was delayed by their disobedience is clear from Judges ii. 20—23.

(20) **What mean the testimonies, and the statutes, and the judgments.**—These three words appear for the first time together in the introduction to this discourse (chap. iv. 45). The Law, or *Torah*, includes *charges*, and *institutions*, and *requirements*. The Decalogue itself is primarily the *Torah* ; the charge which follows may come under the head of "testimony." The "statutes" and "judgments" more properly describe the contents of the chapters from chaps. xi.—xxvi. inclusive.

(21) **The Lord brought us out of Egypt.**— The simple explanation of the obligations of the Law given in these verses is based upon the message of Jehovah to Israel from Sinai, in Exod. xix. 3—6 : " Ye have seen what I did unto the Egyptians, and how I bare you on eagles' wings, and brought you unto my-

upon Egypt, upon Pharaoh, and upon all his household, before our eyes: ⁽²³⁾ and he brought us out from thence, that he might bring us in, to give us the land which he sware unto our fathers. ⁽²⁴⁾ And the LORD commanded us to do all these statutes, to fear the LORD our God, for our good always, that he might preserve us alive, as *it is* at this day. ⁽²⁵⁾ And it shall be our righteousness, if we observe to do all these commandments before the LORD our God, as he hath commanded us.

CHAPTER VII.—⁽¹⁾ When the ^aLORD thy God shall bring thee into the land whither thou goest to possess it, and hath cast out many nations before thee, the Hittites, and the Girgashites, and the Amorites, and the Canaanites, and the Perizzites, and the Hivites, and the Jebusites, seven nations greater and mightier than thou; ⁽²⁾ and when the LORD thy God shall deliver them before thee; thou shalt smite them, *and* utterly destroy them; ^b thou shalt make no covenant with them, nor shew mercy unto them: ⁽³⁾ neither shalt thou make marriages with them; thy daughter thou shalt not give unto his son, nor his daughter shalt thou take unto thy son. ⁽⁴⁾ For they will turn away thy son from following me, that they may serve other gods: so will the anger of the LORD be kindled against you, and destroy thee suddenly. ⁽⁵⁾ But thus shall ye deal with them; ye shall destroy their altars, and break down their ¹ images, and cut down their groves, and burn their

a ch. 31. 1.

b Ex. 23. 32 & 34. 12.

1 Heb., *statues,* or, *pillars.*

---

self. Now therefore, if ye will obey my voice indeed, and keep my covenant, then ye shall be a peculiar treasure unto me." The keeping of the Law of Jehovah by Israel as a nation in the land that He gave them was the final cause of their national existence. This fundamental fact must never be forgotten. This alone would justify what had been done to Egypt. Hence the neglect of the Law must inevitably bring down the Divine vengeance.

⁽²⁵⁾ **And it shall be our righteousness.**—In one Targum, "It shall be *merit* to us," or more fully, in the other, "It shall be merit laid up for us against the world to come." In the LXX., "It shall be alms to us." This conjunction of ideas will help to explain why in Matt. vi. 1 "alms" and "righteousness" occur as alternative readings. We have "alms" in the Authorised Version, "righteousness" in the Revised Version. To this day the Jews call alms *ts'dâkah*, "righteousness."

VII.

⁽¹⁾ **When the Lord thy God shall bring thee into the land** . . .—The former chapter applies the Decalogue to the love of Jehovah and of His word, and to faith in Him as the God of Israel; and thus it may be regarded as an expansion of the first commandment. The exhortation in this chapter concerns the treatment of idolaters in the conquest of Canaan, and the avoidance of all such intercourse or union with them as might tend to turn Israel from Jehovah. Obviously, this may be connected both with the first and with the second commandment.

⁽²⁾ **And when the Lord thy God shall deliver them before thee** . . . .—It would be possible to read, "*Then* the Lord thy God shall deliver them before thee, and thou shalt smite." Or the sentence might also be divided thus: "When the Lord thy God shall bring thee in, and shall have delivered the nations from before thee, and thou hast smitten them, *then* thou shalt utterly destroy them"—*i.e.,* shalt make them *chérem,* a devoted or accursed thing. Perhaps this last way of dividing the clauses is, upon the whole, to be preferred. But in any case it should be noted that *Jehovah's deliverance of the nations into Israel's* hand is to precede their defeat and extermination. Indiscriminate attack and massacre are not to be thought of. (See for a further Note on this, Joshua xiii.) All the operations described in Joshua—the sieges of Jericho and Ai, the southern campaign and the northern campaign—were alike undertaken under Divine direction. The same may be said of the battles in Moses' lifetime, whether against Amalek, Sihon, Og, Arad, or Midian. The same is true of the judges, and of David's operations against the Philistines after he came to the throne (2 Sam. v. 19, &c.). The principle was acknowledged by Ahab in his attack on Ramoth-gilead (1 Kings xxii.).

Thou shalt make no covenant with them. —The reason for this is too obvious to need comment. If Israelites and idolaters were united—still more if they were intermingled in marriage—there was an end to the distinction of race and religion—an end to the supremacy of Israel or the isolation of the people of Jehovah, as exhibiting His Law and the blessings of His government to mankind. It must be remembered, however, that the isolation here commanded was only a means to an end; it was not the end itself. It may be further observed that as soon as the danger of idolatry was at an end, the isolation of Israel in a great measure ceased. The object of giving the people a land of their own, and supremacy among the surrounding nations, was to enable them to develop the religion which was to prepare the way for Christianity. When the religious principles of the nation were sufficiently fixed to make their political supremacy unnecessary, this supremacy was taken away.

⁽⁵⁾ **Ye shall destroy their altars** . . . .— This course, if adopted in a conquered territory, would be certain to bring matters to a crisis. The inhabitants must rise in defence of the objects of their worship—a course which would end in their extermination—or they must adopt the worship of Jehovah.

Their groves.—Here the grove itself in which the idol was worshipped, and so in chap. xvi. 21. Sometimes the word is used for the image.

Burn their graven images with fire.—David treated the images of the Philistines thus (1 Chron. xiv. 12). Compare Isa. xxxvii. 19.

graven images with fire. *(6) ^a For thou *art* an holy people unto the LORD thy God: ^b the LORD thy God hath chosen thee to be a special people unto himself, above all people that *are* upon the face of the earth. (7) The LORD did not set his love upon you, nor choose you, because ye were more in number than any people; for ye *were* the fewest of all people: (8) but because the LORD loved you, and because he would keep the oath which he had sworn unto your fathers, hath the LORD brought you out with a mighty hand, and redeemed you out of the house of bondmen, from the hand of Pharaoh king of Egypt. (9) Know therefore that the LORD thy God, he *is* God, the faithful God, which keepeth covenant and mercy with them that love him and keep his commandments to a thousand generations; (10) and repayeth them that hate him to their face, to destroy them: he will not be slack to him that hateth him, he will repay him to his face. (11) Thou shalt therefore keep the commandments, and the statutes, and the judgments,

<small>a ch. 14. 2 & 26. 19.

b Ex. 19. 5; 1 Pet. 2. 9.

1 Heb., *because.*

c Ex. 23. 26, &c.

d Ex. 9. 14 & 15. 26.</small>

which I command thee this day, to do them.

(12) Wherefore it shall come to pass, ¹ if ye hearken to these judgments, and keep, and do them, that the LORD thy God shall keep unto thee the covenant and the mercy which he sware unto thy fathers: (13) and he will love thee, and bless thee, and multiply thee: he will also bless the fruit of thy womb, and the fruit of thy land, thy corn, and thy wine, and thine oil, the increase of thy kine, and the flocks of thy sheep, in the land which he sware unto thy fathers to give thee. (14) Thou shalt be blessed above all people: ^c there shall not be male or female barren among you, or among your cattle. (15) And the LORD will take away from thee all sickness, and will put none of the ^d evil diseases of Egypt, which thou knowest, upon thee; but will lay them upon all *them* that hate thee.

(16) And thou shalt consume all the people which the LORD thy God shall deliver thee; thine eye shall have no pity upon them: neither shalt thou

---

(6) **An holy people.**—Not merely "a holy nation" (as in Exod. xix. 6), but "a holy *people*," *i.e.*, a *state* of which holiness to Jehovah was the very constitution. If God pleased to establish such a state, manifestly its laws could allow no toleration of anything displeasing to Him. And it is also manifest that nothing but Divine revelation would authorise the establishment of such a constitution.

A special people.—The same word with the "peculiar treasure" of Exod. xix. 5 and the "jewels" of Mal. iii. 17. The private property of King David is described by the same word (1 Chron. xxix. 3), "mine own proper good." (See also Deut. xiv. 2, xxvi. 18; Ps. cxxxv. 4.)

(7) **The Lord did not . . . choose you, because ye were more.**—The danger lest Israel's peculiar relation to the Most High should beget national pride is so obvious, that Moses takes special pains to counteract it by asserting God's sovereignty in the choice.

Ye were the fewest of all people.—It may be observed that the development of the Moabites, Ammonites, Ishmaelites, and Edomites (all, like Israel, descended from Terah), was far more rapid than that of the chosen line. Abraham had twelve grandsons through Ishmael, but only the same number of *great*-grandsons through Isaac and Jacob. Edom, Moab, and Ammon all preceded Israel in the conquest of territory. Kings reigned in Edom "before there reigned any king over the children of Israel" (Gen. xxxvi. 31). It was only "when the time of the promise drew nigh" that "the (chosen) people grew and multiplied in Egypt." The Scripture is throughout consistent in representing their development as due to the special providence of God. (See also on chap. x. 22.)

(8) **But because the Lord loved you.**—And this, again, was not due to themselves, as he points out fully in chap. ix. 4, &c.

(9—11) These verses are a direct comment upon the second commandment. The "thousands of them that love Him" are here expanded into a "thousand generations." The "hatred," too, is the same thing denoted there: "Thou shalt therefore keep the commandments."

(12) At this point begins the third of the Hebrew divisions of the book.

If ye hearken.—Literally, *as a return for your hearkening.* (See Note on chap. viii. 19.)

(13) **The flocks.**—The word here employed for flocks is peculiar to Deuteronomy in this sense. It occurs in chap. xxviii. 4, 18, 51. It is in form identical with Ashtaroth, and signifies "increase," or progeny.

(14) **All people.**—Literally, *all the peoples*: *i.e.*, all other states and communities.

(15) **Evil diseases.**—The word for diseases here used is found only in Deuteronomy (see chap. xxviii. 60). It must not be forgotten that the law of Moses was in many of its details a sanitary quite as much as a moral code. Some of the associations of this word and the root from which it is derived would seem to point to those "languors" and "infirmities" which arise from neglect and violation of the laws of God, both moral and physical.

(16) **Thou shalt consume** (literally, *eat up*) **all the people which the Lord thy God shall deliver thee.**—When delivered to Israel, they are delivered for execution; but the time of delivery is in the hand of Jehovah. (Comp. the words of Caleb and Joshua in Num. xiv. 9: "*They are bread for us*: their shadow is departed from them, and the Lord is with us.")

God will Help them   DEUTERONOMY, VIII.   *against the Heathen.*

serve their gods; for that *will be* ᵃ a snare unto thee. ⁽¹⁷⁾ If thou shalt say in thine heart, These nations *are* more than I; how can I dispossess them? ⁽¹⁸⁾ thou shalt not be afraid of them: *but* shalt well remember what the LORD thy God did unto Pharaoh, and unto all Egypt; ⁽¹⁹⁾ the great temptations which thine eyes saw, and the signs, and the wonders, and the mighty hand, and the stretched out arm, whereby the LORD thy God brought thee out: so shall the LORD thy God do unto all the people of whom thou art afraid. ⁽²⁰⁾ ᵇ Moreover the LORD thy God will send the hornet among them, until they that are left, and hide themselves from thee, be destroyed. ⁽²¹⁾ Thou shalt not be affrighted at them: for the LORD thy God *is* among you, a mighty God and terrible. ⁽²²⁾ And the LORD thy God will ¹ put out those nations before thee by little and little: thou mayest not consume them at once, lest the beasts of the field increase upon thee. ⁽²³⁾ But the LORD thy God shall deliver them ² unto thee, and shall destroy them with a mighty destruction, until they be destroyed. ⁽²⁴⁾ And he shall deliver their kings into thine hand, and thou shalt destroy their name from under heaven: there shall no man be able to stand before thee, until thou have destroyed them. ⁽²⁵⁾ The graven images of their gods ᶜ shall ye burn with fire: thou ᵈ shalt not desire the silver or gold *that is* on them, nor take *it* unto thee, lest thou be snared therein: for it *is* an abomination to the LORD thy God. ⁽²⁶⁾ Neither shalt thou bring an abomination into thine house, lest thou be a cursed thing like it: *but* thou shalt utterly detest it, and thou shalt utterly abhor it; ᵉfor it *is* a cursed thing.

CHAPTER VIII.—⁽¹⁾ All the commandments which I command thee this day shall ye observe to do, that ye may live, and multiply, and go in and possess the land which the LORD sware unto your fathers. ⁽²⁾ And thou shalt remember all the way which the LORD thy God led thee these forty years in the wilderness, to humble thee, *and* to

a Ex. 23. 33.

b Ex. 23. 28; Josh. 24. 12.

1 Heb., *pluck off.*

2 Heb., *before thy face.*

c ch. 12. 3.

d Josh. 7. 1, 21; 2 Mac. 12. 40.

e ch. 13. 17.

⁽¹⁸⁾ **Thou shalt not be afraid of them: but shalt well remember . . . Egypt.**—No free nation could ever have the same ground for terror as a nation of slaves rising up against its masters. If Israel had been delivered by Jehovah in *that* position, it was a security for all time that He would give them the victory in every enterprise He called them to undertake.

⁽¹⁹⁾ **The great temptations.**—The several repetitions of the summons to Pharaoh that he should let Israel go, accompanied and enforced by plagues, may well be called "temptations" in the sense of *trials* of his character. The word "temptation" in the sense of "inducement to sin" is very rare, if not absolutely wanting, in the Old Testament.

⁽²⁰⁾ **The hornet.**—To be understood literally. (See on chap. i. 44, and Josh. xxiv. 12.) The "land flowing with (milk and) honey" may well have swarmed with bees and hornets.

⁽²²⁾ **The Lord thy God will put out.**—The word for "putting out" is illustrated by its use in chap. xix. 5, of the axe-head flying off from the handle in the midst of a blow, and of the olive "casting" his fruit in chap. xxviii. 40. (Comp. also 2 Kings xvi. 6, and 1 Sam. xxv. 29, for a similar thought.)

By little and little.—This confirms the view already expressed, that the expulsion of each particular nation was contingent upon the Divine decree, and that none were to be attacked by Israel except when the Lord should deliver them into Israel's hand.

⁽²⁴⁾ **He shall deliver their kings into thine hand.**—In the summary of Joshua's conquest (Josh. xii.) the kings are reckoned for the cities. Special mention is made of seven of them, who were hanged.

There shall no man be able to stand before thee.—A promise personally renewed to Joshua (chap. i. 5), and fulfilled to Israel under his command (Josh. xx. 44).

⁽²⁵, ²⁶⁾ These words are a special warning against the sin which Achan committed (Josh. vii. 21): "I coveted them, and took them." They also describe the consequences which he experienced, together with his whole household, being made *chérem*, devoted or accursed by the spoil which he took from Jericho. (See on Josh. vii.)

VIII.

⁽¹⁾ **All the commandments.**—Perhaps this verse should be placed at the conclusion of the preceding paragraph rather than at the commencement of the next. The second verse of this chapter introduces a fresh branch of the subject.

That ye may . . . go in and possess.—This does not refer simply to the passage of Jordan and the first conquest under Joshua so much as to that work of possession in detail which Joshua left for Israel to do after their first establishment in the country. On this distinction, see Josh. xiii. 1, 7 (Note).

THE REMEMBRANCE OF THE EXODUS.

⁽²⁾ **And thou shalt remember.**—The whole of the remainder of this exhortation, to the end of chap. x., is chiefly taken up with this topic. Israel must remember (1) the leading of Jehovah, and (2) their own rebellious perversity in the journey through the wilderness. The same recollection is made the occasion for a separate note of praise in Ps. cxxxvi. 16: "To him which *led his people through the wilderness*; for his mercy endureth for ever."

The way which the Lord thy God led thee these forty years.—Not so much the literal journey,

prove thee, to know what *was* in thine heart, whether thou wouldest keep his commandments, or no. (3) And he humbled thee, and suffered thee to hunger, and fed thee with manna, which thou knewest not, neither did thy fathers know; that he might make thee know that man doth *a* not live by bread only, but by every *word* that proceedeth out of the mouth of the LORD doth man live. (4) *b* Thy raiment waxed not old upon thee, neither did thy foot swell, these forty years. (5) Thou shalt also consider in thine heart, that, as a man

a Matt. 4. 4; Luke 4. 4.

b Neh. 9. 21.

but "the way:" *i.e.*, the manner. The details of the actual journey are of course included, but only as incidents of "the way." In the Acts of the Apostles the Christian life is in several passages called "the way." In all these things the Israelites were types of us.

To humble thee, and to prove thee.—The way in itself is described as "three days' journey into the wilderness," so far as the leading to Sinai is concerned (Exod. iii. 18), and "eleven days' journey from Horeb to Kadesh-barnea" (Deut. i. 2). It was in the power of Jehovah to bring Israel from Egypt to Canaan, had He so willed it, without delay, in a very little time. And just so with "the way" of salvation. There is no intrinsic or necessary impossibility in the *immediate* turning of mankind, or of any individual, from darkness to light. And this change might be followed by immediate removal from "this present evil world" into the place which Christ has gone before to prepare for us. But manifestly the formation of human character by probation and training would vanish in such a process as this. There could be no well-tried and deliberate purpose to serve our Creator and Redeemer in any of us—or, at least, *no proof* of our deliberate preference for His service—under such circumstances. Nor, again, could there be that *humility* which arises only out of self-knowledge. The transitory nature of all mere human resolutions and impressions for good demonstrates to the man who knows himself, better than anything else could do, the power and patience of his Redeemer, and the moral cost of his redemption. This human *transitoriness* and feebleness is strikingly illustrated by the story of the Exodus.

To know what was in thine heart.—"To know" is not simply that *He* might know ("Hell and destruction are before the Lord; how much more then the hearts of the children of men!"), but *that the knowledge may arise*—to *determine*, disclose, discover. So in 2 Chron. xxxii. 31: "God left him (Hezekiah) to try him, *to know* all that was in his heart." What God Himself knows by omniscience He sometimes brings to light by evidence for the sake of His creatures. (Comp. Ephesians iii. 10: "To the intent that now unto the principalities and powers in heavenly places *might be known* by (by means of) the church the manifold wisdom of God.")

(3) **And he ... suffered thee to hunger, and fed thee.**—A process naturally humbling. He might easily have fed them without "suffering them to hunger." But He did not give them the manna until the sixteenth day of the second month of the journey (see Exodus xvi. 1, 6, 7); and for one whole month they were left to their own resources. When it appeared that the people had no means of providing sustenance during their journey, "they saw the glory of the Lord" in the way in which He fed them; and for thirty-nine years and eleven months "He withheld not His manna from their mouth."

Manna, which thou knewest not.—Its very name (but see Note on Exod. xvi. 15) commemorates the fact "unto this day." All the natural things which have been called manna (and Dr. Cunningham Geikie, in "Hours with the Bible," has described several) do not afford the least explanation of the bread which God gave Israel to eat.

That man doth not live by bread only, but by every word that proceedeth out of the mouth of the Lord.—Not here alone, but throughout the Law, as in the Gospel, we are taught that life is to do the will of God. Our Saviour called that "My meat." *What* the visible means of subsistence may be is a secondary matter. Man's life is to do the will of God: "My commandments, which, if a man do, he shall even live in them." "He that doeth the will of God abideth for ever."

But the special interest of these words arises from our Lord's use of them in the hour of temptation. He also was led forty days (each day for a year of the Exodus) in the wilderness, living upon the word of God. At the end of that time it was proposed to Him to create bread for Himself. But He had learnt the lesson which Israel was to learn; and so, even when God suffered Him to hunger, He still refused to live by His own word. He preferred that of His Father. "And the angels came and ministered unto Him." It is noticeable that *all* our Lord's answers to the tempter are taken from this exhortation upon the Decalogue in Deut. vi.—x.

(4) **Thy raiment waxed not old upon thee.** —The Jewish commentators say that it grew with their growth, from childhood to manhood. We cannot say that anything miraculous is certainly intended, though it is not impossible. It may mean that God in His providence directed them to clothe themselves in a manner suitable to their journey and their mode of life, just as He taught them how to make and clothe His own tabernacle with various fabrics and coverings of skin. This tabernacle, which was God's dwelling, was (like the Temple) a figure of man. (Comp. Ezek. xvi. 10: "I clothed thee also with broidered work, and shod thee with badgers' skin.")

Neither did thy foot swell.—Just as those who were to die in the wilderness could not live, so those who were to enter Canaan were preserved in health through the journey thither. It seems allowable to point out the spiritual interpretation of the passage also. If "the way" that God leads any of His children through this present evil world should seem long, and should entail constant need of renewal and cleansing in His sight, He provides us with "raiment that waxes not old," in the everlasting righteousness of His Son, and also in the good works which He prepares for us to walk in—that "fine linen which is the righteousness of saints." He also says of those that wait on the Lord that they shall "walk, and not faint" (Isa. xl. 31).

(5) **As a man chasteneth his son.**—This is the foundation of many similar sayings in Holy Scripture: Prov. xiii. 24, "He *seeketh* chastening for him," *i.e.*, seeks it early. All our ideas of training necessarily imply time; it cannot be done in a moment. But the main point of the illustration is to *prove God's love.*

They are to Remember   DEUTERONOMY, VIII.   *God's Goodness to them.*

chasteneth his son, so the LORD thy God chasteneth thee. ⁽⁶⁾ Therefore thou shalt keep the commandments of the LORD thy God, to walk in his ways, and to fear him.

⁽⁷⁾ For the LORD thy God bringeth thee into a good land, a land of brooks of water, of fountains and depths that spring out of valleys and hills; ⁽⁸⁾ a land of wheat, and barley, and vines, and fig trees, and pomegranates; a land [1] of oil olive, and honey; ⁽⁹⁾ a land wherein thou shalt eat bread without scarceness, thou shalt not lack any *thing* in it; a land whose stones *are* iron, and out of whose hills thou mayest dig brass.

⁽¹⁰⁾ *a* When thou hast eaten and art full, then thou shalt bless the LORD thy God for the good land which he hath given thee. ⁽¹¹⁾ Beware that thou forget not the LORD thy God, in not keeping his commandments, and his judgments, and his statutes, which I command thee this day: ⁽¹²⁾ lest *when* thou hast eaten and art full, and hast built goodly houses, and dwelt *therein;* ⁽¹³⁾ and *when* thy herds and thy flocks multiply, and thy silver and thy gold is multiplied, and all that thou hast is multiplied;

⁽¹⁴⁾ then thine heart be lifted up, and thou forget the LORD thy God, which brought thee forth out of the land of Egypt, from the house of bondage; ⁽¹⁵⁾ who led thee through that great and terrible wilderness, *wherein were* fiery serpents, and scorpions, and drought, where *there was* no water; *b* who brought thee forth water out of the rock of flint; ⁽¹⁶⁾ who fed thee in the wilderness with *c* manna, which thy fathers knew not, that he might humble thee, and that he might prove thee, to do thee good at thy latter end; ⁽¹⁷⁾ and thou say in thine heart, My power and the might of *mine* hand hath gotten me this wealth. ⁽¹⁸⁾ But thou shalt remember the LORD thy God: for *it is* he that giveth thee power to get wealth, that he may establish his covenant which he sware unto thy fathers, as *it is* this day.

⁽¹⁹⁾ And it shall be, if thou do at all forget the LORD thy God, and walk after other gods, and serve them, and worship them, I testify against you this day that ye shall surely perish. ⁽²⁰⁾ As the nations which the LORD destroyeth before your face, so shall ye perish; because ye would not be obedient unto the voice of the LORD your God.

[1 Heb., *of olive trees of oil.*]
[a ch. 6. 12, 13.]
[b Num. 20. 11.]
[c Ex. 16. 15.]

" Whom the Lord loveth, He chasteneth; " else, why should He be at the pains to chasten at all?

⁽⁷⁾ **For the Lord thy God bringeth thee into a good land.**—The description in this and the following verses is most attractive; but it is a long time since any one has seen Palestine in that condition. Its desolation, no less than its beauty, is a proof of the truth of the Divine word.

Of fountains and depths that spring out. —Rather, *that go forth in the valley and on the hill.* The watercourse down the mountain-side, and the deep lake or still pool below, are both described here.

⁽⁹⁾ **Whose stones are iron, and out of whose hills thou mayest dig brass.**—We do not hear of mining operations in Palestine from sacred history. "Brass," *i.e.*, copper; and in all passages.

⁽¹⁰⁾ **When thou hast eaten.**—Literally, *and thou shalt eat and be satisfied, and shalt bless the Lord thy God.* There is a saying in the Talmud (*Berachoth*, p. 35 a.), "It is forbidden to any man to take any enjoyment from this present world without thanksgiving; and every one who does so is a transgressor."

⁽¹¹⁾ **Beware that.**—From verse 11 to verse 18 inclusive is one long sentence in the Hebrew, and may be taken thus: " Take heed to thyself *lest* thou forget Jehovah thy God (so that thou keep not, &c.); *lest* thou eat and be satisfied (while thou buildest, &c.); and thine heart be lifted up, and thou forget Jehovah (thy deliverer, thy leader, thy sustainer), and say in thine heart, My power, &c.; and (take heed) *that thou remember* Jehovah thy God, that it is He that giveth thee power to get wealth," &c. The caution is prophetic, as may be seen by the following examples:—

" When Rehoboam had . . . strengthened himself, he forsook the law of the Lord, and all Israel with him " (2 Chron. xii. 1).

" But when he (Uzziah) was strong, his heart was lifted up to his destruction " (2 Chron. xxvi. 16).

" Hezekiah rendered not again according to the benefit done unto him; for his heart was lifted up " (2 Chron. xxxii. 25).

Other instances might easily be added.

⁽¹²⁾ **Hast built goodly houses.**—One of the conditions prescribed by Jonadab the son of Rechab to his family was, " All your days ye shall *dwell in tents;* that ye may live many days in the land *where ye be strangers*" (Jer. xxxv. 7).

⁽¹⁵⁾ **The rock of flint.**—The rock in Horeb is called *tsûr;* the rock smitten in Kadesh, *selagh.* The first word conveys the idea of "hardness"; the other is rather a "cliff," or "height," and suggests the idea of inaccessibility. In Num. xx. 10, the words of Moses to the rebels, " Must we fetch you water out of this rock?" seem to help the distinction, whatever its purpose may be. On the associations of the word *tsûr* with flint, see Note on Josh. v. 2. The word *challâmish,* here used for flint, occurs in chap. xxxii. 13, Job xxviii. 9, Ps. cxiv. 8 (an allusion to this passage), and Isa. l. 7.

⁽²⁰⁾ **Because ye would not be obedient.**— In return for your disobedience. The same word is employed in chap. vii. 12. The use of the word in these two places might fairly be taken to mark off the intervening portion as a complete section of the discourse.

CHAPTER IX.—(1) Hear, O Israel: Thou *art* to pass over Jordan this day, to go in to possess nations greater and mightier than thyself, cities great and fenced up to heaven, (2) a people great and tall, *a* the children of the Anakims, whom thou knowest, and *of whom* thou hast heard *say*, Who can stand before the children of Anak! (3) Understand therefore this day, that the LORD thy God *is* he which goeth over before thee; as a *b* consuming fire he shall destroy them, and he shall bring them down before thy face: so shalt thou drive them out, and destroy them quickly, as the LORD hath said unto thee.

(4) Speak not thou in thine heart, after that the LORD thy God hath cast them out from before thee, saying, For my righteousness the LORD hath brought me in to possess this land: but for the wickedness of these nations the LORD doth drive them out from before thee. (5) Not for thy righteousness, or for the uprightness of thine heart, dost thou go to possess their land: but for the wickedness of these nations the LORD thy God doth drive them out from before thee, and that he may perform the word which the LORD sware unto thy fathers, Abraham, Isaac, and Jacob.

(6) Understand therefore, that the LORD thy God giveth thee not this good land to possess it for thy righteousness; for thou *art* a stiffnecked people. (7) Remember, *and* forget not, how thou provokedst the LORD thy God to wrath in the wilderness: from the day that thou didst depart out of the land of Egypt, until ye came unto this place, ye have been rebellious against the LORD. (8) Also in Horeb ye provoked the LORD to wrath, so that the LORD was angry with you to have destroyed you.

(9) When I was gone up into the mount to receive the tables of stone, *even* the tables of the covenant which the LORD made with you, then *c* I abode in the mount forty days and forty nights, I neither did eat bread nor drink water: (10) *d* and the LORD delivered unto me two tables of stone written

a Num. 13. 28.

b ch. 4. 24; Heb. 12. 29.

c Ex. 24. 18 & 34. 28.

B.C. 1491.

d Ex. 31. 18.

IX.

EXHORTATION TO REMEMBER THE SINS OF THE EXODUS.

(1) **Hear, O Israel.**—A fresh portion of the exhortation begins here. The cause of Israel's conquest of Canaan is not to be sought in their own merit, but in the choice of Jehovah.

Thou art to pass.—Literally, *thou art passing*: *i.e.*, just about to pass.

Nations greater and mightier than thyself. —If this is true (and there is no reason to doubt it), the responsibility of the conquest does not rest with Israel; they were the Divine executioners. (See Note on Josh. v. 13, 14.)

Cities . . . fenced up to heaven.—Comp. the expression in Gen. xi. 4, "a city and a tower whose top may reach unto (literally, *is in*) heaven." So here, "cities great and fortified *in the heavens*." Was St. Paul thinking of this expression when he said, "We wrestle against spiritual wickedness *in the heavenly regions?*" (Eph. v. 12).

(2) **Whom thou knowest.**—The pronoun is emphatic. The twelve spies, two of whom were still living, had seen them (Num. xiii. 33), and their fame was doubtless notorious. It seems to have been a common saying, possibly among the Anakim themselves, "Who will stand up to the children of Anak?" No one could be found to face them.

(3) **Understand therefore.**—Literally, the connection seems to be this: "The children of Anakim thou knowest—*thou knowest also* (the same word) to-day, that it is Jehovah thy God Himself that passeth over before thee, a consuming fire. He will destroy them, and He will make them to bow down before thee. And thou shalt make a conquest of them, and speedily annihilate them, according as Jehovah hath commanded thee."

(4) **But for the wickedness.**—"Say not in thine heart, 'in my righteousness,' *when it is* in consequence of their wickedness that Jehovah is dispossessing them from before thee."

(5) **Not for thy righteousness . . . dost thou go.**—The pronoun is emphatic. There is no reason why *thou* of all others shouldest be thus honoured.

(6) **Understand therefore.**—Literally, *and thou knowest*. Three times the formula occurs in these verses. "The children of Anak thou knowest; and thou knowest the Lord thy God; and (thirdly) thou knowest thyself too."

A stiffnecked people.—The metaphor seems to be taken from a camel or other beast of burden, who hardens his neck, and will not bend it for the driver.

(7) **Remember, and forget not.**—More abruptly in the original, "Remember—do not forget—how thou hast stirred the indignation of Jehovah."

Rebellious.—Not simply rebels, as Moses called them (in Num. xx. 10) at Meribah, but *provoking rebels* —rebels who rouse the opposition of Him against whom they rebel.

(8) **Also.**—*Even in Horeb.* In the very sight of the mountain of the Law, the Law was flagrantly violated.

(9) **I neither did eat bread nor drink water.** —This fact is not related in Exodus concerning the *first* forty days which Moses spent in Mount Sinai "with his minister Joshua." It might be supposed or implied, but it is not recorded.

(10) **Two tables of stone.**—Of these tables it is said in Exod. xxxii. 16, "the *tables* were the *work* of God, and *the writing was the writing* of God, graven upon the tables."

with the finger of God: and on them *was written* according to all the words, which the LORD spake with you in the mount out of the midst of the fire in the day of the assembly. (11) And it came to pass at the end of forty days and forty nights, *that* the LORD gave me the two tables of stone, *even* the tables of the covenant. (12) And the LORD said unto me, *a* Arise, get thee down quickly from hence; for thy people which thou hast brought forth out of Egypt have corrupted *themselves;* they are quickly turned aside out of the way which I commanded them; they have made them a molten image.

(13) Furthermore the LORD spake unto me, saying, I have seen this people, and, behold, it *is* a stiffnecked people: (14) let me alone, that I may destroy them, and blot out their name from under heaven: and I will make of thee a nation mightier and greater than they. (15) So I turned and came down from the mount, and the mount burned with fire: and the two tables of the covenant *were* in my two hands. (16) And I looked, and, behold, ye had sinned against the LORD your God, *and* had made you a molten calf: ye had turned aside quickly out of the way which the LORD had commanded you. (17) And I took the two tables, and cast them out of my two hands, and brake them before your eyes. (18) And I fell down before the LORD, as at the first, forty days and forty nights: I did neither eat bread, nor drink water, because of all your sins which ye sinned, in doing wickedly in the sight of the LORD, to provoke him to anger. (19) For I was afraid of the anger and hot displeasure, wherewith the LORD was wroth against you to destroy you. But the LORD hearkened unto me at that time also. (20) And the LORD was very angry with Aaron to have destroyed him: and I prayed for Aaron also the same time. (21) And I took your sin, the calf which ye had made, and burnt it with fire, and stamped it, *and* ground *it* very small, *even* until it was as small as dust: and I cast the dust thereof into the brook that descended out of the mount.

(22) And at *b* Taberah, and at *c* Massah, and at *d* Kibroth-hattaavah, ye provoked the LORD to wrath. (23) Likewise when the LORD sent you from Kadesh-barnea, saying, Go up and possess the land which I have given you;

a Ex. 32. 7.

b Num. 11. 1, 3.

c Ex. 17. 7.

d Num. 11. 34.

---

(12) **Arise, get thee down.**—The words recorded here and in verses 13, 14, are given at length in Exod. xxxii. 7, &c. Moses' intercession at *that time* is recorded also.

(15) **So I turned . . .**—This verse nearly repeats Exod. xxxii. 15.

(16) **Ye had turned aside quickly.**—The words of Jehovah in verse 16, repeated here, and also recorded in Exod. xxxii. 8. There is nothing so sad in human experience as the rapidity with which good resolutions and impressions fade from the natural heart of man.

(17) **I . . . brake them before your eyes.**—This shows that the act was deliberate on Moses' part. He did not simply drop the tables in his passion before they reached the camp; he deliberately broke the material covenant in the face of the people, who had broken the covenant itself. When we remember the effect of hastily touching *not the tables of the Law themselves, but the mere chest that contained them,* in after-times, we may well believe that the breaking of these two tables was an act necessary for the safety of Israel. In Exod. xxxiii. 7, we read that Moses placed the temporary tabernacle outside the camp at the same time. The two actions seem to have had the same significance, and to have been done for the same reason.

(18) **And I fell down before the Lord, as at the first, forty days and forty nights.**—Moses had already interceded for them in Sinai before he came down on the fortieth day (Exod. xxxii. 11—14). He now spent forty days and nights in the work of intercession. We are not to understand that the first forty were so spent. At that time he received the pattern of the tabernacle and the directions for the priesthood, which he did not deliver to Israel until after he descended from Sinai the second time. (See Exod. xxiv. 18 to xxxi., and xxxv. 1, &c.) During the first forty days, Joshua was with Moses in the mount (probably to help in taking the pattern for the tabernacle); during the second forty Moses was alone.

(19) **For I was afraid.**—In Heb. xii. 21, the words " I exceedingly fear " are (in the Greek) identical with these.

(20) **I prayed for Aaron also.**—Jewish commentators ascribe the loss of Aaron's two sons (Lev. x. 1, 2) partly to God's anger at this time.

(21) **I took your sin . . . and I cast the dust thereof into the brook.**—The stream from the rock in Horeb not only gave Israel drink, but bore away their " sin " upon its waters. " And that Rock was Christ." This identification of the sin with the material object is in harmony with the Law in Leviticus, where " sin " and " sin-offering "—" trespass " and " trespass-offering "—are respectively denoted by a single word.

(22) **At Taberah.**—The first place mentioned after they left Sinai.

At Massah.—The last scene described before they reached it. Sinai is made the centre of provocation.

At Kibroth-hattaavah.—The first *encampment* named after Sinai. It is not certain that they halted at Taberah. (See Num. xi.)

(23) **Ye rebelled against the commandment.**—Literally, *the mouth of Jehovah.*

then ye rebelled against the commandment of the LORD your God, and ye believed him not, nor hearkened to his voice. (24) Ye have been rebellious against the LORD from the day that I knew you.

(25) Thus I fell down before the LORD forty days and forty nights, as I fell down *at the first;* because the LORD had said he would destroy you. (26) I prayed therefore unto the LORD, and said, O Lord GOD, destroy not thy people and thine inheritance, which thou hast redeemed through thy greatness, which thou hast brought forth out of Egypt with a mighty hand. (27) Remember thy servants, Abraham, Isaac, and Jacob; look not unto the stubbornness of this people, nor to their wickedness, nor to their sin: (28) lest the land whence thou broughtest us out say, *a* Because the LORD was not able to bring them into the land which he promised them, and because he hated them, he hath brought them out to slay them in the wilderness. (29) Yet they *are* thy people and thine inheritance, which thou broughtest out by thy mighty power and by thy stretched out arm.

CHAPTER X.—(1) At that time the LORD said unto me, *b* Hew thee two tables of stone like unto the first, and come up unto me into the mount, and make thee an ark of wood. (2) And I will write on the tables the words that were in the first tables which thou brakest, and thou shalt put them in the ark. (3) And I made an ark *of* shittim wood, and hewed two tables of stone like unto the first, and went up into the mount, having the two tables in mine hand. (4) And he wrote on the tables, according to the first writing, the ten ¹ commandments, which the LORD spake unto you in the mount out of the midst of the

a Num. 14. 16.

b Ex. 34. 1.

¹ Heb., *words.*

Ye believed him not—when He encouraged you to go up.

Nor hearkened to his voice—when He forbad you. (See on chap. i. 32, 43.)

(24) **Ye have been rebellious against the Lord from the day that I knew you.**—This is one side of the truth. The other may be found in the words of Balaam, which Jehovah Himself put into his mouth: "He hath not *beheld* iniquity in Jacob, nor *seen* perverseness in Israel" (Num. xxiii. 21). (See also Deut. xxxi. 16.)

(25) **Thus I fell down . . .**—Literally, *And I fell down before Jehovah forty days and forty nights, as I had fallen down* (originally on the fortieth day) *when the Lord said He would destroy you:* i.e., when He told Moses of the calf.

(26) **I prayed therefore . . . and said.**—The words that follow are very similar to those which are recorded in Exod. xxxii. 11—13. Moses appears to be alluding to his *first intercession* here, before he descended from Sinai for the first time.

(27) **Remember thy servants, Abraham, Isaac, and Jacob.**—This is found exactly in Exod. xxxii. 13. Very few of the words used by Moses in the *second forty days* are found in Exodus. (See Exod. xxxiv. 9.)

(29) **Thy people . . . which thou broughtest out.**—So Exod. xxxii. 11. It is noticeable that God said to Moses, "*Thy* people which *thou* broughtest out . . . have corrupted themselves" (Exod. xxxii. 7). Moses said, "Lord, why doth thy wrath wax hot against *thy people which thou hast brought forth?*"

X.

(1) **At that time the Lord said unto me.**—The forty days of intercession alluded to in the previous chapter followed this command (Exod. xxxiv. i. 28).

Hew thee two tables of stone . . . and make thee an ark.—The command to make the ark was given in the former period of forty days (Exod. xxv. 10); the command to hew the two tables was given after Moses had seen the glory of God (Exod. xxxiii.) from the cleft in the rock, but before the forty days spent in intercession. Rashi, the Jewish commentator, thinks there were two arks: one to go out to war, and the other to remain in the tabernacle. But there is no foundation for this statement. There may, of course, have been a temporary receptacle for the tables made by Moses (like the temporary tabernacle mentioned in Exod. xxxiii. 7), to receive them until the completion of the ark which Bezaleel was to make. This was not put in hand until after Moses descended with the second pair of tables. (See Exod. xxxv. &c.)

(2) **And I will write on the tables.**—It is a common error to suppose that *Moses wrote* the Law the second time. The mistake arises from the change of person in Exod. xxxiv. 28, where the same pronoun "he" refers first to Moses, and then to Jehovah. But there is no doubt as to the fact or its spiritual meaning. The tables of stone represent the "fleshy tables of the heart," as St. Paul teaches us in 2 Cor. iii. 3. The first pair of tables were like the heart of Adam, which came fresh from the hand of his Maker, with the word of the Law written on them. But this perished by the fall, beneath the mountain of the Law. The humanity which ascended to receive the Spirit for us was prepared by the Mediator on earth. The "second man" receives "the new covenant," "not the letter, but the Spirit," which puts God's laws in men's minds, and writes them in their hearts, making them God's temple. Thus the ark and the tabernacle which received the Law are a figure of God's human temple, and of the renewed heart of man.

(4) **According to the first writing, the ten commandments.**—The words written on the second tables were the same which had been written on the first.

In the day of the assembly.—Or, in New Testament language, "the day of the Church." The Pentecost of the Old Testament was the day when "the letter" was given; the Pentecost of the New

fire in the day of the assembly: and the LORD gave them unto me. ⁽⁵⁾ And I turned myself and came down from the mount, and put the tables in the ark which I had made; and there they be, as the LORD commanded me.

⁽⁶⁾ And the children of Israel took their journey from Beeroth of the children of Jaakan to ᵃ Mosera: ᵇ there Aaron died: and there he was buried; and Eleazar his son ministered in the priest's office in his stead. ⁽⁷⁾ From thence they journeyed unto Gudgodah; and from Gudgodah to Jotbath, a land of rivers of waters.

⁽⁸⁾ At that time the LORD separated the tribe of Levi, to bear the ark of the covenant of the LORD, to stand before the LORD to minister unto him, and to bless in his name, unto this day. ⁽⁹⁾ ᶜ Wherefore Levi hath no part nor inheritance with his brethren; the LORD is his inheritance, according as the LORD thy God promised him. ⁽¹⁰⁾ And I stayed in the mount, according to the ¹ first time, forty days and forty nights; and the LORD hearkened unto me at that time also, and the LORD would not destroy thee. ⁽¹¹⁾ And the LORD said unto me, Arise, ² take thy journey before the people, that they may go in and possess the land, which I sware unto their fathers to give unto them.

a Num. 33. 30.

b Num. 20. 28.

c Num. 18. 20.

¹ Or, *former days*.

² Heb., *go in journey*.

Testament was the day of the "Spirit that giveth life." Each of these aspects of God's covenant produced a Church after its kind.

⁽⁵⁾ **I . . . put the tables in the ark which I (had) made; and there they be.**—Or, *and they were there*, or *they continued there*. According to the narrative in Exodus, the ark in which the tables ultimately remained was made afterwards. The English reader must not be misled by the word "had" in "I *had* made." There is no pluperfect in Hebrew. The time of an action is determined not so much by the form of the verb as by its relation to the context. "I put the tables in the ark which *I made*, and they remained there," is the literal sense. "I made" may very well mean "I caused to be made," and refers to the ark which Bezaleel constructed under Moses' directions.

(6, 7) On these verses, which are among the most difficult in Deuteronomy, see a separate Excursus. The difficulty is two-fold. First, the account of Israel's marches about the time of Aaron's death is given in a different form here to that which we have in Num. xx., xxi., and xxxiii. Secondly, there is the further question why Aaron's death should be recorded here. It appears to have taken place before Moses began the delivery of the discourses in Deuteronomy. It is separated by thirty-nine years from the incidents which Moses is recapitulating in this passage. The Jewish commentator Rashi gives a very curious tale to account for the allusion to Aaron's death in this place. But though his theory is mythical, he seems to hit the main point, which is that Israel *re-visited* in their journey round the land of Edom four places where they had previously encamped, and among them Mosera, or Moseroth, the district in which Mount Hor, where Aaron died, was situated. There is no impossibility in this; in fact, it is highly probable, and would partly account for the statement in Num. xxi. 4, that "the soul of the people was much discouraged because of the way." It was just about this time that the fiery serpents came.

If the connection of these verses with the train of thought in Moses' mind is *spiritual*, the difficulty may be solved. *The death of the priest of Israel*, whose first representative Aaron was, is spiritually identical with the destruction of the first pair of tables, the death of the first Adam and of all mankind in the person of our representative, the Lord Jesus Christ. After that death He "ariseth" as "another priest, made not after the law of a carnal commandment, but after the power of an endless life." Thus the incident is connected with what goes before. The separation of the tribe of Levi "to bear the ark of the covenant of the Lord," i.e., "to bear the burden of the Law," is the same thing in another form. It deprives them of an earthly inheritance, just as He whose representatives they were gave Himself an offering and sacrifice to God; and "His life is taken from the earth."

Further, the names of the places themselves have in this aspect a spiritual significance. From certain "wells of water"—the wells of the children of Jaakan (crookedness)—the people of God take their journey to the scene of the high priest's death. From thence to Hor-hagidgad, or Gudgodah, the mount of the "troop," or "band" (Sinai is the mount of the "congregation" in the Old Testament, Zion in the New), and thence to a *land of rivers of water*. It is only another way of relating how from the wells of the Law we pass to the rivers of living water opened by the Gospel. But we must pass *by way of the cross of Christ*.

⁽⁸⁾ **At that time**—*i.e.*, at Sinai, after Moses' second descent from the mount, not at the time of Aaron's death. Yet the death of Aaron and the separation of the tribe of Levi are similar events in their way: both alike lose territorial inheritance through bearing the burden of the Law.

To bear the ark of the covenant of the Lord, to stand before the Lord to minister unto him, and to bless in his name.—A recent critic has said that the writer of Deuteronomy knows no distinction between priests and Levites. (See on this point chap. xi. 6.) Rashi's note on this verse is better: "To bear the ark (He separated)—*the Levites;* to stand before Jehovah to minister to Him, and to bless in His name—*the priests*."

⁽⁹⁾ **The Lord is his inheritance.**—As He was the inheritance of Aaron, Moses' brother, whom he had recently taken to Himself, and to whose death Moses had just referred.

⁽¹¹⁾ **And the Lord said unto me, Arise, take thy journey before the people, that they may go in.**—"Although ye had turned aside from following Him, and had erred in the (matter of the) calf, He said to me, Go, lead the people" (Rashi).

(12) And now, Israel, what doth the LORD thy God require of thee, but to fear the LORD thy God, to walk in all his ways, and to love him, and to serve the LORD thy God with all thy heart and with all thy soul, (13) to keep the commandments of the LORD, and his statutes, which I command thee this day for thy good? (14) Behold, the heaven and the heaven of heavens is the LORD'S thy God, *a* the earth *also*, with all that therein *is*. (15) Only the LORD had a delight in thy fathers to love them, and he chose their seed after them, *even* you above all people, as *it is* this day. (16) Circumcise therefore the foreskin of your heart, and be no more stiffnecked. (17) For the LORD your God *is* God of gods, and Lord of lords, a great God, a mighty, and a terrible, which *b* regardeth not persons, nor taketh reward: (18) he doth execute the judgment of the fatherless and widow, and loveth the stranger, in giving him food and raiment. (19) Love ye therefore the stranger: for ye were strangers in the land of Egypt. (20) *c* Thou shalt fear the LORD thy God; him shalt thou serve, and to him shalt thou *d* cleave, and swear by his name. (21) He *is* thy praise, and he *is* thy God, that hath done for thee these great and terrible things, which thine eyes have seen. (22) Thy fathers went down into Egypt *e* with threescore and ten persons; and now the LORD thy God hath made thee *f* as the stars of heaven for multitude.

CHAPTER XI.—(1) Therefore thou shalt love the LORD thy God, and keep his charge, and his statutes, and his judgments, and his commandments, alway.

a Ps. 24. 1.

b 2 Chron. 19. 7; Job. 34. 19, Acts 10. 34; Rom. 2. 11; Gal. 2. 6.; Eph. 6. 9; Col. 3. 25; 1 Pet. 1. 17.

c ch. 6. 13; Matt. 4. 10; Luke 4. 8.

d ch. 13. 4.

e Gen. 46. 27; Ex. 1. 5.

f Gen. 15. 5.

(12) **And now, Israel, what doth the Lord thy God require of thee.**—"Although ye have done all this, still His tender mercies and His affection are set upon you, and after all that ye have sinned before Him, He doth not ask anything of you but to fear," &c. (Rashi). The Rabbis have drawn this exposition from hence: "Everything is in the hand of Heaven (to bestow), save only the fear of Heaven." But it is written elsewhere, "I will put my fear in their hearts, that they shall not depart from me." (Comp. also Micah vi. 8; Matt. xxiii. 23.)

(15) **Only.**—"The whole world belongs to Jehovah, and for all that He chose thy fathers above all people."

(16) **Circumcise . . . your heart.**—"For circumcision is that of the heart, in the spirit, and not in the letter" (Rom. ii. 29). The verse literally runs thus: *Circumcise the foreskin of your heart, and ye will harden your neck no more*. It is the same line of thought as St. Paul's (Gal. v. 16) "Walk in the Spirit, and (then) ye will not fulfil the lust of the flesh."

(17, 18) **A great God, a mighty, and a terrible . . . he doth execute the judgment of the fatherless and widow.**—"Behold (says Rashi) His might! And close beside His might thou mayest find His humility." It is not otherwise in later passages of Scripture: "He healeth the broken in heart, and bindeth up their wounds. *He telleth the number of the stars*, and calleth them all by their names."

(18) **And loveth the stranger, in giving him food and raiment.**—An inclusive expression. The whole substance of Jacob our father was included in the prayer for this. "If God will . . . give me bread to eat and raiment to put on" (Rashi).

(19) **For ye were strangers.**—"The blemish which is upon thyself thou shalt not notice in thy neighbour" (Rashi). The provision made for the stranger throughout the Old Testament Scriptures has another cause besides: "For *I was a stranger*, and ye gathered me in." (See a Sermon on "The Stranger" in *Silver Sockets, and other Shadows of Redemption*.)

(20) **Thou shalt fear the Lord thy God; him shalt thou serve.**—In the New Testament, "Thou shalt *worship* the Lord thy God, and him *only* shalt thou serve." It was our Lord's last answer to the tempter in the wilderness. The order of the Hebrew gives the emphasis. "Jehovah thy God shalt thou fear, Him shalt thou serve, and to Him shalt thou cleave;" "and (adds Rashi) after all these qualities are established in thee, *then thou shalt swear by His name*." At least His name would not be profaned in such a case.

(22) **Thy fathers went down.**—The simple and natural form of this allusion conveys a strong impression of the truth of the facts. If the marvellous increase of Israel in the time allowed by the sacred narrative presents a difficulty, we must remember that the Bible consistently represents the multiplication as the *fulfilment of a Divine promise*, and not purely natural. But the testimony of the First Book of Chronicles must not be overlooked. The genealogy of Judah, given in the second and fourth chapters of that book, discloses a very extensive multiplication, a good deal of which must lie within the period of the sojourning in Egypt. The family of Hezron is particularly to be noticed. Of a certain descendant of Simeon it is written (1 Chron. iv. 27), "And Shimei had *sixteen sons and six daughters*; but his brethren had not many children, *neither did all their family multiply like to the children of Judah*." (!) Modern calculations are perhaps not quite adequate to deal with such a rate of increase as this. (See also the Note on chap. xxxii. 8.)

XI.

(1) **Therefore.**—There is no break here in the original. "The Lord thy God hath made thee as the stars of heaven for multitude, and thou shalt love the Lord thy God."

And keep his charge.—Literally, *keep his keeping*, i.e., all that is to be kept in obedience to Him.

Alway.—Literally, *all the days*. (Comp. "I am with you *all the days*" in Matt. xxviii. 25.) Israel must not omit one day in keeping the charge of Jehovah, for

Recitation of — DEUTERONOMY, XI. — *Past Deliverances.*

(2) And know ye this day: for *I speak* not with your children which have not known, and which have not seen the chastisement of the LORD your God, his greatness, his mighty hand, and his stretched out arm, (3) and his miracles, and his acts, which he did in the midst of Egypt unto Pharaoh the king of Egypt, and unto all his land; (4) and what he did unto the army of Egypt, unto their horses, and to their chariots; how he made the water of the Red sea to overflow them as they pursued after you, and how the LORD hath destroyed them unto this day: (5) and what he did unto you in the wilderness, until ye came into this place; (6) and *a* what he did unto Dathan and Abiram, the sons of Eliab, the son of Reuben: how the earth opened her mouth, and swallowed them up, and their households, and their tents, and all the ¹substance that ²*was* in their possession, in the midst of all Israel: (7) but your eyes have seen all the great acts of the LORD which he did. (8) Therefore shall ye keep all the commandments which I command you this day, that ye may be strong, and go in and possess the land, whither ye go to possess it; (9) and that ye may prolong *your* days in the land, which the LORD sware unto your fathers to give unto them and to their seed, a land that floweth with milk and honey.

(10) For the land, whither thou goest in to possess it, *is* not as the land of Egypt, from whence ye came out, where thou sowedst thy seed, and wateredst *it* with thy foot, as a garden of herbs: (11) but the land, whither ye go to possess it, *is* a land of hills and valleys, *and* drinketh water of the rain of heaven: (12) a land which the LORD thy God ³careth for: the eyes of the LORD thy God *are* always upon it, from the beginning of the year even unto the end of the year.

(13) And it shall come to pass, if ye shall hearken diligently unto my commandments which I command you this

a Num. 16. 31 & 27. 3; Ps. 106. 17.
¹ Or, *living substance which followed them.*
² Heb., *was at their feet.*
³ Heb., *seeketh.*

"He that keepeth Israel will neither slumber nor sleep."

(2) **And know ye.**—Or, *and ye know.*

Not with your children which have not known.—It must be remembered that all those who were less than twenty years of age at the date of the Exodus would still be living, and the events of their youth must have left a strong impression on their memories. Every man of forty-five years of age would feel the force of this address.

The chastisement.—Whether of the Egyptians in wrath, or of Israel in love.

His mighty hand . . . .—Or, *His hand in its strength, and His arm in its length.* The position of the adjectives is emphatic.

(6) **What he did unto Dathan and Abiram . . . .**—See Num. xvi. It is impossible to separate the rebellion of *Korah* from that of *Dathan and Abiram*, and seeing that the whole point of Korah's rebellion was *the priesthood,* it is difficult to see how the writer of Deuteronomy could be ignorant of any priesthood save that of the whole tribe of Levi. The object of Korah's rebellion was to abolish the distinction between a *Kohathite* and a *priest.*

(7) **But your eyes have seen.**—Literally, *For your eyes are the witnesses* (literally, *the seers*) *of all the great working of Jehovah which He hath wrought.*

(8) **The commandments.**—Literally, *the commandment.* It is *one course* of action rather than many details which is enjoined.

Go in and possess—*i.e.,* complete the conquest in detail, so as to enjoy the whole profit of the land.

(9) **To give unto them.**—See Note on verse 21, further on.

(10) **Not as the land of Egypt.**—"But much better. And Egypt was praised above all lands, as it is said (Gen. xiii. 10), 'As the garden of the Lord, like the land of Egypt.' And the land of Goshen, where Israel dwelt, is called 'the best of the land of Egypt' (Gen. xlvii. 6). And even this was not so good as the land of Israel" (Rashi).

Wateredst it with thy foot.—An allusion either to the necessity of *carrying* the water or to the custom of turning the water into little channels with the foot, as it flowed through the garden.

(11) **Drinketh water of the rain of heaven.**—Or, as it is prettily expressed by the Jewish commentator, "While thou sleepest on thy bed, the Holy One (blessed be He!) waters it high and low." (Comp. the parable in St. Mark iv. 26, 27.)

(12) **A land which the Lord thy God careth for.**—Literally, *seeketh,* as in the margin of our Bibles. Comp. Ezek. xx. 6: "A land that I had *espied* for them, flowing with milk and honey, which is the glory of all lands." "To *search out* a resting-place for them" (Num. x. 33). It is difficult not to think of the *better* land in this description, and of our Saviour's promise, "I go to prepare a place for you." There "the poor and needy" shall not "*seek* water," for "He shall lead them to living fountains of water." They shall "hunger no more, *neither thirst* any more."

That something unusual is indicated here seems to have occurred to the old Jewish writer, who says— "And does He not seek out *all lands?* as it is said, 'To cause it to rain on the earth where *no man is*'" (Job xxxviii. 26).

(13) **It shall come to pass.**—At this point begins the formal sanction of this charge by a declaration of rewards and punishments. Such sanctions are a characteristic feature of the Law. (Comp. Exod. xxiii. 20— end, at the close of the first code; Lev. xxvi., and Deut. xxviii.; and, in the New Testament, the well-known close of the Sermon on the Mount in St. Matt. vii., and of the parallel sermon in St. Luke vi.)

To love the Lord your God.—"Not that thou shouldst say, 'Behold, I am a disciple in order

day, to love the LORD your God, and to serve him with all your heart and with all your soul, ⁽¹⁴⁾ that I will give *you* the rain of your land in his due season, the first rain and the latter rain, that thou mayest gather in thy corn, and thy wine, and thine oil. ⁽¹⁵⁾ And I will ¹send grass in thy fields for thy cattle, that thou mayest eat and be full.

⁽¹⁶⁾ Take heed to yourselves, that your heart be not deceived, and ye turn aside, and serve other gods, and worship them; ⁽¹⁷⁾ and *then* the LORD's wrath be kindled against you, and he shut up the heaven, that there be no rain, and that the land yield not her fruit; and *lest* ye perish quickly from off the good land which the LORD giveth you.

⁽¹⁸⁾ Therefore shall ye lay up these my words in your heart and in your soul, and *a* bind them for a sign upon your hand, that they may be as frontlets between your eyes. ⁽¹⁹⁾ *b* And ye shall teach them your children, speaking of them when thou sittest in thine house, and when thou walkest by the way,

when thou liest down, and when thou risest up. ⁽²⁰⁾ And thou shalt write them upon the door posts of thine house, and upon thy gates: ⁽²¹⁾ that your days may be multiplied, and the days of your children, in the land which the LORD sware unto your fathers to give them, as the days of heaven upon the earth.

⁽²²⁾ For if ye shall diligently keep all these commandments which I command you, to do them, to love the LORD your God, to walk in all his ways, and to cleave unto him; ⁽²³⁾ then will the LORD drive out all these nations from before you, and ye shall possess greater nations and mightier than yourselves. ⁽²⁴⁾ *c* Every place whereon the soles of your feet shall tread shall be your's: from the wilderness and Lebanon, from the river, the river Euphrates, even unto the uttermost sea shall your coast be. ⁽²⁵⁾ There shall no man be able to stand before you: *for* the LORD your God shall lay the fear of you and the dread of you upon all the land that ye shall tread upon, as he hath said unto you.

1 Heb., *give.*

a ch. 6. 8.

b ch. 4. 10 & 6. 7.

c Josh. 1. 3.

---

that I may become rich: in order that I may be called great: in order that I may receive reward;' but whatsoever ye do, *do from love*" (Rashi).

To serve him with all your heart.—The Jewish commentator says that this refers to prayer, and compares Daniel (chap. vi. 16): "Thy God whom thou *servest* continually, He will deliver thee." There was no religious service for Israel in Babylon except prayer. The thought seems worth preserving, though the words are obviously capable of a wider application.

(14) **The first rain** (after sowing), **the latter rain** (just before harvest). In the ninth month and the first month respectively. (See Ezra x. 9, 13, and Joel ii. 23.)

That thou mayest gather in.—Literally, *and thou shalt gather in.* Rashi reminds us that this may mean "thou, and not thine enemies." "They that have gathered it shall eat it" (Isa. lxii. 8, 9).

(15) **That thou mayest eat and be full.**—The same writer observes that "this is a further blessing, which belongs to the food itself in man's inward parts." It is possible to eat and not be satisfied.

(16) **Take heed to yourselves**—*i.e.,* when you are satisfied. (Comp. chap. viii. 10, 11.)

(18) **Therefore shall ye lay up these my words.**—The same injunctions are found above (chap. vi. 6—9). The Jewish commentator remarks, somewhat sadly, here, that they would remember them in their captivity, if not before. The "therefore" at the commencement of the verse is a simple "and," so that the passage can be read in connection with what precedes: "Ye will perish quickly from off the good land, and ye will lay these my words to your hearts." But the words of verse 21 seem to show that this is not the primary meaning—only an application suggested, like many other applications of Scripture, by the actual event.

(21) **In the land which the Lord sware unto your fathers to give them.**—"It is not written here 'to give *you,*' but 'to give *them.*' Hence we find the resurrection of the dead taught in the Law." If this were the remark of a Christian commentator, it would be thought fanciful; but it is only the comment of a Jew. And *the Jewish belief in the literal fulfilment of these promises to Abraham and Isaac and Jacob, simply on the ground of God's word, is an unquestionable fact,* whatever may be thought of it. Comp. Acts vii. 5, which is singularly pointed. God "gave him (Abraham) none inheritance in it, no, not so much as to set his foot on; yet *He promised that He would give it to him for a possession,* and to his seed after him," besides.

(22) **To walk in all his ways.**—"He is compassionate, and thou shalt be compassionate. He showeth mercies, and thou shalt show mercies." Again Rashi's comment is worthy of the New Testament. What follows shows the need of a mediator.

To cleave unto him.—Is it possible to speak so? Is He not "a consuming fire"? (and how can we cleave unto Him?) "But cleave unto wise men and their disciples (the students of the Law), and I tell thee it will be as though thou didst cleave unto Him." In New Testament language this would read, "Be ye followers of me, as I am of Christ;" and "He that receiveth Me, receiveth Him that sent Me."

(24) **Every place.**—Repeated in Josh. i. 3, 4, where see Note.

(25) **The fear of you and the dread of you.**—Rashi says: "The fear of you on those that are near, and the dread upon those that are far off." It is a very far-reaching prophecy, for it may be read, "upon all the *earth* that ye shall tread upon." (See Esther viii. 2, 3, where it was fulfilled throughout the whole Persian Empire.)

The Blessing and the Curse.   DEUTERONOMY, XII.   *Idolatry to be Put Down.*

(26) Behold, I set before you this day a blessing and a curse; (27) *a* a blessing, if ye obey the commandments of the LORD your God, which I command you this day: (28) and a *b* curse, if ye will not obey the commandments of the LORD your God, but turn aside out of the way which I command you this day, to go after other gods, which ye have not known. (29) And it shall come to pass, when the LORD thy God hath brought thee in unto the land whither thou goest to possess it, that thou shalt put *c* the blessing upon mount Gerizim, and the curse upon mount Ebal. (30) *Are* they not on the other side Jordan, by the way where the sun goeth down, in the land of the Canaanites, which dwell in the champaign over against Gilgal, beside the plains of Moreh? (31) For ye shall pass over Jordan to go in to possess the land which the LORD your God giveth you, and ye shall possess it, and dwell therein. (32) And ye shall observe *d* to do all the statutes and judgments which I set before you this day.

CHAPTER XII.—(1) These *are* the statutes and judgments, which ye shall observe to do in the land, which the LORD God of thy fathers giveth thee to possess it, all the days that ye live upon the earth. (2) *e* Ye shall utterly destroy all the places, wherein the nations which ye shall ¹ possess served their gods: upon the high mountains, and upon the hills, and under every green tree: (3) and *f* ye shall ² overthrow their altars, and break their pillars, and burn their groves with fire; and ye shall hew down the graven images of their gods, and destroy the names of them out of that place.

a ch. 28. 2.
b ch. 28. 15.
c ch. 27. 13; Josh. 8. 33.
d ch. 5. 32.
e ch. 7. 5.
1 Or, *inherit*
f Judg. 2. 2.
2 Heb., *break down.*

---

(26) **Behold.**—Another of the Jewish divisions of Deuteronomy begins here.

A blessing and a curse.—Literally, *blessing and cursing*—the blessing if ye obey, and the curse if ye do not.

(29) **The blessing ... and the curse...**—The Targum of Onkelos says, "Those that bless," and "those that curse." (See chap. xxvii. 12, 13, and Note.*)

(30) **Where the sun goeth down.**—A memorable passage, as attesting the true position of the speaker, east of Jordan, over against Jericho. The sun has been seen by travellers from that very spot going down exactly in the remarkable gap between Ebal and Gerizim.

The plains of Moreh.—Rather, *the oaks or terebinths of Moreh.* (See Gen. xii. 6.)

(31) **For ye shall pass over Jordan.**—In the place of Sichem, by the oak of Moreh, "the Lord appeared to Abram, and said, Unto thy seed will I give *this* land." It is the first recorded promise given to the patriarch that his seed should inherit that particular country. He had gone out from his own country, "not knowing whither he went" (Gen. xii. 6, 7).

Here ends the first portion of the exposition of the Decalogue—that which sets forth the *relation of the people* brought out of Egypt *to Jehovah*. The following chapters set forth the laws of the *land* of Israel—first, as the seat of *worship* of Jehovah; secondly, as the seat of *His kingdom*; thirdly, as the sphere of operation of certain rules of behaviour, intended to form a distinctive character for His people. For a complete analysis of this portion, see the Introduction to this Book. Some modern writers attribute these chapters to a later hand than that of Moses. It is therefore necessary to consider them carefully, not simply as chapters, but in their primary structure and according to their natural divisions.

The land is considered as the seat of Jehovah's worship from chap. xii. 1 to xvi. 17 inclusive.

* The other Targums say, "When they bless they shall turn their faces towards Mount Gerizim; and when they curse they shall turn their faces towards Mount Ebal." This confirms the antiquity of the view taken in the Talmud.

XII.

(1) **These are the statutes and judgments.**—The word *Mitzvah*—commandment, or duty—is not used here. Particular *institutions and requirements* are now before us.

(2) **Ye shall utterly destroy.**—First of all these requirements is the destruction of every vestige of idolatry. In the land of Jehovah there must be no trace of any other god but Him. The non-fulfilment of this command in the early history of Israel has led some to suppose that the command itself belongs to later times. But it must be observed that the destruction of these things is inextricably connected with the conquest of the country *in detail.* It was part of the work assigned to the several tribes of Israel when the land had been divided by Joshua. His work was to conquer the Canaanitish armies, and give Israel possession of their chief cities. He then assigned the land to the several tribes, to make it their own throughout. Obviously, if every tribe had insisted upon destroying all monuments of idolatry in its own territory, one of two results must have followed: either the remnant of the Canaanitish nations must have been excited to fresh acts of rebellion and hostility, resulting in their extermination, or else they must have yielded themselves entirely to the worship of Jehovah. But Israel disobeyed the order. They did not themselves yield to idolatry in Joshua's time. The disturbance made respecting the altar Ed (see Josh. xxii.) is quite sufficient of itself to prove the strictness of the law against strange altars. But the Canaanites being left undisturbed after they ceased to resist openly, and their objects of worship being left unmolested, there were constant temptations to idolatry, to which Israel yielded. And thus it was not until the times of Hezekiah and Josiah that these laws were carried out. But this does not prove the law to have come into existence then, any more than the present condition of the human race proves that man was not made in God's image in Paradise.

(3) **Destroy the names.**—The substitution in later times of *bosheth* for *baal* in the names Jerubbaal

A Fixed Place of   DEUTERONOMY, XII.   *Worship ordered.*

(4) Ye shall not do so unto the LORD your God. (5) But unto the place which the LORD your God shall *a* choose out of all your tribes to put his name there, *even* unto his habitation shall ye seek, and thither thou shalt come: (6) and thither ye shall bring your burnt offerings, and your sacrifices, and your tithes, and heave offerings of your hand, and your vows, and your freewill offerings, and the firstlings of your herds and of your flocks: (7) and there ye shall eat before the LORD your God, and ye shall rejoice in all that ye put your hand unto, ye and your households, wherein the LORD thy God hath blessed thee.

(8) Ye shall not do after all *the things* that we do here this day, every man whatsoever *is* right in his own eyes. (9) For ye are not as yet come to the rest and to the inheritance, which the LORD your God giveth you. (10) But *when* ye go over Jordan, and dwell in the land which the LORD your God giveth you to inherit, and *when* he giveth you rest from all your enemies round about, so that ye dwell in safety; (11) then there shall be a place which the LORD your God shall choose to cause his name to dwell there; thither shall ye bring all that I command you; your burnt offerings, and your sacrifices, your tithes, and the heave offering of your hand, and all ¹your choice vows which ye vow unto the LORD: (12) and ye shall rejoice before the LORD your God, ye, and your sons, and your daughters, and your menservants, and your maidservants, and the Levite that *is* within your gates; forasmuch as *b* he hath no part nor inheritance with you.

(13) Take heed to thyself that thou offer not thy burnt offerings in every place that thou seest: (14) but in the place which the LORD shall choose in one of thy tribes, there thou shalt offer thy burnt offerings, and there thou shalt do all that I command thee.

a 1 Kings 8. 29; 2 Chr. 7. 12.

¹ Heb., *the choice of your vows.*

b ch. 10. 9.

(Jerubbesheth), Eshbaal (Ishbosheth), Meribbaal (Mephibosheth), is a curious example of the literal fulfilment of this command, or, perhaps, rather of the command in Exod. xxiii. 13, of which the spirit and purport agree with this.

(4) **Ye shall not do so**—*i.e.*, shall not serve Him upon the high mountains, and hills, and under every green tree, after the manner of the nations.

(5) **But unto the place which the Lord your God shall choose out of all your tribes.**—The very form of the order proves its antiquity. No one who was acquainted with the removal of that "place" from Shiloh to Nob, from Nob to Gibeon, from Gibeon to Jerusalem, could have written with such utter unconsciousness of later history as these words imply. It is noticeable that in the reading of this precept in the times of our Lord, the Jews seem to have arrived at the same state of unconsciousness. They could not conceive of the presence or worship of Jehovah anywhere but at Jerusalem. (See on this topic St. Stephen's speech in Acts vii., and the incidental proofs it contains of God's presence with Israel *in many places*, in reply to the accusation made against Stephen of preaching the destruction of the one idolized seat of worship at Jerusalem.)

(6) **And thither ye shall bring . . . your tithes**—*i.e.*, what the Jews understand as the "second tithe;" on which see verse 17.

(8) **Ye shall not do after all the things that we do here this day.**—Another precept strongly marked with the condition of Israel in the wilderness. It has been too much overlooked by recent commentators that the law of Moses has a *prophetic side.* It was given to him and to Israel at a time when they were not in a position to keep it. It was the *law of the land* which God would give them. In many ways its observance depended on the completion of the conquest of the land, and upon the quietness of the times in which they lived. This prophetic aspect was certainly not unrecognised by the Jews, or they would not (for example) have neglected to dwell in booths at the Feast of Tabernacles from the time of Joshua to Nehemiah. (See Neh. viii. 17.)*

(9) **Ye are not as yet come to the rest and to the inheritance.**—Nor would the passage of Jordan and the conquest of Joshua bring them to it.

(10) **When he giveth you rest.**—Rashi observes, "This was not until the days of David." He cites 2 Sam. vii. 1: "It came to pass when the king sat in his house, and the Lord had given him rest round about from all his enemies."

(11) **Then there shall be a place.**—The building of Jerusalem and of the Temple brought with it in due time the accomplishment of the law which is appended to the prophecy.

(13, 14) **Take heed to thyself that thou offer not thy burnt offerings in every place that thou seest: But in the place which the Lord shall choose.**—An attempt is made by some modern writers to establish a contradiction between this precept and the one in Exod. xx. 24: "In all places where I record my name I will come unto thee, and I will bless thee." But they are not really contradictory. The choice of Jehovah makes the place of acceptance. He need not always choose the same spot. Either this law in Deuteronomy was written by Moses, or it was not. If it was, it must be taken in the same sense as Exod. xx. 24. If it was the work of later times, the writer must have known perfectly that Jehovah had varied His choice from time to time, and therefore the injunction must still have the same sense. Rashi remarks upon the words "Take heed that thou offer not . . . in every place that thou seest"—*i.e.*, which comes into thy mind—"but thou must offer at

---

* And compare the curious position of the law in Leviticus, which required them to dwell in booths. It occurs as an appendix outside the regular laws of that festival (Lev. xxiii. 37—43).

The Levite to be Remembered.   DEUTERONOMY, XII.   *Blood not to be Eaten.*

(15) Notwithstanding thou mayest kill and eat flesh in all thy gates, whatsoever thy soul lusteth after, according to the blessing of the LORD thy God which he hath given thee: the unclean and the clean may eat thereof, as of the roebuck, and as of the hart. (16) *a* Only ye shall not eat the blood; ye shall pour it upon the earth as water.

(17) Thou mayest not eat within thy gates the tithe of thy corn, or of thy wine, or of thy oil, or the firstlings of thy herds or of thy flock, nor any of thy vows which thou vowest, nor thy freewill offerings, or heave offering of thine hand: (18) but thou must eat them before the LORD thy God in the place which the LORD thy God shall choose, thou, and thy son, and thy daughter, and thy manservant, and thy maidservant, and the Levite that *is* within thy gates: and thou shalt rejoice before the LORD thy God in all that thou puttest thine hands unto. (19) *b* Take heed to thyself that thou forsake not the Levite ¹as long as thou livest upon the earth.

(20) When the LORD thy God shall enlarge thy border, *c* as he hath promised thee, and thou shalt say, I will eat flesh, because thy soul longeth to eat flesh; thou mayest eat flesh, whatsoever thy soul lusteth after. (21) If the place which the LORD thy God hath chosen to put his name there be too far from thee, then thou shalt kill of thy herd and of thy flock, which the LORD hath given thee, as I have commanded thee, and thou shalt eat in thy gates whatsoever thy soul lusteth after. (22) Even as the roebuck and the hart is eaten, so thou shalt eat them: the unclean and the clean shall eat *of* them alike. (23) Only ²be sure that thou eat not the blood: for the blood *is* the life; and thou mayest not eat the life with the flesh. (24) Thou shalt not eat it; thou shalt pour it upon the earth as water. (25) Thou shalt not eat it; that it may go well with thee, and with thy children after thee, when thou shalt do *that which is* right in the sight of the LORD.

(26) Only thy holy things which thou hast, and thy vows, thou shalt take, and go unto the place which the LORD shall

a ch. 15. 23.

b ch. 14. 27; Ecclus. 7. 31.

¹ Heb., *all thy days.*

c Gen. 28. 14; ch. 19. 8.

² Heb., *be strong.*

---

the command of a prophet, as, for instance, Elijah on Mount Carmel." It seems clear that the general principle inculcated here is the same with that of Exod. xx. and of Lev. xvii. The choice of Jehovah makes the place of worship. Details may safely be left to the direction of the authorised Divine representatives at any given time. If the Jews themselves saw no difficulty or discrepancy in these Scriptures, is it any proof of wisdom for us to make difficulties? Do we not rather prove the imperfection of our own understanding?

(15) **Notwithstanding thou mayest kill and eat flesh.**—This may very possibly be intended as a slight modification of a law made for the wilderness journey (Lev. xvii. 3, 4). There the "killing" of an ox, or lamb, or goat is forbidden anywhere except at the door of the tabernacle. The word "kill," though often used sacrificially, cannot be limited to sacrifice in that place, although the animals mentioned are all sacrificial animals. It would seem that the practice of sacrificing those animals elsewhere, very possibly for the sake of the feast which followed, had become so common that it was necessary to forbid the killing of them anywhere but at the door of the tabernacle. But the continuance of this precept in Canaan would stop the eating of flesh altogether. Hence the exception made here.

As of the roebuck, and as of the hart.—The frequent mention of these animals in this connection suggests the idea that the hunting and catching of them may not have been an uncommon thing in the wilderness.

(16) **Ye shall pour it upon the earth.**—This act was a necessary part of every slaughter of an animal for food. The blood, which is the life, must be poured upon the earth for God, whether the victim was consigned to the altar or not. It was a continual reminder of the necessity for the sacrifice of the death of Christ, and to be continued until He should come. Thus the act was, in a sense, sacramental.

(17) **The tithe.**—This is understood by Jewish commentators of what is called "the second tithe." The disposal of it is more particularly specified in chap. xiv. 22—29. (See also on chap. xxvi. 12, &c.)

(18) **The Levite that is within thy gates.**—The distribution of the Levites throughout the several tribes (ordered in Num. xxxv. 1—8), and carried out by Joshua (chap. xxi.), is here anticipated. The Levites had this provision in Israel until Jeroboam and his sons cast them off, when they migrated to the kingdom of Judah (2 Chron. xi. 13, 14).

(20) **When the Lord thy God shall enlarge thy border . . . .**—This and the following verses (20—25) are perfectly intelligible as an expansion of verses 15, 16, and a modification of the strict rule introduced in Lev. xviii. 2, &c. The distance from the central place of worship to the borders of the land would be manifestly too great for all feasting to be limited to that one spot.

(25) **That it may go well with thee.**—Very possibly, the physical as well as the moral effect of the rule is contemplated here.

(26) **Only thy holy things . . . and thy vows.**—The holy things probably mean the firstlings, which were necessarily holy, and must be made burnt offerings (Lev. xxviii. 26). The second tithe was also considered holy. The first tithe, or ordinary provision for the Levites (see Num. xviii.), was not considered holy. The vows might be either burnt offerings or peace offerings.

Strict Obedience enjoined. **DEUTERONOMY, XIII.** *The False Prophet to be Slain.*

choose: ⁽²⁷⁾ and thou shalt offer thy burnt offerings, the flesh and the blood, upon the altar of the Lord thy God: and the blood of thy sacrifices shall be poured out upon the altar of the Lord thy God, and thou shalt eat the flesh.

⁽²⁸⁾ Observe and hear all these words which I command thee, that it may go well with thee, and with thy children after thee for ever, when thou doest *that which is* good and right in the sight of the Lord thy God.

⁽²⁹⁾ When the Lord thy God shall cut off the nations from before thee, whither thou goest to possess them, and thou ¹succeedest them, and dwellest in their land; ⁽³⁰⁾ take heed to thyself that thou be not snared ² by following them, after that they be destroyed from before thee; and that thou enquire not after their gods, saying, How did these nations serve their gods? even so will I do likewise. ⁽³¹⁾ Thou shalt not do so unto the Lord thy God: for every ³ abomination to the Lord, which he hateth, have they done unto their gods; for even their sons and their daughters they have burnt in the fire to their gods. ⁽³²⁾ What thing soever I command you, observe to do it: *^a* thou shalt not add thereto, nor diminish from it.

CHAPTER XIII.—⁽¹⁾ If there arise among you a prophet, or a dreamer of dreams, and giveth thee a sign or a wonder, ⁽²⁾ and the sign or the wonder

1 Heb., *inheritest, or, possessest them.*

2 Heb., *after them.*

3 Heb., *abomination of the.*

a ch. 4. 2; Josh. 1. 7; Prov. 30. 6; Rev. 22. 18.

b ch. 10. 20.

4 Heb., *spoken revolt against the Lord.*

come to pass, whereof he spake unto thee, saying, Let us go after other gods, which thou hast not known, and let us serve them; ⁽³⁾ thou shalt not hearken unto the words of that prophet, or that dreamer of dreams: for the Lord your God proveth you, to know whether ye love the Lord your God with all your heart and with all your soul. ⁽⁴⁾ Ye shall walk after the Lord your God, and fear him, and keep his commandments, and obey his voice, and ye shall serve him, and *^b* cleave unto him. ⁽⁵⁾ And that prophet, or that dreamer of dreams, shall be put to death; because he hath ⁴spoken to turn *you* away from the Lord your God, which brought you out of the land of Egypt, and redeemed you out of the house of bondage, to thrust thee out of the way which the Lord thy God commanded thee to walk in. So shalt thou put the evil away from the midst of thee.

⁽⁶⁾ If thy brother, the son of thy mother, or thy son, or thy daughter, or the wife of thy bosom, or thy friend, which *is as* thine own soul, entice thee secretly, saying, Let us go and serve other gods, which thou hast not known, thou, nor thy fathers; ⁽⁷⁾ *namely*, of the gods of the people which *are* round about you, nigh unto thee, or far off from thee, from the *one* end of the earth even unto the *other* end of the earth; ⁽⁸⁾ thou shalt not consent unto him, nor hearken unto him; neither shall thine eye pity

---

⁽²⁷⁾ **The blood of thy sacrifices**—*i.e.*, peace offerings, the only kind of which the worshipper as well as the priest might partake.

⁽³⁰⁾ **Take heed to thyself that thou be not snared.**—A necessary caution. "The fear" of heathen deities often attached itself to their seats of worship. It was found necessary to caution Israel against the fear of them and the dread of them in much later times. (See Jer. x. 2—5.)

⁽³²⁾ **What thing soever I command you.**—No later writer could put these words into the mouth of Moses, if he had altered the precepts of Moses to any appreciable extent.

XIII.

⁽¹⁾ **If there arise.**—Three cases of instigation to idolatry are considered in this chapter:—

1. The false prophet (verses 1—5).
2. A private individual (verses 6—11).
3. A city (verses 12—18).

In every case the penalty is the same—death without mercy.

Is this law the production of a later age? It may be said to have been more often broken than observed. But there are instances in the history of Israel which seem to require some such law as this in all its three sections. The case of the false prophet justifies the action of Elijah, who took the prophets of Baal from Carmel when proved to be impostors, and "brought them down to the brook Kishon, and slew them there."

⁽⁶⁾ **If thy brother.**—The substance of this law is that individual idolaters might be executed in Israel. It justifies Jehu and Jehoiada in destroying Baal out of Israel and Judah (2 Kings x. 19—27, xi. 18). It also accounts for the covenant made in the time of Asa (2 Chron. xv. 13), that whosoever would not serve the Lord God of Israel should be *put to death*, whether man or woman.

The law may seem harsh, but its *principle* is reproduced in the Gospel: "He that loveth father or mother more than me is not worthy of me" (Matt. x. 37). "If any man come to me, and hate not his father, and mother, and wife, and children, and brethren, and sisters, yea, and his own life also, he cannot be my disciple" (Luke xiv. 26).

It is impossible to deny or escape the identity of the Lord Jesus with the Jehovah of the Old Testament.

him, neither shalt thou spare, neither shalt thou conceal him: ⁽⁹⁾ but ᵃthou shalt surely kill him; thine hand shall be first upon him to put him to death, and afterwards the hand of all the people. ⁽¹⁰⁾And thou shalt stone him with stones, that he die; because he hath sought to thrust thee away from the LORD thy God, which brought thee out of the land of Egypt, from the house of ¹bondage. ⁽¹¹⁾And ᵇall Israel shall hear, and fear, and shall do no more any such wickedness as this is among you.

⁽¹²⁾ If thou shalt hear *say* in one of thy cities, which the LORD thy God hath given thee to dwell there, saying, ⁽¹³⁾ *Certain* men, ² the children of Belial, are gone out from among you, and have withdrawn the inhabitants of their city, saying, Let us go and serve other gods, which ye have not known; ⁽¹⁴⁾ then shalt thou enquire, and make search, and ask diligently; and, behold, *if it be* truth, *and* the thing certain, *that* such abomination is wrought among you; ⁽¹⁵⁾ thou shalt surely smite the inhabitants of that city with the edge of the sword, destroying it utterly, and all that *is* therein, and the cattle thereof, with the edge of the sword. ⁽¹⁶⁾And thou shalt gather all the spoil of it into the midst of the street thereof, and shalt burn with fire the city, and all the spoil thereof every whit, for the LORD thy God: and it shall be an heap for ever; it shall not be built again. ⁽¹⁷⁾And there shall cleave nought of the ³cursed thing to thine hand: that the LORD may turn from the fierceness of his anger, and shew thee mercy, and have compassion upon thee, and multiply thee, as he hath sworn unto thy fathers; ⁽¹⁸⁾when thou shalt hearken to the voice of the LORD thy God, to keep all his commandments which I command thee this day, to do *that which is* right in the eyes of the LORD thy God.

CHAPTER XIV. — ⁽¹⁾ Ye *are* the children of the LORD your God: ᶜye shall not cut yourselves, nor make any baldness between your eyes for the dead. ⁽²⁾ ᵈFor thou *art* an holy people unto the LORD thy God, and the LORD hath

a ch. 17. 7.
¹ Heb., *bondmen.*
b ch. 17. 13.
² Or, *naughty men.*
³ Or, *devoted.*
c Lev. 19. 28.
d ch. 7. 6 & 26. 18.

He does not always put the execution of His judgments into human hands, but He is the same for ever.

⁽⁹⁾ **Thine hand shall be first upon him to put him to death.**—A law tending to prevent false accusation. Where the witness is obliged to carry out himself, or to aid in carrying out, the sentence he demands, secret accusation is impossible; and it is far less easy to pervert the law in order to prosecute a private quarrel.

⁽¹²⁾ **If thou shalt hear say in one of thy cities.**—The only case of this kind is the case of Gibeah. We may fairly assume the abominations done there to have been connected with idolatry, from the allusions in Hos. ix. 9, x. 9. But the outrage rather than the idolatry seems to have excited the indignation of Israel (see Judges xx., xxi.). It is noticeable that in the remonstrance with the Benjamites at Gibeah—(Judges xx. 13): "Now therefore deliver us the men, the children of Belial, which are in Gibeah, that we may *put them to death, and put away evil from Israel*"—there seems to be an allusion to the language of this chapter in verses 5 and 11.

⁽¹³⁾ **Children of Belial.**—The very same expression is used in Judges xx. 13: "Deliver us the men, the children of Belial, that are among you." This is the first place where the expression "sons of Belial" occurs, and Judges xix. 22 is the second. It is generally explained by modern scholars as "worthlessness." Rashi curiously makes it "destroyers of the yoke" (of Jehovah).

⁽¹⁵⁾ **And the cattle thereof.**—So in Judges xx. 48: "The men of every city, the *beast*, and all that were found."

⁽¹⁶⁾ **And shalt burn with fire the city.**—So Gibeah was treated (Judges xx 40).

⁽¹⁷⁾ We seem to hear an echo of this verse in the close of the story of Achan (Josh. vii. 26): "And all Israel stoned him with stones, and burned them with fire after they had stoned them with stones, and they raised over him a great heap of stones unto this day. So *the Lord turned from the fierceness of his anger.*"

XIV.

⁽¹⁾ **Ye are the children of Jehovah.**—This fact is made the foundation of all the laws of ceremonial and moral holiness in the Pentateuch, more especially in the Book of Leviticus, where these laws are chiefly to be found.

Ye shall not cut yourselves.—The precept is repeated with little variation from Lev. xix. 28

Any baldness between your eyes—*i.e.*, apparently, "on your foreheads." The word for baldness in this place is generally used for baldness on the back of the head.

⁽²⁾ **For thou art an holy people.**—This verse is repeated from chap. vii. 6, word for word, except the "and," which is added here. In the former passage, the principle is made the ground for destroying all monuments of idolatry in the land of Israel. Here it is made the basis of outward personal dignity and purity. This recalls the arrangement of the Book of Leviticus somewhat forcibly. The laws of ceremonial holiness stand first in that book, before the law of yearly atonement. Then follow the laws of moral holiness. But the principle and ground of all these laws is the same: "Ye shall be holy, for I am holy, and ye are Mine."

Nations.—Rather, *peoples.* The commonwealth of Israel and its institutions are contrasted with other states and their institutions.

Beasts, Fish, and Birds   DEUTERONOMY, XIV.   *which may be Eaten.*

chosen thee to be a peculiar people unto himself, above all the nations that *are* upon the earth.

(3) Thou shalt not eat any abominable thing. (4) *a* These *are* the beasts which ye shall eat: the ox, the sheep, and the goat, (5) the hart, and the roebuck, and the fallow deer, and the wild goat, and the ¹ ² pygarg, and the wild ox, and the chamois. (6) And every beast that parteth the hoof, and cleaveth the cleft into two claws, *and* cheweth the cud among the beasts, that ye shall eat. (7) Nevertheless these ye shall not eat of them that chew the cud, or of them that divide the cloven hoof; *as* the camel, and the hare, and the coney: for they chew the cud, but divide not the hoof; *therefore* they *are* unclean unto you. (8) And the swine, because it divideth the hoof, yet cheweth not the cud, it *is* unclean unto you: ye shall not eat of their flesh, nor touch their dead carcase.

(9) *b* These ye shall eat of all that *are* in the waters: all that have fins and scales shall ye eat: (10) and whatsoever hath not fins and scales ye may not eat; it *is* unclean unto you.

(11) *Of* all clean birds ye shall eat. (12) But these *are they* of which ye shall not eat: the eagle, and the ossifrage, and the ospray, (13) and the glede, and the kite, and the vulture after his kind, (14) and every raven after his kind, (15) and the owl, and the night hawk, and the cuckow, and the hawk after his kind, (16) the little owl, and the great owl, and the swan, (17) and the pelican, and the gier eagle, and the cormorant, (18) and the stork, and the heron after her kind, and the lapwing, and the *c* bat. (19) And every creeping thing that flieth *is* unclean unto you: they shall not be eaten. (20) But *of* all clean fowls ye may eat.

(21) Ye shall not eat *of* any thing that dieth of itself: thou shalt give it unto the stranger that *is* in thy gates, that he may eat it; or thou mayest sell it unto an alien: for thou *art* an holy people unto the LORD thy God. *d* Thou shalt not seethe a kid in his mother's milk.

(22) Thou shalt truly tithe all the increase of thy seed, that the field bringeth forth year by year. (23) And thou shalt eat before the LORD thy God, in the

a Lev. 11. 2, &c.

1 Or, *bison*.

2 Heb., *dishon*.

b Lev. 11. 9.

c Lev. 11. 19.

d Ex. 23. 19 & 34. 26.

---

(3) **Thou shalt not eat any abominable thing.**—That is, anything which Jehovah has pronounced abominable. The distinctions between His creatures were alike established and removed by the Creator. Yet, no doubt, they had also a sanitary purpose in relation to the chosen people.

(4) **These are the beasts which ye shall eat.**—The following paragraph to the end of verse 8 answers to Lev. xi. 2—8, with this difference. The beasts that *are* to be eaten are specified in Deuteronomy. The *exceptions* are given in Leviticus.

The ox, the sheep, and the goat.—These being sacrificial animals, naturally stand first. "The sheep and the goat" are literally, "a young one of the sheep or of the goats." This may serve to illustrate Exod. xii. 5, "Ye shall take it out from the sheep, or from the goats." According to the letter of the Law in Exodus, the Passover victim might be either lamb or kid. The word *sêh*, used there and in Gen. xxii. 7, 8, is not distinctive of the species. This word is rendered "lamb" in several places in our English Version.

(5) **The wild goat.**—In German the "steinbock" is given as the equivalent for this creature. The pygarg (*dishon*) is sometimes taken to be the buffalo. If all these creatures were then to be found in Palestine, there must have been far more uncleared land than there has been for many centuries past.

(6—8) These directions are the same given in Lev. xi. 3—8.

(9—10) See Lev. xi. 9—12.

(12) **These are they of which ye shall not eat.**—With one exception, the unclean birds are the same described in Lev. xi. 13—19.

(13) **The glede, and the kite, and the vulture.**—In Lev. xi. 14, "the vulture and the kite" alone are named. The Hebrew words are in Leviticus *dāāh* and *ayyah*. In this place they are *rāāh*, *ayyah*, and *dayyah*. The close resemblance between the names is noticeable. For a description of the creatures, see list in Variorum Bible.

(21) **That he may eat it.**—Literally, *and he will eat it*. The common practice, and not the intention of the writer, may be indicated. It should be remembered that these rules and restrictions were intended to raise the Israelites above the common level; not to degrade the other nations in comparison of them. Strangers were not compelled to eat what Israel refused; they were left free to please themselves.

Thou shalt not seethe a kid in his mother's milk.—This is the last appearance of a command repeated twice in Exodus (chaps. xxiii. 19, xxxiv. 26). See Notes there.

(22) **Thou shalt truly tithe.**—The Talmud and Jewish interpreters in general are agreed in the view that the tithe mentioned in this passage, both here and in verse 28, and also the tithe described in chap. xxvi. 12—15, are all one thing—"the second tithe;" and entirely distinct from the ordinary tithe assigned to the Levites for their subsistence in Num. xviii. 21, and by them tithed again for the priests (Num. xviii. 26).

The tithe described in Numbers was called "the first tithe," and was not considered sacred. The second tithe, on the contrary, was always regarded as a holy thing.

(23) **And thou shalt eat before the Lord thy God**—*i.e.*, thou shalt eat the second tithe. This was to be done two years; but in the third and sixth years

The Second Tithe.   DEUTERONOMY, XV.   *The Seven Years' Release.*

place which he shall choose to place his name there, the tithe of thy corn, of thy wine, and of thine oil, and the firstlings of thy herds and of thy flocks; that thou mayest learn to fear the LORD thy God always.

⁽²⁴⁾ And if the way be too long for thee, so that thou art not able to carry it; or if the place be too far from thee, which the LORD thy God shall choose to set his name there, when the LORD thy God hath blessed thee: ⁽²⁵⁾ then shalt thou turn *it* into money, and bind up the money in thine hand, and shalt go unto the place which the LORD thy God shall choose: ⁽²⁶⁾ and thou shalt bestow that money for whatsoever thy soul lusteth after, for oxen, or for sheep, or for wine, or for strong drink, or for whatsoever thy soul ¹desireth: and thou shalt eat there before the LORD thy God, and thou shalt rejoice, thou, and thine household, ⁽²⁷⁾ and ^a the Levite that *is* within thy gates; thou shalt not forsake him; for he hath no part nor inheritance with thee.

⁽²⁸⁾ At the end of three years thou shalt bring forth all the tithe of thine increase the same year, and shalt lay *it* up within thy gates: ⁽²⁹⁾ and the Levite, (because he hath no part nor inheritance with thee,) and the stranger, and the fatherless, and the widow, which *are* within thy gates, shall come, and shall eat and be satisfied; that the LORD thy God may bless thee in all the work of thine hand which thou doest.

CHAPTER XV.—⁽¹⁾ At the end of ^b every seven years thou shalt make a release. ⁽²⁾ And this *is* the manner of the release: Every ²creditor that lendeth *ought* unto his neighbour shall release *it*; he shall not exact *it* of his neighbour, or of his brother; because it is called the LORD's release. ⁽³⁾ Of a foreigner thou mayest exact *it* again: but *that* which is thine with thy brother thine hand shall release; ⁽⁴⁾ ³ save when there shall be no poor among you; for the LORD shall greatly bless thee in the land which the LORD thy God giveth

---

1 Heb., *asketh of thee.*

a ch. 12. 19.

b Lev. 25. 2, 4.

2 Heb., *master of the lending of his hand.*

3 Or, *To the end that there be no poor among you.*

---

there was a different arrangement (see verse 28). In the seventh year, which was Sabbatical, there would probably be no tithe, for there was to be no harvest. The profit of the earth was for all, and every one was free to eat at pleasure.

⁽²⁶⁾ **Thou shalt bestow that money.**—The Jews were very particular in not permitting the second tithe to be expended upon anything not permitted here. The rules as to its disposal form a separate treatise in the Talmud, called *Ma'aser Shêni,* "second tithe."

Or for strong drink.—From this it is clear that the use of strong drink is not sinful in itself. The same word appears in its Greek form (Heb., *shêcar;* Greek, *sikêr*) in Luke i. 15.

⁽²⁸⁾ **At the end of three years thou shalt bring forth all the tithe.**—This is called by the Jews *Ma'aser 'Âni,* "the poor's tithe." They regard it as identical with the second tithe, which was ordinarily eaten by the owners at Jerusalem; but in every third and sixth year was bestowed upon the poor.

⁽²⁹⁾ **And the Levite.**—Rashi says, "the Levite shall come and take the *first tithe* (described in Num. xviii.), and the stranger and the fatherless and the widow the *second tithe.*" But there is no proof whatever that anything except the second tithe is alluded to in the whole of this passage. *The Levite always shared with the poor* (see chap. xvi. 11, 14). Rashi's opinion is worth notice chiefly for the following reason. Some modern critics insist that the Law of Deuteronomy is contradictory to that of Numbers in respect of tithe; but if the Jews, who kept the whole Law strictly, not only saw no discrepancy between its several precepts, but actually took the precept in Deuteronomy to imply the precept in Numbers, why should we go out of our way to make difficulties now? If the precepts were harmonious and compatible, why should they be the work of different men? It is hardly likely that a whole nation would consent to *pay double tithes, and acknowledge the obligation to do so by perpetual enactment, if the laws that commanded the tithe were contradictory.* And the more closely we look at the subject, the more clearly will the distinction between the first and second tithes appear. The first was only an ordinary rate for the support of the Levitical ministry. No sacredness attached to it. The second was a tithe taken for Jehovah, "that thou mayest learn to fear Jehovah thy God always" (chap. xiv. 23). The tithe was either to be a joyful feast for the family, or a special gift to God's poor. It furnished a table spread by the God of Israel for the entertainment of His guests. Why this should be confused with the ordinary rate for the maintenance of the Levitical ministry, it is not easy to understand.

XV.

⁽¹⁾ **At the end of every seven years thou shalt make a release.**—The Law in this place is an extension of that which we find in Exod. xxi. 2, &c., and Lev. xxv. 3, &c. There was not only to be a manumission of Hebrew slaves and a Sabbath for the land in the seventh year, but also *a release of debts,* of which all the Israelites must have the benefit.

⁽⁴⁾ **Save when there shall be no poor (man) among you.**—This clause is the source of a very interesting passage in the Acts of the Apostles, chap. iv. 34, "Great grace was upon them all, *for neither was there among them any (one) that lacked.*" The words at the beginning of the verse in Hebrew, "save when," may also be rendered (as in the Margin) "to the end that," or "to such an extent that there shall be no poor man among you." Those who can well afford to pay need not be excused from their obligations.

Precepts about Lending.   DEUTERONOMY, XV.   *Relieving the Poor.*

thee *for* an inheritance to possess it: ⁽⁵⁾ only if thou carefully hearken unto the voice of the LORD thy God, to observe to do all these commandments which I command thee this day. ⁽⁶⁾ For the LORD thy God blesseth thee, as he promised thee: and *a*thou shalt lend unto many nations, but thou shalt not borrow; and thou shalt reign over many nations, but they shall not reign over thee. ⁽⁷⁾ If there be among you a poor man of one of thy brethren within any of thy gates in thy land which the LORD thy God giveth thee, thou shalt not harden thine heart, nor shut thine hand from thy poor brother: ⁽⁸⁾ *b*but thou shalt open thine hand wide unto him, and shalt surely lend him sufficient for his need, *in that* which he wanteth. ⁽⁹⁾ Beware that there be not a [1] thought in thy [2] wicked heart, saying, The seventh year, the year of release, is at hand; and thine eye be evil against thy poor brother, and thou givest him nought; and he cry unto the LORD against thee, and it be sin unto thee. ⁽¹⁰⁾ Thou shalt surely give him, and thine heart shall not be grieved when thou givest unto him: because that for this thing the LORD thy God shall bless thee in all thy works, and in all that thou puttest thine hand unto. ⁽¹¹⁾ For the poor shall never cease out of the land: therefore I command thee, saying, Thou shalt open thine hand wide unto thy brother, to thy poor, and to thy needy, in thy land. ⁽¹²⁾ And *c*if thy brother, an Hebrew man, or an Hebrew woman, be sold unto thee, and serve thee six years;

a ch. 28. 12.
b Matt. 5. 42; Luke 6. 34.
1 Heb., *word.*
2 Heb., *Belial.*
c Ex. 21. 2; Jer. 34. 14.

For the Lord thy God shall greatly bless thee.—So in Acts iv. 33, "*Great* grace was upon them all." The blessing need not be equal and universal prosperity, if those who have the good things of this world will always remember the poor to such an extent that no member of the community shall be left in want.

⁽⁵⁾ **Only if thou carefully hearken.**—"Then there will be none among thee in want." So Rashi expounds, in the very spirit of the passage in Acts iv.

⁽⁶⁾ **As he promised thee.**—"I will bless thee" was said to Abram (Gen. xii. 2).

Thou shalt lend.—The root of the word in Hebrew is closely connected with the word for "slave." "The borrower is servant to the lender" (Prov. xxii. 7).

⁽⁷⁾ **A poor man.**—"That needeth anything."

Within any of thy gates.—"The poor of thine own city come before the poor of another city."

Thou shalt not harden.—"There are some men who 'grieve' (grudge) whether they give or not; therefore it is said, 'Thou shalt not harden thy heart; there are some who stretch out the hand (to give), and yet close it; therefore it is said, Thou shalt not shut thine hand."

⁽⁸⁾ **Thou shalt open thine hand wide.**—"Even many times."

And shalt surely lend.—"If he does not like to take it as a gift, grant it to him as a loan."

Sufficient for his need.—"But it is not thy duty to make him rich."

In that which he wanteth.—"Even a horse to ride on, and a slave to run before him."

⁽¹⁰⁾ **Thou shalt surely give.**—"Even a hundred times."

Him.—"Between thee and him alone." (Comp. "Let not thy left hand know what thy right hand doeth" in Matt. vi. 3). I have thought it worth while to borrow the comments of Rashi on these verses (7—10) almost entire, to show how well the Jews have understood the true principles of Christian charity from the law of Moses. That people has always been remarkable for kindness to its own poor.

For this thing.—Literally, *this word,* or *this promise.* And Rashi observes, "Even when thou hast promised to give, thou wilt receive the reward of the promise as well as the reward of the deed;" and we may compare St. Paul. "If there be first a willing mind, it is accepted according to that a man hath, and not according to that he hath not." (2 Cor. viii. 12.)

⁽¹¹⁾ **For the poor shall never cease.**—There is no contradiction between this verse and verse 4 above. There will always be some men falling into poverty; but it is our business to see that they do not remain in want. The poor will never cease, except by the provision made for them by their brethren. God will never make all men absolutely equal in this world.

Thy brother, thy poor, and thy needy.—According to Rashi, the word translated "needy" is stronger than the word for "poor." The "poor" are in humble circumstances; the "needy" are actually in want. In commenting on this verse, Rashi asks a similar question to that of the lawyer in St. Luke x. 29, "Who is this brother? Thy poor man." He might have added that "*thy* poor" and "*thy* needy" are expressions teaching the truth that we are "members one of another." We may not pass by our poorer brethren, and say we have nothing to do with them. Jehovah calls them ours—"*thy* poor man," and "*thy* needy man." The words are both in the singular number in the Hebrew. We cannot shake off the relationship or the responsibility in any one case.

⁽¹²⁾ **If thy brother, an Hebrew man, or an Hebrew woman, be sold unto thee.**—This law is expressly referred to in Jeremiah xxxiv. 9, 13, 14, as given in the time of the Exodus, and as applicable both to men and women. It first appears in Exod. xxi. 2—11, where it occupies the first section of the Sinaitic code. There is no need to suppose that anything enacted here is contradictory to the Law as given there; but there are certain peculiarities about the case of the female slave which create exceptions. (See below on verse 17.) Rashi notes two fresh points in the Law as given in Deuteronomy: one concerning the Hebrew woman (an Hebrew "or an Hebrewess"—verse 12; Jer. xxxiv. 9) and another concerning the "furnishing" (verse 14).

⁽¹²⁾ **In the seventh year.**—This is to be understood of the Sabbatical year whenever it came. It would

then in the seventh year thou shalt let him go free from thee. (13) And when thou sendest him out free from thee, thou shalt not let him go away empty: (14) thou shalt furnish him liberally out of thy flock, and out of thy floor, and out of thy winepress: *of that* wherewith the LORD thy God hath blessed thee thou shalt give unto him. (15) And thou shalt remember that thou wast a bondman in the land of Egypt, and the LORD thy God redeemed thee: therefore I command thee this thing to day. (16) And it shall be, if he say unto thee, I will not go away from thee; because he loveth thee and thine house, because he is well with thee; (17) *a* then thou shalt take an aul, and thrust *it* through his ear unto the door, and he shall be thy servant for ever. And also unto thy maidservant thou shalt do likewise.

(18) It shall not seem hard unto thee, when thou sendest him away free from thee; for he hath been worth a double hired servant *to thee*, in serving thee six years: and the LORD thy God shall bless thee in all that thou doest.

(19) *b* All the firstling males that come of thy herd and of thy flock thou shalt sanctify unto the LORD thy God: thou shalt do no work with the firstling of thy bullock, nor shear the firstling of thy sheep. (20) Thou shalt eat *it* before the LORD thy God year by year in the place which the LORD shall choose, thou and thy household. (21) *c* And if there be any blemish therein, *as if it be* lame, or blind, *or have* any ill blemish, thou shalt not sacrifice it unto the LORD thy God. (22) Thou shalt eat it within thy gates: the unclean and the clean *person shall eat it* alike, as the roebuck, and as the

a Ex. 21. 6.

b Ex. 34. 19.

c Lev. 22. 20; ch. 17, 1; Ecclus. 35. 12.

---

rarely happen that the Hebrew slave would serve for the full period of six years.

(14) **Thou shalt furnish him liberally.**—The beneficence of this provision is noticeable. Those who had fallen into poverty, when they had served their time, must be provided with means for a fresh start in life. And since the Jewish commentator regards the slavery of Hebrew men as chiefly a consequence of theft (If he be sold unto thee, "when the supreme court has sold him for his theft "), it would seem that, under Jewish law, even convicted thieves, when the term of their servitude was over, were to be provided with the means of obtaining an honest livelihood. This state of things is above the attainments of Christian England at the present date.

(15) **Thou shalt remember that thou wast a bondman in Egypt.**—"And that I furnished and adorned thee from the spoils of Egypt and the spoils of the sea" (Rashi).

Therefore I command thee.—In Lev. xxv. 42 the reason is given thus: "They are *my* servants, which I brought forth out of the land of Egypt; they shall not be sold as bondmen" (*i.e.*, not for ever). The land was under the same restriction—it "shall not be sold *for ever; for the land is mine*" (Lev. xxv. 16, 17, 23).

(17) **And unto thy maidservant thou shalt do likewise**—*i.e.*, "in furnishing her liberally" (Rashi), and "possibly also in retaining her if she will."

It must not be supposed that this contradicts Exod. xxi. 7, "She shall not go out as the menservants do." She shall not go out *according to the going of the menservants* (*i.e.*, on the same principle). It is not said, She shall not go out at all. The exceptions are given in Exod. xxi. 8—11, which see. The general right of release is stated here. One difference (as stated by Rashi) is that women were not liable to be sold for theft like men, but might be sold by their parents in infancy. If the girl were not marriageable when the first Sabbatical year arrived, she would obtain her freedom absolutely, because the case contemplated in Exod. xxi. 8—10 could not possibly arise. And, generally, we may suppose that the rights of an unmarried female slave would be the same as those of a man, to go out free in the seventh year. (See Jer. xxxiv. 9.)

(19) **All the firstling males . . . . thou shalt sanctify**—*i.e.*, recognise them as the property of Jehovah by not using them for ordinary purposes. In Lev. xxvii. 26 we read, "No man shall sanctify it"—*i.e.*, shall make it the subject of a special vow or dedication, because it already belongs to Jehovah. This is the only interpretation consistent with the context in Leviticus; for chap. xxvii. deals entirely with "voluntary" offerings, which are in a sense outside the Law. (See Notes at the commencement of Deut. xxviii. and xxix.).

(20) **Thou shalt eat it before the Lord thy God year by year.**—This connects the eating of the firstlings with the "second" tithe (chap. xiv. 23). There is some difficulty in understanding the exact relation between this precept and that which assigns the firstlings to the priests (Num. xviii. 15) with the first tithe. The practical solution is to be sought in the practice of the Jews. One suggestion is (that of Rashi), that "thou shalt eat" in this place refers to the priest; another is, that the firstlings without blemish were for the priest; those that were not fit for sacrifice were for the household of the owner. But it is perfectly conceivable that there was a collection of firstlings at one time of the year for the first tithe, and these were given to the priests. At the time of the collection of the second tithe, there might, and generally would, be other firstlings born since, and these, with the second tithe, would be disposed of in the manner indicated in these verses. And this, upon the whole, seems the most probable explanation. If two tithes were a regular institution, they must have been regularly collected at fixed times. And there might easily be firstlings in both of them; in fact, there almost certainly would be. At any rate, no contradiction can be maintained as between laws which were both observed in practice by the Jews. It appears from the Talmud, that tithes and offerings might be presented, more or less, at any of the three great feasts. They would not all be presented at one time. The tithes and first-fruits in some cases were liable to be delayed. The rule was, that everything due

hart. (23) ª Only thou shalt not eat the blood thereof; thou shalt pour it upon the ground as water.

CHAPTER XVI.—(1) Observe the ᵇ month of Abib, and keep the passover unto the LORD thy God: for ᶜin the month of Abib the LORD thy God brought thee forth out of Egypt by night. (2) Thou shalt therefore sacrifice the passover unto the LORD thy God, of the flock and the herd, in the ᵈ place which the LORD shall choose to place his name there. (3) ᵉThou shalt eat no leavened bread with it; seven days shalt thou eat unleavened bread therewith, *even* the bread of affliction; for thou camest forth out of the land of Egypt in haste: that thou mayest remember the day when thou camest forth out of the land of Egypt all the days of thy life. (4) ᶠAnd there shall be no leavened bread seen with thee in all thy coast seven days; neither shall there *any thing* of the flesh, which thou sacrificedst the first day at even, remain all night until the morning.

(5) Thou mayest not ¹sacrifice the passover within any of thy gates, which the LORD thy God giveth thee: (6) but at the place which the LORD thy God shall choose to place his name in, there thou shalt sacrifice the passover at even, at the going down of the sun, at the season that thou camest forth out of Egypt. (7) And thou shalt roast and eat *it* in the place which the LORD thy God shall choose: and thou shalt turn in the morning, and go unto thy tents. (8) Six days thou shalt eat unleavened bread: and on the seventh day *shall be* a ²solemn assembly to the LORD thy God: thou shalt do no work *therein*. (9) ᵍ Seven weeks shalt thou number unto thee: begin to number the seven weeks from *such time as* thou beginnest *to put* the sickle to the corn. (10) And thou shalt keep the feast of weeks unto the LORD thy God with ³a tribute of a freewill offering of thine hand, which thou shalt give *unto the LORD thy God*, according as the LORD thy God hath blessed thee: (11) and thou shalt rejoice

---

a ch. 12, 16, 23.
b Ex. 12. 2, &c.
c Ex. 13. 4.
d ch. 12. 5.
e Ex. 12. 15.
f Ex. 34. 25.
¹ Or, *kill*.
² Heb., *restraint*.
g Lev. 23. 15.
³ Or, *sufficiency*.

---

for three years last past *must* be cleared out of the establishment, and paid over to the proper authorities at the Feast of the Passover in the fourth and eighth years reckoned by the Sabbatical system. (See chap. xxvi. 12, 13, for more on this head.)

XVI.

Verses 1—8. THE PASSOVER. (See on Exod. xii.)

(1) **The month Abib** was so called from the "ears of corn" which appeared in it.

By night.—Pharaoh's permission was given on the night of the death of the first-born, though Israel did not actually depart until the next day (Num. xxxiii. 3, 4).

(2) **Of the flock, and of the herd.**—The Passover victim itself must be either lamb or kid. (See on chap. xiv. 4, and comp. Exod. xii. 5.) But there were special sacrifices of bullocks appointed for the first day of the Feast of Unleavened Bread, which followed the Passover. (See Num. xxviii. 19.)

(6) **At even, at the going down of the sun, at the season that thou camest forth from Egypt.**—The word "season" here is ambiguous in the English. Does it mean the time of year, or the time of day? The Hebrew word, which usually denotes a *commemorative* time, might seem to point to the hour of sunset as the time when the march actually began. If so, it was the evening of the fifteenth day of the month (See Numbers xxxiii. 3). But the word is also used generally of the time of year (Exod. xxiii. 15; Num. ix. 2, &c.); and as the Passover was to be kept on the fourteenth, not the fifteenth day, the time actually commemorated is the time of the slaying of the lamb which saved Israel from the destroyer, rather than the time of the actual march. It is noticeable that, while the Passover commemorated the deliverance by the slain lamb in Egypt, the Feast of Tabernacles commemorated the encampment at Succoth, the first resting-place of the delivered nation after the exodus had actually begun.

(8) **A solemn assembly.**—Literally, as in the Margin, *a restraint*—*i.e.*, a day when work was forbidden. The word is applied to the eighth day of the feast of tabernacles in Lev. xxiii. 36, and Num. xxix. 35, and does not occur elsewhere in the Pentateuch.

Verses 9—12. THE FEAST OF WEEKS, OR PENTECOST.

See also Exod. xxiii. 16, xxxiv. 18—23; Lev. xxiii. 15—22; Num. xxviii. 26—31. The feast itself is ordained in Exodus; the *time* is given in Leviticus; and the *sacrifices* in Numbers.

(9) **From such time as thou beginnest to put the sickle to the corn.**—The word for sickle only occurs here and in chap. xxiii. 25. In Leviticus the weeks are ordered to be reckoned from the offering of the wave sheaf on the sixteenth day of the first month, two days after the Passover. This sheaf was of barley, the first ripe corn. A different view is sometimes taken of the word "Sabbath" in Lev. xxiii. 11; but the view given here is correct according to the Talmud.

(10) **A tribute.**—This word (*missah*) occurs nowhere else in the Bible. The marginal rendering, "*sufficiency*," is its Aramaic or Chaldæan sense. The idea seems to be "a *proportionate* offering"—*i.e.*, a free will offering, proportioned to a man's means and prosperity. In Exod. xxxiv. 20, and xxiii. 15, we read, "None shall appear before me empty." The command is made general for all the three feasts in verses 16, 17 further on.

(11) **Thou shalt rejoice before the Lord thy God.**—This aspect of the feast of weeks is specially insisted upon in Deuteronomy. Its relation to the poor appears also in the command connected with this feast

The Feast of Tabernacles.   DEUTERONOMY, XVI.   *Appointment of Judges.*

before the Lord thy God, thou, and thy son, and thy daughter, and thy manservant, and thy maidservant, and the Levite that *is* within thy gates, and the stranger, and the fatherless, and the widow, that *are* among you, in the place which the Lord thy God hath chosen to place his name there. (12) And thou shalt remember that thou wast a bondman in Egypt: and thou shalt observe and do these statutes.

(13) Thou shalt observe the feast of tabernacles seven days, after that thou hast gathered in thy [1] corn and thy wine: (14) and thou shalt rejoice in thy feast, thou, and thy son, and thy daughter, and thy manservant, and thy maidservant, and the Levite, the stranger, and the fatherless, and the widow, that *are* within thy gates. (15) Seven days shalt thou keep a solemn feast unto the Lord thy God in the place which the Lord shall choose: because the Lord thy God shall bless thee in all thine increase, and in all the works of thine hands, therefore thou shalt surely rejoice.

(16) *a* Three times in a year shall all thy males appear before the Lord thy God in the place which he shall choose; in the feast of unleavened bread, and in the feast of weeks, and in the feast of tabernacles: and *b* they shall not appear before the Lord empty: (17) every man *shall give* [2] as he is able, according to the blessing of the Lord thy God which he hath given thee.

(18) Judges and officers shalt thou make thee in all thy gates, which the Lord thy God giveth thee, throughout thy tribes: and they shall judge the people with just judgment. (19) Thou shalt not wrest judgment; thou shalt not respect persons, *c* neither take a gift: for a gift doth blind the eyes of the wise, and pervert the [3] words of the righteous. (20) [4] That which is altogether just shalt thou follow, that thou mayest live, and inherit the land which the Lord thy God giveth thee.

(21) Thou shalt not plant thee a grove of any trees near unto the altar of the Lord thy God, which thou shalt make thee. (22) *d* Neither shalt thou set thee up *any* [5] image; which the Lord thy God hateth.

Marginal notes:
1 Heb., *floor and thy winepress.*
a Ex. 23. 14 & 34. 23.
b Ecclus. 35. 4.
2 Heb., *according to the gift of his hand.*
c Ex. 23. 8.
3 Or, *matters.*
4 Heb., *Justice, justice.*
d Lev. 26. 1.
5 Or, *statue,* or, *pillar.*

---

in Lev. xxiii. 22, to leave the corners of the fields unreaped for them.

Verses 13—15. The Feast of Tabernacles.

(13) **Thou shalt observe the feast of tabernacles seven days.**—For details of the observance see the passages already referred to in Exodus, Leviticus and Numbers, but more especially Lev. xxiii. 33—43.

(14) **Thou, and thy son . . .**—The rejoicing of the Feast of Tabernacles was proverbial among the Jews. On the persons who are to share the joy, Rashi has an interesting note. "The Levite, the stranger, and the fatherless, and the widow,—My four (Jehovah's), over against thy four—thy son, thy daughter, thy manservant, thy maidservant. If thou wilt make My four to rejoice, I will rejoice thy four."

(15) **Seven days.**—An eighth day is mentioned both in Lev. xxiii. 36 and Num. xxix. 35. But the seven days of this feast are also spoken of in both those passages (Lev. xxiii. 36 and Num. xxix. 12). There is, therefore, no contradiction between the two passages. The eighth day is treated apart from the first seven days of the Feast of Tabernacles, somewhat in the same way as the Passover is always distinguished in the Pentateuch from the six days which followed it, and which are called the Feast of Unleavened bread. The reason for the distinction in that case becomes clear in the fulfilment of the feast by our Lord. The Passover is *His sacrifice and death*. We keep the feast of *unleavened* bread by serving Him in "*sincerity and truth.*" The Feast of Tabernacles has not yet been fulfilled by our Lord like the two other great feasts of the Jewish calendar. Unfulfilled prophecies regarding it may be pointed out, as in Zech. xiv. Our Lord refused to signalise that feast by any public manifestation (John vii. 2—10). There may, therefore, be some reason for separating the eighth and last day of the Feast of Tabernacles from the former seven, which will appear in its fulfilment in the kingdom of God. It is remarkable that the dedication of Solomon's temple, the commencement of the second temple and the dedication of the wall of Jerusalem, all occurred about the time of the Feast of Tabernacles.

Thou shalt surely rejoice.—In the Hebrew this is a somewhat unusual form of expression. Literally, *thou wilt be only rejoicing*. Rashi says it is not a command, but a promise.

(16) **Three times in a year.**—So Exod. xxiii. 17. And in Exod. xxxiv. 23, 24 a promise is added that their land should be safe in their absence.

(18) **Judges and officers.**—A fresh section of the book, as read in the synagogues, begins with these words.

The land is now considered as the *seat of the Kingdom of Jehovah*, to the end of ch. xviii. See Introduction for a complete analysis, and comp. Joshua xxiii. 2, which shows that these magistrates were already appointed.

(19) See Exod. xxiii. 6, 8.

(21) **Thou shalt not plant thee a grove.**—Heb., *ashêrah*, sometimes used of images, but here evidently of the grove itself. The worship of Jehovah allowed of no secret rites; and nothing that could lead to the abominations of heathen idolatry could be permitted near Jehovah's altar.

(22) **Image.**—Explained by Rashi of a single stone, whether statue or pillar.

The Sacrifice to be Unblemished. DEUTERONOMY, XVII. *The Idolater to be Stoned.*

CHAPTER XVII.—⁽¹⁾ Thou shalt not sacrifice unto the LORD thy God *any* bullock, or ¹sheep, wherein is blemish, *or* any evilfavouredness: for that *is* an abomination unto the LORD thy God.

⁽²⁾ If there be found among you, within any of thy gates which the LORD thy God giveth thee, man or woman, that hath wrought wickedness in the sight of the LORD thy God, in transgressing his covenant, ⁽³⁾ and hath gone and served other gods, and worshipped them, either the sun, or moon, or any of the host of heaven, which I have not commanded; ⁽⁴⁾ and it be told thee, and thou hast heard *of it,* and enquired diligently, and, behold, *it be* true, *and* the thing certain, *that* such abomination is wrought in Israel: ⁽⁵⁾ then shalt thou bring forth that man or that woman, which have committed that wicked thing, unto thy gates, *even* that man or that woman, and shalt stone them with stones, till they die. ⁽⁶⁾ ^aAt the mouth of two witnesses, or three witnesses, shall he that is worthy of death be put to death; *but* at the mouth of one witness he shall not be put to death. ⁽⁷⁾ The hands of the witnesses shall be first upon him to put him to death, and afterward the hands of all the people. So thou shalt put the evil away from among you.

⁽⁸⁾ If there arise a matter too hard for thee in judgment, between blood and blood, between plea and plea, and between stroke and stroke, *being* matters of controversy within thy gates: then

1 Or, *goat.*

a Num. 35. 30; ch. 19. 15; Matt. 18. 16; John 8. 17; 2 Cor. 13. 1; Heb. 10. 28.

XVII.

⁽¹⁾ **Thou shalt not sacrifice . . .**—The law concerning the purity of victims is given in full in Lev. xxii. 17—25. It takes its place there among the special laws of holiness. The same principle appears to unite the several topics treated here in Deuteronomy, as the holy days, the administration of justice, the absence of groves and images, with such a precept as this regarding the perfection of sacrifices. The holiness of the God of Israel necessitates them all. Truth, justice, and purity are demanded in all that come nigh Him. The dignity of His *Kingdom* is also concerned here. (See Introduction.)

Sheep.—The Hebrew word is *sêh* (on which see chap. xiv. 4, note). It may be either a lamb or a kid.

The only time in history when the sacrifice of imperfect creatures is complained of to any great extent is the time of the prophet Malachi (see Mal. i. 7—14). The laxity of the priests in his time called forth the prophecy that "in every place incense should be offered to God's name and a pure offering."

Verses 2—7. EVERY IDOLATER TO BE STONED.

⁽²⁾ **If there be found . . . man or woman.**—This section differs slightly from the third section of chap. xiii. The penalty there is directed against the teachers of idolatry, whether prophets, private individuals, or communities in Israel. Here the penalty of death is enacted for every individual, man or woman, found guilty of worshipping any other god but Jehovah. We find traces of this law in the covenant made in the reign of Asa (2 Chron. xv. 13), "that whosoever would not seek the Lord God of Israel should be put to death, whether small or great, whether man or woman."

⁽³⁾ **Either the sun, or moon, or any of the host of heaven.**—The oldest and simplest, and apparently most innocent form of idolatry. If this was punishable with death, obviously no grosser form of idolatry could be spared. The Book of Job, which knows no other idolatry, admits this to be a denial "of the God that is above" (Job xxxi. 26—28).

⁽⁶⁾ **He that is worthy of death.**—Literally, *he that dieth.*

⁽⁷⁾ **The hands of the witnesses . . . first.**—A great safeguard against false testimony.

Put . . . away.—Literally, *consume.* The primary meaning of the word is "burn." *Taberah,* "burning," is a derivative.

The evil.—The Greek version renders this "the wicked man," and the sentence is taken up in this form in 1 Cor. v. 13, "and ye shall put away from among you *that wicked person.*" The phrase is of frequent occurrence in Deuteronomy, and if we are to understand that in all places where it occurs "the evil" is to be understood of an individual, and to be taken in the masculine gender, the fact seems to deserve notice in considering the phrase "deliver us from evil" in the Lord's Prayer. There is really no such thing as wickedness in the world apart from some wicked being or person. We are also reminded of the famous argument of St. Augustine, that evil has no existence except as a corruption of good, or a creature's perverted will.

Verses 8—20. THE SUPREMACY IN ISRAEL OF THE WRITTEN LAW OF GOD.

⁽⁸⁾ **If there arise a matter too hard for thee.**—Literally, *too wonderful.*

Between blood and blood, between plea and plea, and between stroke and stroke.—The "blood" and the "plea" seem to indicate criminal and civil cases. The word "stroke" is the common word for "plague" in the Pentateuch and elsewhere. It may possibly refer to cases of ceremonial purity or impurity, especially in reference to disease. There is an evident allusion to this law in the history of King Jehoshaphat (2 Chron. xix. 8—10). There the words are "between blood and blood, between law and commandment, statutes and judgments." The questions are (1) between two contending parties; (2) between the law as a general rule and its application to particular duties, institutions and requirements. Other passages in the same chapter recall Deut. xvi. 18—20.

Matters of controversy within thy gates—*i.e.,* in the local courts of their several cities. The "gate" was the place of judgment. In 2 Chron. xix. 10, the phrase is more clearly expressed, thus, "what cause soever shall come unto you of your brethren that dwell *in their cities.*"

Into the place which the Lord thy God shall choose.—This implies what was afterwards

shalt thou arise, and get thee up into the place which the LORD thy God shall choose; (9) and thou shalt come unto the priests the Levites, and unto the judge that shall be in those days, and enquire; and they shall shew thee the sentence of judgment: (10) and thou shalt do according to the sentence, which they of that place which the LORD shall choose shall shew thee; and thou shalt observe to do according to all that they inform thee: (11) according to the sentence of the law which they shall teach thee, and according to the judgment which they shall tell thee, thou shalt do: thou shalt not decline from the sentence which they shall shew thee, *to* the right hand, nor *to* the left. (12) And the man that will do presumptuously,[1] and will not hearken unto the priest that standeth to minister there before the LORD thy God, or unto the judge, even that man shall die: and thou shalt put away the evil from Israel. (13) And all the people shall hear, and fear, and do no more presumptuously.

[1] Heb., *not to hearken.*

---

ordered before Moses' death, that the standard copy of the Law would be kept beside the Ark of the Covenant, in the sacred place (chap. xxxi. 26).

(9) **Thou shalt come unto the priests the Levites**—*i.e.*, "the priests that come of the tribe of Levi" (Rashi). Some modern critics say the writer of Deuteronomy knew no distinction between priests and Levites; but see above on chap. xi. 6, and also the notes on chap. xxxi. 9 and 25.

The priests, the Levites, and ... the judge. —The order agrees exactly with the constitution which Moses left behind him at his death. This has been already indicated in Num. xxvii. 15—21. Joshua was to "stand before Eleazar." Eleazar was to ask counsel from Jehovah, and at his word Joshua and all the people were to go in and out. The order, when the two are mentioned together in the Book of Joshua, is invariably "Eleazar the priest and Joshua the son of Nun," not *vice versâ*. The priests are the custodians of the Law; the judge or chief magistrate is the executor of it. (Comp. Mal. ii. 7, 8.) The principle is not altered by the substitution of a king for the judge, or by the addition of a prophet.

That shall be in those days.—Rashi and the New Testament are curiously agreed in the application of this part of the commandment. Our Lord, in Matt. xxiii. 2, 3, says of the Scribes and Pharisees (the judges of His day) that they "sit in Moses' seat: All therefore whatsoever they bid you observe, that observe and do." Rashi says here, "Although he is not like the rest of the judges that were before him, thou must hearken to him. *There is no judge for thee except the judge that is in thy days.*"

(9—11) **And they shall shew thee the sentence of judgment ... According to the sentence of the law ... thou shalt do.**—This passage should be carefully noted. The function of the priest and judge was to *show, inform, teach, and tell the applicant the sentence of the law*, *i.e.*, of the written law. The four English verbs have only three equivalents in Hebrew, viz., *tell, teach and say*. It is not sufficiently observed that this defines the relation between the Church and the Bible from the time the Law (which was the germ of the Bible) was delivered to the Church, and that the relation between the Church and the Bible is the same to this day. The only authority wherewith the Church (of Israel, or of Christ) can "bind" or "loose," is the written Law of God. The binding (or forbidding) and loosing (or permitting) of the Rabbis —the authority which our Lord committed to His Church—was only the application of His written word. The Rabbis acknowledge this from one end of the Talmud to the other by the appeal to Scripture which is made in every page, sometimes in almost every line. The application is often strained or fanciful; but that does not alter the principle. *The written word is the chain that binds.* Nor does the varying relation between the executive and legislative authority alter the principle. Where the law of Jehovah is the law of the land, death may be the penalty of disobedience. Where it is only the law of the Christian community, exclusion may be the extreme penalty that is possible. But still the relation between the written word and the ministers of the Church is the same. The Church is the "witness and keeper of Holy Writ," and can only *shew* from thence the sentence of judgment. The sentence is an application of the law, not a mere invention of the authorities themselves; and it would be easy to show from history how every misapplication of the Divine code brought with it surely, sooner or later, its own refutation, and the overthrow of the unfaithful government. The prophets not seldom took the place of tribunes of the people in cases of oppression. No one lifted up a more distinct protest from the law itself against the misapplication of the law than the Prophet like unto Moses, who formally acknowledged the authority of them that sat in Moses' seat.*

(12) **And the man that will do presumptuously ... shall die.**—This word "presumptuously" occurs for the first time in this place. (See also chap. xviii. 22.) It is connected with "pride," and denotes a proud self-assertion against the law. The penalty of death arises necessarily out of the theocracy. If God is the king of the nation, rebellion against His law is treason, and if it be proud and wilful rebellion, the penalty of death is only what we should expect to see inflicted. As soon as the law of Jehovah is in any way separated from the law of the land, this state of things may be altered. It is remarkable that in Ezra's commission from Artaxerxes we find permission to identify the law of Jehovah with the law of the Persian empire to the full extent of this precept, "Whosoever will not do the law of thy God, and the law of the king, let judgment be executed speedily upon him, *whether it be unto death*, banishment, confiscation of goods, or imprisonment" (Ezra vii. 25, 26.) But such penalties, except in a theocratic government, are obviously out of place in matters connected with religion.

---

* Manifestly, when copies of the Law were scarce, and when a good deal of it, like this Book of Deuteronomy, was general, and even prophetic, a board of authorised interpreters, or *appliers*, of the law to matters of detail was an absolute necessity. (See Introduction to Deuteronomy for more on this head.)

The Law of   DEUTERONOMY, XVII.   *the Kingdom.*

(14) When thou art come unto the land which the LORD thy God giveth thee, and shalt possess it, and shalt dwell therein, and shalt say, I will set a king over me, like as all the nations that *are* about me; (15) thou shalt in any wise set *him* king over thee, whom the LORD thy God shall choose: *one* from among thy brethren shalt thou set king over thee: thou mayest not set a stranger over thee, which *is* not thy brother. (16) But he shall not multiply horses to himself, nor cause the people to return to Egypt, to the end that he should multiply horses: forasmuch as the LORD hath said unto you, Ye shall henceforth return no more that way. (17) Neither shall he multiply wives to himself, that his heart turn not away: neither shall he greatly multiply to himself silver and gold. (18) And it shall be, when he sitteth upon the throne of his kingdom, that he shall write him a copy of this law in a book out of *that which is* before the priests the Levites: (19) and it shall be with him, and he shall read therein all the days of his life: that he may learn to fear the LORD his God, to keep all the words of this law and these statutes,

---

Verses 14—20. THE LAW OF THE KINGDOM.

(14) **When thou art come unto the land.**—These are not the words of a legislator who is already in the land. Those who say that this law dates from later times must be prepared to assert that this clause is expressly framed to suit the lips of Moses, and is thus far a deliberate forgery.

And shalt possess it, and dwell therein—*i.e.*, shalt complete the conquest and settle. It is not contemplated that the king would be desired immediately after the conquest.

I will set a king over me, like as all the nations.—There is an evident allusion to this phrase in 1 Sam. viii. 20, "That we also may be like all the nations." It is noticeable that Moses in this place says nothing in disapproval of the design. In fact his words might easily have been cited by the people in support of their proposal. Moses said we should need a king; why should we not ask for one? Looked at this way, the citation of the words of Deuteronomy in Samuel is perfectly natural. The people confirm their request by presenting it in the very words of Moses. But if we suppose (with some modern writers) that the passage in Deuteronomy was constructed from that in Samuel, there are several difficulties—(1) Why is there no disapproval here of the plan, which Samuel so strongly disapproved? (2) How does the writer in Deuteronomy contrive to be so wholly unconscious either of the royal tribe, or of the royal family? Precisely the same unconsciousness of the locality of the place which Jehovah should choose in Palestine appears in every reference to it in this book. In Moses this is perfectly natural. But that any later writer should be so totally regardless of the claims of Judah, David, and Jerusalem, and say nothing either for or against them, is inconceivable. Samuel could hardly have written about the king without betraying disapproval of Israel's desire for him. No later writer could have avoided some allusion to the choice of David's family, and the promises to David's son.

(15) **Whom the Lord thy God shall choose ... from among thy brethren.**—This precept seems almost needless from the standpoint of later history. As years passed by, the Israelites were less and less tempted to accept the supremacy of foreign princes.* But Moses can never have forgotten that for two-thirds of his own lifetime the Israelites had been subject to the kings of Egypt; and that even since the exodus they had proposed to make a captain to return thither; *whom* we know not, but very possibly an Egyptian. The chief thing dreaded by Moses was a return to Egypt, as appears by the next verse.

(16, 17) **He shall not multiply horses ... wives ... neither shall he greatly multiply ... silver and gold.**—It is not a little remarkable that these are the very things which Solomon did multiply; and that under him the monarchy attained its greatest glory. But the prophecy avenged itself by its literal fulfilment: "When Solomon was old ... *his wives turned away his heart*" (1 Kings xi. 4). Yet it is easier to read the words as prophecy than as later history. What Israelite could have written this sentence after the time of Solomon without some passing allusion to the glories of his reign? Compare the recorded allusion in Neh. xiii. 26: "Did not Solomon, king of Israel, sin by these things? yet among many nations was there no king like him, who was beloved of his God, and God made him king over all Israel; nevertheless even him did outlandish women cause to sin."

The question, how Solomon came to transgress these orders, may easily be met by another—How came David to attempt the removal of the ark of God in a cart? The wealth which Solomon had is represented as the special gift of Jehovah. His many marriages may be partly accounted for by the fact that *only one son is mentioned, and he was born before his father became king.* The question, "Who knoweth whether he shall be a wise man or a fool?" is singularly applicable to this individual. And one of the Psalms, which is by its title ascribed to Solomon, pursues a similar line of thought (Ps. cxxvii).

The caution against multiplying horses marks the profound wisdom of the writer. The Israelitish infantry was Israel's strength. The conquest of Canaan was entirely effected by infantry. There are not many battle-fields in Canaan suited for chariots and cavalry. An army of infantry can choose its own ground.

(18) **He shall write him a copy of this law.**—This phrase is the source of the Greek title of the book, *Deuteronomion*, or in English, Deuteronomy. The word appears also in Josh. viii. 32. The English conveys the right sense of the word, which primarily denotes repetition. In Hebrew it is *Mishneh*, the name afterwards given to the "text" of the Talmud, of which the idea is to repeat the law; though it is a somewhat peculiar repetition, in which *minutiæ* are chiefly dealt with, and weightier matters left out.

There are traces of this direction (1) in the coronation of Joash (2 Chron. xxiii. 11, "they gave him the

---

* But see note on chap. xxxi. 11 for an incident that illustrates the feeling.

The Portions of the Priests, DEUTERONOMY, XVIII. *and of the Levites.*

to do them: ⁽²⁰⁾ that his heart be not lifted up above his brethren, and that he turn not aside from the commandment, *to* the right hand, or *to* the left: to the end that he may prolong *his* days in his kingdom, he, and his children, in the midst of Israel.

CHAPTER XVIII.—⁽¹⁾ The priests the Levites, *and* all the tribe of Levi, *a*shall have no part nor inheritance with Israel: they *b* shall eat the offerings of the LORD made by fire, and his inheritance. ⁽²⁾ Therefore shall they have no inheritance among their brethren: the LORD *is* their inheritance, as he hath said unto them.

⁽³⁾ And this shall be the priest's due from the people, from them that offer a sacrifice, whether *it be* ox or sheep;

a Num. 18. 20; ch. 10. 9.

b 1 Cor. 9. 13.

¹ Heb., *his sales by the fathers.*

and they shall give unto the priest the shoulder, and the two cheeks, and the maw. ⁽⁴⁾ The firstfruit *also* of thy corn, of thy wine, and of thine oil, and the first of the fleece of thy sheep, shalt thou give him. ⁽⁵⁾ For the LORD thy God hath chosen him out of all thy tribes, to stand to minister in the name of the LORD, him and his sons for ever.

⁽⁶⁾ And if a Levite come from any of thy gates out of all Israel, where he sojourned, and come with all the desire of his mind unto the place which the LORD shall choose; ⁽⁷⁾ then he shall minister in the name of the LORD his God, as all his brethren the Levites *do*, which stand there before the LORD. ⁽⁸⁾ They shall have like portions to eat, beside ¹ that which cometh of the sale of his patrimony.

---

testimony;" (2) in the reign of Jehoshaphat, who had the Book of the Law taught to his people (2 Chron. xvii. 9); and (3) in the delivery of the book when discovered in the Temple to Josiah (2 Chron. xxxiv. 18), and in the effect of the perusal of it upon that king. But it is singular that we do not hear of the Book of the Law in connection with David and Solomon. Possibly, as David was a prophet himself, and not only a king, it may be thought unnecessary to make special mention of his study of the law. In many things he acted upon the direct commands of God to himself or to his seers. We must not forget that the true king of Israel is He whose special mission it was "to fulfil the law and the prophets." "Lo, I come, *in the volume of the book it is written of me*, I delight to do thy will, O my God: *yea, thy law is within my heart.*"

⁽²⁰⁾ **To the end that he may prolong his days in his kingdom, he, and his children.**—Shows that the kingdom in Israel would be hereditary only so far as Jehovah willed it to be so. Again we may say that the striking fact that no dynasty except that of David ever continued for more than five generations, and only two dynasties for more than two generations, while David's dynasty was perpetual by promise, could hardly have escaped notice, if known to the writer of this book.

XVIII.

VERSES 1—5. THE PRIESTS' DUE.

⁽¹⁾ **The priests the Levites, (and) all the tribe of Levi.**—The fact that there is no "and" here in the original, and the look of the sentence in English, might dispose a superficial reader to find some ground here for the theory that priest and Levite are not distinguished in Deuteronomy. No such idea occurred to Rashi. He says, "all the tribe of Levi, not only those that are perfect (who can serve), but those who have a blemish (and cannot)." The distinction between priest and Levite has already been sufficiently noted on chap. xi. 6, and xvii. 9. The passage is evidently on the same lines with Num. xviii. 18—21, which see.

⁽³⁾ **The shoulder, and the two cheeks, and the maw.**—This would be from the peace offering.

The shoulder is assigned to them in Lev. vii. 32, 33 (comp. Num. xviii. 18). The "two cheeks and the maw" are not mentioned elsewhere, and the latter word is found in this place only. They are not a valuable part of the sacrifice. An absurd reason for the gift is assigned by Rashi. We know that in the time of Eli, the priests varied their requirements at pleasure, and in the face of the law (see 1 Sam. ii. 13). The "priests' *due* " here, and "the priests' *custom* " there, are the same word in Hebrew, which we have elsewhere translated "requirement."

⁽⁴⁾ **The firstfruit also of thy corn.**—See Num. xviii. 12. The first of the wool is mentioned here only. The quantity in all these cases has been defined by the Rabbis, on grounds somewhat arbitrary.

⁽⁵⁾ **To stand to minister in the name of the Lord.**—This is the office of the priests. The Levites are said, " to stand before the congregation to minister unto them" (Num. xvi. 9). If the writer of Deuteronomy knew no distinction between priest and Levite, it is difficult to see how the Jews could have derived the distinctive privileges of the priests from these enactments.

^(6—8) **And if a Levite come.**—The Levites with the priests were to receive forty-eight cities in Israel, with the suburbs (Num. xxxv. 7). There was as yet no provision made by which all could serve in turn at the tabernacle. When David divided them all into courses, priests, Levites, singers (and porters?) alike, there was no longer any need for this provision. The institutions of David prove its antiquity. The only case in history that illustrates it is that of the child Samuel. His father, Elkanah, was a descendant of Korah. He dwelt in Mount Ephraim, and came up to Shiloh year by year. But Samuel was dedicated by his mother to perpetual service there, and as long as the tabernacle continued in Shiloh, the child Samuel "ministered to the Lord before Eli the priest"—not as a priest, but as a Levite in attendance upon the priests.

⁽⁸⁾ **They shall have like portions to eat, beside that.**—The Levite thus dedicated was to have the same allowance from tithes as the rest who served at the tabernacle, beside the proceeds of the patrimony which he would have had in his own Levitical city.

Wizards &c. Condemned. DEUTERONOMY, XVIII. *A Prophet Promised.*

(9) When thou art come into the land which the LORD thy God giveth thee, thou shalt not learn to do after the abominations of those nations. (10) There shall not be found among you *any one* that maketh his son or his daughter *a* to pass through the fire, *or* that useth divination, *or* an observer of times, or an enchanter, or a witch, (11) *b* or a charmer, or a consulter with familiar spirits, or a wizard, or a *c* necromancer. (12) For all that do these things *are* an abomination unto the LORD: and because of these abominations the LORD thy God doth drive them out from before thee. (13) Thou shalt be ¹perfect with the LORD thy God. (14) For these nations, which thou shalt ²possess, hearkened unto observers of times, and unto diviners: but as for thee, the LORD thy God hath not suffered thee so *to do*.

(15) *d* The LORD thy God will raise up unto thee a Prophet from the midst of thee, of thy brethren, like unto me; unto him ye shall hearken; (16) according to all that thou desiredst of the LORD thy God in Horeb in the day of the assembly, saying, *e* Let me not hear again the voice of the LORD my God, neither let me see this great fire any more, that I die not. (17) And the LORD said unto me, They have well spoken *that* which they have spoken. (18) *f* I will raise them up a Prophet from among their brethren, like unto thee, and will put my words in his mouth; and he shall speak unto them all that I shall command him. (19) And it shall come to pass, *that* whosoever

a Lev. 18. 21.
b Lev. 20. 27.
c 1 Sam. 28. 7.
¹ Or, *upright, or, sincere.*
² Or, *inherit.*
d John 1. 45; Acts 3. 22 & 7. 3.
e Ex. 20. 19.
f John 1. 45; Acts 3. 22 & 7. 37.

(9—14) Certain forms of idolatry to be avoided, especially unlawful means of communication with the unseen world.

(10) **To pass through the fire.**—See Lev. xviii. 21.

Useth divination—(Num. xxii. 7), possibly by sacrifices.

Observer of times.—This is the Rabbinical explanation of the word. In Hebrew the idea of "time" is not so clear. It seems to mean practising *hidden* arts. (See Lev. xix. 26.)

Enchanter.—Whisperer, or serpent charmer. (See Gen. xlix. 5.)

Witch.—One who uses charms or spells (Ex. vii. 11).

(11) **Charmer.**—Literally *one who ties knots*, used here for the first time in Old Testament.

Consulter with familiar spirits.—Literally, *one who consulteth ôb* (see Lev. xix. 31).

A Wizard.—One who *knows* or pretends to know the secrets of the unseen world. (See Lev. xix. 31.)

Necromancer.—One who inquires of the dead. Four of the above practices are ascribed to king Manasseh in 2 Chron. xxxiii. 6. It is hardly possible that all of them were mere imposture and deceit.

(13) **Thou shalt be perfect with the Lord thy God.**—Rashi's note on this is worth preserving: "Thou shalt walk with Him in sincerity, and wait for Him. And thou shalt not pry into the future. But whatsoever cometh upon thee, take it with simplicity, and then thou shalt *be with Him*, and be His portion."

(14) **The Lord thy God hath not suffered thee so to do.**—More literally, *As for thee, not so hath Jehovah thy God given unto thee. A prophet from the midst of thee, of thy brethren, like unto me, will Jehovah thy God raise up unto thee. Him shall ye hear.* The contrast between the miserable resources of idolatrous nations in their anxiety, and the light and comfort promised to Israel and to us, in the One Mediator, is very marked here. Even Israel was better off than the heathen. As Rashi says upon the words "not so," &c., "He hath not left thee to hearken to observers of times and enchanters; for behold He hath given Shechinah to rest upon the prophets, and Urim and Thummim."

Verses 15—20. THE ONE MEDIATOR.

The connection between these verses and the preceding is well illustrated by Isaiah's question (chap. viii. 19): "And when they shall say unto you, Seek unto them that have familiar spirits, and unto wizards that peep, and that mutter: should not a people seek unto their God? for the living to the dead?" Or, as the angels turned the phrase on Easter morning, "Why seek ye Him that liveth among the dead?"

(15) **The Lord thy God will raise up unto thee a Prophet.**—Namely, Him of whom St. Peter spoke in Acts iii. 22—26. "Unto you first God, having raised up His son Jesus, sent Him to bless you." It must not be forgotten that the prophetic office is still continued to our risen Lord. He still "speaketh from heaven." But He "descended first into the lower parts of the earth." He has "the keys of hell and of death;" and knows all their secrets. They who can draw near to Him have no need to look downward, to consult dead relatives, or seek knowledge from spirits whose character, even if *they* are accessible, is beyond our discernment. The Holy Spirit, our Comforter and Advocate on earth, and the Prophet, our Advocate that speaketh from heaven, are enough for all human need. What we cannot learn from them, or from the light they give us, it is better not to know.

(16) **According to all that thou desiredst . . . in Horeb.**—It should never be forgotten that the Prophet like to Moses was promised on "the day of the assembly." The Holy Spirit, who is Christ in us, was promised on the day of the delivery of the "letter that killeth." (See also on chap. v. 28.)

(18) **He shall speak unto them all that I shall command him.**—"The words that I speak unto you I speak not of myself" (our Lord, in John xiv. 10). "He shall not speak of Himself. He shall receive of mine, and shall show it unto you" (the Holy Spirit, John xvi. 13, 14).

(19) **Whosoever will not hearken . . . I will require it of him.**—"For if they escaped not who refused Him that spake on earth, much more shall not

will not hearken unto my words which he shall speak in my name, I will require it of him.

(20) But the prophet, which shall presume to speak a word in my name, which I have not commanded him to speak, or that shall speak in the name of other gods, even that prophet shall die. (21) And if thou say in thine heart, How shall we know the word which the LORD hath not spoken? (22) When a prophet speaketh in the name of the LORD, if the thing follow not, nor come to pass, that is the thing which the LORD hath not spoken, but the prophet hath spoken it presumptuously: thou shalt not be afraid of him.

CHAPTER XIX.—(1) When the LORD thy God *a* hath cut off the nations, whose land the LORD thy God giveth thee, and thou [1] succeedest them, and dwellest in their cities, and in their houses; (2) *b* thou shalt separate three cities for thee in the midst of thy land, which the LORD thy God giveth thee to possess it. (3) Thou shalt prepare thee a way, and divide the coasts of thy land, which the LORD thy God giveth thee to inherit, into three parts, that every slayer may flee thither.

(4) And this is the case of the slayer, which shall flee thither, that he may live: Whoso killeth his neighbour ignorantly, whom he hated not [2] in time past; (5) as when a man goeth into the wood with his neighbour to hew wood, and his hand fetcheth a stroke with the ax to cut down the tree, and the [3] head slippeth from the [4] helve, and [5] lighteth upon his neighbour, that he die; he shall flee unto one of those cities, and live: (6) lest the avenger of the blood pursue the slayer, while his heart is hot, and overtake him, because the way is long, and [6] slay him; whereas he was not worthy of death, inasmuch as he hated him not [7] in time past.

(7) Wherefore I command thee, saying, Thou shalt separate three cities for thee. (8) And if the LORD thy God *c* enlarge thy coast, as he hath sworn unto thy fathers, and give thee all the land which he promised to give unto thy fathers; (9) if thou shalt keep all these commandments to do them, which I

a ch. 12. 29.
[1] Heb., *inheritest, or, possessest.*
b Ex. 21. 13; Num. 35. 10; Josh. 20. 2.
[2] Heb., *from yesterday the third day.*
[3] Heb., *iron.*
[4] Heb., *wood.*
[5] Heb., *findeth.*
[6] Heb., *smite him in life.*
[7] Heb., *from yesterday the third day.*
c ch. 12. 20.

we escape, if we turn away from Him that speaketh from heaven: *whose voice then shook the earth.*" (Heb. xii. 22, 56.)

(20) **That prophet shall die.**—Rashi illustrates this by the case of Hananiah (Jer. xxviii.) who prophesied that Jeconiah, and all that went with him to Babylon, should return within *two years.* He was sentenced by Jeremiah to die that year; and he died accordingly, within *two months.*

(22) **If the thing follow not, nor come to pass.**—This is one form of our Lord's test for all prophets, "*By their fruits* (*i.e.,* the 'results,' of their teaching, not its first impressions) *ye shall know them.*"

XIX.

Here a fresh section of the laws begins. See Introduction for a full analysis.

Verses 1—13. THE CITIES OF REFUGE.
(See for more on this subject, Num. xxxv. 9, &c.; Josh. xx.)

(1) **When the Lord thy God hath cut off the nations.**—We find that the three cities of refuge on the west of Jordan were appointed by Joshua after the conquest (Josh. xx.). The first three on the east of Jordan, namely, Bezer, Ramoth-Gilead, and Golan, had already been selected by Moses (Deut. iv. 41, &c) but Joshua assigned them to their Levitical possessors.

(3) **Thou shalt prepare thee a way.**—Upon this phrase Rashi remarks (from the Talmud) that "*Miklot! Miklot* ('Refuge! Refuge!') was written up at the parting of the ways."

Divide the coasts of thy land . . . into three parts.—So that no part of the country might be too far from any of the cities of refuge.

(5) **As when a man goeth into the wood.**—An obvious instance.

(6) **The avenger of the blood.**—Literally, *the redeemer of the blood.* The Hebrew, *goël,* stands for all the three words, "redeemer," "avenger," "kinsman."

(8, 3) **If the Lord thy God enlarge thy coast . . . thou shalt add three cities**—*i.e.,* thou shalt add three to the six, making *nine* in all. There is no trace of this ever having been done in the history of Israel. The comments of Jewish writers show that nothing is known of the fact in their literature. Some of them point out that only seven nations were assigned to the host of Joshua, and that the land occupied by these seven could not have needed more than the six cities. They lay stress upon the words "If He give thee *all the land which He promised to give thy fathers*" (not merely the seven nations promised to thee). They refer to the Kenites and the Kenizzites and the Kadmonites in particular, as three nations promised to Abraham. It would have been more to the purpose if they had referred to the Hittites. The cities of this people, as recently discovered, from Kedesh on the Orontes to Carchemish, lie to the north of the known territory of Israel. If "all the land of the Hittites" (Josh i. 4) had been conquered, the three additional cities might have been required. But though this land seems to have been tributary to Solomon, it was not so occupied by Israel as to necessitate the appointment of three additional cities of refuge. And Solomon's empire lasted only for his own reign. But without going back to these details, they also take the promise as prophetical; holding that when the Lord has "circumcised their heart" (Deut. xxx. 6), "to love the Lord," and given them "one heart and one way to fear

command thee this day, to love the LORD thy God, and to walk ever in his ways; *a* then shalt thou add three cities more for thee, beside these three: (10) that innocent blood be not shed in thy land, which the LORD thy God giveth thee *for* an inheritance, and *so* blood be upon thee.

(11) But if any man hate his neighbour, and lie in wait for him, and rise up against him, and smite him ¹mortally that he die, and fleeth into one of these cities: (12) then the elders of his city shall send and fetch him thence, and deliver him into the hand of the avenger of blood, that he may die. (13) Thine eye shall not pity him, but thou shalt put away *the guilt of* innocent blood from Israel, that it may go well with thee.

(14) Thou shalt not remove thy neighbour's landmark, which they of old time have set in thine inheritance, which thou shalt inherit in the land that the LORD thy God giveth thee to possess it.

(15) *b* One witness shall not rise up against a man for any iniquity, or for any sin, in any sin that he sinneth: at the mouth of two witnesses, or at the mouth of three witnesses, shall the matter be established. (16) If a false witness rise up against any man to testify against him ²*that which is* wrong; (17) then both the men, between whom the controversy *is*, shall stand before the LORD, before the priests and the judges, which shall be in those days; (18) and the judges shall make diligent inquisition: and, behold, *if* the witness be a false witness, *and* hath testified falsely against his brother; (19) *c* then shall ye do unto him, as he had thought to have done unto his brother: so shalt thou put the evil away from among you. (20) And those which remain shall hear, and fear, and shall henceforth commit no more any such evil among you. (21) And thine eye shall not pity; *but* *d* life *shall go* for life, eye for eye, tooth for tooth, hand for hand, foot for foot.

CHAPTER XX.—(1) When thou goest out to battle against thine enemies, and seest horses, and chariots, *and* a people more than thou, be not afraid of them: for the LORD thy God *is* with thee, which brought thee up out of the land

a Josh. 20. 7.

1 Heb., *in life.*

b Num. 35. 30; ch. 17. 6; Matt. 18. 16; John 8. 17; 2 Cor. 13. 1; Heb. 10. 28.

2 Or, *falling away.*

c Prov. 19. 5, 9; Dan. 6. 24.

d Ex. 21. 23; Lev. 24. 20; Matt. 5. 38.

Him for ever, and shall make an everlasting covenant with them, and put His fear in their hearts (Jer. xxxii. 39, 40) that they shall not depart from Him," then the promises will be fulfilled. All the land will be given to them, and they will need these other cities. One writer adds, "Blessed is he that waiteth, and shall attain to it," from Dan. xii. 12. Thus the Jews take the passage as prophetic of their ultimate restoration. Evidently it is no addition of later times, but the genuine language of Moses. What later writer would have thought of adding it?

(10) **That innocent blood be not shed**—*i.e.*, the blood of the manslayer who can find no refuge, and yet is no murderer.

(11) **But if any man hate his neighbour, and lie in wait for him.**—Rashi's comment upon this is in the spirit of St. John: "By way of hatred he comes to lying in wait: and hence it has been said, when a man has transgressed a light commandment, that he will end by transgressing a greater. Therefore when he has broken the commandment, Thou shalt not hate, he will end by coming to bloodshed." What is this but "He that hateth his brother is a murderer"?

(12) **Deliver him into the hand of the avenger of blood.**—There is as yet no idea of a public trial and execution, which belongs to a more advanced stage of civilisation than this.

(13) **Shalt put away.**—Literally, *consume,* or, as it were, *burn out.*

(14) **Thou shalt not remove thy neighbour's landmark.**—Another law manifestly appropriate here, where it appears for the first time, like the "field" in the tenth commandment (chap. v. 21). But the immediate connection is not obvious. Perhaps the idea is to caution the people to avoid a most certain incentive to hatred and murder. Ancient landmarks are also important and almost sacred *witnesses.*

They of old time.—The first dividers of the land. There is no idea of antiquity about the expression.

Verses 15–21. FALSE TESTIMONY.

The law of retaliation is sternly laid down here; but it must be administered by the judges, not by men acting on their own behalf.

(17) **Both the men . . . shall stand before the Lord, before the priests and the judges.**—This appears to mean that all cases of suspected false testimony were to go before the supreme court (see chap. xvii. 9); that the matter was not to be lightly decided.

(21) **Eye for eye, tooth for tooth.**—This is to be effected by the award of the judges, not as a matter of private revenge. But manifestly it rests with the injured party to press the case.

XX.

LAWS OF WARFARE.

(1) **When thou goest out to battle**—*i.e.*, generally; not only in the immediate conquest of Canaan. Yet it may be observed that in the writings of Moses it is foreseen that the completion of the conquest will be gradual, and that Israel will have to go to battle many times before all enemies are overcome.

Horses and chariots.—The Israelitish army was chiefly, or rather entirely, composed of infantry, in most of the great victories won by them.

Laws to be Observed   DEUTERONOMY, XX.   *in Warfare.*

of Egypt. ⁽²⁾ And it shall be, when ye are come nigh unto the battle, that the priest shall approach and speak unto the people, ⁽³⁾ and shall say unto them, Hear, O Israel, ye approach this day unto battle against your enemies: let not your hearts ¹ faint, fear not, and do not ² tremble, neither be ye terrified because of them; ⁽⁴⁾ for the LORD your God *is* he that goeth with you, to fight for you against your enemies, to save you.

⁽⁵⁾ And the officers shall speak unto the people, saying, What man *is there* that hath built a new house, and hath not dedicated it? let him go and return to his house, lest he die in the battle, and another man dedicate it. ⁽⁶⁾ And what man *is he* that hath planted a vineyard, and hath not *yet* ³ eaten of it? let him *also* go and return unto his house, lest he die in the battle, and another man eat of it. ⁽⁷⁾ ^a And what man *is there* that hath betrothed a wife, and hath not taken her? let him go and return unto his house, lest he die in the battle, and another man take her. ⁽⁸⁾ And the officers shall speak further unto the people, and they shall say, ^b What man *is there that is* fearful and fainthearted? let him go and return unto his house, lest his brethren's heart ⁴ faint as well as his heart. ⁽⁹⁾ And it shall be, when the officers have made an end of speaking unto the people, that they shall make captains of the armies ⁵ to lead the people.

⁽¹⁰⁾ When thou comest nigh unto a city to fight against it, then proclaim peace unto it. ⁽¹¹⁾ And it shall be, if it make thee answer of peace, and open unto thee, then it shall be, *that* all the people *that is* found therein shall be tributaries unto thee, and they shall serve thee. ⁽¹²⁾ And if it will make no peace with thee, but will make war against thee, then thou shalt besiege it: ⁽¹³⁾ and when the LORD thy God hath delivered it into thine hands, thou shalt smite every male thereof with the edge of the sword: ⁽¹⁴⁾ but the women, and the little ones, and ^c the cattle, and all that is in the city, *even* all the spoil thereof, shalt thou ⁶ take unto thyself; and thou shalt eat the spoil of thine enemies, which the LORD thy God hath given thee.

Marginal notes: 1 Heb., *be tender.*   2 Heb., *make haste.*   3 Heb., *made it common.* See Lev. 19. 23.   *a* ch. 24. 5.   *b* Judg. 7. 3.   4 Heb., *melt.*   5 Heb., *to be in the head of the people.*   *c* Josh. 8. 2.   6 Heb., *spoil.*

⁽²⁾ **The priest.**—There is no mention of the Levite here. The priest is named as a distinct personage. The words which the priest are to pronounce are, as it were, the blessing of Jehovah on the campaign. It follows that Israel could not lawfully go to war except when the blessing of Jehovah might be invoked.

⁽³⁾ **Let not your hearts faint, fear not.**—In these words Isaiah strengthened Ahaz (chap. vii. 4): "fear not, neither be faint-hearted."

Tremble.—As in the Margin, "make haste." (Comp. 2 Sam. iv. 4, and 2 Kings vii. 15.)

Be ye terrified.—A strong word. The idea is, "do not even be unnerved, much less *alarmed,* at the sight of them."

⁽⁴⁾ **For the Lord your God is he that goeth with you.**—"They come in the might of flesh and blood; but ye come in the might of the Eternal" (Rashi). So David to Goliath: "Thou comest to me with a sword and with a spear, and with a shield; but I come to thee in the name of the Lord of Hosts, the God of the armies of Israel, whom thou hast defied." (1 Sam. xvii. 45). And so the Psalmist: "Some trust in chariots, and some in horses: but we will remember the name of the Lord our God" (Ps. xx. 7).

⁽⁵⁾ **And the officers.**—The *shôterim* of chap. xvi. 18; the civil magistrates apparently. The organisation of Israel was not military, but military leaders were to be appointed for special services, as appears by verse 9, "they shall make captains of the armies." The captains of thousands, hundreds, fifties and tens were called *shôterim* (chap. i. 15).

^(5—8) **What man is there . . .**—These questions show that, primarily, all Israelites of military age (20 to 50) were expected to attend the muster; then those who were unprepared for the campaign were suffered to depart. The only recorded instance of the observance of these rules is in Judges vii. 3, at the muster of Gideon's army. The proclamation "Whosoever is afraid, let him depart," sent away 22,000 out of 32,000 on that occasion, or rather more than two-thirds of the army!

⁽⁹⁾ **Captains of the armies**—*i.e.,* special leaders for the campaigns, whose command would probably cease when it was over. We may suppose from mention of the "thousands" in the army—"the captain of their thousand" (1 Sam. xvii. 18)—that the military divisions corresponded with the civil organization of the people so far as this, that the men of the same "thousand," according to Jethro's arrangement, would be brigaded together, and have one captain. If, as is also possible, the word "thousand" in military language signifies the contingent furnished by a "thousand" in Israel, irrespective of its number, it would remove many difficulties; for the whole thousand would very rarely be in the field together, and the contingent sent by a given "thousand" might consist of a very few men. If, therefore, the contingent of sixty "thousands" were to be described as 60,000, and the sixty companies were all cut up or annihilated, it might be reported as a slaughter of 60,000 men, while the lives actually lost would be nothing like so many.

Verses 10—20. SIEGES.

⁽¹⁰⁾ **When thou comest nigh . . . proclaim peace.**—Not as the children of Dan did, who massacred the inhabitants of Laish without warning (Judges xviii. 27, 28). Even in the wars of Joshua, the cities that "stood still in their strength" were generally spared (Josh. xi. 13).

Laws of Sieges. **DEUTERONOMY, XXI.** *Undetected Homicide.*

(15) Thus shalt thou do unto all the cities *which are* very far off from thee, which *are* not of the cities of these nations. (16) But of the cities of these people, which the LORD thy God doth give thee *for* an inheritance, thou shalt save alive nothing that breatheth: (17) but thou shalt utterly destroy them; *namely,* the Hittites, and the Amorites, the Canaanites, and the Perizzites, the Hivites, and the Jebusites; as the LORD thy God hath commanded thee: (18) that they teach you not to do after all their abominations, which they have done unto their gods; so should ye sin against the LORD your God.

(19) When thou shalt besiege a city a long time, in making war against it to take it, thou shalt not destroy the trees thereof by forcing an ax against them: for thou mayest eat of them, and thou shalt not cut them down (¹for the tree of the field *is* man's *life*) ²to employ *them* in the siege: (20) only the trees which thou knowest that they *be* not trees for meat, thou shalt destroy and cut them down; and thou shalt build bulwarks against the city that maketh war with thee, until ³it be subdued.

¹ Or, *for, O man, the tree of the field is to be employed in the siege.*
² Heb., *to go from before thee.*
³ Heb., *it come down.*
⁴ Heb., *mouth.*

CHAPTER XXI.—(1) If *one* be found slain in the land which the LORD thy God giveth thee to possess it, lying in the field, *and* it be not known who hath slain him: (2) then thy elders and thy judges shall come forth, and they shall measure unto the cities which *are* round about him that is slain: (3) and it shall be, *that* the city *which is* next unto the slain man, even the elders of that city shall take an heifer, which hath not been wrought with, *and* which hath not drawn in the yoke; (4) and the elders of that city shall bring down the heifer unto a rough valley, which is neither eared nor sown, and shall strike off the heifer's neck there in the valley: (5) and the priests the sons of Levi shall come near; for them the LORD thy God hath chosen to minister unto him, and to bless in the name of the LORD; and by their ⁴ word shall every controversy and every stroke be *tried:* (6) and all the elders of that city, *that are* next unto the slain *man,* shall wash their hands over the heifer that is beheaded in the valley: (7) and they shall answer and say, Our hands have not shed this blood, neither have our eyes seen *it.* (8) Be merciful, O LORD, unto thy people Israel, whom thou

---

(15) **Thus**—*i.e.,* sparing the women and the little ones.

(16—18) **But of the cities of these people . . . thou shalt save alive nothing that breatheth . . . that they teach you not to do after all their abominations.**—Upon the inhabitants of these cities the Israelites executed the sentence of Jehovah. Their abominations are sufficiently indicated in Lev. xviii. 24—28, and xx. 23.

These verses (16—18) are parenthetical; verse 19 returns to the previous subject.

(19) **And thou shalt not cut them down (for the tree of the field is man's life).**—Literally, the passage seems rather to mean this, *Is the tree of the field a man, that it should escape thee and enter into the siege?* It will not run away and fight in the trenches as a man might do. What need is there to cut it down? This seems to be the view of the Targums, the LXX., and the Jewish commentators, besides modern authorities cited in the Variorum Bible. The destruction of the trees around Jerusalem was a notable feature of the Roman war.

XXI.

Verses 1—9. UNDETECTED HOMICIDES.

(1) **If one be found slain.**—It is remarkable that in our own time the most effectual remedy against outrages of which the perpetrators cannot be discovered is a fine upon the district in which they occur.

(2) **Thy elders and thy judges shall come forth.**—Rashi says these were to be special commissioners, members of the great Sanhedrin.

(3—4) **An heifer, which hath not been wrought with . . . a rough valley which is neither eared nor sown.**—Rashi's note on this is curious : " The Holy One, blessed be He! said, ' A yearling heifer which hath borne no fruit shall come and be beheaded in a place which yieldeth no fruit, to atone for the murder of the man whom they did not suffer to bear fruit.' Some have thought that the valley was neither to be eared (ploughed) nor sown from that time forward." The verbs are not past in the Hebrew, and the words *may* bear this meaning. If so, the district in which the murder occurred would be mulcted in that portion of land for ever.

(5) **And the priests.**—See on verse 8.

(7) **Our hands have not shed this blood, neither have our eyes seen it.**—" Not that the chief magistrates of the city are supposed to have shed this blood; but that they have not contrived or procured the murder by any maintenance or partnership in the deed " (Rashi). We cannot but feel how impossible such solemn public declarations would be if the murderer had been harboured by the inhabitants of the place.

(8) **Be merciful, O Lord.**—In the sense of the publican's prayer in St. Luke xviii. " be propitiated," literally, *cover.* The mercy seat is the " covering " of the Law, which protects Israel from it. The sacrifices are a " covering " for the sinner from a punishment of sin. According to Rashi, the prayer in the eighth verse is spoken by the priests; and it seems probable enough. No part in the transaction is assigned to them, unless it be this. And their presence was certainly necessary.

hast redeemed, and lay not innocent blood [1] unto thy people of Israel's charge. And the blood shall be forgiven them. (9) So shalt thou put away the *guilt of* innocent blood from among you, when thou shalt do *that which is* right in the sight of the LORD.

(10) When thou goest forth to war against thine enemies, and the LORD thy God hath delivered them into thine hands, and thou hast taken them captive, (11) and seest among the captives a beautiful woman, and hast a desire unto her, that thou wouldest have her to thy wife; (12) then thou shalt bring her home to thine house; and she shall shave her head, and [2][3] pare her nails; (13) and she shall put the raiment of her captivity from off her, and shall remain in thine house, and bewail her father and her mother a full month: and after that thou shalt go in unto her, and be her husband, and she shall be thy wife. (14) And it shall be, if thou have no delight in her, then thou shalt let her go whither she will; but thou shalt not sell her at all for money, thou shalt not make merchandise of her, because thou hast humbled her.

(15) If a man have two wives, one beloved, and another hated, and they have born him children, *both* the beloved and the hated; and *if* the firstborn son be her's that was hated : (16) then it shall be, when he maketh his sons to inherit *that* which he hath, *that* he may not make the son of the beloved firstborn before the son of the hated, *which is indeed* the firstborn : (17) but he shall acknowledge the son of the hated *for* the firstborn, by giving him a double portion of all [4]that he hath : for he *is* the beginning of his strength; the right of the firstborn *is* his.

(18) If a man have a stubborn and rebellious son, which will not obey the voice of his father, or the voice of his mother, and *that*, when they have chastened him, will not hearken unto them : (19) then shall his father and his mother lay hold on him, and bring him out unto the elders of the city, and unto the gate

[1] Heb., *in the midst.*
[2] Or, *suffer to grow.*
[3] Heb., *make, or, dress.*
[4] Heb., *that is found with him.*

And the blood shall be forgiven them.—Literally, *shall be covered for them.* Not the same expression as Lev. iv. 20, 26, 31, 35. But we can hardly follow the Jewish commentators into the question whether, if the perpetrator of the murder were afterwards discovered, the blood of the heifer which had been shed already could be allowed to atone for it, so that the murderer need not be punished.

Verses 10—14. MARRIAGE OF CAPTIVE WOMEN.

(10, 11) **When thou . . . seest among the captives a beautiful woman.**—This could not be among the seven nations, of whom it is said (chap. xx. 16), "thou shalt save alive nothing that breatheth." But it may well apply to the recent case of the Midianitish maidens (Num. xxxi. 15—18), who had been taken captive in great numbers, and would naturally be reduced to slavery. It is clear from this passage that they could not be treated as concubines.

(12) **Shall shave her head, and pare her nails.**—Rashi's view is that the object of this order is to spoil the beauty of the captive. The long hair is to be cut off, and the nails pared. On this last point the Targums differ; one taking the view that they are to be left to grow and the other the opposite interpretation. In 2 Sam. xix. 24, there are two examples of the use of the word in the sense of attending to the person. The correct interpretation in this place depends upon the purpose for which the thing was to be done. If the intention was any kind of purification, and long or taper nails were considered an ornament (as by some Eastern nations), it is more probable that the nails were to be cut short.

(13) **The raiment of her captivity.**—Rashi takes this to mean the beautiful raiment put on for the purpose of attracting her captors. (Compare Jezebel's attempt to captivate Jehu, 2 Kings ix. 30.) Whatever may be the precise intent of these several instructions, it is clear that the law is intended to encourage lawful marriage, and no other form of union. In this view it throws an important light upon the treatment of the Midianitish captives in Num. xxxi.

(14) **Thou shalt not make merchandise of her.**—This shows that, in ordinary cases, these captives would be sold as slaves, without the restrictions imposed on Israelitish slavery. (See Lev. xxv. 44—46.)

Verses 15—17. THE BIRTHRIGHT.

(15) **One beloved, and another hated**—*i.e.*, one *preferred above the other*, according to the idiomatic use of this phrase in Hebrew.

(17) **A double portion.**—Literally, *the mouth of two*, *i.e.*, two shares. Supposing there were four sons, the estate would be divided into five shares, and the firstborn would take two. So Jacob said to Joseph (Gen. xlviii. 22) : " I have given thee one portion above thy brethren." The birthright of which Reuben was deprived for ill conduct, was given to Joseph's sons (1 Chron. v. 1). So Elisha said to Elijah before they were parted. " I pray thee let a double portion (the first-born's share) of thy spirit be upon me" (2 Kings ii. 9).

Verses 18—21. THE INCORRIGIBLE SON.

(18) **If a man have a stubborn and rebellious son.**—Here we are again reminded that the Law of Jehovah was also the civil and criminal law of Israel. The systematic breach of the first commandment of the second table of the Law, no less than of the first commandment of the first table, entailed the penalty of death. Manifestly this enactment, if carried out, would be a great protection to the country against

of his place; ⁽²⁰⁾ and they shall say unto the elders of the city, This our son is stubborn and rebellious, he will not obey our voice; *he is* a glutton, and a drunkard. ⁽²¹⁾ And all the men of his city shall stone him with stones, that he die: so shalt thou put evil away from among you; and all Israel shall hear, and fear.

⁽²²⁾ And if a man have committed a sin worthy of death, and he be to be put to death, and thou hang him on a tree: ⁽²³⁾ his body shall not remain all night upon the tree, but thou shalt in any wise bury him that day; (for *^a*he that is hanged is ¹accursed of God;) that thy land be not defiled, which the LORD thy God giveth thee *for* an inheritance.

a Gal. 3. 13.

¹ Heb., *the curse of God.*

b Ex. 23, 4.

CHAPTER XXII.— ⁽¹⁾ Thou *^b* shalt not see thy brother's ox or his sheep go astray, and hide thyself from them: thou shalt in any case bring them again unto thy brother. ⁽²⁾ And if thy brother *be* not nigh unto thee, or if thou know him not, then thou shalt bring it unto thine own house, and it shall be with thee until thy brother seek after it, and thou shalt restore it to him again. ⁽³⁾ In like manner shalt thou do with his ass; and so shalt thou do with his raiment; and with all lost thing of thy brother's, which he hath lost, and thou hast found, shalt thou do likewise: thou mayest not hide thyself. ⁽⁴⁾ Thou shalt not see thy brother's ass or his ox fall down by the way, and hide thyself from

---

lawless and abandoned characters, and would rid it of one very large element in the dangerous classes.

⁽²⁰⁾ **Stubborn and rebellious.**—The Hebrew words became proverbial as the worst form of reproach, *sôrêr û-môreh*. This word *môreh* was the one employed by Moses, when, speaking "unadvisedly" (Num. xx. 10), he said to the people, "Hear now, ye *rebels*, must we fetch you water out of this rock?" It appears in the Revised New Testament, in the margin of St. Matt. v. 22, for "thou fool." But the Greek word there employed is true Greek, and has its own affinities in the New Testament. And the word *môreh* is true Hebrew. They may be idiomatically synonymous. They are not etymologically identical.

A glutton and a drunkard.—The same two words are found in Prov. xxiii. 20—22. "Be not among wine *bibbers;* among *riotous eaters* of flesh: For the *drunkard* and the *glutton* shall come to poverty: and drowsiness shall clothe a man with rags. Hearken unto thy father that begat thee; and despise not thy mother when she is old." The context of this quotation seems to make it a distinct reference to the law in Deut. xxi.

⁽²¹⁾ **Shall stone him with stones.**—Rashi says that the Law cuts short the man's career, anticipating what its close will be. When he has spent all his father's money, he will take to the road, and become a public robber. It is better that he die innocent of such crimes than guilty. We can hardly adopt this view of the case; but it contains one feature that is terribly true.

Verses 22, 23.—HANGING.

⁽²²⁾ **And he be put to death.**—Better, *and he hath been put to death*. Hanging *followed* death in Israel (Josh. x. 26, 27).

⁽²³⁾ **His body shall not remain all night.**—Observed by Joshua, but broken by the Gibeonites (2 Sam. xxi. 9, 10, 14).

He that is hanged is accursed of God.—In the LXX., "Cursed of God *is every one that hangeth upon a tree*," and cited in this form by St. Paul (Gal. iii. 13). We cannot see why he should be pronounced cursed, except for the sake of that which was designed by "the determined counsel and foreknowledge of God," that His Son Jesus Christ should bear our sins in His own body on the tree, and redeem us from the curse of the Law, by being "made a curse for us."

Rashi's note upon this shows how strangely the rays of truth are sometimes refracted in the Jewish mind: "'He that is hanged is the curse of God'—that is, he is *the King's disgrace*. For man was made in the likeness of His image. And Israel are his children. There were two twin brothers, who were much alike. One was made king, the other was taken up for highway robbery, and was hanged. Every one who saw him said, 'There hangs the king!'" From this note it is clear that Rashi takes the words to mean, "He that is hanged is *God's disgrace*," because man is "made after the similitude of God." There is no doubt as to the *shame* of the punishment which our Lord endured and despised.

Thou shalt in any wise bury him that day.—Another law, remarkably and providentially fulfilled in our Lord's death. We do not read that the robbers who were crucified with Him were buried, though their bodies were removed from the cross. It is not improbable that this law was also intended to prevent the barbarous practice of leaving men impaled on sharp stakes or suspended upon crosses from day to day until they died of pain and thirst. It certainly is a disgrace to the Divine image to treat it thus.

XXII.
Verses 1—4. LOST PROPERTY.

⁽¹⁾ **Go astray.**—Literally, *being driven away*, as by wild beasts (Jer. l. 17), or by robbers. It is not simply straying. "I will seek that which was lost and bring again that which *was driven away*" (Ezek. xxxiv. 16), and so in many other passages.

Thou shalt not . . . hide thyself from them.—Comp. Prov. xxiv. 12. "If thou sayest, Behold we knew it not . . . doth not He know it?" And Isa. lviii. 7, "that thou hide not thyself from thine own flesh."

⁽³⁾ **In like manner . . . with all lost thing of thy brother's.**—This is only a particular case of the second great commandment. "Thou shalt love thy neighbour as thyself."

⁽⁴⁾ **Thou shalt not see thy brother's ass or his ox fall down . . . and hide thyself.**—In Exod. xxiii. 4, 5, this is put even more strongly. "If thou meet thine *enemy's* ox or his ass going astray, thou shalt surely bring it back to him again. If thou

them: thou shalt surely help him to lift *them* up again.

⁽⁵⁾ The woman shall not wear that which pertaineth unto a man, neither shall a man put on a woman's garment: for all that do so *are* abomination unto the LORD thy God.

⁽⁶⁾ If a bird's nest chance to be before thee in the way in any tree, or on the ground, *whether they be* young ones, or eggs, and the dam sitting upon the young, or upon the eggs, thou shalt not take the dam with the young: ⁽⁷⁾ *but* thou shalt in any wise let the dam go, and take the young to thee; that it may be well with thee, and *that* thou mayest prolong *thy* days.

⁽⁸⁾ When thou buildest a new house, then thou shalt make a battlement for thy roof, that thou bring not blood upon thine house, if any man fall from thence.

⁽⁹⁾ Thou shalt not sow thy vineyard with divers seeds: lest the ¹fruit of thy seed which thou hast sown, and the fruit of thy vineyard, be defiled. ⁽¹⁰⁾ Thou shalt not plow with an ox and an ass together. ⁽¹¹⁾ ᵃ Thou shalt not wear a garment of divers sorts, *as* of woollen and linen together.

⁽¹²⁾ Thou shalt make thee ᵇ fringes upon the four ²quarters of thy vesture, wherewith thou coverest *thyself*.

⁽¹³⁾ If any man take a wife, and go in unto her, and hate her, ⁽¹⁴⁾ and give occasions of speech against her, and bring up an evil name upon her, and say, I took this woman, and when I came to her, I found her not a maid: ⁽¹⁵⁾ then shall the father of the damsel,

---

1 Heb., *fulness of thy seed.*
a Lev. 19. 19.]
b Num. 15. 38.
2 Heb., *wings.*

---

see the ass of him *that hateth thee* lying under his burden . . . thou shalt surely help with him."

(5) **The woman shall not wear . . .**—One of the things of which we may well say with St. Paul, "Doth not nature itself teach you?"

(6) **If a bird's nest.**—On this precept there is a remarkable comment in the Talmud (*Kiddushin*, p. 39, b). "Rabbi Akiba says, You will not find a single duty prescribed in the Law with a promise of reward attached to it, which has not also the resurrection of the dead hanging thereby. In the command to honour thy father and mother, it is written (chap. v.) 'that thy days may be prolonged and that it may go well with thee.' In the liberty of the nest it is written (here), 'that it may be well with thee, and that thou mayest prolong thy days.' Suppose a man's father says to him, Climb up the tower and bring me the young birds. He ascends the tower, lets the dam go, and takes the young. But on his way back, he falls and is killed. Where is the 'going well' in his case, and where is the prolonging of his days? Aye, but that it may go well with thee *in the world where all goes well*, and that thy days may be prolonged in that *world where all is abiding*."

(8) **When thou buildest a new house.**—Obviously the Law refers to houses with flat roofs, upon which it was customary to walk (1 Sam ix. 25, 26; 2 Sam. xi. 2).

(9–11) These precepts appear also in Lev. xix. 19, more briefly.

(9) **Defiled**—or *sanctified*. Different crops become "common" at different times. The year's corn was freed by the wave-sheaf and wave-loaves. The trees not for five years. The rule about the ox and the ass may rest partly on the ground of humanity, the step and the pull of the two creatures being so very unlike. St. Paul gives a spiritual sense to the precept in 2 Cor. vi. 14. "Be not *unequally yoked* together with unbelievers." The ox was a clean animal and fit for sacrifice. The ass was unclean, and must be redeemed with a lamb. The clean and unclean must not till the holy land of Jehovah together.

All these precepts are part of the laws of holiness in Leviticus—rules of behaviour arising from the fact that Israel is the special people of a holy God.

(11) **A garment . . . of woollen and linen together.**—In Ezek. xliv. 17, 18, the priests are altogether forbidden the use of woollen garments during their ministry. "The *fine linen* is the righteousness of saints" (Rev. xix. 8), literally, *their requirements*. That is what they need. But it is said of the priests in Ezekiel, "They shall not gird themselves with anything that causeth sweat: *That which cometh out of the man defileth him*." Again, in God's dwelling-place, the interior or *mishkán*, the tabernacle where He abode, was of fine linen. The outer tent and coverings were of hair and skin and wool. The tabernacle where He dwells, and the *earthly house* of the tabernacle, must be kept distinct, while His tabernacle "remaineth among us in the midst of our uncleanness." (See Lev. xvi. 16).

(12) **Thou shalt make thee fringes.**—See Num. xvi. 32—41 for the origin of this requirement. We may call this fringe (or κράσπεδον, Greek) on the four sides of the square shawl or mantle, a mourning for the *one man who was executed for sabbath breaking in the wilderness*, as well as a reminder to Israel to do all the commandments and be holy unto their God. Of this κράσπεδον, when worn by our Lord on earth, the sick laid hold and were healed. His obedience and His suffering for the transgressions of God's people are perfect and without flaw.

The *principle* of these precepts is evident. Even the dress of God's people must be distinctive. And whether they eat or drink, or *whatsoever* they do, they must do all to the glory of God. These laws have a symbolical and a sanitary side; being made for the physical well-being as well as for the spiritual teaching of God's people.

Verses 13—30. LAWS OF CONJUGAL FIDELITY.

(13–21) **Virginity.**—The law in these verses will be best appreciated by considering its *effects*. The maidens in Israel would be compelled to guard their maidenliness and innocence, as they valued their lives. Jealousy and caprice on the part of the husbands, in view of this law, would be avoided as likely to incur

and her mother, take and bring forth *the tokens of* the damsel's virginity unto the elders of the city in the gate: (16)and the damsel's father shall say unto the elders, I gave my daughter unto this man to wife, and he hateth her; (17)and, lo, he hath given occasions of speech against her, saying, I found not thy daughter a maid; and yet these *are the tokens of* my daughter's virginity. And they shall spread the cloth before the elders of the city. (18)And the elders of that city shall take that man and chastise him; (19)and they shall amerce him in an hundred *shekels* of silver, and give *them* unto the father of the damsel, because he hath brought up an evil name upon a virgin of Israel: and she shall be his wife; he may not put her away all his days. (20)But if this thing be true, *and the tokens of* virginity be not found for the damsel: (21)then they shall bring out the damsel to the door of her father's house, and the men of her city shall stone her with stones that she die: because she hath wrought folly in Israel, to play the whore in her father's house: so shalt thou put evil away from among you. (22)*a* If a man be found lying with a woman married to an husband, then they shall both of them die, *both* the man that lay with the woman, and the woman: so shalt thou put away evil from Israel.

a Lev. 20. 10.

1 Or, *take strong hold of her.*

b Ex. 22. 16.

c Lev. 18. 8.

(23)If a damsel *that is* a virgin be betrothed unto an husband, and a man find her in the city, and lie with her; (24)then ye shall bring them both out unto the gate of that city, and ye shall stone them with stones that they die; the damsel, because she cried not, *being* in the city; and the man, because he hath humbled his neighbour's wife: so thou shalt put away evil from among you.

(25)But if a man find a betrothed damsel in the field, and the man ¹force her, and lie with her: then the man only that lay with her shall die: (26)but unto the damsel thou shalt do nothing; *there is* in the damsel no sin *worthy of* death: for as when a man riseth against his neighbour, and slayeth him, even so *is* this matter: (27)for he found her in the field, *and* the betrothed damsel cried, and *there was* none to save her.

(28)*b* If a man find a damsel *that is* a virgin, which is not betrothed, and lay hold on her, and lie with her, and they be found; (29)then the man that lay with her shall give unto the damsel's father fifty *shekels* of silver, and she shall be his wife; because he hath humbled her, he may not put her away all his days.

(30)*c* A man shall not take his father's wife, nor discover his father's skirt.

---

discredit and serious penalties. A fine of 100 shekels (as in verse 19), or 50 (as in verse 29), was no light matter for a nation who found a quarter shekel sufficient for a present to a great man (1 Sam. ix. 8), and half a shekel too much for a poll-tax on the men of military age (1 Chron. xxi. 3, and Exod. xxx. 15; Neh. x. 32). The law of the jealousy offering in Num. v. 12—31, must also be taken into consideration, as guarding the fidelity of the wife. It would be most unadvisable for either man or woman so to act as to bring themselves under the penalties here described. The tendency of these laws would be to make all men watchful and careful for the honour of their families.

(21) **She hath wrought folly in Israel.**—This expression should be noticed. It appears for the first time in Gen. xxxiv. 7, very shortly after the bestowal of the name *Israel* (Gen. xxxii.). It would almost appear that the name entailed a higher standard of behaviour upon Jacob's family, after the hand of the Holy One had been laid upon their father. A separate code of rules were binding upon the chosen people from the very beginning of their history. Hardly any point is made of more importance, from the birth of Isaac downwards, than the purity of the chosen seed.

(22) **Adultery.**—See Lev. xx. 10. "Moses in the Law commanded us that such should be stoned." It was not disputed by our Saviour (John viii. 5).

Verses 23—27. PURITY OF THE BETROTHED.

(24) **His neighbour's wife.**—It is evident from the language of this precept that a betrothed virgin in Israel is regarded as *a wife*. The man who humbles her "hath humbled *his neighbour's wife.*" This illustrates the language of Matt. i. Joseph, when Mary was found with child, sought to *put her away* (as though she were already his wife). The angel said to him, "Joseph, thou son of David, fear not to take unto thee Mary *thy wife.*" He "took unto him *his wife.*" From the construction of this law it follows that *Jesus* was the *son of Joseph,* according to the Scripture. The Evangelists do not seem to think it worth while to prove that He was the son of David *except through his father* (in law).

Verses 28, 29.—SEDUCTION.

See Exod. xxii. 16, 17. The sin of seduction before marriage is punished by a heavy fine. We have recently amended our own laws in the direction of this very precept. But the fact that marriage was made compulsory in these cases makes the Law stricter still. It seems, however, from Exod. xxii. 17, that the *girl's father* might forbid the marriage, though the seducer could not escape from it in any other way.

(30) See Lev. xviii. 7. A *principle*, not merely a

CHAPTER XXIII.—⁽¹⁾ He that is wounded in the stones, or hath his privy member cut off, shall not enter into the congregation of the LORD. ⁽²⁾ A bastard shall not enter into the congregation of the LORD; even to his tenth generation shall he not enter into the congregation of the LORD. ⁽³⁾ ᵃ An Ammonite or Moabite shall not enter into the congregation of the LORD; even to their tenth generation shall they not enter into the congregation of the LORD for ever: ⁽⁴⁾ because they met you not with bread and with water in the way, when ye came forth out of Egypt; and ᵇ because they hired against thee Balaam the son of Beor of Pethor of Mesopotamia, to curse thee. ⁽⁵⁾ Nevertheless the LORD thy God would not hearken unto Balaam; but the LORD thy God turned the curse into a blessing unto thee, because the LORD thy God loved thee. ⁽⁶⁾ Thou shalt not seek their peace nor their ¹prosperity all thy days for ever. ⁽⁷⁾ Thou shalt not abhor an Edomite; for he *is* thy brother: thou shalt not abhor an Egyptian; because thou wast a stranger in his land. ⁽⁸⁾ The children that are begotten of them shall enter into the congregation of the LORD in their third generation.

⁽⁹⁾ When the host goeth forth against

ᵃ Neh. 13. 1.

ᵇ Num. 22. 5, 6.

¹ Heb., *good*.

---

precept, is implied here, as appears by the details of Lev. xviii.

XXIII.

The old heading of this chapter, "*Who may or may not enter into the congregation*," supplies a good connection with what goes before. From the law of marriage in the *Church of Israel* it is a natural step to the *Children of Israel*, the members of this Church.

⁽¹⁾ The rule that a eunuch should not enter into the congregation was doubtless intended to prevent the Israelitish rulers from making eunuchs of their brethren the children of Israel. As a set off to this apparent harshness towards the man who had been thus treated, we must read Isa. lvi. 3, 4, in which a special promise is given to the eunuchs that keep God's Sabbaths and take hold of His covenant. God will give to them *within His house and within His walls* "*a place and a name better than of sons and of daughters*—an everlasting name that shall not be cut off." As a special calamity it was foretold to Hezekiah that some of his descendants should be eunuchs in the palace of the King of Babylon. But Daniel, Shadrach, Meshach, and Abednego, in whom this prophecy was fulfilled, have ennobled the "children that are of their sort" for evermore.

We have no means of knowing whether the eunuchs that were in the service of the kings of Israel or Judah (1 Sam. viii. 15; 1 Kings xxii. 9; 2 Kings viii. 6, and ix. 32, &c.) were Israelites by birth or not. Ebed-melech, *the Ethiopian*, who received a special blessing from Jeremiah (chap. xxxix. 15—18), was a foreigner, and so very possibly were most, if not all, of his kind in Israel.

As to the second clause of this verse, it must be remembered that circumcision was the sign of the covenant of Jehovah; mutilation a form of heathen self-devotion. (See Gal. v. 12, Revised New Testament, Margin, and Bishop Lightfoot's comment on that place.) St. Paul's words in Galatians receive a double meaning from this law. By doing what he refers to, they would cut themselves off from the congregation of the Lord. Rashi also gives another meaning, which would connect the precept with Lev. xv. 2.

⁽²⁾ **A bastard shall not enter.**—Such a person would not, even now, be circumcised by the Jews, or permitted to marry an Israelitish woman, or be buried with his people; therefore he was excluded from the covenant. It is manifest how efficacious would be the enforcement of this law also in preserving the purity of family life.

⁽³⁾ **An Ammonite or Moabite shall not enter.** According to Rashi, "shall not marry an Israelitish woman." It must be remembered that the children, according to Jewish law, follow the *father*, not the mother. The case of Ruth would not, therefore, be touched by this precept.

⁽⁴⁾ **Because they met you not with bread and with water.**—We learn incidentally from this passage how the Moabites and the Ammonites requited the forbearance shown them by the Israelites (chap. ii. 9, 19, 29). No one not acquainted with the details of Israel's intercourse with these people on their journey could have written thus.

Because they hired against thee Balaam.—See Num. xxii. and xxxi. 16, and xxv.

⁽⁵⁾ **Because the Lord thy God loved thee.**—The contrast between what He says to Israel in this book and what He said by Balaam is very striking. (See on chap. xxxi. 16.)

⁽⁷⁾ **Thou shalt not abhor an Edomite . . . an Egyptian.**—The contrast between these and the Moabite and Ammonite is drawn rather well by Rashi in this passage. "Learn here," he says, "that he who makes a man to sin, treats him worse than he who kills him; for he that kills, kills only in this world, but he who causes him to sin, banishes him both from this world and from the world to come. Edom, therefore, who met them with the sword (Num. xxi. 18, 20) they must not abhor; nor, again, Egypt, that would have drowned them (Exod. i. 22); but those who made them to sin are to be abhorred of them, because of the counsel wherewith they counselled them to cause them to sin." The counsel of Balaam and the whoredoms of Moab are referred to; the Midianites who joined in this effort had been chastised already (Num. xxxi.).

⁽⁸⁾ **The children that are begotten of them.**— From this passage it is clear that it was not only from Egypt that a "mixed multitude" came up with Israel. It seems to have been impossible to prevent some intermarriages between Edom, Moab, and Israel when the Israelites passed through their land. Such a precept is suitable to the circumstances of Moses' time. It would be less necessary when the bulk of the people had gone over the Jordan and left Moab and Edom far behind.

Verses 9—14. PURITY OF THE CAMP.

⁽⁹⁾ **When the host goeth forth against thine enemies . . . keep thee.**—"Because Satan maketh his accusations in the hour of danger" (Rashi).

Uncleanness to be Avoided.   DEUTERONOMY, XXIII.   *Usury—Vows.*

thine enemies, then keep thee from every wicked thing. (10) If there be among you any man, that is not clean by reason of uncleanness that chanceth him by night, then shall he go abroad out of the camp, he shall not come within the camp : (11) but it shall be, when evening [1]cometh on, he shall wash *himself* with water : and when the sun is down, he shall come into the camp *again.* (12) Thou shalt have a place also without the camp, whither thou shalt go forth abroad : (13) and thou shalt have a paddle upon thy weapon; and it shall be, when thou [2]wilt ease thyself abroad, thou shalt dig therewith, and shalt turn back and cover that which cometh from thee: (14) for the LORD thy God walketh in the midst of thy camp, to deliver thee, and to give up thine enemies before thee; therefore shall thy camp be holy : that he see no [3]unclean thing in thee, and turn away from thee.

(15) Thou shalt not deliver unto his master the servant which is escaped from his master unto thee : (16) he shall dwell with thee, *even* among you, in that place which he shall choose in one of thy gates, where it [4]liketh him best: thou shalt not oppress him.

(17) There shall be no [5]whore of the daughters of Israel, nor a sodomite of the sons of Israel. (18) Thou shalt not bring the hire of a whore, or the price of a dog, into the house of the LORD thy God for any vow : for even both these *are* abomination unto the LORD thy God.

(19) *a* Thou shalt not lend upon usury to thy brother; usury of money, usury of victuals, usury of any thing that is lent upon usury : (20) unto a stranger thou mayest lend upon usury ; but unto thy brother thou shalt not lend upon usury: that the LORD thy God may bless thee in all that thou settest thine hand to in the land whither thou goest to possess it.

(21) *b* When thou shalt vow a vow unto the LORD thy God, thou shalt not slack to pay it : for the LORD thy God will surely require it of thee ; and it would be sin in thee. (22) But if thou shalt forbear to vow, it shall be no sin in thee. (23) That which is gone out of thy lips

---

1 Heb., *turneth toward.*
2 Heb., *sittest down.*
3 Heb., *nakedness of anything.*
4 Heb., *is good for him.*
5 Or, *sodomitess.*
a Ex. 22. 25; Lev. 25. 36; Ps. 15. 5.
b Eccles. 5. 4.

---

(10) **Uncleanness that chanceth him by night.**—As in Lev. xv. 16.

(11) **When the sun is down.**—"No man is clean (after ceremonial uncleanness) except at the going down of the sun" (Rashi).

(12) **Without the camp.**—It must not be forgotten that this is the camp of the *army*, not the whole encampment of Israel in the wilderness. The entire passage is continuous from verse 9. Hence the whole discussion raised, after the appearance of Dr. Colenso's work, on the size of the camp of Israel and the possibility of obeying this rule, was simply waste of words, and arose out of a misunderstanding of the matter under consideration. The sanitary value of the rule has been abundantly demonstrated in our own day.

(13) **A paddle**—rather, a pin, or spike, like that with which Jael slew Sisera. The word for "weapon" does not occur elsewhere. The LXX. translates it "a pin or tent-peg *at thy girdle*;" the Hebrew word (*âzên*) being like the Greek (ζώνη). But both Targums interpret the word as "weapon," connecting it with the Hebrew *zayin*, which has that meaning. The *hinder end of the spear* in Abner's hand was sharp enough to strike Asahel a fatal blow when he followed him (2 Sam. ii. 23). Saul's spear also was "stuck in the ground at his bolster" (1 Sam. xxvi. 7), probably with its point upwards, by the same spike.

(14) **For the Lord thy God walketh in the midst of . . . thee.**—A most beautiful argument for purity in every sense. It was evidently present to St. Paul's mind in 2 Cor. vi. 16—vii. 1, "God hath said, I will dwell in them, and *walk in them.* . . . Having therefore these promises . . . let us *cleanse ourselves from all filthiness of the flesh and spirit*, perfecting holiness in the fear of God."

Verses 15, 16.—REFUGEES.

Thou shalt not deliver . . . the servant.—Even on Israelitish ground the escaped slave was free. Rashi adds, "Even a Canaanitish slave who has escaped from abroad into *the land* of Israel."

(17) **Whore and sodomite** seem both intended to be taken in the sense in which they belonged to the temples of Baal and Ashtaroth, of persons dedicated to impurity.

(18) **The hire of a whore.**—Even a lamb or a kid might not be sacrificed for them, if obtained as the wages of sin (Gen. xxxviii. 17).

The price of a dog.—The ass might be redeemed with a lamb, and the lamb could be sacrificed. The dog could not be treated thus. Yet "the dogs under the table eat of the children's crumbs." But there is a "dog that turns to his own vomit again," and of these it is written that "*without are dogs* and sorcerers, and whoremongers, and murderers, and idolaters, and whosoever loveth and maketh a lie" (Rev. xxii. 15).

(19, 20) **Usury.**—See Exod. xxii. 25; Lev. xxv. 35, 36. Some recent writers on this law have thought that it forbids the putting out of money to interest. But it is noticeable that in both the previous passages referred to (in Exod. and Lev.) the loan is supposed to be made to a "poor man" in "real distress." Usury in such cases means oppression; and so it is proved to be by the examples given in Neh. v. 2—5, 10—12. The connection between this exaction and modern investments is not obvious, except in a very few cases. The Mosaic law against usury does not belong to commerce with other nations; it is part of the poor law of the land of Israel.

(21) **When thou shalt vow . . . thou shalt not be slack . . .**—The three yearly feasts are

Divorce. **DEUTERONOMY, XXIV.** *Divers Precepts.*

thou shalt keep and perform; *even a* freewill offering, according as thou hast vowed unto the LORD thy God, which thou hast promised with thy mouth.

(24) When thou comest into thy neighbour's vineyard, then thou mayest eat grapes thy fill at thine own pleasure; but thou shalt not put *any* in thy vessel. (25) When thou comest into the standing corn of thy neighbour, *a* then thou mayest pluck the ears with thine hand; but thou shalt not move a sickle unto thy neighbour's standing corn.

CHAPTER XXIV.—(2) When a *b* man hath taken a wife, and married her, and it come to pass that she find no favour in his eyes, because he hath found [1] some uncleanness in her: then let him write her a bill of [2] divorcement, and give *it* in her hand, and send her out of his house. (2) And when she is departed out of his house, she may go and be another man's *wife.* (3) And *if* the latter husband hate her, and write her a bill of divorcement, and giveth *it* in her hand, and sendeth her out of his house; or if the latter husband die, which took her *to be* his wife; (4) her former husband, which sent her away, may not take her again to be his wife, after that she is defiled; for that *is* abomination before the LORD: and thou shalt not cause the land to sin, which the LORD thy God giveth thee *for* an inheritance.

(5) *c* When a man hath taken a new wife, he shall not go out to war, [3] neither shall he be charged with any business: *but* he shall be free at home one year, and shall cheer up his wife which he hath taken.

(6) No man shall take the nether or the upper millstone to pledge: for he taketh *a man's* life to pledge.

(7) If a man be found stealing any of his brethren of the children of Israel, and maketh merchandise of him, or selleth him; then that thief shall die; and thou shalt put evil away from among you.

(8) Take heed in the *d* plague of leprosy, that thou observe diligently, and do according to all that the priests the Levites shall teach you: as I commanded them, *so* ye shall observe to do. (9) Remember what the LORD thy God did *e* unto

a Matt. 12. 1; Mark 2. 23; Luke 6. 1.
b Matt. 5. 31 & 19. 7; Mark 10. 4.
[1] Heb., *matter of nakedness.*
[2] Heb., *cutting off.*
c ch. 20. 7.
[3] Heb., *not any thing shall pass upon him.*
d Lev. 13. 2.
e Num. 12. 10.

---

mentioned by Rashi and the Rabbis as occasions for the payment of vows. (See 1 Sam. i. 21.) This precept is cited in Eccles. v. 4, but with sufficient verbal variation to prevent its being called a quotation.

(24) **When thou comest into thy neighbour's vineyard.**—Rashi tries to limit both this and the following precept to the labourer engaged in gathering the vintage or the harvest, when vessels are used and sickles employed. But the plain meaning will stand, and is accepted by our Lord in the Gospel. The objection made to His disciples was not that they plucked their neighbour's corn, but that they did it on the Sabbath (a *kind of harvesting,* and therefore unlawful according to the scribes).

XXIV.

Verses 1—4. DIVORCE.

Some uncleanness.—Evidently mere caprice and dislike are not intended here. There must be some real ground of complaint. (See Margin.)

Let him write her a bill of divorcement.— "Moses, because of the hardness of your hearts, suffered you to put away your wives," is the Divine comment upon this. It is a distinct concession to the weakness of Israel—not the ideal standard of the Law, but the highest which it was found practicable to enforce. (See Matt. xix. 2 *seq.*) There are many other particular enactments in the Law of Moses of which the same thing may be said. The ideal standard of morality has never varied. There is no higher ideal than that of the Pentateuch. But the Law which was actually enforced, in many particulars fell short of that ideal.

(2) **If the latter husband hate her.**—Rashi says here that "the Scripture intimates that the end of such a marriage will be that he will hate her." He makes a similar remark on the marriage with the captive in chap. xxi. The result of the marriage will be a hated wife, and a firstborn son of her, who will be a glutton and a drunkard.

(4) **Her former husband . . . may not take her again . . . and thou shalt not cause the land to sin.**—The comment upon this, supplied by Jer. iii. 1, is singularly beautiful. "They say, If a man put away his wife, and she go from him, and become another man's, shall he return unto her again? Shall not that land be greatly polluted? But thou hast played the harlot with many lovers; *yet return again to me, saith the Lord.*"

Verse 5—end of chap. XXV. VARIOUS PRECEPTS OF HUMANITY.

(5) **He shall not go out to war, neither shall he be charged with any business.**—He shall not go forth in warfare, neither shall warfare pass upon him in any form. In Num. iv. 23, 30 the service of the tabernacle is called its "warfare."

He shall be free at home.—Literally, *he shall be clear for his home;* free from all charges, so as to belong to that.

(6) **The nether or the upper millstone.**—Literally, *the two millstones, or even the upper one.*

A man's life.—Literally, *a soul.* This word connects the two verses (6, 7).

(7) **If a man be found stealing (a soul) any of his brethren . . .**—See Exod. xxi. 16.

(8, 9) **Take heed in the plague of leprosy . . . . Remember what the Lord thy God did to Miriam.**—The point here seems to be that though

Miriam by the way, after that ye were come forth out of Egypt.

(10) When thou dost ¹lend thy brother any thing, thou shalt not go into his house to fetch his pledge. (11) Thou shalt stand abroad, and the man to whom thou dost lend shall bring out the pledge abroad unto thee. (12) And if the man *be* poor, thou shalt not sleep with his pledge: (13) in any case thou shalt deliver him the pledge again when the sun goeth down, that he may sleep in his own raiment, and bless thee: and it shall be righteousness unto thee before the LORD thy God.

(14) Thou shalt not oppress an hired servant *that is* poor and needy, *whether* he be of thy brethren, or of thy strangers that *are* in thy land within thy gates: (15) at his day ᵃthou shalt give *him* his hire, neither shall the sun go down upon it; for he *is* poor, and ²setteth his heart upon it: lest he cry against thee unto the LORD, and it be sin unto thee.

(16) ᵇThe fathers shall not be put to death for the children, neither shall the children be put to death for the fathers: every man shall be put to death for his own sin.

(17) Thou shalt not pervert the judgment of the stranger, *nor* of the fatherless; nor take a widow's raiment to pledge: (18) but thou shalt remember that thou wast a bondman in Egypt, and the LORD thy God redeemed thee thence: therefore I command thee to do this thing.

(19) ᶜWhen thou cuttest down thine harvest in thy field, and hast forgot a sheaf in the field, thou shalt not go again to fetch it: it shall be for the stranger, for the fatherless, and for the widow: that the LORD thy God may bless thee in all the work of thine hands.

---

¹ Heb., *lend the loan of any thing to, &c.*

ᵃ Lev. 19. 13; Tob. 4. 14.

² Heb., *he lifteth his soul unto it.*

ᵇ 2 Kings 14. 6; 2 Chron. 25. 4; Jer. 31. 29, 30; Ezek. 18. 20.

ᶜ Lev. 19. 9 & 23. 22.

Miriam was one of the three leaders of Israel ("I sent before thee Moses, Aaron, and Miriam"—Micah vi. 4), yet she was shut out of the camp seven days (Num. xii. 14) when suddenly smitten with leprosy. There might be a tendency to relax the law in the case of great or wealthy persons. But this would be felt keenly by poorer lepers, who could obtain no exemption. Moses, whose own sister had suffered from the leprosy, and had been treated according to the strict letter of the law, would never consent to any relaxation of it.

The priests the Levites.—The law of leprosy was one of the laws which the "priests" in particular were ordered to administer. "*Aaron* looked on Miriam, and, behold, she was leprous." It seems impossible to maintain that the Levites in general are meant here. The writer evidently had personal knowledge of the case of Miriam. Had he or his first readers lived in later times, he would have explained his meaning more fully.

(10–13) **When thou dost lend.**—The law in these verses is evidently the production of primitive and simple times, when men had little more than the bare necessaries of life to offer as security—their own clothing, or the mill-stones used to prepare their daily food, being almost their only portable property. (See Exod. xxii. 26, 27.)

It shall be righteousness.—LXX., *it shall be alms, or mercy.* In other words, "Blessed are the merciful, for they shall obtain mercy."

(14, 15) **Thou shalt not oppress an hired servant.**—So Lev. xix. 13. "The wages of him that is hired shall not abide with thee all night until the morning." (Comp. also Jer. xxii. 13; Mal. iii. 5; James v. 4.)

(16) **The fathers shall not be put to death for the children, neither shall the children be put to death for the fathers.**—A special note of the observance of this precept by Amaziah son of Joash is noticed both in Kings and Chronicles. See marginal references. It was not observed by the Persians in the case of Daniel's accusers (Dan. vi. 24).

The case of Achan, who "perished not alone in his iniquity," falls under a different head. See Notes on Josh. vii.

(17–22) **The stranger, the fatherless, and the widow**—are the subject of all the laws in these verses. For the first two (verses 17, 18), see Exod. xxii. 22–24. As to the harvest, see Lev. xxiii. 22. It is noticeable that this law is connected with the Feast of Pentecost in that place. Never was such care for the widow and the poor manifested as after the day of Pentecost in the New Testament. When "great grace was upon them all," it is written that "neither was there any among them that lacked."

In a very special way and for some special reason, all through the Old Testament, "the Lord careth for the stranger." What the reason is, if we had the Old Testament only, we might find it hard to discover. But when we open the New Testament, we may see that this is one aspect of the love of God the Father to His Son Jesus Christ, who was one day to come among us as "a stranger," when there was "no room for Him in the inn." His coming hither as a stranger could not be unnoticed. And, therefore, the name and mention of the stranger all through the Old Testament is like a path strewn with flowers, in expectation of the coming of one that is greatly beloved. We see angels walking upon the earth, entertained as strangers. The wealthy patriarch, a "prince of God" among the Canaanites, confesses himself a "stranger and pilgrim on the earth." Those that inherit the land are put in the same category, "Ye are strangers and sojourners with Me." The stranger sits beside the Levite at Israel's table. The second great commandment is rehearsed again for his especial benefit. "He shall be unto you as one born among you, and *thou shalt love him as thyself.*" There is only one key to all this combination of tenderness. "*I was a stranger, and ye took me in.*"

(18, 22) **Thou shalt remember that thou wast a bondman in Egypt.**—An exhortation thoroughly in place here, in the writings of Moses. In this form it

(20) When thou beatest thine olive tree, [1] thou shalt not go over the boughs again: it shall be for the stranger, for the fatherless, and for the widow. (21) When thou gatherest the grapes of thy vineyard, thou shalt not glean it [2] afterward: it shall be for the stranger, for the fatherless, and for the widow. (22) And thou shalt remember that thou wast a bondman in the land of Egypt: therefore I command thee to do this thing.

CHAPTER XXV.—(1) If there be a controversy between men, and they come unto judgment, that *the judges* may judge them; then they shall justify the righteous, and condemn the wicked. (2) And it shall be, if the wicked man *be* worthy to be beaten, that the judge shall cause him to lie down, and to be beaten before his face, according to his fault, by a certain number. (3)[a] Forty stripes he may give him, *and* not exceed: lest, *if* he should exceed, and beat him above these with many stripes, then thy brother should seem vile unto thee. (4)[b] Thou shalt not muzzle the ox when he [3] treadeth out *the corn.* (5)[c] If brethren dwell together, and one of them die, and have no child, the wife of the dead shall not marry without unto a stranger: her [4]husband's brother shall go in unto her, and take her to him to wife, and perform the duty of an husband's brother unto her. (6) And it shall be, *that* the firstborn which she beareth shall succeed in the name of his brother *which is* dead, that his name be not put out of Israel. (7) And if the man like not to take his [5]brother's wife, then let his brother's wife go up to the gate unto the elders, and say, [d] My husband's brother refuseth to raise up unto his brother a name in Israel, he will not perform the duty of my husband's brother. (8) Then the elders of his city shall call him, and speak unto him: and *if* he stand *to it,* and say, I like not to take her; (9) then shall his brother's

[1] Heb., *thou shalt not bough it after thee.*

[2] Heb., *after thee.*

[a] 2 Cor. 11. 24.

[b] 1 Cor. 9. 9; 1 Tim. 5. 18.

[3] Heb., *thresheth.*

[c] Matt. 22. 24; Mark 12. 19; Luke 20. 28.

[4] Or, *next kinsman.*

[5] Or, *next kinsman's wife.*

[d] Ruth 4. 7.

---

occurs repeatedly in the Pentateuch, but not elsewhere. It is not the language which would naturally suggest itself to the prophets of later times.

XXV.

Verses 1—3. HUMANITY IN PUNISHMENTS.

(1) **They shall justify the righteous, and condemn the wicked.**—"I will not justify the wicked" (Exod. xxiii. 7). "He that justifieth the wicked, and he that condemneth the just, even they both are abomination to the Lord" (Prov. xvii. 15). It should be noticed that *justify* is here used forensically, not meaning to make righteous, but to *treat as righteous.* Those who object to this sense in St. Paul's Epistles, will find it hard to put any other sense upon the word in the rest of Holy Scripture.

(2) **If the wicked man be worthy to be beaten.**—Literally, *a son of beating,* or *of Haccôth,* according to the Hebrew. The treatise called *Maccôth,* in the Talmud, describes the infliction of the punishment in later times, when "of the Jews five times" St. Paul "received forty stripes save one." The details have been described by Canon Farrar in an appendix to his *Life of St. Paul.*

Shall cause him to lie down.—The Talmud interprets the position as not sitting nor standing, nor exactly lying, but with the body inclined.

Before his face.—This is interpreted as *on the front of his body.* The thirty-nine stripes were given thirteen on one shoulder, thirteen on the other, and thirteen on the breast.

(3) **Forty stripes.**—The Talmud says that they considered first what a man could bear, and flogged him according to their estimate. In some cases, if the whole punishment could not be administered at once, it was divided. It is contemplated as possibly fatal, however.

Lest . . . thy brother should seem vile unto thee.—The punishment was not considered to be any degradation, after it had been inflicted. It was inflicted in the synagogue, and the law was read meanwhile from Deut. xxviii. 58, 59, with one or two other passages.

(4) **Thou shalt not muzzle the ox.**—We have a comment on these words from St. Paul in two places (1 Cor. ix. 9, and 1 Tim. v. 18). It is not only written for the sake of the oxen, but to prove that the "labourer is worthy of his hire;" "they that preach the Gospel should live of the Gospel."

Verses 5—10. LEVIRATE MARRIAGES.

(5) **If brethren dwell together.**—This law is made the subject of a whole treatise in the Talmud, called *Yebâmôth.* The object of the law was held to be attained if the family of the dead man was perpetuated, and did not become extinct. And therefore the marriage specified was not necessarily between the brother and the brother's wife, but might be between other representatives of the two persons in question. (See Ruth iv.)

The law is older than Moses. We first hear of it in the household of Judah the son of Jacob (Gen. xxxviii. 8). The violation of the law then was punished with *death,* not with disgrace only.

But that which makes the law most memorable, is the teaching elicited from the lips of our Saviour by the question which the Sadducees raised upon it (see marginal reference). It is worth while to observe that the law itself demands that in some sense there should be *a resurrection.* Boaz puts it thus (Ruth iv. 5), "to raise up the name of the dead upon his inheritance." Why should the name of the dead be kept up, if the dead has passed out of existence? We may well believe that this law was partly intended (like baptism for the dead, or like giving children the names of their

wife come unto him in the presence of the elders, and loose his shoe from off his foot, and spit in his face, and shall answer and say, So shall it be done unto that man that will not build up his brother's house. (10) And his name shall be called in Israel, The house of him that hath his shoe loosed.

(11) When men strive together one with another, and the wife of the one draweth near for to deliver her husband out of the hand of him that smiteth him, and putteth forth her hand, and taketh him by the secrets: (12) then thou shalt cut off her hand, thine eye shall not pity *her*.

(13) Thou shalt not have in thy bag ¹divers weights, a great and a small. (14) Thou shalt not have in thine house ²divers measures, a great and a small. (15) *But* thou shalt have a perfect and just weight, a perfect and just measure shalt thou have: that thy days may be lengthened in the land which the LORD thy God giveth thee. (16) For all that do such things, *and* all that do unrighteously, *are* an abomination unto the LORD thy God.

1 Heb., *a stone and a stone.*

2 Heb., *an ephah and an ephah.*

(17) *a* Remember what Amalek did unto thee by the way, when ye were come forth out of Egypt; (18) how he met thee by the way, and smote the hindmost of thee, *even* all *that were* feeble behind thee, when thou *wast* faint and weary; and he feared not God. (19) Therefore it shall be, when the LORD thy God hath given thee rest from all thine enemies round about, in the land which the LORD thy God giveth thee *for* an inheritance to possess it, *that* thou shalt blot out the remembrance of Amalek from under heaven; thou shalt not forget *it*.

CHAPTER XXVI.—(1) And it shall be, when thou *art* come in unto the land which the LORD thy God giveth thee *for* an inheritance, and possessest it, and dwellest therein; (2) that thou shalt take of the first of all the fruit of the earth, which thou shalt bring of thy land that the LORD thy God giveth thee, and shalt put *it* in a basket, and shalt go unto the place which the LORD thy God shall choose to place his name there. (3) And thou shalt go unto the priest

a Ex. 17. 8.

---

departed progenitors) for the express purpose of keeping alive the hope of resurrection in the minds of the chosen people.

(11, 12) **When men strive together . . .**—Another precept of humanity. In Exod. xxi. 22, "If men strive and hurt a woman with child," punishment or compensation must follow. The law in this place is the counterpart of that. Men must be protected as well as women.

Putteth forth her hand and taketh him. —"Him," *i.e.*, him that smiteth her husband. The precept is to enforce modesty as well as to protect humanity.

Verses 13—16. JUST WEIGHTS AND MEASURES.

So Lev. xix. 35, 36. Among the laws of moral holiness comes the law of just weights and measures.

(16) **An abomination unto the Lord.**—So in Prov. xi. 1, "a false balance is abomination to the Lord." (See also Amos viii. 4—8.) The protection of the poor is the chief practical end in this; rich men can take care of themselves. Poor men are *doubly* robbed by short weight and measure, because they cannot protect themselves against it. The injustice tends to perpetuate their poverty.

Verses 17—19. AMALEK TO BE EXTERMINATED.

At the end of all the precepts of humanity, the extermination of that people which is presented to us as the incarnation of inhumanity is decreed.

(18) **He . . . smote the hindmost . . .**—These details are not given in Exod. xvii. Amalek's attack follows the appearance of the stream of water from Horeb. There was nothing more natural than that the faint and weary should stay behind at the water side. There the Amalekites appear to have found them and cruelly massacred them.

(19) **Thou shalt blot out the remembrance of Amalek.**—This decree was entrusted to Joshua in the first instance, as the "servant of the Book" (Exod. xvii. 14); here it is enjoined upon the nation of Israel. It was carried out in several stages: by Barak and Gideon (Judges v. 14, vi. 3, vii. 12, &c.), by Saul and Samuel (1 Sam. xv.), by David (1 Sam. xxvii. 8, 9, xxx. 17), by the Simeonites (1 Chron. iv. 42, 43), and lastly by Esther, who exterminated the Agagites in Haman's house. No doubt any remnant of Amalek in the Persian empire under Mordecai would have shared Haman's fate.

XXVI.

Verses 1—11. PRESENTATION OF THE FIRSTFRUITS.

(1) **When thou art come in.**—Rashi says they were not bound to the discharge of this duty until they had conquered and divided the land. But the state of things described in the Book of Joshua (chap. xxi. 43—45) would demand it. From the words of verse 11, "thou shalt rejoice," the Jews gather that the thanksgiving to be said over the firstfruits (in verses 5—10) must be said at some time between the close of the feast of unleavened bread on the twenty-first day of the first month (the "solemn assembly" of Deut. xvi. 8) and the Feast of Tabernacles. If firstfruits were presented between the Feast of Tabernacles and the Passover, this formula was not used (Rashi).

(3) **The priest that shall be in those days.** —No mention is made of the Levite here. The priest

that shall be in those days, and say unto him, I profess this day unto the LORD thy God, that I am come unto the country which the LORD sware unto our fathers for to give us. ⁽⁴⁾ And the priest shall take the basket out of thine hand, and set it down before the altar of the LORD thy God.

⁽⁵⁾ And thou shalt speak and say before the LORD thy God, A Syrian ready to perish *was* my father, and he went down into Egypt, and sojourned there with a few, and became there a nation, great, mighty, and populous : ⁽⁶⁾ and the Egyptians evil entreated us, and afflicted us, and laid upon us hard bondage : ⁽⁷⁾ and when we cried unto the LORD God of our fathers, the LORD heard our voice, and looked on our affliction, and our labour, and our oppression : ⁽⁸⁾ and the LORD brought us forth out of Egypt with a mighty hand, and with an outstretched arm, and with great terribleness, and with signs, and with wonders : ⁽⁹⁾ and he hath brought us into this place, and hath given us this land, *even* a land that floweth with milk and honey. ⁽¹⁰⁾ And now, behold, I have brought the firstfruits of the land, which thou, O LORD, hast given me.

And thou shalt set it before the LORD thy God, and worship before the LORD thy God : ⁽¹¹⁾ and thou shalt rejoice in every good *thing* which the LORD thy God hath given unto thee, and unto thine house, thou, and the Levite, and the stranger that *is* among you.

⁽¹²⁾ When thou hast made an end of tithing all the tithes of thine increase the third year, *which is* ᵃ the year of tithing, and hast given *it* unto the Levite, the stranger, the fatherless, and the widow, that they may eat within thy gates, and be filled ; ⁽¹³⁾ then thou shalt say before the LORD thy God, I have brought away the hallowed things out of *mine* house, and also have given them unto the Levite, and unto the stranger, to the fatherless, and to the widow, according to all thy command-

ᵃ ch. 14. 28.

(though of the tribe of Levi) has an office distinct from the Levite in the Book of Deuteronomy as much as in the rest of the Old Testament.

I profess.—Literally, *I declare.* "To show that thou art not ungrateful for His goodness" (Rashi, from the Talmud).

This day.—The formula was only used once in the year.

⁽⁴⁾ **The priest shall take the basket.**—"To wave it. The priest put his hand under the hand of the owner, and waved it."

⁽⁵⁾ **A Syrian ready to perish.**—The reference is to Jacob, more especially when pursued by Laban, who would have taken from him his all, except for the Divine mercy and protection. We may also recall his danger from Esau (Gen. xxxi., xxxii.), from the Shechemites (xxxiv., xxxv.), and from the famine, until he heard of Joseph.

⁽⁷⁾ **When we cried unto the Lord.**—Samuel in his famous speech (1 Sam. xii. 8) takes up the language of this passage, "When Jacob was come into Egypt, and your fathers cried unto the Lord, then the Lord . . . brought forth your fathers out of Egypt, and made them dwell in this place."

⁽⁶⁻⁷⁾ See Exod. ii. 25, iii. 9, and vi. 5, 6 for the source of this confession.

⁽¹⁰⁾ **And thou shalt set it before the Lord thy God**—*i.e.*, take it up again after it was first waved by the priest, and hold it in the hand while making this confession, and then wave it once more. After this it would become the priest's.

VERSES 12—15. DECLARATION OF THE TITHE.

⁽¹²⁾ **When thou hast made an end.**—The time fixed for making the confession prescribed in verses 13—15, according to Jewish usage, was the Passover-eve of the fourth year, *i.e.*, the first feast after the completion of the year of tithing. It would seem that something was still to be gathered from the trees after the Feast of Tabernacles, and thus there would still be some produce untithed at that feast in any given year. But the tithe of the third year must be separated to the very last item before the Passover of the fourth.

The third year, which is the year of tithing. —See chap. xiv. 28, 29. In the third and sixth years, *the second tithe*, which in other years was eaten by the owners (in kind or value) at Jerusalem, was given *to the poor*, and was called the poor's tithe. In Talmudical language, the *Ma'aser ăni* took the place of *Ma'aser shéni* in these years.

Thus the words "and hast given it unto the Levite," are applied to the *first tithe*, which was never omitted, and which is prescribed by Num. xviii. The words that follow, "the stranger, the fatherless, and the widow," are interpreted of the *poor's tithe*. The prescribed confession is not to be made until *all the tithe* has been given, both *first* and *second, i.e.*, the annual tithe to the Levites, and the second, which was in these years devoted to the poor.

That they may eat within thy gates, and be filled.—The quantity with which they were to be satisfied was duly prescribed by the Jewish scribes !

⁽¹³⁾ **Thou shalt say before the Lord thy God, I have brought away.**—Literally, *I have consumed*, or *burned out*. It is the same strong word used so frequently in this book for "putting away" evil, and from which the name *Taberah*, "burning," is derived. It is taken by Jewish commentators to include everything that could possibly be required as holy under any law, whether tithe, or firstfruit of trees not yet made common, or anything that from any cause had not been brought to Jerusalem during the three previous years.

I . . . have given . . . unto the Levite (the first tithe), **and unto the stranger . . .** (the poor's tithe).—Rashi.

ments which thou hast commanded me: I have not transgressed thy commandments, neither have I forgotten them: (14) I have not eaten thereof in my mourning, neither have I taken away *ought* thereof for *any* unclean *use*, nor given *ought* thereof for the dead: but I have hearkened to the voice of the LORD my God, *and* have done according to all that thou hast commanded me. (15)ᵃ Look down from thy holy habitation, from heaven, and bless thy people Israel, and the land which thou hast given us, as thou swarest unto our fathers, a land that floweth with milk and honey.

(16) This day the LORD thy God hath commanded thee to do these statutes and judgments: thou shalt therefore keep and do them with all thine heart, and with all thy soul. (17) Thou hast avouched the LORD this day to be thy God, and to walk in his ways, and to keep his statutes, and his commandments, and his judgments, and to hearken unto his voice: (18) and ᵇthe LORD hath avouched thee this day to be his peculiar people, as he hath promised thee, and that *thou* shouldest keep all his commandments; (19) and to make thee high above all nations which he hath made, in praise, and in name, and in honour; and that thou mayest be an holy people unto the LORD thy God, as he hath spoken.

CHAPTER XXVII.—(1) And Moses with the elders of Israel commanded

ᵃ Isa. 63. 15.
ᵇ ch. 7. 6.

According to all thy commandments—*i.e.*, "giving everything in its due order" (Rashi). The following words are also taken to refer to the details of the law respecting these matters.

(14) **I have not eaten thereof in my mourning.**—"When I was clean and they were unclean, or when they were clean and I was unclean" (Rashi). The tomb or presence of a dead body made both persons and things unclean (Num. xix.).

Neither have I taken away.—Literally, *consumed any of them in uncleanness.*

Nor given ought thereof for (or to) **the dead.**—Rashi explains, "to provide for him a coffin or graveclothes." Another explanation, which is certainly possible, is, "I have not made any offering to an idol from them." "They joined themselves to *Baal-peor*, and ate the sacrifices *of the dead*" (Ps. cvi. 28).

I have hearkened . . . and have done according to all that thou hast commanded me.—A claim which might be truly made as to outward observances and requirements. I am therefore the more disposed to take the confession in these verses in its most literal sense, and to limit it to the particular things with which it was connected—the tithes and offerings.

(15) **Look down from thy holy habitation, from heaven.**—A phrase like this occurs frequently in Solomon's prayer; but there is a difference there in the Hebrew, which is less beautiful than in this place. The exact phrase is found in 2 Chron. xxx. 27. And in 2 Chron. xxxvi. 15, we have "His dwellingplace" applied to Jerusalem and the Temple. This suggests that the thought here may be twofold. Look down from the dwelling-place of Thy holiness here below, and not only thence, but from thine own dwelling-place in heaven.

And bless thy people Israel, and the land (literally, *the ground*) **which thou hast given us.** —"We have done what Thou hast decreed for us. Do Thou that which it rests with Thee to do" (Rashi).

Verses 16—19. CLOSE OF THE EXHORTATION.

(16) **This day the Lord thy God hath commanded thee.**—These words are not to be taken as part of the service described in the previous verses, but as the words of Moses in bringing his exhortation to a close. Rashi says, "Every day these commandments shall be new before thine eyes, as though on that very day thou hadst received them."

Thou shalt therefore keep and do them.—It is a beautiful thought that the form of this command (as of many others) makes it prophetic of its own fulfilment. "It is the voice from heaven blessing thee," says Rashi. (See also chap. xxx. 6, 8.)

(17, 18) **Thou hast avouched . . . and the Lord hath avouched.**—The Hebrew word is simply the ordinary word for "to say." "Thou hast said," and "He hath said." There is no distinctive word for "to promise" in Hebrew. "To say" is sufficient. "Hath He said, and shall He not do it?" "Let your yea *be* yea, and your nay nay," like His. But Rashi says there is no exact parallel to this use of the verb in the Old Testament, except, perhaps, in Ps. xciv. 4, where it means, "they boast themselves." Let Israel boast in God, and God will boast Himself of them, as His peculiar people.

(19) **And to make thee high.**—Literally, *most high*; Heb., *'Elyôn*, a well-known name of God. Here, and in chap. xxviii. 1, it is (prophetically and in the Divine purpose) applied to Israel. "Thou shalt put *my Name* upon the children of Israel" was the law of blessing for the priests (Num. vi. 27).

In praise, and in name, and in honour.—Perhaps, rather, *to be a praise, and to be a name, and to be an honour, and to become a people of holiness to Jehovah.* There is an allusion to this in Jer. xxxiii. 9, "And it shall be to me *a name* of joy, a *praise*, and an *honour* before all the nations of the earth;" and in Isa. lxii. 6, 7, " Ye that make mention of the name of the Lord, keep not silence, and give Him no rest, till He establish, and till He make Jerusalem a praise in the earth."

But if, as some would have us believe, the Book of Deuteronomy draws these things from the prophets, rather than the prophets from Moses, how is it that there is not the faintest allusion in Deuteronomy to Jerusalem, which in the days of the prophets had become the centre of all these hopes?

XXVII.

THE LAW TO BE ESTABLISHED IN CANAAN AS THE LAW OF THE LAND.

(1) **Moses with the elders.**—Here joined in exhortation for the first time in this book.

An Altar to be set up   DEUTERONOMY, XXVII.   *on Mount Ebal.*

the people, saying, Keep all the commandments which I command you this day. ⁽²⁾ And it shall be on the day when ye shall pass over Jordan unto the land which the LORD thy God giveth thee, that thou shalt set thee up great stones, and plaister them with plaister: ⁽³⁾ and thou shalt write upon them all the words of this law, when thou art passed over, that thou mayest go in unto the land which the LORD thy God giveth thee, a land that floweth with milk and honey; as the LORD God of thy fathers hath promised thee. ⁽⁴⁾ Therefore it shall be when ye be gone over Jordan, *that* ye shall set up these stones, which I command you this day, in mount Ebal, and thou shalt plaister them with plaister. ⁽⁵⁾ And there shalt thou build an altar unto the LORD thy God, an altar of stones: *b* thou shalt not lift up *any* iron *tool* upon them. ⁽⁶⁾ Thou shalt build the altar of the LORD thy God of whole stones: and thou shalt offer burnt offerings thereon unto the LORD thy God: ⁽⁷⁾ and thou shalt offer peace offerings, and shalt eat there, and rejoice before the LORD thy God. ⁽⁸⁾ And thou shalt write upon the stones all the words of this law very plainly.

⁽⁹⁾ And Moses and the priests the Levites spake unto all Israel, saying, Take heed, and hearken, O Israel; this day thou art become the people of the LORD thy God. ⁽¹⁰⁾ Thou shalt therefore obey the voice of the LORD thy God, and do his commandments and his statutes, which I command thee this day.

⁽¹¹⁾ And Moses charged the people the same day, saying, ⁽¹²⁾ These shall stand upon mount Gerizim to bless the people, when ye are come over Jordan; Simeon, and Levi, and Judah, and Issachar, and Joseph, and Benjamin: ⁽¹³⁾ and these

a Josh. 4. 1.

b Ex. 20. 25; Josh. 8. 31.

Keep.—Literally, *to keep.* Possibly we are intended to connect the two verses. In order to keep them, ye shall write them.

Verses 2—4. THE DECALOGUE TO BE WRITTEN ON MOUNT EBAL.

⁽²⁾ **Set . . . up great stones, and plaister them with plaister.**—The idea is to make a smooth surface, on which the Law could be inscribed. "Plaister" only here and in Isa. xxxiii. 12; Amos ii. 2. In both those places it is rendered "lime."

⁽³⁾ **Thou shalt write upon them all the words of this law, when thou art passed over, that thou mayest go in.**—Again it is evident that the "going in" to the land and the "passing over" Jordan are not identical. The "Law of God" was to be set up in the heart of the country, as soon as Israel had entered it, in order that they might complete the conquest of it. It is abundantly clear that Israel's title to Canaan was dependent upon their maintaining the Law of Jehovah as the law of the land.

For the fulfilment of this precept, see Josh. viii. 32—35. The words of this verse are an additional reason for the view taken in the Note on that passage, that the Law was set up on Ebal immediately after the capture of Ai, without waiting for the completion of the conquest (as some suppose).

⁽⁵⁾ **An altar of stones.**—Rashi propounds the theory that these stones were taken from Jordan. But there is nothing to countenance this theory in the words of the text.

⁽⁶⁾ **Burnt offerings.**—The idea of these is the dedication of man's life to God.

⁽⁷⁾ **Peace offerings**—*i.e.*, offerings for health, salvation, or *deliverance already granted.* On this occasion, the passage of Jordan, and the arrival of Israel in the heart of the country, would be good ground for thanksgiving before God.

And shalt eat there, and rejoice.—The peace offerings were the only kind of which the worshipper and his family might partake. They were, therefore, the natural accompaniment of rejoicing and thanksgiving.

⁽⁸⁾ **Thou shalt write upon the stones all the words of this law**—*i.e.*, the ten commandments. All else in the Law of Moses is but an application of the Decalogue to a particular people under particular circumstances. (See Notes on Josh. iii., viii. 32, for more upon the relation of the ten commandments to the conquest of Canaan.)

Very plainly.—See on chap. i. 5. Rashi says, "In seventy (*i.e.*, in all) languages." There is also an idea in the Talmud that when spoken from Sinai, the Law was spoken (or heard) in all languages at the same time. It is a strange refraction of the truth indicated at Pentecost, when the Holy Spirit was given. Men spake in every tongue the wonderful works of God. The foundation of Jerusalem has effects exactly opposite to the foundation of Babylon (Gen. xi.).

⁽⁹⁾ **Moses and the priests.**—As in verse 1, "Moses and the elders."

Take heed.—A word used nowhere else in the Old Testament.

This day thou art become the people.—"Every day His commandments shall be before thine eyes, as though thou hadst that day entered into covenant with Him." It would seem that the passage of Jordan, which is the thing in view here, pledged Israel more completely to God's Law than even the covenant at Sinai did. He had gone farther with them, and given them a more distinct position. It became more necessary than ever that they should remember whose they were.

^(12, 13) **These shall stand upon mount Gerizim to bless . . . and these . . . upon mount Ebal to curse.**—The expressions "to bless" and "to curse" are misleading. It is not meant that six tribes were to bless, and six to curse their brethren. The phrase will be best understood by noticing the manner in which the ceremony was performed, according to Jewish tradition. According to the treatise *Sotah,* six

shall stand upon mount Ebal ¹to curse; Reuben, Gad, and Asher, and Zebulun, Dan, and Naphtali. (14) And ᵃthe Levites shall speak, and say unto all the men of Israel with a loud voice,

(15) Cursed *be* the man that maketh *any* graven or molten image, an abomination unto the LORD, the work of the hands of the craftsman, and putteth *it* in *a* secret *place*. And all the people shall answer and say, Amen. (16) Cursed *be* he that setteth light by his father or his mother. And all the people shall say, Amen. (17) Cursed *be* he that removeth his neighbour's landmark. And all the people shall say, Amen. (18) Cursed *be* he that maketh the blind to wander out of the way. And all the people shall say, Amen. (19) Cursed *be* he that perverteth the judgment of the stranger, fatherless, and widow. And all the people shall say, Amen. (20) Cursed *be* he that lieth with his father's wife; because he uncovereth his father's skirt. And all the people shall say, Amen. (21) Cursed *be* he that lieth with any manner of beast. And all the people shall say, Amen. (22) Cursed *be* he that lieth with his sister, the daughter of his father, or the daughter of his mother. And all the people shall say, Amen. (23) Cursed *be* he that lieth with his mother in law. And all the people shall say, Amen. (24) Cursed *be* he that smiteth his neighbour secretly. And all the people shall say, Amen. (25)ᵇCursed *be* he that taketh reward to slay an innocent person. And all the people shall say, Amen. (26)ᶜ Cursed *be* he that confirmeth not *all* the words of this law to do them. And all the people shall say, Amen.

¹ Heb., *for a cursing.*

ᵃ Dan. 9. 11.

ᵇ Ezek. 22. 12.

ᶜ Gal. 3. 10.

---

tribes went up to the top of Gerizim, and six ascended mount Ebal, and the priests and the Levites and the ark remained below, between the hills. The Levites turned their faces towards Mount Gerizim, and began with the blessing, "Blessed is the man," &c., and both sides answered "Amen." They then turned their faces towards Mount Ebal, and began the curse, saying, "Cursed is the man," &c. The "Amen" again resounded; and the process was repeated until the last curse was reached. The question whether all the blessings preceded all the cursings is discussed; but the opinion preferred is, that each blessing had its corresponding curse, and were pronounced alternately.

If this account be correct, and it seems both intelligible and probable, we see that the tribes were divided equally to "receive" the blessing and the curse, implying that all were equally liable to either, according as they should obey or transgress. If the one side had answered amen to the blessings, and the other to the curses, the tribes would literally have blessed and cursed the people. But the rule is explicit that *all* the people shall say " Amen;" and therefore we seem to gather this meaning from the Hebrew: These shall stand on Mount Gerizim for the blessing of the people, *i.e.,* to receive the blessing on behalf of the whole, and these on Mount Ebal for the curse (*i.e.,* to receive it on behalf of the rest). It is noticeable that "the law" which inflicts the curse, and the altar which represents in its sacrifices Him who bare the curse, are both on the same hill, Ebal. If the tribes redeemed are on the hill of blessing, the tribes that receive the curse are on the same hill with the Redeemer.

(12, 13) **Simeon, and Levi . . . and Naphtali.** —Strictly speaking, there would be seven tribes on Gerizim to receive the blessing, and six on Ebal for the curse; because, tribally, Joseph must include Ephraim and Manasseh. The general position is that of the audience in an amphitheatre, the speakers being in the centre beneath, and the people on either side above. The more honourable tribes of Judah, Joseph, Benjamin, and Levi are posted on the southern hill, Gerizim. The tribes on Ebal are the four sons of the handmaids Bilhah and Zilpah, with Leah's youngest son Zebulun; and the disinherited firstborn, Reuben, is placed at their head. These last tribes, upon the whole, may be said to have occupied the outer circle of Israel's territory, to the east and to the north. The tribes on Gerizim are the more central tribes.

(16) **Cursed be he that setteth light.**—The first curse points to the first two commandments of the first table, and the second to the first commandment in the second table. If we mark off the first offence specified, secret idolatry—the only one which distinctly recalls the *first* commandment of the Law, and also the last general curse which embraces all transgression whatever, the intervening offences seem more easily arranged. We have duty to parents enforced (verse 16) and the rights of neighbours (v. 17), the blind (verse 18), and the unprotected (verse 19) come next. The next four precepts are all concerned with purity, first in the nearer, afterwards in the more distant relations (verses 20—23). The last two precepts concern slander and treachery (verses 24, 25). Evidently the offences specified are examples of whole classes of actions; and the twelve curses may have some reference to the number of the tribes.

(18) **The blind.**—" He that is in the dark upon any matter, when one deceives him with evil counsel" (Rashi).

(24) **That smiteth his neighbour secretly.**— " Spoken of a backbiting tongue " (Rashi).

(26) **Cursed be he that confirmeth not all the words of this law to do them.**—" Here he sums up the whole Law, all of it, and they took it upon them with a curse and an oath " (Rashi). From this verse St. Paul also reasons that "as many as are of the works of the law are under a curse." For no man can do all of them. And therefore it is impossible to secure the blessing of Gerizim except through Him who bare the curse of Ebal. "Christ hath redeemed us from the curse of the law, being made a curse for us, as it is written, *cursed is every one that hangeth on a tree.*" In all these curses the verb is wanting. " Cursed is he," would be a more correct translation in modern English. These curses are not imprecations so much as declarations of fact.

CHAPTER XXVIII.—⁽¹⁾ And it shall come to pass, ^a if thou shalt hearken diligently unto the voice of the LORD thy God, to observe *and* to do all his commandments which I command thee this day, that the LORD thy God will set thee on high above all nations of the earth: ⁽²⁾ and all these blessings shall come on thee, and overtake thee, if thou shalt hearken unto the voice of the LORD thy God. ⁽³⁾ Blessed *shalt* thou *be* in the city, and blessed *shalt* thou *be* in the field. ⁽⁴⁾ Blessed *shall be* the fruit of thy body, and the fruit of thy ground, and the fruit of thy cattle, the increase of thy kine, and the flocks of thy sheep. ⁽⁵⁾ Blessed *shall be* thy basket and thy ¹ store. ⁽⁶⁾ Blessed *shalt* thou *be* when thou comest in, and blessed *shalt* thou *be* when thou goest out.

a Lev. 26. 3.

¹ Or, *dough*, or, *kneading troughs*.

XXVIII.

SANCTIONS OF THE LAW IN DEUTERONOMY. THE BLESSING AND THE CURSE.

Almost every specific portion of the Law in Scripture has a passage of this kind at the end. The code in Exod. xxi.—xxiii. ends with a declaration of rewards and punishments (Exod. xxiii. 20—33). The laws of holiness, ceremonial and moral, in Leviticus, are closed by chapter xxvi. This book of Deuteronomy, more profound and more spiritual in its teaching, and more earnest in its exhortation than all the rest of the Law, closes with this denunication—the most tremendous in all Scripture—of the consequences of disobedience in detail. The Sermon on the Mount, the law of the New Testament, closes with a passage that astonished the hearers by its *authority* (Matt. vii. 21—27). The exhortations of our Lord's ministry, both public and private, have a similar close: for Israel in Matt. xxiii., for the disciples in Matt. xxv. And the Epistle to the Hebrews, the last appeal to the Jewish nation in God's word, has a similar passage in chapter xii., before the final exhortations and salutations. Finally, the Apocalypse itself puts the same kind of close to all Scripture in chapter xxii. 10—19.

We may divide this chapter into four parts.

First, the blessings of obedience to the nation as God's people, verses 1—14.

Secondly, the curses of disobedience, verses 15—48.

Thirdly, the prophecy of the conquest of Israel by a strange nation, and the miseries of the siege of the capital, verses 49—57.

Fourthly, the *continued* and *protracted* misery of the rejected nation, verses 58—68.

The remarkably prophetic character of this chapter is beyond question. Even were Deuteronomy the work (as some recent critics allege) of some later prophet, it is past all dispute that this chapter is older than the destruction of Jerusalem by Titus, and the last dispersion. Eighteen centuries of misery and oppression, with but short intervals, have branded the truth of this Scripture on the mind of Israel. From this argument there is no escape. No thoughtful Jew denies that the present condition of the nation is the fulfilment of this curse. It must be observed, however, as a *most* significant fact, that this chapter does not form the close of the Pentateuch. *Another covenant* is made with Israel *after this*. And Moses departed with words of blessing on his lips. (See on chap. xxix. 1.)

Every one who takes note of the proportions of this chapter according to the fourfold division indicated above, will at once see that, *verbally*, the curse is larger than the blessing. Why is this? Possibly, because the rebellions and disasters of Israel while under the Sinaitic covenant were to cover a larger number of years than their prosperity. But there may be another reason. The curses of God's broken law in this world, however extended and varied in their operation, are describable and finite. But His love is indescribable and infinite, and were all the blessings of His love to be described in detail, the whole Bible would not have sufficed for the first fourteen verses of this chapter of Deuteronomy.

Verses 1—14. BLESSINGS OF OBEDIENCE.

⁽¹⁾ **Will set thee on high.**—Literally, *will make thee Most High*, using a name of God, as in xxvi. 19. Compare what is said of Jerusalem. "She (Jerusalem) shall be called Jehovah-Tzidkenu" (Jer. xxxiii. 16), and "the name of the city from that day shall be Jehovah-Shammah" (Ezek. xlviii. 35), and "I will write upon him the name of my God, and the name of the city of my God" (Rev. iii. 12), and "His Name shall be in their foreheads" (Rev. xxii. 4).

⁽²⁾ **And overtake thee.**—A beautiful expression, *i.e.*, *shall come home to thee*, and impress the heart with the thought of God's love and of His promises, even when it is least expected. Comp. Zech. i. 6. "My words and my statutes, did they not *take hold of* (*i.e.*, overtake) your fathers? and they returned and said, Like as the Lord of hosts *thought* to do unto us . . . so hath he dealt with us." The opposite is true also of the curses (verse 15).

⁽⁵⁾ **Thy basket**—(Only here and in verse 17, and chap. xxvi. 2, 4)—*i.e.*, the portion which is brought out for the present occasion. *Thy store*, that which is left, and put away for future use. But this view rests upon the LXX. translation of the word for "store." All the Targums, and all the Jewish commentators I have been able to consult, and the lexicons also, take a different view. The word is identical in form with that used for "kneading troughs" in Exod. viii. 3, xii. 34. And so the contrast is taken to be, either (1) between firstfruits in their natural condition (chap. xxvi. 2) and the dough offered when already prepared for food, as in the wave-loaves (Lev. xxiii. 17); or (2) between the basket in which the corn is carried and the receptacle for the meal or dough, or (as Rashi takes it) between the vessel for things moist and the vessel for things dry. But the view taken by the LXX. is as old as any, and the contrast indicated by "basket" and "store" is simpler and more comprehensive than that which is drawn from a reference to the details of the law. The Authorised Version is, therefore, distinctly to be preferred, in my opinion. There are other technical reasons, which cannot be given here.

⁽⁶⁾ **When thou comest in . . . and when thou goest out.**—These words may apply to the details of life, or they may have a further meaning, as the eisodus of Christ was His entrance into this world's labour, and His exodus His departure (Acts xiii. 24; Luke ix. 31).

Blessings of Obedience.   DEUTERONOMY, XXVIII.   *Curse of Disobedience.*

⁽⁷⁾ The LORD shall cause thine enemies that rise up against thee to be smitten before thy face: they shall come out against thee one way, and flee before thee seven ways. ⁽⁸⁾ The LORD shall command the blessing upon thee in thy ¹storehouses, and in all that thou settest thine hand unto; and he shall bless thee in the land which the LORD thy God giveth thee. ⁽⁹⁾ The LORD shall establish thee an holy people unto himself, as he hath sworn unto thee, if thou shalt keep the commandments of the LORD thy God, and walk in his ways. ⁽¹⁰⁾ And all people of the earth shall see that thou art called by the name of the LORD; and they shall be afraid of thee. ⁽¹¹⁾ And ᵃthe LORD shall make thee plenteous ² in goods, in the fruit of thy ³ body, and in the fruit of thy cattle, and in the fruit of thy ground, in the land which the LORD sware unto thy fathers to give thee. ⁽¹²⁾ The LORD shall open unto thee his good treasure, the heaven to give the rain unto thy land in his season, and to bless all the work of thine hand: and ᵇthou shalt lend unto many nations, and thou shalt not borrow. ⁽¹³⁾ And the LORD shall make thee the head, and not the tail; and thou shalt be above only, and thou shalt not be beneath; if that thou hearken unto the commandments of the LORD thy God, which I command thee this day, to observe and to do *them*: ⁽¹⁴⁾ and thou shalt not go aside from any of the words which I command thee this day, *to* the right hand, or *to* the left, to go after other gods to serve them.

⁽¹⁵⁾ But it shall come to pass, ᶜif thou wilt not hearken unto the voice of the LORD thy God, to observe to do all his commandments and his statutes which I command thee this day; that all these curses shall come upon thee, and overtake thee: ⁽¹⁶⁾ cursed *shalt* thou *be* in the city, and cursed *shalt* thou *be* in the field. ⁽¹⁷⁾ Cursed *shall be* thy basket and thy store. ⁽¹⁸⁾ Cursed *shall be* the fruit of thy body, and the fruit of thy land, the increase of thy kine, and the flocks of thy sheep. ⁽¹⁹⁾ Cursed *shalt* thou *be* when thou comest in, and cursed *shalt* thou *be* when thou goest out.

1 Or, *barns.*
2 Or, *for good.*
3 Heb., *belly.*

a ch. 30. 9, &c.
b ch. 15. 6.
c Lev. 26. 14; Lam. 2. 17; Mal. 2. 2; Bar. 1. 20.

Rashi says, "So that thy departure from the world shall be like thine entrance into it, sinless." (The Jews, as a whole, do not believe in original sin.)

⁽⁷⁾ **And flee before tnee seven ways.**—" So is the custom of them that are terrified, to flee, scattering in every direction" (Rashi). See the story of the flight of the Midianites (Judges vii. 21, 22), and of the Syrians (2 Kings vii. 7).

⁽⁸⁾ **Thy storehouses.**—The word is only found here and in Prov. iii. 9, 10, "Honour the Lord with thy substance, and with the firstfruits of all thine increase: so shall *thy barns* be filled with plenty, and thy presses shall burst out with new wine." There is the same kind of contrast here which has been already pointed out in verse 5. The "gathering in" to the barn, and the "putting forth" of the hand—the income and the expenditure—are alike blessed. This contrast is clear in the Hebrew words employed.

And he shall bless thee in the land.—Fixity of tenure in the Divine inheritance is promised here.

⁽⁹⁾ **The Lord shall establish thee an holy people**—*i.e.,* shall "maintain" thee in that position or shall "raise thee up" into it, and exalt thee to it, in its fullest sense. The word here employed has branched out into two lines of thought. In Jewish literature it has taken the sense of permanence and perpetuity. Through the LXX. translation it has given birth to the New Testament word for "resurrection." (See Note on chap. xviii. 18, and comp. Acts iii. 26; 2 Sam. vii. 12; 1 Chron. xvii. 11.)

⁽¹⁰⁾ **That thou art called.**—Literally, *that the name of Jehovah has been called upon thee.*

And they shall be afraid of thee.—Comp. Jer. xxxiii. 9: "And they shall *fear* and tremble for all the goodness and for all the prosperity, that I procure unto it" (Jerusalem).

⁽¹¹⁾ **In goods.**—Rather, *in good* or *goodness, i.e.,* in prosperity. "Goodness" in Jer. xxxiii. 9.

⁽¹²⁾ **The Lord shall open unto thee his good treasure, the heaven to give the rain.**—The Jews have a saying that, "There are three keys in the hand of the Holy One, blessed be He! which He hath not intrusted to the hand of a messenger, and they are these, *the key of the rains,* the key of birth, and the key of the resurrection of the dead." The key of the rain, as it is written (Deut. xxviii. 12), "Jehovah shall open to thee His good treasure," &c. (from the Talmudic treatise, *Ta'anith,* p. 20, b).

⁽¹⁴⁾ **And thou shalt not go aside.**—It is possible, of course, to connect this sentence with the "if" in verse 13, "If that thou hearken and do not go aside." But the LXX., and apparently the Targums also, begin a fresh sentence with this verse. The idea that obedience begets obedience is by no means foreign to the Jewish mind. There are many passages in their literature which contain the thought expressed so forcibly in Rev. xxii. 11, "He that is unjust, let him be unjust still . . . and he that is holy, let him be holy still."

Verses 15—48. THE CURSE OF DISOBEDIENCE.

⁽¹⁵⁾ **But it shall come to pass.**—The following verses to the end of 48 are the contrast to the first fourteen, which declare the blessings of obedience.

⁽¹⁶⁻¹⁹⁾ **Cursed . . . .**—Here we have the counterpart of verses 3—6, inclusive. The only difference is in the position of "the basket and the store" which come one place earlier in the curses than in the blessings.

The Curse   DEUTERONOMY, XXVIII.   *of Disobedience.*

(20) The LORD shall send upon thee cursing, vexation, and rebuke, in all that thou settest thine hand unto ¹for to do, until thou be destroyed, and until thou perish quickly; because of the wickedness of thy doings, whereby thou hast forsaken me. (21) The LORD shall make the pestilence cleave unto thee, until he have consumed thee from off the land, whither thou goest to possess it. (22) ª The LORD shall smite thee with a consumption, and with a fever, and with an inflammation, and with an extreme burning, and with the ²sword, and with blasting, and with mildew; and they shall pursue thee until thou perish. (23) And thy heaven that *is* over thy head shall be brass, and the earth that *is* under thee *shall be* iron. (24) The LORD shall make the rain of thy land powder and dust: from heaven shall it come down upon thee, until thou be destroyed. (25) The LORD shall cause thee to be smitten before thine enemies: thou shalt go out one way against them, and flee seven ways before them: and shalt be ³removed into all the kingdoms of the earth. (26) And thy carcase shall be meat unto all fowls of the air, and unto the beasts of the earth, and no man shall fray *them* away. (27) The LORD will smite thee with the botch of Egypt, and with the emerods, and with the scab, and with the itch, whereof thou canst not be healed. (28) The LORD shall smite thee with madness, and

¹ Heb., *which thou wouldest do.*

ª Lev. 26. 16.

² Or, *drought.*

³ Heb., *for a removing.*

---

(20) **Cursing, vexation, and rebuke.** — *Deficiency,* and *anxiety,* and *failure* in every enterprise, would convey the idea, according to another interpretation. There are two views of the derivation of the first of the three words employed. Probably the Authorised Version is right. The three words have each of them the definite article in the original, just as if they were so many diseases. "*The* curse, and *the* terror, and *the* rebuke" of the Almighty are terrible obstacles to any human undertaking.

In all that thou settest thine hand unto for to do. — Literally, *in every putting forth of thine hand which thou makest,* i.e., in every undertaking. This is the opposite of verse 8.

Thou hast forsaken me. — Moses and Jehovah are here identified. This is characteristic. The prophets say, "Thus saith the Lord." Moses, whom the Lord knew face to face, sometimes exhorts Israel in His name without any such introduction. (Comp. the phrase "to forsake Moses" (literally, *apostasy from Moses*) in Acts xxi. 21.)

(21) **The pestilence.** — One of God's four sore judgments to be sent upon Jerusalem (Ezek. xiv. 19–21).

Until he have consumed thee from off the land. — From verses 21–35, inclusive, we seem to be reading of the gradual consumption of Israel "in the land of promise" before any actual captivity.

(22) **Consumption.** — Only here and in Lev. xxvi. 16. "With which the flesh is consumed and puffed out" (Rashi).

Fever. — Only here and in Lev. xxvi. 16, where it is rendered "burning ague." (Comp. chap. xxxii. 22: "A fire *is kindled* in mine anger.")

Inflammation. — Here only. The word is derived from a verb signifying to burn, or pursue hotly, like a fire that hastens on its way. "A heat greater than the fever" (Rashi).

Extreme burning. — Here only. "A disease which heats the body inwardly" (Rashi).

Blasting and mildew. — "I have smitten you with blasting and with mildew" (Amos iv. 9, same words). (See also 1 Kings viii. 37, where "pestilence, blasting, and mildew" are contemplated as possibilities, very probably in view of this curse. Also Hag. ii. 17.)

(23) **Thy heaven . . . shall be brass, and the earth . . . iron.** — Not only in respect of the drought, but of God's refusal to remove it. See Jer. xiv., xv. for a most pathetic intercession for Israel under this misery, answered by the order, "Pray not for this people for their good" (Jer. xiv. 11). Only grief is permitted (verse 17). Relief is not given (chap. xv. 1).

(24) **Powder and dust.** — The great desert, which lies on the eastern frontier of Palestine, makes this only too possible.

(25) The contrary to verse 7.

Removed. — Literally, *a removing.* The LXX. in this place has διασπορά, or dispersion, the word used for the dispersed Israelites in the New Testament. (See Revised Version, John vii. 35; 1 Pet. i. 1.) The threat is repeated in Jer. xv. 4 for the sins of king Manasseh.

(26) **And thy carcase shall be meat.** — Repeated in Jer. vii. 33, and to be fulfilled in Tophet, when they had buried until there was no more room. (Comp. also Jer. xv. 3.)

No man shall fray (*i.e.,* frighten) **them away.** — Not even a woman like Rizpah, who at the foot of the gallows watched her children's bodies for half the year, and "suffered neither the birds of the air to rest on them by day, nor the beasts of the field by night" (2 Sam. xxi. 10). There shall be no one to do it.

(27) **The botch of Egypt.** — The "boil," with which the Egyptians were plagued (Exod. ix. 9, &c.) is the same word. (See also 2 Kings xx. 7; Job ii. 7.) Rashi says of this boil, "It was very bad, being moist on the inside, and dry outside." A learned Dalmatian Jew, with whom I have read this passage, tells me that he has seen many cases of this kind among the Hungarian and Polish Jews, and that it prevails among them, being traceable partly to their uncleanliness.

Emerods — *i.e.,* hæmorrhoids (as in 1 Sam. v. 6).

The scab. — In Lev. xxi. 20, xxii. 22 "scurvy." It would make both a priest and a victim unclean, and unfit for the service of Jehovah.

The itch. — Here only. "A dry ulcer like a sherd" (Rashi).

Whereof thou canst not be healed. — Not that these things are in themselves incurable, but that they should have them incurably.

(28) **Madness, and blindness, and astonishment.** — The three words are all found in Zech. xii. 4.

blindness, and astonishment of heart: (29) and thou shalt grope at noonday, as the blind gropeth in darkness, and thou shalt not prosper in thy ways: and thou shalt be only oppressed and spoiled evermore, and no man shall save *thee*. (30) Thou shalt betroth a wife, and another man shall lie with her: thou shalt build an house, and thou shalt not dwell therein: *a* thou shalt plant a vineyard, and shalt not ¹gather the grapes thereof. (31) Thine ox *shall be* slain before thine eyes, and thou shalt not eat thereof: thine ass *shall be* violently taken away from before thy face, and ²shall not be restored to thee: thy sheep *shall be* given unto thine enemies, and thou shalt have none to rescue *them*. (32) Thy sons and thy daughters *shall be* given unto another people, and thine eyes shall look, and fail *with longing* for them all the day long: and *there shall be* no might in thine hand. (33) The fruit of thy land, and all thy labours, shall a nation which thou knowest not eat up; and thou shalt be only oppressed and crushed alway: (34) so that thou shalt be mad for the sight of thine eyes which thou shalt see. (35) The LORD shall smite thee in the knees, and in the legs, with a sore botch that cannot be healed, from the sole of thy foot unto the top of thy head. (36) The LORD shall bring thee, and thy king which thou shalt set over thee, unto a nation which neither thou nor thy fathers have known; and there shalt thou serve other gods, wood and stone. (37) And thou shalt become *b* an astonishment, a proverb, and a byword, among all nations whither the LORD shall lead thee. (38) *c* Thou shalt carry much seed out into the field, and shalt gather *but* little in; for the locust shall consume it. (39) Thou shalt plant vineyards, and dress *them*, but shalt neither drink *of* the wine, nor gather

a ch. 20. 6.

1 Heb., *profane, or, use it as common meat.*

2 Heb., *'shall not return to thee.*

b 1 Kin. 9. 7; Jer. 24. 9 & 25. 9.

c Mic. 6. 15; Hag. 1. 6.

But in that place the threat seems directed against the enemies of Jerusalem (see chap. xxx. 7).

(29) **Thou shalt not prosper in thy ways.**—The exact opposite is promised to Joshua (chap. i. 8) if he follows the Book of the Law. (Comp. Isa. xxix. 10—14.) When men find it no longer possible to follow the word of God, it is written that "the wisdom of their wise men shall perish, and the understanding of their prudent men shall be hid."

Oppressed.—The children of Israel and of Judah were "oppressed" together (Jer. l. 33). But it is added, "Their Redeemer is strong" (verse 34).

Spoiled.—The word occurs again in verse 31: "Violently taken away."

(31) **Thou shalt have none to rescue.**—Here and in verse 29 the Hebrew literally is, "Thou shalt have no Saviour." The times of oppression before the several judges were raised up, who are called saviours, must often have temporarily fulfilled these anticipations.

(32) **Thy sons and thy daughters.**—The language of this verse is perhaps the most pathetic piece of description in the whole chapter. Many of the nations bordering on Israel were accustomed when they made inroads to take away, not only the cattle, but the children for slaves. Another equally pathetic passage in Jeremiah touches on the very same thing. "A voice was heard in Ramah, lamentation and bitter weeping; Rachel weeping for her children, refused to be comforted for her children, because they were not." And it would not always be said, as it was then, "they shall come again from the land of the enemy" (Jer. xxxi. 15—17).

Thine eyes shall . . . fail—*i.e.*, shall consume. "All longing after that which comes not is called consumption of the eyes" (Rashi).

And there shall be no might in thine hand.—The Hebrew phrase here is very remarkable. It occurs also in Gen. xxxi. 29. "It is *in the power of mine hand* to do you hurt." But it means, literally, *thou shalt have no hand toward God*, *i.e.*, "thou shalt not be able to lift a hand to Him." We may compare Jacob wrestling with the angel, and Moses in the fight with Amalek: "When he held up his hand, Israel prevailed, and when he let down his hand, Amalek prevailed." Some would perhaps explain the phrase in another way; but this explanation is thoroughly in accordance with the genius of the Hebrew language, and I have good authority for it. Hezekiah said, "Mine eyes fail with looking upward." Here the eyes fail with looking, but cannot look up.

(33) **A nation which thou knowest not.**—Comp. Jer. v. 15—17, "*A nation* whose language *thou knowest not* . . . *shall eat up thy harvest and thy bread*," &c.

(35) **A sore botch.**—A boil, as in verse 27.

In the knees.—Comp. Ezek. vii. 17, xxi. 7, "All knees shall be weak as water."

(36) **Thee, and thy king that thou shalt set over thee.**—Comp. chap. xvii. 14. The former passage is not the only one in which Moses shows his foreknowledge that Israel would have a king. But could any later writer have concealed his knowledge that there were two kingdoms, or have avoided all allusion to the throne of David in passages like these?

Several kings went into captivity. Jehoahaz was taken to Egypt; Jeconiah and Zedekiah to Babylon. Hoshea's fate is not recorded in Scripture; but he was taken (apparently) with Samaria by the Assyrians.

Shalt thou serve other gods, wood and stone.—See Note on chap. iv. 28.

(37) **And thou shalt become an astonishment, a proverb, and a byword.**—This verse is the contrary to verse 10. It was verified in the first captivity, and did not wait for the last dispersion. (See 1 Kings ix. 7—9, where the threat is repeated; Jer. xlii. 18; Ezek. xxxvi. 20—22.)

(38—42) These are the contrary to verse 11; and verse 44 is the contrary to verses 12, 13. From the order of the passage it might seem that these particular troubles were to come on Israel after their captivity. And per-

the grapes; for the worms shall eat them. ⁽⁴⁰⁾ Thou shalt have olive trees throughout all thy coasts, but thou shalt not anoint *thyself* with the oil; for thine olive shall cast *his fruit.* ⁽⁴¹⁾ Thou shalt beget sons and daughters, but ¹thou shalt not enjoy them; for they shall go into captivity. ⁽⁴²⁾ All thy trees and fruit of thy land shall the locust ²consume. ⁽⁴³⁾ The stranger that *is* within thee shall get up above thee very high; and thou shalt come down very low. ⁽⁴⁴⁾ He shall lend to thee, and thou shalt not lend to him: he shall be the head, and thou shalt be the tail.

⁽⁴⁵⁾ Moreover all these curses shall come upon thee, and shall pursue thee, and overtake thee, till thou be destroyed; because thou hearkenedst not unto the voice of the LORD thy God, to keep his commandments and his statutes which he commanded thee: ⁽⁴⁶⁾ and they shall be upon thee for a sign and for a wonder, and upon thy seed for ever. ⁽⁴⁷⁾ Because thou servedst not the LORD thy God with joyfulness, and with gladness of heart, for the abundance of all *things;* ⁽⁴⁸⁾ therefore shalt thou serve thine enemies which the LORD shall send against thee, in hunger, and in thirst, and in nakedness, and in want of all *things:* and he shall put a yoke of iron upon thy neck, until he have destroyed thee. ⁽⁴⁹⁾ The LORD shall bring a nation against thee from far, from the end of the earth, *as swift* as the eagle flieth; a nation whose tongue thou shalt not ³understand; ⁽⁵⁰⁾ a nation ⁴of fierce countenance, which shall not regard the person of the old, nor shew favour to the young: ⁽⁵¹⁾ and he shall eat the fruit of thy cattle, and the fruit of thy land, until thou be destroyed: which *also* shall not leave thee *either* corn, wine, or oil, *or* the increase of thy kine, or flocks of thy sheep, until he have destroyed thee. ⁽⁵²⁾ And he shall besiege thee in all thy gates, until thy high and fenced walls come down, wherein thou trustedst, throughout all thy land: and he shall besiege thee in all thy gates throughout all thy land, which the LORD thy God hath given thee. ⁽⁵³⁾ And *ᵃ*thou shalt eat the fruit of thine own ⁵body, the flesh of thy sons and of thy daughters, which the LORD thy God hath given thee, in the siege, and in the straitness, wherewith thine enemies shall distress thee: ⁽⁵⁴⁾ *so that* the man *that is* tender among you, and very delicate, his eye shall be evil toward his brother, and toward the wife of his bosom, and toward the remnant of his children which he shall leave: ⁽⁵⁵⁾ so that he will not give to any of them of the flesh of his

¹ Heb., *they shall not be thine.*

² Or, *possess.*

³ Heb., *hear.*

⁴ Heb., *strong of face.*

ᵃ Lev. 26. 29; 2 Kin. 6. 29; Lam. 4. 10; Bar. 2. 3.

⁵ Heb., *belly.*

---

haps it is not accidental that something very like a fulfilment of verses 38—40 is found in Haggai i. 6—11. (Comp. also Isa. v. 10, "Ten acres of vineyard shall yield one bath, and the seed of an homer shall yield an ephah.")

⁽⁴⁵⁾ **Till thou be destroyed.**—Not exterminated. The root meaning of the word is connected with "smiting," and the idea seems to be to crush. (Comp. 2 Kings xiii. 7: "The king of Syria had destroyed them, and *had made them like the dust by threshing.*") This kind of destruction is consistent with what follows in verse 46, and also at the end of verse 48.

Verses 49—57. CONQUEST OF ISRAEL BY A STRANGE NATION. MISERIES OF THE SIEGE.

⁽⁴⁹⁾ **The Lord shall bring a nation against thee.**—Comp. "Lo, I will *bring a nation upon you from far,* O house of Israel, saith the Lord: it is a mighty nation, an ancient nation, a *nation whose language thou knowest not, neither understandest what they say*" (Jer. v. 15). In this instance the Chaldæans were intended, "that bitter and hasty nation" (Hab. i. 6).

As swift as the eagle flieth.—The eagles of Rome may be alluded to here. And of the Chaldæans it is said, "They shall fly as the eagle that hasteth to eat" (Hab. i. 8).

Whose tongue thou shalt not understand. —I am told by a learned Jewish friend that (excellent linguists as the Jews often are) hundreds of the people never attain the least acquaintance with the tongue of the countries where they are dispersed, and seem to lose the power of doing so. I have myself been surprised by more than one example, even in London, of their being wholly unable to take up the commonest matter of business when presented to them in an English way. It is not from lack of ability, but from a kind of paralysis of the understanding, except within a certain range of thought.

⁽⁵⁰⁾ **Which shall not regard the person of the old, nor show favour to the young.**— Comp. 2 Chron. xxxvi. 17, "The king of the Chaldees had no compassion upon young man or maiden, old man or him that stooped for age;" and Lam. v. 12, "Princes are hanged up by their hand: the faces of elders were not honoured."

⁽⁵²⁾ **And he shall besiege thee in all thy gates.**—The siege of the last two "fenced cities" by Nebuchadnezzar's army is mentioned in Jer. xxxiv. 7. The siege and capture of Jotapata by the Romans, in spite of all the efforts of the Jews to defend it, is specially recorded by Josephus.

⁽⁵³⁾ **Thou shalt eat the fruit of thine own body.**—Specially confirmed in the siege of Samaria by the Syrians (2 Kings vi. 26—29; but see on verse 56), and also in Jerusalem when besieged by Nebuchadnezzar. (See Lam. ii. 20, iv. 10.)

⁽⁵⁵⁾ **So that he will not give to any of them.** —A complication of horrors is here described. They

children whom he shall eat: because he hath nothing left him in the siege, and in the straitness, wherewith thine enemies shall distress thee in all thy gates. (56) The tender and delicate woman among you, which would not adventure to set the sole of her foot upon the ground for delicateness and tenderness, her eye shall be evil toward the husband of her bosom, and toward her son, and toward her daughter, (57) and toward her [1] young one that cometh out from between her feet, and toward her children which she shall bear: for she shall eat them for want of all *things* secretly in the siege and straitness, wherewith thine enemy shall distress thee in thy gates.

(58) If thou wilt not observe to do all the words of this law that are written in this book, that thou mayest fear this glorious and fearful name, THE LORD THY GOD; (59) then the LORD will make thy plagues wonderful, and the plagues of thy seed, *even* great plagues, and of long continuance, and sore sicknesses, and of long continuance. (60) Moreover he will bring upon thee all the diseases of Egypt, which thou wast afraid of; and they shall cleave unto thee. (61) Also every sickness, and every plague, which *is* not written in the book of this law, them will the LORD [2] bring upon thee, until thou be destroyed. (62) And ye shall be left few in number, whereas ye were *as the stars of heaven for multitude; because thou wouldest not obey the voice of the LORD thy God. (63) And it shall come to pass, *that* as the LORD rejoiced over you to do you good, and to multiply you; so the LORD will rejoice over you to destroy you, and to bring you to nought; and ye shall be plucked from off the land whither thou goest to possess it. (64) And the LORD shall scatter thee among all people, from the one end of the earth even unto the other; and there thou shalt serve other gods, which neither thou nor thy fathers have known, *even* wood and stone. (65) And among these nations shalt thou find no ease, neither shall the sole of thy foot have rest: but the LORD shall give thee there a trembling heart, and failing of eyes, and sorrow of mind: (66) and thy life shall hang in doubt before thee; and thou shalt fear day and night, and shalt have none assurance of thy life: (67) in the morning thou shalt say, Would God it were even! and at even thou shalt say, Would God it were morning! for the

1 Heb., *afterbirth.*

2 Heb., *cause to ascend.*

a ch. 10. 22.

---

shall eat some of their children and refuse to share even this food with those that are left.

(56) **The tender and delicate woman.**—This was fulfilled to the very letter in the case of Mary of Beth-ezob in the siege of Jerusalem by Titus. The story is told with horrible minuteness by Josephus, and again by Eusebius in his Church History. The secrecy of the deed was one of its horrors.

(58, 59) See Note on chap. xxv. 2, 3.

This glorious and fearful name, the Lord thy God.—The first Note of the Decalogue is here referred to, as the great curse of the Law draws to its close. It is no light matter when the Almighty says to any people or to any person, "I am Jehovah thy God." They who are His *must* obey Him, love Him, and acknowledge Him. He will not be mocked. Never did He in all history "assay to go and take Him a nation" from the midst of other nations as he took Israel. Hence these tremendous consequences.

Of long continuance.—Eighteen hundred years have they lasted, and seem to be breaking out afresh now (1882) as though they were in full force. "To chastise thee permanently is their mission" (Rashi).

(60) **The diseases of Egypt, which thou wast afraid of.**—Contrast Exod. xv. 26. "If thou wilt diligently hearken to the voice of Jehovah . . . I will put none of these diseases of Egypt which thou knowest, upon thee; for I am *Jehovah, that healeth thee.*" But, on the other hand, it is said (Ezek. vii. 9), "Ye shall know that *I am Jehovah that smiteth.*" *Jehovah-Rophêka* and *Jehovah-Makkeh* are one Jehovah.

(61) **Every sickness and every plague** (or "smiting;" Heb., *Makkah*) **which is not written.** —Well might the Apostle write, "It is a fearful thing to fall into the hands of the living God."

(63) **As the Lord rejoiced over you.**—See on chap. xxx. 9.

(64) **And the Lord shall scatter thee among all people.**—Fulfilled, literally, in this last dispersion.

Thou shalt serve other gods.—We do not know of Israel's falling into actual idolatry in dispersion, except in Egypt (Jer. xliv. 17), and possibly in Babylon (Ezek. xiv. 22, 23. Comp. chap. xxxiii. 25). But they were slaves to the worshippers of other gods.

(65) **And among these nations shalt thou find no ease.**—The repeated persecutions of the Jews by other nations in the time of their dispersion are among the most fearful and wonderful phenomena of history.

And failing of eyes.—"Looking for salvation, and it cometh not" (Rashi). How many years have they gone on praying that they may keep the feast "next year" in Jerusalem? and still the hope is deferred.

(66) **Thy life shall hang in doubt before thee.**—"Perhaps I shall die to-day by the sword that cometh upon me" (Rashi).

(67) **Thou shalt say.**—The Talmud expounds this of the constant increase of trouble. Yesterday evening

fear of thine heart wherewith thou shalt fear, and for the sight of thine eyes which thou shalt see. (68) And the LORD shall bring thee into Egypt again with ships, by the way whereof I spake unto thee, Thou shalt see it no more again: and there ye shall be sold unto your enemies for bondmen and bondwomen, and no man shall buy *you*.

a Ex. 19. 4.

CHAPTER XXIX.—1) These *are* the words of the covenant, which the LORD commanded Moses to make with the children of Israel in the land of Moab, beside the covenant which he made with them in Horeb.

(2) And Moses called unto all Israel, and said unto them, "Ye have seen all that the LORD did before your eyes in the land of Egypt unto Pharaoh, and unto all his servants, and unto all his land; (3) the great temptations which thine eyes have seen, the signs, and those great miracles: (4) yet the LORD hath not given you an heart to perceive, and eyes to see, and ears to hear, unto this day. (5) And I have led you forty years in the wilderness: your clothes are not waxen old upon you, and thy shoe is not waxen old upon thy foot. (6) Ye have not eaten bread, neither have ye drunk wine or strong

---

this morning was longed for. To-day the trouble is more terrible, and every hour adds to the curse. But the description in the text needs nothing to augment its horrors.

(68) **The Lord shall bring thee into Egypt again with ships.**—Josephus says this was done with many of the Jews by Titus.

Thou shalt see it no more again.—Chap. xvii. 16.

Ye shall be sold . . . and no man shall buy you.—Rashi explains thus: "Ye shall desire to be sold—ye shall offer yourselves as slaves to your enemies, and shall be refused, because you are appointed to slaughter and destruction. Or the sellers shall sell you to other sellers, and no one will care to keep you." But the same word is used in the following passage by Nehemiah, "We after our ability have *redeemed* our brethren the Jews, which were sold to the heathen" (Neh. v. 8). Probably the meaning in Deuteronomy is similar: "Ye shall be sold as slaves to your enemies, and there will *be no one to redeem you.*"

XXIX., XXX.

THE SECOND COVENANT.

(1) **These are the words of the covenant.**—The Hebrew Bibles add this verse to the previous chapter, and begin chap. xxix. at the second verse. But they cannot be right in so doing. For though the pronoun "these" in Hebrew has nothing to determine whether it belongs to what precedes or to what follows, yet the context shows that the covenant is described in chap. xxix., not in chap. xxviii. (See verses 12—15 below). It is very significant that this "covenant in the land of Moab" *stands outside* the tremendous sanction appended to the expansion of the Sinaitic covenant in Deuteronomy. The effect of this arrangement may be illustrated by a reference to Lev. xxvi., xxvii. The "sanction" of the law in Leviticus, which is a complete code of ceremonial and moral holiness, is contained in chap. xxvi. But that chapter is followed by a passage respecting vows, which are not compulsory, and therefore obviously lie, as a whole, outside that which is "commanded." The position of Deut. xxix. and xxx. is analogous to that of Lev. xxvii. Thus we see that the tremendous curse of the Sinaitic covenant *is not the end of God's dealings with the chosen people.* After that, there is still another covenant, to the force of which there is no limit (see verse 15 below). The gifts and calling of God are irrevocable. Nothing can destroy the relation between Jehovah and Israel. Their resurrection as a nation may well be described by the words of Moses in Ps. xc., "Thou turnest man to destruction (national death—Deut. xxviii.), and sayest (chaps. xxix., xxx.), *Return,* ye children of men (resurrection). *For* a thousand years in thy sight (though spent in the grave) are but as yesterday when it is past, and as *a watch in the night*" (to be followed by the dawn of morning). "A watch in the night" is not the blackness of darkness for ever.

Beside the covenant which He made with them in Horeb.—It should be carefully noted that the formal repetition of the law in Moses' second great discourse in this book opens with these words (ch. v. 2), "the *Lord our God made a covenant with us in Horeb.*" There is no real break in Deuteronomy from chap. v. 1 to the end of chap. xxvi. And chaps. xxvii. and xxviii. are the "sanction" of that covenant.

(2) **And Moses called all Israel and said unto them.**—The address in this chapter may be compared with that of Joshua to the *people* (as distinct from their heads and officers) in Josh. xxiv. The topics brought before them are simple. In verses 2, 3, the miracles of the Exodus; in verses 5, 7, the wilderness journey; in verses 7, 8, the conquest of Sihon and Og. All are appealed to, from the captains of the tribes (verse 10), to the little ones (verse 11), and the lowest slaves (verse 11). And the point set before them is one simple thing, to accept Jehovah as their God. All this is very closely reproduced in Josh. xxiv. (see Notes in that place).

Ye have seen.—The pronoun is emphatic. Yourselves are witnesses. I need not repeat the story. (Comp. chap. xi. 2—7.)

(4) **Yet the Lord hath not given you an heart to perceive.**—"To mark the mercies of the Holy One, blessed be He! and to cleave unto Him" (Rashi). And so in Ps. cvi. 7, "Our fathers understood not Thy wonders in Egypt; *they remembered not the multitude of Thy mercies.*" (See also on chap. xxxi. 16, &c.)

(5) See on chap viii. 4.

(6) **Ye have not eaten bread**—but manna (chap. viii. 3).

Neither have ye drunk wine or strong drink.—A fact stated here only, and evidently coming from the lips of one who "knew their walking through the wilderness." "They drank of that spiritual rock that followed them; and that Rock was Christ." God

The People Presented before God DEUTERONOMY, XXIX. *to Enter into this Covenant.*

drink: that ye might know that I *am* the LORD your God.

(7) And when ye came unto this place, Sihon the king of Heshbon, and Og the king of Bashan, came out against us unto battle, and we smote them: (8) and we took their land, and gave it for an inheritance unto the Reubenites, and to the Gadites, and to the half tribe of Manasseh. (9) *a* Keep therefore the words of this covenant, and do them, that ye may prosper in all that ye do.

(10) Ye stand this day all of you before the LORD your God; your captains of your tribes, your elders, and your officers, *with* all the men of Israel, (11) your little ones, your wives, and thy stranger that *is* in thy camp, from the hewer of thy wood unto the drawer of thy water: (12) that thou shouldest ¹enter into covenant with the LORD thy God,

a ch. 4, 6; 1 Kin. 2. 3; Josh. 1. 7.

¹ Heb., *pass.*

² Heb., *dungy gods.*

and into his oath, which the LORD thy God maketh with thee this day: (13) that he may establish thee to day for a people unto himself, and *that* he may be unto thee a God, as he hath said unto thee, and as he hath sworn unto thy fathers, to Abraham, to Isaac, and to Jacob.

(14) Neither with you only do I make this covenant and this oath; (15) but with *him* that standeth here with us this day before the LORD our God, and also with *him* that *is* not here with us this day: (16) (for ye know how we have dwelt in the land of Egypt; and how we came through the nations which ye passed by; (17) and ye have seen their abominations, and their ² idols, wood and stone, silver and gold, which *were* among them:) (18) lest there should be among you man, or woman, or family,

---

cared for their physical health and strength by the natural food which He gave them, and made their natural food represent the act of feeding upon Him. It is observable also that God seems to have especially blessed the abstinence from wine and strong drink for His sake in Israel. (See Lam. iv. 7.)

(7, 8) See chap. iii. 1—17.

(9) **Keep therefore the words of this covenant . . . that ye may prosper.**—Comp. Josh. i. 8 (Note); Ps. i. 3.

(10) **Ye stand this day all of you.**—There is no limit to the blessing of following Jehovah and keeping His word. It is open to all, from the highest to the lowest, to take hold of His covenant.

(11) **Your little ones.**—Compare St. Peter's words on the day of Pentecost: "The promise is unto you and to your children" (Acts ii. 39). The covenant with Abraham was that the Almighty would be a God to him and *to his seed* (Gen. xvii. 7), including the child of eight days old (verse 12), and the slave (verse 13), who were to receive the sign of His covenant in their flesh for an everlasting covenant.

From the hewer of thy wood unto the drawer of thy water.—From this Rashi infers that "there were Canaanites who became proselytes in the time of Moses, in the same way as the Gibeonites in the days of Joshua." It may have been so. And we know that there were many female captives of the Midianites who became slaves. (See Num. xxxi.)

(12) **Enter** (literally "pass") **into covenant with the Lord.**—Comp. Ezek. xx. 37: "I will *cause you to pass* under the rod, and I will bring you into the bond of *the covenant.*" Rashi illustrates by Jer. xxxiv. 18, the *passing between* the parts of the divided victim, in order to enter into the covenant. (Comp. Gen. xv. 17, 18.) But no such ceremony is mentioned here, and therefore we can only say that possibly the practice may have given occasion for this use of the word "pass."

His oath.—A word here used for the first time in Deuteronomy. It is rendered "curse" in verses 19—21. It seems to mean an *imprecation in the name of God* (comp. Lev. v. 21; Gen. xxiv. 41), which may bring a curse if the thing sworn to is not fulfilled.

Which the Lord thy God maketh with thee. —Maketh; literally, *cutteth.* The word refers to the "covenant."

(13) **That he may establish thee to day for a people unto himself.**—It must be carefully observed that this is the aspect of the covenant which makes Jehovah responsible for the fulfilment of the whole. "He takes all this trouble for the sake of establishing thee in His presence for a people" (Rashi). The people's part, as described in this verse, is only to accept the position. And thus the covenant of Deut. xxix. is brought into the closest similarity with that which is called the New Covenant in Jer. xxxi. 31, Heb. viii. 8; the form of which is "I will" be to them a God, and "they shall" be to me a people. God undertakes for the people's part of the covenant as well as His own. In Deuteronomy the first half of the New Covenant appears here in chap. xxix., "that He may be unto thee a God." The second part appears in chap xxx. 6—8, "The Lord thy God will circumcise thy heart . . . to love the Lord thy God."

(14, 15) **Neither with you only . . . but . . . also with him that is not here with us this day**—*i.e.*, "also with generations yet to be" (Rashi).

(16, 17) These verses seem rightly placed in a parenthesis. (Comp. Ezek. xx. 7, 8, 18.)

(17) **Their abominations.**—This word occurs here for the first time, but the verb appears in chap. vii. 26 ("utterly detest"), and in Lev. xi. 11, 13, 43, xx. 25. In the later scriptures of the Old Testament this word "abomination" is frequently used to denote an idol.

Their idols.—Either "great blocks," or as in the margin, a term of extreme contempt. (See Lev. xxvi. 30, where the word first occurs.) It is a favourite term with the prophet Ezekiel, who uses it four times as often as other writers in the Old Testament.

(18) **Lest there should be.**—The connection with verse 15 seems to be this. "I make this covenant binding with all your generations, in case there should

or tribe, whose heart turneth away this day from the LORD our God, to go *and* serve the gods of these nations; lest there should be among you a root that beareth ¹ ² gall and wormwood; ⁽¹⁹⁾ and it come to pass, when he heareth the words of this curse, that he bless himself in his heart, saying, I shall have peace, though I walk in the ³imagination of mine heart, to add ⁴drunkenness to thirst: ⁽²⁰⁾ the LORD will not spare him, but then the anger of the LORD and his jealousy shall smoke against that man, and all the curses that are written in this book shall lie upon him, and the LORD shall blot out his name from under heaven. ⁽²¹⁾ And the LORD shall separate him unto evil out of all the tribes of Israel, according to all the curses of the covenant that ⁵are written in this book of the law:

1 Or, *a poisonful herb.*
2 Heb., *rosh.*
3 Or, *stubbornness.*
4 Heb., *the drunken to the thirsty.*
5 Heb., *is written.*
6 Heb., *wherewith the LORD hath made it sick.*
a Gen. 19. 24, 25.
b 1 Kin. 9. 8; Jer. 22. 8.

⁽²²⁾ So that the generation to come of your children that shall rise up after you, and the stranger that shall come from a far land, shall say, when they see the plagues of that land, and the sicknesses ⁶which the LORD hath laid upon it; ⁽²³⁾ *and that* the whole land thereof *is* brimstone, and salt, *and* burning, *that* it is not sown, nor beareth, nor any grass groweth therein, ᵃlike the overthrow of Sodom, and Gomorrah, Admah, and Zeboim, which the LORD overthrew in his anger, and in his wrath: ⁽²⁴⁾ even all nations shall say, ᵇWherefore hath the LORD done thus unto this land? what *meaneth* the heat of this great anger? ⁽²⁵⁾ Then men shall say, Because they have forsaken the covenant of the LORD God of their fathers, which he made with them when he brought them forth out of the land of Egypt:

---

even now be any root of idolatry among you which may grow up and bring forth fruit in later times, and bring a curse upon your whole country." That there were such roots of idolatry is only too plain from chap. xxxi. 16, and from what followed after the death of the elders of this generation. (Comp. Judges ii. 10—12.)

A root that beareth gall and wormwood.— The same two words occur in Lam. iii. 19, and one of them (gall) in Ps. lxix. 21. From whatever root it came, there was One to whom it was given to drink. The LXX. form of this expression, "lest there is among you any *root that springeth up* in gall and *bitterness,*" is incorporated into the warning in Heb. xii. 15: "Looking diligently, lest any man fail of the grace of God; lest any *root of bitterness springing up* trouble you, and thereby many be defiled."

⁽¹⁹⁾ **The imagination.**—Rather the "stubbornness" or "obstinacy." The word is only found here and in Ps. lxxxi. 12 outside the writings of Jeremiah, who uses it eight times.

To add drunkenness to thirst—*i.e.*, the indulgence of the desire to the desire itself; to add sin to temptation. The LXX. have a strange paraphrase, "So that the sinner shall not involve the righteous with him in destruction." The thought seems to be that, perhaps, one idolater would not make so much difference to Israel. He would never involve the whole nation in destruction. The drunkard could not be the ruin of the thirsty, so to speak, and, therefore, he might do as he pleased, and might, in fact, escape punishment, being protected by the general prosperity of Israel. The quotation in the Epistle to the Hebrews meets this mistaken view admirably: "Lest any root of bitterness springing up trouble you, and *thereby many be defiled.*" The Targums render "to add sins of infirmity to sins of presumption," a rendering which partly explains that of the LXX.

⁽²⁰⁾ **Shall smoke.**—Comp. Ps. lxxx. 4, lxxiv. 1. Mount Sinai was altogether "on a smoke" because the Lord descended on it in fire.

Shall lie upon him.—As the beasts lie down in their lairs. The only other place which we can at all compare with this is the difficult expression in Gen. iv. 7, " Sin *lieth* at the door."

⁽²¹, ²²⁾ **And the Lord shall separate him unto evil . . . so that the generation to come . . . shall say . . . of that land.**— It is not a little remarkable that the sin of one man is here represented as growing and spreading devastation over the whole land of Israel—the very thing which the man apparently regards as impossible in his inward reasonings, described in verse 19. Yet is not this the true anticipation of what actually occurred? Comp. 1 Kings xiv. 15, 16: "The Lord shall root up Israel out of this good land, which He gave to their fathers . . . and *He shall give Israel up because of the sins of Jeroboam, who did sin, and who made Israel to sin.*" And what Jeroboam was to Israel, Manasseh was to Judah (Jer. xv. 4): "*I will cause them to be removed into all kingdoms of the earth, because of Manasseh the son of Hezekiah, king of Judah, for that which he did in Jerusalem.*"

⁽²³⁾ **And that the whole land thereof is brimstone, and salt, and burning, that it is not sown, nor beareth, nor any grass groweth therein.**—Can this be a description of the same country of which it was written in chap. viii. 7— 9, "A good land, a land of brooks of water, of fountains and depths that spring out of valleys and hills; a land of wheat, and barley, and vines, and fig trees, and pomegranates; a land of oil olive, and honey; a land wherein thou shalt eat bread without scarceness;" and (chap. xi. 12) "a land which the Lord thy God careth for"? Yet every one knows which of these two descriptions has been nearer to the actual fact for many centuries.

⁽²⁴⁾ **All nations shall say, Wherefore . . .?**— The people of Israel are represented as asking a similar question in Jer. v. 19, "And it shall come to pass, when *ye shall say, Wherefore* doeth the Lord our God all these things unto us? Then shalt thou answer them, Like as ye have forsaken me, and served strange gods in your land; so shall ye serve strangers in a land that is not yours." Compare also the warning given to Solomon after the completion of the Temple (marginal reference).

(26) for they went and served other gods, and worshipped them, gods whom they knew not, and ¹*whom* he had not ²*given* unto them: (27) and the anger of the LORD was kindled against this land, to bring upon it all the curses that are written in this book: (28) and the LORD rooted them out of their land in anger, and in wrath, and in great indignation, and cast them into another land, as *it is* this day.

(29) The secret *things belong* unto the LORD our God: but those *things which are* revealed *belong* unto us and to our children for ever, that *we* may do all the words of this law.

CHAPTER XXX. — (1) And it shall come to pass, when all these things are come upon thee, the blessing and the curse, which I have set before thee, and thou shalt call *them* to mind among all the nations, whither the LORD thy God hath driven thee, (2) and shalt return unto the LORD thy God, and shalt obey his voice according to all that I command thee this day, thou and thy children, with all thine heart, and with all thy soul; (3) that then the LORD thy God will turn thy captivity, and have compassion upon thee, and will return and gather thee from all the nations, whither the LORD thy God hath scattered thee. (4) *a* If *any* of thine be driven out unto the outmost *parts* of heaven, from thence will the LORD thy God gather thee, and from thence will he fetch thee: (5) and the LORD thy God will bring thee into the land which thy fathers possessed, and thou shalt possess it; and he will do thee good, and multiply thee above thy fathers. (6) And the LORD

---

1 Or, who *had not given to them* any portion.

2 Heb., *divided.*

a Neh. 1. 9.

---

(26) **Whom he had not given.**—The latter clause *may* be a change from plural to singular. "They went and served other gods, gods whom they knew not, and *none of whom gave* them any portion."

(28) **And the Lord rooted them out.**—Comp. 1 Kings xiv. 15, "He shall *root up* Israel out of this good land." The word is not uncommon in Jeremiah.

(29) **The secret things belong unto the Lord our God.**—The immediate connection of these words with the context is not clear. Rashi connects the "secret things" with the "imagination of the evil heart of the secret idolater" of verse 19. (The "secret faults" of Ps. xix. 12 is the same expression.) His note runs thus: "And if thou say, What can we do? wilt Thou punish the many for the devices of the one? as it is said (verse 18), 'lest there be among you *man or woman,*' and afterwards (verse 22), 'they shall see the plagues *of that land;*' and yet, Is there any man that knoweth the secrets of his fellow? It is not that I shall punish you for those secrets; they belong to the Lord our God, and He will exact them from the individual sinner; but the things that are *disclosed* belong to us and to our children, to 'put away the evil from the midst of us.' And if judgment is not executed among them, the many will be punished." But it is impossible not to feel that there is more behind the words of this passage than this. We must remember that Moses was delivering to Israel not law only but prophecy. And further, we may be certain that there was more in this latter portion of his prophecy than he could understand. May not this be one of the occasions concerning which the apostle says of the prophets, that they "searched *what or what manner of time* the spirit of Christ which was in them did signify"? All those curses were to come upon Israel, and yet, after that, there was still a covenant with them, embracing every generation to the world's end. Must not Moses have longed to know what would befall his people in the latter days? and if we ourselves, "upon whom the ends of the world are come," do not yet see the future of Israel distinctly, are not the words appropriate still? "The secret things belong unto the Lord our God: the things that are revealed belong to us and *to our children for ever.*" To the very end, what better way is there than this? "Lord, I have *hoped for Thy salvation,* and *done Thy commandments*" (Ps. cxix. 166).

XXX.

(1) **When all these things are come upon thee, the blessing and the curse.**—The curse is still upon them, and therefore this chapter contemplates the possibility of a restoration still to come. Some would go much further than this. But thus much is undeniable.

And thou shalt call them to mind.—An awakening among the people themselves must precede their restoration.

(3) **The Lord thy God will turn thy captivity.**—The word "turn" is not active as we should expect (in the Hebrew), but neuter, and upon this fact the Rabbis have grounded the following observation that "in some way the Shechinah is abiding upon Israel during the stress of their captivity, and whensoever they are redeemed, He has prescribed Redemption for Himself, that He will return with them." And further, that the day of the gathering of the captivity is great, and attended with difficulty; as though He Himself must be there to take hold visibly of the hand of each man, and bring him from his place, as it is said, "And ye shall be gathered one by one, O ye children of Israel" (Isa. xxvii. 12). But it is observed that the same form of the verb is employed in Jeremiah with respect to Moab (Jer. xlviii. 47). This note at least shows that the Jews look for the fulfilment of this prophecy as a thing yet to come.

(4) **If any of thine be driven out.**—In the LXX., "If thy dispersion be."

Unto the outmost parts of heaven.—The LXX. version of these words is traceable in Matt. xxiv. 31, "From the one end of heaven to the other."

(5) **Into the land which thy fathers possessed.**—It is very difficult to interpret these words of any land except Palestine. Comp. Jer. xxix. 13, 14, for their fulfilment in the first restoration, from Babylon.

Mercies to the Penitent. DEUTERONOMY, XXX. *Death and Life set before them.*

thy God will circumcise thine heart, and the heart of thy seed, to love the LORD thy God with all thine heart, and with all thy soul, that thou mayest live. ⁽⁷⁾ And the LORD thy God will put all these curses upon thine enemies, and on them that hate thee, which persecuted thee. ⁽⁸⁾ And thou shalt return and obey the voice of the LORD, and do all his commandments which I command thee this day. ⁽⁹⁾ ^a And the LORD thy God will make thee plenteous in every work of thine hand, in the fruit of thy body, and in the fruit of thy cattle, and in the fruit of thy land, for good: for the LORD will again rejoice over thee for good, as he rejoiced over thy fathers: ⁽¹⁰⁾ if thou shalt hearken unto the voice of the LORD thy God, to keep his commandments and his statutes which are written in this book of the law, *and* if thou turn unto the LORD thy God with all thine heart, and with all thy soul.

⁽¹¹⁾ For this commandment which I command thee this day, it *is* not hidden from thee, neither *is* it far off. ⁽¹²⁾ ^b It *is* not in heaven, that thou shouldest say, Who shall go up for us to heaven, and bring it unto us, that we may hear it, and do it ? ⁽¹³⁾ Neither *is* it beyond the sea, that thou shouldest say, Who shall go over the sea for us, and bring it unto us, that we may hear it, and do it? ⁽¹⁴⁾ But the word *is* very nigh unto thee, in thy mouth, and in thy heart, that thou mayest do it.

⁽¹⁵⁾ See, I have set before thee this day life and good, and death and evil; ⁽¹⁶⁾ in that I command thee this day to love the LORD thy God, to walk in his ways, and to keep his commandments and his statutes and his judgments, that thou mayest live and multiply: and the LORD thy God shall bless thee in the land whither thou goest to possess it. ⁽¹⁷⁾ But if thine heart turn away, so that thou wilt not hear, but shalt be drawn away, and worship other gods, and serve them; ⁽¹⁸⁾ I denounce unto you this day, that ye shall surely perish, *and that* ye shall not prolong *your* days upon the land, whither thou passest

a ch. 28. 11.

b Rom. 10. 6, &c.

⁽⁸⁾ **And thou shalt return and . . . do all his commandments.**—It *is* as certain as anything can be in this world that the laws of Deuteronomy have never been kept perfectly. The minute observances of the Talmudical system took the heart and spirit out of the law of Moses. Christians do not profess to obey any commandments but those which are called moral. If the Law itself is to be fulfilled, a restoration of Israel would seem to be necessary.

⁽¹⁰⁾ **If thou shalt hearken.**—"If" is the LXX. translation. The Hebrew word signifies "for," or "when."

Verses 11—14. THE LAW OF THE RIGHTEOUSNESS WHICH IS OF FAITH.

⁽¹¹⁾ **For this commandment.**—Heb., *Mitzvah.* This duty, this form of obedience to the law.

Is not hidden from thee—*i.e.*, not too hard. Literally, *too wonderful for thee.* (Comp. chap. xvii. 8; Ps. cxxxix. 6.)

⁽¹²⁾ **It is not in heaven.**—St. Paul cites the words thus: "The righteousness which is of faith speaketh on this wise, Say not in thine heart, Who shall ascend into heaven? *that is, to bring Christ down from above*" (Rom. x. 6, 7).

⁽¹³⁾ **Neither is it beyond the sea.**—St. Paul continues, "Or (say not), Who shall *descend* into *the deep?* that is, *to bring up Christ again from the dead.*" The alteration here is remarkable. The LXX. will not account for it. "Beyond the sea" generally suggests the idea of a land on the other side of the surface of the ocean. But a descent into the "abyss," which is what St. Paul indicates, means a passage through the sea to that which is beneath it, "beyond the sea" in a very different sense. No one but Jonah ever went beyond the sea in this way, as he says, "Out of the belly of hell cried I . . . Thou hadst cast me into the deep, in the heart of the seas . . . I went down to the bottoms of the mountains . . . The *deep* (abyss) *closed me about.*" And this descent of Jonah is chosen as the "sign" of Christ's descent into hell.

⁽¹⁴⁾ **But the word is very nigh unto thee.**—Here the difference between the Jewish and the Christian commentator is very striking. "The Law is given you in Scripture and in tradition" (written and orally), says Rashi on this place. But St. Paul continues thus: "But what saith it (the righteousness of faith)? The word is nigh thee, in thy mouth, and in thine heart, that is, the word of faith which we preach; that if thou shalt confess with thy mouth the Lord Jesus, and shalt believe in thine heart that God hath raised Him from the dead, thou shalt be saved." It is worthy of notice that St. Paul in this place contrasts the righteousness of faith with the righteousness of the law, and describes both alike in the words of the Pentateuch. Concerning the righteousness of the law, he says, Moses describeth it, "The man which doeth those things shall live by them." The citation is from Lev. xviii. 5. And there is a similar passage in chap. vi. 25. What could more clearly prove that the covenant of chaps. xxviii., xxix. was meant to present the way of salvation from a different point of view to the Sinaitic covenant, and was "beside the covenant which he made with them in Horeb." Not that we are to suppose there was ever a different way of salvation. The Decalogue itself begins (like the new covenant) with "I am the Lord thy God." But, unlike the new covenant, it makes no provision whereby Israel may keep the laws arising out of the relationship. The new covenant not only asserts the relationship, but provides the means whereby men may walk worthy of it. "I will put my laws in their mind, and write them in their heart." (See Note on chap. xxix. 13.)

over Jordan to go to possess it. (19) *a* I call heaven and earth to record this day against you, *that* I have set before you life and death, blessing and cursing: therefore choose life, that both thou and thy seed may live: (20) that thou mayest love the LORD thy God, *and* that thou mayest obey his voice, and that thou mayest cleave unto him: for he *is* thy life, and the length of thy days: that thou mayest dwell in the land which the LORD sware unto thy fathers, to Abraham, to Isaac, and to Jacob, to give them.

CHAPTER XXXI.—(1) And Moses went and spake these words unto all Israel. (2) And he said unto them, I *am* an hundred and twenty years old this day; I can no more go out and come in: also the LORD hath said unto me, *b* Thou shalt not go over this Jordan. (3) The LORD thy God, he will go over before thee, *and* he will destroy these nations from before thee, and thou shalt possess them: *and* Joshua, he shall go over before thee, *c* as the LORD hath said. (4) And the LORD shall do unto them as he did to Sihon and to Og, kings of the Amorites, and unto the land of them, whom he destroyed. (5) And *d* the LORD shall give them up before your face, that ye may do unto them according unto all the commandments which I have commanded you. (6) Be strong and of a good courage, fear not, nor be afraid of them: for the LORD thy God, he *it is* that doth go with thee; he will not fail thee, nor forsake thee.

(7) And Moses called unto Joshua, and said unto him in the sight of all Israel, Be strong and of a good courage: for thou must go with this people unto the land which the LORD hath sworn unto their fathers to give them; and thou shalt cause them to inherit it. (8) And the LORD, he *it is* that doth go before thee; he will be with thee, he will not fail thee, neither forsake thee: fear not, neither be dismayed.

(9) And Moses wrote this law, and delivered it unto the priests the sons of

a ch. 4. 26.

b Num. 20. 12; ch. 3. 27.

c Num. 27. 21.

d ch. 7. 2.

It is only in the power of this principle that Moses, in the exhortation which he founds on this statement of the way of righteousness through faith, could say as he did in verse 19, "therefore choose life."

(20) **He is thy life, and the length of thy days.**—This is the Old Testament form of a well-known saying in the New Testament, which may yet be fulfilled in Israel, "*I am* the *resurrection* and *the life*. He that believeth in me, though he were dead, yet shall he live; and whosoever liveth and believeth in me *shall never die*" (John xi. 25, 26).

XXXI.

Verses 1—8. MOSES RESIGNS HIS CHARGE AS LEADER TO JOSHUA.

(1) **And Moses went and spake.**—The expression is unusual. Possibly it means "went on to speak." The Palestine Targum has, "He went into the house of instruction and spake." The LXX. have apparently preserved a different reading, and say, "And Moses made an end of speaking these words" (like chap. xxxii. 45), as if the Hebrew were *vay'cal* instead of *vay-yêlek*. A transposition of two letters would make all the difference.

(2) **I am an hundred and twenty years old this day; I can no more go out and come in.**—The description of Moses' death in chap. xxxiv. 7, says, "his eye was not dim, nor his natural force abated." Yet he may have felt within himself that his work was done. "I have no longer authority, for the authority is taken from me and given into the hand of Joshua" is one interpretation. And it suits with what follows. "The Lord hath said unto me, Thou shalt not go over this Jordan."

(3) **The Lord thy God, he will go over before thee . . . Joshua, he shall go over before thee.**—Can it be accidental that Jehovah and Joshua are spoken of in exactly the same language, and that there is no distinguishing conjunction between them, the "and" of the English Version being supplied? "Jehovah, He is going over; Joshua, he is going over." Verbally, the two are as much identified as "The God who fed me all my life long unto this day, the Angel that redeemed me from all evil" (Gen. xlviii. 15, 16). The prophetical truth of this identification is too remarkable to be missed.

(4) **As he did to Sihon and to Og.**—The value of these two conquests, before Israel passed the Jordan, was inestimable, as an encouragement to them to persevere.

(5) **According unto all the commandments.**—The Hebrew word for "commandments" is in the singular, *Mitzvah*, the principle of action.

(6) **Be strong and of a good courage, fear not, nor be afraid.**—Here this is addressed to the people in the plural number. The same thing is said to Joshua in the next verse.

(7, 8) **And Moses called unto Joshua.**—In these words Moses formally delivers the charge of the people to Joshua, to lead them over Jordan.

He will not fail thee, neither forsake thee.—Repeated by Jehovah Himself (Josh. i. 5). "Will not let thee go" is the exact meaning of "fail" here. Comp. chap. ix. 14, "let me alone."

Verses 9—13. MOSES RESIGNS HIS CHARGE AS LAWGIVER TO THE PRIESTS.

(9—11) **And Moses wrote this law, and delivered it unto the priests . . . And . . . commanded them, saying . . . thou shalt read.**—This must be distinguished from the deliverance of the "book" to the Levites in verses 25, 26. The deliverance here must

Levi, which bare the ark of the covenant of the LORD, and unto all the elders of Israel. (10) And Moses commanded them, saying, At the end of *every* seven years, in the solemnity of the *a* year of release, in the feast of tabernacles, (11) when all Israel is come to appear before the LORD thy God in the place which he shall choose, thou shalt read this law before all Israel in their hearing. (12) Gather the people together, men, and women, and children, and thy stranger that *is* within thy gates, that they may hear, and that they may learn, and fear the LORD your God, and observe to do all the words of this law: (13) and *that* their children, which have not known *any thing*, may hear, and learn to fear the LORD your God, as long as ye live in the land whither ye go over Jordan to possess it.

(14) And the LORD said unto Moses, Behold, thy days approach that thou must die: call Joshua, and present yourselves in the tabernacle of the congregation, that I may give him a charge. And Moses and Joshua went, and presented themselves in the tabernacle of the congregation. (15) And the LORD appeared in the tabernacle in a pillar of a cloud: and the pillar of the cloud stood over the door of the tabernacle.

(16) And the LORD said unto Moses, Behold, thou shalt [1] sleep with thy fathers; and this people will rise up, and go a whoring after the gods of the strangers of the land, whither they go *to be* among them, and will forsake me, and break my covenant which I have made with them. (17) Then my anger shall be kindled against them in that day, and I will forsake them, and I will hide my face from them, and they shall be devoured, and many evils and troubles shall [2] befall them; so that they will say in that day, Are not these evils

a ch. 15. 1.

1 Heb., *lie down*.

2 Heb., *find them*.

---

be understood as a charge and a trust conveyed to the priests, making them responsible for the "reading of the law," and for the instruction of the people. This is the special duty of the priests. They are said to "bear" the ark of the covenant here; not because they always carried it (they did sometimes, as in Josh. iii.), but because they were responsible for it, just as they were also responsible for the exposition of the law (chap. xvii. 9). This is another example of the distinction between priests and Levites in the book of Deuteronomy.

(10, 11) **At the end of every seven years, in the . . . year of release, in the feast of tabernacles . . . thou shalt read this law.**—The fulfilment of this command, as far as the reading of the law is concerned, is described in Josh. viii. 34, 35; and again "at the feast of tabernacles" in Neh. viii. That the law read on these occasions was especially the book of Deuteronomy appears from the Talmudical treatise Sotah (p. 41), where the reading of it by the king is described as beginning with chap. i. 1: "These are the words." It is in this connection that the story is told of Agrippa that he wept when he came to chap. xvii. 15, "Thou mayest not set a stranger over thee." But they said, "Fear not, Agrippa, thou art our brother," and he then finished the reading. It was read from a platform erected in the forecourt of the temple. From this passage it is clear that the "reading" was understood to refer specially to the book of Deuteronomy.

(13) **That their children . . . may hear.**—It is obvious from this that the existence of many copies of the law was not contemplated by the writer. Comp. chap. vi. 6, 7: "These words shall be *in thine heart,* and thou *shalt teach them.*"

Verses 14—23. JOSHUA IS APPOINTED BY JEHOVAH TO MOSES' PLACE.

(14) **Thy days approach that thou must die: call Joshua, and present yourselves.**—What Moses had already done before Israel (verses 1—8) is now ratified by Jehovah to Joshua and Moses.

Moses and Joshua went.—We may compare this scene with that which is described in Num. xx. 25—28, when Aaron and Eleazar went up to Mount Hor, in order that the priesthood might be transferred from one to the other. Elijah and Elisha, in like manner, went together over Jordan, when Elijah was about to depart (2 Kings ii.). For the last time it is recorded here that Jehovah met Moses face to face in the tabernacle. Their next meeting was on Mount Nebo, and the next "within the veil!"

(16, 19) **Behold, thou shalt sleep with thy fathers . . . now therefore write ye this song.**—This prophecy that the children of Israel would forsake Jehovah and break His covenant is not a little remarkable, when we consider His dealings with them as a nation. It is one of the many proofs in Holy Scripture that our Creator is not like the man in our Lord's parable, who "intending to build a tower, sitteth not down first and counteth the cost, whether he hath sufficient to finish it." When He chose Israel to be His people, He knew the risk of doing so, and He provided for it beforehand. Not less when He said, "Let us make man in our image, *after our likeness,*" did He provide the means of forming in us the Divine character by all that Christ has done. The fall is recorded in the third chapter of Genesis. Redemption and restoration are exhibited in type and symbol in the second chapter. God brought Israel into Canaan in full foreknowledge of what the people would become when there.

(16) **And break my covenant.**—With this, contrast Judges ii. 1: "I said, *I will never break my covenant* with you." The phrases are identical in Hebrew. Comp. 2 Tim. ii. 13: "If we believe not, yet He abideth faithful: He cannot deny Himself."

(17) **Are not these evils come upon us, because our God is not among us?**—A confession made freely by them at this present day.

85

come upon us, because our God *is* not among us? ⁽¹⁸⁾ And I will surely hide my face in that day for all the evils which they shall have wrought, in that they are turned unto other gods. ⁽¹⁹⁾ Now therefore write ye this song for you, and teach it the children of Israel: put it in their mouths, that this song may be a witness for me against the children of Israel. ⁽²⁰⁾ For when I shall have brought them into the land which I sware unto their fathers, that floweth with milk and honey; and they shall have eaten and filled themselves, and waxen fat; then will they turn unto other gods, and serve them, and provoke me, and break my covenant. ⁽²¹⁾ And it shall come to pass, when many evils and troubles are befallen them, that this song shall testify [1] against them as a witness; for it shall not be forgotten out of the mouths of their seed: for I know their imagination which they [2] go about, even now, before I have brought them into the land which I sware.

⁽²²⁾ Moses therefore wrote this song the same day, and taught it the children of Israel. ⁽²³⁾ And he gave Joshua the son of Nun a charge, and said, *a* Be strong and of a good courage: for thou shalt bring the children of Israel into the land which I sware unto them: and I will be with thee.

⁽²⁴⁾ And it came to pass, when Moses had made an end of writing the words of this law in a book, until they were finished, ⁽²⁵⁾ that Moses commanded the Levites, which bare the ark of the covenant of the LORD, saying, ⁽²⁶⁾ Take this book of the law, and put it in the side of the ark of the covenant of the LORD your God, that it may be there for a witness against thee. ⁽²⁷⁾ For I know thy rebellion, and thy stiff neck: behold, while I am yet alive with you this day, ye have been rebellious against the LORD; and how much more after my death? ⁽²⁸⁾ Gather unto me all the elders of your tribes, and your officers, that I may speak these words in their

[1] Heb., *before*.
[2] Heb., *ao*.
a Josh. i. 6.

⁽¹⁸⁾ **I will surely hide my face.**—"As though I did not see (them) in their distress" (Rashi).

⁽¹⁹⁾ **Put it in their mouths, that this song may be a witness.**—This method of perpetuating the truth was even better adapted to the times and to the condition of the people than the delivery of a written law. It was not possible to multiply copies of the law among them to any great extent; but the rhythmical form of the song would make it easy to be retained in their memories. There is reason to believe that Samuel, the first person who (so far as we know) effected anything of importance towards the establishment of a system of religious education in Israel, employed the same means for the purpose, viz., psalms and spiritual songs. The first companies of prophets were evidently singers and minstrels (see 1 Sam. x. 5, 6, xix. 20—24); hence their remarkable influence over Saul. And if they taught the psalms to the people, as they learnt them under Samuel and David—especially historical psalms, like the 78th, 105th, and 106th—a very efficacious means of spreading the knowledge of God in Israel was in their hands.

⁽²¹⁾ **This song . . . shall not be forgotten out of the mouths of their seed.**—And it is not forgotten now. St. Paul made special use of it in the last days of the second Temple. This song is a favourite piece of Hebrew poetry to this day. Rashi observes: "This is a promise to Israel that the law shall not be utterly forgotten by their seed."

I know their imagination.—Heb., *yêtzer*, the same word employed in Gen. vi. 5, viii. 21. It is the word commonly used in Rabbinical literature for the evil nature or good nature in any man. *The nature which they are forming, or making, this day*, would be a literal rendering of the sentence in this verse. And yet with all this, He made Balaam say, "He hath not beheld iniquity in Jacob nor seen perverseness in Israel" (Num. xxiii. 21). Comp. 1 Chron. xxviii. 9, "The Lord . . . understandeth all the *imaginations* of the thoughts," and Ps. ciii. 14, "He knoweth our *frame* (*yêtzer*); He remembereth that we are dust."

⁽²³⁾ **And he (Jehovah) gave Joshua the son of Nun a charge.**—This is the first record of God's direct communion with Joshua. He was with Moses on the mount during the first forty days, and "departed not out of the Tabernacle" when they came down (Exod. xxiv. 13, xxxiii. 11). But we have no note of any Divine communication made to Joshua apart from Moses before this. It ratifies Joshua's appointment as leader of Israel.

Be strong . . .—Comp. Josh. i. 2, 6.

Verses 24—28. DELIVERY OF THE BOOKS OF MOSES TO THE LEVITES.

⁽²⁴⁾ **When Moses had made an end of writing.**—This means the completion of the books of Moses as he delivered them to Israel; not merely Deuteronomy, as above, in verse 9, but the whole, including the song mentioned in verse 22. The song was probably the end of the book as delivered to them by Moses.

In a book.—'*Al-sêpher;* upon a roll. The Pentateuch is written upon a single roll to this day.

⁽²⁵⁾ **The Levites, which bare the ark.**—Observe this, and comp. verse 9, above.

⁽²⁶⁾ **In the side of the ark.**—More literally, *beside*. Rashi says, "The wise men of Israel differ about this in the treatise Baba Bathra (in the Talmud). Some of them say there was a leaf or slab projecting from the ark outside, and there the book was placed. Others say that it was placed beside the tables of the covenant in the ark itself."

⁽²⁸⁾ **Gather unto me all the elders.**—In like manner Joshua gave a special charge to the elders at the close of his life (Josh. xxiii...

ears, and call heaven and earth to record against them. ⁽²⁹⁾ For I know that after my death ye will utterly corrupt *yourselves*,¹ and turn aside from the way which I have commanded you; and evil will befall you in the latter days; because ye will do evil in the sight of the LORD, to provoke him to anger through the work of your hands.

⁽³⁰⁾ And Moses spake in the ears of all the congregation of Israel the words of this song, until they were ended.

CHAPTER XXXII.—⁽¹⁾ Give ear, O ye heavens, and I will speak; and hear, O earth, the words of my mouth. ⁽²⁾ My doctrine shall drop as the rain, my speech shall distil as the dew, as the small rain upon the tender herb, and as the showers upon the grass: ⁽³⁾ because I will publish the name of the LORD: ascribe ye greatness unto our God. ⁽⁴⁾ *He is* the rock, his work *is* perfect: for all his ways *are* judgment: a God of truth and without iniquity, just and right *is* he.

⁽⁵⁾ ¹They have corrupted themselves, ²their spot *is* not *the spot* of his children:

¹ Heb., *He hath corrupted to himself.*

² Or, *that they are not his children, that is their blot.*

⁽²⁹⁾ **In the latter days.**—A not uncommon prophetical expression, used with some considerable latitude. It occurs for the first time in Gen. xlix. 1. (See also Num. xxiv. 14 and chap. iv. 30.) Some would refer it to the "days of the Messiah," and make it almost a technical term. But a comparison of these few passages will show that it cannot be tied strictly to any one period.

⁽³⁰⁾ **And Moses spake . . . the words of this song.**—The exodus of Israel begins and ends with a song of Moses. The song of Exod. xv. is usually referred to as the "Song of Moses," and is thought to be intended in Rev. xv. 3, 4. But there is a remarkable resemblance between Rev. xv. 3 and Deut. xxxii. 3, 4, which see.

XXXII.

⁽¹⁾ **Give ear, O ye heavens, and I will speak; and hear, O earth, the words of my mouth.**—Comp. the opening of Isa. i. 2, which is almost identical, excepting that the two words for "hearing" are transposed.

⁽²⁾ **My doctrine.**—Or, *my learning, that which I receive*—a not very common, but beautiful expression in the Hebrew. Everything that comes down from the "Father of lights" is handed on by one heavenly messenger to another, until it falls upon the heart of man, in just that form in which he can best receive it. The Son of God says, "My doctrine is not Mine, but His that sent Me." "I speak that which I have seen with my Father." Of the Holy Spirit He says, "He shall *receive of Mine* and shall show it unto you." The apostles speak "in words which the Holy Ghost teacheth." The parallels of the verse appear to be these:—My learning shall drop as the *rain*; My speech shall distil as the *dew*, as the *sweeping showers* upon the tender herb, as the *multitude of drops* upon the grass. The "small rain" of the Authorised Version points to a different and probably untenable derivation of the Hebrew word. The *rain* is more definite than the dew, and therefore the first word in the second half of the verse should be stronger than the second, and not *vice versâ*. The *tender herb* just sprouting can bear heavier showers than the grown grass.

⁽³⁾—
 "For (or when) it is the Name JEHOVAH that I utter;
 Give ye greatness to our God."

⁽⁴⁾ **He is the rock, his work is perfect: for all his ways are judgment: a God of truth and without iniquity, just and right is he.**—No such combination of all the words for *uprightness*, *sincerity*, *equity*, and *reliability* is to be found elsewhere in all Scripture. This is the character of *the Rock*. This name of God (*Tzur*) is one of the characteristics of the song. The word occurs first in Exod. xvii., where the Rock in Horeb was smitten; "and that Rock was Christ." From that time we find that the very names of the leaders in Israel embody this confession. Eli*zur*, my God is a Rock; *Zur*ishaddai, the Almighty is my Rock; and Peda*zur*, redeemed by the Rock (Num. i. 5, 6, 10), are examples. So exclusively is the term in Hebrew (*Tzûr* or *Sêlagh*) used in this sense, that no *man* is ever described by it in the Old Testament. And the LXX., in this song and in many other places, do not translate it at all, but give it as *God* (Θεός). In other places the word *Petra* (never *Petros*) is employed. This fact convinces me that the Petra of Matt. xvi. 18 could only have been understood by Jews as denoting Deity; and that it not only referred to Christ, but to *Christ as God*. No other interpretation will suit the language of Holy Scripture.

This fourth verse, like the third, is a stanza of four lines. The first line is answered by the third, and the second line by the fourth.

⁽⁵⁾—
 "He (Israel) hath destroyed himself.
 Their undutifulness,* that is their blot.
 A froward and crooked generation!"

These first two lines are given up as hopeless by many interpreters, not because the words are difficult of translation, but from the great variety of possible interpretations. After careful consideration of the passage with a learned Christian Hebrew,† I venture to propound this as the true translation. It is *substantially* identical with that of the English margin. The Hebrew consists of five words only (1) "He-hath-corrupted (2) to-him (3) not (4) his-sons (5) their blemish." That the first two ought to be taken together, if the text is correct, seems certain. The same construction is found in Num. xxxii. 15, "ye shall destroy all this people," and also in 1 Sam. xxiii. 10, "to destroy the city." As to the third and fourth words, we have thought that their true relation is the same which we find in verse 21, a "not-God," and a "not-people," and also in verse 5, "not-wise." In like manner Israel are in this verse called "not-sons of His." Their not-sonship, their unfilial, undutiful, ungodly behaviour to Him who is the perfection of truth and sincerity, a very Rock of fidelity to them, that is their great blemish.

* Literally, *they are no sons to Him*. (Comp. verse 20.)
† Mr. Bernhard Maimon, to whom I desire once for all to express my great obligations for assistance in this and many other difficulties.

they are a perverse and crooked generation. ⁽⁶⁾ Do ye thus requite the LORD, O foolish people and unwise? *is* not he thy father *that* hath bought thee? hath he not made thee, and established thee? ⁽⁷⁾ Remember the days of old, consider the years of ¹ many generations: ask thy father, and he will shew thee; thy elders, and they will tell thee. ⁽⁸⁾ When the Most High divided to the nations their inheritance, when he separated the sons of Adam, he set the bounds of the people according to the number of the children of Israel.

⁽⁹⁾ For the LORD'S portion *is* his people; Jacob *is* the ² lot of his inheritance. ⁽¹⁰⁾ He found him in a desert land, and in the waste howling wilderness; he ³ led him about, he instructed him, he kept him as the apple of his eye. ⁽¹¹⁾ As an eagle stirreth up her nest, fluttereth over her young, spreadeth abroad her wings, taketh them, beareth them on her wings: ⁽¹²⁾ *so* the LORD alone did lead him, and *there was* no strange god with him. ⁽¹³⁾ He made him ride on the high places of the earth, that he might eat the increase of the fields;

1 Heb., *generation and generation.*
2 Heb., *cord.*
3 Or, *compassed him about.*

He has said, "Israel is my son, even my firstborn." But all Israel's behaviour gives Him the lie. The contrast between the two descriptions—the faithful God of verse 4, and the unfaithful children of verse 5—is the cardinal point in the verse. In the form of the expression, *lo-bânâv* is strictly parallel to the *Lo-ammi* of Hosea i. 9. The "*froward* and *crooked* generation" supplies two words to Ps. xviii. 26, "with the *froward* thou wilt *shew thyself froward.*" Compare also the context of the two passages. Many other interpretations have been proposed, and some have altered the text. I believe the text to be correct, and that this is the true meaning.

(6)   "It is Jehovah that ye requite thus!
        A people foolish and unwise!
        Is not He thy Father that hath gotten thee?
        He made thee and establisheth thee."

The first line is an exclamatory question. A question and an exclamation have the same name in the Rabbinical writings. "Hath gotten" in the third line is the same expression which Eve used (in Gen. iv. 1) at the birth of Cain, and occurs also in that magnificent saying in the history of Wisdom, Prov. viii. 22, "The Lord *begat* me (as) the beginning of his way."

(7) The fourfold division of this verse is manifest.

(8, 9) Comp. chap. xxi. 16.

"When the Most High made nations to inherit,
When He parted the sons of Adam,
He set the bounds of the peoples,
According to the number of the sons of Israel.
For the portion of Jehovah is His people,
Jacob the cord * of His inheritance"

The allusion is to the dispersion from Babel (Gen. x., xi.). The Jews were accustomed to reckon seventy nations and languages in that dispersion. Seventy members of Jacob's household went down into Egypt. And literally they interpret this passage to mean that in dividing the lands to the peoples, Jehovah left room for His own, so that they might inherit the promised land without any undue pressure upon other nations. It is noticeable that the children of Lot and Esau were carefully preserved from disturbance by Israel (chap. ii.). But this is the bare literal interpretation. The true meaning of the passage is given by St. Paul in his speech at Athens: "He determined (for all nations) times before appointed, and the setting of the boundaries of their habitation, *that they might seek the Lord.*" The nations were so disposed in the world, and so developed, that each might have its opportunity of seeking Jehovah, in due season, through contact with His people—"if, as was certainly not impossible, they might feel after Him and find Him, who is not far from any one of us. For we are even His offspring." Hence He appoints our inheritance. With some such thought as this, the LXX. translate the latter half of verse 8, "He set the bounds of the peoples according to the number *of the angels of God.*" The chosen people were to be His messengers to the nations. He chose Israel for His own portion, that through them He might inherit the world. And yet in the face of this glorious calling and mission, the undutiful behaviour of Israel was their one great blot. They had only to accept the position already prepared for them, and they refused!

(10) The whole of this verse is in the pictorial present in the Hebrew—

"He findeth him in a desert land,
In a waste howling wilderness;
He compasseth him about, He instructeth him,
He guardeth him as the apple of his eye."

He found him.—This beautiful expression is common to the Old and New Testaments as a description of God's first revelation of Himself to man. In the case of Hagar it is written (Gen. xvi. 7), "the angel of Jehovah *found her* by a fountain of water in the wilderness." Concerning Jacob, that "*He found him* in Bethel," when Jacob said "Surely the Lord is in this place, *and I knew it not*" (Hosea xii. 4; Gen. xxviii. 16). A series of similar passages is closed by the three examples of the lost sheep, the lost money, and the son that had been lost, and *was found* (Luke xv.).

He led him about.—The commoner meaning is given in the margin. Rashi has this remark: "He caused them to abide round about His glory (*Shechinah*), the tent of the congregation in the middle, and four standards on the four sides."

(11, 12)   "As an eagle awakeneth her nest,
       Over her young she broodeth,
       She spreadeth out her wings, she taketh up each one of them,
       She beareth him on her pinions:
       Jehovah alone leadeth him,
       And a stranger-god is not with Him."

The eagle in Hebrew is masculine. He is one of the creatures that is honoured with a description by the lips of Jehovah Himself in Job xxxix. 27—30. But beautiful as the simile and the description in these places are, they are surpassed in gentleness by our Saviour when He says, "How often would I have gathered thy children together, *as a hen doth gather her brood under her wings*, and ye would not" (Luke xiii. 34).

Fluttereth.—Or, *broodeth*, is the word in Gen. i. 2, the Spirit of God *brooding* over the face of the waters.

(13, 14) The verbs again are all present. "*He maketh* him to ride," &c.

* *i.e.*, limit.

and he made him to suck honey out of the rock, and oil out of the flinty rock; (14) butter of kine, and milk of sheep, with fat of lambs, and rams of the breed of Bashan, and goats, with the fat of kidneys of wheat; and thou didst drink the pure blood of the grape. (15) But Jeshurun waxed fat, and kicked: thou art waxen fat, thou art grown thick, thou art covered *with fatness*; then he forsook God *which* made him, and lightly esteemed the Rock of his salvation. (16) They provoked him to jealousy with strange *gods*, with abominations provoked they him to anger. (17) They sacrificed unto devils, ¹not to God; to gods whom they knew not, to new *gods that* came newly up, whom your fathers feared not. (18) Of the Rock *that* begat thee thou art unmindful, and hast forgotten God that formed thee.

(19) And when the LORD saw *it*, he ²abhorred *them*, because of the provoking of his sons, and of his daughters. (20) And he said, I will hide my face from them, I will see what their end *shall be*: for they *are* a very froward generation, children in whom *is* no faith. (21) They have moved me to jealousy with *that which is* not God; they have provoked me to anger with their vanities: and *ᵃ I will move them to jealousy with *those which are* not a people; I will provoke them to anger with a foolish nation. (22) For a fire is kindled in mine anger, and ³shall burn unto the lowest hell, and ⁴shall consume the earth with her increase, and set on fire the foundations of the mountains. (23) I will heap mischiefs upon them; I will spend mine arrows upon them. (24) *They shall be* burnt with hunger, and devoured with

1 Or, *which were not God.*

2 Or, *despised.*

a Rom. 10. 9.

3 Or, *hath burned.*

4 Or, *hath consumed.*

---

(14) **Kidneys of wheat.**—The metaphor is literally translated from the Hebrew. The kidneys are enclosed in the very best of the fat of the animal, fat that was strictly reserved for God's altar by the Levitical Law.

(15) **Jeshurun** is a diminutive—a term of endearment. Either "the child of the upright," or "the beloved Israel." The letters of the diminutive of Israel, if slightly abbreviated, would make "Jeshurun." It is peculiar to Deuteronomy (here and in chap. xxxiii. 5, 26) and Isaiah (chap. xliv. 2). Two of the Targums render the word by "Israel here." The third retains the word itself. The LXX. translate it "the beloved one."

Kicked.—Only in 1 Sam. ii. 29: "Wherefore *kick ye* at my sacrifice and mine offering . . . to *make yourselves fat?*"

Grown thick.—As Rehoboam said, "My little finger shall *be thicker* than my father's loins." Both these parallels illustrate the spirit of the verse.

(17) **They sacrificed unto devils, not to God.**—St. Paul repeats this expression in 1 Cor. xi. 20.

Gods that came newly up.—Literally, *that came from close at hand.* Compare the description of the idol in Isa. xliv. 15, easily made from the firewood; and see also Wisdom xiii. 13, "A carpenter taking a crooked piece of wood, and full of knots, hath carved it diligently, *when he had nothing else to do*"—a comment on the passage in Isa. xliv.

(18) **Of the Rock that begat thee.**—"*The Rock hath begotten thee forgetful, and thou hast forgotten God that travailed with thee*," is another possible translation of this verse. The expression in the second clause is found also in Ps. xc. 2 (a prayer of Moses), "Before the mountains were brought forth, while Thou wast yet *in travail with* earth and world, and from eternity unto eternity Thou art God!" The word which I have rendered "forgetful" is usually taken as a verb. But the *verb* is not found elsewhere (*i.e.*, it is invented for the sake of this passage), and the word may not impossibly be an adjective.

(19) **The Lord saw . . . abhorred.**—Comp. Jer. xiv. 21.

(20) **A very froward generation.**—Literally, *a generation of perversities.*

Children in whom is no faith.—Literally, *children!—there is no relying on them.* (Comp. chap. v. 5.) Faith is not used in the sense of "belief" or "confidence," but as in the expression to "keep faith," or to "break faith," children who will keep no faith with one.

(21) "They have made me jealous with a no-god;
They have provoked me with their vanities:
And I will make them jealous with a no-people;
With a foolish nation will I provoke them."

St. Paul comments on this in Rom. x., as proving that Israel was informed of the calling of the Gentiles, and compares Isa. lxv. 1, "I was found of them that sought me not. I made myself manifest unto those that inquired not after me."

Rashi quotes, perhaps not quite inappropriately Isa. xxiii. 13, and gives this explanation, "A no-people," *i.e.*, a nation without a name; as it is said, "Behold the land of the Chaldæans: *this people was not.*"

(22) **For a fire is kindled in mine anger.**—Quoted by Jeremiah (chap. xv. 14, and comp. chap. xvii. 4).

The foundations of the mountains.—Rashi says, "Jerusalem, which is founded on the mountains," as it is said, "Jerusalem, the mountains are about her" (Ps. cxxv. 2).

(23) **Mischiefs.**—Literally, *ills.* Comp. Ezek. v. 16: "I will send upon them *the evil arrows of famine* . . . I will *increase* the famine upon them."

(24, 25)
"Consumed * with hunger, and devoured with pestilence, and bitter destruction—
I will also send the tooth of the beasts upon them, with the poison of crawling things of the dust.
Outside the sword bereaveth, and in the chambers terror;
Both young man and maiden, the suckling with the man of grey hairs."

* Or, possibly, "*Regaled* with hunger, and *fed with bread* of pestilence and bitter destruction," &c.

¹burning heat, and with bitter destruction: I will also send the teeth of beasts upon them, with the poison of serpents of the dust. (25) The sword without, and terror ²within, shall ³destroy both the young man and the virgin, the suckling *also* with the man of gray hairs. (26) I said, I would scatter them into corners, I would make the remembrance of them to cease from among men: (27) were it not that I feared the wrath of the enemy, lest their adversaries should behave themselves strangely, *and* lest they should say, ⁴Our hand *is* high, and the LORD hath not done all this. (28) For they *are* a nation void of counsel, neither *is* there *any* understanding in them.

(29) O that they were wise, *that* they understood this, *that* they would consider their latter end! (30) How should ᵃone chase a thousand, and two put ten thousand to flight, except their Rock had sold them, and the LORD had shut them up? (31) For their rock *is* not as our Rock, even our enemies themselves *being* judges. (32) For their vine ⁵*is* of the vine of Sodom, and of the fields of Gomorrah: their grapes *are* grapes of gall, their clusters *are* bitter: (33) their wine *is* the poison of dragons, and the cruel venom of asps. (34) *Is* not this laid up in store with me, *and* sealed up among my treasures? (35) To me belongeth ᵇ vengeance, and recompence; their foot shall slide in *due* time: for the day of their calamity *is* at hand, and the things that shall come upon them make haste.

(36) For the LORD shall judge his people, and repent himself for his servants, when he seeth that *their* ⁶power is gone, and *there is* none shut up, or left. (37) And he shall say, Where *are* their gods, *their* rock in whom they trusted, (38) which did eat the fat of their sacrifices, *and*

---

¹ Heb., *burning coals.*
² Heb., *from the chambers.*
³ Heb., *bereave.*
⁴ Or, *Our high hand, and not the LORD, hath done all this.*
ᵃ Josh. 23. 10.
⁵ Or, *is worse than the vine of Sodom, &c.*
ᵇ Ecclus. 28. 1; Rom. 12. 19; Heb. 10. 30.
⁶ Heb., *hand.*

God's four sore judgments are all depicted here—"the sword, and the famine, and the noisome beast, and the pestilence." With verse 25 comp. Jer. xiv. 18, "If I go forth into the field, then behold the slain with the sword! and if I enter into the city, then behold them that are sick with famine! yea both the prophet and the priest go about into a land that they know not."

(26, 27) The argument of these verses is such as no man would dare to put into the mouth of the Most High. Moses had pleaded it (in Num. xiv. 13—16; Exod. xxxii. 12), but none but Jehovah Himself would say for Himself, "*I feared the wrath of the enemy.*"

(27) **Behave themselves strangely.**—Possibly, *misunderstand it*, or *take note of it* (as a strange thing).

(28) **Void of counsel.**—Literally, *perishing in counsels*, or, perhaps, *spoiling the plans* of Jehovah. Yet they said, "Come, and let us devise devices against Jeremiah; for the law shall not *perish* from the priest, nor *counsel* from the wise, nor the word from the prophet" (Jer. xviii. 18).

(29) **Consider their latter end.**—Have some discernment as to their *hereafter*, what their destiny was, and what they will miss, if they fail to fulfil it.

(30) **How should one** (of their enemies) **chase a thousand** (of them).—Comp. the verse in chap. xxviii. 25, and more especially Lev. xxvi. 8, 17, 36.

Had sold them.—Here first used of Jehovah. It is a common expression in the book of Judges (chaps. ii. 14, iii. 8, iv. 2, x. 7; 1 Sam. xii. 9).

Had shut them up (into the hand of their enemies).—Comp. Ps. lxxviii. 62, "He shut up His people also unto the sword."

(31) **For their rock.**—Perhaps this may be taken, *For their rock* (the enemies' God) *is not as our Rock* (Jehovah), *and yet our enemies are judges, i.e., lords, over us*. So Rashi takes it. The verse should be read as a parenthesis. The argument would be this: No cause can be found for the defeat of Israel except the displeasure of Jehovah. The enemies have no gods that could fight against Israel.

The word for judges occurs only in Exod. xxi. 22; Job xxxi. 11. The phrase "our enemies themselves being judges" (of the question) is more like Latin than Hebrew, but it *may* be correct.

(32) **Their vine**—*i.e.,* Israel's, not the enemies'; going back to verse 30, "Their Rock," *i.e.,* Israel's Rock, "had sold them . . . for their vine is of the vine of Sodom." Comp. Hosea x. 1: "*Israel is an empty vine; he bringeth forth fruit unto himself;*" and Isa. v. 2, 7: "He looked that it should bring forth grapes, and it brought forth wild grapes . . . He looked for judgment, but behold oppression; for righteousness, but behold a cry."

(34) **Is not this laid up?**—"This" is generally taken to refer to what follows, but it is not clear. It may refer to the fact that "He looked for grapes, and the vine brought forth wild grapes."

(35) **To me belongeth vengeance, and recompence.**—In the Epistle to the Hebrews (chap. x. 30) this sentence is quoted with the first clause of verse 36, "For we know Him that said, Vengeance belongeth unto me. I will recompense, saith the Lord." And so in Rom. xii. 19.

Their foot shall slide in due time.—Rather, *for the time when their foot shall slide.*

(36) **For the Lord shall judge His people.**—Quoted in Heb. x. 30, in connection with the previous verse. According to this view "shall judge" means "shall punish," not "shall defend."

And repent Himself for His servants.—Or, *and will be comforted over His servants*. Comp. Ezek. v. 13, "I will cause my fury to rest upon them, and I *will be comforted;*" and also Isa. i. 24, &c.

None shut up, or left.—Comp. 1 Kings xiv. 10, xxi. 21; 2 Kings ix. 8, and especially chap. xiv. 26.

(37, 38) **He shall say, Where are their gods?** . . . **let them rise up and help you.**—He did say so in Judges x. 14.

The Song — DEUTERONOMY, XXXII. — *of Moses.*

drank the wine of their drink offerings? let them rise up and help you, *and* be ¹your protection. ⁽³⁹⁾ See now that I, *even* I, *am* he, and *there is* no god with me: ᵃI kill, and I make alive; I wound, and I heal: neither *is there any* that can deliver out of my hand. ⁽⁴⁰⁾ For I lift up my hand to heaven, and say, I live for ever. ⁽⁴¹⁾ If I whet my glittering sword, and mine hand take hold on judgment; I will render vengeance to mine enemies, and will reward them that hate me. ⁽⁴²⁾ I will make mine arrows drunk with blood, and my sword shall devour flesh; *and that* with the blood of the slain and of the captives, from the beginning of revenges upon the enemy.

⁽⁴³⁾ ² ᵇRejoice, O ye nations, *with* his people: for he will avenge the blood of his servants, and will render vengeance to his adversaries, and will be merciful unto his land, *and* to his people.

⁽⁴⁴⁾ And Moses came and spake all the words of this song in the ears of the people, he, and ³Hoshea the son of Nun. ⁽⁴⁵⁾ And Moses made an end of speaking all these words to all Israel: ⁽⁴⁶⁾ and he said unto them, ᶜ Set your hearts unto all the words which I testify among you this day, which ye shall command your children to observe to do, all the words of this law. ⁽⁴⁷⁾ For it *is* not a vain thing for you; because it *is* your life: and through this thing ye shall prolong *your* days in the land, whither ye go over Jordan to possess it.

⁽⁴⁸⁾ ᵈAnd the LORD spake unto Moses

1 Heb., *an hiding for you.*
ᵃ 1 Sam. 2. 6; Tob. 13. 2; Wisd. 16. 13.
2 Or, *Praise his people, ye nations.* Or, *Sing ye.*
ᵇ Matt. 7. 6; Rom. 15. 10.
3 Or, *Joshua.*
ᶜ ch. 6. 6 & 11. 18.
ᵈ Num. 27. 12.

⁽³⁹⁾ **I, even I, am he, and there is no God with me.**—There are many very similar passages in Isa. xli.—xlvi.; but none of them *exactly* reproduces this sentence.

I kill, and I make alive.—This was repeated by Hannah in her song, "The Lord killeth and maketh alive" (1 Sam. ii. 6). Comp. also Isa. xliii. 13, "Yea, before the day was *I am he*; and there is *none that can deliver out of my hand.*"

⁽⁴⁰, ⁴¹⁾ **For I lift up my hand.**—This is the form in taking an oath. (Comp. Rev. x. 5.) The two verses may be connected thus: "For I lift up my hand to heaven, and say, As I live for ever, if I whet my lightning sword, and my hand take hold on judgment, I will render vengeance to mine enemies, and repay them that hate me."

⁽⁴²⁾ **My sword shall devour flesh.**—Comp. Isa. lxvi. 16: "For by fire and by *His sword* will the Lord plead with *all flesh*, and *the slain of the Lord shall be many.*"

With blood.—Literally, *from the blood of the slain and of the captivity, from the beginning of revenges upon the enemy.* Judgment must begin at the house of God, as it did in Ezekiel's vision (chap. ix. 6), "and begin at my sanctuary;" but it will not end there.

⁽⁴³⁾ **Rejoice, O ye nations, with his people.***—This is cited by St. Paul to show that the Gentiles must also "glorify God for His mercy" in sending Jesus Christ. But it is not wholly fulfilled yet. "If the fall of God's people was the wealth of the world . . . what will the receiving of them be, but life from the dead?" (See Rom. xi. 12, 15, xv. 10.)

And will be merciful unto.—Literally, *will reconcile or make atonement for His land, the land of His people, or for the land of His people.* He will cleanse, forgive, and be merciful to it. The very last words speak of *local restoration* of the land to the people, and the people to the land. Of no other land has He said "*The land is mine.*" "Israel" alone is called His "firstborn."

* The LXX. have a longer version of this verse, "Rejoice, ye heavens, with Him, and *let all the angels of God worship Him* (Heb. i. 7); Rejoice, ye Gentiles, with His people, and let all the sons of God be strong in Him; for," &c.

JOSHUA TAKES UP THE HISTORY.

⁽⁴⁴⁾ **He, and Hoshea the son of Nun.**—Why should Joshua be called Hoshea in this place? His name was apparently changed to Joshua at the time when he entered the promised land with the eleven others who searched it out (Num. xiii. 8, 16). Now that he is about to lead Israel to the conquest, we are once more reminded of his change of name, and that the "salvation of Jehovah" was to be manifested through him. Possibly the change of name was also at this time confirmed to him. Compare the case of Jacob, whose change of name to Israel was *twice* made the subject of a Divine communication (Gen. xxxii. 28, xxxv. 10). Compare also what was said to him when about to enter into Egypt: "God spake unto *Israel* in the visions of the night, and said, *Jacob, Jacob.*"

We are assured by the mention of Hoshea in this place that the Joshua appointed to succeed Moses is the same person who was faithful among the spies.

It is also possible that this mention of Hoshea may be Joshua's *first mention of himself in the sacred writings.* After the close of the song, the remainder of Deuteronomy is not covered by Moses' signature. It belongs to Joshua, or else the author is unknown.

⁽⁴⁶⁾ **Set your hearts unto all the words.**—Rashi compares Ezek. xl. 4: "Son of man, behold with thine eyes, and hear with thine ears, and *set thine heart upon all* that I shew thee."

Which ye shall command.—Rather, *that ye may command your children to observe to do all the words of this law.* Obviously the knowledge of the law would depend very much on personal instruction for some time to come.

⁽⁴⁷⁾ **For it is not a vain thing for you.**—Not too light a thing for you, not unworthy of your attention.

It is your life.—For the last time in this book the people are assured that the very end of their existence in Canaan was the observance of the law of Jehovah as the law of the land.

⁽⁴⁸⁾ **And the Lord spake unto Moses that selfsame day.**—The day in which he spake the song in the ears of all Israel.

that selfsame day, saying, (49) Get thee up into this mountain Abarim, *unto* mount Nebo, which *is* in the land of Moab, that *is* over against Jericho; and behold the land of Canaan, which I give unto the children of Israel for a possession: (50) and die in the mount whither thou goest up, and be gathered unto thy people; as *a*Aaron thy brother died in mount Hor, and was gathered unto his people: (51) because *b*ye trespassed against me among the children of Israel at the waters of ¹Meribah-Kadesh, in the wilderness of Zin; because ye sanctified me not in the midst of the children of Israel. (52) Yet thou shalt see the land before *thee;* but thou shalt not go thither unto the land which I give the children of Israel.

CHAPTER XXXIII.—(1) And this *is* the blessing, wherewith Moses the man of God blessed the children of Israel before his death. (2) And he said,

The LORD came from Sinai, and rose up from Seir unto them; he shined forth from mount Paran, and he came with ten thousands of saints: from his right hand *went* ²a fiery law for them. (3) Yea, he loved the people; all his saints *are* in thy hand: and they sat down at thy feet; *every one* shall

a Num. 20. 25, 28 & 33. 38.

b Num. 20. 12, 13 & 27. 14.

¹ Or, *Strife at Kadesh.*

² Heb. *a fire of law.*

---

(49) **Get thee up into this mountain Abarim.**—See Num. xxvii. 12. The same command was given there, and was answered by Moses with the prayer for a successor, which was granted. All that is narrated between that passage and this may be considered as preliminary to Moses' departure.

Mount Nebo.—The particular peak of the "Abarim" ("mountains beyond Jordan," or "passages of Jordan"), where Moses was to die, was not mentioned before. "The rugged summit of mount Nebo rises abruptly 4,000 feet above the plain (where the Israelites were encamped), and still retains its name, with unchanged meaning, in the Arabic Neba, or height" (Conder's *Bible Handbook*, p. 254).

(50, 51) **And die in the mount . . . as Aaron thy brother died in mount Hor . . . because ye trespassed against me.**—It may be asked why Moses and Aaron should both have been made to ascend a mountain to die. I believe a clue to the reason may be found in the words and act which constituted their transgression. They were bidden to speak to the rock in Kadesh, and they struck it. The words which Moses used on that occasion were, "Hear now, ye rebels; must we fetch you water *out of this cliff* (*Selagh*)?" The last words of the sentence are emphatic; and the rock is described as a *cliff,* not by the name given to the Rock in Horeb (*Tzûr*). The emphasis laid upon these words has been much discussed by Jewish commentators, though it escapes English readers. I suspect that the mistake Moses and Aaron made, in thinking it needful to *strike* the cliff, also led them to think it necessary to *ascend it,* instead of gathering the congregation together beneath it, and speaking to it from below. This view harmonises with the spiritual significance of the act. The smitten Rock in Horeb was Christ; the Cliff not to be smitten in Kadesh pointed also to Christ, ascended now, needing only the prayer of faith to call down all that He will give. And so Moses himself taught, in some of his latest words. "It is not in heaven that thou shouldest say, Who shall go up for us to heaven, and bring it unto us? . . . But the word is nigh thee, in thy mouth."

The impatient words of Moses, after toiling up the cliff with his brother Aaron, had to be recompensed by their ascending mount Hor and mount Nebo to die. Moses, as the more responsible of the two, had to ascend on each occasion, for his brother's death and for his own. The remembrance of his brother's death in the Lord may well have comforted Moses in the prospect of his own.

XXXIII.
MOSES' LAST BLESSING.

(1) **Moses the man of God blessed the children of Israel.**—The title *man of God* is here used for the first time. Its counterpart is to be found in chap. xxxiv. 5: "Moses the *servant of Jehovah* died." The more any man is a "servant to Jehovah," the more is he a "man of Elohim" to his fellow-men. After Moses, Elijah and Elisha are more especially described by this title ("man of God") in the Old Testament.

Blessed . . . Israel before his death.—"And if not then, when should he?" (Rashi.)

(2) " And he said, Jehovah came from Sinai,
   And dawned upon them from Seir;
   He shone forth from mount Paran.
   And there came from the ten thousands of holiness,
   From His right hand, a fire of law * for them."

The appearance of God on Sinai is described as a sunrise. His light rose from Sinai, and the tops of the hills of Seir caught its rays. The full blaze of light shone on Paran. (Comp. Ps. l. 2: "Out of Zion, the perfection of beauty, God hath shined.") He came *with* ten thousands of saints is a mere mistranslation. The preposition is "from," not "with." If the verb "he came," in the fourth line, is taken to refer to God, we must translate: "He came from ten thousands of saints" (to sinful men). Rashi takes "from" to mean "part of." "There came some of His ten thousands of saints, but not all of them." I believe the true translation is what I have given. The law itself was "ordained by angels in the hand of a mediator" (Gal. iii. 19). It is called "the word spoken by angels" in Heb. ii. 2. The language of Dan. vii. 10—"A *fiery stream issued and came forth from before Him: thousand thousands ministered unto Him*"—supplies a complete parallel. The fiery law came from the ten thousands on "His right hand;" or *from* them, and *from* His right hand. This construction is by far the most simple, and agrees with what we read elsewhere.

(3) **Yea, he loved.**—The connection appears to be this—

" From His right hand went a fire, a law for them (Israel).
   Loving the peoples also;

(*i.e.,* all who should hereafter become His people)

---

* On this expression see an additional note at the end of the book.

receive of thy words. ⁽⁴⁾ Moses commanded us a law, *even* the inheritance of the congregation of Jacob. ⁽⁵⁾ And he was king in Jeshurun, when the heads of the people *and* the tribes of Israel were gathered together.

⁽⁶⁾ Let Reuben live, and not die; and let *not* his men be few.

⁽⁷⁾ And this *is the blessing* of Judah: And he said, Hear, LORD, the voice of Judah, and bring him unto his people: let his hands be sufficient for him; and be thou an help *to him* from his enemies.

⁽⁸⁾ And of Levi he said, *Let* thy Thummim and thy Urim *be* with thy holy one, whom thou didst prove at Massah, *and with* whom thou didst strive at the waters of Meribah; ⁽⁹⁾ who said unto his father and to his mother, I have not seen him; neither did he acknowledge his brethren, nor knew his own children: for they have observed thy word, and kept thy covenant. ⁽¹⁰⁾ ¹ They shall teach Jacob thy judgments, and Israel thy law: ² they shall put incense ³ before thee, and whole burnt sacrifice upon thine altar.

a Ex. 28. 30.

¹ Or, *Let them teach*, &c.

² Or, *let them put incense*

³ Heb., *at thy nose.*

All His saints are in Thy hand:
(the hand of Him who spake on Sinai, and now "speaketh from heaven")
And they are seated at Thy feet;
(the feet of the same heavenly Prophet. Comp. Matt. v. 1, 2)
Every one shall receive of Thy words."

Or, possibly, He, that prophet, *will take* of thy (*i.e.*, of Moses') words. We know he did so.

(4, 5) "[Of] the law which Moses commanded us,
The inheritance of the congregation of Jacob,
When he (Moses) was king in Jeshurun,
In the gathering of the heads of the people,
The tribes of Israel together."

This fourth verse, from its form, is evidently not what Moses said, but an explanatory parenthesis, inserted by the writer, who was probably Joshua. Upon "He was king in Jeshurun," Rashi says, "The Holy One, blessed be He! the yoke of His kingdom is upon them for ever." It may be so. "When the Lord your God was your king," is Samuel's description of the whole history of Israel previous to himself.

The certainty that the King of kings, the Messiah of Israel, was and is the Lawgiver and Teacher, and Keeper of all saints, and that there are none of that character who do not "sit at the feet of Jesus," makes the real meaning of the passage perfectly plain, even though the exact grammatical relation of the clauses may be not beyond dispute.

⁽⁶⁾ **Let Reuben live, and not die.**—"'Live' in this world." says Rashi, "and 'not die' in the world to come." That his misdeed should not be remembered (Gen. xxxv. 22). Rashi also notices the juxtaposition of this record with the sentence, "the sons of Jacob were *twelve*." Reuben was not cut off, but he was disinherited (1 Chron. v. 1), and his father's blessing had so much in it of disapproval, that Moses' prayer for him was not unnecessary.

And let not his men be few.—The sentence is difficult. The LXX. insert Simeon be "let Simeon be many in number." But there is no need for this. The most terrible destruction ever wrought in Israel by the word of Moses came on Dathan and Abiram (who were Reubenites), when "they and all that appertained to them went down alive into the pit." We cannot say how far the tribe was diminished by this terrible visitation and the plague that followed (Num. xvi.), but the fighting men of the tribe had slightly decreased in the second census (Num. i. 21 and xxvi. 7), and only two of all the twelve tribes had a smaller force than Reuben at this time. It seems best, therefore, to take the whole verse as applying to Reuben, and the negative in the first clause as covering the second clause also. "Let not his men be a (small) number." The omission of Simeon may be accounted for by his coming *within the inheritance of Judah*, in Canaan, and enjoying the blessing and protection of that most distinguished tribe. Rashi also takes this view.

⁽⁷⁾ **And this** (he said) **of Judah.**—The words which follow are a kingly blessing: "Hear, Lord, the voice of Judah, and bring him to his people." In other words, when we think of "the Lion of the tribe of Judah," "Thy kingdom come." Rashi reminds us of the many prayers in Old Testament history which were heard from Judah's lips. The prayers of David and Solomon; of Asa and Jehoshaphat; of Hezekiah against Sennacherib;—and, we may add, of King Manasseh, and Daniel the prophet—were all "the voice of Judah." The last line of Old Testament history is a prayer of Judah by the mouth of Nehemiah, "Remember me, O my God, for good." The psalms of David, again, are all "the voice of Judah." And, best of all, every prayer of our Lord's is "the voice of Judah" also. The remainder of the blessing is easily understood. The "hands" of Judah embrace those Hands which were "sufficient" for the salvation of mankind. "His enemies" include all, even to Death, the "last enemy," whom God shall subdue under His feet.

⁽⁸⁾ **And of Levi.**—Next to Joseph, this tribe has the largest share in Moses' last words, as we might naturally expect, it being his own tribe. The *character of the priest* is the principal subject. The blessing may be thus paraphrased: "Let thy Thummim and thy Urim (the chief high-priestly ornaments) be ever with some saintly man of thine, like him whom thou (Israel) didst tempt in Massah, and with whom thou didst strive at the waters of Meribah (Moses' own departed brother Aaron is alluded to, for the people murmured against them both in both places), like him (Eleazar or Phinehas) who said to his father and to his mother, 'I have not seen him,' &c. These are the priests that shall teach Jacob thy judgments and Israel thy law." The conduct of the tribe of Levi at Sinai is alluded to, when they stood by Moses and slew the idolaters. Who headed them on that occasion we are not told. Eleazar or Phinehas may be intended. The conduct of Phinehas (in Num. xxv.) is also a case in point. As Rashi observes, "his father and his mother, his brethren and children" cannot be taken literally, because the tribe of Levi on the whole was faithful. The fathers,

Of Benjamin, and Joseph,   DEUTERONOMY, XXXIII.   *and of Zebulun.*

⁽¹¹⁾ Bless, LORD, his substance, and accept the work of his hands: smite through the loins of them that rise against him, and of them that hate him, that they rise not again.

⁽¹²⁾ *And* of Benjamin he said,
The beloved of the LORD shall dwell in safety by him; *and the LORD* shall cover him all the day long, and he shall dwell between his shoulders.

⁽¹³⁾ And of Joseph he said,
a Blessed of the LORD *be* his land, for the precious things of heaven, for the dew, and for the deep that coucheth beneath, ⁽¹⁴⁾ and for the precious fruits *brought forth* by the sun, and for the precious things ¹*put forth* by the ²moon,

⁽¹⁵⁾ and for the chief things of the ancient mountains, and for the precious things of the lasting hills, ⁽¹⁶⁾ and for the precious things of the earth and fulness thereof, and *for* the good will of him that dwelt in the bush: let *the blessing* come upon the head of Joseph, and upon the top of the head of him *that was* ᵇ separated from his brethren. ⁽¹⁷⁾ His glory *is like* the firstling of his bullock, and his horns *are like* the horns of unicorns: with them he shall push the people together to the ends of the earth: and they *are* the ten thousands of Ephraim, and they *are* the thousands of Manasseh.

⁽¹⁸⁾ And of Zebulun he said,

a Gen. 49. 25.
¹ Heb., *thrust forth.*
² Heb., *moons.*
b Gen. 49. 26.

---

mothers, brethren, and children chiefly belonged to the other tribes.

Let thy Thummim and thy Urim.—See Exod. xxviii. 30. "*Thy* Thummim and *thy* Urim" may refer to Israel, or to Levi, or to Jehovah Himself. In the last case, He must be thought to have *tried* Levi at Massah, and striven with Moses and Aaron at the waters of Meribah. It is not at all easy to distribute the pronouns with certainty in this speech.

If the writer of Deuteronomy was unconscious of any difference between priest and Levite, how is the mention of Urim and Thummim to be explained?

⁽¹¹⁾ **Bless, Lord, his substance.**—This petition is consistent with the enactment that Levi should have *no land.* But a blessing on his substance means a blessing to the whole land of Israel. *Levi's substance was Israel's tithe.*

Accept the work of his hands.—The chief "work of his hands" was mediatorial for all Israel. The "acceptance" of this work was essential to the welfare of the whole race.

Smite through the loins of them that rise against him.—Rashi refers to the great war begun by the Asmonæans. Mattathias, the father of the Maccabees, was "a priest of the sons of Joiarib from Jerusalem" (1 Macc. ii. 1). In the time of Athaliah and of Antiochus Epiphanes alike, the restorers of the worship of Jehovah, and the deliverers of the nation from a foreign yoke, were *priests.*

⁽¹²⁾ **And of Benjamin.**—It is generally agreed that this blessing points to the site of the place which Jehovah chose out of all the tribes of Israel, *Jerusalem, in the tribe of Benjamin.* The Hebrew is divided thus:—

"Unto Benjamin he said, Beloved of Jehovah !
He (Jehovah) will dwell in security upon him,
Covering him over all the day.
And between his shoulders (mountain slopes) He hath taken up His abode."

⁽¹³⁾ **And of Joseph he said.**—The remark of Rashi is especially applicable here. "Thou wilt find in the case of all the tribes, that the blessing of Moses is drawn from the fountain of the blessing of Jacob."

As the *voice* of Judah, the *office* of Levi, and the *situation* of Benjamin are singled out for notice, so the *land* of Joseph is blessed.

The deep that coucheth beneath. — Rashi observes that "the deep ascends in vapour, and also gives moisture from below."

⁽¹⁴⁾ **And for the precious fruits.**—The "increase of the sun," and "precious things put forth from month to month" (or by night when the moon rules), are next alluded to.

⁽¹⁶⁾ **The good will of him that dwelt in the bush**—is a blessing peculiar to Moses. It contains an exquisite piece of interpretation. From the fact that Jehovah *revealed Himself* to Moses in a flame of fire *in a bush,* the man of God drew the thought that He presented Himself as *dwelling in it*; and thus he has furnished God's Church with this comfort for all ages, that His human temple, although it burn with fire, can never be consumed.

The last part of verse 16 is taken direct from Gen. xlix. 26.

Separated from his brethren.—Heb., *nâzir.* Is it altogether unreasonable to suppose that this particular feature in Joseph's history, when he was "sold into Egypt," and "separated from his brethren," may be part of the meaning of "Nazarene" when applied to our Lord in Matt. ii. 23?

⁽¹⁷⁾ **They are the ten thousands of Ephraim, and they are the thousands of Manasseh.**—Rashi refers this to the ten thousands *slain* by Joshua, the Ephraimite leader, and the thousands slain by Gideon, who was of the tribe of Manasseh. He expounds nearly the whole of the verse in reference to Joshua and the conquest of Canaan. There is an obvious similarity in the song of the Israelitish women after the defeat of the Philistines, "Saul hath slain his thousands, and David his ten thousands." The people "pushed to the ends of the earth" are taken to be the thousands and ten thousands of conquered Canaanites and Midianites. For a similar metaphor, see 1 Kings xxii. 11. Otherwise the ten thousands of Ephraim and the thousands of Manasseh would be the two-horned power of Joseph. (Comp. Dan. viii. 3, 20 for a simile of the same kind.)

⁽¹⁸⁾ **Zebulun . . . and Issachar** were united with Judah, in the leading division of Israel in the wilderness. The warlike character of the first of these two, and the more peaceful wisdom of the second, are illustrated by Judges v. 18 and 1 Chron. xii. 32, 33. (Comp. Jacob's blessing of Issachar in Gen. xlix. 14, 15.)

Rejoice, Zebulun, in thy going out; and, Issachar, in thy tents. ⁽¹⁹⁾ They shall call the people unto the mountain; there they shall offer sacrifices of righteousness: for they shall suck *of* the abundance of the seas, and *of* treasures hid in the sand.[1]

⁽²⁰⁾ And of Gad he said,

Blessed *be* he that enlargeth Gad: he dwelleth as a lion, and teareth the arm with the crown of the head. ⁽²¹⁾ And he provided the first part for himself, because there, *in* a portion of the lawgiver, *was he* ¹seated;[2] and he came with the heads of the people, he executed the justice of the LORD, and his judgments with Israel.

⁽²²⁾ And of Dan he said,

Dan *is* a lion's whelp: he shall leap from Bashan.

⁽²³⁾ And of Naphtali he said,

O Naphtali, satisfied with favour, and full with the blessing of the LORD: possess thou the west and the south.

⁽²⁴⁾ And of Asher he said,

Let Asher *be* blessed with children; let him be acceptable to his brethren, and let him dip his foot in oil. ⁽²⁵⁾ ²Thy shoes *shall be* iron and brass; and as thy days, so *shall* thy strength *be*.

⁽²⁶⁾ *There is* none like unto the God of Jeshurun, *who* rideth upon the heaven in thy help, and in his excellency on the sky. ⁽²⁷⁾ The eternal God *is thy* refuge, and underneath *are* the everlasting arms: and he shall thrust out the

---

[1] Heb., *cieleś.*
[2] Or, *Under thy shoes shall be iron.*

⁽¹⁹⁾ **They shall call the people unto the mountain.**—Or, *they shall give the mountain-call to the peoples*—i.e., they shall call the tribes of Israel to Mount Moriah to offer the sacrifices of righteousness. (See 2 Chron. xxx. 11, 18 for an illustration of this.)

⁽²⁰⁾ **Blessed be he that enlargeth Gad.**—The mountains of Gilead shut him in.

He dwelleth as a lion.—See 1 Chron. xii. 8, for eleven Gadites, "whose faces were as the faces of lions."

⁽²¹⁾ **The first part.**—The first territory conquered by Moses was distributed between Reuben and Gad, and the half tribe of Manasseh.

A portion of the lawgiver is interpreted by Rashi as the field of the "burial-place" of the lawgiver. But this can hardly have been in the mind of Moses.

He came with the heads of the people.—The Gadites with their companion tribes passed over Jordan to the conquest of Canaan by Moses' order.

⁽²²⁾ **Dan is a lion's whelp.**—Jacob compared him to a serpent and an adder. The lion of the tribe of Dan is not like the lion of the tribe of Judah.

He shall leap from Bashan.—The taking of Laish is probably referred to. It was a sudden, treacherous surprise, like the spring of a lion on his prey (Judges xviii. 27, 28). The "hill of Bashan" is opposed to God's hill in Ps. lxviii. 15. The "kine of Bashan" are reproved (Amos iv. 1). The "bulls of Bashan" represent the enemies of Christ in Ps. xxii. 12.

O Naphtali ... possess thou the west (literally, *the sea*) **and the south.**—This is not easy to interpret literally. The only sea in Naphtali's inheritance was the Sea of Galilee. If we look on to the days when that sea becomes famous in Holy Scripture, we find our Saviour dwelling in "the land of Zebulun and the land of Naphtali," and through his Galilean followers possessing the west and the south, taking the "nations for his inheritance, and the utmost parts of the earth for His possession."

⁽²⁴⁾ **Let Asher be blessed with children.**—It can be translated "more blessed than all sons." Rashi quotes an old saying, "You will not find among all the tribes one so blest with children as Asher, and I cannot say why."

Let him be acceptable to his brethren, and ... dip his foot in oil.—The fertility of Asher's inheritance is probably alluded to. There is no tribe of which so little is recorded in history. The happiest lives are sometimes the least eventful.

⁽²⁵⁾ **Thy shoes shall be iron and brass.**—Perhaps we should rather read, *thy bars shall be iron and brass*. The word here rendered "shoes" in the Authorised Version does not occur elsewhere. The nearest word to it means "locks" or "fastenings." It is also uncertain whether the whole sentence belongs to the blessing of Asher, or to all Israel. It seems most likely that, as Asher's territory was at the northern end of Palestine, close to the pass by which the most formidable invaders must enter in, an assurance is here given that the frontier of Israel should be safe. "Iron" and "brass" are mentioned together in connection with gates and bars in Ps. cvii. 16; Isa. xlv. 2. But they are not usually connected with "shoes" in the Old Testament.

And as thy days, so shall thy strength be.—The word for "strength" does not occur elsewhere in the Old Testament, but the Targums and the LXX., and other authorities, seem to agree in its interpretation, and the form of the word points to this meaning, "strength," so that there is little doubt as to its correctness. But the meaning of the clause is variously given by Jewish authorities. "Thy strength in old age shall be as the strength of thy youth;" or, "As thou spendest thy days (in doing the will of the Holy One or not), so shall thy strength be."

⁽²⁶⁾ **There is none like unto the God of Jeshurun.**—*Their rock is not as our Rock*. For Jeshurun, see note on chap. xxxii. 15.

⁽²⁷⁾ **The eternal God is thy refuge.**—The word "thy" is not represented in the original. *Mā‘ônah*, the word for refuge, differs very slightly from the "refuge" of Ps. xc. 1, "Lord, thou hast been our *refuge* in generation and generation," which are also the words of Moses. The same word is used of the "habitation of Jehovah" in heaven (chap. xxvi. 15). Perhaps we ought to connect this clause with what precedes, and render the passage thus:—

"There is none like the God of Jeshurun,
Riding on the heavens for thy help,
And in His Majesty on the sky—
The dwelling of the eternal Jehovah (above thee),
And underneath, the everlasting arms!
And He will expel before thee (every) enemy,
And will say (to thee), Destroy them."

enemy from before thee; and shall say, Destroy *them*. ⁽²⁸⁾ ᵃ Israel then shall dwell in safety alone: the fountain of Jacob *shall be* upon a land of corn and wine; also his heavens shall drop down dew. ⁽²⁹⁾ Happy *art* thou, O Israel: who *is* like unto thee, O people saved by the LORD, the shield of thy help, and who *is* the sword of thy excellency! and thine enemies ¹ shall be found liars unto thee; and thou shalt tread upon their high places.

CHAPTER XXXIV.—⁽¹⁾ And Moses went up from the plains of Moab unto the mountain of Nebo, to the top of ² Pisgah, that *is* over against Jericho.

a Jer. 23. 6.

1 Or, *shall be subdued.*

2 Or, *The hill.*

b ch. 3. 27; 2 Mac. 2. 4.

c Gen. 12. 7 & 13. 15.

And the LORD shewed him ᵇ all the land of Gilead, unto Dan, ⁽²⁾ and all Naphtali, and the land of Ephraim, and Manasseh, and all the land of Judah, unto the utmost sea, ⁽³⁾ and the south, and the plain of the valley of Jericho, the city of palm trees, unto Zoar. ⁽⁴⁾ And the LORD said unto him, ᶜ This *is* the land which I sware unto Abraham, unto Isaac, and unto Jacob, saying, I will give it unto thy seed: I have caused thee to see *it* with thine eyes, but thou shalt not go over thither.

⁽⁵⁾ So Moses the servant of the LORD died there in the land of Moab, according to the word of the LORD. ⁽⁶⁾ And he buried him in a valley in the land of

---

⁽²⁸⁾ **Israel then shall dwell in safety**—*i.e.*, in confidence and security. "*In His days* (the days of Messiah) Judah shall be saved, and *Israel shall dwell safely*" (Jer. xxiii. 6), but not until they learn to rest upon "the everlasting arms."

⁽²⁹⁾ **Thine enemies shall be found liars unto thee.**—See Ps. lxvi. 3: "Through the greatness of thy power *shall thine enemies* submit themselves (*i.e., lie*) *unto thee.*" The idea is, that the enemies of the conqueror will hasten to throw themselves at his feet, protesting that they were always his friends. (Compare Shimei's repentance on the occasion of David's return to Jerusalem, 2 Sam. xix. 18.)

XXXIV.

DEATH OF MOSES.

⁽¹⁾ **Pisgah.**—See Num. xxi. 20. The word seems to mean a height.

⁽¹, ²⁾ **The Lord shewed him all the land of Gilead, unto Dan, and all Naphtali . . . unto the utmost sea**—that is, He showed him all the land which was to be given to these several tribes. Whether He then showed it to him under the names which are given here or not is a question we cannot answer. Many deeply interesting queries suggest themselves here. Did Moses go up alone? or did Joshua accompany him? Who wrote these particulars of *what* was shown to him, and how were the particulars known? I am disposed to believe that as Elijah and Elisha "still went on and talked," until that chariot of fire appeared which "parted them both asunder," so it was with Moses and Joshua—that Moses' minister attended him until Jehovah withdrew him from his sight. But it speaks well for Joshua's character—in fact, it is altogether characteristic of the man—that in this record of the death of the great lawgiver he should have concealed himself and every other figure from sight except Jehovah and His servant Moses. Rashi, in his comment on this scene, says that the Lord showed Moses not only the land, but what should happen therein, in every part. But of this we know nothing. We know that the spectacle was complete. Probably "the eye that was not dim" was enabled to see farther than human eye ever saw from such a height before. "The utmost sea" is full fifty miles away from that spot.

⁽³⁾ **And the south**—*i.e.*, the *Negeb*.

And the plain *i.e.*, the plain of Jordan.

The valley of Jericho.—The city of palm trees may or may not be identical with that place.

⁽⁴⁾ **This is the land which I sware unto Abraham, unto Isaac, and unto Jacob, saying, I will give it unto thee: I have caused thee to see it.**—"That thou mayest go and say to Abraham, Isaac, and Jacob, The oath which He sware to you, the Holy One, blessed be He! hath performed it," is Rashi's comment. But in Paradise they scarcely needed Moses to tell them of His faithfulness.

⁽⁵⁾ **So** (better, *and*) **Moses the servant of the Lord died there in the land of Moab, according to the word of the Lord.**—Literally, *upon the mouth of the Lord*, and hence the Jewish interpretation that he died by a kiss! But the language of the sacred narrative is too simple to need even this interpretation. For many years it had been the habit of Moses to do everything "at the mouth of the Lord." Only one fatal mistake mars the record of obedience. It was but one last act of obedience to lie down and die at the word of Jehovah. It is extraordinary, when we consider the story of Moses' last days, how wholly self is cast aside. There is no anxiety about the unseen world, and no positive expression of hope. St. Paul says far more from Moses about his prospects in the life to come. To Moses, death is a source of anxiety on account of his people, and a source of pain to himself, because he cannot go over Jordan and see the works of Jehovah on the other side. Beyond this, his reticence is absolute, and his calm silence is sublime. But he died in the company of Jehovah, and may well have felt that he would not lose His presence in the other world. "Underneath were the everlasting arms," as he had said but just before. Jehovah was with him, and he feared no evil. He was so fearless, that it does not seem to have occurred to him to say that he did not fear.

⁽⁶⁾ **And he buried him.**—Moses is alone in this honour. The Son of God was buried by sinful men. Moses was buried by Jehovah.

But no man knoweth of his sepulchre.—I have always believed that the contention between Michael and the devil about the body of Moses (Jude v. 9) was, in fact, *a struggle for his body*—that Moses was to be raised from the dead, and that Satan re-

Moab, over against Beth-peor: but no man knoweth of his sepulchre unto this day.

(7) And Moses *was* an hundred and twenty years old when he died: his eye was not dim, nor his ¹ natural force ² abated.

(8) And the children of Israel wept for Moses in the plains of Moab thirty days: so the days of weeping *and* mourning for Moses were ended.

(9) And Joshua the son of Nun was full of the spirit of wisdom; for Moses had laid his hands upon him: and the children of Israel hearkened unto him, and did as the LORD commanded Moses.

(10) And there arose not a prophet since in Israel like unto Moses, whom the LORD knew face to face, (11) in all the signs and the wonders, which the LORD sent him to do in the land of Egypt to Pharaoh, and to all his servants, and to all his land, (12) and in all that mighty hand, and in all the great terror which Moses shewed in the sight of all Israel.

1 Heb., *moisture*.

2 Heb., *fled*.

---

sisted his resurrection. *When* the contest took place we cannot say. But Moses, who died and was buried, and Elijah, who was translated, "*appeared in glory*" on the holy mount, and the New Testament gives no hint of difference between them. We do not know how Moses could have *appeared* as a disembodied spirit so as to be seen of men.

(8) **The children of Israel wept for Moses . . . thirty days**. . .—As they did for Aaron, his brother (Num. xx. 29). It is remarkable that the burial and the tomb of Aaron are only alluded to in chap. x. 6. (See Note and Excursus on that passage.) Miriam was buried in Kadesh (Num. xx. 1).

(9) **And Joshua the son of Nun was full of the spirit of wisdom.**— Probably we should connect this with the preceding verse, "The days of mourning for Moses were ended," and ended more naturally because Joshua proved so well able to meet the wants of the people.

Moses had laid his hands upon him.— See Num. xxvii. 18, 23. It is the first example of "ordination" in Holy Scripture.

And did as the Lord commanded Moses. —Not "commanded Joshua." Joshua would not separate himself from the law given by his Master. Is it not true that when the Israel of God *hearken to the true Joshua*, they must needs do *as the Lord commanded Moses?* *

(10) **And there arose not a prophet since in Israel like unto Moses, whom the Lord knew face to face.**—Probably these words are later than the time of Joshua, when longer experience gave men the power to see how far inferior the prophets were to their great predecessor in this respect. The difference is most clearly set forth in Num. xii. 7, 8. (See Notes on that passage.)

---

* It may be worth while to remark that nowhere does this phrase occur so often as in the record of the setting up of the tabernacle in the last chapter of Exodus. *Seven times* it is written there that all was done *as the Lord commanded Moses*. Is it not a figure of the "true tabernacle which the Lord pitched, and not man"—the temple of His Body, which was *prepared* "*to do Thy will, O God*"?

EXCURSUS ON NOTES TO DEUTERONOMY

EXCURSUS ON CHAPTER X. 6, 7.

THESE verses have always seemed to me to present the greatest difficulty in the whole of Deuteronomy. If it were not for their beautiful spiritual connection with the context, I should not know how to account for their presence in this place at all. And even so, the *difference* between this allusion to Aaron's death and the account given in Numbers, and the superficial *resemblance* between the four stages of the journey of Israel here mentioned, and four stages which belong to a different period (in Num. xxxiii. 31—34)—together create a somewhat formidable perplexity. The Samaritan Pentateuch increases the confusion by introducing here the stages mentioned in Num. xxxiii. 34—37—an obvious attempt to harmonise the accounts of two distinct things. The LXX. version of Deuteronomy x. 6, 7 supports the Hebrew text. The fact that the *burial of Aaron is alluded to in this place only*, shows that the verses in Deuteronomy cannot have been taken from those in Numbers. The following comparison will show the difference.

IN THE FOURTH PERIOD OF THE EXODUS. (Num. xxxiii. 30—33.)	IN THE FIFTH PERIOD OF THE EXODUS. (Deut. x. 6, 7.)
"The children of Israel journeyed from *Ha-h-monah* to *Moseroth*; from *Moseroth* to *Bene-jaakan*; from *Bene-jaakan* to *Hor-hagidgad*; from *Hor-hagidgad* to *Jotbathah*." Three other encampments—at Ebronah, Ezion-gaber, and Kadesh—intervened before their arrival at Mount Hor, where Aaron died, in the fifth period of the Exodus, on the first day of the month. N.B.-The fourth period of the Exodus has no *dates* mentioned. The fifth period begins with the death of Miriam at Kadesh in the first month of the fortieth year. Num. xx. 1.	"The children of Israel journeyed from *Beeroth-bene-jaakan* to *Mosera*, (where Aaron died and was buried), from *Mosera* to *Gudgodah*; from *Gudgodah* to *Jotbath*, a land of rivers of waters." Mosera is singular, Moseroth plural in form. Bene-jaakan means "the children of Jaakan"—Beeroth-bene-jaakan the *wells* of the children of Jaakan. Hor-hagidgad means the mount of Gidgad, which differs from Gudgod only in the vowel pointing. Gudgodah may mean the neighbourhood of Gudgod or Gidgad, and Jotbathah may mean simply *to Jotbath*. *Gadgad* and *Etebatha* are found both in Numbers and Deuteronomy in the LXX. The other names are given with some variation.

The places are not mentioned in the same order in the two passages, and the difference in the form of the words shows that neither passage is copied from the other. All four sites are at present unknown. The additional particulars given in Deuteronomy suggest a reason why Israel should re-visit two of the four places; namely, because of the *water* which was to be had from the *wells* of the children of Jaakan, and in Jotbath, the "land of *rivers of waters*."

The return of Israel in the last period of the Exodus to four places previously visited is in no way remarkable. We are told that they were compelled, about the time of Aaron's death, to "journey from Mount Hor to *compass* the land of Edom," which the Edomites would not permit them to cross (Num, xxi. 4, and xx. 21). The return to these former encampments may have enhanced the weariness and annoyance of the people, so that "their soul was much discouraged because of the way," and if they were travelling in a different direction, they may well have revisited these four places in a different order. They need not have *encamped* at all of them the second time. The narrative in Deuteronomy merely says "they *journeyed from*," not "they *encamped in*." There is no reason why the district of Mount Hor may not have been called *Mosera* or *Moseroth*. And the name "chastisement" may have been given to it by Moses, like many other significant names in the Exodus (Meribah, Kibroth-hattaavah &c.), in consequence of what took place there.

Further there is some reason to believe that the number of the "goings out" of Israel in the Exodus, given in Num. xxxiii. is made to be 42 for a special reason, like the forty-two generations of Matt. i., in which there are at least three evidently intentional omissions. And therefore we need not be surprised at the insertion of places elsewhere, which are not included in that list. *No place is mentioned twice in* Num. xxxiii. Yet the children of Israel were certainly twice at Kadesh (for Numb. xiii. 26 and xx. 1, *cannot* refer to the same *time*), and probably twice at many other places.

The real difficulty is not in the *facts* related in Deut. x. 6, 7, but in the question *why they should be narrated there*. Further, they are narrated in the third person, "*the children of Israel journeyed*," but all the other portions of their journey are narrated in the first person (Deut. i. 19, *we* went; and so ii. 1, 8, 13, iii. 1, 26). A reader of Deuteronomy who was not already familiar with the earlier books, would naturally suppose that *at this period of the discourse* the children of Israel did journey, as the narrative says. It is only by close attention that the verses are seen to refer to a time previous to the beginning of the book, but much later than the events recapitulated in Deut. x. 5, 8.

In form, these verses correspond to what may be called the historical or editorial, as distinct from the hortatory portions of Deuteronomy; as the title, chap. i. 1—5; the parenthetical notes, chap. ii. 10—12, and 20—23; chaps. iii. 14, and iv. 41—43, 44—49; with the historical portions of the last six chapters of the book.

Upon the whole, I am disposed to think that the only

reason for the insertion of these verses is the spiritual reason which I have given in the notes.

From the wells of the children of Jaakan, or *perversity*, the people of God removed to Mosera the place of *chastisement*, where their great High Priest* died and was buried; and another priest arose in his stead. From thence they journeyed unto the mount of the *congregation* (Gudgod or Gidgad; compare *Gad*), and from thence to *Jotbath* (of which the root is *good* or *goodness*), a land of *rivers of waters*—the usual symbol in Scripture for the Holy Spirit given on Mount Zion, the "mount of the congregation" of Jehovah. (See St. John vii. 37—39.)

The explanations given by the Jewish commentators are of a spiritual character, and *in principle* I am disposed to think them correct, though the details are far too fanciful for reproduction, or for our present acceptance.

---

* The following passage from the Talmudical treatise, *Pirkê Aboth of Rabbi Nathan* (section 34), may serve to show that the comparison between Christ and Aaron is not peculiar to the New Testament:—"These are the two sons of fresh oil who stand by the Lord of the whole earth" (Zech. iv. 14). "These are Aaron and Messiah. And I cannot say which of them is the best beloved. But when he saith (Ps. cx. 4), Jehovah hath sworn and will not repent, Thou art priest for ever, then I know that the King Messiah is beloved above the Priest of Righteousness."

ADDITIONAL NOTE ON CHAP. XXXIII. 2. "A FIERY LAW."

THE original expression, *eshdath* or *esh dath*, sometimes written as one word, and sometimes as two, has created some difficulty. *Esh* is "fire," and *dath*, if taken as a distinct word, is "law." But *dath* does not appear elsewhere in the *Hebrew* of the Old Testament, until we meet it in the book of Esther, where it occurs frequently. It is also found in Ezra viii. 36. In the *Chaldee* of Daniel and Ezra it occurs six times. Modern authorities assert that it is properly a Persian word. But since it is found in the Chaldee of Daniel, it was in use among the Chaldæans before the Persian empire. The word has Semitic affinities. The Hebrew syllable *thêth* would have nearly the same meaning. A *datum* (or *dictum*) is the nearest equivalent that we have. There seems no reason to doubt that the word *dath* had obtained a place both in Chaldee and in Hebrew at the time of the Captivity. It is perfectly *possible* that its existence in Chaldee dates very much earlier. We must remember that Chaldee was the language of the family of Abraham before they adopted Hebrew. "A *Syrian* ready to perish was my father," is the confession dictated by Moses in Deut. xxvi. 5. Syriac and Chaldee in the Old Testament are names of the same language. In the Babylonish captivity the Jews really returned to their ancestral language. It is therefore quite conceivable that Chaldæan words lingered among them until the Exodus; and this word *dath*, if it be a true Chaldæan word, may be an example. But, obviously, these Chaldæan reminiscences would be fewer as the years rolled on. The three Targums all take *dath* to be "law" in this place. The LXX. has "angels" (ἄγγελοι), instead of the combination *eshdath*. Possibly the word was taken as *ashdoth* (plural of the Chaldee *ashda*), meaning "rays" (of light?) and so "angels." Comp., "He maketh His angels spirits, and *His ministers a flame of fire*;" they "ran and returned as a flash of lightning" (Ps. civ. 4; Ezek. i. 14). It is also possible that the LXX. read *r* instead of *d* in the word which they had before them, and that they arrived at the meaning "angels" through the Hebrew word *shârath*, "to minister." The confusion between *r* and *d*, which are extremely alike in Hebrew, is very common. The parallels referred to in the notes on the verse show that "fiery law" will yield a good sense. The only question is whether *dath*, "law," can be reasonably supposed to have occurred in the Mosaic writings. If the word were at all generally known at that period, to whatever language it properly belonged, it would hardly have escaped such a man as Moses. I think it quite possible that the common translation may be right. The Hebrew commentators accept it. The only alternative I can suggest is that of the LXX., which cannot be verified with certainty.

THE BOOK OF JOSHUA

INTRODUCTION
TO
THE BOOK OF JOSHUA

The Authorship of the Book of Joshua.— The sentence in chap. xxiv. 26 is the only direct statement in the Bible relating to the authorship of this book. "Joshua wrote these words in the book of the law of God." Do "these words" refer merely to the transaction immediately preceding, viz., the covenant made with Israel at Shechem, or have they any wider application? In order to discuss this question fairly, it is necessary to consider parallel passages, and thus to open in some measure the larger question of the authorship of all the historical books. The signature of Moses at the close of the Book of Deuteronomy is as distinct and explicit as that of any ancient author. "Thucydides of Athens wrote the history of the war between the Athenians and the Peloponnesians, how they warred with one another." So he opens his narrative, and no one disputes the fact. Not less distinct is the assertion in Deut. xxxi. 9: "Moses wrote this law, and delivered it unto the priests the sons of Levi, which bare the ark of the covenant of the Lord, and unto all the elders of Israel." Again (v. 24), "When Moses had made an end of writing the words of this law in a book, until they were finished, Moses commanded the Levites, which bare the ark of the covenant of the Lord, saying, Take this book of the law," &c. The chapter that follows (xxxii.) is also said to have been written by Moses (xxxi. 22): "Moses wrote this song the same day." But chaps. xxxiii. and xxxiv., the latter containing the record of Moses' death, are manifestly not covered by Moses' signature. The next signature that we meet with is that of Joshua (xxiv. 26): "Joshua wrote these words in the book of the law of God." The following verses contain the account of Joshua's death, and events subsequent to it. These verses are not covered by Joshua's signature, and are not the work of his hand.

The next note of authorship which we meet with in the Old Testament is found in 1 Sam. x. 25: "Samuel told the people the manner [*i.e.*, the constitution] of the kingdom, and wrote it in the [not *a*] book, and laid it up before the Lord." From the very first mention of the Bible, it appears as "*the book.*" Exod. xvii. 14: "The Lord said unto Moses, Write this for a memorial *in the book*, and rehearse it in the ears of Joshua."

The signature of Samuel does not stand, like those of Moses and Joshua, at the end of a specified portion of history. And this leads us in the next place to observe that the *historical books of the Old Testament are not presented as separate works*, but rather *as chapters in* what is regarded as *a single book* from the very first. Taking them as they stand in our English Bible, they form two volumes : the first including all from Genesis to the end of 2 Kings; the second from Chronicles to Esther, inclusive. Every book in each of these volumes is connected with its predecessor by the copulative conjunction "*And.*"* (In our English Bible it is sometimes a "Now," or "Then," but the Hebrew conjunction is the same throughout, a simple "*And.*") No one writes "And" as the first word of a distinct and separate work. Such a commencement implies that what follows is intended as a *continuation* of what is already begun.

Thus it appears that all the historical books of the Old Testament to the end of 2 Kings, are written as a continuation of the work of *Moses*. Joshua, Samuel, and the rest wrote their portions "in the book of the law of God," and as it were upon the blank pages which Moses had not filled.

A new beginning is made in 1 Chronicles—"Adam Seth, Enos"—and this work is a compendium of the history of God's people from Adam to Cyrus. The end of 2 Chronicles is repeated at the commencement of Ezra. Nehemiah begins in a somewhat peculiar way : "The words of Nehemiah, the son of Hachaliah. *And* it came to pass." Manifestly the first sentence is a title and signature in one. The real beginning is "*And.*" Esther also begins with "And." This, the last portion of the Old Testament history, also contains the significant clause, "*And it was written in the book*," which appears to be a reference to the sacred volume (Esther ix. 32).

Thus the signature of Joshua in chap. xxiv. 26 is seen to be one of *four* sentences in Old Testament history, referring to the authorship of the Bible. There is another series of passages in the Chronicles alluding to the sacred literature of the kingdom of Judah, from David to Zedekiah, and giving the succession of prophetic writers. But the books in this series have distinct titles, and were not in all cases entirely incorporated into *the book.* This is manifest from their titles, which can hardly be names of portions of Old Testament history. The well-known formula, "The rest of the acts of so-and-so," more literally a "*remainder*" (*Anglicè*, "remains") of so-and-so, does not refer to Scripture at all, except in one or two instances. How far, then, can the Old Testament be said to give any distinct account of the authorship of the historical books? We see that, with one or two exceptions, nothing is asserted which could fix with certainty the authorship of a given portion to a particular man. Moses has certainly signed his name at Deut. xxxii. And it is no less certain (despite the critics) that the *Pentateuch is an organic whole.* The inference, then, that the Pentateuch up to the end of Deut. xxxii. is the work of Moses is unquestionably so strong that we seem justified in accepting it as a literary fact. Whether Moses was the first writer of the whole, or compiled portions of it out of documents already existing, is a matter which we here leave to be discussed in its proper place, only observing that the relative length and connection of the several portions of Genesis show that the book cannot be a *mere* compilation. The Book of Nehemiah is introduced, as we have seen, by a title and a signature. But the only other *historical* book which has been presented to us with a signature is the book before us, viz., Joshua.

---
* The Book of Deuteronomy, like that of Nehemiah, has its first title prefixed to the "And." But this is no exception. (See Notes on Deut. i. 1.)

Is the signature intended to fix with absolute certainty the authorship of the entire book *in its present shape*?

One very simple consideration suffices to answer this question provisionally, and brings us a step further on the road. The Book of Joshua, in its present shape, records Joshua's death; and the Book of Deuteronomy records the death of Moses. Thus these books, as delivered to us, show traces of the hand of an *editor*, no less than an *author*. Some prophet's hand must have penned the closing record of the Book of Deuteronomy, before proceeding to write the story of Joshua's conquest in the Book of the Law of God. Another hand, after Joshua laid down the pen, must have traced the story of his death, and before proceeding to the connected narrative of the Judges, must have collected (in part from Joshua itself) the particulars which form the very careful and thoughtful introduction to that book, contained in chaps. i., ii., iii. 1—6.

In the Book of Joshua, no less than in the Pentateuch as it now stands, we recognise the hand of an *author* and of an *editor*. Where does the work of the one end, and the work of the other begin? The discussion of this question might easily introduce the whole subject of the modern literary criticism of the Old Testament. And there are men bold enough to account for every verse in Old Testament history, and acute enough to imagine, describe, and distinguish any number of editors and authors that their view of the requirements of the text may seem to demand.

But our task is much more modest. We shall be satisfied with pointing out, for the present—(1) that the Old Testament itself does recognise the existence of these two human agencies in its formation; in the present instance, by giving us the signature of Joshua near the close of his work, and by adding the account of his death afterwards in the same book, before making a fresh beginning. And (2) that the general reply of the sacred writers to those who inquire particularly as to who is responsible for every separate statement in the pages of Old Testament history, is to the same effect as that of the three Hebrew heroes to Nebuchadnezzar, "We are not careful to answer thee in this matter." But the reason of this apparent indifference must not be misunderstood. Partly it arises from the existence of a long succession of prophetic authors, from Moses to Malachi, who were authorised to declare to the Jewish nation the will of Jehovah, and through whom, in every question demanding revelation, it was possible to appeal to the authority of Israel's God. Not until that "goodly fellowship of the prophets" had passed away, did it become absolutely necessary to separate that which had received the stamp of Divine authority, from what was mere human composition.

But were the prophets authorised to alter as well as to edit the works of their predecessors? A sentence from Deuteronomy and a sentence from Joshua, placed side by side, will indicate the kind of understanding there was between them. "Ye shall not add unto the word which I command you, neither shall ye diminish from it" (Deut. iv. 2). Yet "Joshua wrote these words in the book of the law of God." Clearly Joshua, who obeyed the Book of the Law more strictly than any of his successors, was not the man to alter anything that Moses had enacted. Yet it never seems to have occurred to him that he was transgressing the orders of Moses by adding his own contribution to the Book of the Law of God.

The view of the Bible itself as to the province of the *prophetical editor* is not inconsistent with additions to the work of a Moses or a Joshua, even under the title of the books which bear their name. Is it possible to go a step further and ascertain (from the Bible itself, as distinct from critical speculations *about* it) whether additions were made not only at the end, but also in the body of the text? One such addition seems to have been made in the text of Joshua, viz., the mention of the Danite colony at Laish, chap. xix. 47. For the settlement of this colony is distinctly and inextricably connected with the establishment of *idolatry* (Judges xviii. 30, 31), and it is expressly stated that the people served the Lord all the days of Joshua. The men who remonstrated with the two and a half tribes after the fashion described in Josh. xxii. would never have tolerated what is described in the story of Laish. It does not seem possible to ascribe Josh. xix. 47 to the hand of Joshua himself. It stands quite naturally at the end of the list of Danite cities, an addition to the inheritance assigned to Dan by Joshua, a town which the tribe acquired for itself.

But if we admit a single addition to the text of Joshua by the hand of a later editor, is it possible to limit the operation of the principle thus conceded?

It is necessary to look this question fairly in the face. It seems to have been too often supposed, on the one side, that if anything were allowed to stand part of a book of the Old Testament, which did not come from the original hand, the authority of the Bible would be impaired. And, on the other hand, modern literary critics feel at liberty to assign any portion of the Old Testament to any period whatever, according to their own (momentary) view of the text.

Between these two extremes, it must be surely possible to find a middle alternative. Why should we not suppose that the prophetic editors of the earlier books acted as any faithful and conscientious man among ourselves would act? To add any subsequent particulars which could give completeness to the narrative, insert a note which would clear up an obscure phrase, or a later name which would identify an ancient city; to mark* divisions, parting the Book of Joshua from Deuteronomy on one side and Judges on the other—all this might be done without in any way interfering with the substance of the book, or effacing the individuality of the author. More than this it is not reasonable to ascribe to the prophetic editor. With these exceptions, there is nothing in the Book of Joshua which may not have been the work of Joshua himself.

The conclusion to which we come presents us with this phenomenon. The *writing* of Joshua in the Old Testament very possibly ranges from the beginning of Deut. xxxiii. to a certain point in Josh. xxiv., say verse 26. The *Book of Joshua* has different limits. The moral is, that the sacred writers were not careful to tell us *exactly* who the authors of the separate portions of the Old Testament were. The reason would seem to be this—that *the books, in their quality of Scripture, do not rest solely, or principally, upon the authority of the individual authors*, but upon the collective authority of the prophets, and of Him whose servants they were.

The Style of the Book of Joshua is very much what we should expect from the place it occupies and its claim to be a continuation of the narrative of the Exodus. Moses wrote the journeyings of the Children of

---

* It is not generally known to readers of the English Bible that the divisions between 1 and 2 Samuel, 1 and 2 Kings, and 1 and 2 Chronicles, which are found even in Hebrew Bibles, are the work of Christian hands. "The Christians divided Samuel and Kings into two books respectively." "They also divided Chronicles into two books." (Elias Levita in "Exposition of the Massorah." Dr. Ginsburg. 1867. p. 29.)

JOSHUA.

Israel " according to their goings out " (Num. xxxiii. 2). Joshua wrote, in the book begun by Moses, the story of their " coming in." In the narrative of Joshua there is much that reminds us of the latter part of the Book of Numbers; while the hortatory portions recall the manner of the Book of Deuteronomy, though falling so far short of it as to be perfectly distinct. It would be interesting to know how far Joshua had himself been employed by Moses in the capacity of a scribe or secretary. In one passage (Josh. xv. 4), if the Hebrew may be trusted (the LXX. differs slightly), the very language of the lawgiver seems to have been unconsciously adopted. But in all arguments from style to authorship in the Old Testament, it is necessary to remember the very great difficulty in the way of distinguishing different writers, arising from the employment of one uniform system of vocalisation and punctuation by the Massorites, who have clothed the original language of the whole book.

One phrase which occurs frequently in Joshua may be called characteristic. It appears for the first time in the narrative of chap. iv. 9, respecting the twelve stones set up in Jordan: "they are there unto this day." So it is said of Rahab (chap. vi. 25), " she dwelleth in Israel *unto this day.*" The phrase itself is not unknown in the Pentateuch, and is common in the later historical books. But it strikes us in the Book of Joshua by its constant recurrence in connection with *local monuments and memorials.* It can scarcely be appealed to as an argument for the date of the book or as a token of the hand of an editor. " These many days unto this day " is used of things lying wholly within Joshua's experience in chap. xxii. 3. And in St. Matt. xxviii. 15, it is impossible not to feel that the employment of the very same phrase is a proof of the early origin of the gospel. The phrase is one that may be used of things comparatively recent, but gain in force as the years roll on. What a truly wonderful confirmation of the Scripture narrative it is, to be able to turn to an Ordnance Survey of Palestine, and say of names and boundaries described in the Book of Joshua, " *There they are unto this day !*"

THE TIME OCCUPIED BY THE NARRATIVE IN JOSHUA is not long. The language of Caleb after the conquest of Canaan, at the commencement of the division of the territory (chap. xiv. 10), shows that the conquest was completed in five-and-forty years from the sending of the twelve spies from Kadesh-barnea. Deducting thirty-eight years for the remainder of the Exodus, we have seven years for the great campaigns of Joshua, not an insufficient period when we remember what is elsewhere associated with the phrase " seven years' war." Joshua died at the age of 110, and if he was of the same age with Caleb, this would leave five-and-twenty years for the remainder of the book.

AMONG RECENT COMMENTARIES ON JOSHUA there are three which are very complete in different ways. Bishop Wordsworth's is most full and interesting upon the *spiritual teaching* of the book. Canon Espin, in the *Speaker's Commentary,* has dealt very fully with its *historical bearings.* And Dr. Maclear, in the *Cambridge Bible for Schools,* although his materials are collected from very various sources, and those not always equally reliable, is nearly perfect in his attention to *geographical detail.*

On Joshua as a Type of Christ.—That Joshua is set before us in the Old Testament as a type of Christ is unquestionable. But, since all sound typical interpretation must rest upon strict historical analogy, it becomes necessary to define precisely those relations of Joshua to God's people, and to the work of their salvation, which will bear comparison with the work of Him for whom the name of Joshua was designed.

Joshua then may be regarded as a type of Christ—

(1) In relation to Moses.
(2) In relation to the written Word of God.
(3) In relation to Israel, and in the details of the work that he did for Israel.
(4) In his own personal character.

(1) IN RELATION TO MOSES.—Moses brought Israel out of Egypt: Joshua was ordered to bring them into the promised land. On the whole, it may be said that the Mosaic legislation was designed to bring Israel out from among the nations, and separate them from all mankind. But it was the work of our Lord to bring them into a position above all nations in their relation to God. They have hitherto refused this position, turning their backs upon the true Joshua, as they did upon Moses when he first offered them deliverance. They must, however, be set above all nations when Christ comes again. But Joshua's principal relation to Moses is—

(2) HIS RELATION TO THE WRITTEN WORD OF GOD.—The first mention of Joshua is in Exod. xvii. In that chapter, both he and the Book of the Law are brought before us abruptly and without any introduction for the first time. " Moses said unto *Joshua,* choose us out men, and go out, fight with Amalek." " The Lord said unto Moses, Write this for a memorial *in the book,* and rehearse it in the ears of Joshua: for I will utterly put out the remembrance of Amalek from under heaven." Thus the book is made for Joshua, and Joshua is appointed to be the servant of the book. It is evident that the relation between the two is the principal thing to be noted in that passage, *not* the fulfilment of the sentence on Amalek. In fact, Joshua did not execute that sentence, although it was written for his sake.

It is clear that Moses knew he would be the conqueror of Canaan from the first, because it was when he sent him from Kadesh-barnea to search the land that he gave him the name of Jehoshua (Jehovah Saviour, instead of Oshea or Hoshea, which was his earlier name). For this mission of Joshua and the other spies was intended as a first step to the conquest of the country. And it is in this conquest, in obedience to the law of Moses, that Joshua is a type of the Lord Jesus.

But what is the counterpart of the conquest of Canaan in the work of our Lord? And what is JOSHUA'S WORK—

(3) IN RELATION TO ISRAEL?—The Epistle to the Hebrews suggests that it is the introduction of the people of God into *the rest* which God gives them. Now the Jews as a nation have not yet entered into the rest offered by Christ. For them, therefore, the work of Joshua is unfulfilled by Him. The accomplishment of the type in that sense is future. Joshua went into Canaan by himself forty years before he brought in Israel. And the Jewish nation has hitherto refused to follow the true Joshua into the rest of God. But the Israel of God has followed Him, and thus in His relation to the Church of the redeemed our Lord has fulfilled the things foreshadowed in Joshua, though not in relation to the nation of the Jews.

JOSHUA.

But *what portion of the work of* Christ for us answers to the conquest of Canaan by Joshua?

Two different views of this are possible, and in fact necessary, if we look at the story in its true historical aspect. Joshua stands at the end of one dispensation and the beginning of another. In relation to the previous history of Israel, the work of Joshua is an end. In relation to their later history, it is only a beginning. It is an end of the pilgrim life which they led in Canaan and Egypt and in the wilderness, having no fixed possession, but travelling from place to place, and halting wherever they were bidden. It is the beginning of their life as a nation, occupying a territory of their own, and maintaining in that territory the laws of Jehovah their God.

Now if we regard the *Christian life* as a *pilgrimage*, the counterpart of Israel's sojourn in Canaan, Egypt, and the wilderness, it is evident that the entrance into Canaan is the end of this life, and a passage to a better world. In this view, the comparison between the crossing of Jordan and death is sufficiently familiar.

But inasmuch as Christ gives His people rest when they begin to live in Him, and calls them to enter on a good fight of faith; and since the Christian life may be compared to the life of Israel as a nation in the promised land, we obtain a second view of the work of Joshua in relation to Christ. It answers to the establishment of the believer in Christ in a position where he may fight and conquer, expelling the enemies of Christ from his own heart, or subduing them in it.

In this view, the work of Joshua is introductory and preliminary to a period of warfare, which will end in complete victory, and in the establishment of David's throne.

(4) IN JOSHUA'S OWN PERSONAL CHARACTER.—The chief points seem to be zealous and faithful discharge of duty, and abnegation of self. The absence of personal ambition and vanity is clear. Deeds and not words make up the greater part of his history. Among the twelve spies Caleb is more prominent than Joshua. When Joshua is jealous it is for Moses' honour, not for his own. He is again and again urged to "be strong and of good courage," as though naturally inclined to shrink from responsibility. He takes his own inheritance last, after all the tribes. His family receives no high position. *None of his descendants are even named*, but "*as for me and my house, we will serve the Lord.*" He appears to have grown old comparatively early, a fact which very possibly indicates the laborious character of his life. Yet he must have been a man of strong personal influence. *Israel served the Lord all his days.*

Analysis of the Book.—The contents of the Book of Joshua can be arranged thus:—

(1) THE PASSAGE OF JORDAN (chaps. i. 1 to v. 12), including—

Joshua's commission to lead Israel over Jordan, in obedience to the law (chap. i. 1—9).
Joshua's first orders to the people (chap. i. 10—18).
The spies sent to Jericho, and received by Rahab (chap. ii.).
Passage of Jordan (chaps. iii. 1 to iv. 19).
Encampment in Gilgal; Circumcision and Passover; Manna ceases (chaps. iv. 20 to v. 12).

(2) THE CONQUEST OF CANAAN (chap. v. 13 to the end of chap. xii.).

Appearance of the Captain of the Lord's Host, with the drawn sword. The order to attack Jericho (chaps. v. 13 to vi. 5).
Jericho taken (chap. vi. 6—27).
Achan's trespass discovered in the failure to take Ai (chap. vii.).
Ai taken (chap. viii. 1—29).
The law set up in the heart of the country (chap. viii. 30—35).
The Gibeonites come in and make peace (chap. ix.).
Gibeon attacked by the southern confederacy, which is crushed by Joshua. The south of Palestine conquered (chap. x.).
Jabin king of Hazor and the northern confederacy conquered (chap. xi.).
Summary of the conquest (chap. xii.).

(3) THE DIVISION OF THE TERRITORY (chaps. xiii. to xxii. inclusive).

Boundaries of the territory to be divided (chap. xiii. 1—14).

(*a*) On the east of Jordan. Territory of *Reuben* (xiii. 15—23), *Gad* (24—28), half *Manasseh* (29—31).
(*b*) On the west of Jordan (chap. xiv. 1—5). *Judah* (chap. xiv. 6 to end of chap. xv.), *Joseph* (xvi. 1—4), including *Ephraim* (xvi. 5—10), and *Manasseh* (xvii. 1—12).

The other seven tribes (chap. xviii. 1—10), including *Benjamin* (xviii. 11—28), *Simeon* (xix. 1—9), *Zebulun* (xix. 10—16), *Issachar* (xix. 17—23), *Asher* (xix. 24—31), *Naphtali* (xix. 32—39), *Dan* (xix. 40—48), *Joshua's inheritance* (xix. 49, 50).

The cities of refuge (chap. xx.) and the other Levitical cities (chap. xxi.).
The two and a half tribes dismissed to their inheritance, and their altar *Ed* (chap. xxii.).

(4) JOSHUA'S LAST CHARGE AND DEATH (chaps. xxiii., xxiv.).

(*a*) His charge to the rulers at Shechem (chap. xxiii.).
(*b*) His charge to the people (chap. xxiv. 1—25). His signature (verse 26). Death (verses 29, 30). Conclusion. Burial of Joseph's bones. Death of Eleazar (verses 31—33).

It is observable that in the record of the conquest we have the capture of two cities described in detail, viz., *Jericho* and *Ai*—one in the territory of Benjamin, and one in mount Ephraim. We have also two great battles —one in the south, another in the north—each opening a campaign. It seems likely that no third campaign was needed, from the absence of any strongholds in the centre of the country, where the cities are far fewer than they are in the south and north, and along the sea-side.

It seems clear, upon the whole, that Israel entered the land of Canaan at the weakest part, where there was least possibility of resistance; that they divided their adversaries, and struck fatal blows alternately on either hand; the resistance of the Canaanites being in great measure paralysed by the unusual mode of attack.

THE BOOK OF JOSHUA

CHAPTER I.—⁽¹⁾ Now after the death of Moses the servant of the LORD it came to pass, that the LORD spake unto Joshua the son of Nun, Moses' *a* minister, saying, ⁽²⁾ Moses my servant is dead; now therefore arise, go over this Jordan, thou, and all this people, unto the land which I do give to them, *even* to the children of Israel. ⁽³⁾ *b* Every place that the sole of your foot shall tread upon, that have I given unto you, as I said unto Moses. ⁽⁴⁾ From the wilderness and this Lebanon even unto the great river, the river Euphrates, all the land of the Hittites, and unto the great sea toward the going down of the sun, shall be your coast. ⁽⁵⁾ There shall not any man be able to stand before thee all the days of thy life: as I was with Moses, *so* I will be with thee: *c* I will not fail thee, nor forsake thee. ⁽⁶⁾ *d* Be strong and of a good courage: for ¹ unto this people shalt thou divide for an inheritance the land, which I sware unto their fathers to give them. ⁽⁷⁾ Only be thou strong and very courageous, that thou mayest observe to do according to all the law,

B.C. 1451.

a Deut. 1. 38.

b Deut. 11. 24; ch. 14. 9.

c Heb. 13. 5.

d Deut. 31. 23.

¹ Or, *thou shalt cause this people to inherit the land*, &c.

JOSHUA'S COMMISSION (chap. i. 1—9).

⁽¹⁾ **After the death of Moses . . . the Lord spake unto Joshua . . . Moses' minister.**—Joshua's commission was the first of its kind, but not the last. No man before Joshua had received orders to regulate his conduct by the words of a written book. Abraham and his household had kept God's laws. Moses had acted by Divine commission. But Abraham and Moses received their orders from the mouth of Jehovah. Joshua and all his successors must fulfil the orders of "this book of the law." Thus Joshua was Moses' *minister* in more than one sense. He was Moses' confidential agent and personal attendant while he lived, and afterwards the executor of that which Moses had written. But the position of Joshua, though at first unique and without precedent, was the position designed for all his successors, more especially for that great Personage whose name Joshua was the first to bear. Joshua and the Book of the Law come before us together, without introduction, in the same passage of the law (Exod. xvii. 9), "Moses said *unto Joshua*, Choose us out men, and go out, fight with Amalek;" and in verse 14, "Write this for a memorial *in a book*, and rehearse it in the ears of Joshua." The book was prepared for Joshua; Joshua came to fulfil the words of the book. Compare Psalm xl. 7, "Lo, I come: in the volume of the book it is written of me, I delight to do thy will, O my God." "Jesus Christ was a minister of the circumcision for the truth of God, to confirm the promises made unto the fathers" (Rom. xv. 8; see also Matt. v. 17).

For the use of the word "minister" (Heb., *m'shârêth*) compare 2 Kings iv. 43, vi. 15; 2 Chron. ix. 4; Ezra viii. 17; Ps. ciii. 21, civ. 4; Prov. xxix. 12; Ezek. xliv. 11. From these references it will be seen that the word may signify a personal attendant, a minister of state, or a minister of religion.

⁽³⁾ **Every place that the sole of your foot shall tread upon, that have I given unto you.**—The conquest of Canaan was the special duty assigned to Joshua by the word of Moses. (Hence the order for the extermination of Amalek was written for Joshua [Exod. xvii. 14] as the representative conqueror, though he did not actually carry it out.) But the conquest of Canaan, as effected by Joshua, must be carefully defined. It was a limited conquest. He took a certain number of strongholds throughout the country, and utterly crushed the armies that were opposed to him in the field. He established the people of Israel in the position that he had won. (See chap. xii. 9—24 for an outline of the position.) He then divided to the tribes of Israel the whole territory, *conquered and unconquered alike* (see chap. xiii. 1—7). The Philistines and Sidonians (or Phœnicians) are examples of two great nations not conquered by Joshua, but assigned to Israel for an inheritance. Thus it appears that what Israel would conquer, *the sole of his foot must tread*. The conquest which Joshua began for the people, must be carried out in detail by the several tribes themselves. For a further discussion of the relation of Joshua's conquest to the whole history of Israel, see Note on chap. xiii. 2.

⁽⁴⁾ **All the land of the Hittites.**—The name Hittites may be used here to represent all the Canaanites; but it seems better to understand the land of the Hittites of the northern districts in which Hamath and Carchemish were situated—between Palestine proper and the Euphrates; but compare Note on Judges i. 26.

⁽⁵⁾ **I will not fail thee, nor forsake thee.**—Compare Gen. xxviii. 15. And consider Heb. xiii. 5 as a combination of the two Old Testament passages.

^(6, 7) **Be strong and of a good courage . . . that thou mayest observe to do according to all the law.**—This command to "be strong," repeated again and again to Joshua, may perhaps be taken as reflecting light upon his natural character, which might not have led him to desire so prominent a position. But it may also be observed that courage was especially needed to carry out the conquest of Canaan *in the way that was ordered by the law.* For

which Moses my servant commanded thee: *ᵃturn not from it *to* the right hand or *to* the left, that thou mayest ¹prosper whithersoever thou goest. ⁽⁸⁾ This book of the law shall not depart out of thy mouth; but thou shalt meditate therein day and night, that thou mayest observe to do according to all that is written therein: for then thou shalt make thy way prosperous, and then thou shalt ²have good success. ⁽⁹⁾ Have not I commanded thee? Be strong and of a good courage; be not afraid, neither be thou dismayed: for the Lᴏʀᴅ thy God *is* with thee whithersoever thou goest.

⁽¹⁰⁾ Then Joshua commanded the officers of the people, saying, ⁽¹¹⁾ Pass through the host, and command the people, saying, Prepare you victuals; for within three days ye shall pass over this Jordan, to go in to possess the land, which the Lᴏʀᴅ your God giveth you to possess it.

⁽¹²⁾ And to the Reubenites, and to the Gadites, and to half the tribe of Manasseh, spake Joshua, saying, ⁽¹³⁾ Remember ᵇ the word which Moses the servant of the Lᴏʀᴅ commanded you, saying, The Lᴏʀᴅ your God hath given you rest, and hath given you this land. ⁽¹⁴⁾ Your wives, your little ones, and your cattle, shall remain in the land which Moses gave you on this side Jordan; but ye shall pass before your brethren ³armed, all the mighty men of valour, and help them; ⁽¹⁵⁾ until the Lᴏʀᴅ have given your brethren rest, as *he hath given* you, and they also have possessed the land which the Lᴏʀᴅ your God giveth them: then ye shall return unto the land of your possession, and enjoy it, which Moses

---

ᵃ Deut. 5. 32. & 28. 14
¹ Or, *do wisely*.
² Or, *do wisely*.
ᵇ Num. 32. 20.
³ Heb., *marshalled by five*.

---

a discussion of this question and its difficulties, see chap. xiii.

⁽⁸⁾ **Thou shalt meditate therein day and night . . . then thou shalt make thy way prosperous.**—These words are taken up again in Ps. i. 2, 3, and a blessing is pronounced on *every* man who takes Joshua's position in relation to the written law of God (see Note, verse 1). Thus the true significance of Joshua's position appears, and also the difference between Moses and all who followed him. Moses was the prophet "whom the Lord knew face to face." Joshua and *all* his successors, from the least to the greatest, find their blessing and their portion in the careful study and fulfilment of the written word of God. It is also worthy of notice that God's Word, from its very first appearance as a collective book (viz., the law), occupies the same position. It is supreme. It is set above Joshua. It is never superseded. And its authority is independent of its quantity. "The law of Moses," "Moses and the prophets," "The law, the prophets, and the Psalms," are descriptions of the Bible differing in the quantity of the matter, but not differing in the authority they exercise or in their relation to the living church. "Blessed is he that readeth and they that hear the words of the prophecy of this book, and keep those things that are written therein," are words that apply to Holy Scripture equally, in every stage, from the completion of the law of Moses to the completion of the entire book.

Joshua's First Orders (chap. i. 10—15).

⁽¹⁰⁾ **Then Joshua commanded the officers of the people.**—Joshua's first orders to the people were to prepare for the passage of Jordan within three days. We may compare this event, in its relation to Joshua, with the giving of the law from Sinai to Moses. Both were preceded by a three days' notice and a sanctification of the people. Both were means employed by God to establish the leaders whom He had chosen in the position which He designed for them. (Comp. Exod. xix. 9, 11 with Josh. i. 11, iii. 7, iv. 14.)

⁽¹¹⁾ **Prepare you victuals.**—The question may be asked, what preparation is intended, since they had the manna, which did not cease until several days after they passed the Jordan. But it does not seem possible to assign any other meaning to the word except that of provision for a journey or for a warlike expedition. Perhaps the order was intended to prepare the Israelites for the transition from the manna to other food. It may be also that the manna which supported them in their pilgrimage through the wilderness was not so fit to sustain them in the warfare which they were about to begin. For the phrase itself, compare Exod. xii. 39: "They were thrust out of Egypt, and could not tarry, neither *had they prepared for themselves any victual.*" When there was a difficulty in obtaining other provision, God gave His people manna. Now, when they could easily provide food for themselves, He would not support them in idleness; and perhaps this is the common-sense view of the order given in the text. If called to any expedition which would take them far from the camp, the manna would not be within reach of all.

⁽¹²⁾ **To the Reubenites, and to the Gadites, and to half the tribe of Manasseh, spake Joshua.**—The reference to Num. xxxii. explains this order. We have only to observe that these two tribes and a half were not forbidden to leave a sufficient number of their fighting men to protect their homes and families. (See on chap. iv. 12.)

⁽¹³⁾ **Hath given you rest.**—Observe this phrase, as applied to the settlement of Israel in the land of promise, on either side of Jordan. Those who condemn the two and a half tribes (or the, persons whom they suppose to be spiritually represented by them) for not going far enough, should notice that on both sides of Jordan equally there was the "rest of God." But this "rest" is only the first stage of several in Israel's history. We find it again in the reign of David (2 Sam. vii. 1), Solomon (1 Chron. xxii. 9), Esther (chap. ix. 16, 17, 18, 22), and we must not forget the comment in Heb. iv., obtained from Ps. xcv.: "For if Joshua had given them rest, then would He not afterward have spoken of another day." "These all received not the promise." "*There remaineth* therefore *a rest* to the people of God." The last rest is Sabbatical;

the LORD's servant gave you on this side Jordan toward the sunrising. ⁽¹⁶⁾ And they answered Joshua, saying, All that thou commandest us we will do, and whithersoever thou sendest us, we will go. ⁽¹⁷⁾ According as we hearkened unto Moses in all things, so will we hearken unto thee: only the LORD thy God be with thee, as he was with Moses. ⁽¹⁸⁾ Whosoever *he be* that doth rebel against thy commandment, and will not hearken unto thy words in all that thou commandest him, he shall be put to death: only be strong and of a good courage.

CHAPTER II.—⁽¹⁾ And Joshua the son of Nun sent out of Shittim two men to spy secretly, saying, Go view the land, even Jericho. And they went, and ᵃcame into an harlot's house, named Rahab, and ¹lodged there.

⁽²⁾ And it was told the king of Jericho, saying, Behold, there came men in hither to night of the children of Israel to search out the country. ⁽³⁾ And the king of Jericho sent unto Rahab, saying Bring forth the men that are come to thee, which are entered into thine house: for they be come to search out all the country.

⁽⁴⁾ And the woman took the two men, and hid them, and said thus, There came men unto me, but I wist not whence they *were*: ⁽⁵⁾ and it came to pass *about the time* of shutting of the gate, when it was dark, that the men went out: whither the men went I wot not: pursue after them quickly; for ye shall overtake them. ⁽⁶⁾ But she had brought them up to the roof of the house, and hid them with the stalks of flax, which she had laid in order upon the roof. ⁽⁷⁾ And the men pursued after them the way to Jordan unto the fords: and as soon as they which pursued after them were gone out, they shut the gate.

⁽⁸⁾ And before they were laid down, she came up unto them upon the roof; ⁽⁹⁾ and she said unto the men, I know

a Heb. 11. 31; Jam. 2. 25.

¹ Heb., *lay*.

---

the rests that precede it are halting-places on the way.

⁽¹⁶⁾ They answered Joshua, saying, All that thou commandest us we will do.—This promise of obedience may be taken as the reply of the whole people to Joshua's orders, not that of the two and a half tribes alone. It is remarkable that they repeat to him the words of Jehovah, as most appropriate in their judgment: "Be strong and of a good courage" (verse 18).

II.

THE SPIES AND RAHAB.

⁽¹⁾ **Joshua . . . sent out of Shittim.**—That is, he sent the spies before the people left the place where they had been encamped for some months (Num. xxii. 1 and xxxiii. 49). Shittim was the last stage of the Exodus under Moses. Probably the sending of these two spies was simultaneous with the issue of the general orders to Israel to prepare for the passage of Jordan within three days. The three days of chaps. i. 11 and ii. 22 appear to be the same period of time.

Two men to spy.—The sending of these spies should be compared, as to the general effect and character of the measure, with other similar events. There are three instances of sending spies in reference to Canaan—viz., (1) the sending of the twelve by Moses from Kadesh-barnea; (2) the instance before us; (3) the sending of men to view Ai. The present instance is the only one in which the measure had a good effect. In the case of the twelve, Moses describes the action as a manifestation of unbelief. The spies took upon them to discover the right path for Israel to take, a thing which was God's prerogative, not theirs (Deut. i. 22, 32, 33). The men who viewed Ai (chap. vii. 2, 3) came back and presumed to instruct Joshua how to proceed against it, with disastrous results. In this instance the two men brought back a report of the state of things in Jericho (exactly what they were ordered to do), which encouraged all Israel to proceed. Compare the effect of Gideon and Phurah's visit to the camp of Midian (Judges vii. 11), "Thou shalt hear what they say, and afterwards shall thine hands be strengthened."

Into an harlot's house, named Rahab.—The attempts to show that Rahab was *not* "an harlot" are not justified by the word used in Hebrew, or in the Greek of the LXX., or in the Epistle to the Hebrews (chap. xi. 31), or in that of St. James (chap. ii. 25). But there is no harm in supposing that she was also an innkeeper, which the Targum calls her in every place; indeed, it is very probable that the spies would resort to a place of public entertainment, as most suitable for ascertaining the state of the public mind. How far they were disguised, how they came to be discovered, whether the king of Jericho knew of the impending march of Israel from Shittim, are questions of detail which the narrative leaves unanswered, and which the imagination may discuss at pleasure. The point of the story is not in these.

⁽⁴⁾ **There came men unto me, but I wist not whence they were.**—A falsehood which evidently left no stain on Rahab's conscience, although all falsehood is sin. The same may be said of Jael's slaying Sisera. The Divine standard of sin and holiness never varies; but the standard of man's conscience, even when faith is a dominant principle in the character, may vary to a very considerable degree. In Jesus Christ "all that believe are justified from all things;" but "by the deeds of the law" no one. Here, as elsewhere, the application of the law only brings the discovery of sin.

⁽⁶⁾ **The stalks of flax.**—It is remarked that flax and barley are both early crops (Exod. ix. 31), and that the first month (see chap. iv. 19) was the time of barley-harvest. (Comp. 2 Sam. xxi. 9.)

⁽⁹⁻¹¹⁾ She said unto the men, I know that the Lord hath given you the land . . . .—

JOSHUA, II.

that the LORD hath given you the land, and that your terror is fallen upon us, and that all the inhabitants of the land [1] faint because of you. (10) For we have heard how the LORD [a] dried up the water of the Red sea for you, when ye came out of Egypt; and what ye did unto the two kings of the Amorites, that *were* on the other side Jordan, [b] Sihon and Og, whom ye utterly destroyed. (11) And as soon as we had heard *these things*, our hearts did melt, neither [2] did there remain any more courage in any man, because of you: for the LORD your God, he *is* God in heaven above, and in earth beneath. (12) Now therefore, I pray you, swear unto me by the LORD, since I have shewed you kindness, that ye will also shew kindness unto my father's house, and give me a true token: (13) and *that* ye will save alive my father, and my mother, and my brethren, and my sisters, and all that they have, and deliver our lives from death.

(14) And the men answered her, Our life [3] for your's, if ye utter not this our business. And it shall be, when the LORD hath given us the land, that we will deal kindly and truly with thee. (15) Then she let them down by a cord through the window: for her house *was* upon the town wall, and she dwelt upon the wall. (16) And she said unto them, Get you to the mountain, lest the pursuers meet you; and hide yourselves there three days, until the pursuers be returned: and afterward may ye go your way.

(17) And the men said unto her, We *will be* blameless of this thine oath which thou hast made us swear. (18) Behold, *when* we come into the land, thou shalt bind this line of scarlet thread in the window which thou didst let us down by: and thou shalt [4] bring thy father, and thy mother, and thy brethren, and all thy father's household, home unto thee. (19) And it shall be, *that* whosoever shall go out of the doors of thy house into the street, his blood *shall be* upon his head, and we *will be* guiltless: and whosoever shall be with thee in the house, his blood *shall be* on our head, if *any* hand be upon him. (20) And if thou utter this our business, then we will be quit of thine oath which thou hast made us

[1] Heb., *melt*.
[a] Ex. 14. 21; ch. 4. 23.
[b] Num. 21. 24.
[2] Heb., *rose up*
[3] Heb., *instead of you to die.*
[4] Heb., *gather.*

The words of this confession are memorable in every way. Note the fulfilment of the prophetic song of Moses, which is partly repeated here (Exod. xv. 15, 16, with Josh. ii. 9—11), "All the inhabitants of Canaan shall melt away; fear and dread shall fall upon them." But especially observe the expression of Rahab's own belief, "Jehovah, your God, He is God in heaven above and in earth beneath." Did the faith of the men of Israel go much further than this? Did it always go so far? (Comp. Josh. xxiv. 14; 1 Kings xviii. 21; Jonah i. 9, 10). The prophets themselves could not assert much more. The greatest of them were satisfied if they could bring the people of Israel to acknowledge this. Rahab's confession is also one of a series. The Egyptians, Philistines, Syrians, Assyrians, Babylonians, Persians, were all in turn brought to the same acknowledgment by their contact with Israel. The reason is stated in Josh. iv. 24, "That all the people of the earth may know the hand of Jehovah, that it is mighty."

(13) **Save alive my father, and my mother, and my brethren, and my sisters.**—Whatever Rahab may have been herself, her acknowledgment of all her family is observable. She was in no way separated or degraded from their society. When we remember what Moses describes the Canaanites to have been (in certain passages of the Pentateuch, as Lev. xviii. 24—28; xx. 22, 23) and compare this chapter, we may reasonably conclude Rahab to have been morally not inferior to her countrymen as they were then, but rather their superior. We are reminded that the "publicans and harlots" were not the worst members of the "evil and adulterous generation" to whom the Word of God came. They believed John the Baptist, and were among the most constant hearers of the true Joshua (Matt. xxi. 32; Luke xv. 1).

(15) **Her house was upon the town wall**—Happily for the two spies. Perhaps, indeed, they selected it for this reason, as it enabled them to leave the town without passing the gate.

(16) **Get you to the mountain.**—The mountains between Jerusalem and Jericho have often been a refuge for worse characters than Joshua's two spies (Luke x. 30).

(18) **The window which thou didst let us down by.**—It seems almost needless to observe that the scarlet line and the cord by which the men were lowered are not the same thing, but described by different words in the original. It would have been preposterous to require Rahab to display in her window the means by which the spies had escaped. It would at once have declared the tale to all beholders—the very thing Rahab was pledged not to do. The "line of scarlet thread" and the "stalks of flax" on the roof were probably parts of the same business, and thus there would be nothing unusual in what was exhibited at the window, although it would be a sufficient token to those who were in the secret, to enable them to identify the house.

(19) **Whosoever shall go out of the doors of thy house into the street, his blood shall be upon his head.**—Comp. Exod. xii. 22 (the account of the Passover), "Ye shall . . . strike the lintel and the two side-posts with the blood that is in the bason: and *none of you shall go out at the door of his house until the morning*; for the Lord will pass through to smite the Egyptians." What the blood was to the houses of

to swear. (21) And she said, According unto your words, so *be* it. And she sent them away, and they departed: and she bound the scarlet line in the window.

(22) And they went, and came unto the mountain, and abode there three days, until the pursuers were returned: and the pursuers sought *them* throughout all the way, but found *them* not. (23) So the two men returned, and descended from the mountain, and passed over, and came to Joshua the son of Nun, and told him all *things* that befell them: (24) and they said unto Joshua, Truly the LORD hath delivered into our hands all the land; for even all the inhabitants of the country do ¹faint because of us.

CHAPTER III.—(1) And Joshua rose early in the morning; and they removed from Shittim, and came to Jordan, he and all the children of Israel, and lodged there before they passed over.

(2) And it came to pass after three days, that the officers went through the host; (3) and they commanded the people, saying, When ye see the ark of the covenant of the LORD your God, and the priests the Levites bearing it, then ye shall remove from your place, and go after it. (4) Yet there shall be a space between you and it, about two thousand cubits by measure: come not near unto it, that ye may know the way by which ye must go: for ye have not passed *this* way ²heretofore.

(5) And Joshua said unto the people, ᵃSanctify yourselves: for to morrow the LORD will do wonders among you.

(6) And Joshua spake unto the priests, saying, Take up the ark of the covenant,

1 Heb., *melt.*

2 Heb., *since yesterday and the third day.*

a Lev. 20. 7; Num. 11. 18; ch. 7. 13; 1 Sam. 16. 5.

Israel in Egypt, that the scarlet line in the window was to the house of Rahab. Both alike prefigured "the precious blood of Christ."

(22) **Three days**—*i.e.*, probably until the completion of three days from the commencement of their mission, according to the usual inclusive reckoning of the Old Testament.

(24) **The Lord hath delivered.**—Observe the entirely satisfactory effect of this mission, and compare what was said on verse 1.

III.

THE PASSAGE OF JORDAN (chaps. iii. 1—iv. 18, inclusive).

Chap. iii. 1—6, preliminaries; iii. 7—iv. 14, the passage of the people and *Joshua*; iv. 15—18, the passage of the ark itself.

(1) **They removed from Shittim.**—See Note on chap. ii. 1. Shittim may be called the last stage of the Exodus of Israel, "their journeyings according to their goings out" (Num. xxxiii. 2). The march from Shittim to Jordan is their first march under Joshua—the first stage of their Eisodus or coming in.

(2) **After three days.**—See chap. i. 2.

(2—6) PRELIMINARY ORDERS.—The priests are to bear the ark. This was usually the duty of the Levites of the family of Kohath; but both at the passage of Jordan and the taking of Jericho, the priests were employed as bearers. The people must be sanctified, as they were in preparation for the giving of the law at Sinai (in Exod. xix.). And the ark itself takes, in some sense, a fresh position. The space of 2,000 cubits was left between the head of the column of Israelites and the ark, in order that they might all see it. Up to this time, during the whole of the Exodus, they had been led by the pillar of cloud and fire. The ark had led the van ever since they left Sinai (Num. x. 33, 34). But as the cloud had moved *above* the ark, where all the people could see it, the head of the column might follow the ark as closely as possible, without any inconvenience. Now the cloud was no longer with them. It was a visible token of God's presence especially granted to Moses, and with him it disappeared. The ark was now to be the only leader, and therefore it must be placed in a somewhat more conspicuous position. This difference of arrangement appears to be indicated by the words in verse 4, "Ye have not passed this way heretofore." The words may mean, "You are marching over untrodden ground;" but if so, they are not more applicable to this march than to many previous marches. They may also mean, "You have not marched in this manner heretofore," and this interpretation seems more to the purpose.

It may be of use to consider here, what was the actual significance of the position assigned to the ark in Joshua. What was the ark? It was a chest containing the ten commandments, written with the finger of God on two tables of stone prepared by Moses (Deut. x. 1—5; Exod. xxxiv. 1, 28). But the ark was made for the law, not the law for the ark. The mercy-seat above was the *covering* of the law—the shield between that law and the people. Between the cherubim that formed the mercy-seat, was the throne of Jehovah. But the central thing, the only thing not of human workmanship, that remained in the ark, was "the law written with the finger of God." If we would exactly describe the position before us, we must say that the Israelites marched into Jordan led by the written law of God. The same written law, borne round the walls of Jericho, was the minister of vengeance to the Canaanites, as indeed it became afterwards to Israel when incautiously handled or invoked, as at Eben-ezer (1 Sam. iv.), and as at Beth-shemesh (1 Sam. vi.; comp. 2 Sam. vi.), and also to the Philistines (1 Sam. v.). As soon as the army of Joshua reached the centre of Canaan, this same law was written on great stones in the heart of the country, and became the law of the land. It is consistent with what we have already noted (chap. i. 1) as to the difference between Moses and Joshua, that under Moses the

and pass over before the people. And they took up the ark of the covenant, and went before the people.

⁽⁷⁾ And the LORD said unto Joshua, This day will I begin to magnify thee in the sight of all Israel, that they may know that, *as I was with Moses, so I will be with thee. ⁽⁸⁾ And thou shalt command the priests that bear the ark of the covenant, saying, When ye are come to the brink of the water of Jordan, ye shall stand still in Jordan.

⁽⁹⁾ And Joshua said unto the children of Israel, Come hither, and hear the words of the LORD your God. ⁽¹⁰⁾ And Joshua said, Hereby ye shall know that the living God *is* among you, and *that* he will without fail drive out from before you the Canaanites, and the Hittites, and the Hivites, and the Perizzites, and the Girgashites, and the Amorites, and the Jebusites. ⁽¹¹⁾ Behold, the ark of the covenant of the Lord of all the earth passeth over before you into Jordan. ⁽¹²⁾ Now therefore take you twelve men out of the tribes of Israel, out of every tribe a man. ⁽¹³⁾ And it shall come to pass, as soon as the soles of the feet of the priests that bear the ark of the LORD, the Lord of all the earth, shall rest in the waters of Jordan, *that* the waters of Jordan shall be cut off *from* the waters that come down from above; and they *b* shall stand upon an heap.

⁽¹⁴⁾ And it came to pass, when the people removed from their tents, to pass over Jordan, and the priests bearing the *ark of the covenant before the people; ⁽¹⁵⁾ and as they that bare the ark were come unto Jordan, and the feet of the priests that bare the ark were dipped in the brim of the water, (for *Jordan overfloweth all his banks all the time of harvest,) ⁽¹⁶⁾ that the waters which came down from above stood *and* rose up upon an heap very far from the city Adam, that *is* beside Zaretan: and those that came down toward the sea of the plain, *even* the salt sea, failed, *and* were cut off: and the people passed over right against Jericho. ⁽¹⁷⁾ And the priests that bare the ark of the covenant of the LORD

---

a ch. 1. 5.

b Ps. 114. 2.

c Acts 7. 45.

d 1 Chron. 12. 15; Ecclus. 24. 26.

---

people should follow the cloudy pillar, and under Joshua, *the written law of God.* But it is a strange picture, and one that may well call up our reverent wonder, that the Israelites should pass over Jordan and assail the Canaanites, *with the ten commandments carried before them, and as it were leading the way.* Was not this the direct object of the conquest of Canaan, that God's law should not only have a people to obey it, but a country in which its working might be exhibited to the nations, as the law of the land?

⁽⁷⁾ **The Lord said unto Joshua, This day will I begin to magnify thee . . .**—Compare chap. iv. 14, "on that day the Lord magnified Joshua." These words mark the beginning and end of the section. The details that follow in chap. iv. 15, &c., seem to be added by way of appendix. The passage of Jordan, being the principal event, is exhibited by itself; and other particulars of attendant circumstances are given separately. A somewhat similar plan appears to be adopted in chap. x., but the arrangement of both narratives is at first sight somewhat complex, and not quite clear.

It is here stated that the passage of Jordan was to be to Joshua what the giving of the law at Sinai was to Moses, "that the people may hear when I speak with thee, and believe thee for ever" (Exod. xix. 9). But the power which establishes Joshua is the work of the *written* instead of the *spoken* word.

⁽¹¹⁾ **The ark of the covenant.**—The ten commandments are presented throughout this narrative as a *covenant.* So Exod. xxxiv. 28, "the words of the covenant, the ten commandments." It must be remembered that a promise precedes all the commandments. "I am Jehovah thy God." The "ten words" that follow are the *testimony* to His character who commanded the covenant. (See *Silver Sockets,* p. 28.) The thing signified by the dividing of Jordan does indeed exhibit the law as a covenant in a way that those who followed Joshua can hardly have understood. But history must come before prophecy, if prophecy is to be understood.

⁽¹²⁾ **Take you twelve men.**—These were selected beforehand and kept in readiness, that there might be no delay in the work which they had to do (chap. iv. 3).

⁽¹³⁾ **The soles of the feet of the priests.**—Observe that the priests, the ark-bearers, did not stand in the middle of the *bed* of the river, but at the edge of the flood. They had no need to advance further. As soon as their feet "rested" in the overflow, "Jordan was driven back." The waters descending from the north as it were recoiled and shrank away, and stood up in "one heap."

⁽¹⁶⁾ **Very far from the city Adam, that is beside Zaretan.**—The written text is "*in* Adam," but the Masorites read it "*from* Adam." The reading makes no difference to the literal fact. The two prepositions, *in* and *from,* express the same thought. The heap of water stood up as it were in Adam. From Adam to the place where Israel crossed, the river-bed was dry—the heap was as far away as Adam, but as it was not actually *in* the city, the word *in* was most likely altered to *from.* The more difficult reading, *in,* may very possibly be the best. For Zaretan see 1 Kings iv. 12 and vii. 46. Adam, as the name of a city, does not occur elsewhere. The meaning of the fact has been well pointed out by Bishop Wordsworth on this place. Zaretan was beneath Jezreel, but has not been identified. Adam has been thought to be at the ford Damieh, thirty miles away.

stood firm on dry ground in the midst of Jordan, and all the Israelites passed over on dry ground, until all the people were passed clean over Jordan.

CHAPTER IV.—⁽¹⁾ And it came to pass, when all the people were clean passed *over Jordan, that the LORD spake unto *Joshua, saying, ⁽²⁾ Take you twelve men out of the people, out of every tribe a man, ⁽³⁾ and command ye them, saying, Take you hence out of the midst of Jordan, out of the place where the priests' feet stood firm, twelve stones, and ye shall carry them over with you, and leave them in the lodging place, where ye shall lodge this night. ⁽⁴⁾ Then Joshua called the twelve men, whom he had prepared of the children of Israel, out of every tribe a man: ⁽⁵⁾ and Joshua said unto them, Pass over before the ark of the LORD your God into the midst of Jordan, and take you up every man of you a stone upon his shoulder, according unto the number of the tribes of the children of Israel: ⁽⁶⁾ that this may be a sign among you, *that* when your children ask *their fathers* ¹in time to come, saying, What *mean* ye by these stones? ⁽⁷⁾ then ye shall answer them, That the waters of Jordan were cut off before the ark of the covenant of the LORD; when it passed over Jordan, the waters of Jordan were cut off: and these stones shall be for a memorial unto the children of Israel for ever.

⁽⁸⁾ And the children of Israel did so as Joshua commanded, and took up twelve stones out of the midst of Jordan, as the LORD spake unto Joshua, according to the number of the tribes of the children of Israel, and carried them over with them unto the place where they lodged, and laid them down there. ⁽⁹⁾ And Joshua set up twelve stones in the midst of Jordan, in the place where the feet of the priests which bare the ark of the covenant stood: and they are there unto this day.

⁽¹⁰⁾ For the priests which bare the ark stood in the midst of Jordan, until every thing was finished that the LORD commanded Joshua to speak unto the people, according to all that Moses commanded Joshua: and the people hasted and passed over. ⁽¹¹⁾ And it came to pass, when all the people were clean passed over, that the ark of the LORD passed over, and the priests, in the presence of the people.

a Deut. 27. 2.

b ch. 3. 12.

¹ Heb., *to morrow.*

IV.

⁽³⁾ **Out of the midst of Jordan . . . twelve stones**—⁽⁹⁾ **Twelve stones in the midst of Jordan.**—It would seem that we are to understand two cairns to have been set up, one on either side the river, to mark the place where the Israelites crossed. The western cairn was in Gilgal, the other on the opposite side, at the edge of the overflow, where the priests had stopped. The only difficulty lies in the words above cited, *in the midst of Jordan*. The phrase, like many other Hebrew phrases, is used in a different way from that in which we should use it. The words "in the middle of the Jordan" to an English reader appear to mean half-way between the banks. But if the river were divided, and half of it had recoiled many miles towards the north, and the rest flowed away to the south, any one standing between these two parts of the river might be said to stand *in the midst of Jordan*, the two parts being on either side; and he would be equally in the midst, *as regards them*, whether he were at the edge of the stream or not. It is contrary to common-sense, as well as to the words of the text, to suppose that a cairn was set up in the midst of the river's bed. "They are there unto this day," the writer adds in verse 9. It is perfectly clear from chap. iii. 8 that the priests stood at the brim of the overflow. That spot and no other would be the particular spot which it would be most interesting to mark, the place from which Jordan, in full flood, was driven back.

Further, the words "in the midst" (Hebrew, *b'thôk*) do not necessarily mean more than *within*. In Joshua xix. 1, it is said the inheritance of Simeon was *within* (*b'thôk*) the inheritance of the children of Judah. Yet it was entirely on one edge of it. May not the ark standing in the midst of Jordan represent that suspension of the power of death which is effected by the interposition of our Saviour, and fills the interval between the reign of death "from Adam to Moses," and the "second death" that is to come?

⁽⁷⁾ **The waters of Jordan were cut off before the ark of the covenant.**—Observe that the act is indirectly ascribed to the *ark of the covenant*.

^(8—9) **According to the number of the tribes . . . .**—Every tribe was represented by a stone on either side Jordan. The two cairns represent a complete Israel in the wilderness, and a complete Israel in the promised land. "Thou shalt remember all the way that the Lord thy God led thee." "By the grace of God I am what I am."

⁽¹⁰⁾ **According to all that Moses commanded Joshua.**—It would seem that the passage of Jordan had been made the subject of some directions by Moses, though nothing is written concerning the manner of it in the Pentateuch. It is noticeable that if Israel had gone into the land when Moses brought them to the frontier at Kadesh-barnea, in the second year of the Exodus, they would have had no occasion to pass the Jordan at all. *When* the route was changed we cannot say, unless the compassing of the land of Edom (Num. xxi.), when they left Kadesh the second time, because they were not permitted to cross that territory, marks the decision. If so, the fact suggests some interesting reflections.

JOSHUA, V.

(12) And ᵃthe children of Reuben, and the children of Gad, and half the tribe of Manasseh, passed over armed before the children of Israel, as Moses spake unto them: (13) about forty thousand ¹prepared for war passed over before the LORD unto battle, to the plains of Jericho.

(14) On that day the LORD magnified Joshua in the sight of all Israel; and they feared him, as they feared Moses, all the days of his life.

(15) And the LORD spake unto Joshua, saying, (16) Command the priests that bear the ark of the testimony, that they come up out of Jordan. (17) Joshua therefore commanded the priests, saying, Come ye up out of Jordan. (18) And it came to pass, when the priests that bare the ark of the covenant of the LORD were come up out of the midst of Jordan, *and* the soles of the priests' feet were ²lifted up unto the dry land, that the waters of Jordan returned unto their place, and ³flowed over all his banks, as *they did* before.

(19) And the people came up out of Jordan on the tenth *day* of the first month, and encamped in Gilgal, in the east border of Jericho. (20) And those twelve stones, which they took out of Jordan, did Joshua pitch in Gilgal. (21) And he spake unto the children of Israel, saying, When your children shall ask their fathers ⁴in time to come, saying, What *mean* these stones? (22) then ye shall let your children know, saying, Israel came over this Jordan on dry land. (23) For the LORD your God dried up the waters of Jordan from before you, until ye were passed over, as the LORD your God did to the Red sea, ᵇwhich he dried up from before us, until we were gone over: (24) that all the people of the earth might know the hand of the LORD, that it *is* mighty: that ye might fear the LORD your God ⁵for ever.

CHAPTER V.—(1) And it came to pass, when all the kings of the Amor-

ᵃ Num. 32. 27.

¹ Or, *ready armed*.

² Heb., *plucked up.*

³ Heb., *went.*

⁴ Heb., *to morrow.*

ᵇ Ex. 14. 21.

⁵ Heb., *all days.*

---

(13) **About forty thousand.**—The totals of these three tribes at the last census (Num. xxvi.) were:—Reuben (verse 7), 43,730; Gad (verse 18), 40,500; Manasseh (verse 34), 52,700, or for the exact half, 26,350. Thus the entire force of the two and a half tribes might amount to 110,580. They therefore left more than half their number to protect their families and their dwellings. This does not seem inconsistent with the spirit of their agreement with Moses, or with the interpretation of that agreement by Joshua and their fellow-Israelites. (See Num. xxxii. 16, 17, 24, 26.) The permission to *build* cities implies the right to fortify and defend them.

Reuben, Gad, and Simeon formed the second division on the march in the wilderness (Num. x. 18—20). Why Reuben and Gad discarded Simeon, and associated themselves with part of Manasseh, is not explained. (See *Names on the Gates of Pearl.*—Simeon.)

(14) **All the days of his life.**—This ends the section, as appears by comparison with chap. iii. 7. Observe that Joshua's position, as equal to Moses in the respect of the people, dates from the passage of Jordan, a fact not to be forgotten in considering his Antitype.

(16) **Command the priests . . . that they come up out of Jordan.**—Observe that the removal of the priests and the ark of the covenant from their station in Jordan is made the subject of a distinct section, and treated as a distinct event. It *need* not have been so for the purpose of the mere historical narrative. We might have taken it for granted. But the significance of the event is so marked as to receive a separate notice. We are not suffered to forget by what means Jordan was driven back, and held in check; and the check was not meant to be perpetual. We are reminded that the suspension of the power of death for men has its limits. When the day of grace is over, the waters will "return unto their place and flow over all the banks as before." (Comp. Isa. xxviii. 16—18, 20.)

EVENTS AT GILGAL (chaps. iv. 19—v. 12, inclusive).

(19) **On the tenth day of the first month.**—Of the forty-first year after they left Egypt. Exactly forty years before, on the tenth day of the first month, (Exod. xii. 5), they had been commanded to take them "a lamb for an house," that they might keep the Passover. The forty years of the Exodus were now complete, and on the self-same day they passed over the last barrier, and entered the Promised Land.

(20—v. 9) It would seem that these verses all belong to one section. The use of the first person in chap. v. 1, "until *we* were passed over," is most naturally explained by taking the verse as part of what the Israelites were to say to their children by the command of Joshua. The difficulty has been met in the Hebrew Bible by a Masoretic reading, in which "they" is substituted for "we." But the more difficult reading is to be preferred. There is nothing else in the section that creates any difficulty. The twenty-third verse authorises a comparison between the passage of Jordan and the passage of the Red Sea. As the one is called a "baptising unto Moses," in the New Testament, we may call the other a baptising unto Joshua. (Comp. the "us" in chap. iv. 23, with the "we" of chap. v. 1.) The first person also appears in verse 6, "that he would give *us*." It would appear that, besides explaining the erection of the *stones*, the Israelites were also to explain to their children the meaning of Gilgal, the place where the stones were, and this explanation is not completed until the end of verse 9.

V.

(1) **The Amorites . . . and . . . Canaanites.**—Two principal nations seem to be here mentioned as representatives of the rest.

We.—See Note on verse 6.

Fear of the Canaanites.   JOSHUA, V.   *Circumcision Renewed.*

ites, which *were* on the side of Jordan westward, and all the kings of the Canaanites, which *were* by the sea, heard that the LORD had dried up the waters of Jordan from before the children of Israel, until we were passed over, that their heart melted, neither was there spirit in them any more, because of the children of Israel.

⁽²⁾ At that time the LORD said unto Joshua, Make thee ^{a 1}sharp knives, and circumcise again the children of Israel the second time. ⁽³⁾ And Joshua made him sharp knives, and circumcised the children of Israel at ²the hill of the foreskins. ⁽⁴⁾ And this *is* the cause why Joshua did circumcise: All the people that came out of Egypt, *that were* males, *even* all the men of war, died in the wilderness by the way, after they came out of Egypt. ⁽⁵⁾ Now all the people that came out were circumcised: but all the people *that were* born in the wilderness by the way as they came forth out of Egypt, *them* they had not circumcised. ⁽⁶⁾ For the children of Israel walked forty years in the wilderness, till all the people *that were* men of war, which came out of Egypt, were consumed, because they obeyed not the voice of the LORD: unto whom the LORD sware that ^b he would not shew them the land, which the LORD sware unto their fathers that he would give us, a land that floweth with milk and honey. ⁽⁷⁾ And their children, *whom* he raised up in their stead, them Joshua circumcised: for they were uncircumcised, because they had not circumcised them by the way. ⁽⁸⁾ And it came to pass, ³ when they had done circumcising all the people, that they abode in their places in the camp, till they were whole. ⁽⁹⁾ And the LORD said unto Joshua, This day have I rolled away the reproach of Egypt from off you. Wherefore the name of the place is called ⁴ Gilgal unto this day.

⁽¹⁰⁾ And the children of Israel encamped in Gilgal, and kept the passover on the fourteenth day of the month at even in

a Ex. 4. 25.

¹ Or, *knives of flints.*

² Or, *Gibeah-haaraloth.*

b Num. 14. 23.

³ Heb., *when the people had made an end to be circumcised.*

⁴ That is, *Rolling.*

THE CIRCUMCISION OF ISRAEL BY JOSHUA (verses 2—9).

⁽²⁾ **Make thee sharp knives.**—Authorities are divided between the rendering "sharp knives" and "knives of flint." The first seems best supported, as far as the meaning of the *words* is concerned. The expression is "knives of *tsurim.*" The word *tsûr* does not seem anywhere to be connected with the material of the tool, but rather with the edge of it. *Knives of keen edge* is, therefore, the better translation. At the same time they may have been stone knives in this instance. The idea that they were so is supported by an addition in the LXX. to chap. xxiv. 30: "They put with him (Joshua) into the tomb . . . the knives of stone with which he circumcised the children of Israel . . . and there they are to this day." The ceremony being a kind of special consecration, it is not unlikely to have been performed with special instruments, which were not used before or after. Comp. Ps. lxxxix. 43, "Thou hast turned the *tsûr* (keen edge) of his sword;" 2 Sam. ii. 16, "Helkath Hazzurim"—*i.e.,* the field of keen blades; Exod. iv. 25, "Zipporah took a *tzôr*"; Ezek. iii. 9, "an adamaut harder than *tzôr.*"

⁽⁴⁾ **The cause why Joshua did circumcise.**—As the narrative stands it is not quite obvious why uncircumcision is called "the reproach of Egypt," whereas all the people born in Egypt were circumcised. The uncircumcision attached to those who were born in the wilderness, during the years of wandering. But that period of wandering, between the departure from Kadesh-barnea and the return to Kadesh (thirty-seven and a half years, Num. xv.—xix., inclusive), is a kind of blank in the story of the Exodus. The five chapters which belong to it in the Book of Numbers contain no note of progress as to time or place. The people had "turned back in their hearts to Egypt" (Acts vii. 39; Num. xiv. 4), and were bearing the reproach of their apostasy all those years, "the reproach of Egypt." Suffering under the "breach of promise" of Jehovah (Num. xiv. 34), they appear to have omitted the sign of the covenant, as though they were no longer the people of God. The passage of Jordan was the practical proof of Israel's restoration to Divine favour, and they were brought into covenant with Him once more.

⁽⁶⁾ **Us.**—The first person is used here as in chaps. iv. 23, v. 7. The whole passage from chap. iv. 22 to chap. v. 6 seems intended to be the reply of the fathers to the children.

⁽⁹⁾ **This day have I rolled away . . . .**—Compare Isa. xxv. 8, "He will swallow up death in victory; and the Lord God will wipe away tears from off all faces; and the rebuke (or *reproach*) of *His people shall He take away from off all the earth*: for the Lord hath spoken it"; Col. ii. 11, "In whom (Christ) also ye are circumcised with the circumcision made without hands, in *the putting off the body* of the *sins of the flesh* by the circumcision of Christ, buried with Him in baptism, wherein also ye are risen with Him"; and 1 Cor. xv. 54, "When this corruptible shall have put on incorruption, . . . then . . . Death is swallowed up in victory."

⁽¹⁰⁾ **The passover.**—This is the third Passover in Israel's history. The first two were kept under Moses —(1) in Egypt, when the Lord delivered them; (2) the second at Sinai, when He had "brought them unto Himself." (3) The third is on the other side Jordan under Joshua. Two belong to the Exodus, or going out; one to the Eisodus, or coming in. Compare Luke xxii. 16: "I will not any more eat thereof, until it be fulfilled in the kingdom of God."

Observe the connection between the Passover and circumcision. The law in Exod. xii. 48 is, "no uncircumcised person shall eat thereof." Hence, while they

the plains of Jericho. (11) And they did eat of the old corn of the land on the morrow after the passover, unleavened cakes, and parched *corn* in the selfsame day. (12) And the manna ceased on the morrow after they had eaten of the old corn of the land; neither had the children of Israel manna any more; but they did eat of the fruit of the land of Canaan that year.

(13) And it came to pass, when Joshua was by Jericho, that he lifted up his eyes and looked, and, behold, there stood *a* a man over against him with his sword drawn in his hand: and Joshua went unto him, and said unto him, *Art* thou for us, or for our adversaries? (14) And he said, Nay; but *as* ¹captain of the host of the LORD am I now come. And Joshua fell on his face to the earth, and did worship, and said unto him, What saith my lord unto his servant? (15) And the captain of the LORD's host said unto Joshua, *b* Loose thy shoe from off thy foot; for the place whereon thou standest *is* holy. And Joshua did so.

CHAPTER VI.—(¹ Now Jericho ²was straitly shut up because of the children of Israel: none went out, and none came in. (²) And the LORD said unto Joshua, See, I have given into thine hand Jericho, and the king thereof, *and*

a Ex. 12. 23.

¹ Or, *prince.*

b Ex. 3. 5; Acts 7. 33.

² Heb., *did shut up, and was shut up.*

---

wandered in the wilderness, this uncircumcised generation could not keep the Passover.

(11) **They did eat of the old corn.**—The word occurs nowhere else except in verse 12. It need not have been last year's corn; in fact, it seems to have been the produce of this very harvest. It seems to mean "that which was brought to them," and was "the fruit" or "produce" of the land of Canaan, probably brought to the camp for sale.

(12) **The manna ceased on the morrow after they had eaten of the old corn of the land.**—The date should be noticed. On the fourteenth day was the Passover; on the fifteenth, Israel ate of the produce of the land. From that day the manna fell no more—*i.e.*, on the *sixteenth day* of the first month of the year of their entering the land of Canaan, it was not found. On the *sixteenth day* of the second month of the first year of the Exodus, it first appeared (Exod. xvi. 1, 7, 13, 14). Thirty-nine years and eleven months it fell, except on the Sabbath. It kept Sabbath all through the wilderness, on the seventh day of the week, and it finally ceased, *kept Sabbath* (*vay-yishboth,* Hebrew) *on the very day afterwards marked by our Lord's resurrection, which became the Lord's day.* The coincidence is too remarkable to be overlooked. It is the risen Christ who takes the place of the manna; and in the discourse wherein He calls Himself "the true bread from heaven," He points again and again to resurrection as the end of the life which He gives: "I will raise him up at the last day" (John vi. 39, 40, 44, 54). Then the manna, which is the food of the wilderness, shall keep Sabbath, for "they shall hunger no more." The food of the wilderness is that which Israel ate, *not knowing what it was.* Of the other world it is written, "*then shall I know, even as also I am known.*"

THE CONQUEST OF CANAAN.

(13) At this point commences the second great division of the book. The Passage of Jordan was the great event of the first portion; and for that Joshua received special directions from Jehovah. A vision now appears to him, to inaugurate his second great enterprise, which was to put the inhabitants of Canaan to the sword. The character of this vision should be carefully noted, as it is of the utmost importance to the interpretation of the book.

(13) **There stood a man over against him with his sword drawn in his hand.**—This should be compared with the vision which Moses saw at Horeb (Exod. iii.), when the angel of Jehovah appeared to him in a flame of fire out of the midst of a bush. The equality of the two visions is proved by the use of the same command on both occasions, "Loose thy shoe from off thy foot; for the place whereon thou standest is holy ground" (Exod. iii. 5; Josh. v. 15). But the actual appearances must be contrasted. "The bush burning with fire, but not consumed," presents to us the figure of suffering Israel in the furnace; and "in all their affliction He was afflicted, and the angel of *His presence* saved them." The man with the drawn sword is the sign of victory. Jehovah no longer suffers with and in His people, but He stands forth to lead them with the drawn sword. In regard of this and earlier theophanies, see Excursus on Gen. 16.

Art thou for us, or for our adversaries? (14) **And he said, Nay; but as captain of the host of the Lord am I now come**—*i.e.*, Jehovah will take part in this conflict, *not as an ally or an adversary, but as commander-in-chief.* It is not Israel's quarrel, in which they are to ask the Divine assistance. It is the Lord's own quarrel, and Israel and Joshua are but a division in His host. The wars of Israel in Canaan are always presented by the Old Testament as "the wars of the Lord." It would be well to remember this aspect of the story. The conquest of Canaan is too often treated as an enterprise of the Israelites, carried out with great cruelties, for which they claimed the Divine sanction. The Old Testament presents the matter in an entirely different light. The war is a Divine enterprise, in which human instruments are employed, but so as to be entirely subordinate to the Divine will. Jehovah is not for Israel, nor for Israel's foes. He fights for His own right hand, and Israel is but a fragment of His army. "The sun stood still." "the stars in their courses fought against" His foes. "The treasures of the hail" were opened, which He had "reserved against the time of trouble, against the day of battle and war."

VI.

(¹) **Now Jericho . . .**—This verse should be read parenthetically, and verses 2—5 should be taken as the orders given to Joshua by the captain of the Lord's host.

the mighty men of valour. (3) And ye shall compass the city, all *ye* men of war, *and* go round about the city once. Thus shalt thou do six days. (4) And seven priests shall bear before the ark seven trumpets of rams' horns: and the seventh day ye shall compass the city seven times, and the priests shall blow with the trumpets. (5 And it shall come to pass, that when they make a long *blast* with the ram's horn, *and* when ye hear the sound of the trumpet, all the people shall shout with a great shout; and the wall of the city shall fall down ¹flat, and the people shall ascend up every man straight before him.

(6) And Joshua the son of Nun called the priests, and said unto them, Take up the ark of the covenant, and let seven priests bear seven trumpets of rams' horns before the ark of the LORD. (7) And he said unto the people, Pass on, and compass the city, and let him that is armed pass on before the ark of the LORD.

(8) And it came to pass, when Joshua had spoken unto the people, that the seven priests bearing the seven trumpets of rams' horns passed on before the LORD, and blew with the trumpets: and the ark of the covenant of the LORD followed them. (9) And the armed men went before the priests that blew with the trumpets, and the ²rereward came after the ark, *the priests* going on, and blowing with the trumpets. (10) And Joshua had commanded the people,

¹ Heb., *under it.*

² Heb., *gathering host.*

³ Heb., *make your voice to be heard.*

⁴ Or, *devoted.*

a ch. 2. 4.

saying, Ye shall not shout, nor ³make any noise with your voice, neither shall *any* word proceed out of your mouth, until the day I bid you shout; then shall ye shout. (11) So the ark of the LORD compassed the city, going about *it* once: and they came into the camp, and lodged in the camp.

(12) And Joshua rose early in the morning, and the priests took up the ark of the LORD. (13) And seven priests bearing seven trumpets of rams' horns before the ark of the LORD went on continually, and blew with the trumpets: and the armed men went before them; but the rereward came after the ark of the LORD, *the priests* going on, and blowing with the trumpets. (14) And the second day they compassed the city once, and returned into the camp: so they did six days.

(15) And it came to pass on the seventh day, that they rose early about the dawning of the day, and compassed the city after the same manner seven times: only on that day they compassed the city seven times. (16) And it came to pass at the seventh time, when the priests blew with the trumpets, Joshua said unto the people, Shout; for the LORD hath given you the city. (17) And the city shall be ⁴accursed, *even* it, and all that *are* therein, to the LORD: only Rahab the harlot shall live, she and all that *are* with her in the house, because *ª* she hid the messengers that we sent. (18) And ye, in any wise keep *yourselves* from the accursed thing, lest ye make

---

(4) **Seven trumpets of rams' horns.**—Literally, *trumpets of jubilee*—*i.e.*, of loud or joyful sound.

(7) **Pass on, and compass the city.**—The meaning of this proceeding becomes clearer when we remember that the centre of the procession is the written law of God. The ark is the vessel that contains it. The armed men that precede it are its executioners. The priests who blow the trumpets are its heralds. It was this law that had brought Israel over Jordan; this law that was henceforth to be established in Canaan; this law that was about to take vengeance on the transgressors. The whole law of Moses is but the expansion of the Decalogue; and the Pentateuch contains an ample statement of the transgressions which had brought the inhabitants of Canaan under the ban of the Divine law. The seven days' march round Jericho, in absolute silence, was well calculated to impress on the inhabitants the lesson of "the forbearance of God." "These things hast thou done, and I kept silence." For several generations the long-suffering of God had waited, while "the iniquity of the Amorites was not yet full." In the first year of the Exodus He had threatened them, bringing the sword of Israel to their borders; and then He had drawn back His hand from them, and given them forty years' respite more. But now the long-suffering of God had waited long enough. The shout that burst from the lips of Israel was a signal that He would wait no longer.

Looked at thus, the shout of Israel at the sound of the trumpet on the seventh day becomes no inapt figure of that which is connected with it by the language of Holy Scripture—"the shout," accompanied by "the voice of the archangel and the trump of God," which shall notify to the world our Lord's second coming. "Our God shall come, and shall not keep silence" any more (Ps. l. 3 and 21; 1 Thess. iv. 16).

(13) **The priests going on.**—Literally, *with a going, and a blowing with the trumpets.* "The priests" is inserted by the Targum.

(17) **The city shall be accursed.**—Heb., *shall be chêrem*, "a devoted or accursed thing"; and so verse 18, "from the accursed thing." (See Note on Deut. vii. 26.) The combination of the two ideas of devotion to God and utter destruction may be seen in the sin

yourselves accursed, when ye take of the accursed thing, and make the camp of Israel a curse, and trouble it. ⁽¹⁹⁾ But all the silver, and gold, and vessels of brass and iron, *are* ¹ consecrated unto the LORD: they shall come into the treasury of the LORD.

⁽²⁰⁾ So the people shouted when *the priests* blew with the trumpets: and it came to pass, when the people heard the sound of the trumpet, and the people shouted with a great shout, that ᵃ the wall fell down ² flat, so that the people went up into the city, every man straight before him, and they took the city. ⁽²¹⁾ And they utterly destroyed all that *was* in the city, both man and woman, young and old, and ox, and sheep, and ass, with the edge of the sword.

⁽²²⁾ But Joshua had said unto the two men that had spied out the country, Go into the harlot's house, and bring out thence the woman, and all that she hath, ᵇ as ye sware unto her. ⁽²³⁾ And the young men that were spies went in, and brought out Rahab, and her father, and her mother, and her brethren, and all that she had; and they brought out all her ³ kindred, and left them without the camp of Israel.

⁽²⁴⁾ And they burnt the city with fire, and all that *was* therein: only the silver, and the gold, and the vessels of brass and of iron, they put into the treasury of the house of the LORD.

⁽²⁵⁾ And Joshua saved Rahab the harlot alive, and her father's household, and all that she had; and she dwelleth in Israel *even* unto this day; because she hid the messengers, which Joshua sent to spy out Jericho.

⁽²⁶⁾ And Joshua adjured *them* at that time, saying, ᶜ Cursed *be* the man before the LORD, that riseth up and buildeth this city Jericho: he shall lay the foundation thereof in his firstborn, and in his youngest *son* shall he set up the gates of it.

⁽²⁷⁾ So the LORD was with Joshua; and his fame was *noised* throughout all the country.

CHAPTER VII.—⁽¹⁾ But the children of Israel committed a trespass in the accursed thing: for ᵈ Achan, the son of Carmi, the son of Zabdi, the son of Zerah, of the tribe of Judah, took of the accursed thing: and the anger of the LORD was kindled against the children of Israel.

⁽²⁾ And Joshua sent men from Jericho to Ai, which *is* beside Beth-aven, on the east side of Beth-el, and spake unto

---

¹ Heb., *holiness*.
ᵃ Heb. 11. 30.
² Heb., *under it*.
ᵇ ch. 2. 14; Heb. 11. 31.
³ Heb., *families*.
ᶜ 1 Kin. 16. 34.
ᵈ ch. 22. 20; 1 Chron. 2. 7.

---

offering (Lev. vi. 25), which is called "holy of holies," or most holy, and yet, when offered for the priest or congregation, must be utterly consumed.

⁽¹⁹⁾ **The silver, and gold, and vessels of brass and iron . . . into the treasury of the Lord.**—See Num. xxxi. 22, 23, and 54, where something similar was done with the spoil of the Midianites.

⁽²¹⁾ **And ox, and sheep, and ass.**—Even the animals must be destroyed, that Israel might not seem to be slaughtering the Canaanites for the sake of plunder. Everything was ordered in such a way as to mark the vengeance of God.

⁽²³⁾ **And left them.**—Literally, *caused them to rest.*

⁽²⁵⁾ **And Joshua saved Rahab the harlot alive.**—"By faith the harlot Rahab perished not with them that believed not" (Heb. xi. 31). And so Jesus said to her who had ministered to Him in the house of Simon the Pharisee, "Thy sins are forgiven;" and again, "Thy faith hath saved thee: go in peace" (Luke vii. 48, 50). "Likewise also was not Rahab the harlot *justified by works?*" (James ii. 25).

And she dwelleth in Israel even unto this day.—"Salmon begat Booz of Rachab" seems certainly to refer to her (Matt. i. 5), though why she is called *Rachab* in that place is not obvious. Rachab is not the usual form of the word, either in the LXX. or in the other passages of the Greek text where she is named. It is not simply a variation in the English spelling, but a difference in the original Greek.

⁽²⁶⁾ **Cursed be the man . . . that . . . buildeth this city Jericho.**—As the marginal reference indicates, the curse of Joshua was not incurred until Hiel the Bethelite built the city, in the reign of Ahab. But the "city of palm-trees" is (somewhat doubtfully) identified with Jericho, and this was occupied by the Moabites under Eglon, not very long after the time of Joshua (Judges iii. 13, &c.), and seems to have been Eglon's residence, where he was slain by Ehud.

The curse, fulfilled upon Hiel and his family, appears to have been finally removed by the intercession of Elisha (2 Kings ii. 18—22), at the request of the inhabitants.

VII.

⁽¹⁾ **Achan . . . of the tribe of Judah.**—The tribe of Judah is distinguished in sacred history both for great crimes and great achievements. (See *Names on the Gates of Pearl.*—Judah.)

⁽²⁾ **Joshua sent men from Jericho to Ai.**—Why Ai should be the next town selected for attack after Jericho, is a question which perhaps we cannot answer with certainty. But we may observe that the next step after the capture of Ai, before the further conquest of the country, was to set up the Ten Commandments in Mount Ebal, in the heart of the country,

The Israelites Defeated at Ai.   JOSHUA, VII.   *Joshua's Lamentation.*

them, saying, Go up and view the country. And the men went up and viewed Ai. ⁽³⁾ And they returned to Joshua, and said unto him, Let not all the people go up; but let ¹ about two or three thousand men go up and smite Ai; *and* make not all the people to labour thither; for they *are but* few. ⁽⁴⁾ So there went up thither of the people about three thousand men: and they fled before the men of Ai. ⁽⁵⁾ And the men of Ai smote of them about thirty and six men: for they chased them *from* before the gate *even* unto Shebarim, and smote them ² in the going down: wherefore the hearts of the people melted, and became as water.

⁽⁶⁾ And Joshua rent his clothes, and fell to the earth upon his face before the ark of the LORD until the eventide, he and the elders of Israel, and put dust upon their heads. ⁽⁷⁾ And Joshua said, Alas, O Lord GOD, wherefore hast thou at all brought this people over Jordan, to deliver us into the hand of the Amorites, to destroy us? would to God we had been content, and dwelt on the other side Jordan. ⁽⁸⁾ O Lord, what shall I say, when Israel turneth their ³ backs before their enemies! ⁽⁹⁾ For the Canaanites and all the inhabitants of the land shall hear *of it*, and shall environ us round, and cut off our name from the earth: and what wilt thou do unto thy great name?

⁽¹⁰⁾ And the LORD said unto Joshua, Get thee up; wherefore ⁴ liest thou thus upon thy face? ⁽¹¹⁾ Israel hath sinned, and they have also transgressed my covenant which I commanded them: for they have even taken of the accursed thing, and have also stolen, and dissembled also, and they have put *it* even among their own stuff. ⁽¹²⁾ Therefore the children of Israel could not stand before their enemies, *but* turned *their*

¹ Heb., *about 2,000 men, or, about 3,000 men.*
² Or, *in Morad.*
³ Heb., *necks.*
⁴ Heb., *fallest.*

---

and to pronounce there the blessing and the curse which are the sanction of the law of God. It may well be that the course of the first military operations was directed to this end. The capture of Ai would put the Israelites in possession of the main road running north and south through Palestine, and enable them to reach the centre immediately. Thus the character of the war, which was no mere human enterprise, is maintained; and it is probable that the Divine reason for the movement is that which we are intended to observe. For the first mention of Ai, see Gen. xii. 8. It is noticeable that there Abram first pitched his tent after his return to Canaan out of Egypt. (See also on chap. viii. 1.) Note also that Beth-aven and Bethel are distinct, although adjacent, places. The one is not a later name of the other, as has been sometimes supposed, although one is "the house of vanity" (*i.e.*, perhaps of idols) and the other "the house of God."

⁽³⁾ **Make not all the people to labour thither.**—In these words we see, by a sort of side-glance, the (not unnatural) comment of Israel on the seven days' march round Jericho. They thought it useless labour, and were unable to appreciate the lesson which it taught. Again our attention is directed to the peculiar character of the warfare. It was *not* that kind of war which men would naturally have been disposed to wage. But the narrative is consistent throughout. (See Note on chap. ii. 1.)

⁽⁴⁾ **They fled before the men of Ai.**—A very natural reaction from overweening confidence to utter dismay is exhibited in this incident and its effect (verse 5), "the heart of the people melted and became as water." The demoralisation of Israel was a suitable penalty for their assumption, quite apart from its supernatural cause. It was absolutely necessary that the character of the conquest of Canaan should be vindicated, at whatever cost.

⁽⁵⁾ **Shebarim**—*i.e.*, the crevices, or ravines. A short distance below Ai the road passes the head of steep glens, which open into the plain of Jordan.

In the going down—*i.e.*, until they escaped into these ravines.

⁽⁶⁾ **Joshua rent his clothes . . .**—The words of Joshua and his behaviour on this occasion are consistent with all that we read of him, and confirm the notion that he was not a man of a naturally daring and adventurous spirit, but inclined to distrust his own powers; and yet utterly indomitable and unflinching in the discharge of his duty—a man of moral rather than physical courage.

⁽⁹⁾ **The Canaanites . . . shall environ us round.**—A thing extremely probable in itself, apart from the supernatural character of the invasion.

⁽¹⁰⁾ **Wherefore liest thou thus upon thy face?**—"Why is this, that *thou* art fallen upon thy face? Israel hath sinned." The pronoun "thou" is emphatic.

⁽¹¹⁾ **They have also transgressed my covenant.**—The law is again brought prominently forward in this scene. "The words of the covenant, the ten commandments," are first of all a pledge that Jehovah is the God of Israel. "I am Jehovah, thy God, who brought thee out of the land of Egypt." And He brought them out that He might bring them in—and He made them the executioners of His wrath against the idolaters. They must have no other gods but Him, and they must not treat the things that had been defiled by association with idolatry as their own spoil. The words which specially apply to this case are to be found in Deut. vii. 25, 26: "The graven images of their gods shall ye burn with fire: thou shalt not *desire* (see verse 21) the silver or gold that is on them. . . . Neither shalt thou bring an abomination into thine house, lest thou be *a cursed thing* like it."

The whole spoil of Canaan was not so treated; but concerning that of Jericho there had been express orders, possibly because the city was especially defiled with idolatry. God had proclaimed it abomination. It was *chêrem*—*devoted* or *accursed*—and no Israelite was to appropriate any of it, under penalty of becoming

backs before their enemies, because they were accursed: neither will I be with you any more, except ye destroy the accursed from among you. (13) Up, sanctify the people, and say, Sanctify yourselves against to morrow: for thus saith the LORD God of Israel, *There is* an accursed thing in the midst of thee, O Israel: thou canst not stand before thine enemies, until ye take away the accursed thing from among you. (14) In the morning therefore ye shall be brought according to your tribes: and it shall be, *that* the tribe which the LORD taketh shall come according to the families *thereof;* and the family which the LORD shall take shall come by households; and the household which the LORD shall take shall come man by man. (15) And it shall be, *that* he that is taken with the accursed thing shall be burnt with fire, he and all that he hath: because he hath transgressed the covenant of the LORD, and because he hath wrought ¹ folly in Israel.

(16) So Joshua rose up early in the morning, and brought Israel by their tribes; and the tribe of Judah was taken: (17) and he brought the family of Judah; and he took the family of the Zarhites: and he brought the family of the Zarhites man by man; and Zabdi was taken: (18) and he brought his household man by man; and Achan, the son of Carmi, the son of Zabdi, the son of Zerah, of the tribe of Judah, was taken.

(19) And Joshua said unto Achan, My son, give, I pray thee, glory to the LORD God of Israel, and make confession unto him; and tell me now what thou hast done; hide *it* not from me. (20) And Achan answered Joshua, and said, Indeed I have sinned against the LORD God of Israel, and thus and thus have I done: (21) when I saw among the spoils a goodly Babylonish garment, and two hundred shekels of silver, and a ² wedge of gold of fifty shekels weight, then I coveted them, and took them; and, behold, they *are* hid in the earth in the midst of my tent, and the silver under it.

(22) So Joshua sent messengers, and they ran unto the tent; and, behold, *it was* hid in his tent, and the silver under

¹ Or, *wickedness.*

² Heb., *tongue.*

---

chêrem himself, and making his household *chêrem*. This Achan had done.

(14—18) **In the morning therefore ye shall be brought.**—That is, *brought near*, or *presented*. The word used here, and throughout the passage, is the same that is commonly used for the presentation of an offering.

(14) **The tribe which the Lord taketh.**—There is nothing in the language of the passage, when closely considered, which would lead us to suppose that the discovery of the criminal was by casting lots. The parallel passage—viz., the selection of King Saul from the tribes of Israel (1 Sam. x. 20, 21)—shows that the oracle of God was consulted. "They inquired," and "the Lord answered." So it was, perhaps, in the case of Achan. We seem to see the High Priest of Israel "asking counsel for Joshua after the judgment of Urim before the Lord," as it had been foretold in Num. xxvii. 21; and the elders of Israel standing by, at the door of the tabernacle of the congregation. The representatives of the tribes enter the sacred enclosure in succession, and pass before the High Priest, in awful silence, broken only by the voice of Jehovah, who pronounces at intervals the names of *Judah, Zarhite, Zabdi, Carmi, Achan.* It must have been a terrible ordeal. But all present must have felt that no human partiality, or private animosity, was seeking its victim. The Judge of all the earth was doing judgment. And when the accusation of Jehovah was followed by the explicit confession of the criminal, and this again by the discovery of the stolen spoil of Jericho, which was brought in by the messengers, and "poured out before the Lord," and when this discovery was followed by the execution of the awful sentence, all who were present must have received a lesson, which it was impossible to forget, as to the reality of the covenant of God. And if, as seems most probable, the voice of the oracle was uttered from the inner sanctuary, from between the cherubim, but "heard even to the outer court, as the voice of the Almighty God, when He speaketh" (Ezekiel x. 5), we learn once more the majesty of the law given to Israel. The arrest of Jordan, the overthrow of Jericho, and the discovery of Achan, are all manifestations of power proceeding from the same source.

(19) **Give . . . glory to the Lord God of Israel, and make confession unto him; and tell me.** —We can hardly read these words of Joshua without being reminded of his great Antitype. In New Testament language, to tell Joshua is to "tell Jesus"—the only way in which confession of sin can bring glory. Joshua could only pronounce sentence of death on Achan. But "if we confess our sins, He is faithful and just to forgive us our sins, and to cleanse us from all unrighteousness." The Hebrew word for "confession" also means "thanksgiving." Acknowledgment of sin and mercy are not far apart, in making confession to God. (See Ezra x. 11 for a parallel to the phrase.)

(21) **A goodly Babylonish garment.**—Literally, *A certain goodly mantle of Shinar*.

I coveted them.—The very word employed, not only in the tenth commandment (Deut. v. 21), but also in Deut. vii. 25, the passage which forbids Israel to desire the spoils of idolatry. This coincidence of terms makes it somewhat probable that the whole were found in some idol's temple, and were part of the spoils of the shrine.

it. ⁽²³⁾ And they took them out of the midst of the tent, and brought them unto Joshua, and unto all the children of Israel, and ¹ laid them out before the LORD.

⁽²⁴⁾ And Joshua, and all Israel with him, took Achan the son of Zerah, and the silver, and the garment, and the wedge of gold, and his sons, and his daughters, and his oxen, and his asses, and his sheep, and his tent, and all that he had : and they brought them unto the valley of Achor. ⁽²⁵⁾ And Joshua said, Why hast thou troubled us ? the LORD shall trouble thee this day. And all Israel stoned him with stones, and burned them with fire, after they had

1 Heb., *poured*.

2 That is, *Trouble*.

a Deut. 1. 21, & 7. 18.

b ch. 6. 21.

c Deut. 20. 14.

stoned them with stones. ⁽²⁶⁾ And they raised over him a great heap of stones unto this day. So the LORD turned from the fierceness of his anger. Wherefore the name of that place was called, The valley of ² Achor, unto this day.

CHAPTER VIII.—⁽¹⁾ And the LORD said unto Joshua, *ᵃ* Fear not, neither be thou dismayed : take all the people of war with thee, and arise, go up to Ai : see, I have given into thy hand the king of Ai, and his people, and his city, and his land : ⁽²⁾ and thou shalt do to Ai and her king as thou didst unto *ᵇ* Jericho and her king : only the spoil thereof, and *ᶜ* the cattle thereof, shall ye take

---

⁽²³⁾ **And laid them out before the Lord.**— The silver and the gold, by His order, should have been brought into His treasury (chap. vi. 19). The spoils of Canaan *might* have been consecrated as holiness to Jehovah. But in this instance the spoil of Jericho had become the sin of Israel, and it must therefore be no longer preserved, but consumed.

⁽²⁴⁾ **And his sons, and his daughters, and his oxen, and his asses, and his sheep, and his tent, and all that he had.**—All were evidently destroyed together (comp. xxii. 20). For any other sin but this, Achan must have suffered alone. "The children shall not be put to death for the fathers." But in this case, warning had been given that the man who took of the accursed thing, or *chêrem*, would be an accursed thing like it, if he brought it into his house (Deut. vii. 26), and would make the camp of Israel *chêrem* also (Josh. vi. 18), and thus Achan's whole establishment was destroyed as though it had become part of Jericho. It is not necessary to assert that the family of Achan were accomplices. His cattle were not so, and yet they were destroyed. See also 1 Chron. ii. 7, where his line is not continued. Observe also the incidental reference to the fact in chap. xxii. 20, "*That man perished not alone* in his iniquity." The severity of the punishment must be estimated by the relation of Achan's crime to the whole plan of the conquest of Canaan. If the destruction of the Canaanites was indeed the execution of the Divine vengeance, it must be kept entirely clear of all baser motives, lest men should say that Jehovah gave His people licence to deal with the Canaanites as it seemed best for themselves. The punishment of Saul for taking the spoil of Amalek (1 Sam. xv.), and the repeated statement of the Book of Esther that the Jews who stood for their lives and slew their enemies, the supporters of Haman's project, *laid not their hands on the prey*, are further illustrations of the same principle. The gratification of human passions may not be mingled with the execution of the vengeance of God. (See Esther viii. 11 and ix. 10, 15, 16.)

The valley of Achor.—In 1 Chron. ii. 7, Achan himself is designated *Achar* (one among several examples of the alteration of a name to suit some circumstance of a person's history. Compare Bathsheba for Bathshua, Shallum for Jehoiachin, Ishbosheth for Eshbaal, &c.). There is a double play upon the names in Hosea ii. 15 : "I will give her her vineyards (*Carmêha*. Compare *Carmi*, "my vineyard") from thence, and the valley of trouble (*Achor*) for a door of hope." The valley of Achor is a pass leading from Gilgal towards the centre of the country, or, as it might be represented, from Jericho towards Jerusalem—*i.e.*, from the city of destruction to the city of God. So it was to Israel in the conquest. The future state of Achan is in the hands of the Judge who "doeth judgment." No mercy to his crime on earth was possible. It would have been injustice to all mankind.

VIII.

⁽¹⁾ **Fear not, neither be thou dismayed.**— See chaps. i. 9 and x. 25. In chap. i. 9, "For the Lord thy God is with thee." These words indicate the return of Jehovah to the host of Israel, for the prosecution of the war.

Take all the people.—Not merely "two or three thousand," as before.

Ai.—In Hebrew, *Hâ-ai*. Ai is intended for one syllable, not two as often sounded in English. It means "the heap" (of ruins apparently). In verse 28 we read that Joshua made it "an heap for ever" (*Tel-ôlâm* in Hebrew). Thus its first and last names agree. It is remarked that whereas Palestine is full of "Tels" with other names appended to them (as Tell-es Sultan, and some ten others near Jericho alone), the place called et-Tel by Bethel has no other appendage. It is not the heap of anything, but simply *the heap*, to this day ; and this fact, which is apparently without parallel, seems to fix the site of Ai at *et-Tel*. (See Note on chap. vii. 2.)

And his land.—The capture of Ai was not simply the capture of a town or fortress, but of the chief town of a territory, the extent of which we are not told. If we knew the circumstances of the time more precisely, we might apprehend the strategical reasons which made it desirable to obtain possession of Ai in particular at this stage of the campaign.

⁽²⁾ **Only the spoil thereof, and the cattle thereof, shall ye take**—*i.e.*, the material spoil, not the persons of the inhabitants. (See chap. xi. 14.) Jericho was treated exceptionally, in that the material spoil was made *chêrem*, devoted to destruction, as the thing accursed of God.

Joshua's Army.   JOSHUA, VIII.   *He Attacks Ai.*

for a prey unto yourselves : lay thee an ambush for the city behind it

(3) So Joshua arose, and all the people of war, to go up against Ai: and Joshua chose out thirty thousand mighty men of valour, and sent them away by night. (4) And he commanded them, saying, Behold, ye shall lie in wait against the city, *even* behind the city: go not very far from the city, but be ye all ready: (5) and I, and all the people that *are* with me, will approach unto the city: and it shall come to pass, when they come out against us, as at the first, that we will flee before them, (6) (for they will come out after us) till we have ¹drawn them from the city; for they will say, They flee before us, as at the first: therefore we will flee before them. (7) Then ye shall rise up from the ambush, and seize upon the city: for the LORD your God will deliver it into your hand. (8) And it shall be, when ye have taken the city, *that* ye shall set the city on fire: according to the commandment of the LORD shall ye do. See, I have commanded you. (9) Joshua therefore sent them forth: and they went to lie in ambush, and abode between Beth-el and Ai, on the west side of Ai: but Joshua lodged that night among the people.

(10) And Joshua rose up early in the morning, and numbered the people, and went up, he and the elders of Israel, before the people to Ai. (11) And all the people, *even the people* of war that *were* with him, went up, and drew nigh, and came before the city, and pitched on the north side of Ai: now *there was* a valley between them and Ai. (12) And he took about five thousand men, and set them to lie in ambush between Beth-el and Ai, on the west side ²of the city. (13) And when they had set the people, *even* all the host that *was* on the north of the city, and ³their liers in wait on the west of the city, Joshua went that night into the midst of the valley.

(14) And it came to pass, when the

---

¹ Heb., *pulled.*
² Or, *of Ai.*
³ Heb., *their lying in wait.*

---

(3) **And Joshua chose out thirty thousand mighty men.**—Some difficulty arises from the fact that thirty thousand men are mentioned as having been sent away with general instructions to form an ambush in the first instance, while five thousand were ultimately posted between Bethel and Ai. Were there two distinct bodies in ambush, or only one? It does not seem possible to answer this question with absolute certainty; but we ought to notice in the first place what the aim of Joshua was. He meant to isolate the town of Ai, taking it in front and flank; but there was another town immediately in the rear, less than two miles off. It was necessary, therefore, to employ a sufficient body of men to close the communications between Bethel and Ai from the first.

(4—8) Joshua's general plan of operations is stated in these verses. The following verses explain how it was worked out.

(9) **They went to lie in ambush.**—Or, *they went to the lurking-place;* and remained between Bethel and Ai. The ambush itself (verses 2, 7, 19, 21) is described by a slightly different word.

Among the people—*i.e.,* at Gilgal.

(10) **Joshua . . . numbered.**—Or, rather, *mustered* the people.

He then went up with the elders of Israel at the head of the main body, and made an imposing demonstration with a large force in front of the town.

(11) **On the north side.**—The lurking-place of the thirty thousand was on the west side, between Bethel and Ai. There is a ravine called the Wady Maheesin which runs nearly east and west, on the north of et-Tel, and probably Joshua's main body took up a position on the rising ground to the north of this ravine, for it is added, "*the* ravine (or Gai) was between them and Ai."

(12) **And he took about five thousand men, and set them to lie in ambush . . .**—Is this a fresh body, or only a portion of the thirty thousand mentioned in verse 3? It is, of course, *possible* that the body of thirty thousand, having closed the communications between Bethel and Ai on the first night, and finding that they were more numerous than was necessary, had rejoined Joshua when he came up, and that a small body of five thousand was told off for the service on the next day. But after carefully studying the natural features of the position by the Ordnance map (of which I have been able to enjoy the advantage at this point of my work), I am inclined to think that both forces were employed—the thirty thousand and the five thousand—and for distinct services. There are *two* ravines, which come to a head between Beitin (Bethel) and et-Tel (Ai). The body of men who were to fire the town of Ai were posted in the one nearer to Ai. The larger body, whose business was to prevent any interference from the side of Bethel, were posted in the ravine next to that city, where they had been from the first. If it be remembered, as was before observed, that Joshua was attacking a fortified town, which was protected in flank by another town, and that it was necessary to be prepared for all contingencies from the first, the meaning of his movements will be apparent.

(13) **Joshua went that night into the . . . . valley** (Emek).—Not the ravine (or Gai) before mentioned (verse 11), but a wider and more open part of the valley, probably a little further to the south: the object being to draw the men of Ai into a pursuit in the direction of the road to Gilgal.

(14) **When the king of Ai saw it . . . . the city went out.**—The stratagem succeeded perfectly. Joshua gave them ample time, by his movements in open daylight, to discover what his apparent intentions were, viz., to renew the direct attack upon the city with a larger force. Accordingly, the Canaanites came out *before the plain*—*i.e.,* in the direction of the

king of Ai saw *it*, that they hasted and rose up early, and the men of the city went out against Israel to battle, he and all his people, at a time appointed, before the plain; but he wist not that *there were* liers in ambush against him behind the city. ⁽¹⁵⁾ And Joshua and all Israel made as if they were beaten before them, and fled by the way of the wilderness. ⁽¹⁶⁾ And all the people that *were* in Ai were called together to pursue after them: and they pursued after Joshua, and were drawn away from the city. ⁽¹⁷⁾ And there was not a man left in Ai or Beth-el, that went not out after Israel: and they left the city open, and pursued after Israel. ⁽¹⁸⁾ And the LORD said unto Joshua, Stretch out the spear that *is* in thy hand toward Ai; for I will give it into thine hand. And Joshua stretched out the spear that *he had* in his hand toward the city. ⁽¹⁹⁾ And the ambush arose quickly out of their place, and they ran as soon as he had stretched out his hand: and they entered into the city, and took it, and hasted and set the city on fire. ⁽²⁰⁾ And when the men of Ai looked behind them, they saw, and, behold, the smoke of the city ascended up to heaven, and they had no ¹power to flee this way or that way: and the people that fled to the wilderness turned back upon the pursuers. ⁽²¹⁾ And when Joshua and all Israel saw that the ambush had taken the city, and that the smoke of the city ascended, then they turned again, and slew the men of Ai. ⁽²²⁾ And the other issued out of the city against them; so they were in the midst of Israel, some on this side, and some on that side: and they smote them, so that they ᵃ let none of them remain or escape. ⁽²³⁾ And the king of Ai they took alive, and brought him to Joshua.

⁽²⁴⁾ And it came to pass, when Israel had made an end of slaying all the inhabitants of Ai in the field, in the wilderness wherein they chased them, and when they were all fallen on the edge of the sword, until they were consumed, that all the Israelites returned unto Ai, and smote it with the edge of the sword. ⁽²⁵⁾ And *so* it was, *that* all that fell that day, both of men and women, *were* twelve thousand, *even* all the men of Ai. ⁽²⁶⁾ For Joshua drew not his hand back, wherewith he stretched out the spear, until he had utterly destroyed all the inhabitants of Ai. ⁽²⁷⁾ ᵇ Only the cattle and the spoil of that city Israel took for a prey unto themselves, according unto the word of the LORD which he ᶜcommanded Joshua. ⁽²⁸⁾ And Joshua burnt Ai, and made it

---

1 Heb., *hand.*
ᵃ Deut. 7. 2.
ᵇ Num. 31. 22, 26.
ᶜ ver. 2.

---

plain of Jordan (the *Arabah*. On this word and *Emek* and *Gai* used above, see Stanley, *Sinai and Palestine*)—intending to drive Joshua down by the way he had come up. And accordingly Joshua and his army fled in that very direction by the way of the *Midbar* or wilderness—*i.e.*, the mountainous district betweeen Ai and the Jordan valley, and lying in that direction. (Comp. chap. vii. 5.)

⁽¹⁷⁾ **There was not a man left in Ai or Beth-el.**—Another singular justification of the peculiar strategy of Joshua. The road past Beth-el to Ai had been left open. It passes the north end of the two ravines in which Joshua's ambush was posted. At the same time, it would have been easy to conceal a chain of sentinels that could observe it and tell the 35,000 men in ambush what was going on, so that if any attempt had been made by the men of Beth-el to protect Ai, it could easily have been frustrated. But no one suspected any danger, and therefore no such attempt was made. The men of Beth-el and Ai took the road that was left open to them and pursued the Israelites, probably down the ancient way past Michmash towards the Shebarim, leaving Beth-el and Ai both unprotected. After they had gone some distance, about a mile or a mile and a half from Ai, this road would bring them past the lower end of the ravine in which the ambush was posted. A second chain of outposts would easily take the signal from Joshua when this point had been passed, and then all was over with the town of Ai.

It is curious that we do not hear of the capture of Beth-el at this time, though it would have been perfectly easy to take it. The king of Beth-el is named in the list of those whom Joshua smote (chap. xii. 16). We read of its capture in Judges i. 22, and of the "entrance into the city" being sought for and betrayed. But that can hardly have been the *first* capture of the town.

⁽¹⁸⁾ **And the Lord said unto Joshua, Stretch out the spear.**—In the capture of Ai, as in that of Jericho, each stage of the process must be ordered by the Lord. In the former case the hand of Jehovah alone does the work. The ark is borne round the walls until they fall down before it. Against Ai, the hand of Israel is employed, and first of all in Israel the hand of Joshua. He seems to have stretched it out, with the light spear or javelin which he carried, somewhat as Moses stretched forth the rod of God over the contending hosts of Amalek and Israel, until the enemy was discomfited with the edge of the sword.

⁽²⁷⁾ **The spoil of that city Israel took.**—The spoil of Ai was assigned to Israel, the spoil of Jericho had been claimed for Jehovah alone.

⁽²⁸⁾ **An heap for ever.**—Heb., *Tel-ôlam*; modern name, *Et-tel*.

an heap for ever, *even* a desolation unto this day. (29) And the king of Ai he hanged on a tree until eventide: and as soon as the sun was down, Joshua commanded that they should take his carcase down from the tree, and cast it at the entering of the gate of the city, and *a* raise thereon a great heap of stones, *that remaineth* unto this day.

(30) Then Joshua built an altar unto the LORD God of Israel in mount Ebal, (31) as Moses the servant of the LORD commanded the children of Israel, as it is written in the *b* book of the law of Moses, an altar of whole stones, over which no man hath lift up *any* iron: and they offered thereon burnt offerings unto the LORD, and sacrificed peace offerings. (32) And he wrote there upon the stones a copy of the law of Moses, which he wrote in the presence of the children of Israel. (33) And all Israel, and their elders, and officers, and their judges, stood on this side the ark and on that side before the priests the Levites, which bare the ark of the covenant of the LORD, as well the stranger, as he that was born among them; half of them over against mount Gerizim, and half of them over against mount Ebal; *c* as Moses the servant of the LORD had commanded before, that they should bless the people of Israel. (34) And afterward he read all the words of the law, the blessings and cursings, according to all that is written in the book of the law. (35) There was not a word of all that Moses commanded, which Joshua read not before all the congregation of Israel, *d* with the women, and the little ones, and the strangers that [1] were conversant among them.

CHAPTER IX.—(1) And it came to pass, when all the kings which *were* on this side Jordan, in the hills, and in the valleys, and in all the coasts of the great sea over against Lebanon, the Hittite, and the Amorite, the Canaanite, the Perizzite, the Hivite, and the Jebusite, heard *thereof;* (2) that they gathered themselves together, to fight with

a ch. 7. 25.
b Ex. 20. 25; Deut. 27. 5.
c Deut. 11. 29. & 27. 12.
d Deut. 31. 12.
[1] Heb., *walked.*

---

(29) **And the king of Ai he hanged on a tree.** —(See Note on Deut. xxi. 22, 23.) Heb., *on the tree.* Why "*the* tree"? It would appear from chap. viii. 2 and x. 1, that the king of Jericho was also hanged; possibly both were hanged on the same tree, and were exhibited, each in turn, as "the curse of God." But when we read of this treatment of the enemies of Joshua, we cannot but be reminded of the greater Joshua, who fulfilled the curse of God in His own person, and made a show of the "principalities and powers" by triumphing over them in His cross. (Comp. also Esth. ix. 10, 13.)

Jericho and Ai are the only cities of Canaan of which the capture by Joshua is recorded in detail. Their capture stands in the narrative, as it was in fact, a specimen of the whole conquest of the Canaanite *cities*. Two campaigns in like manner are recorded as specimens of Joshua's battles with the enemy in the open field. In the capture of Jericho and in the southern campaign, the hand of God is more especially manifested. In the capture of Ai and in the northern campaign, the labour of Israel in the conflict is more prominent. The whole work is thus presented to us in a twofold aspect, as the work of Israel and the work of God.

A great heap of stones.—Not only the death, but the burial of the king of Ai is recorded, as also the burial of the five kings in chap. x. 27. The same thing was done to Achan (chap. vii. 26), and to Absalom (2 Sam. xviii. 17). This kind of burial is another form of the curse, and is a fitting sequel to the hanging of the body upon the tree.

THE LAW SET UP IN THE HEART OF THE COUNTRY.

(30) **Then Joshua built.**—The word *then* is not "and" in the Hebrew; as is too often the case where "then" occurs in our English Old Testament. It is a note of time. Josephus places this transaction later. The LXX. places verses 1 and 2 of chap. ix. before this passage. But there seems no reason for moving the transaction from the place where we find it in the text. By the capture of Ai, Joshua had obtained command over the road to Shechem. We hear of no strong place north of Beth-el in that part of the country. From other passages (see on chap. xvii. 18) there seems reason to think that a large part of this district was wooded and uncleared. The confederacy of the southern kings had its centre far to the south of this, and there was a considerable distance between Shechem and the strong places to the north. It is in keeping with what we have already observed regarding the purpose of the conquest of Canaan, that the law of the God of Israel should be as soon as possible proclaimed and set up in the heart of the country, to be thenceforward the law of the land. For the enactment that was here carried out, see Deut. xi. 26—30, xxvii. 2, &c. Observe also that the command there given required the work to be done as soon after the passing of Jordan as possible. The possibility of reading the law from this position, so as to be heard by the whole congregation, has been proved by actual experiment.

(30, 31) **An altar . . . in mount Ebal . . .**—This was explicitly commanded in Deuteronomy. The blessing was put on mount Gerizim, the altar and the curse on mount Ebal. We do not hear elsewhere of any sacrifice on Ebal. But it is certain that God accepted sacrifices in many places in Canaan. (Cf. Exod. xix. 24.)

IX.

PREPARATIONS OF THE CANAANITES FOR WAR.

(1, 2) These verses record the general preparation of the natives of Canaan for the last struggle with Joshua.

Joshua and with Israel, with one [1] accord.

(3) And when the inhabitants of Gibeon heard what Joshua had done unto Jericho and to Ai, (4) they did work wilily, and went and made as if they had been ambassadors, and took old sacks upon their asses, and wine bottles, old, and rent, and bound up; (5) and old shoes and clouted upon their feet, and old garments upon them; and all the bread of their provision was dry *and* mouldy. (6) And they went to Joshua unto the camp at Gilgal, and said unto him, and to the men of Israel, We be come from a far country: now therefore make ye a league with us.

(7) And the men of Israel said unto the Hivites, Peradventure ye dwell among us; and how shall we make a league with you? (8) And they said unto Joshua, We *are* thy servants. And Joshua said unto them, Who *are* ye? and from whence come ye? (9) And they said unto him, From a very far country thy servants are come because of the name of the LORD thy God: for we have heard the fame of him, and all that he did in Egypt, (10) and all that he did to the two kings of the Amorites, that *were* beyond Jordan, to Sihon king of Heshbon, and to Og king of Bashan, which *was* at Ashtaroth. (11) Wherefore our elders and all the inhabitants of our country spake to us, saying, Take victuals [2] with you for the journey, and go to meet them, and say unto them, We *are* your servants: therefore now make ye a league with us. (12) This our bread we took hot *for* our provision out of our houses on the day we came forth to go unto you; but now, behold, it is dry, and it is mouldy: (13) and these bottles of wine, which we filled, *were* new; and, behold, they be rent: and these our garments and our shoes are become old by reason of the very long journey.

(14) And [3] the men took of their victuals, and asked not *counsel* at the mouth of the LORD. (15) And Joshua made peace with them, and made a league with them, to let them live: and the princes of the congregation sware unto them.

(16) And it came to pass at the end of three days after they had made a league with them, that they heard that they *were* their neighbours, and *that* they dwelt among them. (17) And the

[1] Heb., *mouth*.

[2] Heb. *hand* *in your*

[3] Or, *they received the men by reason of their victuals.*

THE GIBEONITES MAKE PEACE WITH JOSHUA (chap. ix. 3—27).

(3) **The inhabitants of Gibeon.**—Hivites, as appears by verse 7. Gibeon was one member of a tetrapolis, or community of four cities, as is seen in verse 17. Their deception of Joshua and the Israelites on this occasion is a curious compensation for what was done by Simeon and Levi to the Hivites long before, when Jacob first came to Shechem from Padan-Aram (see Gen. xxxiv.). On that occasion, the inhabitants of a single city of the Hivites were put to the sword by Israel, by means of a stratagem; on this occasion, a stratagem saved four Hivite cities from destruction by Israel's sword.

(4) **They did work wilily.**—Literally, *and they also dealt with subtilty.* The stratagem does not seem a very profound one, or one that would have been difficult to detect. But we may remember a fact of Israel's experience which puts it in a somewhat different light. The Israelites themselves had come from a far country, but their raiment had not "waxed old upon them," nor did "their feet swell," these forty years. Of bread they had no need, when there was manna, and God gave them water for their thirst. Of worn garments and stale provisions they had no experience, and therefore, when the Gibeonites presented themselves in this extraordinary garb and guise, it is not unnatural that they were not detected by the eyes of Israel.

They . . . made as if they had been ambassadors.—The verb thus translated does not occur elsewhere in the Hebrew Bible. By the alteration of a letter, the Targum, LXX., and some other versions make it mean, "they gat them provision."

(5) **Clouted**—*i.e.*, patched.

(7) **Peradventure ye dwell among us; and how shall we make a league with you?**—Literally, *Peradventure thou art a dweller in the midst of me; and how shall I make a covenant with thee?* The Israelites assume the ownership of Canaan as already theirs.

(9, 10) **All that he did in Egypt, and . . . to the two kings of the Amorites.**—The Gibeonites carefully abstain from referring to more recent exploits, as the passage of Jordan, the taking of Jericho and Ai; they mention only those which might have had time to reach them in the "far country" from which they asserted that they came.

(14) **And the men took of their victuals.**—*And they accepted the men from* (the appearance of) *their provisions.* This, which is the view taken in our marginal reading, seems to be the more probable interpretation, and follows the Targum. "The men" can hardly refer to any one but the ambassadors of the Gibeonites.

(16) **Their neighbours, and they that dwelt among them.**—Literally, *and that they* (the Gibeonites) *were dwellers in the midst of him* (Israel). (So verse 7.)

(17) **Gibeon, and Chephirah, and Beeroth, and Kirjath-jearim.**—The first three of these were assigned to Benjamin (chap. xviii. 25, 26), the last to Judah (xv. 60), in the division of the land. The fact that the larger portion of the territory of the Gibeonites

children of Israel journeyed, and came unto their cities on the third day. Now their cities *were* Gibeon, and Chephirah, and Beeroth, and Kirjath-jearim. ⁽¹⁸⁾ And the children of Israel smote them not, because the princes of the congregation had sworn unto them by the LORD God of Israel.

And all the congregation murmured against the princes. ⁽¹⁹⁾ But all the princes said unto all the congregation, We have sworn unto them by the LORD God of Israel: now therefore we may not touch them. ⁽²⁰⁾ This we will do to them; we will even let them live, lest wrath be upon us, because of the oath which we sware unto them. ⁽²¹⁾ And the princes said unto them, Let them live; but let them be hewers of wood and drawers of water unto all the congregation; as the princes had *promised them.

⁽²²⁾ And Joshua called for them, and he spake unto them, saying, Wherefore have ye beguiled us, saying, We *are* very far from you; when ye dwell among us? ⁽²³⁾ Now therefore ye *are* cursed, and there shall ¹ none of you be freed from being bondmen, and hewers of wood and drawers of water for the house of my God. ⁽²⁴⁾ And they answered Joshua, and said, Because it

a ver. 15.

¹ Heb., *not be cut off from you.*

b Deut. 7. 1.

c ch. 6. 15.

d ch. 8. 2.

² Heb., *cities of the kingdom.*

was certainly told thy servants, how that the LORD thy God ^bcommanded his servant Moses to give you all the land, and to destroy all the inhabitants of the land from before you, therefore we were sore afraid of our lives because of you, and have done this thing. ⁽²⁵⁾ And now, behold, we *are* in thine hand: as it seemeth good and right unto thee to do unto us, do. ⁽²⁶⁾ And so did he unto them, and delivered them out of the hand of the children of Israel, that they slew them not. ⁽²⁷⁾ And Joshua made them that day hewers of wood and drawers of water for the congregation, and for the altar of the LORD, even unto this day, in the place which he should choose.

CHAPTER X.—⁽¹⁾ Now it came to pass, when Adoni-zedec king of Jerusalem had heard how Joshua had taken Ai, and had utterly destroyed it; ^cas he had done to Jericho and her king, so he had done to ^dAi and her king; and how the inhabitants of Gibeon had made peace with Israel, and were among them; ⁽²⁾ that they feared greatly, because Gibeon *was* a great city, as one of the ² royal cities, and because it *was* greater than Ai, and all the men thereof *were*

---

was in the tribe of Benjamin explains how Saul was tempted to confiscate their possessions for the purpose of supplying his followers with fields and vineyards (1 Sam. xxii. 7). He appears to have carried out his purpose in the case of Beeroth (2 Sam. iv. 2, 3), but not as regards all the Gibeonite towns. Gibeon became a city of the *priests* (chap. xxi. 17), and also a principal place of worship and the seat of the tabernacle (as Kirjath-jearim was of the ark) in later times. (See 1 Sam. vi. 21, vii. 1, &c.; 1 Chron. xx. 29; and 2 Chron. i. 3—6.) The fact that the Gibeonites were dedicated to the service of the sanctuary may partly account for this. In Gibeon, Solomon asked and received the wisdom which Joshua and Israel at this time did not ask.

⁽¹⁹⁾ **We have sworn unto them . . . therefore we may not touch them.**—Although the covenant was obtained from the Israelites by false pretences, yet, being made in the name of Jehovah, it could not be broken; it was His covenant. "He that sweareth to his own hurt, and changeth not," is commended in Ps. xv. 4. We should notice that the law of Jehovah had raised the tone of morality in this particular. There are many Christians who would not hesitate to repudiate an agreement concluded under false pretences.

⁽²³⁾ **Bondmen, and hewers of wood and drawers of water for the house of my God.**—The precedent established in regard to the Gibeonites appears to have been followed by Solomon in his dealings with all the remnant of the doomed nations of Canaan who were not destroyed. (See 1 Kings ix. 20, 21;

2 Chron. viii. 7, 8.) It is thought that they are to be recognised in the Nethinim of Ezra and Nehemiah, who come after the Levites, singers, and porters in the enumeration of the restored captives (Ezra ii. 43). Compare also the mention of Solomon's servants (Ezra ii. 58), whose children are coupled with the Nethinim. The existence of this large body of Canaanites should be remembered in considering the edict of the law of Moses, that the seven nations were to be destroyed. The sentence was clearly not executed on the mass of the non-resisting population.

X.

CONQUEST OF THE SOUTHERN CONFEDERACY OF THE NATIONS OF CANAAN.

⁽¹⁾ **Adoni-zedec king of Jerusalem.**—We may compare this name (Lord of Righteousness) with Melchizedek (King of Righteousness). (See Gen. xiv. 18 and Heb. vii. 1.) The similarity of the names makes it probable that the Salem of Gen. xiv. 18 is Jerusalem (see Notes). The title Lord or King of Righteousness may have belonged to the king of Jerusalem, not only as a local title, but also in relation to the surrounding tribes, over whom he may have been a suzerain. But we know nothing of the matter beyond what we find in the sacred text.

⁽²⁾ **As one of the royal cities.**—One of the cities of the kingdom. Gibeon was afterwards the city of the first king of Israel, Saul (1 Chron. viii. 29, 30, 33).

mighty. ⁽³⁾ Wherefore Adoni-zedec king of Jerusalem sent unto Hoham king of Hebron, and unto Piram king of Jarmuth, and unto Japhia king of Lachish, and unto Debir king of Eglon, saying, ⁽⁴⁾ Come up unto me, and help me, that we may smite Gibeon: for it hath made peace with Joshua and with the children of Israel. ⁽⁵⁾ Therefore the five kings of the Amorites, the king of Jerusalem, the king of Hebron, the king of Jarmuth, the king of Lachish, the king of Eglon, gathered themselves together, and went up, they and all their hosts, and encamped before Gibeon, and made war against it.

⁽⁶⁾ And the men of Gibeon sent unto Joshua to the camp to Gilgal, saying, Slack not thy hand from thy servants; come up to us quickly, and save us, and help us: for all the kings of the Amorites that dwell in the mountains are gathered together against us. ⁽⁷⁾ So Joshua ascended from Gilgal, he, and all the people of war with him, and all the mighty men of valour. ⁽⁸⁾ And the LORD said unto Joshua, Fear them not: for I have delivered them into thine hand; there shall not a man of them stand before thee. ⁽⁹⁾ Joshua therefore came unto them suddenly, *and* went up from Gilgal all night. ⁽¹⁰⁾ And the LORD discomfited them before Israel, and slew them with a great slaughter at Gibeon, and chased them along the way that goeth up to Beth-horon, and smote them to Azekah, and unto Makkedah. ⁽¹¹⁾ And it came to pass, as they fled from before Israel, *and* were in the going down to Beth-horon, that the LORD cast down great stones from heaven upon them unto Azekah, and they died: *they were* more which died with hailstones than *they* whom the children of Israel slew with the sword.

⁽¹²⁾ Then spake Joshua to the LORD in

⁽³⁾ **Hebron, Jarmuth, Lachish, and Eglon.**—Hebron, *i.e.*, el-Khalil.
Jarmuth is identified as el-Yarmûk.
Lachish is still uncertain; but see Note on verse 32.
Eglon is identified as Aglân in Philistia.

⁽⁴⁾ **Come up . . . that we may smite Gibeon.**—It is remarkable that we do not read of one direct attack upon Joshua and his army in all the wars of Canaan. The Canaanites seem to have acted strictly upon the defensive; and this fact tallies with what we read of the alarm and depression that spread among them at the passage of Jordan by Israel. And the armies which did take the field were attacked by Joshua in each instance before they had ventured to attack him. In the present instance it was thought necessary to smite Gibeon, not only to make an example of the inhabitants, but also because of its importance as a stronghold in the hands of Israel. The position of the Hivite tetrapolis was strong enough to command the country. The fact that a man of Gibeon was afterwards selected to reign over Israel, and that the tabernacle was stationed there, so that Gibeon became a sort of metropolis during the latter portion of Saul's reign, is a significant comment upon this.

⁽⁶⁾ **The Amorites that dwell in the mountains**—*i.e.*, in the mountainous district lying on the south of Jerusalem.

⁽⁸⁾ **And the Lord said unto Joshua.**—A distinct command is given for the commencement of this attack, as for all the important steps in the conquest of Canaan.

⁽⁹⁾ **And went up.**—Better thus, *And Joshua came upon them suddenly*; (for) *all the night he had marched* (come up) *from Gilgal*. The expression "went up" is geographically correct, because the line of march from Gilgal to Gibeon is an ascent the whole way.

⁽¹⁰⁾ **Beth-horon**—is identified as Beit' Ur.
Azekah—is unknown.
Makkedah.—Probably el-Moghâr.

⁽¹¹⁾ **Great stones from heaven.**—Compare Job xxxviii. 22, 23, "Hast thou seen the treasures of the hail, which I have reserved against the time of trouble, against the day of battle and war?" The employment of the artillery of heaven against Jehovah's enemies was there foretold by Himself.

⁽¹²⁻¹⁵⁾—The whole of this paragraph appears to be a quotation from the Book of Jasher. That book is mentioned also in 2 Sam. i. 18, where the lament of David over Saul and Jonathan appears to be a citation from it. We may compare Num. xxi. 14 and 27, where reference is made to poetical passages either current among the people (as national ballads) or actually written. The name Jasher (upright) is not taken as the name of an author, and what it refers to no one knows. From the fact that all the passages cited in this way are more or less poetical, we may infer that there was a poetical literature among the Hebrews (partly written, partly unwritten) from which the inspired writers occasionally made extracts. The songs of Moses, including the ninetieth Psalm, belong to this literature.

The fact that the great miracle of the Book of Joshua is recorded in this form is, to those who believe that Joshua was the original author of the book, a remarkable proof of the impression which the miracle had made upon the minds of the people. Even before the death of the hero of the story, it had come to be told in a set form of words, in which the ear could tolerate no alteration. As in later times they sang, "Saul hath slain his thousands and David his ten thousands," so they appear to have recited the deed of Joshua. "Then spake Joshua to the Lord." The form of the original sentence, "Then *speaketh* Joshua," &c., is suitable to this view.

⁽¹²⁾ **And he said in the sight of Israel, Sun, stand thou still . . .**—It is not impossible to read thus: "And he said, In the sight of Israel sun in Gibeon be thou still (dumb); and, moon, in the valley of

the day when the LORD delivered up the Amorites before the children of Israel, and he said in the sight of Israel,

"Sun, ¹ stand thou still upon Gibeon; and thou, Moon, in the valley of Ajalon.

(13) And the sun stood still, and the moon stayed, until the people had avenged themselves upon their enemies. Is not this written in the book of ² Jasher? So the sun stood still in the midst of heaven, and hasted not to go down about a whole day. (14) And there was no day like that before it or after it, that the LORD hearkened unto the voice of a man: for the LORD fought for Israel. (15) And Joshua returned, and all Israel with him, unto the camp to Gilgal.

a Isa. 28.21; Ecclus. 46. 4

¹ Heb., *be silent*.

² Or, *The upright?*

Ajalon." But we do not seem to gain anything by supposing that the miracle was only apparent—*i.e.*, that the light of the sun and moon was retained in its position, while the heavenly bodies themselves—viz., earth, moon, and sun—maintained their actual course (for the sun moves). Nor, again, can we accept the view of some, that it was the *night*, not the *day*, that was specially prolonged. The word used for the sun's standing still is peculiar, and signifies to be *dumb* or *silent*. We may compare with this metaphor the words of Ps. xix. 3, 4, "There is no speech nor language, where their *voice* is not heard. Their line is gone out through all the earth, and *their words* to the end of the world." Joshua's command was that the sun should for the time silence that penetrating voice, and be dumb from those all-prevailing words. Translated into technical language, the command would be to suspend the motion of the earth round its axis, and that of the moon round the earth. At the same time the earth was left free to move round the sun, and the moon to revolve (if it does revolve) on its own axis. The objection which we sometimes hear, that if the earth had stopped in its orbit it would have fallen into the sun, is nothing to the purpose (supposing its Maker to have arrested its motion in such an imperfect and clumsy manner), for Joshua did not ask that it should cease to move in its orbit, only that it should cease the revolution which causes day and night to succeed each other at fixed intervals. Gravitation does not touch this.

How the miracle was done we are not informed. But if we understand the narrative literally, the problem is, How to suspend the motion of the earth upon its axis, and the motion of the moon round the earth, for twelve hours, the earth being free to move round the sun, and the moon free to revolve upon her axis, if these motions are independent of the others. And if they are not independent, it is not easy to say why a perfect soli-lunar cycle is not more readily obtained. This problem should be solved before men can assert the thing to be impossible. The late Professor Mozley has well shown, in his Bampton Lectures, that the presumption against a miracle of this kind is not a *reasonable* presumption. For, on the other hand, the presumption that the sun will rise to-morrow, and that the day will be of a given length, is not based upon *reason* at all, however strongly it may be felt by mankind. But many who do not doubt that the Creator *could* perform the miracle (as easily as an engine-driver can stop an engine at full speed, or a skilful finger arrest the progress of a watch without injury to the works), nevertheless hesitate to believe that He *would* have done such a thing under the stated circumstances and for the proposed end. The answer to this objection is, that the history of the chosen people in Holy Scripture is a series of miracles. The miracles of Moses and Elijah and Elisha are not less wonderful than this. The three days' darkness in Egypt, the sign that was given to Hezekiah, which brought inquirers from Babylon (2 Chron. xxxii. 31), the star that conducted the wise men from the East to Bethlehem, and the miraculous darkness at the crucifixion, were wonders of the same kind. Holy Scripture expressly informs us that there will be "signs in the sun and in the moon and in the stars." Astronomers speak calmly of the possibility of the extinction of the solar fires. Can they tell us what would be the effect of a partial, gradual, or momentary extinction? At least Holy Scripture is consistent throughout, in the view that the God of Israel never spared a sign or a wonder that might further His purposes towards His people. As for the remark made by one commentator, that the silence of other contemporary records is a presumption against the miracle in its literal sense, we ask, Where are the contemporary records that are silent?

At the same time, if any one finds it easier to believe that the motions of the earth, sun, and moon were continued, and the light only was arrested in its course, the Scripture does not forbid that view. But there is still a question left unsolved even then. Why did Joshua bid the moon stand still as well as the sun to be silent? In any case, indeed, this is a remarkable feature of the story. It must not be forgotten that while we know the law and rate of the earth's motion, we do not entirely understand what the CAUSE of the motion is, and therefore it is impossible to state what must be done in order to arrest the motion for a time.

Upon Gibeon; and . . . in the valley of Ajalon.—The two prepositions are the same in Hebrew. It seems to be an order that the sun should not go down, and the moon cease to rise.

(13) **And the sun stood still, and the moon stayed.**—Literally, *the sun was silent, and the moon stopped*.

The sun stood still (*i.e.*, stopped) **in the midst of heaven.**—Literally, *in the half of the heavens*—*i.e.*, either " in the midst of heaven," or " in the same hemisphere " (in the one-half of the heavens).

And hasted not to go down (or *to go in*) **about a whole day.**—The word cannot mean *to rise*, or *ascend*, and thus these words absolutely exclude the view that what Joshua desired was to prevent the sun from rising, in order to complete a night attack upon the Amorites.

(14) **And there was no day like that before it or after it.**—These words are meaningless, unless the writer intended to convey the idea that there was really a great miracle. We may compare the prophecy in Isaiah xxx. 26, " Moreover, the light of the moon shall be as the light of the sun, and the light of the sun shall be sevenfold, as the light of seven days, in the day when the Lord bindeth up the breach of His people, and healeth the stroke of their wound."

(15) **Unto the camp to Gilgal.**—This verse relates by anticipation, in the words of the Book of Jasher

(16) But these five kings fled, and hid themselves in a cave at Makkedah. (17) And it was told Joshua, saying, The five kings are found hid in a cave at Makkedah. (18) And Joshua said, Roll great stones upon the mouth of the cave, and set men by it for to keep them: (19) and stay ye not, *but* pursue after your enemies, and ¹smite the hindmost of them; suffer them not to enter into their cities: for the LORD your God hath delivered them into your hand. (20) And it came to pass, when Joshua and the children of Israel had made an end of slaying them with a very great slaughter, till they were consumed, that the rest *which* remained of them entered into fenced cities. (21) And all the people returned to the camp to Joshua at Makkedah in peace: none moved his tongue against any of the children of Israel.

(22) Then said Joshua, Open the mouth of the cave, and bring out those five kings unto me out of the cave. (23) And they did so, and brought forth those five kings unto him out of the cave, the king of Jerusalem, the king of Hebron, the king of Jarmuth, the king of Lachish, *and* the king of Eglon. (24) And it came to pass, when they brought out those kings unto Joshua, that Joshua called for all the men of Israel, and said unto the captains of the men of war which went with him, Come near, put your feet upon the necks of these kings. And they came near, and put their feet upon the necks of them. (25) And Joshua said unto them, Fear not, nor be dismayed, be strong and of good courage: for thus shall the LORD do to all your enemies against whom ye fight. (26) And afterward Joshua smote them, and slew them, and hanged them on five trees: and they were hanging upon the trees until the evening. (27) And it came to pass at the time of the going down of the sun, *that* Joshua commanded, and they *ᵃ* took them down off the trees, and cast them into the cave wherein they had been hid, and laid great stones in the cave's mouth, *which remain* until this very day.

(28) And that day Joshua took Makkedah, and smote it with the edge of the sword, and the king thereof he utterly destroyed, them, and all the souls that *were* therein; he let none remain: and he did to the king of Makkedah *ᵇ* as he did unto the king of Jericho.

(29) Then Joshua passed from Makkedah, and all Israel with him, unto Libnah, and fought against Libnah:

1 Heb., *cut off the tail.*

ᵃ Deut. 21. 23; ch. 8. 29.

ᵇ ch. 6. 21.

(Heb., *Yâshar*, upright), what we find in the narrative of Joshua at verse 43, viz., the return to Gilgal at the close of this campaign. The immediate return, at the end of the miraculous day's operations, was to *Makkedah*, not to Gilgal (see verse 21).

(16) **In a cave.**—Literally, *in the cave in Makkedah*, and so verse 17.

(19) **Smite the hindmost of them.**—See Deut. xxv. 18, the only other place where the same Hebrew verb occurs.

For the Lord your God hath delivered them into your hand.—It is worth while to observe that the command given to Israel to exterminate the Canaanites, though perfectly general, is notwithstanding limited as to time and circumstances by this very condition, in Deut. vii., verses 1, 2, "when the Lord thy God shall bring thee in, . . . and hath cast out . . . before thee . . . seven nations, *and when the Lord thy God shall deliver them before thee*, thou shalt smite them and utterly destroy them." Again, verse 16, "Thou shalt consume all the people which the Lord thy God *shall deliver thee*," and verse 22, "The Lord thy God will put out those nations before thee by little and little; thou mayest not consume them at once." The extermination of each particular army or nation was to be determined (as to time and circumstances) by the mandate of Jehovah, whose guidance Israel must follow on all occasions. The present occasion was one for pursuit and slaughter without respite or delay. But though the army, as an army, was annihilated, a remnant of fugitives escaped into fortified places (verse 20).

(24) **The captains.**—The original word occurs here for the first time (see Judges xi. 6, 11), and seems to mean the *actual leaders*, not merely the official heads, of the people, who had borne the brunt of the battle. These men having laboured, deserved to see the fruits of their labour; and the action of Joshua was well calculated to inspirit them, and to fire them with courage to lead their followers to the charge in battles that were yet to come.

Put your feet upon the necks of these kings. —Comp. 2 Sam. xxii. 41, "Thou hast also given me the necks of mine enemies;" and Gen. xlix. 8.

(25) **Fear not, nor be dismayed, be strong and of good courage.**—The very words spoken to Joshua by Jehovah (chap. i. 9) with the exception of the word for *fear*, which is stronger in chap. i. 9. Even ordinary fear is needless. Alarm is not to be thought of.

(26) **And hanged them.**—Here the hanging appears to have been a token of disgrace after death. Upon the cross of the true Joshua, the enemies of the Israel of God are exhibited. "He made a shew of them openly, triumphing over them in it" (Col. ii. 15).

(28) **Joshua took Makkedah.**—Perhaps better, *had taken—i.e.*, before the execution of the five kings.

(29) **Then.**—Better, simply *and*. The operations against Libnah are the commencement of a further

(30) and the LORD delivered it also, and the king thereof, into the hand of Israel; and he smote it with the edge of the sword, and all the souls that *were* therein; he let none remain in it; but did unto the king thereof as he did unto the king of Jericho.

(31) And Joshua passed from Libnah, and all Israel with him, unto Lachish, and encamped against it, and fought against it: (32) and the LORD delivered Lachish into the hand of Israel, which took it on the second day, and smote it with the edge of the sword, and all the souls that *were* therein, according to all that he had done to Libnah.

(33) Then Horam king of Gezer came up to help Lachish; and Joshua smote him and his people, until he had left him none remaining.

(34) And from Lachish Joshua passed unto Eglon, and all Israel with him; and they encamped against it, and fought against it: (35) and they took it on that day, and smote it with the edge of the sword, and all the souls that *were* therein he utterly destroyed that day, according to all that he had done to Lachish.

(36) And Joshua went up from Eglon, and all Israel with him, unto Hebron; and they fought against it: (37) and they took it, and smote it with the edge of the sword, and the king thereof, and all the cities thereof, and all the souls that *were* therein; he left none remaining, according to all that he had done to Eglon; but destroyed it utterly, and all the souls that *were* therein.

(38) And Joshua returned, and all Israel with him, to Debir; and fought against it: (39) and he took it, and the king thereof, and all the cities thereof; and they smote them with the edge of the sword, and utterly destroyed all the souls that *were* therein; he left none remaining: as he had done to Hebron, so he did to Debir, and to the king thereof; as he had done also to Libnah, and to her king.

(40) So Joshua smote all the country of the hills, and of the south, and of the vale, and of the springs, and all their kings: he left none remaining, but utterly destroyed all that breathed, as the LORD God of Israel *a* commanded. (41) And Joshua smote them from Kadesh-barnea even unto Gaza, and all the country of Goshen, even unto Gibeon. (42) And all these kings and their land

a Deut. 20. 16, 17.

---

stage of the campaign. Libnah has not been identified; but see chap. xv. 42.

(31) **Lachish** has been variously identified, (1) as Um-Làkis; (2) Zukkanjek; (3) Tell-el-Hesy, near Eglon. It cannot have been far from this latter place.

(32) **On the second day.**—With this fact we may connect two other facts of later history. When Sennacherib, king of Assyria, "came up against all the fenced cities of Judah and took them" (2 Kings xviii. 13), although he "laid siege to Lachish, and all his power with him" (2 Chron. xxxii. 9), he had to abandon the siege (2 Kings xix. 8). Again, when Nebuchadnezzar invaded the kingdom of Judah in the reign of Zedekiah, the last king, we read (Jer. xxxiv. 7) of his army fighting "against Jerusalem and against all the cities of Judah that were left, against Lachish and against Azekah, for these defenced cities remained of the cities of Judah." All these notices of Lachish point to its being a fortress of considerable strength. And the undesigned and indirect agreement of these three passages, which lie so far asunder, is worthy of observation.

(33) **Gezer** is identified as Tell-Jezer or Tel-el-Jezar, about four miles from Amwâs or Emmaus.

(38) **Debir** is not identified.

(40) **Of the hills**—*i.e.*, the mountains of Judah and Ephraim.

The south—*i.e.*, the Nêgeb.

The vale—*i.e.*, Shephêlah, the plain of the coast, but not apparently including the Philistine territory, which was not conquered by Joshua.

The springs—or *Ashdoth*. Some render it the slopes or declivities, the country between the high hills and the low plain of the coast.

(41) **From Kadesh-barnea** (on the south-east) **even unto Gaza** (on the west, now Ghazzeh in Philistia), **and all the country of Goshen** (from the south to Gibeon in a northerly direction).

And all the country of Goshen.—This expression creates some difficulty. Goshen has been thought to be the town of that name mentioned in chap. xv. 51; but it is inconceivable that a single place of no importance in the mountains of Judah should give the name to an extensive district, which is manifestly intended here. If we knew the exact northern boundary of the land of Goshen assigned for a distinct residence to Joseph's brethren in Egypt, it might help to clear up the meaning of this passage. That Goshen, at its Egyptian end, bordered upon the Delta is clear. But how far did Goshen extend towards the north? In 1 Chron. vii. 21, 22, we find that Ephraim's children *in his lifetime* made an incursion into Canaan as far as Gath. But this was during the time that Israel dwelt in the land of Goshen. Did they suppose that they were in the land of Goshen when they plundered the men of Gath? If Goshen (frontier) could be the general name for the *border-land* between Egypt and Palestine, we can understand that the borders might vary with the power of the Egyptian monarchy for the time being. The country of Goshen, *unto Gibeon*, seems to be described from south to north; Gibeon being intended as the northern boundary.

did Joshua take at one time, because the LORD God of Israel fought for Israel. ⁽⁴³⁾ And Joshua returned, and all Israel with him, unto the camp to Gilgal.

CHAPTER XI.—⁽¹⁾ And it came to pass, when Jabin king of Hazor had heard *those things*, that he sent to Jobab king of Madon, and to the king of Shimron, and to the king of Achshaph, ⁽²⁾ and to the kings that *were* on the north of the mountains, and of the plains south of Chinneroth, and in the valley, and in the borders of Dor on the west, ⁽³⁾ *and to* the Canaanite on the east and on the west, and *to* the Amorite, and the Hittite, and the Perizzite, and the Jebusite in the mountains, and *to* the Hivite under Hermon in the land of Mizpeh. ⁽⁴⁾ And they went out, they and all their hosts with them, much people, even as the sand that *is* upon the sea shore in multitude, with horses and chariots very many. ⁽⁵⁾ And when all these kings were ¹ met together, they came and pitched together at the waters of Merom, to fight against Israel.

⁽⁶⁾ And the LORD said unto Joshua, Be not afraid because of them: for to morrow about this time will I deliver them up all slain before Israel: thou shalt hough their horses, and burn their chariots with fire. ⁽⁷⁾ So Joshua came, and all the people of war with him, against them by the waters of Merom suddenly; and they fell upon them. ⁽⁸⁾ And the LORD delivered them into the hand of Israel, who smote them, and chased them unto ² great Zidon, and unto ³ ⁴ Misrephoth-maim, and unto the valley of Mizpeh eastward; and they smote them, until they left them none remaining. ⁽⁹⁾ And Joshua did unto them as the LORD bade him: he houghed their horses, and burnt their chariots with fire.

⁽¹⁰⁾ And Joshua at that time turned back, and took Hazor, and smote the king thereof with the sword: for Hazor beforetime was the head of all those kingdoms. ⁽¹¹⁾ And they smote all the souls that *were* therein with the edge of the sword, utterly destroying *them:* there was not ⁵ any left to breathe: and he burnt Hazor with fire. ⁽¹²⁾ And all the cities of those kings, and all the kings of them, did Joshua take, and smote them with the edge of the sword, *and* he utterly destroyed them, ᵃ as Moses the servant of the LORD commanded. ⁽¹³⁾ But *as for* the cities that stood still ⁶ in their strength, Israel burned none of them, save Hazor only; *that* did Joshua burn. ⁽¹⁴⁾ And all the spoil of these cities, and the cattle, the children of Israel took for a prey unto themselves; but every man they smote with the edge of the sword, until they had destroyed them, neither left they any to breathe. ⁽¹⁵⁾ ᵇ As the LORD commanded Moses his servant, so ᶜ did Moses command Joshua, and so did Joshua; ⁷ he left nothing undone of all that the LORD commanded Moses.

¹ Heb., *assembled by appointment.*
² Or, *Zidon-rabbah.*
B.C. 1450.
³ Or, *salt pits.*
⁴ Heb., *burning of waters.*
⁵ Heb., *any breath.*
ᵃ Num. 33. 52; Deut. 7. 2, & 20. 16, 17.
⁶ Heb., *on their heap.*
ᵇ Ex. 34. 11.
ᶜ Deut. 7. 2
⁷ Heb., *he removed nothing.*

⁽⁴³⁾ **The camp to Gilgal.**—A central position, with Jordan and the conquered territory of the two and a half tribes in the rear.

XI.

JOSHUA'S NORTHERN CAMPAIGN.

⁽¹⁾ **Jabin king of Hazor** seems to have been in northern Palestine what Adonizedec, king of Jerusalem, was in the south. For the strength of this monarchy see the story in Judges iv., v. From its formidable character when it recovered strength in the days of the judges, we may gather some notion of what it was at first.

Hazor is identified as *Jebel Hadîrah,* near *Kedes,* in Upper Galilee.

Madon, perhaps *Madîn,* west of the Sea of Galilee.

Shimron is identified as *Simûnieh,* west of Nazareth.

⁽²⁾ **Chinneroth**—*i.e., Ginizer,* the Gennesaret of the New Testament.

Dor is identified as *Tantûra.*

⁽³⁾ **The land of Mizpeh** is thought to be the plain El-Bukei'a, west of Hermon.

⁽⁵⁾ **The waters of Merom.**—The most northerly of the three lakes on the course of the Jordan.

⁽⁶⁾ **Thou shalt hough their horses.**—See Note on verse 9, and observe that the command of Jehovah is the authority for the act.

⁽⁷⁾ **Suddenly.**—On this occasion, as in the former campaign which began at Gibeon, Joshua surprised his adversaries by the rapidity of his movements.

⁽⁸⁾ **Misrephoth-maim** is thought to be the same with Zarephath or Sarepta, now *Sarafend,* near Sidon.

⁽⁹⁾ **He houghed their horses.**—In what particular way this was done we are not informed; we cannot, therefore, be certain whether it was done so as to destroy the lives of the horses, or merely to make them useless for purposes of warfare.

⁽¹³⁾ **The cities that stood still in their strength.**—Literally, *that stood on their mounds* ("quæ erant in collibus et in tumulis sitæ."—Vulg.). Comp. verse 20. We may fairly suppose that Jericho and Ai committed themselves to hostile measures against Israel, though they were not able to send forth armies against Joshua before they were attacked. Those who "stood still *in their strength*" are those who remained absolutely

Divers Wars.   JOSHUA, XII.   *Rest from War.*

(16) So Joshua took all that land, the hills, and all the south country, and all the land of Goshen, and the valley, and the plain, and the mountain of Israel, and the valley of the same; (17) even from ¹the mount Halak, that goeth up to Seir, even unto Baal-gad in the valley of Lebanon under mount Hermon: and all their kings he took, and smote them, and slew them. (18) Joshua made war a long time with all those kings. (19) There was not a city that made peace with the children of Israel, save *a* the Hivites the inhabitants of Gibeon: all *other* they took in battle. (20) For it was of the LORD to harden their hearts, that they should come against Israel in battle, that he might destroy them utterly, *and* that they might have no favour, but that he might destroy them, as the LORD commanded Moses.

(21) And at that time came Joshua, and cut off the Anakims from the mountains, from Hebron, from Debir, from Anab, and from all the mountains of Judah, and from all the mountains of Israel: Joshua destroyed them utterly with their cities. (22) There was none of the Anakims left in the land of the children of Israel: only in Gaza, in Gath, and in Ashdod, there remained. (23) So Joshua took the whole land, according to all that the LORD said unto Moses; and Joshua gave it for an inheritance unto Israel *b* according to their divisions by their tribes. And the land rested from war.

CHAPTER XII.—(1) Now these *are* the kings of the land, which the children of Israel smote, and possessed their land on the other side Jordan toward the rising of the sun, from the river Arnon unto mount Hermon, and all the plain on the east: (2) *c* Sihon king of the Amorites, who dwelt in Heshbon, *and* ruled from Aroer, which *is* upon the bank of the river Arnon, and from the middle of the river, and from half Gilead, even unto the river Jabbok, *which is* the border of the children of Ammon; (3) and from the plain to the sea of Chinneroth on the east, and unto the sea of the plain, *even* the salt sea on the east, the way to Beth-jeshimoth; and from ²the south, under ³*d* Ashdoth-pisgah: (4) and the coast of Og king of Bashan, *which was* of *e* the remnant of the giants, that dwelt at Ashtaroth and at Edrei, (5) and reigned in mount Hermon, and in Salcah, and in all Bashan, unto the border of the Geshurites and the Maachathites, and half Gilead, the border of Sihon king of Heshbon. (6) Them did Moses the servant of the LORD and the children of Israel smite: and *f* Moses the servant of the LORD gave it *for* a possession unto the Reubenites, and the Gadites, and the half tribe of Manasseh.

---

neutral in the war. "The men of Jericho fought against you" (chap. xxiv. 11).

(17) **The mount Halak** is marked as unknown in Conder's Biblical Gazetteer. But "the smooth hill which goeth up to Seir," may very possibly be the salt hill now called *Khasur-Usdum*, which has a glacier-like appearance, and forms a sufficiently striking object to be mentioned as a boundary-mark.

Baal-gad has by some been identified with Baal-hermon, afterwards *Paneas*, and Cæsarea Philippi. Others think it is still unknown.

(18) **A long time.**—See Note on chap. xiv. 10. The war seems to have lasted seven years, a long time when compared with the desultory incursions and single campaigns which made up the greater part of ancient warfare, when there were no standing armies.

(20) **It was of the Lord to harden their hearts . . . that he might destroy them.**—Or rather *to strengthen their heart*—*i.e.*, render them obstinate. These words go to prove what has been said elsewhere, that the conquest of Canaan was not intended to be a massacre of the unresisting inhabitants.

(21) **Anab** is identified with *Anâb*, west of Debir. The death of Ahiman, Sheshai, and Talmai, the three sons of Anak, the chiefs of the Anakim, is recorded in Judges i. 10.

(22) **Only in . . . Gath.**—Goliath of Gath and his gigantic relatives (1 Sam. xvii. and 2 Sam. xxi.) seem to have been a part of this remnant.

XII.
THIRD DIVISION OF THE BOOK.
SUMMARY OF THE CONQUERED TERRITORY.
(*a*) According to kings.

(2) **Sihon king of the Amorites . . .**—For a description of his territory see Deut. ii. 31—37.

(4) **Og king of Bashan.**—See Deut. iii. 59.

(6) **Them did Moses the servant of the Lord . . . smite.**—The continuity of the work of Moses and Joshua should be noticed. The land which God gave to Israel is made up of two portions: (1) a territory on the east of Jordan conquered by Moses, and given by him to two and a half tribes, as the "portion of the law-giver;" (2) a territory on the west of Jordan, of larger extent, conquered by Joshua, and given to nine and a half tribes. But the conquest of Canaan is *one* enterprise, begun by Moses and finished

(7) And these *are* the kings of the country which Joshua and the children of Israel smote on this side Jordan on the west, from .Baal-gad in the valley of Lebanon even unto *ᵃ*the mount Halak, that goeth up to Seir; which Joshua gave unto the tribes of Israel *for* a possession according to their divisions; (8) in the mountains, and in the valleys, and in the plains, and in the springs, and in the wilderness, and in the south country; the Hittites, the Amorites, and the Canaanites, the Perizzites, the Hivites, and the Jebusites: (9) *ᵇ*the king of Jericho, one; *ᶜ*the king of Ai, which *is* beside Beth-el, one; (10) *ᵈ*the king of Jerusalem, one; the king of Hebron, one; (11) the king of Jarmuth, one; the king of Lachish, one; (12) the king of Eglon, one; *ᵉ*the king of Gezer, one; (13) *ᶠ*the king of Debir, one; the king of Geder, one; (14) the king of Hormah, one; the king of Arad, one; (15) *ᵍ*the king of Libnah, one; the king of Adullam, one; (16) *ʰ*the king of Makkedah, one; the king of Beth-el, one; (17) the king of Tappuah, one; the king of Hepher, one; (18) the king of Aphek, one; the king of ¹Lasharon, one; (19) the king of Madon, one; *ⁱ*the king of Hazor, one; (20) the king of Shimron-meron, one; the king of Achshaph, one; (21) the king of Taanach, one; the king of Megiddo, one; (22) the

ᵃ ch. 11. 17.
ᵇ ch. 6. 2.
ᶜ ch. 8. 29.
ᵈ ch. 10. 23.
ᵉ ch. 10. 33.
ᶠ ch. 10. 38.
ᵍ ch. 10. 29.
ʰ ch. 10. 28.
¹ Or, *Sharon.*
ⁱ ch. 11. 10.

by Joshua. And the land of Israel is one country, though divided by Jordan into two portions. The analogy between the work of Moses and Joshua in this literal conquest, and the work of Moses and the true Joshua in respect of the inheritance of the Church of God, which was partly won before the passage of Jordan—*i.e.*, before the death of Christ—but much more afterwards, is too plain to be overlooked.

(7) **And these are the kings of the country which Joshua . . . smote.**—There are two kings reckoned to Moses, and thirty-one to Joshua; making a total of thirty-three. Yet the two slain by Moses are individually represented as far greater than any who are named in this book. And in the Psalms, in more than one place, we have "Sihon king of the Amorites, and Og the king of Bashan" expressed by name, and the rest only summarised, as "all the kingdoms of Canaan" (Pss. cxxxv. 11, 12 and cxxxvi. 19, 20.).

From Baal-gad . . . unto the mount Halak. —See chap. xi. 17.

(9–24) These verses give a list of the thirty-one kings defeated by Joshua. The order of the conquest is followed. We have first the kings of Jericho and Ai; (2) the kings overcome in the southern campaign (chap. x.) from the king of Jerusalem (verse 10) to the king of Makkedah (verse 16). Among these, the kings of Geder, Hormah, Arad, and Adullam have not been previously mentioned in Joshua, nor is the capture of Jarmuth mentioned. The names Hormah and Arad both occur in Num. xxi. 1, 3, where the town of Arad is, after its destruction by Israel, called Hormah. As the *cities* of the king of Arad are mentioned in that place, it is possible that the Hormah and Arad of this chapter may both be of the number. Or they may be different places. It is also just possible that the capture of those cities may be mentioned in Num. xxi. by anticipation, and that the attack of Arad on Israel was not fully avenged until the conquest of Canaan by Joshua. (3) We next read of the kings conquered in the rest of the country, whose cities ranged from Bethel on the south to Hazor on the north. Of the capture of these cities we have no details, with the exception of Hazor (chap. xi. 10). And it should be carefully noticed how very few of them are in the centre of the country.

The cities mentioned in verses 9—16 have all been mentioned before, with the exception of Geder, verse 13 (the Geder of chap. xv. 58), which is identified as *Jedûr*, in the Hebron mountains.

(16–24) The town of Bethel, on the borders of Benjamin and Ephraim, which passed from the one tribe to the other (Josh. xviii. 22 and 1 Kings xii. 29), seems to mark the geographical transition in this list from the territory conquered in the southern campaign of Joshua, to that which he conquered in his northern campaign.

(17) **Tappuah.**—There were two cities of this name —viz., one in Judah (chap. xv. 34) and one in Ephraim (chaps. xvi. 8 and xvii. 8). The latter is probably intended here. This town was on the borders of Ephraim and Manasseh, and nearly *all* the towns that follow, so far as identified, lie in a northerly direction. This confirms the opinion already expressed, that a large portion of the centre of Palestine was comparatively uncleared and unoccupied at the time of the conquest.

Hepher is not identified, unless it could be the same as *Gath-hepher* or *Gittah-hepher* in Zebulun (chap. xix. 13).

(18) **Aphek** is a name belonging to *six* different towns, according to Conder, who does not, however, profess to identify this one. Three of those which he does identify lie in the northern districts.

Lasharon.—Rather, perhaps, *Sharon* (the first syllable seems to be the Hebrew prefix "to the"). Sharon, in every place (except *one*) where the name occurs in the Old Testament, has the definite article, and appears as *Hassharon*; and so in the critical text of Acts ix. 35, *Assaron* rather than Saron. It is *the* Sharon, or plain; and the king of Lasharon seems to mean the king of that district. Madon, Hazor, and Shimron-meron have been identified as northern towns in chap. xi.

(20) **Achshaph** is thought to be *El-Yasif*, in the tribe of Asher.

(21) **Taanach** is Tânah, in the territory of Issachar, but belonging to Manasseh (chap. xvii. 11). Megiddo, though famous in Old Testament history, is not yet identified with certainty, though it appears to survive in *Mujedd'a*, in the plain of Jezreel, near *Beisan* (Bethshan).

(22) **Kedesh** is probably Kedesh-Naphtali, and survives in *Kedes*. There are two others, according to

The Boundaries   JOSHUA, XIII.   *of the Territory*

king of Kedesh, one; the king of Jokneam of Carmel, one; ⁽²³⁾ the king of Dor in the coast of Dor, one; the king of *a* the nations of Gilgal, one; ⁽²⁴⁾ the king of Tirzah, one: all the kings thirty and one.

CHAPTER XIII. — ⁽¹⁾ Now Joshua was old *and* stricken in years; and the LORD said unto him, Thou art old *and* stricken in years, and there remaineth yet very much land ¹to be possessed. ⁽²⁾ This *is* the land that yet remaineth: all the borders of the Philistines, and all Geshuri, ⁽³⁾ from Sihor, which *is* before Egypt, even unto the borders of Ekron northward, *which* is counted to the Canaanite: five lords of the Philistines; the Gazathites, and the Ashdothites, the Eshkalonites, the Gittites, and the Ekronites; also the Avites: ⁽⁴⁾ from the south, all the land of the Canaanites, and ² Mearah that *is* beside the Sidonians, unto Aphek, to the borders of the Amorites: ⁽⁵⁾ and the land of the Giblites, and all Lebanon, toward the sunrising, from Baal-gad under mount Hermon unto the entering into Hamath. ⁽⁶⁾ All the inhabitants of the hill country from Lebanon unto Misrephoth-maim, *and* all the Sidonians, them will I drive out from before the children of Israel: only divide thou it by lot unto the Israelites for an inheritance, as I have commanded thee. ⁽⁷⁾ Now therefore divide this land for an inheritance unto the nine tribes, and the half tribe of Manasseh, ⁽⁸⁾ with whom the Reubenites and the Gadites have received their inheritance, *b* which Moses gave them, beyond Jordan eastward, *even* as Moses the servant of the LORD gave them; ⁽⁹⁾ from Aroer, that *is* upon the bank of the river Arnon, and the

a Gen. 14. 1.

1 Heb., *to possess it.*

B.C. 1445.

2 Or, *the cave.*

b Num. 32. 33; Deut. 3. 13; ch. 22. 4.

Conder. 1 Chron. (vi. 72 and 76) proves that there are *two* places of the name; but is he right in supposing that the Kedesh of Judges iv. 11 differs from Kedesh-Naphtali in Judges iv. 6? Jokneam of Carmel is identified as *Tell Keimûn*.

⁽²³⁾ **Dor**—*i.e.*, *Tantûra*.

Gilgal (there are three places of this name also) is probably Jiljilieh, in the plain of Sharon.

⁽²⁴⁾ **Tirzah** is thought to be *Teiasir*, in the territory of Manasseh.

XIII.

DESCRIPTION OF THE TERRITORY TO BE DIVIDED (verses 1—14).

(b) According to its boundaries.

⁽¹⁾ **Joshua was old and stricken in years.**—Rather, *he had aged, and was advanced in days.* Old is too absolute a word. He did not live beyond a hundred and ten years (chap. xxiv. 29), and this was not a great age for the time. But in several instances the Hebrew word here employed is used not so much in respect of the number of years men lived, but rather in regard to the weakening of the vital powers. So it is said in Gen. xxvii., "Isaac was old," *i.e.*, he had aged, for he lived forty-three years after that. So in regard to David, "the king was very old," *i.e.*, much aged, in 1 Kings i. 15, for he could not have been more than seventy when he died. The hardships and anxieties of his life had aged him. So it was perhaps with Joshua. Moses was a signal exception; he had not aged at one hundred and twenty. But Jehovah constantly talked with Moses, and knew him face to face; and may we not say that *that* heavenly intercourse even sustained the vital powers? The work of the Lord, though it be successfully carried on, as it was by Joshua, may wear men out by its very excitement. But personal intercourse with Him is like eating of the tree of life, and "in His presence is the fulness of joy." In this personal intercourse Moses was more highly favoured than his successor, Joshua.

^(1, 7) **There remaineth yet very much land to be possessed . . . Now therefore divide this land.**—The land had still to be *inherited*—*i.e.*, not overrun, or conquered, as far as it could be said to be conquered by defeating the armies that took the field; all this was done already, but the land had not passed out of the hands of its actual possessors into the hands of Israel. It is remarkable that we have here a distinct order given to Joshua to divide to Israel land which was *not yet conquered*. In these verses several nations are named—viz., the Philistines, the Geshurites, the Avites, the Giblites, the Sidonians, besides anything more which may be included in the sometimes generic, and sometimes more specific, name of the Canaanites. Of these tribes, the Philistines and "all the Sidonians" (or Phœnicians) were certainly not yet conquered. Can we say that they were ever conquered at any period in the history of the kingdom of all Israel, except in so far as they were reduced to the condition of tributaries?

We may say, then, that while the list of kings in chap. xii. represents the territory in that aspect in which it was conquered, by the reduction of a number of fortified posts and strongholds, and the subjugation of all the principal rulers of the country, the description of its boundaries in chap. xiii. represents it as not yet conquered—viz., as still containing several nations whom the Israelites must dispossess when God gave them the opportunity and ordered them to drive them out.

It is important to mark clearly the distinction between the work done by Joshua and the work left for Israel. Joshua overthrew the ruling powers of Palestine, destroyed the kingdoms, defeated the armies, and captured the fortresses to such an extent as to give Israel a firm foothold in the country. But he did not exterminate the population from every portion even of that territory which he distributed to the several tribes. And there were several nations—of whom the Philistines and Phœnicians were the chief—whom he left entirely intact. The purpose of this is

city that *is* in the midst of the river, and all the plain of Medeba unto Dibon; (10) and all the cities of Sihon king of the Amorites, which reigned in Heshbon, unto the border of the children of Ammon; (11) and Gilead, and the border of the Geshurites and Maachathites, and all mount Hermon, and all Bashan unto Salcah; (12) all the kingdom of Og in Bashan, which reigned in Ashtaroth and in Edrei, who remained of ªthe remnant of the giants: for these did Moses smite, and cast them out. (13) Nevertheless the children of Israel expelled not the Geshurites, nor the Maachathites: but the Geshurites and the Maachathites dwell among the Israelites until this day. (14) Only unto the tribe of Levi he gave none inheritance; the sacrifices of the LORD God of Israel made by fire *are* their inheritance, as he said unto them.

(15) And Moses gave unto the tribe of the children of Reuben *inheritance* according to their families. (16) And their coast was from Aroer, that *is* on the bank of the river Arnon, and the city that *is* in the midst of the river, and all the plain by Medeba; (17) Heshbon, and all her cities that *are* in the plain; Dibon, and ¹Bamoth-baal, and Beth-baal-meon, (18) and Jahaza, and Kedemoth, and Mephaath, (19) and Kirjathaim, and Sibmah, and Zareth-

ª Deut. 3. 11; ch. 12. 4.

¹ Or, *The high places of Baal, and house of Baal-meon.*

---

explained in Judges ii. 20—23 and iii. 1—4. The work done by Joshua was thus distinctly limited.

The work left for Israel was partly similar to that which Joshua had done, and partly different. It was the same when any great war broke out between Israel and the unconquered nations: for example, in the time of Deborah and Barak, or in the wars with the Philistines. But for the most part it was entirely different, and was the completion of the conquest of the land in detail throughout the several towns and villages. But how was this to be effected? Certainly *not* after the manner of the capture of Laish by the Danites, described in Judges (chap. xviii. 27), when they came "unto a people that were at quiet and secure; and they smote them with the edge of the sword, and burnt the city with fire." The rules laid down in the law of Moses were to be the guiding principle for Israel, as also for Joshua. The seventh and twelfth chapters of Deuteronomy give them clearly, and they are these.

(1) Utter extermination of the nations *when Jehovah should deliver them up*—*i.e.*, not at the pleasure of Israel, but at the Divine decree. The signal for this extermination was generally a determined and obstinate attack on Israel. "It was of the Lord to harden their hearts that they should come against Israel in battle, that He might destroy them utterly" (chap. xi. 20). But while they "stood still in their strength" (chap. xi. 13) they were usually unmolested.

(2) The destruction of all traces of idolatry in the conquered territory (Deut. xii. 1, 2: "In the land which the Lord God of thy fathers giveth thee to possess it ... ye shall utterly destroy all the places wherein the nations which ye shall possess served their gods ... overthrow their altars, and break their pillars, and ... hew down the graven images of their gods, and destroy the names of them out of that place." So also Deut. vii. 5, 25). All investigation of idolatrous practices and usages was forbidden (Deut. xii. 30).

(3) No covenant or treaty was to be made between Israel and the nations of Canaan, and all intermarriage was prohibited. (Deut. vii. 2, 3; comp. Josh. xxiii. 12, 13.)

Of these rules, the first entails responsibility, chiefly upon the leaders—as Joshua and his successors; the second and third, upon all the people. And on the observance or non-observance of the two latter rules the completion of the conquest in detail very much depended. It is obvious that the persistent and general destruction of objects of Canaanitish worship, with the refusal to make treaties or intermarry, would tend to perpetuate a state of irritation in the minds of the Canaanites. Had these rules been faithfully observed, there would have been constant outbreaks of hostility, terminating in the further and more rapid extermination of the enemies of Israel, or else in their absolute submission to Israelitish law; and thus the entire conquest would have been completed in a comparatively short time. But, in fact, the second and third rules were constantly broken. Mixed marriages were common, and idolatry was maintained instead of being destroyed. Hence Israelites and Canaanites were mingled together, and it became impossible to carry out Rule 1; for one set of inhabitants could not be exterminated without inflicting serious injury upon the other.

When we consider the above rules, it is impossible not to be struck with the wisdom of them when regarded as a means to the proposed end. We are also able to understand more clearly why so much stress was laid upon the necessity of adherence to the *Book of the Law* in Joshua's commission (chap. i. 6—8). The fact that these rules are *not* what human nature would be at all disposed to obey continuously and as a matter of set practice (have they ever been observed yet in any conquest recorded in history?) is worth noting, as a proof of the undesigned veracity of the story. It is a mark of thorough consistency between the law and the history of Israel. And if the authorship of Deuteronomy belonged to the late date which some claim for it, how could we account for the insertion of a law which was never kept, and could not be kept at the time when some suppose it was written? From the days of Solomon and thenceforward, the relation of the remnant of the conquered Canaanites to Israel was fixed. The Phœnicians and Philistines maintained a separate national existence to the last.

DESCRIPTION OF THE TERRITORY DISTRIBUTED BY MOSES ON THE EAST OF JORDAN
(verses 15—33).

(15) **Reuben.**—See also Num. xxxii. 33—42 and Deut. iii. 16, &c.

shahar in the mount of the valley, ⁽²⁰⁾ and Beth-peor, and *^{a 1}Ashdoth-pisgah, and Beth-jeshimoth, ⁽²¹⁾ and all the cities of the plain, and all the kingdom of Sihon king of the Amorites, which reigned in Heshbon, whom Moses smote *^b with the princes of Midian, Evi, and Rekem, and Zur, and Hur, and Reba, *which were* dukes of Sihon, dwelling in the country. ⁽²²⁾ Balaam also the son of Beor, the ² soothsayer, did the children of Israel slay with the sword among them that were slain by them. ⁽²³⁾ And the border of the children of Reuben was Jordan, and the border *thereof.* This *was* the inheritance of the children of Reuben after their families, the cities and the villages thereof.

⁽²⁴⁾ And Moses gave *inheritance* unto the tribe of Gad, *even* unto the children of Gad according to their families. ⁽²⁵⁾ And their coast was Jazer, and all the cities of Gilead, and half the land of the children of Ammon, unto Aroer that *is* before Rabbah; ⁽²⁶⁾ and from Heshbon unto Ramath-mizpeh, and Betonim; and from Mahanaim unto the border of Debir; ⁽²⁷⁾ and in the valley, Beth-aram, and Beth-nimrah, and Succoth, and Zaphon, the rest of the kingdom of Sihon king of Heshbon, Jordan and *his* border, *even* unto the edge of the sea of Chinnereth on the other side Jordan eastward. ⁽²⁸⁾ This *is* the inheritance of the children of Gad after their families, the cities, and their villages.

⁽²⁹⁾ And Moses gave *inheritance* unto the half tribe of Manasseh: and *this* was *the possession* of the half tribe of the children of Manasseh by their families. ⁽³⁰⁾ And their coast was from Mahanaim, all Bashan, all the kingdom of Og king of Bashan, and all the towns of Jair, which *are* in Bashan, threescore cities: ⁽³¹⁾ and half Gilead, and Ashtaroth, and Edrei, cities of the kingdom of Og in Bashan, *were pertaining* unto the children of Machir the son of Manasseh, *even* to the one half of the *^c* children of Machir by their families.

⁽³²⁾ These *are the countries* which Moses did distribute for inheritance in the plains of Moab, on the other side Jordan, by Jericho, eastward. ^{(33) *d*} But unto the tribe of Levi Moses gave not *any* inheritance: the LORD God of Israel *was* their inheritance, *^e* as he said unto them.

CHAPTER XIV.—⁽¹⁾ And these *are the countries* which the children of Israel

---

⁽²¹⁾ **The princes of Midian . . . which were dukes of Sihon, dwelling in the country.**—The conquest of the Midianites is recorded in Num. xxxi. The orders given were, " Avenge the Lord of Midian " (verse 3); " avenge the children of Israel of the Midianites " (verse 2), because they tempted Israel to idolatry and uncleanness. But this verse in Joshua supplies us with a further reason for hostilities between Midian and Israel. The Midianites were " dukes of Sihon," and a part of his government. Through them he appears to have exercised his dominion over the conquered territory which he had taken from Moab. This land Israel had now, in turn, taken from him. But in order to its complete subjugation, the removal of Sihon's dukes, the princes or kings of Midian, was also necessary. This was brought about in the manner described in Num. xxii.—xxv., and xxxi. The relation between Midian and Moab which is *implied*, but not explained in Numbers, is explained by the apparently casual remark in this place. It is another example of undesigned agreement between Joshua and the Pentateuch. Of the same kind is the allusion to Balaam, as (verse 22) *the soothsayer*, or *diviner*. In Numbers we do not read of anything but prophecy and counsel as coming from Balaam's lips; but it is abundantly evident, from hints scattered through the story, that he was a *soothsayer*, or *diviner*, as well as a prophet. The elders of Moab and Midian went to him with the reward of *divination* in their hands (Num. xxii. 7); " Neither is there any *divination* against Israel " (Num. xxiii. 23) : the word in each of these places is radically connected with the epithet applied to Balaam here. (Comp. Num. xxiv. 1: " He went not, *as at other times,* to seek for *enchantments* "—where a different word is employed.) He is thus shown to have been an unscrupulous man, who, if he could not obtain the knowledge that he desired from above, would not hesitate to seek it from below, that he might secure his base gain.

XIV.

FOURTH DIVISION OF THE BOOK.

DIVISION OF THE TERRITORY ON THE WEST OF JORDAN TO NINE TRIBES AND A HALF
(chaps. xiv.—xix., inclusive).

⁽¹⁾ **And these are the countries which . . . Eleazar . . . and Joshua . . . distributed.**—Here we enter upon the record of the third portion of Joshua's great work. He had (1) to bring Israel over Jordan; (2) to conquer the land; (3) to divide it among the tribes.

Eleazar . . . and Joshua.—Not Joshua and Eleazar, observe. This is in strict accordance with the law of Moses, and the form of government which he was ordered to establish in Israel, to continue after his death. See Num. xxvii., where, in answer to Moses' prayer for a shepherd in Israel, the Lord says, " Take thee Joshua (here a figure of the great " Shepherd, the stone of Israel "), and lay thine hand upon him; and

inherited in the land of Canaan, *a* which Eleazar the priest, and Joshua the son of Nun, and the heads of the fathers of the tribes of the children of Israel, distributed for inheritance to them. (2) *b* By lot *was* their inheritance, as the LORD commanded by the hand of Moses, for the nine tribes, and *for* the half tribe. (3) For Moses had given the inheritance of two tribes and an half tribe on the other side Jordan: but unto the Levites he gave none inheritance among them. (4) For the children of Joseph were two tribes, Manasseh and Ephraim: therefore they gave no part unto the Levites in the land, save cities to dwell *in*, with their suburbs for their cattle and for their substance. (5) *c* As the LORD commanded Moses, so the children of Israel did, and they divided the land.

(6) Then the children of Judah came unto Joshua in Gilgal: and Caleb the son of Jephunneh the Kenezite said unto him, Thou knowest the thing that the LORD said unto Moses the man of God concerning me and thee in Kadesh-

a Num. 34. 17.

b Num. 26. 55, & 33. 54.

c Num. 35. 2; ch. 21. 2.

(verse 21) he (Joshua) shall stand before Eleazar the priest, who shall ask *counsel* for him after the judgment of Urim before the Lord; at his (Eleazar's) word they shall go out, and at his word they shall come in, both he (Joshua) and all the children of Israel with him, even all the congregation." (Comp. also Deut. xvii. 9: "Thou shalt come unto the *priests* (at the place which the Lord shall choose), and unto the *judge* that shall be in those days, and enquire; and they shall shew thee the sentence of judgment.") In these passages we see delineated the nature of the government established in Israel by Moses, to continue until there was a king. The priest had the *legislative* authority, the *executive power* rested with the *judge*. Of these judges, Joshua stands first; those who followed, until Samuel, held the same relation to the priest. Joshua was also a prophet. Samuel (a prophet likewise) established a third power in the constitution, and made the supreme executive power continuous and hereditary, giving to Israel a form of government by prophet, priest, and king. For the present, however, Eleazar the priest and Joshua the son of Nun (the answer to Moses' prayer for a shepherd) were the rulers. "To lead them out and to bring them in" was what Moses asked that the shepherd of Israel might do. Joshua had led them out to victory; he was now to bring in each of the tribes into the home that the Lord had chosen for it in the promised land.

And the heads of the fathers of the tribes of the children of Israel.—These men are all *named* in Num. xxxiv. 16—28: one from every tribe, in addition to Eleazar and Joshua. The names were then given by God to Moses, as the narrative states in verses 16—19. But is it not remarkable that before the land was conquered, in view of all the battles that were to be fought before it could be divided, the names of the men who were to divide it should be revealed? Man could not have arranged it so. The bow drawn at a venture, or one false step in the heat of battle, or the hurry of pursuit or flight, might have made a gap in the list. But it was not to be. "The Lord hath kept me alive," says Caleb (the first man after Joshua on this list) in verse 10. But all the twelve commissioners might have said the same. We cannot forbear to ask the question—Is it conceivable that, were the narrative in Num. xxxiv. anything but simple truth, it should contain such an unlikely statement as this? It will not do to say the names in the Book of Numbers were added afterwards; the form of the language in which they are given forbids this, and, with the single exception of Caleb, we know nothing of these twelve commissioners except their names.

(2) **By lot . . . as the Lord commanded . . . Moses.**—See Num. xxvi. 52—56 and xxxiv. 17—29.

The nine tribes, and for the half tribe; and (3) **For Moses had given;** and (4) **For the children of Joseph were two tribes.**—The argument of these verses can only mean that the tribal inheritances were to be *twelve in number*, and therefore the Levites were excluded from any distinct territorial position, for the children of Joseph were to be two tribes. Of Ephraim and Manasseh, Jacob had said to Joseph, "as Reuben and Simeon, they shall be mine:" *i.e.*, though grandsons, they shall count as sons of Jacob, and each one shall be the head of a tribe. Thus there are two ways of counting Jacob's sons, each making twelve; and these two seem to be recognised as distinct in Exod. xxviii. There we are told that the high priest should bear the names of the children of Israel on his shoulders *according to their birth* (*i.e.*, Joseph being counted as well as Levi, but not Ephraim and Manasseh). On his breastplate he must have them *according to the twelve tribes* (*i.e.*, Ephraim and Manasseh being specified, but Joseph and Levi left out). Both ways of reckoning were necessary in order that the complete Israel might be represented by the high priest. And in each way the number *twelve* was preserved and emphasised, as it is evidently intended to be in this place.

INHERITANCE OF JUDAH (verse 6 to chap. xv. 63).

(6) **Caleb the son of Jephunneh.**—Caleb was the commissioner appointed from the tribe of Judah to divide the land (Num. xxxiv. 19). His coming forward on this occasion to ask for his own inheritance first of all might appear to savour of self-interest, if the post of honour for which he applied had not been also the most dangerous and difficult position in the inheritance of his tribe. He applied for the territory of the gigantic sons of Anak, whom he undertook to drive out in the strength of Jehovah. Therefore "Joshua blessed him" and gave him Hebron for his inheritance. It is noticeable that of the two faithful spies whom Moses sent, Caleb received his inheritance *first*, and Joshua *last* of all Israel. (See chap. xix. 49.) The characters of the two men are well seen in this contrast—the one foremost in a service of danger; the other *last* to seek the things that were his own. Thus, "even Christ pleased not Himself" (comp. Joshua); but "the reproaches of them that reproached thee fell on me," as the conquest of the sons of Anak fell to the lot of Caleb. Observe how the slayer of Goliath is said to take away the *reproach* from Israel, 1 Sam. xvii. 26. "Who can stand before the children of Anak?"

barnea. ⁽⁷⁾ Forty years old *was* I when Moses the servant of the LORD sent me from Kadesh-barnea to espy out the land; and I brought him word again as *it was* in mine heart. ⁽⁸⁾ Nevertheless my brethren that went up with me made the heart of the people melt: but I wholly *ᵃ followed the LORD my God. ⁽⁹⁾ And Moses sware on that day, saying, Surely the land whereon thy feet have trodden shall be thine inheritance, and thy children's for ever, because thou hast wholly followed the LORD my God. ⁽¹⁰⁾ And now, behold, the LORD hath kept me alive, as he said, these forty and five years, even since the LORD spake this word unto Moses, while *the children of* Israel ¹wandered in the wilderness: and now, lo, I *am* this day fourscore and five years old. ⁽¹¹⁾ ᵇAs yet I *am as* strong this day as *I was* in the day that Moses sent me: as my strength *was* then, even so *is* my strength now, for war, both to go out, and to come in. ⁽¹²⁾ Now therefore give me

a Num. 14. 24.

¹ Heb., *walked.*

b Ecclus. 46. 9.

c ch. 21. 12, 1 Mac. 2. 56.

d ch. 15. 13.

B. C. 1444.

e Num. 34. 3.

f Num. 33. 36.

this mountain, whereof the LORD spake in that day; for thou heardest in that day how the Anakims *were* there, and *that* the cities *were* great *and* fenced: if so be the LORD *will be* with me, then I shall be able to drive them out, as the LORD said. ⁽¹³⁾ And Joshua blessed him, and gave unto Caleb the son of Jephunneh Hebron for an inheritance. ⁽¹⁴⁾ ᶜHebron therefore became the inheritance of Caleb the son of Jephunneh the Kenezite unto this day, because that he wholly followed the LORD God of Israel. ⁽¹⁵⁾ And ᵈthe name of Hebron before *was* Kirjath-arba; which Arba *was* a great man among the Anakims. And the land had rest from war.

CHAPTER XV. — ⁽¹⁾ *This* then was the lot of the tribe of the children of Judah by their families; *ᵉ even* to the border of Edom the *ᶠ* wilderness of Zin southward *was* the uttermost part of the south coast.

⁽⁷⁾ **Forty years old was I** . . . **and** ⁽¹⁰⁾ **I am this day fourscore and five years old.**—In this speech we have the only direct evidence as to the duration of the wars of Canaan under Joshua. The spies were sent from Kadesh-barnea in the second year of the Exodus, about 38½ years before the passage of Jordan (see Deut. ii. 14). Thus Caleb would be 40+38=78 years old when they crossed the Jordan. He was 85 when they began to divide the country. Therefore the conquest itself must have extended over a period of seven years. It is manifest that the record of the capture of Jericho and Ai, with the two campaigns of Joshua against the southern and northern confederacies, does not give *all* the details of the war.

⁽⁹⁾ **And Moses sware on that day** . . . **the land whereon thy feet have trodden shall be thine.**—Whether Moses referred to Hebron specifically in this promise, it is impossible to say.

⁽¹¹⁾ **As yet I am as strong this day** . . .—But by chap. xiii. 1, "Joshua had aged." Yet Joshua died at the age of 110, only 25 years older than Caleb was at this time. They were contemporaries. But the far greater responsibility lying upon Joshua (with a possible difference of temperament) may very naturally account for the one man's having aged so much more rapidly than the other.

⁽¹⁴⁾ **The Kenezite.**—This epithet seems to be connected with *Kenaz* (chap. xv. 17).

⁽¹⁵⁾ **Kirjath-arba.**—"Arba the father of Anak" (chap. xxi. 11). Arba means *four* in Hebrew, and therefore some have endeavoured to interpret it as the city of four. Rashi, for example, says it was "the city of Ahiman, and Sheshai, and Talmai, and their father." Others have tried to make it one of four confederate cities like Gibeon and its allies. But the text of Joshua seems to leave no doubt that Arba was a man's name, whatever may have been the occasion of his being so named. Unless the Anakim are of the same date as the Zuzim, and Rephaim, and Emim of Gen. xiv. (who are known to be giant races by Deut. ii. and iii.) Hebron must have been named Hebron before it was Kirjath-arba. But the text of Gen. xxiii. 2 seems to make *Kirjath-arba* the name of *the place where Sarah died, at the time of her death*; and it is perfectly possible that it was so. (See Note on Num. xiii. 22.)

A great man.—Rather, *the great man among the Anakim.*

And the land had rest from war.—This clause appears in chap. xi. 23, where its position is perfectly natural. It closes the record of the wars of Joshua. It is not so easily accounted for here. If we were quite certain at what period the Anakim were dispossessed and slain, we might connect it with that portion of the story; but see Note on chap. xv. 14, and also on the next verse.

XV.

⁽¹⁾ **This then was the lot.**—Rather, *And the lot came to the tribe of Judah.* We might perhaps better begin this section with the last sentence of chap. xiv., and read thus: "And the land had rest from war; and the lot fell to the tribe of Judah (*i.e.*, the tribe of Judah received its allotment), according to their families."

The question arises at this point how the position of the tribes of Judah, Ephraim, and Manasseh was determined. As to the remaining seven, see Note on chap. xviii. 5—10. It is noticeable that Hebron appears to have been promised to Caleb (chap. xiv. 12), and Shechem assigned to Joseph by Jacob (Gen. xlviii. 21, 22; Josh. xxiv. 32). Did not this necessarily bring the tribe of Judah into the south, the neighbourhood of Hebron, and Ephraim (with his brother Manasseh) into the centre of the country?

(2) And their south border was from the shore of the salt sea, from the ¹bay that looketh southward: (3) and it went out to the south side to ²Maaleh-acrabbim, and passed along to Zin, and ascended up on the south side unto Kadesh-barnea, and passed along to Hezron, and went up to Adar, and fetched a compass to Karkaa: (4) *from thence* it passed toward Azmon, and went out unto the river of Egypt; and the goings out of that coast were at the sea: this shall be your south coast.

(5) And the east border *was* the salt sea, *even* unto the end of Jordan.

And *their* border in the north quarter *was* from the bay of the sea at the uttermost part of Jordan: (6) and the border went up to Beth-hogla, and passed along by the north of Beth-arabah; and the border went up to the stone of Bohan the son of Reuben: (7) and the border went up toward Debir from the valley of Achor, and so northward, looking toward Gilgal, that *is* before the going up to Adummim, which *is* on the south side of the river: and the border passed toward the waters of En-shemesh, and the goings out thereof were at ᵃEn-rogel: (8) and the border went up by the valley of the son of Hinnom unto the south side of the Jebusite; the same *is* Jerusalem: and the border went up to the top of the mountain that *lieth* before the valley of Hinnom westward, which *is* at the end of the valley of the giants northward: (9) and the border was drawn from the top of the hill unto the fountain of the water of Nephtoah, and went out to the cities of mount Ephron; and the border was drawn to Baalah, which *is* Kirjath-jearim: (10) and the border compassed from Baalah westward unto mount Seir, and passed along unto the side of mount Jearim, which *is* Chesalon, on the north side, and went down to Beth-shemesh, and passed on to Timnah: (11) and the border went out

¹ Heb., *tongue.*

² Or, *The going up to Acrabbim.*

ᵃ 1 Kin. 1. 9.

---

(2) **Their south border.**—The southern boundary of Judah is thus described by Conder (*Bible Handbook*, p. 257):—"The south boundary of Judah is described from east to west, and became afterwards that of Simeon (see chap. xix. 1). Although the points mentioned along the border are not all certainly known, there is no doubt that the great mountain wall which extends from the Dead Sea to the water-shed south of Rehoboth (*Er-Ruheibeh*) formed the natural and recognised boundary of Palestine, while the river of Egypt (verse 4) is generally supposed to be the present *Wâdy-el'-Arish*, the northern boundary between Syria and Egypt. The north branch of this valley (*Wâdy-el-Abiad*) rises near 'Abdeh (*Ebodah*), south of Rehoboth, and thus carries on the boundary from the mountain rampart. A new identification of importance may be here mentioned, namely, *Hezron* (verse 3), the next point to Kadesh-barnea on the west side. Kadesh has been shown to lie probably in the neighbourhood of *Wâdy-el-Yemen*, and immediately west of that valley is the mountain called *Hadireh*, a name radically identical with Hezron."

(4) **This shall be your south coast.**—This phrase does not seem to fit in with the language of the rest of the passage. But it is extremely like a reminiscence of the language of Moses in Num. xxxiv. 3, 6, 9, 12. "This book of the law shall not depart out of thy mouth" was the instruction to Joshua, and in describing the border of Judah, he is really describing also the southern border of all Israel; and he does it throughout in language very like that of Moses in Num. xxxiv. But Moses wrote it in the second person and in the future tense throughout; Joshua wrote it in the third person and in the past tense, with this one exception, in which he seems to have unconsciously adopted the phraseology of the lawgiver instead of the historian.

(5) **Their border in the north quarter.**—This can be followed with the Ordnance Survey of Palestine, and is described by Conder in the following way:—"It started from the Jordan mouth, but did not apparently follow the river, as Beth Arabah (unknown) and Beth Hogla ('*Ain Hajlah*, about two miles west of Jordan—sheet xviii.) belonged to Benjamin. Passing along the valley of Achor (*Wâdy Kelt*), it left Gilgal on the north, and ascended the pass to the going up of Adummim (*Tal'at-ed-Dumm*), the ancient and modern name 'bloody' being apparently derived from the brick-red marls here found amid a district of white chalk." (It is easy to conjecture other reasons.) A line of Roman road on the map is a very fair guide to the boundary here described, and thus far it lies on sheet xviii. En Rogel, the next known point (on sheet xvii.), close to Zoheleth (*Zahweileh*, 1 Kings i. 9), was evidently the present spring '*Ain Umm-ed-Deraj*, in the Kedron Valley (this may be sought in the separate survey of Jerusalem, which is upon a larger scale). Thence the border ran across the slope (Cataph, verse 8, "side"), beside the valley of Ben Hinnom (*Wâdy Rabâby*), south of Jebus, and thus reached the watershed. (Here the boundary-line takes a turn to the northward.) It then apparently passed along the broad vale (Emek, verse 8) of Rephaim ("valley of the giants"), which Josephus makes to extend towards Bethlehem. This valley is identified with *El-Bukeia* (sheet xvii.). The waters of Nephtoah are apparently identical with '*Ain 'Atân*, south-west of Bethlehem.

(9) **Kirjath-jearim** is by Conder identified as '*Arma* (spelt '*Erma* on the Ordnance map), four miles east of Beth-shemesh ('*Ain Shemes*, or *Shems*).

(10) **Mount Seir.**—Of course, entirely distinct from the place in Edom, but not precisely identified.

Chesalon is identified with *Kesla*, two and a quarter miles due north of *Khurbet 'Erma*, on sheet xvii. Timnah is *Tibneh* (on sheet xvi.).

(11) **Ekron** is *Akir* (on sheet xvi.). Here we are in the Shephêlah, or plain of the sea-coast.

unto the side of Ekron northward: and the border was drawn to Shicron, and passed along to mount Baalah, and went out unto Jabneel; and the goings out of the border were at the sea.

(12) And the west border *was* to the great sea, and the coast *thereof*.

This *is* the coast of the children of Judah round about according to their families.

(13) And unto Caleb the son of Jephunneh he gave a part among the children of Judah, according to the commandment of the LORD to Joshua, *even* ᵃ¹ the city of Arbe, the father of Anak, which *city is* Hebron. (14) And Caleb drove thence ᵇ the three sons of Anak, Sheshai, and Ahiman, and Talmai, the children of Anak. (15) And he went up thence to the inhabitants of Debir: and the name of Debir before *was* Kirjath-sepher. (16) And Caleb said, He that smiteth Kirjath-sepher, and taketh it, to him will I give Achsah my daughter to wife. (17) And Othniel the son of Kenaz, the brother of Caleb, took it: and he gave him Achsah his daughter to wife. (18) And it came to pass, as she came *unto him*, that she moved him to ask of her father a field: and she lighted off *her* ass; and Caleb said unto her, What wouldest thou? (19) Who answered, Give me a blessing; for thou hast given me a south land; give me also springs of water. And he gave her the upper springs, and the nether springs.

(20) This *is* the inheritance of the tribe of the children of Judah according to their families.

(21) And the uttermost cities of the tribe of the children of Judah toward the coast of Edom southward were Kabzeel, and Eder, and Jagur, (22) and Kinah, and Dimonah, and Adadah, (23) and Kedesh, and Hazor, and Ithnan, (24) Ziph, and Telem, and Bealoth, (25) and Hazor, Hadattah, and Kerioth, *and* Hezron, which *is* Hazor, (26) Amam, and Shema, and Moladah, (27) and Hazargaddah, and Heshmon, and Beth-palet, (28) and Hazar-shual, and Beer-sheba, and Bizjothjah, (29) Baalah, and Iim, and Azem, (30) and Eltolad, and Chesil, and Hormah, (31) and Ziklag, and Madmannah, and Sansannah, (32) and Lebaoth, and Shilhim, and Ain, and Rimmon: all the cities *are* twenty and nine, with their villages:

a ch. 14. 15.

1 Or, *Kirjath-arba.*

b Judg. 1. 10.

Jabneel is *Yebnah*, west of Ekron, nearer the sea.

(13—19) **And unto Caleb . . .** This paragraph occurs also in Judges i. 10—15, with some slight variations. Which is its original place? In Judges it is connected with the continuation of the conquest of Canaan by the tribe of Judah *after Joshua's death*, and there we read they slew (literally, *smote*) Sheshai, and Ahiman, and Talmai. If this is the death, and not merely the defeat of the Anakim (the Hebrew word is not absolutely decisive), we have two stages in the conquest of Hebron described—viz., (1) the expulsion of the Anakim sufficiently for Caleb to occupy the place; and (2) their final defeat and death. It seems hardly possible to make the narrative in Judges i. a mere repetition of an earlier story, because it is presented as a part of that which happened after Joshua's death. It would seem, then, that the entire conquest of the Anakim was not effected at once, but begun by Caleb and Joshua in Joshua's lifetime, and completed by the tribe of Judah, under the leadership of Caleb, after Joshua's death. It is remarkable that Ahiman, Sheshai, and Talmai are mentioned as apparently living when the twelve spies went up from Kadesh-barnea (Num. xiii. 22), forty years before. But it has been thought that the three names were the names of three clans of the Anakim. (See Notes on Judges i. 10.)

Upon the whole, it seems most reasonable to conclude that the proceedings by which Caleb secured his inheritance, and fulfilled the promise of chap. xiv. 12, have been recorded here for the sake of completeness, though not necessarily belonging to this time.

(15) **Kirjath-sepher.**—"City of books."

(17) **Othniel the son of Kenaz.**—Comp. Judges iii. 9.

(19) **A south land**—*i.e.*, land in the *Negeb*: "a series of rolling hills clad with scanty herbage here and there." Conder does not identify Debir, but others have taken it to be identical with Dewîr-ban, about three miles west of Hebron.

The upper springs, and the nether springs —*i.e.*, the upper and lower "bubblings," or pools of a rivulet in a valley among the hills in this neighbourhood.

(21) **And the uttermost cities.**—The cities of the tribe of Judah are given under four heads: (*a*) *towards Edom*; (*b*) *in the Shephêlah*, or plain of the coast (verse 33, &c.); (*c*) *in the mountains* (verse 48); (*d*) *in the wilderness* (verse 61).

Of those in verses 21—32, the first twenty-nine, Conder identifies only four—viz., Adadah, verse 22 (*Ad'adah*); Kerioth Hezron (some see a trace of Kerioth in the *sobriquet* of Judas Is-cariot, the man of Kerioth), verse 25 (*Hudîreh*); Beer-sheba, verse 28 (*Bir es-seb'a*); and Ain Rimmon, verse 32 (*Umm er-Rumânîn*). It is not easy to say precisely how the twenty-nine are to be obtained from the thirty-three, but evidently some of the *Hazors* are villages attached to the cities.

(31) **Ziklag.**—It is noticeable that Ziklag became the property of the kings of Judah by the *gift of Achish*, who bestowed it on David (1 Sam. xxvii. 6), not by the gift of Joshua to Judah. The partial character of the conquest and the division of *unconquered* territory to the tribes is thus illustrated.

(33) And in the valley, Eshtaol, and Zoreah, and Ashnah, (34) and Zanoah, and En-gannim, Tappuah, and Enam, (35) Jarmuth, and Adullam, Socoh, and Azekah, (36) and Sharaim, and Adithaim, and Gederah, ¹ and Gederothaim; fourteen cities with their villages: (37) Zenan, and Hadashah, and Migdal-gad, (38) and Dilean, and Mizpeh, and Joktheel, (39) Lachish, and Bozkath, and Eglon, (40) and Cabbon, and Lahmam, and Kithlish, (41) and Gederoth, Beth-dagon, and Naamah, and Makkedah; sixteen cities with their villages: (42) Libnah, and Ether, and Ashan, (43) and Jiphtah, and Ashnah, and Nezib, (44) and Keilah, and Achzib, and Mareshah; nine cities with their villages: (45) Ekron, with her towns and her villages: (46) from Ekron even unto the sea, all that lay ² near Ashdod, with their villages: (47) Ashdod with her towns and her villages, Gaza with her towns and her villages, unto the river of Egypt, and the great sea, and the border thereof:

(48) And in the mountains, Shamir, and Jattir, and Socoh, (49) and Dannah, and Kirjath-sannah, which is Debir, (50) and Anab, and Eshtemoh, and Anim,

¹ Or, or.

² Heb., by the place of.

³ Or, Janus.

a ch. 14. 15.

⁴ Heb., went forth.

(51) and Goshen, and Holon, and Giloh; eleven cities with their villages. (52) Arab, and Dumah, and Eshean, (53) and ³ Janum, and Beth-tappuah, and Aphekah, (54) and Humtah, and ᵃ Kirjath-arba, which is Hebron, and Zior; nine cities with their villages: (55) Maon, Carmel, and Ziph, and Juttah, (56) and Jezreel, and Jokdeam, and Zanoah, (57) Cain, Gibeah, and Timnah; ten cities with their villages: (58) Halhul, Beth-zur, and Gedor, (59) and Maarath, and Beth-anoth, and Eltekon; six cities with their villages: (60) Kirjath-baal, which is Kirjath-jearim, and Rabbah; two cities with their villages: (61) in the wilderness, Beth-arabah, Middin, and Secacah, (62) and Nibshan, and the city of Salt, and En-gedi; six cities with their villages.

(63) As for the Jebusites the inhabitants of Jerusalem, the children of Judah could not drive them out: but the Jebusites dwell with the children of Judah at Jerusalem unto this day.

CHAPTER XVI.—(1) And the lot of the children of Joseph ⁴ fell from Jordan by Jericho, unto the water of Jericho

(33) **In the valley**—i.e., the Shephêlah, or plain of the coast. Of the fourteen that follow in verses 33—36, Conder identifies ten.

Eshtaol, and Zoreah, were afterwards assigned to Dan (chap. xix. 41).

(41) Of the sixteen towns in verses 37—41, Conder identifies seven.

(44) Of the nine towns in verses 42—44, Conder identifies five.

(45) Ekron was afterwards given to Dan (chap. xix. 43).

(46, 47) Ekron, Ashdod, and Gaza are all identified. Observe that the Philistine territory is assigned to Judah here.

(48—51) Nine of these eleven are identified.

(51) **Goshen** is thought by some to give a name to the land of Goshen in chap. x. 41, but the place is insignificant, and not identified; and to take the land of Goshen as frontier or border land seems a very much more reasonable interpretation.

Giloh—the home of Ahithophel the *Gilonite*, David's and Absalom's counsellor (2 Sam. xv. 12, &c.).

(54) Of this total of nine, six have been found.

(57) The four first and the four last of these are all found. Maon, Carmel, and Ziph became famous in David's wanderings (see the story of Nabal, 1 Sam. xxv.); and the Ziphites have covered themselves with infamy by their repeated efforts to betray him to Saul, who sought his life (1 Sam. xxiii. 19, and xxvi. 1).

(59) Five of these six have been identified.

(60) **Kirjath-jearim** has been already pointed out on the boundary-line of the tribe (verse 9). Rabbah is marked as *Rubba*.

(61) **In the wilderness**—i.e., in the mountains near the Dead Sea three places have been identified—viz., Secacah (*Sikkeh*), the City of Salt (*Tell el-Milh*), and En-gedi (*Ain Jidy*). (See 1 Sam. xxiv. 1, &c.)

(63) **Could not drive them out.**—It is observable that the failure of the three great tribes of Judah and Joseph (Ephraim and Manasseh) to clear the inheritance assigned to them is specially noticed in the Book of Joshua—viz., Judah in this place, and Ephraim and Manasseh in chaps. xvi. 10 and xvii. 11, 12. A list of the failures of all the tribes is given in Judges i.

XVI.

INHERITANCE OF JOSEPH—i.e., of Ephraim and Manasseh (chaps. xvi. 1—xviii. 1, inclusive).

(1) **The lot of the children of Joseph.**—The order of precedence among the tribes of Israel was always Judah first and the sons of Joseph second. In the words of 1 Chron. v. 2, "Judah prevailed above his brethren, and of him came the chief ruler; but the birthright was Joseph's." Accordingly in the division of the land of Canaan under Joshua, there are three successive stages: *first*, the settlement of the tribe of Judah in the strongholds of the south of Palestine; *secondly*, the establishment of Ephraim and Manasseh in the centre of the country, and in some strong positions towards the north; *thirdly*, the settlement of the remaining tribes, so as to fill up the gaps left between Judah and Joseph, and also upon the outskirts of their territory, so as to be, as it were, under the shadow of their wings.

In the inheritance of Ephraim and Manasseh we observe some features which distinguish this description

The Lots of Joseph,   JOSHUA. XVII.   *Ephraim, and Manasseh.*

on the east, to the wilderness that goeth up from Jericho throughout mount Beth-el, (2) and goeth out from Beth-el to *a* Luz, and passeth along unto the borders of Archi to Ataroth, (3) and goeth down westward to the coast of Japhleti, unto the coast of Beth-horon the nether, and to Gezer: and the goings out thereof are at the sea. (4) So the children of Joseph, Manasseh and Ephraim, took their inheritance.

(5) And the border of the children of Ephraim according to their families was *thus*: even the border of their inheritance on the east side was Ataroth-addar, unto Beth-horon the upper; (6) and the border went out toward the sea to Michmethah on the north side; and the border went about eastward unto Taanath-shiloh, and passed by it on the east to Janohah; (7) and it went down from Janohah to Ataroth, and to Naarath, and came to Jericho, and went out at Jordan. (8) The border went out from Tappuah westward unto the river Kanah; and the goings out thereof were at the sea. This *is* the inheritance of the tribe of the children of Ephraim by their families. (9) And the separate cities for the children of Ephraim *were* among the inheritance of the children of Manasseh, all the cities with their villages. (10) And they drave not out the Canaanites that dwelt in Gezer: but the Canaanites dwell among the Ephraimites unto this day, and serve under tribute.

CHAPTER XVII.—(1) There was also a lot for the tribe of Manasseh; for he *was* the *b* firstborn of Joseph; *to wit*, for Machir the firstborn of Manasseh, the father of Gilead: because he was a man of war, therefore he had Gilead and Bashan. (2) There was also *a lot* for *c* the rest of the children of Manasseh by their families; for the children of Abiezer, and for the children of Helek, and for the children of Asriel, and for the children of Shechem, and for the

a Judg. 1. 26.

b Gen. 41. 51, & 46. 20, & 50. 23; Num. 32. 39.

c Num. 26. 29.

---

from that of Judah's inheritance in chap. xv. The boundaries of the territory are given, but there is no catalogue of cities. There is also another peculiarity: the tribe of Ephraim is interlocked with the tribe of Manasseh, and the tribe of Manasseh again with Issachar and Asher, by the possession of cities in the territory of these other tribes.

(1—3) Comp. chap. xviii. 12—14. The south border of Joseph was the north border of Benjamin. (See Conder's *Bible Handbook*, p. 260, and Ordnance Map, sheets xiv., xv., and xviii.)

    Archi is *'Ain 'Arik* (sheet xiv.).
    Ataroth is *Ed-Dârieh* (sheet xviii.).
    Japhleti is not identified.
    Beth-horon is *Beit 'Ur.*
    Gezer is *Tell Jezer.*

(5—8) **The border (of Ephraim's inheritance) on the east side.**—The words "on the east side" are not easy to understand. If Ataroth-addar is rightly identified as *Ed-Dârieh*, and Mickmethah as the plain of *Mukhnah*, then the line from Ataroth-addar and Beth-horon to Michmethah is a line running due north, and separating the territory of Ephraim on the east from that of Dan on the west. The line from Michmethah to Taanath-shiloh (*Tana*, sheet xii.) and Janohah (*Yánún*, south of *Tana*, sheet xv.), and so to Jordan, is a line running from north-west to south-east. The brook Kanah is (roughly) continuous with this line, but in a westerly direction, and leads us towards the sea. We thus obtain for the territory of Ephraim four boundary-lines—viz.: (*a*) the plain of Jordan on the east; (*b*) the line of hills bordering the Shephelah on the west; (*c*) the brook Kanah, and the line passing through Taanath-shiloh and Janohah to Jordan on the north; and (*d*) the north border of Benjamin (verses 1, 2, 3, and chap. xviii. 12—14) on the south.

(9) **The separate cities for the children of Ephraim were among the inheritance of the children of Manasseh**; and chap. xvii. 10, 11: "Manasseh had in Issachar and in Asher, Beth-shean," &c. This fact would manifestly tend to produce a *solidarity* among the several tribes, and to prevent disunion by creating common interests. The interest of the stronger tribes would be served by completing the conquest of the territory assigned to the weaker. And the general formation thus produced would resemble that which was known by the name of the *testudo*, or tortoise, in Roman warfare. When a body of soldiers approached the wall of a town which it was intended to assault, they sometimes held their shields over them, overlapping like scales, each man's shield partly sheltering his own, and partly his neighbour's body, so that no missile could penetrate. Thus it may be said not only of Jerusalem, but of all the tribes in the land of their possession, that they were built as a city that is compact together, and at unity in itself: united by joints and bands, so that if one member of the body politic should suffer, all the members must suffer with it. For a further illustration of the same topic, see on the inheritance of Benjamin (chap. xviii. 11) and of Simeon (chap. xix. 1).

(10) **They drave not out.**—The failure of Ephraim here is noticed, as was the failure of Judah above (chap. xv. 63).

XVII.

(2) **Shechem.**—It is noteworthy that according to the boundary of Ephraim and Manasseh, described in chap. xvi., the town of Shechem appears to have lain within the border of Manasseh (Conder, p. 263), but as "the separate cities" of Ephraim were among the inheritance of Manasseh (chap. xvi. 9), this may have been the case with Shechem, the first metropolis of the Israelites in Palestine.

The Daughters of Zelophehad.   JOSHUA, XVII.   *The Border of Manasseh.*

children of Hepher, and for the children of Shemida: these *were* the male children of Manasseh the son of Joseph by their families.

(3) But *a* Zelophehad, the son of Hepher, the son of Gilead, the son of Machir, the son of Manasseh, had no sons, but daughters: and these *are* the names of his daughters, Mahlah, and Noah, Hoglah, Milcah, and Tirzah. (4) And they came near before Eleazar the priest, and before Joshua the son of Nun, and before the princes, saying, The LORD commanded Moses to give us an inheritance among our brethren. Therefore according to the commandment of the LORD he gave them an inheritance among the brethren of their father. (5) And there fell ten portions to Manasseh, beside the land of Gilead and Bashan, which *were* on the other side Jordan; (6) because the daughters of Manasseh had an inheritance among his sons: and the rest of Manasseh's sons had the land of Gilead.

(7) And the coast of Manasseh was from Asher to Michmethah, that *lieth* before Shechem; and the border went along on the right hand unto the inhabitants of En-tappuah. (8) *Now* Manasseh had the land of Tappuah:

a Num. 26, 33, & 27, 1, & 36. 2.

1 Or, *brook of reeds.*

but Tappuah on the border of Manasseh *belonged* to the children of Ephraim; (9) and the coast descended unto the ¹river Kanah, southward of the river: these cities of Ephraim *are* among the cities of Manasseh: the coast of Manasseh also *was* on the north side of the river, and the outgoings of it were at the sea: (10) southward *it was* Ephraim's, and northward *it was* Manasseh's, and the sea is his border; and they met together in Asher on the north, and in Issachar on the east. (11) And Manasseh had in Issachar and in Asher Beth-shean and her towns, and Ibleam and her towns, and the inhabitants of Dor and her towns, and the inhabitants of Endor and her towns, and the inhabitants of Taanach and her towns, and the inhabitants of Megiddo and her towns, *even* three countries. (12) Yet the children of Manasseh could not drive out *the inhabitants of* those cities; but the Canaanites would dwell in that land. (13) Yet it came to pass, when the children of Israel were waxen strong, that they put the Canaanites to tribute; but did not utterly drive them out.

(14) And the children of Joseph spake unto Joshua, saying, Why hast thou given me *but* one lot and one portion to

---

(3) **Daughters.**—On the case of the daughters of Zelophehad, see Num. xxviii. and xxxvi.

(5) **Ten portions**—*i.e.*, five for the sons named in verse 2, excepting Hepher, and five for Hepher's five grand-daughters.

(7) **From Asher to Michmethah.**—Literally, *from Asher-ham-Michmethah*, a double name; Michmethah being taken as the plain of *Mukhnah*. The exact spot is not identified; but the plain of *Mukhnah* runs nearly due south from Shechem.

The inhabitants of En-tappuah—*i.e.*, *Yeshebi-En-tappuah*, or *Yasûf* (sheet xiv.), otherwise *Yeshepheh*. From this place a line drawn westward will bring us into the *Wâdy Kanah*, and so on to the river *'Aujeh*, which falls into the sea north of Jaffa.

(10) **In Asher on the north**—*i.e.* (according to Conder) Asher-ham-Michmethah (verse 7), not the tribe of that name.

And in Issachar on the east—*i.e.*, the tribe of Issachar. The joint border of Issachar and Manasseh is not described. But, having regard to the following verse, it seems more probable on the whole that the meaning is this: "Toward the south (of the brook Kanah) it belonged to Ephraim, and on the north to Manasseh, and the sea was his (Manasseh's) border; and they (*i.e.*, the Manassites) touched Asher on the north, and Issachar on the east." For (by chap. xix. 26) the territory of Asher extended southwards as far as Carmel; and the tribe of Manasseh had in Issachar and Asher the cities specified in verse 11.

Territorially, the tribe of Manasseh had the largest share of Palestine.

(11) **Even three countries.**—The word for "countries" does not occur elsewhere. If taken as in our version, which follows the Targum, we may observe that the places named in this verse do happen to lie on three distinct sheets of the map—viz., Bethshean (*Beisan*), Megiddo (*Khurbet-el-Mujedda*), and Endor (*Endûr*) on sheet ix.; Taanach (*Tana*) and Ibleam (Bileam, 1 Chron. vi. 70), *Wâdy Bel'ameh*, on sheet viii., and Dor (*Tantûra*) on sheet vii. Or it may mean the triple height—viz., Endor, Taanach, and Megiddo—three cities on hills in one district, which make very nearly an equilateral triangle.

(12) **Could not drive.**—Note the defalcation of Manasseh.

(14, 15) **Why hast thou given me but one lot . . . seeing I am a great people . . . If thou be a great people, then get thee up . . . and cut down for thyself . . . in the land of the . . . giants.**—The request and the answer are both characteristic. The words of the proud Ephraimites and the deeds of the humble Joshua, the true hero of the tribe of Ephraim, should never be forgotten. Joshua's own greatness was emphatically of that kind which is proved by deeds, and not by words. There are not many famous sayings recorded from his lips. The arrogance of the Ephraimites, on the other hand, may be abundantly illustrated from Old Testament history, by the stories of their behaviour to Gideon

inherit, seeing I *am* a great people, forasmuch as the LORD hath blessed me hitherto? (15) And Joshua answered them, If thou *be* a great people, *then* get thee up to the wood *country*, and cut down for thyself there in the land of the Perizzites and of the ¹giants, if mount Ephraim be too narrow for thee. (16) And the children of Joseph said, The hill is not enough for us: and all the Canaanites that dwell in the land of the valley have chariots of iron, *both they* who *are* of Beth-shean and her towns, and *they* who *are* of the valley of Jezreel. (17) And Joshua spake unto the house of Joseph, *even* to Ephraim and to Manasseh, saying, Thou *art* a great people, and hast great power: thou shalt not have one lot *only:* (18) but the mountain shall be thine; for it *is* a wood, and thou shalt cut it down: and the outgoings of it shall be thine: for thou shalt drive out the Canaanites, though they have iron chariots, *and* though they *be* strong.

CHAPTER XVIII.— (1) And the whole congregation of the children of Israel assembled together at Shiloh, and set up the tabernacle of the congregation there. And the land was subdued before them.

(2) And there remained among the children of Israel seven tribes, which had not yet received their inheritance. (3) And Joshua said unto the children of Israel, How long *are* ye slack to go to possess the land, which the LORD God of your fathers hath given you? (4) Give out from among you three men for *each* tribe: and I will send them, and they shall rise, and go through the land, and describe it according to the inheritance of them; and they shall come *again* to me. (5) And they shall divide it into seven parts: Judah shall abide in their coast on the south, and the house of Joseph shall abide in their coasts on the north. (6) Ye shall therefore describe the land *into* seven parts, and bring the *description* hither to me, that I may cast lots for you here before the LORD our God. (7) But the Levites have no part among you; for the priesthood of the LORD *is* their inheritance: and Gad, and Reuben, and half the tribe of Manasseh, have received their inheritance beyond Jordan on the east, which

¹ Or, *Rephaims.*

---

and Jephthah, and even to David in later times. They were constantly asserting their right to the supremacy in Israel, without exhibiting any qualification for it.

But the incident in this chapter is the key to several difficulties in the Book of Joshua. It is plain, from what is here stated, that a large portion of the centre of Palestine consisted of uncleared forest: that the cities and inhabitants of that district were far fewer than those of the valley of Esdraelon, or of the territory assigned to Judah on the south. And this fact justifies the strategy of the attack of Israel under Joshua upon the centre of the country, so that the forces of the Canaanites were necessarily divided, and the Israelites could strike first with their whole force at the southern armies, and then turn round upon their enemies in the north. It helps to explain the ease with which they set up the law on Ebal at the commencement of the invasion, and the selection of Shechem for the capital afterwards.

(15) **Perizzites and . . . Rephaim** (giants) are mentioned together in Gen. xv. 20. It is thought that a trace of the name Perizzite may be found in the name *Ferasin* (? *Feráta*), west of Shechem (sheet xi.).

XVIII.

(1) **At Shiloh.**—*Seilûn* (sheet xiv.), about ten miles due south of Shechem, in the territory of Ephraim. The inheritance of the tribe of Judah was determined in Gilgal. The assignment of the central part of the country to Ephraim and Manasseh brought the leaders of Israel into that district, and as soon as the position of Ephraim, Joshua's tribe, was settled, the tabernacle was set up there. For the situation of Shiloh, see Judges xxi. 19.

(2) **And there remained . . . seven tribes, which had not yet received . . . inheritance.** —This statement is well worthy of notice, as illustrating the character of the Israelites in a manner which is thoroughly true to nature. The conquest of the Canaanitish armies being completed, the two leading divisions of the host of Israel took possession of their shares of the conquered territory. The house of Judah and the house of Joseph were satisfied. This done, the weaker tribes were left to take care of themselves. They did not venture to select their own portions; the others did not come forward to offer them anything. Thus there remained, for a time, seven tribes which had not received their inheritance.

(3) **And Joshua said . . .**—Joshua, who took no inheritance for himself until all the tribes had received their portions, was free from the selfishness of the other leaders. He could not rest until he had finished the work that was given him to do. He therefore ordered that the rest of the territory should be surveyed, and divided, according to the number of the cities, into seven portions, which were then to be allotted according to the instructions given by Moses.

(5–10) **They shall divide it into seven parts.** —The several tribes were not permitted to choose their own portions. In Num. xxvi. 54, 55, we read: "To many thou shalt give the more inheritance, and to few thou shalt give the less inheritance . . . . notwithstanding the land shall be divided by lot." These words imply that there must be unequal portions of territory for larger and smaller tribes, but that the particular position of each tribe must be settled by the lot, whereof "the whole disposing is of the Lord." We

Moses the servant of the LORD gave them.

(8) And the men arose, and went away: and Joshua charged them that went to describe the land, saying, Go and walk through the land, and describe it, and come again to me, that I may here cast lots for you before the LORD in Shiloh. (9) And the men went and passed through the land, and described it by cities into seven parts in a book, and came *again* to Joshua to the host at Shiloh: (10) And Joshua cast lots for them in Shiloh before the LORD: and there Joshua divided the land unto the children of Israel according to their divisions.

(11) And the lot of the tribe of the children of Benjamin came up according to their families: and the coast of their lot came forth between the children of Judah and the children of Joseph.

(12) And their border on the north side was from Jordan; and the border went up to the side of Jericho on the north side, and went up through the mountains westward; and the goings out thereof were at the wilderness of Beth-aven. (13) And the border went over from thence toward Luz, to the side of Luz, which *is* Beth-el, southward; and the border descended to Ataroth-adar, near the hill that *lieth* on the south side of the nether Beth-horon.

(14) And the border was drawn *thence*, and compassed the corner of the sea southward, from the hill that *lieth* before Beth-horon southward; and the goings out thereof were at Kirjath-baal, which *is* Kirjath-jearim, a city of the children of Judah: this *was* the west quarter.

(15) And the south quarter *was* from the end of Kirjath-jearim, and the border went out on the west, and went out to the well of waters of Nephtoah: (16) and the border came down to the end of the mountain that *lieth* before the valley of the son of Hinnom, *and* which *is* in the valley of the giants on the north, and descended to the valley of Hinnom, to the side of Jebusi on the south, and descended to En-rogel, (17) and was drawn from the north, and went forth to En-shemesh, and went forth toward Geliloth, which *is* over against the going up of Adummim, and descended to *a*the stone of Bohan the son of Reuben, (18) and passed along toward the side over against ¹Arabah

a ch. 15. 6.

1 Or, *The plain*.

---

are not told how this rule was carried out in the case of Judah, Ephraim, and Manasseh, who received their inheritance first. Possibly a sufficient extent of territory was surveyed at first to provide three large allotments. The three tribes might then cast lots, first between Judah and Joseph for the northern or southern portions, and then between Ephraim and Manasseh for the two sections of the northern territory. This would carry out the instructions of Num. xxvi. But see above (chap. xv. 1).

THE INHERITANCE OF BENJAMIN.

(11—28) **The lot of the tribe of the children of Benjamin.**—It can have been by no accident that their lot came forth "between Judah and Joseph." No wiser method could have been devised to secure an united Israel than thus to make Benjamin the link between the two most powerful and naturally rival tribes. In the story of Joseph, the brethren are reconciled through the mutual affection of Judah and Joseph for Benjamin as their father's youngest and best-loved son.

The position thus given to Benjamin under Joshua was still further developed by circumstances. The tribe was almost exterminated in the time of the judges; the survivors were united in marriage with women of Ephraim and Manasseh (?). On the other hand, the city of Jerusalem, although assigned by Joshua to Benjamin, was first a joint possession of Judah and Benjamin (1 Chron. viii. 28, 32; Judg. i. 8, 21), then the royal city of the kings of the house of Judah. The selection of the first king of Israel from Benjamin, and the ultimate planting of the religious and political centre of all the tribes on the confines of Judah and Benjamin in Jerusalem, would have been two masterstrokes of policy if they had been schemes of man's devising. They were really links in the long chain of God's providential dealing with the chosen people.

(12) **And their border.**—This is first described on the north side, where it coincided with the southern border of Ephraim. Conder draws it from *El 'Aujeh* (sheet xv.), five miles north of Jericho, towards Beth-el (*Beitin*), perhaps going along the *Wâdy 'Aujeh*, Beth-el lying within the territory of Benjamin (verse 22), and so on to Archi (chap. xvi. 2), now *Ain 'Arik* (near the top of sheet xvii.), and thence to Ataroth-addar (*Ed-Dârieh*), near Beth-horon the nether (*Beit-ûr-et-Tahta*). This line is from east to west.

(14) **And the border was drawn thence . . .**—At this point it turns southward, and runs from the neighbourhood of Beth-horon to Kirjath-jearim (*Khurbet 'Erma*, in sheet xvii.: very small, and not easily found).

Corner of the sea.—*Ph'ath Yâm*, "the west side."

(15) **And the south quarter.**—Here the borderline again turns to the east, and runs to *Ain Atân* (the waters of Nephtoah), near Bethlehem. Thence it turns to the north-east, and follows the line described above (chap. xv. 6—8) as the northern boundary of Judah.

(17) **The stone of Bohan the son of Reuben** must have been near the Jordan. Is it possible that Bohan, the son of Reuben, did on his own account what was done for all Israel by the command of Joshua? (chap. iv. 8).

northward, and went down unto Arabah: ⁽¹⁹⁾ and the border passed along to the side of Beth-hoglah northward: and the outgoings of the border were at the north ¹bay of the salt sea at the south end of Jordan: this *was* the south coast.

⁽²⁰⁾ And Jordan was the border of it on the east side.

This *was* the inheritance of the children of Benjamin, by the coasts thereof round about, according to their families.

⁽²¹⁾ Now the cities of the tribe of the children of Benjamin according to their families were Jericho, and Beth-hoglah, and the valley of Keziz, ⁽²²⁾ and Beth-arabah, and Zemaraim, and Beth-el, ⁽²³⁾ and Avim, and Parah, and Ophrah, ⁽²⁴⁾ and Chephar-haammonai, and Ophni, and Gaba; twelve cities with their villages: ⁽²⁵⁾ Gibeon, and Ramah, and Beeroth, ⁽²⁶⁾ and Mizpeh, and Chephirah, and Mozah, ⁽²⁷⁾ and Rekem, and Irpeel, and Taralah, ⁽²⁸⁾ and Zelah, Eleph, and Jebusi, which *is* Jerusalem, Gibeath, *and* Kirjath; fourteen cities with their villages. This *is* the inheritance of the children of Benjamin according to their families.

CHAPTER XIX.—⁽¹⁾ And the second lot came forth to Simeon, *even* for the tribe of the children of Simeon according to their families: and their inheritance was within the inheritance of the children of Judah. ⁽²⁾ And they had in their inheritance Beer-sheba, and Sheba, and Moladah, ⁽³⁾ and Hazar-shual, and Balah, and Azem, ⁽⁴⁾ and Eltolad, and Bethul, and Hormah, ⁽⁵⁾ and Ziklag, and Beth-marcaboth, and Hazar-susah, ⁽⁶⁾ and Beth-lebaoth, and Sharuhen; thirteen cities and their villages: ⁽⁷⁾ Ain, Remmon, and Ether, and Ashan; four cities and their villages: ⁽⁸⁾ and all the villages that *were* round about these cities to Baalath-beer, Ramath of the south. This *is* the inheritance of the tribe of the children of Simeon according to their families. ⁽⁹⁾ Out of the portion of the children of Judah *was* the inheritance of the children of Simeon: for the part of the children of Judah was too much for them: therefore the children of Simeon had

¹ Heb., *tongue*.

⁽²¹⁾ **The cities of the tribe of . . . Benjamin.**—The following are identified: viz., in verse 21, *'Ain-es-Sultan, 'Ain Hajlah* (sheet xviii.); verse 22, *Khurbet es-Súmnrah, Beitín* (sheet xviii.); verse 23, *Fârah* (sheet xviii.), *Taiyibêh* (sheet xiv.); verse 24, *Jeb 'a* (sheet xvii.).

⁽²²⁾ Beth-el seems to have passed into the hands of Ephraim without question when the tribe of Benjamin was all but exterminated. In the division of the kingdoms, though the tribe of Benjamin followed the house of Judah, the town of Bethel was regarded as part of the kingdom of Israel, and Jeroboam's southern boundary. He set up two golden calves, one in Bethel and the other in Dan, at the northern and southern extremities of his kingdom.

⁽²⁵⁾ *El-Jêb, Er-Râm, Bireh* (all in sheet xvii.).

⁽²⁶⁾ *Sh'afât, Kefireh, Beit Mizzeh* (Kefîreh, *i.e.*, Kefriyeh, sheet xiv.); the others are in sheet xvii.

⁽²⁷⁾ *Râfât* (sheet xvii.).

⁽²⁸⁾ *Lifta, El-Kuds, Jebi'a, Kuriet-el-'anab* (all in sheet xvii.).

⁽²⁸⁾ **Jebusi, which is Jerusalem.**—When "Jerusalem, Jerusalem, which killed the prophets, and stoned them that were sent unto her," was called to account for "all the righteous blood shed upon the earth," *the cup was found in Benjamin's sack*, having been put there, as we see, by Joshua, the steward (after Moses) of the true Joseph's house. (See *Names on the Gates of Pearl*—Benjamin, p. 131.) Jerusalem is always thought of as the capital of Judah. Probably few readers of the Bible would answer, if asked for its position, that it was originally a Benjamite city. And we may add that no later writer than Joshua would be likely to have placed it in the territory of Benjamin.

XIX.

INHERITANCE OF SIMEON (chap. xix. 1—9).

⁽¹⁾ **Their inheritance was within the inheritance of the children of Judah.**—The southern part of the inheritance of Judah was given up to Simeon. (See Judges i. 3 and 17.) In this fact a prophecy was fulfilled; for the effect of the allotment was to separate Simeon from the tribes with whom he had been united in the journey through the wilderness (viz., Reuben and Gad), who had cast off Simeon, and united themselves with the half tribe of Manasseh instead. Being also separated from Levi, Simeon was still further isolated: with the result that in the final separation of Israel and Judah, after Solomon's death, the tribe of Simeon, though adhering to the kingdom of the ten tribes (for the children of Simeon were counted *strangers* in Judah—2 Chron. xv. 9), was separated from the territory of that kingdom by the whole breadth of the kingdom of Judah. Thus were Jacob's words brought to pass, which he spoke on his death-bed regarding Simeon and Levi: *I will divide them in Jacob, and scatter them in Israel.*

⁽²⁾ **Beer-sheba.**—*Bir-es-seba.* Sheba (Shema).

⁽⁷⁾ **Ain, Remmon.**—*Umm er-Rumâmin.*

The rest of the cities of Simeon are not identified in Conder's Biblical Gazetteer, with the exception of Sharuhen (*Tell esh-Sheri'ah*, north-west of Beer-sheba).

⁽⁹⁾ **The part of the children of Judah was too much for them.**—In Judges i. we read that Judah invoked the assistance of Simeon to complete the conquest of his inheritance, and also assisted Simeon to conquer his. This fact illustrates the character of the

The Lot of Zebulun.   JOSHUA, XIX.   *The Lot of Issachar.*

their inheritance within the inheritance of them. ⁽¹⁰⁾ And the third lot came up for the children of Zebulun according to their families: and the border of their inheritance was unto Sarid: ⁽¹¹⁾ and their border went up toward the sea, and Maralah, and reached to Dabbasheth, and reached to the river that *is* before Jokneam; ⁽¹²⁾ and turned from Sarid eastward toward the sunrising unto the border of Chisloth-tabor, and then goeth out to Daberath, and goeth up to Japhia, ⁽¹³⁾ and from thence passeth on along on the east to Gittah-hepher, to Ittah-kazin, and goeth out to Remmon-methoar¹ to Neah; ⁽¹⁴⁾ and the border compasseth it on the north side to Hannathon: and the outgoings thereof are in the valley of Jiphthah-el: ⁽¹⁵⁾ and Kattath, and Nahallal, and Shimron, and Idalah, and Beth-lehem: twelve cities with their villages. ⁽¹⁶⁾ This *is* the inheritance of the children of Zebulun according to their families, these cities with their villages.

⁽¹⁷⁾ And the fourth lot came out to Issachar, for the children of Issachar according to their families. ⁽¹⁸⁾ And their border was toward Jezreel, and Chesulloth, and Shunem, ⁽¹⁹⁾ and Haphraim, and Shihon, and Anaharath, ⁽²⁰⁾ and Rabbith, and Kishion, and Abez, ⁽²¹⁾ and Remeth, and En-gannim, and En-haddah, and Beth-pazzez; ⁽²²⁾ and the coast reacheth to Tabor, and Shahazimah, and Beth-shemesh; and the outgoings of their border were at Jordan: sixteen cities with their villages. ⁽²³⁾ This *is* the inheritance of the tribe of the children of Issachar according to their families, the cities and their villages.

⁽²⁴⁾ And the fifth lot came out for the

¹ Or, *which is drawn.*

---

conquest of Canaan by Joshua, and shows that when his work was done, something was still left for the individual tribes to do.

THE BORDER OF ZEBULUN.

(10) **The third lot . . . for the children of Zebulun . . .** Sarid (Syriac, Asdod; LXX., Seddouk) should be apparently spelt with consonants S, D, D. It is identified as *Tell Shadûd* (sheet viii.). From this point a line is drawn westward (past *M'alûl*, sheet v.) to Jokneam (*Tell Keimûn*, same sheet), a place at the south-east end of the Carmel ridge. This is the south boundary. We may note that it does not touch the sea, but leaves room for the territory of Asher to interpose (comp. chap. xvii. 10, 11). Returning to Sarid, the boundary is next (verse 12) drawn eastward to Chisloth-tabor (*Iksâl*, sheet vi.), Daberath (*Dabûrieh*, sheet vi.), Japhia (*Yâfa*, sheet v.), Gittah-hepher (*El-Mesh-hed*, sheet vi.).

(12) **And goeth up to Japhia.**—Better, *and had gone up to Japhia*, which lies west of the two places previously named. Daberath is the south-east boundary. El-Mesh-hed lies north of this.

(13) **Remmon-methoar to Neah.**—Better, *Remmon that stretcheth to Neah.* Remmon is identified as *Rummâneh*, due north of Gittah-hepher (sheet vi.).

(14) **Hannathon** (*Kefr-'Anân*, sheet ix.) is the north-east corner of the boundary. The valley (ravine) of Jiphthah-el (God's opening) seems to be the gorge running south-west from the north of Hannathon towards the plain.

(15) **Nahallal.**—(*'Ain Mahil*, sheet vi.).

Shimron.—(*Simûnieh*, west of Nazareth, sheet v.).

Idalah.—(*El Huwârah*, a ruin just south of Bethlehem, sheet v.).

Beth-lehem.—(*Beit-Lahm*, sheet v.). It seems right to refer Ibzan of Bethlehem (Judges xii. 8, 10) to this town. The other Bethlehem is called in Judges and Ruth, Bethlehem-Judah; and in Micah, Bethlehem-Ephratah (Judges xvii. 7, xix. 1; Ruth i. 1; Micah v. 2). Bethlehem-Judah is designated Bethlehem only when it is impossible to mistake it for Bethlehem of Zebulun (*e.g.*, Ruth i. 19, and 1 Sam. xvi. 4).

Twelve cities.—Ittah-kazin, Neah, Dabbasheth, and Kattath have not been identified, and they may not all be names of towns.

(17) **The fourth lot . . . to Issachar.**—These two tribes were located next to the house of Joseph on the north. It should be remembered that Issachar and Zebulun had been associated with Judah to form the same camp and division of the army in the wilderness. This association, lasting forty years, must have created many ties between these two tribes and their leader Judah. It was no ordinary wisdom that placed the descendants of Rachel (Ephraim, Benjamin, and Manasseh) between Judah on the south and Judah's two associates on the north—to cement the union of all Israel, and as far as possible to prevent discord.

With regard to Judah and Zebulun, it is noticeable that we find their union reproduced in the earthly history of our Lord. Mary, who was of the house of David, and Joseph of the same lineage, are found dwelling in Nazareth, in the tribe of Zebulun. Thus the north and the south alike had "part in David," and inheritance in David's Son. There is a Bethlehem (verse 15) in Zebulun as well as in Judah. The name is not found in any other tribe.

(18) *Zerin* (sheet viii.), *Iksal* (sheet vi.), *Sûlem* (sheet ix.).

(19) *El-Farrîyeh* (sheet vi.), *En-N'aûrah* (sheet ix., near Endor).

(20) *Râba* (sheet xii.), *El Beida* (sheet v.).

(21) *Er-Rameh* (sheet xi.), *Jenin* (sheet viii.), *Kefr-adân* (sheet viii.).

(22) Tabor (? *Deburieh*, sheet vi.). Beth-shemesh (*'Ain Esh-shemsiyeh*, near Beth-shean). The rest are not identified. Of these places, *Shunem* and *Jezreel* are famous in later history: Shunem especially in the story of Elisha (2 Kings iv.).

(24) **The fifth lot . . . for . . . Asher . . .** (and verse 32) **the sixth . . . for . . . Naphtali.** —Asher and Naphtali had been associated with Dan in

tribe of the children of Asher according to their families. (25) And their border was Helkath, and Hali, and Beten, and Achshaph, (26) and Alammelech, and Amad, and Misheal; and reacheth to Carmel westward, and to Shihor-libnath; (27) and turneth toward the sunrising to Beth-dagon, and reacheth to Zebulun, and to the valley of Jiphthah-el toward the north side of Beth-emek, and Neiel, and goeth out to Cabul on the left hand, (28) and Hebron, and Rehob, and Hammon, and Kanah, *even* unto great Zidon; (29) and *then* the coast turneth to Ramah, and to the strong city ¹Tyre; and the coast turneth to Hosah; and the outgoings thereof are at the sea from the coast to Achzib: (30) Ummah also, and Aphek, and Rehob: twenty and two cities with their villages. (31) This *is* the inheritance of the tribe of the children of Asher according to their families, these cities with their villages.

¹ Heb., *Tzor*.

(32) The sixth lot came out to the children of Naphtali, *even* for the children of Naphtali according to their families. (33) And their coast was from Heleph, from Allon to Zaanannim, and Adami, Nekeb, and Jabneel, unto Lakum; and the outgoings thereof were at Jordan : (34) and *then* the coast turneth westward to Aznoth-tabor, and goeth out from thence to Hukkok, and reacheth to Zebulun on the south side, and reacheth to Asher on the west side, and to Judah upon Jordan toward the sunrising. (35) And the fenced cities *are* Ziddim, Zer, and Hammath, Rakkath, and Chinnereth, (36) and Adamah, and Ramah, and Hazor, (37) and Kedesh, and Edrei, and En-hazor, (38) and Iron, and Migdal-el, Horem, and Beth-anath, and Beth-shemesh; nineteen cities with their villages. (39) This *is* the inheritance of the tribe of the children of Naphtali according to their families, the cities and their villages.

---

the exodus, and with him had encamped on the north side of the tabernacle, and had brought up the rear. These two, each dissociated from his *own* brother (viz., Asher from Gad and Naphtali from Dan), are paired together in their inheritance in Palestine (comp. Naphtali and Manasseh in Rev. vii., and see *Names on the Gates of Pearl*, pp. 199, 200). The tribe of Asher was more akin to the house of Judah, for Zilpah, the mother of Asher, was Leah's handmaid; and the tribe of Naphtali to the house of Joseph, for Bilhah, Naphtali's mother, was Rachel's handmaid. But in all cases the lot of the inheritance of the tribe seems to have fallen in such a way as to favour the construction of a united Israel—a *Dodecaphulon*, to use St. Paul's word—an organised body of twelve tribes.

(25) **Their border.**—The border of Asher on the west is the Mediterranean. On the east of Asher lies the tribe of Naphtali, but most of the towns named in these verses lie well within the territory of Asher. The northern end of the territory of this tribe lies beyond the limits of the Ordnance Survey, for it reaches " unto great Zidon" (verse 28). The southern boundary is said to be Carmel (verse 26), but no *town* is identified south of Cabul (*Kabûl*, south-east of *Akkah*, sheet v.).

The towns identified are as follows :—

(25) *El B'aneh*, *El-Yasif* or *Kefr Yasif* (sheet iii.).

(26) *Khurbet-el-Amûd*, and *M'aisleh* (? *Kh.-Muslih*) (sheet iii.).

Shihor-libnath (river of glass), the river Belus (sheet v.).

(27) **Beth-dagon** (*Tell-'Daûk*), near the mouth of the Belus.

Neiel.—(*Y'Arûn*, sheet v.).

Cabul.—(*Kabûl*, south-east of *Akkah*, sheet v.).

(28) **Hebron.**—(*Abdon*, *Kh.-Abdeh*, sheet iii.). Hammon (*El Hama*, sheet iii.).

Kanah (south-east of Tyre, sheet i.).

(29) **Tyre.**—(*es-Sûr*, sheet i.). Hosah (*'Ozziyeh*, sheet i.). Achzib (*es-Zib*, sheet iii., on the coast). (See Josh. xv. 44 for another place of same name.) Ummah (*Kh.-Almah*, north of Achzib).

(33) **And their coast was . . .**—This verse is thus translated by Conder, "Their coast was from Heleph and the Plain of Bitzanannim and Adami, Nekeb, and Jabneel, unto Lakum, and the outgoings were at Jordan."

The east border of the tribe is Jordan, including the waters of Merom and the Sea of Galilee. The tribe of Issachar on the south, and the tribes of Zebulun and Asher on the west, are conterminous with Naphtali.

The places mentioned are identified as follows :—

Heleph.—(*Beit Lif*, sheet iv.). The plain of Bitzanannim (*Kh.-Bessum*, sheet vi.). Adami (*Kh.-Admah*, sheet ix.) : this is the southernmost of all the towns named. Nekeb (*Kh.-Seiyâdeh*, sheet ii.). Jabneel (*Yemma*, sheet v.). All the above places, except Heleph, lie near the Sea of Galilee, on the south-west side.

(34) **Hukkok** (*Yakûk*, sheet vi.), in the same region as the above, but a little further north, near the north-east boundary of Zebulun. Of Judah upon Jordan we can say nothing with certainty.

(35) **The fenced cities.**—Observe the protection of the northern border by fortresses. Ziddim (*Hattin*), Hammath (*Hammâm Tabarîya*), Rakkath (*Tiberias*), and Chinnereth (not identified, but giving a name to the Sea of Galilee, and therefore evidently close by), are all in sheet vi., near the lake.

(36, 37) **Adamah** (*Ed-Dâmeh*, ? *Daimah*, sheet vi.), Ramah (*Râmeh*), Hazor (*Hadîreh*), Kedesh (*Kudes*), Edrei (*Y'ater*), En-hazor (*Hazireh*), and Iron (*Y'arûm*), are all in sheet iv., north of the above. The town of Hazor has been variously identified by previous writers, but Conder expresses no doubt as to its being Hadîreh, which certainly occupies a commanding position above a stream that flows into Lake Merom.

(38) **Migdal-el and Horem** are identified as *Kh.-Mujeidil* and *Hârah* on sheet ii., further north again ; and Beth-anath as *'Ainatha* (sheet iv.).

The Lot of Dan. JOSHUA, XIX. *They Take Leshem.*

(40) And the seventh lot came out for the tribe of the children of Dan according to their families. (41) And the coast of their inheritance was Zorah, and Eshtaol, and Ir-shemesh, (42) and Shaalabbin, and Ajalon, and Jethlah, (43) and Elon, and Thimnathah, and Ekron, (44) and Eltekeh, and Gibbethon, and Baalath, (45) and Jehud, and Bene-berak, and Gath-rimmon, (46) and Me-jarkon, and Rakkon, with the border ¹before ²Japho. (47) And the coast of the children of Dan went out *too little for them*: therefore the children of Dan went up to fight against Leshem, and took it, and smote it with the edge of the sword, and possessed it, and dwelt therein, and called Leshem, *ᵃ* Dan, after the name of Dan their father. (48) This *is* the inheritance of the tribe of the children of Dan according to their families, these cities with their villages.

(49) When they had made an end of dividing the land for inheritance by their coasts, the children of Israel gave an inheritance to Joshua the son of Nun among them: (50) according to the word of the LORD they gave him the

¹ Or, *over against.*
² Or, *Joppa*; Acts 9. 36.
ᵃ Judg. 18. 29.

---

(40) **The seventh lot ... of the children of Dan.**—Dan was the most numerous tribe, next to Judah, in each census taken during the exodus. (See Num. i. and xxvi.) This tribe had also had a post of honour in being commander of the rear-guard during the march. A similar post is here assigned to Dan in Palestine, viz., next to Judah, on the side of the Philistine territory. The Philistines were the most powerful and warlike of the unconquered nations of Palestine. The wisdom of guarding Israel on their frontier by the two strongest of the tribes is manifest. It was Samson, a Danite, who began to deliver Israel from them, and David completed the work. Though there were Philistine wars in the time of the later kings, they never had dominion over Israel after David's time.

(41) **And the coast ...**—Zorah and Eshtaol, in the tribe of Dan, had been originally assigned to Judah (chap. xv. 33); so also Ekron. But it is not clear whether they are mentioned here as marking the border of Dan and Judah, or actually in the territory of the former. However, Dan is wedged in, as it were, between the powerful tribes of Judah and Ephraim, the unconquered Philistines, and the sea. It is not surprising that their coast " went out from them " (verse 47) when it was partly unconquered, partly taken from other tribes in the first instance. Conder says it was carved out of the country of Ephraim.

(41–46) All the towns mentioned here are identified by Conder.

Zorah—*Sur'ah*
Eshtaol—*Eshú'a*
Ir-shemesh—*Ain Shemes*
Shaalabbin—*Selbit*
Ajalon—*Yálo*
Jethlah—(Ruin) *Beit Tul*
} Are all in sheet xvii.

Elon—*Beit Ello*
Thimnathah—(Ruin) *Tibneh*
} Sheet xiv.

Ekron—(*Akir*, sheet xvi.)
Gibbethon—(*Kibbiah*, sheet xiv.)
Baalath—(*Belain*, sheet xiv.)

Jehud—*El-Yehudíyeh*
Bene-berak—*Ibn Ibrak*
} Sheet xiii.

For Gath-rimmon, Conder suggests Gath; but this he identifies with *Tell-es-Safi*, which is well within the territory of Judah (to the south of sheet xvi.).

Me-jarkon, "the yellow water," is thought to be the river *'Aujeh* (sheet xiii.), and Rakkon, *Tell-er-Rakkeit*, to the north of the mouth of it. Japho is *Jaffa*, on the same sheet.

(47) **And the coast of the children of Dan went out too little for them.**—The words "too little" are not in the original; and it seems better to translate literally: *And the coast of the children of Dan went out from them*—*i.e.*, their territory was partly re-conquered by the Philistines. Something similar seems to have occurred in several districts of the country. The Israelites not taking advantage of the impression produced by Joshua's great victories to occupy the territory assigned to them, the nations of Canaan re-possessed themselves of their former abodes, and held them against Israel. The Philistines are expressly said to have been left to prove Israel. Joshua was not permitted to exterminate them. And although Dan and Judah, numerically the two strongest of all the tribes (both in the census in the plains of Moab and at Sinai), were placed next to the Philistines, and had the task of conquering that nation assigned to them, still it was not effected. We read in Judges i., "The Amorites forced the children of Dan into the mountains, for they would not suffer them to come down into the valley."

Hence the Danites, instead of attacking the Philistines and Amorites in their inheritance, preferred to form a new settlement in the north, and put to the sword "a people quiet and secure," who "had no deliverer," rather than "run with patience the race set before them." They were not minded to resist unto blood, striving against their foes. (See the narrative in Judges xviii., especially verses 27 and 28.)

(49, 50) **When they had made an end ... gave an inheritance to Joshua ... according to the word of the Lord they gave him the city which he asked, even Timnath-serah in mount Ephraim** (*Kefr Hâris*, sheet xiv.).—Historically and *typically* the fact is noticeable. (*a*) Historically. Joshua waited for his own inheritance until the last. He sought not his own interest, but that of the people. He asked no kingdom for himself or his family, only a city, which he built, and dwelt therein. (*b*) Typically. "They gave him the city which he asked, according to the word of the Lord." What does this mean in the case of the true Joshua? "*Ask of me*, and I shall give thee the nations for thine inheritance, and the utmost parts of the earth for thy possession." He must reign till God hath put *all enemies under His feet*. Then, and not till then, will He take His own personal inheritance, and be subject to Him that put all things under Him. Timnath-serah means an abundant portion, a portion of abundance. Though small, it was *enough* for Joshua. It will be enough for his Antitype, when "He shall see of the travail of His soul, and *be satisfied*." It is afterwards called Timnath-heres, the portion of city which he asked, even *Timnath-serah in mount Ephraim: and he built the city, and dwelt therein.

(51) *These are* the inheritances, which Eleazar the priest, and Joshua the son of Nun, and the heads of the fathers of the tribes of the children of Israel, divided for an inheritance by lot in Shiloh before the LORD, at the door of the tabernacle of the congregation. So they made an end of dividing the country.

CHAPTER XX.—(1) The LORD also spake unto Joshua, saying, (2) Speak to the children of Israel, saying, *Appoint out for you cities of refuge, whereof I spake unto you by the hand of Moses: (3) that the slayer that killeth *any* person unawares *and* unwittingly may flee thither: and they shall be your refuge from the avenger of blood. (4) And when he that doth flee unto one of those cities shall stand at the entering of the gate of the city, and shall declare his cause in the ears of the elders of that city, they shall take him into the city unto them, and give him a place, that he may dwell among them. (5) And if the avenger of blood pursue after him, then they shall not deliver the slayer up into his hand; because he smote his neighbour unwittingly, and hated him not beforetime. (6) And he shall dwell in that city, until he stand before the congregation for judgment, *and* *until the death of the high priest that shall be in those days: then shall the slayer return, and come unto his own city, and unto his own house, unto the city from whence he fled.

(7) And they ¹appointed Kedesh in Galilee in mount Naphtali, and Shechem in mount Ephraim, and Kirjath-arba, which *is* Hebron, in the mountain of Judah. (8) And on the other side Jordan by Jericho eastward, they assigned *Bezer in the wilderness upon the plain out of the tribe of Reuben, and Ramoth in Gilead out of the tribe of Gad, and Golan in Bashan out of the tribe of Manasseh. (9) These were the cities appointed for all the children of Israel, and for the stranger that sojourneth among them, that whosoever killeth *any* person at unawares might flee thither, and not die by the hand of the avenger of blood, until he stood before the congregation.

---

the Sun. "His going forth is from the end of heaven, and his circuit unto the ends of it, and there is nothing hid from the heat thereof."

XX.

THE INHERITANCE OF LEVI.

(*a*) Six cities of refuge (chap. xx.).
(*b*) Forty-two other cities (chap. xxi.).

(*a*) THE CITIES OF REFUGE.

(2) **Appoint out for you cities of refuge.**—The law in Num. xxxv. appointed that the Levites should have (verse 6) six cities of refuge, and forty-two others. This connection is not always observed, but it has an important bearing on the institution here described. The law of the cities of refuge is given in full in Num. xxxv. and Deut. xix. (See Notes on those passages.)

(6) **Until the death of the high priest.**—The fact is familiar, and the meaning appears to be this: Man being the image of God, all offences against the person of man are offences against his Maker, and the shedding of man's blood is the greatest of such offences. "The blood defileth the land, and the land cannot be cleansed of the blood that is shed therein but by the blood of him who shed it" (Num. xxxv. 33). If, however, the man-slayer did not intend to shed the blood of his neighbour, he is not worthy of death, and the Divine mercy provides a shelter wherein he may still live without offence to the Divine Majesty. Such a shelter is the city of refuge, a city of priests or Levites, whose office was to *bear the iniquity of the children of Israel*, to shield their brethren from the danger they incurred by the dwelling of Jehovah in the midst of them, "dwelling among them in the midst of their uncleanness." Hence the man-slayer must always remain, as it were, under the shadow of the sin-bearing priest or Levite, that he might live, and not die for the innocent blood which he had unintentionally shed. But how could the death of the high priest set him free? Because the high priest was the representative of the whole nation. What the Levites were to all Israel, what the priests were to the Levites, that the high priest was to the priests, and through them to the nation: the individual sin-bearer for all. Into his hands came year by year "all the *iniquities* of the children of Israel, and all their *transgressions* in all their *sins*," and he presented a sin-offering for all.

While the high priest still lived he would still be *legally* tainted with this load of sin, *for the law provides no forgiveness for a priest*. But "he that is dead is justified from sin," and at his death the load which was laid on the high priest might be held to have passed from him, for he had paid the last debt a man can pay on earth. But the high priest being justified, the sinners whom he represents are justified also, and therefore the man-slayers go free. The sentence we have often heard in the explanation of this fact, "Our High Priest can never die," is beside the mark, for if He could never die, we must always remain marked criminals, in a species of restraint. Rather let us say, He has died, having borne our sins in His own body on the tree, that we may be *free* to serve Him, not in guilt and dread and bondage, but in liberty and life.

CHAPTER XXI.— (1) Then came near the heads of the fathers of the Levites unto Eleazar the priest, and unto Joshua the son of Nun, and unto the heads of the fathers of the tribes of the children of Israel; (2) and they spake unto them at Shiloh in the land of Canaan, saying, *The LORD commanded by the hand of Moses to give us cities to dwell in, with the suburbs thereof for our cattle. (3) And the children of Israel gave unto the Levites out of their inheritance, at the commandment of the LORD, these cities and their suburbs.

(4) And the lot came out for the families of the Kohathites: and the children of Aaron the priest, *which were* of the Levites, had by lot out of the tribe of Judah, and out of the tribe of Simeon, and out of the tribe of Benjamin, thirteen cities. (5) And the rest of the children of Kohath *had* by lot out of the families of the tribe of Ephraim, and out of the tribe of Dan, and out of the half tribe of Manasseh, ten cities.

(6) And the children of Gershon *had* by lot out of the families of the tribe of Issachar, and out of the tribe of Asher, and out of the tribe of Naphtali, and out of the half tribe of Manasseh in Bashan, thirteen cities.

(7) The children of Merari by their families *had* out of the tribe of Reuben, and out of the tribe of Gad, and out of the tribe of Zebulun, twelve cities.

(8) And the children of Israel gave by lot unto the Levites these cities with their suburbs, as the LORD commanded by the hand of Moses.

(9) And they gave out of the tribe of the children of Judah, and out of the tribe of the children of Simeon, these cities which are *here* ¹ mentioned by name, (10) which the children of Aaron, *being* of the families of the Kohathites, *who were* of the children of Levi, had: for their's was the first lot. (11) And they gave them ² the city of Arba the father of Anak, which *city is* Hebron, in the hill *country* of Judah, with the suburbs thereof round about it. (12) But the fields of the city, and the villages thereof, gave they to ᵇCaleb the son of Jephunneh for his possession. (13) Thus they gave to the children of Aaron the priest Hebron with her suburbs, *to be* a city of refuge for the slayer; and Libnah with her suburbs, (14) and Jattir with her suburbs, and Eshtemoa with her suburbs, (15) and Holon with her suburbs, and Debir with her suburbs, (16) and Ain with her suburbs, and Juttah with her suburbs, *and* Beth-shemesh with her suburbs; nine cities out of those two tribes. (17) And out of the tribe of Benjamin, Gibeon with her

a Num. 35. 2.

¹ Heb., *called.*

² Or, *Kirjath-arba.*

b ch. 14. 14; 1 Chr. 6. 56.

XXI.

(*b*) THE REST OF THE LEVITICAL CITIES.

(2) **Suburbs.**—The extent of these is described in Num. xxxv. (See on that passage.)

(4–8) The order of the distribution—viz., (1) to priests, (2) to Kohathites, (3) to Gershonites, (4) to Merarites—is in strict agreement with the order of priority observed in the exodus. In the camp of Israel there were two squares surrounding the tabernacle: an inner square of priests and Levites, an outer square of the tribes of Israel, three on each side. The inner square was arranged thus:—The priests, with Moses and Aaron, on the east, by the entrance of the tabernacle; the Kohathites on the south, the Gershonites on the west, and the Merarites on the north. On the march the priests were the chief officers of this portion of the army. The Kohathites carried the sacred vessels, the Gershonites the curtains and various fabrics of the tent and tabernacle, and the Merarites the bars and boards. When they received their inheritances in Palestine, the same relative order was preserved.

INHERITANCE OF THE PRIESTS (verses 9–19).

(9) **Out of the tribe of . . . Judah . . . and Simeon;** and (17) **out of the tribe of Benjamin.** —It is worthy of notice that, with the exception of a single city in the tribe of Simeon (viz., Ain, verse 16), *all the priestly cities are so arranged as to fall ultimately within the kingdom of Judah,* of which the capital was Jerusalem, the city which the Lord had chosen out of all the tribes of Israel to put His name there. The Levites also left their cities and their suburbs in the reign of Jeroboam (2 Chron. xi. 14), and came over to Judah. But the fact that all the priests, with the trifling exception noted above, were already settled in that kingdom, must have been a great attraction.

When these facts are observed, it is hardly possible not to be struck with the undesigned agreement between the Book of Joshua and the later history, as well as with the Divine foresight which arranged the distribution of the people thus.

(13) **Hebron** (*El Khalil*).

(14) **Jattir** (*Attir*).

Eshtemoa (*Es Semû'a*).

(15) **Debir.**—Probably identical with the town of this name in chap. xv. 49 (*Edh. Dhâheriyeh*), south-west of Hebron.

(16) **Juttah** (*Yuttah*).

Beth-shemesh (*Ain Shemes*).

(17) **Gibeon** (*El Jib*).

Geba (*Jeb'a*).

suburbs, Geba with her suburbs, (18) Anathoth with her suburbs, and Almon with her suburbs; four cities. (19) All the cities of the children of Aaron, the priests, *were* thirteen cities with their suburbs.

(20) And the families of the children of Kohath, the Levites which remained of the children of Kohath, even they had the cities of their lot out of the tribe of Ephraim. (21) For they gave them Shechem with her suburbs in mount Ephraim, *to be* a city of refuge for the slayer; and Gezer with her suburbs, (22) and Kibzaim with her suburbs, and Beth-horon with her suburbs; four cities. (23) And out of the tribe of Dan, Eltekeh with her suburbs, Gibbethon with her suburbs, (24) Aijalon with her suburbs, Gath-rimmon with her suburbs; four cities. (25) And out of the half tribe of Manasseh, Tanach with her suburbs, and Gath-rimmon with her suburbs; two cities. (26) All the cities *were* ten with their suburbs for the families of the children of Kohath that remained.

(27) And unto the children of Gershon, of the families of the Levites, out of the *other* half tribe of Manasseh *they gave* Golan in Bashan with her suburbs, *to be* a city of refuge for the slayer; and Beesh-terah with her suburbs; two cities. (28) And out of the tribe of Issachar, Kishon with her suburbs, Dabareh with her suburbs, (29) Jarmuth with her suburbs, En-gannim with her suburbs; four cities. (30) And out of the tribe of Asher, Mishal with her suburbs, Abdon with her suburbs, (31) Helkath with her suburbs, and Rehob with her suburbs; four cities. (32) And out of the tribe of Naphtali, Kedesh in Galilee with her suburbs, *to be* a city of refuge for the slayer; and Hammoth-dor with her suburbs, and Kartan with her suburbs; three cities. (33) All the cities of the Gershonites according to their families *were* thirteen cities with their suburbs.

(34) And unto the families of the children of Merari, the rest of the Levites, out of the tribe of Zebulun, Jokneam with her suburbs, and Kartah with her suburbs, (35) Dimnah with her suburbs, Nahalal with her suburbs; four cities. (36) And out of the tribe of Reuben, Bezer with her suburbs, and Jahazah with her suburbs, (37) Kedemoth with her suburbs, and Mephaath with her suburbs; four cities. (38) And out of the tribe of Gad, Ramoth in Gilead with her suburbs, *to be* a city of refuge for the slayer; and Mahanaim with her suburbs, (39) Heshbon with her suburbs, Jazer with her suburbs; four cities in

---

(18) **Anathoth** (*'Anâta*).
Almon (*'Almit*).

(20) **The children of Kohath ... had the cities ... out of the tribe of Ephraim.**—In this instance the most honoured among the families of the Levites (after the house of Aaron) is grouped with the tribe next in honour after Judah. The tribes of Dan and Manasseh (verses 23—25) also were highly honoured, as they received Kohathites to settle among them.

(21) **Shechem ... in mount Ephraim, to be a city of refuge.**—The metropolis of Israel for the time being is made a city of refuge; and there is an obvious convenience in this. In the same way Solomon made Jerusalem a city of refuge for Shimei, binding him not to leave the city under penalty of death (1 Kings ii. 36—46).

Gezer (*Tell Jezer*).

(22) **Kibzaim** (*Tell el-Kabûs*).
Beth-horon (*Beit-'Ur*).

(23, 24) For these Danite cities, see chap. xix. 40—46.

(25) **Tanach**—*i.e.*, Taanach—a city of Manasseh, in the territory of Issachar.

(27) **Unto the children of Gershon ... out of the other half tribe of Manasseh ... in Bashan, and** (28) **out of the tribe of Issachar, and** (30) **out of the tribe of Asher.**—Each of the four divisions of the house of Levi is made a bond to cement three of the twelve tribes together. Sometimes the association is obvious. In this case the two sides of Jordan are bound together by the Gershonites.

(28) **Dabareh**—*i.e.*, Daberath (*Debûrieh*).

(29) **Jarmuth**—*i.e.*, Remeth.
En-gannim (*Jenin*).

(30) **Mishal.**—See chap. xix. 46.
Abdon.—Also mentioned there.

(32) For **Kedesh** see chap. xix. 37. The other two are not identified with any certainty.

(34) **Unto the .... children of Merari .... out of the tribe of Zebulun, and** (36) **out of the tribe of Reuben, and** (38) **out of the tribe of Gad.**—In the case of the Gershonites, we saw two tribes on the west of Jordan united to one on the east. The Merarites are employed to connect two tribes on the east of Jordan with one upon the west, and the south-east of the Israelitish territory with the north. Thus "the whole body by joints and bands" was "knit together, that it might grow with a growth of God." It is not a little interesting to observe that Joshua's work of dividing the land of Canaan was so much directed to preserve the union of the several parts. The name of Levi (*joined*) thus received a spiritual emphasis. He was divided in Israel that he might be a bond of union, bringing the tribes of Israel together, and joining all of them to their God.

Jokneam (*Tell Keimûn*, near Carmel).

(35) **Nahalal** (*'Ain Mahil*).

all. ⁽⁴⁰⁾ So all the cities for the children of Merari by their families, which were remaining of the families of the Levites, were by their lot twelve cities.

⁽⁴¹⁾ All the cities of the Levites within the possession of the children of Israel were forty and eight cities with their suburbs. ⁽⁴²⁾ These cities were every one with their suburbs round about them: thus were all these cities.

⁽⁴³⁾ And the LORD gave unto Israel all the land which he sware to give unto their fathers; and they possessed it, and dwelt therein. ⁽⁴⁴⁾ And the LORD gave them rest round about, according to all that he sware unto their fathers: and there stood not a man of all their enemies before them; the LORD delivered all their enemies into their hand. ⁽⁴⁵⁾ *a* There failed not ought of any good thing which the LORD had spoken unto the house of Israel; all came to pass.

CHAPTER XXII.—⁽¹⁾ Then Joshua called the Reubenites, and the Gadites, and the half tribe of Manasseh, ⁽²⁾ and said unto them, Ye have kept all that Moses the servant of the LORD commanded you, and have obeyed my voice in all that I commanded you: ⁽³⁾ ye have not left your brethren these many days unto this day, but have kept the charge of the commandment of the LORD your God. ⁽⁴⁾ And now the LORD your God hath given rest unto your brethren, as he promised them: therefore now return ye, and get you unto your tents, *and* unto the land of your possession, *b* which Moses the servant of the LORD gave you on the other side Jordan. ⁽⁵⁾ But take diligent heed to do the commandment and the law, which Moses the servant of the LORD charged you, *c* to love the LORD your God, and to walk in all his ways, and to keep his commandments, and to cleave unto him, and to serve him with all your heart and with all your soul.

⁽⁶⁾ So Joshua blessed them, and sent them away: and they went unto their tents. ⁽⁷⁾ Now to the *one* half of the tribe of Manasseh Moses had given *possession* in Bashan: but unto the *other* half thereof gave Joshua among their brethren on this side Jordan westward. And when Joshua sent them away also unto their tents, then he blessed them, ⁽⁸⁾ and he spake unto them, saying, Return with much riches unto your tents, and with very much cattle, with silver, and with gold, and with brass, and with iron, and with very much raiment: divide the spoil of your enemies with your brethren.

⁽⁹⁾ And the children of Reuben and the children of Gad and the half tribe of Manasseh returned, and departed from the children of Israel out of Shiloh, which *is* in the land of Canaan, to go unto the country of Gilead, to the land of their possession, whereof

a ch. 23. 14, 15.

b Num. 32. 33; ch. 13. 8.

c Deut. 10. 12.

⁽⁴³⁾ **And the Lord gave unto Israel.**—Although the conquest of Canaan was not completed in the time of Joshua, as it was afterwards under David, yet we see by this statement that the expectations of Israel were abundantly satisfied. They received all that they hoped for.

XXII.

DISMISSAL OF THE TWO AND A HALF TRIBES TO THEIR INHERITANCE ON THE EAST OF JORDAN.

(1–6) Charge to the two and a half tribes by Joshua. The words of verses 2 and 3 recall the promise of chap. i. 16, and Joshua's charge in verse 5 recalls that which he himself had received at first (chap. i. 7), and finds a further parallel in what he said to Israel before his death (chaps. xxiii., xxiv.).

(7, 8) Joshua blesses the half tribe of Manasseh that dwelt on the west of Jordan.

⁽⁷⁾ **When Joshua sent them away also unto their tents, then he blessed them.**—It is noteworthy that of all the tribes of Israel who followed Joshua, and remained with him, this half tribe alone is mentioned as receiving a special blessing. We cannot fail to observe that both in ancient times, and also among ourselves, the conduct of the two and a half tribes in choosing their inheritance on the east of Jordan has been regarded as laying them open to some blame. Historically, this is incorrect. God delivered the land of Sihon and Og to Israel; some one must inherit it. Again, the true eastern boundary of Palestine is not the Jordan, but the mountain range of Gilead, which parts it from the desert that lies beyond. Really the two and a half tribes were as much in Palestine as the rest, only their position does not take advantage of that wonderful miracle by which Jordan was driven back, and the Israelites were enabled to strike at the heart of their Canaanitish foes. They themselves, however, were compelled to cross the Jordan before they could obtain the *rest* which they seemed to have won before they crossed it—"that they without us should not be made perfect." In the spiritual world these two and a half tribes answer to the people who received their inheritance from Moses (*i.e.*, from the law); the others are those who received nothing until they followed Joshua, *i.e.*, the Captain of salvation, Jesus Christ, who gives rest to *all*. When He came, His own people were divided,

The Altar of Testimony.   JOSHUA, XXII.   *The Israelites Offended.*

they were possessed, according to the word of the LORD by the hand of Moses. ⁽¹⁰⁾ And when they came unto the borders of Jordan, that *are* in the land of Canaan, the children of Reuben and the children of Gad and the half tribe of Manasseh built there an altar by Jordan, a great altar to see to.

⁽¹¹⁾ And the children of Israel heard say, Behold, the children of Reuben and the children of Gad and the half tribe of Manasseh have built an altar over against the land of Canaan, in the borders of Jordan, at the passage of the children of Israel. ⁽¹²⁾ And when the children of Israel heard *of it,* the whole congregation of the children of Israel gathered themselves together at Shiloh, to go up to war against them. ⁽¹³⁾ And the children of Israel sent unto the children of Reuben, and to the children of Gad, and to the half tribe of Manasseh, into the land of Gilead, Phinehas the son of Eleazar the priest, ⁽¹⁴⁾ and with him ten princes, of each ¹ chief house a prince throughout all the tribes of Israel; and each one *was* an head of the house of their fathers among the thousands of Israel. ⁽¹⁵⁾ And they came unto the children of Reuben, and to the children of Gad, and to the half tribe of Manasseh, unto the land of Gilead, and they spake with them, saying, ⁽¹⁶⁾ Thus saith the whole congregation of the LORD, What trespass *is* this that ye have committed against the God of Israel, to turn away this day from following the LORD, in that ye have builded you an altar, that ye might rebel this day against the LORD? ⁽¹⁷⁾ *Is* the iniquity ^a of Peor too little for us, from which we are not cleansed until this day, although there was a plague in the congregation of the LORD, ⁽¹⁸⁾ but that ye must turn away this day from following the LORD? and it will be, *seeing* ye rebel to day against the LORD, that to morrow he will be wroth with the whole congregation of Israel. ⁽¹⁹⁾ Notwithstanding, if the land of your possession *be* unclean, *then* pass ye over unto the land of the possession of the LORD, wherein the LORD's tabernacle dwelleth, and take possession among us: but rebel not against the LORD, nor rebel against us, in building you an altar beside the altar of the LORD our God. ⁽²⁰⁾ ^b Did not Achan the son of

Marginal notes: 1 Heb., *house of the father.* — *a* Num. 25. 4. — *b* ch. 7. 1, 5.

---

like the tribe of Manasseh. Some could not forsake Moses, a sacrifice which they thought He required of them; some gave up all, and followed Him. "Forgetting (Heb., *M'násheh—i.e.,* Manasseh) the things that were behind, and reaching forth unto the things before," they would take nothing but what He gave. These are they who receive special blessing from Him. (See *Names on the Gates of Pearl—*Manasseh, p. 165, &c.)

⁽¹⁰⁾ **The borders of Jordan, that are in the land of Canaan.**—As far as these words go, the site of the altar *might* be either east or west of Jordan; but it seems to be more probable that it was on the east bank. And thus the phrase above would be a reminder of the very thing the altar was intended to enforce, viz., the fact that *both borders of Jordan* are part of the promised land. But Kurn Surtabeth, twenty miles north of Jericho, on the west side of Jordan, has been thought to be the place.

⁽¹¹⁾ **Have built an altar.**—Rather, *have built the altar.* As appears by verse 28, it was a representation of the altar of Jehovah: a copy of the one altar which He had given to Israel for sacrifice. The design was to set up on the east of Jordan a likeness of that altar which was established on the west, that the tribes on the other side of Jordan might appeal to it as a proof that they also were the people of Jehovah.

⁽¹²⁾ **To go up to war against them.**—There is no more striking proof of Israel's obedience to the law and veneration for it in the days of Joshua than this. A single altar to Jehovah, besides the one in Shiloh, is sufficient cause for *war* against the builders of it. But see what is the language of the prophet. "According to the number of thy cities were thy gods, O Judah; and *according to the number of the streets of Jerusalem have ye set up altars to Bosheth* (disgrace), *even altars to burn incense to Baal*" (Jer. xi. 13). What stronger proof could we require of the veracity of the narrative in this place, and that it is genuine contemporary history? What writer of the days of Jeremiah, to which date some have referred the Book of Deuteronomy and its requirements, could have conceived such a scene as this, when altars to Jehovah on the high places were hardly regarded as illegal, and altars to Baal were as numerous as the very streets?

Another passage in a different part of the Old Testament corroborates indirectly, but in a striking manner, the tone of this (Neh. viii. 17): "The congregation . . . . made booths, and sat under the booths" (as required by the law of Moses in the Feast of Tabernacles); "for *since the days of Joshua the son of Nun* unto that day *had not the children of Israel done so.*"

⁽¹³⁾ **Phinehas . . . and** ⁽¹⁴⁾ **ten princes.**—According to the constitution established by Moses, a government by *priests and judges.* Phinehas in particular was well suited to the office of "defender of the faith" (see Num. xxv.).

⁽¹⁷⁾ **The iniquity of Peor.**—A very natural subject for reference on the part of Phinehas, who had distinguished himself by his zealous opposition to it.

⁽¹⁹⁾ **If the land of your possession be unclean.**—This suggests that they might have built the altar in it to sanctify it. But it would hardly be intelligible unless the altar was, as we supposed, on the eastern side.

⁽²⁰⁾ **That man perished not alone.**—His whole household was exterminated. (See on chap. vii. 24.)

The Two Tribes and a Half JOSHUA, XXII. *Justify their Conduct.*

Zerah commit a trespass in the accursed thing, and wrath fell on all the congregation of Israel? and that man perished not alone in his iniquity.

(21) Then the children of Reuben and the children of Gad and the half tribe of Manasseh answered, and said unto the heads of the thousands of Israel, (22) The LORD God of gods, the LORD God of gods, he knoweth, and Israel he shall know; if *it be* in rebellion, or if in transgression against the LORD, (save us not this day,) (23) that we have built us an altar to turn from following the LORD, or if to offer thereon burnt offering or meat offering, or if to offer peace offerings thereon, let the LORD himself require *it*; (24) and if we have not *rather* done it for fear of *this* thing, saying, ¹In time to come your children might speak unto our children, saying, What have ye to do with the LORD God of Israel? (25) For the LORD hath made Jordan a border between us and you, ye children of Reuben and children of Gad; ye have no part in the LORD: so shall your children make our children cease from fearing the LORD. (26) Therefore we said, Let us now prepare to build us an altar, not for burnt offering, nor for sacrifice: (27) but *that* it *may be* ªa witness between us, and you, and our generations after us, that we might do the service of the LORD before him with our burnt offerings, and with our sacrifices, and with our peace offerings; that your children may not say to our children in time to come, Ye have no part in the LORD. (28) Therefore said we, that it shall be, when they should *so* say to us or to our generations in time to come, that we may say *again*, Behold the pattern of the altar of the LORD, which our fathers made, not for burnt offerings, nor for sacrifices; but it *is* a witness between us and you. (29) God forbid that we should rebel against the LORD, and turn this day from following the LORD, to build an altar for burnt offerings, for meat offerings, or for sacrifices, beside the altar of the LORD our God that *is* before his tabernacle.

(30) And when Phinehas the priest, and the princes of the congregation and heads of the thousands of Israel which *were* with him, heard the words that the children of Reuben and the children of Gad and the children of Manasseh spake, ²it pleased them. (31) And Phinehas the son of Eleazar the priest said unto the children of Reuben, and to the children of Gad, and to the children of Manasseh, This day we perceive that the LORD *is* among us, because ye have not committed this trespass against the LORD: ³now ye have delivered the children of Israel out of the hand of the LORD.

(32) And Phinehas the son of Eleazar the priest, and the princes, returned from the children of Reuben, and from the children of Gad, out of the land of Gilead, unto the land of Canaan, to the children of Israel, and brought them word again. (33) And the thing pleased

---

(26) **An altar.**—Rather, *the altar*. It was not *an* altar (verse 23), but *the* altar, *i.e.*, the pattern or copy of the altar of Jehovah, to prove that the two and a half tribes had the same right to approach Him as all the rest.

(27) **Ye have no part in the Lord.**—Something of the kind was insinuated in the abuse of the Gileadites by the men of Ephraim (Judges xii. 4), when they said, "Ye Gileadites are fugitives of Ephraim among the Ephraimites, and among the Manassites." That taunt cost the Ephraimites the lives of 42,000 men. The person who made it the law of Israel to have no part in Jehovah was "Jeroboam the son of Nebat, who made Israel to sin" by setting up the calves, and thus diverting the stream of national worshippers from Jerusalem, the place chosen by the Lord. It may be further observed that Joshua's efforts under the direction of Jehovah for the establishment of national unity in Israel are proved by the narrative in this chapter to have taken considerable effect. At whatever cost, it was felt that the unity of national worship must be maintained. Rebellion "against Jehovah" is treated by the heads of Israel (verse 19) as rebellion "against us."

(28) **The altar of the Lord, which our fathers made, not for burnt offerings, nor for sacrifices.**—The words suggest the reflection that there are many other "altars" so called in the present day, also an occasion of dispute; and it would tend greatly to peace and acquiescence in their existence if we could be assured that, like this altar, they are "*not for sacrifice*," but for a witness to that common worship of Christ as God which is an essential feature of Christianity.

(31) **We perceive that the Lord is among us, because ye have not committed this trespass** . . .—The best token of the Divine presence *among* men is the Divine likeness and holiness *in* men. "If we say that we have fellowship with Him, and walk in darkness, we lie . . . but if we walk in the light, we have fellowship one with another."

(33) **Did not intend**—*i.e.*, they decided not (Heb. *they did not say to go up against them*).

the children of Israel; and the children of Israel blessed God, and did not intend to go up against them in battle, to destroy the land wherein the children of Reuben and Gad dwelt.

(34) And the children of Reuben and the children of Gad called the altar ¹ *Ed*: for it *shall be* a witness between us that the LORD *is* God.

CHAPTER XXIII.—(1) And it came to pass a long time after that the LORD had given rest unto Israel from all their enemies round about, that Joshua waxed old *and* ² stricken in age. (2) And Joshua called for all Israel, *and* for their elders, and for their heads, and for their judges, and for their officers, and said unto them, I am old *and* stricken in age: (3) and ye have seen all that the LORD your God hath done unto all these nations because of you; for the *ᵃ* LORD your God *is* he that hath fought for you. (4) Behold, I have divided unto you by lot these nations that remain, to be an inheritance for your tribes, from Jordan, with all the nations that I have cut off, even unto the great sea ³ westward. (5) And the LORD your God, he shall expel them from before you, and drive them from out of your sight; and ye shall possess their land, as the LORD your God hath promised unto you. (6) Be ye therefore very courageous to keep and to do all that is written in the book of the law of Moses, *ᵇ* that ye turn not aside therefrom *to* the right hand or *to* the left; (7) that ye come not among these nations, these that remain among you; neither *ᶜ* make mention of the name of their gods, nor cause to swear *by them*, neither serve them, nor bow yourselves unto them: (8) ⁴ but cleave unto the LORD your God, as ye have done unto this day. (9) ⁵ For the LORD hath driven out from before you great nations and strong: but *as for* you, no man hath been able to stand before you unto this day. (10) *ᵈ* One man of you shall chase a thousand: for the LORD your God, he *it is* that fighteth for you, as he hath promised you.

(11) Take good heed therefore unto your-⁶selves, that ye love the LORD

Marginal notes:
1 That is, A witness.
2 Heb., *come into days.*
ᵃ Ex. 14. 14.
3 Heb., *at the sunset.*
B.C. cir. 1427.
ᵇ Deut. 5. 32 & 28. 14.
ᶜ Ps. 16. 4.
4 Or, *For if you will cleave,* &c.
5 Or, *then the LORD will drive.*
ᵈ Lev. 26. 8; Deut. 32. 30.
6 Heb., *souls.*

---

(34) **That the Lord** (*i.e.*, Jehovah) **is God** (of all the twelve tribes alike).

XXIII.
JOSHUA'S LAST CHARGE.

(*a*) To the rulers (chap. xxiii.).
(*b*) To the people (chap. xxiv. to verse 25).

(*a*) TO THE RULERS.
(1) **Joshua waxed old and stricken in age.**—The same expression employed in chap. xiii. 1. It is possible that we ought to translate thus: "It came to pass, a long time after the Lord had given rest ... *and* (after) Joshua had grown old, advanced in days, *that* Joshua called ... " Or it may be that we have here, as it were, "the two evenings" of Joshua's life: the early evening, when his sun began to decline—the afternoon; and the late evening, just before its glorious setting in the service of Jehovah on earth, to "serve Him day and night in His temple."
(Our Lord fed the five thousand between the two evenings—Matt. xiv. 15 and 23. So Joshua gave Israel their inheritance between the two evenings of his life.)

(2) **Joshua called for all Israel** (*i.e.*, first) ... **for their elders ... heads ... judges, and ... officers.**—The first "and" in the English Version of this verse should be omitted.

And said unto them ... —The address which follows should be contrasted with that in chap. xxiv. The first is suited to men of education, authority, and position in Israel, and concerns the duty of the rulers; the second contains one plain lesson for all the people, and makes no demand upon their intellect, nor does it require any position of influence or authority to carry out the instructions which it gives.

(4) **Behold, I have divided unto you by lot these nations that remain.**—Here, as in chap. xiii. 1—7, and afterwards, in Judges ii. 23, the preliminary and partial nature of the conquest achieved by Joshua is distinctly recognised. He gave Israel the land to possess, and gave them the vantage-ground from which they might possess it. In verses 4 and 5 he bids them continue the work which he had begun.

(6) **Be ye therefore very courageous to keep and to do all that is written in the book of the law of Moses.**—As Joshua was the servant of the law himself, so must his successors be. No higher position was attainable than this. It has been the same with the successors of the greater Joshua. With them, and with those who follow them, nothing can ever supersede the authority of *the written word.*

(7) **Come not among these nations**—*i.e.*, do not mix with them; literally, *do not go in unto them.* (See on chap. xiii. 2—7, for the rules to be observed in dealing with the nations.) It must always be remembered that, in proposing the extermination of the seven nations, Jehovah reserved to Himself the ordering of the details of the conquest and extermination. "When the Lord thy God shall deliver them before thee, thou shalt smite them and utterly destroy them." He did not propose to deliver them all to Israel at once, for reasons set forth in Judges ii., iii. Meantime, it was a trial of Israel's faith and obedience to live among idolaters without making any peace with them, or lending any countenance to their idolatry.

(9) **No man hath been able to stand before you.**—Comp. chap. i. 5.

(10) **One man of you shall chase a thousand.**—See Deut. xxviii. 7.

your God. (12) Else if ye do in any wise go back, and cleave unto the remnant of these nations, *even* these that remain among you, and shall make marriages with them, and go in unto them, and they to you: (13) know for a certainty that the LORD your God will no more drive out *any of* these nations from before you; *a* but they shall be snares and traps unto you, and scourges in your sides, and thorns in your eyes, until ye perish from off this good land which the LORD your God hath given you.

(14) And, behold, this day I *am* going the way of all the earth: and ye know in all your hearts and in all your souls, that *b* not one thing hath failed of all the good things which the LORD your God spake concerning you; all are come to pass unto you, *and* not one thing hath failed thereof. (15) Therefore it shall come to pass, *that* as all good things are come upon you, which the LORD your God promised you; so shall the LORD bring upon you all evil things, until he have destroyed you from off this good land which the LORD your God hath given you. (16) When ye have transgressed the covenant of the LORD your God, which he commanded you, and have gone and served other gods, and bowed yourselves to them; then shall the anger of the LORD be kindled against you, and ye shall perish quickly from off the good land which he hath given unto you.

CHAPTER XXIV.—(1) And Joshua gathered all the tribes of Israel to Shechem, and called for the elders of Israel, and for their heads, and for their judges, and for their officers; and they presented themselves before God.

(2) And Joshua said unto all the people, Thus saith the LORD God of Israel, *c* Your fathers dwelt on the other side of the flood in old time, *even* Terah, the father of Abraham, and the father of Nachor: and they served other gods. (3) And I took your father Abraham from the other side of the flood, and led him throughout all the land of Canaan, and multiplied his seed, and *d* gave him Isaac.

a Ex. 23. 33; Num. 33. 55; Deut. 7. 16.

b ch. 21. 45.

c Gen. 11. 31; Judith 5. 6, 7.

d Gen. 21. 2.

(12, 13) **If ye ... make marriages with them ... the Lord your God will no more drive out.**—The common-sense of this warning is manifest. The God of Israel cannot treat as His enemies those whom Israel has united with itself, unless He also makes war on Israel. It was a long time before Israel learned the lesson how to live *in* the world without being *of* the world. It was not learnt until after the Babylonish captivity, and when learnt, it soon developed into a Pharisaical exclusiveness, which produced the very opposite effect to that which the law was intended to have.

(14) **Ye know ... that not one thing hath failed.**—These words, as well as the similar statement in chap. xxi. 43—45, show that though the conquest of Canaan by Joshua was in one way a limited conquest, yet it fully satisfied the hopes of Israel for the time: *i.e.*, that they understood the Divine promises in that sense in which we see them to have been actually fulfilled.

(15) **As all good things are come upon you ... so shall ... all evil things.**—Comp. Deut. viii. 19, 20, and xxx. 17, 18, and xxviii. throughout.

The above exhortations are upon matters that lie within the province of the ruler. The law must be forgotten if the magistrates will not enforce it. Marriages and treaties and public worship are matters under the control of the law. What the rulers will not tolerate, the people will find it hard to maintain.

(16) The resemblance between this verse and an exhortation in Deuteronomy should be noticed, chap. xi. 16, 17, "Take heed to yourselves, lest . . ye turn aside and serve other gods and worship them; and then the Lord's wrath be kindled against you . . . and ye perish quickly from off the good land which the Lord giveth you."

XXIV.

(*b*) JOSHUA'S LAST CHARGE TO THE PEOPLE.

(1, 2) **Joshua gathered all the tribes . . .**—At the former address the rulers alone appear to have been present; on this occasion *all Israel* was gathered. And what is spoken is addressed to the people in the hearing of the rulers. In the speech that now follows Joshua briefly recapitulates the national history; he had not thought this necessary for the rulers. To them he had said, "Ye know;" but "the people" embraced many persons of but little thought and education, whom it was necessary to inform and remind and instruct, even as to the leading events of their national history. The simple lesson which Joshua's words are intended to enforce is the duty of *serving Jehovah*, and *serving Him alone*. It is the first great lesson of the old covenant. "I am Jehovah, thy God; thou shalt have no other gods beside Me." The ark of this covenant had brought them over Jordan into the promised land.

(2) **Your fathers dwelt on the other side of the flood.**—The flood, *i.e.*, the river—probably Euphrates, though it may be Jordan, or both. Flood in our English Bible has been used for river in several places: *e.g.*, Job. xxii. 16, "whose foundation was overflown with a *flood*," *i.e.*, a river; Psalm lxvi. 6, "He turned the sea into dry land: they went through the *flood* (the river, *i.e.*, Jordan) on foot;" Matt. vii. 25, 27, "The rain descended, and the *floods* (*i.e.*, the *rivers*) came."

They served other gods.—They, *i.e.*, Terah, Abraham, and Nachor.

(3) **The flood**—*i.e.*, the river, as in verse 2; and so also in verse 15.

(4) And I gave unto Isaac *Jacob and Esau: and I gave unto *Esau mount Seir, to possess it; *but Jacob and his children went down into Egypt. (5) *I sent Moses also and Aaron, and I plagued Egypt, according to that which I did among them: and afterward I brought you out. (6) And I *brought your fathers out of Egypt: and ye came unto the sea; and the Egyptians pursued after your fathers with chariots and horsemen unto *the Red sea. (7) And when they cried unto the LORD, he put darkness between you and the Egyptians, and brought the sea upon them, and covered them; and your eyes have seen what I have done in Egypt: and ye dwelt in the wilderness a long season. (8) And I brought you into the land of the Amorites, which dwelt on the other side Jordan; *and they fought with you: and I gave them into your hand, that ye might possess their land; and I destroyed them from before you. (9) Then Balak the son of Zippor, king of Moab, arose and warred against Israel, and *sent and called Balaam the son of Beor to curse you: (10) but I would not hearken unto Balaam; therefore he blessed you still: so I delivered you out of his hand. (11) And ye went over Jordan, and came unto Jericho: and the men of Jericho fought against you, the Amorites, and the Perizzites, and the Canaanites, and the Hittites, and the Girgashites, the Hivites, and the Jebusites; and I delivered them into your hand. (12) And *I sent the hornet before you, which drave them out from before you, *even* the two kings of the Amorites; *but* not with thy sword, nor with thy bow. (13) And I have given you a land for which ye did not labour, and cities which ye built not, and ye dwell in them; of the vineyards and oliveyards which ye planted not do ye eat.

(14) Now therefore fear the LORD, and serve him in sincerity and in truth: and put away the gods which your fathers served on the other side of the flood, and in Egypt; and serve ye the LORD. (15) And if it seem evil unto you to serve the LORD, choose you this day whom ye will serve; whether the gods which your fathers served that *were* on the other side of the flood, or the gods of the Amorites, in whose land ye dwell: but as for me and my house, we will serve the LORD.

(16) And the people answered and said, God forbid that we should forsake the LORD, to serve other gods; (17) for the LORD our God, he *it is* that brought us up and our fathers out of the land of Egypt, from the house of bondage, and which did those great signs in our sight, and preserved us in all the way wherein we went, and among all the people through whom we passed: (18) and the LORD drave out from before us all the people, even the Amorites which dwelt in the land: *therefore* will we also serve the LORD; for he *is* our God.

(19) And Joshua said unto the people,

---

(9) **Warred against Israel.**—The sending for Balaam was a distinct act of hostility. Whether Balak himself ever led an army against Israel we are not informed. In the war with the Midianites, Balaam was slain; and there may have been Moabites allied and acting with the Midianites in the war in Num. xxxi.

(12) **The hornet.**—There appears no reason for taking this word in any other than a literal sense. The possibility of what is recorded here has been abundantly illustrated by events reported in our own times.

The two kings of the Amorites.—Apparently, but not *necessarily*, Sihon and Og are intended. There were kings of the Amorites on both sides of Jordan.

(14) **Fear the Lord.**—It should be remembered throughout the whole of this passage that Lord stands for JEHOVAH, the covenant God of Israel.

(15) **The Amorites.**—Here used generically for the inhabitants of Canaan.

As for me and my house, we will serve the Lord.—For Joshua himself the service of Jehovah on earth was nearly over. He pledges his "house" to the same service. What is known of his family? It is a singular fact that *no descendant of the great conqueror, no member of his household, is named in the Bible.* In the genealogies of Ephraim in 1 Chron. vii., Joshua's name is the last in his own line (ver. 27: "Non his son, Jehoshuah his son"). I cannot but regard the silence of Scripture under this head as profoundly significant. It is one more analogy between the Joshua of the Old Testament and his great Antitype in the Gospel: "*whose house are we, if we hold fast the confidence and the rejoicing of the hope firm unto the end*" (Heb. iii. 6). The house of Joshua embraces all the faithful servants of the Lord.

(16) **God forbid that we should forsake the Lord, to serve other gods.**—The feelings of the people are naturally shocked by the bare mention of apostasy. They will not *forsake* Jehovah on any account. But their answer only betrayed their want of intelligence. They missed the point of Joshua's argument, as may be seen by his reply.

(19) **And Joshua said . . . Ye cannot serve the Lord: for he is . . . jealous . . .**

Ye cannot serve the LORD: for he *is* an holy God; he *is* a jealous God; he will not forgive your transgressions nor your sins. (20) If ye forsake the LORD, and serve strange gods, ᵃthen he will turn and do you hurt, and consume you, after that he hath done you good.

(21) And the people said unto Joshua, Nay; but we will serve the LORD.

(22) And Joshua said unto the people, Ye *are* witnesses against yourselves that ye have chosen you the LORD, to serve him. And they said, *We are* witnesses. (23) Now therefore put away, *said he,* the strange gods which *are* among you, and incline your heart unto the LORD God of Israel. (24) And the people said unto Joshua, The LORD our God will we serve, and his voice will we obey.

(25) So Joshua made a covenant with the people that day, and set them a statute and an ordinance in Shechem. (26) And Joshua wrote these words in the book of the law of God, and took a great stone, and set it up there under an oak, that *was* by the sanctuary of the LORD. (27) And Joshua said unto all the people, Behold, this stone shall be a witness unto us; for it hath heard all the words of the LORD which he spake unto us: it shall be therefore a witness unto you, lest ye deny your God. (28) So Joshua let the people depart, every man unto his inheritance.

(29) And it came to pass after these things, that Joshua the son of Nun, the servant of the LORD, died, *being* an hundred and ten years old. (30) And they buried him in the border of his inheritance in ᵇTimnath-serah, which *is* in mount Ephraim, on the north side of the hill of Gaash.

(31) And Israel served the LORD all the days of Joshua, and all the days of the elders that ¹overlived Joshua, and which had known all the works of the LORD, that he had done for Israel.

a ch. 23. 15.

b ch. 19. 50; Judg. 2. 9.

B.C. cir. 1426.

¹ Heb., *prolonged their days after Joshua.*

Jehovah will not consent to be served as one God among many: the very thing which Israel was doing at the moment, which they meant to do, and did do, with rare intervals, down to the Babylonish captivity, when the evil spirit of (literal) idolatry was expelled for evermore. Israel always maintained the worship of Jehovah (except in *very evil* times) as the national Deity, but did not abstain from the recognition and partial worship of other national deities of whom they were afraid, and whom they thought it necessary to propitiate. Therefore Joshua's argument is perfectly intelligible, and was entirely necessary for those times.

(21) **Nay; but we will serve the Lord.**—Being brought to the point, no other answer was possible. If they must give up Jehovah or the idols, the idols must go first.

(22, 23) **Ye are witnesses . . . that ye have chosen you the Lord . . . Now therefore put away . . . the strange gods.**—This was the practical conclusion to which Joshua desired that they should come. But we do not read that they *did anything* in obedience to these words. We read of no images being buried or burned, as in the days of Jacob by David (Gen. xxxv. 4; 2 Sam. v. 21). There is only a verbal promise: "The Lord our God will we serve, and His voice will we obey."

(25) **So Joshua made a covenant**—*i.e.*, a covenant that idolatry should not be tolerated in Israel, or suffered to exist. We read of similar covenants in the reign of Asa (2 Chron. xv. 12, 13), in the reign of Joash, by Jehoiada (2 Chron. xxiii. 16), and of Josiah (2 Chron. xxxiv. 31, 32).

(26) **And Joshua wrote these words in the book of the law of God.**—Primarily "these words" appear to refer to the transaction just recorded. But it must be observed that this is also the second signature among the sacred writers of the Old Testament. The first is that of Moses, in Deut. xxxi. 9: "Moses wrote this law, and delivered it unto the priests," &c. The next signature after Joshua's is that of Samuel (1 Sam. x. 25): "Samuel told the people the manner of the kingdom, and wrote it in the [not *a*] book, and laid it up before the Lord." We have here a clue to the authorship of the Old Testament, and to the view of the writers who succeeded Moses in what they did. They did not look upon themselves as writers of distinct books, but as authorised to add their part to the book already written, to write what was assigned to them "in the book of the law of God." The *unity* of Holy Scripture is thus seen to have been an essential feature of the Bible from the very first.

(28—31) **So Joshua let the people depart . . .** —This passage is recited in Judges ii. 6—9.

(29) **An hundred and ten years old.**—The mention in verse 31 of "elders that prolonged their days after Joshua" seems to suggest that Joshua's death was comparatively an early death.* Had he thought and laboured more for himself and less for Israel, he also might have prolonged his days. But, like his Antitype, he pleased not himself, and, like a good and faithful servant, he entered all the sooner into the joy of his Lord.

(31) **Israel served the Lord all the days of Joshua, and . . . of the elders that over-lived Joshua.**—It cannot surprise us that the personal influence of the man and of the events of his day was so difficult to efface. There was a *primitive* Church in Canaan as well as in the Roman Empire. The short duration of the one seems to have an analogy in the case of the other.

* Yet Brugsch states that the Egyptians "addressed to the host of the holy gods the prayer to preserve and lengthen life, if possible, to the most perfect old age of 110 years." This may be a reminiscence of the life of Joseph, which reached this length (Gen. l. 26).

(32) And ᵃthe bones of Joseph, which the children of Israel brought up out of Egypt, buried they in Shechem, in a parcel of ground which Jacob bought of ᵇthe sons of Hamor the father of Shechem for an hundred ¹pieces of silver: and it became the inheritance of the children of Joseph.

(33) And Eleazar the son of Aaron died; and they buried him in a hill *that pertained to* Phinehas his son, which was given him in mount Ephraim.

ᵃ Gen. 50. 25; Ex. 13. 19.
B.C. cir. 1420.
ᵇ Gen. 33. 19.
¹ Or, *lambs*.

---

(32) **The bones of Joseph,** and also of his brethren, as appears by Acts vii. 16. The precedent set by Joseph is exceedingly likely to have been followed.

And it became the inheritance of the children of Joseph.—It may be that this fact helped to fix the position of Ephraim and Manasseh in the centre of the country.

(33) **And Eleazar the son of Aaron died.**—"Eleazar the priest, and Joshua the son of Nun," were the Moses and Aaron of this period. It is fitting that the Book of Joshua should close with the death of Eleazar, who was Joshua's appointed counsellor; for when Joshua was given as a shepherd to Israel, in answer to the prayer of Moses, Eleazar was also given to Joshua for a counsellor (Num. xxvii. 21). At Eleazar's word he was to go out and come in, "both he and all the children of Israel with him, even all the congregation." It is rather singular that nothing but this has been recorded of Eleazar's personal history. Everything stated about him in his lifetime is official. Not a word that he uttered has been preserved.

A hill . . . . given him in mount Ephraim.—The inheritance of Phinehas as a priest would lie within the tribe of Judah (chap. xxi. 13, &c.) or Benjamin. This gift to Phinehas in Mount Ephraim, near the seat of government, seems to have been a special grant to him over and above his inheritance. But inasmuch as the tabernacle itself was at Shiloh, in Mount Ephraim, it was altogether suitable and natural that some place of abode should be assigned to the priests in that neighbourhood, where they were compelled to reside.

Although Phinehas himself was "zealous for his God," he lived to see the tribe of Benjamin nearly exterminated from Israel for repeating the sin of the Canaanites. (See Judges xx. 28.) We can hardly say that the people served Jehovah all the days of Phinehas. With Eleazar and Joshua the spirit of strict obedience to the law seems to have, in a great measure, passed away.

EXCURSUS TO NOTES ON JOSHUA

THE DEFEAT OF THE FIVE KINGS AT GIBEON (Chap. x. 10—12).

It was not until I had an opportunity of verifying the course of the combatants on the large Ordnance Map with the sheets fitted together that I was able to form a clear and connected notion of the proceedings of that memorable day. It appears to me that the scene described is this:—

When the five kings of the Amorites besieged Gibeon, the Gibeonites sent a hasty appeal to Joshua for help. Joshua replied by a night march from Gilgal, which brought the host of Israel to Gibeon at early dawn. The Amorite army was surprised, and speedily took to flight. Being attacked from the east, they naturally fled westward, and took the road to Beth-horon. An ancient road from Gibeon (El-Jîb) still passes both the Beth-horons, first the upper (Beit'ur El-Foka), then the lower (Beit'ur Et-Tahta). They are about two miles apart. The road then turns southward (the Beth-horons lie slightly to the north-west of Gibeon), and leads to the border of Philistia. Beth-horon the upper is 2,022 feet above the sea; Beth-horon the nether 1,310 feet above the sea; the points about Gibeon varying from 2,300 to 2,500 feet in height. But the road from Gibeon to Beth-horon appears at first to ascend slightly, and then to descend. From Beth-horon the upper there is a steep descent of nearly 600 feet in the first half mile, and from Beth-horon the nether a continuous slope towards Philistia. Ajalon (Yâlo), about five miles south-west of Beth-horon the nether, is only 940 feet above the Mediterranean. Azekah is not identified, but was probably somewhere near Amwâs. Makkedah is thought by Conder to be El-Mughâr, in Philistia, the only place in the district where there are caves. Ajalon and Gibeon are about nine miles apart in a straight line, due east and west of each other, and El-Mughâr (Makkedah) is about eighteen miles from Beth-horon the nether. These are the geographical data. Now as to what occurred.

When Joshua and his army were in pursuit of the Amorites from Gibeon towards the west, the sun was rising behind them. They presently saw—what we so often see in the early morning—the moon in front of them on the west, just setting in the valley of Ajalon, and the sun behind them over Gibeon on the east. It was the height of summer (as appears by the date of the passage of Jordan, and the commencement of the war, chaps. v., vi.), and in a little while the heat would prevent or greatly retard further operations. A sudden inspiration now seized Joshua, and he requested that the cool morning hours—the best time for battle—might be prolonged. Let the sun remain in the east, and the moon in the west, until the discomfiture of the Amorite army was complete. "So the sun stood still in the one-half of the heavens"—in the eastern hemisphere—"and hasted not to go down about a whole day." It may be observed that the book which mentions the sun oftener than any other in the Old Testament describes his course thus : "*The sun ariseth, and the sun goeth down*, and hasteth to his place where he arose" (Eccles. i. 5). Between his rising and setting nothing else is named. So the sun arose on Joshua and on Joshua's enemies. He arose, and his course was then arrested. He was not permitted to go down, or to pass over to the western side of the heavens, until the enemies of Israel had disappeared. We may add that the sun's position in the east over Gibeon was the very best for Israel, and the worst possible for the Amorites. The pursuit being westward, whenever the flying Amorites attempted to turn and rally, the level or slant rays of the sun were full in their faces, and they could not see to fight, while their pursuers had the best possible view of them. Presently, in the descent of Beth-horon (not "the going down to Beth-horon," as in the English Version; but either in the steep descent from the upper to the lower town, or more probably in the long descent from the lower Beth-horon to Azekah, on the borders of Philistia), a storm of hail burst upon them, and followed them to the plain. "They were more that died with hailstones than they whom Israel slew with the sword." At length, after a flight of some five-and-twenty miles, the kings found shelter in the cave at Makkedah. Even then the pursuit was not ended. Under the shadow of the clouds that had obscured the heavens, while the sun made his way westward, the Israelites still hunted down their beaten foes, until the remnant found shelter in the fortresses. Then, in the afternoon, Joshua and his warriors returned to Makkedah, and unearthed the five kings to die. Even for the trained soldiers of the wilderness, that day's work must have been a severe trial. The night march from Gilgal to Gibeon, and the pursuit to Makkedah, cover forty miles of country, measured in a direct line. The time is some thirty-six hours, allowing for the miraculous prolongation of the day. But the whole story is consistent; and Makkedah was an admirable starting-point for the attack upon the fortresses which followed, and which occupied the Israelitish army during the remainder of the campaign.

In Dean Stanley's account of the battle, the sun is made to stand still *at noon*—in the middle of the day. But the mid-day sun does not appear to be "upon" any place in particular; the *morning and evening suns do*. Gibeon and Ajalon are only about nine miles apart. To see the sun upon Gibeon and the moon upon Ajalon it must be early morning, and one must be between the two places. Five miles from Gibeon would soon be accomplished. If the battle began at daybreak, a single hour after sunrise would be sufficient to bring the pursuers and pursued to the required spot. "The midst of heaven" (Hebrew, *the one half of the heaven*) does not seem to mean the meridian, but the one hemisphere as opposed to the other.

Again, Dean Stanley makes the hail come up from the westward. But the narrative says, "As they were in the going down of Beth-horon, the Lord cast down great stones from heaven upon them *unto Azekah*." All down the slope the hail followed them, for some seven or eight miles. It is much more natural for a storm of hail to come from the hills towards the plain than *vice versâ*. Do not the hail and snow in Palestine more generally come from the north and east than from the sea?

THE BOOK OF JUDGES

INTRODUCTION
TO
THE BOOK OF JUDGES

Name of the Book.—The English name "Judges" corresponds with the Hebrew *Shophetim*, as with the Greek *Kritai*, and the Latin *Liber judicum*. A similar magistracy (*suffetes*) existed among the Phœnicians. Officers of this title are mentioned in Num. xxv. 5, Deut. i. 16, xvi. 18, &c., but they were only appointed for subordinate civil functions, whereas the judges whose history is recorded in this book were chiefly summoned to their great work by Divine appointment (chaps. iii. 15, iv. 6, vi. 12, &c.), and were "deliverers" from foreign bondage (chaps. iii. 9, xviii. 28) rather than civil rulers. (See note on chap. ii. 16.) In fact, the very necessity for their call and their deeds arose from the anarchy which rendered all ordinary functions unavailing against the prevalent corruption and misery. The most remarkable of their number were national heroes rather than civil or religious guides.

Plan.—The Book of Judges falls into five well-marked sections, namely:—

I. GENERAL INTRODUCTION (chaps. i.—ii. 5).—In the note on chap. i. 1 reasons will be given for believing that this section is entirely retrospective. It furnishes a sketch of the imperfect conquest of the land previous to the death of Joshua, in order to show the want of faithfulness and obedience which was the cause of all subsequent troubles. It ends with the solemn reproach addressed by God's messenger to the assembled people at Bochim.

II. SECOND INTRODUCTION (chaps. ii. 6—iii. 6).—It is the object of this section to show that the neglect which had begun before the great conqueror passed away continued after his death, and that it was the cause of deep religious degeneracy. The people even sank into idolatry, and provoked the Divine retribution, from which they were delivered by successive judges. In spite of this, they constantly relapsed when the judgment was removed. In this section the moral purpose of the book is most distinctly sketched in outline. It shows that the presence of the Canaanites and the revival of their dominion were alike the cause and the consequence of the troubles of Israel, while, at the same time, God was so far from having utterly forsaken His people that even their sins and sufferings were made to subserve the purposes of their Divine education, and were overruled for their ultimate advantage. (See chaps. ii. 22, iii. 1—4.)

III. MAIN SECTION OF THE BOOK (chaps. iii. 7—xvi. 31).—This section contains notices of the history of twelve judges. The heroic deeds of six of these deliverers are related in detail, and six are mentioned with brief allusion. The episode of Abimelech's usurpation is given at length, partly perhaps—as in the later story of Eli—to point the lesson of the perils which result from imperfect paternal control, but mainly to warn the people of the perilous and abortive character of a royalty unsanctioned by Jehovah (Deut. xvii. 15).

The sub-sections are:—

1. The servitude to Cushan-rishathaim, and the judgeship of Othniel (chap. iii. 5—11).
2. The servitude to Eglon, and the deliverance wrought by Ehud (chap. iii. 12—30). Brief reference to Shamgar (chap. iii. 31).
3. The servitude to Jabin, and the deliverance wrought by Deborah and Barak (chaps. iv., v.).
4. The oppression of the Midianites, and the deliverance wrought by Gideon (chaps. vi.—viii.). Episode of Abimelech, the bramble-king (chap. ix.). Brief notices of Tola and Jair (chap. x. 1—5).
5. The oppression of the Ammonites, and the deliverance wrought by Jephthah (chaps. x. 6—xii. 13), with the sequel of Jephthah's history (chaps. xi. 34—xii. 7). Brief notices of Ibzan, Elon, and Abdon (chap. xii. 8—15).
6. The servitude to the Philistines, and the deeds of Samson (chaps. xiii.—xvi.).

IV. APPENDIX I.—The story of Micah's idolatry; of Jonathan, grandson of Moses; and of the conquest of Laish by the Danites (chaps. xvii., xviii.).

V. APPENDIX II.—The story of the deed of Gibeah, and the vengeance inflicted on Benjamin, with the means taken to save that tribe from extirpation.

It is clear that the Book of Judges is formed on one general plan, because it is intended to illustrate definite moral facts, and to narrate the providence of God as shown continuously in a long series of different events. The arrangement is not strictly chronological, for (as will be seen by the notes on chaps. xvii.—xxi.) the appendices belong to an epoch antecedent to the earliest judge. Nor, again, is the arrangement intended to be geographical, for the earlier notices of the book refer mainly to the south of Palestine; the story of Deborah takes us to the north, and that of Gideon to the central region; that of Jephthah to the west, and that of Samson once more to the south. Three of the chief judges—Othniel, Ehud, Samson—were southrons; two—Barak, Gideon—belong to the north; one—Jephthah—to western Palestine.

Unity.—The subordination of all the incidents of the history to the inculcation of definite religious lessons shows that the book, in its present form, was arranged by one person. On the other hand, it is nearly certain that he performed the functions of a compiler rather than those of author. For it seems clear that he not only consulted various sources of information, but that he actually incorporated several documents, such as the words of the Divine messenger at Bochim (chap. ii. 1—5), the song of Deborah (chap. v.), the parable of Jotham (chap. ix. 8—16), and various traditional fragments of Samson's festive words (chaps. xiv. 14, xv. 16). But further than this, the style points to the conclusion that the body of the book (chaps. iii. 7—xvi. 31) is not by the same author as the appendices (chaps. xvi., xvii., xviii.—xxi.), and that the author of these two memorable narratives is the same as the author of the preface (chaps. i.—iii. 6). The preface and appendices, referring as they do to the same epoch, present special points of view, and abound in identical phrases, which are not found in the main narrative. Thus Judah (chaps. i., xx. 18) and places in Judah (Bethlehem, Jerusalem) are prominent in these sections, and are hardly alluded to in the rest of the book; the migration of Dan is also touched upon in both these sections (chaps. i. 34, xviii.). The general aspect of society and government is also alike in both sections (chaps. i. 1, 2, ii. 4, xx. 26—28), and both allude to the twelve tribes (chaps. i., xix. 29, xx. 1, xxi. 3). For resemblance of phrases, compare chaps. i. 8, xx. 48; i. 21, xix. 30; i. 12, xxi. 14; i. 1, xx. 23; i. 23, xviii. 2; i. 11, &c., xviii. 29. (See note on chap. i. 1.) In the appendices "judges" are not once mentioned; while the characteristic phrase which occurs again and again, "In those days there was no king in Israel, but every man did that which was right in his own eyes" (chaps. xvii. 6, xviii. 1, xix. 1, xxi. 25), is not once used in the body of the book. On the other hand, the characteristic phrases of the main narrative, "The anger of the Lord was hot against Israel . . . and He sold them into the hands of their enemies" (chaps. ii. 14, iii. 8, iv. 2, x. 7), and "The Spirit of the Lord came upon" (chaps. vi. 34, xi. 29, xiv. 6, 19, xv. 14), do not occur in the other parts.*

We are, therefore, naturally led to infer that the main section of the book is a homogeneous narrative, which has, however, been compiled with a free incorporation of older documents; and that the two prefaces and two appendices, which come from a different hand, were added to it, with the Book of Ruth as a third appendix, by some early editor, or perhaps by the author himself. The efforts to trace parallel Jehovistic and Elohistic documents, even in the history of Gideon, much more in other parts of the book, fail to establish any probable result.

Date.—The freshness, vividness, and minuteness of the details with which some of the stories of the judges abound show that the writer was in possession of almost contemporaneous records, or had access to very early traditions. There is an Homeric plainness in the description of many of the events, as well as in the clear delineation of the leading characters. The character and the circumstance of each hero are completely different from those of all the rest. Ehud first acts independently, and then arms the people; Barak stands at the head of a confederacy; Gideon at first only invites the aid of his immediate neighbours; Jephthah is a chief of freebooters; Abimelech avails himself of Canaanite jealousies against Israel, and Ephraimite jealousies against Manasseh; Samson only engages in a series of personal adventures. Local traditions and records have evidently been utilised. The style is inimitably graphic in its very simplicity. We smile at the grim humour which alludes to the "fatness" of Eglon and his Moabites; we hear the shrill accents of the daughter of Caleb; we see the very flash of Ehud's dagger; even the rough jests of Samson, and the trenchant irony of the Danites, and the shadows cast by the troops of Abimelech, and the female vanity of the ladies of Sisera's harem are, with many other minute incidents, immortalised in a few strokes. Again, the picture of the manners prevalent at the epoch described is such as could not have been delineated so naturally at a later period. In its primitive hospitality, its awful degradation, and its terrible savagery, it recalls some of the earliest annals of the Scripture history. (Comp. chap. vi. 19 with Gen. xviii. 1—8; chap. vi. 21 with Gen. xv. 17; chap. xix. with Gen. xix.; chaps. viii. 16, ix. 38 with Gen. xxxiv., &c.)

But while there can be no doubt as to the antiquity of the documents utilised by the writer, it is not so easy to determine with precision the date at which the book was drawn up *in its present form*. The phrase "to this day" (chaps. i. 21, xix. 30) shows that some years must have elapsed since the events recorded. That the appendices could not have been written earlier than the reign of Saul is clear from their constant formula: "In that day there was no king in Israel" (chap. xvii. 6, &c.). On the other hand, the absence of any allusion to the exploits of David confirms the decisive inference, suggested by chap. i. 21, that the book existed, in part at any rate, before his days; for in chap. i. 21, as well as in chap. xix. 10—12, Jerusalem is still called Jebus, and is regarded as a city of the Canaanites, and as *nominally* belonging to Benjamin (chap. i. 21). The attempts to connect chap. i. 27—29 with events in the reign of Solomon (1 Kings iv. 7—19, ix. 16) are entirely futile. On the other hand, the expression in chap. xviii. 30, "until the captivity of the land," would bring the date of the redaction of the book down to a very late period, if that phrase certainly referred to either the Assyrian or the Babylonian captivity. But even if we do not accept the very slight change in two Hebrew letters which will make it mean "to the captivity of *the ark*" (see note on chap. xviii. 30, 31), it seems almost demonstrable that the allusion may be to that Philistine invasion which culminated in the massacre at Shiloh, of which the terrible incidents are preserved for us in Ps. lxxviii. 60—65. In chap. xxi. 12 we find the expression "Shiloh, *which is in the land of Canaan*," and this, too, has been pressed into an indication that the book is not earlier than the time of the exile. It is much more obvious to explain it by way of contrast to Jabeshgilead, which was on the other side of Jordan; or possibly the phrase may point to the circumstance that after the sack and massacre of Shiloh the very site of the place seems to have sunk into an oblivion from which it has never since emerged. But if these phrases are of later origin, the evidences of antiquity which confront us on every page of this book would lead to the conclusion that a few expressions were merely added by way of glosses in the final edition of the sacred canon by Ezra and his school. The expressions and sentiments which are common to the Book of Judges, with the other historical books (see 1 Sam. xiii. 6, 20; 2 Kings ii. 17, viii. 12, xii. 20, xvii. 20, xxi. 15, xxii. 14; and especially comp. chap. ii. 11—23 with 2 Kings xvii. 7—23, and chap. ii. 1—3 with 2 Kings xvii. 35—39), may easily have been borrowed by the later from the earlier writers. The pure Hebrew of the Book of Judges is far too untainted with Chaldaisms and modernisms to allow any probability to the theory of its late authorship. Its many isolated expressions (*hapax legomena*, chaps. i. 15, iii. 22, iv. 4—19, v. 10—28, xv. 8, xviii. 7) show the use of ancient records, and the Aramaisms which have been pointed out (*e.g.*, the prefix ש in chaps. v. 7, vi. 17, and expressions in chaps. xvii. 2, xix. 1, &c.), since they occur in those parts which are incontestably the oldest, are now generally admitted to be poetic forms, and forms peculiar to the idiom of Northern Palestine.

The general conclusion, then, as to the date of the

---

* See Ewald, i. 186, *seq*.

JUDGES.

book in its earlier shape is that it was compiled in the reign of Saul; and if there was any recorder (*mazkir*) in his primitive court, as there subsequently was at the court of David (2 Sam. viii. 16), these histories might have been drawn up from older sources by such an officer; or possibly even by the Prophet Samuel (see below). With this would agree very well the almost unbroken silence respecting Judah (which would otherwise be inexplicable); the prominence of Gibeah and of Benjamin, with the narrative which explained why it was "the smallest of the tribes" (1 Sam. ix. 21), and the tone of hostility towards Ephraim (chaps. viii., xi., xii.). With this hypothesis would also agree the absolutely *unsacerdotal* character of the book. In David's reign the priesthood rose into great prominence and activity, whereas in the days of the judges and of Saul it seems to have sunk to the very nadir of inefficiency and neglect. Not once in the *main* narrative of the Book of Judges are priests appealed to. After Phinehas, they did not furnish one national hero from their ranks; nor did they once strike a blow for freedom or religion. The Levites shared in their decadence. The name of the wandering Levite of Bethlehem-Judah (chap. xix.) has already been forgotten; and the other Levite, though no less a person than a grandson of Moses himself (see note on chap. xviii. 30), is content to serve a shrine of private idolatry for the reward of a few shillings a year.

The Author.—We have already seen sufficient to dispose of the fancy that the book was written by Ezra, although it is quite possible that he or his school may have added some trivial explanatory touches here and there. De Wette has entirely refuted* the conjecture of Stähelin that it is by the same author as the Book of Deuteronomy. Nor could it have been written by the author of the Book of Joshua, because it differs from that book not only in style, but in the two marked particulars that it barely makes any allusion to the Mosaic law, and that it abounds in moral utterances of a character which are not found in the previous book. The Rabbis generally follow the conjecture of the Talmud (*Baba Bathra*, f. 14, b) that it was written by the prophet Samuel. That is a sufficiently obvious conjecture; and though it can neither be proved nor disproved, it accords with many of the facts. From what we know of the character of Samuel, even in what seem to us to be its more dubious or less enlightened features, we see that there is a moral affinity between his views and those expressed in the Book of Judges. The man who so greatly disliked the establishment of royalty (1 Sam. viii.) may well have written the story of Abimelech. The man who commanded the extermination of the Amalekites (1 Sam. xv. 3) was in that stage of as yet imperfect enlightenment (Matt. v. 38) which would have viewed without reprobation the vengeance inflicted by Israel on his enemies. The man who hewed Agag in pieces before the Lord in Gilgal (1 Sam. xv. 33) would have felt no difficulty in commending the deeds of Ehud, of Jael, and of Gideon. The book may have been drawn up by him, or in the school of the prophets of which he was the founder. That he was well acquainted with the incidents of this period we see from his appeal to them in his speech to the people (1 Sam. xii. 11). The mention of "Bedan" with Jerubbaal, Jephthah, and Samson † in this verse has always been a source of perplexity. The notion that Bedan can mean Samson, as though it were "in Dan," is now abandoned. Perhaps "Barak" (as in the LXX., Syriac, and Arabic) is the true reading; but if "Bedan" be a corruption for "Abdon," it would point to the possession on Samuel's part of many particulars respecting the judges which are now quite lost to us.

There are other allusions to the judges in 2 Sam. xi. 21; Pss. lxxviii. 56—64, lxxxiii. 7—11, cvi. 34—45; Isa. ix. 4, x. 26; Hosea x. 9; Neh. ix. 25—31.

Chronology.—The chronology of the Book of Judges offers immense difficulties, and the difficulties are increased by the uncertainties which affect both the reading and interpretation of the passages which bear upon it.

The elements of decision are briefly as follows:—

I. If the stories of the judges are taken to be consecutive, and the periods of forty or eighty years' rest (chaps. iii. 11, 30, v. 31, viii. 28) are supposed to be stated accurately, and not in round numbers, then, adding up the separate totals, we get:—

Servitude under Cushan	. 8 years	iii. 8
Rest under Othniel	. 40 „	iii. 11
Servitude under Moab	. 18 „	iii. 14
Rest under Ehud	. 80 „	iii. 30
Servitude under Jabin	. 20 „	iv. 3
Rest under Deborah and Barak	. 40 „	v. 31
Oppression of the Midianites	. 7 „	vi. 1
Rest under Gideon	. 40 „	viii. 28
Tyranny of Abimelech	. 3 „	ix. 22
Judgeship of Tola	. 23 „	x. 2
Judgeship of Jair	. 22 „	x. 3
Oppression of the Ammonites	. 18 „	x. 8
Judgeship of Jephthah	. 6 „	xii. 7
„ of Ibzan	. 7 „	xii. 9
„ of Elon	. 19 „	xii. 11
„ of Abdon	. 8 „	xii. 14
Oppression of the Philistines	. 40 „	xiii. 1
Judgeship of Samson	. 20 „	xv. 20
	410 years.	

If to this 410 years we add 40 years for Saul's reign, and 40 years for David's, we get 490 years; and as (on this principle of consecutiveness) we must allow about 10 years for the events before Cushan's tyranny (chap. iii. 10) began, and 20 for the judgeship of Samuel, and 1 for Shamgar (chap. iii. 31), we get at once at the traditional Jewish reckonings, which is the basis of much of our received chronology, and which assigns to the epoch between Joshua and Solomon a period of five centuries, in round numbers twelve generations.

II. In 1 Kings vi. 1 we find that Solomon built the Temple "*in the 480th year* after the children of Israel were come out of Egypt." It is doubtful whether the words are genuine, since they are omitted by Origen and other Fathers, were unknown to Josephus, and furnish the only Old Testament passage in which an era is taken as a starting-point. If genuine, there is no obvious way of reconciling them with the previous computation, though it has been suggested that "after the children of Israel came out of Egypt" may mean "after their settlement in Canaan."

III. In Acts xiii. 20 St. Paul says that "the judges unto Samuel the prophet" occupied a period of 450 years. But here, again, the reading is not certain, and the order of the words seems to have been tampered with.

---
* *Einleitung*, p. 142.
† In 1 Sam. xii. 11 "Samson," not Samuel, is the much more probable reading of the Peshito.

IV. In chap. xi. 20 Jephthah says that Israel had lived in Heshbon and the coasts of Arnon 300 years. Now, doubtless, by a certain amount of ingenuity and manipulation, and by lengthening or curtailing those elements in the reckoning which are not specified—such as the length of Samuel's judgeship, the interval between Joshua's death and Cushan's tyranny, &c.—we may give to these different data sufficient semblance of accordance to look plausible. But it is quite obvious that we can arrive at no certainty, and, in point of fact, scarcely two of the authors who have elaborately gone into the question come to the same conclusion. Further than this, these scattered data have to be reconciled with those which we gather from *no less than ten genealogies*—those of David, Zadok, Abiathar, Saul, Heman, Ahimoth, Asaph, Etham, Zabad, and the kings of Edom, which are found scattered chiefly in the Books of Chronicles, and of which some are repeated two, three, and even four times. Now it appears from every one of these genealogies, as they have been thoroughly examined by a former Bishop of Bath and Wells,* that seven and eight generations are assigned to the period between the conquest of Canaan and the accession of David.† The time allowed for a generation is usually thirty years, and this seems to show conclusively that the period covered by the judges was much shorter than that demanded by the received reckoning. For allowing even eight generations, this gives us 240 years, from which we have to subtract for the actual period covered in the Book of Judges, the reign of Saul, the judgeships of Eli and Samuel, and the latter years of Joshua. Now this curtailment of the period, though impossible to reconcile exactly and literally with 1 Kings vi. 1, Judges xi. 20, and Acts xiii. 20 (in which, as we have seen, the reading may be wrong), does coincide remarkably with many indications of the Book of Judges itself. There is not the least warrant for supposing that the numbers 40 and 80 are meant to be stated with precision,‡ nor is there anything to bar the very reasonable hypothesis that parts both of the servitudes and the deliverances may have been synchronous in different parts of Israel : so that, for instance, the movements of Ehud, of Barak, and of Gideon may have taken place in the same fifty years. Thus no high priest is recorded in any genealogy or historical references between Phinehas and Eli, and Jewish legend says that Phinehas was deposed for having sanctioned the offering of Jephthah's daughter. Similarly Boaz, in the Book of Ruth, is the son of Rahab, and the Levite of Judges xvii., xviii. is a grandson of Moses. By thus curtailing the period of the judges many serious difficulties are avoided, and the uncertain meaning and reading of the passages on which the received chronology is founded cannot for a moment be set against the distinct information derived from such a multitude of genealogies. The subject is, however, still involved in obscurity, as may be seen in the notes on chaps. iii. 10, iv. 2, &c. It is clear that many of the fifty schemes of chronology which have been proposed must be completely mistaken, and we must be content with the general conclusion that the whole period covered some 250 years.

* Lord Arthur Hervey, *On the Genealogies*.
† There are five generations between Moses and David in Ruth iv. 18 ; and we may be sure that when there are so many genealogies, and so often repeated, there are no omissions.
‡ Reuss points out the curious circumstance that these round numbers added together—Othniel, 40 ; Ehud, 80 ; Jabin, 20 ; Barak, 40 ; Gideon, 40 ; Philistines, 40 ; Samson, 20—make 280, which is exactly the number required to make 480, if we add the Wanderings, 40 ; Joshua, 40 ; Eli, 40 ; Samuel and Saul, 40 ; David, 40 = 200 (1 Kings vi. 1).

Characteristics of the Epoch.—The Book of Judges gives us an insight into a definite and well-marked epoch of Israelitish history, and we shall understand the book and its object better if we summarise the peculiarities of that age. We mark—

I. The *deepening disunion* between the tribes. While some of them pursued that agricultural mode of life which was specially fostered by the Mosaic institutions, others of them—as Dan, Asher, and the northern tribes—began to engage in navigation and commerce. This may have been one of the tendencies which led each tribe to act more and more as an independent body, while the fierce claim to the leading position advanced by Ephraim (chaps. viii., xii.) was only partially conceded, and at last entirely rejected. There were even separate towns—like Shechem—that could successfully assert their independence of the body of the nation, and choose their own rulers. Shechem thus stood at the head of a confederacy, like those of the German and Italian towns in the Middle Ages. under the protection of Baal-berith—the lord of the covenant—whose temple also served as a strong fortress (chap. ix.).

II. This civil disunion resulted in part from the *religious disintegration*. There was, indeed, a central sanctuary at Shiloh, but the ark itself was at Bethel; and since in these wild times it became all but impossible to carry out the regulations of the Levitic law—which seems, indeed, to have fallen into absolute abeyance—all sorts of local sanctuaries and high places sprang up. Altars were freely raised at any place hallowed by Divine messages or providences, and the irregular and reprehensible, if not directly idolatrous, cult of ephods and teraphim (chaps. viii. 27, xviii. 18) proved to be an irresistible temptation. A nation which had gone so far would be hardly likely to hold out against the manifold seductions and fascinations of the wild forms of nature-worship by which they were on every side surrounded. The sensual temptations of these

"Gay religions, full of pomp and gold,"

could only be effectually resisted by the influence of one religion, firmly established and faithfully obeyed.

III. Another element of degeneracy lay in the extreme *depression of the priesthood* and Levite-hood. The only priest of whom we hear is Phinehas (chap. xx. 28). The grandson of Aaron towers immeasurably above the dreadful degeneracy of Jonathan, the grandson of Moses (chap. xviii. 30). It is with a positive sense of pity that we witness the pauperism and homelessness into which the near descendant of the great lawgiver had fallen (chap. xvii. 8—10). If for a mere pittance he could be induced to give his office and his life to the service of a private and semi-idolatrous chapel, we cannot but see that the salt of his order must have lost its savour. The splendid zeal which Phinehas had shown on former occasions (Num. xxv. 11, xxxi. 6 ; Ps. cvi. 30 ; Josh. xxii. 13) would have led us to expect from him the exertion of an influence which should have rendered impossible the state of degradation which marks the whole story of "the deed of Gibeah." It is clear, however, that he had sunk into impotence or into apathy. We never hear of him after this time ; and it is a mysterious and unexplained circumstance that the next high priest who is mentioned—Eli—does not even belong to the line of Eleazar and Phinehas, but to the younger line of Ithamar. The elder line was only restored to its rights in the reign of David, and in the person of Zadok.

IV. "*Like people, like priest.*" If the priests and

JUDGES.

Levites had not abnegated their true functions, the people could hardly have sunk to a moral standpoint so low as that which is involved in the conduct of the tribe of Benjamin, or in Jephthah's vow; much less into the condition which left unpunished the hideous massacre by Abimelech of his father's sons. Even Ehud and Samson, though they were redeemed into nobleness by the faith and patriotism which animated their deeds, adopted methods which are regarded by purer ages as deeply reprehensible.

V. *Sin is weakness*, and the spiritual degeneracy of the people reduced them to that state of feebleness which made them the easy prey of the Canaanites in the north, the Ammonites in the west, the Midianites and Amalekites whose hordes overran the Plain of Jezreel, and the Philistines in the south, who in course of time extended their authority beyond the confines of the tribe of Judah.

VI. And yet, amid all this distress and degeneracy, the sacred fire did not wholly die out from the hearts of the Israelites. Had it been otherwise, these hero-figures could hardly have risen among them, nor could such a burning song as the song of Deborah have been poured forth from the nation's heart. So many lessons of Divine education could hardly have been in vain. Ten times over in the Book of Judges are repeated the formulæ, "the children of Israel did evil in the sight of the Lord," and each repetition is like the sound of a bell which tolls some approaching ruin. Ten times over recurs the formulæ, "the children of Israel cried unto the Lord," and each time of its recurrence introduces a breathing-space of deliverance and of hope. As the years sped on, such lessons sank more and more deeply into the hearts of the people, until at last the time was ripe for reunion, the moral guidance of prophets, and the restoration of the national religious life.* In the hour of its worst peril and weakness Israel was preserved by the memory of its past, and was being prepared by a loving and guiding Providence for the grandeur of its future.

Moral Characteristics.—In considering the moral characteristics of the Book of Judges, we must distinguish between its general purport and the details of its special narratives.

Its general purport, as the incomplete record of a transitional period, is to illustrate certain broad propositions, which are of the utmost importance to mankind. It is meant to prove that righteousness exalteth a nation, but sin is the reproach of any people; that evil companionships ruin good dispositions; that moral degeneracy always brings with it national weakness; that the affairs of the chosen people were under the immediate care of Divine Providence; that national sin is never left unpunished; that the punishment which it involves is intended always to be educational, not vindictive; that the retribution is withdrawn when it has produced sincere repentance; that the deliverance never comes from unaided human efforts, but from the strength and enthusiasm inspired by the Spirit of God. These and similar lessons elevate the Book of Judges into the position of a sacred philosophy of history, which clearly explains the laws and the objects of a sacred Nemesis. They are summed up not only in the Book of Judges (especially in chap. ii. 11—22), but also in other passages which have been suggested or deeply influenced by its teachings; such as Ps. cvi. 34—45; 2 Kings xvii., xxiv. 2—4; 2 Chron. xxvi. 11—21; Jer. xi. 2—10; Neh. ix. 16—38. The whole book may be regarded as an historical comment on the promises and threatenings of the Book of Deuteronomy.

But when we look from the general lessons to the special deeds even of heroes who were summoned by God's calling to the work of deliverance, we see abundant traces of the imperfection of that moral enlightenment which God vouchsafed to the chosen people only by slow degrees as the result of ever-deepening experiences. Both in its pathos and in its passion, the book is intensely human, aid its heroes are the children of their own day, alike in their wrath and their tenderness, their laxity and their superstition. It must be now clear to every Christian that the exterminating wars of Joshua, the fearful and indiscriminate vengeance inflicted by Israel on the offending tribe of Benjamin, the treachery of Ehud and of Jael, the wild revenge of Samson, the blood-vengeance of Gideon, and other events herein narrated, are not to be quoted as examples for modern times. They are entirely alien to the whole drift of all that is best and highest in the moral teaching even of the Old Testament Scriptures, and still more alien to all the teachings of Christ. The view which we take of these actions will be found in the notes; and it will be seen that while no attempt is made to gild with imaginary sanction deeds which in themselves were due to times of ignorance and the passions of men on whose minds the full light had not yet dawned, yet, on the other hand, the faith and the courage by which these old heroes were animated receive their full recognition, and they are judged solely by the standard prevalent in their own age and country. In adopting this line of judgment we follow the example set us by Christ Himself (Matt. v. 38, xix. 8, &c.). We recognise the nobleness and courage of these heroes of faith, while we guard against the dangerous error of admiring their ignorance or consecrating their imperfections.

Among the books consulted in writing the following commentary I may mention Josephus, *Antiquities*, bk. v.; Rosenmüller's *Scholia*; Ewald, *Gesch. d. Volkes Israel*; Eisenlohr's *Das Volk Israel*; Stanley's *Jewish Church* and *Sinai and Palestine*; Reuss, *Hist. des Israelites*; Bertheau, *Das Buch der Richter* (*Kurzgef. Exeget. Handbuch*); Keil and Delitsch; Prof. Cassel in Lange's *Bibelwerk*; Lord Arthur Hervey, *On the Genealogies*, and in the Speaker's *Commentary*; Bishop Wordsworth's *Commentary*; Davidson's *Introd. to the Old Testament*; articles in Dr. Smith's *Bible Dictionary*; Kitto's *Bible Cyclopædia*; Herzog's *Real. Encyclop.*, &c.

---

* See note on chap. iii. 22.

THE BOOK OF JUDGES

CHAPTER I.—⁽¹⁾ Now after the death of Joshua it came to pass, that [B.C. cir. 1425.] the children of Israel asked the LORD, saying, Who shall go up for us against

"And concerning the Judges, every one by name, whose heart went not a whoring, nor departed from the Lord, let their memory be blessed. Let their bones flourish out of their place, and let the name of them that were honoured be continued upon their children" (Ecclus. xlvi. 11, 12).

"Temporibus Judicum, sicut se habebant peccata populi et misericordia Dei, alternabant prospera et adversa bellorum" (Aug. *De Civ. Dei.* xvi. 43).

1—8. Wars of Judah and Simeon. Defeat of Adonibezek. Temporary capture of Jerusalem. 9, 10. Judah and Caleb drive the Anakim out of Hebron. 11—13. Debir conquered by Othniel. 14, 15. The request of Achsah. 16. Notice of the Kenites. 17—20. Further successes of Judah. 21. Partial success of Benjamin at Jerusalem. 22—26. Ephraim gains Bethel by treachery. 27—36. Partial successes of Manasseh, Ephraim, Zebulon, Asher, Naphtali, and Dan.

⁽¹⁾ **Now.**—The "now" should rather be rendered *And*, as in Lev. i. 1, Num. i. 1, Josh. i. 1, 1 Sam. i. 1, 2 Sam. i. 1, 2 Kings i. 1. The word connects this book with the last, "as a link in the chain of books which relate in unbroken connection the sacred history of the world from the Creation to the Exile" (Bertheau).

After the death of Joshua.—In these first words we are met by a difficulty, for there can be little reasonable doubt that most, at any rate, of the events narrated from this verse to chap. ii. 5 took place *before* the death of Joshua, whose death and burial are accordingly mentioned in chap. ii. 8—9. For (1) the whole passage (chap. i. 1 to chap. ii. 5) evidently describes the first movements of the Israelites after their establishment on the western side of the Jordan. (See Josh. xviii. 1—3, xxi. 43, xxii. 32, xxiv. 28.) (2) It is inconceivable that the Israelites should have remained inactive during the long life of Joshua, who attained the age of 110 years. (3) The events in chap. i. 10—36 are evidently identical with those in Josh. xii. 9—24, xiv., xix. (4) The angel's message (chap. ii. 1—5) and the subsequent notices (6—18) are closely parallel with, and sometimes verbally the same as, those in Josh. xxiv. 24—33. That these should be records of different and yet most closely analogous series of circumstances is all but impossible. Various ways of accounting for the difficulty have been suggested. (1) Some suppose that many events narrated or touched upon in the Book of Joshua (especially chaps. xv. 14—19, xvi., xvii., &c.) are narrated by anticipation. (2) Clericus arbitrarily supplies the words, "After the death of Joshua *the Canaanites recovered strength*, but in his lifetime *the children of Israel.*" (3) Schmidt renders the verbs as pluperfects: "It came to pass after the death of Joshua, the children of Israel had consulted Jehovah," &c. (4) A more recent conjecture is that the name "*Joshua*" has here crept in by an error of the scribes.

If we read, "After the death of Moses," all becomes clear and coherent; and if the book, in its *original* form, possibly began at chap. iii. 7, with the words, "And it came to pass, after the death of Joshua, that the children of Israel did evil in the sight of the Lord," &c., the clerical error may have been caused by the addition of prefatory matter to the book at the same time that the appendix (chaps. xvii.—xxi.) was added. It is in favour of the possibility of this suggestion that there are close resemblances between the style and the allusions of the preface, or perhaps we may say of the two prefaces (chaps. i. 1—ii. 10; ii. 11—23), and the style and allusions of the last five chapters: *e.g.*, in the references to Judah, Jerusalem, and Bethlehem (chaps. i. 1—21, xix., xx. 18), Dan (chaps. i. 34, xviii. 1—31) and the Twelve Tribes (*passim*); the consultations of the Lord by Urim (chaps. i. 1, 2, xx. 26—28); the silence as to the existence of Judges; and the recurrence of various phrases, such as "set on fire," and "with the edge of the sword" (chaps. i. 8, xx. 48), "unto this day" (chaps. i. 21, xix. 30), "give his daughter to wife" (chaps. i. 12, xxi. 1, 14, 18), &c. (5) On the other hand, the conjecture can only be regarded as *possible*, since it is not supported by a single MS. or suggested by any ancient commentator. It is perhaps simpler to suppose that the book originally began with the words, "Now after the death of Joshua," and that this beginning was left unaltered as a *general* description of the book when the prefatory matter and appendix were attached to it.

The children of Israel.—Mainly, it would seem, the western tribes.

Asked the Lord.—The phrase is peculiar, meaning, literally, *enquired in Jehovah* (as we find it in the LXX.). The usual construction is "*Shaal eth-Jehovah*" ("asked the Lord"). This phrase (*shaal be*) is only found again in chap. xx. 23—27. Rabbi Tanchum (whose commentary on this book has been edited by Schnurrer and Haarbrücker) says that the phrase implies the consultation of Jehovah through the high priest by means of the Urim and Thummim. "To ask of *Elohim*" occurs in chaps. xviii. 5, xx. 18. Similarly in Greek, "to ask God" (Xen. *Mem.* viii. 3) means to consult an oracle. If the narrative of this chapter be *retrospective*, the high priest must have been Eleazar, the son of Aaron (Josh. xiv. 1); if not, it must have been his son Phinehas (Josh. xxiv. 33), as Josephus seems to imply (Jos. *Antt.* v. 2, § 1). On this method of inquiring of God, in the absence of any authoritative declaration on the part of a prophet, see Num. xxvii. 21, Josh. ix. 14. On the Urim and Thummim, which was *not* the jewelled "breastplate of judgment," but something which was put "in it," see Ex. xxviii. 30. It is probably useless to inquire as to the method by which the will of God was revealed by the Urim and Thummim. The words mean "lights and perfections," or something closely

Advance of Judah and Simeon.   JUDGES, I.   *The Canaanites defeated.*

the Canaanites first, to fight against them? ⁽²⁾ And the LORD said, Judah shall go up: behold, I have delivered the land into his hand.

⁽³⁾ And Judah said unto Simeon his brother, Come up with me into my lot, that we may fight against the Canaanites; and I likewise will go with thee into thy lot. So Simeon went with him. ⁽⁴⁾ And Judah went up; and the LORD delivered the Canaanites and the Perizzites into their hand: and they slew of them in Bezek ten thousand men. ⁽⁵⁾ And they found Adoni-bezek

---

resembling those conceptions. The Rabbis were themselves ignorant as to the exact nature of the Urim and Thummim, and the mode in which they were used. One favourite theory is that adopted by Milton, when he speaks of Aaron's breastplate as having been "ardent with gems oracular." It identifies the Urim with the twelve gems, and supposes that the answers of God were spelt out by a mystic light which gleamed over these gems. But not to dwell on the fact that the names of the tribes did not contain all the letters of the Hebrew alphabet, this explanation is not consistent with the distinction made between the breastplate which was on the ephod, and the Urim and Thummim that were placed *inside* it (Ex. xxviii. 30). Another theory supposes that the mind of the high priest was abstracted from earthly things by gazing on the gems until the will of God was revealed to him. A third regards the Urim and Thummim as cut and uncut gems, kept in the folds of the breastplate, and used almost like lots. These are but theories, and in all probability the exact truth, which has now been forgotten for thousands of years, will never be discovered.

Who shall go up for us . . . ?—At the solemn investiture of Joshua, as the successor of Moses, Moses is directed to "set him before Eleazar the priest," who was "to ask consent for him after the judgment of Urim before the Lord: *at his word they shall go out, and at his word they shall come in*" (Num. xxvii. 18—21).

⁽²⁾ **The Lord said.**—The answer is given to the priest by the Urim, and he announces it to the people.

Judah shall go up.—The phrase "go up" is used in a military sense (Josh. vi. 5). The question had not been, "Who shall be our leader?" but, "Which *tribe* shall fight first?" The reason why Judah is chosen is from the eminence and power of the tribe, which was also the most numerous at both of the censuses taken in the wilderness (Num. i. 26, xxvi. 19—22). Jacob's blessing on the tribe had been, "Judah, thou art he whom thy brethren shall praise: thy hand shall be in the neck of thine enemies" (Gen. xlix. 8). (Comp. Num. xxxiv. 19; Josh. xv. 1.) In the arrangement of the camp, Judah was stationed at the east, with Issachar and Zebulon, and always started first on the march (Num. ii. 3—9), with its lion-standard, which was a symbol of its lion-courage (Gen. xlix. 9; Rev. v. 5). The same answer is given by Urim in chap. xx. 18.

⁽³⁾ **Unto Simeon his brother.**—Both Judah and Simeon were sons of Leah. It was natural that the two tribes should help one another, because their lots were conterminous; indeed, the lot of the Simeonites is said to lie "*within* the inheritance of the children of Judah" (Josh. xix. 1), and was given them "out of the portion of the children of Judah" (*ib.*, verse 9), because a larger territory had been assigned to the tribe of Judah than it required. The tribe of Simeon was remarkable for its fierce valour (1 Chron. iv. 24—37, 38—43), of which we find a trace even in Judith, who belonged to that tribe (Judith ix. 2). It would, however, have been helpless without the assistance of Judah; for we see from a comparison of the first with the second census in the Desert that Simeon had decreased in strength from 59,300 to 22,200. This fearful diminution seems to have been due to the plague, which may have fallen most heavily on them from their greater guilt, as we may infer from the shamelessness of their prince Zimri (Num. xxv. 14, i. 23, xxvi. 14). Hence the tribe is omitted in the blessing of Moses (Deut. xxxiii.). They seem to have melted away among the nomad tribes of the south, but we see them showing a last flash of vitality in the days of Hezekiah (1 Chron. iv. 41).

Into my lot—*i.e.*, into the territory assigned me by lot ("Crœsus devasted the *lots* (*klerous*) of the Syrians" (Herod. i. 76). The lots of Judah and Simeon fell within two lines drawn to the Mediterranean from the northern and southern extremities of the Dead Sea (Josh. xv.).

⁽⁴⁾ **And Judah went up.**—Under the leadership of Caleb (Josh. xiv. 6).

The Canaanites and the Perizzites. — See Gen. xiii. 7, xxxiv. 30. The former seem to have been *lowlanders*—"by the sea and by the coast of Jordan" (Num. xiii. 29), "on the east and on the west" (Josh. xi. 3, xvii. 16). The Perizzites were the mountain and forest tribes (Josh. xi. 3, xvii. 15). Their antiquity and importance appear from the allusions to them in Gen. xiii. 7, xxxiv. 30; 1 Kings ix. 20; 2 Esdr. i. 21. The name itself seems to imply "open villages" (1 Sam. vi. 18; Deut. iii. 5), and may imply that they were agriculturists. The name does not occur in the genealogy of nations in Gen. x.

In Bezek.—The name means "lightning." There seems to be no adequate reason to distinguish this town from the one mentioned in 1 Sam. xi. 8. Saul numbered the people there before his expedition to deliver Jabesh Gilead. At first sight the mention of this town is surprising, for we have no information of any Bezek except the two villages of that name referred to by Eusebius and Jerome, which were seventeen miles from Shechem, and therefore in the lot of Ephraim. It is, however, needless to conjecture that there was another Bezek in the lot of Judah. We must suppose that the two warlike tribes began their conquest by marching into the centre of Palestine to strike a blow at the main stronghold of Canaanitish power. Ewald conjectures that in this expedition they took Shiloh, and refers Gen. xlix. 8—12 to this fact, rendering "till he come to Shiloh" (*Hist. Isr.* i. 284, E. Tr.). If this chapter does not refer retrospectively to events which occurred before the death of Joshua, it might well be considered strange that this powerful king is not mentioned among those attacked by the Israelites in Joshua's lifetime. It is, however, possible, as Ewald suggests, that a new power may have sprung up.

⁽⁵⁾ **They found.**—The expression perhaps alludes to the suddenness of their march, which enabled them to take the lord of Bezek by surprise.

in Bezek: and they fought against him, and they slew the Canaanites and the Perizzites. ⁽⁶⁾ But Adoni-bezek fled; and they pursued after him, and caught him, and cut off his thumbs and his great toes. ⁽⁷⁾ And Adoni-bezek said, Threescore and ten kings, having ¹their thumbs and their great toes cut off, ²gathered *their meat* under my table: as I have done, so God hath requited me. And they brought him to Jerusalem, and there he died.

⁽⁸⁾ Now the children of Judah had fought against Jerusalem, and had taken it, and smitten it with the edge of the sword, and set the city on fire.

1 Heb., *the thumbs of their hands and of their feet*.
2 Or, *gleaned*.

Adoni-bezek.—This is not a proper name, but a title, meaning "lord of Bezek," as Adoni-zedek, in Josh. x. 1, and perhaps Melchi-zedek, in Gen. xiv. 18.

They slew the Canaanites and the Perizzites.—This seems to refer to a second battle, or perhaps to the slaughter in the city after the battle described in the last verse.

⁽⁶⁾ **Cut off his thumbs and his great toes.**—The cutting off of his thumbs would prevent him for ever again drawing a bow or wielding a sword. Romans who desired to escape conscription cut off their thumbs (Suet. *Aug.* 24). The cutting off of his great toes would deprive him of that speed which was so essential for an ancient warrior, that "swift-footed" is in Homer the normal epithet of Achilles. Either of these mutilations would be sufficient to rob him of his throne, since ancient races never tolerated a king who had any personal defects. This kind of punishment was not uncommon in ancient days, and it was with the same general object that the Athenians inflicted it on the conquered Æginetans. Mohammed (Koran, *Sur.* viii. 12) ordered the enemies of Islam to be thus punished; and it used to be the ancient German method of punishing poachers (Ælian, *Var. Hist.* ii. 9). The peculiar appropriateness of the punishment in this instance arose from the *Lex talionis*, or "law of equivalent punishment," which Moses had tolerated as the best means to limit the intensity of those blood-feuds (Lev. xxiv. 19, 20; Deut. xix. 21; comp. Judges xv. 10, 11), which, "because of the hardness of their hearts," he was unable entirely to abolish.

⁽⁷⁾ **Threescore and ten kings.**—The number might seem incredible, were it not that the title "king" was freely given to every petty Emir, and even to village Sheykhs. The "seventy" kings may have been the rulers of the towns which Adoni-bezek had taken in extending the territory of Bezek. Josephus says seventy-two kings (*Antt.* v. 2, § 2), and this common variation is found in some MSS. of the LXX. The Persians treated their Greek captives in this way (Curtius, v. 5, 6). Mutilation in the East was so common that it was hardly accounted cruel (Xen. *Anab.* i. 9—13). Cutting off the hand or foot was the prescribed Mohammedan punishment for theft in British India (Mill, iii. 447), and many mutilated persons are still to be seen in Northern Scinde (see Grote's *Greece*, xii. 235).

Gathered their meat under my table.—The words "their meat" are wanting in the original. Adoni-bezek, with cruel insolence, treated these subject Sheykhs like dogs "which eat of the fragments that fall from the table of their lords" (Matt. xv. 27). Posidonius says that the king of Parthia used to fling food to his courtiers, who seized it like dogs (Athen. iv. 152). The existence of these feuds among the Canaanites would render the task of the Israelites more easy.

As I have done, so God hath requited me.—Comp. chap. viii. 19; 1 Sam. xv. 33, "As thy sword hath made women childless, so shall thy mother be childless among women;" Judg. xv. 11, "As they (the Philistines) did unto me, so have I (Samson) done unto them;" Jer. li. 56, "The Lord God of recompences shall surely requite thee;" Ex. xviii. 11, "For the thing wherein they sinned came upon them." (See Matt. vii. 2; Gal. vi. 7; Jas. ii. 13.) The word used for God is *Elohim*. In Greek theology this punishment of like by like is called "the retribution of Neoptolemus," who murdered Priam at an altar, and was himself murdered at an altar (Pausan. v. 17, 3). The fate of Phalaris, burnt in his own brazen bull (Ovid, *De Art. Am.* i. 653), and of Dionysius (Ælian, *Var. Hist.* ix. 8), were also prominent illustrations of the law. We must not suppose that this Canaanite prince worshipped Jehovah, but only that he recognised generally that a Divine retribution had overtaken him. It is one of the commonest facts of history that

"Even-handed justice
Commends the ingredients of the poisoned chalice
To our own lips."

This truth, "that wherewithal a man sinneth, by the same also shall he be punished," is magnificently, if somewhat fancifully, worked out in Wisd. xi., xvii., xviii.

They brought him to Jerusalem.—Rabbi Tanchum, author of the celebrated traditional Midrash (or "exposition"), says that this notice must be *prospective*, *i.e.*, it must refer to a time subsequent to the conquest of Jerusalem mentioned in the next verse. It may, however, merely mean that they kept him with them in their camp when they advanced to the siege of Jerusalem; or the "*they*" may refer to his own people. The Israelites may have contemptuously spared his life, and suffered him to join his own people, as a living monument of God's vengeance. In any case the name Jerusalem is used by anticipation, for it seems to have been called Jebus till the days of David. As it is also called Jebusi (*i.e.*, "the Jebusite") in Josh. xv. 8, xviii. 16, probably the name of the town comes from that of the tribe, and the derivation of it is unknown. The meaning "dry" suggested by Ewald is very uncertain.

⁽⁸⁾ **Now.**—Rather, *And*.

Had fought against Jerusalem, and had taken it.—Our version here most unwarrantably interpolates the word "had," meaning it perhaps as a sort of explanatory gloss to imply that the conquest took place before the fact mentioned in the last verse. If we are right in supposing that these chapters refer in greater or less detail to events already touched upon in the Book of Joshua, we must then supplement this brief notice by Josh. xii. 8—10, xv. 63, from which it appears that though the people of Jerusalem were slaughtered, the king conquered, and the city burnt, yet the Jebusites either secured the citadel (as Josephus implies) or succeeded in recovering the city. In chap. xix. 11, 12, the city is called Jebus (with the remark, "which is Jerusalem"), and the Levite expressly re-

(9) *And afterward the children of Judah went down to fight against the Canaanites, that dwelt in the mountain, and in the south, and in the ¹valley. (10) And Judah went against the Canaanites that dwelt in Hebron: (now the name of Hebron before was ᵇKirjath-arba:) and they slew Sheshai, and Ahiman, and Talmai. (11) And from thence he went against the inhabitants of Debir: and the name of Debir before was Kirjath-sepher:

(12) And Caleb said, He that smiteth Kirjath-sepher, and taketh it, to him

a Josh. 10. 36; & 11. 21; & 15. 13.
¹ Or, low country.
B.C. 1444.
b Josh. 15. 13.

---

fuses to enter it, because it is a "city of the Jebusites," "the city of a stranger."

With the edge of the sword. — Literally, *with the mouth of the sword* (Gen. xxxiv. 26; Josh. viii. 24, x. 28. Comp. chaps. iv. 15, xx. 37). It seems to mean that no quarter was given.

Set the city on fire. — Literally, *sent the city into fire*, as in chap. xx. 48; 2 Kings viii. 12; Ps. lxxiv. 7. The phrase does not occur elsewhere. And at a later period Josephus tells us that the siege occupied a long time, from the strength of the position (2 Sam. v. 7).

(9) **Went down to fight.** — "Went up" is the phrase applied to military expeditions (see verse 2); "went down" is the phrase for special battles (1 Sam. xxvi. 10, xxix. 4), like the Latin *descendere in aciem*. No doubt the phrase arose from the custom of always encamping on hills when it was possible to do so.

In the mountain, and in the south, and in the valley. — These are three marked regions of Palestine — the "hill-country" (*ha-Har*, Josh. ix. 1), in which were Hebron and Debir (verses 10, 11); the south or *Negeb* (Josh. xv. 21), in which were Arad and Zephath; and the valley, or rather low lands (*Shephelah*, Josh. xi. 16, xv. 33), in which were the three Philistine towns of Gaza, Askelon, and Ekron (verse 18). The *Har* is the central or highland district of Palestine, which runs through the whole length of the country, broken only by the plain of Jezreel. The *Negeb*, derived from a root which means "dry," was the region mainly occupied by the tribe of Simeon. The *Shephelah*, or low maritime plains (of which the root is perhaps also found in *Hi-Spalis*, Seville—see Stanley, *Sin. and Pal.* 485), is Palestine proper, *i.e.*, the region of Philistia, the sea-coast south of the Plain of Sharon. In the E.V. the name is sometimes rendered as here, "the valley" (Deut. i. 7; Josh. ix. 1, &c.), sometimes we find it as "the plain" (Obad. 19, &c.), or "the low plains" (1 Chron. xxvii. 28).

(10) **That dwelt in Hebron.** — See Josh. x. 36, 37. Hebron is midway between Jerusalem and Beersheba, and twenty miles from either. The first name of the city, which is one of the most ancient in the world (Num. xiii. 22), was Mamre (Gen. xiii. 18), from the name of its chief (*ib.* xiv. 24). It is now called El-Khulil ("the friend"), from Abraham. It was a city of refuge (Josh. xxi. 11—13). If the view taken as to the chronology of this chapter is correct, this assault is identical with those touched upon in Josh. xi. 21, xiv. 6—15, xv. 13, 14. The LXX. have, "Hebron came forth against Judah." For later references to Hebron, see Neh. xi. 25; 1 Macc. v. 65.

Kirjath-arba. — That is, "the *city* of Arba." The word afterwards became archaic and poetical (Ps. xlviii. 2; Isa. xxv. 2). All the cities thus named (Kirjath-huzoth, Kirjath-jearim, &c.) existed *before* the conquest of Palestine. We find the root in Iskariot (*i.e.*, man of Kerioth, a town in the south of Judah). Arba was the father of Anak (Josh. xv. 13, xiv. 15), and Fürst interprets the name "hero of Baal." Some, however, take Arba for the numeral "four," so that Kirjath-arba would mean Tetrapolis; and connect the name Hebron with the Arabic "*Cherbar*," a confederation, "the *cities* of Hebron" (2 Sam. ii. 3).

Sheshai, and Ahiman, and Talmai. — Possibly the names of three *clans* of the Anakim (Num. xiii. 22, 23). The Anakim are connected with the Nephilim—giant races sprung from the union of the sons of God with the daughters of men. Josephus says that giant bones of the race were shown in his day (*Antt.* v. 2, § 3). They were doubtless the bones of extinct animals, and being taken for human remains might well lead to the conclusion of Josephus, that these giants "had bodies so large, and countenances so entirely different from other men, that they were surprising to the sight."

(11) **Debir.** — See Josh. xv. 15, 49. In Josh. x. 38, 39, its conquest is assigned to Joshua. The name means "the oracle." It afterwards became a Levitic town. There seem to have been two other Debirs (Josh. xv. 7, xiii. 26). This one is identified by Dr. Rosen with *Dewirban*, near the spring *Ain Nunkûr*, south-west of Hebron.

Kirjath-sepher. — The name is curious and interesting. It means "the city of the book," and is rendered in the LXX. by "city of letters." It was also called Kirjath-sannah (Josh. xv. 49), which, according to Bochart, means "city of learning." Perhaps, therefore, we may consider that it was a famous centre of Canaanite culture and worship. All further attempts to explain its three names must be purely conjectural. We may compare with it the name of the Egyptian Byblos (Ewald). The LXX. here fall into mere confusion.

(12) **And Caleb said.** — See Josh. xv. 16. Caleb was a "Kenizzite," which seems to imply that he was descended from Kenaz, a grandson of Esau (Gen. xxxvi. 11). In Num. xiii. 6 he is mentioned as being a prince (*nasi*, or chief, *rosh*) of the tribe of Judah. He was certainly affiliated to that tribe; but if the name "Caleb" means "dog," it would seem a very unlikely name for a pure Jew, for I cannot think that the effort to trace a sort of *totem* system (or naming of tribes from animals) among the ancient Jews (*Journ. of Philology*, June, 1880) is successful. His father's name, Jephunneh, is of uncertain derivation. Fürst and Meier derive Caleb from a root meaning "valiant;" but the peculiarity of the expressions used respecting him in Josh. xv. 13, xiv. 14, together with certain marked names and features in the genealogies of his family, at least give some probability to the conjecture that he was of foreign origin.

Will I give Achsah my daughter to wife. — Comp. 1 Sam. xvii. 25 and xviii. 17. So the Messenian hero Aristomenes gave a peasant woman, who had saved his life, in marriage to his son. This story shows the strength and importance of this fastness of the south, which is also proved by the fact that Caleb has to refer to his unbroken strength before he gains permission to win the region by the sword (Josh. xiv. 11).

will I give Achsah my daughter to wife. ⁽¹³⁾ And Othniel the son of Kenaz, Caleb's younger brother, took it: and he gave him Achsah his daughter to wife. ⁽¹⁴⁾ And it came to pass, when she came *to him,* that she moved him to ask of her father a field: and she lighted from off *her* ass; and Caleb said unto her, What wilt thou? ⁽¹⁵⁾ And she said unto him, Give me a blessing: for thou hast given me a south land; give me also springs of water. And Caleb gave her the upper springs and the nether springs.

⁽¹⁶⁾ And the children of the Kenite, Moses' father in law, went up out of the city of palm trees with the children of Judah into the wilderness of Judah,

---

⁽¹³⁾ **Othniel.**—Josh. xv. 15—17. It is here added that he was Caleb's younger brother. (See chap. iii. 9.) The Hebrew may mean either that Othniel was "son of Kenaz and brother of Caleb" (in which case he married his niece); or "son of Kenaz, who was Caleb's brother" (as in "Jonadab, the son of Shimeah David's brother," 2 Sam. xiii. 3), in which case Achsah was his cousin. The Masoretes, to whom is due the punctuation, &c., of our Hebrew Scriptures, show by their pointing that they understood the words in the *former* sense. But though Ben-kenaz may simply mean Kenezite (Josh. xiv. 6; Num. xxxii. 12), it is strange in that case that Othniel should never be called a son of Jephunneh. If he was a brother of Caleb's, he must have lived to extreme old age, and have been an old man when he married Achsah. For the importance of Caleb's family, see 1 Chron. xxvii. 15. The Rabbis identify Othniel with the Jabez who is so abruptly introduced in 1 Chron. iv. 9, 10, and connect Achsah's petition with the prayer there recorded; and they suppose that he founded the school of scribes at Jabez (1 Chron. ii. 55), and was a teacher of law to the Kenites.

⁽¹⁴⁾ **When she came to him.**—When she first reached his house as a bride.

She moved him.—He was too modest to ask for himself, and he declined her request; but she will not enter till she has gained her way.

A field.—Rather, *the field.* In the passage in Josh. xv. 18 there is no definite article, but by the time this book was written the field then obtained by Achsah had become historical.

Lighted.—Not merely in sign of reverence (like Rebecca in Gen. xxiv. 64, and Abigail in 1 Sam. xxv. 25), but "leaped off" with eager impetuosity. The Hebrew verb *tsanach* here used occurs in chap. iv. 21, where it is rendered "fastened," *i.e.,* "drove it firmly by a blow." The LXX. render it "screamed" or "shouted from the ass;" the Vulg., "sighed as she was sitting on the ass;" but they probably had a different reading. "Suddenly," says Ewald, "*as if some accident had happened to her,* she fell from her ass, and on being embraced by her anxious father, she adjured him as if in words of inspiration" (*Hist. Isr.* ii. 366).

What wilt thou?—Caleb was unable to understand her conduct in refusing to enter the house of her bridegroom.

⁽¹⁵⁾ **A blessing**—*i.e.,* "a present" (Gen. xxxiii. 11).

A south land.—The word also means "a dry and barren land" (Ps. cxxvi. 4). The LXX. read "hast given me (in marriage) into a south land."

Springs of water.—In thus asking for the fertile land which lay at the foot of the mountain slope, she showed herself at once more provident and less bashful than her husband.

The upper springs and the nether springs. —The word here rendered "springs" is *gulloth, i.e.,* "bubblings." Probably the district for which she asked was called "the upper Gulloth" and "the lower Gulloth," just as we have "the upper and the nether Beth-horon" (*Beit-ur el-foka* and *el-tahti*). The addition of "the deep green glen" to the arid mountain tract of Debir enormously increased the value of her portion. "The source of this incident," says Dean Stanley, "was first discovered by Dr. Rosen. . . . The word *gulloth* well applies to this beautiful rivulet. The spots are now called *Ain-Nunkúr* and *Dewîr-ban,* about one hour south-west of Hebron. Underneath the hill on which Debir stood is a deep valley, rich with verdure from a copious rivulet, which, rising at the crest of the glen, falls with a continuity unusual in Judean hills down to its lowest depth" (*Jewish Church,* ii. 264, and *Sin. Palest.,* p. 165. Mr. Wilton, in his *Negeb,* p. 16, identifies it with Kurnuil). Othniel had a son, Hathath (1 Chron. iv. 13), and his posterity continued to late times (Judith vi. 15).

⁽¹⁶⁾ **The children of the Kenite, Moses' father in law.**—It is difficult to disentangle the names Jethro, Reuel, or Raguel, and Hobab (chap. iv. 11); but in my article on Jethro in Kitto's *Bible Cyclopædia* I have shown that Jethro and Reuel are identical, the latter name ("friend of God") being his local title as a priest of Midian; and that he was the father of Zipporah and Hobab. When Jethro refused to stay with the Israelites (Ex. xviii. 27), Hobab consented to accompany them as their *hybeer* or caravan-guide. He is well known in the Mohammedan legends as *Schoeib,* but is confounded with Jethro.

The Kenites were the elder branch of the tribe of Midianites. They lived in the rocky district on the shores of the gulf of Akabah (Num. xxi. 1, xxiv. 21; 1 Sam. xv. 6). They seem to have been named from a chieftain *Kain* (Gen. xv. 19; Num. xxiv. 22; *Heb.,* where there is a play on Kenite and *Kinneka,* "thy rest"). They were originally a race of troglodytes or cave-dwellers. The Targum constantly reads *Salmaa* for Kenite, because the Kenites were identified with the *Kinim* of 1 Chron. ii. 55. Jethro, they say, was a Kenite, who gave to Moses a house (*Beth*) and bread (*lehem*) (Ex. ii. 20, 21). They identify Jethro with Salmaa, because in 1 Chron. ii. 5 *Salma* is the father of *Bethlehem.* They also identify Rechab, the ancestor of the Rechabites—who were a branch of the Kenites—with Rechabiah, the son of Moses.

Went up.—Probably, in the first instance, in a warlike expedition.

The city of palm trees.—Probably Jericho (see chap. iii. 13; Deut. xxxiv. 3; 2 Chron. xxviii. 15). When Jericho was destroyed and laid under a curse, it would be quite in accordance with the Jewish feeling, which attached such "fatal force and fascination" to words, to avoid even the mention of the name. The Kenites would naturally attach less importance to the curse, or at any rate would not consider that they were

Capture of the   JUDGES, I.   *Canaanite Cities.*

which *lieth* in the south of Arad; and they went and dwelt among the people. (17) And Judah went with Simeon his brother, and they slew the Canaanites that inhabited Zephath, and utterly destroyed it. And the name of the city was called *Hormah. (18) Also Judah took Gaza with the coast there-

a Num. 21. 3.

1 Or, *he possessed the mountain.*

b Num. 14. 24; Josh. 14. 13; & 15. 14.

of, and Askelon with the coast thereof, and Ekron with the coast thereof. (19) And the LORD was with Judah; and ¹he drave out *the inhabitants of* the mountain; but could not drive out the inhabitants of the valley, because they had chariots of iron. (20) And they gave Hebron unto Caleb, *b*as Moses said:

---

braving it when they pitched their nomad tents among those beautiful groves of palms and balsams, which once made the soil "a divine country" (Jos. *B. J.* i. 6, § 6; iv. 8, § 3; *Antt.* v. 1, § 22), though they have now entirely disappeared. Rabbinic tradition says that Jericho was assigned to Hobab. From the omission of the name Jericho, some have needlessly supposed that the reference is to *Phaenico* (a name which means " palm-grove "), an Arabian town mentioned by Diod Sic. iii. 41 (Le Clerc, Bertheau, Ewald); but there is no difficulty about the Kenites leaving Jericho when Judah left it.

The wilderness of Judah.—The Midbar—not a waste desert, but a plain with pasture—was a name applied to the lower Jordan valley and the southern hills of Judea (Gen. xxi. 14; Matt. iii. 1, iv. 1; Luke xv. 4). The Kenites, like all Bedouins, hated the life of cities, and never lived in them except under absolute necessity (Jer. xxxv. 6, 7).

In the south of Arad.—Our E.V. has, in Num. xxi. 1, King Arad; but more correctly, in Josh. xv. 14, " the king of Arad." It was a city twenty miles from Hebron, on the road to Petra, and the site is still called Tell-Arad (Wilton, *Negeb*, p. 198). They may have been attracted by the caves in the neighbourhood, and, although they left it at the bidding of Saul (1 Sam. xv. 6), they seem to have returned to it in the days of David (1 Sam. xxx. 29).

Among the people.—It seems most natural to interpret this of the Israelites of the tribe of Judah; but it may mean "the people to which he belonged," *i.e.*, the Amalekites (Num. xxi. 21), and this accords with 1 Sam. xv. 21. For the only subsequent notices of this interesting people, see chap. iv. 11; 1 Sam. xv. 6; 1 Chron. ii. 55; Jer. xxxv. They formed a useful frontier-guard to the Holy Land.

(17) **Zephath.**—This name is only mentioned elsewhere in 2 Chron. xiv. 10, as the scene of Asa's battle with Zerah the Ethiopian.

Hormah—*i.e.*, "a place devoted by ban." The name *Chormah* is derived from *Cherem* (anathema or ban), and the verb rendered "utterly destroyed" means " executed the ban upon it." By their conquest the Israelites fulfilled the vow which they had made in consequence of the " defeat inflicted on them by the king of Arad," as a punishment for their disobedient attempt to force their way into Palestine (see Num. xiv. 45, xxi. 1—3). The town belonged to Simeon (Josh. xix. 4; 1 Chron. iv. 28—32), and was close to the lands of the Kenites (1 Sam. xxx. 29, 30).

(18) **Took Gaza . . Askelon . . Ekron.**—Three of the five Philistian lordships, to which the LXX. add Ashdod (Azotus). In Josh. xiii. 3 these five townships are mentioned as still *unconquered*, and here the LXX. put in a negative—" Judah did *not* inherit Gaza, nor," &c. St. Augustine had the same reading. It is, however, possible that "not" may have been conjecturally added because of the apparent discrepancy

between this passage and chap. iii. 8; or, again, " did not inherit" may be a sort of explanatory gloss on the " took." Josephus (*Antt.* v. 2, § 4) says that Askelon and Ashdod were taken in the war, but that Gaza and Ekron escaped, because their situation in the plains enabled them to use their chariots; yet in 3, § 1, he says that the Canaanites *re-conquered* Askelon and Ekron. In any case, the conquest was very transitory. (See Josh. xi. 22; Judg. iii. 3, xiii. *seq.*)

(19) **The Lord was with Judah.**—The Targum here has " The Word of the Lord." The expression is frequently used to imply insured prosperity (Gen. xxxix. 23; 1 Sam. xviii. 14; 2 Kings xviii. 7. Comp. Matt. xviii. 20).

But.—Rather, *for* (*ki*) : *i.e.*, they only dispossessed their enemies of the mountain, for, &c.

Could not.—The Hebrew seems purposely to avoid this expression, and says "*there was no driving out.*" Judah could have driven them out; but their faith was cowed by the (verse 19) iron chariots.

The valley.—Here *Emek*, not *Shephelah*. "Broad sweeps between parallel ranges of hills," like, *e.g.*, the " valley of Jezreel," *i.e.*, the plain of Esdraelon. It differs from *Gî*, which means a gorge or ravine.

Chariots of iron.—See chap. iv. 3; Josh. xi. 6—9, xvii. 16; 1 Sam. xiii. 6. R. Tanchum makes it mean " very strong chariots;" but the phrase means either " chariots with iron-bound wheels," or "*scythed* chariots." Ktesias attributes scythed chariots to Ninus, but none are seen on the Nineveh sculptures, and it is doubtful whether they were known so early. Xenophon says that scythed chariots were invented by Cyrus, which would not be till five centuries after this period. For this clause the LXX. have, " because Rechab resisted them," mistaking *rekeb*, " chariot," for a proper name (as they often do with other words). Hence the notion of Theodoret of the Kenites, to which Rechab belonged (2 Kings x. 15—23; Jer. xxxv. 2), secretly helped the Philistines, is quite groundless. We see a reason for the partial failure of the Israelites in the fact that at this time they had not attained to the same level of civilisation as the Canaanites in arts and arms. This advantage could only have been rendered unavailing by more faith and faithfulness than they showed in their conduct. " Their warriors often rather overran than subdued the land. . . . The chariots and better arms of the Canaanites rendered the conquest of the valleys and plains long and laborious, especially to Joseph, Judah, and Dan. . . . The Hebrews 'walked upon the high places of the land' (Ps. xviii. 33; 2 Sam. xxii. 34; Hab. iii. 19; Is. lviii. 14; Deut. xxxii. 13, 29, 33); but these heights were often encompassed like islands by the inhabitants of the valleys" (Ewald, ii. 264).

(20) **Hebron.**—See Josh. xiv. 12—15, xv. 13, 14.

As Moses said.—Num. xiv. 21.

It is remarkable that after this time Judah is only mentioned in chaps. x. 9, xv. 10, xx. 18. The tribe

The Tribe of Joseph   JUDGES, I.   *take Bethel.*

and he expelled thence the three sons of Anak.

(21) And the children of Benjamin did not drive out the Jebusites that inhabited Jerusalem; but the Jebusites dwell with the children of Benjamin in Jerusalem unto this day.

(22) And the house of Joseph, they also went up against Beth-el: and the LORD *was* with them. (23) And the house of Joseph sent to descry Beth-el. (Now the name of the city before *was* ᵃLuz.) (24) And the spies saw a man come forth out of the city, and they said unto him, Shew us, we pray thee, the entrance into the city, and ᵇwe will shew thee mercy. (25) And when he shewed them the entrance into the city, they smote the city with the edge of the sword; but they let go the man and all his family. (26) And the man went into the land of the Hittites, and built a city, and called the name thereof Luz: which *is* the name thereof unto this day.

(27) ᶜNeither did Manasseh drive out *the inhabitants of* Beth-shean and her

a Gen. 28. 19.
b Josh. 2. 14.
c Josh. 17. 11, 12.

---

produced no judge, with the possible exception of Ibzan (see chap. xii. 8), nor is it mentioned in the song of Deborah. Perhaps we may see a reason for this in the strength which had won for Judah so secure a position. On the other hand, their conduct towards Samson was of the most abject kind (chap. xv. 13). "As the nation gained in settled position and command of the soil it lost in unity and strength of external action. Each tribe looked out for itself" (Ewald, ii. 264).

(21) **The children of Benjamin did not drive out the Jebusites.**—In Josh. xv. 63 we find the same statement respecting the children of Judah. (See verse 8.) Jerusalem was on the borders of Judah (Josh. xvi. 8) and Benjamin (chap. xviii. 28). It belongs more properly to the latter, but the conquest of Zion by David (2 Sam. v. 7) naturally caused its closer identification with Judah. The Jebusites were tolerated inhabitants ever after this conquest, and had their own prince—Araunah (2 Sam. xxiv. 18)—"Araunah the king." We even find traces of them after the exile (Ezra ix. 1). Jerusalem is a remarkable exception to the rule that the Israelites conquered "the hill-country," but not the plain.

Unto this day.—The assignment of Jerusalem to Benjamin shows that *this* narrative, though not contemporaneous, is older than the conquest of Jerusalem by David.

(22) **The house of Joseph.** — Ephraim and Manasseh. The narrative now leaves the conquest of southern for that of central Palestine (Josh. xvi., xvii.).

Beth-el.—The position of this town on the "highway" between Hebron and Shechem—the main thoroughfare of Palestine (chaps. xx. 31, xxi. 19)—gave it great importance, as did also its sacred connection with events in the life of Abraham (Gen. xii. 8, 9, xiii. 3, 4, xii. 8) and Jacob (Gen. xxviii. 10—17). For its subsequent history, see chap. xx. 18—26, and the history of the northern kingdom, Hos. x. 8; Amos v. 21—23, vii. 10; 1 Kings xii. xiii.; 2 Kings ii. 3, &c. It is now the wretched village of *Beitin*. Bethel belonged properly to Benjamin (Josh. xviii. 22), but possibly, as in the case of Jerusalem, the border of Ephraim and Benjamin separated the upper from the lower town.

(23) **To descry Beth-el.**—The word perhaps implies a regular siege, and it is so understood by the LXX. (Cod. Alex.) and the Vulgate.

Luz.—We are also told that this was the original name of the city in Gen. xxviii. 19; but there seems to be in that verse a distinction between the *city* and the *place* of Jacob's dream. (Comp. Josh. xvi. 2.) The name means either "hazel," or "sinking," *i.e.*, a valley-depression.

(24) **The spies.** — Perhaps, rather, *the scouts* of the blockading squadron. The Israelites, like most ancient nations, were little able to take cities by storm, and relied either on blockade or on internal treachery.

Saw a man come forth.—Probably he stole out secretly, and was seized by the scouts. Similarly the Persians took Sardis by seizing a path used by a man who had dropped his helmet, and descended the hill-fortress to pick it up (Herod. i. 84).

We will shew thee mercy.—They bribed him with the promise of personal safety. (Compare Josh. ii. 12, vi.)

(26) **Into the land of the Hittites.**—Probably the inhabitants of Bethel belonged to this tribe of Canaanites. In Josh. i. 4 their name is used for all the inhabitants of Canaan, but probably it means the coast-dwellers. They are often conjecturally classed with the inhabitants of Citium, in Cyprus. They first appear as "children of Heth," in Gen. xxiii. 19, but seem at that time to have been only a small tribe. Abraham, as Ewald observes, went to the Amorites for his allies, but to the Hittites for his grave. The Talmud says that *this* Luz was famous for its purple dye, and partly on this account Thomson identifies it with Kulb Louzy, not far from Antioch. It was not uncommon in ancient days for the fugitives from a city to build another city elsewhere of the same name. Thus Teucer, when driven from Salamis, built a new Salamis in Cyprus:

"Ambiguam tellure novâ Salamina futuram "(Hor. *Od.* i. 7).

Although the site of this new Luz has not been certainly identified, it was probably in some northern district on the Phœnician frontier (Ewald).

Unto this day.—This formula implies the lapse of some time between the event and this record of it.

(27) **Neither did Manasseh.**—The sacred historian is glancing at the conquest of Canaan, advancing from the southern tribes upwards to central and northern Palestine. (See Josh. xvii. 11—13.)

Beth-shean.—The town to the walls of which the victorious Philistines nailed the bodies of Saul and Jonathan after the battle of Gilboa, and from which they were recovered by the gratitude of the brave people of Jabesh Gilead (1 Sam. xxxi. 8 ; 2 Sam. xxi. 12). It is again mentioned in 1 Kings iv. 12, and in later days was well known under the name of Scythopolis, or "city of Scythians" (2 Macc. xii. 29), a name contemptuously given to it from the barbarism of its inhabitants (Jos. *Vit.* 6). Though conquered by Manasseh, it was in the lot of Issachar (Josh. xvii. 11). It is now called *Beisan*. It was in a district so rich

towns, nor Taanach and her towns, nor the inhabitants of Dor and her towns, nor the inhabitants of Ibleam and her towns, nor the inhabitants of Megiddo and her towns: but the Canaanites would dwell in that land. (28) And it came to pass, when Israel was strong, that they put the Canaanites to tribute, and did not utterly drive them out.

(29) *a* Neither did Ephraim drive out the Canaanites that dwelt in Gezer; but the Canaanites dwelt in Gezer among them.

(30) Neither did Zebulun drive out the inhabitants of Kitron, nor the inhabi-

a Josh. 16. 10.

---

and fruitful that the Rabbis describe it as the gate of Paradise.

And her towns.—Literally, *and her daughters*.

Taanach.—The name means "the sandy." It was a town of Issachar assigned to the Levites, and was famous for Barak's victory over Sisera. It is still called Taanuk (Robinson, *Bibl. Res.* i. 316).

Dor.—Properly in Asher, it seems to have been attacked by Manasseh, and was ultimately won by Ephraim (Josh. xi. 2, xvii. 11; 1 Chron. vii. 29). It long continued to be an important place (1 Macc. xv. 11; Jos. *Antt.* xiv. 5, § 3). It lies near the foot of Carmel, and is now called *Tantura*. Endor ("the fountain of Dor") was probably one of its dependencies.

Ibleam.—Also called Bileam (1 Chron. vi. 70). It was a Levitical town (Josh. xxi. 25). The only event connected with it in Scripture is the death of Ahaziah (2 Kings ix. 27). Perhaps Khirbet-Belameh.

Megiddo.—Near Taanach. It is now called *Lejjûn*, from having been a station of the Romans. See verse 19; 2 Kings ix. 27 (the death of Ahaziah); and 2 Kings xxiii. 29; Zech. xii. 11 (the defeat of Josiah by Pharaoh Necho). It was fortified by Solomon (1 Kings ix. 15). From this town is derived the famous name Armageddon (Rev. xvi. 16) as a scene of battle and wailing.

The Canaanites would dwell in that land—*i.e.*, the old inhabitants obstinately and successfully held their own (Josh. xvii. 12).

(28) **Did not utterly drive them out.**—This is mentioned by way of blame, as the cause of their future sins and disasters (chap. ii. 2; Josh. xvi. 16, xvii. 13). As to the morality of these exterminating wars, we must bear in mind that men and nations must alike be judged by the moral standard of their own day, not by the advanced morality of later ages. We learn from unanimous testimony that the nations of Canaan had sunk to the lowest and vilest depths of moral degeneracy. When nations have fallen thus low, the cup of their iniquity is full; they are practically irreclaimable. To mingle with them would inevitably be to learn their works, for their worst abominations would find an ally in the natural weakness and corruption of the human heart. The Israelites therefore believed that it was their positive duty to destroy them, and the impulse which led them to do so was one which sprang from their best and not from their worst instincts. It must not be forgotten that the teaching of Christ has absolutely changed the moral conceptions of the world. It intensified, to a degree which we can hardly estimate, our sense of the inalienable rights of humanity and of the individual man. In these days there is scarcely any amount of evidence which would convince us that we were bidden to exterminate a whole population, and involve women and children in one indistinguishable massacre. But neither the Israelites nor any other ancient nations, at this early stage of their moral development, had any conception corresponding to those which would in our minds rightly excite horror, were we to receive a command like that given by Moses, that "thou shalt save nothing alive that breatheth" (Deut. xxii. 16), or by Samuel, "Slay both man and woman, *infant and suckling*, ox and sheep, camel and ass" (1 Sam. xv. 3). We should instantly declare it to be *impossible* that God—as Christ has revealed to us the character of our Father in heaven—should give us commands which would militate against our sense of justice no less than against our sense of compassion. To quote such commands as an excuse for, or an incentive to, such horrible acts of wickedness as the Sack of Beziers, or the Massacre of St. Bartholomew, is ignorantly and recklessly to obliterate the whole results of God's progressive moral education of our race. It is to ignore the fact that we are living under a wholly different dispensation, and to disavow every blessing which has accrued to humanity from the broadening light and divine revelation of three thousand years. But the ancient Israelites, living as they did in the "days of ignorance" which God "winked at" (Acts xvii. 30), had never attained to that idea of human individuality—that sense of the independence and infinite worth of each human life—which would have shown them that they knew not what manner of spirit they were of (Luke ix. 56). The wild and passionate sense of severe justice, the comparative indifference to human life, the familiarity with pain and death which blunted the keen edge of pity, "the deficient sense of individuality, the exaggerated sense of the solidarity which united a criminal with all his surroundings and possessions," prevented them from regarding the execution of their ban on guilty nations, cities, or families in any other light than that of the zeal for righteousness by which it was impelled. Their deeds must be estimated by the elements of nobleness which mingled with them, and not indiscriminately condemned by standards of judgment of which neither they nor the age in which they lived had any conception. They firmly believed that in exterminating Canaan they were acting under Divine commands; and there was nothing in such commands which would in that day have shocked the moral sense of the world. "They did not look unnatural to the ancient Jew; they were not foreign to his standard; they excited no surprise or perplexity; they appealed to a genuine but rough idea of justice which existed, when the longing for retribution upon crime in the human mind was not checked by the strict sense of human individuality" (Mozley, *Lectures on the Old Test.*, p. 103).

(29) **Neither did Ephraim.**—See Josh. xvi. 10.

Gezer.—This town was not won from the Canaanites till its capture by Pharaoh, who gave it as a present to his daughter, the wife of Solomon (1 Kings ix. 16).

(30) **Neither did Zebulun.**—See Josh. xix. 10—16. Nothing is known of the towns here mentioned. It is remarkable that Issachar is not mentioned, but it may perhaps be accounted for by the condition of contented subjection in which this tribe "bowed his shoulder to the yoke" (Gen. xlix. 14, 15).

tants of Nahalol; but the Canaanites dwelt among them, and became tributaries.

(31) Neither did Asher drive out the inhabitants of Accho, nor the inhabitants of Zidon, nor of Ahlab, nor of Achzib, nor of Helbah, nor of Aphik, nor of Rehob: (32) but the Asherites dwelt among the Canaanites, the inhabitants of the land: for they did not drive them out.

(33) Neither did Naphtali drive out the inhabitants of Beth-shemesh, nor the inhabitants of Beth-anath; but he dwelt among the Canaanites, the inhabitants of the land: nevertheless the inhabitants of Beth-shemesh and of Beth-anath became tributaries unto them.

(34) And the Amorites forced the children of Dan into the mountain: for they would not suffer them to come down to the valley: (35) but the Amorites would dwell in mount Heres in Aijalon, and in Shaalbim: yet the hand of the house of Joseph [1] prevailed,

[1] Heb., *was heavy.*

---

(31) **Neither did Asher.**—See Josh. xix. 24—31.
Accho.—The seaport so famous under the names of Ptolemais (Acts xxi. 7; Macc. v. 15, x. 1), Acre, and St. Jean d'Acre (now Acca). Josephus called it Ako (*Antt.* ix. 14, § 2).
Zidon.—(Josh. xi. 8.) Asher never succeeded in conquering Zidon, which was the capital of Phœnicia, though eclipsed by its neighbour Tyre. (2 Sam. v. 11; Is. xxiii.; Jer. xxvii., xlvii.; Matt. xi. 22, &c.) It is now called *Saida.*
Ahlab.—An unknown town.
Achzib.—(See Josh. xix. 29.) Better known as Ecdippa (Jos. *B. J.* i. 13, § 4), the modern Zib, about nine miles north of Akka. There was a less well-known Achzib in Judah (Chezib)—Gen. xxxviii. 5; Micah i. 14; Josh. xv. 44.
Helbah.—The name is rendered "the coast" in Josh. xix. 29. The site is unknown.
Aphik.—The Aphek of Josh. xix. 30, now Afka (Robinson, *Bible Res.*, iii. 606). The name means "strength." It was famous for a Temple of Venus, destroyed by Constantine. (Euseb. *Vit. Const.*) There seems to have been another Aphek near Hebron. (Josh. xii. 18.)
Rehob.—A Levitical city (Josh. xxi. 21; 1 Chron. vi. 75).

(32) **The Asherites dwelt among the Canaanites.**—The change of phrase from verse 30 implies that in these districts the Canaanites had the upper hand. Thus Asher reached the climax of degradation. The best summary of the moral lesson involved in the narrative is in Ps. cvi. 34—36: "They did not destroy the nations concerning whom the Lord commanded them: but *were mingled among the heathen and learned their works.* And they served their idols, which were a snare unto them."

(33) **Neither did Naphtali.**—See Josh. xix. 32—38.
Beth-shemesh.—The name means "house of the sun," and the place was probably a great centre of Baal-worship; but this Beth-shemesh in Naphtali is not the same as Ir-shemesh ("city of the sun") in Josh. xv. 10, which was on the borders of Judah. It is the "mount of the sun" (Har-cheres) in verse 35. In Is. xix. 18, alluding to another "city of the sun" (On, *i.e.,* Heliopolis), the prophet calls it not Is-ha-Cheres, "the city of the sun," but Ir-ha-Heres, "the city of overthrow," with one of those scornful plays on words of which the Jews were fond.
Beth-anath.—Nothing is known of this town. The name perhaps means "house of echo," and some identify it with Baneas or Paneas, a place at which the echo was famous.

Nevertheless.—The tribe of Naphtali was in the same unhappy condition as that of Asher, living in the midst of a Canaanite population of superior strength to themselves. They had, however, so far succeeded as to reduce the two chief towns (out of nineteen—Josh. xix. 38) to a tributary condition.

(34) **The Amorites.**—They were the Highlanders of Palestine (Josh. x. 6; Num. xiii. 29; Deut. i. 44).
Forced.—Literally "squeezed" or "pressed."
Forced the children of Dan into the mountain.—The condition of this tribe was, therefore, the worst of all. So far from reducing under tribute the Canaanites of its assigned possession, as the central tribes did, the Danites did not even succeed in establishing a tolerated neutrality among them, like the northern tribes, but were driven into a few mountain-strongholds. It was probably this failure, and the consequent pressure of space under which the tribe laboured, which induced them to undertake the successful northern expedition alluded to in Josh. xix. 47 and described in Judg. xviii.

(35) **Mount Heres.**—(See verse 33.) Cheres is used for the sun in Job ix. 7. The Vatican Codex of the LXX. has the strange rendering, "in the mountains of potsherds" (comp. the Monte Testaccio at Rome), and Jerome follows them in reading חֶרֶשׂ for חֶרֶס. The Alexandrian Codex renders it, "the mountain of the myrtle-grove," reading *Haras.*
Aijalon.—The name means "gazelles," and is still preserved in the name *Yalo,* a village on the south side of the beautiful valley, Merj Ibn Omeir. It is mentioned in the story of the battle of Beth-horon (Josh. x. 12), and as a scene of the defeat of the Philistines by Saul (1 Sam. xiv. 31). It was a Levitical town (Josh. xxi. 24).
Shaalbim.—The name means "jackals" (comp. Judg. xv. 4; and *Hazar-shual,* Josh. xv. 28; and *Shalim,* 1 Sam. ix. 4). The LXX. render this and Aijalon by "*where the bears and foxes are.*" Not far off is Zeboim, *i.e.* "Hyænas."
Yet the hand of the house of Joseph prevailed.—This may imply that when Dan was unable to dislodge the Amorites they were effectually aided by the tribes of Ephraim and Manasseh. Hence the LXX. render it, "The hand of the house of Joseph was heavy on the Amorites." (Comp. 1 Sam. v. 6; Ps. xxxii. 6.)
Tributaries.—Not to Dan, but to their conquerors, the Ephraimites; so that the assistance rendered by the house of Joseph to their weak brother was, at the best, somewhat selfish, although it enabled Dan to hold the sea-coast (verse 17).

so that they became tributaries. (36) And the coast of the Amorites *was* from ¹the going up to Akrabbim, from the rock, and upward.

CHAPTER II.—(1) And an ²angel of the LORD came up from Gilgal to Bochim, and said, I made you to go up out of Egypt, and have brought you

¹ Or, *Maale-Akrabbim.*

² Or, *messenger.*

B.C. cir. 1425.

a Deut. 7. 2.
b Deut. 12. 3.

unto the land which I sware unto your fathers; and I said, I will never break my covenant with you. (2) And *a*ye shall make no league with the inhabitants of this land; *b*ye shall throw down their altars: but ye have not obeyed my voice: why have ye done this? (3) Wherefore I also said, I will not drive them out from before you;

---

(36) **The coast of the Amorites.**—This notice is added to account for the obstinate resistance of the Amorites, by showing the extent of their domain, which reached far to the south of Petra. Hazezon Tamar, "the sanctuary of the palm," afterwards called Engedi, "the goat's fountain," belonged to them (Gen. xiv. 7; 2 Chron. xx. 2; Tristram, *Land of Israel*, p. 784). Another opinion given is, that the verse is added to sum up the chapter, by showing that neither the northern, eastern, nor western boundaries were thoroughly secured, but only that of the southern tribes.

From the going up to Akrabbim.—The same as Maaleh Akrabbim (Josh. xv. 3), and "the ascent of scorpions" (Num. xxxiv. 4), probably the *Wady-es-Zuweirah* (De Saulcy, *La Terre Sainte*, i. 528), where scorpions abound to this day under every stone; or the *Wady-es-Sufah*. Robinson supposes it to be the line of rocks which crosses the Jordan valley at right angles, eleven miles south of the Dead Sea (*Bibl. Res.* ii. 120). It is the Akrabattine of 1 Macc. v. 3. It formed the southern boundary of the Holy Land, being a wall of cliffs which separates the Jordan valley from the wilderness.

From the rock.—From "Ras-Selah," *i.e.*, from Petra, the famous capital of Idumea (2 Kings xiv. 7; Is. xvi. 1; Obad. 3). Keil and Delitzsch refer it to the well-known rock at Kadesh-Meribah (Num. xx. 8—10).

And upward.—It is uncertain whether this means "and beyond," *i.e.*, their border extended even farther south; or, "and northwards," *i.e.*, this was their extreme southern limit.

The history of the Twelve Tribes is nowhere separately drawn out in Scripture. The reader will find the character and career of each tribe graphically sketched in Dean Stanley's *Sinai and Palestine*, chap. iii.—xi.; and more briefly in the *Lectures on the Jewish Church*, i. 261—281.

II.

1—5. The messenger of the Lord rebukes the people at Bochim. 6—10. Faithfulness of the Israelites during the lives of Joshua and his generation. 11—13. Their subsequent apostasy. 14, 15. The retribution which fell upon them. 16—19. Failure of their deliverance by Judges to wean them from idolatry. 20—23. Consequences of their apostasy.

(1) **An angel of the Lord.**—The words "*Maleak Jehovah*" are used of Haggai, in Hag. i. 13; of prophets in Is. xlii. 19; Mal. iii. 6; of priests in Mal. ii. 7. Hence from very ancient times these words have been interpreted as, "a messenger of the Lord" (as in the margin of our Bible). The Targum paraphrases it by "a prophet with a message from Jehovah." R. Tanchum, from verse 6, infers that it was Joshua himself. Kimchi and others have supposed that it was Phinehas.

No indications are given of anything specially miraculous. On the other hand, there is much room to suppose that the writer intended "the Angel of the Presence," because (1) he constantly uses the phrase in this sense (chaps. vi. 11, 12, 21, 22; xiii. 3, 13, 15, &c.); (2) the same phrase occurs in this sense elsewhere, as in Gen. xvi. 7; xxii. 11; Ex. ii. 2, 6, 14; Num. xxii. 22, &c.; (3) the angel speaks in the first person, and does not introduce his words by "Thus saith Jehovah," as the prophets always do (but see below). It seems probable, therefore, that by "the angel of the Lord" the writer meant "the captain of the Lord's host," who appeared to Joshua at Jericho (Josh. v. 13—15). Against this conclusion may be urged the fact that in no other instance does an angel appear to, or preach to, multitudes. Angels are sent to individuals, but prophets to nations.

Came up from Gilgal to Bochim.—This notice is by no means *decisive* against the conclusion that an angel is intended. The writer may mean to intimate that the Angel Prince of the host (Ex. xxiii. 20—23), the Angel of the Covenant, left his station in the camp of Gilgal and came up to the new camp or assembly of the people in Central Palestine (Josh. iv. 19; v. 9, 10; x. 7, 15, 33; xiv. 6). Ha-Bochim means "the weepers." The locality is not known, but the LXX. render it "to the weeping-place," and add "and to Bethel, and to the House of Israel." Hence it has been inferred that Bochim was near Bethel. Possibly, however, the LXX. may have been led to this interpretation by the vicinity to Bethel of Allon-Bachuth, "the oak of weeping" (Gen. xxxv. 8).

And said, I made you to go up out of Egypt.—The LXX. have "the Lord, the Lord brought you out of Egypt" (Cod. Alex.). Houbigant, from the repetition of the word, precariously conjectures the loss of some words, "*Thus saith the Lord,* I the Lord," &c., as in the Peshito; and, indeed, in some MSS. a blank (*Piska*) is left, implying at least a suspicion that this formula has accidentally fallen out of the text.

I will never break my covenant with you. —See Gen. xvii. 7; xxix. 12; Ps. lxxxix. 28, 34; Luke i. 54, 55, &c; Ex. iii. 6—8.

(2) **And ye shall make no league.**—This is the *condition* of the Covenant, quoted from Deut. vii. 2; xii. 2, 3. Comp. Ex. xxiii. 31—33; xxxiv. 12, 13.

Why have ye done this?—Comp. Gen. iii. 13; xii. 18.

(3) **Wherefore I also said.**—Rather, *And now I have said.*

I will not drive them out.—The withdrawal of the conditional promises in Ex. xxiii. 31.

They shall be as thorns in your sides.—The Hebrew is, "they shall be to you for *sides.*" The words "*as thorns*" are conjecturally supplied from Num. xxxiii. 55. In Josh. xxiii. 13 we have "*scourges*

Sorrow of the People.   JUDGES, II.   *The Death of Joshua*

but they shall be *ᵃas thorns* in your sides, and their gods shall be a *ᵇ*snare unto you. ⁽⁴⁾ And it came to pass, when the angel of the LORD spake these words unto all the children of Israel, that the people lifted up their voice, and wept. ⁽⁵⁾ And they called the name of that place ¹Bochim: and they sacrificed there unto the LORD.

⁽⁶⁾ And when Joshua had let the people go, the children of Israel went every man unto his inheritance to possess the land. ⁽⁷⁾ And the people served the LORD all the days of Joshua, and all the days of the elders that ²outlived Joshua, who had seen all the great works of the LORD, that he did for Israel. ⁽⁸⁾ And Joshua the son of Nun, the servant of the LORD, died, *being* an hundred and ten years old. ⁽⁹⁾ And they buried him in the border of his inheritance in Timnathheres, in the mount of Ephraim, on the north side of the hill Gaash. ⁽¹⁰⁾ And also all that generation were gathered unto their fathers: and there arose another generation after them, which knew not the LORD, nor yet the works which he had done for Israel.

⁽¹¹⁾ And the children of Israel did evil in the sight of the LORD, and served

ᵃ Josh. 23. 13

B.C. cir. 1426.

ᵇ Ex. 23. 33. & 34. 12.

¹ That is, *Weepers.*

B.C. cir. 1444.

² Heb., *prolonged days after Joshua.*

B.C. cir. 1406.

---

in your sides." The LXX. render "for pressures," and the Vulgate "that you may have enemies." The Hebrew word for "sides" is *tsiddim*, and would differ little from *tsarim* ("nets"), which is the conjecture of R. Jonas; and this root is found in the verb, "and they shall *vex* you," in Num. xxxii. 55. Whether we adopt this reading, or *tsinnim* ("thorns"), or suppose that a word has dropped out, the general sense is the same.

Their gods shall be a snare unto you.—See verses 12, 13; Ps. cvi. 36.

⁽⁵⁾ **Bochim.**—(Comp. Gen. xxxv. 8; l. 11.) It was like "the Jews' wailing-place" in modern Jerusalem.

They sacrificed there unto the Lord.—It is not *necessary* to infer from this that Bochim must have been near the sanctuary at Bethel, Shechem, or Shiloh. Not only did kings and prophets seem to be tacitly excepted from the general rule against offering sacrifice at any place except the chosen sanctuary, but also sacrifice was always freely offered at places where there had been any manifestation of the Divine Presence—chap. vi. 20 (Gideon); xxii. 19 (Manoah); 2 Sam. xxiv. 25 (David), &c. On the other hand, it is improbable that all Israel would have been assembled at some unknown place, or that the memory of such a spot should not have been preserved.

⁽⁶⁾ **When Joshua had let the people go.**—Rather, *And Joshua let the people go.* This passage strongly tends to support the view that the events of the previous chapter, and the message at Bochim, occurred before Joshua's death. (Comp. Josh. xxii. 6, xxiv. 28.)

⁽⁷⁾ **All the days of Joshua.**—Compare the whole passage (verses 6—10) with Josh. xxiv. 28—33, which is almost verbally identical with it. It is usually supposed that Joshua was about eighty at the time of the conquest of Canaan, because that was the age of his comrade Caleb (Josh. xiv. 7); if so, he had lived thirty years after the conquest. The gradual tendency to deteriorate after the removal of a good ruler is but too common (Acts xx. 29; Phil. ii. 12).

The great works of the Lord.—The crossing of the Jordan, the falling of the walls of Jericho, the battles of Beth-horon, Merom, &c.

⁽⁸⁾ **The servant of the Lord.**—Deut. xxxiv. 5 (Moses); Ps. xviii. (David); 2 Tim. ii. 24 (ministers in general), &c.

An hundred and ten years old.—The same age as Joseph (Gen. l. 26). Moses attained the age of 120 (Deut. xxxiv. 7), Jacob, of 130 (Gen. xlvii. 9), Isaac, of 180 (Gen. xxxv. 28).

⁽⁹⁾ **They buried him.**—This circumstance is usually added in the case of kings, heroes, &c. (Gen. xxiii. 19; Jer. xxii. 18, &c.), and this care about burial seems to point to at least a dim hope of that immortality which had not as yet been fully "brought to light."

In the border of his inheritance.—(See Josh. xix. 49, 50.) It was in Mount Ephraim, and in a rugged and barren district—a circumstance which raised the astonishment of Paula at the self-denial of Joshua (Jer., *Ep.* cviii.): "She was much astonished that the distributor of possessions had chosen rough mountain districts for himself."

Timnath-heres.—"The portion of the sun." This seems to be a mere "slip of the pen" (Ewald)—an accidental transposition of letters for *Timnath-serah* ("the portion that remains"), which is the reading of Josh. xix. 50, and of the best versions, and of some MSS. here. The mistake is, however, ancient, for it originated the Rabbinic story that it is a reference to "the sun standing still upon Gibeah," and that the image of the sun (*temunath ha-cheres*) was sculptured on his tomb. The LXX., after Josh. xxiv. 30, add the interesting *Hagadah* (traditional legend), that the people buried in Joshua's tomb the flint knives with which they had performed the neglected rite of circumcision, after the passage of the Jordan (Josh. v. 2). The name Timnath has been, perhaps, preserved in the modern *Tibneh*, about six miles from Shiloh. Its ruins yet contain some richly decorated tombs. There was another Timnath in Dan.

The hill Gaash.—The name means "mount earthquake." Its torrent beds are mentioned in 2 Sam. xxiii. 30. It has not been identified.

⁽¹⁰⁾ **Gathered unto their fathers.**—See 2 Kings xxii. 20, and for similar phrases, Gen. xv. 15; 1 Kings i. 21; Acts xiii. 36, &c. Another common phrase is, "gathered unto his people" (Gen. xv. 8, &c.); and "sleep with fathers" (Deut. xxxi. 16), &c.

Which knew not the Lord.—"They proceed from evil to evil, and they know not me, saith the Lord" (Jer. ix. 3; comp. Tit. i. 16).

⁽¹¹⁾ **Did evil in the sight of the Lord.**—Rather, "*the* evil." Used especially of apostasy (see chaps. iii. 7—12; iv. 1; vi. 1; x. 6; xiii. 1). They fell into the very idolatry against which they had been emphatically warned (Deut. iv. 19).

Apostasy of the People.   JUDGES, II.   *The Anger of the Lord.*

Baalim: (12) and they forsook the LORD God of their fathers, which brought them out of the land of Egypt, and followed other gods, of the gods of the people that *were* round about them, and bowed themselves unto them, and provoked the LORD to anger. (13) And they forsook the LORD, and served Baal and Ashtaroth.

(14) And the anger of the LORD was hot against Israel, and he delivered them into the hands of spoilers that spoiled them, and *a*he sold them into the hands of their enemies round about, so that they could not any longer stand before their enemies. (15) Whithersoever they went out, the hand of the LORD was against them for evil, as the LORD had said, and *b*as the LORD had sworn unto them: and they were greatly distressed.

(16) Nevertheless the LORD raised up judges, which ¹delivered them out of the hand of those that spoiled them.

---

a Ps. 44. 12; Isa. 50. 1.

b Lev. 26; Deut. 28.

¹ Heb., *saved*.

Baalim.—Rather, "*the* Baalim." Baal means "lord," or "possessor," and in its idolatrous sense was applied especially to the sun, that was worshipped as the great nature-power, under a multitude of different names and attributes. Baal-worship was evidently Phœnician (Mövers, *Phönizier,* 184, § 9), and the traces of it are still seen in the Carthaginian names, Hasdru*bal*, Hanni*bal*, Maher*bal*, Adher*bal*, &c.

> "With these came they who, from the bordering flood
> Of old Euphrates to the brook that parts
> Egypt from Syrian ground, had general names
> Of Baalim and Ashtaroth: those male,
> These feminine."
>   Milton, *Par. Lost*, i. 420.

The splendour of the worship, as well as its sensual and orgiastic character, made it very attractive to the *backsliding* Israelites (1 Kings xvi. 32; xxviii. 26; 2 Kings xi. 18; x. 22; Jer. vii. 9; xix. 5). In Scripture we read of Baalzebub ("lord of filth, or flies"); a Jewish term of scorn for Baalzebul, ("lord of the heavenly habitation"); Baal-samîn (Cant. viii. 11; Plaut. *Poem.* v. 2, 67; chap. x. 10; Num. xxxii. 28); Baal-berith ("lord of the covenant," chap. viii. 33), &c. In Hos. ii. 16, 17 there seems to be a warning against the too facile use of the word, "And it shall be in that day, saith the Lord, that thou shalt call me Ishi (my husband), and shalt call me no more Baali (my lord). For I will take away the names of Baalim out of her mouth, and they shall no more be remembered by their name." (Comp. Jer. xxiii. 27; Zech. xiii. 2.) It is at least doubtful whether the name has any philological connection with the Babylonian Bel.

(12) **Forsook the Lord God of their fathers.**—(Deut. xxxi. 16, 17.) It seems, however, that the sin of the Israelites was a breach rather of the *second* than of the *first* commandment. It was not so much a worshipping of other gods as a worshipping of Jehovah under false symbols adopted from the surrounding nations by a spurious syncretism. Similarly, the calf-worship of the northern tribes was originally intended to be an adoration of Jehovah, under the form of cherubic symbols, but naturally lapsed with dangerous facility into actual Baal-worship (Ex. xxxii. 5; 1 Kings xxii. 6).

(13) **Baal and Ashtaroth.**—Literally, "the Baals and the Ashtareths."

Ashtaroth.—The plural of the feminine word Ashtareth, or Astarte, "the goddess of the Sidonians" (1 Kings xi. 5), the Phœnician Venus—identified sometimes with the moon (*e.g.*, in the name Ashtaroth Karnaim, "the city of the two-horned moon," the name of Og's capital, Deut. i. 4), and sometimes with the planet Venus (2 Kings xxiii. 4; Cic. *De Nat. Deor.* iii. 23; Euseb. *Praep. Evang.* i. 10). She is called the "queen of heaven," in Jer. vii. 10; xliv. 17, and was called Baalti ("my lady") by the Phœnicians. The plural form may be, as Ewald thinks, the plural of excellence, or like Baalim an allusion to the different forms and attributes under which the goddess was worshipped. The worship of Baalim and Ashtaroth naturally went hand in hand. (See chap. x. 6; 1 Sam. vii. 4; xii. 10.) Ashtaroth is not to be confused with the Asheroth (rendered "groves" in the E. V.) mentioned in chap. iii. 7. The words resemble each other less in Hebrew, as Ashtaroth begins with ע, not with א. Milton's allusions to these deities are not only exquisitely beautiful but also very correct, as he derived his information from Selden's learned *Syntagma de Dis Syriis*:

> "With these in troop
> Came Ashtoreth, whom the Phœnicians call'd
> Astarte, queen of heaven, with crescent horns,
> To whose bright image nightly by the moon
> Sidonian virgins paid their vows and songs;
> In Zion also not unsung, where stood
> Her temple."
>   *Par. Lost*, i. 439.

The derivation of the word is very uncertain. It probably has no connection with the Greek *Aster*, or the Persian Esther.

(14) **The anger of the Lord was hot.**—(Ps. lxxviii. 59.) The language of the sad summary which follows should be compared with that of very similar passages which we find in various parts of the Bible (Ps. cvi. 34—45; Deut. xxxii.; 2 Kings xvii.; xxiv. 2—4; 2 Chron. xxxvi. 11—21; Jer. xi. 2—10).

He sold them.—We find the same expression in chap. iii. 8; iv. 2; x. 7; Deut. xxxii. 33; Ps. xliv. 12; Is. l. 1; comp. 2 Kings xvii. 20.

So that they could not any longer stand.—Comp. Lev. xxvi. 17, "Ye shall be slain before your enemies"; Deut. xxviii. 15—68.

(15) **The hand of the Lord was against them.**—Contrast this with Josh. i. 9.

As the Lord had said.—Lev. xxvi. 17—36; Deut. xxviii. 25, &c.

(16) **Nevertheless.**—Rather, *And.*

The Lord raised up judges.—Acts xiii. 20; 1 Sam. xii. 10, 11. This is the key-note to the book. (See chap. iii. 10; iv. 4; x. 2; xii. 7, &c.; xv. 20.) The word for *Judges* is *Shophetim*. The ordinary verb "to judge," in Hebrew, is not *Shaphat*, but *dayyân*. Evidently their deliverers (comp. Deut. xvii. 8, 9; Ps. ii. 10; Amos ii. 3) are of higher rank than the mere tribe-magistrates mentioned in Ex. xviii. 26; Deut. i. 16, &c. Artemidorus (ii. 14) says that to judge (*Krinein*) signified among the ancients "to govern." Of the judges in this book some—*e.g.*, Tola, Ibzan, Elon, and Abdon—are not said to have performed any warlike

(17) And yet they would not hearken unto their judges, but they went a whoring after other gods, and bowed themselves unto them: they turned quickly out of the way which their fathers walked in, obeying the commandments of the LORD; *but* they did not so. (18) And when the LORD raised them up judges, then the LORD was with the judge, and delivered them out of the hand of their enemies all the days of the judge: for it repented the LORD because of their groanings by reason of them that oppressed them and vexed them. (19) And it came to pass, ᵃwhen the judge was dead, *that* they returned, and ¹corrupted *themselves* more than their fathers, in following other gods to serve them, and to bow down unto them; ²they ceased not from their own doings, nor from their stubborn way.

(20) And the anger of the LORD was hot against Israel; and he said, Because that this people hath transgressed my covenant which I commanded their fathers, and have not hearkened unto my voice; (21) I also will not henceforth drive out any from before them of the nations which Joshua left when he died: (22) that through them I may prove Israel, whether they will keep the way of the LORD to walk therein, as their fathers did keep *it*, or not. (23) Therefore the LORD ³left those nations, without driving them out hastily; neither delivered he them into the hand of Joshua.

ᵃ ch. 3. 12.
¹ Or, were corrupt
² Heb., they let nothing fall of their.
³ Or, suffered.

---

deeds. They *may*, however, have been warriors, like Jair, whose exploits are only preserved in tradition. Samuel, though not himself a fighter, yet roused the military courage of his people. They received no salary, imposed no tributes, made no laws, but merely exercised, for the deliverance of Israel, the personal ascendency conferred upon them by "the Spirit of God." Perhaps they find their nearest analogy in the Greek *Aisymnetai* (elective princes) or the Roman *Dictators*. The name is evidently the same as that of the Phœnician *Suffetes*, who succeeded the kings and were the Doges of Tyre after its siege by Nebuchadnezzar. (Jos. *c. Ap.* i. 21.) Livy tells us that the Suffetes of Carthage had a sort of consular power in the senate (Liv. xxx. 7; xxviii. 57; xxxiii. 46; xxxiv. 61). So, too, in the Middle Ages, Spanish governors were called "judges," and this was the title of the chief officer of Sardinia. The judges of Israel, at any rate in their true ideal, were not only military deliverers (chap. iii. 9), but also supporters of divine law and order (Gen. xviii. 25). The abeyance of normally constituted authority during this period is seen in the fact that one of the judges is the son of a "stranger" (chap. xi. 2), another a woman (chap. iv. 4), and not one of them (in this book) of priestly or splendid birth.

(17) **Went a whoring.**—Idolatry throughout the Bible is regarded as a spiritual adultery. (Ex. xxxiv. 15; Is. liv. 5; Jer. iii. 8; Ezek. xxiii. 37; Hos. ii. 7; 2 Cor. xi. 2, &c.)

The way which their fathers walked in.—As described in verse 7.

(18) **It repented the Lord**—*i.e.*, Jehovah was grieved. (Comp. Jonah iii. 10, "God repented of the evil that He had said He would do unto them; and He did it not"—Gen. vi. 6; Ex. xxxii. 14; 1 Sam. xv. 35; Amos vii. 3; Joel ii. 13, &c.) The simple anthropomorphism of early ages never hesitates to describe the ways and thoughts of Jehovah by the analogy of human lives; nor is it easy to see how the sacred writers could have otherwise expressed their meaning. Yet they were, even in using this language, perfectly aware that it was only an imperfect and approximate method of explaining God's dealings with man; and when they are using the language of calm and unmetaphorical instruction they say, "God is not a man . . . . that he should repent" (Num. xxiii. 19); "He is in one mind, and who can turn Him?" (Job xxiii. 13); "I am the Lord, I change not" (Mal. iii. 6).

(19) **They ceased not from their own doings.**—Literally, as in the margin, "they let nothing fall of their deeds."

Stubborn.—They are called "stiff-necked" in Ex. xxxii. 9; Deut. x. 16; Acts. vii. 51. The prophets and sacred writers are always careful to impress upon the Jews that they are chosen by God's free grace to work out His purpose, and that their selection for this service was in no sense due to any merits of their own (Is. lxv. 2; Ps. lxxxi. 11, 12; Matt. xxiii. 37; Acts vii. 51). It is to be noted that in the Bible there is none of the extravagant national self-satisfaction which defaces so much of the Talmud.

(20) **This people.**—Comp. Is. vi. 9, 10, "Go, and tell this people"; viii. 12.

Hath transgressed my covenant.—The same expression is used in Josh. xxiii. 16.

(22) **That through them I may prove Israel.**—Yet in this as in all God's punishments there was an element of mercy mingled with the judgment, as we see from Ex. xxiii. 29, 30; Deut. vii. 22; and *infr.* chap. iii. 1, 2. If in one point of view the non-extermination of Canaan at first led the Israelites into temptation and brought down retributive punishments upon them, yet out of these evils God raised the two-fold good, that they meanwhile increased sufficiently in numbers to be able effectually to till the soil and keep down the wild beasts, and were also being trained in bravery and warlike skill, while the aborigines were being driven out "by little and by little." Further, we see that a real growth was going on during this period of suffering and anarchy. The peril of internal discord was partly averted by the noble life, and inspiring memories, and treasures of infinite truth which they had acquired in the free air of the desert. "They learned by perpetual struggle to defend their new home, and the free exercise of their religion, and so they prepared for coming generations a sacred place where that religion and national culture might develop. During the long pause of apparent inaction a hidden movement was going on, and the principles and truths so marvellously brought to light were taking firm root." (Ewald.)

CHAPTER III.—⁽¹⁾ Now these *are* the nations which the LORD left, to prove Israel by them, *even as many of Israel* as had not known all the wars of Canaan; ⁽²⁾ only that the generations of the children of Israel might know, to teach them war, at the least such as before knew nothing thereof; ⁽³⁾ *namely*, five lords of the Philistines, and all the Canaanites, and the Sidonians, and the Hivites that dwelt in mount Lebanon, from mount Baal-hermon unto the entering in of Hamath. ⁽⁴⁾ And they were to prove Israel by them, to know whether they would hearken unto the commandments of the LORD, which he commanded their fathers by the hand of Moses.

⁽⁵⁾ And the children of Israel dwelt among the Canaanites, Hittites, and Amorites, and Perizzites, and Hivites, and Jebusites: ⁽⁶⁾ and they took their daughters to be their wives, and gave their daughters to their sons, and served their gods. ⁽⁷⁾ And the children of Israel did evil in the sight of the LORD,

B.C. cir. 1406.

III.

1—4. Canaanite nations left to try, and train, the Israelites. 5—7. Evil effects of intermarriages. 8. Tyranny of Chushan-rishathaim. 9—11. The Israelites delivered by Othniel. Rest of forty years. 12—14. Tyranny of the Moabites and allied nations under Eglon for eighteen years. 15—30. Assassination of Eglon and deliverance of Israel by Ehud; rest of eighty years. 31. Heroic action of Shamgar.

⁽¹⁾ **To prove Israel.**—The verb here used is the same as in chap. ii. 22 and verse 4, but, as R. Tanchum observes, it is used in a slightly different sense, meaning " to train them." Symmachus renders it *askēsai*.

As many of Israel as had not known all the wars of Canaan.—This expression clearly implies the generation after that of Joshua. " The wars of Canaan " are equivalent to " the wars of the Lord," and refer to the struggles of the actual conquest.

⁽²⁾ **Only that the generations of the children of Israel might know, to teach them war.**—The LXX. here render,. " Only because of the generations of the children of Israel to teach them war." The Vulgate is here a mere paraphrase, and the translations vary. The meaning seems to be, " Only that *He* (Jehovah) might know the generations of the children of Israel, to teach them war." The expression resembles 2 Chron. xxxii. 31. The "teaching them war" doubtless implies the lesson that they could only learn successfully by the help of God.

As before knew nothing thereof.—That is, " knew nothing of those nations, or of those wars."

⁽³⁾ **Five lords of the Philistines.**—The princes of the Pentapolis, Gaza, Ashdod, Askelon, Gath, Ekron. The word rendered "lords" is evidently a technical or local title—*Seranim*. It is rendered by the LXX. "satrapies," and by the Vulgate, "satraps." It is variously derived from *seren*, " a hinge" (comp. "cardinal" from "cardo"); from *sar*, " a prince," being interchanged with *sarim*, in 1 Sam. xiii. 30; xxix. 6 (Ewald, i. 332); and from some Phœnician root. For the Philistines, see chap. xiii. 1.

All the Canaanites.—Of the *shephēlah* or maritime plain.

The Sidonians.—In Gen. x. 15 " Sidon " is the eldest son of Canaan. They maintained their complete independence to the last.

The Hivites that dwelt in Mount Lebanon. —In Josh. xi. 3 they are described as living "under Hermon, in the land at Mizpeh," whence Mizpeh has been identified with " el-Mutalleh," which also means " the look-out " or " watch-tower." The name has been derived from *Havvah*, a circular encampment or village, because they lived (as they do to this day in northern Syria) in circular villages, with enclosures for cattle in the centre. Ewald (i. 318) supposes that the word means " midlanders," and Gesenius " villagers." The Hivite is the sixth son of Canaan, in Gen. x. 17.

Mount Baal-hermon unto the entering in of Hamath.—In Josh. xiii. 5 we have " from Baal-gad under mount Hermon unto," &c. Baal-gad is also mentioned in Josh. xii. 7; xi. 17, and is usually supposed to be Paneas or Cesarea Philippi. It was probably a temple of Baal, but must be farther south than Baalbek. The hill of Paneas is therefore, in all probability, " *Mount* Baal-hermon," and Baal-hermon may be only another name for Baal-gad. Fürst supposes that both Gad and Gedi (in Engedi) are names of Astarte.

The entering in of Hamath.—This is the usual phrase to describe the northern boundary of Canaan. The LXX. take it as a proper name, *Laboemath*.

⁽⁴⁾ **To prove Israel.**—See chap. ii. 22.

⁽⁵⁾ **Dwelt among the Canaanites . . .**—These nations are enumerated also in Ex. xxxiii. 2; xxxiv. 1. In Josh. xxiv. 11 the Girgashites are added; in Ezra ix. 1 the Ammonites and Moabites. (See Notes on those places.) At this verse begins the second great section of the book (chap. iii. 5—xvi.), which Prof. Cassel summarises as " a history of sin repeating itself, and of Divine Grace constantly devising new remedies."

⁽⁶⁾ **And they took their daughters. —** This beginning of intermarriages shows that we are now a generation removed from the days of Joshua. Such marriages had been forbidden in Deut. vii. 3. but are not among the sins denounced by the Angel-messenger at Bochim (chap. ii. 1).

⁽⁷⁾ **Did evil in the sight of the Lord.**—Rather, *did the evil*, as in chap. ii. 11.

And the groves.—Rather, *and the Asheroth*, *i.e.*, the wooden images of the nature-goddess, Asherah (which are called also Asherim). The LXX. render the word Asherah by *alsos*, " a grove," and other versions follow them. (See Ex. xxxiv. 13; Deut. viii. 5; xvi. 21; 2 Kings xxiii. 14, &c.) Thus Luther renders it *die Hainen*, and it used to be erroneously supposed that the word pointed to tree-worship. The Vulgate renders it "Astaroth." It seems, however, to be clear from the researches of Mövers and others that Asherah and Astarte were different though allied deities. For the latter, see chap. ii. 13. Asherah is from a root which means upright (like *Orthia* or *Orthosia*, a designation of Artemis, *Herod*. iv. 87), and her images are generally mentioned in connection with altars and images of

and forgat the LORD their God, and served Baalim and the groves. ⁽⁸⁾ Therefore the anger of the LORD was hot against Israel, and he sold them into the hand of Chushan-rishathaim king of ¹Mesopotamia: and the children of Israel served Chushan-rishathaim eight years. ⁽⁹⁾ And when the children of Israel cried unto the LORD, the LORD raised up a ²deliverer to the children of Israel, who delivered them, *even* Othniel the son of Kenaz, Caleb's younger brother. ⁽¹⁰⁾ And the Spirit of the LORD ³came upon him, and he judged Israel, and went out to war: and the LORD delivered Chushan-rishathaim king of ⁴Mesopotamia into his hand; and his hand prevailed against Chushan-rishathaim. ⁽¹¹⁾ And the land had rest forty

¹ Heb., *naharaim*. Aram-
B.C. cir. 1394.
² Heb., *saviour*.
³ Heb., *was*.
B.C. cir. 1402.
⁴ Heb., *Aram*.

Baal (Ex. xxxiv. 13; Deut. vii. 5, xii. 3; 1 Kings xiv. 23, &c.; Mic. vi. 12).

⁽⁸⁾ **Into the hand of Chushan-rishathaim.**—If the reading of all the MSS. be correct, this must be a term of hatred rather than a name, for it means "Cushan of the double wickedness." Some MSS. of the LXX. have Chousarsathaim. Josephus (*Antt.* v. 3, § 3) shortens it into *Chousarthes*; and St. Clemens of Alexandria (*Strom.* i. 21) into *Chousachar*. Syncellus (*Chronogr.* i. 158) says that Paphos was founded by those who fled from this Mesopotamian conqueror (Ewald). Cushan only occurs elsewhere in Hab. iii. 7, "I saw the tents of Cushan in affliction." Cush was a son of Nimrod (Gen. x. 8), and our translators, in the margin of Hab. iii. 11, render Cushan by Ethiopia. It is quite possible that Rishathaim may be the distorted form of the name of some town. It is always the tendency of a people to re-stamp a word which they receive into their current phraseology, because no nations like to use a term which they do not understand. Thus in our London streets, "Hangman's Gains" is a corruption of Hammes et Guynes, and Blind Chapel Court, of Blanch Appleton.

The Jews were not only accustomed thus to re-stamp (*sur-frapper*) the names of foreign kings, peoples, and idols, but they especially rejoiced in using terms of hatred. Thus the Romans in the Talmud are called Idumeans; Beelzebul was changed into Beelzebub; Bethel into Bethaven; Ptolemy into Talmai; Ir-Cheres into Ir-Heres (see Note on i. 33), &c. In an ancient Rabbinic commentary the "*two* wickednesses" are supposed to be those of Balaam and Cushan, or that of Laban repeating itself in his descendants. The Targum and Syriac render it "the criminal Cushan."

King of Mesopotamia.—In the original Aram-naharian, "the highland of the two rivers" (Euphrates and Tigris), or, as the LXX. render it, "Syria of the rivers." His invasion, like that of Chedorlaomer, king of Elam, and Amraphel, king of Shinar, was from the south. Hence it is repelled by Othniel, whose inheritance was in the tribe of Judah. We find no other invaders from the far east till the close of the monarchy.

⁽⁹⁾ **Cried unto the Lord.**—"In the time of their trouble, when they cried unto Thee, Thou heardest them from heaven; and according to Thy manifold mercies Thou gavest them saviours" (Neh. ix. 27). "Then they cried unto the Lord in their trouble, and He saved them out of their distresses" (Ps. cvii. 13; see, too, Pss. xxvi. 5, lxxviii. 34, cvi. 44).

A deliverer.—Heb., *moshia*; LXX., "a saviour." (Comp. Luke i. 69; Acts. xiii. 23.) The same word is used for the judges in Heb. ix. 27.

Othniel.—The name means "lion of God." St. Jerome makes it mean "my time of God," and spells it Athaniel.

The son of Kenaz.—(See chap. i. 13.) Josephus, to escape the apparent improbability of a brother of Caleb being young enough to marry Caleb's daughter, when Caleb was past eighty-five, calls him "a person of the tribe of Judah." He rightly regards the events of chaps. xvii.—xxi. as preceding the judgeship of Othniel; but they can hardly have happened during the oppression of Cushan-Rishathaim.

⁽¹⁰⁾ **The Spirit of the Lord came upon him.**—Here the Targum has "the spirit of prophecy" (comp. Is. lxi. 1), perhaps with reference to Num. xi. 25. They render the same phrase in chap. vi. 34, "spirit of courage from Jehovah." This expression constantly recurs in this book (chaps. vi. 34, xi. 29, xiii. 25). For "came upon him" (literally "*was upon* him"), a stronger phrase is "clothed him" (chap. vi. 34; 1 Chron. xii. 18; 2 Chron. xxiv. 20). The Jews, however, placed Othniel highest among the judges, and applied to him the words of Cant. iv. 7, "Thou art all fair; there is no spot in thee," because he alone of the judges is represented as irreproachable. Further than this, they followed some dim traditional data in identifying him with Jabez (1 Chron. iv. 10), and regarding him as a learned teacher of the law. (See chap. i. 13.)

He judged Israel.—Some of the Rabbis explain "judged" (*yishhab*) here to mean "avenged," as in Ps. xliii. 1, "Avenge me, O God" (*Shapetêni*), possibly from disliking the notion of a Kenizzite, however distinguished, holding the office of a *suffes*, or judge. There is a difficulty about Othniel's age; Caleb was eighty-five at the conquest, and, if Othniel was his brother, he could not have been less than fifty or sixty at that time. But even supposing him to have been Caleb's nephew, and aged forty at his marriage, then, since Joshua lived to be 110, and Cushan-Rishathaim's oppression did not begin till after the death of the elders who outlived Joshua, and lasted eight years, if Othniel was judge for forty years, this would make him quite 143 years old at his death. It is only another sign that the chronological data of the Book of Judges are not sufficiently definite to enable us to construct a system out of them.

⁽¹¹⁾ **The land had rest forty years.**—Rabbi Tanchum interprets this to mean, "till forty years after the death of Joshua." For the very difficult chronology of this period, see the Introduction. Many questions have been raised, such as—Do the forty years *include* or *exclude* the period of servitude? Is forty meant to be an exact or a general number? Are the various periods of rest and servitude continuous and successive, or do they refer to different parts of the Holy Land, and do they synchronise? Perhaps no final answer to these questions is as yet possible, and no less than fifty schemes of the chronology of the period of the judges have been attempted, which fact alone proves how insufficient are the data on which to decide.

years. And Othniel the son of Kenaz died.

(12) And the children of Israel did evil again in the sight of the LORD: and the LORD strengthened Eglon the king of Moab against Israel, because they had done evil in the sight of the LORD. (13) And he gathered unto him the children of Ammon and Amalek, and went and smote Israel, and possessed the city of palm trees. (14) So the children of

¹ Or, *the son of Jemini.*

B.C. cir. 1336.

B.C. cir. 1354.

² Heb., *shut of his right hand.*

Israel served Eglon the king of Moab eighteen years.

(15) But when the children of Israel cried unto the LORD, the LORD raised them up a deliverer, Ehud the son of Gera, ¹a Benjamite, a man ²lefthanded: and by him the children of Israel sent a present unto Eglon the king of Moab. (16) But Ehud made him a dagger which had two edges, of a cubit length; and he did gird it under his raiment upon

---

Died.—Probably *during* the forty years, unless we suppose that he attained a most unusual age. After this event the tribe of Judah sinks into the background till the days of David.

(12) **Did evil again.**—Literally, "added to do evil." We find this Hebraism even in the New Testament. "He added (*prosetheto*) to send" (Luke xx. 11, 12).

Evil.—Literally, *the evil*, with special reference to idolatry, as in chap. ii. 11, &c.

Strengthened Eglon the king of Moab.—See this event referred to by the prophet Samuel, in 1 Sam. xii. 9. Eglon was a successor of Balak. We have seen that *Rishathaim* is probably a term of hatred or scorn; is the name Eglon due to the same tendency? It may be so, since Eglon means "a fat bullock" (comp. Ps. xxii. 12; Amos iv. 1).

(13) **The children of Ammon.**—They were closely allied with the Moabites by affinities of race and character. (Gen. xix. 37, 38.) We find them united with Moab against Jehoshaphat in 2 Chron. xx. 1. (See chap. xi. 24.) It has been supposed that *Chepharhaammonai* (Josh. xviii. 24), or "the village of the Ammonites," is a memorial of this conquest (Stanley, *Jewish Church*, ii. 316).

Amalek.—The wild desert clans, which are united under this name, had been from the first the bitterest enemies of Israel. They had attacked the sick and feeble of their rearguard in the wilderness, and, after the battle of Rephidim, had called down on themselves the internecine anger of Israel (Ex. xvii. 8—16; Deut. xxv. 17), which finally found expression in the reign of Saul (1 Sam. xv. 2—8). They are first mentioned in Gen. xiv. 7, and it is probable that there was a tribe of Amalekites older than those descended from Eliphaz.

The city of palm trees.—No doubt Jericho. (See chap. i. 16.) The verb "possessed" by no means implies that the whole city was necessarily re-built, still less that it was fortified. The "palace" of king Eglon was probably a wooden structure.

(14) **Served Eglon.**—One instance of that receiving of "a yoke of iron" which had been threatened as a punishment of apostasy (Deut. xxviii. 47, 48). The narrative, however, shows that the Moabite dominion did not extend beyond the borders of Ephraim (verse 13).

(15) **Ehud the son of Gera.**—In Gen. xlvi. 21 Gera is a son of Benjamin; in 1 Chron. viii. 3 he is a son of Bela, son of Benjamin. The name Gera was hereditary in the tribe of Benjamin (see 2 Sam. xix. 18; 1 Chron. viii. 1—7), and the Jews so constantly omit steps in their genealogies that we can never be sure that "son" means more than "descendant." Ehud seems to be another form of Abihud (1 Chron. viii. 1—8). St. Jerome explains it to mean "one who praises" or "is praised." Josephus calls him a young man, and even "a youth" (*neaniskos*).

A Benjamite.—"Ben-ha-jeminî," as in Ps. vii. 1. The word is generally written undivided, so that here the LXX., Vulgate, and Luther have "son of Jemini." No doubt the Syriac, Arabic, and Chaldee rightly understood it to mean a Benjamite, but still there seems to be an intentional play on words, for "Ben-ha-jeminî" may also mean "*a son of the right hand*, who," as the writer adds, "was *helpless with his right hand*" (*Ben-ha-jeminî eesh ittêr jad-jeminî*).

Lefthanded—Marg., "Shut of his right hand." Luther also renders it "*links*," but the LXX. and the Vulgate take it to mean "ambidextrous," *i.e.*, able to use his left hand as well as his right (LXX., *amphoterodexion*; Vulg., *qui utraque manu pro dexterâ utebatur*). Josephus says that he was "best skilled in using his left hand, in which was his whole strength" (*Antt.* v. 4, § 2). This rendering is merely an inference, from the fact that in chap. xx. 15, 16 (comp. 1 Chron. xii. 2) there are "700 chosen men left-handed." (See the Note on that verse.) The Hebrew *ittêr*, however, is correctly rendered " shut" in the margin of our version (comp. Ps. lxix. 16, "lest the pit *shut* her mouth upon me"), and cannot possibly mean "ambidextrous." No doubt Ehud, like other Benjamites, might have been trained to use the sling with the left hand, but it does not follow that he may not have had some accident which maimed the right hand; and if so it would avert all suspicion from him in his dreadful purpose. Ehud in that case was a Hebrew *Scævola*. Stobæus mentions some African tribes which, like the Benjamites, were "left-hand fighters" (*aristeromachoi*), and for the same cause an Egyptian tribe was known as the *Euonymitae*. The Greek *Laius* has the same meaning.

By him.—Either because he was the chief of one of their houses (1 Chron. viii. 6), or perhaps because he had intimated to them his design. The narrative in chap. xx. falls chronologically in the days of Phinehas and, therefore, Ehud's act occurred at a still earlier period after the conquest; for Ehud would hardly have been chosen for this honourable function after the terrible degradation and decimation of the tribe of Benjamin. Possibly Eglon's invasion occurred soon after Joshua's death.

Sent a present.—The Hebrew word is *minchah*, here euphemistically used for "tribute," as it is elsewhere. (2 Sam. viii. 6: "And the Syrians became servants to David, and *brought gifts*." 1 Kings iv. 21: "They [the Philistines] *brought presents* and served Solomon." Ps. lxxii. 10: "The kings of Sheba and Seba shall *bring gifts*.")

(16) **Made him a dagger which had two edges.**—Probably, as in other servitudes, the children of Israel had been disarmed. The "two edges" (comp.

his right thigh. (17) And he brought the present unto Eglon king of Moab: and Eglon *was* a very fat man. (18) And when he had made an end to offer the present, he sent away the people that bare the present. (19) But he himself turned again from the ¹quarries that *were* by Gilgal, and said, I have a secret errand unto thee, O king: who said, Keep silence. And all that stood by him went out from him. (20) And Ehud came unto him; and he was sitting in ²a summer parlour, which he had for himself alone. And Ehud said, I have

¹ Or, *graven images.*

² Heb., *a parlour of cooling.*

Rev. i. 16) show that it was not a mere knife (comp. Ps. cxliv. 6; Heb. iv. 12). Jerome, in the Vulgate, after rightly rendering the word *ancipitem*, adds, "having a handle in the midst," which seems useless and meaningless, and has no equivalent in the Hebrew.

A cubit length.—The LXX. and Vulgate render it *a span long* (*spithamēs, palmæ*; Luther, *eine elle lang*). The Hebrew word is not *ammāh*, the usual word for a cubit, but *gómed*. A dagger of *a span long* hardly, however, suits the following narrative, and perhaps *gómed* is an archaic word for *ammāh*. It meant originally "a staff."

Under his raiment.—The LXX. and Vulgate have "under his war-cloak" (LXX. *manduan*, Vulg. *sagum*). The LXX., however, are only adopting a method very common with them—of choosing a Greek or, as in this case, a Persian (Hesych.) word which *resembles* the Hebrew word (*maddim*) in sound. The root of the Hebrew word shows that a long flowing robe (*vestis talaris*) is intended. Dean Stanley suggests that he wore it as leader of the tribe. Prudentius describes Discord as "hiding a dagger under her robe."

Upon his right thigh.—This would avert all suspicion. Doubtless the war-cloak was flung in folds over the left shoulder, and Eglon, unaware that the bearer of the tribute was left-handed, would see that the side at which arms were usually worn was covered with a flowing robe, and would not suspect the dagger hidden at the *right* side. Daggers were often, however, worn at the right side, when a sword was slung to the left. Amasa fell by a similar act of treachery. Joab, advancing to kiss him, clasped his beard with his *right* hand, while with his unsuspected left he gave the deadly thrust (2 Sam. xx. 9, 10).

(17) **He brought the present.**—Literally, "caused it to come near." Josephus, in his version of the story, evidently means to insinuate a parallel between the deed of Ehud and that of Harmodius and Aristogiton. He calls Ehud a young man who lived in familiarity with Eglon, and who had won his favour by frequent presents (*Antt.* v. 4).

A very fat man.—Vulg., *Crassus nimis*. Such seems to be the undoubted meaning, and the notice is inserted with reference to verse 22. The LXX. render it by the word *asteios*, a word which may mean either "graceful," or, as more probably in this place, "ridiculous."

(18) **The people.**—The tribute-bearers, headed by Ehud, would carry their offerings in long and pompous array, according to the fashion of the East, which always aims at making a present seem as large as possible (see Gen. xxxii. 16). "Fifty persons often bear what one man could easily carry" (Chardin, iii. 217).

(19) **But he himself turned again.**—The plan of Ehud was deeply laid. He wished (1) to secure his end, which would be more difficult amid the soldiers and attendants who would guard the king during the presentation of the tribute; (2) to avoid endangering his comrades; (3) to provide, if possible, for his own escape. By going away with the deputation of serfs which he had introduced, he would still more lull suspicion asleep.

From the quarries.—The Hebrew word is *pesîlim*. The LXX., followed by our margin, render it "graven images;" and the Vulgate, "from Gilgal, where were idols." (Luther, *Götzen*.) Such is the meaning of *pesîlim* in Deut. vii. 5; 2 Kings xvii. 41; Ps. xcvii. 7, &c. The rendering, "stone quarries," is derived from the Chaldee and Rabbi Jarchi; but it probably means idols of some kind—probably those of Moab. Some explain it of the twelve stones which were taken out of Jordan, and pitched at Gilgal (Josh. iv. 2). The LXX. (in some MSS.) make it mean that Eglon returned, but this is clearly a mistake. Gilgal was near Jericho, and when Ehud had accompanied his comrades to some well-known landmark at Gilgal, he returned to Jericho. Josephus says he had "two attendants" with him; but the word "people" in verse 18 implies that many more had accompanied him.

By Gilgal.—Ewald thinks that Gilgal belonged to Ephraim, and that "he went to see if all was safe at this frontier-post." If the *pesîlim* were sacred stones to mark a boundary (cp. v. 26), they would, like the Greek Hermæ, have been condemned by the Jews as idolatrous.

I have a secret errand unto thee, O king.—Something in Ehud's position and antecedents enabled him to reckon on the king's credulity. Eglon, aware of discontent among the Israelites, may have supposed that Ehud had some secret to betray. Similarly Darius obtained an interview with the Pseudo-Smerdis, for the purpose of assassinating him, by pretending to have a secret message to him; and, in explaining it to his comrade, says, "When lying is necessary, lie" (Herod. iii. 72). In Josephus's version of the story, Ehud pretends that he has a *dream* to narrate.

Who said, Keep silence.—Rather, "And he said, Hush!" (Heb., *Hâs*.) The narrative is very graphic, but it does not appear whether the "Hush!" was addressed to Ehud, to prevent him from saying anything more in the presence of the attendants, or as an intimation to the attendants to retire. They at once understood that the king wished to be left alone.

All that stood by him.—Courtiers always *stand* in the presence of Eastern kings.

(20) **Ehud came unto him.**—The previous message had either been spoken at some distance, in a loud voice, or had been merely a message sent to the king by the attendants.

In a summer parlour.—Literally, *a parlour of cooling* (comp. Amos iii. 15). The room is one of the kind known in the East as *alijah* (Greek, *huperōon*; Mark xiv. 15), the coolest part of an Eastern house. *Obergemache der Kühlung* (De Wette). *Sommerlaube* (Luther). The expression reminds us that the scene of the incident is placed in the Ghôr—the Jordan valley, which lies nearly a thousand feet below the level of the Mediterranean, and is probably the hottest district in the world. Eglon had retired into this room after the public reception of the present, and Ehud had anticipated this as part of his deeply-laid design.

a message from God unto thee. And he arose out of *his* seat. (21) And Ehud put forth his left hand, and took the dagger from his right thigh, and thrust it into his belly: (22) and the haft also went in after the blade; and the fat closed upon the blade, so that he could not draw the dagger out of his belly; and [1] the dirt came out. (23) Then Ehud went forth through the porch, and shut the doors of the parlour upon him, and locked them. (24) When he was gone out, his servants came; and when they saw that, behold, the doors of the parlour *were* locked,

[1] Or, *it came out at the fundament.*

Which he had for himself alone.—Rather, "in his solitude." The words merely mean (as in the LXX. and Vulg.) that he was sitting alone.

I have a message from God unto thee.—Josephus makes him say that he had a dream to impart to Eglon, by command of God. The whole narrative implies that Ehud was, to some extent, an honoured person even among the Moabites. Probably he was reckoned as a prophet. In the East sacred claims are readily conceded, even to enemies. The Mohammedans received St. Francis of Assisi with entire respect.

He arose out of his seat.—Probably out of reverence, to receive the Divine message, which would naturally be delivered in low and reverent tones. "He rose from his throne (and came) near him" (LXX.). Josephus says that he "leaped out of his throne for joy of the dream." Thus Cimber pressed close upon Cæsar (Plut. *Cæs.* 86), and Cleander upon Parmenio (Curt. vii. 2, 27) (Cassel).

(21) **Thrust it into his belly.**—This would involve *certain*, though not necessarily instant death. Josephus says, inaccurately, that he stabbed him to the heart (*Antt.* v. 4, § 2). The assassination is *exactly* similar to that of Henry III. of France, by the Dominican monk, Jacques Clement, who had provided himself with a commission from a friend of the king: "On Tuesday, Aug. 1, at 8 a.m.," says L'Estoile, "he was told that a monk desired to speak with him. The king ordered him to be admitted. The monk entered, having *in his sleeve a knife, unsheathed*. He made a profound reverence to the king, who had just got up, and had nothing but a dressing-gown on, and presented him despatches from the Comte de Brienne, saying that *he had further orders to tell the king privately something of importance.* Then the king ordered those who were present to retire, and began reading the letter. The monk, seeing his attention engaged, *drew his knife from his sleeve, and drove it right into the king's small gut, below the navel, so home that he left the knife in the hole.*"—Guizot, "Hist. of France," iii. 479.

(22) **The haft also went in after the blade.**—The tremendous violence of the blow marks that resoluteness of character which Ehud shows throughout. The Hebrew for "blade" is "flame," as the LXX. here render it. It is as though the vivid narrator would make us see the flash of the dagger ere it is buried, hilt and all, in the huge body. So in Nahum iii. 3 we have, "The horseman lifteth up the flame of the sword and the lightning of the spear." The only other passage where the word occurs is to describe the polished head of the spear of Goliath (1 Sam. xvii. 7).

So that he could not draw the dagger out.—Thus he had disarmed himself by the force of his own blow; but the original only says, "for he did not draw the dagger out."

And the dirt came out.—The meaning of this clause is excessively doubtful, because the Hebrew word rendered "dirt" (*parsedonah*) occurs here and here only. (i.) Our E.V. follows the Chaldee and the Vulgate with the alternative rendering (ii.) "it came out at the fundament" (*marg.*), which is the view of Gesenius. The Jews were themselves uncertain of the meaning, and even in Rabbi Tanchum's commentary we find that some understood it to mean (iii.) "he (Ehud) ran out into the gallery." (iv.) A fourth guess—that of the Syriac version—is, "he went out hastily." The LXX. omit it altogether, either because they thought that they were consulting propriety—a tendency which they constantly show—or because they could not rightly explain it. The resemblance of the word *parsedonah* to the word *misderōnah* ("porch"), in the next clause, is certainly in favour of its meaning some part of the house. Ewald renders it, "he rushed out into the gallery," which runs round the roof. He refers to Ezek. xlii. 5. To understand it more exactly, we should require to know the structure of the house. Following the analogy of other Eastern houses, as described by Shaw, it seems that Eglon's *alijah* was a separate building (*domation*, Jos.), or part of a building, with one door opening on a balcony, and another on a private staircase and closet (verse 24). It was an *inner* room, and its outer door communicated with the house.

(23) **Then Ehud went forth through the porch.**—Rather, *into*. The word rendered "porch"—*misderōnah*—is derived from *seder* ("order"). The Chaldee represents it by a transliteration of the Greek word *exedra*, "a hall decorated with pillars." Kimchi supposes it to mean an ante-chamber where people waited to see the king, standing in order; and this seems to be the view of the LXX. (in the Vatican Codex), who render it, "he went out through those set in order" (*tous diatetagmenous*). If this be the meaning, it can only refer to his walking boldly out through the attendants after he had fastened the doors. But the fact is that the ancient versions were as uncertain of the meaning as ourselves. The Syriac has, "through the xystos" or colonnade; the Arabic, "through the window."

Shut the doors of the parlour upon him.—*i.e.*, upon Eglon.

Locked them.—The LXX. have "wedged them" (*esphēnose*). The lock was probably of a character similar to that used by all ancient nations, namely, wooden slides which entered into a hole in the doorpost, and were secured by catches cut into it. See Jahn, *Archæol. Bibl.* ii. 6—37.

(24) **Behold, the doors of the parlour were locked.**—It never occurred to them to suppose that they could have been fastened from without. "They were not strictly on the watch, both because of the heat and because they had gone to dinner" (Jos.).

Surely he covereth his feet.—They assumed that the king had fastened the door inside for the sake of privacy. The margin correctly explains the phrase "covereth his feet," following the LXX. in *both* their readings (*apokenoi tous podas* B. *pros diphrous kathētai.* A) and the Vulgate (*purgat alvum*), the Chaldee, and the Syriac. Josephus gives the same explanation when

they said, Surely he ¹covereth his feet in his summer chamber. (25) And they tarried till they were ashamed: and, behold, he opened not the doors of the parlour; therefore they took a key, and opened *them*: and, behold, their lord *was* fallen down dead on the earth. (26) And Ehud escaped while they tarried and passed beyond the quarries, and escaped unto Seirath. (27) And it came to pass, when he was come, that he blew a trumpet in the mountain of Ephraim, and the children of Israel went down with him from the mount, and he before them. (28) And he said unto them, Follow after me: for the LORD hath delivered your enemies the Moabites into your hand. And they went down after him, and took the fords of Jordan toward Moab, and suffered not a man to pass over. (29) And they slew of Moab at that time about ten thousand men, all ²lusty, and all men of valour; and there escaped not a man. (30) So Moab was subdued that day under the hand of Israel. And the land had rest fourscore years.

(31) And after him was Shamgar the son of Anath, which slew of the Philis-

1 Or, *doth his easement.*

2 Heb., *fat.*

---

alluding to the scene described in 1 Sam. xxiv. 4 (Jos., *Antt.* vi. 13, § 3), though here (*Antt.* v. 4, § 2) he explains it erroneously of "lying down to sleep." It is an Eastern euphemism taken from spreading out the garments while relieving the needs of nature (Bochart, *Hierozoicon*, i. 677).

In his summer chamber.—The word used for "chamber" (*cheder*) is not the same as in verse 20. It may mean either *gynæceum, i.e.,* "women's apartments," or some "retiring place," as rendered by the Alexandrian Codex of the LXX.

(25) **Tarried till they were ashamed.**—See 2 Kings ii. 17, viii. 11. It is a dangerous matter to intrude on the privacy of an Oriental king.

A key.—Literally, *the opener.* The ancient key was simply a bar of wood, hooked at the end, which passed through a hole in the door and caught the bolt inside.

Their lord was fallen down dead.—Comp. chap. iv. 22.

(26) **Unto Seirath.**—Perhaps, rather, *into the bush,* or *woodland,* as the word has the article, and does not occur again. When he had got beyond the frontier-post of Gilgal, into the district of Ephraim, he was safe from pursuit.

(27) **He blew a trumpet.**—The word for "trumpet" is *shophar.* The LXX. have "he trumpeted with a horn" (*Esalpisen en keratinē*).

In the mountain of Ephraim.—The hill-country of Ephraim was always the fastness of Israelitish freedom (chaps. iv. 5, x. 1; 1 Sam. i. 1, xiii. 6, xiv. 22).

He before them.—He assumed the leadership.

(28) **The Lord hath delivered your enemies the Moabites into your hand.**—Comp. chap. vii. 9–15; 1 Sam. xvii. 12; 1 Kings xxii. 47.

Took the fords of Jordan.—This was a matter of extreme importance. The fords of Jordan were few, and far distant from each other. (Josh. ii. 7.) The steep ravine through which it flows forms a natural barrier to Western Palestine, and by securing the fords they cut off from the Moabites all chance of succour. The vehement rapidity of Ehud's movements had rendered their escape impossible.

Suffered not a man to pass over.—Comp. chap. xii. 5, 6. It was a massacre of vengeance, like the Sicilian Vespers, or the massacre of the English of the Pale in Ireland, or that of the Danes in England on St. Brice's day.

(29) **At that time.**—Apparently in the first surprise of the Moabite forces and garrisons.

All lusty.—Literally, *every fat man and every soldier of strength,* the word being the same as that used in verse 17 to describe the fatness of Eglon. The choice of the word seems to be dictated by a certain grim sense of humour. "The narrative ends, as it had begun, with its half-humorous allusion to the well-fed carcases of those who, corpulent like their chief, lay dead along the shore of the river." (Stanley.)

(30) **The land.**—Meaning, probably, the southern tribes.

Fourscore years.—The LXX. add, "And Ehud judged them till he died." Josephus (*Antt.* v. 5, § 1) seems to have read "eight years."

As to the moral aspect of the assassination committed by Ehud, it is only necessary to say that while his courage, and capacity, and readiness to sacrifice himself, if need be, for the deliverance of his country were thoroughly noble, the act by which he achieved his end was unjustifiable. To quote his example in defence of the principle of assassination is a gross abuse of Scripture. Those who defend the murder do so by assuming that the Divine call to Ehud to deliver his people sanctioned and possibly even suggested the *means* by which it was accomplished. But such methods of inferential exegesis undermine the very bases of morals. It is not in the least surprising that, when adopted, they are liable to the grossest abuse, and made to cover the most horrible crimes. Thus, when Jacques Clement asked whether a priest might kill a tyrant, he was told that "*it was not a mortal sin, but only an irregularity*"; and when Pope Paul V. heard of the murder of Henry IV. by Ravaillac, he said, "*The God of nations did this, because he was given over to a reprobate mind.*" If it has been always true that

"The devil can quote Scripture for his purpose,"

he has done so not rarely by the lips of those who have professed to teach it. "Worse than the dagger," says Prof. Cassel, "is such doctrine."

(31) **Shamgar.**—Mentioned here alone, and alluded to in chap. v. 6.

The son of Anath.—There was a Beth-anath in Naphtali, but Shamgar could hardly have belonged to Northern Israel. We know nothing of Shamgar's tribe or family, but, as neither his name nor that of his father is Jewish, it has been conjectured that he may have been a Kenite; a conjecture which derives some confirmation from his juxtaposition with Jael in chap. v. 6. Shamgar means "name of a stranger" (comp. Gershom, "a stranger there"). Samgar-Nebo is the name of a Babylonian general (Jer. xxxix. 3).

tines six hundred men with an ox goad: and he also delivered Israel.

CHAPTER IV.—⁽¹⁾ And the children of Israel again did evil in the sight of the LORD, when Ehud was dead. ⁽²⁾ And the LORD sold them into the hand of Jabin king of Canaan, that reigned in Hazor; the captain of whose host *was* Sisera, which dwelt in Harosheth of the

---

Six hundred men.—It has been most needlessly assumed that he slew them single-handed, and not, as is probable, at the head of a band of peasants armed with the same rude weapons as himself. If he slew 600 with his own hand, the *whole* number that perished would almost certainly have been added. There is, indeed, no impossibility (even apart from Divine assistance, which is implied though not expressly attributed to him) in the supposition that in a battle which may have lasted for more than one day a single chief may with his own hand have killed this number, for we are told that in a night battle against Moawijah, Ali raised a shout each time he had killed an enemy, and his voice was heard 300 times in one night; and a story closely resembling that of Shamgar is narrated of a Swedish peasant; but the question here is merely one of interpretation, and nothing is more common in Scripture, as in all literature, than to say that a leader personally did what was done under his leadership, *e.g.*, "Saul has slain his thousands, and David his ten thousands" (1 Sam. xviii. 7).

With an ox goad.—The LXX. (Codex B) and Vulgate have "with a ploughshare;" and the Alexandrian Codex of the LXX. renders it "besides the oxen." These translations are not tenable. The phrase occurs here alone—*bemalmad ha bākār*; literally, "with a thing to teach oxen." There can be little doubt that an ox-goad is meant. In the East they are sometimes formidable implements, eight feet long, pointed with a strong sharp iron head. The use of them—since whips were not used for cattle—is alluded to in Sam. xiii. 21; Acts ix. 5. Being disarmed, the Israelites would be unable to find any more effective weapon (chap. v. 6, 8). Disarmament was the universal policy of ancient days (1 Sam. xiii. 19); and this reduced the Israelites to the use of inventive skill in very simple weapons (1 Sam. xvii. 40, 43). Samson had nothing better than the jawbone of an ass (chap. xv. 15). Similarly the Thracian king Lycurgus is said to have chased the Bacchanals with an ox-goad (*bouplēgi, Il.* vi. 134), and that in this very neighbourhood ("near Carmel," Nonnus, *Dionys.* xx.). The Athenians, in their painting of Marathon, in the Pœcile, represented the gigantic rustic, Echetlus, who was supposed to have slain so many of the Persians, with his ploughshare (Pausan. i. 15, § 4). Comp. Hom. *Iliad*, vi. 134.

He also delivered Israel.—Josephus (*Antt.* v. 4, § 3), following some Jewish *hagadah*, says that Shamgar was chosen judge, but died in the first year of his office. This may have been a mere inference, from his being passed over in chap. iv. 1. He does not mention his deed of prowess.

IV.

1—3. Fresh apostasy of Israel, and their consequent oppression by Jabin. 4, 5. Deborah, the prophetess. 6—9. She summons Barak to deliver Israel, and accompanies him at his request. 10. Army of Barak. 11. Heber the Kenite. 12, 13. Gathering of Sisera's host. 14—16. Their defeat. 17. Flight of Sisera. 18—22. His murder by Jael. 23, 24. Complete triumph of Israel.

⁽¹⁾ **Again did evil in the sight of the Lord.**—"They turned their backs, and fell away like their forefathers, starting aside like a broken bow" (Ps. lxxviii. 57); see chap. iii. 12.

When Ehud was dead.—See chap. iii. 31.

⁽²⁾ **Sold them.**—See chap. ii. 14.

Jabin.—The name means, "he is wise." It may have been a dynastic name, like Abimelech, Melchizedek, Pharaoh, Hadad, Agag, &c.

King of Canaan—*i.e.*, of some great tribe or nation of the Canaanites. In Josh. xi. 1 Jabin is called king of Hazor, and sends messages to all the other Canaanite princes.

Reigned in Hazor.—See Josh. xi. 1. Hazor was in the tribe of Naphtali (Josh. xix. 36), and overlooked the waters of Merom (Jos., *Antt.* v. 5, § 1). We find from Egyptian inscriptions of Rameses II., &c., that it was a flourishing town in very ancient days. Owing to its importance, it was fortified by Solomon (1 Kings ix. 15). Its inhabitants were taken captive by Tiglath-pileser (2 Kings xv. 29); and it is last mentioned in 1 Macc. ix. 27. (Comp. Jos., *Antt.* xiii. 5, § 7.) De Saulcy discovered large and ancient ruins to the north of Merom, which he identifies with this town. The Bishop of Bath and Wells (Lord A. Hervey *On the Genealogies*, p. 28) has pointed out the strange resemblance between the circumstances of this defeat and that recorded in Josh. xi. In both we have a Jabin, king of Hazor; in both there are subordinate kings (chap. v. 19; Josh. xi. 29); in both chariots are prominent, which, as we conjecture from Josh. xi. 8, were burnt at Misrephoth-maim ("burnings by the waters"); and in both the general outline of circumstances is the same, and the same names occur in the list of conquered kings (Josh. xi. 21, 22). This seems to be the reason why Josephus, in his account of the earlier event (*Antt.* v. 1, § 18), does not mention either Jabin or Hazor, though strangely enough he says, in both instances, with his usual tendency to exaggeration, that the Canaanites had 300,000 foot, 10,000 horse, and 3,000 chariots. It is again a curious, though it may be an unimportant circumstance, that in 1 Sam. xii. 9 the prophet mentions Sisera *before* Eglon. Of course, if the received view of the chronology be correct, we must make the not impossible supposition, that in the century and a half which is supposed to have elapsed since the death of Joshua, Hazor had risen from its obliteration and its ashes (Josh. xi. 11; Jos., *Antt.* v. 5, § 4), under a new Canaanite settlement, governed by a king who adopted the old dynastic name. If, on the other hand, there are chronological indications that the whole period of the Judges must be greatly shortened, we may perhaps suppose that the armies of Joshua and Barak combined the full strength of the central and northern tribes in an attack from different directions, which ended in a common victory. In that case, the different tribal records can only have dwelt on that part of the victory in which they were themselves concerned. It is remarkable that even so conservative a critic as Bishop Wordsworth holds "that some of the judges of Israel were only judges of portions of Canaan, and that the years run parallel to those of

Sisera Captain of the Host.   JUDGES, IV.   *Deborah the Prophetess.*

Gentiles. ⁽³⁾ And the children of Israel cried unto the LORD: for he had nine hundred chariots of iron; and twenty years he mightily oppressed the children of Israel.

B.C cir. 1316.

⁽⁴⁾ And Deborah, a prophetess, the wife of Lapidoth, she judged Israel at that time. ⁽⁵⁾ And she dwelt under the palm tree of Deborah between Ramah and Beth-el in mount Ephraim: and

---

other judges in other districts of the same country." If there are difficulties in whatever scheme of chronology we adopt, we must remember the antiquity and the fragmentary nature of the records, which were written with other and far higher views than that of furnishing us with an elaborate consecutive history.

The captain of whose host.—In Eastern narratives it is common for the king to play a very subordinate personal part. In the last campaign of Crœsus we hear much more of Surenas, the general of the Parthians, than of Orodes (Arsaces, xiv.).

Sisera.—The name long lingered among the Israelites. It occurs again in Ezra ii. 53, as the name of the founder of a family of Nethinim (minor servants of the Levites, of Canaanite origin, 2 Sam. xxi.; Ezra ii. 43; 1 Chron. ix. 2); and in the strange fashion which prevailed among some of the Rabbis of claiming a foreign descent, the great Rabbi Akhivah professed to be descended from Sisera.

Harosheth.—The name means "wood-cutting." The Chaldee renders it, "In the strength of citadels of the nations." It was an ingenious and not improbable conjecture of the late Dr. Donaldson, that the town was named from the fact that Sisera made the subject Israelites serve as "hewers of wood" in the cedar-woods and fir-woods of Lebanon. The site of Harosheth has been precariously identified with *Harsthieh,* a hill on the south-east of the plain of Akka. (Thomson's *Land and Book,* ch. xxix.)

Of the Gentiles—*i.e.,* of the nations; of mixed inhabitants; lying as it did in "Galilee of the Gentiles." (Comp. "Tidal, king of *nations,*" Gen. xiv. 1, and "The king of the nations in Gilgal," Josh. xii. 23.)

⁽³⁾ **Cried unto the Lord.**—Chap. iii. 9, 15; Ps. cvii. 13.

Nine hundred.—Josephus magnifies the number to 3,000.

Chariots of iron.—Chap. i. 19; Josh. xvii. 10. We may notice that as the children of Israel *burnt* these chariots at Misrephoth-maim (Josh. xi.), they could not have been of solid iron throughout.

Mightily oppressed.—The word "mightily" is rendered "sharply" in chap. viii. 1; "by force" in 1 Sam. ii. 16.

⁽⁴⁾ **Deborah.**—The name means "bee," like the Greek Melissa. The names of Jewish women were often derived from natural objects, as Rachel, "a lamb," Tamar, "a palm," &c. It has been sometimes regarded as a title given to her as a prophetess, just as the priestesses of Delphi were called Bees (Pindar, *Pyth.* iv. 106); and priests were called by the title Malebee (*Essēn*). But the fact that Rachel's nurse (Gen. xxxv. 8) had the same name is against this supposition, though Josephus (*Antt.* v., § 5) accepts it. She had, as Cornelius à Lapide quaintly says, "a sting for foes, and honey for friends." The pronunciation Debŏrah is now so deeply-rooted in England (possibly from the Vulgate, Debbora) that it would, perhaps, be pedantic to alter it; but properly the "ō" is long (דְּבוֹרָה; LXX., Deborra and Debbōra).

A prophetess.—Literally, *a woman, a prophetess;* like Miriam (Ex. xv. 20), Huldah (2 Kings xxii.

14), Noadiah (Neh. vi. 14), Anna (Luke ii. 36), &c. She is the only female judge, or, indeed, female ruler of any kind in Jewish history, except the Phœnician murderess, Athaliah. She is also the only judge to whom the title "prophet" is expressly given. "Prophetess" (like the Latin *Vates*) implies the possession of poetic as well as of prophetic gifts (Ex. xv. 20); and we see her right to such a title, both in her predictions (chap. iv. 9), her lofty courage (chap. v. 7), and the splendour of her inspired song (chap. v.). She has modern parallels in the Teutonic prophetesses, Veleda and Alaurinia (Tac., *Germ.* viii.), and Joan of Arc, the "Inspired Maid of Domremi." Among the Jews prophetesses were the exception; among the ancient Germans they were the rule.

The wife of Lapidoth.—This is probably the meaning of the phrase, although some ancient commentators make it mean "a woman of Lapidoth;" as does Tennyson (*Princess*), "Like that great dame of Lapidoth." The phrase closely resembles "Miriam the prophetess, the sister of Aaron," "Huldah the prophetess, wife of Shallum." The name Lapidoth, which occurs nowhere else, means "flames," "lamps," or "splendours;" and Rashi says that she was called "a woman of lamps," from making the wicks for the lamps of the sanctuary; while others, with equal improbability, interpret it of her shining gifts and of her fiery spirit. The parallels which are adduced to support this view (Is. lxii. 1; Job xli. 2; Nah. ii. 5) are inadequate; as also is Ecclus. xlviii. 1, "The word of Elias burnt like a torch;" and the Midrash, which says of Phinehas, that "when the Holy Ghost filled him, his countenance glowed like torches" (Cassel). Perhaps there was a fancy that such a prophetess could only be a virgin. The name Lapidoth has a feminine termination, but this does not prove that it may not have been, like Naboth, Shelomith, Koheleth, &c., the name of a man. It is uncertain whether Deborah was of the tribe of Ephraim or Issachar (chap. v. 15; Ewald, ii. 489).

She judged Israel.—We see from the next verse that up to this time her functions had mainly consisted of peaceful arbitration and legal decision (Deut. xvii. 8).

⁽⁵⁾ **She dwelt under the palm tree of Deborah.** —Similarly Abraham is said to have lived under the oak of Mamre (Gen. xiv. 13), and Saul under the pomegranate of Migron (1 Sam. xiv. 2). "Such tents the patriarchs loved" (Coleridge). Dean Stanley (*Jewish Chron.* i. 318) draws a fine contrast between the triumphant "mother of Israel" (chap. v.) under her palm, full of the fire of faith and energy, and Judæa Captiva, represented on the coins of Titus as a weeping woman sitting under a palm-tree, "with downcast eyes and folded hands, and extinguished hopes." The words "she dwelt" are literally *she was sitting,* which may merely mean that she took her station under this well-known and solitary palm when she was giving her judgment (comp. Ps. ix. 3); just as St. Louis, under the oak-tree at Vincennes (Stanley, *Jewish Chron.* i. 218), and as Ethelbert received St. Austin and his monks under an oak. The tree won its name as the

Deborah calls Barak   JUDGES, IV.   *to go against Sisera.*

the children of Israel came up to her for judgment. ⁽⁶⁾ And she sent and called Barak the son of Abinoam out of Kedesh-naphtali, and said unto him, Hath not the LORD God of Israel commanded, *saying,* Go and draw toward mount Tabor, and take with thee ten thousand men of the children of Naphtali and of the children of Zebulun? ⁽⁷⁾ And I will draw unto thee to the *a* river Kishon Sisera, the captain of Jabin's army, with his chariots and his multitude; and I will deliver him into thine hand. ⁽⁸⁾ And Barak said unto her, If thou wilt go with me, then I will go: but if thou wilt not go with me, *then* I will not go. ⁽⁹⁾ And she said, I will surely go with thee: notwithstanding the journey that thou takest shall not be for thine honour; for the LORD shall sell Sisera

B.C. cir. 1296.

a Ps. 83. 9, 10.

"Deborah palm" from her, and may also have originated the name Baal-Tamar, "the lord of the palm" (chap. xx. 33). Near it was another very famous tree—Allon-Bachuth—the oak or terebinth of weeping; so called from the weeping at the burial of the other Deborah (Gen. xxxv. 8), which is alluded to in 1 Sam. x. 3, if the true reading there be "the oak of Deborah," and not of Tabor, as Thenius conjectures.

Between Ramah and Beth-el.—Both towns were on the confines of Benjamin and Ephraim (see Josh. xviii. 25, xvi. 2).

In mount Ephraim.—The one secure spot in Palestine. (See Note on chap. iii. 27.) The Chaldee prosaically amplifies this into "she lived in Ataroth (Josh. xv. 2), having independent means, and she had palm-trees in Jericho, gardens in Ramah, olive-yards in the valley, a well-watered land in Bethel, and white clay in the king's mount."

Came up.—A technical term for going before a superior (Num. xvi. 12; Deut. xxv. 7). Deborah, unlike the German Veleda—who lived in a tower, in awful seclusion—allowed the freest access to her presence as she sat beneath her palm.

⁽⁶⁾ **Barak.**—The name means "lightning" (Jos., *Antt.*), as does Barca, the family name of Hannibal and Hasdrubal. So in Virgil, the Scipios are called "two lightnings of war." (Comp. Boanerges, Mark iii. 17.)

Kedesh-naphtali.—The name "Kedesh" means a *holy* city. There were, therefore, many towns of the name, as Kadesh-Barnea (Num. xx. 1; Josh. xv. 23), and Kedesh in Issachar (Josh. xii. 22). Jerusalem is called "the holy, the noble" (*El kuds, es shereef*). This sanctuary of Naphtali was a Levitical refuge city in Galilee (Josh. xix. 35, xx. 7, xxi. 32). Josephus says that it was not far from Phœnicia (Jos., *Antt.* xiii. 5, § 6). The site of it is probably at Kades, four miles north-west of Lake Merom. The reading of the Syriac and Arabic versions here—*Rakam*—is inexplicable. The fact that the fame of Barak had penetrated from the northern city to the southern limits of Ephraim shows that he must have been a man of great mark.

Draw.—The meaning of the word is uncertain. The Rabbis understand "the people," others understand "thy steps," referring to Gen. xxxvii. 21; Ex. xii. 21 (Heb.). The LXX. has "thou shalt depart;" the Vulgate, "*lead;*" the Chaldee, "spread out," as in chap. xx. 37. There, however, our version gives in the margin the alternative "*made a long* sound with the trumpet," and the verb is used in that sense in Ex. xix. 13; Josh. vi. 5, but there the substantive is added. The word probably implies that Barak is to draw his troops together in small contingents to prevent suspicion.

Mount Tabor.—The broad flat top of this strong, beautiful, and easily fortified mountain (which is nearly a mile in circumference) would serve the double purpose of a watch-post and a stronghold. It was in the district of Issachar, about six miles from Nazareth, and its peculiarities attracted notice in very early days (see Josh. xix. 22; Ps. lxxxix. 12; Jer. xlvi. 18). Josephus calls it Itaburion; he held it for some time successfully against Placidus and the Romans (Jos., *B. J.* iv. 1, § 8). Its huge truncated cone of limestone rises isolated from the plain to the height of nearly nineteen hundred feet, and its sides are clothed with oaks and terebinths. It is now called Jebel et Tur. It was long regarded as the scene of the Transfiguration, but it must yield this glory to Mount Hermon. But the sacred character of the hill seems to be distinctly intimated in Deut. xxxiii. 19: "They (Zebulon and Issachar) shall call the people unto the mountains; there they shall offer sacrifices of righteousness;" Jer. xlvi. 18: "As I live, saith the King, whose name is the Lord of Hosts, surely as Tabor is among the mountains . . . so shall he come."

Of the children of Naphtali and of the children of Zebulun.—The northern tribes would feel most painfully the tyranny of Jabin, and these were the two most energetic of them.

⁽⁷⁾ **To the river Kishon.**—This word rendered "river" is *nachal,* which means rather "a torrent-bed" or "water-course," the Arabic *wady,* the Italian *fiumara*—such as the bed of the Kedron and the Rhinocolura. (LXX. *cheimarrous,* Vulg. *torrens.*) The river is always prominently mentioned in connection with this great victory (Ps. lxxxiii. 9), because the overwhelming defeat of Canaan was due in great measure to the providential swelling of the torrent-waters, which turned its banks into a morass and rendered the iron chariots worse than useless. It contributed in the same way to the defeat of the Turks in the battle of Mount Tabor, April, 1799. The river is now called the Mukatta, *i.e.,* "the river of slaughter." It rises partly in Mount Tabor and flows into the Bay of Acre, under Mount Carmel. (Comp. 1 Kings xviii. 40.) The plain of Jezreel (Esdraelon), through which it flows, has been in all ages the battle-field of Palestine.

⁽⁸⁾ **If thou wilt go with me.**—The enterprise seemed so daring and so hopeless, that if not for his own sake, yet for the sake of his army, Barak felt how much would be gained by the presence of the inspired prophetess. The LXX. has the remarkable addition, "Because I know not the day in which the Lord prospers the angel with me." This is a sort of excuse for his want of perfect faith. He depends on Deborah to give him the immediate augury of victory. "In the Messenian war the soldiers fought bravely because their seers were present" (Pausan. iv. 16—Cassel).

⁽⁹⁾ **I will surely go with thee.**—Literally, *Going, I will go.*

Shall not be for thine honour.—Literally, *thy pre-eminence* (LXX. "*proterēma*"; Luther, "*der Preis*") *shall not be on the path which thou enterest.*

Heber the Kenite.   JUDGES. IV.   *Sisera gathers his Army.*

into the hand of a woman. And Deborah arose, and went with Barak to Kedesh. ⁽¹⁰⁾ And Barak called Zebulun and Naphtali to Kedesh; and he went up with ten thousand men at his feet: and Deborah went up with him.

⁽¹¹⁾ Now Heber the Kenite, *which was* of the children of *a*Hobab the father in law of Moses, had severed himself from the Kenites, and pitched his tent unto the plain of Zaanaim, which *is* by Kedesh.

a Num. 10. 29.

⁽¹²⁾ And they shewed Sisera that Barak the son of Abinoam was gone up to mount Tabor. ⁽¹³⁾ And Sisera ¹ gathered together all his chariots, *even* nine hundred chariots of iron, and all the people that *were* with him, from Harosheth of the Gentiles unto the river of Kishon.

⁽¹⁴⁾ And Deborah said unto Barak, Up; for this *is* the day in which the LORD hath delivered Sisera into thine hand: is not the LORD gone out before thee? So Barak went down from mount Tabor,

¹ Heb., *gathered by cry, or, proclamation.*

Of a woman.—To enter into the force of this we must remember the humble and almost down-trodden position of women in the East, so that it could hardly fail to be a humiliation to a great warrior to be told that the chief glory would fall to *a woman*. He may have supposed that the woman was Deborah herself; but the woman was not the great prophetess, but Jael, the wife of the nomad chief (R.Tanchum, and Jos., *Antt.* v. 5, § 4). Compare the feeling implied in chap. ix. 24.

⁽¹⁰⁾ **Called.**—The word used is the technical word for summoning an army (2 Sam. xx. 4, 5). Naturally Zebulun and Naphtali would be more difficult to arouse than the central tribes, because, though they felt the oppression most, they would have to bear the brunt of the vengeance in case of defeat. Ephraim and Benjamin (chap. v. 14), being more strong and secure, could raise their contingents without the personal help of Deborah, especially if that view of the chronology be admissible which avoids other difficulties by the difficult supposition that this event took place before the death of Joshua.

Zebulun and Naphtali.—(See chap. v. 18.) Of course it is only meant that in the first instance the *leaders* of those tribes were invited to a conference, like those of the Swiss on the Rütli in 1307.

At his feet.—That is simply "after him," as it is rendered in verse 14. (Comp. chaps. v. 15, viii. 5; Ex. xi. 8; 1 Kings xx. 10.)

Deborah went up with him.—A trace of this fact may yet be preserved in the name *Debarieh*, given to a village at the foot of Tabor.

⁽¹¹⁾ **Heber the Kenite.**—See chaps. i. 16, iii. 31; Num. x. 29.

Which was of the children of Hobab.—Rather, *had separated himself from Kain, from the children of Hobab*. Nomadic settlements are constantly liable to send off these separate colonies. The life and movements of the Kenites resembled those of gipsies, except that they had flocks and herds. To this day a small Bedouin settlement presents very nearly the same aspect as a gipsy camp.

The father in law of Moses.—Rather, *the brother-in-law*. The names for these relationships are closely allied. (See Note on chap. i. 16.)

Pitched his tent.—(Gen. xii. 8, &c.) The "tents" of the Bedouin are not the bell-shaped tents with which we are familiar, but coverings of black goats' hair, sometimes supported on as many as nine poles. The Arab word for tent is *beit*, "house."

Unto the plain of Zaanaim.—Rather, *unto the terebinth in Zaanaim*. (See Josh. xix. 33.) Great trees are often alluded to in Scripture. (Allon-Bachuth, Gen. xxxv. 8, "the oak of Tabor"; 1 Sam. x. 3, "the oak of the house of grace"; 1 Kings iv. 9, "the enchanters' oak"; chap. ix. 37; Josh. xxiv. 26, &c.) This terebinth is again alluded to in Josh. xix. 33; and the size and beauty of the terebinths on the hills of Naphtali, to which we find allusion in the blessing of Jacob, probably led to its adoption as the symbol of the tribe. "Naphtali is a branching terebinth" (Gen. xlix. 21). The word *elon* (אֵלוֹן) is constantly rendered "plain" by our translators (chap. ix. 6—37; Gen. xii. 6, xiii. 18; 1 Sam. x. 3, &c.), because they were misled by the Targums and the Vulgate, which render it sometimes by *vallis* and *convallis*. They always render the cognate word *allon* by "oak," and, in the looseness of common nomenclature, the "oak" and the "terebinth" were not always carefully distinguished. There is a large terebinth, called *Sigar em-Messiah*, six miles north-west of Kedes. The word Zaanaim (also written Zaannanim) means "wanderings," or "unlading of tents," with possible reference to this nomad settlement. The LXX. render it "the oak of the covetous," because they follow another reading. In contrast with these "wandering tents" of the Bedouin, Jerusalem is called in Is. xxxiii. 20 "a tent that wanders not."

Ewald, following the Targum, makes it mean "the plain of the swamp," and this is also found in the Talmud, which seems to indicate this place by *Aquizah hak-Kedesh* ("swamp of the holy place").

Which is by Kedesh.—Oaks and terebinths are still found abundantly in this neighbourhood; and such a green plain studded with trees would be a natural camping-ground for the Kenites.

⁽¹²⁾ **They shewed Sisera.**—The previous verse has been introduced by way of anticipation, that the reader—who has last heard of the Kenites in the south of Judah (chap. i. 16)—may not be surprised at verse 17 to find them in Naphtali. It is not, therefore, necessary to suppose that the "they" means the Kenites. It may be an impersonal expression (as it is rendered in the LXX. and Vulg. "it was told").

⁽¹³⁾ **All his chariots.**—He saw at once that this very sudden revolt had assumed formidable proportions, and he would need all his forces to dislodge Barak from his strongly entrenched position on Tabor.

Harosheth of the Gentiles.—This is simply the name of the town Harosheth-haggoïm. (See verse 2.)

⁽¹⁴⁾ **This is the day.**—See the addition of the LXX. to verse 8. The ancients attached the utmost importance to fortunate and unfortunate days, and Barak was guided by a prophetess, not by idle auguries.

Is not the Lord gone out before thee?—"Then shall the Lord go forth and fight against those nations, as when He fought in the day of battle" (Zech. xiv. 3; comp. Deut. ix. 3).

Went down from mount Tabor.—As he had neither cavalry nor chariots, it required no little faith

and ten thousand men after him. ⁽¹⁵⁾ And ^a the LORD discomfited Sisera, and all *his* chariots, and all *his* host, with the edge of the sword before Barak; so that Sisera lighted down off *his* chariot, and fled away on his feet. ⁽¹⁶⁾ But Barak pursued after the chariots, and after the host, unto Harosheth of the Gentiles: and all the host of Sisera fell upon the edge of the sword; *and* there was not [1] a man left.

⁽¹⁷⁾ Howbeit Sisera fled away on his feet to the tent of Jael the wife of Heber the Kenite: for *there was* peace between Jabin the king of Hazor and the house of Heber the Kenite. ⁽¹⁸⁾ And Jael went out to meet Sisera, and said unto him, Turn in, my lord, turn in to me; fear

a Ps. 83. 10.

[1] Heb., *unto one.*

---

in Barak to abandon his strong post and assume the aggressive against the kind of forces which struck most terror into the Israelites (Heb. xi. 32). Hence the emphatic addition, "at his feet" (Heb., and see ver. 10). If the beginning of the battle was at Taanach, the Israelites had to march thirteen miles along the caravan road. Probably the Canaanites watched this bold and unexpected movement with as much astonishment as the huge Persian host saw the handful of Athenians charge down from the hill-sides into the plain of Marathon.

⁽¹⁵⁾ **Discomfited.**—The same word as in Ex. xiv. 24; Josh. x. 10. The LXX. *exestēse*, and the Vulg. *perterruit*, imply the element of immediate Divine aid in the battle.

Sisera, and all his chariots.—"Some trust in chariots and some in horses, but we will remember the name of the Lord our God" (Ps. xx. 7; comp. Ps. xxxiii. 16, 17; Prov. xxi. 31).

And all his host.—"Do unto them . . as to Sisera, as to Jabin at the brook of Kison, which perished at Endor, and became as the dung of the earth" (Ps. lxxxiii. 9, 10). Considering the allusion to the swollen waters of the Kishon and the storm in chap. v. 20—22, it seems probable that Josephus is following a correct Jewish tradition when he describes the battle thus:— "They joined battle, and as the ranks closed a violent storm came on, and much rain and hail; and the wind drove the rain against the faces of the Canaanites, darkening their outlook, so that their archeries and their slings were rendered useless, and their heavy-armed soldiers, because of the cold, were unable to use their swords. But since the storm was behind the Israelites, it caused them less harm, and they further took courage from their belief in God's assistance, so that, driving into the midst of the enemy, they killed many of them," &c. (*Antt.* v. 5, § 4). The battle thus closely resembled that of Timoleon against the Carthaginians at the Crimessus (Grote, xi. 246), and the English victory at Creçy, as has been graphically described by Dean Stanley (*Jew. Church*, i. 329). We may add that similar conditions recurred in the battle of Cannæ, except that it was the storm of *dust* and not of rain that was blown in the faces of the Romans by the *Scirocco* (Liv. xxii. 46; Plut. *Fab.* 16).

Sisera lighted down off his chariot.—We find an Homeric hero, Idæus (*Il.* v. 20), doing the same thing. On this the frivolous critic Zoilus made the objection, "Why did he not fly in his chariot?" The answer is the same as here: Sisera would have far more chance of escaping into concealment if he left the well-known chariot of a general. Besides this, his chariot—like those of the Egyptians at the Red Sea—was probably struggling in the trampled morass. "It was left to rust on the banks of the Kishon, like Roderick's on the shores of the Guadelete" (Stanley).

⁽¹⁶⁾ **There was not a man left.**—The massacre in all battles in which the fugitives have to escape over a river and contend with a storm is always specially fatal. The memory of this terrible carnage was preserved for years, together with the circumstance that the soil was enriched by the dead bodies (Ps. lxxxiii. 10). Similarly at Waterloo, the year after the battle a blaze of crimson poppies burst out over the plain, and the harvests of the subsequent years were specially rich.

"The earth is covered thick with other clay,
Which her own clay shall cover."

The scene of the battle of Marius at Aquæ Sextiæ was long called *Pourrières* (a corruption of Campi Putridi) for the same reason; and the site of Cannæ is still known as *Pezzo di Sangue*.

⁽¹⁷⁾ **Fled away on his feet to the tent of Jael.** —In a different direction from that taken by his army, which fled towards Harosheth (Kimchi). The expression is probably used by anticipation. He could hardly have meant to fly to Jael rather than to Heber, until Jael came to meet him, unless there are circumstances unknown to us. Women had separate tents (Gen. xviii. 6), and these were regarded as inviolably secure. He thought that there he would lie unsuspected till the pursuers passed (comp. Gen. xxiv. 67). The name Jael means "gazelle" (like Tabitha, Dorcas), "a fit name for a Bedouin's wife—especially for one whose family had come from the rocks of Engedi, the spring of the wild goat or chamois" (Stanley).

For there was peace.—This enabled Sisera boldly to appeal to these nomads for *dakheel*—the sacred duty of protection. A poor strolling Bedouin tribe might well be left by Jabin to its natural independence; tribute can only be secured from Fellahin—*i.e.*, from settled tribes. Three days must have elapsed since the battle before it would be possible for Sisera to fly on foot from the Kishon to "the nomad's terebinth." It may well be conceived that the unfortunate general arrived there in miserable plight—a starving and ruined fugitive.

⁽¹⁸⁾ **Jael went out to meet Sisera.**—This makes it probable that her design was already formed, unless we suppose that Jael as a chieftainess was placed above the ordinary rules which regulate the conduct of Oriental women. As nothing is said of Heber, he may have been absent, or he may have kept out of the way in order to further his wife's designs.

Turn in to me.—Without that special invitation Sisera would not have ventured to violate every law of Oriental propriety by entering the privileged sanctuary of the *harem*.

Fear not.—Treachery is far too common among Bedouin tribes to render the exhortation needless.

She covered him with a mantle.—Rather, *with the tent-rug*. Evidently, the moment he was satisfied that her intentions were honest the weary and unfortunate fugitive flung himself down on the ground,

not. And when he had turned in unto her into the tent, she covered him with a ¹mantle. (19) And he said unto her, Give me, I pray thee, a little water to drink; for I am thirsty. And she opened ᵃa bottle of milk, and gave him drink, and covered him. (20) Again he said unto her, Stand in the door of the tent, and it shall be, when any man doth come and enquire of thee, and say, Is there any man here? that thou shalt say, No. (21) Then Jael Heber's wife took a nail of the tent, and ²took an hammer in her hand, and went softly unto him, and smote the nail into his temples, and fastened it into the ground: for he was

¹ Or, *rug*, or, *blanket*.

^a ch. 5. 25.

² Heb., *put*.

---

or on a divan, to sleep. The word used for "mantle"— *semîcah* (Vulg., "pallio"; Luther, "*mit einan Mantel*")—occurs nowhere else; from its root it probably means "a coverlet" (LXX., *epibolaion*, for which the Alexandrine Codex reads *derrhis*, "a skin"). A large "tent-rug" of goat's hair is usually a part of the furniture of an Arab tent.

(19) **Give me, I pray thee, a little water.**—The request was natural enough; but, as he had not made it at first, we may suspect that he wanted to taste food in the tent, as a way of rendering still more secure the inviolable laws of Eastern hospitality. Saladin refuses to let Reginald of Chatillon drink in his tent, because he means to kill him.

A bottle of milk.—Rather, *the skin of milk*. The word "bottle" means, of course, a leathern bottle or skin. Josephus says that the milk was "already corrupted," *i.e.*, that it was butter-milk (*Antt.* v. 6, § 5). This is quite probable, because butter-milk (*lebban*) is a common drink in Arab tents. When R. Tanchum adds that butter-milk inebriates, and Rashi that it produces deep sleep, and that it was her object to stupefy him, they are simply giving reins to their imagination. Josephus says, "He drank so immoderately that he fell asleep." It might have been supposed that she would naturally offer him *wine*; but it is far from certain that even "must" or "unfermented wine"— much less fermented wine, which requires considerable art to make—would have been found in those poor tents; and, further, these Kenites may have been abstainers from wine, as their descendants the Rechabites were. (Jer. xxxv. 2.)

(20) **Stand.**—The imperative here used has the masculine, not the feminine termination, but probably only because it is used generally.

That thou shalt say, No.—In that age, and among those nations, and under such circumstances, a lie would have been regarded as perfectly natural and justifiable; even under the Christian dispensation, many casuists declare a lie for self-preservation to be venial, though it is to be hoped that there are millions who, without condemning such a falsehood in *others*, would suffer any extremity rather than be guilty of it themselves. Under any circumstances, it would be very unfair to judge by the standard of Christianity the words and actions of ignorant nomads and idolatrous Canaanites, more than a thousand years before Christ. Sisera and Jael would have acted, without the faintest sense of conscientious scruple, on the heathen advice of Darius—"When it is necessary to lie, lie" (*Herod.* iii. 72).

(21) **Then.**—Many commentators have ventured to assume that at this instant Jael received a Divine intimation of what she was to do. To make such an assumption as a way of defending an act of assassination peculiarly terrible and peculiarly treacherous seems to be to the last degree unwarrantable. If any readers choose to adopt such methods for themselves they ought not to attempt the enforcement of such "private interpretations" on others. The mind which is unsophisticated by the casuistry of exegesis will find little difficulty in arriving at a fair estimate of Jael's conduct without resorting to dangerous and arbitrary interpolations of supposition into the simple Scripture narrative.

Heber's wife.—This addition, being needless, might be regarded as emphatic, and as involving an element of condemnation by calling prominent attention to the "peace between Jabin and the house of Heber," which has been mentioned where last his name occurs (verse 17). It is, however, due in all probability to the very ancient and inartificial character of the narrative.

A nail of the tent.—Probably one of the great tent-pegs used to fasten down the cords which keep the tent in its place (Ex. xxvii. 19; Is. xxii. 23, liv. 2, &c.). Josephus says an iron nail, but there is nothing to show whether it was of iron or of wood, and the LXX., by rendering it *passalon* ("a wooden plug"), seem to have understood the latter.

An hammer.—Rather, *the hammer*. The ponderous wooden mallet kept in every tent to beat down the cord-pegs. The word is *Makkebeth*, from which is derived the word *Maccabee*. The warrior-priests, to whom that title was given, were the "hammers" of their enemies, and Karl received the title of *Martel* for a similar reason.

Went softly unto him.—So as not to awake him. The description of Sisera's murder is exceedingly graphic, but as far as the prose account of it is concerned, the silence as to any condemnation of the worst and darkest features of it by no means necessarily excludes the idea of the most complete disapproval. The method of the narrative is the same as that found in all ancient literature, and is a method wholly different from that of the moderns, which abounds in subjective reflections. Thus Homer sometimes relates an atrocity without a word of censure, and sometimes indicates disapproval by a single casual adjective.

Smote.—With more than one blow, if we take the poet's account (chap. v. 26) literally.

Fastened it into the ground.—Rather, *it* (the nail) *went down into the ground*. The verb used is rendered "lighted off" in chap. i. 14.

For he was fast asleep and weary.—The versions here vary considerably, but the English version seems to be perfectly correct. The verb for "he was fast asleep" is the same as in the forcible metaphor of Ps. lxxvi. 6: "The horse and chariot *are cast into a deep sleep*." The description of his one spasm of agony is given in chap. v. 27. There is no authority in the original for the gloss found in some MSS. of the LXX.: "And he was convulsed (ἀπεσκάρισεν) between her knees, and fainted and died." The words here used are only meant to account for his not being awakened by the approach or preparations of Jael (Kimchi), unless they involve a passing touch of pity or disapproval. Similarly it was, when Holofernes was "filled with wine," that Judith "approached to his bed, and took hold of the hair of his head . . . and smote twice upon his neck

Death of Sisera.   JUDGES, V.   *Jabin Destroyed.*

fast asleep and weary. So he died. ⁽²²⁾ And, behold, as Barak pursued Sisera, Jael came out to meet him, and said unto him, Come, and I will shew thee the man whom thou seekest. And when he came into her *tent*, behold, Sisera lay dead, and the nail *was* in his temples.

⁽²³⁾ So God subdued on that day Jabin the king of Canaan before the children of Israel. ⁽²⁴⁾ And the hand of the children of Israel ¹ prospered, and prevailed against Jabin the king of Canaan, until they had destroyed Jabin king of Canaan.

¹ Heb., *going went und was hard.*

CHAPTER V.—⁽¹⁾ Then sang Deborah and Barak the son of Abinoam on that day, saying,

---

with all her might, and she took away his head from him." (Judith xiii. 2, 7, 8.)

⁽²²⁾ **Behold, Sisera lay dead.**—Thus the glory, such as it was, of having slain the general of the enemy passed to a woman (verse 9). The scene which thus describes the undaunted murderess standing in the tent between the dead and the living chieftains—and glorying in the decision which had led her to fling to the winds every rule of Eastern morality and decorum—is a very striking one.

⁽²³⁾ **So God subdued.**—The word used for God is here *Elohim*, while Jehovah occurs through the rest of the narrative. We are not yet in a position to formulate the law which regulates the interchange of these names. It need hardly be added that this attribution of the deliverance of Israel to God's providence and aid does not necessarily involve the least approval of the false and cruel elements which stained the courage and faith of Jael. Though God overrules even criminal acts to the fulfilment of His own purposes, the crimes themselves meet with their own just condemnation and retribution. This may be seen decisively in the case of Jehu. His conduct, like that of Jael, was of a mixed character. He was an instrument in the hands of God to punish and overthrow the guilty house of Ahab, and in carrying out this Divine commission, he, too, showed dauntlessness and faith, yet his atrocious cruelty is justly condemned by the voice of the prophet (Hos. i. 4), just as that of Baasha had been (1 Kings xvi. 7), though he, too, was an instrument of Divine retribution. To explain this clause, and the triumphal cry of Deborah—"So let all thine enemies perish, O Lord"—as Bishop Wordsworth does, to mean that "*the work of Jael* is represented by the sacred writer as *the work of God*," is to claim Divine sanction for a wish that wicked or hostile powers should always "so" perish by cruel and treacherous assassination. At the same time, Jael must not be classed with women actuated only by a demoniacal thirst for vengeance, like Criemhild, in the Niebelungen; or even with Aretophila, of Cyrene, whom Plutarch so emphatically praises (*On the Virtues of Women*, p. 19, quoted by Cassel); but rather with women like Judith in ancient, or Charlotte Corday in modern times, who regarded themselves as the champions of a great and good cause.

⁽²⁴⁾ **The hand of the children of Israel prospered, and prevailed.**—Literally, as in the margin, *The hand . . . . going went, and was hard*—*i.e.*, "became heavier and heavier in its pressure." The battle of the Kishon was the beginning of a complete deliverance of Israel from the yoke of the Canaanites.

V.

The song of Deborah is one of the grandest outbursts of impassioned poetry in the Bible. It is a song of victory, or what the Greeks would have called an Epinician ode. Attempts have been made to show that it cannot have been the work of Deborah, but must belong to a later age, because it contains certain forms which are asserted to be of late occurrence. It is now, however, generally admitted that these may be provincial or colloquial usages of great antiquity, though they only found their way later into the written style. The peculiar splendour and intensity of the poetic passion which breathes throughout the ode, the archaic simplicity of its structure, and the fact that it refers to many circumstances not preserved in the parallel prose narrative, leave little or no doubt as to its perfect genuineness.

It has been arranged in various ways; but the arrangement adopted by Ewald (which may be seen in Dean Stanley's *Jewish Church*, ii. 334), with some modifications, seems to be the most satisfactory. It consists there of a prelude, followed by three main sections, each divisible into three unequal strophes, and ended by a triumphant aspiration, as follows:—

The Prelude (2, 3).

I.

The Significance of the Victory (4—11).
    α. Israel's glorious Redemption of old (4—5).
    β. Israel's recent Degeneracy (6—8).
    γ. The Crisis of Deliverance (9—11).

II.

Second Prelude (12).
The Muster and the Battle (13—21).
    α. The Gathering of the Loyal (13—15a).
    β. The Malingerers and the Brave (15b—18).
    γ. The Victory (19—22).

III.

The Issues of the Victory (24—30).
    α. The Faithless City (23).
    β. The Avenger (24—27).
    γ. The Mother's Frustrated Hope (28—30).
The Cry of Triumph (31).

Although the structure of the ode may not have been intended to be exactly regular, the above scheme fairly represents it. It is characterised throughout by an intense and scathing irony and passion, which gains fresh force from the alliterative form in which it resembles the old Scandinavian and Teutonic poems. There are similar Epinician odes in Exodus (xv.), Numbers (xxi. 27—30), Deuteronomy (xxxii.), 1 Samuel (xviii. 7), and 2 Samuel (i.); but this is incomparably finer than any of those, and has never been equalled, much less surpassed. In energy, scorn, and pathos it rises immensely above the loftiest flights of the "Theban Eagle" (Pindar), whose odes were regarded as unequalled in Greek poetry.

⁽¹⁾ **Then sang Deborah.**—She was a prophetess, and the word for "prophet," like the Latin *vates*, in-

(2) Praise ye the LORD for the avenging of Israel, when the people willingly offered themselves. (3) Hear, O ye kings; give ear, O ye princes; I, *even* I, will sing unto the LORD; I will sing *praise* to the LORD God of Israel.

(4) LORD, *a* when thou wentest out of Seir, when thou marchedst out of the field of Edom, the earth trembled, and the heavens dropped, the clouds also dropped water. (5) *b* The mountains ¹melted from before the LORD, *even c* that Sinai from before the LORD God of Israel.

(6) In the days of *d* Shamgar the son of Anath, in the days of *e* Jael, the highways were unoccupied, and the ²travellers walked through ³byways.

a Deut. 4. 11.
b Ps. 97. 5.
1 Heb., *flowed*.
c Ex. 19. 18.
d ch. 3. 31.
e ch. 4. 18.
2 Heb., *walkers of paths*.
3 Heb., *crooked ways*.

---

volved gifts which were closely allied to those of the poet.

And Barak.—Doubtless Deborah was the sole author of the song, as is implied by the singular verb (ver. 3); but no doubt Barak joined in antiphon when it was sung, just as Moses, at the head of the warriors, and Miriam, at the head of the women, sang the song of Moses, in Ex. xv. As the English version requires some correction, I have appended a translation at the end of the chapter, which must be regarded as a kind of running commentary.

(2) **For the avenging of Israel.**—The Hebrew word *peraoth* cannot have this meaning, though it is found in the Syriac and implied by the Chaldee. The word only occurs in Deut. xxxii. 42, and there, as here, implies the notion of *leading*; so that the LXX. are doubtless right in rendering it, " In the leading of the leaders of Israel." God is praised because both *leaders* and *people* (verses 9, 13) did their duty. *Peraoth* is derived from *perang*, "hair"; and whether the notion which it involves is that of *comati*, "nobles, who wear long hair" (comp. Homer's "long-haired Greeks," and Tennyson's "his beard a yard before him, and his hair a yard behind"), or "hairy champions," or the hair of warriors streaming behind them as they rode to battle ("His beard and hoary hair streamed like a meteor to the troubled air": Gray), *leadership* seems to be the notion involved.

When the people willingly offered themselves.—Comp. Ps. cx. 3: "Thy people shall be willing in the day of thy power."

(3) **Hear, O ye kings.**—There were no kings or princes in Israel, but the appeal is to the "kings of the earth," as in Ps. ii. 10; for which reason the LXX. render "princes" by *satraps*. The Chaldee refers it to the kings allied with Jabin.

(4) **Lord, when thou wentest out of Seir.**—See Ps. lxviii. 7—9; Hab. iii. 3—12. The majority of commentators, both ancient and modern, suppose that the reference is to the promulgation of the law on Sinai, as described in Ex. xix. 16—18, Deut. xxxiii. 3. But the mention of Seir and Edom seems to show that this is not the case, and, indeed, the imagery is different, and the context requires a more pertinent allusion. If the thunders and lightnings of the fiery law are alluded to, we can only suppose that a contrast is intended between the glory which Israel derived from that revelation and their recent abject condition; but the train of thought is clearer if we explain the allusion of the march of Israel from Kadesh Barnea to their first great conquest on the east of the Jordan. This march seems to have been signalised, and the battles of Israel aided, by the same majestic natural phenomena as those which had helped them to defeat Sisera, as though Jehovah Himself were the leader of their vanguard. Though the earthquakes and rains which made so deep an impression upon them are not recorded in the Pentateuch, the memory of the circumstances is preserved in these three passages.

(5) **Melted.**—Literally, *flowed away*—a powerful poetic image. (Comp. Is. lxiii. 19, lxiv. 3; Ps. xcvii. 5—"melted like wax.")

Even that Sinai.—Rather, *even this Sinai*, as though Deborah actually saw the sacred mountain before her. The boldness of the expression leaves no difficulty in supposing the meaning to be that " even as Sinai was moved " (Ps. lxviii. 8), so the mountains of Edom seemed to melt away before the march of Jehovah and the banners of Israel.

(6) **In the days of Shamgar.**—In this and the two next verses is described the misery and dejection of Israel; and the names of Shamgar and Jael are mentioned to enhance the glory of Deborah, by showing that even the presence among the Israelites of two such heroic souls as Shamgar and Jael was unavailing to deliver them until Deborah arose. That Shamgar is thus (apparently) alluded to as a contemporary of Jael has an important bearing on the chronology; for it at least shows that simultaneous struggles may have been going on against the Philistines in the south and the Canaanites in the north.

In the days of Jael.—It has been thought so strange that Deborah should mention the name of the Bedouin chieftainess as marking the epoch, that some have supposed " Jael " to be the name of some unknown judge; and some have even proposed to read Jair. Others render it "the helper," and suppose that Ehud, or Shamgar, is referred to. But (1) Jael is essentially a woman's name (see chap. iv. 17; Prov. v. 19); (2) she is mentioned prominently in this very song as having put the finishing stroke to the victory of Israel; and (3) she may have been—and various incidents in the history lead us to suppose that she was—a woman of great importance and influence, even independently of her murder of Sisera.

The highways were unoccupied.—Literally, *kept holiday*. This had been foretold in Lev. xxvi. 22. The grass grew on them; there was no one to occupy them. "The highways lie waste, the wayfaring man ceaseth" (Is. xxxiii. 8). "The land was desolate after them, that no man passed through nor returned" (Zech. vii. 14). (Comp. 2 Chron. xv. 5; Lam. i. 4, iv. 18.)

Travellers.—Literally, as in the margin, *walkers of paths*. Those of the unhappy conquered race whose necessities obliged them to journey from one place to another could only slink along, unobserved, by twisted —*i.e.*, tortuous, devious—bye-lanes. A traveller in America was reminded of this verse when he saw the neutral ground in 1780, with "houses plundered and dismantled, enclosures broken down, cattle carried away, fields lying waste, the roads grass-grown, the country mournful, solitary, silent."—(Washington Irving's " Life of Washington," ch. cxxxvii.)

Triumphal Song   JUDGES, V   *of Deborah and Barak.*

(7) The inhabitants of the villages ceased, they ceased in Israel, until that I Deborah arose, that I arose a mother in Israel. (8) They chose new gods; then *was* war in the gates: was there a shield or spear seen among forty thousand in Israel? (9) My heart *is* toward the governors of Israel, that offered themselves willingly among the people. Bless ye the LORD. (10) ¹ Speak, ye that ride on white asses, ye that sit in judgment, and walk by the way. (11) *They that are delivered* from the noise of archers in the places of drawing water, there shall they rehearse the ²righteous acts of the LORD, *even* the

¹ Or, *Meditate.*

² Heb., *righteousnesses of the LORD.*

---

(7) **The inhabitants of the villages ceased.**—The one Hebrew word for "the inhabitants of the villages" is *perâzôn*. The rendering of our version is supported by the Chaldee, and by the meaning of the analogous words in Deut. iii. 5, 1 Sam. vi. 18, &c. But this cannot be the meaning in verse 11; and it is far more probable that the LXX. (Cod. B) is right in rendering it "princes" (*dunatoi*; Vulgate, *fortes*), though the difficulty of the word is shown by its being simply transliterated (*phrazon*) in the Alexandrine MS. The meaning probably is "warlike chiefs" (comp. Hab. iii. 14). Luther renders it "peasants."

A mother in Israel.—For this metaphor, comp. 2 Sam. xx. 19; Job xxix. 16; Gen. xlv. 8.

(8) **They chose new gods.**—The Chaldee and the LXX. agree in this interpretation, which is strongly supported by Deut. xxxii. 16, 17. The Syriac and Vulgate render it "God chose new things," or "wars" (*nova bella elegit Dominus*, Vulg.); but this gives a poorer sense, and is open to the objection that *Jehovah*, not *Elohim*, is used throughout the rest of the song. It alludes to the idolatry (Jer. ii. 11) which brought the retribution described in the next clause. Ewald and his pupil, Bertheau, render "gods" (Elohim) by "judges;" but this is very doubtful, though the word has that meaning in Ex. xxi. 6, xxii. 7, 8.

Then was war in the gates.—The Canaanites drove the Israelites from the city gates, where judgments were given, and expelled them from their towns; so the Targum explains it to mean, "the storming of gates," and so too Rabbi Tanchum. One MS. of the LXX. and the Syriac and Arabic versions have the strange rendering, "they chose new gods *like barley bread*," which Theodoret explains to mean, "as though after eating wheaten bread, men would voluntarily descend to coarse barley bread"; but this is only due to an inferior reading.

Was there a shield or spear.—This is usually, and not unnaturally, explained to mean that there had been a general disarmament (comp. chap. iii. 31; 1 Sam. xiii. 19); we must then assume that the Israelites had only bows, slings, and swords. But (1) there is no indication whatever (but rather the reverse, chap. iv. 15) that Barak's army—which, moreover, consisted of 10,000, not 40,000—was unarmed; and (2) the context seems to favour the meaning that, in spite of these degradations, there was not a warrior in all Israel who dared to put on his armour.

Among forty thousand.—Even if the number is meant as a round or general number, it is remarkable. It is true that though Barak only had 10,000 men with him, the contingents of Ephraim, Benjamin, and Manasseh are not counted; but even then the number shows that Israel was weakened and disunited, for the Transjordanic tribes alone had sent 40,000 men to help Joshua in the conquest of Canaan (Josh. iv. 13).

(9) **My heart is toward the governors of Israel.**—The fact that even in this extremity Israel had men (literally, *law-givers*) who were willing to brave any danger to rescue their people fills Deborah with gratitude to them and to God.

Among the people.—When the leaders moved, the people moved with them.

(10) **Speak.**—Rather, *Think of it*, or, perhaps, "Meditate the song." It is placed in the original in far more forcible position at the end of the verse.

Ye that ride on white asses.—That is, nobles and wealthy (chaps. x. 4, xii. 14). The word can hardly mean "white," because there are no such things as white asses. It means rather "bright-coloured" (Ezek. xxvii. 18), "glossy-skinned," or "dappled" (*super nitentes asinos*, Vulg.). These were the more valuable sort of asses, and were used by the rich and great. It is only because this was not understood among the Greeks and Romans, who despised the ass, that the LXX. and Josephus so often disguise the word in writing for Gentiles, using *pōlon*, "steed," or the general word *hupozugion*, "beast of burden," instead. No incident was more derided among the Gentiles than the riding to Zion of her king, "meek and sitting upon an ass" (Zech. ix. 9), (see the *Life of Christ*, ii. 197). Here though the Alexandrine MS. of the LXX has "on female asses of the South"—*i.e.*, of Ethiopia—we find in other MSS. "on beasts of burden."

Ye that sit in judgment.—Rather, *ye that sit on rich divans*, though our version follows the Vatican MS. of the LXX., the Chaldee, and the Vulgate. The Hebrew is, "ye that sit on *middin*," and some Jews understood it to mean "at *Middin*"—*i.e.*, ye inhabitants of the town Middin (which is mentioned in Josh. xv. 61, and which they suppose may have been peculiarly oppressed and insulted by the enemy). Others, again, suppose that *middin* is saddle-cloths (comp. Matt. xxi. 7). The Alexandrine MS. of the LXX. has *epi lampēnôn*—*i.e.*, on sedans or covered chariots. There can be little doubt that it means "bright carpets" (compare *mad* in Ps. cix. 18).

And walk by the way.—Rather, *ye that walk in the way*. Deborah appeals (1) to the wealthy, riding through the safe highways: (2) to those of all classes who now sit at ease on divans, bright with carpets, of which Easterns are so fond: and (3) to foot-passengers in the ordinary life—to join in the thought and song of praise. On the phrases "sitting at home" and "walking on the roads" to describe the ordinary avocations of life, see Deut. vi. 7: "When thou sittest in thine house, and when thou walkest by the way."

(11) **They that are delivered from the noise of archers in the places of drawing water.**—This is usually explained to mean that in the time of oppression the shepherds and the women could not go to the wells to draw water without being disturbed by the enemy's archers; and the construction in that case is changed in the middle of the verse, to remind them that they can now sing God's praises by the safe wellsides. The meaning is highly uncertain. The "they that are delivered" is a conjectural addition of our version. The Hebrew only has "from the noise."

Triumphal Song   JUDGES, V.   *of Deborah and Barak.*

righteous acts *toward the inhabitants* of his villages in Israel: then shall the people of the LORD go down to the gates.

(12) Awake, awake, Deborah: awake, awake, utter a song: arise, Barak, and lead thy captivity captive, thou son of Abinoam. (13) Then he made him that remaineth have dominion over the nobles among the people: the LORD made me have dominion over the mighty.

(14) Out of Ephraim *was there* a root of them against Amalek; after thee, Benjamin, among thy people; out of Machir came down governors, and out of Zebulun they that [1] handle the pen of the writer. (15) And the princes of Issachar *were* with Deborah; even Issachar, and

[1] Heb., *draw with the pen, &c.*

The Vulgate renders it, "where the chariots clashed together, and the army of the enemy was strangled." The LXX. (some MSS.) connect the clause with the last verse: "Sing," or "tell it from (*i.e.* by) the voice of those who strike up their tunes in the midst of the water-drawers." The Chaldee is here utterly vague. Ewald renders it, "from the shoutings of the spoil-dividers between the water-troughs." Amid these uncertainties we have nothing better to offer than the conjecture of our translators.

Righteous acts.—Where these words first occur, the Hebrew is *Tsidkôth*; but in the second recurrence of the English words, "even the righteous acts towards the inhabitants of the villages"—in which they are guided by the Chaldee Targum—we have only the Hebrew words, *Tsidkôth pirzônô*. Here, as in verse 7, the versions were perplexed by the word *perâzôn*; but it is now generally agreed that the meaning is either "the righteous acts of his governance in Israel" (Ewald), or "towards the leaders in Israel" (Rosenmüller, &c.).

Then shall the people of the Lord go down to the gates.—After singing the just deeds of God, they resumed their usual pursuits, unabashed and unterrified.

(12) **Awake, awake, Deborah.**—The prophetess rouses herself in this verse—which forms an introduction to the second section of the song—to describe the loyalty of the tribes and the grandeur of the victory.

Lead thy captivity captive.—Lead in triumph thy long train of captives. For the expression, comp. Rev. xiii. 10.

(13) **Then he made him that remaineth have dominion.**—The translation, reading, and punctuation of this verse is uncertain. The MSS. of the LXX. vary, and the Vulgate merely gives a paraphrase. The Alexandrine MS. of the LXX. may be correct: "Then descended a remnant against the mighty." Ewald renders it, "Then descended a remnant of the nobles of the people." They were only "a remnant," because at least six of the tribes—Judah, Simeon, Dan, Asher, Reuben, Gad—held aloof.

The Lord made me have dominion over the mighty.—Rather, *Jehovah descended to me among the heroes.* The LXX. (Cod. B) and others connect "people" with this clause: "The people of Jehovah descended," &c., and perhaps correctly.

(14) **Out of Ephraim was there a root of them against Amalek.**—The LXX. and Vulgate render it, "Ephraim uprooted them in Amalek." But the meaning seems to be, "Out of Ephraim (came down to the battle) those whose root is in Amalek," or, "among the Amalekites." Ephraim had firmly rooted himself (comp. Is. xxvii. 6; Ps. lxxx. 10) in the country which had been the stronghold of the Amalekites. (See chap. xii. 15.)

After thee, Benjamin, among thy people.—Ephraim is here addressed by a sudden change of person (comp. Is. i. 29, xlii. 20, &c.). After thee, O Ephraim, came down Benjamin, mingled with thy people. The forces of "little Benjamin" are overshadowed by, and almost lost in, the crowded ranks of its powerful neighbour-tribe. In after days Benjamin clung to the skirts of Judah, but at this period his fortunes were more allied with those of Ephraim. "After thee, Benjamin," seems to have become (perhaps from this allusion) a war-cry of the tribe (Hos. v. 8).

Out of Machir came down governors.—Machir was the only son of Manasseh (Gen. i. 23; Num. xxvii. 1), and is here used for the Western Manassites (Josh. xvii. 5). The Eastern half-tribe, no doubt, held aloof with Gad and Reuben. The silence respecting Judah is remarkable. We may conjecture that Judah and Simeon were sufficiently occupied in keeping off the Philistines, or that, having secured their own territory, they remained in selfish isolation. The word rendered "governors" (LXX., "searchers out"; Vulgate, "princes") is more strictly "law-givers" (Symmachus, *entassontes*).

They that handle the pen of the writer.—Literally, *they who draw with the staff* (*shêbet*) *of the scribe* (*sophêr*). *Sophêr* may mean scribe (literally, "one who counts"), and the verb rendered "handle" is, literally, "draw;" but *shêbet* can hardly mean "pen"; nor is it easy to say of what special use "the pen of the writer" would be in the gathering of clans to battle; nor have we the faintest indication that Zebulon had any literary pre-eminence. There can be little doubt that the meaning is, "They who lead (so in Latin, *traho* sometimes has the meaning of *duco*) with the staff of the marshal." The *sophêr* is the officer (2 Kings xxv. 19) who musters, and therefore naturally counts and enrols, the host (Jer. lii. 25), and the staff is his natural "rod of power," or ensign of office; just as it was (*vitis*, Plin., *H. N.* xiv. 1, § 3) of Roman centurions (Vulgate, *De Zebulon qui exercitum ducerent ad bellandum*).

(15) **And the princes of Issachar.**—The ordinary reading of the Hebrew gives the meaning, "And *my* princes in Issachar (came down to battle) with Deborah." If this be the right reading, Deborah calls them "my princes" with a touch of pride, and hence some have assumed that she belonged to the tribe of Issachar, not to that of Ephraim. But a very slight change gives the meaning of "the princes in Issachar." Deborah did not take actual part in the battle, like Boadicea or Joan of Arc, but seems to have been close at hand, in the rear, to encourage the combatants, as the ancient British and German women used to do, and as Arab women do to this day.

Even Issachar, and also Barak: he was sent on foot into the valley.—Rather, *even Issachar.*

also Barak: he was sent on ¹foot into the valley. ²For the divisions of Reuben *there were* great ³thoughts of heart. (16) Why abodest thou among the sheepfolds, to hear the bleatings of the flocks? ⁴ For the divisions of Reuben *there were* great searchings of heart. (17) Gilead abode beyond Jordan : and why did Dan remain in ships? Asher continued on the ⁵sea shore, and abode in his ⁶breaches. (18) Zebulun and Naphtali *were* a people that ⁷jeoparded their lives unto the death in the high places of the field.

(19) The kings came *and* fought, then fought the kings of Canaan in Taanach by the waters of Megiddo ; they took no gain of money. (20) They fought from heaven ; the stars in their ⁸courses

¹ Heb., *his feet.*
² Or, *In the divisions, &c.*
³ Heb., *impressions.*
⁴ Cr, *In.*
⁵ Or, *port.*
⁶ Or, *creeks.*
⁷ Heb., *exposed to reproach.*
⁸ Heb., *paths.*

---

as well as Barak, rushed down at his feet (*i.e.*, after Barak) *into the plain* (*emek*)." It is a pity that the verse does not end here, for the next clause begins the description of "the malingerers," whose cowardice or selfishness is triumphantly contrasted with the heroic daring of Zebulon and Naphtali in verse 18.

For the divisions of Reuben there were great thoughts of heart.—The word for "divisions" (*pelagoth*) might mean "families" or "clans," as the LXX, or "factions," as the Vulgate seems to have understood it; but it almost certainly means *streams*, as in Job xx. 17 (margin, "streaming brooks"), where alone it recurs. The allusion is to the Jabbok and its numerous affluents. "Thoughts of heart" only occurs elsewhere in Is. xii. 1, where it is rendered "decrees," with the epithet "empty," or "vain." Possibly, therefore, an ironic contrast is intended between the magnanimous "decisions" (*chikekey* lēbh) of Reuben and his evanescent "projects" (*chikerey* lēbh). The play of words is almost certainly contemptuous, and there may be some lurking scorn in the word *pelagoth* to imply either "rivers" or "factions." Reuben debated and stayed at home on frivolous pretences, as Sparta did in the days of Marathon. But even then the sting of the reproach lies in the taunting question of the next verse.

(16) **Sheepfolds.**—Literally, *hurdles* (*mishpethaim*), the dual form being due to some method of their construction. Hence the Vulgate renders, *inter duos terminos.*

The bleatings of the flocks.—Rather, *the sounds of shepherds' flutes* or *pastoral pipings* ("Shepherds delighting in syrinx-pipes," Hom., *Il.* xviii. 525). There is a contrast between these peaceful flutings and the battle-horns to which they ought to have been listening. It is as though Deborah would say to Reuben—

"Sound, sound the clarion, shrill the fife;
To all the sensual world proclaim,
One crowded hour of glorious life
Is worth an age without a name."

For the divisions.—It should be, as before, "By the streams of Reuben."

Searchings of heart.—Reuben sent magnanimous debates and promises, but they only ended in sloth and vacillation. They decided to go, and—stayed at home.

(17) **Gilead abode beyond Jordan.**—Gilead was the son of Machir, and grandson of Manasseh. The name is here probably meant to include Gad, as well as the half-tribe of Manasseh. The word "abode" means "stayed quietly" (Ps. xvi. 9), and is rendered *quiescebat* in the Vulgate.

Why did Dan remain in ships?—The sudden question is very picturesque. The other rendering, "Why did Dan fear the ships (of the enemy) ?" is untenable. The possession of Joppa, one of the few seaports of Palestine, naturally influenced the pursuits of the tribe (Josh. xix. 46 ; 2 Chron. ii. 16 ; Ezr. iii. 7) ; but whether they are here reproached for absorption in commerce, or for cowardice in taking refuge in their ships, is uncertain. The word rendered "remain" often involves a notion of "alarm" (Deut. xxxii. 27). If the Danite migration (chap. xviii.) had by this time occurred, it is almost impossible that they should not have rendered some assistance to the revolt of the northern tribes. The fact that it is not here alluded to shows the extremely early date at which this narrative must be placed.

Asher continued on the sea shore.—Asher was the other great maritime tribe (Josh. xix. 28, 29). The word "continued" is, literally, "sat."

Abode in his breaches.—The word rendered "breaches" is, literally, "clefts," or "fissures." The Chaldee curiously paraphrases it by "rebuilt and dwelt in the cities which the Gentiles destroyed." Le Clerc renders it, "Sits in his precipitous rocks," referring it to that part of the coast known as "the Ladder of Tyre ; " and this is perhaps meant by the *diakopas* of the LXX. (Cod. Alex.). The Vulgate renders, *in portibus.* Probably the "creeks" of the margin of our Bibles is the correct rendering.

(18) **Jeoparded their lives.**—Comp. chap. ix. 7 ; Is. liii. 12. The courage of Zebulon and Naphtali is contrasted with the empty debates of Reuben, the sloth of Gilead, the cowardly selfishness of Dan and Asher.

In the high places of the field.—That is, on Mount Tabor. The Hebrew word is *the Meroms;* hence the Vulgate has *in regione Merome.* (Comp. Josh. xi. 5, 7.)

(19) **The kings.**—Comp. Josh. xi. 1. Jabin did not stand alone.

In Taanach.—See chap. i. 27. The word means "sandy soil."

By the waters of Megiddo.—The affluents of the Kishon, or the swollen waves of the river itself. There is a copious spring at *Lejjûn*, the ancient Megiddo, which in rainy seasons rapidly turns the plain into a morass (Thomson's *Land and Book*, ch. xxix.).

They took no gain of money.—Literally, *fragment of silver they did not take.* They had doubtless hoped, if not for much actual spoil, at least for ransom from the numerous captives which they expected to win, or from the gain derived by selling them into slavery.

(20) **They fought from heaven.**—The "they" is impersonal—the powers above. (Comp. Luke xii. 20, Greek, and for the fact, iv. 22.)

The stars in their courses.—This is probably a general reference to the providential storms which had secured the victory to Israel. To understand the "stars" as meaning "angels" is a mistaken inference from Job xxxviii. 7. There is a striking parallel in Claudian's poem on the Consulship of Honorius :—

"Oh nimium dilecte Deo, cui militat aether
Et conjurati veniunt ad classica venti."

fought against Sisera. (21) The river of Kishon swept them away, that ancient river, the river Kishon. O my soul, thou hast trodden down strength. (22) Then were the horsehoofs broken by the means of ¹ the pransings, the pransings of their mighty ones.

(23) Curse ye Meroz, said the angel of the LORD, curse ye bitterly the inhabitants thereof; because they came not to

¹ Or, *tramplings*, or, *plungings*.

the help of the LORD, to the help of the LORD against the mighty.

(24) Blessed above women shall Jael the wife of Heber the Kenite be, blessed shall she be above women in the tent. (25) He asked water, *and* she gave *him* milk; she brought forth butter in a lordly dish. (26) She put her hand to the nail, and her right hand to the workmen's hammer; and with the hammer

---

Similarly, Æschylus represents "water and fire, in ruin reconciled," fighting against the Greek fleet.

(21) **The river of Kishon.**—Chap. iv. 7; Ps. lxxxiii. 9. Either from this massacre, or that of the Baal priests of Elijah, the Kishon is now called the *Nahr Mukatta*, or "river of slaughter" (1 Kings xviii. 40).

That ancient river.—The Vulgate renders this, "the torrent Kedumim," and the LXX. (Cod. Vat.), "the river of the ancients" (comp. Deut. xxxiii. 15). The Chaldee paraphrases it, "the torrent on whose banks illustrious deeds have been done from the ancient times of Israel." As the Plain of Jezreel has been in all ages the battle-field of Israel, the Kishon must always have played an important part in these struggles, as when the Turks were drowned in its swollen waves on April 16th, 1799. We know, however, of no ancient fame of Kishon before these events; and some render it. "the torrent of meeting armies," or "of slaughters" (Ewald), deriving *Kedumim* from an Arabic root; or "the torrent of succours," connecting the word with *Kiddeem* (see Ps. lxxix. 8, &c., Heb.). Aquila renders it by "the torrent of siroccos" (*Kausŏnōn*); and Symmachus, "the torrent of goats" (wild waves, egers, and bores).

O my soul, thou hast trodden down strength. —These sudden exclamations, which break the flow of the poem, add greatly to its fire and impetuosity. The verb may be an imperative, and the Vulgate renders it, "Trample down, O my soul, the mighty." The word "trample" recalls the image of treading the vintage.

(22) **By the means of the pransings.**—Rather, *the stampings*. In crossing the Kishon after moderate rains, I had an opportunity of observing by personal experience how easily a horse might be hopelessly disabled in the muddy morass formed by the river. The word is forcibly repeated by the figure known as *anadiplosis*.

Their mighty ones.—The great lords in their iron chariots, trying to goad their frightened steeds through the flood. There is a scathing taunt in the words. Their "might" was exhibited in valiantly running away. It may, however, mean the strong steeds themselves (comp. Jer. viii. 15, li. 11). Vandevelde speaks of the Kishon as being the most dangerous river of the land, from its quicksands.

(23) **Curse ye Meroz.**—The guilt of Meroz was worse than that of the tribes which held aloof, because, whatever may have been its exact site, it was evidently in the very heart of the country which had been thus inspired to strike a blow for freedom. Possibly it would have been in the power of the inhabitants at least to cut off the retreat of the enemy. We may conjecture, from the ban thus laid on Meroz, that it felt the vengeance of the victorious Israelites, and was destroyed or punished like Succoth and Penuel. Their crime was *detrectatio militiae*, which the ancients regarded with special indignation. The case of Jabesh Gilead, in chap. xxi. 9, 10, may account for the difficulty of ascertaining the site of the town; it is not mentioned elsewhere. By some it is identified with Kefr Musr, a village to the south of Tabor (v. Raumer); by others with Marussus, north of Bethshean. It has been conjectured that the true reading may be Merom, and Dr. Thomson identifies it with Marom, as Eusebius alludes to it under the name Merran, and Jerome calls it Merrom. They, however, place it near Dothan, twelve miles from Shechem —a very unlikely locality.

Said the angel of the Lord.—The *Maleak Jehovah*, as in chap. iii. i. Here, as in that passage, some (referring to Hagg. i. 13; Mal. ii. 7) suppose that Deborah is herself the angel or messenger of the Lord. However that may be, she certainly speaks as the mouthpiece of Jehovah's messenger (chap. iv. 4).

(24) **Blessed above women.**—Jael would be regarded as a patriotic heroine, whose daring had secured to Israel the fruits of their victory. The morals of that early age were not sufficiently enlightened to understand that treachery and assassination are *never* justifiable, however good may be the end in view. But, as serious moralists, even in the nineteenth century, have held up to admiration the murder of Marat by Charlotte Corday, and have even given to her the title of "the Angel of Assassination," we can hardly be surprised that Deborah should exult in Jael's heroism, and her choice of the right side, without expressing—perhaps even without the degree of later moral enlightenment which would have led her to feel—any moral reprobation of the means by which the end was accomplished. But to compare this outburst of patriotic approval for such a deed with the salutation of "Blessed art thou among women," addressed by the angel to the blessed Virgin Mary (as is done by some commentators), seems to me a most dangerous way of handling the mere words of Scripture, apart from their context and true significance.

Above women in the tent.—The honour paid to her because of her deed would raise her far above the common mass of ignorant and downtrodden nomad women. Instead of a Kenite woman, she would be lauded and honoured as a heroine of Israel.

(25) **Butter.**—Rather, *curdled milk*.

In a lordly dish.—Rather, *in a dish of the nobles*: *sephel*, a splendid bowl, reserved for great occasions. All this was done to lull his suspicions into a false security.

(26) **Nail . . . . workmen's hammer.**—See on chap. iv. 21.

Smote.—*Hammered*.

Smote off his head.—Rather, *shattered his head*. The Hebrew is onomatopoetic, *i.e.*, the sound echoes the sense, recalling the smashing and crashing blows of the hammer. The repetition of these terrible alliterative

she ¹smote Sisera, she smote off his head, when she had pierced and stricken through his temples. ⁽²⁷⁾ ²At her feet he bowed, he fell, he lay down : at her feet he bowed, he fell : where he bowed, there he fell down ³ dead.

⁽²⁸⁾ The mother of Sisera looked out at a window, and cried through the lat-tice, Why is his chariot *so* long in coming ? why tarry the wheels of his chariots ? ⁽²⁹⁾ Her wise ladies answered her, yea, she returned ⁴ answer to herself, ⁽³⁰⁾ Have they not sped ? have they *not* divided the prey ; ⁵ to every man a damsel *or* two ; to Sisera a prey of divers colours, a prey of divers colours

1. Heb., *hammered.*
2. Heb., *Between.*
3. Heb., *destroyed.*
4. Heb., *words.*
5. Heb., *to the head of a man.*

---

verbs, "hammered," "shattered," "battered," "transfixed," the signs that the imagination of the prophetess seems to revel in the description, have been ascribed to "the delight of a satisfied thirst for revenge." This is hardly a right view of her character. It must be remembered that the feelings of modern times are far more refined and complex than those of previous ages. The sense of tenderness, the quickness of compassion, the value set on human life, are immeasurably increased, and with them the power of realising by universal sympathy the position and sufferings of others. In ancient days no close moral analysis was applied to acts of which the general tendency was approved as right and beneficial. Cæsar was not inherently a cruel man, yet he records without a shudder the massacre and misery of multitudes of Gaulish men, women, and children at Alesia; and he suffered the brave Vercingetorix to be led away from his triumph, to be strangled in the Tullianum, without the slightest qualm of pity. Deborah, in the spirit of her day, seems to regard with pitiless exultation the wild throes of Sisera's death, and the agonising frustration of his mother's hopes. only because she views those events in the single aspect of the deliverance of Israel. The tenderness of the Mother of Israel was absorbed in the thought of her own long-afflicted, but now rescued, race. "She was a mother in Israel, and with the vehemency of a mother's and a patriot's love, she had shot the light of love from her eyes, and poured the blessings of love from her lips on the people that had jeopardised their lives unto the death against the oppressors, and the bitterness awakened and borne aloft by the same love she precipitates in curses on the selfish and cowardly recreants who came not to the help of the Lord against the unjust" (Coleridge); and we may add, on all connected with the cruel oppressor.

⁽²⁷⁾ **At her feet.**—Literally, *between her feet,* as though the dauntless woman had stridden over him as he lay in the dead sleep of weariness.

He bowed.—The word means that he suddenly curled up his knees in one contortion of agony.

He fell.—Rolling, perhaps, off the divan on which he was resting.

He lay down.—Motionless in death, after that one convulsive movement.

Dead.—Rather, *slaughtered,* or *murdered.* With this one terrific word the scene ends, as with a blow.

⁽²⁸⁾ **The mother of Sisera.**—With a bold poetic impetuosity the scene is changed, and the prophetess, with a few broad touches, sets before us the last scene of the strange eventful history. The mother of Sisera and her attendant princesses had looked for the triumph and return of the host as confidently as the ladies of Spain expected the return of the Armada, or as the ladies of Aberdeen sat, "with their fans into their hand," looking out for the sails of Sir Patrick Spens. We have a similar scene in the *Persians* of Æschylus, where the great Atossa wails over the miserable flight of her defeated son Xerxes. In that, however, there is more of pity and less of derision, though, no doubt, the spectacle was meant to be pleasing to the victorious Athenians. This exulting description of the cruel but blighted hopes of the *women* of Sisera's family is an inimitable touch of genuineness; it shows a woman's authorship (Ewald).

Looked out at a window.—Watching for the first glimpse of her son's return. In Eastern courts the queen-mother is a more important person than the wife.

And cried.—Rather, *wailed* (Vulgate, *ululavit,* an onomatopœia, like the Hebrew *yabhabh*). It is the wail of impatience passing into anxiety.

⁽²⁹⁾ **Her wise ladies.**—Literally, *the wise of her princesses.* There is unconcealed scorn in this, showing that the wisest were most utterly mistaken. Their "wisdom" is the seductive flattery of delusive hopes.

Answered her.—The verb is in the singular, implying that one spoke after another. The Vulgate renders it, "One of his wives, wiser than the rest, answered."

Yea, she returned answer to herself.—The meaning of the clause is very uncertain. It may be, "yea, she repeats their answer to herself," accepting their flattering surmises; or, on the contrary, "but she repeats her words to herself," entirely unconsoled; or, again—but this is less likely—"yea, she retracted her own (anxious) words." The anxious foreboding or the inextinguishable hope would be equally true to nature, according to the temperament of the Canaanite princess.

⁽³⁰⁾ **Have they not sped? have they not divided the prey?**—Literally, *Are they not finding? are they not dividing the spoil? Is not the wealth of their booty the cause of their delay?* (Comp. Ex. xv. 9 : "The enemy said, I will pursue, I will overtake, I will divide the spoil.")

To every man.—Literally, as in the margin, *to the head of a man.* (Comp. Ex. xvi. 16 ; Num. i. 2; 1 Chron. xii. 23.)

A damsel or two.—Literally, *a maiden, two maidens;* only that the word used is strongly contemptuous, as though a captive Hebrew girl could only be described by a term of scorn. In these internecine wars the men were killed and the women reserved as slaves (Num. xxxi. 17, 18). Commentators quote a remarkable parallel from Gibbon (ii., ch. 11), where he says that two or three Gothic female captives fell to the share of each of the soldiers of Claudius II. ("Tantum mulierum cepimus, ut *binas et ternas mulieres* victor sibi miles possit adjungere."—Trebellius Pollio, viii.) The reading of the Peshito is, "a heap, two heaps," as in chap. xv. 16.

Of divers colours.—Literally, *of dyed robes.*

Of divers colours of needlework.—*Of dyed robes of embroidered webs.*

Of divers colours of needlework on both sides.—*A dyed robe, two embroidered webs.*

of needlework, of divers colours of needlework on both sides, *meet* ¹for the necks of *them that take* the spoil?
⁽³¹⁾ So let all thine enemies perish, O LORD: but *let* them that love him *be* as the sun when he goeth forth in his might.

And the land had rest forty years.

¹ Heb., *for the necks of the spoil.*

Meet for the necks of them that take the spoil?—Literally, as in the margin, *for the necks of the spoil.* As this gives no good sense, our version follows those which here understand "spoil" as equivalent to "spoiler." The old versions take "spoil" in apposition to the rest of the sentence: *e.g.,* the LXX. have, "dyed robes of embroidered webs for his neck, as spoils," and a similar meaning is involved in the loose paraphrase of the Vulgate. Others explain it to mean that the dyed robes are to be carried on the necks of the female slaves and the captive cattle. Ewald reads *shegal* ("queen") for *shellal* ("prey")—a brilliant and probable conjecture; for if the booty of the soldiers and the general is mentioned, the royal ladies would be hardly likely to forget themselves. In any case, the mother of Sisera is characteristically described (as Bishop Lowth has pointed out) as talking neither of the slaughter of the enemy nor the prowess of the warriors, but only of the gay and feminine booty. (Comp. "Faemineo praedae et spoliorum arderet amore," *Æn.* xi. 728.) Nothing can exceed the power and skill with which in a few words the vanity, levity, and arrogance of these "wise princesses" are described, as they idly talk of colours and embroidery, and, as it were, gloat over the description; while, at the same time, an unwomanly coarseness (*racham,* for "maiden") mingles with their womanly frivolity. Only we must bear in mind that they too, like Deborah and Jael, though in an ignobler way, are the creatures of their age and circumstances.

⁽³¹⁾ **So let all thine enemies perish, O Lord.**—The abrupt burst in which the song rushes, as it were, to its conclusion, is very grand. The total frustration of the hopes of the princesses is all the more forcibly implied by the scorn with which it is left unexpressed. The one word "so" sums up the story in all its striking phases; and this passionate exclamation accounts, in part, for the intensity of feeling which runs through the whole poem, by showing that Deborah regards the battle as part of one great religious crusade. The completeness of the overthrow caused it to be long remembered as an example of Israel's triumph over God's enemies (Ps. lxxxiii. 9, 10, 12—15). When the Christian warriors of the first crusade were riding deep in the blood of the murdered Saracens, after the capture of Jerusalem, they were fully convinced that they were "doing God service;" and so filled were they with religious emotion, that at vesper-time they all suddenly fell upon their knees with streaming tears. The general dissemination of a feeling of pity—pity even for our worst enemies—is a very modern feeling, and still far from universal.

But let them that love him.—This is probably the right reading, though it was early altered into "they that love thee."

As the sun when he goeth forth in his might.—For the metaphor, comp. Pss. xix. 4, 5, lxviii. 1—3; Dan. xii. 3; Matt. xiii. 43.

And the land had rest.—This is not a part of the song, but concludes the whole story (chaps. iii. 11, 30. viii. 28). This is the last we hear of any attempt of the Canaanites to re-conquer the land which they had lost, although we see a small and spasmodic outbreak of this race in the story of Abimelech (chap. ix.).

TRANSLATION OF THE SONG OF DEBORAH.

I.

THE PRELUDE (2, 3).

2. For the leading of the leaders of Israel,
   For the self-devotion of the people—praise ye the Lord.
3. Hear, O kings; attend, O princes;
   I to the Lord, even I, will sing,
   I will sound the harp to the Lord, the God of Israel.

I.

ISRAEL'S GLORIOUS REDEMPTION OF OLD (4, 5).

4. O Lord, in Thy going forth from Seir,
   In Thy marching forth from Edom's field,
   The earth trembled; yea, the heavens dropped:
   Yea, the clouds poured down water.
5. The mountains flowed away before the face of the Lord.
   This Sinai before the Lord, the God of Israel.

II.

ISRAEL'S RECENT DEGENERACY (6, 7).

6. In the days of Shamgar, son of Anath,
   In the days of Jael, the highways ceased,
   The wayfarers walked in winding ways.
7. Ceased the warriors in Israel, ceased
   Until I arose—Deborah—
   I arose, a mother in Israel.

III.

THE CRISIS OF DELIVERANCE (8—11).

8. They chose new gods;
   Then was there war in the gates.
   Shield nor spear was seen
   Among forty thousand in Israel!
9. My heart is with the reformers of Israel,
   With the self-devoted of the people—Praise the Lord.
10. Ye that ride on bright she-asses,
    Ye that sit on rich divans,
    Ye that walk in the way,
    Think of it!
11. Instead of the hallooings of the archers
    Among the water-drawers,
    Then let them praise the righteous acts of the Lord.
    The righteous acts of His governance in Israel.
    Then to the gates went down the people of the Lord.

II.

NEW PRELUDE (12).

12. Awake, awake, Deborah!
    Awake, awake; utter a song!
    Up, Barak! lead captive thy captives, son of Abinoam!

THE MUSTER AND THE BATTLE (13—22).

I.

THE GATHERING OF THE LOYAL (13—15).

13. Then came down to battle a valiant few of the nobles of the people;
    The Lord came down to me among the heroes;
14. Out of Ephraim (came) those whose root is in Amalek
    Behind thee (came) Benjamin, among thy people;
    Out of Machir came masters;
    And from Zebulon chieftains, with the marshal's staff.
15. And the princes of Issachar, with Deborah,
    Even Issachar, as well as Barak,
    Rushed down at his heels into the plain.

II.

THE MALINGERERS AND THE BRAVE (16—18).

16. By the streams of Reuben was courage of word.
    Why stayest thou within the sheepfolds,
    To hear the sounds of shepherds' flutes?
    By the streams of Reuben was cowardice in deed.
17. Gilead beyond Jordan lingered,
    And Dan, why did he cower in ships?
    Asher sat by the shore of the sea,
    And by his rocky bays reposed.
18. Zebulon—a people flinging its soul to death!
    And Naphtali—on the heights of the field!

III.

THE VICTORY (19—22).

19. They came—the kings they fought;
    They fought, the kings of Canaan.

Israel oppressed   JUDGES, VI.   *by the Midianites.*

CHAPTER VI.—⁽¹⁾ And the children of Israel did evil in the sight of the LORD: and the LORD delivered them into the hand of Midian seven years. ⁽²⁾ And the hand of Midian [1] prevailed against Israel: *and* because of the Midianites the children of Israel made them the dens which *are* in the mountains, and caves, and strong holds. ⁽³⁾ And *so* it was, when Israel had sown, that the Midianites came up, and the Amalekites, and the children of the

B. C. cir. 1256.

1 Heb., *was strong.*

In Taanach, on Megiddo's waters,
No dust of silver did they win.
From heaven they fought;
The stars in their courses fought against Sisera!
21. The torrent Kishon swept them away;
The torrent of slaughters, the torrent Kishon.
Trample, my soul, on strength!
22. Then stamped the hoofs of the steeds
With the plungings, the plungings of the mighty ones!

III.
THE ISSUES OF THE VICTORY (23—30).
I.
THE FAITHLESS CITY (23).

23. Curse ye Meroz, said the angel of the Lord;
Curse ye with a curse the inhabitants thereof;
Because they came not to the help of the Lord,
To the help of the Lord among the heroes.

II.
THE AVENGER (24—27).

24. Blessed among women be Jael,
Heber, the Kenite's wife;
Among women in the tent blessed be she.
25. Water asked he, milk she gave:
In a bowl of the nobles she brought him cream.
26. Her left hand to the tent-peg she stretched forth,
And her right hand to the workman's hammer.
And she hammered Sisera, shattered his head,
And battered and crashed through his temples.
27. Between her feet he writhed, he fell, he lay;
Between her feet he writhed, he fell;
Where he writhed there he fell down—dead!

III.
THE MOTHER'S FRUSTRATED HOPES (28—30).

28. Through the window looked forth and wailed
The mother of Sisera, through the lattice-work.
"Why lingers his chariot to come?
Why tarry the pacings of his chariots?"
29. The wise of her princesses answer her;
Yea, she repeats their words to herself—
"Are they not finding? are they not sharing the spoil?
A maiden, two maidens, to each man."
30. Prey of dyed robes for Sisera,
Prey of red robes, of embroidery;
One dyed, two of embroidery, for the neck of the princess.

THE EPILOGUE.
31. So perish thine enemies, O Lord!
But let those who love Thee be as the sun's rising in his strength.

VI.

1—6. A new apostasy, punished by the oppression of Midian. 7—10. The rebuke delivered by a prophet. 11—14. An angel appears to Gideon and bids him deliver Israel, and (15—18) removes his doubts. 19—23. The offering to the angel, and his disappearance. 24. Gideon builds the altar Jehovah-shalom, and (25—27) hews down his father's Baal and Asherah in the night. 28—32. Joash pacifies the Abi-ezrites by appealing to them to let Baal plead his own cause. 33—35. Gideon rouses Manasseh and northern tribes against a new Midianite invasion. 36—40. The double sign of the fleece.

⁽¹⁾ **Did evil.**—Chaps. ii. 11, iii. 12, iv. 1.

Midian.—Midian was the son of Abraham and Keturah (Gen. xxv. 2), and from him descended the numerous and wealthy nomadic tribes which occupied the plains east of Moab (Num. xxxi. 32—39). The name belongs, properly, to the tribes on the south-east of the Gulf of Akabah (1 Kings xi. 18). Moses himself had lived for forty years among them (Exod. iii. 1, xviii. 1); but the Israelites had been bidden to maintain deadly hostility against the nation because of the shameful worship of Baal-peor, to which, under the instigation of Balaam, the Midianites had tempted them (Num. xxv. 1—18).

⁽²⁾ **The hand of Midian prevailed.**—See chap. iii. 10. This oppression is wholly different from that with which we have been dealing in the last chapter. That was the last great attempt of the old inhabitants to recover their lost country; this is a foreign invasion.

The dens which are in the mountains.—The word *mineharoth*, rendered *dens* (LXX., *mandrai*), occurs here only. Rashi and Kimchi render it, "caves lighted from above," deriving it from *neharah*, "light" (Job iii. 4). They were probably thinking of the subterranean galleries like those found by Wetzstein in the *Hauran* (p. 45). R. Tanchum and others take it to mean *fire-signals*. But the more probable derivation is *nahar*, "a river," and then the meaning is "torrent-gullies," which they easily converted into places of concealment, since the limestone hills of Palestine abound in caves. Josephus understood it to mean *mines* and *caverns* (*Antt.* v. 6, § 1). (Comp. 1 Sam. xiii. 6: "When the men of Israel saw that they were in a strait, then the people did hide themselves in caves, and in thickets, and in rocks, and in high places, and in pits." Heb. xi. 38: "in dens and caves of the earth.") Three places of hiding are mentioned: (1) The *mineharoth*, perhaps catacombs and galleries in the rocks, which, as the article shows, were pointed out long afterwards. (2) Craggy peaks, like Rimmon, Magada, &c. (3) "Limestone caves, here first mentioned, and afterwards often used, like the Corycian cave in Greece during the Persian invasion, and the caves of the Asturias in Spain during the occupation of the Moors. It was returning to the old troglodyte habits of the Horites and Phœnicians" (Stanley, i. 340). These caves were used, long afterwards, by the brigands whom Herod and the Romans found it so hard to extirpate.

⁽³⁾ **When Israel had sown.**—The invasions of these Arab tribes were of the most crushing and irritating kind. Living in idleness and marauding expeditions, they let the Israelites sow their corn, and came themselves to reap and carry it away. They said, "Let us take to ourselves the pastures of God"—*i.e.*, the rich, blessed pastures—"in possession" (Ps. lxxxiii. 12). Alyattes, king of Lydia, treated the people of Miletus in exactly the same way, leaving their houses undestroyed, solely that they might be tempted to return to them, and plough and sow once more (Herod. i. 17). The same thing goes on to this day. The wretched Fellahin, neglected and oppressed by the effete and corrupt Turkish Government, sow their corn, with the constant dread that they are but sowing it for the Bedouin, who yearly plunder them, unrepressed and unpunished. Hence the squalid towns and villages of the Fellahin abound in huge subterranean places of concealment, in which they stow away their corn, and everything else of value which they possess, to save them from these wild marauders.

The Lord sends   JUDGES, VI.   *a Prophet to them.*

east, even they came up against them; ⁽⁴⁾ and they encamped against them, and destroyed the increase of the earth, till thou come unto Gaza, and left no sustenance for Israel, neither ¹sheep, nor ox, nor ass. ⁽⁵⁾ For they came up with their cattle and their tents, and they came as grasshoppers for multitude; *for* both they and their camels were without number: and they entered into the land to destroy it. ⁽⁶⁾ And Israel was greatly impoverished because of the Midianites; and the children of Israel cried unto the LORD.

⁽⁷⁾ And it came to pass, when the children of Israel cried unto the LORD because of the Midianites, ⁽⁸⁾ that the LORD sent ²a prophet unto the children of Israel, which said unto them, Thus saith the LORD God of Israel, I brought you up from Egypt, and brought you forth out of the house of bondage; ⁽⁹⁾ and I delivered you out of the hand of the Egyptians, and out of the hand of all that oppressed you, and drave them out from before you, and gave you their land; ⁽¹⁰⁾ and I said unto you, I *am* the LORD your God; *a* fear not the gods of the Amorites, in whose land ye dwell: but ye have not obeyed my voice.

⁽¹¹⁾ And there came an angel of the LORD, and sat under an oak which *was* in Ophrah, that *pertained* unto Joash the Abi-ezrite: and his son *b*Gideon threshed

---

Marginal notes: ¹ Or, *goat.*   ² Heb., *a man a prophet.*   B.C. cir. 1249.   *a* 2 Kings 17. 35, 38; Jer. 10. 2.   *b* Heb. 11. called Gedeon. 32.

The Amalekites.—See chap. iii. 13; Gen. xxxvi. 12.

The children of the east.—Beni Kedem (Gen. xxv. 6; Job i. 3) is a general name for Arabs, as Josephus rightly calls them. From chap. viii. 26 we can derive a picture of their chiefs in their gorgeous robes and golden ear-rings, mounted on dromedaries and camels, of which the necks were hung with moon-shaped ornaments of gold.

⁽⁴⁾ **They encamped against them.**—It is not implied that there were any battles. The Israelites were too wretched and helpless to offer any resistance. These Arabs would swarm over the Jordan, at the fords of Bethshean, about harvest-time, and would sweep away the produce of the rich plain of Jezreel and the whole Shephelah, even as far south as Gaza. (Comp. the Scythian invasion, alluded to in Zeph. ii. 5, 6.)

Destroyed the increase of the earth.—" Ye shall sow your seed in vain, for your enemies shall eat it" (Lev. xxvi. 16). (Comp. Deut. xxviii. 30, 51; Micah vi. 15.)

No sustenance for Israel.—No support of life, or, as some render the word, "nothing alive."

Sheep.—The margin has, "or goat." The word means "smaller cattle."

⁽⁵⁾ **As grasshoppers.**—See chap. vii. 12. Rather, *as locusts.* The magnificent imagery of Joel ii. 2—11 enables us to realise the force of the metaphor, and Exod. x. 4—6 the number of locusts, which are a common metaphor for countless hordes. Aristophanes (*Ach.* 150) speaks of an army so numerous that the Athenians will cry out, "What a mass of locusts is coming!" The Bedouin call the locusts *Gurrud Allah,* " Host of God" (Wetzstein, *Hauran,* p. 138).

Their camels.—These were very uncommon in Palestine, and were brought by the invaders from the Eastern deserts.

Without number.—This is Oriental hyperbole. "When Burckhardt asked a Bedouin, who belonged to a tribe of 300 tents, how many brothers he had, he flung a handful of sand into the air, and replied, 'Equally numberless'" (Cassel).

⁽⁶⁾ **Impoverished.**—The LXX. render it, "was reduced to pauperism." The word implies flaccidity and helplessness, "as of a door hanging loose on its hinges, or a sere leaf shaking on a tree."

Cried unto the Lord.—See chaps. iii. 9, 15, iv. 3; Ps. cvii. 13; Hosea v. 15.

⁽⁸⁾ **A prophet.**—He is here left nameless, but Jewish legend says that he was Phinehas, the son of Eleazar. Their *Hagadah* (legendary information) generally enables them to name these nameless prophets. Thus they say that the prophet who came to Bethel was Iddo (1 Kings xiii.), and that the young man who anointed Jehu was Jonah.

Unto the children of Israel.—Perhaps assembled at some solemn feast, like the Passover.

I brought you up.—With the prophet's message compare chap. ii. 1—3; 2 Kings xvii. 36—38.

Out of the house of bondage.—A clear reference to Exod. xx. 2. (Comp. Ps. xliv. 1, 2.)

⁽¹⁰⁾ **The gods of the Amorites.**—See Josh. xxiv. 15; 1 Kings xxi. 26. As the Amorites seem to have been the highlanders of Palestine, and the most powerful of all the Canaanitish tribes, their name is sometimes used for that of all the Canaanites (Josh. xxiv. 15). Thus Heber says:—

"As when five monarchs led to Gibeon's fight
In rude array the harnessed Amorite."

No deliverance can be promised till repentance has begun. When the warnings of the prophet are heeded the mission of the deliverer begins.

⁽¹¹⁾ **There came an angel of the Lord.**—It is obviously absurd to suppose, as some have done, that a prophet is intended, like the one in chap. vi. 8. There the word is *Nabi,* here it is *Maleak-Jehovah,* as in chap. ii. 1. Josephus, when he says that "a phantasm stood by him in the shape of a youth," is merely actuated by his usual desire to give the story as classical an aspect as possible for his Gentile readers.

Under an oak. — Rather, *under the terebinth (haëlah)*:—some well-known tree beside the altar in Ophrath. (Comp. Gen. xxxv. 4.)

Ophrah.—This Ophrah was in Western Manasseh. There was another in Benjamin (Josh. xviii. 23). The name means "fawn," and the place is identified by Van de Velde with Erfai, near the north border of Ephraim.

Joash the Abi-ezrite.—Joash was the head of the family which descended from Abiezer, the son of Gilead, the son of Machir, the son of Manasseh (Num xxvi. 30; Josh. xvii. 2).

Gideon.—The name means "hewer."

Threshed wheat by the winepress.—Perhaps,

Gideon chosen   JUDGES, VI.   *as a Deliverer.*

wheat by the winepress, [1] to hide *it* from the Midianites. (12) And the angel of the LORD appeared unto him, and said unto him, The LORD *is* with thee, thou mighty man of valour. (13) And Gideon said unto him, Oh my Lord, if the LORD be with us, why then is all this befallen us? and where *be* all his miracles which our fathers told us of, saying, Did not the LORD bring us up from Egypt? but now the LORD hath forsaken us, and delivered us into the hands of the Midianites. (14) And the LORD looked upon him, and said, Go in this thy might, and thou shalt save Israel from the hand of the Midianites: have not I sent thee? (15) And he said unto him, Oh my Lord, wherewith shall I save Israel? behold, [2] my family *is* poor in Manasseh, and I *am* the least in my father's house. (16) And the LORD said unto him, Surely I will be with thee, and thou shalt smite the Midianites as one man. (17) And he said unto him, If now I have found grace in thy sight, then shew me a sign that thou talkest with me. (18) Depart not hence, I pray thee, until I come unto thee, and bring forth my [3] present, and set *it* before thee. And he said, I will tarry until thou come again.

[1] Heb., *to cause it to flee.*

[2] Or, *my thousand is the meanest.*

[3] Or, *meat offering.*

---

rather, *beating it out* than threshing it, as in Ruth ii. 17 (LXX., *rhabdizōn*). There would hardly be room for regular threshing in the confined space of a winepress, for wine-presses were vats sunk in the ground.

To hide it.—Literally, *to make it fly* (Exod. ix. 20). The threshing-floors—open circular places in the fields where the corn was trodden out by oxen—would naturally be the first places where an invading enemy would come to forage, as in 1 Sam. xxiii. 1.

(12) **The Lord is with thee, thou mighty man of valour.**—Three words in the Hebrew: *Jehovah immekā, Gibbōr*. It was once a salutation and a blessing. (Comp. Josh. i. 5; Luke i. 28). The address seems to show that Gideon had already distinguished himself by bravery in war; it can hardly refer to the vigour with which he was wielding the flail. Only the second and third of the three epochs of his life are narrated; but we see from scattered glimpses that he and his brothers had possibly taken part already in some battle on Mount Tabor—possibly even (so scanty are all our details, and so little certain is the chronology) in the struggle against the Canaanites (chaps. viii. 18, iv. 6); that he was a man of kingly presence, and had a youthful son; that he had numerous slaves, and even an armour-bearer (chaps. vii. 10, viii. 20).

(13) **Oh my Lord.**—The title is here only one of courtesy (*adoni*, like *kurie*; "sir" in John xx. 19, &c.), for Gideon only saw in the angel a stranger seated beneath the terebinth which overshadowed the rock-hewn winevat in which he was working.

Why then is all this befallen us?—See Deut. xxxi. 17: "Are not these evils come upon us, because our God is not among us?" The words "all this" sound like an echo of Gideon's gloomy thoughts—the thoughts of his country and his brothers, which had been darkening his soul amid his hard toil. "A mighty indication of God's favour to me that I am forced to use this wine-press instead of a threshing-floor" (Jos.).

Where be all his miracles?—See Ps. lxxviii. 12, lxxxix. 49.

The Lord hath forsaken us.—See Ps. xiii. 1; 2 Chron. xv. 2: "If ye forsake him, he will forsake you."

(14) **The Lord looked upon him.**—Here, as in Gen. xviii. 13, 17, 20, the angel speaks as the Lord, and it has been hence inferred that this angel was no created angel, but "the angel of the covenant," "the captain of the Lord's host." The only other possible conclusion is to say that the angel only speaks as the mouth of God (comp. Rev. xxi. 15, xxii. 6, 7).

No doubt the expression is here literal, but it involves the sense of favour and acceptance (Ps. xxv. 6; Vulg., *respexit*). The look inspired him with fresh force. The reason why the LXX. retain the phrase "the angel of the Lord" throughout is because they had the true Alexandrian dislike for all anthropomorphic expressions—*i.e.*, for all expressions which seemed to them to lower the invisible and unapproachable majesty of the Almighty.

Have not I sent thee?—See 1 Sam. xii. 11: "The Lord sent Jerubbaal."

(15) **Oh my Lord.**—Here our version deliberately adopts the reading *adoni*, as in verse 13, and the reason for this reading is that Gideon does not appear to have fully recognised the angel till his disappearance (verse 22). The reading of the Hebrew MSS., however, is *Adonai*, "Lord;" and if it be correct, we must suppose that Gideon addresses God as recognising that the message came from Him.

Wherewith shall I save Israel?—We repeatedly find this preliminary diffidence of humility in those whom God selects for His service. (Comp. Exod. iv. 1–13; 1 Sam. ix. 21; Isa. vi. 5; Jer. i. 6, 7, &c.)

My family.—Literally, *my thousand* (Exod. xviii. 21; 1 Sam. x. 19).

Poor.—Rather, *the meanest*, as is shown by the article "my thousand is *the* mean one," just as David is called "*the* little one" of his brethren (1 Sam. xviii. 14). What had caused this depression of the house of Abiezer we do not know, but it may have been due in part to the overweening pride of Ephraim.

I am the least in my father's house.—He was also the last of his father's house. All his brethren had been slain.

(16) **I will be with thee.**—See Exod. iii. 12; Josh. i. 5.

Smite the Midianites as one man.—See Chap xix. i. 8; Num. xiv. 15.

(17) **I have found grace in thy sight.**—A phrase found both in the Old and New Testament. (See Gen. vi. 8; Esth. v. 8.)

Shew me a sign that thou talkest with me.—Give me some clear proof that this is no mere vision, and that thy message is really from God, and portends me favour. (See Ps. lxxxvi. 17; Isa. vii. 11.)

Depart not hence.—Comp. 1 Kings xiii. 15.

My present.—My *minchah*. The word means first "an offering," but specially "an offering to God," as throughout the Book of Leviticus for the meat-offering of flour, &c. Hence the LXX. render it "the sacrifice": "and I will sacrifice before thee." Gideon seems, how-

(19) And Gideon went in, and made ready ¹a kid, and unleavened cakes of an ephah of flour: the flesh he put in a basket, and he put the broth in a pot, and brought it out unto him under the oak, and presented it. (20) And the angel of God said unto him, Take the flesh and the unleavened cakes, and lay them upon this rock, and pour out the broth. And he did so. (21) Then the angel of the LORD put forth the end of the staff that was in his hand, and touched the flesh and the unleavened cakes; and there rose up fire out of the rock, and consumed the flesh and the unleavened cakes. Then the angel of the LORD departed out of his sight. (22) And when Gideon perceived that he was an angel of the LORD, Gideon said, Alas, O Lord GOD! ᵃ for because I have seen an angel of the LORD face to face. (23) And the LORD said unto him, Peace be unto thee; fear not: thou shalt not die. (24) Then Gideon built an altar there unto the LORD, and called it ²Jehovah-shalom: unto this day it is yet in Ophrah of the Abi-ezrites. (25) And it came to pass the same night, that the LORD said unto him, Take thy father's young bullock, ³ even the second

¹ Heb., *a kid of the goats*.

ᵃ Ex. 33. 20; ch. 13. 22.

² That is, *The LORD send peace*.

³ Or, *and*.

---

ever, purposely to use a neutral word, suspecting, but not yet being convinced, that the stranger under the terebinth is something more than man. The desire to be hospitable may have mingled with his deepening sense of awe. (Comp. chap. xiii. 15; Gen. xviii. 6.)

(19) **Unleavened cakes.**—Because these were most quickly made, as by Lot for the angels, and by the Witch of Endor for Saul (Gen. xix. 3; 1 Sam. xxviii. 24).

Of an ephah of flour.—About 22¼ lbs. A homer would have been sufficient, as we see from Exod. xvi. 16. An ephah is *ten* homers; but Eastern hospitality considers nothing to be too lavish.

Presented it.—See chap. xiii. 19. The Vatican MS. of the LXX. renders it "approached," which is inadequate, and the other MSS. "worshipped," which is too strong. The word has a middle sense: "offered it with respect and reverence."

(20) **The angel of God.**—Here alone in the chapter called "the angel of Elohim" and not "of Jehovah."

Upon this rock.—Rather, *upon yonder crag*. The living rock (Exod. xx. 22) served well as an altar.

Pour out the broth.—Comp. Gen. xxxv. 14; Exod. xxx. 9; 1 Kings xviii. 34. In the first of these instances the "drink offering" is used as a libation; in the last Elijah pours the sea-water on the sacrifice, to show the impossibility of any deception. In 2 Macc. i. 20—36 Nehemiah pours the "thick water," called "Naphthaï," on the sacrifice, and when the sun shone "there was a great fire kindled, so that every man marvelled."

(21) **The staff that was in his hand.**—The ordinary accompaniment of an Eastern traveller (Gen. xxxii. 10; Matt. x. 10).

There rose up fire.—The common sign of God's presence and of His acceptance of an offering. (See Lev. ix. 24; 1 Kings xviii. 24; 1 Chron. xxi. 26; 2 Chron. vii. 1.) Water is brought out of the rock for the blessing of man, and fire to show the presence of God.

Departed.—It is not said, as in chap. xiii. 20, that he ascended in the flame.

(22) **When Gideon perceived.**—The last sign gave him a deeper sense than before of the grandeur of the messenger who had come to him.

Alas!—There is no need to supply "I shall die" at the end of the clause, but that this was the apprehension in Gideon's mind is shown by his cry of alarm.

For because.—Rather, *for to this end*. The belief that death or misfortune would be the result of looking on any Divine being was universal among the Jews. We find it in chap. xiii. 22; Gen. xvi. 13, xxxii. 30; Exod. xx. 19; Deut. v. 24, 25. He said, "Thou canst not see my face: for there shall no man see me, and live" (Exod. xxxiii. 20; Isa. vi. 5; Luke v. 8). The existence of the same belief among the heathen is shown in the legends of Semele, Actæon, Psyche, &c.; and Callimachus sings, "Whosoever, save by God's own choice, looks on any of the immortals, sees them only to his own great cost."

(23) **The Lord said unto him.**—How this intimation was given we are not told. The LXX. do not here change "the Lord" into "the angel of the Lord."

Peace be unto thee; fear not.—Comp. Dan. x. 7—9, 19; Ezek. i. 28—ii. 1; Mark xvi. 8; Luke i. 13, ii. 10; Rev. i. 17, &c.

(24) **Built an altar.**—Altars, like the altar Ed (Josh. xxii. 34), built by the Transjordanic tribes, were not always intended for purposes of sacrifices, but to witness some great event or Divine appearance (Gen. xxxii. 48, xxvi. 25; Exod. xvii. 15).

Jehovah-shalom.—"The Lord is peace." We find similar names in *Jehovah-jireh*, "the Lord will provide" (Gen. xxii. 14); *Jehovah-nissi*, "the Lord my banner" (Exod. xvii. 15); and *Jehovah-tsidkenn*, "the Lord our righteousness" (Jer. xxiii. 6). (Comp. Ezek. xlviii. 35.) See Pearson on the Creed, Art. ii.

(25) **The Lord said unto him.**—Luther rightly observes that by such expressions we are not at all meant to understand a voice in the air. It is useless, and therefore undesirable, to speculate as to the exact manner in which the Divine intimation came to him. When God speaks it is not possible for man to mistake His voice. It was distinctly revealed to Gideon that he must be an iconoclast before he could be a deliverer.

Even the second bullock.—It has been disputed whether the true rendering is "*even*" or "*and*." Ewald makes it mean "even," and explains *shani* (second) to mean "old" (*Gesch.* ii. 498). The LXX., the Vulgate, Luther, &c., render it "*and*," as in the margin of our version. This seems to be the right rendering; for (i.) the labour of two bullocks would not be too much for the task before Gideon; (ii.) a bullock (*shor*) of seven years old would hardly be called a *young* bullock: literally, "a heifer (*par*), son of an ox."

Of seven years old.—The Chaldee renders it, "which has been fattened for seven years," and there is very possibly an allusion to the seven years of the Midianite oppression (verse 1). The law had not pre-

bullock of seven years old, and throw down the altar of Baal that thy father hath, and cut down the grove that is by it: (26) and build an altar unto the LORD thy God upon the top of this ¹rock, ²in the ordered place, and take the second bullock, and offer a burnt sacrifice with the wood of the grove which thou shalt cut down. (27) Then Gideon took ten men of his servants, and did as the LORD had said unto him: and so it was, because he feared his father's household, and the men of the city, that he could not do it by day, that he did it by night. (28) And when the men of the city arose early in the morning, behold, the altar of Baal was cast down, and the grove was cut down that was by it, and the second bullock was offered upon the altar that was built. (29) And they said one to another, Who hath done this thing? And when they enquired and asked, they said, Gideon the son of

¹ Heb., *strong place.*

² Or, *in an orderly manner.*

---

scribed any fixed age for burnt offerings. Why the bullock is called "the second bullock" is very uncertain, but this minute and unexplained detail shows that we are not moving in the region of legend. The first bullock is said to belong to Joash, and we must, therefore, probably suppose that the second was Gideon's own. Possibly in this circumstance we may see an explanation of these minute directions, and the significance which they were intended to bear. The first bullock had been intended by Joash as a sacrifice to Baal, and is used in the destruction of his altar; the *second* had, perhaps, been reserved by Gideon as a sacrifice to the Lord when better times should come—a votive offering, which was being fattened for the longed-for day of deliverance. This bullock is sacrificed to Jehovah, and the fact that it, too, has been used for the destruction of the Canaanite idols is a sign to Gideon that the day for which he had hoped has come

Throw down.—As commanded in Exod. xxxii. 13; Deut. vii. 5.

The altar of Baal.—Rather, *of the Baal,* i.e., of that particular Phœnician idol which your father worships. (Comp. 1 Kings xvi. 32.)

That thy father hath.—This shows that Joash had joined with other Israelites in the apostasy, which had provoked the Midianite oppression. The words are literally, *which is to thy father,* as in the previous clause; and the pointed repetition of these words tends to confirm the conjecture mentioned in the previous note. It is called especially Joash's altar because, though used by the whole city (verse 28), he was the head of the Abi-ezrites.

The grove.—Rather, *the Asherah,* as in chap. iii. 7. Baal, "the sun," and the nature goddess Asherah —who is often confused with Astarte—were worshipped in conjunction (1 Kings xvi. 31, 32; 2 Kings xiii. 6, xviii. 16, xxiv. 3—6).

That is by it.—Rather, *that is upon it.* No mention is made of the image of Baal. Possibly the sun was worshipped at this altar without any idol, and the Asherah—perhaps a mere wooden pillar or gross emblem of phallic nature-worship—was placed upon it. It was the first law of God's worship that He was *one* God and therefore "jealous" against that easy combination of idolatries which is common to all forms of Polytheism. "Baal's altar must be overthrown before God's altar is built."

(26) **Of this rock.**—The word is not *selah,* as in verse 20, or *tsor,* as in verse 21, but *malioz,* "stronghold," probably the citadel of Ophrah. The LXX. render it as a proper name (*maoz*), or in some MSS., "on the top of this mountain." The word only occurs elsewhere in Hebrew poetry.

In the ordered place.—The margin reads, "in an orderly manner;" but probably neither version is quite correct. The Hebrew word is *bammaarachah* (comp. Lev. xxiv. 6; 2 Chron. ii. 4); and as the particle *be* is used of the *materials* with which a thing is built in 1 Kings xv. 22, some here render it, "with the materials." That the Jews themselves were not quite certain of the meaning appears from the various versions. The LXX. render it, "in the arrangement," and the Vulg., "on which you have before placed the sacrifice." It means "with the Asherah pillar hewed down, and split up into firewood." The Jews point out the peculiar features of this burnt offering: (1) It was not at Shiloh; (2) it was not offered by a priest; (3) it was offered at night; and (4) the fire was kindled with the unhallowed materials of an idol. The Divine command was, of course, more than sufficient to justify these merely ritual irregularities; and, indeed, it is clear that in these rude times, when the country was in the hands of the heathen, the Levitic order of worship became, for the time, impossible in many particulars. Prophets and those directly commissioned by heaven were tacitly regarded as exempt from the strict rules of outward ritual which were necessary for the mass of the nation.

(27) **Ten men of his servants.**—This shows Gideon's independent position, and also that he had tried to keep his own household free from the guilt of idolatry amid the all but universal defection.

His father's household.—The Abi-ezrites.

The men of the city.—Of whom many may have been of Canaanite race.

(28) **Arose early in the morning.**—The habits of Orientals are early, and Baal-worship may well have involved some adoration of the rising sun.

Cast down.—They observed three things: viz., the demolished altar of Baal; the stump of the destroyed Asherah; and a new altar, with the remains of a burnt offering smoking upon it.

The second bullock.—It has been supposed that Gideon offered both bullocks, the first as a burnt offering for his family, and the second for the nation. Nothing, however, is said of the fate of the young bullock; and, apart from express direction, Gideon may have hesitated to offer to the Lord a sacrifice which may have been devoted to Baal.

(29) **They said.**—We are not told that Gideon's servants betrayed his secret, but suspicion would naturally fall on so brave and prominent a worshipper of Jehovah as Gideon was; and it is rarely that actions which require so much effort and so many coadjutors can be kept secret. Gideon had proved himself to be what his name signifies—"a hewer." A man so brave and so patriotic must have stood almost alone among a cringing and apostate people.

Gideon accused. JUDGES, VI. *He is called Jerubbaal.*

Joash hath done this thing. (30) Then the men of the city said unto Joash, Bring out thy son, that he may die: because he hath cast down the altar of Baal, and because he hath cut down the grove that *was* by it. (31) And Joash said unto all that stood against him, Will ye plead for Baal? will ye save him? he that will plead for him, let him be put to death whilst *it is yet* morning: if he *be* a god, let him plead for himself, because *one* hath cast down his altar. (32) Therefore on that day he called him Jerubbaal, saying, Let Baal plead against him, because he hath thrown down his altar.

(33) Then all the Midianites and the Amalekites and the children of the east were gathered together, and went over, and pitched in the valley of Jezreel. (34) But the Spirit of the LORD¹ came upon Gideon, and he ᵃ blew a trumpet;

1 Heb., *clothed.*

a Num. 10. 3; ch. 3. 27.

---

(30) **The men of the city said unto Joash.**—It is difficult to conceive that these could have been Israelites (see on verse 27).

Bring out thy son, that he may die.—For the phrase, see Gen. xxxviii. 24; 1 Kings xxi. 10; Luke xix. 27.

(31) **Unto all that stood against him.**—The meaning of these words is very uncertain. They may mean, "to all that stood around."

Will ye plead for Baal?—The pronoun *ye* is very emphatic, being twice expressed in the Hebrew.

He that will plead for him, let him be put to death.—These words of Joash were extraordinarily bold and cunning. Possibly the brave act of his son may have roused his conscience, and Gideon may have told him that he had acted under Divine guidance. But he saves his son's life, not by excusing his act, but by feigning such a zeal for Baal as to denounce it as a blasphemous impiety to suppose that Baal will not avenge his own insult—an impiety *so* monstrous, that the man who was guilty of it should be at once put to death. Thus he made Baal-worship a plea for *not* avenging the insult offered to Baal. He was well aware that if he thus gained time, the fact that Baal did *not* interfere to protect himself from such fearful outrage would weigh powerfully with all his worshippers. Among idolaters the sight of an act of open contempt for their idol often shakes their superstitious reverence. Aristophanes, Persius, and Lucian sneer at the inability of Jupiter to defend his own temple, golden locks, and golden beard. When Olaf had the huge image of Odin destroyed, and when the high priest Coifi at Saxmundham, clad in armour and mounted on horseback (two things which were forbidden to a priest), rode up to the Saxon idols and hurled them down, the people, seeing that no thunder followed, but that all went on as well as usual, were quite ready to embrace Christianity.

Whilst it is yet morning.—The Hebrew is *ad habbōker* ("until morning"); LXX., *heōs prōi*, which may mean, "before to-morrow's sun has dawned." (*Antequan lux crastina veniat*, Vulg.; as also the Syriac, Arabic, and Chaldee.) It is a much more likely rendering than that of the E.V., for it implies, "Let us wait till to-morrow, to see whether Baal will avenge himself." Joash knew that in popular outbreaks procrastination means security.

If he be a god.—Compare the language of Elijah to the Baal and Asherah priests (1 Kings xviii. 21, 27).

(32) **He called him.**—Rather, *people called him, he got the name of.* The phrase is impersonal. (*Vocatus est*, Vulg.; *hiess man ihn*, Luther.)

Jerubbaal.—The name meant, "Let Baal strive;" but might also mean, "let it be striven with Baal," or "Baal's antagonist," and this gave the name a more ready currency. It is possible that the name may have been yet more allusive, since from the Palmyrene inscriptions it appears that there was a deity named *Jaribolos* (Mover's *Phönizier*, i. 434). If in 2 Sam. xi. 21 we find the name *Jerubbesheth*, this is only due to the fondness of the Jews for avoiding the names of idols, and changing them into terms of insult. It was thus that they literally interpreted the law of Exod. xxiii. 13 (comp. Josh. xxiii. 7). It was a part of that *contumelia numinum* with which the ancients charged them (Plin. xiii. 9). I have adduced other instances in *Language and Languages*, p. 232. (Longmans.) Bosheth means "shame," *i.e.*, "that shameful thing," and was a term of scorn for Baal (Hosea ix. 10; Jer. xi. 13). **We** have two other instances of this change in the case of the sons of Saul. Whether from a faithless syncretism, or a tendency to downright apostasy, he called one of his sons Esh-baal, *i.e.*, "man of Baal," and another Merib-baal (1 Chron. viii. 33, 34); but the Jews angrily and contemptuously changed these names into Ishbosheth and Mephibosheth (2 Sam. ii. 10, iv. 4). Ewald, however, and others have conjectured that both Baal and Bosheth may, at one time, have had more harmless associations (see especially 2 Sam. v. 20), and it appears that there was a Baal among the ancestors of Saul (1 Chron. viii. 30). The LXX. write the name Hierobalos; and Eusebius (Praep. Evang. i. 9), quoting from Philo Byblius, tells us that a Gentile historian named Sanchoniatho, of Berytus, whom he praises for his accuracy in Jewish history and geography, had received assistance "from Hierombalos, the priest of the god Iao." Some have supposed that this is an allusion to Gideon, under the name Jerubbaal.

(33) **Then all the Midianites.**—See verse 3. They came down for their usual annual raid to get the wheat which, doubtless, thousands besides Gideon had been gathering in and threshing in secret places as soon as it was barely ripe.

In the valley of Jezreel.—As the Philistines did afterwards (1 Sam. xxix. 1, 11). Crossing the fords near Bethshan, they were probably encamped, not in the broad part of the plain of Jezreel, but in the valley between Gilboa and Little Hermon. The word Jezreel means "God's sowing." (See Hosea ii. 22.)

(34) **Came upon Gideon.**—Literally, *clothed Gideon*. See chap. iii. 10 (Othniel); chap. xi. 29 (Jephthah); chap. xiii. 25 (Samson). This forcible figure is found also in 1 Chron. xii. 18 (Amasai); 2 Chron. xxiv. 20 (Zechariah); Ps. lix. 17; and in the New Testament, Luke xxiv. 49 (*endusēsthe*); Gal. iii. 27 (*enedusasthe Christon*); 1 Peter v. 5 (*enkombōsasthe*).

Blew a trumpet.—See chap. iii. 27. The trumpet is *shophar*, or ram's horn (LXX., *keratinē*). Gideon's call was two-fold: the first he had already obeyed in destroying the Baal-worship at Ophrah; he now

and Abi-ezer [1] was gathered after him. (35) And he sent messengers throughout all Manasseh; who also was gathered after him: and he sent messengers unto Asher, and unto Zebulun, and unto Naphtali; and they came up to meet them.

(36) And Gideon said unto God, If thou wilt save Israel by mine hand, as thou hast said, (37) behold, I will put a fleece of wool in the floor; *and* if the dew be on the fleece only, and *it be* dry upon all the earth *beside*, then shall I know that thou wilt save Israel by mine hand, as thou hast said. (38) And it was so: for he rose up early on the morrow, and thrust the fleece together, and wringed the dew out of the fleece, a bowl full of water. (39) And Gideon said unto God, *Let not thine anger be hot against me, and I will speak but this once: let me prove, I pray thee, but this once with the fleece; let it now be dry only upon the fleece, and upon all the ground let there be dew. (40) And God did so that night: for it was dry upon the fleece only, and there was dew on all the ground.

CHAPTER VII.—(1) Then Jerubbaal, who *is* Gideon, and all the people that *were* with him, rose up early, and

[1 Heb., *was called after him*.]
[a Gen. 18. 32.]

---

begins to obey the second, which was to deliver his country.

(35) **Throughout all Manasseh.**—The loyalty with which his own clan, the Abi-ezrites, rallied round him gave him a right to claim still wider support.

Asher.—This tribe, by faithfulness on this occasion, partly redeemed its honour from the tarnish attached of its former defection. This time Asher did not linger on the sands of Accho or the rocks of the Tyrian Ladder. Issachar, however, as before, " bowed his shoulder to the yoke." Perhaps the fact that the Plain of Jezreel, the battle-field of Palestine, was in the domains of this tribe, though not far from the border of Manasseh (Josh. xvii. 16), was unfavourable to their independence and strength. The fierce and haughty character of the tribe of Ephraim, and their jealousy of any leader who did not come from themselves, may have prevented Gideon from risking a rebuff by sending to them.

Zebulun, Naphtali.—These tribes again distinguished themselves, as in the campaign against Jabin (chap. v. 18).

(36) **If thou wilt save Israel.**—This diffidence and hesitation show the seriousness of the crisis. Gideon saw that by human strength alone he would be utterly helpless to repel the countless hosts of the marauders. He had already shown his faith, but now he needed fresh encouragement in his dangerous task.

(37) **A fleece of wool.**—In works of art this is sometimes represented as an entire sheepskin, probably from an erroneous explanation of the Vulgate, *Vellus lanae*, and from Luther's rendering, *ein Fell mit der Wolle*. But the English version is correct.

In the floor.—*i.e.*, on the open threshing-floor. (See Note on verse 11, and comp. Ps. i. 4; Hosea xiii. 3.)

If the dew be on the fleece only.—The very fact that this circumstance might be a purely natural result only shows the simple truthfulness of the narrative. Gideon would hardly have asked for *this* sign if he had been aware that, taken alone, it would be no sign of supernatural guidance. Bishop Hervey quotes Lord Bacon, who says (*Nat. Hist.*) that "Sailors have used every night to hang fleeces of wool on the sides of their ships towards the water, and they have crushed fresh water out of them in the morning." Every one must have noticed flocks of wool on the hedges, sparkling with dewdrops long after the dew on the leaves around them has evaporated. In Ps. lxxii. 6 (Prayer Book), "He shall come down like the rain *into a fleece of wool*,"

the Hebrew word is the same as here, and the ancient version takes it in the same sense (LXX., *epi pokon*; Vulg., *in vellus*); but perhaps the true sense is there "mown grass," as in Amos vii. 1 (*mowings*).

(38) **A bowl full of water.**—The word used for bowl is *sēphel*, as in v. 25.

(39) **Let not thine anger be hot against me, and I will speak but this once.**—The phrase is the same as in Gen. xviii. 32. The word rendered "anger" is literally *nose*. The Hebrew language is very picturesque in its metaphors, and "anger" is so often expressed by the dilatation of the nostrils, that "nose" became a graphic term for anger, as it is to this day in many Eastern languages. I have given some illustrations in my *Language and Languages*, p. 197, &c.

(40) **It was dry upon the fleece only.**—Such a result as this—not being in accordance with natural circumstances—could only have arisen from direct interposition. Besides the simple narrative, which tells us of these results as a sign granted to Gideon in accordance with his prayer, it is of course possible to allegorise the dew as the sign of God's grace, and to say that the first sign represented Israel as replenished with God's love when all was dry around (Hosea xiv. 5, "I will be as the dew unto Israel;" Micah v. 7, "Jacob shall be as the dew"); and the second, the fact that "God manifested himself in the weakness and forsaken condition of His people, while the nations were flourishing all around." Similarly St. Ambrose (*De Sp. Sanct.*, Prol. in i.) sees in the fleece full of dew the Hebrew nation hiding the mystery of Christ within itself, and in the dry fleece that mystery extended to all the world, but leaving the Hebrew nation dry. It would be equally possible to give a mystic significance to the threshing-floor, as a type of the universal Church (Matt. iii. 12, &c.). But these allegoric applications of simple narratives are, to say the least, precarious; nor is there much value in Ewald's comparison of the fleece to Gideon's character, cool amid the general passion, dry amid the general damp of fear.

VII.

1. The two camps. 2, 3. Gideon is bidden to dismiss all who are afraid. 4—8. The remaining ten thousand are tested by the way in which they drink at the fountain of Harod, and only 300 are left. 9—14. The Lord encourages Gideon by suffering him to overhear the narration of a dream in the camp of the Midianites. 15—18. Gideon's stratagem with lamps and torches.

pitched beside the well of Harod: so that the host of the Midianites were on the north side of them, by the hill of Moreh, in the valley. ⁽²⁾ And the LORD said unto Gideon, The people that *are* with thee *are* too many for me to give the Midianites into their hands, lest Israel vaunt themselves against me, saying, Mine own hand hath saved me. ⁽³⁾ Now therefore go to, proclaim in the ears of the people, saying, ᵃ Whosoever *is* fearful and afraid, let him return and depart early from mount Gilead. And there returned of the people twenty and two thousand; and there remained ten thousand.

⁽⁴⁾ And the LORD said unto Gideon, The people *are* yet *too* many; bring them down unto the water, and I will try them for thee there: and it shall be, *that* of whom I say unto thee, This shall go with thee, the same shall go with thee; and of whomsoever I say unto thee, This shall not go with thee, the same shall not go. ⁽⁵⁾ So he brought down the people unto the water: and the LORD said unto Gideon, Every one that lappeth of the water with his tongue, as a dog

ᵃ Deut. 20. 8; 1 Mac. 3. 56.

19—21. Panic and slaughter in the host of Midian. 22, 23. Their disastrous flight, and their pursuit by the Israelites. 24, 25. Capture of Oreb and Zeeb.

⁽¹⁾ **Jerubbaal, who is Gideon.**—Abraham, Sarah, Jacob, Joseph, Esther, Daniel, St. Paul, &c., are other instances of Scriptural characters who have two names.
Beside.—Rather, *above*. It would have been foolish and dangerous to encamp on the plain.
The well of Harod.—The name "Harod" means "trembling," with an obvious allusion to the timidity of the people (*chareed*, verse 3), to which there may be again an allusion in 1 Sam. xxviii. 5. The name is here used by anticipation. It occurs here only, though two *Harodites* are mentioned in 2 Sam. xxiii. 25; and the same fountain is obviously alluded to in 1 Sam. xxix. 1. From the fact that Gideon's camp was on Mount Gilboa there can be little doubt that Harod must be identified with the abundant and beautiful fountain at the foot of the hill now known as *Ain Jalûd*, or "the spring of Goliath," from a mistaken legend that this was the scene of the giant's death; or possibly from a mistaken corruption of the name Harod itself. There is another reading, " Endor" (comp. Ps. lxxxii. 10).
By the hill of Moreh.—Bertheau renders it, "stretching from the hill of Moreh into the valley." The only hill of this name which we know from other sources is that at Shechem (Gen. xii. 6; Deut. xi. 30), but that is twenty-five miles south of Mount Gilboa. There can be no doubt that Moreh is here used for Little Hermon, now Jebel ed-Duhy. The Vulgate renders it " of a lofty hill," perhaps to avoid a supposed difficulty. The word Moreh means "archer," and Little Hermon may have been called " the Archer's Hill," from the bowmen of the Amalekites.
⁽²⁾ **The people that are with thee are too many for me.**—This must have put the faith of Gideon to a severe trial, since the Midianites were 135,000 in number (chap. viii. 10), and Gideon's forces only 32,000 (verse 4).
Lest Israel vaunt themselves.—See Deut. viii. 17.
⁽³⁾ **Whosoever is fearful and afraid.**—This proclamation is in exact accordance with Deut. xx. 8 (and the other general directions in that chapter). It is there founded on the psychological observation that cowardice is exceedingly contagious, so that the presence of timid men in an army is a source of direct danger. The same rule was rigidly observed by the faithful Judas Maccabæus (1 Macc. iii. 56). Epaminondas, for the same reason, made the same proclamation before the battle of Leuctra. In this instance there was the further reason given in the previous verse. "The ancients had observed that even when there are many legions it is always the few that win the battle" (Tac. *Ann.* xiv. 36).
Depart early.—The Hebrew word *tsaphar* occurs here only. The Chaldee explains it by *tsiphra*, "in the morning;" and Abarband says that this injunction was given in order that they might not incur shame when they retired. The rendering "hastily" is explained to mean "like a bird" (*tsippor*). Keil, connecting it with an Arabic root, makes it mean " slink away by bye-paths." It seems to involve a shade of contempt—" Let him take himself off." (*Trolle* sich: Cassel.)
From mount Gilead.—This expression has caused great difficulty, but the Hebrew cannot mean "*to* mount Gilead," nor yet " *beyond* mount Gilead." The only tenable solution of the difficulty is, (1) to alter the text into " mount Gilboa" (Clericus), or from *meehar*, " from mount," to *maheer*, "speedily" (Michaelis); or (2) to suppose that " mount Gilead" was a rallying-cry of the Manassites in general, for Gilead was a son of Abiezer (Num. xxvi. 30, where Jeezer is merely an error); and hence was derived the name "Gilead" of the trans-Jordanic district which fell to the half-tribe of Manasseh (Josh. xvii. 5, 6). If this be a true conjecture, the phrase " let him depart from mount Gilead" means "let him leave the camp of Manasseh." One more conjecture is that Gilead is an ancient name for Gilboa (Schwarz).
There returned of the people twenty and two thousand.—No detail could more decisively show the terror struck into them by the sight of the Midianite host. They looked on them with the same alarm with which the Greeks, before Marathon, used to gaze on the Persian dress. It must not, however, be supposed that all the defaulters went straight to their homes. Doubtless many of them took part in the pursuit which made the victory decisive.
⁽⁴⁾ **The people are yet too many.**—A fresh trial of faith; but small numbers were essential for the method of victory by which God intended that the deliverance should be achieved.
Unto the water.—*i.e.*, to the spring of Harod.
I will try them.—The LXX. render it (*Cod. Vat.*), " I will *purge* them," as gold from dross, and this is the literal sense of the word (Isa. i. 25, xlviii. 10).
⁽⁵⁾ **Every one that lappeth of the water with his tongue.**—Josephus (*Antt.* v. 6, § 4) says that Gideon led them down to the spring in the fiercest heat

The Men who Lapped Water.   JUDGES, VII.   *Gideon Sent to the Midianite Host.*

lappeth, him shalt thou set by himself; likewise every one that boweth down upon his knees to drink. ⁽⁶⁾ And the number of them that lapped, *putting their hand to their mouth,* were three hundred men: but all the rest of the people bowed down upon their knees to drink water. ⁽⁷⁾ And the LORD said unto Gideon, By the three hundred men that lapped will I save you, and deliver the Midianites into thine hand: and let all the *other* people go every man unto his place. ⁽⁸⁾ So the people took victuals in their hand, and their trumpets: and he sent all *the rest of* Israel every man unto his tent, and retained those three hun-

¹ Or, *ranks by five.*

a ch. 6. 33.

dred men: and the host of Midian was beneath him in the valley.

⁽⁹⁾ And it came to pass the same night, that the LORD said unto him, Arise, get thee down unto the host; for I have delivered it into thine hand. ⁽¹⁰⁾ But if thou fear to go down, go thou with Phurah thy servant down to the host: ⁽¹¹⁾ and thou shalt hear what they say; and afterward shall thine hands be strengthened to go down unto the host. Then went he down with Phurah his servant unto the outside of the ¹ armed men that *were* in the host: ⁽¹²⁾ and the Midianites and the Amalekites and ^a all the children of the east lay along in the

---

of the noonday, and that he judged those to be the bravest who flung themselves down and drank, and those to be the cowards who lapped the water hastily and tumultuously. Theodoret also thinks that the Divine aid was shown by the fact that the greatest cowards were chosen. This may have been a Jewish legend (Hagadah); but it seems more reasonable to suppose that greater self-control would be shown by stooping and drinking the water out of the hand than by flinging themselves at full length to drink, which would be the natural instinct of a thirsty man. Rashi says that those who went down on their knees to drink were secret *idolators,* who had "bowed the knee to Baal" (1 Kings xix. 18).

As a dog lappeth.—Some commentators fancy that this is an allusion to Egyptian dogs, who, out of fear for the Nile crocodiles, only venture to lap the water while they are running along the banks.

⁽⁶⁾ **That lapped, putting their hand to their mouth.**—Literally, *licked with their hand to their mouth.*

All the rest of the people—*i.e.,* 9,700 men.

⁽⁷⁾ **Every man unto his place.**—*i.e.,* home, as in Num. xxiv. 11.

⁽⁸⁾ **So the people took victuals in their hand, and their trumpets.**—The E.V. here differs from most of the ancient versions (*e.g.,* the LXX., the Chaldee, the Vulgate, &c.), which render it, "And they (the 300) took the provisions and trumpets of the people (the 9,700) in their hands." This is also the explanation of Rabbi Kimchi, Levi Ben Gerson, &c. Provisions would be scarce in the neighbourhood of so vast a host, and it would be the desire of all that the brave 300 should be well supplied. The reason for taking 300 rams' horns would soon appear; and, indeed, but for this verse we might well wonder how each of the 300 came to have a horn of his own. Their "pitchers" were probably those in which the provisions had been carried.

⁽⁹⁾ **I have delivered it into thine hand.**—Comp. chap. iv. 14.

⁽¹⁰⁾ **To go down.**—If thou fear to make the attack at once, without still further encouragement. Let it be borne in mind that the courage required by Gideon and his men was in many respects far beyond that of the much more vaunted 300 at Thermopylæ—(1) because they were to *attack,* not to defend; (2) because they were to attack a host in the plain, not to hold a narrow valley; (3) because they had not a large number of allies and attendants with them, as the 300 Spartans had (Grote's *Greece,* v. 103, 121).

Phurah thy servant.—The name Phurah means "branch"; the word for "servant" is literally *boy,* but here means the armour-bearer. The classical reader will recall the night-raid of Diomedes and Odysseus into the camp of the Thracians at Troy (*Il.* x. 220, *et seqq.*).

⁽¹¹⁾ **And thou shalt hear what they say.**—This was the kind of omen known by the Jews as the Bath Kol, or "Daughter of a Voice." For a similar instance see 1 Sam. xiv. 6 (Jonathan and his armour-bearer). The word is used in slightly different senses. Sometimes it means a voice from heaven (Matt. iii. 17, &c.): such voices from heaven are described in the Talmud; sometimes it means the first chance words which a man hears after being bidden to look out for them as a Divine intimation; sometimes it means an actual echo (see Hamburger's *Talmud. Wörterb., s.v.*).

It was one of the four recognised modes of Divine direction (viz., prophets, dreams, Urim, and the Bath Kol, 1 Sam. xxviii. 6—15), but stood lowest of the four. It was also known to the Greeks, among whom the oracle sometimes bade a man to take as his answer the first casual words which he heard spoken on leaving the Temple.

The armed men.—Literally, *ranks by five,* the word (*chamooshim*) rendered "harnessed" in Ex. xiii. 18, "armed" in Josh. i. 14. Probably here the word means "foreposts," or "sentries"; and the Vulgate renders it "vigiliae." The LXX. curiously render it "to the beginning," (or in other MSS.) "to part of *the fifty,*" following a wrong punctuation.

That were in the host.—Probably "the host" was in some respects more like a temporary nomad migration, such as is so common among all wandering tribes. If so, it would not be by any means entirely composed of "armed men," but would, like the Persians under Xerxes, trail with it a vast mass of camp followers, &c., who would probably be encamped in the centre with the baggage.

⁽¹²⁾ **Like grasshoppers.**—Comp. chap. vi. 5; Num. xxii. 4, 5.

Their camels.—Which constitute the chief wealth of Arab tribes. "The multitude of camels shall cover thee, the dromedaries of Midian and Ephah" (Isa. lx. 6).

As the sand.—See Josh. xi. 4, and frequently in the Bible. (See Gen. xxii. 17; Isa. xlviii. 19, &c.)

valley like grasshoppers for multitude; and their camels *were* without number, as the sand by the sea side for multitude. (13) And when Gideon was come, behold, *there was* a man that told a dream unto his fellow, and said, Behold, I dreamed a dream, and, lo, a cake of barley bread tumbled into the host of Midian, and came unto a tent, and smote it that it fell, and overturned it, that the tent lay along. (14) And his fellow answered and said, This *is* nothing else save the sword of Gideon the son of Joash,

¹ Heb., *the breaking thereof.*

² Heb., *trumpets in the hand of all of them.*

³ Or, *firebrands, or, torches.*

a man of Israel: *for* into his hand hath God delivered Midian, and all the host. (15) And it was *so*, when Gideon heard the telling of the dream, and ¹ the interpretation thereof, that he worshipped, and returned into the host of Israel, and said, Arise; for the LORD hath delivered into your hand the host of Midian. (16) And he divided the three hundred men *into* three companies, and he put ²a trumpet in every man's hand, with empty pitchers, and ³ lamps within the pitchers.

---

(13) **Behold, I dreamed a dream.**—Since dreams, no less than the Bath Kol, were recognised channels for Divine intimations (Gen. xli. 12; Num. xii. 6; 1 Sam. xxviii. 6; Joel ii. 28, &c.), Gideon would feel doubly assured.

A cake.—The Hebrew word *tsalol* (or *tselil* in the Keri, or margin) is a word which occurs nowhere else. Rabbis Kimchi and Tanchun derive it from *tsalal*, "he tinkled" (as in *tselselim* and other names for musical instruments), or "he overshadowed." Neither derivation yields any sense. The Chaldee, Syriac, and Rashi render it "a cake baked on coals," and so, too, the LXX. (since such is the meaning of *magis*), the Vulgate (*panis subcinericius*), and Josephus (*maza krithinē*); this seems to be the true sense. Ewald makes it mean "a dry rattling crust." Niebuhr tells us that the desert Arabs thrust a round lump of dough into hot ashes, then take it out and eat it. (*Arab.*, p. 52.)

Of barley bread.—Josephus helps us to see the significance of the symbol by adding, "which men can (hardly) eat for its coarseness." It must be remembered that the Israelites had been reduced to such poverty by these raids that the mass of them would have nothing to subsist on but common barley bread such as that used to this day, with bitter complaints, by the Fellahin of Palestine. Among the Greeks also "barley bread" was proverbial as a kind of food hardly fit to be eaten, although such was the poverty which the Saviour bore for our sakes that it seems to have been the ordinary food of Him and His apostles (John vi. 9). "A cake of barley bread" would, therefore, naturally recall the thought of the Israelites, who were no doubt taunted by their enemies with being reduced to this food; just as Dr. Johnson defined oats as "food for horses in England, and for men in Scotland." Thus, in 1 Kings iv. 28, the "barley" is only for the horses and dromedaries. "If the Midianites were accustomed to call Gideon and his band 'eaters of barley bread,' as their successors, the haughty Bedouins, often do to ridicule their enemies, the application would be the more natural" (Thomson, *Land and Book*, p. 447). Josephus makes the soldier say that, as barley is the vilest of all seed, so the Israelites were the vilest of all the people of Asia.

Tumbled.—Rather, *was rolling itself.*

Unto a tent.—Rather, *into the tent*, which doubtless means (as Josephus says) the tent-royal—the tent of Zebah and Salmanah.

Smote it.—Perhaps the dream involved that it also (as Josephus says) "threw down the tents of all the soldiers."

Overturned it, that the tent lay along.—The latter words are involved in the first verb, and are only added for emphasis in accordance with the full picturesque Hebrew style. (Comp. "A bullock that hath horns and hoofs;" "I am a widow woman, and my husband is dead," &c.) This leisurely stateliness of description is found again and again in the Bible. (See my *Origin of Language*, p. 168, and *Brief Greek Syntax*, p. 200.)

(14) **This is nothing else save the sword of Gideon.**—The sort of dread which revealed itself by this instant interpretation of the dream shows that Israel was formidable even in its depression, doubtless because the nations around were well aware of the Divine aid by which they had so often struck terror into their enemies. The fact that this Bath Kol echoed the promise which Gideon had already received (verse 9) would give it additional force.

(15) **The interpretation thereof.**—Literally, *its breaking*. The word is a metaphor from breaking a nut—*enucleation*.

(16) **Into three companies.**—See chap. ix. 43. This division of the attacking force was a common stratagem. We find it in Job i. 17—"the Chaldæans made out three bands"—and it was adopted by Saul against the Ammonites (1 Sam. xi. 11), and by David against Absalom (2 Sam. xviii. 2). (Comp. Gen. xiv. 15.)

A trumpet.—Hearing the sound of three hundred rams' horns, the Midianites would naturally suppose that they were being attacked by three hundred *companies*.

Pitchers.—The Hebrew word is *caddim*, which is connected with our *cask*—the Greek, *kados*. They were of earthenware (verses 19, 20), (LXX., *hydrias*), and hence the Vulgate rendering (*lagenas*) is mistaken.

Lamps.—The LXX., perhaps, chose the word *lampadas* from its resemblance to *lappidim*—a principle by which they are often guided. *Lampadas*, however, here means not "lamps," but (as the margin gives it) "firebrands," or "torches." The best illustration is furnished by a passage in Lane's *Modern Egyptians* (I., chap. iv.), where he tells us that the zabit or agha of the police in Cairo carries with him at night "a torch, which burns, soon after it is lighted, without a flame, excepting when it is waved through the air, when it suddenly blazes forth: it therefore answers the same purpose as our dark lantern. The burning end is sometimes concealed in a small pot or jar, or covered with something else when not required to give light." These torches are simply of wood dipped in turpentine or pitch, which are not easily extinguished.

(17) And he said unto them, Look on me, and do likewise: and, behold, when I come to the outside of the camp, it shall be *that*, as I do, so shall ye do. (18) When I blow with a trumpet, I and all that *are* with me, then blow ye the trumpets also on every side of all the camp, and say, *The sword* of the LORD, and of Gideon.¹ (19) So Gideon, and the hundred men that *were* with him, came unto the outside of the camp in the beginning of the middle watch; and they had but newly set the watch: and they blew the trumpets, and brake the pitchers that *were* in² their hands. (20) And the three companies blew the trumpets, and brake the pitchers, and held the lamps in their left hands, and the trumpets in their right hands to blow *withal*: and they cried, The sword of the LORD, and of Gideon. (21) And they stood every man in his place round about the camp: and all the host ran, and cried, and fled. (22) And the three hundred blew the trumpets, and ᵃ the LORD set every man's sword against his fellow, even throughout all the host: and the host fled to Bethshittah ¹ in Zererath, *and* to ² the border of Abel-meholah, unto Tabbath.

a Isa. 9. 4.

¹ Or, *towards*.

² Heb., *lip*.

---

(17) **Look on me.**—He showed all the three hundred the way in which he wished them, at a given signal, to break the pitchers, wave the torches, and shout. The signal would be given by the one hundred whom he himself headed.

(18) **The sword of the Lord, and of Gideon.**—Literally, *for Jehovah and for Gideon* (LXX., Τῷ Κυρίῳ καὶ τῷ Γεδεών; Vulg., *clangite et conclamate Domino et Gedeoni*), but the particle *le* often has the meaning *of*, as in "a Psalm *to* David," which is found at the beginning of many Psalms. Our version here understands the word "sword" (*chereb*) from chap. vi. 20, as is also done in some MSS. of the LXX. It is better to omit it. The watchword and war-cry, then, resembles that given by Cyrus to his soldiers—"Zeus, our ally and leader" (*Cyrop*. iii. 28). The mention of his own name was only for the purpose of terrifying the enemy (verse 14).

(19) **The middle watch.**—The Jews anciently divided the night, from 6 P.M. to 6 A.M., into three watches (Exod. xiv. 24; 1 Sam. xi. 11). The subsequent division into four watches of three hours each was borrowed from the Romans (Matt. xiv. 25; Mark vi. 48). At the beginning of the middle watch—*i.e.*, soon after 10 at night—would be the time at which the host would be buried in their first sleep.

They had but newly set the watch.—Literally, *scarcely*—or, "just in rousing they roused the watch." The attack took place at the moment of confusion caused by changing the watch.

(20) **The trumpets in their right hands . . .**—Thus they were comparatively defenceless, though, if they had any armour at all, doubtless they could still hold the shield on the left arm, while the sword was girded on the thigh. The effect of the sudden crash and glare and shout upon the vast unwieldy host of the Bedouins may be imagined. Startled from sleep in a camp which, like Oriental camps, must have been most imperfectly protected and disciplined, they would see on every side blazing torches, and hear on every side the rams' horns and the terrible shout of the Israelites. (Comp. Tac. *Ann*. i. 68.) The instant result was a wild panic, such as that which seized the camp of the Persians at Platæa. The first thought which would rise in their minds would be that there was some treachery at work among the motley elements of the camp itself. Even a well-disciplined camp is liable to these outbursts of panic. One such occurred among the Greeks in the camp of the Ten Thousand during their retreat. To shame these groundless alarms, Klearchus next morning caused a reward to be proclaimed for any one who would give information "who had let the ass loose;" and this seems to have been a standing joke to shame Greek soldiers from such panics (Xen. *Anab*. ii. 2, 20). Several stratagems similar to that of Gideon are recorded in history. Polyænus, in his book on the "Art of War," tells us that Diœtas, when attacking Heræa, "ordered the trumpeters to stand apart, and sound a charge opposite to many quarters of the city; and that the Heræans, hearing the blasts of many trumpets from many directions, thinking that the whole region was crowded with enemies, abandoned the city." Frontinus also tells us that the Tarquinians and Faliscans tried to frighten the Romans with torches, and Minucius Rufus terrified the Scordisci by trumpets blown among the rocks (*Strateg*. ii. 3). Hannibal on one occasion escaped from Fabius Maximus by tying torches to the heads of cattle, and having them driven about the hills. The Druids waved torches to repel the attack of Suetonius Paulinus on the island of Mona (Tac. *Ann*. xiv. 30). An Arab chief (Bel-Arab) in the eighteenth century used trumpets in exactly the same manner as Gideon did on this occasion, and with the same success (Niebuhr, *Beschr. von Arabien*, p. 304). Ewald alludes to similar stratagems in Neapolitan and Hungarian wars, the latter so recently as 1849 (*Gesch*. ii. 503).

(21) **Ran, and cried, and fled.**—They ran about to discover the meaning of the trumpet-blast. Their "cries" were either the wail of despair (Vulg., *ululantes*), or a number of confused shouts and words of command (LXX., *esémainan*); their flight would be a natural result of the hopeless terror and confusion which prevailed. The word, however, in the Kethibh, or written text, is *yanîsoo*, which means "caused to fly"—*i.e.*, "carried off their tents," &c.

(22) **Blew the trumpets.**—They continued to blow incessantly, to add to the panic.

The Lord set every man's sword against his fellow.—We have an exact parallel to this in the mutual slaughter of the Ammonites, Moabites, and Edomites, when stricken with a similar panic before the army of Jehoshaphat, in 2 Chron. xx. 21, 22; and on a smaller scale in the camp of the Philistines at Gibeah (1 Sam. xiv.). The tremendous tragedy of their flight can only be appreciated by the vivid impression which it made on the national imagination (Isa. ix. 4, x. 26). In Ps. lxxxiii. 13, 14, it is compared to the whirling flight of dry weeds before a rush of flame and wind, recalling the Arab imprecation, "May you be whirled like the akûkb ('wild artichoke,' 'a wheel,'

(23) And the men of Israel gathered themselves together out of Naphtali, and out of Asher, and out of all Manasseh, and pursued after the Midianites. (24) And Gideon sent messengers throughout all mount Ephraim, saying, Come down against the Midianites, and take before them the waters unto Beth-barah and Jordan. Then all the men of Ephraim gathered themselves together, and took the waters unto Beth-barah and Jordan. (25) And they took ᵃ two princes of the Midianites, Oreb and Zeeb; and they slew Oreb upon the rock Oreb, and Zeeb they slew at the winepress of Zeeb, and pursued Midian, and brought the heads of Oreb and Zeeb to Gideon on the other side Jordan.

ᵃ Ps. 83. 11; Isa. 10. 26.

CHAPTER VIII.—(1) And the men of Ephraim said unto him,¹ Why hast thou served us thus, that thou calledst us not,

¹ Heb., What thing is this thou hast done unto us?

'a rolling thing') before the wind, until you are caught in the thorns or plunged into the sea" (Thomson, *Land and Book*, chap. xxxvi.).

Beth-shittah.—It should be rather, *Beth hash-shittah*, "the house of the acacia"—a place named from the trees which are still abundant in that neighbourhood, just as we have such names as Burntash, Sevenoaks, Nine Elms, &c. (Comp. Abel-Shittim, Num. xxxiii. 49; Josh. ii. 1.) If *Beth hash-shittah* was the village *Shultah*, with which Robinson (*Bibl. Reg.*, iii. 219) identifies it, some of the host must have fled northwards. It is improbable that it was another name for Beth-shean, though the LXX. have Bethsead in some MSS. It is, however, by no means unlikely that some of the marauders would fly towards the fords of the Jordan near Bethshean (comp. Jos. *Antt.* v. 6, § 5), as others fled south to the fords near Succoth, which lay to the south of the Jabbok.

In.—Rather, *towards*, as in the margin.

Zererath.—Rather, *Zererah*. This is omitted in the Vulgate; the LXX. have the extraordinary reading *Tagaragatha*, or in some MSS. "and he led them." The final *th* is no part of the name, but the mode of connecting the name with the particle of motion. Zererath is not again mentioned, but the distinction between the Hebrew letters *r* (ר) and *d* (ד) is so slight that the reading *Zeredath* may here be correct; and if so, it may be the Zeredath in Ephraim, which was the birthplace of Jeroboam (1 Kings xi. 26), and the Zaretan of Josh. iii. 16, 1 Kings vii. 46, which is sixteen miles north of Jericho.

To the border.—Literally, as in the margin, *to the lip*, or *brink*, as in Gen. xxii. 17; Exod. iv. 30. It does not, however, necessarily prove that Abelmeholah was on the edge of the Jordan valley.

Abel-meholah.—"The meadow of the dance." It was in Ephraim, and was the native place of Elisha (1 Kings xix. 16; see, too, 1 Kings iv. 12). Eusebius and Jerome place it ten miles south of Bethshean, at Wady Maleb. *Abel* means "a moist, grassy meadow."

Unto Tabbath.—Literally, *upon Tabbath*. The name seems to mean "famous," but the site is unknown, unless it be the remarkable bank called *Tubukhat Fahil*.

(23) **Out of Naphtali.**—Doubtless these pursuers were some of those who had left Gideon's camp before the victory. Those of Naphtali and Asher might pursue the flying Midianites northwards (if Beth-shittah is the same Shultah), and those of Manasseh might pursue those who fled southwards to the lower fords.

(24) **Throughout all mount Ephraim.**—He had not ventured to summon these haughty clansmen before his victory was assured.

Take before them the waters.—*i.e.*, "intercept their flight unto Beth-barah and Jordan." The "waters" are probably the marshes formed by streams which flow from the watershed of the hills of Ephraim into the Jordan.

Beth-barah.—"House of the waste," not, as Jerome says, "of the well." It can hardly be the Bethabara (house of the passage) of John i. 28, which seems to be too far south.

(25) **Oreb and Zeeb.**—The names mean "raven" and "wolf"; but these are common names for warriors among rude tribes, and there is no reason to look on them as names given in scorn by the Israelites. Such names are common among nomads. The capture of these two powerful sheykhs was the result of the second part of the battle, and was not accomplished without a terrible slaughter. See Ps. lxxiii. 9—12, where the word rendered "houses" of God should be "pastures" of God. It is remarkable that in this passage there seems to be almost an identification of the victories of Barak and Gideon, as though they were the result of one great combined movement. In the phrase "became as the dung of the earth" we see that tradition preserved a memory of the fertilisation of the ground by the dead bodies (see Note on chaps. iv. 16, v. 21). The completeness of the victory is also alluded to in Isa. ix. 4: "Thou hast broken the yoke of his burden . . . as in the day of Midian"; and Isa. x. 26. The brief narrative of Judges perhaps hardly enables us to realise the three acts of this great tragedy of Midianite slaughter —at Gilboa, the Fords, and Karkor.

Upon the rock Oreb.—Rather, *at the raven's rock*. Only again mentioned in Isa. x. 26: "according to the slaughter of Midian at the rock of Oreb." Reland identifies it with Orbo, near Bethshean.

To Gideon on the other side Jordan.—*i.e.*, beyond the Jordan ("trans fluenta Jordani," Vulg.). This notice is given by anticipation, for Gideon's crossing the Jordan is not mentioned till chap. viii. 4. The words literally mean "*from* beyond the Jordan," as the LXX. render them (*apo peran*), but this is idiomatic for "*from* one place to another," as in Josh. xiii. 22, &c.

VIII.

1—3. Gideon's soft answer to the Ephraimites. 4, 5. Unfaithfulness of Succoth. 6—9. And of Penuel. 10—12. Victory over Zebah and Zalmunna. 13—17. Gideon punishes Succoth and Penuel. 18—21. He puts Zebah and Zalmunna to death. 22, 23. The Israelites offer him the kingdom. 24—26. He requests the gift of the golden ear-rings of their prey; 27. And makes an ephod, which becomes a snare to Israel. 28—31. His last days, children, and death. 32—35. Apostasy and ingratitude of Israel.

(1) **The men of Ephraim.**—The arrogance of this tribe was derived partly from its strength, and partly

when thou wentest to fight with the Midianites? And they did chide with him ¹ sharply. ⁽²⁾ And he said unto them, What have I done now in comparison of you? *Is* not the gleaning of the grapes of Ephraim better than the vintage of Abi-ezer? ⁽³⁾ God hath delivered into your hands the princes of Midian, Oreb and Zeeb: and what was I able to do in comparison of you? Then their ² anger was abated toward him, when he had said that.

⁽⁴⁾ And Gideon came to Jordan, *and* passed over, he, and the three hundred men that *were* with him, faint, yet pursuing *them.* ⁽⁵⁾ And he said unto the men of Succoth, Give, I pray you, loaves of bread unto the people that follow me; for they *be* faint, and I am pursuing after Zebah and Zalmunna, kings of

¹ Heb., *strongly.*

² Heb., *spirit.*

---

from the memories of their ancestor Joseph; from the double portion which Joseph had received in memorial of his pre-eminence; from the fact that Jacob, in his blessing, had preferred the younger Ephraim before his elder brother, Manasseh; and from the almost regal influence which had been so long exercised by their tribesman, Joshua. This arrogance was destined, as we shall see later, to bring on them a terrible humiliation (chap. xii. 1). The complaint was fiercely urged, probably at the time when, by bringing the heads of Oreb and Zeeb (chap. vii. 25), they had proved both their power and their fidelity to the national cause. What they wanted was the acknowledgment of their claims (their *hegemony,* as the Greeks would have called it) by all the tribes.

They did chide with him sharply.—Literally, *with force* or *violence,* as in 1 Sam. ii. 16, so that the Vulg. renders it, *jurgantes fortiter, et prope vim inferentes,* "strongly reproaching him, and almost treating him with violence."

⁽²⁾ **What have I done now in comparison of you?**—Since Gideon was by no means a man of very placable and pacific disposition, we see the strong and noble self-control which this answer manifests. He was not in a condition, even had he wished it, to humble the fierce jealousy of this kindred tribe, as the more independent Jephthah, who was not so closely bound to them, did not scruple to do. He remembered that Zebah and Zalmunna were still safe; the Midianites were as yet by no means finally crushed. Patriotism as well as right feeling demanded that at such a moment there should be no civil discord.

Is not the gleaning . . . ?—The answer has a proverbial sound. (Comp. Deut. xxiv. 21.) It here implies that Ephraim, by a mere subsequent and secondary effort, had achieved more (as yet) than Gideon himself had done, or perhaps that the two bloody heads which were their "gleaning" were better than the "vintage" of obscure thousands. In admitting this, in waiving all self-assertion, Gideon was setting an example of the spirit which is content to suffer wrong, and to take less than its proper due (*elassousthai,* Thuc. i. 77). Nor was there any irony or wilful sacrifice of truth in his remark, for there can be no doubt that the Ephraimites had wrought a splendid victory (Isa. x. 26). The Chaldee renders it, "Are not the weak of the house of Ephraim better than the strong of the house of Abiezer?"

⁽³⁾ **Then their anger was abated towards him.**—The soft answer turned away wrath (Prov. xv. 1). The word for anger is *ruach,* "wind," or "spirit"— anger expressed by fierce breathing through the nostrils, "the *blast* of the terrible ones" (Isa. xxv. 4). (Comp. Eccl. x. 4: "If the spirit (*ruach*) of the ruler rise up against thee, leave not thy place; for *yielding pacifieth great offences.*") "Gideon's good words were as victorious as his sword."—Bp. Hall.

⁽⁴⁾ **And Gideon came to Jordan.**—This verse resumes the narrative of chap. vii. 23. The intermediate verses are an episode, and they are only here introduced by anticipation, in order to close the notice about the tribe of Ephraim.

And passed over.—Literally, *passing over;* but the English Version is correct as to the meaning, and it may be regarded as certain that Succoth was to the east of Jordan.

Faint, yet pursuing.—It may be doubted whether the usual application of these words is accurate. The LXX. render them, "fainting and hungry," and the Vulg., "and for weariness they could not overtake the fugitives." Literally it is, *faint* and *pursuing,* where the *and* is explanatory. "Exhausted and pursuing," *i. e.,* exhausted with pursuing (Keil). "In 1815 Mehemet Ali pursued the Arabs with such haste as to find himself without provisions, and had to be content with a few dates; but the result was a great success" (Ritter xii. 932).

⁽⁵⁾ **Unto the men of Succoth.**—The name Succoth means "booths," and the place was so named, or re-named, because of the "booths" which had been erected there by Jacob on his return from Padan-aram (Gen. xxxiii. 17; Josh. xiii. 27). It was situated in the tribe of Gad, and is probably the *Sukkot* mentioned by Burckhardt as on the east of Jordan, southwards from Bethshean. The "valley of Succoth" is mentioned in Pss. lx. 6, cviii. 7.

Loaves of bread.—The loaves are round cakes (*ciccar*). His request was a very modest and considerate one. He did not "requisition" them for forces, or for intelligence, or for any active assistance, because he might bear in mind that they on the east of Jordan would, in case of any reverse or incomplete victory, be the first to feel the vengeance of the neighbouring Midianites. But to supply bread to their own hungry countrymen, who were fighting their battles, was an act of common humanity which even the Midianites could not greatly resent.

Unto the people that follow me.—Literally, *which is at my feet,* as in chap. iv. 10.

Zebah and Zalmunna.—These were Emirs of higher rank than the Sheykhs Oreb and Zeeb, though Josephus calls them only "leaders," while he calls Oreb and Zeeb "kings." *Zebah* means "a sacrifice," perhaps one who had been consecrated by his parents to the gods of Midian. *Zalmunna* seems to mean "shadow of an exile," or, according to Gesenius, "shelter is denied him"—an unintelligible name, but perhaps due to some unknown incident. They are called "kings of Midian" (*malkai Midian*), as in Num. xxxi. 8. Oreb and Zeeb are only called *Sarim,* the same title as that given to Sisera (chap. iv. 2), and in the next verse to the elders of Succoth.

Midian. ⁽⁶⁾ And the princes of Succoth said, *Are* the hands of Zebah and Zalmunna now in thine hand, that we should give bread unto thine army? ⁽⁷⁾ And Gideon said, Therefore when the LORD hath delivered Zebah and Zalmunna into mine hand, then I will ¹tear your flesh with the thorns of the wilderness and with briers. ⁽⁸⁾ And he went up thence to Penuel, and spake unto them likewise: and the men of Penuel answered him as the men of Succoth had answered *him*. ⁽⁹⁾ And he spake also unto the men of Penuel, saying, When I come again in peace, I will break down this tower.

⁽¹⁰⁾ Now Zebah and Zalmunna *were* in Karkor, and their hosts with them, about fifteen thousand *men*, all that were left of all the hosts of the children of the east: for there fell ²an hundred and twenty thousand men that drew sword. ⁽¹¹⁾ And Gideon went up by the way of them that dwelt in tents on the east of

¹ Heb., *thresh.*

² Or, *an hundred and twenty thousand, every one drawing a sword.*

⁽⁶⁾ **Are the hands of Zebah and Zalmunna now in thine hand?**—Literally, *Is the fist (caph) of Zebah and Zalmunna now in thy hand (yad)*? The general meaning, of course, is clear: "Are you so completely victor as to secure us from the vengeance of these kings?" (Comp. 1 Kings xx. 11.) But what the exact shade of meaning is in this proverbial expression we do not know. Perhaps it is an allusion to the chained hands of captives. Nor do we know whether the tone of the elders of Succoth was one of derision or only of cowardice. In any case, they were guilty of inhumanity, want of faith, want of courage, and want of patriotism.

That we should give bread unto thine army. —They use the exaggerated term "army," as though to magnify the sacrifice required of them. Gideon had only said "my followers."

⁽⁷⁾ **And Gideon said.**—Notice in this verse the mixture of heroic faith and barbarous severity. It was this courage and faith (Heb. xi. 32) which ennobled Gideon and made him an example for all time. The ruthlessness of the punishment which he threatened to inflict belongs to the wild times in which he lived, and the very partial spiritual enlightenment of an imperfect dispensation (Matt. v. 21, xix. 8; Acts xvii. 30). It is no more to be held up for approval or imitation than his subsequent degeneracy; while, at the same time, Gideon must, of course, be only judged by such light as he had.

I will tear your flesh.—Rather, as in the margin, *I will thresh* (LXX., *aloēsō*, which is better than the other reading, *kataxanō*, "will card"; Vulg., *conteram*). It has usually been supposed that they were scourged with thorns, which would be terrible enough; but the verb here used is stronger, and seems to imply that they were "put under harrows" after thorns and briers had been scattered over them. That Gideon should inflict a retribution so awful cannot be surprising if we remember that David seems to have done the same (2 Sam. xii. 31; 1 Chron. xx. 3; Amos i. 3). In this case, however, the torture was more terrible, because it was inflicted not on aliens, but on Israelites. It must be borne in mind that every man is largely influenced by the spirit of the age in which he lives, and that in the East to this day there is (1) far greater indifference than there is in Europe to the value of human life, and (2) far greater insensibility to the infliction of pain; so that the mere mention of punishments inflicted, even in this century, by such men as Djezzar and Mehemet Ali makes the blood run cold. It was only by slow degrees that (as we can trace in the writings of their prophets and historians) the Jews learnt that deeper sense of humanity which it was certainly the object of many precepts of the Mosaic Law to inspire. The defections of Succoth and Penuel were even worse than that indifference of Meroz which had called forth the bitter curse of chap. v. 23.

With the thorns of the wilderness.—These thorns (*kotsim*) are again mentioned in Hosea x. 8. Rabbi Tanchum could not explain what plant was meant. It is not impossible (as Kimchi suggests) that the form of the punishment was suggested by another wild play on words; for *Succoth* (סכות), though it means "booths," suggests the idea of "thorns" (סלון).

Briers.—This word, *barkanim*, which the LXX. merely transliterate, occurs nowhere else. The Rabbis rightly understood it of thorny plants which grow among stones. Some modern Hebraists explain it to mean harrows formed of flints, deriving it from an obsolete word, *barkan*, "lightning" (see on chap. iv. 6), and so meaning "pyrites." In that case we must suppose that the elders were laid on some open area, and harrows set with flints driven over them.

⁽⁸⁾ **He went up thence to Penuel.**—Penuel was also in the tribe of Gad, on the heights above the Jordan valley, on the southern bank of the Jabbok. The name means "face of God," from Jacob's vision (Gen. xxxii. 30). It is again mentioned as a fortified town in 1 Kings xii. 25, but the site has not been identified.

⁽⁹⁾ **When I come again in peace.**—Comp. 1 Kings xxii. 27.

I will break down this tower.—If the strength of their citadel emboldened them to refuse food to Gideon's fainting warriors, it would also have helped to protect them against the dreaded vengeance of Midian.

⁽¹⁰⁾ **In Karkor.**—This was the scene of the third battle, or massacre. When they had reached this distant point they probably felt secure. *Karkor* means, "a safe enclosure," and the Vulg., regarding it as an ordinary noun, renders it, "where Zebah and Zalmunna were resting." Eusebius and Jerome identify Karkor with a fortress named *Karkaria*, a day's journey north of Petra; but, from the mention of Nobah and Jogbehah in the next verse, this seems to be too far south. If so, it may be *Karkagheisch*, not far from Amman (Rabbath Ammon), mentioned by Burckhardt. It was, however, "at a very great distance" (Jos., *Antt.* viii. 6, § 5) from the original scene of battle.

⁽¹¹⁾ **By the way of them that dwelt in tents.** —He seems to have taken a wide circuit, through some nomad district, leaving the main road, which runs through Nobah and Jogbehah, so as once more to make up for his inferior numbers (for there were still 15,000 left of these children of the East) by surprise and stratagem.

Nobah.—In Gilead, belonging to the half-tribe of Manasseh (Num. xxxii. 42). It was originally called Kenath, but the name was altered in honour of a

Nobah and Jogbehah, and smote the host: for the host was secure. ⁽¹²⁾ And when Zebah and Zalmunna fled, he pursued after them, and took the two kings of Midian, Zebah and Zalmunna, and¹ discomfited all the host.

⁽¹³⁾ And Gideon the son of Joash returned from battle before the sun *was* up, ⁽¹⁴⁾ and caught a young man of the men of Succoth, and enquired of him: and he² described unto him the princes of Succoth, and the elders thereof, *even* threescore and seventeen men. ⁽¹⁵⁾ And he came unto the men of Succoth, and said, Behold Zebah and Zalmunna, with whom ye did upbraid me, saying, Are the hands of Zebah and Zalmunna now in thine hand, that we should give bread unto thy men *that are* weary? ⁽¹⁶⁾ And he took the elders of the city, and thorns of the wilderness and briers, and with them he ³taught the men of Succoth. ⁽¹⁷⁾ And he beat down the tower of *a*Penuel, and slew the men of the city.

⁽¹⁸⁾ Then said he unto Zebah and Zalmunna, What manner of men *were they* whom ye slew at Tabor? And they answered, As thou *art*, so *were* they; each

---

1 Heb., *terrified.*

2 Heb., *writ.*

3 Heb., *made to know.*

a 1 Kings, 12. 25.

Manassite hero, who is otherwise unrecorded. Jewish tradition says that he was born in Egypt, and died during the passage of the Jordan (*Seder Olam Rabba*). The original name displaced its rival, for the site is now called *Kenâwat.*

Jogbehah.—In Gad (Num. xxxii. 34). It is not mentioned elsewhere, and has not been identified.

The host was secure.—They would have thought it most unlikely that the Israelites, with their mere handful of men, would pursue so large an army for so long a distance. They fancied themselves beyond the reach of pursuit because they mis-calculated the energy and powers of Gideon, who, not improbably, once more attacked them by night.

⁽¹²⁾ **When Zebah and Zalmunna fled.**—In Ps. lxxxiii. 13, 14, we, perhaps, find a reminiscence of the precipitancy of their flight, "like a wheel," *i.e.*, like a winged, rolling seed, and like stubble before a hurricane, and like a conflagration leaping through a mountain forest. (*Dict. of Bible*, s. v. *Oreb*; Stanley, i. 347.)

Discomfited.—Rather, as in the margin, *terrified*. It was the infliction of a second panic which enabled him to seize the two principal Emirs.

⁽¹³⁾ **Before the sun was up.**—If the rendering were certain, it would prove that he had made a night attack on Karkor; but it seems more probable that the words should be rendered "from the ascent of Heres," or "of Hechares," as in the LXX., Peshito, and Arabic. If so, it implies that he came round by some other road to attack Succoth. The word for "going up" is *maaleh*, as in *Maaleh Akrabbim*, "the ascent of scorpions" (see Note on i. 36), which is also applied to sunrise. (Gen. xix. 15.) It cannot possibly mean "before *sunset*" (*ehe die Sonne heraufgekommen war*), as Luther renders it, following the Chaldee and various Rabbis. The ordinary word for "sun" is *shemesh*, not *cheres*; but the latter word occurs in various names (see on chap. i. 35, ii. 9), which makes it perhaps more probable that this also is the name of some place. It might, indeed, be prudent for Gideon to desist from further pursuit when the dawn revealed the paucity and exhaustion of his followers; and in poetic style (Job. ix. 7) *cheres* may mean "sun," so that here the phrase *might* be an archaism, as *cheresah* is in chap. xiv. 18; but the preposition used (*min*) cannot mean "before." Aquila renders it "from the ascent *of the groves*," and Symmachus "of the *mountains*;" but this is only due to a defective reading.

⁽¹⁴⁾ **Caught a young man.**—Comp. chap. i. 24.

Described.—Marg. *writ*, *i.e.*: the boy wrote down their names (LXX., *apegrapsato*; Vulg., *descripsit*).

Threescore and seventeen.—Perhaps a sort of local Sanhedrin of Seventy (Num. xi. 16), with their presiding sheykhs. The number shows that Succoth was a place of considerable importance.

⁽¹⁵⁾ **That are weary.**—The addition of these words enhances the guilt of these elders, though the exhaustion of Gideon's force may have seemed to them a reason for alarm, lest their pursuit should end in rout.

⁽¹⁶⁾ **He taught.**—Literally, *made to know* (Prov. x. 9); but יְדַע may be a misreading for וַיָּדָשׁ, "he threshed," as in vi. 7. (Vulg. *contrivit atque comminuit*.)

The men of Succoth.—*i.e.*, the elders. Gideon would be well aware that in an Oriental city the mass of the people have no voice in any decision. Ewald takes it to mean, "By them (the slain elders) he taught the (rest of the) people of Succoth to be wiser in future."

⁽¹⁷⁾ **Beat down the tower.**—The importance of the place led to its re-fortification by Jeroboam (1 Kings xii. 25).

⁽¹⁸⁾ **Then said he unto Zebah and Zalmunna.** —They had been kept alive in order to answer the cowardly taunt of the elders of Succoth. There is nothing to show whether they were put to death at Succoth, as Josephus says, or taken to Ophrah (*Antt*. iv. 7, § 5). Perhaps Gideon reserved their death for the place where he had once lived with his brothers, whom they had slain.

What manner of men were they.—Literally, *where (are) the men?* Evidently this colloquy is only related in a shortened form, and Gideon's enquiry is rather a taunt or an expression of grief (Job xvii. 15), to show them that he now meant to act as the *goel*, or blood-avenger of his brothers. Up till this time these great chiefs seem to have been led in triumph on their camels, in all their splendid apparel and golden ornaments; and they may have thought, with Agag, that the bitterness of death was passed.

Whom ye slew at Tabor?—We are left completely in the dark as to the circumstances of this battle, or massacre. In the complete uncertainty as to all the details of the chronology, it is not impossible that Gideon's brothers—at least three or four in number—may have perished in Barak's "battle of Mount Tabor," or in some early struggle of this Midianite invasion, or in the first night battle (chap. vii. 22).

As thou . . . so they.—A similar phrase occurs in 1 Kings xxii. 4.

Resembled the children of a king.—We learn from this reference that Gideon added to his other gifts

one ¹resembled the children of a king. (19) And he said, They *were* my brethren, *even* the sons of my mother: *as* the LORD liveth, if ye had saved them alive, I would not slay you. (20) And he said unto Jether his firstborn, Up, *and* slay them. But the youth drew not his sword: for he feared, because he *was* yet a youth. (21) Then Zebah and Zalmunna said, Rise thou, and fall upon us: for as the man *is, so is* his strength. And Gideon arose, and slew Zebah and Zalmunna, and took away the ²ornaments that *were* on their camels' necks.

(22) Then the men of Israel said unto Gideon, Rule thou over us, both thou, and thy son, and thy son's son also: for thou hast delivered us from the hand of Midian. (23) And Gideon said unto them, I will not rule over you, neither shall my son rule over you: the LORD shall rule over you.

(24) And Gideon said unto them, I would desire a request of you, that ye would give me every man the earrings of his prey. (For they had golden earrings, because they *were* Ishmaelites.) (25) And they answered, We will willingly give *them*. And they spread a garment, and did cast therein every man the earrings of his prey. (26) And the weight of the golden earrings that he requested was a thousand and seven hundred *shekels* of gold; beside ornaments, and

1 Heb., *according to the form, &c.*

2 Or, *ornaments like the moon.*

---

that tall, commanding presence which always carried weight in early days (1 Sam. x. 24, xvi. 6, 7). In *Iliad*, iii. 170, Priam says: "One so fair I never saw with my eyes, nor so stately, for he is like a king" (βασιλῆι γὰρ ἀνδρὶ ἔοικεν).

(19) **The sons of my mother.**—Comp. Gen. xliii. 29.

As the Lord liveth.—Ruth iii. 13; 1 Sam. xiv. 41. (Comp. *Æn.* xii. 949.)

(20) **And he said unto Jether.**—By the *jus talionis*, as well as by every other consideration of that time, Gideon, as the last survivor of all his kingly brothers, would hold himself justified in putting his captives to death. Jether also would inherit the duties of goel (Num. xxxv. 12; 2 Sam. ii. 22, &c.), and Gideon desired both to train the boy to fearlessness against the enemies of Israel (Josh. x. 24, 25), to give him prestige, and to add to the disgrace of the Midianite kings. Again, Gideon must only be judged by the standard and the customs of his own day. (Comp. 1 Sam. xv. 33, Samuel and Agag; 2 Sam. i. 15, David and the Amalekite.) The name Jether is another form of Jethro, and means "pre-eminence."

(21) **Rise thou, and fall upon us.**—They deprecated the pain and shame of falling by the irresolute hands of a boy.

For as the man ... his strength.—Deut. xxxiii. 25, "As thy days, so shall thy strength be."

Ornaments.—*Saharonim*, "little moons," crescent-shaped ornaments of gold and silver, still in common use to decorate animals. Isa. iii. 18, "round tires like the moon." "Niveo *lunata monilia* dente" (*Stat. Theb.* ix. 689). After one of his battles Mohammed found a slain camel adorned with these *lunulæ* and with strings of emeralds. The Roman senators (for another reason) wore silver crescents on their shoes.

(22) **Then the men of Israel.**—Here begins the third great phase of the life of Gideon, which was characterised by his noblest act—the refusal of the kingdom—and his most questionable act—the setting up of a schismatic worship.

Rule thou over us.—The energy and success of Gideon had shown them the advantage of united action under one great leader; but they forgot that Gideon had received a special call from God, and that, as Gideon reminded them, God was their king. Yet no doubt the memory of Gideon deepened the wish which Samuel was afterwards commanded to grant (2 Sam. viii. 5—7, xii. 12, 17).

(23) **The Lord shall rule over you.**—Num. xxiii. 21; Deut. xxxiii. 5; 1 Sam. vi. 12. Gideon refused the splendid temptation of an hereditary crown, though, in strict accordance with Divine guidance, he was willing to be their judge (*Shaphat*, as in chaps. x. 2, 3, xii. 7, &c.). Cassel compares the remark of Washington when he accepted the Presidency, because he would "obey the voice of the people," saying that "no people could be more bound to acknowledge and adore the invisible hand which conducts the affairs of men than the people of the United States" (Marshall's *Life of Washington*, ii. 146). The day anticipated in Deut. xvii. 14—20 had not yet come. Up to this point "we feel all the goodness of Gideon. There is a sweetness and nobleness mingled with his courage, something of the past greatness of Joshua, something of the future grace of David." He reminds us in some respects of Henry V. of England, and Henry IV. of France.

(24) **I would desire a request of you.**—Not unfrequently the magnanimity which has just stood firm under a great trial succumbs to a weaker one. His case did not exactly resemble that of Abraham (Gen. xiv. 21—23), but it would have been better for his glory if he had acted in a similar spirit.

The earrings of his prey.—*Nezem* means a ring which, sometimes at least, was worn, especially by women, in the *nose* (Gen. xxiv. 47; Isa. iii. 21; Ezek. xvi. 12; Job xlii. 11). In the absence of any regular currency, these gold rings served as a sort of coinage.

Because they were Ishmaelites.—"Ishmaelites" and "Midianites" occur as convertible terms in Gen. xxxvii. 28.

(25) **We will willingly give.**—Literally, *giving, we will give.*

They spread.—Perhaps the true reading should be "*he* spread," as in the LXX. (*aneptuxe*).

A garment.—Perhaps his own upper garment (*Simlah*), or "a large general's cloke" (Ewald, *Gesch.* ii. 506).

(26) **A thousand and seven hundred shekels of gold.**—About seventy pounds of gold. This would imply a very large number of nose-rings or earrings (Gen. xxiv. 22), and therefore a slaughter of many leading Midianites. It is analogous to the "three bushels of knights' rings" which Mago carried to Car-

¹collars, and purple raiment that *was* on the kings of Midian, and beside the chains that *were* about their camels' necks. ⁽²⁷⁾ And Gideon made an ephod thereof, and put it in his city, *even* in Ophrah: and all Israel went thither a whoring after it: which thing became a snare unto Gideon, and to his house.

⁽²⁸⁾ Thus was Midian subdued before the children of Israel, so that they lifted up their heads no more. And the country was in quietness forty years in the days of Gideon.

⁽²⁹⁾ And Jerubbaal the son of Joash went and dwelt in his own house. ⁽³⁰⁾ And Gideon had threescore and ten sons ² of his body begotten: for he had many wives. ⁽³¹⁾ And his concubine that *was* in Shechem, she also bare him a son, whose name he ³ called Abimelech.

1 Or, *sweet jewels.*
2 Heb., *going out of his thigh.*
3 Heb., *set.*

---

thage, and emptied upon the floor of the Carthaginian Senate, after the massacre of the Romans at Cannae (Liv. xxiii. 12).

Beside ornaments.—Rather, *beside the golden crescents* (verse 21). Gideon seems to have gratified his love of vengeance, as goel, before he thought of booty.

And collars.—Marg., *sweet jewels*. Rather, *and the eardrops* (*netiphoth*, Isa. iii. 19). Wellsted, in his *Travels in Arabia*, says that the Arab women are accustomed to load themselves and their children with earrings and ornaments, of which he sometimes counted as many as fifteen on each side.

Purple raiment.—Comp. Exod. xxv. 4.

⁽²⁷⁾ **Made an ephod.**—The high priest's ephod is described in Exod. xxviii. 6—14. It was a sleeveless coat of gold, blue, purple, scarlet, and fine twined linen, with two ouches of onyx on the shoulders, bound by a rich girdle. Over this was worn the splendid jewelled breastplate, the *choshen*, with the Urim and Thummim. This ephod, with its "oracular gems," was by far the most splendid and sacred adjunct of worship which the Israelites possessed, and hence was regarded with extreme reverence (1 Sam. xxi. 9, xxiii. 9, xxx. 7), and it seems clear that Gideon's object was to provide a counter-attraction to it in an ephod of equally precious materials. It is a mistake to suppose (as Gesenius and others do, following the Peshito and Arabic versions) that *ephod* here means an idol or some unauthorised symbol of Jehovah, like the later "calves." Ewald, too (*Alterthümer*, p. 232), assumes that the "ephod" was really "a gilded household idol." But we may hope that Gideon, though guilty of a great sin, had not sunk quite so low as Jeroboam did. On the other hand, we cannot believe, with the Rabbis, that his ephod was only intended as a memorial of his victory.

Thereof.—This does not necessarily imply that he devoted the *whole* of his mass of gold to this object. In Hosea ii. 13, "decking herself with earrings" is one of the signs of the "days of Baalim." Hence, perhaps, an earring is called in Chaldee *kaddisha*.

Put it in his city, even in Ophrah.—This gives us a clue to Gideon's motive. Shiloh, the national sanctuary, was in the precincts of the fierce tribe of Ephraim, and Gideon may have been as anxious as Jeroboam afterwards was to keep some direct hold on the nation's worship, as one of the secrets of political power. It was the endeavour to secure and perpetuate by unworthy political expedients a power which he had received by Divine appointment.

Went thither a whoring after it.—The phrase and the metaphor are sufficiently explained in verse 33, chap. ii. 12; Lev. xvii. 17, xx. 5; Hosea i. 2; Ps. cvi. 39, &c. As to the nature of the schismatic service we are told nothing further. The strange narrative of chap. xviii. shows us the decadence and disintegration of the national worship at this period, and it is far from improbable that Gideon may have associated his worship with an unauthorised priesthood and modes of divination, if not with teraphim, &c. (chap. xvii. 5; Hosea iii. 4). (See on chap. xvii. 3.) His already existing altar (chap. vi. 24) would promote his object. It does not seem likely that the high priest at Shiloh would abandon the use of his own proper "breastplate of judgment;" but his acquiescence during this epoch of oppression would go far to invalidate his authority. If Hierombalos be meant for Jerubbaal (see chap. vi. 32), he is represented as having been *a priest*.

A snare.—The word used is *mokesh*, which implies not only a stumbling-block (LXX., *skandalon*), but also "a cause of ruin" (*in ruinam*., Vulg., Exod. x. 7, xxiii. 33).

⁽²⁸⁾ **Thus was Midian subdued.**—This verse closes the second great epoch of Gideon's life. The separate phrases occur in chaps. i. 2, iv. 23, 24, v. 31. The remaining verses of the chapter furnish us with a few notices of the third and last period of his life.

⁽²⁹⁾ **Jerubbaal.**—The sudden reversion to this name may be significant. Baal had failed to "plead," but nevertheless Gideon was not safe from idolatrous tendencies.

⁽³⁰⁾ **Threescore and ten sons.**—According to Oriental fashion, no account is taken of his daughters.

He had many wives.—It is clear that Gideon was a king in all but name. This is the most magnificent, but the least honourable, period of his career. In Deut. xvii. 17 it had been said of the future king, "Neither shall he multiply wives to himself . . . neither shall he greatly multiply to himself silver and gold." Polygamy was only adopted on a large scale by rulers (chaps. x. 4, xii. 9).

⁽³¹⁾ **His concubine that was in Shechem.**—In chap. ix. 18 she is contemptuously called his "maidservant." The sequel (chap. ix. 1—4) seems to show that she belonged to the Canaanite population of Shechem. If so, Gideon's conduct in making her a concubine was as much against the Mosaic law as that of Solomon, though it may have had the same colour of worldly expediency. But it is probable that the requirements of the Mosaic law were much better known in the reign of Solomon, when the priests had once more become influential, than they were in this anarchical period. This concubine exercised an influence sufficiently important to cause the preservation of her name by tradition—Drumah (Jos. *Antt.* v. 7, § 1).

Whose name he called Abimelech. — For "called" the margin has *set*. The phrase is not the ordinary one, and perhaps implies that Abimelech (Father-king—"a king, my father") was a surname given him by his father on observing his ambitious and boastful character. It seems more probable that the name was given by the Shechemites and his mother, and it may

Death of Gideon. **JUDGES, IX.** *Abimelech's Conspiracy.*

(32) And Gideon the son of Joash died in a good old age, and was buried in the sepulchre of Joash his father, in Ophrah of the Abi-ezrites.

(33) And it came to pass, as soon as Gideon was dead, that the children of Israel turned again, and went a whoring after Baalim, and made Baal-berith their god. (34) And the children of Israel remembered not the LORD their God, who had delivered them out of the hands of all their enemies on every side: (35) neither showed they kindness to the house of Jerubbaal, *namely*, Gideon, according to all the goodness which he had shewed unto Israel.

B.C. cir. 1209.

1 Heb., *What is good? whether*, &c.

CHAPTER IX.—(1) And Abimelech the son of Jerubbaal went to Shechem unto his mother's brethren, and communed with them, and with all the family of his mother's father, saying, (2) Speak, I pray you, in the ears of all the men of Shechem, ¹Whether *is* better for you, either that all the sons of Jerubbaal, *which are* threescore and ten

---

not have been without some influence for evil upon his ultimate career. The name has exactly the same significance as Padishah and Attalik, the title of the Khan of Bokhara (Gesenius). Being a well-understood dynastic title (Gen. xx.; Ps. xxxiv. title), it would be all the more significant. He was like a bad reproduction of Gideon, with the courage and energy of his father, but with none of his virtues.

(32) **And Gideon . . . died.**—Gideon died in peace and prosperity (Gen. xv. 15, xlix. 29, &c.), in a good old age (Job v. 26), but the evil seed which he had sown bore bitter fruit in the next generation.

(33) **Turned again.**—*Ad vomitum redierunt* (Serarius) (Ps. cvi. 13, 21).

Went a whoring after Baalim.—It was shown again afterwards, in the reign of Ahab, how rapidly unauthorised symbols degenerate into positive idolatry. After all that had occurred it would have been impossible for a Jerubbaal to be a Baal-worshipper, but his little deflection from the appointed ritual soon became a wide divergence from the national faith.

Made Baal-berith their god.—Baal-berith means "Lord of the covenant." The Hebrew will bear the meaning given it by some of the versions: "They made a covenant with Baal that he should be their god" (comp. Josh. xxiv. 25, Heb.), but the E.V. is probably correct. Bochart vainly tries to represent Baal-berith as some female deity of Berytus.

(34) **Remembered not the Lord their God.**—According to chap. ix. 46, they looked on Baal as their *Elohim*, and forgot that Jehovah was the one God. There was always this tendency to syncretism, as a half-way step towards idolatry. Zephaniah (chap. i. 5) mentions them "that swear by the Lord, and that swear by Malcham" (*i.e.*, Moloch), and the Samaritans "feared the Lord and served their own gods" (1 Kings xvii. 33).

(35) **Jerubbaal, namely, Gideon.**—It is doubtful whether we should not join the two names (Jerubbaal-Gideon), as in the Vulgate. Both names may be here allusive. He had been the "hewer" of their enemies and a "pleader against Baal," yet they were ungrateful to him, and apostatised to Baal-worship.

According to all the goodness which he had shewed unto Israel.—See chap. ix. 17, 18.

IX.

1—4. Abimelech induces the Shechemites to join in a conspiracy. 5, 6. The murder of his brethren. 7—15. Jotham's parable of the trees seeking to anoint a king. 16—20. Application of the parable. 21. Escape of Jotham. 22—25. Disaffection of the Shechemites, (26—29) fostered by Gaal. 30—33. Abimelech is informed of the conspiracy by Zebul. 34—40. Defeat of Gaal. 41—45. His assault on Shechem, which he captures and destroys. 46—49. Burning of the temple and fortress of Baal-berith. 50—52. Siege of Thebez. 53—55. Death of Abimelech. 56, 57. The moral of the episode.

(1) **And Abimelech.**—This narrative of the rise and fall of Abimelech, "the bramble king," is singularly vivid in many of its details, while at the same time material facts are so briefly touched upon that parts of the story must remain obscure. The general bearing of this graphic episode is to illustrate the slow, but certain, working of Divine retribution. The two main faults of the last phase of Gideon's career had been his polygamy and his dangerous tampering with unauthorised, if not idolatrous, worship. The retribution for both errors falls on his house. The agents of their overthrow are the kinsmen of his base-born son by a Canaanite mother. Abimelech seems to have taken his first steps very soon after Gideon's death. Doubtless he had long been secretly maturing his plans. The narrative bears on its surface inimitable marks of truthfulness. We can trace in the character of Abimelech a reflection of his father's courage and promptitude, overshadowed by elements which he must have drawn from his maternal origin.

Unto his mother's brethren.—His Canaanite kith and kin, who doubtless had great influence over the still powerful aboriginal element of the Shechemite population.

(2) **All the men of Shechem.**—Rather, *the lords* (*Baali*) *of Shechem*. These seem to be the same as "the men" (*anoshi*), or "lords (*Baali*) of the tower of Shechem," in verses 46, 49. It is by no means impossible that the Canaanites may have still held possession of the fortress, though the Israelites were nominally predominant in the town. At any rate, this particular title of "lords," as applied to the chief people of a town, seems to have been Canaanite rather than Hebrew: the "lords" of Jericho (Josh. xxiv. 11), the "lords" of Gibeah (Judges xxi. 5), of Keilah (1 Sam. xxiii. 11). The term is applied also to the Hittite Uriah (2 Sam. xi. 20). What is clear is that, as in so many other towns of Palestine at this epoch (see chap. i. 32, &c.), there was a mixed population living side by side in a sort of armed neutrality, though with a mutual dislike, which might at any time break out in tumults. The Israelites held much the same position in many towns as the Normans among the English during the years after the conquest. The Israelites had the upper hand, but they were fewer in numbers, and might easily

persons, reign over you, or that one reign over you? remember also that I *am* your bone and your flesh. ⁽³⁾ And his mother's brethren spake of him in the ears of all the men of Shechem all these words: and their hearts inclined ¹ to follow Abimelech; for they said, He *is* our brother. ⁽⁴⁾ And they gave him threescore and ten *pieces* of silver out of the house of Baal-berith, wherewith Abimelech hired vain and light persons, which followed him. ⁽⁵⁾ And he went unto his father's house at Ophrah, and slew his brethren the sons of Jerubbaal, *being* threescore and ten persons, upon one stone: notwithstanding yet Jotham the youngest son of Jerubbaal was left; for he hid himself.

⁽⁶⁾ And all the men of Shechem gathered together, and all the house of

¹ Heb., *after.*

---

be overborne at any particular point. It must be borne in mind also that Abimelech, as a Shechemite, would more easily win the adherence of the proud and jealous Ephraimites, who disliked the *hegemony* (see on chap. viii. 1, and comp. 2 Sam. xx. 1, 1 Kings xii. 16) which Manasseh had acquired from the victories of Gideon. The plans of Abimelech were deep-laid. In counsel no less than in courage—though both were so grievously mis-directed—he shows himself his father's son.

That all the sons of Jerubbaal . . . reign over you.—It seems to have been the merest calumny to suggest that they ever dreamt of making their father's influence hereditary in this sense. Gideon had expressly repudiated all wish and claim to exercise "rule" (*meshol*, viii. 23) of this kind. The remark of Abimelech is quite in the ancient spirit—

οὐκ ἀγαθὸν πολυκοιρανίη, εἷς κοίρανὸς ἔστω.

(Comp. Eur. *Suppl.* 410.)

Your bone and your flesh.—The same phrase is found in Gen. ii. 23, xxix. 14; 2 Sam. v. 1, xix. 12. He was akin to both the elements of the population: to the Ephraimites, from the place of his birth, or at any rate of his mother's residence; and to the Canaanites (as the whole narrative implies), from her blood. The plea was "like that of our Henry II., the first Norman son of a Saxon mother" (Stanley).

⁽⁴⁾ **Pieces.**—Rather, *shekels*, which is the word normally understood in similar phrases (chap. viii. 26). "Neither the citizens of Shechem nor the ignobly-ambitious bastard understood what true monarchy was, and still less what it ought to be in the commonwealth of Jehovah" (Ewald, ii. 389).

Out of the house of Baal-berith.—Like most temples in ancient days (*e.g.*, that of Venus on Mount Eryx, the Parthenon, and that of Jupiter Latiaris), this served at once as a sanctuary, a fortress, and a bank. Similarly the treasures amassed at Delphi enabled the three Phocian brothers, Phayllus, Phalaekus, and Onomarchus, to support the whole burden of the sacred war (Diodor. xvi. 30; comp. Thuc. i. 121, ii. 13). (Comp. also 1 Kings xv. 18.)

Vain and light persons.—These are exactly analogous to the *doruphoroi*—a body-guard of spear-bearers, which an ambitious Greek always hired as the first step to setting up a tyranny (Diog. Laert. i. 49). We find Jephthah (chap. xi. 3), and David (1 Sam. xxii. 2), and Absalom (2 Sam. xv. 1), and Rezon (1 Kings xi. 24), and Adonijah (1 Kings i. 5), and Jeroboam (2 Chron. xiii. 7) doing exactly the same thing. Who these "vain" persons were is best defined in 1 Sam. xxii. 2. They were like the *condottieri*, or free-lances. The word vain (*rikim*) is from the same root as Raca; it means *vauriens*. The word for "light persons" (*pochazim*) occurs in Gen. xlix. 4 (applied to Reuben) and Zeph. iii. 4. It is from a root which means to *boil over*.

⁽⁵⁾ **And he went unto his father's house at Ophrah.**—Probably, like Absalom, he seized the opportunity of some local or family feast at which all his brethren would be assembled (2 Sam. xiii. 23); it may even have been the anniversary of Gideon's vision.

Slew his brethren . . .—This is the first mention in Scripture of the hideous custom, which is so common among all Oriental despots, of anticipating conspiracies by destroying all their brothers and near kinsmen. (Comp. Pope, *Epistle to Arbuthnot*: "Bear, like the Turk, no brother near the throne.") There is little affection and much jealousy in polygamous households. Abimelech by this vile wickedness set a fatal precedent, which was followed again and again in the kingdom of Israel by Baasha (1 Kings xv. 29), Zimri (1 Kings xvi. 11), Jehu (2 Kings x. 7), and probably by other kings (2 Kings xv.); and by Athaliah (2 Kings xi. 1) in the kingdom of Judah. Herod also put to death most of his kinsmen, and some of his sons (see *Life of Christ*, i. 43). Seneca says, "Nec regna socium ferre, nec taedae sciunt"—nor realms nor weddings admit a sharer (*Agam.* 259).

Threescore and ten persons.—Jotham is counted in this number.

Upon one stone.—Perhaps on the rock on which was built Gideon's altar; at any rate, by some formal execution. How ruthlessly these murders were carried out we see from 2 Kings x. 7, and from many events in Eastern history. On one occasion, at a banquet in Damascus, Abdallah-Ebn-Ali murdered no less than *ninety* of the rival dynasty of the Ommiades.

⁽⁶⁾ **The house of Millo.**—It cannot be determined whether Beth Millo is here a proper name, or whether *Beth* means the family or inhabitants of Millo. The Chaldee renders Millo by "a rampart;" and if this be correct, the "house of the rampart" was perhaps the same as the "tower of Shechem" (verses 46—49). There was a Millo on Mount Zion (2 Sam. v. 9), which was also called a Beth Millo (2 Kings xii. 21).

Made Abimelech king.—He was the first Israelite who ever bore that name. It does not appear that his royalty was recognised beyond the limits of Ephraim. Gideon had not only refused the title of king (*melek*), but even the title of ruler (chap. viii. 23).

By the plain of the pillar that was in Shechem.—Rather, *near the terebinth of the monument which is in Shechem*. The word rendered "by" is *im*, which properly means *with*, but may mean "near," as in Gen. xxv. 11. The word rendered "the pillar" is *mutsabh*, which the Syriac and Arabic versions take for a proper name, and the Chaldee renders "the corn-field" or "statue." Luther renders it the "lofty oak," and the Vulg. follows another reading. The LXX. take it to mean "a garrison" (LXX., *stasis*), which is the meaning it has in Isa. xxix. 3; but as the terebinth is doubtless that under which Joshua had raised his

Abimelech made King.   JUDGES, IX.   *Jotham's Parable.*

Millo, and went, and made Abimelech king, [1] by the plain of the pillar that *was* in Shechem.

(7) And when they told *it* to Jotham, he went and stood in the top of mount Gerizim, and lifted up his voice, and cried, and said unto them, Hearken unto me, ye men of Shechem, that God may hearken unto you. (8) The trees went forth *on a time* to anoint a king over them; and they said unto the olive tree, Reign thou over us. (9) But the olive tree said unto them, Should I leave my fatness, wherewith by me they honour God and man, and [2] go to be promoted over the trees? (10) And the trees said to the fig tree, Come thou, *and* reign over us. (11) But the fig tree said unto them, Should I forsake my sweetness, and my good fruit, and go to be promoted over

[1] Or, *by the oak of the pillar.* See Josh. 24. 26.

[2] Or, *go up and down for* other *trees.*

"stone of witness" (Josh. xxiv. 26). the *mutsabh* is perhaps a name for this stone. If so, the neighbourhood of that pledge of faithfulness would add audacity to his acts. There can be little doubt that the terebinth was the celebrated tree under which Jacob had made his family bury their idolatrous earrings and amulets (Gen. xxxv. 4), and the terebinth (E.V., *plain*) of Moreh, near Shechem, under which Abraham had spread his tent and where he had built an altar (Gen. xii. 6). Possibly, too, it may be the "terebinth of the enchanters" mentioned in verse 37. The veneration attached to old trees lasted from generation to generation in Palestine, and the terebinth of Mamre was celebrated for a thousand years.

(7) **In the top of mount Gerizim.**—Unless Shechem is *not* to be identified with Neapolis (*Nablous*), and was rather, as De Saulcy decides, on Mount Gerizim itself, at a spot still marked by extensive ruins, it would have been entirely impossible for Jotham to be heard at Shechem from the actual summit of Gerizim. But over the town of Nablous is a precipitous rock, to the summit of which the name Gerizim might be loosely given. Here Jotham might well have stood; and it seems certain that in the still clear air of Palestine the rhythmical chant adopted by Orientals might be heard at a great distance. A traveller mentions that standing on Gerizim he heard the voice of a muleteer who was driving his mules down Mount Ebal; and on the very summit of Mount Gerizim I heard a shepherd holding a musical colloquy with another. who was out of sight on a distant hill. "The people in these mountainous countries are able from long practice to pitch their voices so as to be heard at distances almost incredible" (Thomson, *Land and Book*, p. 473).

And cried.—It may be asked how Jotham ventured to risk his life by thus upbraiding the Shechemites. No certain answer, but many probable ones, may be offered. At the summit of a precipitous crag far above the city, and on a hillside abounding with caverns and hiding-places, he would have sufficient start to have at least a chance of safety from any pursuit; or he may not have been without some followers and kindly partisans, who, now that the massacre of his brethren was over, would not be too willing to allow him to be hunted down. Indeed, the pathos of his opening appeal may have secured for him a favourable hearing. Josephus says that he seized an opportunity when there was a public feast at Shechem, and the whole multitude were gathered there. "He spoke like the bard of the English ode, and before the startled assembly below could reach the rocky pinnacle where he stood, he was gone" (Stanley, p. 352).

(8) **The trees went forth.**—As in this chapter we have the first Israelite "king" and the first massacre of brethren, so here we have the first fable. Fables are extremely popular in the East, where they are often current, under the name of the slave-philosopher Lokman, the counterpart of the Greek Æsop. But though there are many apologues and parables in Scripture (*e.g.,* in the Old Testament, "the ewe lamb," 2 Sam. xii. 1—4; Ps. lxxx.; Isa. v. 1—6, &c.), there is only one other "fable," and that is one closely akin to this (2 Kings xiv. 9). St. Paul, however, in I Cor. xii. 14—19, evidently refers to the ancient fable of Menenius Agrippa, about the belly and the members (Liv. ii. 30). A "fable" is a fanciful story, to inculcate prudential morality. In the Bible "trees" seem to be more favourite *dramatis personæ* than the talking birds and beasts of other nations. "Went forth" is the emphatic phrase "going, they went." The scenery immediately around Jotham would furnish the most striking illustration of his words, for it is more umbrageous than any other in Palestine, and Shechem seems to rise out of a sea of living verdure. The aptitude for keen and proverbial speech seems to have been hereditary in his family (Joash, chap. vi. 31; Gideon, chap. viii. 2).

To anoint a king over them.—Evidently the thought of royalty was, so to speak, "in the air." It is interesting to find from this passing allusion that the custom of "anointing" a king must have prevailed among the neighbouring nations.

Unto the olive tree.—This venerable and fruitful tree, with its silvery leaves and its grey cloud-like appearance at a distance, and its peculiar value and fruitfulness, would naturally first occur to the trees.

(9) **Wherewith by me they honour God and man.**—The words may also mean, *which gods and men honour in me* (Vulg., *quâ et dii utuntur et homines;* Luther, *meine Fettigheit, die beide Götter und menschen an mir preisen*; and so some MSS. of the LXX.). In either case the mention of gods or God (Elohim) refers to the use of oil in sacrifices, offerings, consecrations, &c. (Gen. xxviii. 18; Exod. xxx. 24; Lev. iii. 1—16). Oil is used in the East as one of the greatest luxuries, and also as possessing valuable medicinal properties. (James v. 15; Luke x. 34).

Go to be promoted over the trees.—The English Version here follows the Vulg. (*ut inter ligna promovear*); but the verb in the original is much finer and more picturesque, for it expresses the utter scorn of the olive for the proffered honour. The margin renders it, *go up and down for other trees,* but it means rather "float about" (LXX., *kineisthai;* Vulg., *agitari*); as Luther admirably renders it, *dass ich uber den Baümen Schwebe.* (Comp. Isa. xix. 1 (be moved), xxix. 9 (stagger); Lam. iv. 14 (wander), &c.) When, in 1868, the crown of Spain was offered to Ferdinand of Portugal, he is reported to have answered, *Pour moi pas si imbécile.*

(10) **The fig tree.**—The luscious fruit and broad green shade of the ancient fig would naturally make it the next choice; but it returns the same scornful answer.

The Application   JUDGES, IX.   *of the Parable*

the trees? ⁽¹²⁾ Then said the trees unto the vine, Come thou, *and* reign over us. ⁽¹³⁾ And the vine said unto them, Should I leave my wine, which cheereth God and man, and go to be promoted over the trees? ⁽¹⁴⁾ Then said all the trees unto the ¹bramble, Come thou, *and* reign over us. ⁽¹⁵⁾ And the bramble said unto the trees, If in truth ye anoint me king over you, *then* come *and* put your trust in my shadow: and if not, let fire come out of the bramble, and devour the cedars of Lebanon.

⁽¹⁶⁾ Now therefore, if ye have done truly and sincerely, in that ye have made Abimelech king, and if ye have dealt well with Jerubbaal and his house, and have done unto him according to the deserving of his hands; ⁽¹⁷⁾ (for my father fought for you, and ²adventured his life far, and delivered you out of the hand of Midian: ⁽¹⁸⁾ and ye are risen up against my father's house this day, and have slain his sons, threescore and ten persons, upon one stone, and have made Abimelech, the son of his maidservant, king over the men of Shechem, because he *is* your brother;) ⁽¹⁹⁾ if ye then have dealt truly and sincerely with Jerubbaal and with his house this day, *then* rejoice ye in Abimelech, and let him also rejoice in you: ⁽²⁰⁾ but if not, let fire come out from Abimelech, and devour the men of Shechem, and the house of Millo: and let fire come out from the men of Shechem, and from the house of Millo, and devour Abimelech.

⁽²¹⁾ And Jotham ran away, and fled, and went to Beer, and dwelt there, for fear of Abimelech his brother.

1 Or, *thistle*.

2 Heb., *cast his life*.

⁽¹²⁾ **Unto the vine.**—We might have felt surprise that the vine was not the first choice, but the low-growing, trellised vine, which needs support for its own tendrils, might seem less suitable. Indeed, ancient nations talked of the *female* vine—

"Or they led the vine
To wed her elm; she round about him flings
Her marriageable arms," &c.—*Milton*.

⁽¹³⁾ **My wine.**—The Hebrew word is *tirôsh*, which sometimes means merely "grape-cluster."

Which cheereth God and man.—For explanation, see Exod. xxix. 40; Num. xv. 7, 10, &c. If *Elohim* be here understood of God, the expression is, of course, of that simply anthropomorphic character which marks very ancient literature.

⁽¹⁴⁾ **Unto the bramble.**—Despairing of their best, they avail themselves of the unscrupulous ambition of their worst. The bramble—*atad*—is rather the rhamnus, or buckthorn, which Dioscorides calls the *Carthaginian atadin*. There seems to be an echo of this fable in Æsop's fable of the fox and the thorn, where the fox is dreadfully rent by taking hold of the thorn to save himself from a fall, and the thorn asks him what else he could expect.

Reign over us.—They seem to address the thorn in a less ceremonious imperative—not *mālekah*, as to the olive, or *mālekî*, as to the fig-tree and vine, but a mere blunt *melāk*!

⁽¹⁵⁾ **If in truth**—*i.e.*, with serious purpose. The bramble can hardly believe in the infatuation of the trees.

Put your trust in my shadow.—The mean leaves and bristling thorns of the rhamnus could afford no shadow to speak of, and even such as they could afford would be dangerous; but the fable is full of fine and biting irony.

If not.—The bramble is not only eager to be king, but has spiteful and dangerous threats—the counterpart of those, doubtless, which had been used by Abimelech — to discourage any withdrawal of the offer.

Let fire come out of the bramble.—Some suppose that there is a reference to the ancient notions of the spontaneous ignition of the boughs of the bramble when rubbed together by the wind. The allusion is far more probably to the use of thorns for fuel: Exod. xxii. 6, "If fire break out, and catch in thorns, so that the stacks of corn . . . be consumed;" Ps. lviii. 9, "Or ever your pots be made hot with thorns;" Eccles. vii. 6, "the crackling of thorns under a pot."

⁽¹⁶⁾ **Now therefore.**—Here follows the *epimuthion*, or application of the fable. Verses 16—18 are the *protasis* of the sentence, which is a long and parenthetic series of premisses; the conclusion, or *apodosis*, follows in verse 19.

If ye have done truly and sincerely.—A bitterly ironical supposition with a side glance at the phrase used by the bramble (see verse 15).

⁽¹⁷⁾ **Adventured his life.**—Literally, as in the margin, *cast his life* (LXX., ἔρριψε), like the Latin *projicere vitam* (Lucan, *Phars.* iv. 516). Comp. the reading *paraboleusamenos* in Phil. ii. 30 and Isa. liii. 12: "He hath poured out his soul unto death."

⁽¹⁸⁾ **Threescore and ten persons.**—See Note on verse 5.

The son of his maidservant.—The term is intentionally contemptuous. It seems clear from chaps. viii. 31, ix. 1, that she was not a slave, but even of high birth among the Canaanites.

⁽¹⁹⁾ **If ye then have dealt truly.**—If your conduct be just and right, I wish you all joy in it.

⁽²⁰⁾ **Let fire come out.**—The malediction is that they may perish by mutual destruction. It was exactly fulfilled (verses 45—49). So when Œetes is crucified as he had crucified Polykrates, Herodotus notices the similarity of the Nemesis (iii. 128).

⁽²¹⁾ **Went to Beer.**—Since Beer means a "well," it was naturally a very common name in Palestine. There is nothing to show with certainty whether this Beer is Beeroth in Benjamin (Josh. ix. 17), now *el Bireh*, about six miles north of Jerusalem (see my *Life of Christ*, i. 73), or the *el Bireh* which lies on the road from Shechem to Askalon, or the *el Bireh* near Endor. Probably Jotham would be safe anywhere in the territories of Judah or Benjamin, without going, as Ewald supposes, to the Beer of Num. xxi. 16, on the frontiers of Moab, an ancient sanctuary on the other side of the Jordan, possibly the Beer-elim (palm-well) of Isa. xv. 8.

(22) When Abimelech had reigned three years over Israel, (23) then God sent an evil spirit between Abimelech and the men of Shechem; and the men of Shechem dealt treacherously with Abimelech: (24) that the cruelty *done* to the threescore and ten sons of Jerubbaal might come, and their blood be laid upon Abimelech their brother, which slew them; and upon the men of Shechem, which ¹ aided him in the killing of his brethren. (25) And the men of Shechem set liers in wait for him in the top of the mountains, and they robbed all that came along that way by them: and it was told Abimelech. (26) And Gaal the son of Ebed came with his brethren, and went over to Shechem: and the men of Shechem put their confidence in him. (27) And they went out into the fields, and gathered their vineyards, and trode *the grapes*, and made ² merry, and went into the house of their god, and did eat and drink, and cursed Abimelech. (28) And Gaal the son of Ebed said, Who *is* Abimelech, and who *is* Shechem, that we should serve him? *is* not *he* the son of Jerubbaal? and Zebul his officer? serve the men of Hamor the father of Shechem: for why should we serve him? (29) And would to God this people were under my hand! then would I remove Abimelech. And he

B.C. cir. 1206.

1 Heb., *strengthened his hands to kill.*

2 Or, *songs.*

For fear of Abimelech.—Literally, *from the face of Abimelech.*

(22) **Had reigned.**—The verb is here *sûr*, not *malak*, as in verse 6; but whether the change of word is meant to be significant we cannot say.

Over Israel—*i.e.,* over all the Israelites who would accept his authority—mainly the central tribes.

(23) **An evil spirit.**—Whether the word used for spirit (*ruach*) is here meant to be *personal* or not we cannot say. Sometimes it seems to mean an evil being (1 Sam. xvi. 14), sometimes only an evil temper (Num. xiv. 24). The later Jews would have made little or no difference between the two, since they attributed almost every evil to the direct agency of demons.

Dealt treacherously.—The word is used for the beginning of a defection.

(24) **That the cruelty . . . might come . . . upon Abimelech.**—Scripture is always most emphatic in the recognition of the Divine Nemesis upon wickedness, especially upon bloodshed.

Their blood be laid upon Abimelech.—Comp. 1 Kings ii. 5, Matt. xxiii. 35, and the cry of the Jews in Matt. xxvii. 25.

(25) **Set liers in wait for him.**—The "for him" does not necessarily mean "to seize him," but to his disadvantage. The disaffection began to show itself, as has so often been the case in Palestine from the days of Saul to those of Herod, by the rise of brigandage, rendering all government precarious, and providing a refuge for all dangerous and discontented spirits. Josephus says that Abimelech was expelled from Shechem, and even from the tribe of Ephraim (*Antt.* v. 1, § 3).

In the top of the mountains.—Especially Ebal and Gerizim.

(26) **Gaal the son of Ebed.**—We are not told any further who he was; but the context leads us to infer that he was one of these freebooters, and probably belonged to the Canaanite population. His "brethren" may have formed the nucleus of a marauding band. Josephus says he was "a certain chief, with his soldiers and kinsmen." For Ebed some MSS. and versions read Eber, and some Jobel. "Gaal Ben-Ebed" ("loathing son of a slave") sounds like some contemptuous distortion of his real name.

Went over to Shechem.—Possibly he had been practising brigandage on the other side of the Jordan.

(27) **And made merry.**—The vintage was the most joyous festival of the year (Isa. xvi. 9, 10; Jer. xxv. 30).

The word rendered "merry" is *hillûlim*, and occurs only here and in Lev. xix. 24, where it is rendered "praise." Some render it "offered thank-offerings." The Chaldee renders it "dances," and the Vulg. "choirs of singers." The word evidently involves the notion of triumphant songs (LXX., *elloulim* and *chorous*).

Of their god.—Baal-berith.

Did eat and drink.—In some public feast, such as often took place in idol temples (chap. xvi. 23; 2 Kings xix. 37; 1 Cor. viii. 10). It is evident that this was a sort of heathen analogue of the Feast of Ingathering. The apostasy would be facilitated by a transference of customs of worship from Elohim to Baal.

Cursed Abimelech.—Rather, *abused*. This seems to have been the first outburst of rebellion among the general population, and Gaal took advantage of it.

(28) **Who is Abimelech?**—This is obviously contemptuous, like "Who is David? and who is the son of Jesse?" in 1 Sam. xxv. 10.

Who is Shechem?—The meaning of this clause is very obscure. It can hardly be a *contrast* between the insignificance of Abimelech and the grandeur of Shechem (Vulg., *quæ est Shechem?*). Some say that "Shechem" means "Abimelech;" but there is no trace of kings assuming the name of the place over which they rule, nor does the LXX. mend matters much by interpolating the words, "who is *the son of* Shechem?"

The son of Jerubbaal?—And, therefore, on the father's side, disconnected both with Ephraimites and Canaanites; and the Baal-fighter's son has no claim on Baal-worshippers.

And Zebul his officer?—We are not even under the rule of Abimelech, but of his underling.

Serve the men of Hamor.—Here the LXX., Vulg., and other versions adopt a different punctuation and a different reading. But there is no reason to alter the text. The Canaanites were powerful; the Ephraimites had apostatised to their religion; even Abimelech bears a Canaanite name (Gen. xxvi. 1), and owed his power to his Hivite blood. Gaal says in effect. "Why should we serve this son of an upstart alien when we might return to the allegiance of the descendants of our old native prince Hamor, whose son Shechem was the *hero eponymos* of the city?" (Gen. xxxiii. 19; Josh. xxiv. 32).

(29) **Would to God this people were under my hand!**—Comp. 2 Sam. xv. 4.

And he said to Abimelech.—The "he said" may be the impersonal idiom (comp. Josh. vii. 26, &c.),

said to Abimelech, Increase thine army, and come out. ⁽³⁰⁾ And when Zebul the ruler of the city heard the words of Gaal the son of Ebed, his anger was ¹kindled. ⁽³¹⁾ And he sent messengers unto Abimelech ²privily, saying, Behold, Gaal the son of Ebed and his brethren be come to Shechem; and, behold, they fortify the city against thee. ⁽³²⁾ Now therefore up by night, thou and the people that *is* with thee, and lie in wait in the field: ⁽³³⁾ and it shall be, *that* in the morning, as soon as the sun is up, thou shalt rise early, and set upon the city: and, behold, *when* he and the people that *is* with him come out against thee, then mayest thou do to them ³as thou shalt find occasion.

⁽³⁴⁾ And Abimelech rose up, and all the people that *were* with him, by night, and they laid wait against Shechem in four companies. ⁽³⁵⁾ And Gaal the son of Ebed went out, and stood in the entering of the gate of the city: and Abimelech rose up, and the people that *were* with him, from lying in wait. ⁽³⁶⁾ And when Gaal saw the people, he said to Zebul, Behold, there come people down from the top of the mountains. And Zebul said unto him, Thou seest the shadow of the mountains as *if they were* men. ⁽³⁷⁾ And Gaal spake again and said, See there come people down by the ⁴ middle of the land, and another company come along by the plain of ⁵Meonenim. ⁽³⁸⁾ Then said Zebul unto him, Where *is* now thy mouth, wherewith thou saidst, Who *is* Abimelech, that we should serve him? *is* not this the people that thou hast despised? go out, I pray now, and fight with them. ⁽³⁹⁾ And Gaal went out before the men of Shechem, and fought with Abimelech. ⁽⁴⁰⁾ And Abimelech chased him, and he fled before him, and many were overthrown *and* wounded, *even* unto the entering of the gate.

1 Or, *hot.*

2 Heb., *craftily, or, to Tormah.*

3 Heb., *as thine hand shall find.*

4 Heb., *navel.*

5 Or, *The regarders of times.*

---

meaning "it was told" (Vulg., *Dictum est*). It is less likely that "he" means Zebul, or that it is Gaal's drunken vaunt to the absent Abimelech. Another reading is, "And I would say to Abimelech," &c.

⁽³⁰⁾ **The ruler of the city.**—The word *sar* seems to imply that he was the military commandant.

⁽³¹⁾ **Privily.**—The Hebrew is *betormah*, which may mean "to Tormah," or Arumah, where Abimelech was living (verse 41). The word occurs nowhere else, and the versions differ (LXX., *in secret*; Cod. B, with *gifts*; Cod. A reading *batherumah*). Whether "craftily" be the right rendering or not, it is clear that the message was a secret one, for Zebul dissembled his anger until he was strong enough to throw off the mask.

They fortify.—Rather, perhaps, *they tyrannise over the city because of thee*.

⁽³²⁾ **Lie in wait in the field.**—To surprise the Shechemites when they went out to finish their vintage operations, which they would do securely under the protection of Gaal's forces.

⁽³³⁾ **As thou shalt find occasion.**—Literally, as in the margin, *as thine hand shall find*, as in 1 Sam. x. 7, xxv. 8.

⁽³⁴⁾ **Four companies.** — Literally, *four heads*. (Comp. chap. vii. 16.)

⁽³⁵⁾ **Stood in the entering of the gate of the city.**—This was the ordinary station of kings, judges, &c.; but Gaal only seems to have gone there in order to keep a look-out (Josh. xx. 4).

⁽³⁶⁾ **He said to Zebul.**—The narrative is too brief to enable us to understand clearly the somewhat anomalous position of Zebul. He seems to have been deposed from his office, and yet to have retained the confidence of Gaal and the Shechemites.

Thou seest the shadow of the mountains.—The shadow advancing as the sun rose. It was, of course, Zebul's object to keep Gaal deceived as long as possible. But it is evident that Gaal's suspicions were by no means lulled. Zebul treats him almost as if he were still suffering from the intoxication of his vaunting feast.

⁽³⁷⁾ **By the middle of the land.**—Literally, *by the navel of the land*. Probably the expression means some gently-swelling hill, but it perplexed the translators. The Chaldee renders it "the strength," and the Syriac "the fortification of the land." In Ezek. xxxviii. 12 it is rendered "in the midst of the land." The LXX. here have the strangely blundering addition, "by sea."

Another company.—Literally, *one head* (Vulg., *cuneus unus*).

By the plain of Meonenim.—Rather, *from the way to the Enchanters' Terebinth* (LXX., "of the oak of those that look away;" Vulg., "which looks toward the oak;" Luther, more correctly, "*zur Zaubereiche*"). *Meonen* in Lev. xix. 28 is rendered "enchantment," and means especially the kind of "enchantment" which affects the eye (the "evil eye," &c.), and therefore implies the use of amulets, &c. Hence, though the terebinth is nowhere else mentioned by this particular name, it is at least a probable conjecture that it may be the ancient tree under which Jacob's family had buried their idolatrous amulets (Gen. xxxv. 4).

⁽³⁸⁾ **Where is now thy mouth . . . ?**—"Mouth" here means *boastfulness*. This is usually taken as a bitter taunt, as though Zebul could now safely throw off his deceitful acquiescence in Gaal's plans. It may be so, for the narrative gives us no further details; but unless Zebul was in some way secured by his own adherents from Gaal's immediate vengeance, it seems better to take it as a sort of expostulation against Gaal's past rashness.

⁽³⁹⁾ **Before the men of Shechem.**—Not merely "in the presence of the Shechemites," as some of the versions understand it, but as leader of the "lords" of Shechem. (Comp. verse 23.)

⁽⁴⁰⁾ **Abimelech chased him . . .**—He won a complete victory; but Gaal and his forces were able to secure themselves in Shechem. They succeeded in closing the gates against Abimelech, but only at the cost of many lives.

(41) And Abimelech dwelt at Arumah: and Zebul thrust out Gaal and his brethren, that they should not dwell in Shechem. (42) And it came to pass on the morrow, that the people went out into the field; and they told Abimelech. (43) And he took the people, and divided them into three companies, and laid wait in the field, and looked, and, behold, the people *were* come forth out of the city; and he rose up against them, and smote them. (44) And Abimelech, and the company that *was* with him, rushed forward, and stood in the entering of the gate of the city: and the two *other* companies ran upon all *the people* that *were* in the fields, and slew them. (45) And Abimelech fought against the city all that day; and he took the city, and slew the people that *was* therein, and beat down the city, and sowed it with salt.

(46) And when all the men of the tower of Shechem heard *that*, they entered into an hold of the house of the god Berith. (47) And it was told Abimelech, that all the men of the tower of Shechem were gathered together. (48) And Abimelech gat him up to mount Zalmon, he and all the people that *were* with him; and Abimelech took an axe in his hand, and cut down a bough from the trees, and took it, and laid *it* on his shoulder, and said unto the people that *were* with him, What ye have seen [1] me do, make haste, *and* do as I *have done*. (49) And all the people likewise cut down every man his bough, and followed Abimelech, and put *them* to the hold, and set the hold on fire upon them; so that all the men of the tower of Shechem died also, about a thousand men and women.

(50) Then went Abimelech to Thebez,

[1] Heb., *I have done*.

---

(41) **Dwelt at Arumah.**—Eusebius and Jerome identify Arumah with Remphis or Arimathea, near Lydda, which is most improbable on every ground. It is clearly some place at no great distance from Shechem which he was still determined to punish.

Zebul thrust out Gaal and his brethren.—Josephus seems here to supply us with the proper clue, for he says that Zebul accused Gaal to the Shechemites of military cowardice and mismanagement. He seems to have been a deep dissembler. Gaal, however, escaped the fate of the Shechemites by their expulsion of him.

(42) **On the morrow.**—This is surprising. Possibly, however, there were important agricultural labours to be finished, and Abimelech had lulled them into security by ostentatiously withdrawing his forces.

Into the field.—"The wide corn-fields at the *opening* of the Valley of Shechem" (Stanley).

(43) **Into three companies.**—Why he only made *three* companies this time can only be matter of conjecture.

He rose up against them, and smote them.—He was evidently a man of ruthlessly vindictive temperament, for these people whom he slew were mere husbandmen, not an armed host.

(44) **In the entering of the gate of the city.**—This time he was able to intercept the people before they could get back, and he had reserved the post of honour and peril for himself.

(45) **Beat down the city.**—Comp. 2 Sam. xvii. 13; Micah iii. 12.

Sowed it with salt.—Nothing can better show his deadly execration against the populace to whom he owed his elevation, and who had been the instrument of his crimes. By this symbolic act he devoted the city to barrenness and desolation. (See Ps. cvii. 34; Deut. xxix. 23; Job xxxix. 6, and marg.) "When Milan was taken, in A.D. 1162, it was sown with salt, and the house of Admiral Coligny, A.D. 1572, was sown with salt by the command of Charles IX., king of France" (Wordsworth).

(46) **The men of the tower of Shechem.**—Evidently the garrison of the house of Millo (verse 6).

Entered into an hold.—The word for "hold" occurs in 1 Sam. xiii. 6 ("high place"). The LXX. render it "a fortress" (*ochuroma*); Luther, "*Festung.*" In the Æthiopic Version of Mark xvi. 15 a similar word is used for "upper room." The Vulg. has, "They entered the fane of their god Berith, where they had made their league with him, and from this the place had received its name, and it was strongly fortified."

Of the house of the god Berith.—Similarly, Arcesilas burnt the Cyrenæns in a tower (*Herod.* iv. 164), and in 1 Macc. v. 43 the defeated enemy fly for refuge to the temple of Ashtaroth in Karnaim, which Judas takes and burns.

(48) **To mount Zalmon.**—Evidently the nearest spot where he could get wood for his hideous design. Zalmon means *shady.* In Ps. lxviii. 14 we find "as white as snow in Zalmon," but whether the same mountain is referred to we cannot tell. It may be any of the hills near Gerizim.

An axe.—Literally, *the axes*—i.e., he took axes for himself and his army.

Cut down a bough.—The word for "a bough" is *socath*, which does not mean "a bundle of logs," as the LXX. render it. Every one will recall the scene in *Macbeth* where Malcolm says:—

"Let every soldier hew him down a bough,
And bear't before him; thereby shall we shadow
The numbers of our host, and make discovery
Err in report of us."—Act v., sc. 4.

But Abimelech merely wanted combustible materials.

What ye have seen me do.—Comp. what Gideon says in chap. vii. 17.

(49) **Set the hold on fire.**—The words of Jotham (verse 20) had proved prophetic. (For a similar incident see 1 Kings xvi. 18—Zimri burnt in the palace at Tirzah.)

Died.—The Vulgate renders it, *Were killed with the smoke and fire.*

(50) **Thebez.**—One of the cities in the league of "Baal of the Covenant," perhaps, *Tubas*, ten miles north-east of Shechem, on a mound among the hills.

and encamped against Thebez, and took it. ⁽⁵¹⁾ But there was a strong tower within the city, and thither fled all the men and women, and all they of the city, and shut *it* to them, and gat them up to the top of the tower. ⁽⁵²⁾ And Abimelech came unto the tower, and fought against it, and went hard unto the door of the tower to burn it with fire. ⁽⁵³⁾ And a certain woman *a* cast a piece of a millstone upon Abimelech's head, and all to brake his skull. ⁽⁵⁴⁾ Then he called hastily unto the young man his armourbearer, and said unto him, Draw thy sword, and slay me, that men say not of me, A woman slew him. And his young man thrust him through, and he died. ⁽⁵⁵⁾ And when the men of Israel saw that Abimelech was dead, they departed every man unto his place.

⁽⁵⁶⁾ Thus God rendered the wickedness of Abimelech, which he did unto his father, in slaying his seventy brethren: ⁽⁵⁷⁾ and all the evil of the men of Shechem did God render upon their heads: and upon them came the curse of Jotham the son of Jerubbaal.

CHAPTER X.—⁽¹⁾ And after Abimelech there arose to ^{1 2} defend Israel Tola the son of Puah, the son of Dodo, a man of Issachar; and he dwelt in Shamir in

a 2 Sam. 11. 21.

1 Or, *deliver.*

2 Heb., *save.*

⁽⁵¹⁾ **There was a strong tower within the city.**—This constant mention of towers and strongholds (chap. viii. 9, &c.) shows the disturbed state of the country, which probably resembled the state of England in the days of King Stephen.

To the top of the tower.—"Standing about the battlements upon the roof of the tower" (Vulg.).

⁽⁵²⁾ **Went hard unto the door.**—Hard, *i.e.*, close. Like other bad men, Abimelech was not lacking in physical courage. He had all his father's impetuous energy. The peril of such rashness served the Israelites as a perpetual warning (2 Sam. xi. 21).

To burn it with fire.—He naturally anticipated another hideous success like that at Millo.

⁽⁵³⁾ **A piece of a millstone.**—The word for millstone is *receb*, literally, *runner, i.e.*, the upper millstone, or *lapis vector*, which is whirled round and round over the stationary lower one, *sheceb* (Deut. xxiv. 6).

And all to brake his skull.—This is a mere printer's error for *all-to* or *al-to, i.e.*, utterly, and it has led to the further misreading of "brake." Others think that it should be printed "all to-brake," where the *to* is intensive like the German *ge*—as in Chaucer's "All is to-broken thilke regioun" (*Knight's Tale*, 2,579). But in Latimer we find "they love, and all-to love him" (see *Bible Word-book*, § 5). The meaning of the verb is "smashed" or "shattered" (LXX., *suneklase*; Vulg., *confregit*; Luther, *zerbrach*). The death of Pyrrhus by a tile flung down by a woman as he rode into the town of Argos is an historic parallel (Pausan. i. 13). The ringleader of an attack on the Jews, who had taken refuge in York Castle in 1190, was similarly killed.

His armour.—*Celim*, literally, *implements.* (Comp. chap. xviii. 11; Gen. xxvii. 3.)

⁽⁵⁴⁾ **A woman slew him.**—He did not, however, escape the taunt (2 Sam. xi. 21). We see also from the narrative of the death of Saul in 2 Sam. i. 9, 1 Sam. xxxi. 4, how sensitive the ancients were about the manner of their death. The same feeling finds ample illustration in Homer and classic writers (Soph. *Trach.*, 1,064). It was a similar feeling which made Deborah exult in the death of Sisera by the hand of a woman, and the Jews in the murder of Holofernes by Judith. It is remarkable that *both* of the first two Israelite kings die by suicide to avoid a death of greater shame.

⁽⁵⁵⁾ **They departed.**—The death of a leader was generally sufficient to break up an ancient army (1 Sam. xvii. 51). "With Abimelech expired this first abortive attempt at monarchy. . . . The true King of Israel is still far in the distance" (Stanley).

^(56, 57) **Thus.**—These impressive verses give the explanation of the whole narrative. They are inserted to show that God punishes both individual and national crimes, and that men's pleasant vices are made the instruments to scourge them. The murderer of his brothers "on one stone" is slain by a stone flung on his head, and the treacherous idolaters are treacherously burnt in the temple of their idol.

X.

1, 2. Tola of Issachar judges Israel for twenty years. 3—5. Jair of Gilead for twenty-two years. 6. Fresh apostasies of Israel, 7—9 and their punishment in the oppression of the people by enemies. 10—14. Repentance of Israel, and God's answer to them. 15, 16. They put away their idols 17. Gathering of Ammonites. 18. Anxiety of the Gileadites.

⁽¹⁾ **After Abimelech.**—This is merely a note of time. Abimelech is not counted among the judges, though it is not improbable that, evil as was the episode of his rebellions, he may have kept foreign enemies in check.

To defend Israel.—Rather, *to deliver*, as in the margin and elsewhere (chaps. ii. 16, 18, iii. 9, &c.).

There arose.—The phrase implies a less direct call and a less immediate service than that used of other judges (chaps. ii. 18, iii. 9).

Tola.—The name of a son of Issachar (Gen. xlvi. 13). It means "worm" (perhaps the *kermes*-worm), and may, like Puah, be connected with the trade in purple dyes. He seems to have been the only judge furnished by this indolent tribe, unless Deborah be an exception. Josephus omits his name.

Puah.—Also a son of Issachar (1 Chron. vii. 1).

The son of Dodo.—The LXX. render it "the son of his uncle," but there can be little doubt that Dodo is a proper name, as in 1 Chron. xi. 12; 2 Sam. xxiii. 9, 24. It is from the same root as David, "beloved." Since Tola was of Issachar, he could not be nephew of Abimelech a Manassite.

He dwelt in Shamir.—The name has nothing to do with Samaria, as the LXX. seem to suppose. It may be *Sanûr*, eight miles north of Samaria.

In mount Ephraim.—As judge, he would have to fix his residence in a town more central than any in

Tola and Jair.   JUDGES, X.   *Idolatry of Israel.*

mount Ephraim. (2) And he judged Israel twenty and three years, and died, and was buried in Shamir.

(3) And after him arose Jair, a Gileadite, and judged Israel twenty and two years. (4) And he had thirty sons that rode on thirty ass colts, and they had thirty cities, which are called ¹ Havoth-jair unto this day, which *are* in the land of Gilead. (5) And Jair died, and was buried in Camon.

(6) And ᵃ the children of Israel did evil again in the sight of the LORD, and served Baalim, and ᵇ Ashtaroth, and the gods of Syria, and the gods of Zidon, and the gods of Moab, and the gods of the children of Ammon, and the gods of the Philistines, and forsook the LORD, and served not him. (7) And the anger of the LORD was hot against Israel, and he sold them into the hands of the Philistines, and into the hands of the children of Ammon. (8) And that year they vexed and ² oppressed the children of Israel: eighteen years, all the children of Israel that *were* on the other side Jordan in the

<small>¹ Or, *The villages of Jair*
ᵃ ch. 2. 11; & 3. 7. & 4. 1; & 6. 1; & 13. 1.
ᵇ ch. 2. 13.
B.C. cir. 1161.
² Heb., *crushed.*</small>

---

his own tribe. There was another Shamir in Judah (Josh. xv. 48).

(2) **He judged Israel.**—The recurrence of the normal verb (to judge) shows that Tola was an honourable "Suffes," not a despot, like Abimelech. Nothing further is known about Tola.

(3) **Jair, a Gileadite.**—In Num. xxxii. 41 we are told of a Jair, the son of Manasseh, who "took the small towns" of Gilead, and called them Havoth-jair. This earlier Jair, with Nobah, plays a splendid part in Jewish legend, which is only alluded to in Scripture (see Deut. iii. 14). In what relation the Jair of these verses stood to him we cannot, in the uncertain data of the chronology, decide. The Jair of Num. xxxii. 41 was descended from Judah on the father's side, and on the mother's was a great-grandson of Manasseh.

(4) **Had thirty sons.**—An indication of his rank and position, which assumed an ostentatious polygamy. (Comp. chap. viii. 30.)

That rode on thirty ass colts.—Comp. chap. v. 10; see on chap. xii. 14. Implying that Jair was able to bring up his numerous household in wealth. The horse was little used in Palestine—for which, indeed, it is little suited—till the days of Solomon (1 Kings iv. 26), and its introduction was always discouraged by the prophets (Deut. xvii. 16; Josh. xi. 6—9; Ps. xxxiii. 17, &c.). There is a curious play of words on Jair (*yair*), "ass-colts" (*ayārim*), and "cities," which ought to be *arim*, but is purposely altered for the sake of the paronomasia. (See on chap. xv. 16.) Such plays on words in serious narratives point to a very early form of literature —but probably they then rose from some popular proverb. The LXX., like Josephus, writing for Gentiles, who did not understand the value attached to asses in Palestine, almost always euphemise the word into "colts," or "foals" (*pōlous*), which here enables them happily to keep up the play of words with "cities" (*poleis*).

Thirty cities, which are called Havoth-jair.—Havoth means villages (LXX., *epauleis*), and since they are here called "cities," and *thirty* are named, we must suppose that this Jair (if he was a different person from the other) had increased the number of the villages originally wrested from Og from twenty-three to thirty (Num. xxxii. 41; Deut. iii. 14; 1 Chron. ii. 22. In the latter passage the Jair there mentioned is spoken of as a son of Segub, and a *great-grandson* of Manasseh).

Unto this day.—Chap. i. 26.

(5) **In Camon.**—There seems to have been a Kamon six miles from Megiddo (Euseb. *Jer.*), but it is far more probable that this town was in Gilead, as Josephus says (*Antt.* v. 6, § 6), and there is a Kamon mentioned as near Pella by Polybius (*Hist.* v. 70, § 12).

(6) **Did evil again.**—Literally, *added to do evil*: "joining new sins to their old ones," as the Vulg. paraphrases it (chaps. ii. 11, iii. 7, &c.).

Served Baalim, and Ashtaroth.—Chap. ii. 19. Seven kinds of idols are mentioned, in obvious symmetry with the seven retributive oppressions in verses 11, 12.

The gods of Syria.—Heb. *Aram.* (See Gen. xxxv. 2, 4.) Manasseh seems to have had an Aramean concubine (1 Chron. vii. 14), who was mother of Machir. Of Syrian idolatry we hear nothing definite till the days of Ahaz (2 Kings xvi. 10, 12):—

> "Thammuz came next behind,
> Whose annual wound in Lebanon allured
> The Syrian damsels to lament his fate
> In amorous ditties all a summer's day."—*Par. Lost,* i.

The gods of Zidon.—1 Kings xi. 5. As Milton borrowed his details from the learned *Syntagma de Diis Syris* of Selden, we cannot find better illustration of these allusions than in his stately verse:—

> "Ashtoreth, whom the Phœnicians call
> Astarte, queen of heaven, with crescent horns,
> To whose bright image nightly by the hour
> Sidonian virgins paid their vows and songs."—*Id.*

The gods of Moab.—1 Kings xi. 7.

> "Chemosh, the obscene dread of Moab's sons.
> From Aroer to Nebo, and the wild
> Of southmost Abarim
> Peor his other name."—*Id.*

The gods of the children of Ammon.—Lev. xviii. 21; 1 Kings xi. 7.

> "First Moloch, horrid king. . . . Him the Ammonite
> Worshipped in Rabba and his watery plain,
> In Argob and in Basan, to the stream
> Of utmost Arnon."—*Id.*

The gods of the Philistines.—1 Sam. v. 2, xvi. 23.

> "One
> Who mourned in earnest when the captive ark
> Maimed his brute image; head and hands lopt off
> In his own temple on the grunsel edge,
> Where he fell flat and shamed his worshippers.
> Dagon his name—sea-monster—upwards man
> And downwards fish."—*Id.*

(7) **The anger of the Lord.**—For the phrases in this verse see chaps. ii. 14—20, iii. 8; comp. 1 Sam xii. 9.

Of the Philistines.—Chap. iii. 31.

(8) **That year.**—The narrative is evidently imperfect, as no year is specified.

Vexed and oppressed.—This again is a *paronomasia*, or assonance, like "broke to yoke" in English.

228

God's Anger against the People. JUDGES, XI. *Invasion by the Ammonites.*

land of the Amorites, which *is* in Gilead. [a Deu. 32. 15. Jer. 2. 13.] (9) Moreover the children of Ammon passed over Jordan to fight also against Judah, and against Benjamin, and against the house of Ephraim; so that Israel was sore distressed.

(10) And the children of Israel cried unto the LORD, saying, We have sinned against thee, both because we have forsaken our God, and also served Baalim. (11) And the LORD said unto the children of Israel, *Did* not *I deliver you* from the Egyptians, and from the Amorites, from the children of Ammon, and from the Philistines? (12) The Zidonians also, and the Amalekites, and the Maonites, did oppress you; and ye cried to me, and I delivered you out of their hand. (13) *a* Yet ye have forsaken me, and served other gods: wherefore I will deliver you no more. (14) Go and cry unto the gods which ye have chosen; let them deliver

[1 Heb., *is good in thine eyes.*]
[2 Heb., *gods of strangers.*]
[3 Heb., *was shortened.*]
[4 Heb., *cried together.*]
[b ch. 11. 6.]
[c Heb., 11. 32, *called Jephthae.*]

you in the time of your tribulation. (15) And the children of Israel said unto the LORD, We have sinned: do thou unto us whatsoever ¹ seemeth good unto thee; deliver us only, we pray thee, this day. (16) And they put away the ² strange gods from among them, and served the LORD: and his soul ³ was grieved for the misery of Israel.

(17) Then the children of Ammon were ⁴ gathered together, and encamped in Gilead. And the children of Israel assembled themselves together, and encamped in Mizpeh. (18) And the people *and* princes of Gilead said one to another, What man *is he* that will begin to fight against the children of Ammon? he shall *b* be head over all the inhabitants of Gilead.

CHAPTER XI.—(1) Now *c* Jephthah the Gileadite was a mighty man of

---

The land of the Amorites.—The kingdoms of Og and Sihon.

(9) **Moreover.**—Rather, *and.* Eighteen years' oppression of the Trans-jordanic tribes emboldened them to attack the others.

Was sore distressed.—The same expression is used in chap. ii. 19.

(10) **Cried unto the Lord.**—Chap. vi. 6; 1 Sam. xii. 10.

And the Lord said.—The method of the Divine communication is not specified. A stern experience might have spoken to the national conviction with prophetic voice.

From the Egyptians.—Exod. i.–xiv.

From the Amorites.—Num. xxi. 3–21; Josh. x.

From the children of Ammon.—Chap. iii. 13.

From the Philistines.—Chap. iii. 32; 1 Sam xii. 9.

(12) **The Sidonians.**—Chaps. iii. 3, xviii. 7–28. Nothing very definite is recorded of deliverance from the Sidonians; but (as we have seen) the narrative of the book is typical rather than exhaustive. (Comp. Ps. cvi. 42, 43.)

The Amalekites.—Exod. xvii. 8, vi. 33, iii. 13.

The Maonites.—As the LXX. here read *Madian* (and in some MSS. *Canaan*; Vulg., *Chanaan*), it seems probable that there has been an early corruption of the text. In the Arabic version we have "Moabites." There was a town Maon in the desert of Judah (Josh. xv. 55; 1 Sam. xxiii. 24, xxv. 2), but this cannot be meant. There is also a Beth Meon in the tribe of Reuben (Num. xxii. 38; Baal Meon, Jer. lxviii. 23), and a Meon in Arabia Petræa. *Mehunims* are also mentioned in 2 Chron. xxvi. 7, and Meonim in 1 Chron. iv. 41. If this is an allusion to some disaster of which we have no record given we must suppose that Meon was once the capital of some tribe which subsequently dwindled into insignificance.

(13) **I will deliver you no more.**—A threat which, as the sequel proves, was (as in other passages of Scripture) to be understood *conditionally* (Jer. xviii. 7, 8).

(14) **Go and cry unto the gods.**—With this bitter reproach comp. Deut. xxxii. 37, 38; 2 Kings iii. 13; Jer. ii. 28.

In the time of your tribulation.—Comp. 1 Kings xviii. 27; Prov. i. 26.

(15) **Deliver us only, we pray thee, this day.**—The invariable cry of the soul in trouble. With the former half of the verse comp. 1 Sam. iii. 18, xv. 26.

(16) **They put away the strange gods.**—The moment the sincerity of their repentance was proved, God hears them (Gen. xxxv. 1; 1 Sam. vii. 3; 2 Chron. xv. 8).

His soul was grieved.—Literally, *was shortened.* (Comp. Zach. xi. 8).

(17) **Then.**—Rather, *and,* a general note of time.

Were gathered together.—Literally, *were cried together. Conclamati sunt.*

In Mizpeh.—A very common name, since it means "watch-tower." This is doubtless the Mizpeh in Gilead (chap. xi. 29; Josh. xi. 3), also called Ramoth-Mizpeh, or Ramoth-Gilead (Josh. xiii. 26, xx. 8). (Comp. Gen. xxxi. 49).

(18) **The people and princes.**—There is no "and" in the original; but it cannot be a case of apposition, because the term "people" is never applied to "princes."

Head.—Comp. chap. xi. 11.

XI.

1—3. Expulsion of Jephthah from his home. 4—11. The Gileadites offer him the headship of their tribe if he will lead them in war. 12. His embassy to the Ammonites. 13. Their untenable claims refuted. 14—27, by Jephthah on historical and legal grounds. 28. Their refusal of peace. 29—31. Jephthah's vow. 32, 33. His victory over the Ammonites. 34, 35. His daughter comes forth to meet him. 35—40. Fulfilment of his vow.

(1) **The son of an harlot.**—The words are so rendered in all the versions, and can hardly have any other

valour, and he *was* the son of ¹ an harlot: and Gilead begat Jephthah. ⁽²⁾ And Gilead's wife bare him sons; and his wife's sons grew up, and they thrust out Jephthah, and said unto him, Thou shalt not inherit in our father's house; for thou *art* the son of a strange woman. ⁽³⁾ Then Jephthah fled ² from his brethren, and dwelt in the land of Tob: and there were gathered vain men to Jephthah, and went out with him.

⁽⁴⁾ And it came to pass ³ in process of time, that the children of Ammon made war against Israel. ⁽⁵⁾ And it was so, that when the children of Ammon made war against Israel, the elders of Gilead went to fetch Jephthah out of the land of Tob: ⁽⁶⁾ and they said unto Jephthah, Come, and be our captain, that we may fight with the children of Ammon. ⁽⁷⁾ And Jephthah said unto the elders of Gilead, Did not ye hate me, and expel me out of my father's house? and why are ye come unto me now when ye are in distress? ⁽⁸⁾ And the elders of Gilead said unto Jephthah, Therefore we turn again to thee now, that thou mayest go with us, and fight against the children of Ammon, and be our head over all the inhabitants of Gilead. ⁽⁹⁾ And Jephthah said unto the elders of Gilead, If ye bring me home again to fight against the children of Ammon, and the LORD deliver them before me, shall I be your head? ⁽¹⁰⁾ And the elders of Gilead said unto Jephthah, The LORD ⁴ be witness between us, if we do not so according to thy words. ⁽¹¹⁾ Then Jephthah went with the elders of Gilead, and the people made him head

¹ Heb., *a woman an harlot.*
² Heb., *from the face.*
³ Heb., *after days.*
⁴ Heb., *be the hearer between us.*

---

meaning. If an inferior wife had been meant, the word used would not have been *zonah*, but *pilgesh*, as in chap. viii. 31. The word may, however, be used in the harsh sense of the brethren of Jephthah, without being strictly accurate. (Comp. 1 Chron. ii. 26.)

Gilead begat Jephthah.—We are here met by the same questions as those which concern Tola and Jair. That Gilead is a proper name, not the name of the country mythically personified, may be regarded as certain. But is this Gilead the son of Machir, the son of Manasseh, or some later Gilead? or does "begat" mean "was the ancestor of?" The answer to these questions depends mainly upon the insoluble problem of the chronology; but we may note (1) that since no *other* Gilead is mentioned, we should naturally infer that *this* is the grandson of Manasseh; and (2) that the fact referred to in the obscure genealogy of 1 Chron. vii. 14—17 seems to show that the family of Manasseh had Syrian (Aramean) connections, and Jephthah's mother may have been an Aramitess from the district of Tob. The name Jephthah means "he opens" (the womb).

⁽²⁾ **They thrust out Jephthah.**—This was in perfect accordance with the law (Deut. xxiii. 2, 3), and with family rules and traditions. Abraham had sent the son of Hagar and the sons of Keturah to found other settlements (Gen. xxi. 10, xxv. 6).

⁽³⁾ **Dwelt in the land of Tob.**—A Syrian district on the north-east of Peræa (2 Sam. x. 6). It is referred to in 1 Macc. v. 13; 2 Macc. xii. 17. The name means "good," but lends no sanction to the idle allegories which have been based upon it.

Vain men.—Chap. ix. 4.

Went out with him.—Jephthah simply became a sort of Syrian freebooter. His half-heathen origin, no doubt, influenced his character unfavourably, as it had done that of Abimelech.

⁽⁴⁾ **In process of time.**—Marg., *after days*, implying the time between Jephthah's expulsion in early youth and his mature manhood.

The children of Ammon made war.—The fact that this is introduced as a new circumstance, though it has been fully related in chap. x. 8, 9, 17, 18, probably arises from the use of some new, and probably Gileadite, document in these two chapters.

⁽⁵⁾ **When the children of Ammon made war.** —The allusion is to some special threat of invasion (*acriter instantibus*, Vulg.) at the close of the eighteen years of oppression (chap. x. 9).

To fetch Jephthah.—Because by this time he had made himself a great name as a brave and successful chieftain of marauders, who would doubtless come with him to lead the Gileadites.

⁽⁶⁾ **Our captain.**—The word used is *katzin* (Josh. x. 24; Isa. i. 10, xxii. 3), which is specially a leader in time of war; but Jephthah demands something more— namely, to be their "head" (*rosh*) in time of peace also.

⁽⁷⁾ **Did not ye hate me?**—The elders of Gilead must at least have permitted his expulsion by his brethren.

⁽⁸⁾ **Therefore.**—*i.e.*, with the express desire to repair the old wrong.

⁽⁹⁾ **Shall I be your head?**—We must not be surprised if Jephthah does not display a disinterested patriotism. He was only half an Israelite; he had been wronged by his father's kin; he had spent long years of his manhood among heathens and outlaws, who gained their livelihood by brigandage or mercenary warfare. "As Gideon is the highest pitch of greatness to which this period reaches," says Dean Stanley, "Jephthah and Samson are the lowest points to which it descends." Since, then, we have marked elements of ferocity and religious ignorance and ambition even in the noble character of Gideon, we must remember that we might naturally make allowance for a still lower level of attainment in one who had been so unfavourably circumstanced as Jephthah. Apart from the Syrian influences which had told upon him, the whole condition of the pastoral tribes on the east of the Jordan was far below that of the agricultural western tribes.

⁽¹⁰⁾ **The Lord be witness.**—Rather, *be hearing* (*Dominus, qui haec audit ipse Mediator ac testis sit*, Vulg.).

⁽¹¹⁾ **The people made him head and captain.** —The people ratified the promise of the elders, and solemnly inaugurated him as both the civil and military leader of the Trans-jordanic tribes.

Jephthah's Message to   JUDGES, XI.   *the King of Ammon.*

and captain over them: and Jephthah uttered all his words before the LORD in Mizpeh.

(12) And Jephthah sent messengers unto the king of the children of Ammon, saying, What hast thou to do with me, that thou art come against me to fight in my land? (13) And the king of the children of Ammon answered unto the messengers of Jephthah, ^a Because Israel took away my land, when they came up out of Egypt, from Arnon even unto Jabbok, and unto Jordan: now therefore restore those *lands* again peaceably.

(14) And Jephthah sent messengers again unto the king of the children of Ammon: (15) and said unto him, Thus saith Jephthah, ^b Israel took not away the land of Moab, nor the land of the children of Ammon: (16) but when Israel came up from Egypt, and walked through the wilderness unto the Red sea, and came to Kadesh; (17) then ^c Israel sent messengers unto the king of Edom, saying, Let me, I pray thee, pass through thy land: but the king of Edom would not hearken *thereto*. And in like manner they sent unto the king of Moab: but he would not *consent*: and Israel abode in Kadesh. (18) Then they went along through the wilderness, and compassed the land of Edom, and the land of Moab, and came by the east side of the land of Moab, and pitched on the other side of Arnon, ^d but came not within the border of Moab: for Arnon *was* the

a Num. 21. 13.

B.C. cir. 1143.

b Deut. 2. 9.

c Num. 20. 14.

d Num. 21. 13, 24

Uttered all his words.—It probably means that he took some oath as to the condition of his government.

Before the Lord in Mizpeh.—Some have supposed that this must mean that the oath was taken before the Tabernacle or Ark, or Urim and Thummim, because the phrase has this meaning elsewhere (Exod. xxxiv. 34; Josh. xviii. 8; and *infra*, xx. 26, xxi. 2);—and consequently that the scene of this covenant must be the *Western* Mizpeh, in Benjamin (Josh. xviii. 26; 1 Macc. iii. 46, "for in Maspha was the place where they prayed aforetime in Israel"). There are, indeed, no limits to the possible irregularities of these disturbed times, during which the priests seem to have sunk into the completest insignificance. The Ark may therefore have been transferred for a time to Mizpeh, in Benjamin (chap. xx. 1), as tradition says. But if that Mizpeh had been meant, it would certainly have been specified, since the Mizpeh of our present narrative (chap. x. 17, 34) is in Gilead. Nor is it at all likely that the High Priest would have carried the sacred Urim into the disturbed and threatened Eastern districts. "Before Jehovah" probably means nothing more than by some solemn religious utterance or ceremony; and Mizpeh in Gilead had its own sacred associations (Gen. xxxi. 48, 49).

(12) **What hast thou to do with me?**—Literally, *What to me and to thee?* (Josh. xxii. 24; 2 Sam. xvi. 10, &c.). Jephthah speaks in the name of Israel, as an acknowledged prince. His message resembles the preliminary negotiations of the Roman generals when they sent the Fetiales to proclaim the justice of their cause (*Liv.* i. 24).

(13) **Because Israel took away my land.**—This was a very plausible plea, but was not in accordance with facts. The Israelites had been distinctly forbidden to war against the Moabites and Ammonites (Deut. ii. 9, 19); but when Sihon, king of the Amorites, had refused them permission to pass peaceably through his land, and had even come out to battle against them, they had defeated him and seized his territory. It was quite true that a large district in this territory had *originally* belonged to Moab and Ammon, and had been wrested from them by Sihon (Num. xxi. 21—30; Josh. xii. 25); but that was a question with which the Israelites had nothing to do, and it was absurd to expect that they would shed their blood to win settlements for the sole purpose of restoring them to nations which regarded them with the deadliest enmity.

From Arnon even unto Jabbok.—The space occupied by Gad and Reuben. The Arnon ("noisy") is now the Wady Modjeb. It was the southern boundary of Reuben, and its deep rocky ravine separated that tribe from Moab. The Jabbok ("pouring out") was originally the "border of the children of Ammon" (Deut. iii. 16; Num. xxi. 24). It is nearly midway between the Dead Sea and the Sea of Galilee, and is now called the *Wady Zurka*.

(14, 15) **And Jephthah sent messengers again.** —Jephthah disputes the king of Ammon's facts, and supports his denial of them by an historic retrospect (verses 16—24).

(15) **Took not away the land of Moab . . .**— What they took was the territory of Sihon, which they had never been forbidden to take, and had indeed been forced to take by Sihon's attack on them. It was not likely that they could enter into discussion as to the *previous* owners of the land.

(16) **When Israel came up from Egypt.**— Compare with this narrative Num. xx., xxi.

Walked through the wilderness.—In the second year of the wanderings (Deut. i. 19).

Unto the Red sea.—Num. xiv. 25. The name for this sea in the Old Testament is *Yam sooph*, "the sea of weeds." They reached Kadesh Barnea from Ezion Geber ("the Giant's backbone"), in the Gulf of Akaba (Num. xxxiii. 36).

To Kadesh.—Num. xx. 1, xxxiii. 16.

(17) **Unto the king of Edom.**—As narrated in Num. xx. 14, *seq.* Even if Jephthah had no written documents before him to which he could refer, the events which he recounts were not so distant as to have been forgotten.

Unto the king of Moab.—This is not recorded in the Pentateuch, but the Israelites did not enter the territory of Moab (Deut. ii. 9, 36). The Arnon bounded Moab from the Amorites (Num. xxi. 13), and Israel encamped upon its banks.

Abode in Kadesh.—"Many days" (Deut. ii. 1). Probably they were encamped at Kadesh during a great part of the forty years (Deut. ii. 14).

border of Moab. (19) And ^a Israel sent messengers unto Sihon king of the Amorites, the king of Heshbon; and Israel said unto him, Let us pass, we pray thee, through thy land into my place. (20) But Sihon trusted not Israel to pass through his coast: but Sihon gathered all his people together, and pitched in Jahaz, and fought against Israel. (21) And the LORD God of Israel delivered Sihon and all his people into the hand of Israel, and they smote them: so Israel possessed all the land of the Amorites, the inhabitants of that country. (22) And they possessed all the ^b coasts of the Amorites, from Arnon even unto Jabbok, and from the wilderness even unto Jordan. (23) So now the LORD God of Israel hath dispossessed the Amorites from before his people Israel, and shouldest thou possess it? (24) Wilt not thou possess that which Chemosh thy god giveth thee to possess? So whomsoever the LORD our God shall drive out from before us, them will we possess. (25) ^c And now art thou any thing better than Balak the son of Zippor, king of Moab? did he ever strive against Israel, or did he ever fight against them, (26) while Israel dwelt in Heshbon and her towns, and in Aroer and her towns, and in all the cities that be along by the coasts of Arnon, three hundred years? why therefore did ye not recover them

a Deu. 2. 26.

b Deu. 2. 36.

c Num. 22. 2; Deu. 23. 4.; Josh. 24. 9.

---

(19) **Unto Sihon.**—Num. xxi. 21; Deut. ii. 26—29 (where see the Commentary).

The King of Heshbon.—He was king of the Amorites by birth, but king of Heshbon only by conquest. The town was assigned to Reuben (Num. xxxii. 37).

Into my place.—The conquest of the territories of Reuben, Gad, and half-Manasseh had not entered into the original plan of Israel, but had been providentially determined by the hostility of Sihon and Og (Deut. ii. 29). The Vulg. renders it "unto the river" (*usque ad fluvium*).

(20) **Trusted not Israel.**—Sihon did not believe their promise to pass peacefully through his land.

Pitched in Jahaz.—Num. xxi. 33; Isa. xv. 4; Jer. xlviii. 3. The site of the battle has not been ascertained.

(21) **The Lord God of Israel.**—This is evidently a cardinal point in the mind of Jephthah. The God of Israel has decided against the gods of Ammon.

All the land of the Amorites.—All the land, therefore, which they took from the Amorites was theirs by the immemorial law of nations, irrespective of any who had been its previous owners (Grot., *De Jure Belli*, iii. 6, § 7).

(23) **Shouldest thou possess it?**—Is it likely that Israel would fight battles solely to benefit Ammon and Moab?

(24) **Chemosh thy god.**—The expression shows the close connection between Ammon and Moab. Chemosh was distinctively the god of Moab, and Moloch of Ammon; but the two nations were of kindred blood and allied institutions (chap. iii. 12, 13). The name Chemosh means "subduer," and there is here, perhaps, a tacit reference to the wild popular song of triumph over the conquest of Heshbon, in which Chemosh is taunted by name (Num. xxi. 29; comp. Jer. xlviii. 7). The clause might be rendered, "Whatever Jehovah our God hath dispossessed before us, that take we in possession."

(25) **Art thou anything better than Balak?**—Literally, *Are you the good, good in comparison with?* It is one of the Hebrew ways of expressing the superlative. Jephthah here argues from prescriptive right, which even the contemporary king Balak had not ventured to challenge, showing, therefore, that he admitted the claim of Israel, deadly as was his hatred against them.

Did he ever fight against them?—This may seem at first sight to contradict Josh. xxiv. 9. There "Balak the son of Zippor arose and warred against Israel"; and we might infer that it was in some Moabite battle that Balaam had been slain (Num. xxxi. 8; Josh. xiii. 22). But this would not affect Jephthah's argument. Balak had fought against Israel out of pure hatred, not from any pretensions to claim their conquests from them.

(26) **While Israel dwelt in Heshbon.**—See Num. xxi. 25. This is an argument from undisputed possession.

In Aroer and her towns.—These had been assigned to the tribe of Gad (Num. xxxii. 34).

In all the cities that be along by the coast of Arnon.—The LXX. read Jordan.

Three hundred years.—There is an almost insuperable difficulty in making out any reasonable scheme of chronology even by accepting this as a round number, because it is difficult to reconcile with nine or ten genealogies which have been preserved to us, and which represent the period between the conquest and David by seven or eight generations. Now the period covered by these genealogies includes the judgeship of Samuel and the reign of Saul—at least seventy years; and seven or eight generations cannot possibly span 370 years. The hypothesis that in *all* these genealogies—even the four times repeated genealogy of David—generations are always omitted is very improbable. The chronology of the Jews is confessedly loose and uncertain, and it seems quite possible that "three hundred years" may be a marginal gloss which has crept into the text. What makes this more probable is that the words not only create an immense chronological difficulty, but (1) are quite needless to Jephthah's argument, and (2) actually conflict with the rest of the sentence, which refers to Balak alone; the argument being, If Balak, "*at that time*" (as the words should be rendered), did not advance any claim, what right have you to do so *now?* If, however, in spite of these difficulties, the clause be genuine, and if there has not been one of the clerical errors which are so common where numerals are concerned, it seems possible that 300 years may be counted inclusively, *e.g.*, 100 full years since the death of Joshua and nominal completion of the conquest of Canaan. with parts of a century before and after it.

within that time? ⁽²⁷⁾ Wherefore I have not sinned against thee, but thou doest me wrong to war against me: the LORD the Judge be judge this day between the children of Israel and the children of Ammon.

⁽²⁸⁾ Howbeit the king of the children of Ammon hearkened not unto the words of Jephthah which he sent him. ⁽²⁹⁾ Then the Spirit of the LORD came upon Jephthah, and he passed over Gilead, and Manasseh, and passed over Mizpeh of Gilead, and from Mizpeh of Gilead he passed over *unto* the children of Ammon.

⁽³⁰⁾ And Jephthah vowed a vow unto the LORD, and said, If thou shalt without fail deliver the children of Ammon into mine hands, ⁽³¹⁾ then it shall be, that ¹ whatsoever cometh forth of the doors of my house to meet me, when I return in peace from the children of

1 Heb., *that which cometh forth, which shall come forth.*

Certainly this is a recognised mode of reckoning time among the Jews. For instance, if a king began to reign on December 30, 1879, and died on January 2, 1881, they would say that he had reigned three years. Whatever explanations we may adopt, there is nothing but conjecture to go upon. (See Introduction.)

Within that time.—This is a mis-translation, due probably to the perplexity caused by the "three hundred years." The Hebrew has "in that time," *i.e.*, at that crisis. It was obvious, without special mention, that they had remained in possession ever since Balak's day, and in the most ancient times it was admitted that lapse of time secured possession (Isocr. *Ep. ad Aechid.*, p. 121; Tac. *Ann.* vi. 31).

⁽²⁷⁾ **The Lord the Judge be judge this day.**—An appeal to the arbitrament of Jehovah to decide on the justice of an appeal to arms. (Comp. Gen. xvi. 5, xxxi. 53, xviii. 25; 1 Sam. xxiv. 15.)

These verses contain a deeply interesting specimen of what may be called ancient diplomacy, and very powerful and straightforward it is—at once honest, conciliatory, and firm. Jephthah maintains the rights of Israel on three grounds, viz., (i.) Right of direct conquest, not from Ammon but from the Amorites (15—20); (ii.) The decision of God (verses 21—23), which he supports by an *argumentum ad hominem*—namely, the acquiescence in this decision of the Moabite god Chemosh (verse 24); (iii.) Undisputed possession from the first (verses 25, 26). He ends by an appeal to God to approve the justice of his cause.

⁽²⁸⁾ **Hearkened not.**—We are not told of any counter-arguments. Probably the king of Ammon cared only for the argument of the sword—

"The good old rule
Contented him, the simple plan
That they should get who have the power,
And they should keep who can."

⁽²⁹⁾ **The Spirit of the Lord came upon Jephthah.**—A weaker expression is used than that which is applied to Gideon in chap. vi. 34. It implies, as R. Tanchum rightly says, that he was endowed with the courage and wisdom without which success would have been impossible. The phrase no more involves a complete inspiration of Jephthah than it does in the case of Samson; nor is it meant to imply the least approval of many of his subsequent actions. It furnished the power which he needed to work out the deliverance—and that only. To hold up characters like Jephthah and Samson as religious examples, *except* (as is done in Heb. xi. 32) in the one special characteristic of faith displayed at memorable crises, is to sacrifice the whole spirit of Scripture to the mis-interpretation of a phrase.

⁽²⁹⁾ **He passed over Gilead and Manasseh.**—Rather, *he went through* (Vulg., *circuiens*). His object clearly was to collect levies and rouse the tribes —"He swept through the land from end to end to kindle the torch of war and raise the population" (Ewald).

Passed over Mizpeh.—Perhaps, as in the next clause, *to Mizpeh*.

Passed over unto the children of Ammon. —*i.e.*, went to attack them.

⁽³⁰⁾ **Jephthah vowed a vow.**—This was a practice among all ancient nations, but specially among the Jews (Gen. xxviii. 20—22; 1 Sam. i. 11; 2 Sam. xv. 8; Ps. lxvi. 13).

⁽³¹⁾ **Whatsoever cometh forth.**—The true rendering undoubtedly is, *Whosoever cometh forth* (LXX., ὁ ἐμπορευόμενος; Vulg., *quicunque*). Nothing can be clearer than that the view held of this passage, from early Jewish days down to the Middle Ages, and still held by nearly all unbiassed commentators, is the true one, and alone adequately explains the text: viz., that Jephthah, ignorant as he was—being a man of semi-heathen parentage, and long familiarised with heathen surroundings—contemplated a human sacrifice. To say that he imagined that *an animal* would "come forth of the doors of his house to meet him" on his triumphant return is a notion which even St. Augustine ridicules. The offer to sacrifice a single animal—even if we *could* suppose an animal "coming forth to meet" Jephthah—would be strangely inadequate. It would be assumed as a matter of course that not one, but *many* holocausts of animals would express the gratitude of Israel. Pfeiffer sensibly observes (*Dub. vexata*, p. 356): "What kind of vow would it be if some great prince or general should say, 'O God, if Thou wilt give me this victory, the first calf that meets me shall be Thine?'" Jephthah left God, as it were, to choose His own victim, and probably anticipated that it would be some slave. The notion of human sacrifice was all but universal among ancient nations, and it was specially prevalent among the Syrians, among whom Jephthah had lived for so many years, and among the Phœnicians, whose gods had been recently adopted by the Israelites (chap. x. 6). Further than this, it was the peculiar worship of the Moabites and Ammonites, against whom Jephthah was marching to battle; and one who had been a rude freebooter, in a heathen country and a lawless epoch, when constant and grave violations of the Law were daily tolerated, might well suppose in his ignorance that Jehovah would need to be propitiated by some offering as costly as those which bled on the altars of Chemosh and Moloch. Human sacrifice had been "the first thought of Balak in the extremity of his terror" (Micah vi. 7), and "the last expedient of Balak's successor" (2 Kings iii. 27)—Stanley, i. 358. If it be urged that after the great lesson which had been taught to Abraham at Jehovah-jireh the very

Jephthah returning Victorious   JUDGES, XI.   *is Met by his Daughter.*

Ammon, shall surely be the Lord's, ¹ and I will offer it up for a burnt offering. ⁽³²⁾ So Jephthah passed over unto the children of Ammon to fight against them; and the Lord delivered them into his hands. ⁽³³⁾ And he smote them from Aroer, even till thou come to Minnith, *even* twenty cities, and unto ² the plain of the vineyards, with a very great slaughter. Thus the children of Ammon were subdued before the children of Israel. ⁽³⁴⁾ And Jephthah came to Mizpeh unto his house, and, behold, his daughter came out to meet him with timbrels and with dances: and she *was* his only child; ³ ⁴ beside her he had neither son nor daughter. ⁽³⁵⁾ And it came to pass, when he saw her, that he rent his

¹ Or, *or I will offer it, &c.*
² Or, *Abel.*
³ Or, *he had not of his own either son or daughter.*
⁴ Heb., *of himself.*

---

notion of human sacrifice ought to have become abhorrent to any Israelite, especially as it had been expressly forbidden in the Law (Lev. xviii. 21; Deut. xii. 31, &c.), one more than sufficient answer is that *even in the wilderness* Israel had been guilty of Molochworship (Ezek. xx. 26; Jer. xlix. 1; *Melcom*, Amos v. 26; Acts vii. 43). The Law was one thing; the knowledge of it and the observance of it was quite another. During this period we find the Law violated again and again, even by judges like Gideon and Samson; and the tendency to violate it by human sacrifices lasted down to the far more enlightened and civilised days of Ahaz and Manasseh (2 Chron. xxviii. 3, xxxiii. 6). Indeed, we find the priests expressly sanctioning, even in the palmiest days of David's reign, an execution which, to the vulgar, would bear an aspect not far removed from human sacrifice, or (rather) which might easily be confused with the spirit which led to it (2 Sam. xxi. 1—9). If, again, it be said that the possibility of Jephthah's being guilty of so rash and evil a vow is excluded by the phrase that "the Spirit of the Lord came upon him," such reasoning is to substitute idle fancies for clear facts. The Spirit of the Lord " clothed " Gideon, yet he set up an illegal worship. The "Spirit of the Lord" came upon Saul (1 Sam. xix. 23), yet Saul contemplated slaying his own son out of regard for no less foolish a vow (1 Sam. xiv. 44). The "Spirit of the Lord" came upon David "from that day forward " on which Samuel anointed him (1 Sam. xvi. 13), yet he could sink into adultery and murder. The phrase must not be interpreted of high or permanent spiritual achievement, but of Divine strength granted for a particular end.

And I will offer it up for a burnt offering.—The margin gives the alternative reading *or* instead of *and*. This is due to the same feeling which made our translators adopt the rendering "*what*soever." They are practically following R. Kimchi in the attempt to explain away, out of deference to modern notions, the plain meaning of the Bible. It is true that *vau*, "and," is sometimes *practically* disjunctive (or, rather, is used where a disjunctive might be used), but to take it so here is to make nonsense of the clause, for if any person or thing was made "a burnt offering" it was necessarily "the Lord's" (Exod. xiii. 2, &c.), so that there *can* be no *alternative* here. The "and" is exactly analogous to the "and" between the two clauses of Jacob's (Gen. xxviii. 21, 22) and of Hannah's vow (1 Sam. i. 11). The "*it* will I offer" ought to be, "I will offer *him*."

⁽³²⁾ **So.**—Rather, *And*. The clause does not refer in any way to Jephthah's vow, but merely resumes the narrative.

⁽³³⁾ **To Minnith.**—According to Eusebius and Jerome, this is Maanith, four miles from Heshbon (Ezek. xxvii. 17).

Unto the plain of the vineyards.—Rather, *unto Abel-ceramim.* The place is either Abela, a few miles beyond Maanith, or another Abela, twelve miles from Gadara (Euseb., Jer.).

Were subdued before.—Chaps. iii. 30, viii. 28.

⁽³⁴⁾ **Behold, his daughter came out to meet him with timbrels and with dances.** — As Miriam went to meet Moses (Exod. xv. 20), and the women to meet Saul and David (1 Sam. xviii. 6, 7).

His only child.—This is added because the narrator feels the full pathos of the story. (Comp. Gen. xxii. 2; Jer. vi. 26; Luke ix. 38.) The term used (*yechidah*) is peculiarly tender. The "beside *her*" is, literally, *beside him;* but this is only due to a Hebrew idiom, which is also found in Zech. viii. 10.

⁽³⁵⁾ **He rent his clothes.**— Comp. Josh. vii. 6. By one of the curious survivals which preserve customs for centuries after the meaning is gone out of them, every Jew on approaching to Jerusalem for the first time has to submit to the *krie*—*i.e.*, to a cut made in his sleeve, as a sort of symbol of rending his clothes.

Thou hast brought me very low.—Literally, *crushing, thou hast crushed me.*

I have opened my mouth unto the Lord.—A vow was not deemed binding unless it had been actually expressed in words (Num. xxx. 2, 3, 7; Deut. xxiii. 23). There were two kinds of vows among the Hebrews—the simple vow, *neder* (Lev. xxvii. 2—27), and the "devotion," or "ban," *cherem* (*id*. 28, 29). Anything devoted to Jehovah by the *cherem* was irredeemable, and became "a holy of holies" (*kodesh kadashim*) to Him, and was to be put to death (*id*. 29).

I cannot go back.—Num. xxx. 2. Jephthah had not understood until now the horror of human sacrifice. He would neither wish nor dare to draw back from his *cherem* (Eccles. v. 4, 5; Matt. v. 33; Jonah ii. 9; Pss. lxxii. 25, xxvi. 11) merely because the anguish of it would fall so heavily upon himself. The Hebrews had the most intense feeling about the awfulness of breaking an oath or vow, and they left no room for any mental reservations (Lev. xxvii. 28, 29). Saul was determined to carry out his ban even at the cost of the life of his eldest son, and even Herod Antipas felt obliged to carry out his oath to Herodias, though it involved a deep pang and a haunted conscience. It is clear that not for one moment did it occur to Jephthah to save himself from the agony of bereavement by breaking his "ban" (*cherem*) as a mere redeemable vow (*neder*). The Jews shared in this respect the feelings of other ancient nations. Thus the Greeks believed that the house of Athamas were under an inexpiable curse, because when the Achæans had been bidden to offer him up for a sacrifice for compassing the death of Phryxus, Kytissorus, the son of Phryxus, had intercepted the sacrifice (Herod. vii. 197, § 3; Plat. *Minos*, 5). It must be remembered that though his

clothes, and said, Alas, my daughter! thou hast brought me very low, and thou art one of them that trouble me: for I have opened my mouth unto the LORD, and I cannot go back. ⁽³⁶⁾ And she said unto him, My father, *if* thou hast opened thy mouth unto the LORD, do to me according to that which hath proceeded out of thy mouth; forasmuch as the LORD hath taken vengeance for thee of thine enemies, *even* of the children of Ammon. ⁽³⁷⁾ And she said unto her father, Let this thing be done for me: let me alone two months, that I may go ¹up and down upon the mountains, and bewail my virginity, I and my fellows. ⁽³⁸⁾ And he said, Go. And he sent her away *for* two months: and she went with her companions, and bewailed her virginity upon the mountains. ⁽³⁹⁾ And it came to pass at the end of two months, that she returned unto her father, who did with her *according* to his vow which he had vowed: and she knew no man.

¹ Heb., *go, and go down.*

---

cherem had taken an unusual and unlawful (though far from unknown) form, the notion of such a vow would come far more naturally to a people which in very recent times, as well as afterwards, had devoted whole cities—men, women, children, cattle, and goods—to absolute destruction (Num. xxi. 2, 3).

⁽³⁶⁾ **And she said unto him.**—To explain this the LXX. add the words, "I have opened my mouth to the Lord *against* or *concerning* thee." There is, however, no need for the addition. His words would fatally explain themselves, even if he added nothing more.

If thou hast opened thy mouth unto the Lord.—The needless and incorrect insertion of the *if* in the English Version a little weakens the noble heroism of her answer.

Do to me according to that which hath proceeded out of thy mouth.—While Jephthah, living in times of ignorance which "God winked at," must not be judged for that terrible ignorance of God's nature which led him to offer a sacrifice which, as Josephus says, was "neither lawful nor acceptable to God," we may well rejoice in the gleam of sunlight which is flung upon the sacred page by his faithfulness in not going back from his vow, though it were to his own hurt (Ps. xv. 4), and in the beautiful devotion of his daughter, cheerfully acquiescing in her own sacrifice for the good of her country. Compare the examples of Iphigenia; of Macaria (Pausan. i. 32); of Auchurus, the son of Midas; of Curtius; of the Decii; of Marius offering his daughter for victory more the Cimbri; and of the Romans during more than one national panic. Our modern poets have happily seized this aspect of the event (see Dante, *Parad.* v. 66):—

"Though the virgins of Salem lament,
Be the judge and the hero unbent;
I have won the great battle for thee,
And my father and country are free."—*Byron.*

"When the next moon was rolled into the sky,
Strength came to me that equall'd my desire.
How beautiful a thing it was to die
For God and for my sire!"—*Tennyson.*

"It was not a human sacrifice in the gross sense of the word, not a slaughter of an unwilling victim, but the willing offering of a devoted heart, to free, as she supposed, her father and her country from a terrible obligation. . . The heroism of father and daughter are to be admired and loved in the midst of the fierce superstition round which it plays like a sunbeam on a stormy sea."

⁽³⁷⁾ **Let me alone two months.**—There was nothing which forbade this postponement for a definite purpose and period of the fulfilment of the vow. For the phrase "let me alone," see Deut. ix. 14; 1 Sam. xi. 3.

And bewail my virginity.—The thought which was so grievous to the Hebrew maiden was not death, but to die unwedded and childless. This is the bitterest wail of Antigone also, in the great play of Sophocles (*Ant.* 890); but to a Hebrew maid the pang would be more bitter, because the absence of motherhood cut off from her, and, in this instance, from her house, the hopes which prophecy had cherished. Josephus makes the expression mean no more than "to bewail *her* youth," *neoteta* (Jos. *Antt.* v. 7, § 10).

⁽³⁹⁾ **Who did with her according to his vow.**—In this significant euphemism the narrator drops the veil—as though with a shudder—over the terrible sacrifice. Of course, "did with her according to his vow" can only mean "offered her up for a burnt offering" (verse 31). "Some," says Luther, "affirm that he did not sacrifice her; but the text is clear enough." The attempt, first started by Rabbi Kimchi, to make this mean "kept her unmarried until death" —*i.e.*, shut her up in a sacred celibacy — is a mere sophistication of plain Scripture. That he did actually slay her in accordance with his *cherem* is clear, not only from the plain words, but also for the following reasons:—(1) The customs of that day knew nothing about treating women as "nuns." If there had been any institution of vestals among the Jews we should without fail have heard of it, nor would the fate of Jephthah's daughter been here regarded and represented as exceptionally tragic. (2) There are decisive Scriptural analogies to Jephthah's vow, taken in its most literal sense—Abraham (Gen. xxiii. 3), Saul (1 Sam. xiv. 44), &c. (See on verse 31.) (3) There are decisive Pagan analogies, both Oriental (2 Kings iii. 27; Amos ii. 1) and classical. Thus Idomeneus actually sacrificed his eldest son (Serv. *ad Æn.* iii. 331) in an exactly similar vow, and Agamemnon his daughter Iphigenia. (4) The ancient Jews, who were far better acquainted than we can be with the thoughts and customs of their race and the meaning of their own language, have always understood that Jephthah did literally offer his daughter as "a burnt offering." The Targum of Jonathan adds to the words "it was a custom in Israel" the explanation, "in order that no one should make his son or his daughter a burnt offering, as Jephthah did, and did not consult Phinehas the priest. Had he done so, he would have redeemed her with money"—*i.e.*, Phinchas would have decided that it was *less* crime to redeem such a *cherem* than to offer a human sacrifice. It is curious to find that another legend (*hagadah*) connects Phinehas with this event in a very different way. It says that Phinehas sanctioned, and even performed the sacrifice, and that for this very reason he was superseded by the indignation of the Israelites, which is the

And it was a ¹custom in Israel, ⁽⁴⁰⁾ that the daughters of Israel went ²yearly ³to lament the daughter of Jephthah the Gileadite four days in a year.

CHAPTER XII.—⁽¹⁾ And the men of Ephraim ⁴gathered themselves together, and went northward, and said unto Jephthah, Wherefore passedst thou over to fight against the children of Ammon, and didst not call us to go with thee? we will burn thine house upon thee with fire. ⁽²⁾ And Jephthah said unto them, I and my people were at great strife with the children of Ammon; and when I called you, ye delivered me not out of their hands. ⁽³⁾ And when I saw that ye delivered *me* not, I put my life in my hands, and passed over against the children of Ammon, and the LORD delivered them into my hand: wherefore then are ye come up unto me this day, to fight against me?

¹ Or, *ordinance.*
² Heb., *from year to year.*
³ Or, *to talk with.*
⁴ Heb., *were called.*

reason they offer for the fact that Eli was of the house, *not* of Phinehas, but of Ithamar (Lightfoot, *Works*, i. 12—18). In the same way Idomeneus, after sacrificing his eldest son, is punished by the gods with plague and by his citizens with banishment. Josephus agrees with these Jewish authorities, and says that Jephthah offered (*holokautôsen*) his daughter (see on verse 31); and so does Rabbi Tanchum. The opinion was undisputed till a thousand years after Christ, when Rabbi Kimchi invented the plausible hypothesis which has pleased so many commentators who carry their own notions to the Bible ready made, and then find them there. Ewald contents himself with saying that this "timid modern notion needs no refutation." It is remarkable that we find a similar vow as late as the sixth century after Christ. Abd Almuttalib, grandfather of Mohammed, vows to kill his son Abd Allah if God will give him ten sons. He had twelve sons; but when he wishes to perform his vow the Koreish interfere, and Abd Almuttalib, at the bidding of a priestess, gives one hundred camels as a ransom (Weil, *Mohammed*, p. 8).

It was a custom. — Or, *ordinance*—namely, to lament Jephthah's daughter. Probably the custom was local only, for we find no other allusion to it.

⁽⁴⁰⁾ **To lament.**—Rabbi Tanchum makes it mean "to praise," or "celebrate." The feelings of the Israelites towards Jephthah's daughter would be much the same as that of the Romans towards Claelia, and of other nations towards heroines whose self-sacrifice has helped them to victory.

XII.

1. Fierce and jealous conduct of the Ephraimites. 2, 3. Jephthah's expostulation with them. 4. Their defeat. 5, 6. The fugitives, tested by the word "Shibboleth," are massacred. 7. Death and burial of Jephthah. 8—10. The judgeships of Ibzan, (11, 12) Elon, and (13—15) Abdon.

⁽¹⁾ **Gathered themselves together.**—Literally, *were called.* Hence the Vulg. renders it "a sedition arose in Ephraim." No doubt the phrase arose from the circulation of some warlike summons—whether watchword or token—among the tribe (chaps. vii. 23, 24, x. 17).

Northward.—Mizpeh in Gilead lay to the north-east of the tribe of Ephraim. The Hebrew word is *Tsaphonah*, rendered *Sephenia* in some MSS. of the LXX. (Cod. A., *Kephenia*). Hence some suppose that it means "towards Tsaphon," a town in the Jordan valley not far from Succoth, which the Jews identified with Amathus (Josh. xiii. 27).

And didst not call us.—The tribe of Ephraim throughout the Book of Judges is represented in a most unenviable light—slothful and acquiescent in time of oppression, and turbulently arrogant when others have taken the initiative and won the victory (Josh. xvii. 14—18; Judges viii. 1). They brought on their own heads the terrible disgrace and humiliation which Jephthah inflicted on them. They resembled Sparta in dilatoriness, and perhaps in courage; but when Athens had won Marathon, Sparta had at least the generosity to congratulate her (Herod. v. 20).

We will burn thine house upon thee with fire—*i.e., we will burn thee alive in thy house.* They regarded it as an unpardonable offence that Jephthah should have delivered Israel without recognising their *hegemony* (see chap. viii. 1). The horrible threat shows the wild manners of the times (chaps. xiv. 15, xv. 6, xx. 48); and if a whole tribe could be guilty of such conduct, it shows how little cause we have for surprise at the much less heinous aberrations of individual men like Gideon and Jephthah and Samson.

⁽²⁾ **I and my people were at great strife with the children of Ammon.**—Literally, *I was a man of strife, I and my people, and the children of Ammon exceedingly.* We have a similar phrase in Jer. xv. 10. Jephthah adopts the tone of a recognised chief, as he had done to the Ammonites.

And when I called you, ye delivered me not.—Ephraim was not immediately affected by the Ammonite oppression, any more than it had been by the Midianite. The effect of those raids was felt chiefly by Manasseh and by the Eastern tribes. Hence the Ephraimites held themselves selfishly aloof. That we are not told of this previous appeal of the Gileadites to Ephraim illustrates the compression of the narrative. We cannot tell whether it took place before or after the summons of the Gileadites to Jephthah.

⁽³⁾ **I put my life in my hands.**—Rather, *in the hollow of my hand* (*caph*). (See for the phrase, Ps. cxix. 109; Job xiii. 14; 1 Sam. xx. 5, xxviii. 21.) It expresses extreme peril.

The Lord delivered them into my hand.—Here the word for "hand" is *yad*. Here, as he had done in arguing with the king of the Ammonites (chap. xi. 21—24), Jephthah appeals to the decision of Jehovah, as proving that he had done rightly.

Wherefore then are ye come up . . ?—For the phrase "come up" see chap. i. 1—16. Jephthah's answer is as moderate as Gideon's (chap. viii. 2, 3), though it does not display the same happy tact, and refers to topics which could not but be irritating. Whether it was made in a conciliatory spirit or not, we cannot tell. Certainly if Ephraim persisted in aggressive violence after these explanations, they placed themselves so flagrantly in the wrong that civil war became inevitable.

Jephthah Fights with Ephraim.   JUDGES, XII.   *The Test of Shibboleth.*

(4) Then Jephthah gathered together all the men of Gilead, and fought with Ephraim: and the men of Gilead smote Ephraim, because they said, Ye Gileadites *are* fugitives of Ephraim among the Ephraimites, *and* among the Manassites. (5) And the Gileadites took the passages of Jordan before the Ephraimites: and it was *so*, that when those Ephraimites which were escaped said, Let me go over; that the men of Gilead said unto him, *Art* thou an Ephraimite? If he said, Nay; (6) then said they unto him, Say now Shibboleth: and he said Sibboleth: for he could not frame to pronounce *it* right. Then they took him,

---

(4) **All the men of Gilead.**—This probably implies the Eastern tribes generally.

And the men of Gilead smote Ephraim because they said . . .—The translation and the meaning are here highly uncertain. It seems to be implied that in spite of Jephthah's perfectly reasonable answer the Ephraimites advanced to attack Gilead, and goaded the Gileadites to fury by intolerable taunts, which prevented the Gileadites from giving any quarter when they had won the victory.

Ye Gileadites are fugitives of Ephraim.—If the English Version is here correct, the meaning is, "You people of the eastern half of the tribe of Manasseh are a mere race of runaway slaves, *who belong neither to Ephraim nor to Manasseh*" (1 Sam. xxv. 10). It is very possible that fierce jealousies may have sprung up between the Eastern Manassites and their tribal brethren of the West, and that these may have mainly originated in the fact that the Eastern Manassites less and less acknowledged the lead of Ephraim, but changing their character and their habits, threw in their lot more and more with the pastoral tribes of Reuben and Gad. The taunt sounds as if it had sprung from a schism in clanship, a contemptuous disclaimer on the part of Ephraim of any ties with this Eastern half-tribe. Indeed, the taunt may have been so far true that very probably any who fell into debt or disgrace in Ephraim and Eastern Manasseh might be as likely to fly to Western Manasseh as an English defaulter might escape to New York. And if the Ephraimites indulged in such shameful jibes, it might well be deemed sufficient to account for the ruthless character of the fighting. But the rendering of the English Version is very uncertain, and the versions vary in the view they take of the meaning, punctuation, and even of the reading of the passage. On the whole, the best view is to render the words thus: *The men of Gilead smote Ephraim* [not only in the battle, but in the far more fatal pursuit] *because they* [the men of Gilead] *said, Ye are fugitives of Ephraim* (see on verse 5). Then follows the geographical explanation and historical illustration of the clause, which is, "It was possible for the Gileadites to inflict this vengeance, for (1) Gilead [lies] between Ephraim and [Eastern] Manasseh." [Part, at any rate, of Gilead belonged to Gad, and lies geographically between the district of Eastern Manasseh and the district of Ephraim, as is sufficiently clear since Ephraim has advanced "northwards," or *towards Tsaphon* (verse 1), for the attack.] Then (2) there follows the seizure of the fords, which led to the total slaughter of all these Ephraimite fugitives. One slight circumstance which adds probability to this view is that "fugitives" (comp. Jer. xliv. 14) is a term which could hardly be applied to a *whole tribe*.

(5) **Took the passages of Jordan.**—Only through these fords could the Ephraimites escape to their own tribe. (Comp. chaps. iii. 28, vii. 24.) But while it was excusable to cut off all escape from a dangerous foreign invader, it showed a terrible exasperation to leave no chance of flight to Israelites in a civil war.

Before the Ephraimites.—Literally, *to Ephraim*, which perhaps means "towards, or in the direction of, Ephraim" (*per quæ Ephraim reversurus erat*, Vulg.).

When those Ephraimites which were escaped.—The fact that the Hebrew phrase is exactly the same as in verse 4, "fugitives of Ephraim," adds great additional force to the view which we have adopted. If the rendering of the English Version be adopted in verse 4, we can only suppose that there is a bitter retribution implied in the words. The Ephraimites had taunted the Eastern Manassites with being "fugitives of Ephraim," and in the next verse they themselves appear to be in another, but fatal, sense "fugitives of Ephraim."

Art thou an Ephraimite?—There must have been considerable traffic across the Jordan fords, and the object was to distinguish between Ephraimite fugitives and harmless travellers and merchants.

(6) **Say now Shibboleth.**—The word means "a ford;" (Ps. lxix. 2) "depth of waters;" (verse 15) "water flood;" (Isa. xxvii. 12) "channel." The LXX. render it (Cod. B) "an ear of corn." (Vulg., *quod interpretatur spica*), and the word might have this meaning also (as it has in Gen. xli. 5), because the root from which it is derived means both "to flow" and "to spring." In the Alexandrian MS. of the LXX. the rendering is, "Tell us then the watchword;" but that is rather an explanation than a translation.

And he said Sibboleth.—

"And how ingrateful Ephraim
Had dealt with Jephthah—who by argument
Not worse than by his shield and spear
Defended Israel from the Ammonite—
Had not his prowess quelled their pride
In that sore battle where so many died,
Without reprieve, adjudged to death
For want of well pronouncing Shibboleth."
Milton, *Sams. Agon.* 282—289.

The word *Shibboleth* has become a proverb for the minute differences which religious parties thrust into exaggerated prominence, and defend with internecine ferocity. In this instance, however, the defective pronunciation was not the reason for putting men to death, but only the sign that the man is an Ephraimite. In theological warfare the differences of watchword or utterance have sometimes been the actual cause of the hatred and persecution; and sometimes the two opposing parties have been in agreement in every single essential fact, but have simply preferred other formulæ to express it, which has failed to cause any diminution in the fierceness of opinions. "It was," says South, "the very *shibboleth* of the party, nothing being so much in fashion with them as the name, nor more out of fashion, and out of sight too, as the thing itself" (*Sermons*, vi. 128).

For he could not frame to pronounce it right.—This is a most singular circumstance, and it is one

and slew him at the passages of Jordan: and there fell at that time of the Ephraimites forty and two thousand.

⁽⁷⁾ And Jephthah judged Israel six years. Then died Jephthah the Gileadite, and was buried in *one of* the cities of Gilead.

⁽⁸⁾ And after him Ibzan of Beth-lehem judged Israel. ⁽⁹⁾ And he had thirty sons, and thirty daughters, *whom* he sent abroad, and took in thirty daughters from abroad for his sons. And he judged Israel seven years. ⁽¹⁰⁾ Then died Ibzan, and was buried at Beth-lehem.

⁽¹¹⁾ And after him Elon, a Zebulonite, judged Israel; and he judged Israel ten years. ⁽¹²⁾ And Elon the Zebulonite died, and was buried in Aijalon in the country of Zebulun.

⁽¹³⁾ And after him Abdon the son of Hillel, a Pirathonite, judged Israel. ⁽¹⁴⁾ And he had forty sons and thirty ¹ nephews, that rode on threescore and ten ass colts: and he judged Israel eight

B.C. cir. 1130.
B.C. cir. 1137.
B.C. cir. 1120.

¹ Heb., *sons' sons.*

---

which, if it stood alone, would have decisive weight in the question of chronology. Nothing is more natural or more analogous with common linguistic phenomena than that differences of dialect and pronunciation should develop themselves between tribes divided by the deep barrier of the Jordan valley; and these differences would arise all the more rapidly if the Eastern tribes were powerfully subjected to Syrian and other foreign influences. (Comp. Neh. xiii. 24.) Still, it must have required a certain lapse of time before a difference so marked as the inability of the Western tribes to pronounce the letter *sh* could have arisen (Vulg., *eâdem literâ spicam exprimere non valens*). Cassel quotes an interesting parallel from the war of the Flemish against the French. On May 25, 1802, all the French were detected by their inability to pronounce the words *Scilt ende friend*. In the LXX. and Vulg. *Shibboleth* could not be reproduced, because the sound *sh* is unknown in Greek and Latin. Hence the LXX. use *stachus*, "wheat-ear," for Shibboleth, and leave out *Sibboleth* altogether.

Slew him.—We might wish that the meaning were that assigned to the word by the Arabic version, "they led him across." The word means, rather, *massacred, butchered*; Vulg., *jugulabant*. (Comp. Jer. xxxix. 6.) The LXX. render it "sacrificed"—almost as though each Ephraimite were regarded as a human sacrifice.

Forty and two thousand.— This immense slaughter effectually reduced the strength and arrogance of this overweening tribe. It is not, of course, meant that 42,000 were butchered at the fords, but only that that was the number of the invading army, or the number of those who fell in the campaign.

⁽⁷⁾ **Judged Israel.**—The word implies that he was one of the recognised *Shophetim*, but there are no details to show in the case of any of the judges either what were the limits of their jurisdiction or what amount of authority it implied.

In one of the cities of Gilead.—The Hebrew only says, "in *cities* of Gilead." This may, no doubt, mean "one of the cities of Gilead," as in Gen. xix. 29 "the cities *in the which* Lot dwelt" means "in *one of which* Lot dwelt." But the burial-place of so renowned a hero as Jephthah was not likely to be forgotten, and the reading adopted by the LXX. and Vulg., "in his city, Gilead" (*i.e.*, Ramoth-Gilead or Mizpeh of Gilead), is furnished by a mere change of ' into ו. The *Sebee*, in which Josephus says he was buried, may be a corruption of Mizpeh.

⁽⁸⁾ **Ibzan.**—Nothing more is known of Ibzan than is detailed in these three verses. The notion that Ibhtsam (אִבְצָן) is the same as Boaz (בֹּעַז) has nothing to support it.

Of Beth-lehem.—Usually assumed, as by Josephus (*Antt.* v. 7, § 13), to be Bethlehem in Judah. There are, however, two reasons against the identification: (1) That Bethlehem is even in this book distinguished as Bethlehem Judah (chap. xvii. 7, 9; Ruth i. 2; 1 Sam. xvii. 12), or Bethlehem Ephratah (Micah v. 1); (2) Judah seems at this epoch to have stood entirely aloof from the general life of the nation. There was a Bethlehem in Zebulon (Josh. xix. 15), and as the next judge was a Zebulonite (verse 11), and that tribe had been recently powerful and prominent (chaps. iv. 10, v. 18), it may be the town here intended.

⁽⁹⁾ **Thirty sons, and thirty daughters.**—Implying polygamy, wealth, and state (chap. viii. 30).

Whom he sent abroad—*i.e.*, whom he gave in marriage "out of his house" (Vulg., *quas emittens foras maritis dedit*). The only reason for recording the marriage of his sons and daughters is to show that he was a great man, and sought additional influence by intermarriages with other families. It showed no little prosperity that he lived to see his sixty children married.

⁽¹¹⁾ **Elon.**—The name means "a terebinth." Orientals to this day are often named from trees. (One of the author's muleteers in Palestine was named *Abû Zeitûn*, "father of olives.")

⁽¹²⁾ **Was buried in Aijalon.**—There is a play of words between אֵילוֹן (Elon) and אַיָּלוֹן (Ayalon), which is precisely the same word, though with different vowel-points. It means not "a terebinth," but "gazelle." Ajalon is not *Yalo*, which is in the tribe of Dan (Josh. x. 12; 1 Sam. xiv. 31); and it is at least doubtful whether it should not be read Elon, as in the LXX. (*Ailon*, both for the judge and his burial-place), in which case we must suppose that the place was named from him. It is not mentioned elsewhere.

⁽¹³⁾ **Abdon.**—The name means "servant." Some suppose that he is the unknown Bedan of 1 Sam. xii. 11.

Hillel.—The first occurrence of a name ("praising") afterwards destined to be so famous in the annals of Jewish theology. Hillel, the rival of Shammai, shortly before our Lord's day, may be regarded, with all his faults, as by far the greatest and best of the Rabbis.

A Pirathonite.—And, therefore, of the tribe of Ephraim.

⁽¹⁴⁾ **Thirty nephews.**—The Hebrew has "sons of sons" (*beni bhanim*), and the word *nephews* in our version always means "grandsons" (*nepoles*), *e.g.*, in Job xviii. 19, Isa. xiv. 22, 1 Tim. v. 4, as in old English generally; similarly *nieces* means "granddaughters" in Wiclif's Bible (Gen. xxxi. 43, &c.). "The Emperor Augustus . . . saw ere he died the *nephew* of his *niece*, that is to say, *his progenie to the fourth degree of lineal descent*" (Holland's *Pliny*, vii. 13; *Bible Word Book*).

That rode on threescore and ten ass colts.— Riding on asses' foals in trappings of state implies that

years. ⁽¹⁵⁾ And Abdon the son of Hillel the Pirathonite died, and was buried in Pirathon in the land of Ephraim, in the mount of the Amalekites.

CHAPTER XIII.—⁽¹⁾ And the children of Israel ^{1a}did evil again in the sight of the LORD; and the LORD delivered them into the hand of the Philistines forty years. ⁽²⁾ And there was a certain man of Zorah, of the family of the Danites,

B.C. cir. 1112.

1 Heb., *added to commit*, &c.
a ch. 2. 11; & 3. 7; & 4. 1; & 6. 1; & 10. 6.

B.C. cir. 1161.

---

they were all wealthy and distinguished persons (chap. x. 4)—perhaps, like the Turkish pennon on the horsetail, that they commanded a division (Ewald, ii. 38, 39). Again the LXX. euphemise the ass-colts into the grand and poetic word *pōlous*. Josephus says that Abdon used to ride in state with his seventy sons and grandsons, "who were all very skilful in riding horses."

⁽¹⁵⁾ **In Pirathon.**—The city of David's hero, Benaiah (2 Sam. xxiii. 30; 1 Macc. ix. 50; Jos. *Antt.* xiii. 1, § 3). It is now *Feratah*, six miles west of Shechem.

In the mount of the Amalekites.—The phrase is explained in verse 14. It points to an early settlement of Amalekites in Central Palestine.

XIII.

THE BIRTH OF SAMSON.

1. Fresh apostasy of Israel. 2—5. Appearance of an angel to the wife of Manoah, and prophecy that she is to bear a son, who is to be a Nazarite and a deliverer. 6, 7. She tells her husband. 8—10. At the prayer of Manoah the angel again appears. 11—14. His conversation with Manoah. 15—18. Manoah offers a kid. 19, 20. Disappearance of the angel. 21—23. Fears of Manoah set at rest by his wife. 24, 25. Birth and first actions of Samson.

Endeavours have been made to arrange the acts of Samson in the following four chapters in the form of a drama in five acts, each containing three incidents (Ewald); but the arrangement is arbitrary, for it counts chap. xiii. 25 as one of the incidents, and supposes that two are accidentally omitted after the carrying away of the gates of Gaza. Nor can it be made out, without arbitrary combination, that *twelve* of his acts are recorded (Bertheau). The attempts to draw out a parallel (as Roskoff has done) between the acts of Samson and the labours of Hercules is entirely valueless and unsuccessful, although, as will be seen from the notes on chaps. xiv. 6—12, xv. 4—14, xvi. 6, parts of his story may have crept into Greek legends through the agency of Phœnician traders, and though certain features in his character—*e.g.*, its genial simplicity and amorous weakness—resemble those of the legendary Greek hero. The narrative is in great measure biographical. It illustrates Samson's dedication to God as the source of his strength (chaps. xiv., xv.), and his own personal sins and follies as the source of his ruin (chap. xvi.). The first section contains six incidents:—(1) The slaying of a lion (chap. xiv. 5). (2) The slaughter of the Philistines (chap. xiv. 19). (3) The burning of the Philistines' corn-fields (chap. xv. 4, 5). (4) Slaughter of the Philistines (chap. xv. 8). (5) The breaking of the cords (chap. xv. 14). (6) Slaughter of a thousand Philistines (chap. xv. 14—17). The chief incidents in the second section are:—(1) The gates of Gaza (chap. xvi. 3). (2) The breaking of the Philistines' bonds (chap. xvi. 6—14). (3) The pulling down the temple of Dagon (chap. xvi. 22). Samson shows greater personal prowess than any of the judges, but a less noble personal character.

⁽¹⁾ **Did evil again.**—Chaps. iii. 7, iv. 1, vi. 1—11, x. 6.

Of the Philistines.—Hitherto the nation has only been cursorily mentioned (chaps. iii. 31, x. 7—11); from this time to the reign of David they play an important part. They were not Canaanites, but foreign conquerors. The district which they held, and from which the name of "Palestine" has been derived, was originally in the hands of the Avim (Deut. ii. 23). The name means "emigrants." They seem to have been also called Caphtorim (Jer. xlvii. 4), from living in Caphtor, *i.e.*, Crete (Tac. *Hist.* v. 3); but it is uncertain whether they were Semitic (Ewald, Mövers), or Hamitic (see Gen. x. 14), or Aryan (Hitzig). Their connection with Crete is inferred from the name *Cherethites* (LXX., *Kretes*). They were in Palestine by Abraham's time (Gen. xxi. 32).

Forty years.—These terminated with the battle of Ebenezer (1 Sam. vii. 13). The ark had been taken and sent back about twenty years before this battle, and the acts of Samson probably fall within those twenty years, so that Eli died about the time that Samson came of age.

⁽²⁾ **There was a certain man . . . .**—The narrative of the birth of Samuel (1 Sam. i. 1) is similarly introduced.

Zorah.—The name means "place of hornets." In Josh. xv. 33 it is mentioned with Eshtaol among the towns north-east of the Shephelah, and it belonged to Dan (Josh. xix. 41). Robinson identifies it with *Surah*, fourteen miles from Jerusalem, seven miles south of Yalo, west of Kirjath-jearim. It is mentioned again in 1 Chron. xi. 10; Neh. xi. 29. Its conical hill and abundant fountain made it a strong and convenient place.

Of the family of the Danites.—There seems to be no clear distinction between "family" (*mispachath*) and "tribe" (*shebet*), since they are used interchangeably in chap. xviii. 1, 2, 11, 30. The same word is used of the house of Levi (Zech. xii. 13). It has, however, this appropriateness, as applied to Dan, that the tribe seems to have consisted of the single family of Shuham (Num. xxvi. 42).

Manoah.—The name ("rest") perhaps expressed the yearning of the Israelites in these troubled days.

His wife was barren.—We find the same circumstance mentioned of Sarah (Gen. xvi. 1), Rebekah (Gen. xxv. 21), Hannah (1 Sam. i. 2) Elizabeth (Luke i. 7). Many of the phrases here used occur in Luke i. 7, 11, 15, 31, ii. 23. The Talmud (*Babha Bathra*, 91) says that the name of Samson's mother was Hazelelponi, or Zelelponi (for which they refer to 1 Chron. iv. 3), and that she was of the tribe of Judah. Zelelponi means "the shadow falls on me."

And bare not.—The pleonastic addition is common in the forms of ancient literature. "Sarai was barren; she had no child" (Gen. xi. 30). "I am a widow woman, and my husband is dead." It often takes the form of both a positive and negative statement, as "Thou shalt live, and not die." "It is He that hath made us, and not we ourselves," &c.

whose name *was* Manoah; and his wife *was* barren, and bare not. (3) And the angel of the LORD appeared unto the woman, and said unto her, Behold now, thou *art* barren, and bearest not: but thou shalt conceive, and bear a son. (4) Now therefore beware, I pray thee, and *a* drink not wine nor strong drink, and eat not any unclean *thing*: (5) for, lo, thou shalt conceive, and bear a son; and *b* no razor shall come on his head: for the child shall be a Nazarite unto God from the womb: and he shall begin to deliver Israel out of the hand of the Philistines. (6) Then the woman came and told her husband, saying, A man of God came unto me, and his countenance *was* like the countenance of an angel of God, very terrible: but I asked him not whence he *was*, neither told he me his name: (7) but he said unto me, Behold, thou shalt conceive, and bear a son; and now drink no wine nor strong drink, neither eat any unclean *thing*: for the child shall be a Nazarite to God from the womb to the day of his death. (8) Then Manoah intreated the LORD, and said, O my Lord, let the man of God which thou didst send come again unto us, and teach us what we shall do unto the child that shall be born. (9) And God hearkened to the voice of Manoah; and the angel of God came again unto the woman as she sat in the field: but Manoah her husband *was* not with her. (10) And the woman made haste, and ran, and shewed her husband, and said unto him, Behold, the man hath appeared unto me, that came unto me the *other* day. (11) And Manoah arose, and went after his wife, and came to the man, and said unto him, *Art* thou the man that spakest unto the woman? And he said, I *am*. (12) And Manoah said, Now let thy words come to pass. ¹How shall we order the child, and ²³ *how* shall we do unto him? (13) And the angel of the LORD said unto Manoah, Of all that I said unto the woman let her beware. (14) She may not eat of any *thing* that cometh of the vine, neither let her drink wine or strong drink, nor eat any unclean *thing*: all that I commanded her let her observe.

a Num. 6. 2, 3.
b Num. 6. 5; 1 Sam. 1. 11.
¹ Heb., *What shall be the manner of the*, &c.
² Or, *what shall he do?*
³ Heb., *what shall be his work?*

---

(3) **The angel of the Lord.**—On this expression see chap. ii. 1. Rabbi Levi Ben Gershom says that this "messenger of the Lord" was Phinehas; but nothing can be clearer than that, as in chap. vi. 11, Gen. xviii. 10, Luke i. 11—28, a supernatural being is meant.

(4) **Drink not wine.**—The mother is to share for a time in part of the Nazarite vow.

Strong drink.— *Sheekar* (LXX., *Sikera*) means *intoxicating liquor not made from grapes* (Luke i. 15).

Eat not any unclean thing. — Lev. xi. The law applied to all Israelites, but is to be specially observed by the wife of Manoah, to impress on her and on the nation the separated character of her son.

(5) **No razor shall come on his head.**—The law of the Nazarite is laid down in Num. vi., and when that chapter is read as the *Parashah* (or first lesson) in the synagogue-worship, this account of the birth of Samson, the first recorded Nazarite, is read as the *Haphtarah* (or second lesson).

Shall begin to deliver.—The weaknesses of Samson's own character rendered him unfit to achieve that complete deliverance which was carried out by Samuel. In the cases of Jephthah and Samson the Israelites learnt the power which rests in individual vows to display the occult and mysterious heroism of the human spirit, and to save people from sinking into the lowest depths (Ewald, ii. 397). The vow became a new force of the age. In Jephthah's case it had been an isolated vow, but in Samson's it was the devotion of a life, and developed an indomitable energy and power.

(6) **A man of God.**—Angels always appeared in human form, and Manoah's wife, though awe-struck by the majesty of the angel's appearance, did not know him to be other than a prophet. Josephus, writing to please the coarse tastes of Gentile readers, describes the messenger as a tall and beautiful youth, who excited the jealousy of Manoah (*Antt.* v. 8, § 2).

Very terrible.—Comp. Matt. xxviii. 3, 4.

I asked him not whence he was.—The LXX. omit the negative.

(7) **The child shall be a Nazarite.**— Comp. Luke i. 15. Since Samuel was also a Nazarite, we see that the distress of the people had led mothers to meditate on the old law of life-dedication to God. In Samson's case this vow was imposed on him from his birth, perhaps to teach the Israelites a moral lesson. Other Nazarites were John the Baptist and James, the Lord's brother. It is not impossible that Joseph was a Nazarite, for in Gen. xlix. 26 this word is used, though in the English Version it is rendered "separated" from his brethren. The order was highly valued in later days (Lam. iv. 7; Amos ii. 11).

(8) **And teach us.**—Manoah, yearning for the deliverance of his race, desired further guidance as to the training of the child, which he receives in verses 13, 14.

(12) **How shall we order the child . . . ?**—The literal rendering is given in the margin, *What shall be the ordering* (*mishpat*; LXX., *krima*) *of the child, and his work?*

(14) The object of this message only seems to have been to give certainty to Manoah.

Any thing that cometh of the vine.—In Num. vi. 3—5 it is emphatically added, "He shall separate himself from wine . . . and shall drink no vinegar of wine . . . neither shall he drink any liquor of grapes, nor eat moist grapes or dried. All the days of his separation shall he eat nothing that is made of the vine, *from the kernels even to the husk.*"

(15) And Manoah said unto the angel of the LORD, I pray thee, let us detain thee, until we shall have made ready a kid [1] for thee. (16) And the angel of the LORD said unto Manoah, Though thou detain me, I will not eat of thy bread: and if thou wilt offer a burnt offering, thou must offer it unto the LORD. For Manoah knew not that he *was* an angel of the LORD. (17) And Manoah said unto the angel of the LORD, What *is* thy name, that when thy sayings come to pass we may do thee honour? (18) And the angel of the LORD said unto him, Why askest thou thus after my name, seeing it *is* [2] secret? (19) So Manoah took a kid with a meat offering, and offered *it* upon a rock unto the LORD: and *the angel did* wonderously; and Manoah and his wife looked on. (20) For it came to pass, when the flame went up toward heaven from off the altar, that the angel of the LORD ascended in the flame of the altar. And Manoah and his wife looked on *it*, and fell on their faces to the ground. (21) But the angel of the LORD did no more appear to Manoah and to his wife. Then Manoah knew that he *was* an angel of the LORD.

(22) And Manoah said unto his wife, "We shall surely die, because we have seen God. (23) But his wife said unto him, If the LORD were pleased to kill us, he would not have received a burnt offering and a meat offering at our hands, neither would he have shewed us all these *things*, nor would as at this time have told us *such things* as these.

(24) And the woman bare a son, and called his name Samson: and the child grew, and the LORD blessed him. (25) And the Spirit of the LORD began to move him at times in the camp of Dan between Zorah and Eshtaol.

[1 Heb., *before thee.*]
[2 Or, *wonderful.*]
[a Ex. 38. 20; ch. 6. 22.]

---

(15) **A kid for thee.**—Literally, *before thy face.* The narrative is closely analogous to that of the appearance of the angel to Gideon, and there is the same uncertainty in the terms used, so that we cannot certainly decide whether Manoah's object was to offer a sacrifice or to offer hospitality. The verb *gnasoth*, like the Greek *rezein* (LXX., *poiein*) and the Latin *facere*, means either "to do" or "to sacrifice." A kid was a special delicacy (Gen. xxvii. 9; 1 Sam. xvi. 20). (See Augustine, *Quaest.*, in Jud. vii. 53.)

(16) **Thou must offer it unto the Lord.**—Rather, *a burnt offering unto the Lord thou mayest offer it.* (Comp. chap. vi. 20.) Angels invariably discourage and reprove that "worship of angels" (Col. ii. 18), which was the tendency of early Gnostic sects (Dan. x.; Rev. xix. 10, xxii. 8). The angel might have partaken of earthly food, as we see from Gen. xviii. 8, xix. 3. Hence Milton says:—

"Food alike these pure
Intelligential substances require,
As doth your rational."—*Par. Lost*, v. 418.

(17) **What is thy name?**—Comp. Gen. xxxii. 29; Exod. iii. 13; Prov. xxx. 4.

We may do thee honour.—Especially by a gift, which is the commonest Eastern notion of the word (Num. xxii. 17; Jos. *Antt.* v. 8, § 3).

(18) **Seeing it is secret.**—The word is *peli*, which in Isa. ix. 5 is rendered "wonderful." The word is an adjective, not the actual name of the angel. The only angel who names himself in Scripture is Gabriel.

(19) **Did wonderously.**—With a reference to the word *peli* in the previous verse. (Comp. chap. vi. 20—26.)

(20) **From off the altar.**—The rock (*tsor*) of verse 19 is now hallowed into an altar (*mizbeach*).

Fell on their faces.—Comp. Lev. ix. 24; Num. xiv. 5; Ezek. i. 28.

(22) **We shall surely die.**—See on chap. vi. 22.

We have seen God.—*As seeing Him who is invisible*; by seeing a manifestation of Him in human form. "Thou canst not see my face: for there shall no man see me and live" (Exod. xxxiii. 20). (Comp. Gen. xxxii. 30; Deut. v. 24.)

(24) **Samson.**—Josephus renders the word "strong" (ἰσχυρός), deriving it from a root (*shameem*), and perhaps not unwilling to suggest an analogy between Samson and the Greek Hercules. St. Jerome, rendering it "strength of the sun," derives it from *shemesh*, "sun," and *on*, "strength." It is more probable that it means "sunny." In Ezra iv. 8 we have the name Shimshai, perhaps from the same root. The connection of "the sun" with strength was very natural (chap. v. 31; Ps. xix. 5, 6). The Rabbis say that he was "named after the name of God, who is called sun and shield of Israel" (Ps. lxxxiv. 12). The mother gave the name in this instance. (Comp. Gen. xxix. 32—35, xxxv. 18; Luke i. 60.) Ewald refers it to an Egyptian root, and makes it mean "servant of God," in reference to his being a Nazarite.

The child grew, and the Lord blessed him.—God has many different kinds of blessings, and those here alluded to appear to be the gifts of health, strength, courage, &c. These blessings by no means place Samson on a level with Samuel (1 Sam. ii. 21—26, iii. 19) or John the Baptist (Luke ii. 80).

(25) **The Spirit of the Lord.**—Chap. iii. 10. The Targum of Jonathan paraphrases it rightly, "The spirit of courage from Jehovah." Amos (ii. 11) ranks Nazarites with prophets. "Different as may be their mode of action, they agree in a belief, which strings up every power to its highest tension, that they are Jehovah's very own, consecrated to Him by a wholly special calling" (Ewald).

Began to move him.—Literally, *to agitate* or *thrust him* (*paham*, Gen. xli. 8; Dan. ii. 1). The word implies vehement and overwhelming impulses to noble deeds ("*fing an ihn zu treiben*," Luther), which, however, only came over him "at times" (chaps. xiv. 6, xv. 14, xvi. 20). The LXX. rendering, "to go with him," comes from a wrong reading.

In the camp of Dan.—Rather, *in Mahaneh-dan.* Doubtless the name originated in the migration of

JUDGES, XIV.

CHAPTER XIV.—⁽¹⁾ And Samson went down to Timnath, and saw a woman in Timnath of the daughters of the Philistines. ⁽²⁾ And he came up, and told his father and his mother, and said, I have seen a woman in Timnath of the daughters of the Philistines: now therefore get her for me to wife. ⁽³⁾ Then his father and his mother said unto him, *Is there* never a woman among the daughters of thy brethren, or among all my people, that thou goest to take a wife of the uncircumcised Philistines? And Samson said unto his father, Get her for me; for ¹ she pleaseth me well. ⁽⁴⁾ But his father and his mother knew not that it *was* of the LORD, that he sought an occasion against the Philistines: for at that time the Philistines had dominion over Israel.

⁽⁵⁾ Then went Samson down, and his father and his mother, to Timnath, and came to the vineyards of Timnath: and, behold, a young lion roared ² against him. ⁽⁶⁾ And the Spirit of the LORD came mightily upon him, and he rent him as he would have rent a kid, and *he had* nothing in his hand: but he told not his

B.C. cir. 1141.

¹ Heb., *she is right in mine eyes.*

² Heb., *in meeting him.*

---

this hard-pressed tribe, which is mentioned in chap. xviii. 11, 12, but which took place long before this time. The sites of Mahaneh-dan and Eshtaol have not been identified. In his hatred to the enemies of his country, Samson is the Hannibal of the Hebrews.

XIV.

1—4. Samson desires a woman of Timnath to wife. 5—7. He kills a lion on his way. 8, 9. He finds honey in the carcase. 10, 11. The wedding feast. 12—14. Samson's riddle. 15—18. It is treacherously revealed by his wife. 19, 20. He slays thirty Philistines, and so pays the forfeit.

⁽¹⁾ **To Timnath.**—This town, of which the site still retains the name Tibneh, is perhaps the same as that in Gen. xxxviii. 12, unless that be a town in the mountains of Judah, as Judah is there said to have "gone *up*," not as here, "*down*" to it. In Josh. xv. 10 it is assigned to Judah, but appears to have been afterwards ceded to Dan (chap. xix. 45). The name means "a portion," and is found also in Timnath-serah, where Joshua was buried (Josh. xxiv. 30).

Of the daughters of the Philistines.—This was against the spirit of the law, which forbad intermarriages with Canaanites (Exod. xxxiv. 16; Deut. vii. 3, 4). The sequel showed the wisdom of the law (2 Cor. vi. 14).

⁽²⁾ **Get her for me to wife.**—These arrangements were always left to parents, who paid the marriage dower (Gen. xxxiv. 4—12). (Comp. chap. xii. 9; Neh. x. 30, &c.)

⁽³⁾ **Of the uncircumcised Philistines.**—This on the lips of Israelites was a term of peculiar hatred (1 Sam. xvii. 36). How repugnant such a marriage would be in the eyes of Manoah and his wife we may see from the story of Simeon, Levi, and the Shechemites (Gen. xxxiv).

She pleaseth me well.—Literally, *she is right in my eyes* (verse 7; 1 Kings ix. 12).

⁽⁴⁾ **That it was of the Lord.**—All that can be meant is that in this marriage God was overruling the course of events to the furtherance of His own designs. He makes even the weakness and the fierceness of man redound to His praise. (Comp. Josh. xi. 10; 2 Chron. xxv. 20.) See the same phrase in the story of Rehoboam's folly (1 Kings xii. 15). "Behold this evil is of the Lord," says Elisha in 2 Kings vi. 33. It is the strong sense of the Divine rule which we find even in heathen writers, so that in the very opening lines of Homer we find the poet saying, "that amid all the crimes and passions of men the counsel of Zeus was being accomplished."

"Achilles' wrath, to Greece the direful spring
 Of woes unnumbered, heavenly goddess sing:
 That wrath which hurled to Pluto's gloomy reign
 The souls of mighty chiefs unnumbered slain,
 Whose limbs, unburied on the naked shore,
 Devouring dogs and hungry vultures tore,
 Since great Achilles and Atrides strove,—
 Such was the sovereign doom, and such the will of Jove!".

That he sought an occasion.—Some commentators explain "he" to mean Jehovah, which seems most unlikely. The word rendered "an occasion" is rather, "a quarrel" (LXX., "retribution," or "vengeance").

⁽⁵⁾ **The vineyards of Timnath.**—All this part of Palestine, and especially the neighbouring valley of Sorek (chap. xvi. 4), was famous for its vines (Isa. v. 2; Jer. ii. 21). The hills of Judah, which at that time were laboriously terraced up to the summit, like the hill-sides of the Italian valleys, were peculiarly favourable for vineyards (Gen. xlix. 11). Now they are bleak and bare by the denudation of centuries, but might by labour be once more rendered beautiful and fruitful.

A young lion.—Literally, *a lion of lions*, like "a kid of goats" (chap. xiii. 15). That lions and other wild beasts were still common in Palestine, we see, both from the direct statement of the fact (1 Kings x. 19; 2 Kings xvii. 25, &c.), from the incidents which show it to have been so (1 Sam. xvii. 34; 2 Sam. xxiii. 20; 1 Kings xiii. 25, xx. 36), and from the names Arieh (2 Kings xv. 6), Lebaoth ("lionesses," Josh. xv. 32), Beth Lebaoth (*id.* xix. 6), Shaalbim ("jackals"), Zeboim ("hyenas"), &c.

⁽⁶⁾ **The Spirit of the Lord.**—Implying here an access of courage and strength. The verb rendered "came mightily" literally means *pervaded*, as in verse 19, chap. xv. 14; 1 Sam. x. 10. (Comp. 1 Sam. xviii. 10—of the evil spirit rushing upon Saul; LXX., "leapt upon him;" Vulg., *irruit*.)

Rent him.—Josephus (with the intention of making his Greek readers think of Hercules and the Nemean lion) says "he *throttled* him." Of course this was a most heroic exploit, but it is not unparalleled. Pausanias, in his *Eliaca* (ap. Suid. *Lex.* s.v. Polydamas), related a feat of the athlete Polydamas, who in his youth slew, while unarmed, a great and strong lion in Olympus, B.C. 400. Cases are recorded in which Arabs have done the same. Similar acts of prowess are attributed to David (1 Sam. xvii. 54) and to Benaiah (2 Sam. xxiii. 28).

father or his mother what he had done. (7) And he went down, and talked with the woman; and she pleased Samson well. (8) And after a time he returned to take her, and he turned aside to see the carcase of the lion: and, behold, *there was* a swarm of bees and honey in the carcase of the lion. (9) And he took thereof in his hands, and went on eating, and came to his father and mother, and he gave them, and they did eat: but he told not them that he had taken the honey out of the carcase of the lion.

(10) So his father went down unto the woman: and Samson made there a feast; for so used the young men to do.

(11) And it came to pass, when they saw him, that they brought thirty companions to be with him. (12) And Samson said unto them, I will now put forth a riddle unto you: if ye can certainly declare it me within the seven days of the feast, and find *it* out, then I will give you thirty [1] sheets and thirty change of garments: (13) but if ye cannot declare *it* me, then shall ye give me thirty sheets and thirty change of garments. And they said unto him, Put forth thy riddle, that we may hear it. (14) And he said unto them,

Out of the eater came forth meat, and out of the strong came forth sweetness.

[1] Or, *shirts*.

He told not his father or his mother.—This reticence shows how free he was from all boastfulness.

(7) **Talked with the woman.**—His father and mother seem to have preceded him, and made the betrothal arrangements; otherwise he would not have been allowed by Eastern custom to talk with her. It cannot mean "talked *about* the woman," as Rosenmüller says.

(8) **After a time.**—There is nothing to show how long this time was. A betrothal might last a year. In chap. xi. 4 the same phrase ("after days") is used of many years.

To take her.—To lead her to his own home after the bridal feast.

A swarm of bees and honey in the carcase of the lion.—This incident has been questioned, because it is truly said that bees hate all putrescence and decomposition, and that the notion of bees being generated in the rotting bodies of oxen (which we find in Virgil, *Georgic* iv., &c.) is a vulgar error. But it is overlooked that the word "carcase" here means (as the Syriac renders it) "skeleton." The fierce sun of the East dries up all the animal moisture of a dead body, and reduces it to a skeleton with extreme rapidity, and bees have no dislike to dried bones as a place in which to swarm. Thus Herodotus tells us (v. 114) that when the Amathusians cut off the head of Onesilus, because he besieged them, and hung it over their gates, a swarm of bees filled the skull with their combs and honey. Rosenmüller also quotes the authority of the physician Aldrovand for the story that swarms of bees built their combs between the skeletons of two sisters who were buried in the Church of Santa Croce, at Verona, in 1566. (Comp. Plin. *H. N.*, xi. 24; Varro, *R. R.*, iii. 16.)

(9) **He took thereof in his hands.**—Unless he considered that a skeleton could not be regarded as a dead body, he could not have done this without breaking the express conditions of his Nazarite vow (Num. v. 6).

He told not them.—Perhaps from the general reticence of his character, but more probably because they might have been more scrupulous than he was about the ceremonial defilement involved in eating anything which had touched a carcase. Possibly, too, he may have already made the riddle in his head, and did not wish to give any clue to its solution.

(10) **Went down unto the woman.**—Formally, to claim her as the bride of his son.

Made there a feast.—According to the universal custom in all ages (Gen. xxix. 22; Rev. xix. 9). The LXX. add the words "seven days." (Comp. Gen. xxix. 27.)

(11) **When they saw him.**—The reason why this clause is added is somewhat obscure, and this is perhaps the reason why the LXX. and Josephus, without any warrant, render it "when they were afraid of him," which would involve a change in the reading.

They brought thirty companions.—It was necessary to the splendour of the marriage feast that there should be these paranymphs (*shoshbenim*, or "children of the bride-chamber," Matt. ix. 15). The fact that Samson had brought none with him seems to prove that his marriage was highly unpopular among his own countrymen. *Thirty*, however, was a most unusual number.

(12) **I will now put forth a riddle unto you.** —*Chidah*, "a riddle," comes from *chud*, "to knot." The use of riddles at feasts is of great antiquity both among the Jews (1 Kings x. 1, &c.) and Greeks (Athen. x. 457; Pollux, vi. 107, &c.). Jewish legends have much to tell us of the riddles which passed between Solomon and the Queen of Sheba, and between Solomon and Hiram (Dius *ap.* Jos., *Antt.* viii. 5, § 3); and as large sums often depended on the discovery of the answer, they were very much of the nature of wagers. A sharp boy named Abdemon helped Hiram, just as the Greek sage Bias is said to have helped Amasis to solve the riddles of the Ethiopian king, which would otherwise have caused heavy losses. The Sphinx of Theban legend devoured those who could not solve her riddle. Mirth and riddles are also connected with the rites of Hercules (Müller, *Dorians*, ii. 12).

Sheets.—Rather, as in the margin, *shirts*; but it means shirts of fine linen (*sedinim*; LXX., Vulg., *sindones*), such as are only worn by the wealthy (Isa. iii. 23; Mark xiv. 51). Samson's offer was fair enough, for if defeated, each paranymph would only have to provide one *sindon* and one robe, whereas Samson, if they guessed his riddle, would have to provide thirty.

(14) **Out of the strong came forth sweetness.** —The antithesis is not perfect, but we cannot strain the word "strong" to mean "bitter," as the LXX. and Syriac do. Josephus gives the riddle in the form, "the all-devouring having generated sweet food from itself, though itself far from sweet" (*Antt.* v. 8, § 6). The whole of Samson's life has been described by Ewald as "a charming poetic picture, in which the interspersed

And they could not in three days expound the riddle. (15) And it came to pass on the seventh day, that they said unto Samson's wife, Entice thy husband, that he may declare unto us the riddle, lest we burn thee and thy father's house with fire: have ye called us ¹ to take that we have? *is it* not so? (16) And Samson's wife wept before him, and said, Thou dost but hate me, and lovest me not: thou hast put forth a riddle unto the children of my people, and hast not told *it* me. And he said unto her, Behold, I have not told *it* my father nor my mother, and shall I tell *it* thee? (17) And she wept before him ² the seven days, while their feast lasted: and it came to pass on the seventh day, that he told her, because she lay sore upon him: and she told the riddle to the children of her people. (18) And the men of the city said unto him on the seventh day before the sun went down,

What *is* sweeter than honey? and what *is* stronger than a lion?

And he said unto them, If ye had not plowed with my heifer, ye had not found out my riddle. (19) And the Spirit of the LORD came upon him, and he went down to Ashkelon, and slew thirty men of them, and took their ³ spoil, and gave change of garments unto them which expounded the riddle.

And his anger was kindled, and he went up to his father's house. (20) But Samson's wife was *given* to his companion, whom he had used as his friend.

¹ Heb., *to possess us, or, to impoverish us.*
² Or, *the rest of the seven days, &c.*
³ Or, *apparel.*

---

verses gleam forth like the brightest pearls in a circlet." It must be confessed that the riddle was hardly a fair one, for the event to which it alluded was most unusual, and no one could have guessed such a riddle without some clue; for—

"'Tis seldom when the bee doth leave her comb
In the dead carrion."
Shakespeare: *Henry V.*, ii. 4.

Cassel quotes a curious parallel from the legends of North Germany. The judges offer a woman her husband's life if she can make a riddle which they cannot guess. On her way to the court she had found the carcase of a horse in which a bird had built its nest and hatched six young ones, which she took away. Her riddle was (I venture rudely to translate the rude old lines):—

"As hitherwards on my way I sped,
I took the living out of the dead,
Six were thus of the seventh made quit:—
To rede my riddle, my lords, 'tis fit."

The judges failed, and the husband was spared (Mullenhof, *Sagen*, p. 506).

In three days.—It is hard to see why this is mentioned if it was only on the *seventh* day (verse 15) that they tried the unfair means of inducing Samson's wife to reveal the secret. Bishop Hervey conjectures, with much probability, that we should read *shesheth* "six," for *shelsheth*, "four." The LXX. and Syriac read "on the fourth day," and ו (7) may easily have been confused with ד (4).

(15) **On the seventh day.**—When they were in despair.

Lest we burn thee and thy father's house with fire.—As, indeed, they ultimately did (chap xv. 6). If Samson appears in no very favourable light in this chapter, the Philistines show themselves to be most mean, treacherous, and brutal.

To take that we have.—The Hebrew expression is stronger—"to spoil us," or "make us paupers." The "is it not so?" is added to show the vehemence of the question.

(16) **Wept before him.**—Samson's riddle had the effect of making the whole wedding-feast of this ill-starred marriage one of the most embittered and least joyous that ever fell to a bridegroom's lot. This was a just punishment for his lawless fancies, though God overruled them to His own ends. A weeping, teazing, fretting bride and sullen guests might have served as a warning that Philistine marriages were not good for the sons of Israel.

(17) **The seven days.**—The margin suggests that it may mean *the rest of the seven days*. If not, it can only imply that mere feminine curiosity had induced Samson's wife to weary her husband to tell her the secret from the first.

On the seventh day.—Perhaps he hoped that he might prevent her from finding an opportunity to betray his secret.

He told her.—"Keep the door of thy mouth from her that lieth in thy bosom" (Micah vii. 5).

She lay sore upon him—*i.e.*, she grievously troubled him (LXX., Vulg.).

She told the riddle.—Perhaps she might have done so in any case, but she now had the excuse of violent menaces.

(18) **What is sweeter than honey?**—Their answer is given in the same rhythmical form as the riddle itself.

If ye had not plowed with my heifer.—Many commentators, following Rabbi Levi Ben Gershom, read in this proverbial phrase an implication that Samson suspected his wife of adultery; but there is no sufficient reason for this view.

(19) **To Ashkelon.**—Probably he seized the opportunity of some great feast to Dagon, or even of another marriage festival, since the linen robes and rich garments would not be such as would be worn every day.

Took their spoil.—The Hebrew werd *chalisah* is rendered "armour" in 2 Sam. ii. 21 (LXX., *panoplia*), and the Targum on verse 13 seems to understand "suits of armour."

Gave . . . unto them which expounded the riddle.—They were unaware whence he had obtained the means to discharge his wager. The morality of the act can, of course, only be judged from the standpoint of the time.

(20) **To his companion, whom he had used as his friend**—*i.e.*, to the chief of the paranymphs (the bride-conductor, LXX.); "the friend of the bride-

Samson's Wife Given to Another.   JUDGES, XV.   *He Burns the Philistines' Corn.*

CHAPTER XV.—(1) But it came to pass within a while after, in the time of wheat harvest, that Samson visited his wife with a kid; and he said, I will go in to my wife into the chamber. But her father would not suffer him to go in. (2) And her father said, I verily thought that thou hadst utterly hated her; therefore I gave her to thy companion: is not her younger sister fairer than she? ¹ take her, I pray thee, instead of her.

(3) And Samson said concerning them, ² Now shall I be more blameless than the Philistines, though I do them a displeasure. (4) And Samson went and caught three hundred foxes, and took ³ firebrands, and turned tail to tail, and put a firebrand in the midst between two tails. (5) And when he had set the brands on fire, he let *them* go into the standing corn of the Philistines, and burnt up both the shocks, and also the

B. C. cir. 1140.

1 Heb., *let her be thine*

2 Or, *Now shall I be blameless from the Philistines, though*, &c.

3 Or, *torches.*

---

groom" (John iii. 29). Hence, even if the suspicion as to the meaning of Samson's words in verse 18 be unfounded, it is clear that there was treachery and secret hostility at work. Bunsen renders the phrase, " to his companion, whose friend (*amica*) she was."

XV.

1, 2. Samson, desiring to return to his wife, learns that she has been betrothed to another. 3—5. He revenges himself by setting fire to the crops of the Philistines by means of jackals and fire-brands. 6. The Philistines burn his wife and her father. 7, 8. He inflicts a massacre upon them. 9—13. He is handed over to them by the people of Judah. 14—17. He breaks his cords, and slaughters a thousand with the jaw-bone of an ass. 18, 19. The Fountain of the Crier.

(1) **Within a while after.**—" After days " (chaps. xi. 4, xiv. 8).

In the time of wheat harvest.—This, in the *Shephelah*, would be about the middle of May.

Visited his wife with a kid.—We find the same present given by Judah to Tamar in Gen. xxxviii. 17. We may compare the complaint of the elder brother of the prodigal, that his father has never given him a kid (Luke xv. 29).

I will go in to my wife.—Uxoriousness was the chief secret of the weakness and ruin of Samson, as it was afterwards of a very different type of man, Solomon.

Into the chamber.—Cant. i. 4, iii. 4.

(2) **Verily thought . . . utterly hated.**—In the emphatic simplicity of the Hebrew style it is, *Saying I said that hating, thou hatest her.* As Samson had left his wife in anger immediately after the wedding feast, the father might have reasonably supposed that he meant finally to desert her.

I gave her.—This must mean *I have betrothed her*, for otherwise she would not have still been living in her father's house. But if the father had been an honourable man he could not under these circumstances have done less than restore the dowry which Manoah had given for her.

To thy companion.—See on chap. xiv. 20.

Her younger sister.—The father sought in this way to repair the wrong he had inflicted, and to offer some equivalent for the dower which he had wrongly appropriated.

(3) **Concerning them.**—There is no reason for this rendering. It should be *to them.* The Vulg. has *cui*, and the LXX. " to them," or " to him."

Now—*i.e.*, This time. He means that his second act of vengeance will at least have more excuse than his assault on the Askelonites.

More blameless than the Philistines.—Rather, *innocent as regards the Philistines.* The words are somewhat obscure. Ewald renders them—

" This time I am quit of the Philistines,
If 'tis evil I think of doing them."

(4) **Caught three hundred foxes.**—Rather, *three hundred jackals.* The word *Shualim* is used for both; but it would be difficult to catch three hundred foxes, whereas the jackals are still heard howling in herds about these very regions at night. They must have been still more common in Palestine in ancient days, and hence we find such names as " the land of Shual " (1 Sam. xiii. 17), Hazar-shual (" jackal's enclosure," Josh. xv. 28), Shalim (1 Sam. xi. 4), Shaalabbin (" place of foxes or jackals," Josh. xix. 42). There would be no difficulty in trapping them; nor is it said that they were all let loose at once.

Turned tail to tail.—This implies that he tied the tails together (LXX., *sunedēsen*; Vulg., *junxit*).

Put a firebrand in the midst.—The firebrands were pieces of resinous wood, like Gideon's torches (chap. vii. 20), which were loosely trailed between the tails of the jackals. The object of tying *two* together was to impede their motion a little, so that they might not dart away so violently as to extinguish the torch.

(5) **Into the standing corn of the Philistines.**—He probably did this at night, when his actions would be unobserved, and no one would be at hand to quench the flames. We may imagine him watching the trails of fire from his rocky fastness, and exulting as the conflagration reddened the night. The heat of a tropical country makes everything so dry that his plan would be certain to succeed. To burn the crops of an Arab is to this day the deadliest of all injuries (Burckhardt). This was the method adopted by Absalom, in 2 Sam. xiv. 30, to gain an interview with Joab. It is needless to point out that the adoption of these rough, coarse, and cruel expedients must be as little judged by a later and better standard as his thirst for the revenge of personal wrongs. There can be no ground to question the literal truth of the narrative. It is in entire accordance with the custom of the East, and it finds curious confirmation from the story in Ovid's *Fasti*, that every year, at the Cerealia, torches were tied to the tails of foxes, and they were let loose in the Roman circus, to commemorate the incident that on one occasion a young man at Carseoli, to punish a fox for depredations on his hen-coops, had wrapped it up in straw, and set it on fire, and that the creature had escaped into the corn-fields and burnt down the standing crops (Ovid, *Fasti*, iv. 681—711). The attempt of Bochart to establish any connection between this custom and the revenge of Samson is quite untenable, but the incident itself throws

standing corn, with the vineyards *and* olives. ⁽⁶⁾ Then the Philistines said, Who hath done this? And they answered, Samson, the son in law of the Timnite, because he had taken his wife, and given her to his companion. And the Philistines came up, and burnt her and her father with fire.

⁽⁷⁾ And Samson said unto them, Though ye have done this, yet will I be avenged of you, and after that I will cease. ⁽⁸⁾ And he smote them hip and thigh with a great slaughter: and he went down and dwelt in the top of the rock Etam.

⁽⁹⁾ Then the Philistines went up, and

---

light on the possibility of the narrative. Ewald refers to *Mêghadúta*, liv. 4; Babrius, *Fab.*, xi.

Both the shocks, and also the standing corn. —Literally, *from the heap, even up to the standing.* The extent of the vengeance and its terrible future consequences would be fully, and we fear ruthlessly, estimated by Samson, as he saw the rivers of fire running and spreading through that vast plain of corn-land in harvest-time. (Comp. Exod. xxii. 6.)

With the vineyards and olives.—Literally, *and to vineyard, to olive.* There may be some slight corruption in the text, or it may be an abbreviation of "from vineyard to vineyard, and from olive to olive." (Comp. Micah vii. 12.) The low vines festooning the trees and trellis-work, and the olives with their dry trunks, would be sure to suffer injury.

⁽⁶⁾ **They answered.**—The phrase is impersonal; but Samson had quite openly threatened vengeance in speaking to the Timnites, and is not likely to have done his work unaided or to have been very reticent about it; nor would the poor oppressed Israelites be inclined to keep his secret when they were confronted with the fury of the Philistines.

Burnt her and her father with fire.—Was this meant as a way of revenging themselves on Samson, or of avenging him for the wrongs which he had received from the Timnite? The latter seems to be most unlikely. Looking with despair and fury at the blackened fields which but a few days before had been thick with golden corn, it is inconceivable that the Philistines would be in a mood to perform an act of justice for the sake of the deadly enemy who had inflicted this loss upon them. Their motive is clear enough. They wished to insult and injure Samson, and, at the same time, vent their fierce spleen on the man whose family and whose conduct had led to all these troubles. That they thought about "burning as the punishment of adultery among the Jews" (Gen. xxxviii. 24, &c.) is still more improbable. To burn a person, and his house and his family, seems to have been the ordinary revenge of these barbarous days. (See chaps. xii. 1, xiv. 15.)

⁽⁷⁾ **Though ye have done this.**—The rendering of these words is involved in the same obscurity as other details of the narrative. They may mean, " If ye act thus, then will I be avenged on you before I have done;" and perhaps the verse implies, "as long as you avenge yourselves, I mean to retaliate."

⁽⁸⁾ **Hip and thigh.**—There is no doubt that the expression intensifies the words "with a great slaughter;" but the origin of the phrase is a matter of conjecture. It may be purely general, like the German expression "*Arm und Bein*," or "*er hieb den Feind in die Pfanne*," or "*in Kochstücke*" ("A blow strikes a fugitive on the hip, and that would be enough; another blow on the thigh ends him"). "Hence," says Ewald, "it means thigh over and above"—*i.e.*, besides the hip. It cannot possibly mean "cavalry and infantry," as the Chaldee renders it, or be a reference to wrestling (Greek, *huposkelizein*); nor is it likely to have a sacrificial origin (" good and bad pieces "). It is hard to see what St. Jerome means by his gloss "*ita ut stupentes suram femori imponerent.*" Literally it is, *thigh upon hip*, or *leg upon thigh* (LXX., κνήμην ἐπὶ μηρόν). May it not have had its origin in some such fierce custom as that known to the Greeks as *akroteriasmos*, or *maschalismos*, in which the extremities of a corpse were cut off and placed under the arm-pits? (Æsch. *Cho.* 439; Soph. *El.* 445.) Thus in Hesychius and Suidas *maschalismata* means "mutilated limbs," and also "the flesh of the shoulders laid on the haunches at sacrifices."

With a great slaughter.—It is not said, nor is it necessarily implied (any more than in the case of Shamgar), that Samson was absolutely alone in these raids. There is nothing either in the narrative or in the ordinary style of Hebrew prose which makes any such inference necessary, nor, indeed, is there any such inference drawn in many similar passages (*e.g.*, chap. i. 20, &c.).

In the top of the rock Etam.—It should undoubtedly be *in a ravine* (or cave) *of the cliff Etam.* For instance, in verse 11 the men of Judah could not go *down* to the top of a rock, and the same word is rendered " cleft" in Isa. lvii. 5, and should be so rendered for " top " in Isa. iii. 21 (LXX., "in a hole of the rock," and " in the cave of Etam;" Vulg., *in spelunca petrae*). This explains the expression " went down " in this verse, and " brought him up " in verse 13. Such cliff-caves are the natural refuge of oppressed peoples (chap. vi. 2; 1 Sam. xiii. 6; 1 Kings xviii. 13). These caves, like the cave of Adullam, are often supplied with water by natural springs, and one man may defend them against a multitude. The LXX. (Cod. A) add the words " by the torrent." The site of Etam is uncertain; but it is in the tribe of Judah, which Samson only enters once, or, possibly (chap. xvi. 3), twice, and then only as a fugitive.

⁽⁹⁾ **Then the Philistines went up.** — They "went up" in hostile array against the hill-country of Judea to take vengeance for the dreadful injury which Samson had inflicted on them.

Spread themselves in Lehi.—The use of the name before the incident from which a place is said to have received the name is found also in the case of Hormah (Num. xiv. 45, xxi. 3). It was called in full Ramath-Lehi. (See on verse 17.) The character of the narrative suggests the question whether the name may not have existed previously, and the play on words may not have been *adapted* by Samson to the incident. For the name of the place is *Lechi* (לחי), and "a jawbone" is *Lehi* (לחי). *Shen*, "tooth," is the name of an isolated sharp rock (1 Sam. xiv. 4), and therefore " jaw" would not be an unnatural name for a range of such rocks. Josephus, however, says that before Samson's exploit the place " had no name." It may be again alluded to in 2 Sam. xxiii. 11, where the words rendered "into a troop" may mean " to Lehi," as it is understood by

pitched in Judah, and spread themselves in Lehi. (10) And the men of Judah said, Why are ye come up against us? And they answered, To bind Samson are we come up, to do to him as he hath done to us. (11) Then three thousand men of Judah [1] went to the top of the rock Etam, and said to Samson, Knowest thou not that the Philistines *are* rulers over us? what *is* this *that* thou hast done unto us? And he said unto them, As they did unto me, so have I done unto them. (12) And they said unto him, We are come down to bind thee, that we may deliver thee into the hand of the Philistines. And Samson said unto them, Swear unto me, that ye will not fall upon me yourselves. (13) And they spake unto him, saying, No; but we will bind thee fast, and deliver thee into their hand: but surely we will not kill thee. And they bound him with two new cords, and brought him up from the rock. (14) *And* when he came unto Lehi, the Philistines shouted against him: and the Spirit of the LORD came mightily upon him, and the cords that *were* upon his arms became as flax that was burnt with fire, and his bands [2] loosed from off his hands. (15) And he found a [3] new jaw-

[1] Heb., *went down.*
[2] Heb., *were melted.*
[3] Heb., *moist.*

Josephus (*Antt.* vii. 12, § 4) and some MSS. of the LXX.

(10) **Why are ye come up against us?**—Samson was not of the tribe of Judah, which seems to have been living in contented servitude.

(11) **Went to the top of the rock Etam.**—Rather, *went down to the cave of the rock Etam.* They would easily gain information as to Samson's hiding-place.

What is this that thou hast done unto us?—The abject condition into which the Lion Tribe had sunk can best be estimated by this *reproach* against the national hero, and still more by their baseness in betraying him. He finds no sympathy. There are no patriots in search of heroes. What might not this 3,000 have achieved if they had been like Gideon's 300?

(12) **Swear unto me, that ye will not fall upon me yourselves.**—It seems as if Samson were parleying with them from some point of vantage which he could easily have defended for a time.

(13) **Brought him up from the rock.**—Again the details are uncertain. Was Samson's cave down the steep side of a cliff? Such caves are common in Palestine, and such a situation would explain these expressions. (See Josephus, *Antt.* xiv. 15, § 5, where he says that the brigands' caves were inaccessible against a few defenders, either from below or from above, and that Herod could only attack the robbers by letting down soldiers in chests from the top of the precipices.)

(14) **Shouted against him.**—Rather, *cheered as they came to meet him* (LXX., ἠλάλαξαν εἰς ἀπάντησιν αὐτοῦ; Vulg., *cum vociferantes occurrissent ei*). The verb *heerioo* is an onomatopœia, like our "hurrah." This was not a war cry, as in 1 Sam. xvii. 20, but a shout of joy.

The cords that were upon his arms became as flax.—It seems clear that the poetical colour and rhythmic structure of the narrative are influenced by some poem which described the deeds of Samson.

That was burnt with fire.—In both the LXX. and the Vulg. we find the metaphor, "flax when it has *smelt* the fire."

His bands loosed.—Literally, *melted,* or *flowed off,* a highly poetic expression. A legend of Hercules in Egypt, who suddenly burst his bonds and slew the Egyptians who were leading him to sacrifice, may possibly have been coloured by this event in the life of Samson. (See Rawlinson's *Herodotus*, ii., p. 70.)

(15) **A new jawbone.**—Literally, *a moist jawbone* —*i.e.,* the jawbone of an animal recently dead, and before the bone had become brittle. In this instance, at any rate, Samson might feel himself absolved from the rule of ceremonial cleanness, which forbad him as a Nazarite to touch carcases. A jawbone is a mighty magic weapon in one of the Polynesian legends (Grey, *Polyn. Mythology,* p. 35), but that throws no light on this narrative.

Slew a thousand men.—The verb is rather *smote* than "slew," and the expression (whether due to poetry or not) is to be taken generally, like "Saul has slain his thousands, and David his ten thousands." If Goliath was able single-handed to strike terror into the whole army of Israel, Samson with his long locks and colossal strength would be still more likely to strike a terror into the Philistines, and all the more because a supernatural awe was doubtless attached by this time to his name and person. The very fact that, though armed only with this wretched weapon of offence, he yet dared to rush upon the Philistines would make them fly in wilder panic (Josh. xxiii. 10). "One man of you shall chase a thousand; for the Lord your God He it is that fighteth for you, as He hath promised you." (Comp. Lev. xxvi.; Deut. xxxii. 30.) So we read that one of David's heroes slew three hundred men (1 Chron. xi. 11; comp. 2 Sam. xxiii. 8). The Philistines, dull and superstitious, seem to have been peculiarly liable to these panics (1 Sam. xiv. 4—18). Bishop Patrick quotes a striking parallel from a song on the Emperor Aurelian.

(16) **And Samson said, With the jawbone of an ass.**—Here we once more find ourselves in very primitive regions of poetry and paronomasia. Samson's exultation over his extraordinary achievement finds vent in a sort of punning couplet, which turns entirely on the identity of sound between *chamor,* a heap, and *chamor,* an ass, and the play of *meaning* between *aleph,* a thousand, and *aleph,* an ox. In the Hebrew the couplet runs :—

"Bi-lechi *ha-chamor chamor chamorathaim.*
Bi-lechi *ha-chamor* hicceythi *eleph* eesh."

Literally, with some attempt, however clumsy, to keep up the play of words,

"With jaw of the ass, a (m)ass two (m)asses,
With jaw of the ass I smote an ox-load of men."

The versions are, of course, unable to preserve these rough paronomasias, which are characteristic of the age. It would be quite a mistake to infer that they show any levity of spirit in Samson. On the contrary, such peculiarities of expression often arise out of deep emotion.

He Slays them with   JUDGES, XVI.   *the Jawbone of an Ass.*

bone of an ass, and put forth his hand, and took it, and slew a thousand men therewith. (16) And Samson said,

With the jawbone of an ass, ¹heaps upon heaps, with the jaw of an ass have I slain a thousand men.

(17) And it came to pass, when he had made an end of speaking, that he cast away the jawbone out of his hand, and called that place ³Ramath-lehi.

(18) And he was sore athirst, and called on the LORD, and said, Thou hast given this great deliverance into the hand of thy servant: and now shall I die for thirst, and fall into the hand of the un-

circumcised? (19) But God clave an hollow place that *was* in ³the jaw, and there came water thereout; and when he had drunk, his spirit came again, and he revived: wherefore he called the name thereof ⁴En-hakkore, which *is* in Lehi unto this day.

(20) And he judged Israel in the days of the Philistines twenty years.

XVI.

(1) Then went Samson to Gaza, and saw there ⁵an harlot, and went in unto her. (2) *And it was told* the Gazites, saying, Samson is come hither. And they

---

1 Heb., *an heap, two heaps.*
2 That is, *The lifting up of the jawbone, or, casting away of the jawbone.*
3 Or, *Lehi.*
4 That is, *The well of him that called, or, cried.*
B.C. cir. 1120.
5 Heb., *a woman an harlot.*

When John of Gaunt begins his dying speech to Richard II. with—

"Old Gaunt, indeed ! and gaunt in being old," &c.,

the king asks :—

"Can sick men play so nicely with their names?"

and the dying prince makes the striking answer :—

"No ; misery makes sport to mock herself."

I have fully examined the whole subject in *Chapters on Language,* pp. 227—238. These sallies of playful fancy tended no less than the flashes of military prowess to prepare the nation for better times by keeping up their buoyant mood. "The nation felt unsubdued in mind and body, while its sons could flow out in such health and vivacity ;" and thus Samson *began* to deliver them, though his actual deeds were casual—"a sort of teasing, reiterated mark of mortifying humiliation" (Ewald).

(17) **Ramath-lehi.**—The marginal rendering, " the lifting up of the jawbone " is found in the LXX. and Vulg., and derives Ramath from the verb *rûm*, "to be high." The more natural explanation is, "the hill of Lehi." The other marginal rendering, "the casting away of the jawbone," derives Ramath from the verb *ramah,* "he cast." This would require the form *Remath.*

(18) **He was sore athirst.**—It was in the heat of harvest time, and he had pursued the Philistines till he was exhausted.

Into the hand.—Rather, *by the hand.*

(19) **Clave an hollow place that was in the jaw.**—Rather, *the (fountain called the) "socket," which is in Lehi.* The notion that God made a miraculous fountain in one of the tooth-sockets of the jawbone of the ass is one of the childish misinterpretations with which Scripture exegesis is constantly defaced. Lehi is here the name of the place, and if the fountain is said to have sprung up in *Hammaktesh,* " the toothsocket" (Vulg., *molarem*), that is only due to the play on words which characterises the narrative. When the cliff had got the name of " Jawbone," the spring would naturally be called a " tooth-socket." The word *maktesh* properly means " a mortar " (Greek, *holmiskos* ; Lat., *mortariolum*) (Prov. xxvii. 22), and this name was transferred to the sockets of teeth. We find another place with the same name in Zeph. i. 11. Milton understood the passage rightly :—

"God, who caused a fountain at thy prayer
From the dry ground to spring thy thirst to allay."

For similar instances in the Bible, see Gen. xxi. 19 (Hagar); Exod. xvii. 6 (the smitten rock); Is. xli. 17, 18 (" When the poor and needy seek water, and there is none, and their tongue faileth for thirst, I the Lord will hear them. I will open rivers in high places, and fountains in the midst of the valleys . . . I will make the wilderness a pool of water, and the dry land springs of water"). Josephus says that God caused to spring up for Samson " a plentiful fountain of sweet water at a certain rock."

He called the name thereof.—Rather, *the name thereof was called.*

En-hakkoré.—*The Spring of the Crier.* These names have vanished, but perhaps traces of them may still be discovered " in the abundant springs and numerous eminences of the district round Urtas," the place from which Solomon's pleasure-gardens and the Temple and Bethlehem were supplied with water.

(20) **And he judged Israel.**—Probably, as Jephthah had done, with the sort of vague prerogatives of a military hero. Why the verse is found here, as though to close the narrative (comp. chap. xii. 7, &c.), and is again repeated in chap. xvi. 31, we cannot say. The next chapter belongs mainly to Samson's fall and humiliation. These twenty years probably fell within the contemporary judgeship of Eli.

XVI.

1—3. Samson's escape from Gaza. 4, 5. Delilah, bribed by the Philistine lords, endeavours to entrap him. 6—14. He thrice deceives her. 15—21. At last he reveals to her the secret of his strength, is seized, blinded, and forced to grind for the Philistines. 22—31. His final revenge, death, and burial.

(1) **Then went Samson to Gaza.**—Rather, *And Samson, &c.* The narrative is brief and detached. Gaza is near the sea, and was the chief town of the Philistines, in the very heart of their country. It is useless to inquire how Samson could venture there in safety, or whether he went in disguise, or what was his object in going there ; to such side-questions the narrative gives us no reply.

(2) **And it was told.**—Our version rightly supplies these words. They are found in all the versions, and there can be no doubt that the word *vayyuggar* (Gen. xxii. 20) has in this case accidentally dropped out of the text.

They compassed him in.—They apparently did not know in what house he was. The word might mean

compassed him in, and laid wait for him all night in the gate of the city, and were ¹quiet all the night, saying, In the morning, when it is day, we shall kill him. ⁽³⁾ And Samson lay till midnight, and arose at midnight, and took the doors of the gate of the city, and the two posts, and went away with them, ²bar and all, and put *them* upon his shoulders, and carried them up to the top of an hill that *is* before Hebron.

⁽⁴⁾ And it came to pass afterward, that he loved a woman ³in the valley of Sorek, whose name *was* Delilah. ⁽⁵⁾ And the lords of the Philistines came up unto her, and said unto her, Entice him, and see wherein his great strength *lieth*, and by what *means* we may prevail against him, that we may bind him to ⁴afflict him: and we will give thee every one of us eleven hundred *pieces* of silver.

⁽⁶⁾ And Delilah said to Samson, Tell me, I pray thee, wherein thy great strength *lieth*, and wherewith thou

¹ Heb., *silent.*
² Heb., *with the bar.*
³ Or, *by the brook.*
⁴ Or, *humble.*

"they went round the city" (Ps. lix. 7), *i.e.*, to look for him.

Were quiet—*i.e.*, they made no attack. Thinking that they had secured him, they seem to have retired to rest. (Comp. Acts ix. 23, 24.)

⁽³⁾ **Arose at midnight.**—Apparently — but here again the narrative omits all details—he had been told of the plot, and found the gates unguarded; unless we are to suppose that he slew the guards, without awaking the city.

Took.—Rather, *grasped* or *seized.*

The two posts—*i.e.*, the side-posts.

Went away with them, bar and all.—Rather, *tore them up, with the bar*; the bar was the bar which fastened the two valves together. Gaza, as we see from the site of its walls, had *several* gates. The site of the gate traditionally pointed out is on the south-east. It may have been the smaller gate, by the side of the main gate, which he thus tore up. In Mohammedan legend Ali uses the gate of Chaibar as a shield, which may be a sort of confused echo and parallel of this event (Pococke, *Hist. Arab.*, p. 10).

That is before Hebron.—It is not implied that Samson walked with the gates and bars on his shoulders nine miles to Hebron; but probably (as the local tradition says) to El Montar, a hill in the direction of Hebron, from which the hills of Hebron are visible. Pliny, in his *Natural History* (vii. 19), adduces many instances of colossal strength, but in this narrative it is distinctly implied that the strength of Samson was a supernatural gift, arising from his dedication to God. The carrying away the *gate* of his enemies would be understood in the East as a very peculiar insult. "When Almansor took Compostella, he made the Christians carry the gates of St. James's Church on their shoulders to Cordova in sign of his victory" (Ferraras, *Gesch. von Spanier*, iii. 145, quoted by Cassel).

⁽⁴⁾ **He loved a woman.**—Delilah was not, as Milton represents, his wife. Josephus (*Antt.* v. 8, § 11) says that she was one who played the harlot among the Philistines, and the fathers all speak of her in similar terms. Nor is it at all clear—as is generally assumed —that she was a Philistine.

In the valley of Sorek.—The English Version here follows the Vulgate, but the word for valley is *nachal*, and the words may mean (as the LXX. take them) "on the brook of Sorek." Sorek was not in the Philistine district, but was near Samson's native town of Zorah (chap. xiii. 2). It seems to have derived its name from the "choice vines" that grew there (Gen. xlix. 11; Isa. v. 2; Jer. ii. 21, *Hebr.*).

Delilah.—The "tender" or "delicate." Ewald thinks it means "the traitress," referring to *Journ.*

Asiat., ii. 389. The Rabbis refer it to the root *daldal*, "to debilitate."

⁽⁵⁾ **The lords of the Philistines.** — The five "satraps." (See Note on chap. iii. 3.) If she were what Josephus asserts, the Philistines might both get access to her, and tempt the cupidity of an unprincipled and degraded mind. Had she been of their own race, threats would probably have been even more effectual with her than with the lady of Timnath (chap. xiii. 15). The LXX. here begin to call the Philistines *allophuloi*, or "aliens."

Entice him.—See Prov. ii. 16, 18, 19.

Wherein his great strength lieth.—Rather, *wherein his strength is great.* They attributed his strength to some amulet which might be removed.

Eleven hundred pieces of silver.—That is, "eleven hundred silver shekels." The same sum recurs in chap. xvii. 2 as the amount laid by for the construction of teraphim by the mother of Micah. If the five lords each gave 1,100 shekels, the amount would be nearly two talents of silver (Exod. xxxviii. 25, 26)—a most enormous bribe for that age, and especially to such a woman as Delilah. It may be regarded as an almost conclusive proof that Milton is mistaken in making her a Philistine.

⁽⁶⁾ **And wherewith thou mightest be bound.** —The narrative, if taken as a full account of all that took place, would leave in the mind an impression of almost incredible fatuity on the part of Samson. The general lesson is that of 1 Esdras iv. 26: "Many have gone out of their wits for women, and have become slaves on account of them; many have perished and erred and sinned by reason of women." (Comp. Prov. vii. 26.) Eastern legends constantly show how women have deceived even prophets. But there was no reason why the sacred historian should linger over the details of scenes so unworthy. If Delilah spoke thus plainly at once, we can only imagine that she was professing to treat the whole matter as a jest. Josephus says: "When Samson was drinking, or at other moments, expressing admiration of his deeds, she kept scheming how to ascertain in what way he was so pre-eminent in valour." An illustration may be found in 1 Esdras iv. 29: "I saw Apame taking the crown from the king's head and setting it on her own head; she also struck the king with her left hand, and yet for all that the king gaped and gazed upon her with open mouth. If she laughed upon him, he laughed; if she took displeasure at him, he flattered her, that she may be reconciled to him." The genius of a great poet has depicted such wiles in the idyll of Merlin and Vivienne, and it is only by supposing that such wiles were put forth in this instance that we can retain credit for even the most ordinary sense on the part of the Danite

mightest be bound to afflict thee. ⁽⁷⁾ And Samson said unto her, If they bind me with seven ¹`²green withs` that were never dried, then shall I be weak, and be as ³another man. ⁽⁸⁾ Then the lords of the Philistines brought up to her seven green withs which had not been dried, and she bound him with them. ⁽⁹⁾ Now *there were* men lying in wait, abiding with her in the chamber. And she said unto him, The Philistines *be* upon thee, Samson. And he brake the withs, as a thread of tow is broken when it ⁴toucheth the fire. So his strength was not known.

⁽¹⁰⁾ And Delilah said unto Samson, Behold, thou hast mocked me, and told me lies: now tell me, I pray thee, wherewith thou mightest be bound. ⁽¹¹⁾ And he said unto her, If they bind me fast with new ropes ⁵that never were occu-pied, then shall I be weak, and be as another man. ⁽¹²⁾ Delilah therefore took new ropes, and bound him therewith, and said unto him, The Philistines *be* upon thee, Samson. And *there were* liers in wait abiding in the chamber. And he brake them from off his arms like a thread.

⁽¹³⁾ And Delilah said unto Samson, Hitherto thou hast mocked me, and told me lies: tell me wherewith thou mightest be bound. And he said unto her, If thou weavest the seven locks of my head with the web. ⁽¹⁴⁾ And she fastened *it* with the pin, and said unto him, The Philistines *be* upon thee, Samson. And he awaked out of his sleep, and went away with the pin of the beam, and with the web.

⁽¹⁵⁾ And she said unto him, How canst thou say, I love thee, when thine heart

---

¹ Or, *new cords.*
² Heb., *moist.*
³ Heb., *one.*
⁴ Heb., *smelleth.*
⁵ Heb., *wherewith work hath not been done.*

---

hero. But his fault was not stupidity—it was sensual infatuation; and in the ruin and shame which this sensual weakness brought upon him, and the way in which, step by step, it led him to forfeit the great gift of God, lies the chief moral of the story. We find the same lesson in the legend of Hercules and Omphale; and even if this legend was not influenced by the story of Samson's life, yet there is a general analogy between the character of the Greek and the Jewish hero. Samson was no Solomon, and yet the heart of even Solomon—

"... though large,
Beguiled by fair idolatresses, fell."

⁽⁷⁾ **Green withs.**—The meaning of the words is uncertain. Probably the LXX. and the Vulg. are right in taking them to mean *moist, i.e., fresh sinews* (Ps. xi. 2) (LXX., *Neurais hugrais*; Vulg., *Nerviceis funibus necdum siccis et adhuc humentibus*). Josephus says "vine shoots," but fresh vine shoots would be ridiculously inadequate. The number *seven* is used as the sacred number implying perfectness; and it is one of the signs that even thus early Samson is playing about on the confines of his secret.

As another man.—Literally, *as one man, i.e.,* as an ordinary man.

⁽⁹⁾ **Men lying in wait.**—Literally, *and the spy sat in the room for her, i.e.,* to help her. It is doubtful whether there was more than one spy, who could be easily concealed. It is implied that she bound Samson while he slept, as in verse 19.

When it toucheth the fire.—Literally, *when it smelleth the fire.* (See Note on chap. xv. 14.) So in Job xiv. 9: "through the *scent* of water it will bud." Of course the writer leaves us to infer that the spy or spies did not appear, seeing that the plan had failed.

⁽¹⁰⁾ **Now tell me, I pray thee.**—Delilah would, of course, tell Samson that the scene had been merely a playful jest, and that she had said "Philistines upon thee, Samson!" only to be delighted with one fresh exhibition of his great strength, if he really had not revealed the secret. She would represent her desire to know as due only to loving curiosity.

⁽¹¹⁾ **New ropes.**—As in chap. xv. 13.
That never were occupied.—"Occupied" is an old word for "used." (See Exod. xxxviii. 24, "All the gold that was occupied for the work;" Luke xix. 13; Heb. xiii. 9; "Like a new bright silver dish never *occupied*"—Ascham, *Schoolmaster*.) Here, again, Samson distantly touches on the consecration which is the secret of his strength.

⁽¹³⁾ **If thou weavest the seven locks of my head with the web.**—The illustrious and "sunny locks of the Nazarite" did not, as Milton imagines, "lie waving and curling about his god-like shoulders," but were plaited into seven locks. The word for "locks" —*machelephoth*—occurs here only. The LXX. render it "curls" (*bostruchous*) and *seiras*, which appears to mean "plaits," like the Greek *plokamous*. The word for "web" is a technical word, and perhaps means warp. The LXX. and the Vulg. add, "and drive them with the peg into the wall," which is implied in the next verse. With almost incredible levity and folly, Samson here goes to the very verge of the true secret, and suffers his sacred hair to be woven in a harlot's loom. (*Tertio de mysterio deprompsit jam lapsuro propior.* St. Ambrose.)

⁽¹⁴⁾ **She fastened it with the pin.**—Unless the additions of the Vulg. and the LXX. to the last verse were in the original text, she had not been told by Samson to do this, but did it to make assurance doubly sure. The versions add that she drove the pin "into the wall" (LXX.) or "into the ground" (Vulg.).

Went away with.—Rather, *tore up,* as in verse 3.
With the pin of the beam, and with the web. —The words are technical, but the "pin" or "plug" seems to be the wooden peg with which the web was fastened down; and the "beam" was certainly not the "weaver's beam" of 1 Sam. xvii. 7, but apparently "the comb." The loom was doubtless one of a simple kind in ordinary domestic use (like that described in *Livingstone's Travels*), and Samson, startled from sleep, tore away his locks with the plug which fastened them down and the warp into which they were woven.

⁽¹⁵⁾ **How canst thou say, I love thee . . . ?**— Samson had undergone all these wiles before, and

is not with me? thou hast mocked me these three times, and hast not told me wherein thy great strength *lieth*. (16) And it came to pass, when she pressed him daily with her words, and urged him, so that his soul was ¹vexed unto death; (17) that he told her all his heart, and said unto her, There hath not come a razor upon mine head; for I *have been* a Nazarite unto God from my mother's womb: if I be shaven, then my strength will go from me, and I shall become weak, and be like any *other* man.

(18) And when Delilah saw that he had told her all his heart, she sent and called for the lords of the Philistines, saying, Come up this once, for he hath shewed me all his heart. Then the lords of the Philistines came up unto her, and brought money in their hand. (19) And she made him sleep upon her knees; and she called for a man, and she caused him to shave off the seven locks of his head; and she began to afflict him, and his strength went from him. (20) And she said, The Philistines *be* upon thee, Samson. And he awoke out of his sleep, and said, I will go out as at other times before, and shake myself. And he wist not that the LORD was departed from him. (21) But the Philistines took him, and ²put out his eyes, and brought him down to Gaza, and bound him with fetters of brass; and he did grind in the prison house. (22) Howbeit the hair of his head began to grow again ³after he was shaven.

(23) Then the lords of the Philistines gathered them together for to offer a great sacrifice unto Dagon their god, and to rejoice: for they said, Our god

¹ Heb., *shortened.*
² Heb., *bored out.*
³ Or, *as when he was shaven.*

---

experienced their hollowness (chap. xiv. 16), yet he had not learnt wisdom.

(16) **His soul was vexed.**—He at last reveals the secret, because he is wearied—literally, *his soul is shortened*—to death. (Comp. Num. xxi. 4, 5.) Even the dangerous use which Delilah had made of his last revelation did not rouse his mind from its besotted stupefaction.

"Swollen with pride, into the snare I fell
Of fair fallacious looks, venereal trains,
Softened with pleasure and voluptuous life,
At length to lay my head and hallowed pledge
Of all my strength in the lascivious lap
Of a deceitful concubine."—Milton, *Sams. Agon.*

If he thrice proved his vast strength, he also thrice proved his immense folly. To use his strength in the mere saving of his own life was to squander it, and now, " as if possessed by insanity, he madly trifles with the key of his secret. He risks even the tampering with his hair. From this there is but one step to the final catastrophe " (Ewald).

(18) **Saw that he had told her all his heart.**—She could not mistake the accent of truthfulness, nor was Samson so far gone as to be able to reveal the great secret without some sense of awe and shame.

Money.—Rather, *the silver* (verse 5).

(19) **Made him sleep upon her knees.**—As his locks could hardly be shaved off without awaking him from any ordinary sleep, the expression looks as if she had administered some "drowsy syrup," like mandragora.

She called for a man.—Probably the concealed spy (verse 9). " Laying down his head amongst the strumpet flatteries . . . while he sleeps and thinks no harm, they, wickedly shaving off all those bright and weighty tresses . . . which were his ornament and his strength, deliver him over . . . " (Milton, *Reason of Church Government*). Whether the pagan legends of the lock of Nisus or Pterolaus were distant echoes of this incident we cannot say. But the hair of Samson was no magical amulet. It was only a sign of dedication to God. While he kept his vow the strength remained; it only departed when the vow was shamefully broken.

She began to afflict him.—Rather, *to humble him* (chap. xix. 24). We cannot tell the exact meaning of the clause, since it is only in the next verse that Samson is said to awake. (Comp. Prov. vii. 26.)

(20) **And he wist not that the Lord was departed from him.**—A deeply tragic clause. Men do not know how much they are changed "when the Lord departs from them" until they feel the effects of that departure in utter shame and weakness. (Comp. Num. xiv. 43; 1 Sam. xvi. 14.) Samson was under a vow, but was, alas! too weak to resist the current which ran counter to his vow, particularly when he had come to rely on the mere external sign of it. For his strength was in no sense in his hair, but only in the dedication to God of which it was the symbol.

(21) **Put out his eyes.**—The margin, "bored out," is more correct. The Arabic version has the curious gloss that they burnt out his eyes with the red-hot style with which *stibium* (see Job xlii. 14) is applied to the eyes. To blind a man was the most effectual humiliation (2 Kings xxv. 7). The story of Evenius, a priest of the sun-god, who is blinded by the people of Apollonia, who thereby incur the anger of the gods, seems to move in a similar circle of ideas to this.

Fetters of brass.—Literally, *two brasses — i.e., pairs of brazen fetters* (*nechushtarim*).

He did grind in the prison house.—This was the degrading work of slaves and females (Exod. xi. 5; Isa. xlvii. 2). Grotius in a curious note says that slaves thus employed were blinded by the Scythians to save them from giddiness (see Herod. iv. 2). The end of Samson was mournful; " his whole powerful life was only like a light, blazing up brightly at moments, and shining afar, but often dimmed, and utterly extinguished before its time " (Ewald).

(23) **Unto Dagon their god.**—Comp. 1 Sam. v. 1, 2; 1 Chron. x. 10. This was the

"Sea-monster:—upward man,
And downward fish."

In 1 Sam. v. 4 we have an allusion to his stump or fish-part. **Dag** means "fish," and the same root is found in *Tagus*. A goddess of similar form and attributes was worshipped under the name of Atargatis or Derceto (2 Macc. xii. 26). How widely the worship was spread we see from the commonness of the name Beth-dagon

hath delivered Samson our enemy into our hand. (24) And when the people saw him, they praised their god: for they said, Our god hath delivered into our hands our enemy, and the destroyer of our country, ¹which slew many of us. (25) And it came to pass, when their hearts were merry, that they said, Call for Samson, that he may make us sport. And they called for Samson out of the prison house; and he made ²them sport: and they set him between the pillars. (26) And Samson said unto the lad that held him by the hand, Suffer me that I may feel the pillars whereupon the house standeth, that I may lean upon them. (27) Now the house was full of men and women; and all the lords of the Philistines *were* there; and *there were* upon the roof about three thousand men and women, that beheld while Samson made sport. (28) And Samson called unto the LORD, and said, O Lord GOD, remember me, I pray thee, and strengthen me, I pray thee, only this once, O God, that I may be at once avenged of the Philistines for my two eyes. (29) And Samson took hold of the two middle pillars upon which the house stood, and ³on which it was borne up, of the one with his right hand, and of the other with his left. (30) And Samson said, Let ⁴me die with the Philistines. And he bowed himself with *all his* might; and the house fell upon the lords, and upon all the people that *were* therein. So the dead which he slew at his death were more than *they* which he slew in his life.

(31) Then his brethren and all the house of his father came down, and took him, and brought *him* up, and buried him between Zorah and Eshtaol in the buryingplace of Manoah his father. And he judged Israel twenty years.

¹ Heb., *and who multiplied our slain.*
² Heb., *before them.*
³ Or, *he leaned on them.*
⁴ Heb., *my soul.*

---

in the Shephelah (Josh. xv. 41). His chief temple at Azotus was burned by Judas Maccabeus (1 Macc. x. 83). The only other Philistine god mentioned in Scripture is Baal-zebub, god of Ekron (2 Kings i. 2—16).

(25) **When their hearts were merry.**—Comp. chap. ix. 27; 1 Sam. xxv. 36; Esther i. 10.

That he may make us sport.—Whether by his forced jests, or by feats of strength, or merely by being made to submit to insults, we cannot tell. Josephus says that they sent for Samson "that they might insult him over their wine."

He made them sport.—The LXX says (Cod. B), "And he played before them, and they beat him with rods."

(26) **That I may feel the pillars.**—The temple of Dagon had a flat roof; but further than this we are unable to conjecture what was its architecture. An attempt to explain it is found in Stark's *Gaza*, p. 332, *seq.*

(27) **The house was full of men and women ... upon the roof about three thousand men and women.**—The words for "men and women" in the first clause are *anashim* and *nashim*, and in the second *eesh* and *eeshsha.* The more distinguished people were with the lords in the house itself; the common people were on the flat roof.

There were upon the roof.—The temple may have been like a Turkish kiosk, "a spacious hall, of which the roof rested in front upon four columns, two of them standing at the ends, and two close together in the centre. Under this hall the chief Philistines celebrated a sacrificial meal, whilst the people were assembled above upon the top of the roof, which was surrounded by a balustrade" (Faber, *Archäol. d. Hebr.*, quoted by Keil). "His puissant locks," as Milton says, "sternly shook thunder with ruin upon the heads of those his evil counsellors, but not without great affliction to himself." In the life of Samson and the incidents of chap. xviii. we find the chief illustrations of the character of his tribe as described in Jacob's blessing (Gen. xlix. 16, 17). Hence, perhaps, he is called *Bedan* in 1 Sam. xii. 11, if we follow the improbable gloss of the Targum in making the word there mean a Danite.

(28) **O Lord God ... O God.**—Three names of God—Adonai, Jehovah, Elohim.

That I may be at once avenged of the Philistines.—Again we see that Samson stood at a comparatively low level of spiritual enlightenment as well as of moral purity. One cannot help feeling that Milton has read into the hero's character an austere grandeur which it did not possess. His Samson of the *Samson Agonistes* is rather Milton himself than the Jewish hero. That stern classic poem is the "thundering reverberation of a mighty spirit, struck by the plectrum of disappointment."

For my two eyes.—The words rendered "at once" in the previous clause may be rendered "that I may avenge myself *the revenge of one* of my two eyes." If so, there seems to be in the words a grim jest, as though no vengeance would suffice for the fearful loss of both his eyes (LXX., "one revenge for my *two* eyes"), "one last tremendous deed, one last fearful jest." There is a curious parallel to this achievement of Samson in the story of Cleomedes of Astypalæa, who in revenge for a fine pulls down a pillar, and crushes the boys in a school (Pausan. *Perieg.* vi. 2, 3). Cassel tells us that on July 21st, 1864, many people were killed by the breaking of a granite pillar in the Church of the Transfiguration at St. Petersburg.

(29) **And on which it was borne up.**—Rather, as it is given in the margin, *and he leaned himself upon them.*

(31) **His brethren and all the house of his father.**—Probably Manoah and his wife were dead. The religious terror caused by the catastrophe may well have prevented the people of Gaza from offering any opposition to the removal of his body.

"Samson hath quit himself
Like Samson, and heroically has finished
A life heroic."—*Milton.*

CHAPTER XVII.—⁽¹⁾ And there was a man of mount Ephraim, whose name was Micah. ⁽²⁾ And he said unto his mother, The eleven hundred *shekels* of silver that were taken from thee, about which thou cursedst, and spakest of also in mine ears, behold, the silver *is* with me; I took it. And his mother said, Blessed *be thou* of the LORD, my son. ⁽³⁾ And when he had restored the eleven hundred *shekels* of silver to his mother, his mother said, I had wholly dedicated the silver unto the LORD from my hand for my son, to make a graven image and

B.C. cir. 1406.

XVII.

1, 2. An Ephraimite, named Micah, first steals eleven hundred shekels from his mother, and then restores them. 3—5. She blesses him, and uses them, with his assistance, for the establishment of an idolatrous form of worship. 6. Anarchy of the times. 7—13. A wandering Levite comes from Bethlehem to the house of Micah, and consents to become priest of the new worship.

The two narratives which occupy the five remaining chapters of the Book of Judges are disconnected from one another and from what precedes. They are, in fact, two Appendices, which serve the purpose of showing the social anarchy, religious confusion, and moral degradation to which tribes and individuals were liable during this period. In date they belong to an earlier time than most of the preceding chapters, and they are connected by various terms of phraseology with the preface (verse 1, chap. ii. 5). The migration of Dan in chap. xviii. (Josh. xix. 47, 48) is accounted for by the pressure to which the tribe was subjected by the Amorites, as related in chap. i. 34. The story of Micah, so valuable and interesting as a sketch of manners, seems to have been preserved solely from its bearing on the fortunes of this tribe. The fact that Jonathan, the grandson of Moses (chap. xviii. 30), and Phinehas, the grandson of Aaron (chap. xx. 28), are prominent characters in the two narratives shows that the events must have happened (as Josephus states) at a time shortly subsequent to the death of Joshua, and previous to the career of many of the judges. The first narrative (chaps. xvi., xvii.) still bears on the fortunes of Dan, the tribe of Samson; and in both the narratives the tribe of Judah—which has been almost unnoticed in the body of the book—occupies an important position (chaps. xvi. 9, xviii. 12, xix. 1, 2, 10, xx. 18). These chapters belong, in fact, mainly to the annals of Dan and Judah. It is somewhat remarkable that both of them turn on the fortunes of a Levite of Bethlehem-Judah (chaps. xvii. 7, xix. 1).

⁽¹⁾ **There was.**—The Vulg. has, "there was *at that time*," which is an error, for these events happened before the days of Samson.

A man of mount Ephraim.—The hill-district of Ephraim, as in chap. ii. 9. The Talmud (*Sanhedr.* 103, *b*) says that he lived at Garab, not far from Shiloh, but the name ("a blotch") is probably a term of scorn (Deut. xxviii. 27). Similarly, we find in *Perachim*, 117, *a*, that he lived at *Bochi*. (See chap. ii. 1—5.) Most of the idolatrous violations of the second commandment occurred in the northern kingdom (Gideon, chap. viii. 27; Micah, chap. xvii.; Jeroboam, 1 Kings xii., xiii.). These apostasies were not a worship of other gods, but a worship of the true God under unauthorised conditions, and with forbidden images.

Whose name was Micah.—Scripture does not deem it necessary to say anything more about him. His very name—here *Micayehû*, "Who is like Jehovah"—seems to show that he had been trained by pious parents. The contraction Micah is adopted throughout the rest of the story.

⁽²⁾ **He said unto his mother.**—The story is singularly abbreviated, and all details as to how she had acquired the money, &c., are left to conjecture.

The eleven hundred shekels of silver.—The value of eleven hundred shekels would be about £136. It is the same sum which each of the lords of the Philistines promised to give Delilah (chap. xvi. 5), and only six hundred shekels less than the entire mass of the earrings given to Gideon—only that those were golden shekels. It is hard to say whence this Ephraimitish lady could have amassed so large a sum.

That were taken from thee.—This is probably the true rendering. The LXX. (Cod. B) have "which thou tookest for thyself," and (Cod. A) "those taken by thee," as though she had stolen them.

About which thou cursedst.—Literally, *and thou didst adjure*. The LXX. (Cod. B) add, "dost adjure me." The adjuration was clearly that commanded in Lev. v. 1: "And if a soul sin, and hear the voice of swearing, and is a witness, whether he hath seen or known of it; *if he do not utter it, then he shall bear his iniquity.*" (Comp. Ecclus. iii. 9: "The curse of a mother rooteth out foundations."

I took it.—Micah is terrified into confession by his mother's adjuration. He shows throughout a singular mixture of superstition and ignorance.

Blessed be thou of the Lord, my son.—Because of his penitence and confession.

⁽³⁾ **I had wholly dedicated the silver.**—Literally, *Consecrating, I consecrated*—either, "I have now consecrated it" as a thanksgiving for its restoration, or "I had done so before it was stolen."

For my son—*i.e.*, for your benefit.

To make a graven image and a molten image.—Whether in the universal decadence of religion, the people, untaught by a careless priesthood, had become ignorant of the second commandment, or whether she justified her conduct by the same considerations which have been used even in the Christian Church in favour of image-worship, we cannot tell. The word used for a graven image is *pesel*, and for a molten image is *massecah*. They are the very words used in the curse against idolaters in Deut. xxvii. 15. Some suppose the two words to be used by Hendiadys (like "cups and gold" for "golden cups") to describe *one silver image* adorned with sculptured ornament. All that is clear is that the *pesel* is the more prominent, but the details are left quite vague. It is therefore impossible to determine whether the graven and molten image consisted of one or of two silver "calves," like that of the wilderness, and those afterwards set up by Jeroboam at Dan and Bethel. *This*, however, was a form which the violation of the second commandment was constantly liable to take, and it probably involved much less blame than other violations of it—*not*, as is often stated, because the Israelites had become familiar with the worship of Apis and Mnevis in Egypt, but

a molten image: now therefore I will restore it unto thee. ⁽⁴⁾ Yet he restored the money unto his mother; and his mother took two hundred *shekels* of silver, and gave them to the founder, who made thereof a graven image and a molten image: and they were in the house of Micah. ⁽⁵⁾ And the man Micah had an house of gods, and made an ᵃephod, and ᵇteraphim, and ¹consecrated one of his sons, who became his priest. ⁽⁶⁾ ᶜIn those days *there was* no king in Israel, *but* every man did *that which was* right in his own eyes.

⁽⁷⁾ And there was a young man out of Beth-lehem-judah of the family of Judah, who *was* a Levite, and he sojourned there. ⁽⁸⁾ And the man departed out of the city from Beth-lehem-judah to sojourn where he could find *a place*: and he came to mount Ephraim to the house of Micah, ²as he journeyed. ⁽⁹⁾ And Micah said unto him, Whence comest thou? And he said unto him, I am a Levite of Beth-

a ch. 8. 27.
b Gen. 31. 19; Hosea 3. 4.
1 Heb., *filled the hand.*
c ch. 18. 1 & 21. 25.
2 Heb., *in making his way.*

---

because the calf was a recognised cherubic emblem, and had consequently been deliberately sanctioned in the symbolism of the Temple. (See Exod. xx. 4, 23, xxxii. 4, 5; 1 Kings vii. 25, &c.) Some suppose that the *massecah* was the pedestal of the *pesel*, and that it was too heavy for the Danites to carry away, since it is not mentioned among the things which they seized.

Now therefore I will restore it unto thee.—Rather, *for thee*—in which case "I will restore it" may possibly mean "use it for its original purpose for thy advantage." If not, a slight correction would give us the much simpler reading of the Syriac, "restore it to me."

⁽⁴⁾ **Yet.**—Rather, *And.*

Two hundred shekels of silver.—Bertheau supposes that these two hundred shekels were not *a part of the eleven hundred*, but the trespass-money of one-fifth, which by the law Micah had to pay for his theft (Lev. v. 24). But apart from the sum not being exact, no such impression is given by the narrative. It is left to be understood that the remaining nine hundred shekels were spent in other parts of the idolatrous worship. (It may be mentioned, by way of passing illustration, that when Sir John Hawle was murdered in Westminster Abbey, the £200 paid in penance by his murderers seem to have been expended upon the purchase of a costly image, which was placed in the Chapel of St. Erasmus.)

Gave them to the founder.—An illustration of the folly which Isaiah pursues with such a storm of irony and contempt (Isa. xlvi. 6—20). These *pesilim* were originally of all sorts of materials (*e.g.*, wood, brass, stone, and clay, Dan. ii. 33, v. 23; Deut. vii. 5, xii. 3, &c.), but usually of metal (Isa. xl. 19, xliv. 10, &c.), adorned with plates and chains of precious metal, and embroidered robes (Jer. x. 9; Ezek. xvi. 18, &c.). (See *Excursus I.: Calf-Worship*.)

⁽⁵⁾ **Had an house of gods.**—The Hebrew is *Beth Elohim*, which may mean equally well "a house of God" (Vulg., *œdiculam Deo*, and so too the LXX.). It is quite clear that Micah did not abandon the worship of God under the names of Jehovah and Elohim, by which He was known to the Israelites. How he co-ordinated this worship with his grossly idolatrous symbols, or whom those symbols were intended to represent, it is impossible to say. The fact remains that in the Beth-Micah we find "a house of gods"—"a whole chapel of idols"—consecrated to Jehovah as a pious act (chaps. xvii. 2, 5, 13, xviii. 6).

An ephod.—No doubt the ephod was nothing more than a gorgeous priestly garment, though possibly it may have been used for oracular purposes. (See chap. viii. 27.)

And teraphim.—These were Syrian images (Gen. xxxi. 19), the use of which among the Israelites seems to have lasted for a long period, until it was put down by King Josiah in his great reformation (2 Kings xxiii. 34; Ezek. xxi. 26; Hosea iii. 4; Zech. x. 2). I have entered upon the interesting question of the use of Teraphim in an article on the subject in *Kitto's Cyclopædia*. (See *Excursus II.: Teraphim*.)

Consecrated.—The curious Hebrew phrase is "filled the hand" (see Exod. xxviii. 41, xxix. 24; Lev. vii. 37), *i.e.*, gave him the office by putting certain offerings in his hands. It is rather *installed* than "consecrated."

⁽⁶⁾ **In those days there was no king.**—This shows that these narratives were written, or more probably edited, in the days of the monarchy. (See chaps. xviii. 1, xix. 1, xxi. 25.)

Did that which was right in his own eyes.—The notice is added to show why there was no authoritative interference of prince or ruler to prevent idolatrous or lawless proceedings. (Deut. xii. 8: "Ye shall not do after all the things which we do here this day, *every man what is right in his own eyes*.")

⁽⁷⁾ **A young man.**—Later on in the story we, as it were incidentally, make the astonishing discovery that this young man was no other than a grandson of Moses.

Out of Beth-lehem-judah.—So called to distinguish it from the Bethlehem in Zebulon (Josh. xxix. 15). (See Note on chap. xii. 8.) In later times, when Bethlehem was famous as David's birthplace, and the other Bethlehem had sunk into insignificance, the descriptive addition is often dropped.

Of the family of Judah.—It may be doubted whether this refers to the "young man" or to Bethlehem, or whether it ought not, as in some MSS. and versions (LXX., Cod. B, and Syriac), to be omitted. If it applies to the young Levite, it must mean that he did not live in one of the Levitic cities, which belonged to his own family (the family of Gershom), which were in the northern and eastern tribes (Josh. xxi. 6), but in Judah, and therefore was ranked in civil matters as belonging to that tribe. Homes in the tribe of Judah were assigned to the priests alone (Josh. xxi. 9—42).

He sojourned there.—Comp. chap. xix. 1. The curse had been pronounced on the tribe of Levi: "I will divide them in Jacob, and scatter them in Israel" (Gen. xlix. 7).

⁽⁸⁾ **To sojourn where he could find.**—Or, as we should say, *to get his living*. It may easily be supposed that in the disorganisation of these days, the due support of the Levites would be much neglected. The same neglect occurred in the troubled days of Nehemiah: "*I perceived that the portions of the Levites had not been given them*: for the Levites and the singers, that did the work, were fled every one to his field," &c. (Neh. xiii. 10, 11).

lehem-judah, and I go to sojourn where I may find *a place*. ⁽¹⁰⁾ And Micah said unto him, Dwell with me, and be unto me a father and a priest, and I will give thee ten *shekels* of silver by the year, and ¹²a suit of apparel, and thy victuals. So the Levite went in. ⁽¹¹⁾ And the Levite was content to dwell with the man; and the young man was unto him as one of his sons. ⁽¹²⁾ And Micah consecrated the Levite; and the young man became his priest, and was in the house of Micah. ⁽¹³⁾ Then said Micah, Now know I that the LORD will do me good, seeing I have a Levite to *my* priest.

CHAPTER XVIII.—⁽¹⁾ In ªthose days *there was* no king in Israel: and in those days the tribe of the Danites sought them an inheritance to dwell in; for unto that day *all their* inheritance had not fallen unto them among the tribes of Israel. ⁽²⁾ And the children of Dan sent of their family five men from their coasts, ³men of valour, from Zorah, and from Eshtaol, to spy out the land, and

1 Or, *a double suit, &c.*

2 Heb., *an order of garments.*

a ch. 17. 6 & 21. 25.

3 Heb., *sons.*

To the house of Micah.—Probably he was induced to go there by the rumour of Micah's chapel and worship.

⁽¹⁰⁾ **Be unto me a father and a priest.**—The title "father" is here ecclesiastical, like "papa," "pope," &c., and this title was given to spiritual directors, as we find in several other passages in the Bible (2 Kings ii. 12, v. 13, vi. 21; Isa. xxii. 21, &c.). Micah knew enough of the law to be aware of the extreme irregularity of his conduct in making one of his own sons his priest.

Ten shekels of silver.—Thus the grandson of Moses became priest of an idolatrous worship at a salary of 25s. a year!

By the year.—Literally, *by days*. (Comp. Lev. xxv. 29.)

A suit of apparel.—The Vulgate renders these words "a double robe." It seems to mean either "an order of garments" or "the value of garments," *i.e.*, "your clothes."

⁽¹¹⁾ **Was unto him as one of his sons.**—The words are added by way of reflection on his subsequent ingratitude.

⁽¹³⁾ **That the Lord will do me good.**—In this anticipation we find a very little further on that he was rudely undeceived, and we are hardly in a position to know whether it was due to hypocrisy or to mere ignorance. So far as Micah was devout and sincere, we must feel that the Lord did him good by stripping him of his gorgeous instruments of superstition and humbling his pride.

I have a Levite to my priest.—Rather, *the Levite*. The article may be generic, meaning "one of the Levites;" but Jonathan, as a son of Gershom, has a special right to be called "*the* Levite," as a representative of the tribe. It is at least doubtful whether the priestly functions expected of him in this instance included sacrifice; but, in any case, Micah could hardly have been entirely unaware that the Levites were incapable of priestly functions ("Seek ye the *priesthood* also?"—Num. xvi. 10), or of the fact that the authorised worship of the nation was to be confined to the place which God should choose, which in this instance was Shiloh. In any case, however, the passage furnishes us with a fresh proof of the utter neglect of the Mosaic law, as represented in the Book of Leviticus, from a very early period. His "house of God" seems to have resembled the high places, which even the faithful kings of Israel were unable or unwilling to clear away. They were ultimately cleared away by Hezekiah, but not without so great a shock to the then established custom, that Rabshakeh actually appeals to the fact in proof of Hezekiah's impiety, and as a sign that he has forfeited the favour of Jehovah (2 Kings xviii. 22).

XVIII.

1, 2. Five Danites are sent out as spies for their tribe. 3—6. They are encouraged by the young Levite. 7—10. They bring home a favourable report of Laish. 11—13. Emigration of six hundred Danites. 14—18. They rob the house of Micah of its images. 19—21. Jonathan consents to accompany them. 22—26. Micah is forced to acquiesce. 27—29. They conquer Laish, and (30, 31) set up the idolatrous worship.

⁽¹⁾ **In those days . . .**—The repetition of the phrase does not necessarily prove the use of different documents. It may only emphasise the reason for the occurrence of such disorders and irregularities.

The tribe.—*Shebet* sometimes means a whole tribe, and sometimes apparently the division of a tribe (chap. xx. 12).

The tribe of the Danites.—There seems to be a difference between "tribe of Dan" (*Shebet Dan*) and "tribesmen of the Danites" (*Shebet had-Dani*). In verse 11 they are called *Mishpecath had-Dani*; but the distinctions between *Mishpecath* ("family") and *Shebet* ("tribe") do not seem to be accurately kept. (See Notes on verse 19 and chap. xx. 12.)

Sought them an inheritance.—See chap. i. 34; Josh. xix. 47, 48.

Unto that day all their inheritance had not fallen unto them.—Their inheritance is described in Josh. xix. 40—46. The inheritance had been *assigned* to them; but they had not been able to conquer it, owing to the opposition of the Philistines and the Amorites. The English Version interpolates the words "all their" before "inheritance," apparently to avoid difficulties. But these glosses, however well meant, are almost always a violation of the primary duty of translation, which is to be rigidly faithful to the original. The failure of the Danites to conquer their allotment, and the low condition to which they dwindled, are the more remarkable because in the wilderness they were the strongest of all the tribes, numbering 62,700, and because they received the *smallest* assignment of land of all the tribes.

⁽²⁾ **From their coasts.**—Literally, *their ends* (Gen. xix. 4; 1 Kings xii. 31). Some explain it to mean "from their whole number."

Men of valour.—Literally, *sons of force* (chap. xxi. 10).

To spy out the land.—As in Josh. ii. 1.

They come to Micah's House.   JUDGES, XVIII.   *They Search Laish.*

to search it; and they said unto them, Go, search the land: who when they came to mount Ephraim, to the house of Micah, they lodged there. ⁽³⁾ When they *were* by the house of Micah, they knew the voice of the young man the Levite: and they turned in thither, and said unto him, Who brought thee hither? and what makest thou in this *place*? and what hast thou here? ⁽⁴⁾ And he said unto them, Thus and thus dealeth Micah with me, and hath hired me, and I am his priest. ⁽⁵⁾ And they said unto him, Ask counsel, we pray thee, of God, that we may know whether our way which we go shall be prosperous. ⁽⁶⁾ And the priest said unto them, Go in peace: before the LORD *is* your way wherein ye go.

⁽⁷⁾ Then the five men departed, and came to Laish, and saw the people that *were* therein, how they dwelt careless, after the manner of the Zidonians, quiet and secure; and *there was* no ¹magistrate in the land, that might put *them* to shame in *any* thing; and they *were* far from the Zidonians, and had no business with *any* man. ⁽⁸⁾ And they came unto their brethren to Zorah and Eshtaol: and their brethren said unto

¹ Heb., *possessor*, or, *heir of restraint*.

They came to mount Ephraim.—It would have been an easier journey to pass along the *Shephelah*, but that was mainly in the hands of the original inhabitants.

To the house of Micah.—There is no necessity for the supposition that they did not actually lodge in the house, or, at any rate, in the khan which doubtless formed part of the settlement. The centre of a new and gorgeous worship was sure to have places around it where those could lodge who came to consult the *pesel-ephod* (see verse 18), just as even the ordinary synagogues had lodgings for wayfarers.

⁽³⁾ **By the house of Micah.**—Literally, *with*—*i.e.*, lodging in it, as in Gen. xxvii. 43.

They knew the voice of the young man the Levite.—Again the narrative is too much compressed to enable us to fill up its details with any certainty. The youthful Jonathan had lived in Bethlehem. The grandson of Moses could not be wholly unknown, and at this time there was close intercourse between the tribes of Dan and Judah. Possibly, therefore they were personally acquainted with him; nor do they ask (as Micah had done), " Whence cometh thou?" They recognised his voice, possibly by some dialectic peculiarity, but more probably by hearing him performing in the upper room his service before the *pesel*. Cassel renders " voice " by " sound," and refers it to the bells on the priestly dress, as in Exod. xxviii. 35. We notice that Micah had been reticent about the ephod, &c., perhaps out of suspicion as to their intentions.

Turned in thither.—Not necessarily into the house, but into the room—the oratory (*aedicula*), or Beth-Elohim (chap. xvii. 5). It seems to have been a kind of spurious Shiloh.

What makest thou in this place?—The accent of extreme surprise in their queries shows that they knew Jonathan, and did not expect to find a Judæan Levite in Ephraim.

⁽⁴⁾ **Thus and thus.**—Literally, *according to this and according to that,* as in 2 Sam. xi. 25; 1 Kings xiv. 5.

I am his priest.—See chap. xvii. 13. Similarly in the dearth of genuine priests Jeroboam was forced to make even Levites out of the lowest of the people (1 Kings xii. 31).

⁽⁵⁾ **Ask counsel . . of God.**—Doubtless Jonathan showed them the glittering ephod. There were no prophets of whom to inquire, as in 1 Kings xxii. 5; but their unauthorised inquiry was liable to the strong censure expressed in Isa. xxx. 1, Hosea iv. 12. They might have at least consulted the high priest Phinehas, or some other national representative.

⁽⁶⁾ **Before the Lord is your way**—*i.e.*, *Jehovah looks favourably upon it.* (Comp. Prov. v. 21; Ezra viii. 21.) The answer had, however, some of the oracular ambiguity. Jonathan did not stake his own credit or that of his ephod on any definite details, or even on any distinct promise.

⁽⁷⁾ **Laish.**—It is called *Leshem* in Josh. xix. 47, and is now called *Tel el-Kadi*, " the mound of *the judge*," possibly (though not probably) with some reference to the name of Dan (Gen. xlix. 16). It is four miles from Paneas and Cæsarea Philippi, and was the northernmost city of Palestine (chap. xx. 1). As such, its name recurs in Isa. x. 30, if our version is there correct. It is sometimes called *el-Leddan*, because it is at the source of the Leddan, the chief stream of the Jordan. The position of the town, on a round hill girt with trees, is very striking, and fully bears out the description of this chapter (Robinson, *Bible Res.* iii. 392). The *name* " Dan " in Gen. xiv. 14 may have been altered from Laish at a later date (Ewald, *Gesch.* i. 73).

After the manner of the Zidonians—*i.e., in luxurious commercial ease.* There can be little doubt that they were a colony from Zidon.

Quiet and secure . . . There are three peculiarities in this clause:—(1) Although the word for " people " (*am*) is masculine, yet the word for " dwelling " (*yoshebeth*) is feminine, perhaps because the writer had the word " city " in his mind, just as αὐτήν is feminine in Acts xxvii. 14, though the word for " ship " has been neuter, because the writer has ναῦς in his mind. (2) The word for " careless " and the word for " secure " are from the same root, and are tautological. (3) The clause " no magistrate," &c., is curiously expressed. It is difficult not to suppose that the text is in some way corrupt.

There was no magistrate . . . This difficult clause seems to mean, " no one possessing wealth " (LXX., " heir of treasure ") " among them doing harm in the land in any matter." The various versions differ widely from each other, and the text is almost certainly corrupt.

They were far from the Zidonians.—As Josephus says, the town is a day's journey distant from Zidon.

No business with any man.—The reading of some MSS. of the LXX., " They had no business with Syria," rises from reading *Aram* for *Adam*.

them, What *say* ye? ⁽⁹⁾ And they said, Arise, that we may go up against them: for we have seen the land, and, behold, it *is* very good: and *are* ye still? be not slothful to go, *and* to enter to possess the land. ⁽¹⁰⁾ When ye go, ye shall come unto a people secure, and to a large land: for God hath given it into your hands; a place where *there is* no want of any thing that *is* in the earth.

⁽¹¹⁾ And there went from thence of the family of the Danites, out of Zorah and out of Eshtaol, six hundred men ¹appointed with weapons of war. ⁽¹²⁾ And they went up, and pitched in Kirjath-jearim, in Judah: wherefore they called that place Mahaneh-dan unto this day: behold, *it is* behind Kirjath-jearim. ⁽¹³⁾ And they passed thence unto mount Ephraim, and came unto the house of Micah. ⁽¹⁴⁾ Then answered the five men that went to spy out the country of Laish, and said unto their brethren, Do ye know that there is in these houses an ephod, and a teraphim, and a graven image, and a molten image? now therefore consider what ye have to do. ⁽¹⁵⁾ And they turned thitherward, and came to the house of the young man the Levite, *even* unto the house of Micah, and ²saluted him. ⁽¹⁶⁾ And the six hundred men appointed with their weapons of war, which *were* of the children of Dan, stood by the entering of the gate. ⁽¹⁷⁾ And the five men that went to spy out the land went up, *and* came in thither, *and* took the graven image, and the ephod, and the teraphim, and the molten image: and the priest stood in the entering of the gate with the six hundred men *that were* appointed with weapons of war. ⁽¹⁸⁾ And these went into Micah's house, and fetched the carved image, the ephod, and the teraphim, and the molten image. Then said the priest unto them, What do ye? ⁽¹⁹⁾ And they said unto him, Hold thy peace, lay thine hand upon thy mouth,

¹ Heb., *girded*.

² Heb., *asked him of peace*.

⁽⁹⁾ **Behold, it is very good.**—Comp. Num. xiv. 7; Josh. ii. 23, 24. The beauty of the site well bears out the description—"the rich and beautiful seclusion of that loveliest of the scenes of Palestine" (Stanley). It was by a similar statement that Anaxilaus of Rhegium persuaded the Messenians to seize Zankle (Pausan. iv. 23, quoted by Cassel).

Are ye still?—1 Kings xxii. 3; 2 Kings vii. 9.

⁽¹⁰⁾ **To a large land.**—Literally, *wide on both hands* (Gen. xxxiv. 11). This well describes the position of Tel el-Kadi. (See Notes on verses 7 and 28.)

God hath given it into your hands.—Of this they feel confident, from the interpretation which they put upon the oracular response given them by Jonathan in verse 6.

⁽¹¹⁾ **Appointed.**—Literally, *girded*. This was not a mere raid of warriors, but the migration of a section from the tribe, accompanied by their wives and children, and carrying their possessions with them (verse 21). The numbers of the whole tribe at the last census had been 64,400 (Num. xxvi. 43).

⁽¹²⁾ **In Kirjath-jearim.**—Josh. ix. 17. The name means "city of forests." The modern name is "city of grapes" (*Kuriet el Enab*). It is nine miles from Jerusalem, on the Jaffa road. Its original names were Baalah and Kirjath-Baal (Josh. xv. 9, 60). It was here that the ark remained for twenty years when sent back by the Philistines (1 Sam. vi. 20, 21, vii. 2). "We found it *in the fields of the wood*" (Ps. cxxxii. 6).

Mahaneh-dan—*i.e.*, the camp of Dan (chap. xiii. 25). They must have probably encamped here for some little time, as we can hardly suppose that the place would have received the name permanently from the bivouac of one night.

Behind—*i.e.*, *to the west of*. So "the *hinder* sea" is the western or Mediterranean Sea (Deut. ix. 24; Zech. xiv. 8). The site of Mahaneh-dan cannot be identified with certainty, as the position of Eshtaol is unknown.

⁽¹³⁾ **Unto the house of Micah.**—Probably the precincts of the new sanctuary gave their name to a sort of village—Beth-Micah.

⁽¹⁴⁾ **Answered.**—Equivalent to *they said*, as in Job iii. 2, Zech. i. 10.

Consider what ye have to do—*i.e.*, *whether*, *and how, you would possess yourselves of them.* We notice in these Danite freebooters the same strange mixture of superstition and lawlessness, robbery, and devotion which has often been observed in Greek and Italian brigands.

⁽¹⁵⁻¹⁸⁾ In these verses we have a graphic description of the whole nefarious proceeding. The five spies, knowing Jonathan, salute him, and inveigle him to the entrance of the court to talk to their six hundred companions. While the chiefs of this little army detain him in conversation, without any show of violence the five slip away unobserved to the *aliyah*, or upper room, which serves as the chapel, and steal all the essentials of the worship—namely, (1) the ephod; (2) the teraphim; (3) the graven image; (4) the molten image. It is true that in verses 20–30 the *massecah* is not mentioned; but it may be regarded as belonging to the *pesel*. It is only when he sees them in actual possession of these that Jonathan asks the alarmed question, "What do ye?"

⁽¹⁸⁾ **The carved image, the ephod.**—In the Hebrew this is *pesel ha-ephod*—*i.e.*, the "pesel-ephod." Very possibly, however, the ephod may, as a rule, have hung on the carved image, so that to carry off the pesel was also to carry off the ephod, which ordinarily covered it.

⁽¹⁹⁾ **Hold thy peace, lay thine hand upon thy mouth.**—Comp. Job xxi. 5, xxix. 9; Prov. xxx. 32. The laying of the finger on the lip is one of the most universal of gestures. It is the attitude of Horus, the Egyptian god of silence. (See Apul. *Metamorph.* i.: *at ille digitum, a pollice proximum ori suo admovens . . . tace, tace, inquit.*)

and go with us, and be to us a father and a priest: *is it* better for thee to be a priest unto the house of one man, or that thou be a priest unto a tribe and a family in Israel? (20) And the priest's heart was glad, and he took the ephod, and the teraphim, and the graven image, and went in the midst of the people. (21) So they turned and departed, and put the little ones and the cattle and the carriage before them.

(22) *And* when they were a good way from the house of Micah, the men that *were* in the houses near to Micah's house were gathered together, and overtook the children of Dan. (23) And they cried unto the children of Dan. And they turned their faces, and said unto Micah, What aileth thee, [1]that thou comest with such a company? (24) And he said, Ye have taken away my gods which I made, and the priest, and ye are gone away: and what have I more? and what *is* this *that* ye say unto me, What aileth thee? (25) And the children of Dan said unto him, Let not thy voice be heard among us, lest [2]angry fellows run upon thee, and thou lose thy life, with the lives of thy household. (26) And the children of Dan went their way: and when Micah saw that they *were* too strong for him, he turned and went back unto his house.

(27) And they took *the things* which Micah had made, and the priest which he had, and came unto Laish, unto a people *that were* at quiet and secure: and they smote them with the edge of the sword, and burnt the city with fire. (28) And *there was* no deliverer, because it

[1] Heb., *that thou art gathered together.*

[2] Heb., *bitter of soul.*

A father and a priest.—Chap. xvii. 10.

Unto a tribe and a family.—Both to a *shebet* and a *mishpecah*. (See Note on verse 1.)

(20) **The priest's heart was glad.**—Chap. xix. 6, 9; Ruth iii. 7. The disgraceful alacrity with which he sanctions the theft, and abandons for self-interest the cause of Micah, is very unworthy of a grandson of Moses. Dean Stanley appositely compares the bribe offered in 1176 to the monk Roger of Canterbury:—"Give us the portion of St. Thomas's skull which is in thy custody, and thou shalt cease to be a simple monk; thou shalt be Abbot of St. Augustine's."

In the midst of the people.—That they might guard his person. It is not necessarily implied that he carried *all* these sacred objects himself; he *may* have done so, for the molten image, which was perhaps the heaviest object, is not here mentioned.

(21) **The little ones and the cattle.**—It is only in this incidental way that the fact of this being a regular migration is brought out. (Comp. Exod. xii. 37.) The women are, of course, included, though not mentioned (Gen. xxxiv. 29; 2 Chron. xx. 13).

And the carriage—*i.e.*, "the baggage." (Comp. Acts xxi. 15.) The word is *hakkebodah*, which the LXX. (Cod. A) render "their glorious possession," and the Vulg. "everything which was precious," *i.e.*, the valuables. But as *cabid* means "to be heavy," the rendering of the Vatican MS. of the LXX.—"the weight," *i.e.*, "the heavy baggage" (*impedimenta*)—may be right. The word has no connection with that similarly rendered in 1 Sam. xvii. 22.

Before them.—Because they expected pursuit.

(22) **A good way from the house of Micah.**—It took some time to raise the alarm and collect a sufficient force. The Beth-Micah was probably strong enough to resist any ordinary robbers, but no one could have expected a raid of 600 men. Yet they would easily overtake the Danites, because their march was delayed and encumbered with women, children, and cattle.

Were gathered together.—See chap. vi. 34.

(23) **What aileth thee?**—There is again a certain grim humour in the narrative, with some sense of irony for the total discomfiture and pathetic outcries of Micah. Dan showed himself in this proceeding like "a serpent on the way, an adder in the path" (Gen. xlix. 17). (Comp. Deut. xxxiii. 22.)

(24) **My gods which I made.**—He does not scruple to call the pesel and teraphim "gods" (his Elohim), any more than the idolater Laban had done (Gen. xxx. 31). The expression seems to be intended to show scorn for Micah; and perhaps it is from missing this element that the LXX. soften it down into "my graven image," and the Chaldee to "my fear." "My gods which I made" would be a very ordinary expression for the Greeks, who called a sculptor a "god-maker" (*theopoios*), but was startling on the lips of an Israelite. Micah pathetically asks "What have I more?" but we may well hope that his present loss was his ultimate gain, and that he found the true God in place of the lost gods which he had made.

(25) **Lest angry fellows run upon thee.**—Literally, *lest men bitter of soul fall upon thee*. (Comp. chaps. viii. 21, xv. 12; 2 Sam. xvii. 8, "chafed in their minds.")

Thou lose thy life.—Literally, *thou gather thy life*, as in Ps. xxvi. 9.

(27) **Burnt the city with fire.**—This was unusual, for we are told that Hazor was the only city which Joshua burnt (Josh. xi. 13). Perhaps they had devoted the city by a ban, as Jericho was devoted (Josh. vi. 24); or the burning may have been due to policy or to accident. Probably the notion that such conduct was cruel and unjustifiable never occurred to them; nor must we judge them by the standard of Christian times. But Dan was no gainer. His name disappears from the records of 1 Chron. iv. 1, and he is not mentioned among the elected tribes in Rev. vii. Blunt (*Undesigned Coincidences*, pt. ii., 4) conjectures, from 2 Chron. ii. 14, that the cause of their disappearance from Israelite records—the latest mention of them as a tribe being in 1 Chron. xxvii. 22—was due to their intermarriages with the Phœnicians.

(28) **In the valley that lieth by Beth-rehob.**—At the foot of the lowest range of Lebanon, and at the sources of the Jordan (Num. xiii. 21), north of Lake Huleh. It is probably the Rehob of chap. i. 31, Josh. xix. 30; and later it belonged to Syria (2 Sam. x. 6). The name means "house of spaciousness." Robinson

was far from Zidon, and they had no business with *any* man; and it was in the valley that *lieth* by Beth-rehob.

And they built a city, and dwelt therein. ⁽²⁹⁾ And they called the name of the ᵃcity Dan, after the name of Dan their father,

a Josh. 19. 47.

who was born unto Israel: howbeit the name of the city *was* Laish at the first. ⁽³⁰⁾ And the children of Dan set up the graven image: and Jonathan, the son of Gershom, the son of Manasseh, he and his sons were priests to the tribe of Dan

---

(*Bibl. Res.* iii. 371) identifies it with *Hunîn*, a fortress which commands the plain of Huleh.

⁽²⁹⁾ **They called the name of the city Dan.**—Just as the Messenians changed the name Zankle into Messene.

⁽³⁰⁾ **Set up the graven image.**—If this *pesel* was in the form of a calf, the tradition of this cult may have given greater facility to the daring innovation of Jeroboam (1 Kings xii. 30). In any case, it would make the inhabitants more ready to accept a cherubic symbol of Jehovah; for we may fairly assume that the "image" was not dissociated from the worship of God, whether as Elohim or Jehovah. Jonathan and the Danites both acknowledged Him under the name Elohim (chap. xviii. 5, 10), and Micah, in spite of his images, acknowledged God as Jehovah (chaps. xvii. 2, 13, xviii. 6), to whom, indeed, the very name of Jonathan ("gift of Jehovah") bore witness. Whether this, or rather the smallness of Dan, is the reason for its exclusion from Rev. vii. 4 must remain uncertain. The Fathers thought, for this reason, that Antichrist would spring from the tribe of Dan.

Jonathan, the son of Gershom, the son of Manasseh.—The extreme reluctance to admit this fact —the disgrace involved against the memory of Moses by this rapid and total degeneracy of his grandson—is probably the reason why up to this point in the narrative the name has been withheld. There can, however, be no doubt that Jonathan was the young Levite who has all along been spoken of. The reading of MANASSEH for MOSES is by the confession of the Jews themselves due to the same cause. Moses is in Hebrew מֹשֶׁה, Manasseh is מְנַשֶּׁה. It will thus be seen that (without the points) the names only differ by the letter *n* (נ). But in what is called the Masoretic text—*i.e.*, the text edited by the Jewish scribes—the נ is not boldly inserted, but is timidly and furtively suspended—thus מֹ^נשֶׁה MSSH—and is called *nun thalûyah* (n suspended). This was done to conceal from the uninitiated the painful fact. It was known to St. Jerome, and accordingly the Vulg. reads "son of Moses," which is also found in some MSS. of the LXX. Theodoret has "son of Manasseh, son of Gershom, son of Moses." The Jews distinguish between the "text" (*Kethib* "written") and the margin (*Keri* "read"), and Rabbi Tanchum admits that here "Moses" is *written*, though "Manasseh" is *read*. The Talmud says that he was grandson of Moses; but "because he did the deeds of Manasseh" (the idolatrous king, 2 Kings xxi.), "the Scripture assigns him to the family of Manasseh" (*Babha Bathra*, f. 109, 2); and on this a later Rabbi remarks that "the prophet"—*i.e.*, the sacred author—"studiously avoided calling Gershom the son of Moses, *because it would have been ignominious to Moses to have had an ungodly son;* but he calls him the son of Manasseh, suspending the *n* above the line to show that he was *the son of Manasseh* (in a metaphorical sense) by imitating his impiety, though a son of Moses by descent." The Talmudists account for the distasteful fact by saying that the degeneracy was due to the *wife*

of Moses, who was a Midianite, so that there was a taint in the blood of the family. It is not, however, the sacred author who is guilty of this "pious fraud," but the Masoretic editors. The rarity of the name Gershom (which means "a stranger there," Exod. ii. 22) would alone be sufficient to betray the secret. The extravagant and superstitious letter-worship of the scribes did not suffice to prevent them from tampering with the *letter*, any more than it prevented the Rabbis from entirely explaining away the obvious *spirit* of the Law which they professed to adore. The only uncertainty in the matter is whether this wandering Levite, this young Jonathan, who for less than thirty shillings a year becomes the priest of an idolatrous worship, was the actual *grandson*, or only a later descendant of Moses, since the Jews often omit steps in their genealogies. There is, however, no reason why he should not have been the actual grandson, since he is contemporary with Phinehas (chap. xx. 28) who was, without any question, the actual grandson of Aaron. This rapid degeneracy may perhaps account for the obscuration of the family of Moses, which never seems to have subsequently risen into any importance, and of which no more names are preserved. Jonathan's name is excluded, perhaps deliberately, from 1 Chron. xxiii. 15, 16. Or is he indeed Shebuel, as St. Jerome avers, probably from Jewish tradition?—and has his name been purposely altered? It is probably from a similar dislike to reveal the disgrace which thus fell on the family of the great law-giver that Josephus entirely omits the story. It is impossible that he should not have been perfectly acquainted with it. The identity of Jonathan with Shebuel in 1 Chron. xxiii. 16 is asserted in the Targum, which says that "Shebuel, that is, Jonathan, the son of Gershom, the son of Moses, *returned to the fear of Jehovah*, and when David saw that he was skilful in money matters, he appointed him chief over the treasures."

Until the day of the captivity of the land.—(1) If the expression meant "the captivity," as ordinarily understood, the meaning could only be that these descendants of Moses continued also to be priests of the calf-worship for nearly two centuries, until the ten tribes were carried captive by Shalmaneser and Tiglath-pileser. (Comp. 1 Chron. v. 22.) If so, there would be a strong additional reason for identifying this worship with the calf-worship, and the fact might then be supposed to account for there being no mention of non-Levitic priests at Dan, but only at Bethel (1 Kings xii. 33). (2) Some suppose that we should read "ark" (*aron*) for "land" (*arets*). (See 1 Sam. iv. 21, 22.) But this conjecture of Houbigant is not supported by a single MS. or version. (3) It is far from impossible that "the captivity" may mean the Philistine captivity, which resulted from their terrible sack of Shiloh after the battle of Aphek (1 Sam. iv. 11, 22). It is called "a captivity" in the passage which so graphically describes the scene in Ps. lxxxviii. 58—61. Otherwise we may suppose (4) that "the land" has here a circumscribed sense, and that "the captivity" alluded to is one inflicted on the Danites by the kings of Zobah, or some other Syrian invasion (1 Sam. xiv. 47). The

until the day of the captivity of the land. ⁽³¹⁾ And they set them up Micah's graven image, which he made, all the time that the house of God was in Shiloh.

CHAPTER XIX.—⁽¹⁾ And it came to pass in those days, *when there was no king in Israel*, that there was a certain Levite sojourning on the side of mount Ephraim, who took to him ¹a concubine out of Beth-lehem-judah. ⁽²⁾ And his concubine played the whore against him, and went away from him unto her father's house to Beth-lehem-judah, and was there ^{2 3}four whole months. ⁽³⁾ And her husband arose, and went after her, to speak ⁴friendly unto her, *and* to bring her again, having his servant with him, and a couple of asses: and she brought him into her father's house: and when the father of the damsel saw him, he rejoiced to meet him. ⁽⁴⁾ And his father in law, the damsel's father, retained him; and he abode with him three days: so they did eat and drink, and lodged there. ⁽⁵⁾ And it came to pass on the fourth day, when they arose early in the morning, that he rose up to depart: and the damsel's father said unto his son in law, ⁵Comfort thine heart with a morsel of bread, and afterward go your way. ⁽⁶⁾ And they sat down, and did eat and drink both of them together: for the damsel's father had said unto the man, Be content, I pray thee, and tarry all night, and let thine heart be merry. ⁽⁷⁾ And when the man rose up to depart, his father in law urged him: therefore he lodged there again. ⁸ And he arose

a ch. 17. 6; & 18. 1; & 21. 25.

1 Heb., *a woman a concubine, or, a wife a concubine.*

2 Or, *a year and four months.*

3 Heb., *days, four months.*

4 Heb., *to her heart.*

5 Heb., *Strengthen.*

---

third explanation is, however, rendered almost certain by the following verse.

⁽³¹⁾ **And they set them up Micah's graven image.**—Rather, *entrusted to them,* i.e., to Jonathan's descendants. The phrase "set them up" can only have been used by inadvertence by our translators in this verse, since the verb used, *yasimo* (LXX., *etaxan heautois*; but Vulg., *mansitque apud eos,* i.e., there remained with *them* the descendants of Jonathan), is wholly different from the verb *yakimu,* rendered "set up" (LXX., *anestēsan*) in verse 30.

All the time that the house of God was in Shiloh—i.e., till Samuel's early manhood, when the Philistines sacked Shiloh, to which place the Ark and Tabernacle never returned (1 Sam. iii. 31, iv. 3, vi. 21, vii. 1). This verse may probably have been added by a later hand to prevent any mistake in the interpretation of the former. It may have been written in Saul's reign, when the Tabernacle and ephod had been removed to Nob for greater safety. The last mention of the town of Dan is in 2 Chron. xvi. 4

XIX.

1—4. A Levite of Mount Ephraim goes to Bethlehem to bring back his unfaithful concubine, and is hospitably received by her father. 5—9. The afternoon of the fifth day after his arrival he sets out to return. 10—15. Unwilling to stop at the heathen town of Jebus, he proceeds to Gibeah, where at first no man gives him shelter. 16—21. An old Ephraimite offers him hospitality. 22—28. Infamous conduct of the inhabitants of Gibeah, resulting in the woman's death. 29, 30. The Levite, by sending her dismembered body to the tribes, rouses them to vengeance.

In this chapter we see the unutterable depth of profligacy and shamelessness into which some of the Israelites had sunk. At the same time, we see that the moral sense of the nation was still sufficiently keen to be aroused by the glare of unnatural illumination thus flung upon their consciences. This narrative, like the former, belongs to the period between the death of Joshua and the rise of the greater Judges (Theodoret, *Quæst.* xxvii.; Jos. *Antt.* v. 2, § 8).

⁽¹⁾ **On the side of mount Ephraim.**—Literally, *on the two thighs* (*yarcethaim*). (Comp. Ps. cxxviii. 3; Isa. xxxvii. 24.) As to the residence of the Levite at Mount Ephraim, see Note on chap. xvii. 8. It is probably a fortuitous coincidence that both this Levite and Jonathan have relations with Mount Ephraim and with Bethlehem.

Took to him a concubine.—Such connections were not legally forbidden; yet it is probable that in the case of all but princes or eminent men they were looked on with moral disapprobation. She is called "a wife or concubine"—i.e., a wife with inferior rights for herself and her children.

⁽²⁾ **Four whole months.**—Literally, *days, four months,* which some interpret to mean "a year (see Note on chap. xvii. 10) and four months." The incident has, however, little bearing on the general story.

⁽³⁾ **To speak friendly unto her.**—Literally, *to speak to her heart*—i.e., to bring about a kindly reconciliation (Gen. xxxiv. 3, l. 21; Ruth ii. 13).

A couple of asses.—One was meant to convey back his wife on her return.

⁽⁴⁾ **Retained him.**—One motive of the father-in-law would doubtless be to practise the full rights of hospitality, which are in the East so specially sacred; but he probably desired further to win back the Levite's heart to his erring daughter.

⁽⁵⁾ **Early in the morning.**—Except in winter, most journeys are performed in the early morning or late evening, in order to avoid the burning heat.

Comfort thine heart.—Literally, *Prop up thy heart,* as in Gen. xviii. 5. This resembles the Latin expression *cor fulcire.*

⁽⁶⁾ **Let thine heart be merry.**—Chap. xvi. 25, xviii. 20.

⁽⁷⁾ **His father in law urged him.**—Considering the remorselessly savage revenge which is to this day permitted to an Eastern husband in punishment of unfaithfulness, the father might well desire to be thoroughly assured that the Levite was not dissembling, and did not desire to inflict some sanguinary retribution on his wife.

⁽⁸⁾ **And they tarried until afternoon.**—The verb is perhaps an imperative: *and linger* (as in Isa.

early in the morning on the fifth day to depart: and the damsel's father said, Comfort thine heart, I pray thee. And they tarried ¹until afternoon, and they did eat both of them. ⁽⁹⁾ And when the man rose up to depart, he, and his concubine, and his servant, his father in law, the damsel's father, said unto him, Behold, now the day ²draweth toward evening, I pray you tarry all night: behold, ³the day groweth to an end, lodge here, that thine heart may be merry; and to morrow get you early on your way, that thou mayest go ⁴home. ⁽¹⁰⁾ But the man would not tarry that night, but he rose up and departed, and came ⁵over against Jebus, which *is* Jerusalem; and *there were* with him two asses saddled, his concubine also *was* with him.

⁽¹¹⁾ *And* when they *were* by Jebus, the day was far spent; and the servant said unto his master, Come, I pray thee, and let us turn in into this city of the Jebusites, and lodge in it. ⁽¹²⁾ And his master said unto him, We will not turn aside

1 Heb., *till the day declined.*
2 Heb., *is weak.*
3 Heb., *it is the pitching time of the day.*
4 Heb., *to thy tent.*
5 Heb., *to over against Jebus.*

hither into the city of a stranger, that *is* not of the children of Israel; we will pass over to Gibeah. ⁽¹³⁾ And he said unto his servant, Come, and let us draw near to one of these places to lodge all night, in Gibeah, or in Ramah. ⁽¹⁴⁾ And they passed on and went their way; and the sun went down upon them *when they were* by Gibeah, which *belongeth* to Benjamin. ⁽¹⁵⁾ And they turned aside thither, to go in *and* to lodge in Gibeah: and when he went in, he sat him down in a street of the city: for *there was* no man that took them into his house to lodging.

⁽¹⁶⁾ And, behold, there came an old man from his work out of the field at even, which *was* also of mount Ephraim, and he sojourned in Gibeah: but the men of the place *were* Benjamites. ⁽¹⁷⁾ And when he had lifted up his eyes, he saw a wayfaring man in the street of the city: and the old man said, Whither goest thou? and whence comest thou? ⁽¹⁸⁾ And he said unto him, We *are* passing from Beth-lehem-judah toward the side of

---

xix. 9) *till the day turns.* So the LXX., Chaldee, and Vulg. take it.

⁽⁹⁾ **The day draweth toward evening.**— Literally, *is weak,* or *has slackened to evening.* The father had purposely detained the Levite till late, in the hopes of inducing him to spend one more night under his roof. The forms of Eastern politeness would render it difficult for the Levite to resist these importunities.

The day groweth to an end.—Literally, *it is the bending* or *declining of the day,* not, as in the margin of our version, "the pitching time of the day."

Home.—Literally, *to thy tent,* which may be something more than a mere reminiscence of the earlier stage of the national existence. (Comp. "To your tents, O Israel," 1 Kings xii. 16, &c.) The Levite is conscious that if the father has been too pressing he has himself been too self-indulgent, and too fond of good living. "His experience is that of all weak and vacillating people: first, unnecessary delay, and then overstrained hurry."

⁽¹⁰⁾ **Jebus, which is Jerusalem.**—See chap. i. 8; Josh. xv. 8.

Saddled.—Rather, *loaded* (Vulg., *onustos*).

⁽¹¹⁾ **The day was far spent.**—Jerusalem is only two hours distant from Bethlehem. The father of the woman, by his unwise neglect to "speed the parting guest," had greatly added to the perils of their journey in a half-conquered country, and in such wild times.

Unto his master.—Literally, *to his lord,* a mere form of respect, as in Gen. xxxix. 2.

This city of the Jebusites.—Their complete and undisturbed possession shows that this narrative falls at an early date (chap. i. 7, 8, 11, 21; Josh. xv. 63). The travellers would reach the town from Bethlehem at about five o'clock.

⁽¹²⁾ **To Gibeah.**—This is the "Gibeah of Saul," where the first king of Israel was born (1 Sam. xi. 4). It was one of the fourteen cities of Benjamin (Josh.

xviii. 28), and is the modern *Tuleil el Ful.* It only involved a journey of four miles more (Jos. *Antt.* v. 2, § 8).

⁽¹³⁾ **Or in Ramah.**—This town, now *el-Ram,* is only two miles beyond Gibeah. The two places are often mentioned together (Hosea v. 8). The Levite is naturally anxious to push on homewards as fast as he can. Perhaps he knew that Gibeah did not bear a good character, and that it would be better to get as far as Ramah if possible. In countries where there are no public inns, each town and village gets a character of its own from the reports of travellers.

⁽¹⁴⁾ **The sun went down upon them.**—They were evidently reluctant to stop at Gibeah; but it was dangerous to travel after dark, and the twilight in Palestine is very brief.

Which belongeth to Benjamin.—There were many other Gibeahs in Palestine, and for that reason Jibah and el-Jib are common names.

⁽¹⁵⁾ **In a street.** — Rather, *in the open place* (*Rechob*)—*i.e.,* the square or market-place of the city, often a space *outside* the walls (Deut. xiii. 16). (Comp. Gen. xix. 1, 2; "The stranger did not lodge in the street"—Job xxxi. 32.)

No man that took them into his house.— The same neglect would have been experienced by the angels at Sodom but for the care of Lot. This neglect of the very first duty of the East was sufficient at once to prove the base condition into which Gibeah had fallen (Deut. x. 19; Matt. xxv. 35).

⁽¹⁶⁾ **Which was also of mount Ephraim.**— He was therefore a fellow-countryman of the Levite, but his hospitable feelings were aroused before he had been informed of this fact.

⁽¹⁸⁾ **Toward the side of mount Ephraim.**— Rather, *the depths of the hill-country of Ephraim.*

I am now going to the house of the Lord. —We are not told anywhere else in the story that

mount Ephraim; from thence *am* I: and I went to Beth-lehem-judah, but I *am now* going to the house of the LORD; and there *is* no man that ¹receiveth me to house. (19) Yet there is both straw and provender for our asses; and there is bread and wine also for me, and for thy handmaid, and for the young man *which is* with thy servants: *there is* no want of any thing. (20) And the old man said, Peace *be* with thee; howsoever *let* all thy wants *lie* upon me; only lodge not in the street. (21) So he brought him into his house, and gave provender unto the asses: and they washed their feet, and did eat and drink.

(22) *Now* as they were making their hearts merry, behold, the men of the city, certain sons of Belial, beset the house round about, *and* beat at the door,

1 Heb., *gathereth*.

a Gen. 19. 6.

2 Heb., *the matter of this folly*.

and spake to the master of the house, the old man, saying, Bring forth the man that came into thine house, that we may know him. (23) And *a*the man, the master of the house, went out unto them, and said unto them, Nay, my brethren, *nay*, I pray you, do not *so* wickedly; seeing that this man is come into mine house, do not this folly. (24) Behold, *here is* my daughter a maiden, and his concubine; them I will bring out now, and humble ye them, and do with them what seemeth good unto you: but unto this man do not ²so vile a thing. (25) But the men would not hearken to him: so the man took his concubine, and brought her forth unto them; and they knew her, and abused her all the night until the morning: and when the day began to spring, they let her go.

---

the Levite was going to Shiloh (chap. xviii. 31; Josh. xviii. 1), but that he was returning to his home in Mount Ephraim. Hence some render the words, "I walk at the house of Jehovah"—*i.e.*, I am a Levite, engaged in the service of the Tabernacle at Shiloh. It is true that this would be no answer to the question, "Whither goest thou?" On the other hand, the phrase is not a usual one for going *to* a place, and the Levite perhaps meant to imply an additional reason why the inhospitable reception was very unworthy. His office ought to have procured him a welcome, yet he who belongs to God's house cannot find shelter in any house in Gibeah. The LXX. adopt another reading, and render it "to my house" (reading *Bithi*). The reading of the MSS. may have come from regarding the last letter as an abbreviation of Jehovah.

(19) **Straw and provender.**—Comp. Gen. xxiv. 25—32. All that the Levite asked was shelter. He would provide for all his own wants.

Thy servants.—The ordinary language of Eastern obsequiousness.

(20) **Peace be with thee.**—The words are not here a greeting, but an assurance of help.

Only lodge not in the street.—Gen. xix. 2.

(21) **Gave provender unto the asses.**—Notice the humane Eastern custom of attending first the wants of the animals.

They washed their feet.—One of the first necessities for personal comfort after a journey in hot countries, and where only sandals are worn (Gen. xviii. 4, xxiv. 32, xliii. 24; Luke vii. 44; John xiii. 5; 1 Tim. v. 10).

(22) **Sons of Belial.**—It is only by a deeply-rooted misconception that Belial is written with a capital. The word is not the name (as is supposed) of an evil spirit, but an ordinary noun, "sons of worthlessness," *i.e.*, "worthless fellows." (See Deut. xiii. 14; Ps. xviii. 5.) Later (comp. 2 Cor. vi. 15) it became a kind of proper name. Josephus dishonestly suppresses all the darkest features of the story (*Antt.* v. 11, § 7).

Beset the house.—There is a close resemblance to the equally hideous narrative of Gen. xix. 8.

Beat at the door.—The word implies continuous knocking and gradual increase of noise (Cant. v. 2).

We cannot wonder that the intense horror excited by this scene of infamy lasted for centuries afterwards. "They have deeply corrupted themselves, as in the days of Gibeah" (Hosea ix. 9). "O Israel, thou hast sinned from the days of Gibeah" (Hosea x. 9).

"And when night
Darkens the streets, then wander forth the sons
Of Belial, flown with insolence and wine.
Witness the streets of Sodom, and that night
In Gibeah, when the hospitable door
Exposed a matron to avoid worse rape."—*Milton.*

(23) **Do not this folly.**—It is from no deficiency of moral indignation that the word "folly" (*nebalah*) is used. Sometimes when crime is too dark and deadly for ordinary reproach the feelings are more deeply expressed by using a milder word, which is instantly corrected and intensified by the hearer himself. (See Gen. xxxiv. 7; Deut. xxii. 21.) Thus Virgil merely gives the epithet "unpraised" ("*illaudati* Busiridis aras") to the cannibal tyrant, which serves even better than a stronger word. (Comp. "Shall I praise you for these things? I *praise you not*," 1 Cor. xi. 17—22.) (See the author's *Brief Greek Syntax,* p. 199.) This figure of speech takes the various form of antiphasis, litotes, meiosis, &c.

(24, 25) **Behold, here is my daughter . . .**—The main horror of these verses lies, and is meant to lie, in the nameless infamy to which these men had sunk, of whom we can only say,

"Non ragionam di lor ma guarda è passa."

But we must not omit to notice that the conduct of the old man and the Levite, though it is not formally condemned, speaks of the existence of a very rudimentary morality, a selfishness, and a low estimate of the rights and sacred dignity of women, which shows from what depths the world has emerged. If it was possible to frustrate the vile assault of these wretches in this way it must have been possible to frustrate it altogether. There is something terribly repulsive in the selfishness which could thus make a Levite sacrifice a defenceless woman, and that woman his wife, for a whole night to such brutalisation. The remark of St. Gregory is very weighty: "*Minus peccatum admittere ut gravius evitetur est a scelere victimas offerre Deo.*"

The Concubine's Body Divided   JUDGES, XX.   *and Sent to the Twelve Tribes.*

⁽²⁶⁾ Then came the woman in the dawning of the day, and fell down at the door of the man's house where her lord *was*, till it was light. ⁽²⁷⁾ And her lord rose up in the morning, and opened the doors of the house, and went out to go his way: and, behold, the woman his concubine was fallen down *at* the door of the house, and her hands *were* upon the threshold. ⁽²⁸⁾ And he said unto her, Up, and let us be going. But none answered. Then the man took her *up* upon an ass, and the man rose up, and gat him unto his place.

⁽²⁹⁾ And when he was come into his house, he took a knife, and laid hold on his concubine, and divided her, *together* with her bones, into twelve pieces, and sent her into all the coasts of Israel. ⁽³⁰⁾ And it was so, that all that saw it said, There was no such deed done nor seen from the day that the children of Israel came up out of the land of Egypt unto this day: consider of it, take advice, and speak *your minds*.

CHAPTER XX.—⁽¹⁾ Then all the children of Israel went out, and the congregation was gathered together as one man, from Dan even to Beer-sheba, with the land of Gilead, unto the LORD in Mizpeh. ⁽²⁾ And the chief of all the people, *even* of all the tribes of Israel, presented themselves in the assembly of

---

⁽²⁶⁾ **Then came the woman . . . .**—It would be scarcely possible to enhance the depth of pathos and of horror which the sacred writer throws into these simple words. If to the wretched woman punishment had come in the guise of her sin (Wisd. xi. 16, "that they might know that wherewithal a man sinneth, by the same also shall he be punished") which had been the prime cause of the whole catastrophe, the Levite was punished both for his condonation of an offence which could not be condoned, and for the unmanly cowardice or heartless self-absorption which could alone have rendered it possible for him to accept personal safety at such a price.

⁽²⁷⁾ **Her hands were upon the threshold.**—As though they had been stretched out towards her husband in one last agony of appeal (Vulg., *sparsis in limine manibus*).

⁽²⁸⁾ **But none answered.**—The sacred writer, in his horror, will not say that she was dead.

Upon an ass.—Rather, *the ass*, which had borne her while she was living. The omission of every detail, the narration of the naked facts in the simplest words, without pausing to say so much as a single word respecting the Levite's or the old man's feelings, is a striking example of the difference of the historic method of ancient and modern times.

⁽²⁹⁾ **Divided her.**—We see again that the narrative is taking us back to wild times, when the passions of men expressed themselves in wild and fierce expedients. A similar method of arousing a nation, but different in its details, is narrated in 1 Sam. xi. 7, when Saul sends round the pieces of an ox, as was done by the ancient Scythians (Lucian, *Toxaris*, chap. xlviii.). Many analogous customs existed among the ancient Highlanders, and have been repeated within recent days among the Arab tribes (Stanley, i. 301).

With her bones.—Literally, *according to her bones*.

Into twelve pieces.—One for each tribe. Benjamin was probably thus appealed to as well as the other tribes. It is needless to suppose that one was sent to Eastern Manasseh or to Levi.

⁽³⁰⁾ The verse shows that the Levite had successfully gauged the depths of moral indignation that still lay in the hearts of his countrymen. The story of the deed thrilled through all Palestine, and awoke a determined desire for retribution upon the guilty inhabitants of Gibeah. The whole nation felt the stain and shame (Hosea ix. 9, x. 9).

XX

1—7. The tribes meet at Mizpeh, and the Levite tells the story of the crime at Gibeah. 8—11. The people rise like one man, and determine to punish Gibeah. 12—14. The Benjamites espouse the cause of the guilty city. 15—17. The forces on both sides. 18—25. The Israelites twice defeated by Benjamin. 26—28. Victory promised them after a day of fast at Bethel. 29—41. Their stratagem and its success. 42—46. Destruction of the Benjamites. 47, 48. The tribe extirpated except six hundred men.

⁽¹⁾ **The congregation was gathered together.**—This phrase is one which was familiar to the Israelites in the desert. It disappears after the days of Solomon (1 Kings xii. 20).

From Dan even to Beer-sheba.—This expression would be like "from John o' Groat's house to Land's End" for England and Scotland (1 Sam. iii. 18, xvii. 11, &c.). Unless it be added by an anachronism, because it had become familiar when the Book of Judges was written, we should certainly infer from it that, early as were these events, they were subsequent to the migratory raid of the tribe of Dan to Laish.

With the land of Gilead.—The Trans-jordanic tribes obeyed the summons, with the exception of the town of Jabesh-Gilead.

Unto the Lord.—See Note on chap. xi. 11. There is not, however, the same difficulty in supposing that the ark and Urim was taken to this Mizpeh, for we see in verse 27 that it was taken to Bethel.

In Mizpeh.—See Note on chap. xi. 11. This Mizpeh is not the same as the one there mentioned, but is probably the bold hill and watch-tower now known as *Nèby Samwil*, and called Mountjoie by the Crusaders, from which the traveller gains his first glimpse of Jerusalem. In the Hebrew the name has the article, "the watch-tower." It was the scene of great gatherings of the tribes in the days of Samuel (1 Sam. vii. 2, x. 17) and of Solomon (2 Chron. i. 3, probably), and even after the captivity (2 Kings xxv. 23).

⁽²⁾ **The chief.**—The Hebrew word is *pinnoth*, "corner-stones," as in 1 Sam. xiv. 38; Isa. xix. 13.

Four hundred thousand.—Hence we learn the interesting fact that in their struggles against the Canaanites the number of the people had been diminished

the people of God, four hundred thousand footmen that drew sword. (3) (Now the children of Benjamin heard that the children of Israel were gone up to Mizpeh.)

Then said the children of Israel, Tell us, how was this wickedness? (4) And ¹the Levite, the husband of the woman that was slain, answered and said, I came into Gibeah that *belongeth* to Benjamin, I and my concubine, to lodge. (5) And the men of Gibeah rose against me, and beset the house round about upon me by night, *and* thought to have slain me : and my concubine have they ²forced, that she is dead. (6) And I took my concubine, and cut her in pieces, and sent her throughout all the country of the inheritance of Israel : for they have committed lewdness and folly in Israel. (7) Behold, ye *are* all children of Israel; give here your advice and counsel.

(8) And all the people arose as one man, saying, We will not any *of us* go to his tent, neither will we any *of us* turn into his house. (9) But now this *shall be* the thing which we will do to Gibeah; *we will go up* by lot against it; (10) and we will take ten men of an hundred throughout all the tribes of Israel, and an hundred of a thousand, and a thousand out of ten thousand, to fetch victual for the people, that they may do, when they come to Gibeah of Benjamin, according to all the folly that they have wrought in Israel.

(11) So all the men of Israel were gathered against the city, ³knit together as one man.

(12) And the tribes of Israel sent men through all the tribe of Benjamin, saying, What wickedness *is* this that is done among you? (13) Now therefore deliver us the men, the children of Belial, which *are* in Gibeah, that we may put them to death, and put away evil from Israel. But the children of Benjamin would not hearken to the voice of their brethren the children of Israel :

1 Heb., *the man the Levite.*
2 Heb., *humbled.*
3 Heb., *fellows.*

---

one-third—*i.e.*, to a far greater extent than they had been diminished by the wanderings in the wilderness. For at the census in the first year of the wanderings their numbers were (including 35,400 of Benjamin) 603,550 (Num. i. 46); and in the census in the last year they were 601,730, excluding the Benjamites, who, unlike the other tribes, had *increased* in numbers, for they were then 45,600 in number.

Footmen.—The Israelites were forbidden to use either chariots or cavalry. (See Notes on chaps. i. 19, iv. 3.)

That drew sword.—Chap. viii. 10.

(3) **Heard.**—Probably the Benjamites had received the same summons as the other tribes (see chap. xix. 29), but insolently refused to notice the summons.

Tell us.—Literally, *Tell ye us.* The request is addressed to any who could give the necessary information.

(5) **The men of Gibeah.**—Literally, *the lords of Gibeah*, as in chap. ix. 2. We cannot infer that they were heathen inhabitants of the town, though they behaved as if they were. If the phrase implies that they were men in *positions of authority*, it perhaps shows why there was no rescue and little resistance. This is also probable, because there could not have been the same unwillingness to give up to justice a few lawless and insignificant offenders.

Thought to have slain me.—Obviously some circumstances of the assault have been omitted in chap. xix. 22—25. The Levite colours the whole story in the way most favourable to himself.

(7) **Ye are all children of Israel.**—There would not be much point in this remark. Rather, *ye are all here, children of Israel.*

Your advice and counsel.—Chap. xix. 30. "In the multitude of counsellors there is wisdom."

(8) **Arose as one man.**—The same words are rendered "with one consent" in 1 Sam. xi. 7.

To his tent . . . . into his house.—Possibly many of the Trans-jordanic Israelites, who were chiefly graziers, were obliged by the necessities of nomadic life to live in tents, not in villages or cities.

(9) **We will go up by lot against it.**—The English Version follows the LXX. and other versions in supplying "we will go up." This is like the decision of the Amphictyonic counsel against the guilty city of Crissa (Grote, iv. 85). But perhaps it should be rendered "we will cast the lot upon it," to divide its territory when conquered.

(10) **Ten men of an hundred.**—A tenth of the nation, chosen probably by lot, is to be responsible for the commissariat. They do not anticipate any other difficulty.

(11) **Knit together as one man.**—The Hebrew word for "knit together" (marg., *fellows*) is *chabeerim.* It means that they were all as united as if they belonged to one *cheber*, or club. It is the spirit of *clubbism* (Greek, ἑταιρεία), displayed in this instance in a good cause.

(12) **Through all the tribe of Benjamin.**—It was equitable to send this embassy, although the Benjamites had not come to the sacred gathering at Mizpeh. The word for "tribe" is in the plural, so that it is, "the tribes of Israel sent men through all the *tribes* of Benjamin." Clearly, in the latter instance *shebet* means a family. (See Note on chap. xviii. 19, and Num. iv. 18 : "the *tribe* of the *families* of Kohath.") There were ten families in the tribe of Benjamin (Gen. xlvi. 21).

(13) **The children of Benjamin would not hearken.**—They were actuated by the same bad spirit of solidarity which has often made Highland clans defend a member of their body who has committed some grave outrage. That they should have preferred an internecine civil war to the giving up their criminals illustrates the peculiarly fierce character of the tribe (Gen. xlix. 27). Their determination to hold out against

(14) but the children of Benjamin gathered themselves together out of the cities unto Gibeah, to go out to battle against the children of Israel. (15) And the children of Benjamin were numbered at that time out of the cities twenty and six thousand men that drew sword, beside the inhabitants of Gibeah, which were numbered seven hundred chosen men. (16) Among all this people *there were* seven hundred chosen men *a*lefthanded; every one could sling stones at an hair *breadth*, and not miss. (17) And the men of Israel, beside Benjamin, were numbered four hundred thousand men that drew sword: all these *were* men of war.

(18) And the children of Israel arose, and went up to the house of God, and asked counsel of God, and said, Which of us shall go up first to the battle against the children of Benjamin? And the LORD said, Judah *shall go up* first.

(19) And the children of Israel rose up in the morning, and encamped against Gibeah. (20) And the men of Israel went out to battle against Benjamin; and the men of Israel put themselves in array to fight against them at Gibeah. (21)And the children of Benjamin came forth out of Gibeah, and destroyed down to the ground of the Israelites that day twenty and two thousand men.

(22) And the people the men of Israel encouraged themselves, and set their battle again in array in the place where

a ch. 3. 15.

---

united Israel is analogous to the courage in a bad cause of the Phocians in the sacred wars of Greece (Grote, iv. 85).

(15) **Out of the cities.**—They could only live in cities, because the Jebusites still held Jerusalem, and the Canaanites around them were very incompletely subdued.

Twenty and six thousand.—This seems to be the correct number, and is found in the Chaldee, Syriac, and Arabic. Josephus, however (*Antt.* v. 2, § 10), has 25,000, as also has Codex A of the LXX., and Codex B has 23,000 (see Note on verse 46). We see generally that the Benjamites, like the rest of the Israelites, in spite of their exceptional increase in the wilderness, had been now diminished by about a third since the last census (Num. xxvi. 41). (See Note on verse 2.)

Seven hundred chosen men.—There seems to be some uncertainty or confusion in the text here. It is difficult to imagine that, as the text stands, the single city of Gibeah furnished to the Benjamites their one choice contingent of seven hundred slingers, and it would be a curious coincidence that the force of Gibeah and the slingers should each be exactly seven hundred.

(16) **Seven hundred chosen men.**—These words are omitted in the LXX. and Vulg.

Lefthanded.—The same phrase as that employed in chap. iii. 15.

Could sling stones at an hair breadth, and not miss.—The expression is perfectly simple, and merely implies extreme accuracy of aim. Bochart's attempt (*Hieroz.* ii. 162) to explain it by a passage in *Quintus Smyrnæus*, which says that archers used to contend which should be able to shoot off the horsehair crest of a helmet, is a mere specimen of learning fantastically misapplied. Skill with the sling was not confined to the Benjamites, as we see from the case of David (1 Sam. xvii. 49). The sling is the natural weapon of a people which is poor and imperfectly armed. Cyrus valued his force of 400 slingers (Xen. *Anab.* iii. 3—6). The inhabitants of the Balearic Isles were as skilful as the Benjamites, and children were trained to sling their breakfasts down from the top of high poles. They once prevented the Carthaginian fleet from coming to anchor by showers of stones (Liv. xxviii. 37, *solo eo telo utebantur*). Practice made them so expert that the stones they slung came with as much force as though hurled by a catapult, and pierced shields and helmets (Diod. Sic. *Bibl.* v. 18). Exactly similar tales are told of the trained skill of our English archers. The advantage of slinging with the *left* hand was very obvious, for it enabled the slinger to strike his enemy on the *right*, *i.e.*, the undefended side.

(18) **To the house of God.**—Rather, *to Bethel* (as in the LXX., Syriac, Arabic, and Chaldee). The reason why our translators adopted their translation is shown by the Vulgate, which renders it "to the house of God *that is in Shiloh*." But *Beth El* cannot mean "house of God," which is always either *Beth ha-Elohim* or *Beth Adonai* (house of the Lord). Why they did not meet at the more central Shiloh we cannot say.

Asked counsel of God.—Namely, by the Urim and Thummim. Apparently the high priest was not prevented by any scruple from taking the ephod, with its jewelled breastplate and Urim and Thummim, to any place where its use was needed. The ark was similarly carried from place to place, and had been brought (verse 27) to the venerable sanctuary of Bethel with the high priest. It is not necessary to suppose that the tabernacle was itself removed. It *may* have been—for Shiloh was never understood to be more than its temporary resting-place. Bethel—as being a sacred place and near Gibeah—would be a convenient place of rendezvous.

Which of us . . ?—Chap. i. 1, 2.

Judah . . . first.—This is remarkable as indicating that the Urim and Thummim were something more than a pair of lots, and that the questions with which God was consulted by its means were other than those which admitted a mere positive or negative answer.

(21) **Came forth out of Gibeah.**—The whole armed force of the tribe had therefore assembled to save the wicked town from assault. Like many of the towns of Palestine (as their names indicate), it was on a hill, and therefore easily defensible against the very imperfect siege operations of the ancients.

Destroyed down to the ground—*i.e.*, laid them dead on the ground, as in chap. vi. 25.

Twenty and two thousand men.—This immense slaughter shows the extraordinary fierceness of the battle. The Benjamite force must have nearly killed a man apiece.

(22) **Encouraged themselves.**—Trusting, as the Vulgate adds, in their courage and numbers.

they put themselves in array the first day. ⁽²³⁾ (And the children of Israel went up and wept before the LORD until even, and asked counsel of the LORD, saying, Shall I go up again to battle against the children of Benjamin my brother? And the LORD said, Go up against him.) ⁽²⁴⁾ And the children of Israel came near against the children of Benjamin the second day. ⁽²⁵⁾ And Benjamin went forth against them out of Gibeah the second day, and destroyed down to the ground of the children of Israel again eighteen thousand men; all these drew the sword.

⁽²⁶⁾ Then all the children of Israel, and all the people, went up, and came unto the house of God, and wept, and sat there before the LORD, and fasted that day until even, and offered burnt offerings and peace offerings before the LORD. ⁽²⁷⁾ And the children of Israel enquired of the LORD, (for the ark of the covenant of God *was* there in those days, ⁽²⁸⁾ and Phinehas, the son of Eleazar, the son of Aaron, stood before it in those days,) saying, Shall I yet again go out to battle against the children of Benjamin my brother, or shall I cease? And the LORD said, Go up; for to morrow I will deliver them into thine hand. ⁽²⁹⁾ And Israel set liers in wait round about Gibeah. ⁽³⁰⁾ And the children of Israel went up against the children of Benjamin on the third day, and put themselves in array against Gibeah, as at other times. ⁽³¹⁾ And the children of Benjamin went out against the people, *and* were drawn away from the city; and they began ¹to smite of the people, *and* kill, as at other times, in the highways, of which one goeth up ²to the

¹ Heb., *to smite of the people wounded as at,* &c.

² Or, *Beth-el.*

⁽²³⁾ **And the children of Israel.**—This verse is parenthetical and retrospective. The whole narrative is arranged in a very simple manner, and shows an unformed archaic style.

Against the children of Benjamin my brother.—The words "my brother" show a sort of compunction, an uneasy sense that possibly, in spite of the first answer by Urim, God did not approve of a fratricidal war.

⁽²⁴⁾ **The second day.**—This does not mean the day after the first battle. One full day at least—the day of supplication—must have intervened between the two battles.

⁽²⁵⁾ **Destroyed ... eighteen thousand men.**—This second defeat seems to have been due, like the first, to overweening confidence and carelessness. Thus in two battles the eleven tribes lost 40,000 men—*i.e.*, 13,300 *more than the entire Benjamite army, which was only* 26,700. Such a hideous massacre can only be accounted for by the supposition that the Benjamite slings did deadly execution from some vantage-ground. Similarly at Crecy "1,200 knights and 30,000 footmen —a number equal to the whole English force—lay dead upon the ground" (Green, i. 419).

⁽²⁶⁾ **And all the people**—*i.e.*, the non-combatants as well as the fighting men.

Unto the house of God.—Rather, *to Bethel*, as in verse 18.

And wept.—These two battles must have caused an almost universal bereavement. (Comp. Lam. ii. 10; Ps. cxxxvii. 1; Joel i. 8—14, ii. 12—17, &c.)

Fasted ... until even.—As is still common in the East. (Comp. 1 Sam. xiv. 24, &c).

Burnt offerings and peace offerings.—The former were burnt entire, and therefore could not be used for food; of the latter, only a part was consumed, and the rest might be eaten by the worshippers. The distinction between the two was that the burnt offerings typified absolute self-dedication, whereas the peace offerings were mainly eucharistic.

⁽²⁷⁾ **Enquired of the Lord**—*i.e.*, of Jehovah, as in verse 23. On the occasion of their first general inquiry (verse 18) it is said that they "enquired of *Elohim*,"

but it is impossible to draw any certain inferences from this change of expression. It is clear, however, that the nation had been thoroughly and beneficially humiliated by these two terrible reverses, and that their approach to Jehovah on this occasion was far more solemn and devout than it had been at first.

Was there—*i.e.*, at Bethel, though Bethel has not been mentioned in the English Version, owing to the erroneous rendering of the name by "House of God" in verses 18—26.

⁽²⁸⁾ **Phinehas.**—The fact that the high priest is still the grandson of Aaron, who had shown such noble zeal in the desert (Num. xxv. 8; Ps. cvi. 30), is an important note of time, and proves decisively that this narrative, like the last, is anterior to much that has been recorded in the earlier chapters. It is remarkable that the chief personages in these two wild scenes are the grandson of Moses and the grandson of Aaron, and it is a strange illustration of the disorder of the times. that while the latter fulfils the supreme functions of the high priest, the former, who has sunk to the condition of a poor wandering Levite, does not go to his powerful cousin, but serves an unknown and schismatic image for a most paltry pittance.

To morrow.—Comp. chap. iv. 14; Josh. viii. 1. This is the first promise of success. The people needed to be taught that even in a religious war they could by no means rely on their own strength. How often has history laughed to scorn the cynical remark of Napoleon that "Providence usually favours the strongest battalion!"

⁽²⁹⁾ **Set liers in wait.**—This exceedingly simple and primitive stratagem had also been successful against Ai (Josh. viii. 4) and against Shechem (chap. ix. 43). Here, as in verses 22, 23, the narrative follows a loose order, the general fact being sometimes stated by anticipation, and the details subsequently filled in.

⁽³¹⁾ **To smite of the people, and kill.**—Rather, *to smite the wounded or beaten of the people.* It means, apparently, that when some of the Israelites had been wounded with slings, the Benjamites began to rush on them, for the purpose of killing them, and they feigned flight along two highways, of which

house of God, and the other to Gibeah in the field, about thirty men of Israel. ⁽³²⁾ And the children of Benjamin said, They *are* smitten down before us, as at the first. But the children of Israel said, Let us flee, and draw them from the city unto the highways. ⁽³³⁾ And all the men of Israel rose up out of their place, and put themselves in array at Baal-tamar: and the liers in wait of Israel came forth out of their places, *even* out of the meadows of Gibeah. ⁽³⁴⁾ And there came against Gibeah ten thousand chosen men out of all Israel, and the battle was sore: but they knew not that evil *was* near them. ⁽³⁵⁾ And the LORD smote Benjamin before Israel: and the children of Israel destroyed of the Benjamites that day twenty and five thousand and an hundred men: all these drew the sword.

⁽³⁶⁾ So the children of Benjamin saw that they were smitten: for the men of Israel gave place to the Benjamites, because they trusted unto the liers in wait which they had set beside Gibeah. ⁽³⁷⁾ And the liers in wait hasted, and rushed upon Gibeah; and the liers in wait ¹drew *themselves* along, and smote all the city with the edge of the sword. ⁽³⁸⁾ Now there was an appointed ²sign between the men of Israel ³and the liers

¹ Or, *made a long sound with the trumpet.*

² Or, *time.*

³ Heb., *with.*

---

one led to Bethel, and the other to a place which, to distinguish it from Gibeah, seems to have been called "Gibeah in the field." In this feigned flight thirty Israelites were killed. "Gibeah in the field" seems to be Jeba, and the main road from Gibeah (*Tuleil el Fûl*), at about a mile's distance from the hill, branches off into two, of which one leads to Beitin (Bethel), and the other to Jeba ("Gibeah in the field").

The highways.—(*Mesilloth*.) Roads like the Roman *viae regiae*, regularly built.

⁽³²⁾ **Said, Let us flee.**—In a later historical style the *plan* of the feigned flight would have been mentioned earlier.

Unto the highways. — This would have the double effect of allowing the ambuscade to cut off their retreat, and of dividing their forces at the point where the roads branched off.

⁽³³⁾ **Put themselves in array at Baal-tamar.** This is either a detail added out of place (so that we might almost suppose that there has been some accidental transposition of clauses), or it means that when the Israelites in their pretended rout had got as far as Baal-tamar ("Lord of the Palm") they saw the appointed smoke-signal of the ambuscade, and at that point rallied against their pursuers. What makes this probable is that Baal-tamar can only have derived its name from some famous, and therefore isolated, palm-tree. Now there was exactly such a palm-tree—the well-known "Palm of Deborah" (see Note on chap. iv. 5)—"between Ramah and Bethel," and therefore at a little distance from the spot where the roads branch. The place was still called Bathamar in the days of Eusebius and Jerome. The Chaldee rendering, "in the plains of Jericho" ("the palm city," chap. i. 16), is singularly erroneous.

Out of the meadows of Gibeah.—The word *maareh*, rendered "meadows," occurs nowhere else. Some derive it from *arah*, "to strip." The LXX., not understanding it, render it as a name, *Maraagabe*, and in Cod. A (following a different reading), "from the west of Gibeah," as also does the Vulg. Rashi renders it, "because of the stripping of Gibeah," and Buxtorf, "after the stripping of Gibeah." It is, however, clear that the words are in apposition to and in explanation of "out of their places." The Syriac and Arabic understand *maareh* to mean "a cave" or "caves," printing it *maarah* instead of *maareh*. Similarly the reading "from the west" only involves the change of a single letter (*maarab*). If the text be left unaltered, the "meadows" may have been concealed from the town by intervening rocks. In Isa. xix. 7 *aroth* means "pastures."

⁽³⁴⁾ **Ten thousand chosen men.**—Though the verse is obscurely expressed, the meaning probably is that this was the *number of the ambuscade of picked warriors.* If it means that this was the Israelite force left after the slaughter of 40,000, we are not told the number of the ambush.

The battle was sore.—It would be a battle in which the Benjamites were now attacked both in front and rear.

But.—Rather, *and.*

They knew not that evil was near them —*i.e.*, as we should say, "that the hour of their ruin had come," or, as the Vulg. has it, *quod ex omni parte illis instaret interitus,* "that destruction was threatening them on every side." (Comp. Isa. xlvii. 10.)

⁽³⁵⁾ **Destroyed of the Benjamites . . .** Here again we have a summary of the final result, followed by details, in a manner which proves either that the narrative was compiled from various sources (one of which seems to have been a poem), or that it was penned before the "periodic style" of history (*lexis katestrammene*) had been invented. If written consecutively, and not compiled, the writer must have been one whose method bore the same resemblance to that of later writers, as the style of Hellanicus did to that of Herodotus and Thucydides. It is the style to which Roman writers would have applied the epithet *inconditus*—the style of the oldest annals. Verses 36—46 are not, as has been conjectured by some writers, necessarily a different account of the battle, but contain a loose assemblage of details, which has been added to explain the general result.

⁽³⁶⁾ **That they were smitten.**—The "they" refers to the Israelites. The rest of the verse gives the reason for the feigned flight.

⁽³⁷⁾ Results of the ambuscade. (Comp. Josh. viii. 15, 19, 20.)

Drew themselves along.—The marginal suggestion, *made a long sound with the trumpet,* is untenable (See chap. iv. 6.)

With the edge of the sword.—See chap. i. 8; Josh. viii. 24.

⁽³⁸⁾ The signal which had been agreed upon.

That they should make.—Literally, *multiply to cause to ascend.* The actual words of the agreed on signal are quoted. For the word *hereb* (which is an imperative) some MSS. read *chereb,* "a sword," and

in wait, that they should make a great ¹flame with smoke rise up out of the city. (39) And when the men of Israel retired in the battle, Benjamin began ²to smite *and* kill of the men of Israel about thirty persons: for they said, Surely they are smitten down before us, as *in* the first battle. (40) But when the flame began to arise up out of the city with a pillar of smoke, the Benjamites looked behind them, and, behold, ³the flame of the city ascended up to heaven. (41) And when the men of Israel turned again, the men of Benjamin were amazed: for they saw that evil ⁴was come upon them. (42) Therefore they turned *their backs* before the men of Israel unto the way of the wilderness; but the battle overtook them; and them which *came* out of the cities they destroyed in the midst of them. (43) *Thus* they inclosed the Benjamites round about, *and* chased them, *and* trode them down ⁵with ease ⁶over against Gibeah toward the sunrising. (44) And there fell of Benjamin eighteen thousand men; all these *were* men of valour. (45) And they turned and fled toward the wilderness unto the rock of Rimmon: and they gleaned of them in the highways five thousand men; and pursued hard after them unto Gidom, and slew two thousand men of them. (46) So that all which fell that day of Benjamin were twenty and five thousand men that drew the sword; all these *were* men of valour. (47) ᵃBut six hundred men turned and fled to the wilderness unto the rock Rimmon, and abode in the rock Rimmon four months.

(48) And the men of Israel turned again upon the children of Benjamin, and smote them with the edge of the sword, as well the men of *every* city, as the beast, and all that ⁷came to hand: also they set on fire all the cities that ⁸they came to.

---

1 Heb., *elevation.*
2 Heb., *to smite the wounded.*
3 Heb., *the whole consumption.*
4 Heb., *touched them.*
5 Or, from *Menuchah, &c.*
6 Heb., *unto over against.*
a ch. 21. 13.
7 Heb., *was found.*
8 Heb., *were found.*

---

this is adopted by the LXX. (Cod. A). But the flash of a sword would not be seen at such a distance, and the word gives no good sense. Otherwise it would remind us of the shield, which was seen to flash in the sun as a traitorous signal from Athens to the Persians, just before the battle of Marathon.

A great flame with smoke.—The margin gives *elevation* for "flame." It means a column of smoke, or "beacon." (Comp. Jer. vi. 1: "Set up a sign of fire in Beth-haccerem.")

(39) **And when the men of Israel retired.**—This merely repeats with more graphic details the fact already mentioned in verse 31. The "when" should be omitted, and from "Benjamin began" to the end of the next verse is parenthetic.

(40) **When the flame began to arise up.**—Rather, *when the column* (of smoke), as in verse 38.

The flame of the city.—Literally, *the whole of the city*—i.e., the universal conflagration—a very powerful expression. (LXX., συντέλεια τῆς πόλεως.)

(41) **And when the men of Israel turned again.**—Another detail of the rally described in verse 33, and its effect (verse 34).

(42) **Unto the way of the wilderness.**—The wilderness is that known as "the wilderness of Bethaven" (Josh. xviii. 12). It is described in Josh. xvi. as "the wilderness that goeth up from Jericho throughout Mount Bethel." (See Robinson, *Bibl. Res.* i. 572.) The first thought of fugitives in Eastern Palestine was to get to one of the fords of the Jordan (2 Sam. xv. 23; 2 Kings xxv. 4, 5).

Them which came out of the cities they destroyed in the midst of them.—This obscure clause is rendered differently in different versions. If the English Version be correct, as it probably is, the meaning must be that the Benjamites fled to their own cities, and were pursued thither and slain by the Israelites.

(43) A strong and poetic description of the total rout and massacre which ensued.

With ease.—There is no "with" in the Hebrew, but perhaps it may be understood. The LXX. and Luther make it mean "from Noria." Others render it "in their rest," *i.e.*, in the places to which they fled for refuge. The Vulg. paraphrases it: "Nor was there any repose of the dying." But the whole verse is obscure.

(45) **Unto the rock of Rimmon**—*i.e.*, of the pomegranate. As the tree is common in Palestine (Num. xx. 25; Deut. viii. 8, &c.), the name is naturally common. There was one Rimmon in Zebulon (Josh. xix. 13), another in Judah (Josh. xv. 32), south of Jerusalem (Zech. xiv. 10; and see Josh. xxi. 25; Neh. xi. 29). This Rimmon is a steep conical hill of white limestone (Robinson, i. 440), not far from Gibeah, and fifteen miles north of Jerusalem, six miles east of Bethel ("towards the sun-rising"). It is still called Rimmon.

They gleaned.—A metaphor from the vintage, like the "trode down" of verse 43. (See Jer. vi. 9: "They shall glean the remnant of Israel as a vine.")

Unto Gidom.—A place entirely unknown, and hence omitted in the Vulg.

(46) **Twenty and five thousand men.**—Eighteen thousand killed in battle, + 5,000 on the paved roads (*mesilloth*), + 2,000 near Rimmon, + 600 survivors, makes 25,600. But as the Benjamites were 26,700 (see verse 15), either the total in verse 15 is wrong, or we must make the much more natural supposition that 1,000 Benjamites, as against 40,000 Israelites (which would only be 1 to 36), had fallen in the two first battles.

(47) **In the rock Rimmon.**—This may be quite literally taken, for there are four large caverns in the hill.

(48) **As well the men of every city, as the beast.**—The phrase is literally, *from the city, men down to beast,* reading *methim*, "men," for *methom*, "entire." The dreadful meaning which lies beyond these short and simple words is *the absolute extermination of* a whole tribe of Israel, MEN, WOMEN, AND CHILDREN, CITIES

CHAPTER XXI.—⁽¹⁾ Now the men of Israel had sworn in Mizpeh, saying, There shall not any of us give his daughter unto Benjamin to wife. ⁽²⁾ And the people came to the house of God, and abode there till even before God, and lifted up their voices, and wept sore; ⁽³⁾ and said, O LORD God of Israel, why is this come to pass in Israel, that there should be to day one tribe lacking in Israel? ⁽⁴⁾ And it came to pass on the morrow, that the people rose early, and built there an altar, and offered burnt offerings and peace offerings.

⁽⁵⁾ And the children of Israel said, Who *is there* among all the tribes of Israel that came not up with the congregation unto the LORD? For they had made a great oath concerning him that came not up to the LORD to Mizpeh, saying, He shall surely be put to death. ⁽⁶⁾ And the children of Israel repented them for Benjamin their brother, and said, There is one tribe cut off from Israel this day. ⁽⁷⁾ How shall we do for wives for them that remain, seeing we have sworn by the LORD that we will not give them of our daughters to wives?

⁽⁸⁾ And they said, What one *is there* of the tribes of Israel that came not up to Mizpeh to the LORD? And, behold, there came none to the camp from

---

AND CATTLE, with the exception of 600 fugitives. There is something almost inconceivably horrible and appalling in the thought of thousands of poor women and innocent children ruthlessly butchered in cold blood in this internecine war between brother Israelites. The whole tribe were placed under the ban of extirpation, as though they had been Canaanites, just as mercilessly as Sihon and his people had been extirpated (Deut. ii. 34, xiii. 15, 16), or Jericho (Josh. vi. 17, 21), or Ai (Josh. viii. 25, 26). Their feelings were doubtless exasperated by the fearful destruction which Benjamin had inflicted upon them, as well as by religious horror at the conduct of the tribe; and for the rest, we can only say that "the times of this ignorance God winked at." The good side of the deed lies in its motive: it expressed an intense horror against moral pollution. The evil side lay in its ruthless savagery. In both aspects it agrees both with the recorded and the traditional character of Phinehas (Num. xxv. 8, xxxi. 6). (See Note on chap. xi. 39.)

XXI.

1—7. Remorse of the Israelites at the extirpation of a tribe in consequence of their oath not to give their daughters in marriage to the Benjamites. 8—15. Expedient of destroying Jabesh-Gilead to furnish wives from thence. 16—25. As there was still an insufficient number of wives, they persuade the Benjamites to seize the virgins of Shiloh at a sacred dance.

⁽¹⁾ **Had sworn.**—The circumstance has not been mentioned in the account of the proceedings at Mizpeh. It is clear from the sequel (verse 18) that the oath was not only an oath but "a vow under a curse," as in Acts xxiii. 14.

⁽²⁾ **To the house of God.**—Rather, *to Bethel*, as in chap. xx. 18, 27.

Wept sore.—As after their defeat (chap. xx. 26); but this time they were remorseful for the fate of those whom they were then pledged to destroy.

⁽³⁾ **Why is this come to pass . . ?**—This is not so much an inquiry into the cause, which was indeed too patent, but a wail of regret, implying a prayer to be enlightened as to the best means of averting the calamity. The repetition of the name "Israel" three times shows that the nation had not yet lost its sense of corporate unity, often as that unity had been rent asunder by their civil dissensions. Their wild justice is mingled with a still wilder mercy.

One tribe lacking.—The number twelve had an almost mystic significance, and is always preserved in reckoning up the tribes, whether Levi is included or excluded.

⁽⁴⁾ **Built there an altar.**—We find David doing the same at the threshing-floor of Araunah (2 Sam. xxiv. 25), and Solomon at Gibeon. Unless the entire tabernacle had, for the time, been removed to Bethel, there was no regular altar there. It has been suggested that in any case this altar must have been necessitated by the multitude of sacrifices required for the holocausts and the food of the people. (See Note on chap. xx. 26.) Probably there is some other reason unknown to us.

⁽⁵⁾ **Who is there . . . ?**—This verse is anticipatory of verse 8.

They had made a great oath.—Another detail which has been omitted up to this point. The spirit of this *cherem* was exactly the same as that which we find in chap. v. 23: "Curse ye Meroz . . . because they came not to the help of the Lord, to the help of the Lord against the mighty." Now that these victories had been so complete, they probably were sick with slaughter, and would not have inquired after any defaulters but by way of finding an expedient to mollify the meaning of their rash oath. We see once more in this narrative both the force derivable from a vow and the folly and wickedness of fierce vows rashly taken in moments of passion. It is obvious that the direct *meaning* of the vow, taken in connection with the curse under which they had placed the Benjamites, had been to annihilate the tribe.

⁽⁸⁾ **There came none to the camp from Jabesh-gilead.**—Jabesh-Gilead, which Josephus calls the metropolis of Gilead (*Antt.* vi. 5, § 1), is probably to be identified with the ruins now called El-Deir in the Wady Yabes (Robinson, iii. 319). It was six miles from Pella, on the top of a hill which lies on the road from Pella to Gerasa. For some reason with which we are unacquainted, there seems to have been a bond of intense sympathy between the inhabitants of this town and Benjamin. If their abstinence from the assembly of vengeance was not due to this, we must suppose that the sort of companionship in misery caused by these wild events itself created a sense of union between these communities, for it is the peril of Jabesh which first arouses King Saul to action (1 Sam. xi.), and in memory of the deliverance which he effected the men of Jabesh alone save the bodies of Saul and Jonathan from the indignity of rotting on the wall of Bethshan

Jabesh-gilead to the assembly. (9) For the people were numbered, and, behold, *there were* none of the inhabitants of Jabesh-gilead there. (10) And the congregation sent thither twelve thousand men of the valiantest, and commanded them, saying, Go and smite the inhabitants of Jabesh-gilead with the edge of the sword, with the women and the children. (11) And this *is* the thing that ye shall do, *a* Ye shall utterly destroy every male, and every woman that ¹hath lain by man. (12) And they found among the inhabitants of Jabesh-gilead four hundred ²young virgins, that had known no man by lying with any male: and they brought them unto the camp to Shiloh, which *is* in the land of Canaan.

(13) And the whole congregation sent *some* ³to speak to the children of Benjamin that *were* in the rock Rimmon, and to ⁴call peaceably unto them. (14) And Benjamin came again at that time; and they gave them wives which they had saved alive of the women of Jabesh-gilead: and yet so they sufficed them not. (15) And the people repented them for Benjamin, because that the LORD had made a breach in the tribes of Israel.

(16) Then the elders of the congregation said, How shall we do for wives for them

---

a Num. 31. 17.

¹ Heb., *knoweth the lying with man.*

² Heb., *young women virgins.*

³ Heb., *and spake and called.*

⁴ Or, *proclaim peace.*

(1 Sam. xxxi. 11), which gained them the blessing of David (2 Sam. ii. 5, 6). We see from these later incidents that Jabesh recovered from the extermination now inflicted on its inhabitants.

(9) **For the people were numbered.** — It is doubtful whether this implies another numbering besides that at Mizpeh (chap. xx. 1—17). In the tale which had then been made up, the absence of inhabitants of a single town might for the present escape notice. It would be sufficient now merely to refer to the lists then made (chap. xx. 1—17).

(10) **Twelve thousand men.** —The Vulgate has 10,000, but it is doubtless meant to imply that each tribe sent a thousand "valiant men" (Gen. xlvii. 6, &c.), as in the war against the Midianites, in which Balaam was slain and at which Phinehas had been present (Num. xxxi. 6).

(11) **Ye shall utterly destroy.** —The verb is *tacharîmû*—*i.e.,* Ye shall place under the ban (*cherem*), ye shall devote to destruction. The words of the *cherem* are almost identical with those of the indignant command of Moses after the war with Midian alluded to in the last verse (Num. xxxi. 17, 18), and there the same exception is made. (Comp. Lev. xxvii. 21—28; Num. xxi. 2, 3.) The words are easy to read; it is needless to dwell on the horror of the massacre which they describe. We are dealing throughout with the fierce passions of men living in times of gross spiritual darkness; for we cannot doubt that the oath against Jabesh-Gilead was carried out, though the writer drops a veil over all but the result. The vow of destruction (*cherem, anathema,* Lev. xxvii. 28, 29) was quite different from the vow of devotion (*neder*) and the vow of abstinence (*corban*).

(12) **They brought them.** —It can hardly be doubted that the "them" means the young virgins, although the pronoun is masculine (*otham*), as in verse 22. If so, the idiom is like the Greek one in which a woman speaking of herself in the plural uses the masculine (*Brief Greek Syntax,* p. 61). There is no other trace of this idiom in Hebrew, but we can hardly suppose that many Jabesh-Gileadite captives were brought to Shiloh, and then put to death in cold blood in accordance with the ban.

Unto the camp to Shiloh. —The Israelites, now that the war with Benjamin was over, appear to have moved their stationary camp to Shiloh, the normal and more central seat of the tabernacle at this period (chap. xviii. 31).

Which is in the land of Canaan. —We find the same addition in Josh. xxi. 2, xxii. 9. Perhaps there was another Shiloh on the east of the Jordan; but see Note on verse 19. The mere fact of Jabesh being in *Gilead* does not seem sufficient to account for it.

(13) **To call peaceably**—*i.e.,* proclaim peace.

(14) **Came again**—*i.e.,* returned to their desolate towns.

Yet so they sufficed them not. —There would still be 200 Benjamites left without wives.

(15) **The Lord had made a breach.** —The breach (*perets,* 1 Kings xi. 24) had been caused by their own headstrong fury and unreasoning passion, even though it had been in a righteous cause; but in the Hebrew conception the results even of man's sin and follies is referred to Jehovah as overruled by Him (Amos iii. 6; Isa. xlv. 7). It was therefore needless, and not quite honest of St. Jerome in the Vulg., to omit "the Lord."

(16) **How shall we do . . . ?**—They want to keep their vow in the letter, while they break it in the spirit. The sense of the binding nature of the "ban" was intensely strong (Exod. xx. 7; Ezek. xvii. 18, 19), but, as is so often the case among rude and ignorant people, they fancied that it was sufficient to keep it *literally,* while in effect they violated it. Similarly in Herodotus (chap. iv. 154), Themison having sworn to throw Phronima into the sea—the *intention* having been that she should be drowned—feels himself bound to throw her into the sea, but has her drawn out of it again. Their want of moral enlightenment revealed itself in this way, and still more in having ever taken this horrible oath, which involved the butchery of innocent men, and of still more innocent women and children. In point of fact, the *cherem* often broke down under the strain which it placed on men's best feelings (1 Sam. xiv. 45) as well as on their lower temptations. The guilt of breaking a guilty vow is only the original guilt of ever having made it. What the Israelites should have done was not to bathe their hands in more rivers of fraternal blood, but to pray to God to forgive the brutal vehemence which disgraced a cause originally righteous, and to have allowed the remnant of the Benjamites to intermarry with them once more. As it was, they were led by ignorance and rashness into several vows which could not be fulfilled without horrible cruelty and bloodshed, and the fulfilment of which they after all casuistically evaded, and that at the cost of still more bloodshed. As all these events took place under the guidance of Phinehas, they give us a high estimate indeed of the

Wives Taken from   JUDGES, XXI.   *the Daughters of Shiloh.*

that remain, seeing the women are destroyed out of Benjamin? ⁽¹⁷⁾ And they said, *There must be* an inheritance for them that be escaped of Benjamin, that a tribe be not destroyed out of Israel. ⁽¹⁸⁾ Howbeit, we may not give them wives of our daughters: for the children of Israel have sworn, saying, Cursed *be* he that giveth a wife to Benjamin.

⁽¹⁹⁾ Then they said, Behold, *there is* a feast of the LORD in Shiloh [1] yearly *in a place* which *is* on the north side of Bethel, [2] on the east side [3] of the highway that goeth up from Beth-el to Shechem, and on the south of Lebonah. ⁽²⁰⁾ Therefore they commanded the children of Benjamin, saying, Go and lie in wait in the vineyards; ⁽²¹⁾ and see, and, behold, if the daughters of Shiloh come out to dance in dances, then come ye out of the vineyards, and catch you every man his wife of the daughters of Shiloh, and go to the land of Benjamin. ⁽²²⁾ And it shall be, when their fathers or their brethren come unto us to complain, that we will say unto them, [4] Be favourable unto them for our sakes: because we reserved not to each man his wife in the war: for ye did not give unto them at this time, *that* ye should be guilty.

[1] Heb., *from year to year.*

[2] Or, *towards the sunrising.*

[3] Or, *on.*

[4] Or, *Gratify us in them.*

---

zeal which was his noblest characteristic (Ps. cvi. 30), yet a very low estimate of his state of spiritual insight; and clearly to such a man the fulfilment of Jephthah's *cherem* by sacrificing his daughter (see Note on chap. xi. 39) would have seemed as nothing compared to the extermination of tribes and of cities, involving the shedding of rivers of innocent blood. But why should we suppose that the grandson of Aaron, in such times as these —when all was anarchy, idolatry, and restlessness, against which he either did not strive or strove most ineffectually—should stand on so much higher a level than his schismatical and semi-idolatrous cousin, the wandering grandson of Moses?

⁽¹⁷⁾ **There must be an inheritance.**—Rather, *possession of the remnant shall be for Benjamin*—*i.e.*, We will leave untouched their land and possessions. "We give you leave to take the whole land of Benjamin to yourselves" (Jos. *Antt.* v. 3, § 12).

That a tribe be not destroyed.—Benjamin never quite recovered this crushing blow. Even though it furnished the second judge (Ehud) and the first king (Saul) to Israel, and was advantageously situated, and was often honoured by the residence of Samuel, it became a mere satellite to the more powerful tribe of Judah. Perhaps in the quiescence and permanence derived from the close association with its powerful neighbour we see in part the fulfilment of the blessing in Deut. xxxiii. 12.

⁽¹⁹⁾ **A feast of the Lord in Shiloh.**—It is unlikely that the reference is to a local feast; but it is impossible to say which of the three yearly feasts is meant. The most natural would be the Feast of Tabernacles. We see from 1 Sam. i. 3 that even among pious families the trying custom of going up to the Tabernacle three times a year had fallen into complete abeyance.

A place which is on the north side of Beth-el . . .—This elaborate description of the site of Shiloh, a place which is so often mentioned elsewhere without any addition, is extremely curious. There can be little doubt that it is due to the marginal gloss of some Masoretic scribe, perhaps in the editing of the sacred books by Ezra. That it is a gloss seems clear, because it comes in as a parenthesis in the speech of the elders, and, of course, in their day such a description was needless. Indeed, it was spoken at Shiloh itself, and the site was well known to all Israel. But by the time that the story was committed to writing in the days of the kings, or finally edited in the days of Ezra, Shiloh had long been desolate, and probably the very site was unknown to thousands. Hence this very valuable and interesting description was added, which has alone enabled us to identify Shiloh in the modern *Seilûn*.

South of Lebonah.—Lebonah, now *Lubban*, is not mentioned elsewhere.

⁽²⁰⁾ **They commanded.**—Rather, *they gave notice.* This is the *keri* or marginal reading of the Hebrew; the *kethib*, or written text, has the verb in the singular, in which case we must take it impersonally, "It was bidden," and suppose that some leading personage— probably Phinehas, the impress of whose character and reminiscences is observable throughout—is the speaker.

⁽²¹⁾ **To dance in dances.**—Possibly the dances of the vintage festival. There is a fountain in a narrow dale, at a little distance from Shiloh, which was very probably the scene of this event. It is a needless conjecture that the feast was the Passover, and the dances a commemoration of the defeat of the Egyptians, like those of Miriam. There seems to have been no regular town at Shiloh; at least, no extensive ruins are traceable. It was probably a community like the Beth-Micah (see Note on chap. xviii. 2), which was mainly connected with the service of the Tabernacle. The "daughters of Shiloh" would naturally include many women who were in one way or other employed in various functions about the Tabernacle, and not only those who came there to worship (1 Sam. ii. 22, where "assembled" should be rendered *served*, as in Num. iv. 23; "the handmaid" of the priests is mentioned in 2 Sam. xvii. 17). But the traces of female attendants in the sanctuary are more numerous in Jewish traditions than in Scripture.

Catch you every man his wife.— The scene is very analogous to the famous seizure of the Sabine women at the Consualia, as described in Liv. i. 9. St. Jerome (*adv. Jovin.* i. § 41) quotes another parallel from the history of Aristomenes of Messene, who once, in a similar way, seized fifteen Spartan maidens, who were dancing at the Hyacinthia, and escaped with them.

⁽²²⁾ **Be favourable unto them for our sakes.**— Rather, *Present them* (*otham*, masc., as in verse 12) *to us*; or (as in the margin), *Gratify us in them.* The verse is somewhat obscure, but its general drift is a promise to pacify the parents of the damsels, by showing them that thus they did not violate the *cherem*, and that the cause was pressing. Perhaps they would be more readily consoled, because the land of these six hundred Benjamites must now have been far more than was necessary for their wants. They had become possessors of the lot of the whole tribe. Perhaps the reading should be, *Gratify us as regards these damsels, for they* (the

(23) And the children of Benjamin did so, and took *them* wives, according to their number, of them that danced, whom they caught: and they went and returned unto their inheritance, and repaired the cities, and dwelt in them. (24) And the children of Israel departed thence at that time, every man to his tribe and to his family, and they went out from thence every man to his inheritance. (25) *a* In those days *there was* no king in Israel: every man did *that which was* right in his own eyes.

a ch. 17. 6; & 18. 1; & 19. 1.

Benjamites) have not received every man his wife through the war.

At this time.—Rather, perhaps, *in that case* (*i.e.*, "if you had *given* them your daughters in marriage, ye would be guilty"). We are left to assume that the appeal of the elders to the parents whose two hundred daughters were thus seized was sufficient to pacify them.

(25) **In those days** ... This verse, already occurring in chaps. xvii. 6, xviii. 1, xix. 1, is here added once more by way of apology for the lawless crimes, terrible disasters, evaded vows, and unhallowed excesses of retribution, which it has been the painful duty of the sacred historian thus faithfully and impartially to narrate. Out of these depths the subsequent Judges, whose deeds have been recorded in the earlier chapters, partially raised their countrymen, until the dread lessons of calamity had been fully learnt, and the nation was ripe for the heroic splendour and more enlightened faithfulness of the earlier monarchy.

EXCURSUS ON NOTES TO JUDGES

EXCURSUS I.—ON CHAPTER XVII. 4. (CALF-WORSHIP.)

IT may be regarded as certain, from the testimony of Scripture itself, that the calf of Aaron and those by which the rebel king

"Doubled that sin in Bethel and in Dan,
Likening his Maker to the grazed ox,"

were not idols in the ordinary sense of the word, but were intended as symbols of the one God. The calf-worship was a violation not of the first, but of the second commandment. The main element of the four-fold cherub was certainly an ox, as is clear from the comparison of Ezek. x. 14 with chap. i. 7, 8; and the knowledge of this cherubic emblem was not confined to the Jews, but was spread at least through all Semitic races. That the calf was intended to be an emblem of God seems to be the opinion of Josephus, who in such a matter would represent creditable Jewish traditions (*Antt.* viii. 8, § 4). Aaron in proclaiming the feast at the inauguration of his golden calf distinctly calls it a feast to Jehovah (Exod. xxxii. 5). It was the well-understood purpose of Jeroboam not to introduce a new worship, but to provide a convenient modification of the old; and it appears from 1 Kings xxii. 16 that the prophets of the calf-worship still regarded themselves, and were regarded, as the prophets of Jehovah; but the fate of Amos is sufficient to show that they must have sanctioned, or at least tolerated, the use of these unauthorised symbols, against which, so far as we are informed, not even Elijah or Elisha ever raised their voices, though the former was so implacable a foe to all idolatry, and the latter lived on terms of close friendship with at least one of the northern kings. (See the article "Calf," by the present writer, in Smith's *Dictionary of the Bible*.)

EXCURSUS II.—ON CHAPTER XVII. 5. (TERAPHIM.)

THE Hebrew word *Teraphim* is always simply transliterated as in our version, or rendered by "images," with "teraphim" in the margin, except in 1 Sam. xv. 23, Zech. x. 2, where it is represented by "idolatry," "idols." The singular of the word, "a teraph," does not occur in Scripture, although it is clear that only one can have been put into David's bed (1 Sam. xix. 13—16). The LXX. adopt many different renderings, as does the Vulg., but they all point to idolatrous images or the implements of necromancy, as do the two renderings of the Targums, images and (Hosea iii. 4) "announcers."

1. Teraphim are first mentioned in Gen. xxxi. 19, where Rachel steals her father's "images," and successfully hides them from his search under the *hiran* on which she was sitting—the coarse carpet used to cover the wicker-work pack-saddle of her camel. Josephus supposes that she was actuated by idolatrous reverence; Iben Ezra that she expected oracular guidance from them; others that she stole them because of their

intrinsic value. She probably shared the superstitions of her father, and regarded them as sacred (Gen. xxx. 14, xxxi. 30), as being the figures of ancestral divinities (Gen. xxxi. 53). It is not impossible that they were among the "strange gods" which Jacob ordered his family to bury under "the sorcerer's oak"—*Allon Meonenim* (chap. ix. 37). But that Jacob's right feeling in the matter was not permanent is proved only too clearly by the conduct of Micah (chap. xvii. 5) and the Danites (chap. xviii. 3), although, unlike Jeroboam, they could not even plead the poor palliation of political motives.

2. The next definite notice of teraphim occurs in 1 Sam. xix. 13—16, where Michal, in the dark eastern chamber, conceals her husband's absence by putting the teraphim in his bed, with a bolster of goat's hair for a pillow. The use of the article shows that even in David's family the use of the "teraphim" was perfectly well known. Nor can we rely on the vague conjecture of Thenius, that barren women (Rachel and Michal) were especially addicted to their worship, or on that of Michaelis, that Michal may have possessed them unknown to David. The passage seems to show that they had at least some rude resemblance to the human shape, whence Aquila renders the word by *protomai* ("busts"), which is used of figures like the ancient Hermae. This is not the place to enter into the curious reading of the LXX. on this verse, by which they seem to connect the worship of teraphim with what the ancients called *extispicium*—i.e., divination by means of the liver of sacrifices, as in Ezek. xxi. 21. Josephus follows the same reading, and dishonestly suppresses all mention of the teraphim.

3. The next important passage is Hosea iii. 4, where the *primâ facie* view of every unbiassed reader would be that the "image" (*matsêbah*) and the teraphim are mentioned without blame as ordinary adjuncts to religious worship. Hence, perhaps, arose the notion that the teraphim were in some way connected with the Urim and Thummim, which led to the rendering of the word in this passage by δῆλοι (LXX., "bright gems"), and by φωτισμούς ("enlightenments," Aquila), and by "implements of priestly dress" (St. Jerome). This is the theory maintained most unconvincingly, though with great learning, by Spencer in his *De Legibus Hebræorum*, lib. iii., pp. 920—1038.

But if these passages show that even in religious families teraphim were sometimes tolerated as material adjuncts to an Elohistic worship, on the other hand we find them unequivocally condemned by Samuel (1 Sam. xv. 23), by Josiah (2 Kings xxiii. 24), and by the prophet Zechariah (Zech. x. 2); and in Ezek. xxi. 21 the use of them is attributed to the heathen Nebuchadnezzar.

The general inference seems to be that the use of the teraphim involved a violation of the second commandment, but that this use of symbols, this *monotheistic idolatry*, which is very different from polytheism, arises from a tendency very deeply ingrained in human nature, and which it took many years to eradicate. If centuries elapsed before the Jews were cured of their propensity to worship "other gods," we can feel no surprise that "image worship" continued to linger among them, in spite of the condemnation of it by the stricter prophets. The calf-worship, the toleration of teraphim and consecrated stones (*baetylia*) and high places, the offering of incense to the brazen serpent, the glimpses of grave irregularities even in the worship of the sanctuary, show that it was only by centuries of misfortune and a succession of prophets that Israel was at last educated into the spiritual worship of the true God.

The reader will find further remarks on this subject in the article on "Teraphim," by the present writer, in Kitto's *Biblical Cyclopædia*.

INTRODUCTION
TO
THE BOOK OF RUTH

I. Contents.—In the book of Ruth is presented to us a family, consisting of father, mother and two sons, which under the pressure of a famine in the days of the Judges, migrated from Bethlehem to the land of Moab. Here the two sons, Mahlon and Chilion, took two Moabitesses, Ruth and Orpah, to wife. After a ten years' sojourn, Elimelech the father, and the two sons having died, and tidings having come of the change of famine to plenty in the land of Judah, Naomi and her two daughters-in-law set off to return. In spite, however, of her evident affection for them, and of their unwillingness to leave her, she unselfishly urges them to seek their own kindred, and not to venture on what must have been a long toilsome journey. After a struggle Orpah yields, but Ruth, with a devotedness which says almost as much for Naomi as herself, sinks all ties of home and kindred in the outburst, "Thy people shall be my people, and thy God my God." Thus she takes her last look at the fertile fields of Moab, to enter a strange land, where the result of her devotion to her mother-in-law was to be, that from her line in ages to come should be born, David, the sweet psalmist of Israel, Solomon, the wisest of the sons of men, Zerubbabel, the later Moses, and the Messiah, the son of David, whom all these prefigured.

When Bethlehem is reached, the barley harvest is beginning, and Ruth, going to glean, chances upon the field of Boaz, a wealthy kinsman of the family of Elimelech. Learning that the unknown woman was the daughter-in-law of Naomi, and having clearly been much impressed with the story of her devotedness, he bids her to continue to glean in his fields, and to make use of the food provided for his own people. Through the kindness of Boaz, she gleans barley, which when beaten out, is about an ephah, and so first the barley and then the wheat harvest pass by.

The end of the harvest having come, Naomi bids Ruth to claim a kinsman's help from Boaz in his threshing floor, where he had been winnowing barley, and accordingly at midnight when Boaz awoke he found Ruth lying at his feet. He promises then to discharge the kinsman's duty unless a still nearer relative should claim to do it. The case was brought into judgment on the following morning. The next kinsman, afraid of "marring his own inheritance," declines to redeem the land that was Elimelech's. Accordingly Boaz himself redeems it, taking therewith Ruth to wife to raise up the name of the dead Mahlon on his inheritance. The offspring of the marriage was Obed the father of Jesse, the father of David.

II. Date of events recorded.—It may be asked next, when are we to fix the period when the events here recorded happened. Here our *data* are sufficiently vague, being indeed but two. The famine broke out in the days "when the judges judged," and if the genealogy be complete, Ruth was the great-grandmother of David, that is, probably lived a hundred years before him. Of this last point, however, we can be by no means certain, both because we undoubtedly find sometimes gaps in the genealogies in the Bible, (see *e.g.*, three generations omitted in Matt. i. 8) and because the number of generations from Pharez to David (given as ten, Ruth iv. 18—22) seems insufficient to fill up the intervening space of over 900 years. It is probable that if there are any omissions in the genealogy, they are to be assigned to the period before Boaz.

It may be noticed that the father of Boaz is given as Salmon, (iv. 21) who (Matt. i. 5) was the husband of Rahab, so that we should thus have Boaz born no great number of years after the taking of Jericho.

Josephus (*Ant.* v. 9. 1) refers the events to a time after Samson, in the days of Eli, but this must certainly be too late; and at any rate the date given above may be taken as fairly probable.

The various attempts to fix the date more closely (as for example, to connect the famine with the ravages of the Midianites, Judges vi. 1 *seq.*) involve mere guesses, and rest on too uncertain grounds to warrant our entering into the discussion.

III. Date of composition.—We cannot speak with any degree of certainty as to the time at which the book was written. From chap. i. 1, the reference to the Judges would suggest that they had now been replaced by the Monarchy, and from chap. iv. 17 it is clear that the book is not to be put before the time of David. Whether we are to fix it later than David's time, and if so, how much later, must be considered very doubtful. The Talmud (*Baba Bathra*, f. 14 b.) tells us, "Samuel wrote his own book, and Judges and Ruth." This gives the earliest date possible, and in our opinion there is nothing in the phenomena of the book itself which renders this view inadmissible, though, on the other hand, it cannot be held that any great amount of positive probability attaches to it. Most critics have fixed the date later, and some much later, as for example Ewald, who supposes the book to have been written during the Babylonian captivity. The various arguments, however, on which these theories are built, are many of them most arbitrary, and need not be entered upon here. One point sometimes relied upon to prove the late date is the presence of a certain Aramæan element in the Hebrew of Ruth. To discuss this at length would be beside our present purpose, but it may be remarked here that it is at least as likely that these alleged Aramæisms are to be considered as dialectic varieties, mere provincialisms, or in some cases even as archaisms. It is curious also, that these occur in the dialogues exclusively, the narrative proper being in the purest Hebrew.

On the whole, then, the book may indeed belong to a comparatively late period, but this certainly has not been proved; nor has anything been satisfactorily established by those who have maintained, as Ewald, that Ruth is a section of a larger work, the solitary surviving fragment, or that it is really part of the book of Judges, from which it somehow got separated. Such arbitrary theorising can only be considered as guessing pure and simple.

The main reason why the Book of Ruth is included in the Old Testament seems sufficiently obvious, namely on account of David, of whose lineage it may be remarked the books of Samuel make no mention. This definite association of the book with David may perhaps be taken as evidence of a comparatively early date, prior to the books of Samuel, in which it was not considered necessary to repeat matter already given.

IV. **Place in Canon.**—In the Hebrew Bible, Ruth forms the second of the five so called *Megilloth* [*i.e.*, Rolls] (the others being, Song of Solomon, Lamentations, Ecclesiastes, Esther). It has been thought by some, however, that this was not its original position, for Josephus (*contr. Apion.* i. 8) as well as some important early Christian witnesses to the Jewish Canon, as Melito, Bishop of Sardis in the second century, (cited by Eusebius, *Hist. Eccles.* iv. 26), and Origen, (cited by Eusebius, *Hist. Eccles.* vi. 25), reckoned the number of books of the Old Testament as twenty-two, counting Judges and Ruth as one book.* This might rather suggest that the original position of Ruth was immediately after the book of Judges. On the other hand, the Talmud (*l. c.*) includes Ruth in the Hagiographa, and mentions it first, preceding the Psalms. In the LXX. and Vulgate, the book of Ruth follows the Judges, and the same order is found in the English Bible, and in that of Luther.

* This was doubtless with the view of making the number of the books agree with the number of the letters of the Hebrew alphabet.

THE BOOK OF RUTH

CHAPTER I.—⁽¹⁾ Now it came to pass in the days when the judges ¹ruled, that there was a famine in the land. And a certain man of Beth-lehem-judah went to sojourn in the country of Moab, he, and his wife, and his two sons. ⁽²⁾ And the name of the man *was* Elimelech, and the name of his wife Naomi, and the name of his two sons Mahlon and Chilion, Ephrathites of Beth-lehem-judah. And they came into the country of Moab, and ²continued there.

⁽³⁾ And Elimelech Naomi's husband died; and she was left, and her two sons. ⁽⁴⁾ And they took them wives of the women of Moab; the name of the one *was* Orpah, and the name of the other Ruth: and they dwelled there about ten years. ⁽⁵⁾ And Mahlon and Chilion died also both of them; and the woman was left of her two sons and her husband.

⁽⁶⁾ Then she arose with her daughters in law, that she might return from the country of Moab: for she had heard in the country of Moab how that the LORD

B.C. cir. 1322.

1 Heb. *judged.*

2 Heb. *were.*

⁽¹⁾ **When the judges ruled.**—Literally, *when the judges judged.* This note of time is by no means definite. As we have seen, some have proposed to connect the famine with the ravages of the Midianites (Judges vi. 1); or, supposing the genealogy to be complete (which is more likely, however, to be abridged, if at all, in the earlier generations), then since Boaz was the son of Salmon (Salma, 1 Chron. ii. 11) and Rahab (Matt. i. 5), whom there can be no reasonable grounds for supposing to be other than the Rahab of Jericho, the events must be placed comparatively early in the period of the judges.

Beth-lehem.—See note on Gen. xxxv. 19. Judah is added by way of distinction from the Bethlehem in the tribe of Zebulun (Josh. xix. 15).

Moab.—See notes on Gen. xix. 37; Num. xxi. 13; Deut. ii. 9. The land of Moab seems to have been of exceptional richness and fertility, as allusions in the threats of Isaiah xvi., Jeremiah xxxviii., indicate. It was divided from the land of Israel by the Dead Sea, and on the north by the river Arnon, the old boundary between Moab and the Amorites (Num. xxi. 13). The journey of the family from Bethlehem would probably first lead them near Jericho, and so across the fords of the Jordan into the territory of the tribe of Reuben. Through the hilly country of this tribe, another long journey would bring them to the Arnon, the frontier river.

How far Elimelech was justified in fleeing, even under the pressure of the famine, from the land of Jehovah to a land where Chemosh was worshipped and the abominations practised of Baal-peor, may well be doubted, even though God overruled it all for good. It was disobeying the spirit of God's law, and holding of little value the blessings of the land of promise.

⁽²⁾ **Naomi.**—The name is derived from the Hebrew root meaning *to be pleasant* (see below, ver. 20). Mahlon and Chilion mean *sickness* and *wasting*, it may be in reference to their premature death, the names being given by reason of their feeble health. It is not certain which was the elder: Mahlon is mentioned first in chap. i. 2, 5, and Chilion in chap. iv. 9. It is probable, however, that Mahlon was the elder.

Ephrathites.—See note on Gen. xxxv. 19. Ephrath was the old name of Bethlehem. Why, in the present passage, the town is called Bethlehem-judah, and the inhabitants Ephrathites, does not appear.

⁽⁴⁾ **They took them wives.**—This seems to have been after the father's death. The fault of settling on a heathen soil begun by the father is carried on by the sons in marrying heathen women, for such we cannot doubt they must have been in the first instance. The Targum (or ancient Chaldee paraphrase) says: "They transgressed against the decree of the Word of the Lord, and took to themselves strange wives." This act was to incur a further risk of being involved in idolatry, as King Solomon found.

Ruth.—This name will mean either "comeliness" or "companion," according to the spelling of which we suppose the present name to be a contraction. The Syriac spelling supports the latter view. Ruth was the wife of Mahlon (chap. iv. 10), apparently the elder son. The Targum calls Ruth the daughter of Eglon, king of Moab, obviously from the wish to exalt the dignity of Ruth.

⁽⁵⁾ **And they died.**—Clearly as quite young men. It is not for us to say how far those are right who see in the death of Elimelech and his sons God's punishment for the disregard of His law. Thus Naomi is left alone, as one on whom comes suddenly the loss of children and widowhood.

⁽⁶⁾ **That she might return.**—Literally, *and she returned.* Clearly, therefore, the three women actually began the journey; and when the start has been made, Naomi urges her companions to return. Then, as with Pliable in the *Pilgrim's Progress*, so with Orpah: the dangers and difficulties of the way were too much for her affection.

The Lord had visited His people.—The famine had ceased, and Naomi's heart yearns for the old home. Perhaps, too, the scenes where everything reminded her of her husband and sons, filled her with sadness (for it would appear that she set out immediately after her

Naomi returns Home. **RUTH.** *Ruth cleaves to her.*

had visited his people in giving them bread. ⁽⁷⁾ Wherefore she went forth out of the place where she was, and her two daughters in law with her; and they went on the way to return unto the land of Judah. ⁽⁸⁾ And Naomi said unto her two daughters in law, Go, return each to her mother's house: the LORD deal kindly with you, as ye have dealt with the dead, and with me. ⁽⁹⁾ The LORD grant you that ye may find rest, each *of you* in the house of her husband. Then she kissed them; and they lifted up their voice, and wept. ⁽¹⁰⁾ And they said unto her, Surely we will return with thee unto thy people. ⁽¹¹⁾ And Naomi said, Turn again, my daughters: why will ye go with me? *are* there yet *any more* sons in my womb, that they may be your husbands? ⁽¹²⁾ Turn again, my daughters, go *your way*; for I am too old to have an husband. If I should say, I have hope, ¹*if* I should have an husband also to night, and should also bear sons; ⁽¹³⁾ would ye ²tarry for them till they were grown? would ye stay for them from having husbands? nay, my daughters; for ³it grieveth me much for your sakes that the hand of the LORD is gone out against me. ⁽¹⁴⁾ And they lifted up their voice, and wept again: and Orpah kissed her mother in law; but Ruth clave unto her.

⁽¹⁵⁾ And she said, Behold, thy sister in law is gone back unto her people, and unto her gods: return thou after thy sister in law. ⁽¹⁶⁾ And Ruth said, ⁴Intreat me not to leave thee, *or* to return from following after thee: for whither thou goest, I will go; and where thou lodgest, I will lodge: thy people *shall be* my people, and thy God my God: ⁽¹⁷⁾ where thou diest, will I die, and there will I be buried: the LORD do so to me, and more also, *if* ought but death part thee and me. ⁽¹⁸⁾ When she saw that she ⁵was stedfastly minded to go with her, then she left speaking unto her.

⁽¹⁹⁾ So they two went until they came to Beth-lehem. And it came to pass, when they were come to Beth-lehem,

---

1 Or, *if I were with an husband.*
2 Heb. *hope.*
3 Heb. *I have much bitterness.*
4 Or, *be not against me.*
5 Heb. *strengthened herself.*

---

sons' death), and perhaps, too, her conscience smote her for distrusting the mercies of the God of Israel.

⁽⁷⁾ **Her two daughters in law with her.**—Both clearly purposing to go with Naomi to the land of Israel (verse 10), not merely to escort her a little way. Naomi had obviously won the affections of her daughters-in-law, and they were loth to part with her, since such a parting could hardly but be final.

⁽⁸⁾ **Return.**—Naomi's love is all unselfish. The company of Ruth and Orpah would clearly have been a great solace to her, yet she will not sacrifice them to herself. They each had a mother and a home; the latter, Naomi might fail to secure to them.

⁽⁹⁾ **The Lord grant you . . .**—A twofold blessing is invoked by Naomi on her daughters-in-law, made the more solemn by the twofold mention of the sacred name Jehovah. She prays first for the general blessing, that God will show them mercy, and secondly for the special blessing, that they may find rest and peace in a new home.

⁽¹¹⁾ The advice of Naomi thus far is insufficient to shake the affectionate resolve of the two women. She then paints the loneliness of her lot. She has no more sons, and can hope for none; nay, if sons were to be even now born to her, what good would that do them? Still her lot is worse than theirs. They, in spite of their great loss, are young, and from their mothers' houses they may again go forth to homes of their own. She, old, childless, and solitary, must wend her weary way back to live unaided as best she may.

⁽¹³⁾ **It grieveth me much for your sakes.**—A much more probable translation is, *it is far more bitter for me than for you.* An exact parallel to the construction is found in Gen. xix. 9. The ancient versions are divided, the LXX., Peshito Syriac, and Targum support this translation; the Vulg. is rather loose in its rendering.

⁽¹⁴⁾ **Kissed.**—Orpah, though unwilling to leave her mother-in-law, and though warmly attached to her, still thinks of the hardships of the journey, of the hardships when the journey is done; and the comforts of home detain her.

⁽¹⁵⁾ Naomi, now armed with a fresh argument, urges Ruth to follow her sister-in-law's example.

Her gods.—Naomi doubtless views the Moabite idols as realities, whose power is, however, confined to the land of Moab. She is not sufficiently enlightened in her religion to see in the Lord more than the God of Israel.

⁽¹⁶⁾ **Intreat me not.**—Ruth's nobleness is proof against all. The intensity of her feeling comes out all the more strongly now that she pleads alone: "I will undertake with thee the toilsome journey, I will lodge with thee however hardly, I will venture among a strange people, and will worship a new god."

⁽¹⁷⁾ **The Lord do so to me.**—Ruth clinches her resolutions with a solemn oath, in which, if we are to take the words literally, she swears by the name of the God of Israel. With this Naomi yields; after so solemn a protest she can urge no more.

⁽¹⁹⁾ **They went.**—The journey for two women apparently alone was long and toilsome, and not free from danger. Two rivers, Arnon and Jordan, had to be forded or otherwise crossed; and the distance of actual journeying cannot have been less than fifty miles. Thus, weary and travel-stained, they reach Bethlehem, and neighbours, doubtless never looking to see Naomi again, are all astir with excitement. It would seem that though the news of the end of the famine had reached Naomi in Moab, news of her had not reached Bethlehem.

that all the city was moved about them, and they said, *Is* this Naomi? (20) And she said unto them, Call me not ¹Naomi, call me ²Mara: for the Almighty hath dealt very bitterly with me. (21) I went out full, and the LORD hath brought me home again empty: why *then* call ye me Naomi, seeing the LORD hath testified against me, and the Almighty hath afflicted me? (22) So Naomi returned, and Ruth the Moabitess, her daughter in law, with her, which returned out of the country of Moab: and they came to Beth-lehem in the beginning of barley harvest.

CHAPTER II.—(1) And Naomi had a kinsman of her husband's, a mighty man of wealth, of the family of Elimelech; and his name *was* Boaz. (2) And Ruth the Moabitess said unto Naomi, Let me now go to the field, and glean ears of corn after *him* in whose sight I shall find grace. And she said unto her, Go,

¹ That is, *Pleasant.*

² That is, *Bitter.*

³ Heb. *hap happened.*

⁴ Called, Matt. 1. 5, *Booz.*

my daughter. (3) And she went, and came, and gleaned in the field after the reapers: and her ³hap was to light on a part of the field *belonging* unto ⁴Boaz, who *was* of the kindred of Elimelech. (4) And, behold, Boaz came from Beth-lehem, and said unto the reapers, The LORD *be* with you. And they answered, The LORD bless thee. (5) Then said Boaz unto his servant that was set over the reapers, Whose damsel *is* this? (6) And the servant that was set over the reapers answered and said, It *is* the Moabitish damsel that came back with Naomi out of the country of Moab: (7) and she said, I pray you, let me glean and gather after the reapers among the sheaves: so she came, and hath continued even from the morning until now, that she tarried a little in the house.

(8) Then said Boaz unto Ruth, Hearest thou not, my daughter? Go not to glean in another field, neither go from hence,

---

They said . . .—The Bethlehemite women, that is, for the verb is feminine. Grief and toil had doubtless made her look aged and worn.

(20) **Call me not Naomi, call me Mara.**—Here we have one of the constant plays on words and names found in the Hebrew Bible. *Naomi*, we have already said, means *pleasant*, or, perhaps, strictly, *my pleasantness*. *Mara* is *bitter*, as in Exod. xv. 23. The latter word has no connection with Miriam or Mary, which is from a different root.

The Almighty.—Heb., *Shaddai*. According to one derivation of the word, "He who is All Sufficient," all sufficing; the God who gives all things in abundance is He who takes back (see Note on Gen. xvii. 1).

Hath dealt very bitterly.—Heb., *hemar*, referring to the preceding Mara. The pleasantness and joys of life are at an end for me, my dear ones passed away, bitterness and sadness are now my lot.

(22) **Barley-harvest.**—God had restored plenty to His people, and the wayfarers thus arrive to witness and receive their share of the blessing. The barley harvest was the earliest (Exod. ix. 31, 32), and would ordinarily fall about the end of April.

II.

(1) **Boaz.**—It has been already said that if there are any gaps in the genealogy, these are most probably to be referred to its earlier portion. According to the line, however, given in chap. iv. 18 *seq.*, Boaz is grandson of the Nahshon who was prince of the tribe of Judah during the wanderings in the desert, and son of Salmon and Rahab of Jericho. It may be noted that the difficulty of date may be lessened by supposing that in the last two generations we have children of their fathers' old age.

(2) **Let me now go.**—The character of Ruth comes out strongly here. She does not hesitate to face the hard work necessary on her mother-in-law's account; nor is she too proud to condescend to a work which might perhaps seem humiliating. Nor does she hanker after her old home in the land of Moab and the plenty there. Energy, honesty of purpose, and loyalty are alike evinced here.

(3) **Her hap was to light on.**—Literally, *her hap happened*. A chance in outward seeming, yet a clear shaping of her course by unseen hands. Her steps were divinely guided to a certain field, that God's good purposes should be worked out.

(4) **The Lord be with you.**—There is a trace here of the good feeling prevailing between Boaz and his servants. Though he has come to his field to supervise the work, it is not in a fault-finding spirit, but with true courtesy and friendliness; nor is it a frivolous jesting manner that he displays, but with gravity and soberness he presents a true gentleman in his intercourse with his inferiors.

(6, 7) The steward gives a detailed account of Ruth. She is "the (rather "a") Moabitish damsel," she is a foreigner [as such she had a *special* claim to the gleaning, Lev. xix. 9, 10]. She is the daughter-in-law of Naomi; and he adds that her behaviour has been praiseworthy, for she asked leave before beginning to glean, and she has worked hard all day, save for a short interval of rest. It would seem that Boaz's visit to the field fell at the time when Ruth was thus resting: "This is her tarrying for a little in the house"; apparently, that is, some rude shelter from the heat set up in the field, like the *lodge* of Isa. i. 8.

(8) **My daughter.**—This address suggests that Boaz was no longer a young man; clearly the account he had heard of Ruth, both from his servant and from general report, as well as her appearance and behaviour, and doubtless a feeling of pity at her condition, had prepossessed him in her favour.

Abide here fast by my maidens.—Literally, *cleave to* (Gen. ii. 24). The true courtesy of Boaz's character shows itself in the mention of the maidens. He will not have the stranger even run the chance of

but abide here fast by my maidens: ⁽⁹⁾ *let* thine eyes *be* on the field that they do reap, and go thou after them: have I not charged the young men that they shall not touch thee? and when thou art athirst, go unto the vessels, and drink of *that* which the young men have drawn. ⁽¹⁰⁾ Then she fell on her face, and bowed herself to the ground, and said unto him, Why have I found grace in thine eyes, that thou shouldest take knowledge of me, seeing I *am* a stranger? ⁽¹¹⁾ And Boaz answered and said unto her, It hath fully been shewed me, all that thou hast done unto thy mother in law since the death of thine husband: and *how* thou hast left thy father and thy mother, and the land of thy nativity, and art come unto a people which thou knewest not heretofore. ⁽¹²⁾ The LORD recompense thy work, and a full reward be given thee of the LORD God of Israel, under whose wings thou art come to trust. ⁽¹³⁾ Then she said, ¹ Let me find favour in thy sight, my lord; for that thou hast comforted me, and for that thou hast spoken ² friendly unto thine handmaid, though I be not like unto one of thine handmaidens. ⁽¹⁴⁾ And Boaz said unto her, At mealtime come thou hither, and eat of the bread, and dip thy morsel in the vinegar. And she sat beside the reapers: and he reached her parched *corn*, and she did eat, and was sufficed, and left.

⁽¹⁵⁾ And when she was risen up to glean, Boaz commanded his young men, saying, Let her glean even among the sheaves, and ³ reproach her not: ⁽¹⁶⁾ and let fall also *some* of the handfuls of purpose for her, and leave *them*, that she may glean *them*, and rebuke her not. ⁽¹⁷⁾ So she gleaned in the field until even, and beat out that she had gleaned: and it was about an ephah of barley. ⁽¹⁸⁾ And she took *it* up, and went into the city: and her mother in law saw what she had gleaned: and she brought forth, and gave to her that she had reserved after she was sufficed.

⁽¹⁹⁾ And her mother in law said unto her, Where hast thou gleaned to day? and where wroughtest thou? blessed be he that did take knowledge of thee. And she shewed her mother in law with whom she had wrought, and said, The man's name with whom I wrought to day *is* Boaz. ⁽²⁰⁾ And Naomi said unto her daughter in law, Blessed *be* he of the LORD, who hath not left off his kindness to the living and to the dead. And Naomi said unto her, The man *is* near

¹ Or, *I find favour.*

² Heb. *to the heart.*

³ Heb. *shame her not.*

---

rudeness, by being away from the company of her own sex. As the next verse shows, he had already given orders to his men on the subject.

⁽⁹⁾ **Have drawn.**—Literally, *shall (from time to time) draw.* Possibly from that self-same well at Bethlehem from which David desired to drink (2 Sam. xxiii. 15).

⁽¹⁰⁾ **A stranger.**—A foreigner. Note, however, that the Moabite language, though having its own peculiarities, really differed but little from Hebrew, as may be seen, for instance, from the famous inscription of King Mesha discovered in the land of Moab in 1868.

⁽¹¹⁾ **Heretofore.**—The curious Hebrew phrase thus rendered is literally, *yesterday and the day before.*

⁽¹²⁾ Boaz prays that God will recompense Ruth's dutifulness to her mother-in-law, and the more seeing that she herself has put herself under His protection. Faith in Divine help and grace will win an undoubted recompense.

⁽¹³⁾ **Friendly.**—Literally, *unto the heart.* The same phrase is rendered *comfortably* (Isa. xl. 2).

⁽¹⁴⁾ **At meal-time.**—This should apparently be joined to what precedes: Boaz now shows a fresh act of kindness.

Vinegar.—By this term is to be understood wine which had become sour (Proverbs x. 26). As such, Nazarites were forbidden to use it (Num. vi. 3). Similar to this was the vinegar of the Gospel narrative, a sour wine generally mixed with water, which was offered to our Saviour (Matt. xxvii. 48, &c.).

Left.—Had to spare. In verse 18, we find that this superfluity was put by for her mother-in-law.

⁽¹⁷⁾ **Beat out.**—That is, she threshed it herself, so as to save the labour of carrying away the straw. She then found she had an ephah, that is, rather more than four pecks.

⁽¹⁹⁾ **Blessed be he that did take knowledge of thee.**—Naomi easily perceives that the quantity of corn brought home is unusually large, and that therefore some special kindness must have been shown. Her own, therefore, as well as her daughter's thanks are due to this benefactor.

⁽²⁰⁾ **Who hath not . . .**—It is not clear whether the grammatical antecedent is God or Boaz. Either way a good sense is obtained. As our lost dear ones had kindness shown them of old, so we too now. If Boaz is the antecedent, it may seem curious that Naomi (knowing that she was dwelling near to a kinsman of her husband's, and, further, one who had shown kindness before they departed to Moab) should not have made herself known to him. It is, at any rate, a proof of the independence of her character. However, the name once named evidently suggests the train of thought which at length leads Naomi to appeal to him for a kinsman's special aid, the aid of the *Goel* or redeemer.

One of our next kinsmen.—One of those who must redeem.

of kin unto us, ¹one of our next kinsmen. (21) And Ruth the Moabitess said, He said unto me also, Thou shalt keep fast by my young men, until they have ended all my harvest. (22) And Naomi said unto Ruth her daughter in law, *It is* good, my daughter, that thou go out with his maidens, that they ²meet thee not in any other field. (23) So she kept fast by the maidens of Boaz to glean unto the end of barley harvest and of wheat harvest; and dwelt with her mother in law.

CHAPTER III.—(1) Then Naomi her mother in law said unto her, My daughter, shall I not seek rest for thee, that it may be well with thee? (2) And now *is* not Boaz of our kindred, with whose maidens thou wast? Behold, he winnoweth barley to night in the threshingfloor. (3) Wash thyself therefore, and anoint thee, and put thy raiment upon thee, and get thee down to the floor: *but* make not thyself known unto the man, until he shall have done eating and drinking. (4) And it shall be, when he lieth down, that thou shalt mark the place where he shall lie, and thou shalt go in, and ³uncover his feet, and lay thee down; and he will tell thee what thou shalt do. (5) And she said unto her, All that thou sayest unto me I will do.

(6) And she went down unto the floor, and did according to all that her mother in law bade her. (7) And when Boaz had eaten and drunk, and his heart was merry, he went to lie down at the end of the heap of corn: and she came softly, and uncovered his feet, and laid her down. (8) And it came to pass at midnight, that the man was afraid, and ⁴turned himself: and, behold, a woman lay at his feet. (9) And he said, Who *art* thou? And she answered, I *am* Ruth thine handmaid: spread therefore thy skirt over thine handmaid; for thou *art* ⁵a near kinsman. (10) And he said,

---

1 Or, *one that hath right to redeem.*

2 Or, *fall upon thee.*

3 Or, *lift up the clothes that are on his feet.*

4 Or, *took hold on.*

5 Or, *one that hath right to redeem.*

---

(21) **My young men ... my harvest.**—Emphatic in the Hebrew. As long as my reaping lasts, cleave steadily to us.

(22) **That they meet thee not.**—*It is good ... and that people meet thee not.* This would not only be throwing away genuine kindness, but would be contemptuously proclaiming the fact.

Maidens.—Naomi speaks of the young women, whereas Ruth had spoken of the young men. We need not suppose that any distinction is intended: Ruth names the young men as the chief workers; Naomi, the young women as those with whom Ruth would be specially thrown.

(23) **And dwelt.**—Unspoiled by mixing with her new society, she stops on quietly at the end of her task, and tends her mother-in-law at home with the same fidelity with which she had worked for her abroad.

III.

(1) **Rest.**—Although Naomi had already (chap. i. 12) repudiated any thought of marriage for herself, still she felt it her duty to do what she could to provide a home for the daughter-in-law who had so loyally followed her, lest her own death should leave her young companion specially unprotected and friendless. But there is clearly a second thought. The marriage of Boaz and Ruth will not only ensure *rest* for the latter, but will also raise up the seed of her dead son and preserve the family name.

That it may be well with thee.—The object of the marriage is for Ruth's good, and thus should it be with every marriage; it must be for the good, and comfort, and abiding peace, not of the body only, but of the soul.

(3—5) The plan suggested by Naomi seems peculiar, yet some thoughts may give a certain colouring to it. (1) Naomi seems to have believed that Boaz was the nearest kinsman, being ignorant of the yet nearer one (verse 12). Consequently, according to Israelite law (Deut. xxv. 5 *sqq.*), it would be the duty of Boaz to marry Ruth to raise up seed to the dead. (2) The general tone of Naomi's character is clearly shown in this book to be that of a God-fearing woman, so that it is certain that, however curious in its external form, there can be nothing counselled here which really is repugnant to God's law, or shocking to a virtuous man such as Boaz, otherwise Naomi would simply have been most completely frustrating her own purpose. (3) Her knowledge by long intimacy of Ruth's character, and doubtless also of that of Boaz by report, would enable her to feel sure that no ill effects could accrue.

(4) **Uncover his feet.**—More literally, as the margin, *lift up the clothes that are on his feet;* so LXX. and the Vulgate. We are told that the custom still prevails in Palestine of owners of crops sleeping on their threshing-floors, lying with their clothes on, but with their feet covered with a mantle.

(5) **I will do.**—Ruth's obedience here is an intelligent obedience. She knew in what relation Boaz stood to her family, and the duties attaching to the relationship (chaps. ii. 20, iii. 9). Thus with obedient trust, implicitly but not blindly, she follows her mother-in-law's orders; strong in conscious innocence she risks the obloquy that may attend her duty.

(8) **Was afraid.**—Was startled. See the use of the word in Gen. xxvii. 33.

Turned.—Literally, *bent himself.* (Comp. Judges xvi. 29.) He wakes with a start, and in turning sees a woman at his feet.

(9) **Skirt.**—Literally *wing;* Heb. *canaph,* as in chap. ii. 12. The Targum treats this as in itself the claim to espousal on her part. The metaphor may be illustrated from Ezek. xvi. 8, and more generally from Matt. xxiii. 37.

(10) **Blessed be thou of the Lord.**—This answer of Boaz's is in itself a sufficient proof of the view he

Blessed be thou of the LORD, my daughter: for thou hast shewed more kindness in the latter end than at the beginning, inasmuch as thou followedst not young men, whether poor or rich. (11) And now, my daughter, fear not; I will do to thee all that thou requirest: for all the ¹city of my people doth know that thou *art* a virtuous woman. (12) And now it is true that I *am thy* near kinsman: howbeit there is a kinsman nearer than I. (13) Tarry this night, and it shall be in the morning, *that* if he will perform unto thee the part of a kinsman, well; let him do the kinsman's part: but if he will not do the part of a kinsman to thee, then will I do the part of a kinsman to thee, *as* the LORD liveth: lie down until the morning.

(14) And she lay at his feet until the morning: and she rose up before one could know another. And he said, Let it not be known that a woman came into the floor. (15) Also he said, Bring the ²vail that *thou hast* upon thee, and hold it. And when she held it, he measured six *measures* of barley, and laid *it* on her: and she went into the city.

(16) And when she came to her mother in law, she said, Who *art* thou, my daughter? And she told her all that the man had done to her. (17) And she said, These six *measures* of barley gave he me; for he said to me, Go not empty unto thy mother in law. (18) Then said she, Sit still, my daughter, until thou know how the matter will fall: for the man will not be in rest, until he have finished the thing this day.

CHAPTER IV.—(1) Then went Boaz up to the gate, and sat him down there: and, behold, the kinsman of whom Boaz spake came by; unto whom he said, Ho, such a one! turn aside, sit down here. And he turned aside, and sat down. (2) And he took ten men of the elders of the city, and said, Sit ye down here. And they sat down. (3) And he said unto the kinsman, Naomi, that is come

¹ Heb. *gate.*

² Or, *sheet,* or, *apron.*

---

took of her conduct, and of the integrity of his own. We note, too, that this blessing follows immediately on the avowal of her name. His own feelings had already been attuned to due honour and respect for Ruth; he is prepared not only to discharge the duty of next of kin, but to do it in no perfunctory spirit, but with a sincere loyal affection. The Targum on verse 15 supposes that to Ruth, the distant ancestress of the Saviour, was vouchsafed the knowledge, as in its fulness to the Virgin hereafter, of the birth of the Messiah through her. Origen compares Ruth to the Gentile Church, the engrafted wild olive.

Thou hast shewed ....—Literally, *thou hast done well thy latter kindness above the former.*

(11) **City.**—Literally, *gate*: the constant meeting-place of persons going in and out. (See Gen. xix. 1, xxxiv. 20, 24; Deut. xvi. 18, xxi. 19, &c.)

(13) **Until the morning.**—You have made clear the object of your plea, and I fully assent to it; but do not run the risk of going now, in the dead of night, back to your home.

(14) **One could know another.**—Literally, *a man could recognise his friend;* i.e., before daylight, in the early dusk.

A woman.—Literally, *the woman*—i.e., this woman. Thus it is of Ruth, not of himself, that Boaz is here thinking. A sensible man like Boaz knows "that we must not only keep a good conscience, but keep a good name; we must avoid not only sin but scandal." (Henry.)

(15) **Vail**—Rather a *mantle,* so in Isa. iii. 22.

She went.—This should be, if we follow the current Hebrew text, *he went.* The verb is masculine (*yabho*), and the distinction is shewn in the Targum, which inserts the name Boaz as the nominative. It must be allowed that a fair number of Hebrew MSS., as well as the Peshito and Vulgate, take the verb in the feminine. The LXX. is from the nature of the Greek language unable to mark the distinction. The clause, if we accept the current reading, will mean that Boaz went to the city to find the kinsman whose claim lay before his own, while Ruth, laden with six measures of barley, goes to her mother-in-law.

(16) **Who art thou?**—We can hardly view this as a simple question as to Ruth's identity, but rather as meaning, *how hast thou fared?*

(18) **Will not be in rest.**—*i.e., will not keep quiet.*

IV.

(1) **Went up.**—Inasmuch as the town stood on a hill: so in chap. iii. 3, Ruth is bidden to *go down* to the threshing-floor.

The kinsman.—The *Goel.* (See chap. iii. 12).

Turn aside.—The form of the imperative is such as to give a hortatory turn, pray turn aside and sit down.

Such a one.—Heb., *p'loni almoni.* This phrase is used like the English so-and-so, such-and-such, of names which it is thought either unnecessary or undesirable to give. The derivation is probably from *palah,* to mark out, to separate, to distinguish, and *alam,* to hide, giving the twofold notion of one who is indicated, though in a certain sense concealed. The phrase is used of places, 1 Sam. xxi. 2, 2 Kings vi. 8; see also Dan. viii. 13. Why the name is not recorded here does not appear; possibly it was not known to the writer, or it may have been thought unworthy of recording, since he neglected his plain duty in refusing to raise up seed to the dead. We know nothing of this unnamed person save the fact of the offering of the redemption set before him, and his refusal of it, an offer which involved the glory of being the ancestor of the Christ who was to be born in the far-off ages.

(3) **Naomi selleth . . .**—Rather, *the portion of land, which belonged to our brother Elimelech, has Naomi sold.* The present tense of the English

again out of the country of Moab, selleth a parcel of land, which *was* our brother Elimelech's: ⁽⁴⁾ and ¹I thought to advertise. thee, saying, Buy *it* before the inhabitants, and before the elders of my people. If thou wilt redeem *it*, redeem *it*: but if thou wilt not redeem *it*, then tell me, that I may know: for *there is* none to redeem *it* beside thee; and I *am* after thee. And he said, I will redeem *it*. ⁽⁵⁾ Then said Boaz, What day thou buyest the field of the hand of Naomi, thou must buy *it* also of Ruth the Moabitess, the wife of the dead, to raise up the name of the dead upon his inheritance. ⁽⁶⁾ And the kinsman said, I cannot redeem *it* for myself, lest I mar mine own inheritance: redeem thou my right to thyself; for I cannot redeem *it*. ⁽⁷⁾ ᵃNow this *was the manner* in former time in Israel concerning redeeming and concerning changing, for to confirm all things; a man plucked off his shoe, and gave *it* to his neighbour: and this *was* a testimony in Israel. ⁽⁸⁾ Therefore the kinsman said unto Boaz, Buy *it* for thee. So he drew off his shoe.

⁽⁹⁾ And Boaz said unto the elders, and unto all the people, Ye *are* witnesses this day, that I have bought all that *was* Elimelech's, and all that *was* Chilion's and Mahlon's, of the hand of Naomi. ⁽¹⁰⁾ Moreover Ruth the Moabitess, the wife of Mahlon, have I purchased to be my wife, to raise up the name of the dead upon his inheritance, that the name of the dead be not cut off from among his brethren, and from the gate of his place: ye *are* witnesses this day. ⁽¹¹⁾ And all the people that *were* in the gate, and the elders, said, *We are* witnesses. The LORD make the woman that is come into thine house like Rachel and like Leah, which

1 Heb. *I said I will reveal*, in thine ear.

a Deut. 25. 7, 9.

Version seems to suggest that the sale is taking place at this particular time, but the meaning clearly is that Naomi, as the representative of the dead Elimelech had, so far as it was possible for an Israelite to part with a family estate, sold the land to obtain in some sort the means of living. In the year of Jubilee, the property would return to the family, on which it was, so to speak, settled, but Boaz proposes to the *Goel* that he should redeem the property at once. We might perhaps compare this to the owner of a freehold buying from a leaseholder under him the residue of his lease, so that he may occupy his own estate.

⁽⁴⁾ **And I thought . . .**—literally, *and I said I will uncover thy ear.*

The inhabitants.—This should perhaps rather be, *those who are sitting here* [the Hebrew word *yashabh* has the two meanings of *dwelling* and *sitting*, see *e.g.*, Gen. xxiii. 10, where the latter meaning should certainly be taken]. So the LXX., Peshito and Vulg.

If thou wilt not.—The current Hebrew text has here, *if he will not*, which is clearly an error for the second person, which is read by a large number of Hebrew MSS., and by all the ancient versions.

I will redeem it.—He is willing enough to redeem the land as a good investment, forgetting, until reminded, the necessary previous condition. It involves marrying Ruth, and this he declines to do.

⁽⁵⁾ **What day . . .**—When the person had been bought out to whom Naomi had sold the land until the year of Jubilee should restore it to her family, there remained Naomi's own claim on the land, and afterwards that of Ruth, as the widow of the son of Elimelech. But further, this last carried with it the necessity of taking Ruth to wife, so that a child might be born to inherit, as the son of Mahlon, Mahlon's inheritance.

⁽⁶⁾ **Lest I mar . . .**—The redemption of the land would involve the spending of money, drawn away from the *Goel's* own estate; but the land thus acquired would not belong to the *Goel* himself, but to the son he should have by Ruth, who would yet be, in the eyes of the law, the son of Mahlon. It would, therefore, be like mortgaging one's own estate, and that for the benefit of another. Josephus and the Targum explain it by saying that he already had a wife, and feared the discord that might arise.

⁽⁷⁾ **In former time.**—Arguments have been built on this word in favour of our assigning a late date to the book, but the inference seems hardly warranted. The same Hebrew word occurs in Deut. ii. 10, Judges i. 10, &c.

Plucked off his shoe.—The idea of this act apparently is that the man resigns the right of walking on the land as master, in favour of him to whom he gives the shoe. A similar but not identical custom is prescribed in Deut. xxv. 9.

A testimony. — *The* testimony, the manner in which the solemn witness is born.

⁽⁸⁾ **Drew.**—The same word in the Hebrew as *plucked* in verse 7.

⁽¹¹⁾ **The Lord . . .**—In this way is the nuptial blessing invoked.

Is come.—Rather, *is coming.*

Rachel—though the younger sister and the junior wife—is put first, probably from her death and burial having associated her with Bethlehem (see Gen. xxxv. 16, 19). In this way, too, we should explain the prophecy of Jeremiah as applied by St. Matthew (Jer. xxxi. 15; Matt. ii. 18).

Build.—From the Hebrew word to *build* are derived the words for *son* and *daughter*, thus a twofold aspect in the word sometimes appears as here. (See also Gen. xvi. 2, xxx. 3).

Do thou worthily.—The Hebrew phrase (*asah khayil*) thus rendered, involves the notion of doing a thing with vigour and might. The *khayil* of a soldier is his valour—of a land, its material resources, and (Prov. xxxi. 10) the "virtuous woman" of the English Version is literally, *woman of khayil*. The good wish for Boaz here is that by his energy he may command continual prosperity.

Be famous.—Literally, *proclaim a name.*

Boaz Marries Ruth. RUTH, IV. *Birth of Obed.*

two did build the house of Israel: and ¹do thou worthily in Ephratah, and ²be famous in Beth-lehem: ⁽¹²⁾ and let thy house be like the house of Pharez, ᵃwhom Tamar bare unto Judah, of the seed which the LORD shall give thee of this young woman.

⁽¹³⁾ So Boaz took Ruth, and she was his wife: and when he went in unto her, the LORD gave her conception, and she bare a son. ⁽¹⁴⁾ And the women said unto Naomi, Blessed *be* the LORD, which hath not ³left thee this day without a ⁴kinsman, that his name may be famous in Israel. ⁽¹⁵⁾ And he shall be unto thee a restorer of *thy* life, and ⁵a nourisher of ⁶thine old age: for thy daughter in law, which loveth thee, which is better to thee than seven sons, hath born him. ⁽¹⁶⁾ And Naomi took the child, and laid it in her bosom, and became nurse unto it. ⁽¹⁷⁾ And the women her neighbours gave it a name, saying, There is a son born to Naomi; and they called his name Obed: he *is* the father of Jesse, the father of David.

⁽¹⁸⁾ Now these *are* the generations of Pharez: ᵇPharez begat Hezron, ⁽¹⁹⁾ and Hezron begat Ram, and Ram begat Amminadab, ⁽²⁰⁾ and Amminadab begat Nahshon, and Nahshon begat ⁷Salmon, ⁽²¹⁾ and Salmon begat Boaz, and Boaz begat Obed, ⁽²²⁾ and Obed begat Jesse, and Jesse begat David.

Marginal notes:
1 Or, *get thee riches, or, power.*
2 Heb. *proclaim thy name.*
a Gen. 38. 29; 1 Chron. 2. 4; Mat. 1. 3.
3 Heb. *caused to cease unto thee.*
4 Or, *redeemer.*
5 Heb. *to nourish.*
6 Heb. *thy gray hairs.*
b 1 Chron. 2. 4; Matt. 1. 3.
7 Or, *Salmah.*

⁽¹²⁾ **Pharez.**—(See Gen. xxxviii. 29). Judah having, though unwittingly, fulfilled the Levirate obligation to the widow of his eldest son, the child thus born becomes the heir of that eldest son, and therefore the head of the house of Judah.

⁽¹⁴⁾ **Left thee without.**—Literally, *not allowed to cease to thee.*

A kinsman.—That is, *the child* (See next verse). The word *kinsman* here is Goel, a redeemer.

⁽¹⁵⁾ **A nourisher.**—(See marginal renderings).

Daughter-in-law.—The position of the nominative is emphatic.

Loveth.—The verb is a perfect, *which hath ever loved thee.*

⁽¹⁶⁾ **Nurse.**—The verb (*aman*) here is that used in Isa. xlix. 23, "and kings shall be thy *nursing fathers.*" That ordinarily used for the natural nursing of a woman is different.

⁽¹⁷⁾ **Obed.**—*i.e.*, a serving one.

⁽¹⁸⁻²²⁾. This short genealogy, abruptly added, may be due to a later hand, it being thought necessary to connect David's line fully with Judah.

⁽¹⁸⁾ **Hezron.**—See Gen. xlvi. 12.

⁽¹⁹⁾ **Ram.**—See 1 Chron. ii. 9; St. Matt. i. 3.

Amminadab.—It was to his daughter Elisheba that Aaron was married. (Exod. vi. 23).

⁽²⁰⁾ **Nahshon** was the prince of the children of Judah in the wilderness. (See Num. i. 7, &c).

Salmon—Heb., *Salmah*, though called Salmon in the next verse. In 1 Chron. ii. 11 he is called *Salma*. Salmon may very probably have been one of the two spies sent to Jericho, who having been sheltered by Rahab, had repaid her kindness by marrying her.

It has been observed above that the smallness of the number of the generations hardly suits the long period of years here implied, and on the whole we are disposed to believe that some links of the chain have been dropped, and if so, then doubtless in the period before Boaz. Thus we may suppose that we have here the distinguished names, others of less note being passed over. Unless this is done we are forced to increase largely the average length of a generation, and suppose that most of these generations were children of their fathers' old age. We know from 1 Kings vi. 1 that from the Exodus to the fourth year of Solomon was 480 years. If we deduct from this forty years for the wanderings in the desert, then, seeing that David died at the age of seventy, we have for the period from the entrance into Canaan to the birth of David, 480—40—70—4 = 366 years. But if Rahab bears Boaz to Salmon only a few years after the beginning of this period, we have to cover nearly 366 years with three generations, Boaz, Obed, Jesse, which entails upon us the conclusion that each of the above three begat the specified son at the age of over a hundred, and that Salmon was also well advanced in years at his marriage. This, however, seems hardly credible, and the theory that one or two generations have dropt from the list is, at any rate, reasonable.

INTRODUCTION TO THE FIRST BOOK OF SAMUEL

I. The Contents and Design of the (First) Book of Samuel.

—In the reign of King Rehoboam,* the son of Solomon—at the instance, probably, of the chief of the then flourishing prophetic schools—a learned son of the prophets, one (his name is not recorded) who in later days would have been termed a scribe, undertook to compose, from materials preserved in these schools, a general history of the events connected with the chosen people for some 120—130 years prior to the accession of the great Solomon, whose memory was still fresh in Israel.

It was well, surely, that the renowned centres of Hebrew education should possess a connected story of that marvellous century which had witnessed so mighty a change in the people. In its first years, Israel, without culture, almost without religion, seemed fast degenerating into a loose aggregation of Bedouin tribes, perpetually harassed by the neighbouring races, especially by a growing and powerful nation—the Philistines—who were constantly recruited from countries beyond the seas.

The last years of the same century witnessed a different state of things. Israel, having completely vanquished the neighbouring races, had developed into a great and united nation. Its tribes were no longer confined to the narrow limits of Canaan; its influence was acknowledged over a great extent of the continent of South-western Asia. It had become, strange to relate, one of the great world-kingdoms, and under David and Solomon scarcely acknowledged a rival power in the East. The internal life of the people had undergone no less a change. Arts and literature were cultivated; great prosperity and a comparatively high state of culture and learning were to be found in the dominion ruled by the famous Solomon. An elaborate system of government had been established, and a powerful standing army, of which the twelve tribes formed the nucleus, gave a seeming stability to the marvellous structure of Hebrew power. On one of the old sacred hills, in the centre of the land originally conquered by the tribes, on a spot hallowed among the race by primeval tradition, the great king had built a temple to their God—the unseen Protector of the people—a building of magnificence and grandeur never surpassed, probably never equalled, in any land, though some 3,000 years have passed over the world since the dedication morning.

What strange chain of events had led up to this marvellous change in the condition of the Hebrew people? The sacred "scribe" begins his story of these "events" about 170 years before the death of Solomon, with a picture of the life of the people in the days of the aged Eli, high priest and judge of Israel.

1. THE DAYS OF ELI.—The introduction is abrupt. It says nothing of the early history of the old priestly judge, who, however, in his youth and vigorous manhood, must have been a distinguished hero and administrator; for his high post, which he retained to the end of his days, was not inherited by him, but won: Eli belonged only to the younger branch of the house of Aaron, and therefore the transfer to him of the high-priestly and judicial office, of which the historian tells us nothing, must have been the result of his own merit.

In his old age, as represented in this book, he appears as a benevolent, kindly man, but utterly incapable of controlling the wild passions of the people. His own sons, themselves priests, are represented as being covetous and utterly lawless; and a terrible picture of the shame and degradation of the people is painted for us in the brief, but vivid, recital of the doings at Shiloh in the old age of Eli, the high priest—in Shiloh, the chief religious centre of the race.

But though the people, as a whole, were deeply tainted, even in the highest ranks, with all the vices most hateful to the pure religion of their God, yet there were some families in Israel pious, simple, honest folk. Of these the writer gives us a specimen in the account of the house of Elkanah, and especially in the carefully drawn picture of the inner life of his wife, Hannah, the mother of Samuel.

At this time Israel was still contending for bare existence with the neighbouring nations and tribes; its very life and existence as a people (as has been related in another compilation, called the "Judges") had long been threatened. One of these neighbouring peoples—the warlike Philistines—as it grew in power, directed its energies especially to the conquest of the Hebrew race, whom they seem to have hated with a fierce and jealous hatred.

In the old age of Eli, each year the Philistine encroachments seem to have grown more intolerable; each year the people seem to have been less capable of offering to these encroachments any effectual resistance. The patriot scribe who compiled our history, with stern grief, very shortly recounts a terrible sequence of national disasters—the utter defeat of his people; the loss of their prized and sacred symbol, the Ark of the covenant; the death of Eli, the high priest and judge, caused by shame and grief;

---

* The earlier date—that of the reign of Rehoboam—is adopted by Thenius, Keil, Erdmann in *Lange, Commentary*.

Dr. Payne Smith, for reasons suggested in his Introduction to the First Book of Samuel, in the *Pulpit Commentary*, puts the date a little later—somewhere in the time of Jehoshaphat.

The Rabbinical view is that Jeremiah was the author. Grotius adopts this view.

Stähelin suggests Hezekiah's reign as the period of this composition.

Haevernich prefers the early years of Solomon.

Ewald places the first production as late as the second half of the Babylonian exile, but assumes that this was only a partial revision of a much earlier history.

I. SAMUEL.

The nation had now reached its lowest pitch of degradation. It appeared as though nothing could now save Israel from being wiped out from among nations: for even worse, we know, happened to the "chosen race" than our historian tells us in this Book of Samuel. He recounts enough, surely, in his sorrowful narrative, for us to picture Israel's deep distress—her armies beaten, her strong places taken, her people little better than trodden-down subjects of the idolatrous Philistines—but here he pauses; he refrains from dwelling on the sacking of Shiloh, on the destruction of the sanctuary, on the awful scenes which evidently followed the taking of the Ark in battle, and the death, through shame, of the aged Eli. It was a horror too great for the patriot scribe to dwell on. But Asaph, the psalmist, darkly speaks of this dread period in his mournful poem, where it speaks so eloquently of the time " when God greatly abhorred His Israel, so that He forsook the tabernacle of Shiloh." The psalmist draws with a few masterly strokes a vivid picture of the utter desolation of the land—a prey to fire and sword:—

> "He was wroth,
> And greatly abhorred Israel:
> So that He rejected the tabernacle in Shiloh—
> The tent (which) He pitched among men.
> And He gave His strength into captivity,
> And His beauty into the adversary's hand.
> Yea, He gave over His people to the sword,
> And was wroth with His inheritance.
> Their young men the fire devoured,
> And their maidens were not praised in the marriage song.
> Their priests fell by the sword,
> And their widows made no lamentation."—Ps. lxxviii.

The memory of the awful disaster seems never to have been lost in Israel. Far on in the history of the chosen people the prophet Jeremiah refers to this terrible judgment, which inaugurates in so stern a manner the public career of Samuel: "For go now to my place which was in Shiloh, where I made my name to dwell at the first, and see what I have done to it because of the wickedness of my people Israel" (Jer. vii. 12. See also verse 14 and chap. xxvi. 6 of the same prophet).

2. THE DAYS OF SAMUEL.—The prophet-scribe proceeds then to give an account of the times which immediately succeed the catastrophe of Shiloh and the death of Eli. In the period of the deepest degradation of the people (again to use Asaph's words in Ps. lxxviii.), "the Lord awakened as one out of sleep," and gave them Samuel. To the divinely-guided labours of this prophet-judge—no doubt, after Moses, the greatest of the sons of Israel—was owing all the matchless prosperity which the people enjoyed in the latter part of David's life, and during the reign of his son Solomon. Our historian—educated, no doubt, in one of Samuel's prophet schools—gives us some account of the Restorer's early days. Brought up by the high priest Eli, under the shadow of the sanctuary at Shiloh, the child Samuel was early trained to love the glorious national traditions of the past, and to share in the yet more glorious national hopes for the future. He was too—living as he did at Shiloh—a sorrowful witness of the moral degradation of the lives of the foremost men of the land. Their fatal example in Shiloh was but too faithfully copied in all the coasts of Israel. He shared, too, in the terrible disaster which overwhelmed high priest and sanctuary, and which threatened the total ruin of his nation. From that sad day Samuel, the pupil of Eli, became the foremost man among the scattered and disorganised tribes. For long years he laboured with all his great powers, ever helped with the consciousness that the Glorious Arm of the Holy One who loved Israel was beside him. For long years he laboured to restore the dying life of the people, by infusing into it the old trust in the Eternal Friend — by restoring throughout the harassed land a respect for morality, and a reverence for the religion of their fathers.

And to a certain extent Samuel was successful. His steady, ardent faith held together in their darkest hours the shattered remnant of the race, at a time when total absorption among the Philistines and the neighbouring tribes seemed imminent. But as he worked and prayed, slowly,* against his own wishes and pre-conceptions, the conviction forced itself upon him that the whole existing system had become hopelessly unsound, and the community would only be saved by a totally new organisation.

The historian, in simple, eloquent language, gives us the picture of Samuel's inward struggles here, and relates how the noble-minded statesman, always under Divine guidance, founded the monarchy, chose a king, and quietly yielded up the supreme power in the State. Nor was this all; in his long wanderings up and down among the people, during the years of his toil in the course of his vast labour of religious restoration, he had seen how deep was the ignorance of the children of Israel. In the troublous days of the judges the arts, music, poetry, history, were unknown. The chosen race cared for none of these things. In matters of religion a wild and gloomy superstition had taken the place of the pure and spiritual belief taught by Moses. To remedy this state of things, Samuel founded the schools of the prophets,† in order that, by their agency, the mental condition of the people might be raised, and men trained to serve God in Church and State. In these schools the founder did not expect his students to receive the gift of inspiration. That, the most rare and precious of gifts, the great seer knew was to be obtained by no education or training, but was the gift of God alone, from whom it might come to a herdman, with only such learning as could be picked up in a village (Amos vii. 14, 15); he knew that it was never bestowed except for high purposes, and in cases where there was a special internal fitness on the part of the receiver. But the words prophet and prophecy have a wide meaning in Holy Scripture.

The instruction was essentially free, was open to all comers, and, when educated, the prophet might return to his farm, or to some occupation connected with city life. But he was from henceforth an educated man; and he had been taught too the nature of Jehovah: how He was to be worshipped, and what was the life which every member of a covenant nation ought to lead.

Thus Samuel's schools not only raised Israel to a higher mental level, but were the great means of maintaining the worship of Jehovah among the people. As such, we find future prophets earnest in maintaining them.‡ But the prophetic order had in Samuel's mind another important function. It was to be a permanent public power alongside of the priesthood which already existed, and of the kingly office which he, Samuel, had inaugurated. It was intended especially to offer to the latter, when inclining to tyranny, a powerful opposition, founded on the Divine Word. Throughout the history of Israel we find the prophetical order not merely the preachers of a high and pure morality, and a lofty, spiritual religion, but

---
* Ewald, *History of Israel*, Book II., Section III., chap. iii.—Samuel.
† Dean Payne Smith, *Introduction to the Book of Samuel* (*Pulpit Comm.*).
‡ Dr. Erdmann in *Lange, Introduction*, Section IV.

I. SAMUEL.

we see in them "the tribunes of the people," the protectors of the oppressed subjects against the despotic monarch, the steady defenders of the down-trodden poor against the exacting and covetous rich.

In one sense, they filled the position which the priesthood ought to have occupied, had the representatives of that order done their duty, but who—as Samuel well knew, not only from the past sad history of the period of the judges, but from his own personal observation at Shiloh during the life-time of Eli—had been tried, and had been found miserably wanting.

This was the first part of the prophetic historian's work. Up to 1 Sam. vii. 14, the life and work of Samuel, the pupil of Eli, was his theme. Here a new period in the story of Israel begins. The king—the creation of Samuel—from henceforth fills the central position: on him now all eyes are turned. The judge of Israel—Samuel—with dignified composure quits the office he had so well filled, and makes room for the leader of the new Israel. In this place (chap. vii. 14—17) the historian summarily condenses all that had still to be said about Samuel, and in the succeeding chapters the great judge only fills the subordinate, but still important, position which he may be said to have created—that of chief of the prophetic order.

3. THE DAYS OF SAUL.—The writer of our book now brings a new figure—King Saul—on the stage of his history; round this personage, for some seven chapters, the whole interest centres. Already a considerable change in the state of Israel has been effected during the quarter of a century of Samuel's work and influence. The people had been able to stem the tide of invasion during that period; they had more than held their own. A feeling of national unity had once more been created, and the tribes agreed to acknowledge the object of their loved prophet's choice as their king; and now, in the first records of the new state of things under a king, we see the result of Samuel's toil in the spirit of energy with which the people seconded the efforts of Saul to free the land from the enemy. The chronicle of the years that followed is the chronicle principally of wars—successful wars, on the whole. Israel is depicted as slowly rising into a new independent position. One by one the great predatory tribes of the border lands, crushed and defeated, are driven back into their native deserts; the old nations of Canaan, who had begun in good earnest during the troublous times of the judges to assert anew their independence, fell again into servitude; while the most dangerous of all—the warlike Philistines—had to contend no longer for supremacy, but for very existence. Under the first king the military education of the people was completed. It has been in almost all ages customary to condemn the royal hero who led Israel with such consummate skill and splendid valour during the restless years of those wars, necessary for the existence of Israel as a distinct people; but this is by no means the spirit of the writer of the book. He represents Saul as a great hero, better fitted than any of his contemporaries for the royal dignity—represents him as possessing warlike courage and skill, indomitable energy to push his conquests in all directions, a sense of honour ever watchful for the welfare of his people against their many and powerful foes, zeal and tenacity in carrying out his plans. He reiterates that, under his successful generalship, a really heroic school of great warriors arose—the warriors who later formed and led the great conquering armies of David and Solomon; he dwells on his power of attracting noble souls to himself; and with loving pen he lingers on that infinite charm which the name "anointed of Jehovah" carried with it in all succeeding centuries, and shows us how this strange and mighty kingly influence was first inspired by King Saul. The writer closes the "Saul" division in chap. xiv. 47—52, where, as before, in the case of Samuel (chap. vii. 14—17), so now here, in the case of King Saul, he brings together everything that remains to be said in general about the first king—his prowess, his wars, even his family and private matters. From this point forward another—David—is chosen as the true central figure of the national history, round which all interest henceforth gathers. And here a tinge of sadness characterises the great national epic, for Saul, in spite of his great and heroic qualities, fell short of his true destiny; in spite of his skill and valour, he failed to satisfy the invisible Guardian of Israel. It is hard at this distance of time to trace the real causes which led to the fall, and to the final rejection of his house. He seems, however, to have sickened with that strange sickness which so often among men is the result of supreme power: the sickness of despotism—that terrible malady which has marred so many noble souls. Saul forgot altogether the Glorious Arm which originally lifted him up, and set him on his throne, and then fought for him, and strengthened him in all his ways. He ceased to hold communion with the Spirit of the Eternal God, and so the Spirit left him. The writer then begins the fourth division of his history, in which the central figure is no longer Saul, but the new choice of the Lord—the brave shepherd-boy, the loving friend of Saul and his noble son Jonathan, the gallant chief, the king of the future—David, the son of Jesse.* Throughout the remaining portion of our book (1 Samuel),† the gradual *ascent* of David, through conflict and suffering, to the throne, along with the slow heartrending *descent* of Saul, till his sorrowful death in battle, is the writer's theme.

4. THE DAYS OF DAVID.—In this First Book of Samuel we have only the memoirs of some of the early days of the mighty king, the days of his hard and painful trials; but it was in these times that the foundation stories of that character, loved of God, were laid. It was in the long wanderings with the ever-increasing band of his devoted men, who followed him in his exile, that he first showed that firm and unshaken trust in the Lord, who had chosen him out of the sheepfolds to be His servant—that simple, pure striving never to be untrue to Him—those longing efforts to return to Him after error and transgression—the trust, the striving, and the efforts, which were the mainsprings of that chequered, but still glorious, golden-hued life. We see, too, in the prophet-scribe's selection of passages out of the first period of David's career (in the First Book of Samuel), how deep and true was the enthusiasm which the young chieftain kindled in all those Jewish heroes who—driven from Saul's court by Saul's fatal mistakes—rallied round the hero, the friend, and pupil of Samuel. With rare power, by a few master-touches in the simple narrative, the scribe-writer shows us how the name of David became dearer and ever dearer to the people; and although the last chapter of our book ends with the account of the great military disaster which closed the reign of Saul, the reader feels no

---

* Dr. Erdmann in *Lange, Comm.: Introduction to the Book of Samuel*, Section IV.
† Ewald. *History of Israel*, Book III.—B. David, I.

I. SAMUEL.

apprehension any longer for the fate of the chosen people, knowing that David was ready to step into the breach, conscious that to such a hero-king—strong in the devoted love of the nation—a splendid future indeed lay before Israel. That future is painted in the Second Book of Samuel, which describes at length the splendour and glory of the reign of David, the man after God's own heart.

In this inspired chronicle of our book the youth of Israel, in the days of the kings, would find an answer to the question, "What changed their nation from 'the loose aggregate of Bedouin tribes' of the days of Eli into the mighty, world-famed Israel of the magnificent Solomon?" It was a noble story, and one well fitted to inspire a new, bright confidence in the mighty arm of Jehovah.

II. The Original Sources of the Book.

—Two well-known passages in the Book of Chronicles— referred to below—inform us of certain original writings which issued most probably from the prophetic schools founded by Samuel. These writings, or memoirs, without doubt, form the basis of the two Books of Samuel.

To these written records we must add a mass of well-authenticated oral traditions, which — assuming the Books of Samuel were written, as we suppose, in the reign of King Rehoboam, or even a little later, in the reign of Jehoshaphat—must have been well known to the prophetic scribes. We read also in 1 Chron. xxvii. 24 of an historical work relating to the government of David, entitled, "The Chronicles of King David" (Diaries or Annals of King David).* We may safely infer that all the principal events of his reign were included in these chronicles. These annals—probably of a statistical, historical character, since the reference to them occurs in the midst of lists of state and military officials—were, no doubt, also in the possession of the writer of the Books of Samuel.

In 1 Chron. xxix. 29 the following statement concerning contemporary literature occurs: "Now the acts of David the king, behold they are written in the acts of Samuel the seer (the *Roëh*), and in the acts of Nathan the prophet (the *Nabi*), and in the acts of Gad the seer (the *Chozeh*)." We conclude then that for the narrative of Eli's times, for the details respecting himself, for much of Saul's story, for many of the events related (in the First Book of Samuel) of David's early career— the principal written authority was the Books of the Acts of Samuel the Seer (*Roëh*). The acts of Gad the seer (*Chozeh*) were, there is little doubt, the foundation of a large portion of the narrative of the desert wanderings of David. Nathan the prophet (*Nabi*) supplies materials for the life and work of David in the so-called Second Book of Samuel. Each of the prophets, it is evident, recorded the events of his own times. But besides these written contemporary memoirs, and the well-authenticated oral traditions which were current in his time, the prophet-writer has incorporated in his history certain songs and verses of songs from poems, such as the "Song of Hannah," "the folk-song respecting the victories of Saul," and the still more glorious deeds of David; and notably, in the second book, "the elegy of David on Saul and Jonathan," taken directly from the Book of the Upright (*Yashar*); he has also made use of certain psalms and songs composed by David.

Guided by the "Spirit of the Lord," the unknown son of the prophets in his college home—possibly in the Naioth of Ramah—out of these materials made his selection, and wrote down, for the teaching of the Israel of his own time and—unconsciously, no doubt, as far as he was concerned—for the instruction of a long series of generations yet unborn, the strange story of the rise of his people to grandeur and to power.

1. DATE OF WRITING.—In the first section of this Introduction the probable date has been assumed to be the reign of King Rehoboam, the son of Solomon (see too the Note on p. 1). There are a few notes of time in the two Books of Samuel, which were most probably written or compiled by one hand—for instance, the statement, "Ziklag pertaineth unto the kings of Judah unto this day" (1 Sam. xxvii. 6), plainly tells us the separation of Israel had already taken place; in the six stories respecting some of the principal heroes of David's army, at the end of the Second Book (chap. xxiii. 8—39), the compiler is evidently uncertain as to their proper place in the life of David: thus a considerable time must have elapsed before the tradition of the *exact* period when these events happened could have died out. The chronology, too, of Saul's reign is also indefinite. All this points to a date for the composition some time *after* David's death. But, on the other hand, the language is pure, and virtually free from Chaldaisms and later forms of Hebrew, being in this respect different from the Books of Kings, where the Hebrew used belonged evidently to a later date. There are absolutely no hints as to the subsequent disasters of the people and the exile. Thenius, Keil, and Erdmann place the composition in the times of Rehoboam; Dean Payne Smith, a little later, probably in the days of King Jehoshaphat. On the whole, it seems most probable that in the latter days of King Rehoboam our book was compiled in its present form.

2. CHARACTER OF THE BOOK.—It is more than a mere historic record of the fortunes of Israel during the momentous period of their rapid rise from semi-barbarism to a state of comparatively high civilisation— more than a brilliant and vivid biography of certain of the most gifted and famous of the children of Israel: Eli, Samuel, David, and Saul. Careful students of the book have particularly noticed *its deep religious spirit*, in which respect it is said to take* the highest rank among the historical books of the Old Testament. Samuel—by far the most prominent figure—is throughout the instrument of the Divine working; Saul the king is anointed by Divine command, and prospers with his doings only so long as "the Spirit of the Lord" remains with him; the instant that "Spirit," whose blessed influence was quenched by Saul's self-will and reliance, departs, success departs too from Saul's armies, and peace and prosperity from his house. From the sad moment of the separation from the king of the Spirit of the Lord, the course of the royal life is downwards. No gallantry or determination can avert the catastrophe, and the life of the disobedient "anointed of the Lord" closes in clouds and thick darkness.

His divinely appointed successor, in his first great deed of arms, and in his subsequent military successes is ever assisted to victory by the "glorious arm" of the Lord; by the same protection he is preserved through numberless persecutions and deadly perils, and is led higher and higher by the same Almighty Hand, till,

---

* Keil, *Introduction to the Books of Samuel*.

* Dr. Erdmann, in *Lange, Comm.: Introduction*, Section IV.

I. SAMUEL.

without crime or plotting, he mounts his fallen predecessor's throne.

Throughout the book, the work and power of a new order or class in Israel is dwelt on with peculiar insistence. The first notice of this "order of prophets"—which was the name by which those enrolled in its ranks were known—is made in the compilation now under our consideration. And that great servant of the Lord, Samuel, who was the mainspring of all the mighty changes wrought at this period among the people, was undoubtedly the founder of the famous "order." From the period of the death of Eli, related in the early chapters of this book, for more than 800 years, during all the changing fortunes of the people, the prophetic order continued an enduring public power. It acted as the mediating agency between God and His people, and was the organ of the Spirit of the Lord to the children of Israel during the whole period of the monarchy and the captivity. After the sorrowful return from Babylon, the priesthood—which from the days of Eli onward had continued to exist, though shorn of its old splendour and influence—seems to have recovered some of its ancient power and consideration, and during the last melancholy age of the existence of Israel as a people once more filled the chief position in the nation.

Throughout the Book of Samuel the influence of the new order of prophets is depicted as ever growing. Samuel, the prophet and seer, chooses the first king, and during Saul's period of loyalty to God stands by him as friend and counsellor. The successor to the faithless Saul is selected and anointed again by the prophet Samuel, and the young "anointed of the Lord," David, receives his training and education evidently in Samuel's prophetic school. All the days of Samuel's life, the seer remained David's counsellor and friend. When Samuel had passed away, another of the order, Gad the seer, trained by Samuel, took his place by David's side; and later we see the prophet Nathan occupying the same position when David had become a mighty monarch. Here and there, too, in our book, we come upon casual references to the growing influence of the prophetic order; and it was, be it remembered, the spirit of the first chief of the prophets that King Saul, in his dire necessity, invoked as the only Being who could give him real help or true advice. The documents referred to above (Section II.) as the main sources of the writing were mostly, if not entirely, the work of distinguished and well-known members of the great prophetic schools; and we may, therefore, with some certainty conclude that * this Book of Samuel—at least, the greater part—was taken from a tradition of which the centre and starting-point was in the mighty and influential prophetic order.

---

* Erdmann, *Introduction to Samuel*, Section IV.

III. **Messianic Teaching.** — In the Book of Samuel there is little which *directly* touches upon Messianic hopes, although the history is frequently quoted in the New Testament, especially in the writings of St. Paul and St. Luke.

Two fine passages, written by contemporary theologians of our own Church of England, sum up the Messianic teaching of our book.

"It is the first book in Holy Scripture which declares the incarnation of Christ as King in a particular family—the family of David. It is the first book in Scripture which announced that the kingdom founded in Him, raised up from the seed of David, would be universal and everlasting. Here also the prophetic song of Hannah gives the clue to the interpretation of this history. 'The Lord,' she says, 'shall judge the *ends of the earth*,' that is, His kingdom shall be established in *all nations*. 'He shall give strength unto His *King*, and exalt the horn of His *Anointed*'—the Messiah, or Christ, who was come of David—and sit on His throne for ever."—*Bishop Wordsworth.*

"It was thus Samuel's lot to sketch out two of the main lines of thought which converge in Christ. The idea of the prophet and the idea of the king gain under him their shape and proportion. This is especially true as regards the latter. The king is ever in Samuel's eyes 'the Messiah,' Jehovah's Anointed One. Again and again the word occurs with marked prominence. It was the pregnant germ of a great future with the Jew. He never lost the idea, but carried it onward and onward, with David's portrait for its centre, as of one in whom Messiah's lineaments were marked in outline—feebly indeed, and imperfectly, but with the certainty that a Messiah would come who would fill up with glorious beauty that faint, blurred sketch."—*Dean Payne Smith.*

IV. **The Name.**—Abarbanel writes—"All the contents of both books may, in a certain sense, be referred to Samuel: even the deeds of Saul and David, because both, having been anointed by Samuel, were, so to speak, the works of his hands." In other words, the writing is called after Samuel not because he wrote it all, but on account of it describing his great work for the chosen people. The two Books of Samuel really form one book. In Hebrew MSS. they form one undivided work, and are called "the Book of Samuel." The present division in the Hebrew Bible into two books under the same name dates only from the sixteenth century, and was introduced by Daniel Bomberg, after the example of the LXX. and Vulg. Versions.

In the LXX. and Vulg., however, these books are reckoned as belonging to the Book of the Kings. In the LXX. they are called "the Book of the Kingdoms."

THE FIRST BOOK OF SAMUEL

OTHERWISE CALLED

THE FIRST BOOK OF THE KINGS

CHAPTER I.—⁽¹⁾ Now there was a certain man of Ramathaim-zophim, of mount Ephraim, and his name was Elkanah, the son of Jeroham, the son of Elihu, the son of Tohu, the son of Zuph, an Ephrathite: ⁽²⁾ and he had two wives; the name of the one was Hannah, and the name of the other Peninnah: and Peninnah had children, but Hannah had no children.

⁽³⁾ And this man went up out of his city ^{a 1} yearly to worship and to sacrifice

B.C. cir. 1171.
a Deut. 16. 16.
1 Heb., from year to year.

(1—8) The Home Life of the Family of the future Prophet-judge of Israel. (9—28) Interview of Hannah with Eli—Birth and Dedication of Samuel.

Somewhere about the year 1140 B.C. (or, as some suppose, thirty years earlier), the Levitical family of Elkanah, of the house of Kohath, lived in Ramathaim-zophim, a little city of Benjamin, built on the slopes of Mount Ephraim. The supposed date of the Trojan War coincides with this period of Jewish history. We may then fairly assume that the events related in the Homeric epic took place during the time treated of in these Books of Samuel.

⁽¹⁾ **Now there was a certain man.**—Literally, *And there was, &c.* These introductory words do not signify that this history is the continuation of the Book of Judges or of any preceding writing. It is a common historical introductory formula. We find it at the commencement of Joshua, Judges, Ruth, 1 Kings, Esther, Ezra, Ezekiel, &c. The circumstances under which this record was probably compiled are discussed elsewhere.

Of Ramathaim-zophim.—The name Ramathaim —literally, *The Two Ramahs*—is the dual of the well-known Ramah, the appellation by which this city is usually known. The old city was, no doubt, built on two hills, which looked one on the other: hence perhaps the name Zophim, *the watchers.* Possibly at an early date watch-towers or outlooks, to enable the citizens to guard against surprise, were built on the summit of these hills. Either of these suppositions would account for the suggestive name by which Ramah was once known, the "Ramahs of the Watchers."

Others would connect the appellation "Zophim" with the family of Zuph, from whom Elkanah descended. (See 1 Chron. xxvi. 35, and 1 Sam. ix. 5, where the land of Zuph is mentioned.) An interesting, though fanciful, derivation refers Zophim, *watchers*, to the "prophet-watchmen" of the house of Israel, as Ramah in after years was a school of the prophets.

On the whole, the simplest and least strained explanation is the one given above, which refers the name to the hills so placed that they watched one another, or better still, to the watch-towers built at an early date on the two summits.

Ramah lay among the mountains of Ephraim, which extended into the territory of Benjamin, in which tribe the city of Ramah lay.

His name was Elkanah.—Elkanah, the father of the future prophet-judge, was a Levite of the family of Kohath (compare the genealogy given here with 1 Chron. vi. 22). He is here termed an Ephrathite: that is, an Ephraimite, because, as far as his civil standing was concerned, he belonged to the tribe of Ephraim.

Some have found a difficulty in reconciling the Levitical descent of Samuel with his dedication to the Lord by his mother, supposing that in the case of a Levite this would be unnecessary; but the dedication of Samuel, it should be remembered, was a life-long one, whereas the Levitical service only began when the Levite was twenty-five years old; and even then the service was not continuous.

⁽²⁾ **And he had two wives.**—The primeval Divine ordination, we know, gave its sanction alone to monogamy. The first who seems to have violated God's original ordinance appears to have been Lamech, of the family of Cain (Gen. iv. 19). The practice apparently had become general throughout the East when the Mosaic Law was formulated. In this Divine code it is noticeable that while polygamy is accepted as a custom everywhere prevailing, it is never approved. The laws of Moses—as in the case of another universally accepted practice, slavery—simply seek to restrict and limit it by wise and humane regulations. The inspired writer in this narrative of the home life of Elkanah of " Ramah of the Watchers" quietly shows up the curse which almost invariably attended this miserable violation of the relations of the home life to which in the old Eden days the eternal law had given its sanction and blessing. The Old Testament Book contains many of these gently-worded but fire-tipped rebukes of sin and frailty—sins condoned and even approved by the voice of mankind.

Peninnah.—Hannah signifies grace or favour, and has ever been a favourite name among the women of the East. It was the name of the Punic Queen Dido's sister, Anna. The traditional mother of the Virgin Mary was named Anna. (See Luke ii. 36.) Peninnah is translated by some scholars "coral;" according to others it signifies "pearl." We have adopted the same name under the modern "Margaret."

⁽³⁾ **Went up out of his city yearly.**—The Hebrew expression rendered yearly, is found in Exodus

unto the LORD of hosts in Shiloh. And the two sons of Eli, Hophni and Phinehas, the priests of the LORD, *were* there. (4) And when the time was that Elkanah offered, he gave to Peninnah his wife, and to all her sons and her daughters, portions: (5) But unto Hannah he gave ¹a worthy portion; for he loved Hannah: but the LORD had shut up her womb. (6) And her adversary also ²provoked her sore, for to make her fret, because the LORD had shut up her womb. (7) And as he did so year by year, ³ ⁴when she went up to the house of the LORD, so

1 Or, *a double portion.*
2 Heb., *angered her.*
3 Or, *from the time that she, &c.*
4 Heb., *from her going up.*

---

xiii. 10, and there refers to the Feast of Unleavened Bread, the Passover. There is little doubt but that this great national festival is here referred to. It was the Passover that the whole family were accustomed to keep at the sanctuary of the Eternal. The writer places in strong contrast the piety and devotion which evidently still existed in the family life of many in Israel with the fearful disorders and crime which disfigured the priestly life in those days. There were not a few, doubtless, in Israel who, like Elkanah and his house, honoured the name of the Lord, while the recognised rulers and religious guides of the people, like the sons of Eli the high priest, too often lived in open and notorious sin.

Unto the Lord of hosts.—This is the first time in the Old Testament Book that we find the well-known appellation of the Eternal "Jehovah Sabaoth," Lord of hosts.

It is computed that this title of God occurs 260 times in the Old Testament, but it is not found in any of the books written or compiled before this time. In the New Testament it is only once used (see Jas. v. 4).

The glorious title, with which Isaiah, who uses it some sixty times, and Jeremiah some eighty times, have especially made us familiar, represented Jehovah, the Eternal One, as ruler over the heavenly hosts: that is, over the angels and the stars; the stars being conceived to be the dwelling-places of these deathless beings.

The idea of their invisible God-Friend being the sovereign Master of a host of those innumerable glorious beings usually known as angels, or messengers, was no strange one to Hebrew thought. For instance, already in the story of Jacob we find the patriarch calling the angels who appeared to him the "camp of God" (Gen. xxxii. 1, 2).

In the blessing of Moses in the magnificent description of the giving of the law on Sinai (Deut. xxxiii. 2), we read of "ten thousands of saints" (Kodesh). The glorious Angel who allowed Joshua to worship him under the towers of Jericho (Josh. v. 14) speaks of himself as "captain or prince of the host of the Lord." It is especially noteworthy that here in these Books of Samuel, which tell of the establishment of an earthly sovereignty over the tribes, this stately title of the real King in Israel, which afterwards became so general, first appears. It was the solemn protest of Samuel and his school against any eclipsing of the mighty but invisible sovereignty of the Eternal by the passing splendours and the outward pomp of an earthly monarchy set up over the people.

It told also the strange and the alien peoples that the God who loved Israel was, too, the star ruler, the Lord of the whole universe, visible and invisible.

In Shiloh.—That is, *rest*. This sacred city was situated in Ephraim. It became the sanctuary of Israel in the time of Joshua, who pitched the tent of the Tabernacle there. Shiloh, as the permanent seat of the Ark and the Tabernacle, was the religious centre of Israel during the whole period of the judges. On rare occasions the sacred tent, and all or part of the holy furniture, seems to have been temporarily moved to such places as Mizpah and Bethel, but its regular home was Shiloh. At the time of the birth of Samuel, and during his younger days, the high priest resided there, and the religious families of the people were in the habit of making an annual pilgrimage to this, the central sanctuary of the worship of Jehovah.

The priests of the Lord.—The mention of these two priests of the Lord by no means suggests that the ritual of the Tabernacle had become so meagre and deficient as only to require the services of two or three ministers: indeed, the contrary is signified by the description of one portion only of the ceremonies given in the next chapter. These two, Hophni and Phinehas, are here alluded to specially by name. First, on account of their rank and connection with the high priest Eli, to whose high dignity one of the brothers would probably succeed. Secondly, because these unhappy men figured in one of the great historical disasters of the people. Thirdly, the writer, out of many servants of the sanctuary, chose two prominent figures to illustrate the terrible state of corruption into which the priesthood had fallen. Bishop Wordsworth here draws a curious but suggestive lesson. "Although Hophni and Phinehas were among the priests, yet Elkanah and Hannah did not separate themselves from the service of the sanctuary when they ministered—a lesson against schism."

(5) **A worthy portion.**—Literally, *one portion for two persons*: *i.e.*, a double portion. It was an expression of his deep love for her. As Von Gerlach puts it, "Thou art as dear to me as if thou hadst borne me a child." Some scholars would translate the difficult Hebrew expression here by, "But to Hannah he gave a portion of anger or sadness," thus intensifying the natural sorrow of Hannah by representing her husband as unkind. The Vulgate, Luther, and Abarbanel favour this singular interpretation; but the one adopted by the English Version, and explained above, is in all respects grammatically and exegetically to be preferred.

(6) **And her adversary also provoked her sore.**—Jealousy, grief, anger, malice, the many bitter fruits of this way of living, so different to God's original appointment, here show themselves. The one sin of polygamy poisons the whole home life of the family, in all other respects apparently a quiet, God-fearing, orderly household.

(7) **And as he did so year by year.**—That is, Elkanah, on the occasion of every yearly visit to the national sanctuary, was in the habit of publicly giving the childless Hannah the double gift, to show his undiminished love; while the happier mother of his children, jealous of her rival, every year chose this solemn occasion of offering thank-offerings before the Tabernacle, especially to taunt the childless wife, no doubt referring the absence of children, which among the mothers of Israel was considered so deep a calamity, to the special anger of God.

she provoked her; therefore she wept, and did not eat. ⁽⁸⁾ Then said Elkanah her husband to her, Hannah, why weepest thou? and why eatest thou not? and why is thy heart grieved? *am* not I better to thee than ten sons?

⁽⁹⁾ So Hannah rose up after they had eaten in Shiloh, and after they had drunk. Now Eli the priest sat upon a seat by a post of the temple of the LORD. ⁽¹⁰⁾ And she *was* ¹in bitterness of soul, and prayed unto the LORD, and wept sore. ⁽¹¹⁾ And she vowed a vow, and said, O LORD of hosts, if thou wilt indeed look on the affliction of thine handmaid, and remember me, and not forget thine handmaid, but wilt give unto thine handmaid ²a man child, then I will give him unto the LORD all the days of his life, and ᵃthere shall no razor come upon his head.

⁽¹²⁾ And it came to pass, as she ³continued praying before the LORD, that Eli marked her mouth. ⁽¹³⁾ Now Hannah, she spake in her heart; only her lips moved, but her voice was not heard: therefore Eli thought she had been drunken. ⁽¹⁴⁾ And Eli said unto her, How long wilt thou be drunken? put away thy wine from thee. ⁽¹⁵⁾ And Hannah answered and said, No, my lord; I *am* a woman ⁴of a sorrowful spirit: I have drunk neither wine nor strong drink, but have poured out my soul be-

¹ Heb., *bitter of soul.*
² Heb., *seed of men.*
ᵃ Num. 6. 5; Judg. 13. 5.
³ Heb., *multiplied to pray.*
⁴ Heb., *hard of spirit.*

⁽⁸⁾ **Than ten sons.**—Merely a round number to express many. The simple narration evidently came from Hannah, who, no doubt, in after years loved to dwell on her past sorrowful life, contrasted with her present strange blessedness as mother of the Restorer of the people.

⁽⁹⁾ **After they had eaten in Shiloh, and after they had drunk.**—This was the solemn sacrificial meal, at which the whole family were present.

Now Eli the priest sat upon a seat.—Eli, the high priest of Israel at this time, was a descendant of Ithamar, the younger son of Aaron (see 1 Chron. xxiv. 3, where it is stated that his great-grandson, Ahimelech, was of the sons of Ithamar). The circumstances which led to the transfer of the dignity from the line of Eleazar, who succeeded his father Aaron in the office, are unknown. It has been suggested that at the death of the last high priest of the line of Eleazar, Ozi, there was no son of sufficient age and experience to succeed, and so the office passed to the next of kin, Eli, a son of the house of Ithamar. (See Josephus, *Antt.* v., 2, § 5.)

The seat upon which Eli is represented as usually sitting (see chap. iv. 18) was evidently a chair or throne of state, where the high-priestly judge sat at certain times to administer justice and to transact business. The Hebrew word rendered here "post," and the expression "doors of the house" (chap. iii. 15), seem to suggest that now a permanent home had been erected for the sanctuary: something of a building, possibly of stone, surrounding the Tabernacle had been built.

The "temple of the Lord," rather, *palace of the Lord*, so called not from any external magnificence but as being the earthly place where at times the visible glory of the Eternal King of Israel, the Shekinah, was pleased to manifest itself.

⁽¹¹⁾ **And she vowed a vow.**—The vow of Hannah contained two solemn promises—the one pledged the son she prayed for to the service of the Eternal all the days of his life. The mother looked on to a life-long service in the ritual of the Tabernacle for him, but the Being who heard her prayer destined her son for higher work; in his case the priestly duties were soon merged in the far more responsible ones of the prophet—the great reformer of the people. The second promise undertook that he should be a Nazarite. Now the Nazariteship included three things—the refraining from intoxicating drinks, the letting the hair grow, and the avoiding all ceremonial defilement by corpses even of the nearest kin. Samuel was what the Talmud calls a perpetual Nazarite.

These strange restrictions and customs had an inner signification. The abstinence from wine and strong drink typified that the Nazarite determined to avoid all sensual indulgence which might cloud the mind and render the man unfit for prayer to, and work for, the Lord; the avoiding contact with the dead was a perpetual outward protest that the vower of the solemn vow renounced all moral defilement, that he gave up every thing which could stain and soil the life consecrated to the Eternal's service; the untouched hair, which here is especially mentioned, was a public protest that the consecrated one had determined to refrain from intercourse with the world, and to devote the whole strength and fulness of life to the Lord's work. The LXX. (Greek) Version here inserts the words, "and he shall drink neither wine nor strong drink," wishing to bring the passage into stricter accordance with Numbers vi. The original Hebrew text, however, contents itself with specifying merely the outward sign of the untouched hair, by which these solemnly consecrated ones were publicly known.

⁽¹³⁾ **Now Hannah, she spake in her heart.**—Eli was watching the worshippers, and, as Bunsen well remarks, was struck with dismay at her silent earnestness, such heartfelt prayer being apparently not usual at that time, and remembering the condition of the moral life in the precincts of the sanctuary over which he ruled with so weak and vacillating a rule, and how sadly frequent were disorders at the sacrificial meal, at once suspected that the weeping, praying one was a drunken woman. He, however, quickly atoned for his unworthy suspicion.

⁽¹⁴⁾ **And Eli said unto her.**—The LXX. or Septuagint attempts to soften the harshness of the high priest to Hannah by inserting before Eli the word "servant," or "young man," thus suggesting that the hard, unjust words were spoken by an attendant. But it is clear that the English Version represents the true text here, for in the next verse Hannah replies directly to Eli with the simple words "No, my lord."

⁽¹⁵⁾ **No, my lord, I am a woman of a sorrowful spirit . . .**—Calvin, quoted by Erdmann, well remarks here:—"Consider the modesty of Hannah, who,

Birth and Dedication   I. SAMUEL, I.   of Samuel.

fore the LORD. (16) Count not thine handmaid for a daughter of Belial: for out of the abundance of my ¹complaint and grief have I spoken hitherto. (17) Then Eli answered and said, Go in peace: and the God of Israel grant *thee* thy petition that thou hast asked of him. (18) And she said, Let thine handmaid find grace in thy sight. So the woman went her way, and did eat, and her countenance was no more *sad*.

(19) And they rose up in the morning early, and worshipped before the LORD, and returned, and came to their house to Ramah: and Elkanah knew Hannah his wife; and the LORD remembered her. (20) Wherefore it came to pass, when ²the time was come about after Hannah had conceived, that she bare a son, and called his name ³Samuel, *saying*, Because I have asked him of the LORD.

(21) And the man Elkanah, and all his house, went up to offer unto the LORD the yearly sacrifice, and his vow. (22) But Hannah went not up; for she said unto her husband, *I will not go up* until the child be weaned, and *then* I will bring him, that he may appear before the LORD, and there abide for ever. (23) And Elkanah her husband said unto her, Do what seemeth thee good; tarry until thou have weaned him; only the LORD establish his word. So the woman abode, and gave her son suck until she weaned him.

(24) And when she had weaned him, she took him up with her, with three bullocks, and one ephah of flour, and

1 Or, *meditation*.

2 Heb., *revolution of days*.

3 That is, *Asked of God*.

B.C. cir. 1165

---

though she had received injury from the high priest, yet answers with reverence and humility."

On these words of Hannah the Talmud says:—" Some think that Hannah spake in the following sense. Thou art neither lord, nor does the Holy Spirit rest upon thee, because thou dost suspect me in this matter, and hast formed such an uncharitable opinion of me. Neither the Shekinah nor the Holy Spirit are with thee."—Treatise *Berachoth*, fol. 31, col. 2.

(17) **The God of Israel grant thee thy petition.**—The character of Eli is a deeply interesting one. Weak and over-indulgent to his headstrong, wicked sons, probably too self-indulgent, and a lover of ease, yet in the brief record we possess we catch sight of not a few noble thoughts and wishes: flashes of true nobility, real generosity and self-forgetfulness, of intense, devoted patriotism, light up a life which closed in failure and disaster. Here the old man is quick to see that he had been insulting a blameless woman, so at once he retracts his cruel accusation, and silently accuses himself of precipitancy and injustice in his graceful, courteous words of farewell; adding too his fatherly wish, he almost promises that what she wished so ardently should be hers.

(18) **Let thine handmaid find grace.**—In other words, Hannah's reply to his loving farewell asked the old man to think kindly of her, and to pray for her with his mighty power of prayer.

Did eat, and her countenance was no more sad.—A beautiful example of the composing influence of prayer. "Hannah had cast her burden upon the Lord, and so her own spirit was relieved of its load. She now returned to the family feast, and ate her portion with a cheerful heart."—*Speaker's Commentary.*

(19) **And they rose up.**—Another notice of the pious customs of the house of Elkanah. This is a striking picture of one of the many holy homes in Israel, even in the wild, disorderly days of the Judges, and of the deep degradation of the priests of the sanctuary.

"The house at Ramah," the usual short name by which the city, "The Ramahs of the Watchers," *Ramathaim-zophim*, was known.

(20) **And called his name Samuel.**—The words translated " because I have asked him of the Lord," do not explain the meaning of the name "Samuel;" they simply give the reason for his mother so calling him. The name Sh'muel (Samuel) is formed from the Hebrew words *Sh'mua El* (*a Deo exauditus*), "heard of God."

(21) **And his vow.**—Elkanah too had vowed a vow unto the Lord, in case his wife Hannah should have a son. It has been remarked that vows are characteristic of that particular age of the Judges; for instance, we have detailed accounts of Samson and Jephthah's vows, the oath in the Benjamite vow, &c.

(22) **Until the child be weaned.**—Weaning, we know, took place very late among the Hebrews. From 2 Macc. vii. 27, it appears that Hebrew mothers were in the habit of suckling their children for three years. The mother proposed, when the weaning had taken place, to leave her son as a servant of the sanctuary, there to remain all his life.

On the late period of weaning among the Oriental nations, Kalisch refers to the Persian custom of suckling boys two years and two months, and girls two years.

(23) **Only the Lord establish his word.**—No special word or promise of the Eternal in the case of the infant Samuel is recorded in this history; but there was an ancient Rabbinical tradition that a direct revelation respecting the future destiny of Samuel was made. " The Bath-kol (Daughter of the Voice) went forth, saying, There shall arise a just one, whose name shall be Samuel. Then every mother who bore a son called him Samuel; but when they saw his actions, they said, This is not Samuel. But when this one was born, they said, This is that Samuel, and this is what the Scripture means when it says, 'The Lord confirmed his word that Samuel may be that just one.'"—*Rashi.*

If we decline to accept the Rabbinical tradition, Bunsen's simple comment will explain the difficult words of the text, "establish his word": that is, may the Lord fulfil what He designs with him, and has promised by his birth.

(24, 25) **With three bullocks . . . And they slew a bullock.**—There at first sight seems a discrepancy here, and the LXX. translators seem to have felt it, for they read, instead of " three bullocks,"

Hannah's Offering.   I. SAMUEL, II.   *Her Song of Joy.*

a bottle of wine, and brought him unto the house of the LORD in Shiloh: and the child *was* young. ⁽²⁵⁾ And they slew a bullock, and brought the child to Eli. ⁽²⁶⁾ And she said, Oh my lord, *as* thy soul liveth, my lord, I *am* the woman that stood by thee here, praying unto the LORD. ⁽²⁷⁾ For this child I prayed; and the LORD hath given me my petition which I asked of him: ⁽²⁸⁾ therefore also I have ¹lent him to the LORD; as long as he liveth ²he shall be lent to the LORD. And he worshipped the LORD there.

CHAPTER II. — ⁽¹⁾ And Hannah prayed, and said, My heart rejoiceth in the LORD, mine horn is exalted in the LORD: my mouth is enlarged over mine enemies; because I rejoice in thy salvation. ⁽²⁾ *There is* none holy as the LORD: for *there is* none beside thee: neither *is there* any rock like our God. ⁽³⁾ Talk no more so exceeding proudly; let *not* ³ar-

Marginal notes:
1 Or, *returned him, whom I have obtained by petition, to the LORD.*
2 Or, *he whom I have obtained by petition shall be returned.*
3 Heb., *hard.*

"a bullock of three years old." The true explanation, however, is that the one bullock alluded to in verse 25 was the burnt offering by which the child was consecrated to the Lord. The other two were the yearly festival offering, the presentation of which being the usual gift, the chronicler did not think it here worth while to mention again.

⁽²⁶⁾ **O my lord, as thy soul liveth.** — "This oath is peculiar to the Books of Samuel, in which it occurs six times, and to the Books of Kings, in which, however, it is found only once. The similar oath, *as Pharaoh liveth* (by the life of Pharaoh), occurs in Gen. xlii. 15; and *as the Lord liveth* is found almost exclusively in the books of which Judges is the first and 2 Kings the last, being especially frequent in the Books of Samuel. This accords with the fact of the age of the Judges and Saul being characteristically the age of vows."—*Speaker's Commentary.*

⁽²⁸⁾ **I have lent him to the Lord.**—The rendering of the Hebrew here, "I have lent," and in Exod. xii. 36, is false. The translation should run: "Therefore I also make him one asked of the Lord; all the days that he liveth he is asked of the Lord." The sense is: "The Lord gave him to me, and now I have returned him whom I obtained by prayer to the Lord, as one asked or demanded."

And he worshipped the Lord there.—"He," that is, the boy Samuel: thus putting his own child-seal to his mother's gift of himself to God.

II.

(1–10) The Song of Hannah.

⁽¹⁾ **And Hannah prayed, and said.**—"Prayed," not quite in the sense in which we generally understand prayer. Her prayer here asks for nothing; it is rather a song of thanksgiving for the past, a song which passes into expressions of sure confidence for the future. She had been an unhappy woman; her life had been, she thought, a failure; her dearest hopes had been baffled; vexed, tormented, utterly cast down, she had fled to the Rock of Israel for help, and in the eternal pity of the Divine Friend of her people she had found rest, and then joy; out of her own individual experience the Spirit of the Lord taught her to discern the general laws of the Divine economy; she had had personal experience of the gracious government of the kind, all-pitiful God; her own mercies were a pledge to her of the gracious way in which the nation itself was led by Jehovah—were a sign by which she discerned how the Eternal not only always delivered the individual sufferer who turned to Him, but would also at all times be ever ready to succour and deliver His people.

These true, beautiful thoughts the Spirit of the Lord first planted in Hannah's heart, and then gave her lips grace and power to utter them in the sublime language of her hymn, which became one of the loved songs of the people, and as such was handed down from father to son, from generation to generation, in Israel, in the very words which first fell from the blessed mother of the child-prophet in her quiet home of "Ramah of the Watchers."

My heart rejoiceth.—The first verse of four lines is the introduction to the Divine song. She would give utterance to her holy joy. Had she not received the blessing at last which all mothers in Israel so longed for?

Mine horn is exalted.—She does not mean by this, "I am proud," but "I am strong"—mighty now in the gift I have received from the Lord: glorious in the consciousness "I have a God-Friend who hears me." The image "horn" is taken from oxen and those animals whose strength lies in their horns. It is a favourite Hebrew symbol, and one that had become familiar to them from their long experience—dating from far-back patriarchal times—as a shepherd-people.

⁽²⁾ **Neither is there any rock.**—This was a favourite simile among the inspired song-writers of Israel. The image, doubtless, is a memory of the long desert wandering. The steep precipices and the strange fantastic rocks of Sinai, standing up in the midst of the shifting desert sands, supplied an ever present picture of unchangeableness, of majesty, and of security. The term rock, as applied to God, is first found in the Song of Moses (Deut. xxxii. 4, 15, 18, 30, 31, 37), where the juxtaposition of rock and salvation in verse 15—*he lightly esteemed the rock of his salvation*—seems to indicate that Hannah was acquainted with this song or national hymn of Moses. The same phrase is frequent in the Psalms.

That the term was commonly applied to God so early as the time of Moses we may conclude from the name Zurishaddai: "My rock is the Almighty" (Numb. i. 6); and Zuriel: "My rock is God" (Numb. iii. 35).—*Speaker's Commentary.*

⁽³⁾ **A God of knowledge.**—The Hebrew words are placed thus: *A God of knowledge is the Lord.* The Talmud quaintly comments here as follows:— Rabbi Ami says: "Knowledge is of great price, for it is placed between *two* Divine names; as it is written (1 Sam. ii. 3), 'A God of knowledge is the Lord,' and therefore mercy is to be denied to him who has no knowledge; for it is written (Isa. xxvii. 11), 'It is a people of no understanding, therefore He that made them will not have mercy on them.'"—Treatise *Berachoth*, fol. 33, col. 1.

rogancy come out of your mouth: for the LORD *is* a God of knowledge, and by him actions are weighed. ⁽⁴⁾ The bows of the mighty men *are* broken, and they that stumbled are girded with strength. ⁽⁵⁾ *They that were* full have hired out themselves for bread; and *they that were* hungry ceased: so that the barren hath born seven; and she that hath many children is waxed feeble. ⁽⁶⁾ ᵃThe LORD killeth, and maketh alive: he bringeth down to the grave, and bringeth up. ⁽⁷⁾ The LORD maketh poor, and maketh rich: he bringeth low, and lifteth up. ⁽⁸⁾ He ᵇraiseth up the poor out of the dust, *and* lifteth up the beggar from the dunghill, to set *them* among princes, and to make them inherit the throne of glory: for the pillars of the earth *are* the LORD's, and he hath set the world upon them. ⁽⁹⁾ He will keep the feet of his saints, and the wicked shall be silent in darkness; for by strength shall no man prevail. ⁽¹⁰⁾ The adversaries of the LORD shall be broken to pieces; ᶜout of heaven shall he thunder upon them:

ᵃ Deut. 32. 39; Tob. 13. 2; Wis. 16. 13.
ᵇ Ps. 113. 7.
ᶜ ch. 7. 10.

And by him actions are weighed.—This is one of the fifteen places reckoned by the Masorites where in the original Hebrew text, instead of "lo" with an aleph, signifying *not*, "lo" with a vaw, signifying *to*, or *by him*, must be substituted. The amended reading has been followed by the English Version. The meaning is that all men's actions are weighed by God according to their essential worth, all the motives which led to them are by Him, the All-knowing, taken into account before He weighs them.

⁽⁴⁾ **The bows of the mighty men are broken.**—God reverses human conditions, bringing low the wicked, and raising up the righteous.

Von Gerlach writes of these verses that "Every power which will be something in itself is destroyed by the Lord: every weakness which despairs of itself is transformed into power." "The bows of the heroes," that is to say, *the heroes of the bow*, the symbol of human power being poetically put first instead of the bearer of the symbol. The next line contains the antithesis: while the heroes rejoicing in their strength are shattered, the tottering, powerless ones are by Him made strong for battle.

⁽⁵⁾ **They that were full.**—Another image to illustrate the vicissitudes of human affairs is sketched, one very familiar to the dwellers among the cornfields and vineyards of Canaan.

The barren hath born seven.—Here the thought of the inspired singer reverts to herself, and the imagery is drawn from the story of her own life. Seven children are mentioned as the full number of the Divine blessing in children (see Ruth iv. 15; Jer. xv. 9). There is a curious Jewish legend which relates how for each boy child that was born to Hannah, two of Peninnah's died.

⁽⁶⁾ **The Lord killeth, and maketh alive.**—Death too and life come from this same omnipotent Lord: nothing in the affairs of men is the sport of blind chance. The reign of a Divine law administered by the God to whom Hannah prayed is universal, and guides with a strict unerring justice what are commonly called the ups and downs, the changes and chances, of this mortal life. The following lines of the 7th, 8th, and 9th verses enforce by varied instances the same solemn truth.

The Babylonian Talmud on these words has a curious and interesting tradition:—"Three classes appear on the day of judgment: the perfectly righteous, who are at once written and sealed for eternal life; the thoroughly bad, who are at once written and sealed for hell: as it is written (Dan. xii. 2), 'And many of them that sleep in the dust of the earth shall awake, some to everlasting life, and some to shame and everlasting contempt;' and those in the intermediate state, who go down into hell, where they cry and howl for a time, whence they ascend again: as it is written (Zech. xiii. 9), 'And I will bring the third part through the fire, and will refine them as silver is refined, and will try them as gold is tried; they shall call on my name, and I will hear them.' It is of them Hannah said (1 Sam. ii. 6), 'The Lord killeth, and maketh alive: he bringeth down to hell, and bringeth up.'"—Treatise *Rosh Hashanah*, fol. 16, col. 2.

⁽⁸⁾ **The pillars of the earth.**—And the gracious All-Ruler does these things, for He is at once Creator and Upholder of the universe. The words of these Divine songs which treat of cosmogony are such as would be understood in the childhood of peoples. The quiet thinker, however, is tempted to ask whether after 3,000 or 4,000 years, now, with the light of modern science shining round us, we have made much real progress in our knowledge of the genesis and government of the universe.

The pillars.—Or *columns*—Jerome, in the Vulgate, translates this unusual word by "hinges"—*cardines terræ.*

Gesenius prefers the rendering "foundations." On the whole, the word used in the English Version, "pillars," is the best.

⁽⁹⁾ **He will keep the feet.**—This was the comforting deduction Hannah drew from the circumstances of her life: this the grave moral reflection the Spirit of the Lord bade her put down for the support and solace of all true servants of the Eternal in coming ages. Seeing that Jehovah of Israel governs the world, the righteous have nothing really to fear; it is only the wicked and rebellious who have reason to be afraid. The Babylonian Talmud has the following comment on these words:—"If any man has passed the greater part of his years without sin, he will sin no more. If a man has been able to resist the same temptation once or twice, he will sin no more; for it is said (1 Sam. ii. 9), 'He will keep the feet of his saints.'"—Treatise *Yoma*, fol. 38, col. 2.

By strength shall no man prevail.—The same thought is expressed very grandly by the prophet, "Not by might, nor by power, but by my Spirit, saith the Lord of hosts" (Zech. iv. 6). The Holy Ghost, in one of the sublime visions of St. Paul, taught the suffering apostle the same great truth, "My grace is sufficient for thee: for my strength is made perfect in weakness" (2 Cor. xii. 9).

⁽¹⁰⁾ **His king . . . of his anointed.**—A

the LORD shall judge the ends of the earth; and he shall give strength unto his king, and exalt the horn of his anointed.

(11) And Elkanah went to Ramah to his house. And the child did minister unto the LORD before Eli the priest.

(12) Now the sons of Eli *were* sons of Belial; they knew not the LORD. (13) And the priest's custom with the people *was, that,* when any man offered sacrifice, the priest's servant came, while the flesh was in seething, with a fleshhook of three teeth in his hand; (14) and he struck *it* into the pan, or kettle, or caldron, or pot; all that the fleshhook brought up the priest took for himself. So they did in Shiloh unto all the Israelites that came thither. (15) Also before they burnt the fat, the priest's servant came, and said to the man that sacrificed, Give flesh to roast for the priest; for he will

---

Lapide, quoted by Wordsworth, wrote here, "*haec omnia spectant ad Christum*," "all these things have regard to Christ." Jewish expositors, too, have generally interpreted these words as a prophecy of King Messiah. The words received a partial fulfilment in the splendid reigns of David and Solomon; but the pious Jew looked on the golden halo which surrounded these great reigns as but a pale reflection of the glory which would accompany King Messiah when He should appear.

This is the first passage in the Old Testament which speaks of "His Anointed," or "His Messiah." The LXX. render the words "*Christou autou.*"

This song was soon evidently well known in Israel. The imagery, and in several passages the very words, are reproduced in the Psalms. See *Excursus* A and B at the end of this Book.

(11—26) The Service of the boy Samuel in the Sanctuary—The Dissolute Life of the Sons of Eli—The Doom of the House of Ithamar.

(11) **Elkanah went to Ramah.**—These simple words just sketch out what took place after Hannah left her boy in Shiloh. Elkanah went home, and the old family life, with its calm religious trustfulness, flowed on in the quiet town of "Ramah of the Watchers" as it did aforetime; the only disturbing sorrowful element was removed in answer to the mother's prayers, and little children grew up (verse 21) round Hannah and Elkanah. But the life of the dedicated child Samuel was a different one; he lived under the shadow of the sanctuary, *ministering* with his child powers before the altar of the Invisible, and trained, we may well assume, in all the traditions and learning of Israel by the old high priest. The word "minister" is the official term used to signify the duties performed by priests and Levites in connection with the service of God.

(12) **Sons of.**—The word Belial is printed here and chap. i. 16, as though Belial were the name of some pagan deity, but it simply signifies "worthlessness." It is a common term in these records of Samuel, being used some nine or ten times. It is rarely found in the other historical books. "Sons of Belial" signifies, then, merely "sons of worthlessness," worthless, good-for-nothing men. The *Speaker's Commentary* ingeniously accounts for the use of Belial in the English Version here, and in other places in the Old Testament, by referring to the contrast drawn by St. Paul between Christ and Belial, as if Belial were the name of an idol, or the personification of evil (2 Cor. vi. 15).

They knew not the Lord.—The whole conduct of these high priestly officials showed they were utter unbelievers. They used their sacred position merely as affording an opportunity for their selfish extortions; and, as is so often the case now, as it was then, their unbelief was the source of their moral worthlessness (see verse 22). "Hophni and Phinehas (the two sons of Eli) are, for students of ecclesiastical history, eminently suggestive characters. They are true exemplars of the grasping and worldly clergy of all ages.

"It was the sacrificial feasts that gave occasion for their rapacity. It was the dances and assemblies of the women in the vineyards and before the sacred feast that gave occasion for their debaucheries. They were the worst development of the lawlessness of the age, penetrating, as in the case of the wandering Levite of the Book of Judges, into the most sacred offices.

"But the coarseness of these vices does not make the moral less pointed for all times. The three-pronged fork which fishes up the seething flesh is the earliest type of grasping at pluralities and Church preferments by base means, the open profligacy at the door of the Tabernacle is the type of many a scandal brought on the Christian Church by the selfishness or sensuality of the ministers."—Dean Stanley, *On the Jewish Church,* Lecture xvii., Part I.

(13) **The priest's custom.**—That is to say, the custom or practice introduced under these robber-priests, who were not content with the modest share of the offerings assigned to them by the Law of Moses. (See Lev. vii. 31, 35; Deut. xviii. 3.)

(15) **Before they burnt the fat.**—This was a still graver offence against the ritual of the sacrifice. A contemptuous insult was here offered to the Lord. This fat was not to be eaten or taken by any one; it was God's portion, to be burnt by the priest on the altar (Lev. iii. 16, vii. 23, 25, 30, 31).

In all these strange rites and ceremonies there was a higher symbolism involved. This was ruthlessly set at nought and trampled on by these reckless, covetous guardians of the worship of Israel.

Portions of the sacrifice fell legally to the ministering priests in lieu of fee. It was fair "that they which ministered at the altar should live of the altar." The "heave leg" and the "wave breast" of the slaughtered victim were theirs by right, and these the sacrificing priest was to receive *after* the fat portion of the sacrifice had been burnt upon the altar. But to take the flesh of the victim, and roast it before the symbolic offering had been made, was a crime which was equivalent to robbing God. It dishonoured the whole ceremony.

He will not have sodden flesh.—The meaning of this is, these priests and their attendants insisted on having the best part of the sacrificed victim *raw,* not boiled—that is, fresh, full of juice and strength—before the offering had been made.

not have sodden flesh of thee, but raw. ⁽¹⁶⁾ And *if* any man said unto him, Let them not fail to burn the fat ¹presently, and *then* take *as much* as thy soul desireth; then he would answer him, *Nay; but* thou shalt give *it me* now: and if not, I will take *it* by force. ⁽¹⁷⁾ Wherefore the sin of the young men was very great before the LORD: for men abhorred the offering of the LORD.

⁽¹⁸⁾ But Samuel ministered before the LORD, *being* a child, ᵃgirded with a linen ephod. ⁽¹⁹⁾ Moreover his mother made him a little coat, and brought *it* to him from year to year, when she came up with her husband to offer the yearly sacrifice. ⁽²⁰⁾ And Eli blessed Elkanah and his wife, and said, The LORD give thee seed of this woman for the ²loan which is lent to the LORD. And they went unto their own home. ⁽²¹⁾ And the LORD visited Hannah, so that she conceived, and bare three sons and two daughters. And the child Samuel grew before the LORD.

⁽²²⁾ Now Eli was very old, and heard all that his sons did unto all Israel; and how they lay with the women that ³assembled *at* the door of the tabernacle of the congregation. ⁽²³⁾ And he said unto them, Why do ye such things? for ⁴I hear of your evil dealings by all

---

1 Heb., *as on the day.*

a Ex. 28. 4.

2 Or, *petition which she asked,* &c.

3 Heb., *assembled by troops.*

4 Or, *I hear evil words of you.*

⁽¹⁶⁾ **And if not, I will take it by force.**—The solemn ritual of the sacrifice was not only transgressed by these covetous, greedy, ministering priests, but the worshippers were compelled by force to yield to these new lawless customs, probably introduced by these sons of the high priest Eli.

⁽¹⁷⁾ **The sin of the young men was very great.** —*Grave peccatum sacerdotum ob scandalum datum laicis* ("the sin of the priests was a great one, because it put a stumbling-block in the way of the people").—A. Lapide, quoted by Wordsworth. Religion was being brought into general disrepute through the conduct of its leading ministers; was it likely that piety, justice, and purity would be honoured and loved in the land of Israel when the whole ritual of the sacrifices was openly scoffed at in the great sanctuary of the people by the chief priests of their faith?

⁽¹⁸⁾ **Ministered . . . being a child.**—A striking contrast is intended to be drawn here between the covetous, self-seeking ministrations of the worldly priests and the quiet service of the boy devoted by his pious mother and father to the sanctuary service.

Girded with a linen ephod.—The ephod was a priestly dress, which Samuel received in very early youth, because he had, with the high priest's formal sanction, been set apart for a life-long service before the Lord. This ephod was an official garment, and consisted of two pieces, which rested on the shoulders in front and behind, and were joined at the top, and fastened about the body with a girdle.

⁽¹⁹⁾ **A little coat.**—The "little coat"—Hebrew, *m'il*—was, no doubt, closely resembling in shape the *m'il,* or robe worn apparently by the high priest, only the little *m'il* of Samuel was without the costly symbolical ornaments attached to the high priestly robe.

This strange, unusual dress was, no doubt, arranged for the boy by his protector and guardian, Eli, who looked on the child as destined for some great work in connection with the life of the chosen people. Not improbably the old man, too, well aware of the character of his own sons, hoped to train up the favoured child —whose connection with himself and the sanctuary had begun in so remarkable a manner—as his successor in the chief sacred and civil office in Israel.

⁽²⁰,²¹⁾ **And Eli blessed Elkanah and his wife . . . And the Lord visited Hannah.**— The blessing of Eli, a blessing which soon bore its fruit in the house of the pious couple,—his training of Samuel, and unswerving kindness to the boy (see following chapter),—his sorrow at his priestly sons' wickedness,—his passionate love for his country, all indicate that the influence of the weak but loving high priest was ever exerted to keep the faith of the people pure, and the life of Israel white before the Lord. There were evidently two parties at Shiloh, the head-quarters of the national religion: the reckless, unbelieving section, headed by Hophni and Phinehas; and the God-fearing, law-loving partisans of the old Divine law, under the influence of the weak, but religious, Eli. These latter kept the lamp of the loved faith burning—though but dimly—among the covenant people until the days when the strong hand of Samuel took the helm of government in Israel.

⁽²²⁾ **Now Eli was very old.**—The compiler of these Books of Samuel was evidently wishful to speak as kindly as possible of Eli. He had, no doubt, deserved well of Israel in past days; and though it was clear that through his weak indulgence for his wicked sons, and his own lack of energy and foresight, he had brought discredit on the national sanctuary, and, in the end, defeat and shame on the people, yet the compiler evidently loved to dwell on the brightest side of the old high priest's character—his piety, his generous love for Samuel, his patriotism, &c.; and here, where the shameful conduct of Hophni and Phinehas is dwelt on, an excuse is made for their father, Eli. "He was," says the writer, "very old."

The women that assembled.—These women were evidently in some way connected with the service of the Tabernacle; possibly they assisted in the liturgical portion of the sanctuary worship. (Compare Ps. lxviii. 11: "The Lord gave the word, great was the company of female singers.") Here, as *so* often in the world's story, immorality follows on unbelief.

In Ps. lxxviii. 60—64, the punishment of the guilty priests and the forsaking of the defiled sanctuary is recorded. The psalmist Asaph relates how, in His anger at the people's sin, God greatly abhorred Israel, so that He "forsook the Tabernacle at Shiloh—even the tent that He had pitched among men. He delivered their power into captivity, and their beauty into the enemy's hand. The fire consumed their young men, and their maidens were not given to marriage. Their priests were slain with the sword, and there were no widows to make lamentation."

this people. (24) Nay, my sons; for *it is* no good report that I hear; ye make the LORD's people ¹to transgress. (25) If one man sin against another, the judge shall judge him: but if a man sin against the LORD, who shall intreat for him? Notwithstanding they hearkened not unto the voice of their father, because the LORD would slay them.

(26) And the child Samuel grew on, and was in favour both with the LORD, and also with men.

(27) And there came a man of God unto Eli, and said unto him, Thus saith the LORD, Did I plainly appear unto the house of thy father, when they were in Egypt in Pharaoh's house? (28) And did I choose him out of all the tribes of Israel *to be* my priest, to offer upon mine altar, to burn incense, to wear an ephod before me? and *a*did I give unto the house of thy father all the offerings made by fire of the children of Israel? (29) Wherefore kick ye at my sacrifice and at mine offering, which I have commanded *in my* habitation; and honourest thy sons above me, to make yourselves fat with the chiefest of all the offerings

1 Or, *to cry out.*

a Lev. 10. 14.

---

(24) **Ye make the Lord's people to transgress.**—The life led by the priests publicly in the sanctuary, with their evident scornful unbelief in the divinely established holy ordinances on the one hand, and their unblushing immorality on the other, corrupted the inner religious life of the whole people.

(25) **Sin against the Lord.**—This touches on the mystery of sin. There are transgressions which may again and again receive pardon, but there seems to be a transgression beyond the limits of Divine forgiveness. The pitiful Redeemer, in no obscure language, told His listeners the same awful truth when He warned them of the sin against the Holy Ghost.

They hearkened not . . . because the Lord would slay them.—Here the mysteries connected with God's foreknowledge and man's free-will are touched upon. The Lord's resolution to slay them was founded on the eternal foreknowledge of their persistence in wrong-doing.

There seems to be a period in the sinner's life when the Spirit of the Eternal ceases to plead; then the man is left to himself, and he feels no longer any remorse for evil done; this is spoken of in Exod. iv. 21 as "hardening the heart." This period in the life of Hophni and Phinehas apparently had been reached when the Lord resolved to slay them.

(26) **Grew on, and was in favour.**—The very expressions of the biographer of Samuel were adopted by St. Luke when, in the early chapters of his Gospel, he wishes to describe in a few striking words the boyhood and youth of Him who was far greater than the child-prophet of Israel.

(27) **There came a man of God.**—Of this messenger of the Highest, whom, from his peculiar title, and also from the character of his communication, we must regard as one of the order of prophets, we know nothing. He appears suddenly on the scene at Shiloh, nameless and—as far as we know—homeless, delivers his message of doom, and disappears.

The term "man of God" we find applied to Moses and to different prophets some forty or more times in the Books of Judges, Samuel, and Kings. It occurs, though but rarely, in Chronicles, Ezra, and Nehemiah, and in the prophetical books only once.

Until the sudden appearance of this "man of God," no mention of a prophet in the story of Israel had been made since the days of Deborah.

Did I plainly appear . . . ?—The interrogations in this Divine message do not ask a question with a view to a reply, but simply emphatically appeal to Eli's conscience. To these questions respecting well-known facts the old man would reply with a silent "Yes." The "house of thy father" refers to the house of Aaron, the first high priest, from whom, through Ithamar, the fourth son of Aaron, Eli was descended.

The Talmud has a beautiful note on this passage:— Rabbi Shimon ben Yochi said, "Come and see how beloved Israel is by the Holy One! Blessed be He! Wherever they are banished, there the Shekinah is with them; as it is said (1 Sam. ii. 27): 'Did I (God) plainly appear unto the house of thy fathers when they were in Egypt?' &c. When they were banished to Babylon, the Shekinah was with them; as it is said (Isa. xliii. 14): 'For your sakes was I sent to Babylon.' And when they will be redeemed the Shekinah will be with them; as it is said (Deut. xxx. 3): 'Then the Lord thy God will return with thy captivity;' it is not said, He will cause to return (transitively), but He will return (intransitively)."—Treatise *Megillah,* fol. 29, col. 1.

(28) **Did I choose him out of all the tribes of Israel? . . .** —After such glorious privileges had been conferred on this favoured house, and such ample provision for all its wants had been made for it, it was indeed a crime of the blackest ingratitude that its leading members should pour dishonour on their invisible King and Benefactor.

To wear an ephod before me.—This included the privilege, which belonged to the head of the house of Aaron, the reigning high priest, of entering the Holy of Holies—that lightless inner sanctuary where the visible presence of the Eternal was ever and anon pleased to dwell—and also the possession of the mysterious Urim and Thummim, by which enquiry could be made of the will of the invisible King of Israel.

(29) **Wherefore kick ye at my sacrifice.**—The imagery of the words are taken from Deut. xxxii. 15: "Jeshurun waxed fat, and kicked . . . then he forsook God which made him, and lightly esteemed the Rock of his salvation." The image is one drawn from the pastoral life of the people: the ox or ass over-fed, pampered, and indulged, becomes unmanageable, and refuses obedience to his kind master.

And honourest thy sons above me.—Although Eli knew well what was right, yet foolish fondness for his sons seems in part to have blinded his eyes to the enormity of their wickedness. It is also probable that he was influenced not by feelings of weak affection, but also by unwillingness to divert from his own family the rich source of wealth which proceeded from the offerings of the pilgrims from all parts of the

of Israel my people? ⁽³⁰⁾ Wherefore the LORD God of Israel saith, I said indeed *that* thy house, and the house of thy father, should walk before me for ever: but now the LORD saith, Be it far from me; for them that honour me I will honour, and they that despise me shall be lightly esteemed. ⁽³¹⁾ Behold, the days come, that I will cut off thine arm, and the arm of thy father's house, that there shall not be an old man in thine house. ⁽³²⁾ And thou shalt see ¹an enemy *in my* habitation, in all *the wealth* which *God* shall give Israel: and there shall not be an old man in thine house for ever. ⁽³³⁾ And the man of thine, *whom* I shall not cut off from mine altar, *shall be* to consume thine eyes, and to grieve thine heart: and all the increase of thine house shall die ²in the flower of their age. ⁽³⁴⁾ And this *shall be* a sign unto thee, that shall come upon thy two sons, on Hophni and Phinehas; in one day they shall die both of them. ⁽³⁵⁾ And I will raise me up a faithful priest, *that* shall do according to *that* which *is* in mine heart and in my mind: and I will build him a sure house; and he shall

¹ Or, *the affliction of the tabernacle, for all the wealth which God would have given Israel.*

² Heb., *men.*

---

land. These considerations induced him to maintain these bad and covetous men as his acknowledged representatives in the national sanctuary of Shiloh. Eli then allowed things, which gradually grew worse and worse, to drift, and merely interfered with a weak rebuke; but the day of reckoning was at hand.

⁽³⁰⁾ **. . . but now the Lord saith, Be it far from me.**—But the fulfilment of the glorious and gracious promise which involved the walking of the favoured house for ever in the light of the Lord in the blessed courts of the sanctuary with no worldly cares —were they not amply provided for without sowing and reaping?—were they not invested with high honours and universal consideration?—was necessarily dependent upon those that walked, the favoured house carrying out their share of the covenant. To be honoured of God, they for their part must be His faithful servants. Now the life and conduct of the priestly house had wrought the gravest dishonour and brought the deepest shame on the worship and sanctuary of the "King in Jeshurun."

⁽³¹⁾ **I will cut off thine arm.**—"The arm" signifies power and strength: "Thy power and strength, and that of thy house is doomed." (See for the figure Job xxii. 9; Ps. xxxvii. 17.)

And there shall not be an old man in thine house.—No one more in thy house, O High Priest, who hast so signally failed in thy solemn duty, shall attain to old age; sickness or the sword shall ever early consume its members. This strange denunciation of the "man of God" is emphasised by being repeated in the next (32) verse, and in different words again in verse 33.

⁽³²⁾ **And thou shalt see an enemy.**—Some—*e.g.,* the Vulgate—understand by enemy a "rival": thou shalt see thy rival in the Temple. The words, however, point to something which Eli would live to see with grief and horror. The reference is no doubt to the capture of the Ark by the Philistines in the battle where his sons were slain. The earthly habitation of the Eternal was there robbed of its glory and pride, for the ark of the covenant was the heart of the sanctuary.

In all the wealth which God shall give Israel. —"The affliction of God's house from the loss of the ark remained; while under the lead of Samuel there came blessing to the people."—*Erdmann.*

There is another explanation which refers the fulfilment of this part of the prophecy to the period of Solomon's reign, when Abiathar, of the house of Eli, was deposed from the High Priestly dignity to make room for Zadok, but the reference to the capture of the ark is by far more probable.

⁽³³⁾ **To consume thine eyes and to grieve thine heart.**—The *Speaker's Commentary* well refers to verse 36 for an explanation of these difficult words. "Those who are not cut off in the flower of their youth shall be worse off than those who are, for they shall have to beg their bread."

And all the increase of thine house shall die. —In the Babylonian Talmud the Rabbis have related that there was once a family in Jerusalem the members of which died off regularly at eighteen years of age. Rabbi Jochanan ben Zacchai shrewdly guessed that they were descendants of Eli, regarding whom it is said (1 Sam. ii. 33), "And all the increase of thine house shall die in the flower of their age;" and he accordingly advised them to devote themselves to the study of the Law, as the certain and only means of neutralising the curse. They acted upon the advice of the Rabbi; their lives were in consequence prolonged; and they thenceforth went by the name of their spiritual father.—*Rosh Hashanah,* fol. 18, col. 1.

⁽³⁴⁾ **In one day they shall die both of them.** —See for a literal fulfilment the recital in chap. iv. 11. This foreshadowing of terrible calamity which was to befal Israel was to be a sign to Eli that all the awful predictions concerning the fate of his doomed house would be carried out to the bitter end.

⁽³⁵⁾ **A faithful priest.**—Who here is alluded to by this "faithful priest," of whom such a noble life was predicted, and to whom such a glorious promise as that "he should walk before mine anointed for ever," was made? Many of the conditions are fairly fulfilled by Samuel, to whom naturally our thoughts at once turn. He occupies a foremost place in the long Jewish story, and immediately succeded Eli in most of his important functions as the acknowledged chief of the religious and political life in Israel. He was also eminently and consistently faithful to his master and God during his whole life. Samuel, though a Levite, was not of the sons of Aaron; yet he seems, even in Eli's days, to have ministered as a priest before the Lord, the circumstances of his early connection with the sanctuary being exceptional. *After* Eli's death, when the regular exercise of the Levitical ritual and priesthood was suspended by the separation of the ark from the tabernacle, Samuel evidently occupied a priestly position, and we find him for a long period standing as mediator between Jehovah and His people, in sacrifice, prayer, and intercession, in the performance of which high offices his duty, after the solemn anointing of Saul as king, was to walk before the anointed of the Lord (Saul), while (to use the words of Von Gerlach, quoted by Erdmann), the

walk before mine anointed for ever. ⁽³⁶⁾ And it shall come to pass, *that* every one that is left in thine house shall come *and* crouch to him for a piece of silver and a morsel of bread, and shall say, ¹Put me, I pray thee, into ²one of the priests' offices, that I may eat a piece of bread.

CHAPTER III.—⁽¹⁾ And the child Samuel ministered unto the LORD before Eli. And the word of the LORD was

¹ Heb., *Join.*

² Or, *somewhat about the priesthood.*

Aaronic priesthood fell for a long time into such disrepute that it had to beg for honour and support from him (verse 36), and became dependent on the new order of things instituted by Samuel. (See *Excursus* C at the end of this Book.)

The prediction " I will build him a sure house" is satisfied in the strong house and numerous posterity given to Samuel by God. His grandson Heman was " the king's seer in the words of God," and was placed by King David over the choir in the house of God. This eminent personage, Heman, had fourteen sons and three daughters (1 Chron. vi. 33; xxv. 4, 5).

Samuel also fulfilled the prophecy "He shall walk before mine anointed for ever" in his close and intimate relation with King Saul, who we find, even after the faithful prophet's death — although the later acts of Saul had alienated the prophet from his sovereign—summoning the spirit of Samuel as the only one who was able to counsel and strengthen him (1 Sam. xxviii. 15).

Of the other interpretations, that of Rashi and Abarbanel, and many of the moderns, which supposes the reference to be Zadok, of the house of Eleazar, who, in the reign of Solomon, superseded Abiathar, of the house of Ithamar (the ancestor of Eli), alone fairly satisfies most of the different predictions, but we are met with this insurmountable difficulty at the outset— Can we assume that the comparatively unknown Zadok, after the lapse of so many years, was pointed out by the magnificent promises contained in the words of the "man of God" to Eli? The words of the "man of God" surely indicate a far greater one than any high priest of the time of Solomon. In the golden days of this magnificent king, the high priest, overshadowed by the splendour and power of the sovereign, was a very subordinate figure indeed in Israel; but the subject of this prophecy was one evidently destined to hold no secondary and inferior position.

Some commentators, with a singular confusion of ideas, see a reference to Christ in the "faithful priest," forgetting that this "faithful priest" who was to arise in Eli's place was to walk *before* the Lord's Christ, or Anointed One.

On the whole, the reference to Samuel is the most satisfactory, and seems in all points—without in any way unfairly pressing the historical references—to fulfil that portion of the prediction of the "man of God" to Eli respecting the one chosen to replace him in his position of judge and guide of Israel.

III.

(1—21) The Lord appears to the Boy Samuel.

⁽¹⁾ **The child Samuel ministered unto the Lord.**—The writer of this history, although well aware of the great revolution accomplished in Israel by the prophet whose life and work the Holy Spirit bade him record, gives us but the simplest and shortest possible account of the child-days of him who was only second to Moses in his influence on the eventful story of the chosen people. But short and devoid of detail though the record be, it is enough to show us that the atmosphere in which the child lived was a pure and holy one; the boy was evidently kept apart from Hophni, Phinehas, and their impious self-seeking party. The high priestly guardian was evidently fully conscious of the importance of his charge, and he watched over his pupil with a tender watchful care. Perhaps his sad experiences with his evil headstrong sons had taught the old man wisdom; certainly the training he gave to Samuel was one that educated the boy well for his after-life of stirring public work. The notices of the childhood and boyhood are indeed brief. The first contrasts sharply the lawless profligacy of the priestly houses with the pure holy childhood passed in the sanctuary courts, probably always in the company of the old man. Hophni and Phinehas, *the grown men*, prostituted the holy work to their own vile worldly ends: *the child* ministered before the Lord in his little white robe; and while in the home life of his own mother and father in Ramah, his brothers and sisters were growing up with the sorrows and joys of other Hebrew children, " the child Samuel grew before the Lord" amid the stillness and silence and the awful mystery of the Divine protection, which seems ever, even in the darkest days of the history of Israel, to have surrounded the home of the Ark of the Covenant of the Lord. It was amidst this silent, sacred mystery, apart from the disorders of his priestly sons, that Eli taught the boy the story of his ancestors, with only the dark curtains of the sanctuary hanging between master and pupil and the mystic golden throne of God, on which His glory was sometimes pleased to rest.

The writer wrote his gloomy recital of the wild unbridled life of the wicked priests, wrote down the weak, sorrowful remonstrances of the father and high priest, foreshadowing, however, their certain doom; and then, again, with their life of shame sharply contrasts the pure child-life of the little pupil of the old sorrowstricken high priest—the boy whom all men loved. " And the boy Samuel grew on, and was in favour both with the Lord, and also with men."

Once more Eli, now weak with age, is warned of the sure consequences which would follow the evil licence and the irreligion of his priestly sons; and again the boy Samuel and his life, guided by Eli, his guardian and teacher, is contrasted with the wild, unchecked lawlessness of the priestly sons of Eli perpetually dishonouring religion and the sanctuary—a lawlessness which had just been denounced by the nameless prophet (chap. ii. 27—36).

Josephus tells us that Samuel, when the Lord first called him, was twelve years old. This was the age of the child Jesus when He disputed with the doctors in the Temple.

Was precious in those days.—Precious, that is, *rare*. "The word of the Lord" is the will of the Lord announced by a prophet, seer, or man of God. Between the days of Deborah and the nameless man of God who came with the awful message to Eli, no inspired voice seems to have spoken to the chosen people.

The Lord calls Samuel.   I. SAMUEL, III.   *He tells Eli.*

precious in those days; *there was* no open vision. ⁽²⁾ And it came to pass at that time, when Eli *was* laid down in his place, and his eyes began to wax dim, *that* he could not see; ⁽³⁾ and ere the lamp of God went out in the temple of the LORD, where the ark of God *was*, and Samuel was laid down *to sleep;* ⁽⁴⁾ that the LORD called Samuel: and he answered, Here *am* I. ⁽⁵⁾ And he ran unto Eli, and said, Here *am* I; for thou calledst me. And he said, I called not; lie down again. And he went and lay down. ⁽⁶⁾ And the LORD called yet again, Samuel. And Samuel arose and went to Eli, and said, Here *am* I; for thou didst call me. And he answered, I called not, my son; lie down again. ⁽⁷⁾ ¹Now Samuel did not yet know the LORD, neither was the word of the LORD yet revealed unto him. ⁽⁸⁾ And the LORD called Samuel again the third time. And he arose and went to Eli, and said, Here *am* I; for thou didst call me. And Eli perceived that the LORD had called the child. ⁽⁹⁾ Therefore Eli said unto Samuel, Go, lie down: and it shall be, if he call thee, that thou shalt say, Speak, LORD; for thy servant heareth. So Samuel went and lay down in his place. ⁽¹⁰⁾And the LORD came, and stood, and called as at other times, Samuel, Samuel. Then Samuel answered, Speak; for thy servant heareth.

B.C. cir. 1141.

1 Or, *Thus did Samuel, before he knew the LORD, and before the word of the LORD was revealed unto him.*

The "open vision" refers to such manifestations of the Divinity as were vouchsafed to Abraham, Moses, Joshua, and Manoah, and in this chapter to Samuel. There may possibly be some reference to the appearance of Divine glory which was connected with the Urim and Thummim which were worn by the high priest. This significant silence on the part of the invisible King the writer dwells on as a result of the deep corruption into which the priests and, through their evil example, a large proportion of the nation, had fallen.

^(3, 4) **Ere the lamp of God went out.**—There is a Talmud comment here of singular interest and beauty: "On the day that Rabbi Akiva died, Rabbi (compiler of the Mishnah) was born; on the day when Rabbi died, Rav Yehudah was born; on the day when Rav Yehudah died, Rava was born; on the day when Rava died, Rav Ashi (one of the editors of *Guemara*) was born. It teaches thee, that no righteous man departs this life before another equally righteous is born; as it is said (Eccles. i. 5): 'The sun rises, and the sun goes down.' The sun of Eli had not set before that of Samuel rose; as it is said (1 Sam. iii. 3): 'Ere the lamp of God was out . . . and Samuel laid down.'"—*Tract Kiddushin*, fol. 72, col. 2.

"It was night in the sanctuary. The high priest slept in one of the adjacent chambers, and the attendant ministers in another. In the centre, on the left of the entrance, stood the seven-branched candlestick, now mentioned for the last time; superseded in the reign of Solomon by the ten separate candlesticks, but revived after the Captivity by the copy of the one candlestick with seven branches, as it is still seen on the Arch of Titus. It was the only light of the Tabernacle during the night, was solemnly lighted every evening, as in the devotions of the Eastern world, both Mussulman and Christian, and extinguished just before morning, when the doors were opened.

"In the deep silence of that early morning, before the sun had risen, when the sacred light was still burning, came through the mouth of the innocent child the doom of the house of Ithamar."—Stanley, *Lectures on the Jewish Church*, Part I.

The Lord called Samuel.—It seems probable that the voice came from out of the "visible glory," the Shekinah, which on that solemn night of the calling of the child-prophet, no doubt rested on its chosen earthly throne—the mercy-seat of God—which formed the top of the Ark, and which was overshadowed by the outspread wings of the golden Cherubim.

⁽⁸⁾ **And Eli perceived that the Lord had called the child.**—The whole story of the eventful night is told so naturally, the supernatural wonderfully interwoven with the common life of the sanctuary, that we forget, as we read, the strangeness of the events recorded. The sleeping child is awakened by a voice uttering his name. He naturally supposes it is his half-blind old master summoning him. The same thing occurs a second and a third time. Then it flashed upon Eli the boy had had no dream. We can well fancy the old man, when Samuel again came in, asking, "Where did the voice you thought was mine come from?" and the boy would reply, "From your chamber, master." And the old high priest would remember that in the same direction, only at the extremity of the sanctuary, behind the veil, was the Ark and the seat of God. Was, then, the glory of the Lord shining there? and did the voice as in old days proceed from that sacred golden throne? So he bade his pupil go to his chamber again, and if the voice spoke to him again, to answer, not Eli, but the invisible King—"Speak, Lord; for thy servant heareth."

^(9, 10) **And the Lord came, and stood.**—Then before the boy, as he lay and waited for *the voice*, came *something*, and it stood before him. The question naturally occurs to us, *What* came and stood before the boy's couch? As a rule, we find that generally, when the Lord was pleased to take some form, the form is specified. Now, as in Abraham's case at Mamre, it was a traveller; now, as in Joshua's, an armed warrior; very frequently, as to Manoah, the form was that of an angel; here nothing is specially described. Was it not that simply "the glory" on which Moses gazed when he met the Holy One on Sinai—"the glory" which seemed to rest at times in the lightless Holy of Holies on the golden mercy-seat of the Ark of the Covenant? Was it not this "visible glory"—Shekinah, as the Hebrews termed it—which filled the chamber of the child, and from out of *this* came the voice of the Eternal, and spoke to Samuel? "See how God loves holiness in children. The child Samuel was preferred by Him to Eli, the aged high priest and judge."—*Theodoret*, quoted by Bishop Wordsworth.

(11) And the LORD said to Samuel, Behold, I will do a thing in Israel, at which both the ears of ᵃevery one that heareth it shall tingle. (12) In that day I will perform against Eli all *things* which I have spoken concerning his house: ¹when I begin, I will also make an end. (13) ² ᵇFor I have told him that I will judge his house for ever for the iniquity which he knoweth; because his sons made themselves ³vile, and he ⁴restrained them not. (14) And therefore I have sworn unto the house of Eli, that the iniquity of Eli's house shall not be purged with sacrifice nor offering for ever.

(15) And Samuel lay until the morning, and opened the doors of the house of the LORD. And Samuel feared to shew Eli the vision. (16) Then Eli called Samuel, and said, Samuel, my son. And he answered, Here *am* I. (17) And he said, What *is* the thing that *the* LORD hath said unto thee? I pray thee hide *it* not from me: God do so to thee, and ⁵more also, if thou hide *any* ⁶thing from me of all the things that he said unto thee. (18) And Samuel told him ⁷every whit, and hid nothing from him. And he said, It *is* the LORD: let him do what seemeth him good. (19) And Samuel grew, and the LORD

a 2 Kings 21. 12.
1 Heb., *beginning and ending.*
2 Or, *And I will tell him*, &c.
b ch. 2. 29, 30, 31, &c.
3 Or, *accursed.*
4 Heb., *frowned not upon them.*
5 Heb., *so add.*
6 Or, *word.*
7 Heb., *all the things*, or, *words.*

---

(11) **The ears of every one that heareth it shall tingle.**—The calamity which is here referred to was the capture of the Ark of the Covenant. Neither the death of the warrior priests, Hophni and Phinehas, nor the crushing defeat of the Hebrew army, would have so powerfully affected the people; but that the sacred symbol of the presence and protection of the invisible King should be allowed to fall into the hands of the uncircumcised Philistines, the hereditary foes of the chosen race, was a calamity unparalleled in their annals.

It seemed to say that God had indeed forsaken them.

The expression is a very singular one, and re-occurs in 2 Kings xxi. 12, and Jer. xix. 3, on the occasion of the destruction of Jerusalem by Nebuchadnezzar.

(13) **Because his sons made themselves vile.**—The enormity of the sin of Eli and his house, which was to be so fearfully punished, must be measured by the extent of the mischief it worked; well-nigh all Israel were involved in it. The fatal example the priests had set at Shiloh filtrated through the entire people; the result was, that unbelief in the Eternal was becoming general throughout the land. The old pure religion was rapidly dying out of the hearts of the men, and the profligacy and covetousness of Shiloh would soon have been copied only too faithfully in all the homes of Israel. This fearful state of things was known to the high priest and judge, and still the weak and indulgent father refrained from removing his sons from their high office.

(14) **Shall not be purged with sacrifice.**—No earthly sacrifice, bloody or unbloody, should ever purge on earth the sin of the doomed high priestly house. A great theological truth is contained in these few words. In the sacrificial theory of the Mosaic Law we see there was a *limit* to the efficacy of sacrifice after a certain point in sin and evil example had been reached: a scar was printed on the life which no blood of bullock or of goat could wash away; but the quiet, though sorrowful, resignation with which the old man received the intimation of the certain earthly doom seems to indicate that Eli, sure of the love of the All-Pitiful, looked on to some other means of deliverance, devised in the counsels of the Eternal Friend of Israel, by which his deathless soul, after the earthly penalty, would be reconciled to the invisible King. Did not men like Eli look on in sure and certain trust to the *one hope?* Did not these holy, though often erring, patriarchs and priests see in those far-back days, " as in a glass darkly," the blood of another Victim, which should cleanse the repentant and sorrowing sinner from all sin?

(15) **And opened the doors.**—This is another notice which indicates that the sanctuary of Shiloh was enclosed in a house or temple. We have no record of the building of the *first* house of the Lord, but from the references contained in the record of Samuel's childhood it is clear that the sacred Tabernacle had been for some time enclosed by, and perhaps covered in with, permanent buildings.

Feared.—" Here was Samuel's first experience of the prophet's cross: the having unwelcome truth to divulge to those he loved, honoured, and feared. Jeremiah felt this cross to be an exceedingly heavy one " (Jer. xv. 10, xvii. 15—18, xx. 7—18).—*Speaker's Commentary.*

(18) **It is the Lord.**—Such a reply, and such a reception of the news of the terrible doom twice communicated to him by a direct message from the Eternal, indicates that Eli, in spite of his weakness and foolish partiality for his sons, was thoroughly devoted to the Lord in his heart. He saw how deeply he had failed in his high office, how he had allowed worldly considerations to influence his conduct, how he had been tried and found wanting; and now, without a murmur, he submits to the righteous judgment of his God, he leaves himself in God's hands, and never tries to justify himself and his past conduct. *Now* it was probably too late to attempt any reformation in the priestly life. The influence and power of Hophni and Phinehas were too strong for his enfeebled will to set aside. Eli was probably in his last days little more than a puppet in their hands. He had sown the wind, and now must reap the whirlwind.

(19) **And Samuel grew, and the Lord was with him.**—Again in a brief sentence the life of Samuel was contrasted with another: this time with that of his predecessor in the judgeship. As the boy grew up to manhood, we hear that while, on the one hand, as, no doubt, in earlier days with Eli, so now with Samuel, the Lord was with His servant, giving him strength and wisdom, guiding him and guarding him; and, on the other, different from Eli, we hear how the young prophet let none of the Divine words fall to the ground. In those dark days of sin and shame at Shiloh, in the midst of scenes of temptation, the boy stood firm; his early life was a perpetual protest against covetousness and iniquity.

was with him, and did let none of his words fall to the ground. (20) And all Israel from Dan even to Beersheba knew that Samuel was [1] established *to be* a prophet of the LORD. (21) And the LORD appeared again in Shiloh: for the LORD revealed himself to Samuel in Shiloh by the word of the LORD.

CHAPTER IV.—(1) And the word of Samuel [2][3] came to all Israel.

[1] Or, *faithful*.
[2] Or, *came to pass*.
[3] Heb., *was*.
[4] Heb., *the battle was spread*.
[5] Heb., *the array*.

Now Israel went out against the Philistines to battle, and pitched beside Eben-ezer: and the Philistines pitched in Aphek. (2) And the Philistines put themselves in array against Israel: and when [4] they joined battle, Israel was smitten before the Philistines: and they slew of [5] the army in the field about four thousand men.

(3) And when the people were come into the camp, the elders of Israel said,

---

(20) **A prophet of the Lord.**—Then from the northern to the southern cities of the land the fame of the boy-friend of the Eternal was established. The minds of all the people were thus gradually prepared when the right moment came to acknowledge Samuel as a God-sent chieftain. On this rapid and universal acknowledgment of the young prophet it has been observed, "that the people, in spite of their disruption, yet formed religiously an unit."

IV.

(1–22) Last Days of Eli. Defeat of Israel at Aphek. The Ark leaves the Shiloh Sanctuary. The Battle in which the Ark is taken. Hophni and Phinehas are Slain. The Death of Eli.

(1) **And the word of Samuel.**—To which portion of the narrative does this statement belong? Is it part of that account of the Lord's dealings with Samuel which closed the preceding chapter? Does it close that brief narrative which tells of the Divine voice which called to, and the vision seen by, the young chosen servant of the Highest, with a note simply relating how the word of the boy-prophet was received through the varied tribes of the people? Or does it tell us that at Samuel's word—that is, acting under his advice—Israel commenced this new disastrous war with the Philistines? By adopting the *first* supposition, which understands the words as a general statement respecting Samuel's influence in Israel, the grave difficulty of supposing that Samuel was mistaken in his first advice to the people is, of course, removed; but then we have to explain the separation of this clause from the preceding section in chapter iii., to which it would appear so naturally to belong; we have also to account for the exceeding abruptness with which the announcement of the war with the Philistines follows the clause respecting the "word of Samuel." The *Speaker's Commentary* attempts to solve the problem by suggesting as "the cause of the abruptness" that the account of the battle probably is extracted from some other book in which it came in naturally and consecutively, and that it was here introduced for the sake of exhibiting the fulfilment of Samuel's prophecy concerning Eli's family. Evidently, however, the Hebrew revisers of Samuel did not so understand the clause. They have placed the notice of *Samuel's words coming to all Israel* as introducing the narrative of the battle.

The compiler of the book, in his relation of the young prophet's error, touches upon an important feature of his great life. Anarchy and confusion had long prevailed throughout the tribes, and none of the hero Judges who had as yet been raised to power had succeeded in restoring the stern, rigid form of theocracy which had made the Israel of Moses and Joshua so great and powerful. The high qualities which in his prime had, no doubt, raised Eli to the first place in the nation, in his old age were almost totally obscured by a weak affection for his unworthy sons. A terrible picture of the corruption of the priesthood is presented to us during the last period of Eli's reign. We can well imagine what the ordinary life of many among the people, with such an example from their religious guides and temporal governors, must have been. Individual instances of piety and loyalty to the God of their fathers, such as we see in the house of Elkanah, even though such instances were not unfrequent of themselves, would have been totally insufficient to preserve the nation from the decay which always follows impiety and corruption. In this period of moral degradation the Philistines, part of the original inhabitants of the land, a warlike and enterprising race, taking advantage of the internal jealousies and the weaknesses of Israel, made themselves supreme in many portions of the land, treating the former conquerors often with harshness, and even with contempt.

Samuel grew up to manhood in the midst of this state of things. He was conscious that the invisible King, forgotten by so many of the nation, had chosen him to be the restorer of the chosen people. The boy-prophet, as he passed out of childhood into manhood, does not appear at first to have recognised the depth of moral degradation into which Israel had sunk, or to have seen that it was utterly hopeless to attempt to free the people from the yoke of their Philistine foes until something like a pure national religion was restored. Samuel and the nobler spirits in Israel, who thirsted to restore their nation to freedom and to purity, needed a sharp and bitter experience before they could successfully attempt the deliverance of the people; so the first call to arms resulted in utter disaster, and the defeat at Aphek—the result, we believe, of the summons of Samuel—was the prelude to the crushing blow to the pride of Israel which soon after deprived them of their leaders, their choicest warriors, and, above all, of their loved and cherished "Ark of the Covenant," the earthly throne of their unseen King, the symbol of His ever-presence in their midst.

And pitched beside Eben-ezer.—"The stones of help." The name was not given to the place until later, when Samuel set up a stone to commemorate a victory he gained, some twenty years after, over the Philistines.

In Aphek.—With the article, "the fortress." Perhaps the same place as the old Canaanitish royal city Aphek.

(3) **Wherefore hath the Lord smitten us?**—The people and the elders who, as we have seen above, had undertaken the war of liberty at the instigation of

Wherefore hath the LORD smitten us to day before the Philistines? Let us ¹fetch the ark of the covenant of the LORD out of Shiloh unto us, that, when it cometh among us, it may save us out of the hand of our enemies. ⁽⁴⁾ So the people sent to Shiloh, that they might bring from thence the ark of the covenant of the LORD of hosts, which dwelleth *between* the cherubims: and the two sons of Eli, Hophni and Phinehas, *were* there with the ark of the covenant of God.

¹ Heb., *take unto us*.

⁽⁵⁾ And when the ark of the covenant of the LORD came into the camp, all Israel shouted with a great shout, so that the earth rang again. ⁽⁶⁾ And when the Philistines heard the noise of the shout, they said, What *meaneth* the noise of this great shout in the camp of the Hebrews? And they understood that the ark of the LORD was come into the camp. ⁽⁷⁾ And the Philistines were afraid, for they said, God is come into the camp. And they said, Woe unto us! for there

---

the young man of God, amazed at their defeat, were puzzled to understand why God was evidently not in their midst; they showed by their next procedure how thoroughly they had gone astray from the old pure religion.

Let us fetch the ark of the covenant.—Whether or not Samuel acquiesced in this fatal proposition we have no information. It evidently did not emanate from him, but, as we are expressly told, from the "elders of the people." Probably the lesson of the first defeat had deeply impressed him, and he saw that a thorough reformation throughout the land was needed before the invisible King would again be present among the people.

It may save us.—It was a curious delusion, this baseless hope of the elders, that the unseen God was inseparably connected with that strange and beautiful symbol of His presence, with that coffer of perishable wood and metal overshadowed by the lifeless golden angels carved on the shining seat which closed this sacred Ark—that glittering mercy seat, as it was called, round which so many hallowed memories of the glory vision had gathered. Far on in the people's story, one of the greatest of Samuel's successors, Jeremiah, presses home the same truth the people were so slow in learning, when he passionately urges his Israel, "Trust ye not in lying words, saying The temple of the Lord, the temple of the Lord, the temple of the Lord are these. For if ye thoroughly amend your ways and your doings, then will I cause you to dwell in this place, in the land that I gave to your fathers, for ever and ever" (Jer. vii. 4, 5, 7).

Wordsworth here, with great force, thus writes:—"Probably David remembered this history when, with a clearer faith, he refused to allow the Ark to be carried with him in his retreat before Absalom out of Jerusalem; and even when the priests had brought it forth, he commanded them to carry it back to its place, saying, 'If I shall find favour in the eyes of the Lord, He will bring me again, and show me both it and His habitation.' (2 Sam. xv. 25.)

"David, without the Ark visibly present, but with the unseen help of Him who was enthroned on the mercy-seat, triumphed, and was restored to Jerusalem; but Israel, with the Ark visibly present, but without the blessing of Him whose throne the Ark was, fell before their enemies, and were deprived of the sacred symbol, which was taken by the Philistines."

⁽⁴⁾ **So the people sent to Shiloh.**—There was, no doubt, in the minds of the elders, the memory of many a glorious victory gained in the old heroic days of Moses and Joshua in the presence of their sacred Ark; but *then* God was with His people, and the sacred Ark of the Covenant served as a reminder of His ever-presence with them; now they had been disloyal to their unseen King, His very sanctuary had become infamous as the centre of vice, and His ministers were chiefly known as the prominent examples of covetousness and immorality, and the Ark had become only a symbol of the broken covenant.

It was in vain that the grand battle hymn of Israel was raised as in the old days when the Ark set forward: "Rise up, Lord, and let Thine enemies be scattered, and let them that hate Thee flee before Thee" (Numb. x. 35).

Were there with the ark.—This Note respecting the guardians of the Ark is sufficient to account for the terrible discomfiture of Israel. The conduct and general life and example of their priestly leaders have already been indicated. What a contrast the writer of the Book bitterly puts down in his memoirs here—the glorious but now deserted earthly throne of God, and its guardians, the wicked, abandoned priests!

⁽⁵⁾ **And when the ark . . . came into the camp.**—As far as we know, this was the first time since the establishment of the people in Canaan that the Ark had been brought from the permanent sanctuary into the camp. The shout of joy represented the confidence of the army that now the Ark, which had witnessed so many splendid victories of the chosen race, was among them, discomfiture was out of the question.

⁽⁷⁾ **God is come into the camp.**—The joy manifested by the Israelites at the arrival of the Ark from the sanctuary made the Philistines suspect that their enemies' God was now present with the defeated army.

The city of Aphek, near to which the camp of Israel was pitched, was close to the western entrance of the Pass of Beth-horon. The two defeats of Israel are termed in this Commentary the Battles of Aphek. The name of Eben-ezer, by which the scene was known in after days, was only given to the locality some twenty years later, on the occasion of the victory of Samuel near the same spot.

Philistines and Israelites, then, were equally superstitious in their belief, both supposing that Deity was in some way connected with the lifeless gold and wood of the symbol Ark and Cherubim. But the Philistines had some excuse for their fears. Tradition was, no doubt, current among the old inhabitants of Canaan how this sacred Ark had been carried before the conquering armies of Israel in many a battle and siege in those bygone days, when the strange shepherd hordes under Joshua had first invaded and taken possession of their beautiful land. The next verse explains more clearly some of the reasons for their fear.

Defeat of Israel.   I. SAMUEL, IV.   *The Ark is Captured.*

hath not been such a thing ¹heretofore. ⁽⁸⁾ Woe unto us! who shall deliver us out of the hand of these mighty Gods? these *are* the Gods that smote the Egyptians with all the plagues in the wilderness. ⁽⁹⁾ Be strong, and quit yourselves like men, O ye Philistines, that ye be not servants unto the Hebrews, *a* as they have been to you : ² quit yourselves like men, and fight.

⁽¹⁰⁾ And the Philistines fought, and Israel was smitten, and they fled every man into his tent : and there was a very great slaughter; for there fell of Israel thirty thousand footmen. ⁽¹¹⁾ And the ark of God was taken; and the two sons of Eli, Hophni and Phinehas, ³were slain.

⁽¹²⁾ And there ran a man of Benjamin out of the army, and came to Shiloh the same day with his clothes rent, and with earth upon his head. ⁽¹³⁾ And when he came, lo, Eli sat upon a seat by the wayside watching : for his heart trembled

1 Heb., *yesterday, or, the third day.*

a Judg. 13. 1.

2 Heb., *be men.*

3 Heb., *died.*

⁽⁸⁾ **These are the Gods that smote the Egyptians.**—No doubt the compiler of these "Memoirs of Samuel" has given us the very words of the Philistines, preserved in their national traditions of this sad time. They are the expression of idolaters who knew of "Gods" and dreaded their malevolent influence, but who had no conception of the One Most High God. The plural form Elohim, so often found in the sacred record for God, is used here; but whereas the inspired compilers would have written *their* qualifying adjective in the singular, the Philistine idolaters write *theirs* in the plural—*Elohim addirim* : Mighty Gods.

It is noticeable that the Philistine exclamation of awe and terror is based outwardly upon the Egyptian traditions of the acts of the Lord. They studiedly ignore what they were all in that camp painfully conscious of—His acts in their own land of Canaan. The Septuagint and Syriac Versions, and some commentators, add " and " before the words " in the wilderness," to make the Philistine exclamation more in harmony with history, seeing that the plagues were inflicted *before* the Israelites entered the wilderness ; but the very vagueness of the exclamation of fear speaks for its truth. They were little concerned with exact historical accuracy, and were simply conscious of some terrible judgment having fallen on the foes of this Israel, a judgment they not unnaturally connected with the Ark of the Covenant just arrived in the enemy's camp : that Ark their ancestors remembered so often at the head of the armies of this Israel in their days of triumph.

⁽⁹⁾ **Be strong, . . . O ye Philistines . .**—The ring of these striking words—part of the same Philistine tradition of their splendid success—probably embodied in some well-known hymn of victory, was evidently in St. Paul's mind when he wrote his stirring words of exhortation to his loved Corinthian Church, "Quit ye like men ; be strong."

⁽¹⁰⁾ **And Israel was smitten.**—The result was strictly in accordance with those immutable laws which have ever guided the connection of Israel and their God-Friend. As long as they clave to the invisible Preserver, and served Him with their whole heart and soul, and kept themselves pure from the pollution of the idol nations around them, so long was He in their midst, so long would they be invincible ; but if, as now, they chose to revel in the impure joys, and to delight themselves in the selfish, shameless lives of the idolatrous world around them, and only carried the Ark on their shoulders, with no memory of Him whom the mercy-seat and the overshadowing cherubim of that Ark symbolised, in their hearts, then—to use the solemn words of the hymn of Asaph—" Then God was wroth, and greatly abhorred Israel, and forsook the tabernacle of Shiloh, and delivered his strength into captivity, and his glory into the enemy's hand." (See Psa. lxxviii. 59—61, where the crushing defeat of Aphek and the signal victory of the Philistines is recounted in detail.)

⁽¹¹⁾ **And the ark of God was taken.**—The bare fact, without comment or note, is given of this, the greatest calamity that had yet happened to Israel. All the people would know by this terrible sign that their invisible King had withdrawn His countenance from them ; but the loss of the Ark to the heathen taught another lesson, not merely for the Israel of the days of Eli and Samuel—the eternal truth that " the living God does not bind His presence to a dead thing " (Erdmann). But though it was a dead thing, it was inexpressibly precious to the patriot Israelite. Was it not the ark " which Moses had made by God's command at Sinai, and on which the Divine presence was enshrined in the Holy of Holies ; and which had accompanied Israel in their marches through the wilderness, and before which the waters of Jordan had fled backward, and the walls of Jericho had fallen down?—*that* ark was taken by idolaters."—*Bishop Wordsworth.*

The two sons of Eli . . . were slain.—This was in strict accordance with the saying of the man of God. (See chap. ii. 34.)

⁽¹²⁾ **And there ran a man of Benjamin.**—The Rabbinical tradition relates that this messenger was Saul, who snatched from Goliath the tables of the Law taken out of the Ark, in order to save them. The whole of this account is so vivid, and is so full of detail that it must have come from some eye-witness —probably from Samuel himself. These swift runners are still employed to carry news in war time in the East. In the sacred story we possess several important instances of such messages : for instance, in the account of Absalom's death, Cushi and Ahimaaz bring the tidings from Joab to King David (2 Sam. xviii. 21—27). Asahel, the son of Zeruiah, the sister of David, is mentioned as being famous for his running (2 Sam. ii. 18). Elijah, again, we hear, once outran the chariot of Ahab between Carmel and Jezreel. Phidippides, when sent to urge the people of Sparta to come to the help of the Athenians against the Persians, arrived at Sparta on the second day after his departure from Athens (Herodotus, vi. 105, 6). Running seems to have been an exercise specially cultivated among the athletes of old times.

The rent clothes and the earth upon the head were the usual indications that the news brought by the messenger were tidings of evil.

⁽¹³⁾ **Eli sat upon a seat.**—The text here is a little confused, but the sense is perfectly clear. The best and most accurate rendering would be, *Eli sat by* for the ark of God. And when the man came into the city, and told it, all the city cried out. (14) And when Eli heard the noise of the crying, he said, What *meaneth* the noise of this tumult? And the man came in hastily, and told Eli. (15) Now Eli was ninety and eight years old; and ᵃ his eyes ¹ were dim, that he could not see. (16) And the man said unto Eli, I *am* he that came out of the army, and I fled to day out of the army. And he said, What ² is there done, my son? (17) And the messenger answered and said, Israel is fled before the Philistines, and there hath been also a great slaughter among the people, and thy two sons also, Hophni and Phinehas, are dead, and the ark of God is taken. (18) And it came to pass, when he made mention of the ark of God, that he fell from off the seat backward by the side of the gate, and his neck brake, and he died: for he was an old man, and heavy. And he had judged Israel forty years.

(19) And his daughter in law, Phinehas' wife, was with child, near ³ to be de-

a ch. s. 2.
1 Heb., *stood.*
2 Heb., *is the thing.*
3 Or, *to cry out.*

---

the side of the way of the watchers: i.e., the street or way in Shiloh, so named probably from the watch-tower which was situated in it. (See *Speaker's Commentary* here.) The LXX. renders it, "by the side of the gate watching the way."

The old judge was naturally anxious for news from the army. It must be remembered the people had already (verse 2) suffered a great reverse in the first battle of Aphek, when 4,000 fell, but his chief anxiety was for that sacred Ark which he had allowed —no doubt against his better judgment—to leave the sanctuary. All had gone wrong lately, and the high priest was deeply conscious that he, for his part, with his culpable weakness, and his priestly sons, with their flagrant wickedness, had broken the covenant with the invisible King. Eli knew too much of the Eternal Guardian of Israel to put any real trust in the power of the lifeless Ark. It was a long time, the high priest well knew, since the glory had rested on its golden mercy-seat between the silent cherubim. Had that mysterious light shone in the dark Holy of Holies since the night when the Divine voice spoke to the child, telling him the doom of the house of Ithamar? So he waited with sorrowful forebodings the advent of the messenger, asking himself, Would the Ark ever return to Shiloh?

(14) **What meaneth the noise?**—The blind old man, we must suppose, was seated on his chair of state, surrounded by priests and Levites, who were in attendance on him as high priest and judge. As the runner drew near, and the torn dress and the dust sprinkled on his head— the symbols of disaster—became visible, the wail of woe would soon run through the place. The cry of sorrow was the first intimation to the blind Eli: he was soon to hear the details. His question was probably, in the first place, addressed to the little court standing by his throne. The narrative is so vivid we seem to hear the sound of the cries of grief and terror which Eli heard, and to see the scene of dismay and confusion which those sightless eyes were prevented from looking on.

(15) **Ninety and eight years old.**—The LXX. here reads "ninety" years, the Syriac Version "seventy eight." In the sacred text, where numbers are concerned we usually find these varieties of translation and interpretation. The present system of numerals was invented by the Arabs. The Hebrews use the letters of the alphabet to express numbers. Such a system was naturally fruitful in errors of transcription, and thus numbers, and dates especially, in the earlier books of the Old Testament are frequently confused and uncertain. Many of the difficulties which have given so much trouble to commentators have arisen out of the confusion of copyists substituting, through inadvertence, in Hebrew one letter for another. Instead of "his eyes were dim," the more accurate rendering would be *his eyes were set*—were stiff, so that he could no longer see. This, as Keil observes, is a description of the so-called black cataract (amaurosis), which not unfrequently occurs at a very great age from paralysis of the optic nerves.

(16) **I fled to day out of the army.**—The fatal battle had taken place very early that same morning. The utter rout, the awful slaughter, the death of Hophni and Phinehas, and the loss of the Ark of the Covenant, all this the messenger knew, and with this terrible news had hasted to the seat of the government—the now empty sanctuary.

The very words of the runner were remembered. The whole vivid scene was evidently related by a bystander—some have even suggested that it was Samuel who stood by Eli's side.

(18) **He fell from off the seat backward.**—The compiler of these books was actuated by no feeling of friendship to the high priest Eli. In composing this history of the events which led to the elevation of Samuel to the judgeship, he simply puts together the materials he possessed of the records of these days, and gives us a vivid picture of the calamities of the rule of Eli. As he never spares his weakness, or attempts to veil his blind nepotism, we feel here the perfect truth of this touching incident which closed the old man's life. He loved the Ark, because of its close connection with his God, better, after all, than his two sons. We have seen already that he could bear the stern announcement of the ruin and degradation of the fortune of his proud house, for which he toiled only too faithfully; he could bear to see another—the boy Samuel—preferred before him, the high priest and judge of Israel; he could endure to hear of the defeat and ruin of the country over which he had so long ruled, and which he loved so well; even the news of the death of his sons he could listen to with sad resignation; but when his ears caught the words "the ark of God is taken," the old man's heart broke, and he died. The chronicler of this period, who certainly never favoured Eli, leaves upon us the impression that with all his faults and imperfections he was still a servant of God. Wordsworth quotes here Ps. cxxxvii. 5, 6: "If I forget thee, O Jerusalem, let my right hand forget *her* cunning. If I do not remember thee, let my tongue cleave to the roof of my mouth: *if I prefer not Jerusalem above my chief joy.*"—The dying words of Archbishop Whitgift were, "*Pro ecclesiâ Dei,*"—"For the church of God."

livered: and when she heard the tidings that the ark of God was taken, and that her father in law and her husband were dead, she bowed herself and travailed; for her pains [1] came upon her. (20) And about the time of her death the women that stood by her said unto her, Fear not; for thou hast born a son. But she answered not, [2] neither did she regard *it*. (21) And she named the child [3] I-chabod, saying, The glory is departed from Israel:

[1] Heb., *were turned.*

[2] Heb., *set not her heart.*

[3] That is, *Where is the glory?* or, There is no glory.

because the ark of God was taken, and because of her father in law and her husband. (22) And she said, The glory is departed from Israel: for the ark of God is taken.

CHAPTER V.—(1) And the Philistines took the ark of God, and brought it from Eben-ezer unto Ashdod. (2) When the Philistines took the ark of God, they brought it into the house of Dagon, and

---

And he had judged Israel forty years.—" When I read of Eli the priest, of the sons of Aaron, judging Israel forty years, and of Samuel, certainly a Levite, though not a priest, going circuit as a judge itinerant in Israel (1 Sam. vii. 16), and of others of the families of Levi appointed by King David to be judges and officers, not only in all the business of the Lord, but also for the outward business of Israel (2 Sam. xv. 35; 1 Chron. xxvi. 29—32)—when I observe in the Church stories, ever since the world had Christian princes, how ecclesiastical persons have been employed by their sovereigns in their weightiest consultations and affairs of state, I cannot but wonder at those who inveigh against courts, power, jurisdiction, and the temporalities of bishops and other ecclesiastical persons. I speak it not to justify abuses of men, but to justify the lawfulness of the thing."—Bishop Sanderson, quoted by Wordsworth.

(21 22) **The glory is departed from Israel.**—This singular and circumstantial account of the death of the widow of Phinehas, the evil warrior-priest, the son of Eli, which follows directly after the story of the great national disaster, is introduced from the records of that sad time, not from any special interest in the hapless woman and her sad fate, but solely for the purpose of showing how deeply the heart of Israel was penetrated with a love for their God, His Tabernacle, and its sacred contents. It was not the intelligence of her husband's bloody end on the field of battle, or of her father-in-law's death on his throne, or the downfall of her house, which stirred her so painfully; she could have borne all this better than the news that the Ark of the Covenant was in the hands of the idolatrous enemies of God. Von Gerlach remarks that "the wife of this deeply corrupt man shows how penetrated the whole people then was with the sense of the value of its covenant with God."

The meaning of the term I-chabod is much disputed, owing to the doubt which hangs over the first syllable —"I" followed by "chabod." It is usually taken to mean a simple negative; "not:" chabod signifying "glory:" I-chabod thus represents "not glory:" *i.e.*, there is no glory. Others render the "I" syllable as a query, "Where?" "Where is the glory?" the answer, of course, being, "It is nowhere." But the best rendering seems to be to understand the syllable "I" as an exclamation of bitter sorrow, "Alas!" The name then could be translated, "*Alas! the glory.*"

V.

(1—12) The Ark of God among the Philistines.

(1) **The Philistines took the ark of God.**—The sacred writer concerns himself after the battle of Aphek only with the future of the Ark of the Cove-nant, and says nothing of the fate of Shiloh after the rout of the Israelites and the death of the high priest. We can, however, from Psalm lxxviii. 60—64, and two passages in Jeremiah (chaps. vii. 12, and xxvi. 9), complete the story of the sanctuary city after the death of Eli. After the victory of Aphek, the Philistines, flushed with success, probably at once marched on Shiloh, where, from the words of the above quoted Psalm, they seem to have revenged themselves for past injuries by a terrible massacre, and then to have razed the sacred buildings of the city to the ground. The awful fate of the priestly city seems to have become a proverb in Israel. "This house shall be like Shiloh," wrote Jeremiah, hundreds of years later, and "this city shall be desolate, without inhabitant." Yet, in spite of this crushing blow, the national life of the Hebrew people was by no means exterminated; we shall soon hear of its revival under happier auspices. There were others in Israel like Samuel, who, as we have seen, with all their hearts trusted in that Lord who, "when Israel was a child, then He loved him;" others like that weak but still righteous judge Eli, who for one great weakness had paid so awful a penalty; many others, like the wife of Phinehas, the wicked priest, and Elkanah and Hannah, the pious father and mother of Samuel, who dwelt in "Ramah of the Watchers."

(2) **They brought it into the house of Dagon.**—The conquerors, we are told, in the meantime, with triumph, carried the captured Ark from the battle-field to Ashdod. This was one of the capital cities of the five Philistine princes. It is built on a hill close to the Mediterranean Sea, and was in after days known as Azotus (Acts viii. 40).

In Ashdod they placed it in the temple of the popular Philistine god, Dagon. *This* was their vengeance for the slaughter of the 3,000 Philistine worshippers in the temple of the same deity at Gaza, not many years before, by the blind Hebrew champion Samson.

The princes and Philistine people well remembered how the blind hero on that awful day, when 3,000 perished in the house of Dagon when he with his superhuman strength forced the great temple pillars down, called on the name of the God of Israel, whom they in their idol-trained hearts associated with the golden Ark.

"This only hope relieves me, that the strife
 With me hath end, all the contest now
'Twixt God and Dagon; Dagon hath presumed,
Me overthrown, to enter lists with God,
His deity comparing and preferring
Before the God of Abraham. He, be sure,
Will not connive or linger thus provoked,
But will arise, and His great name assert."—MILTON.

The insulted Dagon and all their murdered countrymen should be avenged by the perpetual humiliation of the "God of Abraham."

The Ark in the Temple of Dagon.   I. SAMUEL, V.   *Ashdod Afflicted with Plagues.*

set it by Dagon. ⁽³⁾ And when they of Ashdod arose early on the morrow, behold, Dagon *was* fallen upon his face to the earth before the ark of the LORD. And they took Dagon, and set him in his place again. ⁽⁴⁾ And when they arose early on the morrow morning, behold, Dagon *was* fallen upon his face to the ground before the ark of the LORD; and the head of Dagon and both the palms of his hands *were* cut off upon the threshold; only ¹ *the stump of* Dagon was left to him. ⁽⁵⁾ Therefore neither the priests of Dagon, nor any that come into Dagon's house, tread on the threshold of Dagon in Ashdod unto this day.

⁽⁶⁾ But the hand of the LORD was heavy upon them of Ashdod, and he destroyed them, and smote them with ᵃ emerods, *even* Ashdod and the coasts thereof. ⁽⁷⁾ And when the men of Ashdod saw that *it was* so, they said, The ark of the God of Israel shall not abide with us: for his hand is sore upon us, and upon Dagon our god. ⁽⁸⁾ They sent therefore and gathered all the lords of the Philistines unto them, and said, What shall we do with the ark of the God of Israel? And they answered, Let the ark of the

¹ Or, *the fishy part.*

ᵃ Ps. 78. 66.

The sacred Ark should henceforth be placed at the feet of their god Dagon.

⁽³⁾ **Dagon was fallen upon his face.**—This Dagon was one of the chief Philistine deities, and had temples not only in Ashdod and in Gaza, but in the cities of Philistia. (See St. Jerome on Is. xlvi. 1.) The idol had a human head and hands, and the body of a fish. Philo derives the word Dagon from *dagan,* "corn," and supposes the worship to have been connected with Nature worship. The true derivation, however, is from *Dag,* a fish, which represents the sea from which the Philistines drew their wealth and power. In one of the bas-reliefs discovered at Khorsabad, and which, Layard states, represents the war of an Assyrian king—probably Sargon—with the inhabitants of the coast of Syria, a figure is seen swimming in the sea, with the upper part of the body resembling a bearded man wearing the ordinary conical tiara of royalty, adorned with elephants' tusks, and the lower part resembling the body of a fish. It has the hand lifted up, as if in astonishment or fear, and is surrounded by fishes, crabs, and other marine animals.

"There can be hardly any doubt," argues Keil, "that we have here a representation of the Philistine Dagon. This deity was a personification of the generative and vivifying principle of nature, for which the fish, with its innumerable multiplication, was specially adapted, and set forth the idea of the Giver of all earthly good."

This strange image the men of Ashdod, on the morrow of their triumphal offering of the Ark of the Lord before the idol shrine, found prostrate on the temple floor, before the desecrated sacred coffer of the Israelites.

They at once assumed that this had taken place owing to some accident, and they raised again the image to its place.

⁽⁴⁾ **When they arose early on the morrow.**—Strange to say, on the next day a new and startling circumstance aroused and disturbed the exultant Philistines. The idol was again fallen, but this time broken. No mere accident could account for what had happened. The head and hands were severed from the image, and thrown contemptuously on the threshold of the temple, upon which the foot of every priest or worshipper as he passed into the sacred house must tread.

Only the stump of Dagon.—The Hebrew, rendered literally, would run, *only Dagon was left to him:* that is to say, only "the fish," the least noble part of the idol image, was left standing; the human head and hands were tossed down for men as they passed in to trample on; "only the form of a fish was left in him."—*R. D. Kimchi.*

⁽⁵⁾ **Unto this day.**—This curious "memory" of the disaster to the Dagon image in this Philistine temple at Ashdod long existed among the worshippers of the fish-god. Zephaniah (chap. i. 9), in the reign of King Josiah, mentions this among idolatrous observances which he condemns: "In the same day I will punish all those that leap on (or over) the threshold."

⁽⁶⁾ **But the hand of the Lord was heavy upon them of Ashdod.**—A painful and distressing sickness, in the form, perhaps, of tumours—(the word *emerods* should be spelt *hemorrhoids*)—broke out among the inhabitants of the Philistine city in which was situated the idol temple, where was placed the Ark of the Covenant. The LXX. has an addition to the Hebrew text here which speaks of a terrible land plague which, apparently from subsequent notices, visited Philistia in addition to the bodily sufferings here spoken of. The Greek Version adds to verse 6 these words: "and mice were produced in the land, and there arose a great and deadly confusion in the city." In chap. vi. 4, &c., among the expiatory offerings sent by the idolators to Israel to appease what they imagined the offended Hebrew God, "golden mice" are mentioned: "images of the mice that mar the land." The mouse, according to Herodotus and the testimony of hieroglyphics, was an old symbol of pestilence. The Greek translators, however, failing to understand the meaning of. the offering of golden mice, added the words—apparently in accordance with a received tradition—by way of explanation.

⁽⁸⁾ **Gathered all the lords of the Philistines unto them.**—The Philistine federation seems to have been a very powerful one, and owing to the disinclination of the Israelites to maritime pursuits and foreign commerce—[the foreign commercial expeditions of King Solomon were apparently quite exceptional]—held in their hands a large proportion of the Mediterranean trade—the Mediterranean being the great highway between Eastern and Western nations; hence, no doubt, the worship of Dagon, the fish-god. It seems to have been something more than mere "Nature worship," the devotion of the Phœnician settlers on the sea-board of Syria and Canaan to a marine deity. The constitution of Philistia was oligarchical: that is, the government was in the hands of a College of Princes, whose decision no individual could oppose. The princes (*seranim*) are the heads of the several city districts, which formed a confederation, each one of the five chief cities

God of Israel be carried about unto Gath. And they carried the ark of the God of Israel about *thither*. ⁽⁹⁾ And it was so, that, after they had carried it about, the hand of the LORD was against the city with a very great destruction: and he smote the men of the city, both small and great, and they had emerods in their secret parts.

⁽¹⁰⁾ Therefore they sent the ark of God to Ekron. And it came to pass, as the ark of God came to Ekron, that the Ekronites cried out, saying, They have brought about the ark of the God of Israel to us, to slay us and our people. ⁽¹¹⁾ So they sent and gathered together all the lords of the Philistines, and said, Send away the ark of the God of Israel, and let it go again to his own place, that it slay us not, and our people: for there was a deadly destruction throughout all the city; the hand of God was very heavy there. ⁽¹²⁾ And the men that died not were smitten with the emerods: and the cry of the city went up to heaven.

B.C. cir. 1140.

CHAPTER VI.—⁽¹⁾ And the ark of the LORD was in the country of the Philistines seven months. ⁽²⁾ And the Philistines called for the priests and the diviners, saying, What shall we do to the ark of the LORD? tell us wherewith we shall send it to his place. ⁽³⁾ And they said, If ye send away the ark of the God of Israel, send it not empty; but in any wise return him a trespass offer-

---

holding a number of places, country cities, or "daughter" cities, as its special district. (See Erdmann in *Lange's Commentary*.) Dr. Payne Smith (Dean of Canterbury) has an ingenious and scholarly derivation for the titular designation of these lords (Hebrew, *seranim*), in which, rejecting the usual root *sar*, a prince, he connects the word with *seren*, a hinge; "just," he says, "as the cardinals of the Church of Rome take their name from *cardo*, which has the same meaning."

⁽¹¹⁾ **Send away the ark.**—The lords of the Philistines were a long time before they could make up their minds to get rid of this deadly trophy of their victory. They had grown up with an undefined awe of the "golden chest," which, as they supposed, had so often in the days of the famous Hebrew conqueror, Joshua, led the armies of Israel to victory; and now at last it was their own. It was indeed a sore trouble for them to yield it up to their enemies again; to see the historical sacred treasure of Israel, so long veiled in awful mystery, at the feet of their fish-god idol, was a perpetual renewal for Philistia of the glorious triumph of Aphek, which avenged so many years of bitter humiliation. The plague and misery which afflicted the cities of Philistia in the day when the sacred Ark dwelt an unhonoured guest in their midst suggest many and grave thoughts. Is there not an unseen power ever protecting God's institutions, His ordinances, and His ritual, the sacred House dedicated to His solemn worship, the vessels of the sanctuary, the very lands and gold consecrated to His service, even though all these things, owing to the faults and errors of His servants, have lost apparently their holy and beneficial influence over the hearts and homes of men?

Does not this old loved story warn rash and careless souls against laying rough hands on *any* ark of the Lord, though the ark in question *seem* to be abandoned by God, and destitute of power and dignity?

VI.

⁽¹⁻²¹⁾ The Philistines return the Ark to Israel. The Citizens of Beth-shemesh forget its Sanctity. Their Punishment.

⁽²⁾ **What shall we do to the ark of the Lord?**—During the seven months which followed the great Philistine victory of Aphek, the Ark remained in the country of the enemies of Israel. It was removed from temple to temple in the various cities, but the same doom always followed it. The inhabitants of the city where was the Ark were smitten with deadly abscesses, in addition to which, from the statement in verse 5, a plague of field-mice during the same period probably desolated the land. In their distress the Philistine rulers, determining to get rid of the fatal trophy of which they were once so proud, consulted their priests and diviners as to the most graceful and effective way of returning the captured Hebrew emblem. The "diviners" in the counsels of all the nations of antiquity occupy a distinguished place. We hear of them under different designations, as magicians, sorcerers, soothsayers, augurs, oracles, &c. They plied their strange trade, now with the aid of arrows, now with the entrails of slain animals, now with observation of the stars, now with the watching of natural signs, the flight of birds, &c. These men, who in one form or other dabbled in occult science, and perhaps here and there were aided by evil and unclean spirits, but who more frequently traded on the credulity and superstition of their fellows, occupied a considerable position among the nations of antiquity. We hear of them frequently among the Israelites, who seem to have adopted this class of advisers from the heathen nations around them. Isaiah (chap. iii. 2) specially mentions them, and reckons these diviners among the leading orders of the State. The English Version, however, with singular inconsistency, renders the word in that same passage by "prudent;" possibly, it has been ingeniously suggested, owing to the translators being displeased at finding the professors of a forbidden art ranked so highly among the chosen people.

In the first verse the LXX. add, "and the land swarmed with mice," another of the many explanatory additions so common in the Greek translation of the Hebrew.

⁽³⁾ **Send it not empty.**—The advice was to propitiate with gifts the powerful Hebrew Deity, whom they imagined was offended and angry at the insult offered Him—the being placed in an inferior position in the Dagon temple.

The priests and diviners evidently thought that the Hebrew Deity, in some way resident in the "golden

The Philistines determine I. SAMUEL, VI. *to Return the Ark.*

ing: then ye shall be healed, and it shall be known to you why his hand is not removed from you. ⁽⁴⁾ Then said they, What *shall be* the trespass offering which we shall return to him? They answered, Five golden emerods, and five golden mice, *according to* the number of the lords of the Philistines: for one plague *was* on ¹you all, and on your lords. ⁽⁵⁾ Wherefore ye shall make images of your emerods, and images of your mice that mar the land; and ye shall give glory unto the God of Israel: peradventure he will lighten his hand from off you, and from off your gods, and from off your land. ⁽⁶⁾ Wherefore then do ye harden your hearts, as the Egyptians and Pharaoh hardened their hearts?

1 Heb., *them.*

2 Or, *reproachfully.*

a Ex. 12. 31

3 Heb., *them*

4 Or, *it.*

when he had wrought ²wonderfully among them, ᵃdid they not let ³the people go, and they departed? ⁽⁷⁾ Now therefore make a new cart, and take two milch kine, on which there hath come no yoke, and tie the kine to the cart, and bring their calves home from them: ⁽⁸⁾ and take the ark of the LORD, and lay it upon the cart; and put the jewels of gold, which ye return him *for* a trespass offering, in a coffer by the side thereof; and send it away, that it may go. ⁽⁹⁾And see, if it goeth up by the way of his own coast to Beth-shemesh, *then* ⁴he hath done us this great evil: but if not, then we shall know that *it is* not his hand *that* smote us; it *was* a chance *that* happened to us.

---

chest," was a childish, capricious deity, like one of their own loved gods—Dagon, or Beelzebub, lord of flies. Their people had insulted Him; He had shown Himself powerful enough, however, to injure His captors, so the insults must cease, and He must be appeased with rich offerings.

⁽⁴⁾ **Five golden emerods, and five golden mice.**—It was a general custom in the nations of antiquity to offer to the deity, to whom sickness or recovery from sickness was ascribed, likenesses of the diseased parts; so, too, those who had escaped from shipwreck would offer pictures, or perhaps their garments, to Neptune, or, as some tell us, to Isis. (See, for instance, Horace, *Carm.* i. 5.) Slaves and gladiators would present their arms to Hercules; captives would dedicate their chains to some deity. This practice has found favour in more modern times. In the fifth century Christians—Theodoret tells us—would often offer in their churches gold or silver hands and feet, or eyes, as a thank-offering for cures effected in reply to prayer. Similar votive offerings are still made in Roman Catholic countries.

⁽⁵⁾ **Images of your mice.**—This is the first mention of the plague of "mice" in the Hebrew text. The Greek Version had (see above) carefully appended to the description of the bodily disease the account of this scourge which devastated the land of Philistia. In these warm countries which border the Mediterranean vast quantities of these mice from time to time seem to have appeared and devoured the crops. Aristotle and Pliny both mention their devastations. In Egypt this visitation was so dreaded that the mouse seems to have been the hieroglyphic for destruction. The curse then weighed heavily in Philistia, both upon man and the land.

⁽⁶⁾ **As the Egyptians and Pharaoh hardened their hearts.**—We have here the traditional account of the deliverance of Israel from Egypt, no doubt, as it was preserved in Philistia. These constant references to the story of Moses and the Exodus are indications of the deep impression those events had made on the surrounding nations; hence the value they set on the Ark, which they looked upon as the visible symbol of the mighty Hebrew God. The argument here used by the priests and diviners is:— "You all remember the well-known story of the obdu-

racy of the powerful Egyptians in connection with these Israelites, yet even they in the end had to let them go. You Philistines have had the experience of one plague; will you, like those foolish Egyptians, harden your hearts till you, like them, have been smitten with ten?"

⁽⁷⁾ **Now therefore make a new cart.**—The note here in the *Speaker's Commentary* is interesting. "This was so ordered in reverence to the Ark, and was a right and true feeling. (See Num. xix. 2; 2 Sam. vi. 3.) So our Lord rode on an ass 'whereon never man sat' (Mark xi. 2), and His holy body was laid in Joseph's 'new tomb, wherein never man before was laid' (Matt. xxvii. 60; Luke xxiii. 53). For the supposed peculiar virtue of *new* things, see Judges xvi. 7—11."

⁽⁸⁾ **In a coffer by the side thereof.**—The reverent awe with which these Philistines treated the Ark, which had, they supposed, wrought them such great evil, presents a strong contrast to the careless curiosity of the men of Beth-shemesh with regard to the same sacred object—a careless curiosity, which was punished, as we so often find in the case of acts of sacrilege, with extreme severity.

⁽⁹⁾ **It was a chance that happened to us.**— The priests and diviners were not certain whether the plague had been sent by the offended God of Israel or had visited Philistia in the ordinary course of nature. This strange experiment would satisfy the minds of the Philistine people. If the cows, contrary to their expectation, kept on the road to Beth-shemesh, this would be a sign that they were driven and guided by a Divine power, and it would be clear to all that the Ark was a dangerous possession, and that they were well rid of it. They would be assured then that the scourge they were suffering from came from the angry Israelite Deity. If, on the other hand, the animals, left to themselves, returned to their own stalls, which, evidently, the diviners expected would be the case—then the Philistines might safely retain the Ark, being confident that their late sufferings were simply the results of natural causes. It will be remembered (verse 7) that these were milch cows, whose calves were shut up in the stall. The diviners felt quite sure that the cows, left to their own instincts, would, unless driven by some Divine power, come back

(10) And the men did so; and took two milch kine, and tied them to the cart, and shut up their calves at home: (11) and they laid the ark of the LORD upon the cart, and the coffer with the mice of gold and the images of their emerods. (12) And the kine took the straight way to the way of Beth-shemesh, *and* went along the highway, lowing as they went, and turned not aside *to* the right hand or *to* the left; and the lords of the Philistines went after them unto the border of Beth-shemesh. (13) And *they of* Beth-shemesh *were* reaping their wheat harvest in the valley: and they lifted up their eyes, and saw the ark, and rejoiced to see *it*. (14) And the cart came into the field of Joshua, a Beth-shemite, and stood there, where *there was* a great stone: and they clave the wood of the cart, and offered the kine a burnt offering unto the LORD. (15) And the Levites took down the ark of the LORD, and the coffer that *was* with it, wherein the jewels of gold *were*, and put *them* on the great stone: and the men of Beth-shemesh offered burnt offerings and sacrificed sacrifices the same day unto the LORD. (16) And when the five lords of the Philistines had seen *it*, they returned to Ekron the same day.

(17) And these *are* the golden emerods which the Philistines returned *for* a trespass offering unto the LORD; for Ashdod one, for Gaza one, for Askelon one, for Gath one, for Ekron one; (18) and the golden mice, *according to* the number of all the cities of the Philistines *belonging* to the five lords, *both* of fenced cities, and of country villages, even unto the ¹great *stone of* Abel, whereon they set down the ark of the LORD: *which stone remaineth* unto this day in the field of Joshua, the Beth-shemite.

1 Or, *great stone.*

---

to their young ones in the stall. What the priests and diviners advised was done, and the next two verses (10 and 11) relate how the restoration of the Ark was carried out in the way prescribed above.

(12) **Went along the highway, lowing.**—But the dumb beasts did what the idol priests and diviners scarcely considered possible, for God's hand drove them. The narrative here throughout is evidently unadorned, very easy and natural, and speaks of primitive customs, telling its story of the Divine interference of the "Glorious Arm" with exquisite simplicity and truth.

The dumb beasts went on their strange way with their golden burden, the princes of the Philistines following them, awe-struck, at a distance.

(13) **And they of Beth-shemesh.**—Beth-shemesh, or "House of the Sun," nearly equivalent to Heliopolis, "City of the Sun," was a priestly city. It would thus have seemed that this was a fitting home for the Ark of the Covenant to rest in for a time. Shiloh, the old sanctuary, was, we know, now desolate and ruined; but the priests and Levites, from what follows, evidently had forfeited their old position as guides and teachers of the people. Beth-shemesh was no fit permanent dwelling for the Ark of God. The story of the priestly life in the once famous Shiloh during the latter years of Eli indicated how utterly incapable the Levitical families were to influence and guide the people. The subsequent conduct of priestly Beth-shemesh on this memorable occasion, therefore, is not to be wondered at; at first they seem to have rejoiced at the sight of their lost sacred treasure, but an act of careless irreverence called down a swift and unexpected punishment.

(14) **The field of Joshua, a Beth-shemite.**—The great stone—most likely a mass of natural rock rising from the soil—was the occasion of the cart being stopped there, Beth-shemesh and its suburbs being a city of the priests (Joshua xxi. 16). The presence of Levites, among whom were doubtless priests, is natural. These were, of course, the principal men of the city and its suburbs, and they were familiar with all sacrificial rites prescribed by the Law. The offering of these sacrifices at Beth-shemesh, although the Tabernacle never had been stationed there, was no transgression against the law, for now the Ark of the Covenant was present, the occasional throne of the glory-presence of the Eternal, before which the sacrifices were really offered.

(16) **They returned to Ekron.**—The five Philistine princes, when they had watched the strange scene from a distance, returned; their mission was accomplished, and the question solved as to the source of the plagues which had visited their country.

(17) **The golden emerods.**—The offering of the golden emerods (or *tumours*), including one for each of the five principal cities. In the preceding chapter only Ashdod, Gath, and Ekron are mentioned as abiding places of the Ark, but there is no doubt that during the "seven months" the sacred chest was for a long or short period located in each of the five towns, in the Dagon temple which each of the cities possessed.

(18) **And the golden mice.**—We have here a far greater number of "golden mice" mentioned as being offered in expiation than appear specified in the directions of the priests and diviners (verse 4). The truth was that whilst the human sickness was confined to the five cities, the plague of field mice no doubt extended over the whole country. The inhabitants of all the villages were anxious to do their part to propitiate the insulted Hebrew God, and to get rid of the plague which was devastating their fields and vineyards; hence this large offering, so much in excess of what was suggested by the diviners.

The great stone of Abel.—The LXX. Version reads here, "And this great stone on which they placed the Ark of Jehovah, which is in the field of Joshua the Beth-shemite, is a witness unto this day." With this reading the Chaldee Targum substantially agrees. The Hebrew text here is hopelessly corrupt; the copies which the Greek translators and the Chaldee Targumist apparently had before them, instead of the word "Ável" (Abel), which signifies mourning, read the word *ǎven*, a stone, and the punctuation of *v'ad*,

(19) And he smote the men of Beth-shemesh, because they had looked into the ark of the Lord, even he smote of the people fifty thousand and threescore and ten men; and the people lamented, because the Lord had smitten *many* of the people with a great slaughter. (20) And the men of Beth-shemesh said, Who is able to stand before this holy Lord God? and to whom shall he go up from us? (21) And they sent messengers to the inhabitants of Kirjath-jearim, saying, The Philistines have brought again the ark of the Lord; come ye down, *and* fetch it up to you.

CHAPTER VII.—(1) And the men of Kirjath-jearim came, and fetched up the

---

"and unto," in the last clause was evidently (*v'ed*), "and a witness." If the reading Avel be the true one ("even unto the great Avel"), then the conjecture of R. D. Kimchi is probably right, that this stone was known as the Great Avel (or Abel), "the great mourning," owing to the terrible judicial calamity, related in the next three verses (19, 20, 21), which happened there. With this slight change a very good sense is obtained.

(19) **They had looked into the ark.**—Some commentators consider that the words here should be rendered, "because they had looked at the Ark" with a foolish irreverent staring, which dishonoured the holiness of the sacred mercy-seat; but it is better far to preserve the rendering of our English Version, which is also the favourite Rabbinical explanation of the original. It seems probable that the chief men of the city, most of whom were priests and Levites, after the festive rejoicings which accompanied the sacrificial feast celebrating the Ark's joyful return, heated with wine, lost all sense of reverence, and determined to use this opportunity of gazing into that sacred chest of which they had heard so much, and into which no profane eye in Israel had ever peered, since the golden cover—on which the glory of the Eternal loved to rest—had sealed up the sacred treasures in the wilderness. Perhaps they wished to see those grey Sinai tablets on which the finger of God had traced His ten solemn commandments; perhaps they excused themselves by a desire to learn if the Philistines had violated the secrets of the holy chest.

Even he smote of the people fifty thousand and threescore and ten men.—Here it is perfectly clear that the present Hebrew text, which the English Version literally renders, is corrupt. The system of writing letters for numbers, as we have seen, constantly has occasioned great discrepancies in the several versions, &c. Here the arrangement of the letters which express this enormous number is quite unusual, and taken by itself would be sufficient to excite grave doubts as to the accuracy of this text. The number of stricken ones, 50,070, is simply inconceivable. Beth-shemesh was never a large or important place; there were, in fact, no *great* cities in Israel, the population was always a scattered one, the people living generally on their farms. Dean Payne Smith computes the population of Jerusalem in its best days as under 70,000. The various versions, LXX., Chaldee, &c., vary in their rendering of these astounding figures. Josephus, *Antt.* vi. 1, § 4, in his account of this occurrence speaks of the smitten as numbering seventy. This is probably the correct number. A strange reading, which the LXX. inserts here, deserves to be quoted; it is another proof of the uncertainty of the text at the close of this sixth chapter: "And the children of Jechoniah among the Beth-shemites were not pleased with the men of Beth-shemesh because they saw the Ark, and he smote them, &c." Erdmann, in *Lange*, is inclined to believe the LXX. Version represents the true text, and thus comments on it: "The reason of the sudden death of the seventy of the race of Jechoniah is their unsympathising and, therefore, unholy bearing towards the symbols of God's presence among His people, which showed a mind wholly estranged from the living God—a symptom of the religious moral degeneracy which had spread among the people, though piety was still to be found."

(20) **Who is able to stand?**—There is some superstition involved in this exclamation, "Whither shall we send this awful visitant?" The men of the priestly city of Beth-shemesh strangely connected their invisible King with that golden Ark, which, sacred though it was, was but a lifeless chest of wood and gold.

Yet through their superstition we can discern a deep consciousness of sin and shortcoming, which argued well for the future reformation of the religious life of the people—a grand work, which we shall soon see Samuel the prophet labouring so faithfully and so successfully to bring about. These poor sinners, discerning the cause of the fatal stroke which had fallen upon their brethren, felt too surely that they were none of them any better really than those who had fallen victims to their impiety, and were fully sensible that sinners could not dwell in the presence of God. Carried away by this feeling of awe before the purity of the invisible King, they cried, "To whom shall He go up from us?"

These poor Hebrews felt the same fear as John was sensible of centuries later, when at the feet of the glorified Son of Man he fell as dead; but they, less blessed than John and the children of the kingdom, had no Redeemer there to raise them up with the loving whisper: "Fear not; I (whom thou dreadest) am He that liveth and was dead." (See Rev. i. 17, 18.)

(21) **Kirjath-jearim.**—Kirjath-jearim should be spelt and pronounced Kirjath-jearim, the "city of woods" (wood-ville, wood-town, wooton). Its modern name is Kurzet-el-Erab, "the city of grapes," the woods being in later days replaced by vines.

VII.

(1—17) The Revival of Israel. The Work of Samuel.

(1) **The ark of the Lord.**—Kirjath-jearim, the home of the Ark for nearly fifty years, was probably selected as the resting-place of the sacred emblem as being the nearest large city to Beth-shemesh then in the hands of the Israelites. It was neither a priestly nor a Levitical city, but it no doubt had preserved something of its ancient character of sanctity even among the children of Israel. In old days

ark of the LORD, and brought it into the house of Abinadab in the hill, and sanctified Eleazar his son to keep the ark of the LORD.

(2) And it came to pass, while the ark abode in Kirjath-jearim, that the time was long; for it was twenty years: and all the house of Israel lamented after the LORD. (3) And Samuel spake unto all the house of Israel, saying, If ye do return unto the LORD with all your hearts, then *a*put away the strange gods and *b*Ashtaroth from among you, and prepare your hearts unto the LORD, and *c*serve him only: and he will deliver you out of the hand of the Philistines.

a Josh. 24. 15, 23.
b Judg. 2. 13.
B.C. cir. 1120.
c Deut. 6. 4; Matt. 4. 10; Luke 4. 8.

---

before the Hebrew invasion, it was a notable "high place," and a seat of worship of Baal. This was also, no doubt, taken into account when it was resolved to locate the Ark there. The words "in the hill" remind us that the old "high place" was still marked, and was from its sacred associations looked on as a fitting temporary resting-place for the sacred treasure of Israel.

Eleazar—It is most likely that this Abinadab was a Levite. The names Eleazar and Uzzah, and Ahio of the same family (2 Sam. vi. 3), are Levitical appellations. Samuel—who, though he is not named in this transaction, was, no doubt, the director—would, of course, have endeavoured to find a man of the tribe of Levi for the sacred trust. "This Eleazar was constituted not priest, but watchman at the grave of the Ark by its corpse, till the future joyful resurrection."—*Hengstenberg*, quoted in *Lange*. Here the Ark remained until King David brought it from "the house on the hill," in the city of woods, first to the home of Obed-edom, and then to his own royal Zion. (2 Sam. vi. See too Ps. cxxxii. 6.)

(2) **And it came to pass, while the ark abode in Kirjath-jearim, that the time was long; for it was twenty years.**—Literally, *And it came to pass, from the day that the Ark rested at Kirjath-jearim, that the time was long; for it was twenty years.* There is something very touching in this sad note of time. We think we read Samuel's own words here. The unwearied toiler for God and His dear people found the twenty years a weary period of waiting. We must not, however, by any means suppose that the hungering of Israel after their God-Friend only began after the twenty years of sorrow were over.

It had been a stern trial time. The great victory of Aphek and the destruction of Shiloh had laid all Israel at the feet of their Philistine enemies, and they, we know, made their supremacy bitterly felt. The restoration of the Ark in no wise signified that they loosed their hold on the conquered people. This long time, when the hand of Philistia pressed so heavily on Israel, was the important period of Samuel's life. For these twenty years he must have laboured incessantly to wake up the old worship of the Eternal and the pure life loved by God among the people. The early dreams of his boy days, the hopes excited by his burning enthusiasm, were scattered to the winds.

The fatal battle of Aphek, the capture of the holy Ark, the death of his old guardian, the great high priestly judge Eli, the sack and devastation of Shiloh, the loved sanctuary, the terrible and continued oppression of Philistia, had opened the eyes of the young inspired man of God. Taught by the bitter lessons of adversity, he saw it was by no bold stroke of a few gallant patriots that the nation could be saved; all such efforts Samuel the seer, after the crushing defeat of Aphek, saw would only sink the nation into still lower depths of degradation and misery. Other and different things were needed before the lion standard of Judah could be safely unfurled, or the war-cry of Ephraim raised on her mountains. "What means he used we are not told, or what was his mode of life during those twenty years of waiting and work; but probably the life of the young prophet-judge was that of a fugitive, going stealthily from place to place that he might teach and preach, hiding in the caverns in the limestone ranges of Judæa, emerging thence to visit now one quarter of the country and now another, ever in danger, but gradually stirring up, not merely those districts which were contiguous to the Philistines, but all Israel to a sense of the greatness of their sins, and to the necessity of renewed trust in and return of old love to their God. And so a fresh spiritual life by degrees sprang up among the people, and with it came the certainty of the future restoration of their national independence."—*Dean Payne Smith.*

And all the house of Israel lamented after the Lord.—The English Version is singularly happy here. The Hebrew word Englished by "lamented after" has been variously rendered and paraphrased. The Syriac translates, "they all cast themselves down after Jehovah." Gesenius and some would translate "were assembled together;" others, "the people of Israel quieted themselves, and in quiet devotion followed Jehovah;" but the English Version is best on all grounds. This "lamenting" or "hungering after the Lord" was a gradual result of Samuel's unwearied labours. The assertion of chap. iii. 19, that "none of his words fell to the ground," especially belongs to this period of restless activity, when dangers and apparently insurmountable difficulties hemmed him in; slowly, but surely, the heart of the people, roused by his loving but passionate appeals, returned to their Eternal Friend; sick of crime and folly, gradually they began to hate their impurity and moral degradation; by degrees they began to loathe their idolatry; and when Samuel, after his twenty years of faithful restless work among them, summoned them boldly to declare their abhorrence of the strange Philistine gods, and the life taught and lived by the Philistine peoples, the heart of all Israel responded with intense gladness to the summons.

Then the wise and patriotic statesman-prophet saw the hour of deliverance and national restoration had struck. No longer solitary hamlets and scattered families mourned after the glorious Eternal and His pure holy worship and life; but the heart of a whole people mourned after the Lord, and hungered for His presence among them once more.

(3) **The strange gods.**—The strange gods are in verse 4 described as "Baalim." This plural form of Baal refers to the numerous images of Baal which existed, as does the plural form Ashtaroth to those of the female goddess Astarte. They were both favourite Phœnician deities, known under the familiar names of Baal, Bil, Bel, and Ashtaroth, Astarte, Istar. They represented the productive power of nature, and were generally worshipped throughout the East, usually with a wild and wanton worship.

(4) Then the children of Israel did put away ᵃBaalim and Ashtaroth, and served the LORD only.

(5) And Samuel said, Gather all Israel to Mizpeh, and I will pray for you unto the LORD. (6) And they gathered together to Mizpeh, and drew water, and poured *it* out before the LORD, and fasted on that day, and said there, We have sinned against the LORD. And Samuel judged the children of Israel in Mizpeh.

(7) And when the Philistines heard that the children of Israel were gathered together to Mizpeh, the lords of the Philistines went up against Israel. And when the children of Israel heard *it*, they were afraid of the Philistines. (8) And the children of Israel said to Samuel, ¹Cease not to cry unto the LORD our God for us, that he will save us out of the hand of the Philistines. (9) And Samuel took a sucking lamb, and offered

ᵃ Judg. 2. 11.

¹ Heb., *Be not silent from us from crying.*

Prepare your hearts.—It was, indeed, a desperate venture seemingly, this, to which the prophet summoned unarmed and undisciplined Israel. They were then completely at the mercy of their long victorious foes, who held the chief fortified places in the country with their garrisons; and Samuel challenged Israel to bid defiance to the most cherished institutions of their oppressors, bade them, if they loved the Eternal, to turn aside from reverencing what Philistia held to be sacred and all-powerful. He knew well that what he urged upon the people would at once provoke what appeared to be a dangerous and most unequal contest. If defeated, then Israel would bring upon their devoted heads utter misery, and a ruin hitherto undreamed of even in their unhappy land. Had they courage and faith to plunge unarmed, undisciplined, into so perilous a contest? For twenty years the great patriot-statesman had laboured for this end. He had succeeded at last in opening the eyes of Israel to see the real cause of their misfortunes. He had made them as a nation hunger for the lost presence of the Eternal, who had loved them in past days with so great a love; and now, after twenty long slow years, was his work done at last? They sorrowed indeed for their national sins; but had they faith and courage, all unarmed as they were, to rise against the powerful enemies of purity and God?

(4) **Then the children of Israel did put away Baalim and Ashtaroth.**—The answer of the people showed how well and thoroughly the prophet-statesman had done his Master's work. Through the land of Israel the graven images of the Phœnician idols were thrown down, and their impious worship everywhere was boldly dishonoured, and once more, in bold defiance of the idol-worshipping Philistines, the Invisible and Eternal was throughout the land acknowledged as the one God. These acts, of course, were an open act of rebellion against that warlike people who for so long had ruled them with an iron rule.

(5) **Mizpeh.**—Or, as it should be spelt, *Mizpah,* a common name for lofty situations. It signifies a "watch-tower," a place where an outlook could be kept against an advancing enemy.

Now the assembly of the tribes at Mizpeh marked a new departure for Israel. It was the result of more than twenty years of toil undertaken by the greatest reformer and statesman the chosen race ever knew. The great gathering belonged both to religion and to war. Its first object was solemnly to assure the Lord that the heart of His people, so long estranged from Him, was again His. Its second was to implore that Jehovah might again restore a repentant and sorrowful people to the land of their inheritance. What more likely than that the prophet-statesman—who in that solemn juncture represented priest and judge and seer to Israel—devised on that momentous day new symbolic rites, signifying Israel's new dedication to the Eternal for the future, Israel's repentance for the sad past? The solemn pouring out of water before the Lord symbolised, to a people trained so carefully to watch the meaning and signification of symbols and imagery, the heart and whole inner life poured out before the Lord; the fasting represented the repentant humble sinner bowed down in grief before the one true God. Is it not at least probable that the strange, mysterious custom which we hear of in after days—the high priest filling the golden vessel with the waters of Siloam, and then pouring it out silently before the Lord—was the record of one of the holiest memories of the people—their reconciliation with their God-Friend at Mizpeh? Now, after years of estrangement, they repented and were forgiven. The fasting of Mizpeh being a favourite practice, ever much observed by the worshippers in the Temple and synagogue, needed no special record or reminder.

(6) **And Samuel judged the children of Israel in Mizpeh.**—For some quarter of a century Samuel had been the principal personage among the people, and had, no doubt, long exercised the varied functions of the "judges" of Israel; but the tribes were scattered, their fortresses in the hand of enemies, there was scarcely any national life in that gloomy period in the people. In the first general assembly of the tribes the rank and position which Samuel had long really filled are publicly acknowledged.

(7) **The lords of the Philistines went up against Israel.**—This was what might naturally have been expected. The sudden destruction of the Phœnician idol shrines throughout the country, followed immediately by the summons of a vast popular assembly, held in so conspicuous a place as Mizpeh in Benjamin, aroused at once the warlike nation which had so long kept Israel in servitude. The Philistine leaders promptly assemble a powerful force, and proceed to interrupt the Mizpeh gathering.

(8) **Cease not to cry unto the Lord our God for us.**—The fear on the part of Israel was very natural. Unarmed—or, at least, very poorly armed and equipped —the assembled Israelites saw from the heights the advancing Philistine army. What hope was there for their ill-disciplined masses when they joined battle with that trained host of fighting men? But they remembered the days of old, and how, when Moses prayed, "the Angel of His presence" saved them. Had they not then with them there a seer equal to Moses, greater than Joshua, one with whom the Eternal of Hosts was wont to speak, as friend speaketh with friend? So in that supreme hour of danger they turned to Samuel the seer. We are just going, they said, all unarmed to meet that armed host; "cease not to cry unto the Lord our God for us." And Samuel, we read in the

it for a burnt offering wholly unto the LORD: and Samuel cried unto the LORD for Israel; and the LORD ¹heard him. ⁽¹⁰⁾ And as Samuel was offering up the burnt offering, the Philistines drew near to battle against Israel: but the LORD thundered with a great thunder on that day upon the Philistines, and discomfited them; and they were smitten before Israel. ⁽¹¹⁾ And the men of Israel went out of Mizpeh, and pursued the Philistines, and smote them, until *they came* under Beth-car. ⁽¹²⁾ Then Samuel took a stone, and set *it* between Mizpeh and Shen, and called the name of it ²Ebenezer, saying, Hitherto hath the LORD helped us.

⁽¹³⁾ So the Philistines were subdued, and they came no more into the coast of Israel: and the hand of the LORD was against the Philistines all the days of Samuel. ⁽¹⁴⁾ And the cities which the Philistines had taken from Israel were restored to Israel, from Ekron even unto Gath; and the coasts thereof did Israel deliver out of the hands of the Philistines. And there was peace between Israel and the Amorites.

¹ Or, *answered.*

² That is, *The stone of help.*

---

brief and graphic account before us, hurriedly—for the time was short, and the foe close at hand—and with rites somewhat different from those enjoined in the Law—for the occasion was indeed a critical one—offered up a sacrifice, and raised that weird piercing cry which many in Israel had heard before when Samuel the seer prayed; and while the prophet-statesman was sustaining that loud imploring cry, while the smoke of the slain lamb was still ascending, the first line of the Philistine army appeared on the topmost slope of Mizpeh. Once more, as in old days, the glorious Arm fought with no earthly weapons for the people; an awful thunderstorm burst over the combatant hosts, the storm probably beating in the faces of the advancing Philistines. The tribes welcomed it as the answer to their prophet's prayer, and with a wild enthusiasm charged down and broke the serried ranks of their oppressors. Josephus tells us of an earthquake, which added fresh horrors to the scene of battle. Each crash of thunder, each wild and furious gust of hail and rain, the men of Israel welcomed as a fresh onslaught on the part of an unseen army fighting by their side. The dismayed Philistines fled, and the rout was complete; the defeated army hurried panic-stricken over the same ground in the neighbourhood of Aphek illustrious twenty years before for their signal victory. The scene of carnage now received the significant name of Eben-ezer, or The Stone of Help.

⁽¹¹⁾ **Until they came under Beth-car.**—"House of the Lamb," or, as some would render it, *House of the Field.* Of this place we know nothing; it was, no doubt, a Philistine fortress, where the scattered remains of the beaten host were able to rally and defend themselves.

⁽¹²⁾ **Between Mizpeh and Shen.**—The situation of Ha-Shen, "The Tooth," has not yet been identified. It probably denotes a peak or crag, a prominent rock formation, so named, like the modern French *dent*—a favourite name for a peak in some districts of the Alps and Pyrenees: *e.g., Dent du Midi.*

⁽¹³⁾ **So the Philistines were subdued.**—The work of Samuel had been thorough. It was no mere solitary victory, this success of Israel at Eben-ezer, but was the sign of a new spirit in Israel, which animated the nation during the lifetime of Samuel, and the reigns of David and Solomon and the great Hebrew kings. The petty jealousies had disappeared, and had given place to a great national desire for unity. In the several tribal districts it was no longer the glory and prosperity of Judah, Ephraim, or Benjamin, but the glory and prosperity of Israel that was aimed at. The old idol worship of Canaan, which corrupted and degraded every nationality which practised it, was in a great measure swept away from among the chosen people, while the pure religion of the Eternal of Hosts was no longer confided solely to the care and guardianship of the tribe of Levi, which had shown itself unworthy of the mighty trust. The Levites still ministered in the sanctuary, and when the Temple took its place, alone officiated in its sacred courts; and the chosen race of Aaron, in the family first of Ithamar, then of Eleazar, alone wore the jewels and the official robe of the high priest; but in religious matters the power of the priestly tribe was never again supreme in the Land of Promise. From the days of Samuel a new order—that of the Prophets, whose exact functions with regard to the ritual of the worship of the Eternal were undefined—was acknowledged by the people as the regular medium of communication with the Jewish King of Israel.

The hand of the Lord was against the Philistines.—The Philistines never entirely recovered their supremacy in Canaan. There was, it is true, a long fierce struggle, but with the exception of the short period which immediately preceded the election of Saul, and the temporary disasters of the children of Israel which were the punishments of that king's disobedience—from this time forward the power of the Philistines gradually decayed, while the strength of Israel steadily increased, until King David completely subdued them, and the old oppressors of Israel were absorbed into the subject races of Canaan.

⁽¹⁴⁾ **The cities.**—The immediate result of Samuel's great victory at Eben-ezer, and the renovated national spirit of the people, was their recovery of the towns and villages which during the late disastrous period had fallen into the Philistines' hands.

From Ekron even unto Gath.—It is doubtful whether these words signify that at this period these famous Philistine cities fell into the hands of Samuel. This expression more probably indicates on the Philistine side the direction and limits of the space in which the Israelites recovered their lost territory.

The Amorites.—The Amorites here, as representing the most powerful of the old Canaanite tribes, are especially mentioned. This note respecting them tells us that in these glorious days of the restoration of Israel under Samuel, not only were the Philistines of the coast kept in check and gradually subdued, but that the Canaanite tribes of the interior of the land submitted quietly to the old conditions imposed by Joshua at the time of the conquest.

(15) And Samuel judged Israel all the days of his life. (16) And he went from year to year ¹in circuit to Beth-el, and Gilgal, and Mizpeh, and judged Israel in all those places. (17) And his return *was* to Ramah; for there *was* his house; and there he judged Israel;

1 Heb., *and he circuited.*

B.C. cir. 1112.

and there he built an altar unto the LORD.

CHAPTER VIII.—(1) And it came to pass, when Samuel was old, that he made his sons judges over Israel. (2) Now the name of his firstborn was Joel; and

(15) **And Samuel judged Israel all the days of his life.**—The influence and supreme power of Samuel only ended with his life. For a very long period —probably for at least twenty years after the decisive battle of Eben-ezer—Samuel, as "judge," exercised the chief authority in Israel. The time at length arrived when, convinced by clear Divine monition that it was best for the people that a king should rule over them, Samuel the seer, then advanced in years, voluntarily laid down his high office in favour of the new king, Saul; but his influence remained, and his authority, whenever he chose to exercise it, seems to have continued undiminished, and on momentous occasions (see, for instance, chap. xv. 33) we find king and nation submitting to his counsel and expressed will.

(16) **To Beth-el, and Gilgal, and Mizpeh, and judged Israel.**—These centres, it is observable, were all situated in the southern part of the land, in the tribe of Benjamin. This leads us to the conclusion that the power of Samuel, if not exclusively, was chiefly exercised among the southern tribes. The whole subsequent story of the chosen people seems to tell us that the religion of the Eternal at an early date became corrupted in the north of the Promised Land, and that the restoration of faith and purification of life—the result of the great work of Samuel—was so much less marked in the northern than in the southern tribes, that when the strong hand of Solomon was removed, a formal secession from the southern league at once took place. This was followed by a rapid deterioration both in faith and practice in the northern kingdom of Israel.

The places mentioned as the centres where Samuel "judged" were all holy sites, and at different periods of the year, no doubt, were crowded with pilgrims from distant parts of the land.

(17) **Ramah.**—The same Ramah "of the Watchers" where Elkanah and Hannah had dwelt. After the destruction of Shiloh, Samuel seems to have fixed his abode in his father's city.

And there he built an altar.—Thus following the old custom of the patriarchs. It must be remembered that at this period there was no national sanctuary, no formal seat of worship, where the high priest and his attendant priests and Levites served. The Ark, we know, was in safe keeping in the "city of woods," Kirjath-jearim, but it was in private custody; and we hear of no priests and Levites, of no ritual or religious observances, in connection with the long sojourn of the holy Ark in that place. It is probable that the sacred vessels and furniture had been saved from the destruction of Shiloh by Samuel. These were, very likely, in the prophet-judge's safe keeping at Ramah.

VIII.

(1–22) Israel desires an earthly King. The Elders bring the Request to Samuel. The Eternal sees fit to Grant their Request.

(1) **When Samuel was old.**—We are not able with any precision to fix the dates of Samuel's life.

When the great disaster happened which resulted in the capture of the Ark of God and Eli's death, the young prophet was barely thirty years old. For the next twenty years we have seen how unweariedly he laboured to awaken in the people a sense of their deep degradation and of the real causes of their fallen state. Thus, when the great revolt and the Israelite victory at Eben-ezer took place, Samuel the judge was probably nearly fifty years of age. Another considerable lapse of time must be assumed between the day of the uprising of the people and the throwing off the Philistine yoke and the events related at such length in the present chapter—the request of the people for an earthly king; for we must allow a sufficient lapse of time for the Philistines to have recovered the effects of their defeat at Eben-ezer, and again to have established themselves in power, at least in the southern districts of Canaan. A famous Hebrew commentator suggests seventy years of age as the most likely time of life. This supposition is, likely enough, a correct one.

The following little table, showing the events in the life of Samuel, will assist the student of the Bible story:—

1st period, 12 years.	The child life in the Tabernacle service, under the guardianship of Eli.
2nd period, about 15 to 20 years.	The boy is called by the holy Voice to be a prophet; Josephus states that this happened in his twelfth year. The boy-prophet remains in Shiloh. The people gradually come to the knowledge that a new prophet had risen up among them. He stays with Eli until his death, after the disastrous battle of Aphek and the capture of the Ark. Shiloh was probably destroyed by the Philistines after the battle of Aphek.
3rd period, 20 years.	He works unweariedly up and down among the people, and rouses them to renounce idolatry, and under the Eternal's protection to win their freedom.
4th period, probably nearly 20 years.	Samuel judges Israel, now a free nation, again. The Eternal God-Friend acknowledged by the people as King.
5th period.	Samuel the seer and judge and Saul the king govern Israel.

(2) **They were judges in Beer-sheba.**—It was natural that the father, as the infirmities of old age were beginning to make his toilsome life more burdensome, should turn to his sons, and endeavour to train them up to share in his high duties, but beyond the natural regret of a father that the honours and dignities he had himself so hardly won should pass from his house for ever, no murmur seems to have escaped Samuel's lips when the will of the Eternal was made known to him; and the aged prophet, forgetting he had sons and a house which bore his name, was the principal agent in the establishment of the king, in whom all the powers of the judge were to be

The Elders of Israel I. SAMUEL, VIII. *desire an earthly King.*

the name of his second, Abiah: *they were judges in Beer-sheba.* (3) And his sons walked not in his ways, but turned aside after lucre, and ᵃtook bribes, and perverted judgment.

(4) Then all the elders of Israel gathered themselves together, and came to Samuel unto Ramah, (5) and said unto him, Behold, thou art old, and thy sons walk not in thy ways: now ᵇmake us a king to judge us like all the nations.

(6) But the thing ¹displeased Samuel, when they said, Give us a king to judge us. And Samuel prayed unto the LORD.

(7) And the LORD said unto Samuel, Hearken unto the voice of the people in all that they say unto thee: for they have not rejected thee, but they have

---

a Deut. 16. 19.

b Hos. 13. 10; Acts 13. 21.

1 Heb., *was evil in the eyes of Samuel.*

---

merged. It is probable that at the time when old age was beginning to enfeeble the strength of Samuel, and many of the duties devolved upon his worthless sons, the Philistines recovered much of their lost power over the southern districts of Israel. The names of these sons are especially significant of the holy atmosphere their father lived in. Joel signifies Jehovah is God; and Abiah, Jehovah a Father. But the glorious traditions of Samuel were quickly forgotten by these unworthy men who called him father. Josephus supplements the Biblical record by stating that while one of these sons remained in Beer-sheba, the other "judged" in the north of the land.

(3) **Took bribes, and perverted judgment.**—This sin, at all times a fatally common one in the East, was especially denounced in the Law. (See Exod. xxiii. 6—8; Deut. xvi. 19.) It is strange that the same ills that ruined Eli's house, owing to the evil conduct of his children, now threatened Samuel. The prophet-judge, however, acted differently to the high priestly judge. The sons of Samuel were evidently, through their father's action in procuring the election of Saul, quickly deposed from their authority. The punishment seems to have been successful in correcting the corrupt tendencies of these men, for we hear in after days of the high position occupied at the court of David by the distinguished descendants of the noble and disinterested prophet. (See the notices in 1 Chron. vi. 33, xxv. 4, 5, respecting Heman, the grandson of Samuel, the king's seer, who was chief of the choir of the Psalmist-king in the house of God.)

(4) **All the elders of Israel.**—We have here a clear trace of a popular assembly which seems in all times to have existed in Israel. Such a body appears to have met for deliberation even during the Egyptian captivity (see Exod. iii. 16). Of this popular council we know little beyond the fact of its existence. It seems to have been composed of representatives of the people, qualified by birth or office; these were known as "elders." Ewald sees special allusions to the "Parliament" or Assembly of Elders in Psalms l. and lxxxii. There are, however, various mentions of these councils in the Books of Samuel, Kings, Jeremiah, and Isaiah.

(5) **And said unto him.**—They ground their request—which, however, they framed almost in the very terms used in the prophecy of the Law (Deut. xvii. 14)—upon two circumstances: first, the age of Samuel, and his consequent inability to act as their leader in those perpetual wars and forays with the surrounding hostile nations; secondly, the degeneracy of his sons, who, placed by their father in positions of great trust, naturally looked to succeed him in his high dignity. They felt that the cares and duties of government were too weighty for Samuel, now growing old; and the men who through their kinship to him would naturally succeed him were utterly unfit for his office. The prospect before them was, they felt, a gloomy one. The Philistine power, too, was becoming daily greater in the south.

But what confidence must this assembly of elders have reposed in their aged judge to have used such a plea—his own growing infirmity and the unworthiness of his own sons, whom he had himself appointed to high offices! The elders of the people knew Samuel, the man of God, would do what was right and just—would give them the wisest counsel, utterly regardless of any private interest or feeling. The result justified their perfect confidence.

(6) **The thing displeased Samuel.**—It is clear that it was perfectly justifiable in the elders of the people to come to the resolution contained in their petition to Samuel. The Deuteronomy directions contained in chap. xvii. 14—20 are clear and explicit in this matter of an earthly king for the people, and Moses evidently had looked forward to this alteration in the constitution when he framed the Law. No date for the change is specified, but from the terms of the Deuteronomy words no distant period evidently was looked on to. Then, again, though Samuel was naturally displeased, he at once, as prophet and seer, carried the matter to the God-Friend of Israel in prayer, and the Eternal King at once bids His old true servant to comply with the people's desire.

The displeasure of the prophet-judge was very natural. He felt—this we see from the comforting words his Master addressed to him (see verse 7)—that the people, notwithstanding the vast claims he possessed to their gratitude, craved another and a different ruler, and were dissatisfied with his government. Samuel too was conscious that Israel by its request declined the direct sovereignty of the Eternal. The change to an earthly sovereign had been foreseen, foretold, even arranged for, by Moses, but, in spite of all this, to one like Samuel it was very bitter. It seemed to remove the people from that solitary platform which they alone among nations had been allowed to occupy. They had found by sad experience, as Moses,—"their Rabbi," as the old teachers loved to style him—had predicted, that such a form of government was, alas! unsuited to them, and that they must descend *here* to the level of ordinary peoples. But though all this was undisputably true, it was very bitter for the hero patriot to give up for ever the splendid Hebrew ideal that his people were the subjects of the Eternal King, ruled directly by Him.

(7) **Hearken unto the voice of the people.**—The words spoken to Samuel, probably in a vision, by the Most High are very touching and very sad. *Very touching*, in their extreme tenderness to the noble old man. Take courage, they seem to say, "my old true servant, and be not dismayed at this apparently bitter proof of the ingratitude of the people you loved so well. This deliberate complaint on the part of Israel is directed not against you, the judge, but

rejected me, that I should not reign over them. ⁽⁸⁾ According to all the works which they have done since the day that I brought them up out of Egypt even unto this day, wherewith they have forsaken me, and served other gods, so do they also unto thee. ⁽⁹⁾ Now therefore ¹hearken unto their voice: ²howbeit yet protest solemnly unto them, and shew them the manner of the king that shall reign over them.

⁽¹⁰⁾ And Samuel told all the words of the LORD unto the people that asked of him a king. ⁽¹¹⁾ And he said, This will be the manner of the king that shall reign over you: He will take your sons, and appoint *them* for himself, for his chariots, and *to be* his horsemen; and *some* shall run before his chariots. ⁽¹²⁾ And he will appoint him captains over thousands, and captains over fifties; and *will set them* to ear his ground, and to reap his harvest, and to make his instruments of war, and instruments of his chariots. ⁽¹³⁾ And he will take your daughters *to be* confectionaries, and *to be* cooks, and *to be* bakers. ⁽¹⁴⁾ And he will take your fields, and your vineyards, and your oliveyards, *even* the best *of them*, and give *them* to his servants. ⁽¹⁵⁾ And he will take the tenth of your seed, and of your vineyards, and give to his ³officers, and to his servants. ⁽¹⁶⁾ And he will take your menservants, and your maidservants, and your goodliest young men, and your asses, and put *them* to his work. ⁽¹⁷⁾ He will take the tenth of your sheep: and ye shall be his servants.

¹ Or, *obey*.
² Or, *notwithstanding, when thou hast solemnly protested against them, then thou shalt shew, &c.*
³ Heb., *eunuchs.*

against Me, the invisible King. They have ever been the same—incapable of becoming my true subjects, and of winning on earth the lofty position I would have given them; you must give them now their hearts' desire. It has all been foreseen and provided for; only make them understand *what* they are asking. Then give them their earthly king." Very sad, for it was the deliberate abandonment by the Eternal God of His first intention as regarded Israel — the deliberate lowering of the grand ideal once formed for His chosen people. Here, as is not unfrequent in the Divine records, we have a corner of the veil which hangs between the creature and the Creator lifted for a moment. We see how sadly possible it is for man in the exercise of his perfect freewill to mar the glorious work arranged for him by his God. We see too in the records of such a transaction as this (see Deut. xvii. 14) how all was foreseen by the King of heaven, and we catch sight of the sorrowful regret—if we may use the term—of the Creator for the perverse folly of His creatures.

⁽¹¹⁾ **And he said, This will be the manner of the king that shall reign over you.**—In obedience to the word of the Lord, Samuel, the judge of Israel, without blaming the people for their desire, quietly asks them if they were in real earnest—if they had fully considered the grave changes which such an appointment as that of a sovereign over the nation would bring about in the constitution. Were they willing to exchange their Republican freedom for the condition of subjection to a sovereign who, after the manner of those other kings of foreign nations—the Pharaohs, for instance—would of course govern Israel after his own will? in other words, were they really willing to give up their Republic for a Despotism?

In this whole transaction of the appointment of an earthly king in Israel, we must not forget that although under the present circumstances of Israel it was the *best* course to pursue, and, as such, received the Divine sanction, yet it was giving up the old grand ideal of a nation dwelling on earth ruled over directly by a King whose throne and home were in the eternal heavens. The glorious hope had to be given up, because Israel had been tried and found unworthy to share in the undreamed-of blessings of such a Government.

He will take your sons.—Here follows a graphic picture of the changed life of the people under a despotic monarch. They must be prepared, must those elders, for a court—a gorgeous court such as they had heard of, and perhaps some of them had seen on the banks of the Nile, the Euphrates, or the Tigris; all that was best and choicest in Israel would be summoned there. The old pastoral life would disappear; the dwelling under their own vines and fig-trees would give place to a very different way of living; the pleasures and vices of a gay and brilliant city life would allure the sons and daughters, and tempt them from the old simple way of living, dear to so many in Israel. War, too, on a scale they hitherto had never dreamed of, would be their portion—all these heavy burdens would become the heritage of Israel if they chose to imitate in their government the nations of the world. Had they thought of all *this* when they asked for a king?

⁽¹²⁾ **To ear his ground.**—To ear, that is, to plough. The word is an old word (Anglo-Saxon *earian*), and connected with the Latin *arare*.

⁽¹³⁾ **Confectionaries.**—Better rendered *perfumers*—that is, makers of ointments and scents, of which Orientals are inordinately fond.

⁽¹⁶⁾ **And your goodliest young men.**—The LXX. Greek Version here reads, "your best oxen," which required only the change of one letter of similar sound in the Hebrew word here. This was, no doubt, the reading of the original text, as the young men seem included among the sons in verses 11 and 12, and oxen would naturally precede the asses mentioned in the next clause of this verse.

⁽¹⁷⁾ **And ye shall be his servants.**—This statement generally includes all that has gone before. In other words, " Ye elders and chiefs of the people must make up your minds, in the event of electing a king, to the loss of all political and social freedom." How bitterly the nation, even in the successful and glorious reign of King Solomon, felt the pressure of the royal yoke, so truly foretold by their last judge, is shown in the history of the times which followed the death of Solomon, when the public discontent at the brilliant but despotic rule of the great king led to the revolution which split up the people into two nations. (See 1 Kings xii. 4.) "This whole passage bears internal

(18) And ye shall cry out in that day because of your king which ye shall have chosen you; and the LORD will not hear you in that day.

(19) Nevertheless the people refused to obey the voice of Samuel; and they said, Nay; but we will have a king over us; (20) that we also may be like all the nations; and that our king may judge us, and go out before us, and fight our battles. (21) And Samuel heard all the words of the people, and he rehearsed them in the ears of the LORD. (22) And the LORD said to Samuel, Hearken unto their voice, and make them a king. And Samuel said unto the men of Israel, Go ye every man unto his city.

a ch. 14. 51; Chr. 8. 33.

CHAPTER IX.—(1). Now there was a man of Benjamin, whose name was *a* Kish,

---

evidence of having been written before the establishment of the monarchy."—*Speaker's Commentary.*

(18) **The Lord will not hear you in that day.**—After the separation of the north and the south, when King Solomon was dead, a large proportion of the northern sovereigns—or kings, as they were called, of "Israel," in distinction to the southern monarchs, the kings of "Judah"—fulfilled in their lives and government of the realm the dark forebodings of the seer. The northern tribes broke with all the hallowed associations connected with the Ark and temple, and set up a rival and semi-idolatrous religion in some of their own popular centres. There no holy influences swayed the councils of their despotic kings. The lives of the Israelites who still loved the law of the Lord, and cherished the glorious memories of their fathers, must have been very bitter and hard when men like Omri and Ahab reigned with all their cruel power in Tirzah and Samaria.

But no prayers then availed; one wicked dynasty succeeded another, until the cup of iniquity was filled, and Israel carried away captive for ever out of their fair land.

(19) **The people refused.**—The warning words of the prophet-judge were evidently carefully considered and debated in a formal assembly, but the majority at least abided by the terms of their request.

(20) **Like all the nations.**—There is something strangely painful in these terms with which the elders urged their request—the wish "to be like other nations" seems to have been very strong with them. They forgot, or chose to ignore, the solitary position of lofty pre-eminence God had given them among the nations. They had, it is true, failed to comprehend it in past, as in present days, but this haste to give up their lofty privileges, and to descend from the pedestal on which their God had set them, was in the eye of one like Samuel a strange inexplicable foolishness.

(21) **In the ears of the Lord.**—Again the seer returns from the council chamber, where he had met the elders of the people, to some quiet spot, probably the sanctuary he had set up in his own "Ramah of the Watchers," where he poured out his heart before his God-Friend.

(22) **Hearken unto their voice.**—And for the third time (see verses 7 and 9) the voice of the Eternal, which Samuel the seer knew so well, used the same expression, bidding the reluctant and indignant old man comply with the request of the people. God had allowed His servant to remonstrate, well knowing all the time what would be the result of his remonstrances.

So now, with the self-same words with which He had spoken to the seer when at the first he laid the petition of Israel before the eternal throne, He finally directs Samuel respecting the course of action he was to pursue on this momentous occasion.

The men of Israel.—That is, to the elders. The words which follow, "Go ye every man unto his city," show that these elders were in truth a representative body, drawn from the chief centres of the land.

Attention has already been drawn to the perfect trust which the Eternal must have placed in Samuel the judge, seeing that He entrusted him with all the arrangements connected with this vital change in the Hebrew constitution, although his own downfall from power was necessarily involved in it. The confidence of the God-Friend of Israel in their upright judge was evidently shared in by the people. It was to their ruler, to the earthly head of their republic, that they in the first instance carried, through their representative chiefs, their request, which in other words said, "Let kings for the future, and not judges like yourself, rule over us." The elders of Israel seem to have listened respectfully to the urgent remonstrances of their great judge, and to have deliberated carefully over them, and then, still respectfully, but firmly, to have reiterated their first request, which asked for a king instead of a judge. Again they watched him go alone into the presence of the Eternal, and after the seer's solitary prayer, the "elders," at the bidding of their judge, dispersed quietly, each one journeying to his own city. They loved and trusted the patriot Samuel, and though they were ready to depose him, they waited till he should give them a sign.

IX.

(1—27) The Preparation of Saul the Son of Kish the Benjamite, for his appointment as anointed King of Israel.

(1) **Saul.**— The inspired compiler of these books—having related the circumstances which accompanied the people's request to the last of the judges for a king—closed the first part of the story of this momentous change in the fortunes of the chosen people with the words of the prophet-judge, bidding the representative elders to return to their homes, and wait the result of his solemn communing with the Eternal Friend of Israel on the subject of this king they so earnestly desired.

The Eternal answered His servant either in a vision, or by Urim, or by an angel visitant. We are in most cases left in ignorance respecting the precise method by which God communicated with these highly-favoured men—His elect servants. The chosen Israelite whom Samuel was to anoint as the first king in Israel would meet the prophet—so said the "word of the Lord" to Samuel—on a certain day and hour, at a given place. The ninth chapter begins with a short account of the family of this man chosen for so high an office, and after a word or two of personal description, goes on to relate the circumstances under which he met

The early Life and   I. SAMUEL, IX.   *Family History of Saul*

the son of Abiel, the son of Zeror, the son of Bechorath, the son of Aphiah, ¹a Benjamite, a mighty man of ²power. ⁽²⁾ And he had a son, whose name *was* Saul, a choice young man, and a goodly: and *there was* not among the children of Israel a goodlier person than he: from his shoulders and upward *he was* higher than any of the people.

⁽³⁾ And the asses of Kish Saul's father were lost. And Kish said to Saul his son, Take now one of the servants with thee, and arise, go seek the asses. ⁽⁴⁾ And he passed through mount Ephraim, and

<small>1 Or, *the son of a man of Jemini.*
B.C. cir. 1095.
2 Or, *substance.*</small>

Samuel. Saul, a man in the prime of manhood, distinguished among his fellows by his great stature, and for his grace and manly beauty, was the son of a noble and opulent Benjamite of Gibeah, a small city in the south of the Land of Promise.

The whole of this episode in our ancient book is singularly picturesque. We see the yet unproclaimed king occupied in his father's business, and throwing his whole powers into the every-day transactions of the farm on the slopes of Mount Ephraim. In a few words the historian describes how the modest and retiring Saul was roused from the quiet pastoral pursuits in which his hitherto uneventful life had been spent. The reverent, perhaps slightly reluctant, admiration with which the seer of God gazed at the future king of Israel; the prophet's significant address, the symbol gifts, the graceful hospitality, and, above all, the solemn and, no doubt, burning words of the generous old man, woke up the sleeping hero-spirit, and prepared the young Benjamite for his future mighty work. But there was no vulgar elation at the prospect which lay before him, no hurried grasping at the splendid prize which the seer told him the God of his fathers had destined for him. Quietly he took leave of the famous Samuel; the predicted signs of his coming greatness one by one were literally fulfilled; but Saul returned to the ancestral farm in the hills of Benjamin, and was subject to his father, as in old days; and when at last the public summons to the throne came to him, he seems to have accepted the great office for which he had been marked with positive reluctance and shrinking, nor does he appear materially to have altered his old simple way of living until a great national disgrace called for a devoted patriot to avenge it. Then the heroic heart of the Lord's anointed awoke, and Saul, when the hour came, showed himself a king indeed.

Kish, the son of Abiel.—On comparison with the genealogical summaries given in Gen. xlvi. 21; 1 Sam. ix. 1, xiv. 51; 1 Chron. vii. 6—8, &c., the line of Samuel appears as follows:—

<pre>
        BENJAMIN
           |
        BECHER
           |
   APHIAH (qu. ABIAH)
           |
        BECHORAH
           |
    ZEROR (qu. ZUR)
           |
         ABIEL
           |
          NER
           |
         KISH
           |
         SAUL.
</pre>

Yet even here certain links are omitted, for we hear of one **Matri** in 1 Sam. x. 21, and Jehiel in 1 Chron. ix. 35.

The truth is that in each of the genealogical summaries the transcriber of the original family document left out certain names not needed for his special purpose. The names omitted are not always the same; hence, often in these tables, the apparent discrepancies.

Dean Payne Smith, too, suggests that the hopeless entanglement in the Benjamite genealogies is in a measure due to the terrible civil war which resulted from the crime related in Judges xx. In the confusion which naturally resulted from the massacres and ceaseless wars of this early period, many of the older records of the tribes must have perished.

⁽²⁾ **A choice young man, and a goodly.**—The Hebrew word which is rendered in English by "a choice young man" cannot signify both these epithets. The translators were probably influenced by the Vulg. (Latin) Version, which translates the Hebrew word by *electus*, "chosen, or choice," the more common signification of the Hebrew word being avoided, owing to the fact that at this time Saul appears to have had a son (Jonathan) who must have well-nigh reached his maturity. But the term young was not inappropriate to Saul, who was still in the full vigour of manhood as contrasted with the old age of Samuel, being about forty to forty-five years old. Translate then simply, "a young man," &c. In the childhood of nations heroic proportions were highly valued, and the gigantic stature and the remarkable beauty of the king, no doubt contributed to the ready acceptance on the part of the still semi-barbarous Israel of the young man Saul. (Comp. *Herodotus*, iii. 20, vii. 187; Aristotle, *Polit.*, iv. 29; and Virgil's description of Turnus, *Æneid*, vii. 650, 783; and Homer's words about Ajax, *Iliad*, iii. 226.)

The asses.—Literally, *And the she-asses*. At this period of Jewish history asses were much used by the people. The horse was forbidden by the Law. Asses were used not only for purposes of agriculture, but also for riding; so in the song of Deborah we find, "Speak, ye that ride on white asses" (Judges v. 10); and again we read of the thirty sons of Jair, the Gileadite judge, each one ruler of a city, who rode on thirty ass colts (Judges x. 4). These belonging to the farm of Kish, being probably kept for breeding purposes, were untethered, and so strayed from the immediate neighbourhood, and were lost.

The whole of this chapter and part of the following is full of picturesque details of the pastoral life of the people. In many of the little pictures we see how strongly at this early period the religion of the Eternal coloured almost all parts of the every-day life of Israel.

One of the servants.—The "servant," not "slave;" the Hebrew word for the latter would be different. The servant was evidently a trusty dependant of the house of Saul's father, and was on familiar terms with his young master. We hear of his giving wise advice in the course of the search (verse 6); he was the one in charge of the money (verse 8); and this servant, we are especially told, was treated by Samuel the judge as an honoured guest at the sacrificial feast at Ramah. He was traditionally believed to have been Doeg the Edomite, afterwards so famous as one of the most ruthless of the great captains of King Saul. (See chap. xxii. 18.)

⁽⁴⁾ **And he passed through mount Ephraim.**—The chain of the mountains of Ephraim ran southward into the territory of Benjamin, where were situated the patrimonial possessions of Saul's house.

passed through the land of Shalisha, but they found *them* not: then they passed through the land of Shalim, and *there they were* not: and he passed through the land of the Benjamites, but they found *them* not. ⁽⁵⁾ *And* when they were come to the land of Zuph, Saul said to his servant that *was* with him, Come, and let us return; lest my father leave *caring* for the asses, and take thought for us. ⁽⁶⁾ And he said unto him, Behold now, *there is* in this city a man of God, and *he is* an honourable man; all that he saith cometh surely to pass: now let us go thither; peradventure he can shew us our way that we should go. ⁽⁷⁾ Then said Saul to his servant, But, behold, *if* we go, what shall we bring the man? for the bread ¹is spent in our vessels, and *there is* not a present to bring to the man of God: what ²have we? ⁽⁸⁾ And the servant answered Saul again, and said, Behold, ³I have here at hand the fourth part of a shekel of silver: *that* will I give to the man of God, to tell us our way. ⁽⁹⁾ (Beforetime in Israel, when a man went to enquire of God, thus he spake, Come, and let us go to the seer: for *he that is* now *called* a Prophet was beforetime called a Seer.) ⁽¹⁰⁾ Then said Saul to his servant, ⁴Well said; come, let us go. So they went unto the city where the man of God *was*.

⁽¹¹⁾ *And* as they went up ⁵the hill to the city, they found young maidens going out to draw water, and said unto

1 Heb., *is gone out of,* &c.
2 Heb., *is with us?*
3 Heb., *there is found in my hand.*
4 Heb., *Thy word is good.*
5 Heb., *in the ascent of the city.*

And passed through the land of Shalisha.—Or land " of the Three;" so called because three valleys there united in one, or one divided into three. It is believed to be the region in which Baal-shalisha lay (2 Kings iv. 42), fifteen miles north of Diospolis, or Lydda.

The land of Shalim.—Probably a very deep valley, derived from a Hebrew word, signifying " the hollow of the hand."

⁽⁵⁾ **The land of Zuph.**—This was believed to be in the south-west of Benjamin.

Lest my father . . . take thought for us. —" Saul's tender regard for his father's feelings here is a favourable indication of character."—*Dr. Kitto.*

⁽⁶⁾ **A man of God.**—When Saul determined to give up the search for his father's asses, he was in the neighbourhood of the city of Samuel the seer—" Ramah of the Watchers." The servant points out to him the tower of the then famous residence of the seer and judge, Samuel. " Will you not ask him," suggests the servant, " about the missing beasts?"—the young countryman, in the simplicity of his heart, thinking the occasion of the loss of his master's asses a sufficient one to warrant an intrusion upon the prophet-judge of Israel. The relation, however, between Samuel and the people must have been of a very close and friendly nature, else it would never have occurred, even to a simple countryman—as probably *then* Saul's servant was—to have sought the advice of one so great as Samuel in such a matter. It says, too, much for the old prophet's kindly, unselfish disposition that his name was thus loved and honoured, even in the secluded farms of the Land of Promise.

An honourable man.—Better rendered, *one held in honour.*

⁽⁷⁾ **What shall we bring?**—It would seem at first strange that one like Samuel should be approached by presents, but the custom of offering gifts was in many cases an act of respectful homage to a superior rather than a mere fee. Compare, for instance, the many detailed accounts of presents offered and accepted, chronicled in the varied sacred records—such as the little present of spicery, &c., sent by Jacob to the great minister or vizier of the Pharaoh of Egypt (Gen. xliii. 11), and the ten cheeses Jesse gave to the captain of the thousand in which his sons were serving, and in the days of the highest civilisation and culture known in Israel, the gifts offered by the Queen of Sheba to the magnificent Solomon (1 Kings x. 10).

⁽⁸⁾ **The fourth part of a shekel of silver.**— " Probably this shekel of silver was roughly stamped, and divided into four quarters by a cross, and broken when needed. What was its proportionate value in Samuel's days we cannot tell, for silver then was rare."—*Dean Payne Smith.*

⁽⁹⁾ **Beforetime in Israel.**—This verse was evidently inserted in the original book of memoirs of the days of Samuel by a later hand. Three special words are found in the Divine writings for the inspired messengers or interpreters of the Eternal will; of these, the title seer (*roeh*) was the most ancient. It is the title, evidently, by which Samuel in his lifetime was generally known. " Is the seer here?" we read in this passage; and " Where is the seer's house?" and " I am the seer." As time passed on, the term, in the sense of an inspired man of God, became obsolete, and the word *chozeh*, " a gazer" on strange visions, seemed to have been the word used for one inspired. The title *nabi*—prophet—began to come into *common* use in the time of Samuel, to whom the term is not unfrequently applied. The word *nabi*, or prophet, is found in nearly all the Old Testament books, from Genesis to Malachi, though rarely in the earlier writings. This note was inserted by some scribe who lived comparatively later (perhaps in the time of Ezra), but who must have been a reviser of the sacred text of very high authority, as this " note " has come down to us as an integral part of the received Hebrew text. The reason of the insertion is obvious. The title *roeh*—seer—as time passed on, no longer belonged exclusively to " a man of God." The scribe who put in this expression was desirous of pointing out that when Samuel lived it was *the* word always used for a prophet of the Lord. In those early days it had not deteriorated in meaning.

⁽¹⁰⁾ **Unto the city.**—The name of the city where Samuel and Saul first met in this strange way is not given. Still, the impression which the narrative leaves on the mind is that it was Samuel's usual residence— " Ramah." We know Samuel had built an altar to the Lord at Ramah (chap. vii. 17); on the day of Saul's arrival there was a great sacrifice taking place on the

them, Is the seer here? ⁽¹²⁾ And they answered them, and said, He is; behold, *he is* before you: make haste now, for he came to day to the city; for *there is* a ¹sacrifice of the people to day in the high place: ⁽¹³⁾ as soon as ye be come into the city, ye shall straightway find him, before he go up to the high place to eat: for the people will not eat until he come, because he doth bless the sacrifice; *and* afterwards they eat that be bidden. Now therefore get you up; for about ²this time ye shall find him. ⁽¹⁴⁾And they went up into the city: *and* when they were come into the city, behold,

¹ Or, *feast*.

² Heb., *to day*.

a ch. 15. 1; Acts 13. 21.

³ Heb., *revealed the ear of Samuel*.

⁴ Heb., *restrain in*.

Samuel came out against them, for to go up to the high place.

⁽¹⁵⁾ ᵃNow the LORD had ³told Samuel in his ear a day before Saul came, saying, ⁽¹⁶⁾ To morrow about this time I will send thee a man out of the land of Benjamin, and thou shalt anoint him *to be* captain over my people Israel, that he may save my people out of the hand of the Philistines: for I have looked upon my people, because their cry is come unto me. ⁽¹⁷⁾ And when Samuel saw Saul, the LORD said unto him, Behold the man whom I spake to thee of! this same shall ⁴reign over my people.

---

altar of the high place of the city. Again, in this nameless city the seer had a house of his own (see verses 18 and 25). Samuel, too, was known to Saul's servant as dwelling in this place.

⁽¹²⁾ **He came to-day.**—The little scene—in itself in no way remarkable—is recounted by an eye-witness, evidently as introducing momentous consequences.

Every detail of that day's proceedings was of deep interest to Israel. Some of the maidens of Ramah were at the well side, drawing water for their homes. The two strangers accost them with the words, "Is the seer who dwells among you here just now?" and they eagerly reply, "Yes, this very day he came from his house into the town. It is a festival day—you will find him presiding up there," pointing, no doubt, to the high place, where the sacrifices were being offered. Every word spoken by the girls of Ramah, loving to chatter and exhibit their local knowledge and their interest in their great fellow-citizen, the seer and judge, to whom they, in common with the inhabitants of Ramah, were, no doubt, much attached, was remembered in after time by Saul and his companion.

⁽¹³⁾ **He doth bless the sacrifice.**—It has been well remarked that we have here, in this note of the people's conduct at the sacrificial banquet of "Ramah of the Watchers," a very early instance of the devout practice among the Hebrews of asking a blessing on meals.

⁽¹⁴⁾ **Behold, Samuel came out against them.** —"Saul comes before Samuel, bashfully pursuing his humble quest, in apparent unconsciousness of the power slumbering within him of aspiring and attaining to the highest place; the great seer receives him in a way quite different from all that he could have hoped or feared. At the moment of their meeting the seer has come forth from his house on the way to the solitary sacred heights of Ramah, the city of his residence, where he sacrifices on the altar to Jahveh, or is wont to partake of a sacred sacrificial repast with some of his closest friends. He at once desires to take Saul also with him, telling him beforehand how unimportant was the immediate object of his inquiries, and that the matter was already settled; but that for him and his whole house was reserved a very different and far better destiny in Israel. And though Saul, in his unassuming simplicity, would fain waive the honour which is obscurely hinted (so little does he yet know his better self), the holy man, more discerning, takes him with him to the sacrificial meal, which is already prepared; nay, assigns him the place of honour among the thirty guests before invited, while he is served with a portion of the sacrificial meat, put by, as it were, specially for him: for in like manner a portion other and higher than that of ordinary men had been long reserved for him by heaven."—*Ewald.*

⁽¹⁵⁾ **Had told Samuel in his ear.** — Literally, *had uncovered the ear of Samuel*. The image is taken from the action of pushing aside the head-dress, in order the more conveniently to whisper some words to the ear. This is one of the few more direct intimations in the sacred records of one of the ways in which the Spirit of God communicated Divine thoughts to the human spirit. Here the Eternal Spirit is represented as whispering in the ear of man. "The true spirit of Jahveh (Jehovah), full of compassion, had already on the preceding day whispered to Samuel that for the deliverance of Jahveh's people . . . a Benjamite must be anointed king."—*Ewald.*

⁽¹⁶⁾ **The Philistines.**—This statement evidently points to the fact—of which, a little later, we have such ample evidence—that at this juncture the Philistines were again harassing the Israelite territory with their destructive raids. The power of the Philistines was broken, but by no means destroyed, in the great battle of Mizpeh. We know that all through King Saul's reign, and in the early days of King David, these invasions were repeated with varying success. The statement of chap. vii. 13 must be understood not as representing that the victory of Mizpeh once and for all destroyed the Philistine power, but that from that day the power of these determined enemies of Israel began to decline. The words of chap. vii. 13 must be taken as including the *ultimate* result of the great Hebrew victory. It is clear that the annoyance of these Philistine raids and incursions were the immediate cause of the prayer for a king. The desire for this form of government, no doubt, for a very long while had existed among the people, but this pressing need for a younger and more warlike leader than their old prophet judge prompted the request to Samuel.

⁽¹⁷⁾ **Behold the man.**—This verse, it must be remembered, follows closely on verse 14, the statements of verses 15 and 16 being parenthetical. The young Saul and his servant came up to accost the seer on his way to the sacred height; Samuel, at once impressed by the great stature and splendid beauty of the stranger coming towards him, asks his Master silently, "Lord, is this then he of whom Thou whisperest me yesterday, to whom the destinies of Thy people were to be confided?" The words "Behold the

(18) Then Saul drew near to Samuel in the gate, and said, Tell me, I pray thee, where the seer's house *is*. (19) And Samuel answered Saul, and said, I *am* the seer: go up before me unto the high place; for ye shall eat with me to day, and to morrow I will let thee go, and will tell thee all that *is* in thine heart. (20) And as for thine asses that were lost ¹three days ago, set not thy mind on them; for they are found. And on whom *is* all the desire of Israel? *Is it* not on thee, and on all thy father's house? (21) And Saul answered and said, *Am* not I a Benjamite, of the smallest of the tribes of Israel? and my family the least of all the families of the tribe of Benjamin? wherefore then speakest thou ²so to me? (22) And Samuel took Saul and his servant, and brought them into the parlour, and made them sit in the chiefest place among them that were bidden, which *were* about thirty persons. (23) And Samuel said unto the cook, Bring the portion which I gave thee, of which I said unto thee, Set it by thee. (24) And the cook took up the shoulder, and *that* which *was* upon it, and set *it* before Saul. And Samuel said, Behold that

¹ Heb., *to day three days.*

² Heb., *according to this word?*

man," &c., were the silent answer of God to the silent prayer of His old servant.

Shall reign.—The word "shall reign," which was whispered by the "Spirit" to the listening heart of the seer, should rather have been translated, "shall control," or "shall restrain." It was a word which—looking on to Saul's future reign—represented it as a stern, severe rule.

(18) **In the gate.**—The LXX. (Greek Version) here reads, "in the midst of the city." It is not improbable that this is the original reading, it being very possible for a scribe to write the Hebrew word "gate" for "city."

(19) **Go up before me unto the high place.**—The desiring the young stranger to precede him to the public place of sacrifice was a sign of distinguished honour from one of Samuel's rank to a young unknown wayfarer like Saul. These words of courteous respect were addressed to Saul alone: "Go thou up before me." The prophet-judge then speaks to the two, Saul and his servant: "ye shall eat." The verb here is in the plural, and invites both to the sacrificial banquet; and then again Samuel confines his words to Saul: "I will tell thee all"—"all that is in thine heart." The seer informs him that on the morrow he proposes to make strange disclosures to this young man, who, all unknowing what lay before him, had just come up and accosted him, the aged judge and seer. Yes, he would on the morrow show this young Benjamite that he, Samuel, was indeed a seer; he would tell him all his secret thoughts and aspirations; as for those asses for whose fate he was so anxious, let him dismiss these from his thoughts altogether. They were already found. Far graver thoughts than the everyday weal and woe of a farm on Mount Ephraim had to be discussed on the morrow.

All the desire of Israel.—"All the desire of Israel," or, as the Vulg. renders it, "optima quæque Israel," "the best in Israel" (Luther). The words do not signify the desire of Israel — all that it *desires*—but all that it possesses of what is precious or worth desiring. The obscure dark words of the seer on this, the occasion of his first meeting with Saul, were intended to draw him away from thinking about the asses and the little matters which hitherto had filled his life, and to lift him up to higher thoughts and aspirations. The old seer's words were vague and indefinite, certainly, but coming as they did from the lips of one so high in dignity, known to be the possessor of many a strange secret of futurity hid from the knowledge of mortal men, and holding out a prospect of undreamed of future glory for Saul, amazed the young man; and he, full of wonderment and awe, replied, "Speakest thou of such glories to *me*, a member of an unimportant family of the smallest of the tribes of Israel?"

(22) **And Samuel took Saul.**—The seer gave Saul no answer to this question, in which the young man's wonderment was expressed that one so insignificant should be chosen for so high a destiny. Samuel merely wished, in the first instance, to awaken new and grander thoughts and aspirations in this young heart, and without reply he proceeded to conduct his guests to the scene of the sacrifice on the high place. In the guest-chamber, where thirty of the most distinguished persons present at the solemn sacrifice were assembled, Samuel places Saul and his companion, no doubt to their great surprise, in the principal seats. "The parlour" is an unfortunate rendering of the Hebrew word here, which signifies the "cell," or "chamber" attached to the building on the high place, for such purposes as the present. These solemn sacrificial meals were the usual adjuncts of a solemn sacrifice.

Not only was Saul thus highly honoured in public as the future king, but his servant also. If, as tradition tells us, this servant was Doeg the Edomite, he, too, on this occasion had a foretaste of his future position, an earnest of the rank and power which he would receive when one of Saul's great officers of state.

(23) **And Samuel said unto the cook.**—The meaning of this statement is simply this—all that took place in the meeting of the prophet and Saul at the sacrificial feast, and subsequently in Samuel's house, was arranged for beforehand; every event was foreseen and provided for, even the trivial details—all was symbolical in this preparation for the great change in the constitution of Israel, which, under God's providence, was fraught with such important consequences. The very piece of meat set before Samuel at the Ramah banquet was no chance piece, but one which, owing, no doubt, to its being considered the choicest, had been carefully set aside for him when the sacrificial feast was being prepared.

(24) **And Samuel said.**—There is an error here in the English translation which requires correction. Although the matter is not one of great moment, yet it is important and deeply interesting to notice the little details that the inspired historian has thought it right to preserve in connection with this whole transaction. There was, no doubt, a very early

which is ¹left! set *it* before thee, *and* eat: for unto this time hath it been kept for thee since I said, I have invited the people. So Saul did eat with Samuel that day.

(25) And when they were come down from the high place into the city, *Samuel* communed with Saul upon the top of the house. (26) And they arose early: and it came to pass about the spring of the day, that Samuel called Saul to the top of the house, saying, Up, that I may send thee away. And Saul arose, and they went out both of them, he and Samuel, abroad.

(27) *And* as they were going down to the end of the city, Samuel said to Saul, Bid the servant pass on before us, (and he passed on,) but stand thou still ²a while, that I may shew thee the word of God.

1 Or, *reserved.*

2 Heb., *to day.*

---

and authentic tradition of the circumstance of this anointing of the first king, which was, of course, often rehearsed in the sacred assemblies of Israel. "Samuel's name is not given in the Hebrew, and though inserted by the LXX. and Vulg., it is so only by a manifest error. The Syriac and Chaldee, like the Hebrew, make *the cook* the speaker. The right translation is, And the cook lifted up the shoulder, with that which was upon it, and set it before Saul, and said, Behold that which hath been reserved is set (a participle, and not the imperative) before thee; eat, for it hath been kept for thee unto the appointed time, of which he (*i.e.*, Samuel) spake, saying, I have invited the people. The word translated in the Authorised Version, "since I said," is one which means *saying*, and nothing else; and as what goes before contains no verb to which *saying* can refer, it is plain that there is an ellipse. But if the cook be the speaker, the meaning is plain, as follows:—When, on the previous day, the revelation was made to Samuel that Israel's future king would present himself on the morrow, the prophet at once made preparations to receive him with due solemnity, and for this purpose arranged a sacrifice, and invited thirty of the chief citizens of Ramah to assemble at the high place, and sit at the banquet with him. And then it was, when telling the cook of his invitation, that he gave orders that the portion of honour should be carefully reserved, to be set at the fitting time before the stranger. The chat of the cook is entirely after the manner of ancient times, and would show Saul how completely his coming had been foreseen and provided for."—Dean Payne Smith, in *Pulpit Comm.*

(25) **And when they were come down.**—After the public sacrificial meal at which such signal honours had been shown to the Benjamite stranger and his servant, the prophet-judge detained Saul from continuing his journey homewards, and persuaded him to remain as his guest that night at Ramah. He conducted him to the flat roof of his house, often the favourite locality in the East for quiet conversation or rest, and where frequently the honoured guest was lodged for the night: there the prophet had a long interview with his young guest. The conversation that evening probably did not turn upon the royal dignity, so soon to be conferred on Saul; of that Samuel spoke at length, we know, on the following morning. The solemn words of the old man that evening on the house-top in "Ramah of the Watchers" referred, no doubt, to the sad religious and political decline of the people of God, from which he (Samuel) had laboured, not unsuccessfully, to rescue them, "to the opposition of the heathen nations, the causes of the impotency of Israel to oppose their enemies, the necessity of a religious change in the people, and of a leader thoroughly obedient to the Lord."—Otto von Gerlach, quoted in *Lange.* It has been suggested that this conversation was the connecting link between that on the height (verses 19, 20) and the communication which Samuel made to Saul the following morning. The LXX. reads here, instead of "communed with Saul on the top of the house," "they strewed a couch for Saul on the top of the house, and he lay down." But the Chaldee and Syriac Versions agree with the Hebrew text. The strange LXX. variation is apparently a correction. These Greek translators could not understand a conversation of the prophet and Saul taking place in the evening, when the announcement of the crown was made so formally on the following morning. Why did Samuel not tell Saul of God's intention during that evening spent together?

(26) **And they arose early.**—The English translation of this verse is misleading. It should run thus: "And they arose early, namely, when the morning dawned. Samuel called for Saul upon the roof, Get up, that I may send thee, &c." The English rendering seems to suppose that they rose first, and afterwards, about the spring of the day (the morning dawn), Samuel called Saul—the fact being that, as is frequent in Hebrew narration, the second clause simply related the same event as the first clause had already done, only with greater detail. The sense then is obvious. Saul, evidently weary after the exciting scene and revelations of the day before, slept soundly, probably heavily, on his couch spread on the roof of the prophet's house. From this roof-top Samuel calls Saul in the early morning, wishing to conduct him himself out of the city, as he had a yet more important communication to make to his amazed and awe-struck visitor.

(27) **That I may shew thee the word of God.**—The wonderment of Saul at the strange honour and distinction shown to him, a comparatively unknown Benjamite, by the famous prophet-judge, was, no doubt, increased by this proposal of Samuel to accompany him a little way on his journey homeward. The meaning of all that had happened to him on the day before was, however, now to be revealed: the gracious welcome as a distinguished guest evidently looked for, the courteous hospitality in the judge's house; and, more than all, the long private instructions Samuel had given him in the evening on the state of Israel. The prophet now directs that the servant should be sent on alone, that he might in all solemn confidence impart to Saul "the word of God," that is, all that the God of Israel had revealed to him, the seer, concerning Saul's appointment.

It would have been interesting to have learned something of Saul's state of mind when this startling revelation of the choice of God was first made to him.

The writer here is silent, but in the next chapter (verse 6) we read that the Spirit of the Lord was specially promised to this chosen one. When new duties are imposed by God, He never forgets to bestow the gift of new powers.

CHAPTER X.—(1) Then Samuel took a vial of oil, and poured *it* upon his head, and kissed him, and said, *Is it* not because the LORD hath anointed thee *to be* captain over his inheritance? (2) When thou art departed from me to day, then

a Gen. 35. 20.

1 Heb., *the business.*

thou shalt find two men by *a*Rachel's sepulchre in the border of Benjamin at Zelzah; and they will say unto thee, The asses which thou wentest to seek are found: and, lo, thy father hath left ¹the care of the asses, and sorroweth for

X.

(1—27) Saul is anointed King by Samuel. The Divine Signs given to him. The Election of King Saul.

(1) **Then Samuel took a vial of oil.**—The vial was a narrow-necked vessel, from which the oil flowed in drops. It was, of course, no common oil which the prophet used on this momentous occasion, but the oil of holy ointment, the sacred anointing oil which was used at the consecration of the priests, and also of the Tabernacle and the sacred vessels. (See Exod. xxix. 7, xxx. 23—33, &c.) The solemn anointing took place in the ceremony of consecration in the case of some, but not of all, the Hebrew sovereigns. We hear of it at the accession of David, Absalom, Solomon, Joash, Jehoahaz, and Jehu. In cases of regular succession the anointing was supposed to continue its effect—that is, the regular succession needed no new anointing. Hence it is that only the above named kings are mentioned as having been anointed, all founders of dynasties or irregularly advanced to the throne. (See Erdman in *Lange* here.)

And kissed him.—Rather as a customary sign of reverential homage than as a mark of affection, which at that early date of their acquaintance it was hardly possible to assume that the old man felt for the younger. (Compare Ps. ii. 12: "Kiss the son, lest he be angry": that is, "Do homage, O ye kings of the earth, to Him who is your anointed King.")

The Lord hath anointed thee.—Samuel replies to the look and gesture of extreme astonishment with which the young Saul received the anointing and the kiss with these words: "Do you mutely ask me why I pay you this formal homage? why I salute you with such deep respect? Is it not because *you* are the chosen of the Eternal? Are you still incredulous respecting your high destiny? See now, as you go on your way home, you will meet with three signs; they will prove to you that what I do, I do not of myself, but in obedience to a higher power."

(2) **When thou art departed from me to day, then . . . .**—Here follows Samuel's careful description of the three signs which should meet the future king as he went from Ramah to his father's home in Benjamin. Each of these tokens, which were to strengthen the young Saul's faith, contained a solemn lesson, the deep meaning of which, as his life went on, the future sovereign would be able to ponder over. Each of the three signs from heaven met him at one of the sacred spots which were so plentifully dotted over these southern districts of Canaan, memorable for the life-stories, first of Abraham and the patriarchs, and then of the warriorchieftains of the Israel of the conquest. The selection of localities famous as homes of prayer, or sacred as the resting-place of the illustrious dead, taught the eternal truth "that help comes from the holy place." At the sepulchre of Rachel, the loved ancestress of the warlike tribe of Benjamin, to which the new king belonged, men should meet him on his homeward journey with the news that the lost asses which he had gone to seek were found again. This showed him that henceforth in his new life he was to dismiss all lower cares, and give himself up alone to higher and more important matters. A king must take counsel and thought for the weal of a whole people; he must put aside now and for ever all consideration for himself and his family, all anxiety for the mere ordinary prosperity of life. God, who had chosen him, would provide for these things, as He had now done in the case of the lost asses. Further on in his journey, when he reached the terebinth-tree of Tabor, three men on a pilgrimage to the great Beth-el sanctuary would meet him, and would offer him some of the loaves which they proposed offering at Beth-el. The signification of this peculiar gift was that some portion of the products of the soil, which had hitherto been appropriated exclusively to the service and support of the sanctuary, in future should be devoted to the maintenance of the anointed of the Lord. The third sign which he should perceive would meet him as he approached his home, which was situated near a famous holy place of prayer, known as the "Gibeah," or "Hill of God." A number of prophets belonging to one of the "schools" of the prophets founded by Samuel, coming from the altar on the "hill of God," where sacrifice had just been offered, would meet him. They would be plunged in prophetic raptures, he would hear them chanting hymns to the Eternal, accompanied by the music of their instruments. A new and mighty influence, Samuel told the astonished Saul, would, as he met this company of singers, come upon him, and involuntarily he who evidently had never joined before in any of these solemn choruses would sing his part with the rest. The new influence, said the old seer, which would then come upon him would be the Spirit of the Lord, and from that moment he would be a changed man. Never in his after days of glory and might was the king to forget how, in a moment, the Divine power had swept down and given him—the ignorant shepherd, the humble vine-dresser, the heir to a few asses and sheep, to some fields of corn or vineyards—wisdom, power, and a mighty kingdom. He must remember that in a moment the same Divine power might wing away from him its solemn flight; that was the lesson of the third sign which was to meet him on his homeward journey.

The LXX. and Vulg. have a somewhat long addition to verse 1. It is, however, manifestly an explanatory gloss, and is made up from verses 16 and 17 of chap. ix.

(2) **Thou shalt find two men by Rachel's sepulchre.**—This tomb of the loved wife of the patriarch does not thus appear to have been very far from Ramah, whence Saul started. The words of Jeremiah xxxi. 15, which speak of the future massacre of the Bethlehem innocents by Herod, connects Ramah and Rachel's tomb: "A voice was heard in Ramah, lamentation *and* bitter weeping: Rachel weeping for her children."

At Zelzah.—This locality has never been identified. Some have supposed it was the same as Zela in Benjamin, the place where the bodies of Saul and Jonathan were eventually buried. The LXX. curiously render it as

you, saying, What shall I do for my son? ⁽³⁾ Then shalt thou go on forward from thence, and thou shalt come to the plain of Tabor, and there shall meet thee three men going up to God to Beth-el, one carrying three kids, and another carrying three loaves of bread, and another carrying a bottle of wine: ⁽⁴⁾ and they will ¹salute thee, and give thee two loaves of bread; which thou shalt receive of their hands. ⁽⁵⁾ After that thou shalt come to the hill of God, where *is* the garrison of the Philistines: and it shall come to pass, when thou art come thither to the city, that thou shalt meet a company of prophets coming down from the high place with a psaltery, and a tabret, and a pipe, and a harp, before them;

¹ Heb., *ask thee of peace.*

---

though it were a verb, "dancing (lit. springing) vehemently," or, as Ewald would translate the Greek words, "in great haste," of course, with reference to the two men who brought Saul the news of the recovered asses.

(3) **Thou shalt come to the plain of Tabor.**—The accurate translation of the Hebrew is "to the terebinth or oak of Tabor." There was evidently a history, now lost, connected with the "terebinth of Tabor." Ewald suggests that "Tabor" is a different form for Deborah, and that this historic tree was the oak beneath which Deborah, the nurse of Rachel, was buried (Gen. xxxv. 8).

Going up to God to Beth-el.—This since the old patriarchal days had been a sacred spot. Samuel used to visit it as judge, and hold his court there annually, no doubt on account of the number of pilgrims who were in the habit of visiting it. These men were evidently on a pilgrimage to the old famous shrine.

(5) **After that thou shalt come to the hill of God.**—These words should be rendered to the *Gibeah of God*. The writer here is alluding to Saul's own city, afterwards known as "Gibeah of Saul." The name of Gibeah, or Hill of God, was given to it on account of a well-known high place or sacrificial height in or hard by the town. We know that this sacred place was chosen by Samuel as the site of one of his "schools of the prophets."

Where is the garrison of the Philistines.—These warlike Phœnician tribes seem gradually, after their great defeat at Mizpeh, to have again established themselves in various stations of the land, whence they harried the Israelites. A parallel to these marauding soldiers, so long the plague of Israel, might be found in the countless freebooters' strongholds which, in the Middle Ages, were the curse especially of Germany, the terror of the peaceful trading folk of the rich countries of Central Europe.

A company of prophets.—These evidently belonged to one of those seminaries termed "schools of the prophets," founded by Samuel for the training of young men. The foundation of these schools in different parts of the country was one of the greatest of the works of this noble and patriotic man. These schools seem to have flourished during the whole period of the monarchy, and in no small measure contributed to the moral and mental development of the people. Some of the youth of Israel who received in these schools their training became public preachers of the Word; for after all, this, rather than foretelling future events, was the grand duty of the prophet's calling.

It is a grave mistake to conclude that *all*, or even the greater part, of these young men trained in the "schools of the prophets" were *inspired* in the usual sense of the word. The aim of these institutions, beside high mental culture, seems to have been to train the youth of Israel to love, and then live, noble pure lives. Dean Payne Smith calls attention to the remarkable fact that at David's court all posts which required literary skill were held by "prophets." He considers that it was owing to these great educational institutions which Samuel founded that the Israelites became a highly trained and literary people. "Prophets," in the awful sense of the word as used by us—men who, as compared with their fellows, stood in a different relation to the Most High, who heard things which other men heard not, and saw visions unseen by any save themselves—men before whose eyes the veil which hid the dark future now and again was raised—were, after all, even among the people of God, very rare. In the course of a generation, one or two, or perhaps three, appeared, and were listened to, and their words in many cases, we know, preserved. These, for the most part, we may assume, received their early training in the "schools of the prophets," but these famous institutions were never, as has often been popularly supposed, established in the hope of training up and developing such men, but were founded and supported with the intention of fostering what we should call the higher education in Israel; and in this, we know from the outset, these schools were eminently successful.

Dr. Erdmann, in *Lange's Commentary*, accounts for this especial mention of the music which we know, from this and other passages, was carefully cultivated in these seminaries of the sons of the prophets, by suggesting that in these societies religious feeling was nourished and heightened by sacred music. It would be a mistake to attribute to this carefully cultivated music and singing that condition of ecstatic inspiration into which some of these companies appear to have at times fallen. We understand and know, however, very little respecting this state of ecstasy—what produced it, and how it affected those who had fallen into this strange condition. The object of the musical teaching of the schools of the prophets was, no doubt, to enable those who had studied in the seminaries to guide and direct the religious gatherings of the people, into which—as we know from the subsequent Temple service, the model of all popular sacred gatherings for worship—music and psalmody entered so largely.

With a psaltery, and a tabret, and a pipe, and a harp, before them.—The four instruments here mentioned indicate that even in this—which is often termed a semi-barbarous age—music had been long and carefully studied. The *psaltery* (*nevel*) was a species of lyre with ten strings, in shape like an inverted delta ∇, and was played with the fingers. The *tabret* (*toph*) was a hand-drum—a tambourine. Miriam (Exod. xv. 20) is represented as using it to accompany her triumph song. The *pipe* (*chalil*) was a flute of reed, wood, or horn, and seems to have been ever a favourite instrument among the children of Israel. The *harp* (*cinnor*) was a stringed instrument, like the psaltery, only apparently larger, and was played

| *The Signs given by* | I. SAMUEL, X. | *Samuel to Saul.* |

and they shall prophesy: ⁽⁶⁾ and the Spirit of the LORD will come upon thee, and thou shalt prophesy with them, and shalt be turned into another man. ⁽⁷⁾ And ¹ let it be, when these signs are come unto thee, ² *that* thou do as occasion serve thee; for God *is* with thee. ⁽⁸⁾ And thou shalt go down before me to Gilgal; and, behold, I will come down unto thee, to offer burnt offerings, *and* to sacrifice

¹ Heb., *it shall come to pass, that when these signs, &c.*

² Heb., *do for thee as thine hand shall find.*

---

usually with a plectrum. David, however, is represented in several psalms as playing on the "cinnor" with his fingers.

And they shall prophesy.—In this case the company from the "School of the Prophets" were, no doubt, singing some hymns or psalms in praise of the Eternal to the accompaniment of their musical instruments. Saul, as he drew near his home at Gibeah, would meet these men coming down from sacrificing on the high place of God, and as he listened to the sweet pure sounds he would be sensible of a something indescribable taking possession of his whole being; new thoughts—high grand thoughts—would chase away the aspirations and hopes of the past. Through his *heart* (see verse 9) would flash the memory of what Samuel had told him when alone on the house-top at Ramah—of the glory and future of Israel; a conviction would steal over him that *he* was the man of the future chosen by the Eternal to work His will among His people. The Saul of the vineyards and the corn-fields of the farm on the Ephraim hills would die, and a new hero-Saul would be born; and although quite untrained and untaught in the elaborate music of the choirs of the sons of the prophets, the really inspired Saul would lift up his voice in the choruses singing before him, and join with a new strange power in their glorious hymn to the Eternal—would pour out his whole heart and soul in thanksgiving to his God. Thus would the Spirit of the Lord come upon him.

⁽⁷⁾ **When these signs are come unto thee.**—When these varied circumstances have happened to thee, *then* be sure that the splendid and glorious life which I have foretold as thy lot will assuredly lie before thee in the immediate future. I will give thee no imperious directions by which thou art to shape thy course. Go bravely on; do well and truly whatever thy hand findeth to do, being confident that God will be with thee, and that His glorious Arm shall be thy guide along that road of honour and of peril which thou art destined to travel.

⁽⁸⁾ **And shew thee what thou shalt do.**—Considerable doubt exists among expositors as to the exact meaning and reference of these words of Samuel. In chap. xiii., verses 8 and following, a well-known and most important event in Saul's life and reign is related, in which the circumstances strangely fit in with the words of the warning of Samuel. Only between this first meeting of the seer and the future king and the Gilgal meeting, described in chap. xiii., two years—perhaps even a much longer period—elapsed (the dates of this age are most uncertain); besides which, that famous meeting at Gilgal was not by any means the first meeting of Samuel and Saul at that place. Yet, in spite of these difficulties, it seems best to refer to this meeting between the prophet and king at Gilgal, related in chap. xiii., as the trial of faith especially looked on to by Samuel here. The solemn warning here given was, doubtless, repeated in a much more detailed form by the prophet some time before the appointed Gilgal meeting. So much for the *reference*; the signification of the warning is best explained in the following way:—Samuel had bidden the future king to advance along the paths of glory and difficulty which lay before him in all confidence and trust, acting in each emergency according to the dictates of his own heart—only in *one* thing he must be ever on his guard. In his future great work for the regeneration and advancement of Israel, he must, for the sake of the faith of Israel, be on his guard against infringing the sacred privileges of the religion of the Eternal. In the plenitude of his kingly power, the day would come when the temptation would assault him to disregard the ancient sanctity of the sacrifice, and to assume as king, functions which belonged alone to men like Samuel set apart for the sacred office, and thus publicly to dishonour the commandments of God, and by his reckless example of unbelief in revelation to weaken the faith of the people.

Such a temptation presented itself to Saul, we believe, some two or more years from this time, when, as related in chap. xiii., a solemn assembly of the people was summoned to Gilgal, before the commencement of the war of independence. This great enterprise for the people of the Lord must necessarily be begun with solemn religious rites and sacrifices. These the king was forbidden to officiate at without the presence of the Divinely appointed seer. We shall see how King Saul acted under the temptation to set himself and his royal power above the prophet of the Lord and the direct command of God. Whether or no King Saul with his own hand offered the Gilgal sacrifice is uncertain; at all events, the great sin he, seemed to have been guilty of having committed, is to have declined to wait for the presence of the prophet of the Lord, although publicly required by the word of the Lord to do so. (See Notes on chap. xiii.)

The "heart" is mentioned as changed by God, because, according to the conception of the Divine writings, the *heart* is represented as the centre of the whole mental and physical life—of will, desire, thought, perception, and feeling. It was one thing for Samuel the seer to put before the young Benjamite the brilliant destiny which lay before him, but it was another and different thing to transform one like Saul, brought up to merely agricultural pursuits, into a fit and worthy recipient of such honours and powers. We know how utterly incapable are all such things as wealth and rank and power in themselves of inspiring the heart with any noble patriotic aspirations, or with any high religious longings, or lofty patriotic aims; a higher influence is needed to awaken the heart, or to rouse it from merely earthly and sordid contemplations.

This is the work which God worked in the heart of the young Saul as, in the early morning, he left "Ramah of the Watchers," his ears tingling with the burning words of the great seer all through that day and many succeeding days. In quiet humility, and, no doubt, with many a silent prayer, he watched and waited; when he returned home there was no sign of exultation visible in the man, no mark of impatience. His lips were sealed; he seems to have whispered to no one what the prophet had told him; he made no sign even when events came crowding

sacrifices of peace offerings: *seven days shalt thou tarry, till I come to thee, and shew thee what thou shalt do.

(9) And it was so, that when he had turned his ¹back to go from Samuel, God ²gave him another heart: and all those signs came to pass that day. (10) And when they came thither to the hill, behold, a company of prophets met him; and the Spirit of God came upon him, and he prophesied among them. (11) And it came to pass, when all that knew him beforetime saw that, behold, he prophesied among the prophets, then the people said ³one to another, What is this that is come unto the son of Kish? *Is Saul also among the prophets? (12) And one ⁴of the same place answered and said, But who is their father? Therefore it became a proverb, Is Saul also among the prophets? (13) And when he had made an end of prophesying, he came to the high place.

(14) And Saul's uncle said unto him

a ch. 13. 8.
1 Heb., *shoulder.*
2 Heb., *turned.*
3 Heb., *a man to his neighbour.*
b ch. 19. 24.
4 Heb., *thence.* from

---

thick about him—such as the popular assembly for the choice of a king, presided over by the prophet-judge, whose mind Saul alone in Israel knew: the drawing of the lots: the narrowing of the fateful circle: the designation of his tribe, his family, then himself. We see, indeed, God had changed his heart. Was there not in these early days a promise of a noble king —a man after God's own heart?

And all those signs came to pass that day. —Of the first two signs which were to meet him no further details are given; we are simply told that in the order predicted by Samuel Saul came across them. The third alone gives occasion for a special mention, because it had a great effect on the life of the future king.

(10) **To the hill.**—"To the hill:" more accurately rendered, *to Gibeah.* This was the home of Saul; the estate of the house of Kish lay evidently in the immediate vicinity of Gibeah, henceforward to be known as Saul's royal city, "Gibeah of Saul." "As he walked, the Spirit of God came upon him," we read. The coming of the Spirit of God upon him may be looked on as the sequel of that Divine gift of the new heart bestowed on him in the early morning, when he left Ramah. The changed heart was a fit home for that Divine Spirit which came on him in the eventide, as he drew near to his ancestral city.

(11) **What is this?**—The natural expression of extreme surprise at the sudden change which had come over one so well known at Gibeah as Saul evidently was, shows us that this was *his home*. The words, "What is this that is come unto the son of Kish?" seem to tell us that the life hitherto led by Saul was a life very different in all respects to the life led by the sons of the prophets in their schools. It need not be assumed that the youth and early manhood of the future king had been wild and dissolute, but simply that the way of life had been rough and uncultured—a life spent in what we should call "country pursuits," in contradistinction to the pursuit of knowledge and of higher acquirements. It is evident from the statement here and in the following verse that a considerable respect for these schools had already grown up among the people.

Is Saul also among the prophets?—In chap. xix. 23 we again find Saul, but under changed circumstances, under the influence of a Divine and coercing power, and uttering strange words, and singing hymns as one trained in the prophets' schools. It was probably this recurrence of the same incident in the king's life which gave rise to the saying, or proverb, which expresses amazement at the unexpected appearance of any man in a position which had hitherto been quite strange to him. "Is Saul among the preachers of Christ? was a question of wonder asked by the friends of St. Paul" (Gal. i. 23).—*Wordsworth.*

(12) **Who is their father?**—As an instance of the extreme surprise with which the association of Saul with the sons of the prophets was witnessed by the inhabitants of Gibeah—an association apparently very foreign to his old habits and to the manner of life of his family—a short dialogue between two of the citizens of Gibeah is here related: a conversation important, owing to the words uttered by the second citizen in reply to the amazed question, "What is this that is come unto the son of Kish?" The reply gives us some insight into the deep conviction entertained by the ordinary Israelite of the days of Samuel that the invisible God was ever present, *working* in the midst of His chosen people.

The reply of the second citizen has been well explained by Von Bunsen:—"Is the *son of Kish,* then, a prophet?" asks the first citizen, surprised, apparently, that one so undistinguished, that one so unlikely to train up a "son of the prophets," should have a son associated in this peculiar and sudden manner with a chosen band of scholars and teachers. To this question the second citizen replied—no doubt, pointing to the honoured group from the prophet schools of Gibeah—"Do you wonder that the son of so rough and uncultivated a man as Kish should receive the Divine gift which we all love so well and admire so greatly? Who," pointing to the group singing on the hill-side, "who is *their* father?" They owe their power of persuasive speech, their gift of holy song, to no accident of birth. Surely Saul, like them, may have received the same power as a gift of the Eternal, not as a patrimony. Owing to this obvious meaning not having occurred to them, the LXX., Vulgate, and Syriac Versions alter the original into, "Who is his (instead of their) father?" in other words, "Who is Saul? and who is his father, Kish?" But the Hebrew text and the English Version, as explained above, gives an admirable sense, and teaches besides a great spiritual lesson.

(13) **He came to the high place.**—After he had spent his fervour in the hymn, and probably ecstatic prayer, Saul, before he went to his home, we read, betook himself at once to the high place of Gibeah, whence the sons of the prophets had just come down when he met them on the hill-side. He went there, no doubt, because, conscious of the change that had passed over him, and aware of his new powers, he felt a desire for solitary communing in the quiet of a holy sanctuary with God, who had come so near him.

(14) **Saul's uncle.**—Most probably, this uncle was the subsequently famous Abner—so Ewald, Josephus, and others. Kish, the father of Saul, a quiet, plain man, evidently was quite content that his beasts were found.

and to his servant, Whither went ye? And he said, To seek the asses: and when we saw that *they were* no where, we came to Samuel. (15) And Saul's uncle said, Tell me, I pray thee, what Samuel said unto you. (16) And Saul said unto his uncle, He told us plainly that the asses were found. But of the matter of the kingdom, whereof Samuel spake, he told him not.

(17) And Samuel called the people together unto the LORD to Mizpeh; (18) and said unto the children of Israel, Thus saith the LORD God of Israel, I brought up Israel out of Egypt, and delivered you out of the hand of the Egyptians, and out of the hand of all kingdoms, *and* of them that oppressed you: (19) and ye have this day rejected your God, who himself saved you out of all your adversities and your tribulations; and ye have said unto him, Nay, but set a king over us. Now therefore present yourselves before the LORD by your tribes, and by your thousands.

(20) And when Samuel had caused all the tribes of Israel to come near, the tribe of Benjamin was taken. (21) When he had caused the tribe of Benjamin to come near by their families, the family of Matri was taken, and Saul the son of Kish was taken: and when they sought him, he could not be found. (22) Therefore they enquired of the LORD further,

---

and that his son had returned in safety, and so asks no curious questions about his son's journey. Not so Abner, who was a restless, ambitious man, and who, very probably, had heard something already from the servant who accompanied Saul (traditionally supposed to have been Doeg) of the strange honours paid to his nephew by the great and revered judge of Israel, the famous Samuel, and also of the long private interview between them. Abner, the uncle of the future king, an observant man, might well have been struck with the change that had passed over his nephew since he had last seen him; hence his question, "Tell me what Samuel said unto you?"

(16) **He told him not.**—It has been suggested ingeniously that this reply was prompted by the characteristic Israelite caution—the fear of betraying prematurely an important secret. It is, however, far better to assume that Samuel had given the young Saul to understand that the revelation respecting his future, and the great state change involved in it, was, in the first instance, for him alone; no other man was as yet to share that great secret with him. In His own good time God would signify His sovereign will and pleasure to Israel; till then, Saul was strictly to keep his own counsel in this important matter. To have imparted the secret to any one would have at once opened the door to secret intrigues and party plotting; one like Abner, especially, would not have been slow in devising schemes to compass so great an end as the placing the crown of Israel on the head of one of his own family.

The modesty and humility, as well as the wisdom, of Saul in these early days of his greatness is remarkable. The "changed heart" was indeed an acknowledged fact with him. Wordsworth quotes here how, "in like manner, Samson, in the early days of his humility, told not his parents of the lion. (See Judges xiv. 6.) So Saul of Tarsus spake not of his visions and revelations of the Lord till he was constrained to do so by his enemies." (See 2 Cor. xii. 1.)

(17) **Samuel called the people together.**—"Samuel does all that further lies in his power to promote the great cause. He calls a national assembly to Mizpeh. Here the sacred lot, it is stated, fell, among all the tribes of Israel, upon Benjamin; and, in an ever narrowing circle, at length upon Saul, the son of Kish. If we consider the general use in those ages of the sacred lot, we shall find that, taking the whole account in this connection, it exhibits nothing but the great truth that for the full and auspicious acknowledgment of Saul as king, his mysterious interview with the seer did not alone suffice—publicly, in solemn national assembly, was it necessary for the Spirit of the Eternal to choose him out, and to make him known as the Eternal's man."—*Ewald.*

Mizpah (for so the name should be spelt) was chosen by Samuel for the solemn assembly of the tribes on the occasion of the electing their first king, on account of the glorious memories of his own victory, many years before, at that place. The words, "unto the Lord," probably signify that the mysterious Urim and Thummim, by which inquiry was used to be made of the Eternal, had been brought there by the high priest, or, on the supposition that the office was then vacant, by the priest who temporarily replaced him.

(18) **Thus saith the Lord.**—Before proceeding to the election, Samuel again reminds Israel of its folly and ingratitude in their voluntarily rejecting the glorious Eternal King for an earthly sovereign. It was perfectly true that, under the present circumstances of Israel, the establishment of a mortal king was needful for the development of the Hebrew power, but it was none the less true that such a change in the Hebrew constitution would never have been necessary had not the nation forsaken their own Eternal Sovereign, who in time past had saved them out of far greater perils than any then threatening them. Now a change in the government of Israel was necessary, therefore God gave them their desire; but the change would involve the loss for ever of the higher blessedness for which the people had shown itself utterly unworthy.

(20) **The tribe of Benjamin was taken.**—How the "lots" were taken is not said; usually it was by throwing tablets (Josh. xviii. 6, 8), but sometimes by drawing from a vessel or urn, as in Num. xxxiii. 54. The latter, from the Hebrew word used, was probably the method employed on this occasion.

(21) **The family of Matri was taken.**—In none of the Benjamite genealogies connected with the royal house of Saul does this name occur. We cannot account for the omission. Ewald conjectures that the name Matri is a corruption from "Bikri" (see 1 Chron. vii. 8).

(22) **Therefore they enquired of the Lord further, if the man should yet come thither.**—Saul and Samuel alone, of all the host gathered that

Election of Saul — I. SAMUEL, X. — as King over Israel

if the man should yet come thither. And the LORD answered, Behold, he hath hid himself among the stuff. ⁽²³⁾ And they ran and fetched him thence: and when he stood among the people, he was higher than any of the people from his shoulders and upward. ⁽²⁴⁾ And Samuel said to all the people, See ye him whom the LORD hath chosen, that *there is* none like him among all the people? And all the people shouted, and said, ¹God save the king. ⁽²⁵⁾ Then Samuel told the people the manner of the kingdom, and wrote *it* in a book, and laid *it* up before the LORD. And Samuel sent all the people away, every man to his house.

⁽²⁶⁾ And Saul also went home to Gibeah;

¹ Heb., *Let the king live.*

---

day at Mizpeh, knew on whom the lot would fall. So certain was Saul, after the strange signs had sealed the truth of the prophet's revelation, that he would be designated by the sacred lot, that he shrank from waiting to hear the result, and concealed himself among the baggage and store-tents and waggons of the vast assembly. A second Divine announcement was needed to discover his hiding-place, and draw him forth before the people.

^(23—24) **He was higher than any of the people.** —"How shall this man save us?" was the impatient and angry murmur soon raised by some discontented spirits in Israel, not improbably princes of the leading houses of the great tribes of Judah and Ephraim, who were disgusted at the choice falling on an unknown man of the small and comparatively powerless tribe of Benjamin. But Samuel—whose place in the nation the unknown Benjamite was really to take—with rare nobility and singleness of purpose, had already singled out and called conspicuous attention to the one gift Saul undoubtedly, in an extraordinary degree, possessed—the one gift by which, in that primitive time, a man seemed to be worthy of rule. He was "goodly": "there was not among the children of Israel a goodlier person than he;" from his shoulders and upward he towered above all the people. When he stood among the people, Samuel could say of him, "See ye him? Look at him whom the Lord hath chosen, that there is none like him among all the people." It is in the days of the Judges, as in the Homeric days of Greece; Agamemnon, like Saul, is head and shoulders taller than the people. Like Saul, too, he has that peculiar air and dignity expressed by the Hebrew word which we translate "good," or "goodly." This is the ground of the epithet which became fixed as part of his name, "Saul the chosen," "the chosen of the Lord." In the Mussulman traditions this is the only trait of Saul which is preserved. His name has there been almost lost; he is known only as Thalût, "the tall one." In the Hebrew songs of his own time he was known by a more endearing, but not less expressive, indication of the same grace. His stately towering form, standing under the pomegranate-tree above the precipice of Migron, or on the pointed crags of Michmash, or the rocks of Engedi, claimed for him the title of "wild roe," "the gazelle," perched aloft, the pride and glory of Israel. Against the giant Philistines a giant king was needed. The time for the little stripling of the house of Jesse was close at hand, but was not yet come. Saul and Jonathan, swifter than eagles and stronger than lions, still seemed the fittest champions of Israel. When Saul saw any strong man or any valiant man, he took him unto him. He, in his gigantic panoply, that would fit none but himself, with the spear that he had in his hand, of the same form and fashion as the spear of Goliath, was a host in himself.—Dean Stanley: *Lectures on the Jewish Church*, xxi.

⁽²⁵⁾ **Wrote it in a book.**—The "Law of the Kingdom," which Samuel rehearsed before the people, and which he wrote in a roll, and laid solemnly up and preserved among the State archives, related to the divinely established right and duties of the God-appointed king, and also clearly set forth the limitations of his power. The vice-gerent on earth of the invisible King could be no arbitrary despot, unless he transgressed plainly and openly the "manner of the kingdom" written in a book, and laid up before the Lord by Samuel.

This sacred document, we may assume, contained, too, the exact details of the singular story of the choice of the first king of Israel. It was well, no doubt, thought Samuel, that coming ages should know exactly how it came to pass that he, the seer, anointed the Benjamite of Gibeah as king over the Lord's inheritance. We may, therefore, fairly conclude that from the record laid up among the sacred archives in the sanctuary, the compiler or redactor of this "Book of Samuel" derived his intimate knowledge of every little fact connected with the Divine choice of Saul.

The legal portion of this writing respecting the kingdom was, of course, strictly based upon what Moses had already written on this subject in Deuteronomy (see chap. xvii. 14—20).

We find here, in this writing of Samuel, the first trace of literary composition among the Israelites since the days of Moses. The great revival in letters which began shortly after the days of Saul was due, most probably, to the influence of Samuel and those great schools of the prophets which he had established in the land.

And laid it up before the Lord.—We are not told where this was done, but the words seem to imply that the document, or roll, was placed by the side of the Ark, then in the "city of woods," Kiriath-jearim. Josephus says this writing was preserved in the Tabernacle of the Holy of Holies, where the Book of the Law had been laid up (Deut. xxxi. 26).

And Samuel sent all the people away.—It is noteworthy that even after the formal popular ratification of Saul's election as king, it is *Samuel* who dismisses the assembly. Indeed, throughout the remainder of the great seer's life, whenever he appears on the scene, he is evidently the principal person, occupying a position above king or priest. On the other hand, after this period Samuel made but comparatively few public appearances; of his own free will he seems to have retired into privacy, and only in emergencies to have left his retirement.

⁽²⁶⁾ **And Saul also went home to Gibeah.**—Saul departed for the present to his own home. We may conclude that his fellow citizens, proud of the honour conferred on one of themselves, were among his earliest devoted attendants. The young hero, however, as we shall see, had not long to wait for an opportunity of

and there went with him a band of men, whose hearts God had touched. (27) But the children of Belial said, How shall this man save us? And they despised him, and brought him no presents. But ¹he held his peace.

CHAPTER XI.—(1) Then Nahash the Ammonite came up, and encamped against Jabesh-gilead: and all the men of Jabesh said unto Nahash, Make a covenant with us, and we will serve thee. (2) And Nahash the Ammonite answered them, On this *condition* will I make *a covenant* with you, that I may thrust out all your right eyes, and lay it *for* a reproach upon all Israel.

(3) And the elders of Jabesh said unto him, ²Give us seven days' respite, that we may send messengers unto all the

1 Or, *he was, as though he had been deaf.*

2 Heb., *Forbear us.*

---

displaying his prowess, and of rallying the hearts of the people generally firmly to his standard.

A band of men.—Among these early friends, doubtless, were to be found the names of the distinguished men whom we hear of later surrounding Saul. The highest prudence and sagacity marked all the early period of the reign of the first king. Slow to take offence, we shall see from the next verse how Saul and his valiant adherents busied themselves in conciliating the disaffected, and in preparing for a decisive action against the enemies who were on all sides harrying the land. An opportunity (see the history in the next chapter) soon presented itself of showing that the choice of a king had been wisely made.

(27) **The children of Belial.**—More accurately, *worthless men.* (See Note on chap. ii. 12.)

And they despised him.—As above suggested, these malcontents were probably princes and leading men of the great tribes of Judah and Ephraim, displeased that the new king should be selected from the small unimportant tribe of Benjamin. It will be remembered that the tribe of Benjamin had been almost entirely destroyed in the civil war related in the concluding chapters of Judges. "They despised him," because in no way had he made his mark, either in the arts of war or peace. From what has gone before (see verses 11 and 12 of this chap.) it is evident that Saul was a man of no special culture; his early years had been spent in agriculture and work on his father's lands in the neighbourhood of Gibeah.

And brought him no presents.—These gifts were, in the East, the token of submission and homage; not to offer them to Saul was almost the same thing as to ignore his authority. Although not stated, it is clear that these malcontents were among the chiefs of the greater tribes who had assisted at the election.

But he held his peace.—Literally, *he was a deaf man,* acting as though he had not heard the murmurs. This prudent conduct showed great self-control and self-denial on the part of the new king and his counsellors.

XI.

(1–15) King Saul shows himself worthy of the Kingdom by his prompt action in the case of the Siege of Jabesh-gilead by the Ammonites. He is universally acknowledged Sovereign.

(1) **Nahash the Ammonite.**—Nahash was king of the children of Ammon (see chap. xii. 12). This royal family was in some way related to David (see 2 Sam. xvii. 25; 1 Chron. ii. 16, 17). At the time of David's exile owing to the rebellion of Absalom, a son of Nahash the Ammonite is specially mentioned as showing kindness to the fugitive king.

Jabesh-gilead was a city situated in Northern Gilead, in the territory assigned to Manasseh. Josephus states that it was the capital of the country of Gilead. The Ammonites were a kindred race to the Moabites, being descended from the same ancestor, the patriarch Lot. They asserted that a portion of their territory had been taken from them by Israel, and in the days of the judges sorely harassed the people. The Judge Jephthah attacked and defeated them with great slaughter.

It was, no doubt, to avenge the disgrace they had suffered at the hands of Jephthah that their warlike monarch, Nahash,—deeming the opportunity a favourable one, owing to the old age of the reigning judge, Samuel,—invaded the Israelitic country bordering upon his kingdom, and besieged the city of Jabesh-gilead.

Make a covenant with us.—The citizens of Jabesh-gilead, feeling their isolation and comparative remoteness from the chief centre of the people, were willing to pay a tribute to the Ammonite king, and made him overtures to this effect.

(2) **On this condition.**—The horrible cruelty of this scornful proposal gives us an insight into the barbarous customs of this imperfectly civilised age. Indeed, many of the crimes we read of in these books—crimes which, to modern ears, justly sound shocking and scarcely credible—are referable to the fact that civilisation and its humanizing influences had made but little way as yet among the nations of the world.

The object of Nahash's cruelty was to incapacitate the inhabitants of Jabesh from ever further assisting his enemies in war; they would henceforth be blinded in the right eye, while the left eye would be concealed by the shield which fighting-men were in the habit of holding before them.

(3) **Give us seven days' respite.**—This kind of proposal has always in time of war been a common one; such a request from a beleaguered fortress we meet with constantly, especially in mediæval chronicles. It was, no doubt, made by the citizens in the hope that Saul the Benjamite, in whose election as king they had recently taken a part, would devise some means for their rescue. Between Benjamin and the city of Jabesh-gilead there had long existed the closest ties of friendship. How far back this strange link between the southern tribe and the distant frontier town dated, we know not. When Israel was summoned "as one man" (Judges xxi.), probably under the direction of Phinehas, the grandson of Aaron, to avenge on Benjamin the crime committed by the men of Gibeah, Jabesh-gilead alone, among the cities of Israel—no doubt, out of its friendship for the sinning tribe—declined to obey the imperious summons, and for this act of disobedience was rased to the ground, and its inhabitants put to the sword. The tribes, however, subsequently regretted their remorseless cruelty in their punishment of Benjamin, and feared lest their

335

coasts of Israel: and then, if *there be* no man to save us, we will come out to thee. (4) Then came the messengers to Gibeah of Saul, and told the tidings in the ears of the people: and all the people lifted up their voices, and wept. (5) And, behold, Saul came after the herd out of the field; and Saul said, What *aileth* the people that they weep? And they told him the tidings of the men of Jabesh.

(6) And the Spirit of God came upon Saul when he heard those tidings, and his anger was kindled greatly. (7) And he took a yoke of oxen, and hewed them in pieces, and sent *them* throughout all the coasts of Israel by the hands of messengers, saying, Whosoever cometh not forth after Saul and after Samuel, so shall it be done unto his oxen. And the fear of the LORD fell on the people, and they

---

brother's name might perish out of the land; mindful, then, of the old loving feeling which existed between the city of Jabesh-gilead and the tribe of Benjamin, they gave the maidens of the ruined city spared in the judicial massacre perpetrated on the citizens, to the fighting remnant of Benjamin, still defending themselves on the impregnable Rock of the Pomegranate, "Rimmon," and did what was in their power to restore the ruined and broken tribe. Jabesh-gilead seems to have risen again from its ashes, and Benjamin once more held up its head among the tribes of Israel, and just now had given the first king to the people. No wonder, then, that the city in the hour of its sore need and deadly peril should send for succour to Gibeah in Benjamin, and to Saul, the Benjamite king. Neither the tribe nor the king failed them in their distress.

(4) **Then came the messengers to Gibeah.**—In the preceding verse we read that it was resolved by the beleaguered city to send messengers to all the coasts of Israel, but we only hear of the action taken by Saul in Gibeah. It therefore may be assumed that this was the first city they sent to, not only on account of their ancient friendship with Benjamin, but because Gibeah was the residence of the newly-elected sovereign, Saul.

And all the people lifted up their voices, and wept.—This is exactly what might have been expected from Benjamites hearing of the terrible straits into which the city they all loved so well, and which was united to them by such close bonds of friendship and alliance, was reduced; but though they grieved so deeply, they do not seem of themselves to have been able to devise any plan for its relief, until their great fellow-citizen took the matter in hand.

(5) **And, behold, Saul came after the herd out of the field.**—Saul was still busied with his old pursuits. At first this would seem strange, but it must be remembered that the regal authority was something quite new in republican Israel, and that the new king's duties and privileges at first were vague, and but little understood; besides which, jealousies, such as have already been noticed (chap. x. 27), no doubt induced Saul and his advisers to keep the royalty in the background till some opportunity for bringing it to the front should present itself. It is, therefore, quite to be understood that the newly-elected king should be spending at least a portion of his time in pursuits which hitherto had occupied his whole life. He was not the first hero summoned from agricultural labours to assume, in a national emergency, the command of an army. Gideon, we read, was called from the threshing-floor to do his great deeds; and to quote from profane history, one of the noblest of the sons of Rome, like Saul, was ploughing when the Senate fetched him to be the dictator and the general of their armies; and to the plough we know that that great man returned when his work was successfully accomplished and his country saved.

(6) **And the Spirit of God came upon Saul.**—Nothing, perhaps, could have moved Saul so deeply as this news respecting the distress of Jabesh-gilead; he was affected not merely by the disgrace to Israel over which the Eternal had so lately directed him to be anointed king, but by the sore peril which menaced the ancient friend and ally of his tribe. On Saul's heart, thus prepared for action, the Holy Spirit fell, and endued him with extraordinary wisdom, valour, and power for the great and difficult work which lay before him.

We read of the Spirit of the Lord coming upon men like Othniel (Judges iii. 10) and the other great Israelitic judges, who were raised up to be in their day the deliverers of the people; and the immediate result of the Spirit of the Lord coming upon them was to impart new and unusual power to their spirit, power which enabled them successfully to surmount every danger and difficulty which barred the progress of the great work they were specially called upon to do.

(7) **A yoke of oxen.**—In a moment all the great powers of Saul, hitherto dormant, woke up, and he issued his swift commands in a way which at once showed Israel that they had got a hero-king who would brook no trifling. In that self-same hour, striking dead the oxen standing before his plough, he hews them in pieces, and handing a bloody strip to certain of the men standing around him, weeping for grief and shame and the wrong done to Israel, bade them swiftly bear these terrible war-signals throughout the length and breadth of the land, and by these means to rouse the nation to prompt action.

On this strange war-signal of king Saul, Ewald, in his *History of Israel*, Book II., section iii. 1 (note), remarks, "how in like manner it was formerly the custom in Norway to send on the war-arrow; and in Scotland a fire-brand, with both ends dipped in blood, was dispatched as a war-token."

Not improbably Saul cut the oxen into eleven pieces, and sent one to each of the other tribes.

And the fear of the Lord fell on the people.—It was some such mighty awakening under the influence of the Spirit of the Eternal, as is here related of King Saul, which suggested to the poet Asaph the bold but splendid image of the seventy-eighth Psalm, when, after describing in moving language the degradation and bitter woe of fallen Israel, the singer, struck with a new inspiration, bursts forth with "Then the Lord awaked as one out of sleep, and like a mighty man that shouteth by reason of wine. And he smote his enemies," &c. (Ps. lxxviii. 65). "The people rose as one man" (see margin) against the enemies of their national freedom. It was the same Spirit of the Lord which inspired Saul to put himself at the head of the children of

Saul Defeats the Ammonites   I. SAMUEL, XI.   *before Jabesh-gilead.*

came out ¹with one consent. ⁽⁸⁾ And when he numbered them in Bezek, the children of Israel were three hundred thousand, and the men of Judah thirty thousand.

⁽⁹⁾ And they said unto the messengers that came, Thus shall ye say unto the men of Jabesh-gilead, To morrow, by *that time* the sun be hot, ye shall have ²help. And the messengers came and shewed *it* to the men of Jabesh; and they were glad. ⁽¹⁰⁾ Therefore the men of Jabesh said, To morrow we will come out unto you, and ye shall do with us all that seemeth good unto you.

⁽¹¹⁾ And it was *so* on the morrow, that Saul put the people in three companies; and they came into the midst of the host in the morning watch, and slew the Ammonites until the heat of the day: and it came to pass, that they which remained were scattered, so that two of them were not left together.

⁽¹²⁾ And the people said unto Samuel, Who *is* he that said, Shall Saul reign over us? bring the men, that we may put them to death. ⁽¹³⁾ And Saul said, There shall not a man be put to death this day: for to day the LORD hath wrought salvation in Israel.

⁽¹⁴⁾ Then said Samuel to the people, Come, and let us go to Gilgal, and renew

1 Heb., *as one man.*

2 Or, *deliverance.*

Israel which now laid hold of all the people, lifting them up, and giving them new strength and resistless courage, and the mighty feeling that God was with them.

It was owing to some influence of a similar nature that with scanty numbers, ill-armed and ill-trained, the Swiss won for their land centuries of freedom on memorable fields like Laupen and Morat, though the proudest chivalry of Europe was arrayed against them. It was the same Spirit which impelled the peace-loving traders of the marshes of Holland to rise as one man, and to drive out for ever from their loved strip of fen land the hitherto invincible armies of Spain. No oppressor, though backed by the wealth and power of an empire, has ever been able to resist the smallest people in whose heart has burned the flame of the Divine fire of the "fear of the Lord."

⁽⁸⁾ **Bezek.**—Bezek was in the tribe of Issachar, in the plain of Jezreel, an open district, well adapted for the assembling of the great host which so promptly obeyed the peremptory summons of the war-signal of King Saul.

The children of Israel were three hundred thousand, and the men of Judah thirty thousand.—It has been suggested that this verse was the addition of some late reviser of the book, who lived in the northern kingdom after the final separation of Israel and Judah, but such a supposition is not necessary to account for the separate mention of Judah and Israel, or for the apparently great disproportion in the numbers supplied by the great southern tribe. The chronicler, with pardonable exultation, specially mentions the splendid result of the young hero's first summons to the tribes, adding, with perhaps an undertone of sadness, that the rich and populous Judah to that great host only contributed 30,000. There is no doubt, as Dean Payne Smith well observes, that "as a matter of fact Judah always stood apart until there was a king who belonged to itself. Then, in David's time, it first took an active interest in the national welfare, and it was its vast power and numbers which made the shepherd-king, who sprang from Judah, so powerful." In the reign of King Asa of Judah, the numbers of the men of war of that proud tribe amounted to 300,000. It is, however, to be remembered that in the Old Testament Books, owing to the mistakes of copyists, *numbers* are not always to be strictly relied upon.

⁽⁹⁾ **To morrow, by that time the sun be hot.**—That is, about noon the army of rescue will be at hand. The distance from Bezek to Jabesh was not much over twenty miles.

⁽¹¹⁾ **The morning watch.**—The morning watch was the last of the three watches, each lasting for four hours; this was the old Hebrew division of the night. Thus the first onslaught of the men of Israel under Saul would have taken place some time between two and six a.m. The battle, and subsequent rout of Ammon, continued evidently for many hours.

⁽¹²⁾ **And the people said unto Samuel.**—The great weight and influence of the seer among the people is strikingly shown by this record of their turning to him, even in the first flush of this great victory of Saul's. It was Samuel to whom the people looked to bring to punishment the men who had dared to question the wisdom of electing Saul as king. It should be remembered, too, that the royal summons to Israel which accompanied the bloody war-signal of King Saul, ran in the joint names of Saul and Samuel. (See verse 7.)

⁽¹³⁾ **And Saul said, There shall not a man be put to death this day.**—A wise, as well as a generous, decision; anything like a bloody vengeance would have been the commencement of future feuds and bitter heart-burnings between the new king and the powerful families of the other tribes, who misliked and opposed his election. Saul began his reign with wise discretion, as well as with heroic valour. By this determined refusal to avenge the cruel affront showed to him, he taught "kings to be" how truly a royal virtue was forgiveness of all past wrongs.

For to day the Lord hath wrought salvation in Israel.—And as yet unspoiled, the king's heart was full of humble reverent piety. By this first public act of pardon, he "not only signified that the public rejoicing should not be interrupted, but reminded them of the clemency of God, and urged that since Jehovah had shown such clemency upon that day, that He overlooked their sins, and had given them a glorious victory. it was only right they should follow His example, and forgive their neighbours' sins without bloodshed." (Seb. Schmidt, quoted by Keil and Delitsch.)

⁽¹⁴⁾ **Then said Samuel to the people, Come, and let us go to Gilgal.**—This was the well-known sanctuary of that name, and was selected as the place of solemn assembly, no doubt, because it was in the now royal tribe of Benjamin. It is situated in the Jordan Valley, not far from Jericho, and has been the scene of many of the most striking events in Israelitic history.

the kingdom there. ⁽¹⁵⁾ And all the people went to Gilgal; and there they made Saul king before the LORD in Gilgal; and there they sacrificed sacrifices of peace offerings before the LORD; and there Saul and all the men of Israel rejoiced greatly.

CHAPTER XII.—⁽¹⁾ And Samuel said unto all Israel, Behold, I have hearkened unto your voice in all that ye said unto me, and have made a king over you. ⁽²⁾ And now, behold, the king walketh before you: and I am old and greyheaded; and, behold, my sons *are* with

And renew the kingdom there.—There had been, as Samuel and Saul well remembered, many murmurings on the occasion of the original royal election at Mizpeh. Then the people had by no means unanimously accepted as sovereign the Benjamite who was now crowned with the glory of a splendid success. The seer, with striking generosity to one who superseded him in his position as judge, again presented the hero Saul to Israel as their anointed king.

(15) And there they made Saul king before the Lord in Gilgal.—We must not understand with the LXX. Version that Saul was anointed afresh at Gilgal. The Greek Version reads, "and Samuel anointed Saul king there." The Gilgal convention was nothing more than a solemn national confirmation of the popular election at Mizpeh. The words "before the Lord," imply the presence of the Ark, or of the high priest with the mystic Urim and Thummim. Bishop Wordsworth understands the words "they made Saul king" to signify that after this "the people would not allow him any longer to lead a private life, but they made him to assume the royal state and authority to which he had been appointed by God."

XII.

(1—25) Samuel's Defence of his past Career—He Rehearses the Story of Israel, and shows, in asking for an earthly King, how ungrateful the People are to the Heavenly King—The Miraculous Sign—Samuel urges them to be Loyal to God under their new Government.

(1) And Samuel said unto all Israel.—We believe we possess in this section of our history, in the report the compiler of these memoirs has given us of the dialogue between the judge Samuel and the elders of Israel at the solemn assembly of Gilgal, many of the very words spoken on this momentous occasion by the old man. It is doubtless a true and detailed account of all that took place on that day—the real inauguration of the earthly monarchy; that great change in the life of Israel which became of vast importance in the succeeding generations. In such a recital the words used by that grand old man, who belonged both to the old order of things and to the new, who was the link between the judges and the kings—the link which joined men like Eleazar, the grandson of Aaron, Gideon, and Jephthah, heroes half-veiled in the mists which so quickly gather round an unlettered past, with men like David and Solomon, round whose lives no mist will ever gather—the words used by that old man, who, according to the cherished tradition in Israel, was the accredited minister of the invisible King when the Eternal made over the sovereignty to Saul, would surely be treasured up with a jealous care. This gives an especial and peculiar interest to the present chapter, which contains the summary of the proceedings of the Gilgal assembly. The old judge Samuel, with the hero-king Saul standing by his side, presents the king to the people of the Lord under the title of the "Anointed of the Eternal," and then in a few pathetic words speaks first of his own pure and upright past. The elders reply to his moving words. Then he rehearses the glorious acts of the Eternal King, and repeats how He, over and over again, delivered the people from the miseries into which their own sins had plunged them; and yet, in full memory of all this, says the indignant old man, "in the place of this invisible Ruler, so full of mercy and pity, you asked for an earthly king. The Lord has granted your petition now. Behold your king!" pointing to Saul at his side.—The old man continues: "Even after your ingratitude to the true King, still He will be with you and the man He has chosen for you, if only you and he are obedient to the old well-known Divine commandments." At this juncture Samuel strengthens his argument by invoking a sign from heaven. Awe-struck and appalled, the assembled elders, confessing their sin, ask for Samuel's prayers. The old prophet closes the solemn scene with a promise that his intercession for king and people shall never cease.

Behold, I have hearkened unto your voice in all that ye said unto me, and have made a king over you.—This should be compared with chap. viii. 7, 19, 20, 22, where the proceedings of the deputation of the people to Samuel at Ramah are related at length. Their wishes expressed on that public occasion had been scrupulously carried out by him. He would now say a few words respecting the past, as regards his (Samuel's) administration, would ask the assembled elders of the nation a few grave questions, and then would leave them with their king. The account, as we possess it, of these proceedings at Gilgal on the occasion of the national reception of Saul as king, is in the form of a dialogue between the prophet Samuel and the elders of the people.

(2) And now, behold, the king walketh before you.—No doubt, here pointing to Saul by his side. The term "walketh before you" implied generally that the kingly office included the guiding and governing the people, as well as the especial duty of leading them in war; from henceforth they must accept his authority on all occasions, not merely in great emergencies. Both king and people must understand that the days when Saul could quietly betake himself to his old pursuits on the farm of the Ephraim hills were now past for ever. He must lead, and they must follow. The metaphor is taken from the usual place of a shepherd in the East, where he goes before his flock. Compare the words of our Lord, who uses the same image of a shepherd walking before his sheep (John x. 27): "My sheep hear my voice, and I know them, and they *follow* me."

And I am old and grayheaded.—Here the prophet, with some pathos, refers to the elders' own words at Ramah (chap viii. 5). Yes, said the seer, I am old—grown grey in your service; listen to me while I ask you what manner of service that has been. Can any one find in it a flaw? has it not been pure and disinterested throughout?

Samuel's Defence of   I. SAMUEL, XII.   *his own past Career.*

you: and I have walked before you from my childhood unto this day. ⁽³⁾ Behold, *^a*here I *am*: witness against me before the LORD, and before his anointed: whose ox have I taken? or whose ass have I taken? or whom have I de-frauded? whom have I oppressed? or of whose hand have I received any ¹bribe ²to blind mine eyes therewith? and I will restore it you. ⁽⁴⁾ And they said, Thou hast not defrauded us, nor oppressed us, neither hast thou taken ought

^a Ecclus. 46. 19.

¹ Heb., *ransom.*

² Or, *that I should hide mine eyes at him.*

My sons are with you.—Yes, old indeed, for my offspring are numbered now among the grown men of the people. Possibly, however, a tinge of mortified feeling at the rejection of himself and his family, mixed with a desire to recommend his sons to the favour and goodwill of the nation. is at the bottom of this mention of them.—*Speaker's Commentary.* It is evident that these sons, whose conduct as Samuel's deputies had excited the severest criticism on the part of the elders (chap. viii. 5), had been reduced—with the full consent, of course, of their father, who up to this period exercised evidently supreme power in all the coasts of Israel—to the condition of mere private citizens.

From my childhood unto this day.—Samuel's life had in truth been constantly before the public observation from very early days; well known to all were the details of his career—his early consecration under peculiar and exceptional circumstances to the sanctuary service, the fact of the "word of the Lord" coming directly to him when still a boy, his recognition by the people directly afterwards as a prophet, then his restless, unwearied work during the dark days which followed the fall of Shiloh. It was indeed a public life. He would have Israel, now they had virtually rejected his rule, think over that long busy life of his for a moment, and then pronounce a judgment on it.

⁽³⁾ **Behold, here I am: witness against me before the Lord, and before his anointed.**—I speak in a solemn presence, "before the Eternal," went on the old man, looking up heavenward, "and before His anointed," pointing with a reverent gesture to the kingly form by his side. "His Anointed"—this is the earliest instance of a *king* bearing this title of honour. The high priest, whose blessed office brought him in such close contact with the invisible and eternal King, is in the early Hebrew story styled now and again by this honoured name. But henceforth it seems to be limited to the man invested with the kingly dignity. The infinite charm which the name "Anointed of the Eternal" carried with it for centuries is, no doubt, due to the fact that one greater than any of the sons of men would, in the far future, assume the same sacred designation—"His Anointed," or "His Christ." (The words are synonymous, both being translations of the Hebrew word Messiah.)

Nor has this peculiar reverence for the "Lord's Anointed" been limited to His own people. Since the seer in the early morning on the hill-side, looking on "Ramah of the Watchers," poured out the holy oil on the young Saul's head, and then before all Israel gathered at Gilgal styled the new king by the title of the "Anointed of the Eternal," wherever the one true God has been worshipped, an infinite charm has gone with the name, a strange and peculiar reverence has surrounded every one who could fairly claim to bear it, and for many a century, among all peoples, an awful curse has at once attached itself to any one who would dare lift his hand against the "Lord's Anointed."

Whose ox have I taken? or whose ass have I taken?—The ox and the ass are taken as representative possessions in this primitive age, in a country where agriculture formed the principal source of the national resources. Before the wars and conquests of David and Solomon, there was comparatively little of the precious metals among the Hebrew people, who seem to have traded in those early days but rarely with foreign nations; horses were, too, unknown among them. The law of Exodus xx. 17 especially makes mention of the ox and the ass as things the Israelite was forbidden to covet. On these words of Samuel the Babylonian Talmud has an important note, which well illustrates the doctrine of the "Holy Spirit" as taught in Israel before the Christian era.

"Rabbi Elazer said, on three occasions did the Holy Spirit manifest Himself in a peculiar manner—in the judicial tribunal instituted by Shem, in that of Samuel the Ramathite, and in that of Solomon. In that of Shem, Judah declared, "She is righteous," &c. How could he know it? Might not another man have come to her as well as he did? But an echo of a voice was heard exclaiming: Of me (the word ממני is separated from the preceding word, and taken as a distinct utterance of the Holy Spirit); these things were overruled by me. Samuel said (1 Sam. xii. 3—5), "Behold, here I am: witness against me before the Lord, and before his anointed: whose ox have I taken? or whose ass have I taken? . . . And he said unto them, The Lord is witness against you, &c. . . And he said, He is witness" (ויאמר). It ought to read, "And *they* said." But it was the Holy Spirit that gave that answer. So with Solomon the words "She is the mother thereof" (1 Kings iii. 27) were spoken by the Holy Spirit."—Treatise *Maccoth*, fol. 23, col. 2.

Whom have I defrauded? whom have I oppressed?—Alluding, of course, to his conduct during his long continuance in office as supreme judge in Israel. The "bribe"—literally, *ransom*—alludes to that practice unhappily so common in the East of giving the judge a gift (usually of money) to buy his favour, and thus a criminal who had means was too often able to escape punishment.

The sons of Samuel, we know from chapter viii. 3, "took bribes, and perverted judgment." This accusation, we know, had been preferred by the very elders of the nation before whom the seer was then speaking. The old judge must have been very confident of his own spotless integrity to venture upon such a solemn challenge. The elders had shown themselves by their bold accusation of the seer's sons no respecters of persons, and from the tone of Samuel's address, must have felt his words were but the prelude of some scathing reproaches they would have to listen to, and yet they were constrained with one voice to bear their witness to the perfect truth of his assertion that his long official life had been indeed pure and spotless. The Talmud has a curious tradition respecting the prophets, based apparently upon this saying of Samuel. "All the prophets were rich men. This we infer from the account of Moses, Samuel, Amos, and Jonah. Of Moses, as it is written (Num. xvi. 15), 'I have not taken one ass from them.' Of Samuel, as it is written (1 Sam. xii. 3), 'Behold, here I am; witness against me before the Lord, and before

of any man's hand. ⁽⁵⁾ And he said unto them, The LORD *is* witness against you, and his anointed *is* witness this day, that ye have not found ought in my hand. And they answered, *He is* witness.

⁽⁶⁾ And Samuel said unto the people, *It is* the LORD that [1]advanced Moses and Aaron, and that brought your fathers up out of the land of Egypt. ⁽⁷⁾ Now therefore stand still, that I may reason with you before the LORD of all the [2]righteous acts of the LORD, which he did [3]to you and to your fathers. ⁽⁸⁾ *a* When Jacob was come into Egypt, and your fathers cried unto the LORD, then the LORD *b* sent Moses and Aaron, which brought forth your fathers out of Egypt, and made them dwell in this place. ⁽⁹⁾ And when they forgat the LORD their God, *c* he sold them into the hand of Sisera, captain of the host of Hazor, and into the hand of the Philistines, and into the hand of the king of Moab, and they fought against them. ⁽¹⁰⁾ And they cried

1 Or, *made.*

2 Heb., *righteousnesses, or, benefits.*

3 Heb., *with.*

a Gen. 46. 5, 6.

b Ex. 4. 16.

c Judg. 4. 2.

His anointed. Whose ox have I taken? or whose ass have I taken?' Of Amos, as it is written (Amos vii. 14), 'I was an herdsman and a gatherer of sycamore fruit,' *i.e.,* I am proprietor of my herds and own sycamores in the valley. Of Jonah, as it is written (Jonah i. 3), 'So he paid the fare thereof, and went down into it.' Rabbi Yochanan says he hired the whole ship. Rabbi Rumanus says the hire of the ship amounted to *four thousand* golden denarii."—Treatise *Nedarim,* fol. 38, col. 1.

(5) **The Lord is witness.**—Then Samuel again, with increased solemnity, called the Eternal in the heavens above and His anointed king then standing by his side to witness what the people had just acknowledged concerning his scrupulously just rule.

And they answered, He is witness.—And the assembly of Israel, again with one voice, shouted, Yes, He is witness.

(6) **It is the Lord that advanced Moses and Aaron.**—The Hebrew should be rendered, "even the Eternal that advanced Moses and Aaron." The elders of Israel (verse 5) had with one consent cried out, in reply to Samuel's solemn calling God and the king to witness, *He is witness.* Then Samuel takes up their words with great emphasis, *even the Eternal that advanced Moses, &c.* The English rendering greatly weakens the dramatic force of the original Hebrew. The LXX. has caught accurately the thought by supplying the word "witness": thus, *The Lord is witness, &c.*

The Exodus is mentioned in this and in many places in these ancient records of the people as the great call of love by which the Eternal assumed the sovereignty over Israel. The Talmud here comments: "It is the Lord that made Moses and Aaron" (1 Sam. xii. 6); and it is said (1 Sam. xii. 11), "And the Lord sent Jerubbaal, and Bedan, and Jephthah, and Samuel." Scripture balances in the same scale the three least important with the three most important personages, in order to teach thee that Jerrubbaal in his generation was like Moses in his, Bedan (said to be Samson) like Aaron, and Jephthah like Samuel. Hence the most insignificant man, if appointed a ruler of the congregation, has the same authority as the most important personage.—Treatise *Rosh-Hashanah,* fol. 25, col. 2.

(7) **Now therefore . . .** —Samuel proceeds in his painful work. See now, he says, we have advanced thus far in my solemn pleading. Stand up now, ye elders, while I proceed. My innocence, as your judge, you have thus borne witness to, before God and the king, yet in spite of this you have wished to be quit of me, and of One who stood high above me—of One who has worked for you such mighty deeds, even the Eternal. See now, ye elders, what He has done for your fathers and for you, this invisible King, whom ye have just deliberately replaced by an earthly king.

(8) **When Jacob was come into Egypt.**—Now, in order, Samuel rehearses the deeds of loving-kindness done for Israel by this Eternal King. And first he mentions the wonders of the Exodus, and how, under that Divine guidance, they were guided through so many dangers safe into the land of Canaan, *this place.*

(9) **And when they forgat the Lord their God.** —The idolatry of Israel, and the immorality and shameless wickedness which ever attended it, was simply an act of rebellion against the pure government of the invisible King, and was punished by the withdrawal of the Divine protection. The instances which are here adduced of the people being given up into the hands of strange hostile nations are prominent ones, quoted as they occurred to him, without any careful attention being paid to the order of events and times, which was here not necessary for the course of his argument. Three leading nations out of the neighbouring peoples are mentioned by him as having been allowed, in consequence of Israel's rebellion against the Eternal, to oppress and harass, for a season, the tribes of God's inheritance—the Canaanites, the Philistines, and the Moabites.

Captain of the host of Hazor.—Hazor is mentioned as the capital city of the Canaanites in Josh. xi. 1, 10, 13, &c., and again as a royal residence in Judges iv. 2. Sisera is specially named as the well-known commander of the army against which Israel fought, and as the victim of the sanguinary but patriotic deed of fury of Jael.

Into the hand of the Philistines.—These "Phœnicians," who literally dwelt among the Israelites, were most formidable foes to the chosen people for a long series of years. We have before compared their many strongholds and fastnesses to those robber nests which in the stormy middle ages disturbed the peace, and were the scourge of the commerce and trade, of Central Europe. It was owing especially to these Philistines that for so long a period such slow progress in wealth and the arts of civilisation was made in Israel. The advance of the Hebrew nation, from the days of Samuel, who first really checked these Philistine robbers, was singularly rapid. In an almost incredibly short period, from being a poor, half-barbarous people, the Israelites became a highly cultured, wealthy, and powerful nation. In great measure this strangely rapid progress was owing to the complete subjugation of the Philistines under the rule of Samuel, Saul, and David.

The king of Moab.—The king referred to here is Eglon, who was slain by Ehud. (See Judges iii.)

(10) **And they cried unto the Lord.**—As soon as they were convinced of their sin and rebellion, and accused

Samuel Exhorts the People   I. SAMUEL, XII.   *to Fear the Lord.*

unto the LORD, and said, We have sinned, because we have forsaken the LORD, and have served Baalim and Ashtaroth: but now deliver us out of the hand of our enemies, and we will serve thee. ⁽¹¹⁾ And the LORD sent Jerubbaal, and Bedan, and ^aJephthah, and Samuel, and delivered you out of the hand of your enemies on every side, and ye dwelled safe. ⁽¹²⁾ And when ye saw that Nahash the king of the children of Ammon came against you, ye said unto me, Nay; but a king shall reign over us: when the LORD your God *was* your king. ⁽¹³⁾ Now therefore behold the king whom ye have chosen, *and* whom ye have desired! and, behold, the LORD hath set a king over you. ⁽¹⁴⁾ If ye will fear the LORD, and serve him, and obey his voice, and not rebel against the ¹commandment of the LORD, then shall both ye and also the king that reigneth over you ²continue following the LORD your God: ⁽¹⁵⁾ but if ye will not obey the voice of the LORD, but rebel against the commandment of the LORD, then shall the hand of the

a Judg. 11. 1.

1 Heb., *mouth.*

2 Heb., *be after.*

---

themselves, and returned to their old allegiance, their invisible King, ever full of pity and tender compassion, forgave them, and sent them quick deliverance.

And have served Baalim and Ashtaroth.—Baal and Ashtaroth were the well-known leading Phœnician deities; the worship, with most of its details, was imported probably from Carthage, the great Phœnician centre. The temple of Baal-shemesh, the Sun god, at Carthage, was renowned in that luxurious and splendid city. (For a detailed and picturesque account of the worship and ritual of Baal at Carthage, see M. Gustave Flaubert's romance of *Salômbo*.) Baal and Ashtaroth, the Greek Astarté, were probably originally worshipped simply as the sun and moon. The plural form refers to the various personifications and different titles of the god and goddess.

⁽¹¹⁾ **And the Lord sent Jerubbaal.**—Again the speaker only names a few of the God-sent deliverers, just the most prominent of their great and famous heroes. Gideon was surnamed Jerubbaal out of scorn and derision for the Phœnician deity: "Let Baal then strive or contend with me, Gideon."

Bedan.—This name does not occur in the record of the "judges." We meet with it only in 1 Chron. vii. 17, as a name of one of the descendants of Machir the Manassite, but this Bedan of the Chronicles seems to have been a person of no importance. The LXX. and the Syriac, the two most ancient versions, read, instead of Bedan, *Barak*. The letters forming these two names in the Hebrew are very similar, and a scribe might easily have written the one for the other, and the mistake might well have been perpetuated—at least, this is probable. The famous Hebrew commentator, Rabbi D. Kimchi, suggests Bedan is written for Ben-Dan, the son of Dan *the* Danite. that is, Samson. The list of Hebrew heroes in Heb. xi. 32 noticeably connects Barak with Gideon and Jephthah. Wordsworth curiously prefers to leave the unknown name of Bedan in the hero catalogue, because he argues "that in this very obscurity of the name we have a confirmation of the genuineness of the speech. A forger would not have ventured to insert a name which occurs nowhere else."

And Samuel.—The Syriac Version substitutes Samson for Samuel, finding, doubtless, a difficulty in the quotation of his own name by the speaker. But the other versions uniformly agree with the Hebrew text, and in truth Samuel could well cite himself a signal instance of God's loving pity in sending deliverance, conscious as he was of his own high mission. No judge had accomplished such great things for the people, and none had received more general recognition. It was a most fitting name to bring in at the close of his list.

⁽¹²⁾ **Nahash the king of the children of Ammon.**—It has been suggested, with great probability, that Nahash and the Ammonites had invaded the trans-Jordanic territory of Israel in the period immediately preceding the demand addressed to Samuel for a king, and that the invasion which culminated in the siege of Jabesh-gilead was only one of a series of destructive forays and invasions.

⁽¹³⁾ **Now therefore, behold the king whom ye have chosen.**—The seer now turns from the story of the past and its sad lessons to the present. "You now have your wish—behold your king. The Eternal has seen fit to grant your petition. His—again pointing to Saul—election rests on the will of the invisible King, whom virtually you have rejected."

⁽¹⁴⁾ **If ye will fear the Lord . . .**—The English Version has missed the point of the original Hebrew of this passage. It should run, "If ye will fear the Lord, &c., . . . and if both ye and the king that reigneth over you will follow the Lord your God, *it shall be well with you*." Dean Payne Smith has well caught the spirit of the passage in his note: "Samuel piled up one upon another the conditions of their happiness, and then from the depth of his emotion breaks off, leaving the blessed consequences of their obedience unsaid." The intense wish, "O that you would only fear the Lord! O that you and your king would only continue following!" is contained in the Hebrew particle which introduces these ejaculatory sentences. A similar unfinished sentence will be found in St. Luke xix. 42, where the apodosis is left to be supplied.

Samuel, with mournful earnestness, would drive home to the hearts of the people and their new king the great truth that the past, full of sin and sorrow, was forgiven—that even their present act, which seemed to border on ingratitude to that Mighty One who deigned to concern Himself with the interests of this fickle people, would bring no evil consequences in its track, if only the people and their king would in the future obey the glorious voice of the Eternal.

⁽¹⁵⁾ **But if ye will not obey.**—The English translation here, with several of the versions, accurately and happily understands the Hebrew in the sense of "as:" "as it was against your fathers." Rabbi D. Kimchi prefers to understand "fathers" as put for "kings": "the hand of the Lord shall be against you and your kings." The LXX. reads, "against you and your king."

LORD be against you, as *it was* against your fathers. ⁽¹⁶⁾ Now therefore stand and see this great thing, which the LORD will do before your eyes. ⁽¹⁷⁾ *Is it* not wheat harvest to day? I will call unto the LORD, and he shall send thunder and rain; that ye may perceive and see that your wickedness *is* great, which ye have done in the sight of the LORD, in asking you a king.

⁽¹⁸⁾ So Samuel called unto the LORD; and the LORD sent thunder and rain that day: and all the people greatly feared the LORD and Samuel. ⁽¹⁹⁾ And all the people said unto Samuel, Pray for thy servants unto the LORD thy God, that we die not: for we have added unto all our sins *this* evil, to ask us a king.

⁽²⁰⁾ And Samuel said unto the people, Fear not: ye have done all this wickedness: yet turn not aside from following the LORD, but serve the LORD with all your heart; ⁽²¹⁾ and turn ye not aside: for *then should ye go* after vain *things*, which cannot profit nor deliver; for they *are* vain. ⁽²²⁾ For the LORD will not forsake his people for his great name's sake: because it hath pleased the LORD to make you his people. ⁽²³⁾ Moreover as for me, God forbid that I should sin against the LORD ¹in ceasing to pray for you: but I will teach you the good and

¹ Heb., *from ceasing.*

⁽¹⁶⁾ **This great thing, which the Lord will do.**—Then, to give greater emphasis to his warning words, Samuel adds: "O, ye elders, stand forth. I will show you by means of a Voice from heaven that this very asking for a king, though the Eternal has granted your prayer, is evil in His sight." Their wishing for an earthly king was the crown of a long course of rebellion against the Supreme will. It was, in fact, the breaking up for ever of the glorious ideal which had been for so long before the eyes of the noblest spirits in Israel.

⁽¹⁷⁾ **Is it not wheat harvest day?**—The Canaan wheat harvest is between the middle of May and the middle of June. Rain in that season seldom or never falls, but if it does it is usually severe. This is the testimony of one who spoke as a resident, and his statement is confirmed by the observations of the latest travellers and scholars. The terrible storm of rain accompanied with thunder, at a time of year when these storms of thunder and rain rarely took place, coming, as it did, in direct answer to the seer's invocation, struck the people naturally with great fear, and for the moment they thoroughly repented of the past, and entreated Samuel—who, they felt, stood on strangely familiar terms with that awful yet loving Eternal—to intercede for them.

⁽²⁰⁾ **Fear not: ye have done all this wickedness.**—A very great and precious evangelical truth is contained in these comforting words of the great and good seer. They show how deeply this eminent servant of the Most High had entered into the Eternal thought. No sin or course of sin was too great to be repented of. Afar off these true ministers of the Lord saw, though, perhaps, "in a glass darkly," the Lamb of God, whose blood cleanseth from all sin. Isaiah often pressed home the same truth to the sinning Israel of his own day in such terms as, "Though your sins be as scarlet, they shall be white as snow;" and Samuel's words—bidding the people, *in spite of the guilty past,* yet press on, following the Lord and serving Him with all the heart—were taken up by Samuel's prophet-successors, and repeated in coming ages again and again in such moving exhortations as, "O Israel, return unto the Lord thy God" (Hos. xiv. 1). They were re-echoed by men like Paul, who, with stirring loving words, bade their hearers, forgetting all the things that were behind, their past guilt and failure, press on still fearlessly for the real prize of life.

⁽²¹⁾ **For then should ye go after vain things.**—The passage is more forcible without the "for" and the words in italics supplied in the English translation. The verse without it would run thus: "Turn ye not aside after vain things which cannot profit," &c. Singularly enough, *not one* of the ancient versions translate the Hebrew *ki,* "for": they *all* omit it. It is therefore clear that this "for" has, through some copyist's error, got into the text since the versions were made.

⁽²²⁾ **It hath pleased the Lord to make you his people.**—The simple doctrine of election—as far as we can see, based alone on the arbitrary will of God (though, no doubt, unseen by us, deep reasons exist for every seemingly arbitrary choice)—is here enunciated. The analogy of every-day life teaches the same truth. "He maketh one vessel to honour and another to dishonour." These things are to us inscrutable.

⁽²³⁾ **Moreover, as for me.**—"In this he sets a glorious example to all rulers, showing them that they should not be led astray by the ingratitude of their subordinates or subjects; and give up on that account all interest in their welfare, but should rather persevere all the more in their anxiety for them."—*Berleb. Bible,* quoted in Lange. Moses and Samuel, wrote S. Gregory, are especially brought forward by the Prophet Jeremiah (xv. 1) as having extraordinary power with Him, and why? because they prayed for their enemies. Samuel's impassioned answer when the Elders asked his prayers, "Pray for you!" God forbid that I should sin against the Lord in ceasing to pray for you.

I will teach you.—The old man felt that in the future, although his powers as Judge were not abrogated yet, there would be, comparatively speaking, save on special occasions, but little opportunity for their exercise. In the presence of the regular authority of a king surrounded by armed men, such authority as he had wielded as Judge over the hearts of Israel must fall into abeyance.

But one, and that a still higher office, still remained to him untouched by the great constitutional change that had passed over Israel—*that of prophet.* In this sphere, while he lived, he said he would work ceaselessly on; and the words he used on this solemn occasion tell out to all ages that the true function of the prophet or the preacher of the Eternal is to teach the people the good and the right way; and Samuel's own life of brave self-denial and noble self-effacement showed men that this teaching must be pressed home by something more than mere words. "Only a Samuel could thus quit office, proudly challenging all to convict him of one single injustice in

Early Military Achievements   I. SAMUEL, XIII.   *of Saul and Jonathan.*

the right way: ⁽²⁴⁾ only fear the LORD, and serve him in truth with all your heart: for consider ¹how great *things* he hath done for you. ⁽²⁵⁾ But if ye shall still do wickedly, ye shall be consumed, both ye and your king.

CHAPTER XIII.—⁽¹⁾ Saul ²reigned one year; and when he had reigned two years over Israel, ⁽²⁾ Saul chose him three thousand *men* of Israel; *whereof* two thousand were with Saul in Michmash

¹ Or, *what a great thing, &c.*

² Heb., *the son of one year in his reigning.*

³ Or, *The hill.*

B.C. 1093.

⁴ Heb., *did stink.*

and in mount Beth-el, and a thousand were with Jonathan in Gibeah of Benjamin: and the rest of the people he sent every man to his tent.

⁽³⁾ And Jonathan smote the garrison of the Philistines that *was* in ³Geba, and the Philistines heard *of it.* And Saul blew the trumpet throughout all the land, saying, Let the Hebrews hear. ⁽⁴⁾ And all Israel heard say *that* Saul had smitten a garrison of the Philistines, and *that* Israel also ⁴was had in abomi-

---

his past career; and by the act of resignation gaining, not losing, greatness. No longer judge and ruler, but simple prophet, he is able now to discourse with greater freedom of the monarchy about to be introduced, and he seizes the moment to cast a more distant glance into all the past and future of the community."—Ewald: *History of Israel*, Book III., 1—3.

XIII.

(1–21) Saul's Reign—The Gallantry of Saul and Jonathan—The new King's attempt to Rule as an Absolute Sovereign—His Disregard of the Most High—He and his House are Rejected as Kings of Israel—The Philistine War.

⁽¹⁾ **Saul reigned one year.**—The only possible literal translation of the Hebrew of this verse is, "Saul was the son of one year (*i.e.*, one year old); he began to reign, &c." In several places in the Books of Samuel the numbers are quite untrustworthy (we have another instance of this in the 5th verse of this chapter). The present verse, however, is an old difficulty, the corruption or gap in the text dating from a far back period. The English translation is simply a probable, but conjectural, paraphrase. The Chaldee and some of the Rabbis thus strangely interpret it: "Saul was an innocent child when he began to reign"—that is, was as innocent as a one year old child, &c. The Syriac and others paraphrase much as our English Version. The LXX. omit the verse altogether. The *Speaker's Commentary* thus literally translates the Hebrew, marking with a — where a number probably originally stood: "Saul was — years old when he began to reign, and he reigned — and two years over Israel." On the whole, the usually accepted meaning is that Saul had reigned one year when the events related in the last chapter took place, and after he had reigned two years he chose out the 3,000 men, and did what is related in this chapter.

⁽²⁾ **Saul chose him three thousand men of Israel.**—This is a very important statement, as it tells us of the first beginning of a standing army in Israel. This was the first step towards the development of Israel into a great military power. It was Saul's military genius and foresight which enabled David and Solomon to make those great conquests which raised Israel for a time to the position of one of the greatest Eastern Powers. The really great life of Saul was frittered away in repelling what may be termed Israel's domestic enemies, such as the Philistines, Moabites, Ammonites, and Edomites; but he left behind him a powerful and disciplined army, and a nation carefully trained to war. It has been asked, how was it, considering the position of Israel and the Philistines at that juncture—the latter people possessing evidently not a few strong places in the territories of the tribes, from whence they were in the habit of sallying forth, and harassing and pillaging the people—that Saul, instead of at once declaring war, dismissed the people gathered at Gilgal, only retaining so few? The probability is that Saul, with true military instinct, saw that Israel was at this period by no means trained or armed to undertake a regular war with such an enemy. He therefore adopted the wise course here related.

Whereof two thousand were with Saul in Michmash.—Michmash was a position strongly situated at the head of a pass some nine miles north-east of Jerusalem. The "one thousand" he placed under the command of his son Jonathan, and stationed them in the neighbourhood of his old home, where he would have the benefit of the aid of his family and kinsfolk. This is the first mention of the gallant and chivalrous prince, the story of whose unbroken and romantic friendship with David is one of the most touching episodes of these books. "If the substance of this narrative was written in David's reign, we may perhaps see the effect of David's generous and loving nature in the care taken to give Jonathan his due place of honour in the history."—*Speaker's Commentary.*

⁽³⁾ **And Jonathan smote the garrison.**—Jonathan throughout this history appears as the perfect type of a warrior, according to the requirements of his age; he is everywhere the first in courage and activity and speed, slender also, and of well-made figure. This personal beauty and swiftness of foot in attack or retreat gained for him among the troops the name of "gazelle." (The first lines of the song, 2 Samuel i. 19, can only be explained on the supposition that Jonathan was well known by this name in the army.) "In all this, as in his uprightness and fidelity, he showed himself the right worthy son of a king."—Ewald. Some translate the word rightly rendered "garrison" as "pillar," a sign of the authority of the Philistines; others—*e.g.*, Ewald—as a proper name, supposing that the officer appointed to collect tribute from Israel in that part of the country is meant.

And Saul blew the trumpet.—This was evidently more than a communication of good news to the people. Saul intended it as a summons to Israel to prepare at once for war.

⁽⁴⁾ **And all Israel heard.**—Saul is put for "Jonathan," though the bold deed had been performed by the young prince, Saul being the general-in-chief. The expression "smitten" implies that the garrison in question had been utterly routed, probably put to the sword. The intense hatred with which the Philistines hated the Hebrews is often brought forward. From the first conquest by Joshua they regarded them as

The War with the Philistines.   I. SAMUEL, XIII.   *Saul impatient at Samuel's Delay.*

nation with the Philistines. And the people were called together after Saul to Gilgal. ⁽⁵⁾ And the Philistines gathered themselves together to fight with Israel, thirty thousand chariots, and six thousand horsemen, and people as the sand which *is* on the sea shore in multitude: and they came up, and pitched in Michmash, eastward from Beth-aven.

⁽⁶⁾ When the men of Israel saw that they were in a strait, (for the people were distressed,) then the people did hide themselves in caves, and in thickets, and in rocks, and in high places, and in pits. ⁽⁷⁾ And *some of* the Hebrews went over Jordan to the land of Gad and Gilead. As for Saul, he *was* yet in Gilgal, and all the people ¹ followed him trembling. ⁽⁸⁾ ᵃAnd he tarried seven days, according to the set time that Samuel *had appointed*: but Samuel came not to Gilgal; and the people were scattered from him. ⁽⁹⁾ And Saul said, Bring hither a burnt offering to me, and

¹ Heb., *trembled after him*.

a ch. 10. 8.

---

interlopers and intruders; between the two peoples there was ceaseless warfare, until the Philistines were completely subdued by the greater Hebrew kings. Naturally, such a deed as that of Jonathan's would at once arouse Philistia.

And the people were called together.—Gradually round the King of Israel the fighting men of the nation in great numbers were gathered. This seems to have been by no means a "levée en masse" of all the people; they seem to have come together very slowly, and very quickly again to have dispersed. The hour for a decisive blow was not yet come. Something, as we shall soon see, prevented Saul, with all his gallantry and splendid military skill, from winning popular confidence. (On Gilgal, the place where Saul was trying to assemble the people at this juncture, see Note on verse 8 and *Excursus* E at the end of this Book.)

⁽⁵⁾ **And the Philistines gathered themselves together to fight with Israel.**—The figures here, again, of the numbers of this vast army are perfectly untrustworthy. In the rolls of ancient armies (and we possess many a one in the sacred records) the number of war chariots is always smaller than that of the horsemen; here the chariots are represented as four times as numerous. In the rolls of the most famous armies there never appear anything like this number. For instance, Jabin (Judges iv. 3) had 900 chariots. Pharaoh pursued Israel with 600. When David defeated Syria, the great Syrian army had 40,000 horsemen and 700 chariots. King Solomon is only reported (1 Kings x. 26) to have possessed 1,400 chariots. Zerah the Ethiopian had but 300 in his vast army, and the Pharaoh Shishak 1,200. Here the more probable reading would be "300" not 30,000. Bishop Wordsworth endeavours to explain the vast array by a reference to Josephus, who relates that this Philistine force was composed of various nations; but this would never account for the incredible number of chariots. The Philistines evidently lost no time. While Saul was endeavouring to rally at Gilgal a Hebrew army, Philistia at once, with the aid of foreign allies, took the field, and with a large army—for it is clear their host on this occasion was very large—encamped no great distance from Gilgal, evidently determined once and for all to crush their enemies and their recently-elected daring king.

⁽⁶⁾ **Saw that they were in a strait.**—It was evidently no ordinary Philistine foray or invasion which the Israelites had to make head against. The tradition preserved by Josephus tells us that a host of foreign allies had joined the Phœnician armies in this war. This accounts for the great numbers alluded to in the text: "People as the sand which *is* on the sea shore in multitude" (verse 5). The hearts of the as yet undisciplined Hebrews sank at the tidings of such an invasion.

And in high places.—The word in the original Hebrew is not the same as the one usually rendered "high places" for prayer and sacrifice. The word here signifies towers. It is the same word which in Judges ix. 46, 49 is translated "a hold." In the *Speaker's Commentary* it is suggested that it was applied to a particular kind of tower which was the work of the old Canaanite inhabitants, and which remained as ruins in the time of Saul.

⁽⁸⁾ **And he tarried seven days.**—When was this "set time" appointed? It seems difficult at first to refer back to the day of Saul's mysterious prophetic consecration (chap. x. 8), which took place at least some three or four years—perhaps much longer—before the event here related, especially as we know that Saul and Samuel had been together on one occasion certainly at Gilgal in the meantime (chap. xi. 14, 15); and yet the extraordinary solemnity of the warning of the seer at the time of the anointing at Ramah evidently pointed to some event which should in the future happen at Gilgal, and which would be a most important epoch in King Saul's career. All these conditions are satisfied in the meeting between the prophet and the king, here related. It is best, then, to understand this event as the one alluded to on the day of anointing at Ramah, and to conclude that this grave warning and positive direction had been repeated, probably more than once, since then by the seer to the king. (On the place Gilgal, and on the nature of the "sin of Saul," which was so terribly punished, see *Excursus* E and F at end of this Book.) Saul, we read, waited seven days, but before the seventh expired, gave up waiting, and offered the sacrifice without the seer, and thus, as Josephus says, "he did not fully obey the command." His faith failed him under pressure at the last, and he acted on his own responsibility, quite irrespective of the positive command of God.

The people were scattered from him.—This trial of the king's faith was doubtless a severe one. The panic which pervaded all Israel was every hour thinning the host Saul had gathered round him at Gilgal. The martial king longed for a chance of joining battle: and this he was forbidden to do until the seer had offered sacrifice, and publicly inquired of the Lord; and the day passed by, and Samuel came not. An attack on the part of the Philistine army, encamped at no great distance, seemed imminent, and Saul's forces were rapidly melting away.

⁽⁹⁾ **Bring hither a burnt offering to me.**—It has been supposed by many that the greatness of the sin of Saul consisted in his offering sacrifice with his own hand, but not a hint of this is anywhere given us

peace offerings. And he offered the burnt offering.

(10) And it came to pass, that as soon as he had made an end of offering the burnt offering, behold, Samuel came; and Saul went out to meet him, that he might ¹salute him. (11) And Samuel said, What hast thou done? And Saul said, Because I saw that the people were scattered from me, and *that* thou camest not within the days appointed, and *that* the Philistines gathered themselves together at Michmash; (12) therefore said I, The Philistines will come down now upon me to Gilgal, and I have not ²made supplication unto the LORD: I forced myself therefore, and offered a burnt offering. (13) And Samuel said to Saul,

¹ Heb., *bless him.*

² Heb., *intreated the face.*

³ Heb., *found.*

Thou hast done foolishly: thou hast not kept the commandment of the LORD thy God, which he commanded thee: for now would the LORD have established thy kingdom upon Israel for ever. (14) But now thy kingdom shall not continue: the LORD hath sought him a man after his own heart, and the LORD hath commanded him *to be* captain over his people, because thou hast not kept *that* which the LORD commanded thee.

(15) And Samuel arose, and gat him up from Gilgal unto Gibeah of Benjamin. And Saul numbered the people *that were* ³present with him, about six hundred men.

(16) And Saul, and Jonathan his son, and the people *that were* present with

---

It is more than probable that the sacrifice which was offered so prematurely in the absence of the seer of God was performed by the hand of Ahiah the priest, who, no doubt, was in attendance on the king. No unlawful assumption of priestly functions, as in the case of King Uzziah (2 Chron. xxvi. 18), is anywhere charged on Saul.

(10) **Behold, Samuel came.**—Scarcely does the sacrificial ceremony appear to have been completed when the seer appeared on the scene.

It was the seventh day, according to the solemn injunction given to the king, but Saul, in his impatience, had not waited till the end of the day.

Saul went out to meet him.—The reverence which the king, in spite of his disobedience, felt for Samuel is displayed in his going out to meet him thus publicly. This deep feeling of the king for the great prophet to whom he felt he owed so much existed on Saul's part all the days of Samuel's life, and, as we shall see, even after Samuel's death.

(11) **What hast thou done?**—The deeper aspects of King Saul's sin are discussed in *Excursus* F. On this memorable occasion the king plainly told Samuel that though he would gratefully receive any help which the prophet of the Most High could and would bring him, still, in an emergency like the present, sooner than run any risk, he preferred to act alone, and, if necessary, to go into battle without Divine consecration and blessing. The danger at this juncture was imminent; to ward it off, he considered that the direct Divine intimation which he allowed he had received through Samuel must be disregarded. Acting upon this persuasion, he set it aside, acting according to the ordinary dictates of worldly prudence. He must in his action at Gilgal either have forgotten or disbelieved the story of the Joshua conquest, and of the signal deliverances under the hero Judges, when the Glorious Arm fought by the people, and splendid successes were won in the face of enormous odds through the intervention of no mortal aid.

Saul might have been, and was, a valiant and skilful general, but was no fitting Viceroy of the invisible King in heaven, who required from him before all things the most ardent unquestioning faith.

Saul and his house, it is too clear, would only rule the Israel of God according to the dictates of their own haughty will.

The twice-repeated assertion of Samuel, "Thou hast not kept the commandment of the Lord" (verses 13, 14)—an assertion uncontradicted by Saul—shows us that this whole transaction was an act of overt rebellion against the will of the Eternal.

(14) **Now thy kingdom shall not continue.**—The succession was thus formally transferred elsewhere; still, when the words of doom were spoken by the prophet, David, the son of Jesse, the man after God's own heart, could at that time have been but a mere child. Had King Saul repented what he had done, he might have been forgiven, "for God's threatenings, like His promises, are conditional. There is no fatalism in the Bible, but a loving discipline for man's recovery. But behind it stands the Divine foreknowledge and omnipotence, and so to the prophetic view Saul's refusal to repent, his repeated disobedience, and the succession of David were all revealed as accomplished facts."—*Dean Payne Smith.*

(15) **And Samuel arose.**—Although the close union between the prophet and the king was thus disturbed by the unhappy self-willed conduct of Saul, by which he virtually threw away the power which had been conferred on him, still Samuel does not as yet break off friendly relations with Saul. Perhaps the noble old man still hoped that the brilliant and gallant king would recognise his fatal error.

From Gilgal, we read, Samuel passed to Gibeah of Benjamin, the home of Saul: there, no doubt, he took counsel with and encouraged Jonathan, who was stationed there, and whose splendid gallantry was soon after to be called into action again.

And Saul numbered the people.—The disobedience of Saul had availed nothing. Instead of being able to lead a host against the Philistine army, the camp of Israel became deserted. Even his small division of regulars seems to have melted away; only six hundred answered to the despairing king's roll-call. It would seem as though the Divine punishment had begun already.

(16) **Gibeah of Benjamin.**—Saul and his son, uniting their sadly diminished forces, entrench themselves at Geba, in a strong position at the end of a pass, whence they could watch the movements of the Philistines. Their small numbers forbade any idea of an attack on the enemy.

I. SAMUEL, XIII.

Israel and the Philistines. — *Weakness of Israel.*

them, abode in Gibeah of Benjamin: but the Philistines encamped in Michmash. (17) And the spoilers came out of the camp of the Philistines in three companies: one company turned unto the way *that leadeth to* Ophrah, unto the land of Shual: (18) and another company turned the way *to* Beth-horon: and another company turned *to* the way of the border that looketh to the valley of Zeboim toward the wilderness.

(19) Now there was no smith found throughout all the land of Israel: for the Philistines said, Lest the Hebrews make *them* swords or spears: (20) but all the Israelites went down to the Philistines, to sharpen every man his share, and his coulter, and his ax, and his mattock. (21) Yet they had [1] a file for the mattocks, and for the coulters, and for the forks, and for the axes, and [2] to sharpen the goads. (22) So it came to pass in the day of battle, that there was neither sword nor spear found in the hand of any of the people that *were* with Saul and Jonathan: but with Saul and with Jonathan his son was there found.

(23) And the [3] garrison of the Philistines went out to the passage of Michmash.

[1] Heb., *a file with mouths.*
[2] Heb., *to set.*
[3] Or, *standing camp.*

The English translators wrongly here substitute "Gibeah of Benjamin" for "Geba of Benjamin," probably led astray by the mention of Gibeah in the preceding verse.

(17) **And the spoilers came out.**—The compiler of these Books of Samuel does not profess to give a detailed account of this or any of the wars of Saul. It would seem that the Philistines, with their great armed demonstration (verse 5), had completely cowed the Israelites, certainly in the southern part of Canaan. Probably the allied forces were now suffered to leave the Philistine host, and we next hear of the old raids re-commencing. The three companies spoken of in this and the next verse were directed to ravage districts in the tribe of Benjamin, for in that locality are situated all the places mentioned. Unchecked, they seem to have carried out their plans. These armed companies swept away all the smithies in the south part of the land. The fortunes of Saul now reached their lowest ebb. "The heights of his own tribe . . . and the passes of his own tribe were occupied by hostile garrisons. We see him leaning on his gigantic spear, whether it be on the summit of the Rock Rimmon . . . or under the tamarisk of Ramah . . . or on the heights of Gibeah. There he stood with his small band, the faithful six hundred, and as he wept aloud over the misfortunes of his country . . . another voice swelled the wild, indignant lament—the voice of Jonathan, his son."—Dean Stanley: *Lectures on the Jewish Church.*

(19) **Now there was no smith found.**—We must allow a year, perhaps two or three, to have elapsed while "Saul and Jonathan . . . abode in Gibeah," during which period the Philistine raids went on unchecked, the Israelitish forces being too weak to venture with any hope of success into the open country. The statement respecting the destruction of the smithies probably only specially refers to the southern districts of Canaan—especially the territory of Benjamin, whence Saul and Jonathan, in the earlier years of the former's reign, drew, no doubt, the majority of their men of war. These devastating forays are alluded to in verses 17, 18.

(20) **To sharpen every man his share, and his coulter.**—Porsenna, we read, in the time of the wars of the Republic, allowed the Romans iron implements for agriculture only. *Coulter.* — In Isa. ii. 4, Joel iii. 10, this word is rendered "ploughshares"; so most of the older versions. We cannot now with any precision distinguish between these two implements of tillage.

And his mattock.—Jerome renders the Hebrew word here by "hoe" (*sarculum*). It was probably a kind of heavy hoe, used for turning up the ground.

(21) **Yet they had a file for the mattocks . . .** —This translation, the sense of which is not very clear, is supported by the Targum and by many of the great Hebrew commentators—Rashi, for instance. Gesenius and the majority of modern scholars, however, render the word in the original translated "file" (*p'tsirah*) by "bluntness." The passage then would run: "And there was bluntness (or dulness) of edge to the mattocks;" or, "so that bluntness of the edges occurred to the mattocks." "The forks" were probably an instrument with three prongs, like our trident.

And to sharpen the goads.—The words from "and there was bluntness," &c. (English Version, "they had a file"), down to "axes," form a parenthesis. "This parenthesis indicates that the result of the burthensome necessity of going to the Philistines was that many tools became useless by dulness, so that even these poorer sort of arms did the Israelites not much service at the breaking out of the war."—Bunsen.

The LXX. read this 21st verse with considerable changes: "And the vintage was ready to be gathered, and the tools were three shekels to the tooth [to sharpen], and to the axe and to the scythe there was the same rate" (or, as the Greek has been rendered, "tools cost three shekels apiece [to sharpen]").

(22) **There was neither sword nor spear.**—These words must not be pressed too literally. The general result of the raids alluded to in verses 16, 17 was that in the open valleys of Southern Canaan, especially in the Benjamite territory, the districts whence Saul and Jonathan could most easily recruit their thinned and dispirited forces, there was an absence of arms. This fact is especially dwelt upon, for the Philistines appear to have armed their fighting men to the teeth. (Compare the description of their champion, Goliath, who is described as "clad in armour.")

But with Saul.—These words probably signify that the companies of regulars, who throughout this disastrous period were always with the king and prince, were—in contrast to the country people around—fully armed. (See allusion, for instance, to Jonathan and *his* armour-bearer in the next chapter.)

(23) **The garrison of the Philistines went out.** —These words form an introduction to the recital of the heroic deed of Jonathan related in the following chapter. The Philistines are represented as sending forward an armed detachment, or out-post detachment,

CHAPTER XIV.—(1) Now ¹it came to pass upon a day, that Jonathan the son of Saul said unto the young man that bare his armour, Come, and let us go over to the Philistines' garrison, that *is* on the other side. But he told not his father. (2) And Saul tarried in the uttermost part of Gibeah under a pomegranate tree which *is* in Migron: and the people that *were* with him *were* about six hundred men; (3) and Ahiah, the son of Ahitub, *a* I-chabod's brother, the son of Phinehas, the son of Eli, the LORD's priest in Shiloh, wearing an ephod. And the people knew not that Jonathan was gone. (4) And between the passages, by which Jonathan sought to go over unto the Philistines' garrison, *there was* a sharp rock on the one side, and a sharp rock on the other side: and the name of the one *was* Bozez, and the name of the other Seneh. (5) The ²forefront of the one *was* situate northward over against Michmash, and the other southward over against Gibeah. (6) And Jonathan said to the young man that bare his armour, Come, and let us go over unto the garrison of these uncircumcised: it may

B.C. cir. 1087.

¹ Or, *there was a* d—*t.*

a ch. 4. 21.

² Heb., *tooth.*

---

beyond the camp of Michmash, as a protection against a surprise on the part of the Israelitic force under the king and his son.

XIV.

(1–52) Saul's War with the Philistines — Jonathan becomes the Divinely appointed Hero for the People's Deliverance from their restless Foes—The Battle of Michmash—Saul's Rash Oath—The House of Saul.

(1) **Now it came to pass.**—As if in strong contrast to Saul—who at Gilgal openly made light of the supernatural assistance promised by Samuel, showing plainly by his conduct on that memorable occasion that he hardly believed in the part the invisible King had taken in the history of the people—the action of Jonathan at Michmash, which led to the rout of the Philistine army, is related with some detail. Jonathan was the typical warrior of that wild and adventurous age—recklessly brave, chivalrous, and generous, possessing evidently vast strength and unusual skill in all warlike exercises. He was animated with an intense faith in the willingness and power of the Eternal to help Israel. This mighty faith in the ever-presence of the God who chose Israel, was the mainspring of the victorious power of all the great Hebrew heroes—of men like Joshua and Gideon, Barak and Samson. David, the greatest of them all, we shall see, possessed this sublime spirit of faith in a pre-eminent degree. But King Saul utterly lacked it; hence his rejection.

The young prince's heart burned within him at the degradation which the Philistine occupation brought upon the people. His father was too prudent to engage in battle with his own feeble and disorganised forces, so Jonathan determined, with the help of the Divine Friend of Israel, to strike a blow at these insolent foes. Under any other circumstances—without the consciousness of supernatural help—to attempt such a feat of arms would have been madness; but Jonathan had an inward conviction that an unseen Arm would hold a shield before him. It is noticeable that he never communicated his desperate purpose to his father, Saul.

(2) **Under a pomegranate tree.**—The love of Saul for trees, which was so common among the children of Israel, has been noticed. (See again chap. xxii., verse 6. The king is spoken of as under the tamarisk of Ramah; Deborah is specially mentioned as judging Israel under the palm-tree in Beth-el.)

(3) **Ahiah, the son of Ahitub.**—The Chronicles, rehearsing these facts, show us what a terrible impression the last events in Eli's reign as high priest had made in Israel. The destruction of Shiloh, the death of the high priest, the fall of Phinehas and his brother in battle, the melancholy circumstances of the birth of I-chabod, were still fresh in the memory of the people. Well might Jonathan be ready to sacrifice himself if he could deal an effectual blow upon these hereditary enemies of his country. Of this high priest Ahiah we never hear again in these Books of Samuel. He is generally supposed to be the same as the high priest Ahimelech, who was subsequently murdered by Doeg, by the direction of Saul, with the priests at Nob (chap. xxii. 9, &c.). The name Ahiah signifies "brother," or "friend of the Eternal"; Ahimelech, "brother of the king," may be another form of the same name.

Wearing an ephod.—The ephod here alluded to is not the ordinary priestly vestment of white linen, but that official garment worn alone by the high priest, in which was the breast-plate of gems with the mysterious Urim and Thummim, by which inquiry used to be made of the Lord.

(4) **Bozez . . . Seneh.**—These names are of extreme antiquity. Their signification is disputed. Possibly Bozez signifies "shining," and Seneh "the accacia." These rocks have been identified by modern travellers.

(6) **And Jonathan said.**—This companion in arms answered to the esquire of the knight of the middle ages. Gideon, Joab, David, and others of the famous Israelite warriors, were constantly accompanied in a similar manner by an armour-bearer.

Come, and let us go over.—Although in this history of the great deed of Jonathan there is no mention of the "Spirit of the Lord" having come upon him, as in the case of Gideon (Judges vi. 34), Othniel (Judges iii. 10), Samson, and others—who, in order to enable them to accomplish a particular act, were temporarily endowed with superhuman strength and courage and wisdom—there is no shadow of doubt but that in this case the "Spirit of the Lord" descended on the heroic son of Saul. All the circumstances connected with this event, which had so marked an influence on the fortunes of Israel, are evidently supernatural. The brave though desperate thought which suggested the attack, the courage and strength needful to carry it out, the strange panic which seized the Philistine garrison, the utter dismay which spread over the whole of the Philistine forces, and which caused them to fly in utter confusion before the small bands of Israelites, all belong to the same class of incidents so common in the earlier Hebrew story, when it is clear that the

be that the LORD will work for us: for *there is* no restraint to the LORD ᵃto save by many or by few. ⁽⁷⁾ And his armourbearer said unto him, Do all that *is* in thine heart: turn thee; behold, I *am* with thee according to thy heart. ⁽⁸⁾ Then said Jonathan, Behold, we will pass over unto *these* men, and we will discover ourselves unto them. ⁽⁹⁾ If they say thus unto us, ¹Tarry until we come to you; then we will stand still in our place, and will not go up unto them. ⁽¹⁰⁾ But if they say thus, Come up unto us; then we will go up: for ᵇthe LORD hath delivered them into our hand: and this *shall be* a sign unto us. ⁽¹¹⁾ And both of them discovered themselves unto the garrison of the Philistines: and the Philistines said, Behold, the Hebrews come forth out of the holes where they had hid themselves. ⁽¹²⁾ And the men of the garrison answered Jonathan and his armourbearer, and said, Come up to us, and we will shew you a thing. And Jonathan said unto his armourbearer, Come up after me: for the LORD hath delivered them into the hand of Israel. ⁽¹³⁾ And Jonathan climbed up upon his hands and upon his feet, and his armourbearer after him: and they fell before Jonathan; and his armourbearer slew after him. ⁽¹⁴⁾ And that first slaughter, which Jonathan and his armourbearer made, was about twenty men, within as it were ²an half acre of land, *which* a yoke *of oxen might plow.* ⁽¹⁵⁾ And there was trembling in the host, in the field, and among all the people: the garrison, and the spoilers, they also trembled, and the earth quaked:

a 2 Chr. 14. 11.
1 Heb., *Be still.*
b 1 Mac. 4. 30.
2 Or, *half a furrow of an acre of land.*

Glorious Arm of the Eternal helped them in a way it helped no other peoples.

The term "uncircumcised" is commonly applied to the Philistines, and to other of the enemies of Israel. It is used as a special term of reproach. The enmity between Philistia and Israel lasted over a long period, and was very bitter.

It may be that the Lord will work for us.—These words explain the apparent recklessness of Jonathan's attempt. It was Another who would fight the armed garrison on those tall peaks opposite, and bring him safely back to his people again.

For there is no restraint to the Lord to save by many or by few.—"O Divine power of faith, which makes a man more than men. The question is not what Jonathan can do, but what God can do, whose power is not in the means, but in Himself. There is no restraint in the Lord to save by many or by few. O admirable faith in Jonathan, whom neither the steepness of the rocks nor multitude of enemies can dissuade from such an assault."—*Bishop Hall.*

⁽⁷⁾ **Turn thee.**—The very words of the prince's armour-bearer seem to have been preserved; the expression is a colloquial one, and is rendered here literally. It signifies, "Go on; I will follow."

⁽⁸⁾ **Behold, we will pass over.**—The steep crag upon which the Philistine outpost was entrenched was across a deep ravine, or chasm, which separated the hostile armies.

⁽⁹⁾ **If they say thus unto us.**—He longed for a supernatural sign which should confirm him in his conviction, that the prompting which urged him to this deed of extreme daring was indeed a voice from heaven.

⁽¹¹⁾ **And the Philistines said. . . .**—Easily might the sentinels of the outpost have rolled stones down the steep cliff, and hurled back the daring assailants; but they treated them with utter contempt, probably thinking to take them alive if ever they succeeded in scaling the slippery cliff.

⁽¹³⁾ **And they fell before Jonathan . . .**—The sign he prayed for was given him. There were probably but few sentinels at their posts; the inaccessibility of the craggy fortress had lulled the garrison into security. The few watching him at first mocked, and then, as Jonathan advanced with strange rapidity, they seem to have been, as it were, paralysed—the feat was hardly human—as the man, all armed, sprang over the rocky parapet. "His chief weapon was his bow," writes Dean Stanley; "his whole tribe was a tribe of archers, and he was the chief archer of them all." Arrived at the summit, in rapid succession he shot his deadly bolts, his gallant armour-bearer following his chief's example, and twenty men, so says the record, fell before they had recovered their surprise. In a moment a panic seized the garrison, and a hurried flight ensued, for they felt they had to deal with no mortal strength.

⁽¹⁴⁾ **And that first slaughter . . .**—Considerable doubt exists as to the exact meaning of this verse. The LXX. either had here a different text before them, or else translated, as has been suggested, "conjecturally, what they did not understand;" their rendering is "about twenty men, with darts and slings and stones of the field." Ewald explains the Hebrew words as follows: "At the very beginning he strikes down about twenty men at once, *as if a yoke of land were in course of being ploughed*, which must beware of offering opposition to the sharp ploughshare in the middle of its work." The simplest interpretation seems to be that twenty men were smitten down, one after the other, in the distance of half a rood of land. Bunsen considers this verse an extract from a poet.

⁽¹⁵⁾ **And there was trembling in the host.**—The rest of the outpost garrison, panic-stricken, escaped to the other camp of the main body of the host, spreading dismay as they fled.

And the earth quaked . . .—To add to the dire confusion, an earthquake was felt, which completed the discomfiture of the Philistines; they perceived that some Divine power was fighting against them, and all the stories of the unseen Helper of the Hebrews would flash across their minds. Some would explain the earthquake as a poetical description of the extreme terror and confusion which prevailed far and near, but the literal meaning is far the best. The Eternal fought for Jonathan and Israel that day, and the powers of nature were summoned to the young hero's aid, as

Saul's Victory   I. SAMUEL, XIV.   *over the Philistines.*

so it was ¹a very great trembling. ⁽¹⁶⁾And the watchmen of Saul in Gibeah of Benjamin looked; and, behold, the multitude melted away, and they went on beating down *one another*. ⁽¹⁷⁾ Then said Saul unto the people that *were* with him, Number now, and see who is gone from us. And when they had numbered, behold, Jonathan and his armourbearer *were* not *there*. ⁽¹⁸⁾ And Saul said unto Ahiah, Bring hither the ark of God. For the ark of God was at that time with the children of Israel. ⁽¹⁹⁾ And it came to pass, while Saul talked unto the priest, that the ²noise that *was* in the host of the Philistines went on and increased: and Saul said unto the priest, Withdraw thine hand. ⁽²⁰⁾ And Saul and all the people that *were* with him ³assembled themselves, and they came to the battle: and, behold, *a*every man's sword was against his fellow, *and there was* a very

Marginal notes:
1 Heb., *a trembling of God.*
2 Or, *tumult.*
3 Heb., *were cried together.*
a Judg. 7. 22; 2 Chr. 20. 23.

---

they had been before, when Pharaoh pursued the people at the Red Sea (Exod. xiv. 26, 27), as when Joshua fought the Canaanites at Beth-horon (Joshua x. 11), and as when Barak smote Sisera at Kishon (Judges v. 21).

⁽¹⁶⁾ **And the watchmen of Saul in Gibeah of Benjamin looked . . .**—The distance between the outposts of the little Israelite army and the vast Philistine host was only about two miles, but a deep ravine or chasm lay between them. The watchmen of Saul were well able to see the scene of dire confusion in the outposts, a confusion which they could discern was rapidly spreading through the more distant camp of the main body.

The Hebrew words, *vayēleh vahălom*, in the last clause of the verse, have been variously rendered; the Rabbinical interpretation is the best: "magis magisque pangebatur"—"were more and more broken up." This takes *hălom* as an infinitive absolute. The LXX. considers this word an adverb, and translates *enthen kai enthen*, hither and thither, and does not attempt to give any rendering for *vayēleh*.

⁽¹⁷⁾ **Then said Saul . . .**—When this panic which was taking place in the Philistine army was reported to King Saul, he naturally inquired as to what had caused it, knowing that he, as general-in-chief, had given no directions to any of his men to attack the enemy. In the little Israelitish force, when the roll was called, it was soon discovered who was missing.

⁽¹⁸⁾ **And Saul said unto Ahiah . . .**—The LXX. renders here, "And Saul said to Ahijah, Bring hither the ephod; for he bore the ephod in those days before the children of Israel." This is a statement easily to be understood. Saul was in doubt what to do under the present emergency. Should he—seeing the panic that was evidently increasing in the Philistine camp, and knowing nothing of the cause, only that his son and the armour-bearer were missing—should he risk his little force, and, leaving his strong position, attack that great host of apparently panic-stricken enemies? So he sent for the high priest Ahijah, and bade him consult the Urim and Thummim in his ephod.

But the Hebrew and all the versions read as in our English Version, "Bring hither the Ark of God." What does this mean? Was the Ark, then, with that little band of Saul? We never before, or after, find the slightest hint that the sacred coffer ever left the "city of woods" (Kiriath-jearim) until David bore it to Zion. Then, again, the word preceding "Bring hither" is never used in connection with the Ark. No question or oracle could be asked of the Ark or by the Ark. The Urim and Thummim, whatever these mysterious objects were, alone were used to give answers to questions solemnly asked by king and people, and this Urim and Thummim were connected, not with the Ark, but with the high-priestly ephod. On the whole, the reading of the LXX. probably represents the original Hebrew. The present Hebrew text, with the word "Ark," is, however, clearly of extreme antiquity; the second part of the verse is most likely an explanatory gloss of some ancient scribe. Josephus' account of this transaction shows us that he had before him a text corresponding to the LXX. His words are, "He bid the priest take the garment of his high priesthood and prophesy" (*Antiq.*, vi. § 3). Maurer prefers the present Hebrew text, for he says, At that supreme moment of danger Saul wanted not the advice of an oracle, but rather the help and encouragement which the presence of the sacred Ark would give to his handful of soldiers. But this would rather degrade Saul to the level of the superstitious Hophni and Phinehas, the wicked sons of Eli, who, it will be remembered, exposed and lost the sacred Ark in the fatal battle in which they perished. Saul, with all his faults, was a far nobler type of man than those profligate, though brave, priests.

⁽¹⁹⁾ **Withdraw thine hand.**—The instinct of the general, as we should expect from the character of Saul, soon got the better of his first desire for some Divine guidance. His watchful eye saw that the confusion in the Philistine camp was increasing; now was the moment for his little compact force to throw itself into the melée; so he at once bids Ahijah, the priest of the Lord, to put up the Urim and Thummim, and no longer to seek higher counsel, for the hour was come to fight rather than to pray. This has been the general interpretation of Saul's action here. Wordsworth quotes Bishop Andrewes, saying, "There are some who with Saul will call for the Ark, and will presently cry 'Away with it!' that is, will begin their prayers, and break them off in the midst on every occasion." And Bishop Hall: "Saul will consult the Ark; hypocrites, when they have leisure, will perhaps be holy. But when the tumult was aroused, Saul's piety decreased. 'Withdraw thine hand,' he said; 'the Ark must give place to arms.'"

⁽²⁰⁾ **Assembled themselves.**—In the margin of the English Version we find "were cried together," that is, "were assembled by the trumpet call." The Syriac and Vulg., however, more accurately render the Hebrew *shouted*, that is, raised the war-cry of Israel.

Every man's sword was against his fellow. —The statement in the next verse (21) explains this. Profiting by the wild confusion which reigned now throughout the Philistine host, a portion of their own auxiliaries—unwilling allies, doubtless—turned their arms against their employers or masters. From this moment no one in the panic-stricken army could rightly distinguish friend from foe. In such a scene of confusion the charge of Saul, at the head of his small but

great discomfiture. (21) Moreover the Hebrews *that* were with the Philistines before that time, which went up with them into the camp *from the country* round about, even they also *turned* to be with the Israelites that *were* with Saul and Jonathan. (22) Likewise all the men of Israel which had hid themselves in mount Ephraim, *when* they heard that the Philistines fled, even they also followed hard after them in the battle. (23) So the LORD saved Israel that day: and the battle passed over unto Beth-aven.

(24) And the men of Israel were distressed that day: for Saul had adjured the people, saying, Cursed *be* the man that eateth *any* food until evening, that I may be avenged on mine enemies. So none of the people tasted *any* food. (25) And all *they of* the land came to a wood; and there was honey upon the ground. (26) And when the people were come into the wood, behold, the honey dropped; but no man put his hand to his mouth: for the people feared the oath. (27) But Jonathan heard not when his father charged the people with the oath: wherefore he put forth the end of the rod that *was* in his hand, and dipped it in an honeycomb, and put his hand to his mouth; and his eyes were enlightened. (28) Then answered one of the people, and said, Thy father straitly charged the people with an oath, saying, Cursed *be* the man that eateth *any* food this day. And the people were ¹faint. (29) Then said Jonathan, My father hath troubled

1 Or, *weary.*

---

well-trained soldierly band, must have done terrible execution. Shouting the well-known war-cry of Benjamin, it penetrated wedge-like into the heart of the broken Philistine host.

(21) **Moreover the Hebrews that were with the Philistines.**—These Israelites were, most likely, prisoners who had been compelled to fight against their countrymen, or were levies raised in those parts of the land more immediately under Philistine influence. These, we read, took the first opportunity to go over to Saul. Other Israelites—probably the men of whole villages, who had been compelled, as the result of the late Philistine successes, to desert their homesteads, and seek a precarious living in the hills—joined in the pursuit of the now flying Philistine armies. This is the meaning of the words of the 22nd verse, which speaks of "the men of Israel which had hid themselves in Mount Ephraim."

(23) **So the Lord saved Israel . . .** — The identical words used at the Red Sea, after the deliverance of the people from Egypt. So the battle rolled westward through Beth-aven, past city and village, over Mount Ephraim. It was a decisive victory, crushing in its results to the Philistines, who were driven back so effectually as not to re-appear till the close of Saul's reign. The king was now at liberty to develop the military character of the people; and till the disaster which closed his life and reign, his various campaigns against the idolatrous nations who surrounded Israel generally appear to have gone on from victory to victory.

(24) **And the men of Israel were distressed that day.**—The LXX., between the 23rd and 24th verses, has a somewhat long addition: "And the whole people was with Saul, about ten thousand men; and the battle spread in the whole city, in the mountains of Ephraim; and Saul committed a great error." The number 10,000 is not an improbable one, as the original small force which had kept with Saul and Jonathan had been joined by the Hebrew auxiliaries in the Philistine camp, and also by many of the fugitives from the villages around. They were, we read, "distressed," that is, were wearied out by the long pursuit on the Ephraim hills.

For Saul had adjured the people.—Better, *And Saul, &c.*: that is, the king was so intent upon his vengeance—so bent upon pursuing to the uttermost these Philistines who so long had defied his power, and who had brought him so low—that he grudged his soldiers the necessary rest and refreshment, and, with a terrible vow, devoted to death any one who should on that day of blood slack his hand for a moment, even to take food.

(25) **And all they of the land came to a wood.**—In the wilder parts of the land the old woods were not yet cleared. There seems to have been once in that favoured land an abundance of woods.

And there was honey . . .—The wild bees, as has been often seen in the American forests, fill the hollow trees with honey, till the combs, breaking with the weight, let the honey run down upon the ground.

(26) **Behold, the honey dropped.** — Literally, *Behold, a stream of honey.*

(27) **He put forth the end of the rod.**—Most likely, with the point of his staff took up a piece of the honeycomb. Jonathan in that hurried battle and pursuit had heard nothing of his father's rash oath, and was, no doubt, owing to his exertions in the earlier part of that eventful day, worn out with fatigue and hunger.

And his eyes were enlightened.—This simply means that the natural dimness caused by extreme exhaustion passed away when his long fast was broken; literally, *his eyes became bright.* Hence the Talmud comments: "Whoever suffers from the effects of intense hunger, let him eat honey and other sweet things, for such eatables are efficacious in restoring the light of one's eyes . . . Thus we read of Jonathan, 'See, I pray you, how my eyes have been enlightened because I tasted a little of this honey'" (1 Samuel xiv. 27).—Treatise *Yoma,* fol. 83, col. 2.

(28) **Then answered one of the people.**— Most probably, in reply to Jonathan's pointing out the plentiful supply of honey, and inviting the soldiers near him to refresh themselves with it. The words "and the people were faint," at the close of the verse, should be rendered, *and the people are faint*; they were part of the speech of the soldier who was telling Jonathan of his father's rash oath.

(29) **My father hath troubled the land.**—In other words, "My father's ill-considered vow has done grave harm to us in Israel. Had he not weakened the

the land: see, I pray you, how mine eyes have been enlightened, because I tasted a little of this honey. ⁽³⁰⁾ How much more, if haply the people had eaten freely to day of the spoil of their enemies which they found? for had there not been now a much greater slaughter among the Philistines?

⁽³¹⁾ And they smote the Philistines that day from Michmash to Aijalon: and the people were very faint. ⁽³²⁾ And the people flew upon the spoil, and took sheep, and oxen, and calves, and slew *them* on the ground: and the people did eat *them* ᵃwith the blood. ⁽³³⁾ Then they told Saul, saying, Behold, the people sin against the LORD, in that they eat with the blood. And he said, Ye have ¹transgressed: roll a great stone unto me this day. ⁽³⁴⁾ And Saul said, Disperse yourselves among the people, and say unto them, Bring me hither every man his ox, and every man his sheep, and slay *them* here, and eat; and sin not against the LORD in eating with the blood. And all the people brought every man his ox ²with him that night, and slew *them* there. ⁽³⁵⁾ And Saul built an altar unto the LORD: ³the same was the first altar that he built unto the LORD.

⁽³⁶⁾ And Saul said, Let us go down after the Philistines by night, and spoil them until the morning light, and let us not leave a man of them. And they said, Do whatsoever seemeth good unto thee. Then said the priest, Let us draw near hither unto God. ⁽³⁷⁾ And Saul asked counsel of God, Shall I go down after the Philistines? wilt thou deliver them into the hand of Israel? But he answered

a Lev. 7. 26 & 19. 26; Deut. 12. 16.

¹ Or, *dealt treacherously*.

² Heb., *in his hand*.

³ Heb., *that altar he began to build unto the LORD*.

---

people, by hindering them from taking the needful refreshment, our victory would have been far more complete. Utter exhaustion has prevented us from following up our victory."

⁽³¹⁾ **From Michmash to Aijalon.**—The battle and pursuit had then extended some twenty miles of country. Again the extreme weariness of the Israelites is mentioned. Aijalon, the modern Yālo, is some eighteen or twenty miles from Michmash, where the main body of the Philistine army had been encamped.

⁽³²⁾ **And the people flew upon the spoil . . .**—No doubt, had the men of Israel not been so faint for want of food, and utterly weary, many more of the Philistine host would have fallen: as it was, vast spoil was left behind in the hurried flight; but it was the beasts that the conquerors greedily seized, their hunger was so great. "The moment that the day, with its enforced fast, was over, they flew, like Mussulmans at sunset during the fast of Ramazan, upon the captured cattle, and devoured them, even to the brutal neglect of the Law forbidding the eating of flesh which contained blood."—*Stanley*. (See Leviticus xvii. 10—14, xix. 26.)

⁽³³⁾ **Roll a great stone unto me this day.**—The object of this was that the people should kill their beasts upon the stone, and the blood could run off upon the ground. It was a rough expedient, but it showed the wild soldiers that their king and general determined that the Law of Moses should be kept and honoured, even under circumstances of the direst necessity. This scrupulous care for the "Law of the Lord" at such a time as the evening of the battle of Michmash shows us what a strange complex character was Saul's: now superstitiously watchful lest the letter of the Law should be broken; now recklessly careless whether or not the most solemn commands of God were executed.

⁽³⁵⁾ **The same was the first altar that he built . . .**—More accurately, as in margin, *the same he began to build as an altar*. The great Jewish commentators are divided as to the precise meaning of the old Hebrew language of this verse. Abarbanel interprets the words, "that King Saul began to build, but did not finish." The Midrash prefers to understand the statement as telling how "Saul began among the kings of Israel the building of altars." The more obvious meaning, if we translate as in our English Version, seems to be that this was the first public acknowledgment King Saul made to God for the mercies and goodness vouchsafed to him.

⁽³⁶⁾ **Let us go down after the Philistines by night.**—In the depth of the night, when the rough feasting on the captured beasts was over, King Saul would have had the bloody work begun afresh, and would have hurried after the flying Philistines, and with a wild butchery have completed the great and signal victory. With the implicit obedience which his soldiers seem ever to have shown him—whether a vow of total abstinence, or a desperate charge, or a wild night attack, or a ruthless bloodshed, was enjoined on them by their stern and gloomy king—the army professed themselves at once ready again to fight. Only one man in that army flushed with victory dared, with the bravery which alone proceeds from righteousness, to withstand the imperious sovereign. The high priest, Ahiah, doubted whether such a wholesale bloodshed as would surely have resulted from the conquering troops of Saul pursuing a dispersed and vanquished enemy, was in accordance with the will of God. No command to exterminate these Philistines had ever been given, and that day, so glorious in the annals of Israel, was wholly due to the special interposition of the Eternal Friend of Israel. Ahiah said, "Let us first inquire of the oracles of God"—alluding, of course, to the jewels of Urim and Thummim on his high-priestly ephod.

⁽³⁷⁾ **And Saul asked counsel of God.**—The same phrase is always used in the many passages in the Books of Judges, 1 Sam., 2 Sam., 1 Chron., Hosea, &c. when God was inquired of by the Urim and Thummim. It may be styled the technical term of inquiry of the Oracle of the Most High; there are, however, slight variations in the English translations of this phrase.

But he answered him not . . .—When the mysterious gems refused to shine, or in any way to signify the Divine approbation or disapproval, the high-priestly questioner seems, as in this instance, to have concluded that some public transgression had been committed, and that special atonement must be made before the desired answer could be expected. The sacred gems probably remained dull and lightless; the

him not that day. (33) And Saul said, Draw ye near hither, *all the ¹chief of the people: and know and see wherein this sin hath been this day. (39) For, as the LORD liveth, which saveth Israel, though it be in Jonathan my son, he shall surely die. But *there was* not a man among all the people *that* answered him. (40) Then said he unto all Israel, Be ye on one side, and I and Jonathan my son will be on the other side. And the people said unto Saul, Do what seemeth good unto thee. (41) Therefore Saul said unto the LORD God of Israel, ²Give a perfect *lot*. And Saul and Jonathan were taken: but the people ³escaped. (42) And Saul said, Cast *lots* between me and Jonathan my son. And Jonathan was taken. (43) Then Saul said to Jonathan, Tell me what thou hast done. And Jonathan told him, and said, I did but taste a little honey with the end of the rod that *was* in mine hand, *and*, lo, I must die. (44) And Saul answered, God do so and more also: for thou shalt surely die, Jonathan. (45) And the people said unto Saul, Shall Jonathan die, who hath wrought this great salvation in Israel? God forbid: *as* the LORD liveth, there shall not one hair of his head fall to the ground; for he hath wrought with God this day. So the people rescued Jonathan, that he died not. (46) Then Saul went up from following the Philistines: and the Philistines went to their own place.

(47) So Saul took the kingdom over Israel, and fought against all his enemies on every side, against Moab, and against the children of Ammon, and against

a Judg. 20. 2.

¹ Heb., *corners*.

² Or, *Shew the innocent*.

³ Heb., *went forth*.

---

night was wearing on, and Saul chafed at the unexpected delay, and in his impetuous anger uttered the wild words on which we are about to comment.

(38) **Draw ye near hither.**—Round that rough unfinished altar, in the dark night, King Saul hastily summoned his leading officers and the prominent chiefs of the Israelites who had joined him in the late battle. The word rendered "chief of the people" (*pinnoth*) is literally, *corner stones* (as in Judges xx. 2).

He would ask God's help in the casting of lots, to discover who of these was the transgressor, whose sin made dumb the Divine Oracle.

(39) **Though it be in Jonathan my son.**—"Were Jonathan himself the transgressor, he [Saul] would not spare his life; and so, feeling inwardly bound by his oath, presses for decision by means of the sacred lot, amid the ominous silence of the horror-stricken people."—*Ewald.*

(41) **Give a perfect lot.**—The rendering in the margin, "show the innocent," is a better and more accurate rendering of the Hebrew. "Give a perfect lot" is the translation given by Rabbi D. Kimchi. Dean Payne Smith observes that "there are few mistakes of the English Version which have not some good authority for them, as King James' translators were singularly well versed in Jewish literature, while they seem strangely to have neglected the still higher authority of the ancient versions."

In the forty-first and in the following verse the LXX. version is lengthened out with a long paraphrase, which, however, contains no fact of additional interest.

(43, 44) **Lo, I must die.**—These wild and thoughtless vows are peculiarly characteristic of this half-barbaric period. We have already observed that the age now closing had been peculiarly the age of vows. A similar terrible oath, equalling Saul's in its rashness, had been taken by Jephthah. It is noticeable that not only Saul, who vowed the vow, but Jonathan, its victim, were convinced that the vow, though perhaps hastily and rashly made, must be kept. "Against both these," says Erdman in *Lange* with great force "rises the people's voice as the voice of God, the question (in verse 45), 'Shall Jonathan die?' and the answer, 'Far be it,' expresses the sorrowful astonishment and the energetic protest of the people, who were inspired by Jonathan's heroic deed and its brilliant result. . . . Over against Saul's oath the people set their own: 'As the Lord liveth, there shall not one hair of his head fall to the ground.' Probably Saul was not unwilling in this awful question, when his son's life trembled in the balance, to submit his will for once to the people's."

"Take then no vow at random: ta'en in faith,
Preserve it; yet not bent, as Jephthah once,
Blindly to execute a rash resolve,
Whom better it had suited to exclaim,
'I have done ill,' than to redeem his pledge
By doing worse."—Dante, *Paradise.* v. 63–68.

(46) **Then Saul went up from following the Philistines.**—Saul recognised now that the fault which caused the oracle of the Urim and Thummim to keep silence was his, and not Jonathan's. He seems quietly to have acquiesced with Ahijah's evident reluctance to countenance a public pursuit; he drew off his forces then from the direction of the enemy, and went up, no doubt, to Gibeah; but the power of the Philistines for the time seems to have been utterly broken, and they retreated to their own districts along the sea coasts.

(47) **So Saul took the kingdom over Israel.**—Some expositors closely connect this verse with the successful termination of the Philistine war, considering that it was through this great victory over the nation which had so long harassed and impoverished Israel that Saul really acquired for the first time the regal authority over all Israel, and that previously his rule had only been acknowledged in certain of the tribes. It is, however, better to consider the statement contained in this verse as simply a general view of Saul's reign, which was a reign of perpetual wars. The words, then, of our verse are simply introductory to the list of wars waged from the very beginning of his government. It should be observed that this view is supported by the mention of the Ammonite war, which took place a considerable time before the events just related. Such a mention would, therefore, be out of place, unless we take this verse as containing a general statement—in other words, "Saul assumed the reins of government, and during his reign he waged the following wars."

Edom, and against the kings of Zobah, and against the Philistines: and whithersoever he turned himself, he vexed them.¹ ⁽⁴⁸⁾ And he ¹gathered an host, and smote the Amalekites, and delivered Israel out of the hands of them that spoiled them.

⁽⁴⁹⁾ Now the sons of Saul were Jonathan, and Ishui, and Melchi-shua: and the names of his two daughters *were these;* the name of the firstborn Merab, and the name of the younger Michal: ⁽⁵⁰⁾ And the name of Saul's wife *was* Ahinoam, the daughter of Ahimaaz: and the name of the captain of his host *was* Abner, the son of Ner, Saul's uncle. ⁽⁵¹⁾ And Kish *was* the father of Saul; and Ner the father of Abner *was* the son of Abiel. ⁽⁵²⁾ And there was sore war against the Philistines all the days of Saul: and when Saul saw any strong man, or any valiant man, he took him unto him.

CHAPTER XV.—⁽¹⁾ Samuel also said unto Saul, ªThe LORD sent me to anoint

Marginal notes: 1 Or, *wrought mightily.* — ª ch. 9. 16. — B.C. cir. 1079.

On every side ... Moab ... Ammon ... Edom ... Zobah ... Philistines.—This enumeration of the nations with whom he fought literally included the countries on every side of the Land of Promise. Moab and Ammon bounded the Israelites on the east; Edom on the south; the Philistines on the west, along the coast of the Mediterranean; while Zobah was a district of Syria on the north-east of the territory of the twelve tribes, lying between the Euphrates and the Syrian Orontes.

He vexed them.—The exact sense of the Hebrew word *yar'shia*, rendered in our version "he vexed," has puzzled all commentators. The LXX. evidently read another word here, as they translate it by *esōzeto*, "he was preserved." The majority of the versions and Gesenius, however, give the real sense: "Whithersoever he (Saul) turned himself *he was victorious.*" Luther's rendering is scholarly: "Whithersoever he turned *he inflicted punishment,*" and is adopted by Keil.

⁽⁴⁸⁾ **Smote the Amalekites.**—Out of the many wars the king waged, this war with Amalek is singled out, for in the new development of Hebrew power by which Saul's reign was marked this campaign or series of campaigns was especially prominent. This war is related with some detail in the next chapter, but it is there introduced on account of other considerations. The English translators in their rendering, "he gathered an host," have followed the Syriac and Vulg.; the marginal translation, "he wrought mightily," is the more accurate.

⁽⁴⁹⁾ **The sons of Saul.**—The three brave sons who perished with their father in the battle on Mount Gilboa are apparently mentioned here, the only difficulty being the middle name, "Ishui," which occurs nowhere else, save in two genealogies as that of a son of Asher (Gen. xlvi. 17; 1 Chron. vii. 30). It is supposed to be the same as the Abinadab mentioned in that battle. His two daughters, Merab and Michal, are specially named, probably owing to their connection with the history of David (chap. xviii. 17—21), the elder of them having been promised to him in marriage, and the younger being actually wedded to him.

⁽⁵⁰⁾ **Saul's wife.**—In accordance with a usual practice, the name of the most prominent of the family and royal household of the king are given. We know nothing of Saul's queen besides her name. It has been surmised that she was of the family of Eli, the high priest, owing to the *Ah* (brother) entering into her name and that of her father, Ahimaaz, as this compound was apparently the favourite prefix to names in this great and renowned house. The simplicity and modesty of the king's domestic habits is evident. Ewald thinks from this circumstance that he had only this one wife and one concubine, Rizpah, the daughter of Aiah, afterwards so famous for her sad misfortunes and for her devoted love to her ill-fated children. (See 2 Sam. xxi. 8—12.)

The captain of his host was Abner.—This "cousin"—or, as some have understood the sentence, the uncle—of King Saul was evidently a man of rare powers and ability. The brilliant campaigns of this reign were, no doubt, in no small measure owing to the military skill of this great commander. After the terrible disaster on Mount Gilboa, Abner was the mainstay of the house of the dead King Saul, and when he died the generous David followed the bier, and lamented over him with a lamentation which has come down to us in words ever memorable: "Know ye not that there is a prince and a great man fallen this day in Israel." His son Jaasiel was subsequently allowed the first place in the tribe of Benjamin. (See 1 Chron. xxvii. 21.)

⁽⁵¹⁾ **The son of Abiel.**—For "son" the commentators mostly agree we must read *sons*. Kish and Ner, we know, were both sons of Abiel. (See 1 Chron. ix. 35, 36, where, however, the father's name is given as Jehiel.)

⁽⁵²⁾ **All the days of Saul.**—Although after the rout of Michmash the Philistines were driven out of their fastnesses in the land of Israel back into their own coast districts, yet all through the reign of Saul they continued to be powerful, and were a constant source of danger and trouble to the people. We know that in the end Saul lost his life in an engagement with this warlike and restless race, who were not finally crushed before the days of his successor, David. To keep them in check necessitated the maintenance of a standing army, which, in the days of David, became one of the great armed forces of the East. The reader of this verse is reminded at once of a similar military fancy of King Frederick William of Prussia, the founder of Prussian military greatness, and the father of the Great Frederick.

XV.

⁽¹⁻³⁵⁾ **The War with Amalek.**—Saul's Disobedience to the Will of God in the matter of Sparing the King and the Choicest of the Plunder.—The Last Meeting in Life of Saul and Samuel.—The Prophet reproaches the King.—Death of Agag at the hands of Samuel.

⁽¹⁻³⁾ **Samuel also said unto Saul ...**—The compiler of the history, selecting, no doubt, from ancient state records, chose to illustrate the story of the reign and rejection of Saul by certain memorable incidents as good examples of the king's general life and conduct. The incidents were also selected to show the

thee *to be* king over his people, over Israel: now therefore hearken thou unto the voice of the words of the LORD. (2) Thus saith the LORD of hosts, I remember *that* which Amalek did to Israel, ᵃ how he laid *wait* for him in the way, when he came up from Egypt. (3) Now go and smite Amalek, and utterly destroy all that they have, and spare them not; but slay both man and woman, infant and suckling, ox and sheep, camel and ass.

(4) And Saul gathered the people together, and numbered them in Telaim, two hundred thousand footmen, and ten thousand men of Judah. (5) And Saul came to a city of Amalek, and ¹laid wait in the valley. (6) And Saul said unto the Kenites, Go, depart, get you down from among the Amalekites, lest I destroy you with them: for ye shewed kindness to all the children of Israel, when they came up out of Egypt. So the Kenites departed from among the Amalekites. (7) And Saul smote the Amalekites from Havilah *until* thou comest to Shur, that *is* over against Egypt. (8) And he took Agag the king of the Amalekites alive, and utterly destroyed all the people with the edge of

a Ex. 17. 8; Num. 24. 20.

¹ Or, *fought.*

---

rapid development of the power and resources of Israel at this period.

The sacred war with Amalek is thus introduced without any "note of time."

The Lord sent me to anoint thee.—The account of the Amalekite war is prefaced by the solemn words used by the seer when he came to announce the Eternal's will to Saul. They are quoted to show that the war was enjoined upon Israel in a general official way by the accredited prophet-messenger of the Most High.

(2) **That which Amalek did to Israel.**—The Amalekites were a fierce, untameable race of wanderers, who roamed at large through those deserts which lie between Southern Judea and the Egyptian frontier. They were descended from Esau's grandson, Amalek. Not long after the exodus from Egypt, they attacked and cruelly harassed the almost defenceless rear-guard of Israel in the desert of Rephidim. They were then, at the prayer of Moses, defeated by Joshua; but, for this cowardly unprovoked attack, solemnly doomed to destruction. In the prophecy of Balaam they are alluded to as the first of the nations who opposed the Lord's people. During the stormy ages that followed, the hand of Amalek seems to have been constantly lifted against Israel, and we read of them perpetually as allied to their relentless foes.

(3) **Smite Amalek, and utterly destroy . . .**—For "utterly destroy" the Hebrew has the far stronger expression, "put under the ban" (*cherem*). Whatever was "put under the ban" in Israel was devoted to God, and whatever was so devoted could not be redeemed, but must be slain. Amalek was to be looked upon as accursed; human beings and cattle must be killed; whatever was capable of being destroyed by fire must be burnt. The cup of iniquity in this people was filled up. Its national existence, if prolonged, would simply have worked mischief to the commonwealth of nations. Israel here was simply the instrument of destruction used by the Almighty. It is vain to attempt in this and similar transactions to find materials for the blame or the praise of Israel. We must never forget that Israel stood in a peculiar relation to the unseen King, and that this nation was not unfrequently used as the visible scourge by which the All-Wise punished hopelessly hardened sinners, and deprived them of the power of working mischief. We might as well find fault with pestilence and famine, or the sword—those awful instruments of Divine justice and—though we often fail to see it now—of Divine mercy.

(4) **In Telaim.**—Identical with Telem (Joshua xv. 24), a place on the south border of Judah, near the region where the Amalekites chiefly dwelt.—*Kimchi.* Telaim, however, signifies "lambs;" probably "Beth," house of, is to be understood. Thus it was no town, but the "place or house of lambs"—some open spot, where, at the proper season, the lambs were collected from the pastures in the wilderness.—*Dean Payne Smith.*

Ten thousand men of Judah.—Again the numbers of this great tribe are out of proportion to the numbers furnished by the rest of the tribes. (See Note on chap. xi. 8.)

(5) **A city of Amalek.**—Better rendered, *The city of Amalek*: no doubt, their principal place of arms.

And laid wait in the valley.—Better, in a torrent bed, then dry (Arabic, "Wady"). There is a strange tradition in the Talmud that Saul's mind misgave him when he came to this "torrent bed;" thus he called to mind the command of Deut. xxi. 4 to slay an heifer at a torrent in expiation of a murder, and determined not to carry out the stern charge of Samuel, but to spare rather than to slay.

(6) **And Saul said unto the Kenites.**—The Kenites, like the Amalekites, were a nomad race of Arabs, but seem to have been ever friendly to the Israelites. This kindly feeling sprang up soon after the departure from Egypt, and was, no doubt, in the first instance owing to the fact of Hobab, the father-in-law of Moses, belonging to this people.

(7) **From Havilah until thou comest to Shur.**—The Havilah here alluded to cannot be now identified. Shur, which signifies "wall," probably refers to the wall which crossed the north-east frontier of Egypt, extending from Pelusium, past Migdol, to Hevo. Ebers suggests that this wall gave to Egypt the name of "Mizraim," the enclosed, or fortified.

(8) **And he took Agag . . . alive.**—Agag seems to have been for the sovereigns of Amalek the official title, like Pharaoh in the case of the kings of Egypt, and Abimelech among certain of the Philistine peoples. The meaning of the term Agag is unknown.

Utterly destroyed all the people.—That is to say, Ir-Amalek was sacked, and the nation generally broken up; but many, no doubt, escaped into the desert, for we hear of the people again on several occasions in this book. In 1 Chron. iv. 43 their complete, and probably final, annihilation is recorded.

the sword. ⁽⁹⁾ But Saul and the people spared Agag, and the best of the sheep, and of the oxen, and ¹of the fatlings, and the lambs, and all *that was* good, and would not utterly destroy them: but every thing *that was* vile and refuse, that they destroyed utterly.

⁽¹⁰⁾ Then came the word of the LORD unto Samuel, saying, ⁽¹¹⁾ It repenteth me that I have set up Saul *to be* king: for he is turned back from following me, and hath not performed my commandments. And it grieved Samuel; and he cried unto the LORD all night. ⁽¹²⁾ And when Samuel rose early to meet Saul in the morning, it was told Samuel, saying, Saul came to Carmel, and, behold, he set him up a place, and is gone about, and passed on, and gone down to Gilgal.

⁽¹³⁾ And Samuel came to Saul: and Saul said unto him, Blessed *be* thou of the LORD: I have performed the commandment of the LORD. ⁽¹⁴⁾ And Samuel said, What *meaneth* then this bleating of the sheep in mine ears, and the lowing of the oxen which I hear? ⁽¹⁵⁾ And Saul said, They have brought them from the Amalekites: for the people spared the best of the sheep and of the oxen, to sacrifice unto the LORD thy God; and the rest we have utterly destroyed. ⁽¹⁶⁾ Then Samuel said unto Saul, Stay, and I will tell thee what the LORD hath

¹ Or, *of the second sort*.

⁽⁹⁾ **Agag, and the best of the sheep, and of the oxen.**—It would seem that Saul carried out the awful curse to the letter (with the exception that he spared the king) in the case of the human beings and the less valuable of their beasts. But covetousness seems to have suggested the preservation of the choicest cattle, and pride probably induced the Hebrew king to save Agag alive, that he might show the people his royal captive.

⁽¹⁰⁾ **Then came the word. . .**—Very likely in a dream.

⁽¹¹⁾ **It repenteth me. . .**—"God does not feel the pain of remorse (says St. Augustine in Ps. cxxxi.), nor is He ever deceived, so as to desire to correct anything in which He has erred. But as a man desires to make a change when he repents, so when God is said in Scripture to repent, we may expect a change from Him. He changed Saul's kingdom when it is said He repented of making him king."—*Bishop Wordsworth.*

And it grieved Samuel.—"Many grave thoughts seem to have presented themselves at once to Samuel, and to have disturbed his mind when he reflected on the dishonour which would be inflicted upon the name of God, and the occasion which the rejection and deposition of Saul would furnish to wicked men for blaspheming the invisible King of Israel. . . For Saul had been chosen by God Himself from all the people, and called by Him to the throne; if, therefore, he was deposed, it seemed likely that the worship of God would be overturned, and the greatest disturbance ensue."—*Calvin, quoted by Keil.* Abarbanel tells us respecting Samuel's grief that he was angry and displeased, because he loved Saul for his beauty and heroism, and as his own creature whom he had made king; and that he prayed all night because God had not revealed to him Saul's sin, and he wished to know why sentence was pronounced against him.

And he cried unto the Lord all night.—This was, no doubt, that "piercing shrill cry" peculiar to Samuel. With this strange cry he seems to have on many a solemn occasion spoken with his God. He is often in this book represented as thus "crying unto God." (See Stanley's *Lectures on the Jewish Church*, Vol. I., chap. xviii.)

⁽¹²⁾ **And when Samuel rose early . . .**—After the revelations of that sad night, the prophet rose, and at once went to seek the guilty king. He was told Saul was come to Carmel, identical with Kurmul in Judah, to the south-east of Hebron; there the victorious monarch had erected a monument of his victory, literally, *a hand*. In 2 Sam. xviii. 18, Absalom's Pillar is styled Absalom's Hand (*yad*), not "place," as in the English Version. It has been suggested that very likely these victory cairns or columns erected by the Hebrews had a hand engraved upon them.

⁽¹³⁾ **Blessed be thou of the Lord.**—Saul must have been fully conscious that he had failed to carry out the will and command of the Eternal King of Israel. In the late war, undertaken for the definite and solemn purpose of exterminating a wicked and bloodthirsty people, whose continued existence worked terrible evil upon the adjacent countries, he, disregarding the express instructions of the prophet of the Lord for his own covetous purposes, had not destroyed all, but reserved some of the living spoil for himself. Conscious of all this, he still dared to come forward, and to congratulate the prophet upon the fulfilment of the Lord's command. But Saul's words of self-gratulation were evidently feigned; in his heart he knew he had been faithless.

⁽¹⁴⁾ **What meaneth then this bleating? . . .**—"Saul is convicted of falsehood by the voices of the animals which he has spared, contrary to God's command. Samuel's mode of citing them against him by the question, 'What meaneth these voices?' has an air of holy humour and cutting irony."—*Lange.*

⁽¹⁵⁾ **The people spared the best of the sheep . . .**—At once the king understood the drift of his old friend's words; still more, perhaps, the stern, sorrowful look of reproach which accompanied them. "Yes, I understand your meaning. This bleating and lowing certainly does come from the captured flocks and herds of Amalek, but this reservation, which you condemn, was insisted upon by the people; and their object, for which you blame me for acquiescing in, was to do special honour to God in a great sacrifice." There seems something strangely cowardly in this trying to transfer from himself to the people the blame of disobedience to the Divine commands. It is unlike Saul's old character; but covetousness and vanity invariably lead to moral cowardice.

⁽¹⁶⁾ **Stay, and I will tell thee . . .**—The king was probably turning away, desirous of closing an interview which to him was full of bitterness, when he was arrested

said to me this night. And he said unto him, Say on.

(17) And Samuel said, When thou *wast* little in thine own sight, *wast* thou not *made* the head of the tribes of Israel, and the LORD anointed thee king over Israel? (18) And the LORD sent thee on a journey, and said, Go and utterly destroy the sinners the Amalekites, and fight against them until ¹they be consumed. (19) Wherefore then didst thou not obey the voice of the LORD, but didst fly upon the spoil, and didst evil in the sight of the LORD?

(20) And Saul said unto Samuel, Yea, I have obeyed the voice of the LORD, and have gone the way which the LORD sent me, and have brought Agag the king of Amalek, and have utterly destroyed the Amalekites. (21) But the people took of the spoil, sheep and oxen, the chief of the things which should have been utterly destroyed, to sacrifice unto the LORD thy God in Gilgal.

(22) And Samuel said, Hath the LORD as *great* delight in burnt offerings and sacrifices, as in obeying the voice of the LORD? Behold, ᵃ to obey *is* better than sacrifice, *and* to hearken than the fat of rams. (23) For rebellion *is as* the sin of ²witchcraft, and stubbornness *is as* iniquity and idolatry. Because thou hast rejected the word of the LORD, he hath also rejected thee from *being* king.

¹ Heb., *they consume them.*
ᵃ Eccles. 5. 1; Hos. 6. 6; Matt. 9. 13 & 12. 7.
² Heb., *divination.*

---

by the solemn words, and probably by the commanding gesture, of his old friend and counsellor, who now addressed him with the majesty and power of an accredited servant of the Most High.

(17) **When thou wast little in thine own sight.**— Kimchi's rendering of the Hebrew here is singular: "Though thou seemest to thyself too little and weak to curb the people, yet wast thou the head, and shouldest have done thy duty;" but this, as Lange observes, would imply that Samuel had *accepted* Saul's excuse that it was the people's will to reserve the choicest spoil. The prophet's words, however, were simply to remind Saul that the Lord, whose clearly expressed will he had disregarded, had raised him in bygone days from a comparatively humble station to the proud position he was then occupying as chief of Israel. The old counsellor reminds the king that there had been a time when he judged himself unequal to this great work to which his God summoned him; but now, how strange the contrast! Flushed with success, he was trusting alone in his unaided strength, and openly disobeying the Divine commands.

(18) **The sinners the Amalekites.**—This briefly rehearses the charge of the Most High, which Saul had deliberately disobeyed. It is noticeable that the Amalekites are expressly called "sinners," thus indicating the reason of the Divine wrath against them. The men of Sodom (Gen. xiii. 13) were styled "sinners before the Lord."

(19) **Didst fly upon the spoil.**—The expression used evidently includes the idea of greedy eagerness, as though Samuel detected a spirit of grasping covetousness at the bottom of this disobedient act of Saul's.

(20) **Yea, I have obeyed . . .**—These and the words which follow are simply a repetition of the king's former excuse for his act: but they show us what was the state of Saul's mind: he evidently disbelieved in the power of the Eternal as a heart reader. If he could justify himself before Samuel, that was all he cared for. He asserted his own integrity of purpose and his great zeal for the public sacrifice to God, knowing all the while that low earthly reasons had been the springs of his conduct. He reiterated the plea that what he had done was in accordance with the voice of the people, conscious all the while that the plea was false.

(22) **Behold, to obey is better than sacrifice.**— In this answer it would seem that the Spirit of the Lord descended upon Samuel, and that he here gave utterance to one of those rapt expressions which now and again in the course of each of these Hebrew prophets' lives these famous men were commissioned by the Divine power to give out to their fellows. The words of Samuel here were reproduced, or at least referred to, by other prophets and teachers of the old dispensation; for example, see Pss. l. 8—14, li. 16, 17; Isaiah i. 11; Jer. vi. 20; Micah vi. 6—8; Hosea vi. 6. Our Lord himself, in His words recorded in Matt. ix. 13, if not actually referring to this passage, makes substantially the same declaration.

Irenæus, *Haer*. iv. 32 (quoted by Wordsworth), sees in this great saying of Samuel's a plain intimation that the day would come when the burnt offerings enjoined on Israel would give place to a simple worship of the heart. Wordsworth also quotes a weighty comment from St. Gregory (*Moral*. xxxv. 10): "In sacrifices (per victimas) a man offers only strange flesh, whereas in obedience he offers his own will."

(23) **For rebellion is as the sin of witchcraft.**— Witchcraft, more literally *soothsaying* or *divination*, was a sin constantly held up to reprobation in the Old Testament. It was the greatest of all the dangers to which Israel was exposed, and was in fact a tampering with the idol-worship of the surrounding nations. Impurity, and an utter lack of all the loftier principles of morality which the one true God and His chosen servants would impress on the peoples of the East, characterised the various systems of idol-worship then current in Syria and the adjacent countries. And Samuel here, in this solemn inspired saying, briefly gives the grounds of the Lord's rejection of His Anointed: "Rebellion," or conscious disobedience to the express commands of the Eternal, in the case of Saul, God's chosen king, was nothing else than the deadly sin of idol-worship, for it set aside the true Master of Israel, and virtually acknowledged another. The next sentence still more emphatically expresses the same thought: "Stubbornness," or "intractableness," is in the eyes of the pure God the same thing as worshipping idols and teraphim. The Hebrew word *aven*, rendered iniquity, literally signifies "nothingness;" it is a word used in the late prophets for an idol (Hos. x. 8; Isa. lxvi. 3). The word in the original translated in the English Version "idolatry," is teraphim. Teraphim were apparently small household gods or

Samuel Solemnly Predicts   I. SAMUEL, XV.   *the Fall of Saul's House.*

⁽²⁴⁾ And Saul said unto Samuel, I have sinned: for I have transgressed the commandment of the LORD, and thy words: because I feared the people, and obeyed their voice. ⁽²⁵⁾ Now therefore, I pray thee, pardon my sin, and turn again with me, that I may worship the LORD. ⁽²⁶⁾ And Samuel said unto Saul, I will not return with thee: for thou hast rejected the word of the LORD, and the LORD hath rejected thee from being king over Israel. ⁽²⁷⁾ And as Samuel turned about to go away, he laid hold upon the skirt of his mantle, and it rent. ⁽²⁸⁾ And Samuel said unto him, The LORD hath rent the kingdom of Israel from thee this day, and hath given it to a neighbour of thine, *that is* better than thou. ⁽²⁹⁾ And also the ¹Strength of Israel will not lie nor repent: for he *is* not a man, that he should repent. ⁽³⁰⁾ Then he said, I have sinned: *yet* honour me now, I

¹ Or, *Eternity*, or, *victory.*

---

idols, venerated as the arbiters of good and evil fortune. In Roman life we find similar idols under the name of "Lares." Teraphim is derived from an unused root, *taraph*, signifying "to live comfortably;" Arabic, *tarafa*: compare the Sanscrit *trip*, and the Greek τρέφειν. These idols appear to have been small human figures of various sizes. The image in 1 Sam. xix. 13 was probably nearly life-size. These teraphim were made generally of silver or of wood. It has been suggested that the teraphim which Rachel stole were images of her ancestors. (See Note on Gen. xxxi. 19, and Mr. Whitelaw's comment on *ib.* in the *Pulpit Commentary*.)

⁽²⁴⁾ **I have sinned.**—The grave condemnation of the prophet appalled the king. The grounds of the Divine rejection evidently sank deep into Saul's heart. Such a thought as that, in the eyes of the Invisible and Eternal, he ranked with the idolators and heathen sinners around, was, even for one sunk so low as Saul, terrible.

Because I feared the people.—He, with stammering lips, while deprecating the Divine sentence, still seeks to justify himself; but all that he could allege in excuse only more plainly marked out his unfitness for his high post. He could, after all, only plead that he loved the praise of men more than the approval of his God; that he preferred—as so many of earth's great ones have since done—the sweets of transient popular applause to the solitary consciousness that he was a faithful servant of the Highest.

⁽²⁵⁾ **Now therefore, I pray thee, pardon my sin.**—But, after all, the sorrow of Saul was rather for the immediate earthly consequence which he feared might follow the Divine rejection. He foresaw his power in Israel would sensibly decrease, so he intreats the great prophet not to desert him.

⁽²⁶⁾ **I will not return with thee.**—Samuel too clearly sees what are the true springs of Saul's repentance, and refuses at first. It was only, as C. à Lapide forcibly urges, a fear on the part of the king, of losing the kingdom and of incurring public disgrace. The prophet for reply again repeats the terrible Divine sentence of rejection.

⁽²⁷⁾ **He laid hold upon the skirt of his mantle.**—The king's passionate action indicates a restless, unquiet mind. Not content with intreating words, Saul, perhaps even with some violence, lays hold of the old man as he turns away, to detain him. What Saul laid hold of and tore was not the "mantle" (Authorised Version), but the hem, or outer border, of the "meil," the ordinary tunic which the upper classes in Israel were then in the habit of wearing. The Dean of Canterbury, in a careful Note in the *Pulpit Commentary*, shows that the "mantle," which would be the accurate rendering of the Hebrew *addereth*, the distinctive dress of the Hebrew prophets, was certainly not used in the days of Samuel, the great founder of the prophetic order. Special dresses came into use only gradually, and Elijah is the first person described as being thus clad. Long before his time the school of the prophets had grown into a national institution, and a loose wrapper of coarse cloth, made of camel's-hair, fastened round the body at the waist by a leathern girdle, had become the *distinctive* prophetic dress, and continued to be until the arrival of Israel's last prophet, John the Baptist (Mark i. 6).

⁽²⁸⁾ **The Lord hath rent the kingdom.**—The prophet at once looks upon the garment torn by the passionate vehemence of the king, as an omen for the future, and uses the rent vesture as a symbol, to show Saul that thus had the Lord on that day rent the kingdom from him.

A neighbour of thine.—It had not yet been revealed to the seer who was to replace the rebellious king, so he simply refers to the future anointed one quite indefinitely as "a neighbour."

⁽²⁹⁾ **The Strength of Israel will not lie.**—This title of the Eternal, here rendered "the Strength of Israel," would be better rendered *the Changeless One of Israel*. The Hebrew word is first found in this passage. In later Hebrew, as in 1 Chron. xxix. 2, it is rendered "glory," from the Aramæan usage of speech (Keil). Some, less accurately, would translate it here "The Victory," or "the Triumph of Israel," will not lie, &c. In the eleventh verse of this chapter we read of the Eternal saying, "*It repenteth me* that I have set up Saul to be king," while here we find how "the Changeless One (or Strength) of Israel *will . . . not repent.*" The truth is that with God there is no change. Now He approves of men and their works and days, and promises them rich blessings; *now* He condemns and punishes the ways and actions of the same men; hence He is said "to repent:" but the change springs alone from a change in the men themselves, not in God. Speaking in human language the Lord is said "to repent" because there was what appeared to be a change in the Eternal counsels.

"One instrument," well says Dean Payne Smith, "may be laid aside, and another chosen (as was the case of Saul), because God ordains that the instruments by which He works shall be beings endowed with free will." So God in the case of King Saul—in human language—was said to repent of His choice because, owing to Saul's deliberate choice of evil, the Divine purposes could not in his case be carried out. Predictions and promises in the Scriptures are never absolute, but are always conditional. Still, God is ever the "Changeless One of Israel." "The counsel of the Lord stands for ever" (Ps. xxxiii. 11). "I am Jehovah; I change not" (Mal. iii. 6).

⁽³⁰⁾ **Yet honour me now, I pray thee, before the elders.**—It was a strange penitence, after

pray thee, before the elders of my people, and before Israel, and turn again with me, that I may worship the LORD thy God.

(31) So Samuel turned again after Saul; and Saul worshipped the LORD.

(32) Then said Samuel, Bring ye hither to me Agag the king of the Amalekites. And Agag came unto him delicately. And Agag said, Surely the bitterness of death is past. (33) And Samuel said, *As thy sword hath made women childless, so shall thy mother be childless among women. And Samuel hewed Agag in pieces before the LORD in Gilgal.

(34) Then Samuel went to Ramah; and Saul went up to his house to Gibeah of Saul. (35) And Samuel came no more to see Saul until the day of his death: nevertheless Samuel mourned for Saul: and the LORD repented that he had made Saul king over Israel.

a Ex. 17. 11; Num. 14. 45.

---

all, this sorrow of Saul for his great sin. He was, no doubt, terribly in earnest and in great fear; but his earnestness was based upon a desire to maintain his power and royal state, and his fear sprang from a well-grounded apprehension that if he lost the countenance of Samuel the seer, the revered and honoured servant of the Lord, he would probably forfeit his crown. "If Saul had been really penitent, he would pray to have been humble rather than to be honoured" (*St. Gregory*, quoted by Wordsworth).

(31) **So Samuel turned again after Saul.**—The prophet, after the repeated and pressing request of the king, consents publicly to worship the Lord in his company. There is little doubt but that the principal motive which induced Samuel on this occasion not to withdraw himself from the public thanksgiving was a desire to prevent any disaffection towards the monarchy. His known disapproval of Saul's conduct, and his declining the king's earnest prayer to stay, would probably have been the signal to the discontented spirits in Israel to revolt, under the pretext that such a revolt would be pleasing to the great seer. Such a revolt in those critical times would have been disastrous to the growing prosperity of the chosen people.

It has been well suggested that many blessings came upon the unhappy Saul and the nation over which he ruled in answer to Samuel's intercession on this occasion for him.

The result was what might have been looked for. Saul remained in undiminished power apparently; but the will of God, as declared by His servant Samuel, was slowly, but surely, accomplished. The doom of the reigning family pronounced by the prophet on this momentous occasion was irrevocable.

The story of Israel contained in this book shows how the march of events in solemn procession moved onward, every year bringing the ill-fated rebel king nearer the execution of the stern sentence which his own self-willed conduct had called down on him.

(32) **Bring ye hither to me Agag the king of the Amalekites.**— But in the public service of thanksgiving there was one stern act of judgment still to be done. The King of the Amalekites had been sentenced to die. Saul had spared him for selfish reasons of his own; we need not discuss here the apparent harshness of the doom. There were, no doubt, amply sufficient reasons for the seemingly hard sentence on the people of Amalek: such as their past crimes, their evil example, the unhappy influence which they probably exercised on the surrounding nations. Weighed in the balance of the Divine justice, Amalek had been found wanting; and perhaps—we speak in all reverence—this death which was the doom of Amalek was sent in mercy rather than in punishment: mercy to those whom their evil lives might have corrupted with deep corruption—mercy to themselves, in calling them off from greater evils yet to come, had they been permitted still to live on in sin. Their king, whom Saul had, in defiance of the Divine command, spared, could not be permitted to live. From Samuel's words in verse 33 he seems, even among a wicked race, to have been pre-eminent in wickedness. Ewald suggests a curious, but not wholly improbable, reason for Saul's preserving him alive: "kings, for the honour of their craft, must spare each other." There are other instances in the Sacred Book of prophets and priests acting as the executioners of the Divine decrees: for instance, Phinehas, when he slew Zimri and Cozbi before all Israel (Num. xxv. 8—15); and Elijah, in the case of the slaughter of the prophets of Baal on Mount Carmel (1 Kings xviii. 40). It has been suggested that Samuel did not perform the terrible act of Divine justice with his own hand, but simply handed over Agag to the officers of justice to put to death; but it is far more in harmony with other similar scenes in Hebrew story, and with the stern unflinching character of these devoted servants of the God of Israel, to understand the recital in its literal sense, which certainly leaves the impression on the reader that Samuel himself slew the King of Amalek.

The Hebrew word rendered "delicately" is apparently derived from the same root as "Eden," the garden of joy; the meaning then would probably be "cheerfully, gladly;" another derivation, however, would enable us to render it "in bands or in fetters." This would give a very good sense, but most expositors prefer the idea of "cheerfulness" or "gladness." The LXX. must have found another word altogether in their copies, for they render it "trembling." The Syriac Version omits it—strangely enough—altogether. Another view of the tragical incident is suggested in *Excursus* G at the end of this Book.

(33) **Samuel hewed Agag in pieces.**—It has been suggested, with some probability, that these words refer to a peculiar form of putting to death, like the quartering in vogue during the Middle Ages.

(35) **Came no more to see Saul . . .**—Once more the old friends met together *in life* (see chapter xix. 24), but the interview on this occasion was not of Samuel's seeking; nor does it appear then that any communication passed between them. When next the seer and the king *spoke* together, the seer belonged to another and a different world. "After this, Samuel came no more to him, bearing messages and commands, and giving him counsel and guidance from God. Saul's kingship, though still one *de facto*, yet from this time lost its theocratic relation. God's ambassador was recalled from him; the intercourse of the God of Israel with Saul through His Spirit came to an end, because Saul, sinking step by step away from God, had, by continued disobedience and increasing impenitence, given up communion with God."—*Lange*.

Samuel is ordered by God   I. SAMUEL, XVI.   *to Anoint a Successor to Saul.*

CHAPTER XVI.—⁽¹⁾ And the LORD said unto Samuel, How long wilt thou mourn for Saul, seeing I have rejected him from reigning over Israel? fill thine horn with oil, and go, I will send thee to Jesse the Beth-lehemite: for I have provided me a king among his sons. ⁽²⁾ And Samuel said, How can I go? if Saul hear *it*, he will kill me. And the LORD said, Take an heifer [1] with thee, and say, I am come to sacrifice to the LORD. ⁽³⁾ And call Jesse to the sacrifice, and I will shew thee what thou shalt do: and thou shalt anoint unto me *him* whom I name unto thee. ⁽⁴⁾ And Samuel did that which the

B.C. cir. 1063.

[1] Heb., *in thine hand.*

Nevertheless Samuel mourned for Saul.—The old seer, who had known Saul from the days of his splendid youthful promise, had indeed good reason to mourn. He, no doubt, loved him much, and regarded him as his own adopted child. On Saul he had built up all his hopes for the future of the Israel he loved so well. There was besides so much that was great and noble in the character of that first Hebrew king: he was the bravest of the brave, a tried and skilful general, possessed too of many of those high gifts which belong to men like Saul and David, and which enable them to be the saviours and regenerators of their country. This first great king only lacked one thing: true faith in that God who loved Israel with a peculiar love. Saul through his chequered career never really leaned on the Arm of the Mighty One of Jacob. No doubt, too, Samuel already perceived in the brilliant but headstrong king the first beginning of that terrible malady which over-shadowed the meridian and clouded the latter years of Saul—signs of that dread visitant, insanity, were, no doubt, visible to Samuel when the old man began to mourn for Saul.

XVI.

(1–23) **David.—His early History.—His First Connection with Samuel.—His Meeting with King Saul.**

⁽¹⁾ **How long wilt thou mourn for Saul?**—The constant references to the influence Saul acquired, and the love and admiration he attracted, is a striking feature in this most ancient Book of Samuel, where the fall and ruin of the first Hebrew king is so pathetically related.

Though it tells us how Saul was tried, and found utterly wanting, still the record, which dwells on the evil qualities which ruined the great life, never loses an opportunity of telling how men like Samuel and David mourned for Saul, and how heroes like Jonathan loved the king who *might* have been so great. The ordinary reader of the story, but for these touches of feeling, would be tempted to condemn with far too sweeping a condemnation the unhappy Saul, whose sun, as far as the world was concerned, set amidst clouds and thick darkness. Is it too much to think that for Saul the punishment ended here? that the bitter suffering caused by the solemn anger of his prophet friend, the gloomy last years of unhappiness and distrust, and the shame and defeat of the last campaign, purged away from the noble soul the scars left by the self-will and disobedience? The Divine Voice, so well-known to the seer, at length roused him from his mourning inactivity. Though that instrument, prepared with so much care, was broken, the work of God for which this instrument was created must be done. If Saul had failed, another must be looked for, and trained to fill the place of the deposed disobedient king.

Fill thine horn with oil.—Heb., *the oil;* probably, as Stanley suggests, the consecrated oil preserved in the Tabernacle at Nob. (On the use to be made of this "sacred oil," see Note on verse 3.)

Jesse the Beth-lehemite.—From this day forward the village of Bethlehem obtained a strange notoriety in the annals of the world. David loved the village, where his father, most probably, was the sheik, or head man. "The future king never forgot the flavour," as Stanley graphically reminds us, "of the water of the well of Bethlehem" (1 Chron. xi. 17). It was Bethlehem, the cradle of the great ancestor, that was selected in the counsels of the Most High as the birthplace of Jesus Christ.

This Jesse was evidently a man of some wealth, Mohammedan tradition speaks of him as one who, in addition to his farming pursuits, was famous for his skill in making hair-cloths and sack-cloths.

⁽²⁾ **He will kill me.**—The unhappy mental malady of Saul must have made rapid progress. The jealous king was indeed changed from the Saul who even, in his self-willed rebellion against the Lord, was careful to pay honour to Samuel. But now the aged prophet felt that if he crossed the king's path in any way, even in carrying out the commands of the invisible King of Israel, his life would be forfeited to the fierce anger of Saul.

Take an heifer with thee.—And the Divine voice instructed Samuel how he should proceed. There was to be as yet no public anointing of the successor to Saul, only the future king must be sought out, and quietly, but solemnly, set apart for service before the Lord, and then watched over and carefully trained for his high office.

⁽³⁾ **And thou shalt anoint.**—From very early times the ceremony of anointing to important offices was customary among the Hebrews. In the first instance, all the priests were anointed (Exod. xl. 15; Numb. iii. 3), but afterwards anointing seems to have been reserved especially for the high priest (Exod. xxix. 29). Prophets also seem occasionally to have been anointed to their holy office. Anointing, however, was the principal ceremony in the inauguration of the Hebrew kings. It belonged in so especial a manner to the royal functions that the favourite designation for the king in Israel was "the Lord's anointed." In the case of David, the ceremony of anointing was performed three times—(1) on this occasion by Samuel, when the boy was set apart for the service of the Lord; (2) when appointed king over Judah at Hebron (2 Sam. ii. 4); (3) when chosen as monarch over all Israel (2 Sam. v. 3). All these official personages, the priest, the prophet, and peculiarly the king, were types of the great expected Deliverer, ever known as the "Messiah," "the Christ," "the Anointed One."

Wordsworth curiously considers these three successive unctions of David figurative of the successive unctions of Christ: conceived by the Holy Ghost in the Virgin's womb; then anointed publicly at his baptism; and finally, set at God's right hand as King of the Universal Church in the heavenly Jerusalem.

⁽⁴⁾ **Trembled at his coming.**—The appearance of the aged seer, with the heifer and the long horn of

LORD spake, and came to Beth-lehem. And the elders of the town trembled at his ¹coming, and said, Comest thou peaceably? ⁽⁵⁾ And he said, Peaceably: I am come to sacrifice unto the LORD: sanctify yourselves, and come with me to the sacrifice. And he sanctified Jesse and his sons, and called them to the sacrifice.

⁽⁶⁾ And it came to pass, when they were come, that he looked on Eliab, and said, Surely the LORD's anointed *is* before him. ⁽⁷⁾ But the LORD said unto Samuel, Look not on his countenance, or on the height of his stature; because I have refused him: for *the LORD seeth* not as man seeth; for man looketh on the ²outward appearance, but the LORD looketh on the *ᵃ*heart. ⁽⁸⁾ Then Jesse called Abinadab, and made him pass before Samuel. And he said, Neither hath the LORD chosen this. ⁽⁹⁾ Then Jesse made Shammah to pass by. And he said, Neither hath the LORD chosen this. ⁽¹⁰⁾ Again, Jesse made seven of his sons to pass before Samuel. And Samuel said unto Jesse, The LORD hath not chosen these.

⁽¹¹⁾ And Samuel said unto Jesse, Are here all *thy* children? And he said, There remaineth yet the youngest, and, behold, he keepeth the sheep. And Samuel said unto Jesse, *ᵇ*Send and fetch him: for we will not sit ³down till he come hither. ⁽¹²⁾ And he sent, and brought him in. Now he *was* ruddy, *and* withal ⁴of a beautiful countenance, and goodly to look to. And the LORD said, Arise, anoint him: for this *is* he. ⁽¹³⁾ Then Samuel took the horn of oil, and anointed him in the midst of his brethren: and the Spirit of the LORD came upon David from that day forward. So Samuel rose up, and went to Ramah.

1 Heb., *meeting.*
2 Heb., *eyes.*
a 1 Chr. 28. 9; Ps. 7. 9; Jer. 11. 20 & 17. 10, & 20. 12.
b 2 Sam. 7. 8; Ps. 78. 70.
3 Heb., *round.*
4 Heb., *fair of eyes.*

---

holy oil, at first terrified the villagers of the quiet, secluded Bethlehem. The name and appearance of the old seer was well known in all the coasts of Israel. Why had he come thus suddenly among them? Had their still remote township then been the scene of some unknown and grave crime? What was happening in Israel, which brought Samuel the seer to little Bethlehem?

⁽⁵⁾ **Peaceably: I am come to sacrifice.**—The answer at once re-assured the villagers. He had simply come to perform the usual rite of sacrifice among them. The reasons of his coming were unknown, but his mission was one alone of blessing. There was nothing unusual in his sanctifying Jesse and his sons. This was evidently the principal family in the place, and the village sheik and his sons would be the fittest persons to assist in preparing for, and then carrying out, the sacrificial rites.

⁽⁶⁾ **He looked on Eliab.**—There was something in the tall and stately presence of the eldest born of Jesse which reminded the old man of the splendid youth of Saul. Eliab seemed to Samuel in all respects a fit successor to the great warrior whom the Lord rejected. But the Divine voice gave no reply back to the prophet's mute questioning; and the other sons of Jesse, an imposing band of gallant youths, passed in review before the old seer, and were severally introduced to him; but the Divine voice only warned the seer that these external advantages of mere human beauty and strength, were no marks of true greatness.

⁽¹⁰⁾ **Seven of his sons.**—These seven, with David, the youngest, make eight. In 1 Chron. ii. 13—15 only seven of the family are recorded: one apparently of that bright band of youths died young.

⁽¹¹⁾ **Are here all thy children?**—For a moment the prophet is uncertain. The command from the Eternal Friend to come and anoint "the son of Jesse of Bethlehem" had been definite, but the sons of Jesse had passed before him, and no sign had been vouchsafed to him indicating that God had chosen one of these youths of whom the father was so fond; so the seer asks, "Are these all thy children?"

There remaineth yet the youngest.—Why David was kept in the background is uncertain. He, clearly, was different to the stalwart band of elder brothers who were grouped round their father. Although fair to look on, his beauty was of a very different type to that of his brothers, probably, compared with Saul and his own brothers, little of stature, with reddish-brown hair and a fair complexion. His father and the men in the village thought less of him than of his dark, tall brothers: at all events, Jesse thought him of too little account to present to Samuel. But, as so often, God's thoughts are not our thoughts, and in a moment Samuel saw that in the ruddy shepherd boy—small of stature, and held of little account in his father's house—he beheld the future king of Israel.

⁽¹³⁾ **Anointed him in the midst of his brethren.**—The history here simply relates the bare fact that the young shepherd was anointed in the presence of his brethren. No words of Samuel on this occasion are recorded; we are left, therefore, uncertain whether any reason was given for the choice of David, or any explanation of this peculiar anointing. It would seem most probable that Samuel kept silence for the present respecting the high destinies of the boy standing before him, and that he merely anointed him as one chosen to be his assistant in the sacrifice he was about to offer, stating probably that the Spirit of the Lord had directed him thus to associate the young son of Jesse with himself, and to adopt him in some way as a pupil in his prophetic school. From this time forward much of David's time was doubtless spent in Samuel's company. From him he received his training in poetry and music, for which he subsequently became distinguished; from the wise seer, too, the future king derived those early lessons of wisdom and learning which enabled him later to fill so nobly the great position for which he was thus early marked out. David was, before everything, Samuel's pupil, and the last years of that long and memorable career of the prophet were spent in moulding the life of Israel's greatest king.

Saul's Mental Malady.   I. SAMUEL, XVI.   *David's Music soothes the King.*

(14) But the Spirit of the LORD departed from Saul, and an evil spirit from the LORD ¹troubled him. (15) And Saul's servants said unto him, Behold now, an evil spirit from God troubleth thee. (16) Let our lord now command thy servants, *which are* before thee, to seek out a man, *who is* a cunning player on an harp: and it shall come to pass, when the evil spirit from God is upon thee, that he shall play with his hand, and thou shalt be well. (17) And Saul said unto his servants, Provide me now a man that can play well, and bring *him* to me. (18) Then answered one of the servants, and said, Behold, I have seen a son of Jesse the Beth-lehemite, *that is* cunning in playing, and a mighty valiant man,

B.C. cir. 1065.

¹ Or, *terrified.*

And the Spirit of the Lord came upon David . . . (14) But the Spirit of the Lord departed from Saul.—This "Spirit of the Lord" which on the day of his anointing by Samuel came upon the shepherd boy, was the "Holy Ghost, or good Spirit of God," and is clearly and formally opposed to those evil spirits which (to use the words of Bishop Pearson) "must be acknowledged persons of a spiritual and intellectual subsistence, as *the Spirit of the Lord departed from Saul, and an evil spirit from the Lord troubled him.* Now, what those evil spirits from the Lord were is apparent from the sad example of Ahab, concerning whom we read, *There came out a spirit and stood before the Lord, and said, I will entice him; and the Lord said unto him, Wherewith? and he said, I will go out, and be a lying spirit in the mouth of all his prophets. And the Lord said, Thou shalt entice him, and thou shalt also prevail; go out, and do even so.* From whence it is evident that the evil spirits from God were certain persons—even bad angels—to which the one good Spirit as a person is opposed, departing from him to whom the other cometh" (Bishop Pearson, *Creed*, Art. viii.).

The effect of this *descent* of the Spirit of the Lord upon David was that the shepherd boy grew up into a hero, a statesman, a scholar, and a wise, far-sighted king. The effect of the *departure* of the Spirit from Saul was that from that hour the once generous king became a prey to a gloomy melancholy, and a victim to a torturing jealousy of others, which increased as time went on, and which goaded him now and again to madness, ruining his life, and marring utterly the fair promise of his early years.

(15) **An evil spirit from God.**—The form in which the evil spirit manifested itself in Saul was apparently an incurable melancholy, which at times blazed forth in fits of uncontrollable jealous anger. When Saul's attendants, his officers, and those about his person, perceived the mental malady under which their king was evidently suffering, they counselled that he should try whether the evil influence which troubled him could not be charmed away by music.

There is no doubt but that King Saul's nervous, excitable temperament was peculiarly subject to such influences. We have some striking instances of this power exercised by sacred music over the king in the incidents related in chaps. x. 10, xix. 23, 24, where the songs and chaunts of the pupils of the prophetic schools had so powerful an influence over Saul. The solemn declaration of God through his prophet Samuel, that the kingdom was taken away from him and his house, weighed upon his naturally nervous and excitable mind. He became gloomy, and suspicious of his dearest friends, and, as we know, at times sought to take their lives; at times would command terrible massacres, such as that of the priests at Nob (chap. xxii. 17—19). As the sad life advanced, we see the nobler traits in his character growing fainter, and the evil becoming more and more obvious. It was a species of insanity, fatal alike to the poor victim of the malady and to the prosperity of the kingdom over which he ruled. History gives us not a few similar instances of monarchs given up to the "evil spirit from God," and who, in consequence, became a prey to insanity in one form or other.

(16) **And it shall come to pass . . . thou shalt be well.**—It has been a well-known fact in all ages that music exerts a powerful influence on the mind. We have several instances in ancient Greek literature, where this influence is recommended to soothe the passions or to heal mental disease. Pythagoras, whenever he would steep his mind in Divine power, was in the habit before he slept of having a harp played to him; Æsculapius, the physician, would often restore such sick souls with music. (See reference from Censorinus, *De die natali*, quoted by Keil.)

"Priests would call
On Heaven for aid : but then his brow would lower
With treble gloom. Peace! Heaven is good to all.
To all, he sighed, but one—God hears no prayers for Saul.
At length one spake of *music.*"—HANKINSON.

(18) **Then answered one of the servants.**—The Dean of Canterbury calls attention to the fact that the word in the original here rendered "servants" is not the same as was translated by "servants" in verses 15, 16, 17. In each of these passages the Hebrew word rendered "servant," no doubt signifies officers connected with the royal court. Here the different word *hann'-ārim* lays stress on the royal attendant in question being a *young man*. Probably, the one spoken of in this place was a contemporary of David, very likely a youth trained with David in Samuel's prophetic school at Naioth in Ramah, and consequently able to speak thus in detail about the young shepherd pupil of the great seer.

Cunning in playing.—As a boy, it is certain that David possessed rare gifts of poetry, and, no doubt, of music. It is probable that some of his early Psalms were originally composed while watching his father's sheep among those hills and vales round the village of Bethlehem, where "in later centuries shepherds were still watching over their flocks by night, when the angel host appeared to them to tell them of the birth of a child in Bethlehem."

These gifts of poetry and music were further cultivated and developed in the prophets' school of Samuel, and there the young pupil of the seer no doubt quickly acquired among his companions that reputation and skill which induced the "young man" of the court of Saul to tell his afflicted master of the shepherd son of Jesse, famous for his "cunning in playing."

And a mighty valiant man, and a man of war.—The description of the Bethlehemite David as

David at the Court of Saul.   I. SAMUEL, XVII.   *War with the Philistines.*

and a man of war, and prudent in ¹matters, and a comely person, and the LORD *is* with him. (19) Wherefore Saul sent messengers unto Jesse, and said, Send me David thy son, which *is* with the sheep. (20) And Jesse took an ass *laden* with bread, and a bottle of wine, and a kid, and sent *them* by David his son unto Saul. (21) And David came to Saul, and stood before him: and he loved him greatly; and he became his armourbearer. (22) And Saul sent to Jesse, saying, Let David, I pray thee, stand before me; for he hath found favour in my sight. (23) And it came to pass, when the *evil* spirit from God was upon Saul, that David took an harp, and played with his hand: so Saul was refreshed, and was well, and the evil spirit departed from him.

CHAPTER XVII.—(1) Now the Philistines gathered together their armies to battle, and were gathered together at Shochoh, which *belongeth* to Judah, and pitched between Shochoh and Azekah, in ²Ephes-dammim. (2) And Saul and the men of Israel were gathered together, and pitched by the valley of Elah, and ³set the battle in array against the Phi-

¹ Or, *speech.*
² Or, *The coast of Dammim.*
³ Heb. *ranged the battle.*

---

a mighty valiant man can well be explained from what is related in chap. xvii. 34, 35, about the young shepherd's prowess in the conflicts with the lions and the bears. A question has, however, been raised respecting the expression "a man of war," as it would seem from the narrative of chap. xvii. that the combat with the giant Philistine was David's first great military exploit. It has, however, been suggested that, in addition to the combat with those wild beasts, which we know in those days frequented the thickets of the Jordan, and were a terror to the Israelitish shepherds, David had most likely been engaged in repelling one or more of the Philistine marauding expeditions so common in those wild days. Bethlehem, we know, was a strong place or garrison of these hereditary foes of Israel. (See 2 Sam. xxiii. 14; 1 Chron. xi. 16.)

(20) **And Jesse took an ass.**—It was and is ever customary in the East to acknowledge obedience and subjection with a present. Jesse, the sheik of Bethlehem, would thus be expected on sending his son to the court of Saul to acknowledge his sovereign by some token of homage.

The nature of Jesse's gifts shows how simple and primitive were the customs of the Hebrew people at that time.

(21) **And he became his armour-bearer.**—But probably only for a very short time. David returned, we should conclude, to Samuel, whose pupil and friend we know he was. The seer was watching over the young man with a view to his lofty destiny. Saul apparently, from his question in chap. xvii. 55, "Whose son is this youth?" had forgotten all about him. There is no "note of time," so we are not able to determine how long a period had elapsed between the events narrated in this chapter and the combat with the Philistines told in chap. xvii. It is, however, likely that the king's malady, which was making rapid progress in this period of his reign, had already obscured his once powerful mind; his memory for the past was likely enough to have been treacherous.

(23) **David took an harp, and played with his hand.**—"The music," beautifully writes F. D. Maurice, "was more than a mere palliative. It brought back for the time the sense of a true order, a secret, inward harmony, an assurance that it is near every man, and that he may enter into it. A wonderful message, no doubt, to a king or a common man, better than a great multitude of words, a continual prophecy that there is a deliverer who can take the vulture from the heart, and unbind the sufferer from the rock . . . .

As the boy minstrel played, the afflicted monarch was refreshed, and the dark clouds rolled away."

"He is Saul, ye remember in glory—ere error had bent
  The broad brow from the daily communion, and still, though much spent
Be the life and the bearing that front you, the same God did choose
To receive what a man may waste, desecrate, never quite lose."—BROWNING: *Saul.*

And the evil spirit departed from him.—Many instances besides those recorded above (see note to verse 16) might be quoted of the beneficial effects of music and singing upon a disturbed spirit, or on a mind diseased. The holy Elisha, we are told, when "disturbed in spirit," would call for a minstrel, and after listening to the sweet, soothing strains, would write and speak his prophetic utterances.

In modern times a well-known instance of this strange power over a troubled spirit is that of Philip V. of Spain, who, we are told, was restored from the deepest melancholy and depression by the sweet voice and words of Farinelli. Luther speaks of this power of music over the sick and weary soul as "one of the fairest and most glorious gifts of God, to which Satan is a bitter enemy, for it removes from the heart the weight of sorrow and the fascination of evil thoughts." Basil's words on this subject are worth quoting:—"Psalmody is the calm of the soul, the repose of the spirit, the arbiter of peace. It silences the wave, and conciliates the whirlwind of our passions. It is an engenderer of friendship, a healer of dissension, a reconciler of enemies. It repels demons, lures the ministry of angels, shields us from nightly terrors, and refreshes us in daily toil."

XVII.

(1–58) The First Feat of Arms of David—the Encounter with the Philistine Giant.

(1) **Now the Philistines gathered together their armies to battle.**—There is nothing to tell us how long a time had elapsed since the victory of Saul over Amalek and the other events related in the last chapter. The compiler of the book is henceforth mainly concerned with the story of David, and how he gradually rose in popular estimation. The history does not profess to give anything like a consecutive account of the reign and wars of Saul. It was evidently compiled from documents of the time, but put into its present shape long afterwards. "Probably," writes Dean Payne Smith, "at each prophetic school there

Goliath Defies the   I. SAMUEL, XVII.   *Soldiers of Saul.*

listines. (3) And the Philistines stood on a mountain on the one side, and Israel stood on a mountain on the other side: and *there was* a valley between them.

(4) And there went out a champion out of the camp of the Philistines, named Goliath, of Gath, whose height *was* six cubits and a span. (5) And he had an helmet of brass upon his head, and he *was* ¹armed with a coat of mail; and the weight of the coat *was* five thousand shekels of brass. (6) And *he had* greaves of brass upon his legs, and a ²target of brass between his shoulders. (7) And the staff of his spear *was* like a weaver's beam; and his spear's head *weighed* six hundred shekels of iron: and one bearing a shield went before him. (8) And he stood and cried unto the armies of Israel, and said unto them, Why are ye come out to set *your* battle in array? *am* not I a Philistine, and ye servants to Saul? choose you a man for you, and let him come down to me. (9) If he be able to fight with me, and to kill me, then will we be your servants: but if I prevail against him, and kill him, then shall ye be our servants, and serve us. (10) And the Philistine said, I defy the armies of Israel this day; give me a man, that we may fight together. (11) When Saul and

¹ Heb., *clothed.*

² Or, *gorget.*

---

would be stored up copies of Psalms written for their religious services, ballads such as those in the Book of Jashar, and in the book of the wars of the Lord, narratives of stirring events like this before us, and histories both of their own chiefs, such as was Samuel (the original founder of these famous educational centres), and afterwards Elijah and Elisha, and also of their kings."

Pitched between Shochoh and Azekah.—The locality was some twelve or fifteen miles southwest of Jerusalem, and nine or ten from Bethlehem, the home of the family of Jesse. The name Ephes-dammim, the "boundary of blood," is suggestive, and tells of the constant border warfare which took place in this neighbourhood.

(3, 4) **And the Philistines stood . . . .**—Conder, in his *Tent Work in Palestine*, writing on the spot, gives us a vivid picture of the scene of the well-known encounter between David and the giant Philistine:—"We may picture to ourselves the two hosts covering the low rocky hills opposite to each other, and half hidden among the lentisk bushes. Between them was the rich expanse of the ripening barley, and the red banks of the torrent, with its white shingly bed. Behind all were the distant blue hill-walls of Judah, whence Saul had just come down. The mail-clad warrior advanced from the west through the low corn, with his mighty lance perhaps tufted with feathers, his brazen helmet shining in the sun. From the east a ruddy boy in his white shirt and sandals, armed with a goat's-hair sling, came down to the brook, and, according to the poetic fancy of the Rabbis, the pebbles were given voices, and cried, 'By us shalt thou overcome the giant!' The champion fell from an unseen cause, and the wild Philistines fled to the mouth of the valley, where Gath stood towering on its white chalk cliff, a frontier fortress, the key to the high road leading to the corn-lands of Judah and to the vineyards of Hebron.

Goliath, of Gath.—The Philistine champion belonged to a race or family of giants, the remnant of the sons of Anak (see Josh. xi. 22), who still dwelt in Gath and Gaza and Ashdod. The height mentioned was about nine feet two inches. We have in history a few instances of similar giants. This doughty champion was "full of savage insolence, unable to understand how any one could contend against his brute strength and impregnable panoply; the very type of the stupid 'Philistine,' such as has, in the language of modern Germany, not unfitly identified the name with the opponents of light and freedom and growth."—*Stanley.*

(5) **A coat of mail.**—More accurately, *breastplate of scales.* This armour has been sometimes understood as "chain armour," but it is more probable that the Philistine armour was made of metal scales, like those of a fish, whose defensive coat was, no doubt, imitated at a very early date by this warlike race, who dwelt on the sea-shore, and whose life and worship were so closely connected with the great sea. This coat of mail, or corselet, was flexible, and covered the back and sides of the wearer. The weight of the different pieces of the giant's panoply largely exceeds the weight of mediæval suits of armour.

(8) **Am not I a Philistine?**—The literal rendering here gives a far more forcible reading: *Am not I the Philistine?* the famous warrior whom you know too well? The Targum of Jonathan adds here the proud boast of the giant warrior that it was he who had slain Hophni and Phinehas (the sons of Eli, the high priest), and had carried the Ark to the temple of Dagon. This Targum, although comparatively a late compilation, doubtless embodied many ancient national traditions.

And ye servants to Saul.—Thus taunting the soldiers of Israel with the memory of the former glory of their king. Will none of the famous servants of the warrior king dare to meet me?

Must we not deem it probable that the fact of the separation of the prophet from the king had been made public in Philistia, and that the present daring challenge was owing to their knowledge that the Spirit of the Lord—whom we know these enemies of the Hebrews dreaded with so awful a dread—had departed from Saul and his armies?

(9) **Then will we be your servants.**—Each of the positions which the two opposing armies held was well-nigh impregnable; thus it seemed as though a single combat was the only way of deciding the present campaign: besides which, in those far back times such single combats between renowned chieftains of the opposing armies were not by any means uncommon. The reader of the *Iliad* will ever readily call to mind—in colloquies before the deadly duel—words not altogether unlike the haughty, boastful challenge of the giant Philistine. See, for instance, the speeches of Glaucus and Diomede in Book VI. of the *Iliad*: "Come hither," says Glaucus, "that you may quickly reach the goal of death."

(11) **They were dismayed, and greatly afraid.**—Saul the king, perhaps, was restrained from personally accepting the challenge by motives of dignity, but the

David Visits his Brothers I. SAMUEL, XVII. *in the Camp of Israel.*

all Israel heard those words of the Philistine, they were dismayed, and greatly afraid.

(12) Now David *was* ᵃthe son of that Ephrathite of Beth-lehem-judah, whose name *was* Jesse; and he had eight sons: and the man went among men *for* an old man in the days of Saul. (13) And the three eldest sons of Jesse went *and* followed Saul to the battle: and the names of his three sons that went to the battle *were* Eliab the firstborn, and next unto him Abinadab, and the third Shammah. (14) And David *was* the youngest: and the three eldest followed Saul. (15) But David went and returned from Saul to feed his father's sheep at Beth-lehem. (16) And the Philistine drew near morning and evening, and presented himself forty days.

(17) And Jesse said unto David his son, Take now for thy brethren an ephah of this parched *corn*, and these ten loaves, and run to the camp to thy brethren; (18) and carry these ten ¹cheeses unto the ²captain of *their* thousand, and look how thy brethren fare, and take their pledge.

(19) Now Saul, and they, and all the men of Israel, *were* in the valley of Elah,

ᵃ ch. 16. 1.

¹ Heb., cheeses of milk.

² Heb., captain of a thousand.

---

marked silence on his part, and the utter hopelessness of his army, reads in strange contrast to the former records of Hebrew daring. Where was Jonathan, for instance, ever the bravest of the brave, and his gallant armour-bearer? There had assuredly been a time when neither motives of dignity nor prudence would have restrained Saul and his warriors from accepting the challenge of the uncircumcised enemy. We notice, too, here there is no inquiry of the Urim and Thummim, no mention of prayer to the God of the armies of Israel. An evil spirit was indeed upon the King of Israel.

(12) **Now David was the son of that Ephrathite.**—This verse, and the following verses to the end of verse 31, are left out altogether, with verses 55—58, in the Vatican LXX. This omission was, no doubt, owing to the difficulty connected with this mention of David, where he is apparently introduced for the first time into the history; the LXX. translation not unfrequently adding or subtracting from the text when anything met them which they could not readily understand. The passage, as we find it, is undoubtedly genuine; the probable explanation of what puzzled the LXX. is given below.

It is, however, better (with the Syriac Version) to place all the words after "Beth-lehem-judah" down to the end of verse 14 in a parenthesis. Verse 15, after the parenthesis descriptive of Jesse and his three elder sons, takes up the account of David again, thus: "But David went," &c.

Went among men for an old man.—This rendering follows the translation of Jerome's Vulgate, "Senex et grandævus inter viros," rather than the Hebrew. The literal translation of *ba-baănashim* would be *went among men*. It is best to assume that the verb *ba-* here is used elliptically for *ba-bayamin*, "was advanced in days," that is, "was an old man." Keil renders *baanashim* "among the weak," that is, "Jesse had come to be reckoned among the weak" (or the aged). Maurer and others believe the present Hebrew reading corrupt; the sense, however, is clear.

Jesse is represented in this parenthesis, descriptive of the father of David, for some reason known only to the compiler, as already an old man. Possibly this notice is inserted to explain the reason why the father of the future hero-king of Israel was not among the warriors of Saul.

(15) **Returned from Saul to feed his father's sheep.**—This short statement was, no doubt, introduced by the compiler of the First Book of Samuel to show that, in spite of this apparent introduction of David into the history for the first time in this chapter (see verse 12 and following verses), and the inquiry of King Saul from Abner respecting the young hero's father (see verses 55—58), he, the compiler, was perfectly aware that David had already visited the court of Saul in the capacity of a musician (see chap. xvi. 18—23). As has been already suggested, these historical books of the Old Testament are, no doubt, made up from contemporaneous documents, stored up most probably in one or other of the prophetic schools. It is, therefore, to be expected that certain facts will be found occasionally repeated. The circumstances connected with the healing influence of the music of David in the case of the *soul malady* of King Saul were of course preserved with great care and detail in these "schools," where music and poetry were so highly cultivated and esteemed. We have here many of the very words of the original narrative preserved to us. Similarly the story of the first exploit of David is incorporated in the history probably unchanged. Each of these ancient and favourite "memories" of David, as being complete in themselves, would of course contain some of the same details.

The apparent ignorance of Saul and Abner respecting the young shepherd's family will be discussed in the note on verses 55—58.

(16) **And presented himself forty days.**—Wordsworth, following Augustine, sees here a reference to the temptation of the true David, who "was in the wilderness *forty days*, tempted of the devil." "In David is Christ . . . . do not, therefore, read this history of David as if it did not concern you who are members of Christ." (Aug. in Ps. cxliii.)

(18) **Look how thy brethren fare.**—The same learned commentator (Wordsworth), following out this curious line of Patristic interpretation, remarks on these words: "David is sent by his father to his brethren from Bethlehem. So the Divine David, Jesus Christ, who was born at Bethlehem, was sent to His brethren by his Heavenly Father." He completes the analogy between David and Christ by pointing out how David was ill-received by his brethren, though he came at his father's bidding to show them an act of kindness; so Christ, when sent by His Father from heaven on an embassy of love, was ill-received by His own brethren, the Jews. "He came unto His own, and His own received Him not" (John i. 11).

(19) **In the valley of Elah, fighting with the Philistines.**—The words of this verse, which read in

David Hears the Defiant Words   I. SAMUEL, XVII.   *of Goliath the Philistine.*

fighting with the Philistines. ⁽²⁰⁾ And David rose up early in the morning, and left the sheep with a keeper, and took, and went, as Jesse had commanded him; and he came to the ¹trench, as the host was going forth to the ²fight, and shouted for the battle. ⁽²¹⁾ For Israel and the Philistines had put the battle in array, army against army. ⁽²²⁾ And David left ³his carriage in the hand of the keeper of the carriage, and ran into the army, and came and ⁴saluted his brethren. ⁽²³⁾ And as he talked with them, behold, there came up the champion, the Philistine of Gath, Goliath by name, out of the armies of the Philistines, and spake according to the same words: and David heard *them*. ⁽²⁴⁾ And all the men of Israel, when they saw the man, fled ⁵from him, and were sore afraid.

⁽²⁵⁾ And the men of Israel said, Have ye seen this man that is come up? surely to defy Israel is he come up: and it shall be, *that* the man who killeth him, the king will enrich him with great riches, and *a*will give him his daughter, and make his father's house free in Israel.

⁽²⁶⁾ And David spake to the men that stood by him, saying, What shall be done to the man that killeth this Philistine, and taketh away the reproach from Israel? for who *is* this uncircumcised Philistine, that he should defy the armies of the living God? ⁽²⁷⁾ And the people answered him after this manner, saying, So shall it be done to the man that killeth him.

⁽²⁸⁾ And Eliab his eldest brother heard when he spake unto the men; and Eliab's anger was kindled against David, and he

---

1 Or, *place of the carriage.*

2 Or, *battle array,* or, *place of fight.*

3 Heb., *the vessels from upon him.*

4 Heb., *asked his brethren of peace.*

5 Heb., *from his face.*

a Josh. 15. 16.

---

the English Version as an explanatory parenthesis, are really part of Jesse's direction to his shepherd son, telling him where he would find his brethren. "They are in the valley of the Terebinth (Elah), fighting with the Philistines."

⁽²⁰⁾ **He came to the trench.**—Literally, *to the wagon rampart;* a circle of wagons formed a rude fortification about the camp of Israel. There—that is, within the fortified enclosure—he left (verse 22) his baggage, the ten cheeses, &c., and hastened to the "front," where he knew his brethren and the men of Judah would be posted. (See Num. x. 14.)

⁽²²⁾ **And David left his carriage.**—That is, his baggage. The word "carriage," as signifying baggage, is used in the English Version in this archaic sense in Isaiah x. 28: "At Michmash he hath laid up his carriages;" and in Acts xxi. 15: "We took up our carriages."

⁽²³⁾ **The Philistine of Gath.**—There is a difficulty connected with the Philistine giant's name, for we read in 2 Sam. xxi. 19 how that Goliath of Gath, the giant, "the staff of whose spear *was* like a weaver's beam," was slain by Elhanan, the son of Jaare-oregim, a Bethlehemite, after David had been made king. It is possible that Goliath was a general designation of these monstrous descendants of the ancient Anakim in Gath; but Ewald suggests that the name Goliath really only belongs to the giant slain by Elhanan, some years after the exploit of the youthful son of Jesse, and that it was transferred in error to the "champion" whom David slew (who is, moreover, generally called simply "the Philistine") when his proper name had been lost.

⁽²⁴⁾ **Fled from him, and were sore afraid.**—The student of the history can hardly understand this great fear of a giant Philistine which seems to have come upon the warriors of Saul. When we remember the gallant deeds of the people in former years, it reads like a page out of the story of another race. A dull, cowardly torpor had come over Saul, the punishment for his self-will and disobedience, and the king's helpless lethargy had settled now on the hearts of the soldiers he had trained so well in his earlier and nobler days.

⁽²⁵⁾ **And make his father's house free in Israel.**—Among the lavish offers Saul made to the one who should vanquish the giant was this, "The family of the successful combatant should be free in Israel." The exact signification here of the Hebrew word rendered "free" is disputed. The simple meaning would seem to be freedom from personal service in the army and elsewhere, what in mediæval history is known by the general term *Corvée.* It also probably includes a certain exemption from taxation or enforced contributions to war expenses.

Ewald goes still further, and considers that the royal promise included the elevation of the house of the victorious warrior to noble rank, as henceforth they would be ":free"—"freeholders," a family released from the ordinary service of subjects; and this high distinction, the great German scholar considers, would easily come to be looked upon as hereditary, and thus such favoured houses would form an intermediate stage between the king and the simple subject. Although it is clear that a wonderful advance in the internal development of the kingdom of the children of Israel had taken place in Saul's reign, yet it is doubtful if the government of the first king was as yet sufficiently organised to justify us in accepting, in its fulness, the conclusion of the ingenious comment of Ewald here. It does not appear from the narrative that these promises were ever fulfilled by Saul in the case of the house of Jesse.

⁽²⁶⁾ **And David spake . . .**—Very vividly does the historian here depict the scene that morning in the "front:" the dismayed soldiers of King Saul watching and listening to the boastful, impious words, as the giant champion shouted them across the narrow ravine which parted the outposts of the two armies; the enthusiastic shepherd boy, glowing with religious fervour, going from group to group of the advanced guard in the front, as they stood gloomily leaning on their spears, asking questions, and gleaning all the information possible about this insulter of his God.

⁽²⁸⁾ **And Eliab's anger was kindled against David.**—There were probably many years between the ages of the eldest and youngest of these eight brothers,

said, Why camest thou down hither? and with whom hast thou left those few sheep in the wilderness? I know thy pride, and the naughtiness of thine heart; for thou art come down that thou mightest see the battle. (29) And David said, What have I now done? *Is there not a cause?* (30) And he turned from him toward another, and spake after the same ¹manner: and the people answered him again after the former manner. (31) And when the words were heard which David spake, they rehearsed *them* before Saul: and he ²sent for him. (32) And David said to Saul, Let no man's heart fail because of him; thy servant will go and fight with this Philistine. (33) And Saul said to David, Thou art not able to go against this Philistine to fight with him: for thou *art but* a youth, and he a man of war from his youth. (34) And David said unto Saul, Thy servant kept his father's sheep, and there came a lion, and a bear, and took a ³lamb out of the flock: (35) and I went out after him, and smote him, and delivered *it* out of his mouth: and when he arose against me, I caught *him* by his beard, and smote him, and slew him. (36) Thy servant slew both the lion and the bear: and this uncircumcised Philistine shall be as one of them, seeing he hath defied the armies of the living God. (37) David said moreover, The LORD that delivered me out of the paw of the lion, and out of the paw of the bear, he will deliver me out of the

1 Heb., *word.*

2 Heb., *took him.*

3 Or, *kid.*

---

and this jealous anger was, no doubt, no new thing in Eliab. The casual mention (verse 34) of the boy's prowess, when the lion and the bear attacked his father's flock, tells us that the boyhood and youth of David had been no ordinary one, and Eliab's jealous disposition had been, doubtless, often aroused. Probably, too, the envious elder brother well remembered the visit of the great seer to Bethlehem, and how Samuel had, for some mysterious, and as yet unknown, reason, anointed this young brother of his, and had chosen him to be his pupil and companion. Was he now come with power unknown to him (Eliab) to perform some startling deed of daring?

(29) **Is there not a cause?**—David answers his jealous and over-bearing elder brother with all gentleness and forbearance, but he does not cease to make his inquiries of the soldiers respecting the giant, nor does he refrain from loudly expressing his astonishment at such a public insult to the God of Israel being allowed to continue for so many days. The Hebrew here would be more literally rendered, "Is it not a word," or "It was only a word," thus deprecating his elder brother's anger. "What have I done? It was but a mere word. I was only speaking with holy anger about this impious challenge of the Philistine; nothing more." The ancient versions thus understand this clause.

If we render as the Authorised Version, then the sense is quite clear. "You seem bitterly displeased with my zeal in this matter, but surely, is there not a good cause for my passionate emotion here—such an insult to our God?"

(31) **He sent for him.**—No doubt much more was said by the brave shepherd boy than the compiler of the history has preserved for us in the brief account here. David felt that supernatural strength had been communicated to him by the Spirit of God, which came upon him on the day of his anointing (chap. xvi. 13), and it is probable that he had openly avowed his earnest desire of meeting the dreaded foe face to face. This had been reported to Saul.

(33) **And Saul said to David . . .**—The king evidently looked on the brave boy with love and admiration, but at first doubted in his heart the reality of David's mission. Whether or not Saul recognised the youth as the sweet singer who had charmed away, perhaps more than once, that terrible soul malady of his which was desolating his once vigorous manhood, is doubtful. (See the Note at the end of this chapter.) He—more than any one in that armed camp—evidently felt that David possessed powers not usually bestowed on the sons of men, and was clearly disposed from the first to grant the shepherd boy's startling petition that the honour of Israel might be entrusted to his almost childhands. Still, Saul would talk with him, and set before him the grave perils of the terrible encounter he was so eager to engage in.

(34) **Thy servant kept his father's sheep.**—Here follows in the colloquy between the king and the boy that simple brave narrative which children listen to with glowing cheeks—that simple story, bearing the stamp of truth on every word—of what had happened to him in past days. Fierce wild animals, the terror of the Hebrew shepherds, had attacked his flock: these he had met and slain, almost without arms. *Another* had helped him when he did his brave duty *then*; and he felt that the same invisible Guardian would give him nerve and strength *now* in this more dangerous encounter. Only let him try. There was nothing to fear; he *must* succeed, he and his Divine Helper!

(36) **The lion and the bear.**—The lion and the bear were, in the days of Saul, common in Palestine; the country then was densely wooded. In some of the wilder districts bears are still numerous.

Shall be as one of them.—"He, the idolator, must know that he has not to do with mere men, but with God: with a living God will he have to do, and not with a lifeless idol."—*Berleburger Bible.*

(37) **Go, and the Lord be with thee.**—This permission and blessing of King Saul recalls the Saul of old days, before the covenant between him and the Mighty One of Israel was broken, before the Spirit of the Lord had departed from him. It was a great act of courageous trust in the Glorious Arm which had, Saul knew, so often fought for Israel. We must bear in mind that it was no mere duel between two fighting men, an Israelite and a Philistine, but that the fortunes of the nation for an indefinite period were to be staked on this momentous single combat between a tried warrior of gigantic strength and a boy quite unaccustomed to martial exercises, and, as we shall presently see, a stranger even to a soldier's dress and martial equipment.

hand of this Philistine. And Saul said unto David, Go, and the LORD be with thee.

(38) And Saul ¹armed David with his armour, and he put an helmet of brass upon his head; also he armed him with a coat of mail. (39) And David girded his sword upon his armour, and he assayed to go; for he had not proved *it*. And David said unto Saul, I cannot go with these; for I have not proved *them*. And David put them off him. (40) And he took his staff in his hand, and chose him five smooth stones out of the ²brook, and put them in a shepherd's ³bag which he had, even in a scrip; and his sling *was* in his hand: and he drew near to the Philistine. (41) And the Philistine came on and drew near unto David; and the man that bare the shield *went* before him.

(42) And when the Philistine looked about, and saw David, he disdained him: for he was *but* a youth, and ruddy, and of a fair countenance. (43) And the Philistine said unto David, Am I a dog, that thou comest to me with staves? And the Philistine cursed David by his gods. (44) And the Philistine said to David, Come to me, and I will give thy flesh unto the fowls of the air, and to the beasts of the field. (45) Then said David to the Philistine, Thou comest to me with a sword, and with a spear, and with a shield: but I come to thee in the name of the LORD of hosts, the God of the armies of Israel, whom thou hast defied. (46) This day will the LORD ⁴deliver thee into mine hand; and I will smite thee, and take thine head from thee; and I will give the carcases of the host of the Philistines this day unto the fowls of the air, and to the wild beasts of the earth; that all

¹ Heb., *clothed David with his clothes.*
² Or, *valley.*
³ Heb., *vessel.*
⁴ Heb., *shut thee up.*

---

(38) **And Saul armed David with his armour.**—But the king was determined to omit no earthly means of securing victory to his young champion, and we read how he made him try on his own various pieces of fighting array, doubtless the best-tempered and costliest that the camp of Israel possessed. The word rendered "his armour" literally signifies *his garments*, that is, the dress worn beneath the mail. Upon this was buckled on the heavy metal armour suit, with the great fighting sword and the royal helm. It is not necessary to suppose David was at all of the same proportions as Saul, for much of the dress could have been speedily adjusted to the requirements of one slighter and shorter than the king; besides, the result shows they were, in spite of alteration, far too heavy and cumbersome. "I cannot go with these," simply said the brave boy, his purpose, however, of meeting the Philistine giant quite unshaken, though he found his comparatively weak person unable to bear the weight of the king's panoply or to wield his arms.

(40) **And he took his staff in his hand.**—It was a true stroke of military genius in David, this determination of his to fight only with the weapons, weak and unimportant though they seemed, with which he was familiar, and in the use of which he was so skilful; nor was the issue of the combat, now he had resolved to use the sling, even doubtful. It has been well said he was like one armed with a rifle, while his enemy had only a spear and a sword, and if only he could take sure aim the result was absolutely certain.

Wordsworth, again, on the words "chose him five smooth stones out of the brook," refers to Augustine's Commentary, who finds here a deep mystical signification. It is an admirable specimen of the Patristic School of Exposition, which, although quaint, and not unfrequently "far-fetched," will always, and with good reason, possess great power over the minds of the earnest and devout student. "So our Divine David, the Good Shepherd of Bethlehem, when He went forth at the temptation to meet Satan—our ghostly Goliath—chose *five stones* out of the brook. He took the five books of Moses out of the flowing stream of Judaism. He took what was solid out of what was fluid. He took what was permanent out of what was transitory. He took what was moral and perpetual out of what was ceremonial and temporary. He took stones out of a brook, and with one of these He overthrew Satan. All Christ's answers to the tempter are *moral* precepts, taken from *one* Book of the Law (Deuteronomy), and He prefaced His replies with the same words, '*It is written;*' and with this sling and stone of Scripture He laid our Goliath low, and He has taught us by His example how we may also vanquish the tempter." (See St. Augustine, Sermon xxxii.)

(43) **Am I a dog?**—The Philistine warrior—as the shepherd boy, all unarmed, drew near—rose apparently, for he was seated, as was often the custom with these heavily-clad warriors of antiquity when not actually engaged in combat, and coming towards David, taunted him and his cause with the most contemptuous expressions. "Am I a dog," he asked—and dogs are animals held in many parts of the East in great contempt—"that you come against me with sticks and staves?" The LXX. missed the force of this plural "of contempt," and altering the text, translates " with staff and with stones."

By his gods.—This should be rendered *by his God*. No doubt the idolator here made use of the sacred Name, so dear to every believing Israelite, thus defying the Eternal of Hosts.

(44) **Come to me.**—In similar terms Hector addresses Ajax—

"And thou imperious! if thy madness wait
The lance of Hector, thou shalt meet thy fate.
That giant corse, extended on the shore,
Shall largely feed the fowls with fat and gore."—
Iliad, xiii. 1053.

(46) **I will smite thee.**—David reiterated to the Philistine, as he had done to Saul, his certainty of victory, but in the same breath says that the victory will be that God's whose name the Philistine had just been contemptuously using.

the earth may know that there is a God in Israel. (47) And all this assembly shall know that the LORD saveth not with sword and spear: for the battle *is* the LORD's, and he will give you into our hands.

(48) And it came to pass, when the Philistine arose, and came and drew nigh to meet David, that David hasted, and ran toward the army to meet the Philistine. (49) And David put his hand in his bag, and took thence a stone, and slang *it*, and smote the Philistine in his forehead, that the stone sunk into his forehead; and he fell upon his face to the earth. (50) So *a* David prevailed over the Philistine with a sling and with a stone, and smote the Philistine, and slew him; but *there was* no sword in the hand of David. (51) Therefore David ran, and stood upon the Philistine, and took his sword, and drew it out of the sheath thereof, and slew him, and cut off his head therewith.

And when the Philistines saw their champion was dead, they fled. (52) And the men of Israel and of Judah arose, and shouted, and pursued the Philistines, until thou come to the valley, and to the gates of Ekron. And the wounded of the Philistines fell down by the way to Shaaraim, even unto Gath, and unto Ekron. (53) And the children of Israel returned from chasing after the Philistines, and they spoiled their tents. (54) And David took the head of the Philistine, and brought it to Jerusalem; but he put his armour in his tent.

a Ecclus. 47. 4; 1 Mac. 4. 30.

---

(47) **For the battle is the Lord's** . . .—Although we possess no special ode or psalm composed by David on the occasion of this mortal combat, in which, owing to his sure trust in Jehovah, he won his never-to-be-forgotten victory, yet in many of the compositions attributed to him in the Psalter we find memories of this, his first great triumph. So in Ps. xliv. 6—8 we read—

"I will not trust in my bow,
Neither shall my sword save me.
In God we boast all the day long,
And praise thy Name for ever."

And in Ps. xxxiii. 16—20,

"There is no king saved by the multitude of an host,
A mighty man is not delivered by much strength."
. . . . .
"Our soul waiteth for the Lord,
He is our help and our shield."

(49) **And smote the Philistine in the forehead.**—The LXX. add the words "through the helm." The Greek translators could not understand the fact of the forehead being unprotected. But the head-pieces of the armour then do not appear to have possessed "visors;" the face was covered with the heavy shield, which was borne, we are told (verse 7), before him. No doubt the Philistine, utterly despising his youthful "unarmed" antagonist, advanced towards him without using, as was customary, the face protection of the shield.

Slinging stones had been brought among the Israelites to an extraordinary perfection. Many years before this time we read that in the tribe of Benjamin were "700 chosen men left-handed; every one could sling stones at an hair's *breadth*, and not miss" (Judges xx. 16).

A work by W. Vischer, on "Ancient Slings" (Basel, 1866), quoted by Lange, speaks of slingers who could hit the part of the enemy's face at which they aimed.

(50) **But there was no sword in the hand of David.**—The story of the daring of the son of Jesse dwells, and with good reason, on the extraordinary valour and skill of the young champion of Israel. Had his heart for one instant failed him—as, indeed, it well might; had he not possessed a confidence which nothing could shake in an unseen Helper—or had his skill as a marksman failed him in the slightest degree, the Philistine with one blow would have laid David lifeless at his feet; or had the active shepherd boy eluded his giant antagonist, it must have been by flight. In any case, the single combat upon which Israel had staked so much would have gone against the chosen people.

(51) **And when the Philistines saw their champion was dead, they fled.**—The Philistines had agreed to consider this single combat as decisive. *They* had no fears as to its result, and when they saw their boasted champion fall they were seized with a sudden panic. Their adversaries, the children of Israel, on the other hand, seeing the unarmed shepherd boy with the head of the great warrior who had so long defied them in his hand, felt that the old power had come back to them, and that once more their Invisible King was with them, so they at once, with an irresistible shout, charged their dismayed foes, and the battle, as far as the Philistines were concerned, became a total rout.

(52) **To the valley.**—More accurately, *to a valley*; there is no article in the Hebrew. This want of the article at once suggests that the "valley" here spoken of so indefinitely was not that well-known valley or ravine which divided the two armies; besides which, it is nowhere suggested that the Philistines had ever crossed *the* valley or ravine.

Keil remarks that it is strange that no further mention is made of this "valley" of the pursuit. The LXX. render, instead of "to a valley," "to Gath." These Greek translators probably then had before them the true text: *Gath*, instead of *gai*, a valley. *Gath* is mentioned in the next sentence.

The way to Shaaraim.—This was a town in the lowlands of Judah (see Joshua xv. 36); the name has probably been preserved in the modern Kefr Zakariya. The LXX., however, do not understand Shaaraim as a city at all, but render, instead of "by the way to Shaaraim," "in the way of the gates." The "gates" of Ekron are mentioned as one of the notable places of the flight in the preceding sentence.

If the LXX. interpretation be adopted, we must understand by this expression the space between the outer and the inner gates of Ekron.

(54) **The head of the Philistine.**—There is no real difficulty here, for although the fortress of Jebus,

(55) And when Saul saw David go forth against the Philistine, he said unto Abner, the captain of the host, Abner, whose son *is* this youth? And Abner said, *As* thy soul liveth, O king, I cannot tell. (56) And the king said, Enquire thou whose son the stripling *is*. (57) And as David returned from the slaughter of the Philistine, Abner took him, and brought him before Saul with the head of the Philistine in his hand. (58) And Saul said to him, Whose son *art* thou, *thou* young man? And David answered, *I am* the son of thy servant Jesse the Bethlehemite.

---

on Mount Zion, was in the hands of the Jebusites, and continued to be so until David captured the stronghold, many years later, the city of Jerusalem already belonged to the Israelites. (See Josh. xv. 63; Judges i. 21.) This "place of arms" was naturally selected for the home of the famous trophy, being the nearest stronghold to the scene of the victory.

But he put his armour in his tent.—*Ohel*, the Hebrew word rendered here "tent," is the ancient word for "dwelling." If we understand that David kept for the present the armour of his mighty adversary, we must suppose he took it to his dwelling at Bethlehem, and after a time presented it to the sanctuary at Nob. In chapter xxi. 9 we read of the "sword of Goliath wrapped in a cloth behind the ephod." Abarbanel, however, with great probability, believes that by the expression "in his tent" the "tabernacle of Jehovah" is meant—"*His* tabernacle," so termed pointedly by the compiler of the history, because David, in later days, with great ceremony, "pitched it" in his own city (2 Sam. vi. 17). In Acts xv. 16 the writer of this New Testament Book expressly calls the sacred tent "the Tabernacle of David."

(55) **Whose son is this youth?**—A grave difficulty, at first sight, indisputably exists here. It is briefly this. In the preceding chapter (verses 18—23), David, the son of Jesse, is chosen to play before the mentally sick king; his playing relieved the sufferer, who became attached to the young musician, and in consequence appointed him to a position about his person that certainly would have involved a lengthened, if not a continuous, residence at the court. In this and the following verses we read how this same David, at the time of his great exploit, was apparently unknown to the king and to Abner, the captain of the host. The LXX., fully conscious of the difficulty, determined to solve it by boldly, if not wisely, cutting the knot. They literally expunged from their version all the later passages which they could not easily bring into harmony with the earlier. The Greek Version, then, simply omits these four last verses of chap. xvii., together with the first five verses of chap. xviii., and the whole of the section chap. xvii. 12—31.

Various ingenious explanations have been suggested by scholars.

(a) The mental state of Saul when David played before him was such that the king failed to recognise him on the present occasion, and Abner probably had never seen him before.

(b) Some length of time had elapsed since his last visit to the court, and as he was then in very early manhood, he had, so to speak, grown, in a comparatively speaking short space of time, out of Saul's memory.

(c) The purpose of Saul's inquiry was *not* to find out who David was—that he knew well already—but to ascertain the position and general circumstances of the young hero's father, as, according to the promise (in verse 25), in the event of his success (which evidently the king confidently looked for), the father of the champion and his family would receive extraordinary honours.

The real solution of the difficulty probably lies in the fact that, as has been before stated, this and the other historical books of the Old Testament were made up by the inspired compiler from well-authenticated traditions current in Israel, and most probably preserved in the archives of the great prophetic schools. (See Notes on verses 1 and 15.) There were, no doubt, many of these traditions connected with the principal events of David's early career. Two here were selected which, to a certain extent, *covered the same ground*. The first—preserved, no doubt, in some prophetic school where music and poetry were especially cultivated—narrates the influence which David acquired over Saul through his great gift of music. The power of music and poetry in Saul's mental disease was evidently the great point of interest to the original writer of chap. xvi. 14—23. Now, in the narrative contained in these ten verses *no note of time* occurs. The events related evidently were spread over a considerable, possibly over a very long, period. The afflicted king might have seen the young musician perhaps in a darkened tent once or twice before the Goliath combat, but the great intimacy described in chap. xvi. 21—23, we may well assume, belonged to a period subsequent to the memorable combat with the giant.

Following out this hypothesis, we may with some confidence assume that King Saul failed entirely to recognise the young player whom he had only seen (possibly only heard in his darkened tent) on one or two sad occasions; and Abner probably had never seen him.

As for the great love on the part of the king, and position of royal armour-bearer, these things we have little doubt came to David *after* the victory over the giant Philistine, and very likely indeed in consequence of it.

In the *later* of the two sections of the Goliath history, the compiler cared little for the musical detail; his work was to show that the foundation stone of David's brilliant and successful life was intense faith in the Jehovah of Israel, a perfect child-like trust in the power of the Invisible King.

In the *former* of the two sections the relater—no doubt in his day a famous teacher in some school of prophetic music—was only concerned to show the mighty influence of this Divine art upon the souls and the lives of men, as exemplified in the story of the early days of the sweet Psalmist-King of Israel.

The musical details connected with the early life of David, the composer of so many of the famous hymns sung in the Temple Service and also in the public gatherings of the people, would be—in the eyes of this writer—of the deepest interest to coming generations.

CHAPTER XVIII.—⁽¹⁾ And it came to pass, when he had made an end of speaking unto Saul, that the soul of Jonathan was knit with the soul of David, and Jonathan loved him as his own soul. ⁽²⁾ And Saul took him that day, and would let him go no more home to his father's house. ⁽³⁾ Then Jonathan and David made a covenant, because he loved him as his own soul. ⁽⁴⁾ And Jonathan stripped himself of the robe that *was* upon him, and gave it to David, and his garments, even to his sword, and to his bow, and to his girdle.

⁽⁵⁾ And David went out whithersoever Saul sent him, *and* ¹behaved himself

¹ Or, *prospered*.

XVIII.

(1–30) David with Saul. Jonathan and David. The Envy of Saul is excited by the People's praises of David. He Marries King Saul's daughter Michal.

⁽¹⁾ **The soul of Jonathan was knit with the soul of David.**—We have in this and the following chapters somewhat of a detailed account of David at the Court of Saul. In chap. xvi. this Court life of the future king has been already touched upon, notably in verses 21—23, where the affection of Saul for David was mentioned, where also the appointing of the young shepherd to a post about the king's person is recorded. But this mention in chap. xvi. considerably anticipated the course of events. In relating the results of this affection of Saul for David, the writer of what we may term the episode treating of the influence of music and poetry passed over, so to speak, the story of several years, in the course of which took place the single combat of David with the Philistine giant, and the victorious campaign in which the young hero took so distinguished a part. The history here takes up the thread of the future king's life, after the campaigns which immediately followed the discomfiture of the Philistine champion (verses 6 and following). Verses 1—4 simply relate the beginning of the world-famous friendship between Prince Jonathan and David.

The Hebrew is rendered "was knit," or better, *was bound up*. This is a strong term, and is used in Gen. xliv. 30 of Jacob's love to Benjamin : " seeing that his life is bound up in the lad's life." Aristotle, *Nicom.* ix. 8, has noted that friends are called one soul.

Jonathan loved him as his own soul.—As has been before remarked, the character of the princely son of Saul is one of the most beautiful in the Old Testament story. He was the type of a true warrior of those wild, half-barbarous times—among brave men seemingly the bravest—a perfect soldier, whether fighting as a simple man-at-arms or as the general of an army—chivalrous and generous—utterly free from jealousy—a fervid believer in the God of Israel—a devoted and loyal son—a true patriot in the highest sense of the word, who sealed a devoted life by a noble death, dying as he did fighting for his king and his people. The long and steady friendship of Jonathan no doubt had a powerful and enduring influence on the after life of the greatest of the Hebrew sovereigns. The words, the unselfish, beautiful love, and, above all, the splendid example of the ill-fated son of Saul, have no doubt given their colouring to many of the noblest utterances in David's Psalms and to not a few of the most heroic deeds in David's life.

We read of this friendship as dating from the morrow of the first striking deed of arms performed by David when he slew the giant. It is clear, however, that it was not the personal bravery of the boy hero, or the rare skill he showed in the encounter, which so singularly attracted Prince Jonathan. These things no one would have admired and honoured more than the son of Saul, but it needed more than splendid gallantry and rare skill to attract that great love of which we read. What won Jonathan's heart was the shepherd boy's sublime faith, his perfect childlike trust in the "Glorious Arm" of the Lord. Jonathan and David possessed one thing in common—an intense, unswerving belief in the power of Jehovah of Israel to keep and to save all who trusted in Him.

The two were typical Israelites, both possessing in a very high degree that intense confidence in the Mighty One of Israel which was the mainspring of the people's glory and success, and which, in the seemingly interminable days of their punishment and degradation, has been the power which has kept them still together—a people distinct, reserved yet for some mighty destiny in the unknown future.

⁽³⁾ **Made a covenant.**—The son of the first Hebrew king recognised in David a kindred spirit. They were one in their God, in their faith, in their devotion to the Divine will. Jonathan recognised in the young shepherd, who unarmed went out alone to meet the mighty Philistine warrior, the same spirit of sublime faith in the Invisible King which had inspired him in days far back to go forth alone with his armour-bearer to attack and capture the Philistine stronghold, when he spoke those memorable words which enable us to understand the character of Jonathan: "It may be that the Lord will work for us: for there is no restraint to the Lord to save by many or by few" (chap. xiv. 6).

The great friendship, which has been the admiration of succeeding generations, began with the strong faith in the Eternal common to the two friends. Throughout its duration the link which united them was an intense desire to do the will of Him who, as true Hebrew patriots, they felt loved Israel; and when the friends parted for the last time in the wilderness of Ziph, we are told how the elder (Jonathan) strengthened the younger (David's) "hand in God" (chap. xxiii. 16).

⁽⁴⁾ **Gave it to David.**—It has been suggested that the reason of this gift was to enable his friend David—then poorly clad—to appear at his father's court in a fitting dress; but this kind of present was usual among friends in those remote ages. Glaucus and Diomed, for instance, exchanged armour of a very different value.

"Now change we arms, and prove to either host
We guard the friendship of the line we boast.
 * * * *
For Diomed's brass arms, of mean device,
For which nine oxen paid (a vulgar price),
He gave his own of gold, divinely wrought :
A hundred beeves the shining purchase bought."
Iliad, vi. 286–295.

⁽⁵⁾ **And he was accepted.**—The historian here calls especial attention to the strange power David was able to acquire over the hearts of men. It was not only over Saul and his great son that he rapidly won

King Saul's   I. SAMUEL, XVIII.   *Jealousy of David.*

wisely: and Saul set him over the men of war, and he was accepted in the sight of all the people, and also in the sight of Saul's servants.

(6) And it came to pass as they came, when David was returned from the slaughter of the [1]Philistine, that the women came out of all cities of Israel, singing and dancing, to meet king Saul, with tabrets, with joy, and with [2]instruments of musick. (7) And the women answered *one another* as they played, and said,

[a] Saul hath slain his thousands, and David his ten thousands.

(8) And Saul was very wroth, and the saying [3]displeased him; and he said, They have ascribed unto David ten thousands, and to me they have ascribed *but* thousands: and *what* can he have more but the kingdom? (9) And Saul eyed David from that day and forward.

(10) And it came to pass on the morrow, that the evil spirit from God came upon Saul, and he prophesied in the midst of the house: and David played with his

---

1 Or, *Philistines.*

2 Heb., *three stringed instruments.*

a ch. 21. 11 & 29. 5; Ecclus. 47. 6.

3 Heb., *was evil in his eyes.*

---

influence, but in the case of his colleagues at the Court and in the army, all of whom he was rapidly outstripping in the race for honour and distinction, he seems to have disarmed all jealousy. His rapid rise to high position was evidently looked upon with general favour. This is still farther enlarged upon in the next and following verses.

(6) **When David was returned.**—The triumphant return of the young soldier does not refer to the homecoming after the death of the giant, but to the close of the campaign which followed that event. Evidently a series of victories after the fall of the dreaded champion —perhaps spread over a very considerable period—had for a time restored the supremacy of Israel in Canaan. In this war, David, on whom after his great feat of arms the eyes of all the soldiery were fixed, established his character for bravery and skill.

Singing and dancing.—This was on some grand occasion—probably the final triumph at the end of the war. The *Speaker's Commentary*, on the English rendering "singing and dancing," remarks that "the Hebrew text is probably here corrupt, and suggests that for *vau*, 'and,' we ought to read *beth*, 'with,' and that then the sense would be to sing 'in the dance,' or 'with dancing.' The action was for the women to dance to the sound of the timbrel, and to sing the Epinicium with strophe and antistrophe as they danced and played." (Comp. Exod. xv. 20, 21; Judges xi. 34.)

We know that music and song were originally closely connected with dancing. David, for instance, when a mighty king, on one great occasion in Jerusalem actually himself performed dances before all the people (2 Sam. vi. 14, 16). (See Note on Exod. xv. 20.)

(7) **Saul hath slain his thousands, and David his ten thousands.**—These words, which sing of the early glory of David in battle, are quoted again in chap. xxix. 5. They were, no doubt, the favourite refrain of an old national or folk-song.

(8) **What can he have more but the kingdom?** —In this foreboding utterance of Saul there was involved not only a conjecture which the result confirmed, but a deep inward truth: if the king stood powerless before the subjugators of his kingdom at so decisive a period as this, and a shepherd boy came and decided the victory, this was an additional mark of his rejection.— V. Gerlach, quoted in *Keil*.

Some years had passed since he first heard from the lips of his old prophet-friend the Divine sentence of his rejection from the kingdom. In that sad period he had doubtless been on the look-out for the one destined by the Invisible King to be his successor. This dread expectation of ruin and dethronement had been a powerful factor in the causes which had led to the unhingement of Saul's mind. Was not this gifted shepherd boy—now the idol of the people—the future hope of Israel?

(9) **And Saul eyed David.**—From the hour on which the king listened to the people's lilt in honour of the young hero, in Saul's distempered mind hate alternated with love. He still in his heart longed for the presence of the only human being who could charm away his ever-increasing melancholia, but he dreaded with a fierce jealousy the growing influence of the winning and gifted man whom he had taken from the sheep-folds; and now through the rest of the records of this book we shall see how the hate gradually obscured the old love. All our memories of Saul seem bound up with his life-long murderous pursuit of David.

(10) **The evil spirit.**—The evil spirit comes now over the unhappy king in quite a new form. Hitherto, when the dark hour came upon Saul the madness showed itself in the form of a dull torpor, a hopeless melancholia, an entire indifference to everything connected with life, as well in the lower as in the higher forms. This earlier phase of the *soul's malady* has been exquisitely pictured by Browning in his poem of "Saul." Now the madness assumes a new phase, and the king is consumed with a murderous jealousy, that fills his whole soul, and drives him now to open deeds of ruffianly violence—now to devise dark plots against the life of the hated one. What a fall for the heroking of Israel, the anointed of the Lord, whose reign had begun so brilliantly and successfully!

And he prophesied.—In his wild phrenzy—under the control of a power higher than himself, had he not by his breaking off all communion with God, left his soul defenceless and prepared for the presence of the evil spirit?—in his wild phrenzy we read "Saul prophesied." The Dean of Canterbury well calls attention here to the conjugation employed in the original Hebrew of the word rendered "prophesied"—*the Hithpael*, which is never used by an Old Testament writer of real true prophecy, this being always expressed by the *Niphal* conjugation. This of Saul's was but a bastard imitation.

Saul was in a state of phrenzy, unable to master himself, speaking words of which he knew not the meaning, and acting like a man possessed. In all this there was something akin to the powerful emotions which agitated the true prophet: only it was not a holy influence, but one springing from violent passions.

hand, as at other times: and *there was* a javelin in Saul's hand. (11) And Saul cast the javelin; for he said, I will smite David even to the wall *with it*. And David avoided out of his presence twice.

(12) And Saul was afraid of David, because the LORD was with him, and was departed from Saul. (13) Therefore Saul removed him from him, and made him his captain over a thousand; and he went out and came in before the people. (14) And David ¹behaved himself wisely in all his ways; and the LORD *was* with him. (15) Wherefore when Saul saw that he behaved himself very wisely, he was afraid of him. (16) But all Israel and Judah loved David, because he went out and came in before them.

(17) And Saul said to David, Behold my elder daughter Merab, her will I give thee to wife: only be thou ²valiant for me, and fight the LORD's battles. For Saul said, Let not mine hand be upon him, but let the hand of the Philistines be upon him. (18) And David said unto Saul, Who *am* I? and what *is* my life, *or* my father's family in Israel, that I should be son in law to the king? (19) But it came to pass at the time when Merab Saul's daughter should have been given to David, that she was given unto Adriel the Meholathite to wife.

(20) And Michal Saul's daughter loved

1 Or, *prospered.*

2 Heb., *a son of valour.*

---

(11) **And Saul cast the javelin.**—The Alexandrian MS. of the LXX. and the Chaldee Version translate the Hebrew here "lifted the javelin." The probable meaning of the verb in this place is "brandished," or "aimed." It is hardly credible that if he actually threw it, David would have trusted himself a second time in the king's chamber.

(12) **And Saul was afraid of David.**—Even after the scenes in the royal chamber just related, David remained at Court. He looked on such manifestations of bitter hatred as simple outbursts of a temporary insanity. His loyal nature would not believe in the enduring hate of one so great and noble as Saul; but we read here that even when the king recovered from the paroxysm, he *feared* David. Saul was conscious that his old vigour and ability were deserting him, and in David he recognised the presence of a power he knew had once been his. Not being able, even in his sane hours, to endure the presence of one whom he too surely felt would sooner or later take his place, the king dismissed him honourably from the Court, and invested him with an important military charge. Perhaps already the dark thought which some time later (see verses 17 and 25) influenced the king had entered into his unhappy mind.

(16) **But all Israel and Judah.**—This distinct mention of the two great later divisions of the chosen people seems to point to the fact that the compiler of the Books of Samuel lived after the final separation of the ten tribes from Judah and Benjamin, in the reign of Rehoboam. It is, however, clear from other notices (see, for instance, chaps. xi. 8, xv. 4, in this book) that at a period long anterior to the final disruption between the north and south a marked distinction between the two had begun to exist.

In David's case, however, although he was of Judah, the future king was equally popular with the northern tribes.

(17) **Behold my elder daughter Merab, her will I give thee to wife.**—This was but the fulfilment of a much earlier promise. The king had said he would give his daughter in marriage to the hero who should slay the Philistine giant champion. For one cause or other he had declined, or at least postponed, the carrying out of his pledge; and the dark thought crossed his mind, Could he not endanger the hated life, while seeming to wish to keep the old promise? He speaks of the Philistine war as the Lord's battles. This was a feeling which inspired every patriotic Israelite. "He was," when fighting with the idolatrous nations, "warring for the Lord"—so David felt when he spoke of the Philistine giant as having defied the ranks of the living God, and alluded to the battle as the Lord's (chap. xvii. 26 and 47). The same idea is expressed in the title of that most ancient collection of songs which has not been preserved to us—"Book of the Wars of the Lord" (Numbers xxi. 14).

(18) **What is my life?**—These words in David's modest and wise answer have been variously interpreted. (*a*) They have been taken to refer to David's personal life; but surely *that* has been alluded to in the preceding words, "Who am I?" (*b*) As referring to the condition of life in which he was born and to which he was accustomed; so Keil; but it is doubtful if the Hebrew word here used ever has this significance. (*c*) With a reference to David's family; so Ewald and Lange. Ewald would translate, "What are my folks or relations?" Of these (*c*) is undoubtedly the preferable meaning.

(19) **She was given unto Adriel.**—Saul's capricious wavering nature, so painfully prominent in the last part of his reign, displayed itself in this sudden change of purpose. It may have been brought about owing to some great fit of jealousy of David; or possibly the large gifts in money or valuables offered by the wealthy Adriel for the princess's hand may have occasioned this arbitrary act of Saul. Such gifts to the father in return for the daughter's hand were customary. In the case of such a prize as the Princess Merab, the gift would doubtless have been very costly. David, who was comparatively a poor man, was of course unable to show such liberality; besides, the young hero looked, no doubt, upon the marriage as the fulfilment of the old promise to the victor in the combat with the giant. The marriage, however, of the daughter of King Saul and Adriel was consummated, and was disastrous in its consequences. They had five sons, and they fell victims to the blood revenge exacted by the Gibeonites from the family of Saul: the five hapless youths were "hanged" (we read in 2 Sam. xxi. 9) "in the hill before the Lord." These three verses (17—19) are entirely omitted by the LXX., apparently because they failed to see any reason for Saul's sudden change of purpose.

(20) **And Michal Saul's daughter loved David.**—But the love of the younger of the two royal

David: and they told Saul, and the thing ¹pleased him. ⁽²¹⁾ And Saul said, I will give him her, that she may be a snare to him, and that the hand of the Philistines may be against him. Wherefore Saul said to David, Thou shalt this day be my son in law in *the one of* the twain.

⁽²²⁾ And Saul commanded his servants, *saying*, Commune with David secretly, and say, Behold, the king hath delight in thee, and all his servants love thee: now therefore be the king's son in law. ⁽²³⁾And Saul's servants spake those words in the ears of David. And David said, Seemeth it to you *a* light *thing* to be a king's son in law, seeing that I *am* a poor man, and lightly esteemed? ⁽²⁴⁾And the servants of Saul told him, saying, ²On this manner spake David. ⁽²⁵⁾ And Saul said, Thus shall ye say to David, The king desireth not any dowry, but an hundred foreskins of the Philistines, to be avenged of the king's enemies. But Saul thought to make David fall by the hand of the Philistines. ⁽²⁶⁾ And when his servants told David these words, it pleased David well to be the king's son in law: and the days were not ³expired. ⁽²⁷⁾ Wherefore David arose and went, he and his men, and slew of the Philistines two hundred men; and David brought their foreskins, and they gave them in full tale to the king, that he might be the king's son in law. And Saul gave him Michal his daughter to wife.

⁽²⁸⁾ And Saul saw and knew that the LORD *was* with David, and *that* Michal Saul's daughter loved him. ⁽²⁹⁾And Saul was yet the more afraid of David; and Saul became David's enemy continually. ⁽³⁰⁾ Then the princes of the Philistines went forth: and it came to pass, after they went forth, *that* David behaved himself more wisely than all the servants of Saul; so that his name was much ⁴set by.

CHAPTER XIX.—⁽¹⁾ And Saul spake to Jonathan his son, and to all his ser-

---

1 Heb., *was right in his eyes.*

2 Heb., *According to these words.*

3 Heb., *fulfilled.*

4 Heb., *precious.*

---

princesses for her father's brilliant officer gave the unhappy king a fresh excuse to expose David's life to peril, while at the same time he appeared to be endeavouring to carry out an old formal promise.

(21) **That she may be a snare to him.**—Is it not possible that this dark plot of Saul against a life once so dear to him—a plot which in after days, when the enmity of the king was a matter of general notoriety, became of course known by David—suggested to him (David) the means by which, in the darkest hours of his life, he got rid of the brave Uriah, the husband of Bath-sheba, at the siege of Rabbah? (2 Sam. xi.)

In the one of the twain.—More accurately translated, *in this second time*, or *in this second way*. The LXX. again leaves out this statement, no doubt because it refers back to the omitted passage in verses 17—19.

(22) **Behold, the king hath delight in thee.**—Lange quaintly sees in this fluent discourse of the courtiers "something of the flattering, conciliatory tone usual in such circles."

(23) **I am a poor man.**—David dwells upon this fact of his utter inability to give the expected costly offering for the princess. He evidently attributes to his poverty and his successful rival's wealth his former disappointment in the case of Merab.

And lightly esteemed.—David looked upon himself as a mere successful soldier of fortune among the wealthy chiefs who surrounded Saul. His father—though, no doubt, "head man" or sheik in tiny Bethlehem—was, compared with the elders of Israel who formed the Court of Saul, a poor man.

(25) **An hundred foreskins.**—Wordsworth's note here, which he derives from Theodoret, is curious. *Foreskins!* why not *heads?* Here is a sign of Saul's suspicious and malignant spirit. He, judging for himself, impiously suspects that David would go forth and destroy some of the *Israelites*—Saul's own subjects—as he himself desired to destroy David, his own deliverer; and the foreskins were required as a proof that they who were killed were *not Israelites*. Josephus, however, with a strange exaggeration, mentions 600 heads as the price of Michal.

(26) **It pleased David well.**—The king's design succeeded well, and the prospect of the alliance with Saul spurred on this brave soldier to more daring achievements, and yet wilder feats of arms. The savage, half-barbarous state of the age, however, comes prominently into view when we reflect upon the ferocious cruelty of such an offer being made and accepted, and carried out with even more than the required number of victims.

(28) **Saul saw . . . that the Lord was with David.**—The success of the last savage enterprise, and the return of David with his ghastly spoils, filled the unhappy king with dismay. His daughter's love, too, for the rising soldier contributed to his trouble. Saul felt that all that David undertook prospered—that surely another and a higher Power was helping him. So his fear grew, we read in verse 29, and the paroxysms of jealous hatred deepened into a lifelong enmity.

(30) **Went forth.**—Probably to avenge the last raid of David (recounted in verse 27). Wordsworth, quoting from the Rabbis, suggests that they were emboldened to make this attack, supposing that their successful foe would, according to the Hebrew Law, claim exemption from warfare for a year after marriage (Deut. xxiv. 5).

XIX.

(1—24) The Hatred of Saul for David. The Love of Jonathan and Michal saves David's Life. David Escapes to Samuel. The Influence of the Prophetic Schools on (1) Saul's Men; (2) on Saul himself.

(1) **That they should kill David.**—The literal translation of the original gives a much better sense:

vants, that they should kill David. ⁽²⁾ But Jonathan Saul's son delighted much in David: and Jonathan told David, saying, Saul my father seeketh to kill thee: now therefore, I pray thee, take heed to thyself until the morning, and abide in a secret *place*, and hide thyself: ⁽³⁾ and I will go out and stand beside my father in the field where thou *art*, and I will commune with my father of thee; and what I see, that I will tell thee. ⁽⁴⁾ And Jonathan spake good of David unto Saul his father, and said unto him, Let not the king sin against his servant, against David; because he hath not sinned against thee, and because his works *have been* to thee-ward very good: ⁽⁵⁾ for he did put his ᵃlife in his hand, and slew the Philistine, and the LORD wrought a great salvation for all Israel: thou sawest *it*, and didst rejoice: wherefore then wilt thou sin against innocent blood, to slay David without a cause? ⁽⁶⁾ And Saul hearkened unto the voice of Jonathan: and Saul sware, *As* the LORD liveth, he shall not be slain. ⁽⁷⁾ And Jonathan called David, and Jonathan shewed him all those things. And Jonathan brought David to Saul, and he was in his presence, as ¹in times past.

⁽⁸⁾ And there was war again: and David went out, and fought with the Philistines, and slew them with a great slaughter; and they fled from ²him.

⁽⁹⁾ And the evil spirit from the LORD was upon Saul, as he sat in his house

a Judg. 9. 17 & 12. 3; ch. 28. 21; Ps. 119. 109.

¹ Heb., *yesterday third day*.

B.C. cir. 1062.

² Heb., *his face*.

"that he intended to kill David," or "about killing David." The latter is the rendering of the LXX. and the Syriac. The murderous impulse of the unhappy Saul gradually increased in intensity. First, it showed itself only in the paroxysms of insanity, when the half-distraught king would grasp and poise his heavy spear, as though he would hurl it at the kindly musician as he tried to calm the troubled spirit. Then it would plot and scheme against the hated life, trying to involve this young soldier in some enterprise fraught with deadly peril. Now he speaks openly to his heir and his counsellors of the risk incurred by suffering so dangerous a man to live.

⁽²⁾ **Jonathan told David.**—The danger Jonathan saw was a very present one. A very slight expression on the part of a powerful king of his earnest desire to get rid of an obnoxious subject, however eminent or great, is sufficient to stir up unscrupulous men to commit the murder which they might fancy would be acceptable to their master.

⁽³⁾ **In the field.**—No doubt some garden or quiet place, whither the king was in the habit of resorting with his friends and counsellors.

⁽⁴⁾ **Jonathan spake good of David.**—The heir to the throne—the one above all men likely to be injured by the growing popularity of David—with great power and intense earnestness, represented to his father the king the great virtues, the unrivalled gifts, and, above all, the splendid services of the young soldier whose life Saul was so anxious to cut short. "See,' urged the eloquent pleader for his friend's life, "on that ever memorable occasion when he fought the giant, when he aimed the pebble of the brook from his shepherd's sling, he put his life in his hand. Had he missed a hair's-breadth, the giant would have slain him, and the deliverance then wrought for Israel would never have been accomplished."

⁽⁶⁾ **And Saul hearkened.**—The moving eloquence of Jonathan touched Saul's heart, and for a brief space something of the old noble spirit influenced the king, and he swore he would not attempt his life.

⁽⁷⁾ **As in times past.**—The old life went on as before, and David seemingly was received on terms of intimacy and affection by the king, but a new cause was soon supplied which again lit up the slumbering fires of jealousy in the king's heart. The next verse tells us of a successful campaign against the hereditary foes of Israel, in which, as usual, David was the hero.

⁽⁹⁾ **And the evil spirit . . . was upon Saul.**—Again the terrible malady was upon the king—not unlikely brought on by the wild storm of jealous fury which Saul allowed to sweep unchecked across his soul. Once more—

" Out of the black mid-tent's silence, a space of three days,
Not a sound hath escaped to thy servants of prayer nor of praise,
To betoken that Saul and the spirit have ended their strife,
And that, faint in his triumph, the monarch sinks back upon life."
                                                    BROWNING: *Saul*.

But the time when the skilled musician with his Divine strains had roused him into life again was passed (see chap. xvi. 21—23), not now as in old days, when, to use the words the great poet put into David's mouth—

" ———— I looked up to know
If the best I could do had brought solace: he spoke not, but slow
Lifted up the hand slack at his side, till he laid it with care,
Soft and grave, but in mild settled will, on my brow; through my hair
The large fingers were pushed, and he bent back my head, with kind power—
All my face back, intent to peruse it as men do a flower.
Thus held he me there, with his great eye that scrutinized mine,
And oh, all my heart how it loved him! . . . ."
                                                    BROWNING: *Saul*.

This time, seizing the tall spear which was ever by his side, he hurled it with deadly intent at the sorrow-stricken, loving face, and David fled in hot haste from the doomed presence for ever. The LXX. was offended at the statement "evil spirit of (or from) Jehovah," and cuts the knot by leaving out "Jehovah." It is, no doubt, a hard saying, and no human expositor has ever yet been able fully to explain it.

To the expression *Ruach Jehovah*, "Spirit of Jehovah" (for "of" is more accurate than "from"), and the equivalent phrase, *Ruach Elohim*, "Spirit of God" (chap. xvi. 14, 15), the epithet "evil" is added. We cannot attempt to fathom the mysteries of the spirit world—we have absolutely no data—we simply possess in the sacred book a few scattered notices, which indicate the existence of evil spirits. To suppose that these malignant or evil beings were part of the heavenly host *employed* by the Eternal is a supposition utterly at variance with our conception of the All-Father. We may, how-

Michal saves David from I. SAMUEL, XIX. *the Emissaries of Saul*

with his javelin in his hand: and David played with *his* hand. (10) And Saul sought to smite David even to the wall with the javelin; but he slipped away out of Saul's presence, and he smote the javelin into the wall: and David fled, and escaped that night.

(11) Saul also sent messengers unto David's house, to watch him, and to slay him in the morning: and Michal David's wife told him, saying, If thou save not thy life to night, to morrow thou shalt be slain. (12) So Michal let David down through a window: and he went, and fled, and escaped. (13) And Michal took an image, and laid *it* in the bed, and put a pillow of goats' hair for his bolster, and covered *it* with a cloth. (14) And when Saul sent messengers to take David, she said, He *is* sick. (15) And Saul sent the messengers *again* to see David, saying, Bring him up to me in the bed, that I may slay him. (16) And when the messengers were come in, behold, *there was* an image in the bed, with a pillow of goats' hair for his bolster. (17) And Saul said unto Michal, Why hast thou deceived me so, and sent away mine enemy, that he is escaped? And Michal answered Saul, He said unto me, Let me go; why should I kill thee?

(18) So David fled, and escaped, and came to Samuel to Ramah, and told him

---

ever, safely grant (1) the *existence* of evil spirits—probably beings fallen through sin and disobedience from their high estate; and (2) we may suppose that these evil spirits—all, of course, belonging to the Eternal, even in their deep degradation (so though " evil," still " spirits of God, or Jehovah,")—receive occasional permission, for some wise—though to us unknown—reasons, to tempt and plague for a season the souls of certain men.

The introduction to the Book of Job (Job i. 6, ii. 1—7), and the circumstance which led to the death of King Ahab before Ramoth Gilead (1 Kings xxii. 19—22), at least favour this hypothesis. The presence of those evil spirits, or "devils," who possessed those unhappy ones whom we meet so often in the Gospel story, points to the same conclusion. Why certain souls should have been exposed to this dread experience is, of course, beyond our ken. From the scanty information vouchsafed to us, it seems, however, that the power of the evil spirit was sometimes permitted to be exercised (*a*) as a trial of faith, as in the case of Job; or (*b*) as a punishment incurred by the soul's desertion of God, as in the case of Saul.

(10) **The javelin.**—This is the great spear, which in so many of the scenes in the First Book of Samuel is represented as in the hand of Saul or by his side.

(12) **So Michal let David down.**—The princess, his wife, knew well her father's character, and conscious, now that the veil of his dark design was publicly lifted, that there was no hope for her husband any longer save in his instant flight, she "let David down through a window," because the king's guards were watching the door. With this desperate flight began those long weary wanderings, those perpetual risks of his life, which went on until the death of King Saul released David from his deadly enemy.

(13) **An image.**—An image in the Hebrew is *teraphim*—a plural form, but used as a singular. We have no instance of the singular. The Latin equivalent, "penates," singularly enough, is also only found in the plural form. In this case, probably, it was a life-size figure or bust. The word has been discussed above (chap. xv. 23). It is singular how, in spite of the stern command to avoid idolatry, the children of Israel seemed to love to possess these lifeless images. The teraphim were probably a remnant of the idolatry originally brought by some of Abraham's family from their Chaldæan home. These idols, we know, varied in size, from the diminutive image which Rachel (Gen. xxxi. 34) was able to conceal under the camel saddle to the life-size figure which the Princess Michal here used to make her father's guards believe that her sick husband, David, was in bed. They appear to have been looked on as tutelary deities, the dispensers of domestic and family good fortune. It has been suggested, with some probability, that Michal, like Rachel, kept this teraphim in secret, because of her barrenness.

A pillow of goats' hair.—More accurately, *a goat's skin about its head*. So render the Syriac and Vulgate Versions. The reason of this act apparently was to imitate the effect of a man's hair round the teraphim's head. Its body, we read in the next clause, was covered "with a cloth." Some scholars have suggested that this goat's skin was a net-work of goat's hair to keep off the flies from the supposed sleeper. The LXX., instead of *k'vir* (skin), read in their Hebrew copies *kaved* (liver). As the vowel points were introduced much later, such a confusion (especially as the difference between *d* and *r* in Hebrew is very slight) would be likely enough to occur in the MSS. Josephus, adopting the LXX. reading, explains Michal's conduct thus—"Michal put a palpitating goat's liver into the bed, to represent a breathing sick man."

With a cloth.—Heb., *beged*. This was David's every-day garment, which he was in the habit of wearing. This, loosely thrown over the image, would materially assist the deception. The fifty-ninth Psalm bears the following title—" A michtam (or song of deep import) of David, when Saul sent, and they watched the house to kill him." The internal evidence, however, is scarcely confirmatory of the accuracy of the title. The sacred song in question is very probably one of David's own composition, and it is likely enough that the danger he incurred on this occasion was in his mind when he wrote the solemn words; but there are references in this psalm which must apply to other events in his troubled, anxious life.

(18) **And came to Samuel.**—The influence and authority which Samuel still preserved in the nation, even in the stormy close of Saul's career, must have been very great for the frightened David to have sought a refuge in his quiet home of prayer and learning. The exile, fleeing before his sovereign, felt that in the residence of the old seer he would be safe from

all that Saul had done to him. And he and Samuel went and dwelt in Naioth. (19) And it was told Saul, saying, Behold, David is at Naioth in Ramah. (20) And Saul sent messengers to take David: and when they saw the company of the prophets prophesying, and Samuel standing as appointed over them, the Spirit of God was upon the messengers of Saul, and they also prophesied. (21) And when it was told Saul, he sent other messengers, and they prophesied likewise. And Saul sent messengers again the third time, and they prophesied also. (22) Then went he also to Ramah, and came to a great well that is in Sechu: and he asked and said, Where are Samuel and David? And one said, Behold, they be at Naioth in Ramah. (23) And he went thither to Naioth in Ramah: and the Spirit of God was upon him also, and he went on, and prophesied, until he came to Naioth in Ramah. (24) And he stripped off his clothes also, and prophesied before Samuel in like manner, and [1] lay down naked all that day and all that night. Wherefore they say, *a Is Saul also among the prophets?

[1] Heb., *fell.*

a ch. 10. 11.

---

all pursuit, as in a sanctuary. David's intimate connection with Samuel has been alluded to on several occasions. He stood to the old seer in the relation of a loved pupil.

(19) **Naioth.**—Naioth, or Nevaioth, as it is also written, was not a town, but, as the name denotes, *a cluster of dwellings or abodes.* It is derived from the verb *navah*, to rest or abide. Samuel had his own house in Ramah, and these dwellings, where his prophetic schools were established, were in the immediate neighbourhood, "Naioth in Ramah." It was to this school he took David on this occasion. The Chaldee Targum renders or paraphrases Naioth here by "house of learning."

(20) **The company of the prophets.**—(On the general question of this company of prophets see *Excursus* H, at the end of this Book.) The Hebrew word rendered "company" occurs only in this place, but the ancient versions agree in rendering it "company," or "assembly." The Chaldee paraphrases here "they saw the company of the scribes praising, and Samuel standing over them teaching."

And they also prophesied.—Like so much that happened among the chosen people during their eventful trial period, the circumstance here related does not belong to ordinary natural experience. The words which immediately precede suggest the only possible explanation of the strange occurrence: "The Spirit of God was upon these messengers of Saul." Ewald thus graphically paraphrases the Biblical record of this scene:—"It is related of those who started with the most hostile intentions against the prophets and their pupils, that as they approached they suddenly stood still, spell-bound by the music and solemn dance of the devotees; then, more and more powerfully drawn by the same Spirit into the charmed circle, they broke forth into similar words and gestures; and then, flinging away their upper garments, they joined in the dance and the music, and sinking down into ecstatic quivering, utterly forgot the hostile spirit in which they had come. . . . The same thing befell fresh messengers a second, nay, a third time. Then Saul himself, enraged, rushed to Ramah, . . . and as he looked down from the hill upon the school, and heard the loud pealing songs rising from it, he was seized by the Divine Spirit; and when he at last reached the spot he sank into the same condition of enthusiasm still more deeply than all the messengers whom he had previously despatched."

(21) **And they prophesied likewise.**—Bishop Wordsworth calls attention here to the fact of "this portion of Scripture, from verse 18 to end of the chapter, which relates the illapse of the Spirit on Saul's messengers, and even on Saul himself, the persecutor of David, being appointed by the Church to be read on Whitsun Tuesday (Old Lect.), in order to show the existence and working of the Holy Spirit before the times of the Gospel, and the freedom and power of His Divine agency." (Comp. here Num. xi. 26—31: the history of Eldad and Medad, which we read on Whitsun Monday, New Lect.)

(24) **And he stripped off his clothes also, and prophesied before Samuel in like manner.**—This was certainly not the first time that Saul had experienced a similar influence of the Spirit of God. We are told (chap. x. 10) that directly after his anointing by Samuel, he met a company of prophets, who were prophesying at Gibeah, and that "the Spirit of God came upon him, and he prophesied among them." On *that* occasion he had been changed into another man. What was the meaning of the outpouring upon the faithless king now? The Chaldee, according to Raschi's explanation, says *he was mad.* Is it not, however, better to explain the incident by understanding that once more the pitiful Spirit pleaded with the man whom the Lord had chosen to be His anointed? But, alas! when the moment of strange excitement was over, the blessed pleading was forgotten. Is not this a matter of every-day experience?

And lay down naked.—Not necessarily without any clothes, for under the tunic there was worn by men of the upper ranks certainly a fine-woven shirt of linen or cotton. Lyranus explains the words "stripped off his clothes" as simply denoting that he threw off his upper garment, "his royal robe."

Is Saul also among the prophets?—The same thing having taken place before (see chap. x. 12), this saying gained currency among the people. There seemed something strange to men in one so self-willed and disobedient as was Saul receiving, as it seemed to the by-standers, the Divine and much coveted gift. "Many," says St. Augustine, "are the gifts of God which are possessed by evil men. Evil men have often great talents, great skill, great wealth. . . . The gift of prophesy is a great gift, but it was possessed by Saul. Saul, an evil king, prophesied at the very time he was persecuting holy David. Let not, therefore, men boast if they have God's gifts; those gifts will profit them nothing without charity (1 Cor. xiii. 1—2). But let them think of the fearful account they must one day give to God, if they use not holy things holily."—*St. Augustine*, in Ps. ciii., quoted by Wordsworth.

CHAPTER XX.—(1) And David fled from Naioth in Ramah, and came and said before Jonathan, What have I done? what *is* mine iniquity? and what *is* my sin before thy father, that he seeketh my life? (2) And he said unto him, God forbid; thou shalt not die: behold, my father will do nothing either great or small, but that he will ¹shew it me: and why should my father hide this thing from me? it *is* not so. (3) And David sware moreover, and said, Thy father certainly knoweth that I have found grace in thine eyes; and he saith, Let not Jonathan know this, lest he be grieved: but truly *as* the LORD liveth, and *as* thy soul liveth, *there is* but a step between me and death. (4) Then said Jonathan unto David, ²Whatsoever thy soul ³desireth, I will even do *it* for thee.

(5) And David said unto Jonathan, Behold, to morrow *is* the new moon, and I should not fail to sit with the king at meat: but let me go, that I may hide myself in the field unto the third *day* at even. (6) If thy father at all miss me, then say, David earnestly asked *leave* of me that he might run to Beth-lehem his city: for *there is* a yearly ⁴sacrifice there for all the family. (7) If he say thus, *It is* well; thy servant shall have peace: but if he be very wroth, *then* be sure that evil is determined by him. (8) Therefore thou shalt deal kindly with thy servant;

¹ Heb., *uncover mine ear.*
² Or, *Say what is thy mind, and I will do, &c.*
³ Heb., *speaketh,* or, *thinketh.*
⁴ Or, *feast.*

XX.

(1—42) Jonathan and David Seal their Friendship with a Solemn Covenant—David is Declared a Public Enemy—The Last Interview between David and Jonathan.

(1) **And David fled from Naioth in Ramah, and came and said before Jonathan.**—The strange course of events in the prophetic schools by Ramah, while warning David that even the home of his old master, the great seer, was no permanent sanctuary where he could safely rest, still gave him time to fly, and to take counsel with his loved friend, the king's son. It was, no doubt, by Samuel's advice that he once more betook himself to the city of Saul, but his return was evidently secret.

Alone with his friend, he passionately asserts his entire innocence of the crimes laid to his charge by the unhappy, jealous Saul. His words here are found in substance in not a few of his Psalms, where, in touching language, he maintains how bitterly the world had wronged and persecuted a righteous, innocent man.

(2) **God forbid; thou shalt not die.**—Jonathan even now refuses to believe that his loved father, *when he was himself,* really wished ill to David; all that had hitherto happened the princely Jonathan put down to his father's unhappy malady. He urges upon his friend that if the king in good earnest had designs upon David's life, he would in his calm, lucid days have consulted with him, Jonathan, to whom he ever confided all his State secrets.

Will do nothing.—Here the commentators and the versions—LXX., Vulg., and Chaldee—all agree to read in the Hebrew text, *lo* "not," for *lo* "to him," that is, for a *vau* an *aleph* must be substituted.

(3) **Thy father certainly knoweth that I have found grace in thine eyes.**—David urges that his fall, and even his death, had been decided upon by Saul, who, knowing how Jonathan loved him, would shrink from confiding to his son his deadly plans respecting his loved friend. David, with his clear, bright intellect, looked deeper into Saul's heart than did the heroic, guileless son. He recognised only too vividly the intensity of the king's hatred of him; and we see in the next verse that the mournful earnestness of the son of Jesse had its effect upon the prince, who consented to make the public trial of Saul's real mind which his friend asked for.

(5) **The new moon.**—On the religious ceremonies connected with the day of the new moon at the beginning of each month, see the Mosaic enactments in Numb. x. 10, xxviii. 11—15.

At the court of Saul the feast seems to have been carefully observed, doubtless with the blast of trumpets, and with solemn burnt offerings and sin offerings, for we notice in this narrative that the plea of possible ceremonial uncleanness was at once accepted as an excuse for absence. (See verse 26.)

The sacrificial and ceremonial rites were accompanied by a state and family banquet, at which David, as the king's son-in-law, and also as holding a high post in the royal army, was expected to be present.

Jonathan persisted in looking upon his father's later designs against the life of David as simply frenzied acts, incident upon his distressing malady, and evidently believed that after his strange seizure at Ramah he would return, and treat David with the confidence of old days when he met him at the feast of the new moon. David, however, believed otherwise, and was convinced, to use his own expressive words, that there was but a step between him and death. He would not trust himself, therefore, to Saul's hands until his friend had made the experiment he suggested.

(6) **A yearly sacrifice.**—The Mosaic Law (Deut. xii. 5 and following verses) strictly required these great sacrificial feasts to be kept at the Tabernacle, "unto the place which the Lord your God shall choose out of all your tribes;" but ever since the destruction of the Tabernacle of Shiloh there had been no central sanctuary, and these solemn feasts had been held, most probably, in tribal centres. "In the then disorganised condition of public worship to which David first gave regular form, family usages of this sort, after the manner of other nations, had established themselves, which were contrary to the (Mosaic) prescriptions concerning the unity of Divine worship."—O. von Gerlach, in *Lange*. It is highly probable that the festival in question was at this time being held at Bethlehem. It is, however, clear that David did not purpose being present at it, and therefore the excuse was a feigned one. The morality of this request of David is by no means sanctioned by the compiler of the history; he simply relates the story.

(8) **A covenant of the Lord with thee.**—It may at first sight seem strange that we have these last meetings of David and Jonathan told us in such detail

for ᵃthou hast brought thy servant into a covenant of the LORD with thee: notwithstanding, if there be in me iniquity, slay me thyself; for why shouldest thou bring me to thy father?

(9) And Jonathan said, Far be it from thee: for if I knew certainly that evil were determined by my father to come upon thee, then would not I tell it thee?

(10) Then said David to Jonathan, Who shall tell me? or what *if* thy father answer thee roughly? (11) And Jonathan said unto David, Come, and let us go out into the field. And they went out both of them into the field. (12) And Jonathan said unto David, O LORD God of Israel, when I have ¹sounded my father about to morrow any time, *or* the third *day*, and, behold, *if there be* good toward David, and I then send not unto thee, and ²shew it thee; (13) the LORD do so and much more to Jonathan: but if it please my father *to do* thee evil, then I will shew it thee, and send thee away, that thou mayest go in peace: and the LORD be with thee, as he hath been with my father. (14) And thou shalt not only while yet I live shew me the kindness of

ᵃ ch. 18. 3 & 23. 18.

¹ Heb., searched.

² Heb., uncover thine ear.

—the speaker's very words quoted, and so many apparently trivial circumstances related.

The question, too, might be asked: Whence did the compiler of the book derive his intimate acquaintance with what took place at these meetings, when David was *alone* with Jonathan? But the difficulties are only surface ones, for we must never forget how intensely interesting to the chosen people were all the circumstances connected with their loved king's life—never lose sight of the deathless interest with which they would hear and read the particulars of David's rise through great suffering and long trial to the throne; and this period here related in such detail was the turning-point of a grand career. From this moment, David's way diverged from the every-day life of ordinary duty and prosperity, and became, during a long and weary period, for him the way of almost uninterrupted suffering. The way of suffering and of trial is in all ages the royal road to true greatness. As to the *source* whence the compiler of the book derived his knowledge of what passed at these last meetings of the two friends, Ewald suggests that when in after years David drew to his Court the posterity of Jonathan, *he often told them himself of these last events before their separation* (events with which no one but the two friends could be acquainted).

Slay me thyself.—" This supposes that Jonathan had the right to inflict capital punishment for crimes against his father as king."—*Lange.* This was David's last earnest request to the prince. If Jonathan felt there was any truth in the charges brought against him by Saul—if *he* deemed his friend a traitor to the reigning dynasty—let him slay the betrayer himself there and then.

(9) **Far be it from thee.**—Vulg., *absit hoc a te.* This strong expression bears emphatic testimony to Jonathan's implicit belief in his loved friend's stainless loyalty. He indignantly refuses to take his life, or even to allow that life to be touched by his father. The sentences here are broken ones; the next one following is left, in the Hebrew, incomplete. They betoken the agitation and deep feeling of the chivalrous, indignant speaker.

(10) **Who shall tell me? or what if thy father answer thee roughly?**—The language in the original is here very abrupt and involved. Evidently the very words uttered in the memorable scene by the excited and sorrowful friends are remembered and reported.

The "if" supplied in the English Version probably is nearest the meaning intended to be conveyed by the broken, agitated words. Another rendering is, "If thy father shall answer thee harshly, who will declare it to me?"

"These questions of David were suggested by a correct estimate of the circumstances—namely, that Saul's suspicions would lead him to the conclusion that there was some understanding between Jonathan and David, and that he would take steps, in consequence, to prevent Jonathan from making David acquainted with the result of his conversation with Saul."—*Keil.*

In the next verse Jonathan leads David into a solitary spot—"the field"—where, before saying their last words together, they might agree upon some secret sign by means of which Saul's real mind towards David might be communicated, if necessary, by Jonathan to his friend.

(12) **O Lord God of Israel.**—Now that the two friends have come to a remote solitary spot, Jonathan prefaces his reply to David's piteous request by a very solemn invocation of that God they both loved so well. The vocative, however, "O Lord God," &c., of the English Version has been generally looked upon as an impossible rendering—" there being no analogy for such a mode of address "—*Lange.*

The versions avoid it by supplying different words. So the Syriac and Arabic render "The Lord of Israel is *my witness*"; the LXX., "The Lord God of Israel knows." Others have supplied a word which they find in two Hebrew MSS., "As the Lord God of Israel *liveth.*" The meaning, however, is perfectly clear.

Or the third day.—This statement of time on the part of Jonathan evidently assumes that the festival was continued the day after the "new moon" by a royal banquet. The time is thus reckoned: the present day; the morrow, which was the new moon festival; and the day after, which would reckon as the third day.

Behold, if there be good toward David.—In the event of the news being good—that is, if Saul, contrary to David's expectation, spoke kindly of him—then Jonathan would *send* to him a special messenger; if, on the other hand, the king displayed enmity, in that case Jonathan would come himself and see David (for the last time). This sad message should be brought by no messenger.

(14) **And thou shalt not only while yet I live shew me the kindness of the Lord, that I die not.**—The Hebrew of this and the next verse is again very confused, abrupt, and ungrammatical, but this is evidently to be attributed to the violent emotion of the speaker. We have, doubtless (as above suggested),

the LORD, that I die not: ⁽¹⁵⁾ but *also* thou shalt not cut off thy kindness from my house for ever: no, not when the LORD hath cut off the enemies of David every one from the face of the earth.

⁽¹⁶⁾ So Jonathan ¹made *a covenant* with the house of David, *saying,* Let the LORD even require *it* at the hand of David's enemies. ⁽¹⁷⁾And Jonathan caused David to swear again, ²because he loved him: for he loved him as he loved his own soul.

⁽¹⁸⁾ Then Jonathan said to David, To morrow *is* the new moon: and thou shalt be missed, because thy seat will be ³empty. ⁽¹⁹⁾ And *when* thou hast stayed three days, *then* thou shalt go down ^{4 5}quickly, and come to the place where thou didst hide thyself ⁶when the business was *in hand*, and shalt remain by the stone ⁷Ezel. ⁽²⁰⁾ And I will shoot three arrows on the side *thereof,* as though I shot at a mark. ⁽²¹⁾ And, behold, I will send a lad, *saying*, Go, find out the arrows. If I expressly say unto the lad, Behold, the arrows *are* on this side of thee, take them; then come thou: for *there is* peace to thee, and ⁸no hurt; *as* the LORD liveth. ⁽²²⁾ But if I say thus unto the young man, Behold, the

1 Heb., *cut.*
2 Or, *by his love towards him.*
3 Heb., *missed.*
4 Or, *diligently.*
5 Heb., *greatly.*
6 Heb., *in the day of the business.*
7 Or, *that sheweth the way.*
8 Heb., *not any thing.*

David's own report of what took place, and the words of his dead friend had, no doubt, impressed themselves with a sad accuracy on his heart.

The Syriac and Arabic renderings have been followed by Maurer, Ewald, Keil, Lange, and others, who change *v'lo* ("and not") in the first two clauses of verse 14, into the interjection *v'lu* (and "O that," or "would that"). They render them, "And mayest thou, if I still live, show to me the favour of the Lord, and if I die, not withdraw thy favour from my house for ever, not even when Jehovah shall cut off the enemies of David, every one from the face of the earth."

The last words, "when Jehovah shall cut off," tells us with striking clearness how thoroughly convinced was Jonathan that in the end David's cause, as the cause of their God, would surely triumph. Mournfully he looked on to his father's downfall and his own (Jonathan's) premature death; and in full view of this he bespoke the interest of his friend—though his friend would probably in a few hours become an exile and outlaw—on behalf of his own (Jonathan's) children, who would, he foresaw, before many years had expired, be landless, homeless orphans.

⁽¹⁶⁾ **So Jonathan made a covenant.**—It is not necessary to supply (as in the English Version) "saying," but it is better to understand this verse as a remark interposed in the dialogue by the narrator, and to translate the Hebrew literally, "So Jonathan made a covenant with the house of David, and Jehovah required it at the hand of David's enemies."

⁽¹⁷⁾ **And Jonathan caused David to swear again.**—Throughout this touching interview it is the prince who appears as the suppliant for the outlaw's future kind offices. Jonathan—looking forward with absolute certainty to the day when his persecuted friend would be on the throne, and he in his grave—dreaded for his own fatherless children the fate which too probably awaited them, it having been in all ages a common custom in the East, when the dynasty was violently changed, to put to death the children and near relations of the former king.

⁽¹⁸⁾ **Thou shalt be missed.**—Well then, resumes Jonathan—after the passionate conclusion of the solemn covenant betwixt the friends—the last trial shall be as you propose. At the State banquet of my father tomorrow your seat, as agreed upon, will be empty, then you and I—when King Saul misses you—will know the worst.

⁽¹⁹⁾ **Go down quickly.**—"Quickly" represents, but not faithfully, the Hebrew *m'od*. "Quickly" comes from the Vulg., *descende ergo festinus.* The literal rendering of *m'od* is "greatly," and probably Dean Payne Smith's rendering, "and on the third day go a long way (greatly) down into the valley," represents the meaning of the original, which has been a general stumbling-block with the versions. The Chaldee, Arabic, and Syriac here interpret rather than translate, "on the third day thou wilt be missed the more." "It did not matter," writes the Dean, "whether David went fast or slow, as he was to hide there some time, but it was important that David should be far away, so that no prying eye might chance to catch sight of him."

When the business was in hand.—The expression, *b'yom hammaaseh*, rendered in our version by "when the business was *in hand*," is one hard to understand. Perhaps the best translation is that adopted by Gesenius, De Wette, and Maurer, who render it quite literally "on the day of the deed," and understand by "deed" King Saul's design of killing David (see chap. xix. 2).

By the stone Ezel.—This stone, or cairn, or possibly ruin, is mentioned nowhere else. Some have supposed it to have been a road-stone, or stone guidepost. The following ingenious conjecture is hazarded in the *Speaker's Commentary*:—"The LXX. here, and again in verse 41 (where the spot, but not the stone, is spoken of), read *argab*, or *eryab*, a word meaning *a heap of stones*. If this is the true reading, David's hiding place was either a natural cavernous rock, which was called *argab*, or some ruin of an ancient building equally suited for a hiding place." Ewald, slightly changing the text, understands the word as signifying "the lonely waste."

⁽²⁰⁾ **I will shoot three arrows.**—The two friends agree on a sign. It was a very simple one, and seems to speak of very early primitive times. Jonathan slightly varies from his original purpose. In verse 12 it seems as though he meant to have sent a special messenger had the news been good, but now the arrangement is that in either event he should come himself out from the city into the solitary valley where it was agreed David should remain in hiding by the stone "Ezel." Dean Payne Smith rather strangely conceives that the arrows of the "sign" were to be aimed at the stone Ezel, but the description points to the "mark" as situated on the side of "Ezel," in or behind which David was to be concealed.

The prince agreed that after the feast he would leave the city, as though about to practise shooting at a mark.

Saul misses David at the Feast.   I. SAMUEL, XX.   *The King's Anger with Jonathan.*

arrows *are* beyond thee; go thy way: for the Lord hath sent thee away. ⁽²³⁾ And *as touching* the matter which thou and I have spoken of, behold, the Lord *be* between thee and me for ever.

⁽²⁴⁾ So David hid himself in the field: and when the new moon was come, the king sat him down to eat meat. ⁽²⁵⁾ And the king sat upon his seat, as at other times, *even* upon a seat by the wall: and Jonathan arose, and Abner sat by Saul's side, and David's place was empty. ⁽²⁶⁾ Nevertheless Saul spake not any thing that day: for he thought, Something hath befallen him, he *is* not clean; surely he *is* not clean.

⁽²⁷⁾ And it came to pass on the morrow, *which was* the second *day* of the month, that David's place was empty: and Saul said unto Jonathan his son, Wherefore cometh not the son of Jesse to meat, neither yesterday, nor to day? ⁽²⁸⁾ And Jonathan answered Saul, David earnestly asked *leave* of me *to go* to Beth-lehem: ⁽²⁹⁾ and he said, Let me go, I pray thee; for our family hath a sacrifice in the city; and my brother, he hath commanded me *to be there*: and now, if I have found favour in thine eyes, let me get away, I pray thee, and see my brethren. Therefore he cometh not unto the king's table.

⁽³⁰⁾ Then Saul's anger was kindled against Jonathan, and he said unto him, ^{1 2} Thou son of the perverse rebellious *woman*, do not I know that thou hast chosen the son of Jesse to thine own confusion, and unto the

1 Or, *Thou perverse rebel.*

2 Heb., *Son of perverse rebellion.*

---

and that he would bring with him a servant—probably one of his young armour-bearers—when, at the spot agreed upon in the neighbourhood of David's place of concealment near Ezel, he would post his servant in his place as marker, and then would shoot. After shooting, he would call out to his attendant, "the arrows are on this side of thee" (that is, between the mark and Jonathan himself), then David would know all was well; but if he cried "the arrows are beyond thee," that is, on the further side of the mark, David would understand that all was over, and that he must fly. Jonathan evidently took these precautions not knowing whether or no he would be accompanied by friends of his father from the city, in which case the "sign" agreed upon would be sufficient to tell David what had happened at the feast. As it turned out, Jonathan was able to escape observation, and to go alone with his servant to the place of meeting. He used the sign to attract his friend's attention, and then followed the last sorrowful parting, told in verses 41, 42.

⁽²⁴⁾ **Sat him down.**—The LXX. paraphrases here, "came to the table."

⁽²⁵⁾ **David's place was empty.**—All took place as the two friends had calculated. Saul's seat was by the wall—then, as now, in the East the highest place of honour was opposite the door. The exact meaning of the phrase, "and Jonathan arose," has been disputed. The LXX. translate here from a different text thus: "He (Saul) went before Jonathan." Keil speaks of this, however, as "the senseless rendering of the Greek Version." The sense in which this difficult passage is understood by Abarbanel and Rashi seems on the whole the best. Understanding that Jonathan had already seated himself after Saul, and that David's absence was observed, "he (Jonathan) arose and seated Abner at Saul's side," that is, in the place left vacant by David's absence, in order that the seat next to Saul might not be empty, he himself having taken the seat on the other side of Saul. This rendering considers *vayêshev* as causative, a verb in the Hiphil conjugation, written defectively, as in 2 Chron. x. 2; so Lange, who also quotes Kitto as suggesting an explanation of Saul's expecting David's presence at all at the new moon feast. David, after the strange events at Naioth by Ramah, would suppose (so the king thought) that Saul's feelings towards him had undergone a complete change, and that now, after the ecstasy into which Saul had fallen, he would be once more friendly with him as aforetime.

⁽²⁷⁾ **On the morrow.**—David's continued absence on the second day of the feast awoke Saul's suspicion, and he asked his son, who was sitting by him, what was the reason of his friend's absence, aware that no accident connected with ceremonial defilement would keep him away two following days.

⁽²⁹⁾ **Our family hath a sacrifice in the city; and my brother, he hath commanded me.**—Jonathan answers the king's question in the way previously agreed upon between him and David. He quotes the excuse in David's own words.

The LXX., instead of "my brother," has "my brothers." It thus alters the original, not understanding the singular "brother," Jesse, their father, being still alive. The brothers collectively might, the LXX. seemed to think, have bidden David to the family sacrificial feast. Dean Payne Smith suggests that as the ceremony was not a private family gathering, but one shared in by the district, the "brother" (probably the eldest), likely enough, was the convener of the absent member of the house of Jesse.

⁽³⁰⁾ **Saul's anger was kindled.**—As David expected, his absence kindled into a flame the anger of Saul. Probably he had determined at that very feast, surrounded by his own devoted friends and members of his family, to carry out his evil designs against David's life.

Murder was, probably enough, one of the incidents arranged for at that banquet, but the absence of the intended victim marred the plot; besides which, the king, too, with the cunning which the partially insane so often display, saw through the veil of the specious excuse that David too clearly suspected his wicked design, and purposely stayed away; nay, more, that his own son Jonathan, the heir of his kingdom, suspected him, and openly sympathised with his friend David, for whose pointed absence he thus publicly apologised.

Thou son of the perverse rebellious woman.—These words, spoken in public, in any sense were a bitter insult to the prince. Another and better rendering has, however, been suggested. The word *naävath*, rendered *perverse*, instead of being a feminine adjective,

Jonathan Leaves the Court I. SAMUEL, XX. *to Warn David.*

confusion of thy mother's nakedness? ⁽³¹⁾ For as long as the son of Jesse liveth upon the ground, thou shalt not be established, nor thy kingdom. Wherefore now send and fetch him unto me, for he ¹shall surely die. ⁽³²⁾ And Jonathan answered Saul his father, and said unto him, Wherefore shall he be slain? what hath he done? ⁽³³⁾ And Saul cast a javelin at him to smite him: whereby Jonathan knew that it was determined of his father to slay David. ⁽³⁴⁾ So Jonathan arose from the table in fierce anger, and did eat no meat the second day of the month: for he was grieved for David, because his father had done him shame.

⁽³⁵⁾ And it came to pass in the morning, that Jonathan went out into the field at the time appointed with David, and a little lad with him. ⁽³⁶⁾ And he said unto his lad, Run, find out now the arrows which I shoot. And as the lad ran, he shot an arrow ²beyond him. ⁽³⁷⁾ And when the lad was come to the place of the arrow which Jonathan had shot, Jonathan cried after the lad, and said, *Is* not the arrow beyond thee? ⁽³⁸⁾ And Jonathan cried after the lad, Make speed, haste, stay not. And Jonathan's lad gathered up the arrows, and came to his master. ⁽³⁹⁾ But the lad knew not any thing: only Jonathan and David knew the matter. ⁽⁴⁰⁾ And Jonathan gave his ³artillery unto ⁴his lad, and said unto him, Go, carry *them* to the city.

⁽⁴¹⁾ *And* as soon as the lad was gone, David arose out of *a place* toward the south, and fell on his face to the ground, and bowed himself three times: and

---

1 Heb., *is the son of death.*

2 Heb., *to pass over him.*

3 Heb., *instruments.*

4 Heb., *that was his.*

---

is probably an abstract noun. The translation would then run, "Thou son of perversity of rebellion," a common Hebraism for "a man of perverse and refractory nature;" so Clericus, Lange, and Payne Smith. This avoids the extreme improbability that Saul insulted his *own* wife, Jonathan's mother, which, as has been observed, contradicts the Hebrew family spirit.

The confusion of thy mother's nakedness.—This is far from insulting Jonathan's mother; it is simply an Oriental mode of saying, "she will feel ashamed at having brought such a son into the world."

⁽³¹⁾ **Thou shalt not be established.**—Here the king gives expression to the thought which was ever torturing that poor diseased brain of his—David, his own kind physician, his faithful soldier, and his son's dearest friend and loved companion, was plotting basely against that master for whom he had done so much, and the son whom he loved so well. Saul, in his blind fury, goes on to betray his fell purpose when he exclaims, "he shall surely die." His command, "Send and fetch him unto me," tells us that the murder had been pre-arranged to take place at the feast. Doubtless those rough soldier chiefs sitting round the royal table would be ready at any moment to carry into effect their master's savage behest.

⁽³²⁾ **And Jonathan answered.**—Jonathan, remembering the effect of his quiet, earnest remonstrance on a previous occasion, again tried to deprecate his father's unreasoning jealous anger, but this time to no purpose. A paroxysm of madness seized Saul, and he grasped the long spear leaning by his side, and with hate and fury in his eye raised the great war weapon to strike down his son.

⁽³⁴⁾ **So Jonathan arose.**—"In fierce anger," so runs the too true record. The son of Saul left the presence, and appeared no more at that fatal feast. The hot anger was stirred up, first, no doubt, by the terrible insult offered him, the prince and heir to the throne, before the assembled great ones of Israel. The great spear uplifted to strike, following the harsh and bitter words spoken, was an act not likely soon to be forgotten by the spectators. And secondly, by the determined and relentless enmity of Saul against David, of whose stainless integrity and perfect loyalty Jonathan was firmly convinced. The bitter wrong done to David his friend no doubt affected Jonathan most.

⁽³⁵⁾ **At the time appointed with David.**—This meeting between the friends is not described at any length; all was done as had been pre-arranged, and, alas! everything had come to pass as David in his sad foresight had expected.

⁽³⁶⁾ **He shot an arrow beyond him.**—This was the sign agreed on if all was over for David at the court of Saul. Expositors are in a little difficulty, though, here, as only *one arrow* is mentioned, whereas "three" had to be shot according to the terms of the understanding. We cannot imagine, as some have suggested, that "Jonathan shortened the affair, and shot only once, considering that there was danger in delay," and that every moment was of consequence; had there been such need of haste, the parting scene would have been cut even shorter. It is better, with Keil, to assume that the "singular" here stands in an indefinite general way, the author not thinking it needful, after what he had before said, to state that Jonathan shot three arrows one after another.

⁽³⁸⁾ **Make speed, haste, stay not.**—Although Jonathan, of course, trusted to a certain extent the youth (probably an armour-bearer) who was with him, still he hurried this attendant away, that he might not see David, who was close by in hiding, and who, *after* the sign, would presently appear in sight. The next clause (verse 39) expressly tells us how this meeting was unknown and unwitnessed. The youth was sent to the city that Jonathan might be alone once more with David.

⁽⁴⁰⁾ **His artillery.**—Literally, *his implements.* The word "artillery," expressive though it be, would scarcely now be used in this sense; we should now translate the Hebrew word by "arms."

⁽⁴¹⁾ **David arose out of a place toward the south.**—If the text be correct here, which is very doubtful, we must understand these words as signifying that as soon as David perceived that Jonathan was alone (as soon as the lad was gone), he rose from the south side of the rock, where he had been lying concealed. [The "arrow" sign would have been enough to have warned David; and had he not seen that Jonathan was

David flies to Nob,   I. SAMUEL, XXI.   *the City of the Priests.*

they kissed one another, and wept one with another, until David exceeded. (42) And Jonathan said to David, Go in peace, ¹forasmuch as we have sworn both of us in the name of the LORD, saying, The LORD be between me and thee, and between my seed and thy seed for ever. And he arose and departed: and Jonathan went into the city.

¹ Or, *the* LORD *be witness of that which, &c.*

CHAPTER XXI.—(1) Then came David to Nob to Ahimelech the priest: and Ahimelech was afraid at the meeting of David, and said unto him, Why *art* thou alone, and no man with thee? (2) And David said unto Ahimelech the priest, The king hath commanded me a business, and hath said unto me, Let no man know anything of the business where-

---

alone and waiting for him, David would, from his place of hiding, have made his escape unseen.] The Chaldee here reads, "from the stone of the sign (or the stone Atha) which is on the south;" the LXX. (Vat. MS.), "from the Argab;" Alex. MS., "from sleep." The different versions, more or less, have repeated the statement in verse 19, failing altogether to understand the two Hebrew words *mêêtzel hannegev*, translated in our English Version, "out of a place toward the south."

And fell on his face.—Josephus' words, in his traditional account of the event, explain David's reason for this. "He did obeisance, and called him the saviour of his life."

Until David exceeded.—The expression is a strange one, and apparently signifies either simply that while Jonathan wept bitterly at the parting, David wept *still more*, or else that "David broke down," that is, "was completely mastered by his grief."—*Dean Payne Smith.* The LXX. translators here are quite unintelligible in their rendering, which represents David as weeping "until a (or the) great consummation."

(42) **Go in peace.**—The abruptness of the closing words is most natural, and accords with the evident deep emotion of the speaker. David's heart was too full to reply to his friend's words; blinded with tears, he seems to have hurried away speechless.

"We may indeed wonder at the delicacy of feeling and the gentleness of the sentiments which these two men in those old rough times entertained for one another. No ancient writer has set before us so noble an example of a heartfelt, unselfish, and thoroughly human state of feeling, and none has described friendship with such entire truth in all its relations, and with such complete and profound knowledge of the human heart."—*Phillipson,* quoted by Payne Smith.

XXI.

David in Exile—His Visit to the High Priest Ahimelech at the Sanctuary of Nob—His Sojourn with Achish, the Philistine King of Gath.

(1) **Then came David to Nob.**—Before leaving his native land, David determined once more to see, and if practicable to take counsel with, the old high priest of Israel, with whom, no doubt, in the past years of his close connection with Samuel, he had had frequent and intimate communion. He hoped, too, in that friendly and powerful religious centre to provide himself and his few companions with arms and other necessaries for his exile; nor is it improbable that he purposed, through the friendly high priest, to make some inquiry of the Divine oracle, the Urim and Thummim, concerning his doubtful future. The unexpected presence of Doeg, the powerful and unscrupulous servant of Saul, at the sanctuary, no doubt hurried him away in hot haste across the frontier.

The town of Nob, situated between Anathoth and Jerusalem—about an hour's ride from the latter—has been with great probability identified with the "village of Esau," El-Isaurizeh, a place bearing all the marks of an ancient town, with its many marble columns and ancient stones. There, in these latter days of Saul, "stood the last precious relic of the ancient nomadic times—the tabernacle of the wanderings, round which, since the fall of Shiloh, had dwelt the descendants of the house of Eli. It was a little colony of priests; no less than eighty-five persons ministered there in the white linen dress of the priesthood, and all their families and herds were gathered round them. The priest was not so ready to befriend as the prophet (we allude to David's reception by Samuel at Naioth by Ramah, chap. xix.). As the solitary fugitive, famished and unarmed, stole up the mountain side, he met with but a cold welcome from the cautious and courtly Ahimelech."—Stanley, *Lectures on the Jewish Church,* Lect. xii.

To Ahimelech the priest.—He was the great grandson of Eli, thus—

Died at Shiloh after news of capture of Ark, Eli
|
Slain by Philistines in battle   Phinehas
|
Ahitub   Ichabod
|
Reign of Saul—High Priest, Ahimelech

Reign of David—High Priest, Abiathar. (See chap. xxii. 19, 20.)

He was probably identical with Ahiah (chap. xiv. 3); this, however, is not certain. Dean Payne Smith believes Ahiah was a younger brother of Ahimelech, who, while Ahimelech remained with the Ark, acted as high priest at the camp for Saul, especially in consulting God for him by means of the ephod with the breastplate (the Urim).

Why art thou alone?—The not unfriendly but cautious priest, who, though unaware of the final rupture of Saul and David, was of course cognisant of the strained relations of the king and his great servant, was uneasy at this sudden appearance of the king's son-in-law—the well-known military chieftain, David—alone and travel-stained at the sanctuary.

(2) **The king hath commanded me.**—This is one of the sad episodes in a glorious life. Overwhelmed with dismay at his sudden fall, home and wife, friends and rank, all had been taken from him, and he who had been on the very steps of the throne, the darling of the people, strangely successful in all that he had up to this time put his hand to, was now a proscribed exile, flying for his life. These things must plead as his excuse for his falsehood to Ahimelech, and his flight to and subsequent behaviour among the hereditary enemies of his race, the

about I send thee, and what I have commanded thee: and I have appointed *my* servants to such and such a place. (3) Now therefore what is under thine hand? give *me* five *loaves of* bread in mine hand, or what there is ¹present. (4) And the priest answered David, and said, *There is* no common bread under mine hand, but there is ᵃhallowed bread; if the young men have kept themselves at least from women. (5) And David answered the priest, and said unto him, Of a truth women *have been* kept from us about these three days, since I came out, and the vessels of the young men are holy, and *the bread is* in a manner common, ²yea, though it were sanctified this day in the vessel. (6) So the priest gave him hallowed *bread:* for there was no bread there but the shewbread, that was taken

¹ Heb., *found.*

ᵃ Ex. 25. 30; Lev. 24. 5; Matt. 12. 4.

² Or, *especially when this day there is other sanctified in the vessel.*

Philistines. But here, as in so many places, the Holy Spirit who guided the pen of the compiler of this true history could not lie, but fearlessly tells the repulsive truth which must ever be deeply damaging to the favourite hero of Israel. "The Holy Spirit is become the chronicler of men's foolish, yea, sinful actions. He has narrated the lies of Abraham, the incest of Lot, the simulation of the man after God's heart."—*Lange.*

I have appointed my servants.—This portion of his words to Ahimelech was, no doubt, strictly true. It is unlikely that one in the high position of David at the court of Saul, possessing, too, such powers over men's hearts, would be allowed to go even into exile without any friends or attendants. Those alluded to here probably joined him soon after his parting with Jonathan. Our Lord, in Mark ii. 25, 26, speaks of the priest giving the shewbread to David and to those that were with him, when both he and they that were with him were an hungred.

(4) **There is no common bread.**—The condition of the priests in these days of Saul was evidently a pitiable one. The terrible massacre related in the next chapter seems not to have excited the wail of indignation and woe which such a wholesale murder of the priests of the living God should naturally have called out from the entire people. They were evidently held in little esteem, and their murder was regarded at the time, not as an awful act of sacrilege, but simply as an act of political vengeance—of punishment for what the king was pleased to style treason. Here the almost destitute condition of the ministers of the principal sanctuary of Israel appears from the quiet answer of the high priest to David, telling him they had positively no bread but the stale bread removed from before "the Presence" in the holy building.

This "hallowed bread," or shewbread, five loaves of which David petitioned for, consisted of twelve loaves, one for each tribe, which were placed in the Tabernacle fresh every Sabbath Day. The law of Moses was that this bread, being most holy, could only be eaten by the priests in the holy place. It is probable that this regulation had been relaxed, and that the bread was now often being carried away and eaten in the homes of the ministering priests, and on urgent occasions, perhaps, was even given to the "laity," as in this case, the proviso only being made that the consumers of the bread should be ceremonially pure. Our Saviour, in Matt. xii. 3, especially uses this example, drawn from the Tabernacle's honoured customs, to justify a violation of the letter of the law, when its strict observance would stand in the way of the fulfilment of man's sacred duty to his neighbour.

The natural inference from this incident would be that such a violation of the Mosaic Law was not an uncommon occurrence, as Ahimelech at once gave him the hallowed bread, only making a conditional inquiry about ceremonial purity—a condition which came out so readily that we feel it had often been made before. The Talmud, however, is most anxious that this inference should not be drawn, and points out in the treatise *Menachoth*, "Meat-offerings" (*Seder Kodashim*), that this bread was not newly taken out of the sanctuary, but had been removed on some previous day, and that as, after a week's exposure, it was stale and dry, the priests ate but little of it, and the rest was left. (See Treatise *Yoma*, 39.) It also points out that had such violation of the Levitical Law been common, so much importance would not have been attached to this incident.

(5) **The vessels.**—Their clothes and light, portable baggage—answering to the modern "knapsack." The Vulg. renders the Hebrew word by "*vasa.*" David means to say, "Since we have just left home, you may readily suppose that no impurity has been contracted; it would be different if we were returning home from a journey, when on the way—especially in war—uncleanness might be contracted by the blood of enemies or otherwise."—Seb. Schmid, quoted in *Lange.*

The LXX., by a very slight change in the Hebrew letters, instead of "the vessels of the young men," render, "all the young men."

And the bread is in a manner common.—The original is here very difficult, almost utterly obscure. The English Version of the clause is simply meaningless. Of the many translations which have been suggested, two at least offer a fairly good sense. (*a*) "*And if it is an unholy way* (viz., the way David and his band were going—his purpose or enterprise), *moreover there is also the fact that it becomes holy through the instrument*" (viz., through me, as an ambassador of the anointed of the Lord), on the supposition of the important royal mission upon which David pretended to be sent. So Keil and O. von Gerlach. (*b*) Lange, however, and Thenius, maintain that the words in question must contain a remark by which the priest is to be induced to give the bread, and would translate, "*Though it is an unholy* (ceremonially illegal) *procedure* (to take the shewbread), *yet it is sanctified* (to-day) *through the instrument*" (David or Ahimelech). The instrument is here David, the appointed messenger of the Lord's anointed, or, even better, Ahimelech, the sacred person of the high priest.

No doubt, the words of Lev. xxiv. 9, which speak of the destination of the stale shewbread—"And they (Aaron and his sons) shall eat it in the holy place"—suggested the practice of the Church of England embodied in the Rubric following the "Order of the Administration of the Holy Communion"—"And if any" (of the bread and wine) "remain of that which was consecrated, it shall not be carried out of the church, but the priest, and such other of the communicants as he shall then call unto him, shall immediately after the

from before the LORD, to put hot bread in the day when it was taken away.

(7) Now a certain man of the servants of Saul *was* there that day, detained before the LORD; and his name *was* Doeg, an Edomite, the chiefest of the herdmen that *belonged* to Saul. (8) And David said unto Ahimelech, And is there not here under thine hand spear or sword? for I have neither brought my sword nor my weapons with me, because the king's business required haste. (9) And the priest said, The sword of Goliath the Philistine, whom thou slewest in ᵃthe valley of Elah, behold, it *is here* wrapped in a cloth behind the ephod: if thou wilt take that, take *it*: for *there is* no other save that here. And David said, *There is* none like that; give it me.

(10) And David arose, and fled that

ᵃ ch. 17. 2.

---

blessing reverently eat and drink the same." Among the legendary Jewish lore that has gathered round the history of this transaction is one strange tradition that the holy bread thus given became useless in the hands of the king's fugitive. (See Stanley, *Lectures on the Jewish Church*, Lect. xxii., quoting from Jerome.)

(7) **A certain man.**—Among the personages who surround Saul in the Bible story appears incidentally the keeper of the royal mules, and chief of the household slaves, the "Comes stabuli," "the constable of the king," as appears in the later monarchy. "He is the first instance of a foreigner employed in a high function in Israel, being an Edomite, or Syrian, of the name of Doeg—according to Jewish tradition, the steward who accompanied Saul in his pursuit after the asses, who counselled him to send for David, and who ultimately slew him, according to the sacred narrative—a person of vast and sinister influence in his master's counsels." (Stanley, *Lectures on the Jewish Church*, Lect. xxi.) Some traditions affirm that the armour-bearer who slew Saul on Mount Gilboa was not Doeg, but Doeg's son.

The Hebrew words rendered in the English Version, "the chiefest of the herdmen that *belonged* to Saul," are translated in the LXX. by "feeding the mules of Saul;" and in accordance with this reading, in chap. xxii. 9 also, they have changed "Saul's servants" into "Saul's mules." The Vulg. and the other versions, however, translate as the English Version, "potentissimus pastorum," although in some of the Vulg. MSS. there is an explanatory gloss, evidently derived from the singular interpretation of the LXX., "This (man) used to feed Saul's mules." There can be no foundation in tradition or otherwise for such a reading, as we never read until the days of King David of mules being used by royal princes. (See 2 Sam. xiii. 29, xviii. 9.) Before David's time, the sons of princes used to ride on asses. (See Judges x. 4, xii. 14.) Ewald, disregarding the current Jewish tradition respecting the ancient connection of Doeg with the house of Kish, considers that this influential chieftain of the king probably came over to Saul in his war with Edom.

Detained before the Lord.—Several interpretations have been suggested for these words. (*a*) He was at the sanctuary of the Tabernacle as a proselyte—one who wished to be received into the religious communion of Israel. (*b*) He was detained there for his purification on account of supposed leprosy, or simply in fulfilment of a temporary Nazarite vow. (*c*) According to Ephrem Syrus (who probably referred to some lost tradition), he had committed some trespass, and was detained there till he had offered the appointed sacrifice. Any one of these reasons—all sufficiently probable in themselves—would have occasioned a residence long or short at the sanctuary at Nob. At all events, when the fugitive David recognised the presence of one of Saul's most unscrupulous servants, whom he must have known well, his mind must have misgiven him, and he, probably on this account, hasted to get away, and at once begs the old high priest to furnish him with any arms he might have laid up in the priestly homes.

(8) **Spear or sword?**—We may well suppose *to what* David pointed when he made his request—the famous sword, the trophy of the combat which had for ever made his name illustrious. In the first flush of gratitude to the invisible One who had stood by him in the hour of peril, he had doubtless taken and presented to the sanctuary guardians, as an offering to be kept for ever, a memorial of the victory of Israel over the uncircumcised; but now, in his hour of need and humiliation, he needed all the credentials he could gather together of his ability and power to lead men, so he trusts the priest will let him have his glorious prize back again. This seems to have been really the meaning of his petition to Ahimelech, and so evidently the priest understood David, for at once he suggested restoring the well-known, treasured sword. The sanctuary, he said, possesses no war weapon but that one which hangs up among us, a votive offering.

(9) **The sword of Goliath the Philistine.**— It was in safe guardianship, that trusty sword of the mightiest of the Philistines, stained perhaps with the blood of the brave but unworthy priests, Hophni and Phineas, the sons of Eli, whom Goliath was believed to have slain in the fatal battle when the Ark was taken, and the power of Israel shattered for many a long year. It was wrapped up and lying in a place of honour behind the sacred ephod with the Urim and Thummim—wrapped up, it has been suggested, in the blood-stained war cloak of the dead Philistine, for the word translated "cloth" is used in Isa. ix. 5 of military attire.

Give it me.—David grasped the sword with a child-like expression of joy; its sight and touch revived the old bright faith and the sure trust in the strength of Israel on which he leaned when, as a boy, he fought with the wild beasts which infested the wild pasture-lands where he kept his father's flocks (the Shepherd of David was the Holy One; blessed be He.—*Midrash Rabbah*, 59), and which guided his trembling hand the day he slew the giant in the face of the watching hosts. The sight and touch of the glorious trophy revived the old sure trust which in these dark days of betrayal and persecution was beginning to fail that gallant spirit of David's. It does not appear from the story that the Philistine's sword was of extraordinary size; that it was a tried weapon of approved temper and strength is certain, but its chief preciousness consisted, of course, in its storied associations. The Dean of Canterbury suggests it was probably of the ordinary pattern imported from Greece. The LXX. adds here, "and he gave it to him."

(10) **And David arose and fled.**—The cause of

David flies to   I. SAMUEL, XXI.   *Achish, King of Gath.*

day for fear of Saul, and went to Achish the king of Gath. (11) And the servants of Achish said unto him, Is not this David the king of the land? did they not sing one to another of him in dances, saying, ᵃSaul hath slain his thousands, and David his ten thousands? (12) And David laid up these words in his heart, and was sore afraid of Achish the king of Gath. (13) And he changed his behaviour before them, and feigned himself mad in their hands, and ¹scrabbled on

a ch. 18. 7 & 29. 5; Ecclus. 47. 6.

1 Or, *made marks*.

---

this sudden flight was, of course, the fear of Doeg, one of Saul's most trusted servants. Not an hour must be lost, thought David; my deadly foe will hear that I am here, and I shall be trapped like a hunted beast of prey. It seems at first sight strange that David should dare to go among the Philistines, who had such good cause to hate and fear him, but the son of Jesse ever thought lightly of himself, and had no idea that his person was so well known, or his story so generally current as it subsequently proved to be. (See verse 11.) Of David's humility, so conspicuously exhibited on this occasion, when he ventured among his foes, not dreaming how great a personage they considered him, the Babylonian Talmud strikingly writes:—"No man in Israel despised himself more than David where the precepts of the Lord were concerned, and this is what he said before God (Ps. cxxxi. 1, 2), 'Lord, my heart was not haughty when Samuel anointed me king, nor were mine eyes lofty *when I slew Goliath* . . . *as a child* . . . have I likened myself before Thee, in not being ashamed to depreciate myself before Thee for Thy glory.'"—Treatise *Bamidbar,* chap. iv.

Achish the king of Gath.—The title "king" is somewhat loosely used in this scene among the Philistines. Achish was one of the Philistine lords, perhaps the hereditary lord of Gath. Achish is called Abimelech in the title of Ps. xxxiv., that apparently being the title, the "nomen dignitatis," of the hereditary (or elected) chief among the Philistines, like Agag among the Amalekites. It is quite possible that this Achish, although called king of Gath, was the supreme chief or king of the Philistine nation. Gath was the nearest Philistine city to the sanctuary of Nob where David then was.

(11) **Is not this David?**—Some expositors have supposed, but quite needlessly, that it was the sword of Goliath which betrayed the identity of the hero; but although David in his humility did not suspect how widely spread was his fame, he was evidently as well known in Philistia as in his own land. That popular lilt, the folk-song of the Israelitish maidens, which sang of the prowess of David, the son of Jesse, was no doubt current in frontier towns like Gath, and at once the fugitive was recognised. We hear of no attempt made upon his life, or even against his liberty. The feeling among his generous foes was rather pitiful admiration mingled with wonder at seeing the doer of such splendid achievements being in poverty and in exile.

David the king.—Here, again, the title king is vaguely used. Neither the people of Gath nor his own countrymen—save, perhaps, a few chosen spirits—knew of the sacred anointing by Samuel at Bethlehem. The appellation simply means: Is not this the renowned warrior, the greatest man in Israel of whom the people sing? Saul, our sovereign, has been a valiant captain over us, and has slain his thousands; but this one is greater still, he has slain his ten thousands.

(12) **And David laid up these words.**—Now, for the first time, David saw how widely travelled was a renown of which he in his humbleness of heart had thought so little, and at once a deadly fear took possession of him. The life he held so cheaply when in battle with the enemies of his country now, strange to say, in his deep degradation and poverty, became of real value to him, and he adopted the piteous and humiliating device of feigning madness, hoping thus to change the wondering admiration of the servants of Achish into pitying scorn. What David hoped took place, and he was driven out of Gath with ignominy; but there is no reason for supposing that had he maintained a quiet dignity of behaviour any evil would have happened to him. The Philistines, for those wild times, seem to have been a cultured people, and by no means devoid of generous instincts. Not one word, strangely enough, is reported to have been spoken about the great injury he had done to the Philistine nation when he slew Goliath. It has been suggested with considerable ingenuity that the great name of the dead champion, the hero of so many battle-fields, was never brought forward here, perhaps out of a natural indisposition to recall a grievous calamity, but more likely out of regard for Goliath's family and friends. Singularly little is told us, in fact, about this renowned hero, whom tradition hints at as the great warrior in the decisive battle when the Ark was captured and the sons of Eli were slain. The Talmud has a curious comment on this strange silence—"Not half the praises of Goliath are related in Scripture; hence it follows that it is wrong to tell the praises of the wicked."—Treatise *Soteh,* fol. 42, col. 2.

(13) **He changed his behaviour.**—These very words (with the substitution of Abimelech for Achish, a name which, as has been above suggested, seems to have been the "nomen dignitatis" for generations of Philistine kings) are found in the title of Ps. xxxiv. The poem in question is, however, of a general, not of an historical character, and especially celebrates Jehovah's guardian care of the righteous. Its "acrostic" arrangement, however, suggests a later date than the time of David. If, as is quite possible, the royal psalmist was the original author, and that the deliverance on the present occasion suggested the theme, then it must have been brought into its present form by some later temple musician.

Feigned himself mad.—Literally, *he roamed hither and thither, restless and in terror.*—Dean Payne Smith. "In their hands," that is, "in their presence." Some have supposed that the madness was not "simulated," but *real.* Wrought upon by excitement of fear and terrible anxiety, it has been suggested that the mind for a time lost its balance, and that David became temporarily really insane; but the sense of the narrative plainly indicates that the madness was feigned.

Scrabbled on the doors of the gate.—Scratched on them; "scrabble" being probably a diminutive of "scrape" (Richardson, *Dictionary*). By others it is connected with "scribble," the root in either case being ultimately the same. The LXX. and Vulg. apparently translate from a slightly different word, and instead of "scrabbled," render "drummed" (*impingebat*) on the wings of the doors.

David takes Refuge   I. SAMUEL, XXII.   *in the Cave Adullam.*

the doors of the gate, and let his spittle fall down upon his beard. ⁽¹⁴⁾ Then said Achish unto his servants, Lo, ye see the man ¹is mad: wherefore *then* have ye brought him to me? ⁽¹⁵⁾ Have I need of mad men, that ye have brought this *fellow* to play the mad man in my presence? shall this *fellow* come into my house?

¹ Or, *playeth the mad man.*

² Heb., *had a creditor.*

³ Heb., *bitter of soul.*

CHAPTER XXII.—⁽¹⁾ David therefore departed thence, and escaped to the cave Adullam: and when his brethren and all his father's house heard *it*, they went down thither to him. ⁽²⁾ And every one *that was* in distress, and every one that ²*was* in debt, and every one *that was* ³discontented, gathered themselves unto him; and he became a captain over

---

Let his spittle fall.—That is, allowed the foam which comes from the mouth of a madman to hang about his beard. It has been cleverly suggested that David was only too well acquainted with all the signs of madness, from his long and intimate association with King Saul in his darker hours of insanity. There are other well-authenticated examples in history of great heroes, in seasons of sore danger, feigning madness like David, with a view of escaping from their enemies. For instance, according to the Shâhnâmeh, Kai Khosrev feigned idiocy in face of mortal peril.

⁽¹⁴⁾ **Then said Achish . . . the man is mad.** —The Philistine king would look with peculiar sorrow and repulsion on a madman if, as according to Jewish tradition (see Philippson), *his own wife and daughter were insane.*

The device, however, succeeded, as David hoped it would, and he was suffered to depart in safety—nay, was even hurried out of the Philistine country. In old times, as now, in many parts of the East, the insane are looked upon as persons in some peculiar way possessed by, and therefore under the more immediate protection of, Deity. The life then of the hunted fugitive was perfectly safe from the moment the Philistines considered him mad.

There is a curious legend in the Talmud in which several events recorded in the Biblical account are confused. Part of it apparently refers to this strange choice of his of Philistia as a place of refuge. "One day *Satan* appeared to him (David) in the shape of a gazelle, which, eluding his pursuit, decoyed him into the land of the Philistines. 'Ah!' said Ishbi-benob, when he caught sight of him, 'art thou the man that slew my brother, Goliath?' So saying, he seized and bound him."—Treatise *Sanhedrin*, fol. 95, cols 1, 2. The wild legend goes on to explain how, partly by miracle, partly with the aid of Abishai, David slew Ishbi-benob and escaped.

XXII.

(1–23) David's Life when Bearing Arms against the King at Adullam and Hareth—Saul is informed by Doeg of the Visit of David to the High Priest at Nob—Massacre of all the Priests, and Destruction of the Sanctuary of Nob by Saul—Abiathar, son of Ahimelech, escapes to David.

⁽¹⁾ **The cave Adullam.**—The great valley of Elah forms the highway from Philistia to Hebron. In one especially of the tributary vales or ravines of the Elah valley are many natural caves, some of great extent, roomy and dry, which are still used by the shepherds as dwelling-places, and as refuges for their flocks and herds. David chose one of these natural fastnesses as the temporary home for himself and his followers. The traveller sees that there was ample room for the 400 refugees who gathered under David's skilled leadership. Stanley even speaks of this Adullam Cavern as "a subterranean palace, with vast columnar halls and arched chambers."

The name Adullam was probably given to the largest of these great caverns from its proximity to the old royal Canaanitish city of Adullam (Josh. xv. 35), ruins of which on a rounded hill to the south of the cave are still visible.

His brethren and all his father's house.— They of course soon felt the weight of Saul's anger against the prominent hero of their race, and dreading the fate which often overwhelms whole families for the faults of one of the more distinguished members, fled from their homes, and joined David and his armed force of outlaws.

⁽²⁾ **Every one that was in distress.**—Ewald writes on this statement:—"The situation of the country, which was becoming more and more melancholy under Saul, . . . drove men to seek a leader from whom they might hope for better things for the future. . . David did not send away these refugees, many of them distinguished and prominent Israelites, but organised them into a military force. He foresaw that while commanding such a company as this, he might, without injuring his king and former benefactor, be of the very greatest use to the people, and protect the southern frontiers of the kingdom—sadly exposed in these later years of King Saul—from the plundering incursions of the neighbouring nomadic tribes. This state of things, with a few interruptions, really came to pass, and David won great repute and popularity among the protected districts during these years when he was a warderer and an outlaw—a popularity which in after years stood him in good stead."

These persons "in distress" were especially those who were persecuted by Saul and his men for their attachment to David. The several statements of the refugees who took shelter in David's armed camp, of course go over a considerable time. They did not all flock to his standard at once. Some went to him in the first days of his exile, others after the massacre at the sanctuary at Nob, others later, and thus gradually 400 gathered round him. Soon after, these numbers were swelled to 600, and these probably only were the chosen men-at-arms of the little force, which, no doubt, was numerically far greater.

And every one that was in debt.—Throughout the whole long story of Israel this unhappy love of greed and gain has been a characteristic feature of the chosen race, ever a prominent and ugly sin. In the Mosaic Law, most stringent regulations were laid down to correct and mitigate this ruling passion of avarice among the Jews. (See such passages as Exod. xxii. 25; Lev. xxv. 36; Deut. xxiii. 19.) The poor, improvident, or perhaps unfortunate, debtor was protected by wise laws against the greedy avaricious spirit of his merciless creditor. These beneficent regulations of the great

David's Parents in Moab.   I. SAMUEL, XXII.   *David Admonished by Gad.*

them: and there were with him about four hundred men.

⁽³⁾ And David went thence to Mizpeh of Moab: and he said unto the king of Moab, Let my father and my mother, I pray thee, come forth, *and be* with you, till I know what God will do for me. ⁽⁴⁾ And he brought them before the king of Moab: and they dwelt with him all the while that David was in the hold. ⁽⁵⁾ And the prophet Gad said unto David, Abide not in the hold; depart, and get thee into the land of Judah. Then David departed, and came into the forest of Hareth.

⁽⁶⁾ When Saul heard that David was

---

lawgiver had, under the capricious, faulty rule of King Saul, of course fallen into abeyance, and a terrible amount of misery, no doubt, was the consequence. In the Divine record sad scenes (see 2 Kings iv. 1—7), exemplifying this pitiless spirit, are casually related, but they are so woven into the mosaic of the history, as to show us they were, alas! no uncommon occurrence in the daily life of the people. In Proverbs, for instance, we have some conspicuous instances. The chronicles of the Middle Ages in all countries teem with similar stories about the chosen people. Our own great dramatist, some three centuries ago, evidently without attempt at exaggeration, selects the avaricious, grasping Jew as the central figure of one of his most famous dramas. In our own time the same spirit, as is too well known, is still abroad, and constitutes the bitterest reproach which the many enemies of the strange, deathless race can promulgate against a people evidently walled in by a Divine protection and a changeless eternal love.

And he became a captain over them.—It was evidently no undisciplined band, these outlaws of Adullam and the hold of Moab, of Hareth and Keilah, of Ziph and Engedi. David quickly organised the refugees, among whom, by degrees, many a man of mark and approved valour and ability were numbered.

To complete the picture of this First Book of Samuel, we must unite in one the scattered notices of this same period which occur in the Second Book of Samuel and in the Books of Kings and Chronicles. (See *Excursus I.* at the end of this Book.)

⁽³⁾ **Mizpeh.**—This particular Mizpeh is mentioned nowhere else. The word means *a watch tower*; it was probably some mountain fortress in Moab. It has been suggested that it was the same as Zophim, a word of the same root as Mizpeh (see Num. xxiii. 14). David evidently sought hospitality among his kin in Moab. Jesse, his father, was the grandson of Ruth the Moabitess. The distance from the south of Judah where the fugitives were wandering was not great.

Till I know what God will do for me.—This memory of David's words to the King of Moab shows that the old trust and love, which in his first moments of care and sorrow had failed him, had come back again to the son of Jesse. It is interesting to note that David when addressing the Moabite sovereign speaks of "God" "Elohim," not of Jehovah. This was probably out of deep reverence; an idolator had nothing to do with the awful name by which the Eternal was known to His covenant people—a Name which, as originally uttered, has now passed away from the earth. We read the mystic four letters, but no man, Jew or Gentile, can pronounce the Name of Names. The "Name," however, was not unknown in Moab, for the mystic letters which compose it occur in the inscription of Mesha, dating about 150 years from the days of David's exile.

⁽⁴⁾ **While that David was in the hold.**—This "hold" is, of course, identical with the "hold" of verse 5, from which Gad the prophet directs David to depart, and to return into the land of Judah. It was, most likely, in the Land of Moab.

⁽⁵⁾ **The prophet Gad.**—From this time onward throughout the life and reign of David, Gad the prophet occupied evidently a marked place. He is mentioned as the king's seer in 2 Sam. xxiv. 11; and in 1 Chron. xxix. 29 he appears as the compiler of the acts of David, along with Samuel and Nathan. In 2 Chron. xxix. 25 he is mentioned with his brother prophet Nathan again, as the man who had drawn up the plan of the great Temple services, which have been the model now for eighteen centuries of the countless Christian Liturgies in all the Churches.

It was Gad also who, far on in the golden days of the exile's rule, dared to reprove the mighty king for his deed of numbering the people, which act involved a great sin, or the design of a great sin, not recorded for us, and who brought as a message from the Highest the terrible choice of three evils (2 Sam. xxiv. 11, and following verses). As he appears in the last years of the great king's life, and apparently survived his master and friend, Gad must have been still young, or at all events in the prime of life, when he joined the fugitive and his outlawed band. He had, therefore, not improbably been a fellow student and friend of David's in the Naioth of Samuel by Ramah. It seems hardly a baseless conjecture which sees in Gad a direct messenger from the old prophet Samuel to his loved pupil David, "the anointed," Samuel well knew, "of the Lord." As has been before observed, among the many who were educated and brought up in the Schools of the Prophets as historians, preachers, musicians, and teachers, but very few seem to have received the Divine influence (the Spirit's "afflatus") which was needed to constitute a prophet in the true high sense of the solemn word as we now understand it. Gad, however, appears to have been one of these rarely favoured few, and the presence of such an one in this outlaw camp of David must have been of great advantage to the captain.

Abide not.—The wise advice of the prophet, suggested by a Divine influence, told David not to estrange himself from his own country and people by remaining in a foreign land, but to return with his followers to the wilder districts of Judah. There was work for him and his followers to do in that distracted, harassed land.

The forest of Hareth.—The LXX. and Josephus here read "the city of Hareth." Lieutenant Conder, whose late investigations have thrown so much light upon the geography of the Promised Land, can find no trace of forest on the edge of the mountain chain of Hebron, where Kharas now stands, and he therefore believes the LXX. text the true one. Dean Payne Smith, however, considers that "the thickets," which still grow here abundantly, are what the Hebrew word *yar*, here translated "forest," signifies.

⁽⁶⁾ **When Saul heard.**—No note of time is here given. Probably the return of David with a disci-

discovered, and the men that *were* with him, (now Saul abode in Gibeah under a ¹tree in Ramah, having his spear in his hand, and all his servants *were* standing about him;) ⁽⁷⁾ then Saul said unto his servants that stood about him, Hear now, ye Benjamites; will the son of Jesse give every one of you fields and vineyards, *and* make you all captains of thousands, and captains of hundreds; ⁽⁸⁾ that all of you have conspired against me, and *there is* none that ²sheweth me that my son hath made a league with the son of Jesse, and *there is* none of you that is sorry for me, or sheweth unto me that my son hath stirred up my servant against me, to lie in wait, as at this day? ⁽⁹⁾ Then answered Doeg the Edomite, which was set over the servants of Saul, and said, I saw the son of Jesse coming to Nob, to Ahimelech the son of Ahitub.

1 Or, *grove in a high place.*

2 Heb., *uncovereth mine ear.*

---

plined force to the land, and the pitching of an armed camp in the "forest of Hareth," excited anew Saul's jealous fears.

Now Saul abode in Gibeah.—In Gibeah of Saul, his own royal city. The LXX. wrongly render, instead of Gibeah, "on the hills." The margin of the English Version, "under a grove in a high place," is correct as regards the later words, *baramah* signifying here upon the height. "Under a tree" is, however, nearer the original than "under a grove." The literal rendering would be "under a tamarisk tree." The sentence then should run, "Now Saul abode in Gibeah, under the tamarisk tree on the height." The tamarisk, which grows so abundantly on the sea-shore of England and in warmer climates, develops into a very graceful tree, with long feathery branches and tufts. Saul's love for trees has been noticed before. This solemn council of his, when the darkest deed of his reign was decided upon, was held in the spot Saul loved so well, under the spreading tamarisk branches. There we see him, leaning, as was his wont in peace as in war, upon his tall spear, surrounded by his valiant captains, chosen apparently, with one exception, from his own tribe of Benjamin—the exception being his wicked counsellor, the Edomite Doeg, who was over the royal herds. This is one of the earliest councils we have any definite account of in the world's history. The king, surrounded by his chosen "fideles," complaining of the treason of one of them lately exiled from their midst, bewailing the want of fidelity of his son, the heir to the throne—then the stepping forward of one of these "fideles," one invested with high office, and publicly denouncing the chief religious official of the kingdom—forms a striking and vivid picture.

⁽⁷⁾ **Hear now, ye Benjamites.**—We have here a fair specimen of Saul's manner of ruling in his later years. It is no wonder that the heart of the people gradually was estranged from one of whom in earlier years they had been so proud. The suspicious and gloomy king had evidently—we have it here from his own mouth—gradually given all the posts of honour and dignity to men of his own tribe and family, or to strangers like Doeg. "Hear now, ye Benjamites"—so the "fideles" were evidently men of his own favoured tribe; indeed, he refers to his own weak partiality as the reason why *they* of all men should be loyal. "Who but a Benjamite," he says, "would only honour Benjamites?" Such a sovereign had surely forfeited his kingdom. The consequences of such a weak and short-sighted policy were plainly visible in the thin array he was able in his hour of bitter need to muster together on the fatal field of Mount Gilboa against his sleepless Philistine enemies. (See chap. xxxi.)

⁽⁸⁾ **That all of you have conspired.**—The unhappy, jealous spirit had obtained such complete mastery over the unhappy king that now he suspected even the chosen men of his own tribe. All his tried favourites, the men of his own house, even his gallant son, he charged with leaning towards David the traitor, his supplanter in the hearts of Israel.

My son hath made a league.—It would seem as though Saul had learned something of what passed between Jonathan and David when they met for that farewell interview at the memorable New Moon feast; the words respecting the covenant between the two being too pointed and marked to refer only to the well-known ancient friendship between the prince and the son of Jesse.

There is none of you that is sorry for me.—These words of the sad king—tormented as he was by an evil spirit, ever whispering doubt and jealous thoughts into the poor diseased mind—are here strangely real and pathetic.

⁽⁹⁾ **Then answered Doeg the Edomite.**—This Doeg has already been mentioned in the preceding chapter. His presence in this council meeting under the tamarisk of Gibeah, among the famous Benjamite chieftains, and the previous notice which speaks of him as the officer superintending the royal herds, indicates that he was a personage of no small importance at the Court of Saul. He occupies too a considerable position in the Psalmodic literature. (See, for instance, Ps. lii.)

Here he is spoken of as a wicked and unscrupulous character. Jewish tradition tells us this Doeg was skilled in all the learning of his time. Doeg the Edomite, and Ahitophel (whose counsel was as the oracle of God) are represented in the Talmud as the most learned men of their time. "The Holy One, blessed be He! said to wicked Doeg, what hast thou to do to declare my statutes (Ps. lii.)? When thou comest to the chapter on murderers and on spreading evil reports, what dost thou make of them?"—*Sanhedrin*, fol. 106, col. 2.

It is strange that this renowned man, whom evidently David looked upon as the evil genius of Saul at the period when he wrote the sad, bitter words of Psalm lii., and spoke of the tongue of this Doeg as being like a sharp razor, and dwelt with singular persistence on the wickedness, falsehood, and calumny of this relentless enemy, should have gone down among the noteworthy Talmudical traditions as "the *greatest Rabbinist*" (*i.e.*, the most deeply learned in the Mosaic Law, and in its interpretation) of his time.

Which was set over the servants of Saul.—This statement would be a puzzling one were it the correct rendering. It would be unlikely in the highest degree that Saul would set a foreigner—however able and devoted—over his faithful Benjamite chieftains. The accurate translation is "who stood with the servants of Saul." In verse 6 we read, in the description of the council meeting under the tamarisk of Gibeah, all his

(10) And he enquired of the LORD for him, and gave him victuals, and gave him the sword of Goliath the Philistine.

(11) Then the king sent to call Ahimelech the priest, the son of Ahitub, and all his father's house, the priests that were in Nob: and they came all of them to the king. (12) And Saul said, Hear now, thou son of Ahitub. And he answered, ¹Here I *am*, my lord. (13) And Saul said unto him, Why have ye conspired against me, thou and the son of Jesse, in that thou hast given him bread, and a sword, and hast enquired of God for him, that he should rise against me, to lie in wait, as at this day? (14) Then Ahimelech answered the king, and said, And who *is so* faithful among all thy servants as David, which is the king's son in law, and goeth at thy bidding, and is honourable in thine house? (15) Did I then begin to enquire of God for him? be it far from me: let not the king impute *any* thing unto his servant, *nor* to all the house of my father: for thy servant knew nothing of all this, ²less or more.

(16) And the king said, Thou shalt surely die, Ahimelech, thou, and all thy father's house.

(17) And the king said unto the ³⁴footmen that stood about him, Turn, and slay the priests of the LORD; because their hand also *is* with David, and because they knew when he fled, and did not shew it to me. But the servants of the king would not put forth their hand to fall upon the priests of the LORD.

1 Heb., *Behold me.*
2 Heb., *little or great.*
3 Or, *guard.*
4 Heb., *runners.*

---

servants (that is, his chief dignitaries) stood by (around) him (Saul), and with these, his peers, stood Doeg the Edomite, the hero of the terrible scene which followed.

(9) **Then answered Doeg.**—"Far better," quaintly writes Seb Schmid, "did Saul's other servants who kept silence." The Edomite's witness had the more effect on Saul because he related no hearsay evidence, but what he had absolutely seen.

(10) **And he enquired of the Lord for him.**—This is, however, by no means certain (see below); nothing was said about the Urim and Thummim being brought out and questioned by the high priest on the occasion of David's visit. It is possible that Doeg was misled here by the fact of the high priest's going into the sanctuary, where the ephod was, to fetch the sword of Goliath for David. This famous sword was laid up, we know, *behind the ephod.*

(11) **Then the king sent to call Ahimelech.**—This sending for all the priestly house to Gibeah when alone Ahimelech was to blame—if blame there was—looks as though Saul and Doeg had determined upon the wholesale massacre which followed.

(13) **And hast enquired of God for him.**—This using of the Urim and Thummim for David is again repeated by the king. It seems in Saul's eyes to have been the gravest of the charges imputed to the high priest by Doeg, for Ahimelech specially in his defence recurs to this point with peculiar insistence: the only charge, as it appears, to which Ahimelech deigned to reply, "Did I then begin to enquire of God for him?" (verse 15).

(14) **Who is so faithful among all thy servants?**—The words of the high priest were quiet and dignified, and no doubt spoke the general sentiments of the people respecting David. What he—the guardian of the sanctuary—had done, he had done as a matter of course for one so closely related to the king—for one, too, ever loyal and devoted as David had ever proved himself.

(15) **Did I then begin to enquire?**—The English translation of the Hebrew here would imply that David had on many previous occasions received through him (the high priest) Divine directions from the Urim and Thummim. "Did I that day *begin* to enquire?" Abarbanel gives an alternative rendering: "That was the first day that I enquired of God for him, and I did not know that it was displeasing to thee." Another rendering is: "Did I enquire?" in a negative sense, suggesting the reply "*No, I did not.*" On the whole, the alternative rendering suggested by Abarbanel, quoted in *Lange*, is the best: "That was the first day, &c." And the reason why Ahimelech allowed the sacred Urim to be consulted was that he supposed David was come (as he represented) on a mission direct from King Saul. Surely, thought the blameless high priest, I never supposed my king would have been wroth with me for that.

If we render as in the English Version, which has the support of many scholars and versions, the only possible explanation of the words, "Did I that day begin to enquire?" is to suppose that David had been in the habit of consulting the Urim on special occasions *for the king.* The king, when there was a king in Israel, it is nearly certain, *alone* had this right. The Talmud teaching here is most definite; and it is a point in which the Talmud tradition may be looked on as authoritative. "The Rabbis have taught—How were the Urim and Thummim oracularly consulted? The king or the chief of the legislative administration, who alone had the privilege of consulting the Urim, stood facing the priest, and the priest was facing the Shekinah and the 'Shem-hammephorash,' the ineffable name deposited with the Urim within the breastplate."—Treatise.*Yoma*, fol. 73, cols. 1, 2.

(17) **The footmen.**—"Footmen," literally *runners.* These "guards," or "lictors," were men who ran by the royal chariot as an escort. They are still the usual attendants of any great man in the East. From long habit they were able to maintain a great speed for a long time. (See chap. viii. 11, where Samuel tells the children of Israel how the king of the future, whom they asked for, would take some of them to "run before his chariot." See, too, for an example of the power of running in old times, 1 Kings xviii. 46, when Elijah outstripped the chariot of Ahab.)

But the servants of the king would not put forth their hand.—"And thus they were more faithful to Saul than if they had obeyed his order, which was against the commandment of the Lord, whose servant the king was no less than they."—*Wordsworth.*

(18) And the king said to Doeg, Turn thou, and fall upon the priests. And Doeg the Edomite turned, and he fell upon the priests, and slew on that day fourscore and five persons that did wear a linen ephod. (19) And Nob, the city of the priests, smote he with the edge of the sword, both men and women, children and sucklings, and oxen, and asses, and sheep, with the edge of the sword.

(20) And one of the sons of Ahimelech the son of Ahitub, named Abiathar, escaped, and fled after David. (21) And Abiathar shewed David that Saul had slain the LORD's priests. (22) And David said unto Abiathar, I knew it that day, when Doeg the Edomite was there, that he would surely tell Saul: I have occasioned the death of all the persons of thy father's house. (23) Abide thou with me,

---

(18) **And Doeg the Edomite .... fell upon the priests, and slew on that day fourscore and five persons.**—No doubt, assisted by his own attached servants, Doeg carried out this deed of unexampled barbarity. For this act the Edomite servant of Saul has been execrated in the most ancient Jewish writings perhaps above any other of the famous wicked men who meet us in the Holy Scriptures. For instance, we read in the Babylonian Talmud how "Doeg the Edomite, after his massacre of the priests, was encountered by three destructive demons. One deprived him of his learning (concerning which see above, in Note on verse 9), a second burned his soul, and a third scattered his dust in the synagogues."—Treatise *Sanhedrin*, fol. 106, col. 2. The Babylonian Talmud has a still more curious comment on the iniquity of Doeg, in which David is bitterly reproached by the Most High for being the cause of Doeg's great sin and its terrible consequences. "Rav Yehudah recorded that Rav had said ... The Holy One, blessed be He! had said to David, How long shall this iniquity cling to thee? Through thee the priests of Nob were slain; through thee Doeg the Edomite became a reprobate; and through thee Saul and his three sons were slain."—Treatise *Sanhedrin*, fol. 95, cols. 1, 2.

A linen ephod.—The ordinary priests appear to have worn a linen over garment, similar in form to the high priestly cape or ephod. They came probably from Nob to Gibeah (the distance was not great) clad in their official costume, out of respect to the king who sent for them. The murderous deed assumes a still more awful character when we recollect who were the victims—the priests of the living God, clad in their white ministering robes!

(19) **Nob, the city of the priests, smote he.**—The vengeful king, not content with striking the men, the heads of the priestly houses, in his insane fury proceeded to treat the innocent city where they resided as a city under the ban "cherem," as though it had been polluted with idolatry and wickedness, and therefore devoted to utter destruction. The only crime of Nob had been that its venerable chief citizen, Ahimelech the priest, had shown kindness to David, whom Saul hated with a fierce mad hate. In 2 Samuel xxi. 1 we read of a scourge in the form of a famine afflicting Israel during three years. The cause of this God-sent calamity is told us in the Lord's words: "It was for Saul and his bloody house, *because he slew the Gibeonites.*" Now, this slaughter of the Gibeonites—evidently a dark crime—is nowhere specially related in the Old Testament books. Was it not this awful sequel to the crime of Gibeah, where the hapless Ahimelech and his eighty-five priests were murdered, that was referred to in the above mentioned passage—the awful sequel when Saul smote Nob, the city of the priests, with the sword? In that terrible catastrophe, were not the Gibeonites, *hewers of wood and drawers of water for the Tabernacle* (see Josh. ix. 21—27), slain? for we read how in the destruction of the ill-fated city men, women and children, and all cattle perished. "Only once before had so terrible a calamity befallen the sons of Aaron, and that was when the Philistines destroyed Shiloh. But they were enemies, and had been provoked by the people bringing the Ark to battle; and even then the women and children seem to have escaped. It was left to the anointed king of Israel, who had himself settled the priests at Nob and restored Jehovah's worship there, to perpetrate an act unparalleled in Jewish history for its barbarity."—*Dean Payne Smith*.

(20) **Abiathar.**—Of those who dwelt at Nob, only one single priest, Abiathar, Ahimelech's son, seems to have escaped this general massacre. It has been suggested that when his father and the whole body of priests went to Gibeah, in accordance with the summons of King Saul, Abiathar remained behind to perform the necessary functions in the sanctuary, and when he heard of the death of his father and his brother priests, he made his escape, and eventually joined David. The exact period of his coming to the exiled band under David is uncertain; in many of the recitals in this Book no note of time is given. It is, therefore, probable that the meeting and interview with David —related in verse 20 and following verses—did not take place immediately after the massacre at Gibeah, nor even directly after the destruction of Nob. From the statement in verse 6 of chap. xxiii., it would appear that Abiathar only joined David at Keilah. From that time, however, Abiathar, who became after his father's death high priest, occupies an important place in the story of David's life. Throughout his reign he continued his faithful friend, and seems to have been a worthy holder of his important office. The close of his life, however, was a melancholy one. In the troubles which arose about the succession, in the last days of David's reign, he espoused the side of Adonijah, and was in consequence deposed by the successful Solomon from the high priesthood, and sent into banishment to Anathoth. (See 1 Kings ii. 26.)

(22) **When Doeg the Edomite was there.**—The Talmudical tradition evidently pre-supposes that a bitter enmity existed between David and Saul's too faithful friend Doeg. If the Rabbinical belief that the identity between the family servant, or steward, who accompanied the young man Saul on that journey when we first meet with him (see chap. ix.) be accepted, this enmity would be partly accounted for. The Edomite Doeg, brought up with Saul in the family of Kish, no doubt was jealous for his master and his master's house with the passionate jealousy we so

fear not: for he that seeketh my life seeketh thy life: but with me thou *shalt be* in safeguard.

CHAPTER XXIII.—⁽¹⁾ Then they told David, saying, Behold, the Philistines fight against Keilah, and they rob the threshingfloors. ⁽²⁾ Therefore David enquired of the LORD, saying, Shall I go and smite these Philistines? And the LORD said unto David, Go, and smite the Philistines, and save Keilah. ⁽³⁾ And David's men said unto him, Behold, we be afraid here in Judah: how much more then if we come to Keilah against the armies of the Philistines? ⁽⁴⁾ Then David enquired of the LORD yet again. And the LORD answered him and said, Arise, go down to Keilah; for I will deliver the Philistines into thine hand. ⁽⁵⁾ So David and his men went to Keilah, and fought with the Philistines, and brought away their cattle, and smote them with a great slaughter. So David saved the inhabitants of Keilah.

⁽⁶⁾ And it came to pass, when Abiathar the son of Ahimelech ^a fled to David to Keilah, *that* he came down *with* an ephod in his hand.

a ch. 22. 20.

---

often find in old servants. He would share and probably fan his royal master's envy and fear respecting the brilliant young hero who was so rapidly supplanting Saul and Saul's house in the affections of Israel. So when David, flying for his life from Saul, met Doeg at the Sanctuary of Nob, he was seized with grave misgivings as to what would happen; and now, after the terrible vengeance of Saul, seems to reproach himself with having in Doeg's presence exposed the hapless priest Ahimelech to Saul's furious anger.

The Talmud says the servant (chap. xvi. 18) who first searched out and brought David to play to the sick king was Doeg, anxious to relieve his master's sufferings, but curiously adds that even then the praises bestowed on David by Doeg were unreal: "All the praises of David enumerated by Doeg in 1 Sam. xvi. 18 had a malicious object."—*Sanhedrin,* fol. 93, col. 2.

XXIII.

^(1–28) **David Saves Keilah.**—He enquires of God by means of the Urim and Thummim, and leaves treacherous Keilah.—He sees Jonathan once more.—The Ziphites Betray him to Saul.—He is Saved by an Invasion of the Philistines.

⁽¹⁾ **Then they told David. . . .**—For this and like duties the prophet Gad (chap. xxii. 5) had summoned David to return with his armed band to Judah. There was a great work ready to his hand in his own country at that juncture. Saul was becoming more and more neglectful of his higher duty—that of protecting his people; as time went on and his malady increased, his whole thoughts were concentrated on David's imaginary crimes, and the history of the latter part of his reign is little more than a recital of his sad, bewildered efforts to compass the young hero's destruction. The task of protecting the people from the constant marauding expeditions of the Philistines, and probably of the neighbouring nations, then was entrusted to David. To point this out to the son of Jesse was evidently the first great mission of Gad the seer. Samuel's mind was, no doubt, busied in this matter. It is more than probable that Gad was first dispatched to join David at the instigation of the aged, but still mentally vigorous, prophet.

Keilah.—"This town lay in the lowlands of Judah, not far from the Philistine frontier, some miles south of Adullam, being perched on a steep hill overlooking the valley of Elah, not far from the thickets of Hareth" (Conder: *Tent Life in Palestine*).

⁽²⁾ **David enquired of the Lord.**—The enquiry was not made of the priest wearing the ephod, by means of the Urim and Thummim, for, according to verse 6, Abiathar, the high priest who succeeded the murdered Ahimelech, only joined David at Keilah, the citizens of which place were then asking for his aid against their foes. But Gad the prophet was with David, and the enquiry was made, no doubt, through him. We know that such enquiries were made through prophets, for we possess a detailed account of such an enquiry being made by Jehoshaphat of the prophet Micaiah (1 Kings xxii. 5, 7, 8), in which passage the same formula is used as in this case. The Talmud too, when discussing the enquiries made through the Urim and Thummim, whilst dwelling on the greater weight of the decision pronounced by the sacred stones, assumes that questions were also asked *through the prophets.* "The decree pronounced by a prophet is revocable, but the decision of the Urim and Thummim is irrevocable."—Treatise *Yoma,* fol. 73, col. 1.

⁽³⁾ **Here in Judah.**—This does not imply that Keilah was out of the territory of Judah, but simply that the district in the neighbourhood round Keilah was at that time under Philistine domination. The open country in times of Philistine supremacy first fell under their control; their strong places, like Keilah, would resist for a much longer period.

⁽⁴⁾ **David enquired . . . yet again.**—This second enquiry, made for the sake of inspiring his little army with confidence before embarking on the seemingly desperate attempt, was, as in the previous case mentioned in verse 2, no doubt through the prophet Gad. Abiathar had not yet arrived with the ephod.

⁽⁶⁾ **With an ephod in his hand.**—The difficulty here with the version and commentators is that they failed to understand that enquiry of the Lord could be made in any other mode than through the Urim. (See Note above on verse 2.) Saul in happier days, we know, enquired and received replies "*through prophets,*" for before he had recourse to forbidden arts we read how, in contrast evidently to other and earlier times, the Lord answered him not, neither by dreams, nor by Urim, *nor by prophets* (chap. xxviii. 6). The LXX. here must have deliberately altered the Hebrew text, with the view of escaping what seemed to these translators a grave difficulty. They render, "And it came to pass, when Abiathar the son of Ahimelech fled to David, that he came down with **David**

(7) And it was told Saul that David was come to Keilah. And Saul said, God hath delivered him into mine hand; for he is shut in, by entering into a town that hath gates and bars. (8) And Saul called all the people together to war, to go down to Keilah, to besiege David and his men.

(9) And David knew that Saul secretly practised mischief against him; and he said to Abiathar the priest, Bring hither the ephod. (10) Then said David, O LORD God of Israel, thy servant hath certainly heard that Saul seeketh to come to Keilah, to destroy the city for my sake. (11) Will the men of Keilah deliver me up into his hand? will Saul come down, as thy servant hath heard? O LORD God of Israel, I beseech thee, tell thy servant. And the LORD said, He will come down. (12) Then said David, Will the men of Keilah ¹deliver me and my men into the hand of Saul? And the LORD said, They will deliver *thee* up.

B.C. cir. 1061.

1 Heb., *shut up.*

---

to Keilah, having an ephod in his hand," thus implying that Abiathar had come down *with David* to Keilah, having joined him previously. The Hebrew text is, however, definite and clear, and tells us that Abiathar first joined David when he was at Keilah. But the difficulty which puzzled the LXX. and so many others vanishes when we remember that the enquiry of the Lord was not unfrequently made through the prophet; and this was evidently done by David through Gad, a famous representative of that order, in the case of the enquiry referred to in verses 2 and 4 of this chapter.

(7) **God hath delivered him into mine hand.**—There was little chance, Saul knew, of his being able to capture or slay his foe when he was roaming at large through the desert and forests which lay to the south of Palestine, and which stretched far southward beyond the reach of any armed force that he could collect; but there was a hope of being able to compass his enemy's destruction, either through treachery or a hand-to-hand encounter, in a confined space like a city with bars and gates, such as Keilah. Saul and his counsellors knew too well whom they had to deal with in the case of the citizens of that faithless, thankless city. It is strange, after all that had passed, that Saul could delude himself that *his* cause was the cause of God, and that David was the reprobate and rejected. The Hebrew word here is remarkable: God hath "repudiated or rejected him." The LXX. renders "sold him" (into my hands).

(8) **And Saul called all the people together.**—Such a summons to war on the part of the sovereign has been always a royal right. The plea, of course, alleged for this "summons" was the necessity of an immediate national effort against the hereditary enemies of the people.

(9) **Secretly practised mischief.**—The idea of secrecy suggested in the English translation does not appear in the Hebrew; the accurate rendering would be, "was forging, or devising." It is likely enough that Jonathan contrived to keep his friend informed of these Court plots against him.

Bring hither the ephod.—It is quite clear that a different method of enquiry was used by David on this occasion. In verses 3 and 4 it is merely stated that he enquired of the Lord; here at Keilah his enquiry was prefaced, in verse 6, by a definite statement that Abiathar the priest, *with the ephod,* had arrived here before he asked the question of God. The history tells us he directed Abiathar the priest to "bring hither the ephod," thus pointedly connecting the enquiry in some way with the ephod. In this ephod were set twelve precious stones, one for each of the twelve tribes. The names of the tribes were engraved on these gems, the Rabbis tell us, along with some other sacred words. On important solemn occasions—it seems perfectly certain during a considerable time—that these stones were allowed by the providence of God, who worked so many marvels for His people, to be used as oracles. It has been already stated that according to a most ancient tradition the use of the sacred gems was restricted to the high priest, who could only call out the supernatural power at the bidding of the king or the head of the State for the time being (such an one as Joshua, for instance). The Divine response given by the sacred gems seems to have been the visible response to earnest, faithful prayer.

The common belief is that the ephod stones gave their answer to the royal and high priestly questions by some peculiar shining. But a passage (quoted at length in the *Excursus* M on the Urim and Thummim at the end of this Book) from the Babylonian Talmud (Treatise *Yoma*)—apparently little known—tells us that the Rabbis had two other explanations traditionally handed down from the days when the ephod and its holy gemmed breastplate was questioned on solemn occasions by the high priest.

(11) **Will the men of Keilah deliver me up into his hand? will Saul come down, as thy servant hath heard?**—There is a curious inversion of David's questions here. In their logical sequence, of course the second, respecting Saul's coming down, should have been put first, for the men of Keilah could not have delivered him into Saul's hands if Saul had not come down. Dean Payne Smith suggests that in David's earnest prayer "his two questions are put inversely to the logical order, but in accordance with the relative importance in his mind." The Dean thinks "that when the ephod was brought forward, the questions were of course put, and replied to in their logical sequence.

"And the Lord said, He will come down."
"And the Lord said, They will deliver thee up."

Thus the answer of the Urim and Thummim was given to the questions in their logical order. The Talmud has an interesting comment here. In consulting the Urim and Thummim, the enquirer is not to ask about *two things at a time,* for if he does, he will be answered about *one only,* and only about the one he first uttered, as it is said (1 Sam. xxiii. 11, 12). David asked first "Will the men of Keilah deliver me into his hands?" and then he asked also "Will Saul come down?" The answer was to the *second* query. "And the Lord said He will come down." But it has just been asserted that the enquirer will be answered only about the one thing he first uttered. To this it is replied, David framed his enquiry not *in good order,* but the reply of the

David in the Wilderness.   I. SAMUEL, XXIII.   *He Meets Jonathan.*

(13) Then David and his men, *which were* about six hundred, arose and departed out of Keilah, and went whithersoever they could go. And it was told Saul that David was escaped from Keilah; and he forbare to go forth. (14) And David abode in the wilderness in strong holds, and remained in a mountain in the wilderness of Ziph. And Saul sought him every day, but God delivered him not into his hand.

(15) And David saw that Saul was come out to seek his life: and David *was* in the wilderness of Ziph in a wood. (16) And Jonathan Saul's son arose, and went to David into the wood, and strengthened his hand in God. (17) And he said unto him, Fear not: for the hand of Saul my father shall not find thee; and thou shalt be king over Israel, and I shall be next unto thee; and that also Saul my father knoweth. (18) And they two made

---

Urim and Thummim was as though the enquiry had been *in proper order.* Hence when David became aware that his question had not been put properly, he repeated it again in better order, as it has been said, "Then said David, Will the men of Keilah deliver me and my men into the hand of Saul? And the Lord said, They will deliver thee up."—Treatise *Yoma,* fol. 73, col. 1.

(13) **Which were about six hundred.**—This is the only note we have in this part of the narrative of the rapid increase of the number of "men-at-arms" who joined David.

Whithersoever they could.—That is, the armed camp of David was pitched without any fixed plan or aim. Probably the force was marched in the direction of any Philistine raid, and it carried on thus on behalf of Israel a perpetual border warfare.

(14) **The wilderness of Ziph.**—This wilderness probably lies between Hebron and En-gedi. Some of these "stations" in the wanderings of the future king are only doubtfully identified. Cowper's musical—though perhaps, according to our recent canons of taste, old-fashioned—lines well describe the Psalmist-king's weary wanderings during this portion of his chequered career:—

> "See Judah's promised king bereft of all,
> Driven out an exile from the face of Saul.
> To distant caves the lonely wanderer flies,
> To seek that peace a tyrant's frown denies.
> His soul exults; hope animates his lays;
> The sense of mercy kindles into praise;
> And wilds familiar with the lion's roar
> Ring with ecstatic sounds unheard before."
>   COWPER.

Saul sought him every day, but God delivered him.—This is merely a general remark, and intended to cover a long period of time, including the remaining portion of Saul's reign, during which David was perpetually exposed to Saul's attempts to destroy him. It quietly mentions also that though Saul was armed with all the power of the king in Israel, he was powerless, for the invisible King of Israel declined to give this hated David into his hand.

(15) **In a wood.**—Some have understood this as a proper name, Horesh. There is no trace of the wood now. The land lost its ornament of trees centuries ago, through the desolating hand of man.—*Van der Velde.*

(16) **And Jonathan Saul's son arose, and went to David.**—Some have wished to show that the account of the last interview between the friends really belongs to the secret meeting between David and Jonathan recounted in chap. xx., and that it has got transposed; but such a view is quite untenable, for the narrative here is circumstantial, and even mentions the scene of the interview—"the wood," or, less probable, the town named "Horesh." The expression "strengthened his hand in God" is added by the narrator to show how sorely tried was the king of the future at this juncture, notwithstanding that so many gallant spirits rallied round him. The determined and relentless hostility of the king of the land, his sovereign, and once his friend—the apparent hopelessness of his struggle—the cruel ingratitude of whole bodies of his fellow countrymen, such as the men of Ziph—his homeless, outlawed condition: all these things naturally weighed upon the nervous and enthusiastic temperament of David, which was soon depressed. His sad forebodings in his desolateness and loneliness at this time are breathed forth in not a few of the Psalms which tradition ascribes to him. At such a juncture the warm sympathy, the steady onlook to a sunnier future of one like Jonathan was a real help to David. Jonathan was far-sighted enough when David's fortunes were at their lowest ebb to look confidently forward to a time when all these thick dark clouds of trouble should have passed away. Jonathan, we know (chap. xx. 14, 15) possessed sufficient confidence in David's future fortune even to ask the hunted exile to remember him, the prince, with kindness when he should have come into his kingdom. Such warm sympathy, such glowing trustful words, we may well imagine, raised the spirits of the outlaw, and gave him new courage to face the grave difficulties of his dangerous position.

(17) **And I shall be next unto thee.**—To us—who read a few pages on in the record of these times how this same generous, loving friend found a grave on Mount Gilboa instead of a home with David, whom he admired with so ungrudging an admiration—these words of Jonathan possess a pathetic interest of their own. That brave, romantic career was nearly run when he met David for the last time in the woods of Ziph. As far as we can judge, if Jonathan had lived he would have certainly ceded any rights he had to the throne of his father Saul in favour of David, unlike that other comparatively unknown son of Saul, Ishbosheth, who set up as a rival claimant to the son of Jesse. But his generosity was not to be exposed to any such severe test, and David was spared the presence of such a rival as the gallant and gifted Jonathan would assuredly have been to him.

And that also Saul my father knoweth.—It is very likely by this time that the circumstance of Samuel's mysterious anointing of the son of Jesse years before at Bethlehem had become known to Saul. Now that David had been openly proclaimed a public enemy, and that the king had repeatedly and openly sought his life, there was no reason for any concealment. No doubt, by this time very many in Israel looked on him as the anointed successor of Saul. The covenant alluded to in the next verse was, of course,

a covenant before the LORD: and David abode in the wood, and Jonathan went to his house.

(19) Then came up the Ziphites to Saul to Gibeah, saying, Doth not David hide himself with us in strong holds in the wood, in the hill of Hachilah, which is ¹on the south of ²Jeshimon? (20) Now therefore, O king, come down according to all the desire of thy soul to come down; and our part *shall be* to deliver him into the king's hand. (21) And Saul said, Blessed *be* ye of the LORD; for ye have compassion on me. (22) Go, I pray you, prepare yet, and know and see his place where his ³haunt is, *and* who hath seen him there: for it is told me *that* he dealeth very subtilly. (23) See therefore, and take knowledge of all the lurking places where he hideth himself, and come ye again to me with the certainty, and I will go with you: and it shall come to pass, if he be in the land, that I will search him out throughout all the thousands of Judah.

(24) And they arose, and went to Ziph before Saul: but David and his men *were* in the wilderness of Maon, in the plain on the south of Jeshimon. (25) Saul also and his men went to seek *him*. And they told David: wherefore he came down into a rock, and abode in the wilderness of Maon. And when Saul heard *that*, he pursued after David in the wilderness of Maon. (26) And Saul went on this side of the mountain, and David and his men on that side of the mountain: and David made haste to get away for fear of Saul; for Saul and his men compassed David and his men round about to take them. (27) But there came a messenger unto Saul, saying, Haste thee,

1 Heb., *on the right hand.*
2 Or, *the wilderness?*
3 Heb., *foot shall be.*

---

the old covenant of eternal friendship which they had made when they parted outside Gibeah at the New Moon feast, as we find related at length in chap. xx.

After this meeting David never looked on Jonathan's face in life again.

"Oh, heart of fire! misjudged by wilful man,
Thou flower of Jesse's race!
What woe was thine when thou and Jonathan
Last greeted face to face!
He doomed to die, thou on us to impress
The portent of a blood-stained holiness."
Lyra Apostolica.

(19) **The Ziphites.**—The words of these Ziphites, and the king's grateful reply, show that they were very warm adherents of Saul, entirely devoted to his fortunes, and well aware of his passionate desire to be rid of David.

On the south of Jeshimon.—Jeshimon is not the name of a place, but it signifies a "desert" or "solitude" (see Isaiah xliii. 19). It is used here for the "dreary desert which extends between the Dead Sea and the Hebron Mountains..... It is a plateau of white chalk, terminated on the east by cliffs, which rise vertically from the Dead Sea shore to a height of above 3,000 feet. The scenery is barren and wild beyond all description."—Conder: *Tent Life in Palestine.* This is the wilderness of Judea spoken of in Matt. iii. 1. David was just then encamped with some of his followers in some thickets bordering on this trackless desert. The Ziphites evidently knew the country well, not only the hills, but the solitary wastes stretching out at its base. They were willing and ready, if Saul's trained soldiers marched into their neighbourhood, to act as their guides in the pursuit of the famous outlaw and his men. They kept their promise faithfully, and in the pursuit which followed the arrival of Saul and his forces, David was in extreme danger of capture. The news that the Philistines had invaded the territories of Saul in great force hastily summoned the king from the district, and David was thus saved from a destruction which appeared to be imminent.

(23) **Throughout all the thousands of Judah.**—The "thousands" (Heb., *alaphim*), as we learn from Numbers i. 16, x. 4, were the greater tribal divisions. Judah was especially mentioned by Saul as being "the tribe of David," and where he found probably the larger number of his adherents. It was too, from its importance, the typical tribe, certainly in the southern part of Canaan.

(24) **In the wilderness of Maon.**—Still further to the south. The name of this district is still preserved in the village or small town of Main, which is built on a prominent conical hill.

In the plain.—This accurate description was, no doubt, inserted by the compiler of these books, owing to the intense interest which the wanderings of this favourite hero and king excited among his countrymen. We can well imagine how gladly the dwellers in Judea, especially in later days—after the glorious reign of David had changed the tribes struggling with the surrounding petty nations for very existence into a great and renowned nation—would trace out the itinerary of the great king as he fled for his life before Saul. Is it too much to assume that each of these spots, which to us is little more than a hard, dry name, for a long period were the resort of reverent and curious pilgrims, anxious to gaze on localities made sacred by the weary wanderings and the hair-breadth escapes of the glorious king of Israel?

The plain.—Literally, *the Arabah,* the desert track which extends along the Jordan Valley from the Dead Sea to the Lake of Gennesareth; it is now called El-Ghor. The term is also applied to the desolate valley which lies between the Dead Sea and the Gulf of Akaba. Stanley, in his *Sinai and Palestine,* has given a picturesque description of these weird districts.

(26) **The mountain.**—Conder, in his *Tent Life in Palestine,* identifies this spot with high probability. Indeed, his whole book is most instructive and trustworthy, and to the reader interested in these scenes in the life of David, as well as in those other many events which have taken place in the Storied Land, his book will form an admirable guide.

(27) **The Philistines have invaded the land.**—This, as *Lange* well observes, was "God's plan to save David." The Philistines had probably availed them-

David Dwells in   I. SAMUEL, XXIV.   *the Wilderness of En-gedi.*

and come; for the Philistines have ¹invaded the land. (28) Wherefore Saul returned from pursuing after David, and went against the Philistines: therefore they called that place ²Sela-hammahlekoth. (29) And David went up from thence, and dwelt in strong holds at En-gedi.

CHAPTER XXIV.—(1) And it came to pass, when Saul was returned from ³following the Philistines, that it was told him, saying, Behold, David *is* in the wilderness of En-gedi. (2) Then Saul took three thousand chosen men out of all Israel, and went to seek David and his men upon the rocks of the wild goats. (3) And he came to the sheepcotes by the way, where *was* a cave; and Saul went in to cover his feet: and David

---

1 Heb., *spread themselves upon,* &c.

2 That is, *The rock of divisions.*

3 Heb., *after.*

---

selves of the opportunity which Saul's withdrawal of his forces southward to surround the armed band of David had given them, and were invading in force the more northern provinces.

(28) **Sela-hammahlekoth.**—Literally, as in the margin of our Bibles, *the rock* (or, still better, *the cliff*) *of divisions.* Other scholars, with greater reason, prefer the derivation from a Hebrew word signifying *to be smooth*—the cliff of smoothness: that is, of slipping away or escaping. Ewald rather fancifully interprets the term as the "Cliff of Destiny or of Fate."

XXIV.

(1—22) The Pursuit of David renewed—David Spares Saul's Life in the En-gedi Cave—David's Generosity—Saul for a time Regrets his Persecution of David.

(1) **When Saul was returned.**—How intent Saul was on his bloody purpose with regard to his supposed rival is clear, for no sooner was the Philistine raid repulsed than with sleepless animosity he at once set forth with a force, as the next verse relates, of considerable magnitude to hunt down his foe. Saul was encouraged in this fresh enterprise by the offer of the Ziphites (see preceding chap., verses 19—23). These bitter enemies of David, in the interval of the Philistine war—accustomed to the passes and mountains of the barren region of the south of Canaan—complying with the king's request (chap. xxiii. 23), had taken careful knowledge of the lurking-places where David was hiding, and were now prepared to act as guides to the well-equipped and disciplined forces under Saul in its marches and counter-marches in the deserts bordering on the south of Judah.

En-gedi.—David and his band were now wandering along a lofty plateau, upon the tops of cliffs some 2,000 feet above the Dead Sea. En-gedi—still known as Ain-jedy, the Fountain of the Kid—is a beautiful oasis, in the barren wilderness to the south of Judah. Its original name was Hazazon Tamar—"The Palm Wood" (see 2 Chron. xx. 2)—and was once an ancient settlement of the Amorites (see Gen. xiv. 7). It has in all ages been a favourite spot with the possessors of the land. King Solomon appears to have paid peculiar attention to this garden of the wilderness. He planted the hills round it with vines; from the fountain flows a warm limpid stream, delicious to the taste. The remains of ancient gardens tell us that in the golden days of the kings En-gedi was probably a favourite resort of the wealthy citizen of Jerusalem. Solomon, in his "Song of Songs," writes of it in a strain which shows how he loved it, when he compares his beloved "to a cluster of camphire in the vineyards of En-gedi."—Canticles i. 14. Its present condition, as described by modern travellers, more nearly resembles the En-gedi when Saul hunted David among the rocks and caverns than the En-gedi the resort of the Jerusalem citizens, beautiful with gardens and vines of Solomon.—Conder: *Tent Life.* Dean Stanley and others have described the spot with great care, and left us a vivid picture of the scene. They tell us of the long and weary journey across the desolate valleys and precipitous barren heights, and of the enchanting scene which lay before them when once Ain-jedy was reached. They describe in flowing language the plentiful and rich vegetation, the trees and fruits, the ruins of the ancient gardens, and remains of the beautiful groves, still inhabited by a multitude of singing birds. In the limestone cliffs are numerous caves, some of them very large and deep, well calculated to be the temporary shelter of large bodies of men.

(2) **Three thousand chosen men.**—This large and carefully selected force is an indication how thoroughly impressed Saul was with the power of David at this juncture. He, indeed, evidently looked on him as a rival king, who must be met by a numerous and disciplined force.

Upon the rocks of the wild goats.—"Ibex rocks," so called because probably only these ibexes, the chamois of Syria, would find pasturage on them. Some have suggested that this was a proper name. The ibex is still found among the precipitous cliffs in the neighbourhood of Ain-jedy.

(3) **The sheepcotes.**—Thomson (*The Land and the Book*) saw, he says, hundreds of these sheepcotes around the mouth of the caves, of which there are so many in Palestine. In that land and among these Eastern peoples, whose customs change so little, they are as common now as they were then. "These sheepcotes are generally made by piling up loose stones in front of the cave's entrance in a circular wall, which is covered with thorns as a further protection against thieves and wild animals who would prey on the sheep. During cold storms and in the night the flocks retreat into the cave, but at other times they remain in the enclosed cote. . . . . These caverns are as dark as midnight, and the keenest eye cannot see four paces *inward*; but one who has been long within, and looking *outward* toward the entrance, can observe with perfect distinctness all that takes place in that direction. David, therefore, could watch Saul as he came in . . . . but Saul could see nothing but impenetrable darkness."

From this thorny fence, so universal in the countless sheepcotes of Palestine, was very possibly derived a quaint simile in the strange passage on "Death" in the Talmud:—

"The hardest of all deaths is by a disease (some suppose quinsey), which is like the *forcible extraction of prickly thorns from wool*. . . . The easiest of

and his men remained in the sides of the cave. ⁽⁴⁾ And the men of David said unto him, Behold the day of which the LORD said unto thee, Behold, I will deliver thine enemy into thine hand, that thou mayest do to him as it shall seem good unto thee. Then David arose, and cut off the skirt of ¹Saul's robe privily. ⁽⁵⁾And it came to pass afterward, that David's heart smote him, because he had cut off Saul's skirt. ⁽⁶⁾ And he said unto his men, The LORD forbid that I should

¹ Heb., *the robe which was Saul's.*

all deaths is the Divine kiss, which is like the extracting of hair from milk. Moses, Aaron, and Miriam died by this Divine kiss."—Treatise *Berachoth,* fol. 8, col. 1.

Where was a cave.—The well-known traveller Van de Velde wishes to identify the cave in question with an immense cavern in a rock with many side vaults, near the ruins of Chareitum; the difficulty is, however, that this vast cavern is fifteen or twenty miles from Ain-jedy. In this cave all David's band could well have been gathered: not only his 600 fighting men, but the camp followers and women also. In Pocock we read that the Arabs call this cavern Elmaama (hiding-place), and relate how on one occasion thirty thousand people hid themselves in it to escape an evil wind (the simoom). It is, however, quite possible that the incident here may be related, connected with Saul and David, took place in one of the much smaller caves close to En-gedi. It is not necessary to assume that *all* David's band were with him in one cave. A hundred or so of his more special companions were probably with him on this occasion, the remainder of the little army being dispersed in other similar refuges in the immediate neighbourhood.

And Saul went in to cover his feet.—The meaning of this disputed passage is quite simple. Saul, fatigued with the morning's march, some time about midday withdrew—probably with a very few attendants composing his personal staff—to take a short siesta, or sleep, in one of those dark, silent caves on the hill-side, which offered a cool resting-place after the glare and heat of a long and fatiguing march along the precipitous paths of the region. He lay down, no doubt, near the cave's mouth, and one of his faithful attendants threw lightly over the king's feet the royal manycoloured mantle (*m'il*). The king and his attendants little suspected that in the dark recesses of their midday resting-place were concealed the dreaded freebooter and a great company of his devoted armed followers. As explained in the Note above, in these great rock recesses, coming from *outside*, from the glare of daylight, not five paces forward can be seen, but those already *inside*, and accustomed to the darkness, can, at a considerable distance within the cave, see distinctly all that takes place in the neighbourhood of the cavern mouth. The sharp eyes of David's sentinels, no doubt, far in the cave, quickly saw the little party of intruders. The tall form of the king, his jewelled armour, and perhaps his many-coloured brightly-tinted cloak, betrayed to the amazed watchmen of David the rank of the wearied sleeper.

This interpretation of the words, "Saul went in to cover his feet"—namely, "to sleep"—is adopted by the Peshito Syriac Version, Michaelis, and of late, very positively, Ewald. The ordinary interpretation of the words, besides being an unusual statement, by no means suits the narrative; for it must be remembered that considerable time was necessary for the sentinel to inform David, and for David to have approached and cut off the hem of the royal garment, and again to have retired into the recesses of the cave.

In the sides of the cave.—That is, in the side vaults and passages which exist in the largest of these natural refuges.

⁽⁴⁾ **Behold the day of which the Lord said unto thee.**—This was the version by David's men of such predictions as 1 Sam. xv. 28, xvi. 1, 12. Jonathan's words (chaps. xx. 15, xxiii. 17) show clearly that these predictions were known; and the version of them here given was a very natural one in the mouth of David's men (*Speaker's Commentary*). It is, however, quite possible that a prophet such as Gad had predicted publicly, in the hearing of David's band of followers, that the days would come when their now outlawed captain, the son of Jesse, the "Anointed of Jehovah" —all his enemies being overthrown—would reign in peace and glory over all the land.

Then David arose.—For a moment the "king to be" listened to the seductive voice of the tempter; and we may imagine him, with the sword of Goliath naked in his hand, advancing towards his unconscious adversary, sleeping in the cave's mouth, resolved with one good blow to end the long, cruel war, and then, his great rival being gone, to seat himself at once on the empty throne which he knew the Eternal meant him one day to occupy—but only for a moment; for through the soul of David rapidly passed the thought that the helpless sleeping one was, after all, the "Anointed of Jehovah." How could he, himself "an anointed king," touch another of the same order to do him harm? So with a matchless generosity, unequalled, indeed, in those rough days, he spared the man who so ruthlessly and so often had sought *his* life, and even at that moment, with all the power of the land, was trying to do him to death; and David the outlaw bent over the sleeping king who hated him with so deep a hate, and deftly cut off the skirt, perhaps some of the golden fringe which edged the royal *m'il*, and as he bent over him, and saw once more the face of Saul—from whose brow so often his minstrelsy had chased the dark clouds of madness—we can fancy the son of Jesse once more loving the great hero of his boyhood: loving him as he did in the old days when he played in the king's dark hours.

There is no doubt but that one of the most beautiful characteristics of David's many-sided nature, was this enduring loyalty to Saul and to Saul's house. No jealousy, or even bitter injuries done in after years could affect the old love, the old feeling of loyal reverence, the more than filial affection; it was even proof against time. Years after Saul was in his grave, David gave the most conspicuous proof of his faithful memory of his old, devoted friendship for Saul and his house, when he pardoned Mephibosheth, the grandson of Saul, for his more than suspected treason in the matter of the revolt of Absalom, and restored to him a large portion of his forfeited lands (2 Sam. xix. 24—29).

⁽⁵⁾ **David's heart smote him.**—Not for what he had done to Saul, but his conscience smote him for the momentary thought that had stained his soul of slaying the Lord's Anointed. This is better than with Clericus to say, "David was afraid that Saul would

do this thing unto my master, the LORD's anointed, to stretch forth mine hand against him, seeing he *is* the anointed of the LORD. ⁽⁷⁾ So David ¹ stayed his servants with these words, and suffered them not to rise against Saul. But Saul rose up out of the cave, and went on *his* way. ⁽⁸⁾ David also arose afterward, and went out of the cave, and cried after Saul, saying, My lord the king. And when Saul looked behind him, David stooped with his face to the earth, and bowed himself.

⁽⁹⁾ And David said to Saul, Wherefore hearest thou men's words, saying, Behold, David seeketh thy hurt? ⁽¹⁰⁾ Behold, this day thine eyes have seen how that the LORD had delivered thee to-day into mine hand in the cave: and *some* bade *me* kill thee: but *mine eye* spared thee; and I said, I will not put forth mine hand against my lord; for he *is* the LORD's anointed. ⁽¹¹⁾ Moreover, my father, see, yea, see the skirt of thy robe in my hand: for in that I cut off the skirt of thy robe, and killed thee not, know thou and see that *there is* neither evil nor transgression in mine hand, and I have not sinned against thee; yet thou huntest my soul to take it. ⁽¹²⁾ The LORD judge between me and thee, and the LORD avenge me of thee: but mine hand shall not be upon thee. ⁽¹³⁾As saith the proverb of the ancients, Wickedness

1 Heb., *cut off*.

---

take this, though a clear sign of his [David's] magnanimity, in bad part, and regard it as a violation of his royal majesty." There is no sign at all of David's even regretting he had cut off the fringe of the king's garment. It was the far more terrible thought of slaying the God-anointed king which troubled David. The words of the next verse show us clearly what was passing in his mind when he gravely rebuked his men, and evidently restrained them, with some little trouble, from rushing upon Saul, even after he had left the sleeping form, with the piece of the mantle in his hand. The Hebrew word rendered "stayed" is a forcible one, and, literally, would be *crushed down*. There is a curious Note, however, in the Babylonian Talmud on this passage in the Book of Samuel which tells how David cut off a piece of Saul's robe, in which the act is evidently very strongly condemned. Rabbi Yosi ben Rabbi Chanina on the words, "Then David arose, and cut off the skirt of Saul's robe privily," said, "Whoever treats clothes slightingly will at last derive no benefit from them, for it is said (1 Kings i. 1), 'And they covered him [David] with clothes, but he gat no heat.'" —Treatise *Berachoth*, fol. 62, col. 2.

This is evidently one of the "cryptographs," of which there are such innumerable instances in the Talmud. The lesson intended to be taught by the famous Rabbi was probably intense reverence for the teachers and guides of Israel, here represented by Saul; any act of disrespect shown to one of these, even by injuring the clothes they wore, would be punished by God sooner or later.

⁽⁸⁾ **And cried after Saul.**—The outlaw suffered the king and his companion to proceed some little way —possibly down the deep ascent which led up to the cave's mouth—and then called after Saul, but with an address of the deepest reverence, accompanied too (see next clause) with an act of the profoundest homage which an inferior could pay to a superior. He would show Saul at least he was no rival king.

⁽⁹⁾ **Wherefore hearest thou men's words?**— David had many deadly enemies at the court of Saul, who evidently laboured with success to deepen Saul's jealousy, and to widen the breach which already existed between the king and David. Doeg has been already mentioned as one of the more prominent of these slanderers; another was Cush the Benjamite, who was alluded to in the inscription which heads the seventh Psalm. The Ziphites and their representatives at the royal residence also belonged to this class of malicious foes spoken of here.

⁽¹⁰⁾ **Thine eyes have seen.**—David and a crowd of armed men around him were standing at the entrance of the cave which King Saul had just left; thus the king's eye had seen—nay, was seeing that very moment —that his life had been in his enemy David's hand.

And some bade me kill thee.—The literal translation here would be *Jehovah delivered thee to-day into mine hand in the cave, and bade* [*me*] *kill thee*. And this rendering has been explained by assuming that God's *allowing* Saul to choose the very cavern for his midday slumber where David and his company were lodging was tantamount to *directing* David to slay his bitter foe, thus given over helpless into his hands; but this is contrary to the spirit of the whole narrative. The English Version has followed the Syriac and Chaldee Versions here, and by supplying "some"— better, perhaps, *one*—before "bade me kill thee," has given us the sense in which the Hebrews have always understood the passage. The Vulg. here, with a very slight change in the vowel points, renders "I thought to kill thee."

But mine eye spared thee.—The English Version supplies an obvious subject in "mine eye." Clericus suggests more happily, "my soul," or "my hand," before "spared thee."

⁽¹¹⁾ **My father.**—Not in the sense of "my father-in-law." The Princess Michal before this time probably had been given to Phalti. The *time* when this wicked act was carried out by Saul is left quite indefinite in the notice of chap. xxv. 44; but the relations of David and Saul were evidently far more bitter before than after the En-gedi incident, hence the probability of Michal's being given to Phalti *before* this meeting is great. The expression "my father" is simply the reverence (*pietas*) of the young to the old—of the loyal subject to the sovereign. It is so used in the beautiful lines of Browning already quoted.

See the skirt of thy robe.—Doubtless at this juncture holding up the piece of the royal *m'il* he had so carefully cut off when the king was sleeping in fancied security. "See *this*, how near thou wast to death, had I been pleased to take thy life when I cut *this* off."

⁽¹³⁾ **The proverb of the ancients.**—Clericus, quoted by Lange, explains these words: "David means

proceedeth from the wicked: but mine hand shall not be upon thee. (14) After whom is the king of Israel come out? after whom dost thou pursue? after a dead dog, after a flea. (15) The LORD therefore be judge, and judge between me and thee, and see, and plead my cause, and ¹deliver me out of thine hand.

(16) And it came to pass, when David had made an end of speaking these words unto Saul, that Saul said, *Is* this thy voice, my son David? And Saul lifted up his voice, and wept. (17) And he said to David, Thou *art* more righteous than I: for thou hast rewarded me good, whereas I have rewarded thee evil. (18) And thou hast shewed this day how that thou hast dealt well with me: forasmuch as when the LORD had ²delivered me into thine hand, thou killedst me not. (19) For if a man find his enemy, will he let him go well away? wherefore the LORD reward thee good for that thou hast done unto me this day. (20) And now, behold, I know well that thou shalt surely be king, and that the kingdom of Israel shall be established in thine hand. (21) Swear now therefore unto me by the LORD, that thou wilt not cut off my seed after me, and that thou wilt not destroy

1 Heb., *judge*.

2 Heb., *shut up*.

---

to say, that if he had been guilty of conspiracy against the king, he would not have neglected this favourable opportunity to kill him, since men usually indulge their feelings, and from a mind guilty of conspiracy nothing but corresponding deeds could come forth." So Grotius, who writes how "actions usually correspond to the quality of the mind." Erdmann quotes a Greek proverb: "From a bad raven comes a bad egg."

(14) **After a dead dog, after a flea.**—These homely but vivid similes are very common in Oriental discourse. David certainly, in his protestations of loyalty, could scarcely humble himself more than by drawing a comparison between the king of Israel in his grandeur and power and a poor dead dog—evidently an object held in special loathing by the Hebrews. "After a flea"—the original is even stronger, after "one flea" (a single flea)—"against *a single flea*," which is not easily caught, and easily escapes, and if it is caught, is poor game for a royal hunter.—*Berl. Bible* and *Lange*.

(15) **The Lord therefore be judge, and judge between me and thee, and see, and plead my cause, and deliver me out of thine hand.**—Shall I lay these hands on the Lord's Anointed? God forbid. No; I will not do it for a kingdom. Such wicked feats I leave for wicked men to act. God can and will in His own due time make good His own promise without my sin. I shall be content to wait His leisure, and remain in the sad condition I now am in, till it shall please Him to bring me out of it.—*Bishop Sanderson*, in Wordsworth.

(16) **These words.**—L. Philippson (in the Israelitish Bible, Leipzig) sums up strikingly the general effect of David's moving but natural words to Saul. "This appeal possesses so much natural eloquence, such warmth, such true earnestness, that no one who has any love for the simple beauties of the Bible can read it unmoved. There is a striking grandeur, too, in the whole scene. We see David standing on some peak in this wilderness of rocks, holding up the trophy of his romantic generosity, gazing at and addressing the melancholy Saul, whom he loved as a father, paid homage to as a king, and reverenced as the Lord's Anointed, but who, for his part, hated him without a cause, and hunted him down with a restless, murderous zeal; and (as David stood there and gazed on Saul) he seized the opportunity, and tried to touch his royal enemy's heart with words, hurried, indeed, and quickly spoken, but breathing the intense earnestness of his inward feeling. He was overwhelmed with the consciousness of a sorrow too deep for words, yet he spoke as one inspired with the knowledge of a noble deed just done."

And Saul lifted up his voice, and wept.—And for a time the words, but still more the forbearance, of David in the cave touched Saul to the quick. He not only spoke kindly to the hated David, but even wept. There is nothing strange in this sudden change of feeling in one so nervous and excitable as was Saul. It is clear that for the moment Saul meant to alter his conduct to David, but the sad sequel shows that the impression made was only transitory; and David, by his conduct, clearly saw this, for he made—as the last verse of the chapter shows us—no effort to return to his old home and position with Saul, but maintained his independent, though precarious, position as an outlaw.

(20) **And now, behold, I know well that thou shalt surely be king.**—Clericus (in *Lange*) says: "From this great magnanimity of David, Saul concluded that a man who was much superior in soul to kings could not but reign." This is a good comment, and doubtless expresses something of what was in Saul's mind on this occasion; but more must have been behind to have induced the king to make such a speech to David. Never had he for one moment forgotten his old friend's words—the words of Samuel, whom he too well knew was the prophet of the Most High—when he with all solemnity announced to him, as a message from heaven, that the Lord had rent the kingdom from him, and had given it to a neighbour that was better than he (chap. xv. 21). Since that awful denunciation, the unhappy Saul was only too sensible that the blessing of Jehovah of Hosts no longer rested on his head, no longer blessed his going out and coming in, while the strange, bright career of the son of Jesse seemed to point him out as the neighbour on whom the choice of God had fallen. Rumours, too, of a mysterious anointing must have long ere this reached Saul; this, joined to the passionate advocacy of Jonathan, and the quiet, steady friendship of Samuel, no doubt convinced King Saul that in the son of Jesse he saw Israel's future monarch. Strong, therefore, in this conviction, and for the time humiliated and grieved at the sorry part he had been playing in this restless persecution of one destined to fill so great a position, the king positively entreats the outlaw to swear to him the strange promise contained in the next (21st) verse.

(21) **Swear now therefore unto me.**—So strongly was Saul convinced at this moment that David would at no distant period of time occupy the throne of Israel

my name out of my father's house. **(22) And David sware unto Saul.** And Saul went home; but David and his men gat them up unto the hold.

B.C. cir. 1060.

a ch. 28. 3; Ecclus. 46. 13, 20.

CHAPTER XXV.—(1) And *a* Samuel died; and all the Israelites were gathered together, and lamented him, and buried him in his house at Ramah.

---

that he entreated him, when that day should come, not to destroy all his (Saul's) children. This barbarous custom has been always too common a practice in the jealous East. It seems to have been equally dreaded by Jonathan, who made—it will be remembered—this condition of mercy to be shown by David in his day of power to his (Jonathan's) children a part of the solemn covenant concluded between them. (See chap. xx. 15.) In the frequent dynastic changes which took place in the kingdom of Israel, we have instances of such wholesale massacres of the royal family of the fallen house. (See 1 Kings xv. 29, where Baasha slew King Nadab, the son of Jeroboam, and took his throne. Then Baasha, we read, " smote all the house of Jeroboam; he left not to Jeroboam any that breathed;" and in 1 Kings xvi. 11, where Zimri murdered his master, King Baasha. Zimri, "as soon as he sat on his throne, slew all the house of Baasha: he left him not one, neither of his kinsfolks, nor of his friends.") A similar massacre is described, only with more ghastly details, in 2 Kings x., where "Jehu slew all that remained to Ahab in Samaria." There the story is peculiarly an Oriental scene of history, with the seventy baskets containing the seventy heads of princes presented as an acceptable offering to the new stern king of Israel—Jehu. It was, therefore, no vain dread of what might happen in the future which made King Saul ask this of David. Doubtless the fear of some such awful catastrophe happening to his own loved children and friends was no small part of the punishment of Saul.

(22) **And David sware unto Saul.**—The generous son of Jesse at once complied with Saul's curious request, and for a time, at least, the persecution and pursuit of David ceased. Stricken with remorse, the gloomy king left him to himself; no word, however, seems to have passed as to restoring the exile to his home or rank. Bishop Wordsworth quotes here a characteristic passage from one of Chrysostom's eloquent homilies, in which the Patristic method of allegorising all these famous scenes of Old Testament history is well exemplified.

"Meditate on the example of David, and do thou imitate it: imitate it in his self-control and in his love of his enemy. The cave in which he was became like a Christian Church, and he became like a Christian bishop, who first preaches a sermon and then offers the sacrifice of the altar.

"So David preached a sermon by his example, and offered a true sacrifice—the spiritual sacrifice of himself and of his own anger; he became as it were a priest, a sacrifice, and an altar, and having offered his victims, he gained a glorious victory."—*St. Chrysostom,* tom. iv., p. 761.

XXV.

(1–44) The Death of Samuel—The Story of Nabal and Abigail—An Incident illustrative of the Life which David led when a Captain of Outlaws—Abigail becomes his Wife.

(1) **And Samuel died.**—At this period—namely, about the time when Saul and David met at En-gedi—died Samuel, full of years and honour—perhaps rather than *honours*, for for a long time the old prophet had lived apart from the court, and alienated from the king he had chosen and anointed. Since Moses, none so great as Samuel had arisen. Briefly to recapitulate his work: his influence had in great measure restored the Law of Moses to the affections of the people. Before his time, the words and traditions which the great lawgiver, amidst the supernatural terrors of Sinai, had with some success impressed upon the great nomadic tribe of the Beni-Israel were almost forgotten; and the people among whom, for a long period, no really great leader had sprung up were becoming rapidly mixed up, and soon would have been hardly distinguished from the warlike tribes of Canaan in the neighbouring countries. But Samuel, aided by his great natural genius, but far more by the Glorious Arm, on which he leaned with a changeless trust from childhood to extreme old age, quickened into life again the dying traditions of the race, and taught them who they—the down-trodden Israelites—really were—*the chosen of God.* He restored the forgotten laws of Moses, by the keeping of which they once became great and powerful, and by the creation of an earthly monarchy he welded into one the separate interests of the twelve divisions of the race; so that from Dan to Beersheba there was but one chief, one standard. But his greatest work was the foundation of the Prophetic Schools, in which men were trained and educated carefully, with the view of the pupils becoming in their turn the teachers and guides of the people. (These schools, which exercised so great an influence upon the future of Israel, and their especial character have been already discussed.)

And all the Israelites were gathered together, and lamented him.—"When the hour of his death came, we are told, with a peculiar emphasis of expression, that *all* the Israelites—not one portion or fragment only, as might have been expected in that time of division and confusion—were gathered together round him who had been the father of all alike, and lamented him, and buried him, not in any sacred spot or secluded sepulchre, but in the midst of the home which he had consecrated only by his own long, unblemished career in his house at Ramah."—Stanley, *Jewish Church,* Lect. xviii. Josephus makes especial mention of the public funeral honours paid to the great prophet. "They wept for him a very great number of days, not looking on it as a sorrow for the death of another man, but as that in which they were all concerned. He was a righteous man, and gentle in his nature, and on that account he was very dear to God."—*Antt.* vi. 13, § 5. F. W. Krummacher beautifully writes on this public lamentation. "It was as if from the noble star, as long as it shone in the heaven of the Holy Land, though veiled by clouds, there streamed a mild, beneficial light over all Israel; now the light was extinguished in Israel." It is probable by "in his house," the court or garden attached to the prophet's house is signified. To have buried him literally "in his house" would have occasioned perpetual ceremonial defilement. We read also of Manasseh the king being "buried in his own house" (2 Chron. xxxiii. 20), which is explained in 2 Kings xxi. 18 by the words, "in the garden of his own

And David arose, and went down to the wilderness of Paran. (2) And there was a man in Maon, whose ¹possessions were in Carmel; and the man was very great, and he had three thousand sheep, and a thousand goats: and he was shearing his sheep in Carmel. (3) Now the name of the man was Nabal; and the name of his wife Abigail: and she was a woman of good understanding, and of a beautiful countenance: but the man was churlish and evil in his doings; and he was of the house of Caleb. (4) And David heard in the wilderness that Nabal did shear his sheep. (5) And David sent out ten young men, and David said unto the young men, Get you up to Carmel, and go to Nabal, and ²greet him in my name: (6) and thus shall ye say to him that liveth *in prosperity*, Peace be both to thee, and peace be to thine house, and peace be unto all that thou hast.

1 Or, *business*.

2 Heb., *ask him in my name of peace*.

---

house." In modern times Samuel's grave is pointed out in a cave underneath the floor of the Mahommedan Mosque on Nebi Samuel, a lofty peak above Gibeon, which still bears his honoured name. There is, however, a tradition that his remains—or what purported to be his remains—were removed with royal pomp from Ramah to Constantinople by the Emperor Arcadius, at the beginning of the fifth century.

The wilderness of Paran.—The LXX. (Vatican) read "Maon" instead of "Paran," not conceiving it probable that the scene of David's camp would be so far removed from Maon and Carmel, the localities where the following events took place. "Paran" is properly the south of the Arabian peninsula, west of Sinai; "but it seems to have given its name to the vast extent of pasture and barren land now known as the Desert of El Tih. Of this the wilderness of Judah and Beersheba would virtually form part, without the borders being strictly defined. The LXX. emendation, therefore, is quite unnecessary.—*Dean Payne Smith.*

(2) **Maon.**—Maon mentioned above was in the hill country of Judah. The Carmel here mentioned is not the famous Mount Carmel in the north, but the small town, the modern Kurmeel, near Maon, of which we read in chap. xv. 12, when Saul set up a place or monument after the war with Amalek.

And the man was very great.—The wealthy chief—the subject of the story—was a descendant of Caleb, the friend and comrade of Joshua, who at the time of the conquest of Canaan obtained vast possessions in the valley of Hebron and in the south of Judah. The tradition even has preserved to us the exact number of his flocks, probably to enhance the churlishness of his reply to David when he asked him for some return for the protection his armed bands had afforded to these vast flocks in their pasturage on the edge of the desert. The occasion of David's mission to Nabal was the annual sheep-shearing of the rich sheep-master—always a great occasion, and accompanied usually on large estates by festivities.

(3) **Nabal.**—The word "Nabal" means "fool," connected with *naval*, to fade away. The name was probably a nickname given him on account of his well-known stubborn folly.

Abigail.—The famous beautiful woman who afterwards became David's wife seems to have been, as Stanley calls her, "the good angel of the household" of the ill-starred, boorish southern chieftain. Her name, too, which signifies "whose father is joy," was most likely given her by the villagers on her husband's estate, as expressive of her sunny, gladness-bringing presence. Her early training, and the question respecting the sources whence she derived her wisdom and deep, far-sighted piety—apparently far in advance of her age—is discussed further on in the chapter.

The house of Caleb.—In the original *Kalibi*, i.e., of the house or family of Caleb. Thus the word is *read* in the Hebrew Bible. There is, however, an alternative reading—*K'libi*—with different vowel-points in the written text, which would be read "according to his heart." Josephus, the LXX., and the Arabic and Syriac Versions understand it as derived from *kelev*, a dog, and render—"and he was a cynical man" (that is, "one of a dog-like character"—*anthrōpos kunikos*). The Chaldee "e domo Caleb," and Vulgate "de genere Caleb," follow the text which is read in the Hebrew Bible, and translated in our version, "of the house of Caleb," which seems, on the whole, the preferable and most likely meaning.

(4) **And David heard in the wilderness.**—The question of the support of the large band of devoted followers who obeyed David must have been usually a very anxious one. No doubt, contributions from the farmers and sheep-masters materially aided the supplies David and his men derived from their raids across the Philistine borders. It is likely enough that some of these contributions were not always willingly made; still, there is no doubt that the presence of the armed band of David during the latter years of Saul afforded considerable protection to the border land. His position resembled that of a modern Arab sheik of a friendly Bedaween tribe, and it is clear that on the whole his career as head of an army of free lances tended to popularise him among the southern tribes of Israel. Nabal's conduct appears to have been more than churlish and foolish, for David, according to the showing of Nabal's own shepherds, had on many occasions been of substantial service to them as they tended their flocks in exposed and dangerous localities. The testimony of these shepherd folk may be accepted generally as the popular estimate of David and his acts during this rough and sorely tried period of his life.

(6) **And thus shall ye say.**—On such a festive occasion near a town or village, an Arab sheik of the neighbouring desert would hardly fail to put in a word, either in person or by message; and his message, both in form and substance, would be only the transcript of that of David.—Robinson, *Palestine*, p. 201.

To him that liveth in prosperity.—Considerable diversity of opinion exists as to the meaning of the Hebrew original here, *lechai*. The Vulg. alters the text slightly, and renders "to my brother." The LXX. have an impossible translation—"*eis horas*," for times, or for seasons. It is better, however, to take it as a popular expression of congratulation, not found, as Lange well puts it, in the *literary* language. So Luther, "glück auf," "may it turn out well," "may you be prosperous." The famous Hebrew commentator Raschi, and also the Babylonian Talmud, apparently understand it in this sense.

(7) And now I have heard that thou hast shearers: now thy shepherds which were with us, we ¹hurt them not, neither was there ought missing unto them, all the while they were in Carmel. (8) Ask thy young men, and they will shew thee. Wherefore let the young men find favour in thine eyes: for we come in a good day: give, I pray thee, whatsoever cometh to thine hand unto thy servants, and to thy son David.

(9) And when David's young men came, they spake to Nabal according to all those words in the name of David, and ²ceased. (10) And Nabal answered David's servants, and said, Who is David? and who is the son of Jesse? there be many servants now a days that break away every man from his master. (11) Shall I then take my bread, and my water, and my ³flesh that I have killed for my shearers, and give it unto men, whom I know not whence they be? (12) So David's young men turned their way, and went again, and came and told him all those sayings. (13) And David said unto his men, Gird ye on every man his sword. And they girded on every man his sword; and David also girded on his sword: and there went up after David about four hundred men; and two hundred abode by the stuff.

(14) But one of the young men told Abigail, Nabal's wife, saying, Behold, David sent messengers out of the wilderness to salute our master; and he ⁴railed on them. (15) But the men were very good unto us, and we were not ⁵hurt, neither missed we any thing, as long as we were conversant with them,

¹ Heb., *shamed.*
² Heb., *rested.*
³ Heb., *slaughter.*
⁴ Heb., *flew upon them.*
⁵ Heb., *shamed.*

---

(7) **Neither was there ought missing unto them.**—These words doubtless refer to the protection which David's armed band had afforded to the herdsmen against the frequent raids of the neighbouring people—the Philistines and other more savage and unscrupulous tribes who dwelt on the borders of Palestine. The request was certainly a fair one, for, as Lange and Ewald remark, "apart from the Eastern custom of giving largely at such great merry-makings, according to which such a request would seem in no way strange, David had a certain right to ask a gift from Nabal's wealth. He had indirectly no small share in the festal joy of Nabal and his house. Without some part of the superfluity of the inhabitants whom he protected, he could not have maintained himself and his army."

(9) **And ceased.**—Better rendered, *and they sat down.* The Hebrew word here has been variously translated. Bunsen suggests, "and they waited modestly for an answer;" the Vulg., followed by some scholars, has "and they were silent."

(10) **There be many servants now a days that break away.**—This evident insult indicates that Nabal was of the faction of Saul at this time—was reckoned among those who hated David. It was the report of these words, doubtless, which so furiously excited David. In Nabal, the rich sheep-master, the churlish refuser of the fairly earned gift, he saw a deadly political adversary—one who, with men like Doeg and Cush, would hunt him down like a wild beast. Without this explanation, David's wrath and determination to take such speedy and bloody vengeance on a mere selfish churl is inexplicable. With the light, however, which such an open declaration of deadly hostility on the part of Nabal throws on the transaction, the subsequent passionate conduct of David, although deeply blameable, is not difficult to understand.

(11) **Unto men, whom I know not.**—In other words, "Shall I give largesse to the enemies of my king —to a band of rebel freebooters?"

My water.—The LXX., instead of "water," read "wine." This is one of the countless alterations this version arbitrarily makes in the original sacred text. The Greek translators were puzzled at Nabal's enumeration of "water" as one of the demands of David. Its mention, however, is a mark of the accuracy of the record. Water in many parts of the East is exceedingly precious. The words of Josh. xv. 19 clearly indicate the especial want of this district of Palestine, when Caleb's daughter Achsah specially prayed her father for springs of water. Its mention, however, can scarcely, as Dean Payne Smith observes, "mark the abstemious habits of the people," considering in the same chapter we find the owner of all these flocks prostrate through intoxication.

(13) **Gird ye on every man his sword.**—The formal preparation and the largeness of the force told off for the work showed how terribly David was in earnest, and how bent he was on wiping out the insult of Nabal in blood. From the view we have taken of the transaction above, David's anger is quite to be accounted for, though not to be excused.

(14) **But one of the young men told Abigail.**—The servant of Nabal—accustomed, no doubt, to his master's wild and ungovernable displays of temper—had heard the insulting words which Nabal spoke to the armed messenger of the famous outlaw captain; and probably gathering from the angry demeanour of these warlike followers of David how deadly was the insult— aware, too, how great was the power of the man thus insulted—came at once, and recounted to his mistress what had taken place. Abigail had, no doubt, often acted as peace-maker between her intemperate husband and his neighbours, and on hearing the story and how imprudently her husband had behaved, saw that no time must be lost, for with a clever woman's wit she saw that grave consequences would surely follow the churlish refusal and the rash words, which betrayed at once the jealous adherent of Saul and the bitter enemy of the powerful outlaw.

(15) **But the men were very good unto us.**—The "young man" in question who spoke thus to his mistress, Abigail, was evidently one in high authority in the sheep farms of Nabal. His testimony in verses 15, 16, respecting David is clear and decisive, and occurring as it does in the heart of an episode most discreditable to David, it bears weighty testimony to the admirable discipline and the kind forethought of the son of Jesse in times when lawlessness and pillage

when we were in the fields: (16) they were a wall unto us both by night and day, all the while we were with them keeping the sheep. (17) Now therefore know and consider what thou wilt do; for evil is determined against our master, and against all his household: for he *is such* a son of Belial, that *a man* cannot speak to him.

(18) Then Abigail made haste, and took two hundred loaves, and two bottles of wine, and five sheep ready dressed, and five measures of parched *corn*, and an hundred ¹clusters of raisins, and two hundred cakes of figs, and laid *them* on asses. (19) And she said unto her servants, Go on before me; behold, I come after you. But she told not her husband Nabal. (20) And it was *so, as* she rode on the ass, that she came down by the covert of the hill, and, behold, David and his men came down against her; and she met them.

(21) Now David had said, Surely in vain have I kept all that this *fellow* hath in the wilderness, so that nothing was missed of all that *pertained* unto him: and he hath requited me evil for good. (22) So and more also do God unto the enemies of David, if I leave of all that *pertain* to him by the morning light any that pisseth against the wall.

(23) And when Abigail saw David, she hasted, and lighted off the ass, and fell before David on her face, and bowed herself to the ground, (24) and fell at his feet, and said, Upon me, my lord, *upon me let this* iniquity *be:* and let thine handmaid, I pray thee, speak in thine ²audience, and hear the words of thine handmaid. (25) Let not my lord, I pray thee, ³regard this man of Belial, *even* Nabal: for as his name *is*, so *is* he; Nabal *is* his name, and folly *is* with him: but I thine handmaid saw not the young men of my lord, whom thou didst send.

---

¹ Or, *lumps.*

² Heb., *ears.*

³ Heb., *lay it to his heart.*

---

would have been, if not excusable, certainly to be expected. The great powers of the future king were admirably displayed in this difficult period of his life. Few men could have so moulded a wild company of free lances into a force which, according to the rather unwilling testimony of these shepherds of Nabal's, was positively a blessing to the country, instead of being, as these bands of free lances usually have been, a terrible curse.

(17) **A son of Belial.**—Belial was not a proper name, though it subsequently came to be considered one. It signifies simply worthlessness; here a "son of Belial" is an expression for a bad, worthless fellow.

(18) **Five measures.**—The LXX. alter the measure into five ephahs, thinking the quantity in the text ridiculously small for such an host as followed David. Ewald too, would change 5 into 500; but the truth is that Abigail in her haste, thinking rightly that no time must be lost, as the danger was pressing, simply provided a liberal present for David's own immediate followers, not for the whole force.

An hundred clusters of raisins.—That is, an hundred cakes of dried grapes—what in Italy is called "simmuki."

(20) **The covert of the hill.**—Keil explains the words *sether hahar*—literally, *a hidden part of the mountain*—as probably signifying a hollow between two peaks of the mountain; thus each of the advancing parties would "come down"—Abigail, who approached on one side, and David, who came on the other—and would meet in the hollow between.

(21) **Now David had said.**—This verse and the following (22nd) must be understood as a kind of parenthesis in the narrative. They express what David felt, and, as it were, his justification in his own mind for the violent and vengeful act he was about to carry out. The argument was, Nabal had returned indeed evil for good. For a long time David's band had guarded faithfully his vast scattered flocks, and had preserved them safely, and now, when he asked a small favour in return, the churl repaid him by throwing in his teeth the taunt that he was a rebel and a runaway slave.

(22) **So and more also.**—This is an unusual variation of the common form of imprecation, "God do so to me and more also, if, &c., &c." The Syriac and Arabic Versions, followed by some commentators, instead of "enemies of David," read "his servant David." The LXX., as usual, boldly cuts the knot by leaving out the word of difficulty, and reads "David" simply, omitting "enemies." But there is no doubt that the Hebrew text here is correct. The words signify David himself. If God's anger for the broken vow visited even David's enemies, as distantly connected with him, how much more the guilty oath breaker himself? (This was Raschi's explanation for a similar expression in Jonathan's oath, chap. xx. 16.) "A superstitious feeling probably lay at the root of this substitution of David's enemies for himself, when thus invoking a curse" (Dean Payne Smith, in the *Pulpit Commentary*). Bishop Wordsworth here draws a good lesson on the non-obligation to keep a solemn oath, taken perhaps in a moment of undue excitement, and instances the evil example of Herod Antipas, who considered himself bound to carry out to the bitter end his rash oath to the daughter of Herodias, though it involved the death of John the Baptist, his former friend.

(23) **Fell before David.**—This act of obeisance, and, in fact, the whole tone of the wise wife of Nabal in her address to David, seems to betoken her consciousness that she was addressing the anointed of Jehovah, the future king—at no distant date—of Israel. Her worst fears she found realised when she met David, probably at no great distance from the principal residence of Nabal, accompanied by so large an armed force, evidently bent on some deed of violence. She deprecated his wrath by representing her husband not merely as a bad man, but as one scarcely responsible for his actions. Had *she* only known of the mission of David's followers to Nabal, she implies, very different indeed

(26) Now therefore, my lord, as the LORD liveth, and as thy soul liveth, seeing the LORD hath withholden thee from coming to *shed* blood, and from ¹avenging thyself with thine own hand, now let thine enemies, and they that seek evil to my lord, be as Nabal. (27) And now this ²blessing which thine handmaid hath brought unto my lord, let it even be given unto the young men that ³follow my lord. (28) I pray thee, forgive the trespass of thine handmaid: for the LORD will certainly make my lord a sure house; because my lord fighteth the battles of the LORD, and evil hath not been found in thee *all* thy days. (29) Yet a man is risen to pursue thee, and to seek thy soul: but the soul of my lord shall be bound in the bundle of life with the LORD thy God; and the souls of

1 Heb., *saving thyself.*
2 Or, *present.*
3 Heb., *walk at the feet of*, &c.

had been their reception; they would not, at least, have returned to David empty-handed.

(26) **Seeing the Lord hath withholden.**—This passage, as the *Speaker's Commentary* rightly observes, "since the oath affirmed nothing, should be rendered, 'And now my lord, as the Lord liveth, and as thy soul liveth, it is the Lord that hath withholden thee.' Literally, *As true as that the Lord liveth, so true is it that the Lord hath withholden thee*, &c., from coming into blood-guiltiness." So confident is this pious and wise woman that she is doing the Lord's work, and that He is standing by her, that, in presence of the armed band and their angry leader, she speaks as though the danger to her husband's house was a thing of the past, and that David had real cause for thankfulness in that he had been prevented from doing a wanton, wicked act.

Now let thine enemies . . . be as Nabal.—Nabal, the insulter of David, she dismisses as too insignificant to be considered; she regards him as utterly powerless to harm one like David; and her prayer is that his other enemies may only be like him—equally harmless.

(27) **This blessing.**—That is to say, *gift.* Of this Abigail makes little account—it was simply an expression of her homage and good will. It was not intended, of course, for David, but for his company; but she brought it, as is the custom in the East where an inferior approaches a superior, whether as a visitor or as a suppliant, to bring in the hand gifts. Let it be given, she added, to his companions.

(28) **The trespass of thine handmaid.**—Abigail again takes upon herself the wrong; the gracious act of forgiveness, of which she feels assured beforehand, she reminds David, will be shown *to her.* Thus all the chivalry of David's character—if we may use a term which belongs to another age—was brought out by this wise and beautiful woman.

For the Lord will certainly make my lord a sure house.—Unconsciously, perhaps, without any very definite conception of their far reaching and magnificent meaning, the Israelitish lady repeats the words which she had heard perhaps in Samuel's "Naioth" by Ramah—possibly from some trained or inspired disciple of the prophet's school. She was thinking, perhaps, of the young captain then standing before her in all the pride of his early reputation, as the future hero-king of Israel, sitting on the throne of the insane and gloomy man—her evil husband's friend—King Saul, and it may be of his son reigning after him; but the unconscious prophetess, we may be sure, never dreamed of that glorious and holy One in whose person, far down the stream of ages, the Eternal would make good her words, and indeed found for that outlawed chieftain, before whom she was then kneeling, a sure house.

The battles of the Lord.—Abigail, in common with the pious Israelites of her time, looked on the wars waged by the armies of Israel against the idolatrous tribes and nations around them as the wars of Jehovah. We frequently in these early records meet with the expressions, "fighting the battle of the Lord," "the ranks of the living God," "the battle is the Lord's." We hear, too, of an ancient collection of songs—ballads, perhaps, would be a more accurate designation—now lost, entitled "The Book of the Wars of the Lord" (Num. xxi. 14). For several years now since his famous combat with the great champion of idolatry, Goliath, David had been the popular hero and the favourite subject of those folk-songs which ever loved to sing of these "Wars of Jehovah."

Evil hath not been found in thee.—*Raah*, "evil," here signifies not "wickedness," but "misfortune." The wife of Nabal means to say that all through that stormy, restless life of David's, the Lord had ever held him up. It had given him victory and crowned his efforts with splendid success; and in the later days of bitter persecution, the same invisible One had shielded him, and had turned what seemed to be the certain ruin of his prospects into a still more certain career of usefulness and popularity.

(29) **A man is risen.**—She here refers, of course, to Saul, but with exquisite courtesy and true loyalty refrains from mentioning in connection with evil the name of her king, the "Anointed of Jehovah."

Shall be bound in the bundle of life.—This is one of the earliest and most definite expressions of a sure belief in an eternal future in the presence of God, and Hebrew tradition from the very earliest times down to our day has so regarded it. It is now a favourite and common inscription on Jewish gravestones. Keil beautifully paraphrases the words of the original. "The words," he writes, "do not refer primarily to eternal life with God in heaven, but only to the safe preservation of the righteous on this earth in the grace and fellowship of the Lord. *But whoever is so hidden in the gracious fellowship of the Lord in this life, that no enemy can harm him or injure his life, the Lord will not allow to perish, even though temporal death should come, but will then receive him into eternal life.*"—Keil.

The image, as so often in Eastern teaching, is taken from common every-day life—from the habit, as Dean Payne Smith remarks, of packing up in a bundle articles of great value or of indispensable use, so that the owner may carry them about his person. In India the phrase is common. Thus, a just judge is said to be bound up in the bundle of righteousness; a lover in the bundle of love. Among the striking references in the Babylonian Talmud to this loved and cherished saying of the wife of Nabal, we find how, in one of the Treatises of *Seder Moed*, "Rabbi Ezra says, *The*

thine enemies, them shall he sling out, ¹*as out* of the middle of a sling. ⁽³⁰⁾ And it shall come to pass, when the LORD

¹ Heb., *in the midst of the bought of a sling.*

shall have done to my lord according to all the good that he hath spoken concerning thee, and shall have appointed

souls of the righteous are hidden beneath God's glorious throne: as it is said, The soul of my lord shall be bound in the bundle of life with the Lord thy God."—Treatise *Shabbath*, fol. 152, col. 2.

What student of this verse of the Book of Samuel, and the beautiful Talmud comments on the far-reaching words, can fail to see in them the original of St. John's well-known picture of the "souls of them that were slain for the word of God, and for the testimony which they held?" (Rev. vi. 9)—these souls of the righteous hidden beneath the glorious throne of God.

The thought is embodied in the following extract. "The angel of death came and stood before Moses. Give me thy soul, said he; but Moses rebuked him, and said, thou hast no permission to come where he (Moses) was; and he departed crest-fallen. Then the Holy One—blessed be He!—took the soul of Moses, and hid it under His throne of glory: as it is said (1 Sam. xxv. 29): 'And the soul of my lord shall be bound in the bundle of life.' But when He took it He took it by means of a kiss."—*Avoth. of Rabbi Nathan*, chap. xii.

In the *Seder Moed*, again, in the same Treatise *Shabbath*, there is a remarkable parable, founded on this saying of Abigail: a parable that reminds us of the framework of one of the well-known pictures of the Redeemer. A king once distributed royal robes among his servants; those that were wise folded them up and laid them by in a coffer, and those that were foolish wore them on their working days. When the king demanded back his robes, those given to the wise were returned free from stains, whilst those of the foolish were soiled. The king, pleased with the wise servants, ordered their robes to be deposited in his treasury, and then that they should depart in peace. But he manifested his displeasure at the foolish servants; he sent their robes to be washed, and dispatched them to prison. So the bodies of the righteous "enter into peace, and rest in their beds" (Isa. lvii. 2), and their souls are bound up in the bundle of life; but with reference to the bodies of the foolish there is no peace, saith the Lord, and the wicked (Isa. lvii. 21) and their souls (quoting the next paragraph of this chapter of Samuel) are slung out, as out of the middle of a sling (1 Sam. xxv. 29).—Treatise *Shabbath*, fol. 152, col. 2.

And the souls of thine enemies, them shall he sling out, as out of the middle of a sling.—The simile was one Abigail had with all probability heard from one or other of the prophets or their pupils. It was not unlikely originally suggested by the ever memorable encounter between David and Goliath: as in the case of the souls of the righteous, in the passage just discussed, the reference in the first instance was to the fate of the enemies of God in this life; but Hebrew theologians in all times have understood it in a deeper and more solemn sense, as a reference to the doom after death reserved for all unrighteous. (See, for instance, above in the passage quoted from the Talmud, Treatise *Shabbath*.) In the same most ancient writing—which, most probably, contains the teaching of the great Jewish schools before the Christian era—we read: "The souls of the wicked are incessantly thrown by angels, as with a sling, from one end of the world to the other, as it is said: 'The souls of thine enemies shall he sling out, as out of the middle of a sling;' and what, asks Ravah of Rav. Nachman (this is a later comment), is the lot of those who are neither righteous nor wicked? They, as well as the wicked, are handed over to 'Dumah'—*silence* (see Ps. cxv. 17)—an angel who has charge of disembodied spirits. The former, the neither righteous nor wicked, have rest; the latter, the wicked, have none."—Treatise *Shabbath*, fol. 152, col. 2.

The strange wild statement, as it seems to us, is no doubt a cryptograph; and the great rabbis of old days in their famous schools would now and again unrol its meaning. With that, for the present, we have not to concern ourselves. But the bare text, as we copy it from the Talmud, conveys to us this important fact,—that men and women in the Canaan of Samuel and Saul—people who lived remote, as it would seem, from any famous centre of civilisation, in the midst of shepherds and herdsmen in the long sheep farms of Judah and Benjamin—believed in the glories of the life eternal with God, and looked on to a future state of rewards and punishments, instead of limiting their hopes and fears to the sitting in quiet peace under the vine and the fig tree of their own loved land of promise.

The knowledge of a future state of existence was ever the blessed heritage of the chosen race—but the spread of that knowledge and the re-awakening of that belief we ascribe to the beneficial influence of one man. The Divine record, if we read between its lines, and the mighty wealth of Hebrew tradition, if we take sufficient pains to make it our own, tell us one story—how Samuel, whom, when he was a child, the God of Israel loved: with whom, during his long and blameless life, He used to speak face to face—now by a vision, now by the echo of a voice—tell us how Samuel was the founder of those great Prophetic Schools where the lamp of the knowledge of God was re-lit, and then kept burning with a steady flame through his time and for centuries after: the one bright light during the long, sad record of Israel.

Hero-kings like David, prophets like Gad and Nathan, the great psalm writers and musicians of the Temple of Solomon, were the more prominent results of the peculiar teaching and spirit of these "schools;" but their noblest work, after all, was the high and beneficial influence they exercised over the people of the land—an influence exemplified in such characters as that of Abigail, the sheep-master of Carmel's wife, a page of whose life story we have just been considering.

⁽³⁰⁾ **And shall have appointed thee ruler over Israel.**—The wife of Nabal here speaks of the outlaw captain's future rule over Israel as king as a matter of absolute certainty. This she, in common with other religious persons of the people, had doubtless heard through the Prophetic Schools. We may fairly suppose that not a few of the pupils of Samuel and his associates had been, when the first meeting of David with Abigail took place, for a considerable time working as teachers and preachers throughout the land. It is most likely that the synagogue, or something out of which the synagogue sprang—some kind of assembly for prayer to the God of Israel for instruc-

Nabal is Smitten   I. SAMUEL, XXV.   *with sudden Disease.*

thee ruler over Israel; ⁽³¹⁾ that this shall be[1] no grief unto thee, nor offence of heart unto my lord, either that thou hast shed blood causeless, or that my lord hath avenged himself: but when the LORD shall have dealt well with my lord, then remember thine handmaid. ⁽³²⁾ And David said to Abigail, Blessed *be* the LORD God of Israel, which sent thee this day to meet me: ⁽³³⁾ and blessed *be* thy advice, and blessed *be* thou, which hast kept me this day from coming to *shed* blood, and from avenging myself with mine own hand. ⁽³⁴⁾ For in very deed, *as* the LORD God of Israel liveth, which hath kept me back from hurting thee, except thou hadst hasted and come to meet me, surely there had not been left unto Nabal by the morning light any that pisseth against the wall. ⁽³⁵⁾ So David received of her hand *that* which she had brought him, and said unto her, Go up in peace to thine house; see, I have hearkened to thy voice, and have accepted thy person.

⁽³⁶⁾ And Abigail came to Nabal; and, behold, he held a feast in his house, like the feast of a king; and Nabal's heart *was* merry within him, for he *was* very drunken: wherefore she told him nothing, less or more, until the morning light. ⁽³⁷⁾ But it came to pass in the morning, when the wine was gone out of Nabal, and his wife had told him these things, that his heart died within him, and he became *as* a stone.

[1] Heb., *no staggering,* or, *stumbling.*

---

tion and exhortation—had already taken root among the people. The "sons of the prophets," we may still with fair probability assume, were the first Teachers—the first *rabbis* in Israel. It must be remembered that at this time, and even before the murder of the priests at Nob, the central Sanctuary exercised comparatively small influence over the religious life of the people; even the Ark of the Covenant never seems to have been kept there. The religious life, when Samuel had grown up to manhood, had well-nigh died out of the people.

⁽³¹⁾ **Then remember thine handmaid.**—With exquisite grace Abigail wound up her earnest simple words to the king of the future with a reference to the period when those happy days, to which she looked forward with such certainty, should have arrived— *then* David must have no deeds of violence, of furious passion, and of shed blood to look back upon. When that golden time should have come—as come it surely would—he must remember then that Abigail, who was now speaking to him, had saved him from the commission of a wild and sinful act, and, in grateful memory for the good service, must then look kindly on her from his throne.

⁽³³⁾ **And blessed be thy advice.**—David, with his usual frank generosity, allows he has been in the wrong in giving way to wild, ungovernable passion, and openly confesses that if Abigail had not met him and reasoned with him, he would have carried out his purpose, and stained his fair fame for ever with a terrible crime. His dark purpose was to cut off, root and branch, the whole house of Nabal, amongst others the woman standing before him there. It is noticeable how, in this age of deeper religion and of higher culture, the old superstitious reverence for vows, taken in moments of frenzy or of extreme excitement, had given place to a calmer and more reasonable spirit. Never had a more solemn vow been taken than David's that morning, when he took a solemn oath that he would murder the whole house of Nabal; and yet, before the sun set he is convinced of the wickedness of his purpose, and sooner than carry it out he deliberately breaks the oath. Some years before, Saul—had he not been forcibly hindered by the people—would, by the murder of his son, the hero-prince Jonathan, have fulfilled the rash oath which he swore at the battle of Michmash (1 Sam. xiv. 24, 45); and Jephthah, the judge of Israel, we know, in the person of his loved daughter, ruthlessly carried out his wild, useless oath (Judges xi. 34, 40).

⁽³⁶⁾ **He held a feast in his house.**—This completes the picture of the wealthy sheep-master. The contrast between him and his wife, the high-minded and wise Abigail, is very striking. The husband, churlish, obstinate, a friend of Saul and the old disorderly state of things, haughty, unyielding, selfish, and indulging to excess in the coarse pleasures of the table, falling a victim in the end to his own untamed passions; the wife—"the good angel of the household," as Stanley phrases it—thoughtful, prudent, far-seeing, a patient listener, and an apt pupil evidently of the new masters of learning and culture in Israel, a beautiful example of the highest type of the devout Hebrew woman who during the long chequered story of the chosen race exercised so often a holy influence on the life of the people. Nabal may be taken as an extreme, though not an uncommon, example of the leading Israelites of the days *before* Samuel; Abigail as the representative of the nobler spirit among the higher classes *after* the spirit of Samuel had influenced the inhabitants of the land.

⁽³⁷⁾ **When the wine was gone out.**—Simply, when the brutish, selfish reveller had become sober by lapse of time.

His heart died within him.—These words are generally understood as signifying that an attack of apoplexy had seized the intemperate man. Commentators are a little divided as to the immediate cause of the stroke. (*a*) It was brought on by fear, hearing to what a terrible danger he had been, through his reckless, unguarded language and churlish conduct, exposed. In that drunken sleep, out of which he was then scarcely awakened, he and all his family would have perished miserably had it not been for his wife's forethought. In his enfeebled state, feverish and excited still with the strong drink, terror and horror seized him, and the "stroke" followed. (*b*) A furious burst of anger at his wife's intelligence swept over him: that she should have humiliated herself before one whom he evidently hated, like David, was to him unbearable; and the wild burst of anger acting on the ruined, drink-shattered frame completed the mischief, and the

Death of Nabal. I. SAMUEL, XXVI. *David Marries Abigail.*

(38) And it came to pass about ten days after, that the LORD smote Nabal, that he died. (39) And when David heard that Nabal was dead, he said, Blessed be the LORD, that hath pleaded the cause of my reproach from the hand of Nabal, and hath kept his servant from evil: for the LORD hath returned the wickedness of Nabal upon his own head.

And David sent and communed with Abigail, to take her to him to wife. (40) And when the servants of David were come to Abigail to Carmel, they spake unto her, saying, David sent us unto thee, to take thee to him to wife. (41) And she arose, and bowed herself on *her* face to the earth, and said, Behold, *let* thine handmaid *be* a servant to wash the feet of the servants of my lord. (42) And Abigail hasted, and arose, and rode upon an ass, with five damsels of her's that went [1]after her; and she went after the messengers of David, and became his wife.

(43) David also took Ahinoam *a*of Jezreel; and they were also both of them his wives. (44) But Saul had given *b*Michal his daughter, David's wife, to Phalti the son of Laish, which *was* of Gallim.

CHAPTER XXVI. — (1) And the Ziphites came unto Saul to Gibeah, say-

[1] Heb., *at her feet.*
a Josh. 15. 56.
b 2 Sam. 3. 14, 15.

result was the stroke of apoplexy. The first is, however, the more probable.

(38) **The Lord smote Nabal.**—That is to say, that after ten days had passed the Lord put an end to the base life by a second apoplectic stroke. Although the death was a sequel to the selfishness, the passion, and the intemperance, it does not appear that anything more than the operation of natural causes occasioned the end here. In the language of these old divinely inspired writers, disease and sickness are often spoken of as the special "shafts" aimed by the Most High, as in fact they are.

(40) **When the servants of David were come to Abigail.**—The time that had elapsed between the death of Nabal and this mission of David to Abigail is not specified. The legal time of mourning was fixed at only seven days, but a very considerable period may have elapsed in this case. S. Ambrose allegorises here, as is usual in Patristic expositions, and compares the espousals of Abigail to David after Nabal's death to the union of the Church (*i.e.*, the Gentile world) to Christ after the cessation of its connection with heathenism.—*S. Ambrose*, Ep. 31 (quoted in Wordsworth).

(43) **David also took Ahinoam of Jezreel.**—Jezreel is not the city in Issachar (Josh. xix. 18), but a town in the southern part of Canaan, situate in the hill country of Judah, near Maon. The fatal results of this disastrous and unhappy Oriental custom of polygamy, as time went on, showed themselves in King David's household—a plentiful crop of intrigues, crimes, and murders in the royal palace were the sad fruits of his yielding to the miserable practice, which has ever been one of the curses of the East.

(44) **Michal his daughter.**—The marriage of the Princess Michal to Phalti (Michal, we read, "loved David," chap. xviii. 20) had taken place probably some time before. This high-handed act showed on the part of Saul a fixed determination to break utterly and for ever with David. Phalti was presumably a chieftain whom Saul was desirous of attracting to his fortunes. But the story of Michal does not end here. After King Saul's death, Abner, the uncle (or perhaps the cousin) of the late king, the well-known captain of his host, made overtures to David. David, however, only consented to a friendship with Abner if his young kinswoman, the Princess Michal, Saul's daughter, was taken away from Phalti, and restored to him as his wife. Abner, we read, complied with the condition, and Michal was taken from Phaltiel—as he is called in the account of this transaction, contained in 2 Sam. iii. 13, 16—and restored to David. An interesting and curious tradition respecting this man Phalti, or Phaltiel, is contained in the Talmud. In 1 Sam. xxv. 44 the second husband of David's wife is called Phalti, and in 2 Sam. iii. 15 he is called Phaltiel. Rabbi Jochanan said his name received that extension (el=God) to indicate that *God* had *saved* him from transgression. (The name *Phalti* being derived from the root *palat*—to cause to escape, Michal and Phalti never having lived together as man and wife.)—Treatise *Sanhedrin*, fol. 19, col. 2.

Once more the daughter of Saul appears in the sacred history. (See 2 Sam. vi. 20—23.) It was the greatest day in David's life—the Ark of the Covenant was being brought up with solemn pomp from its place of long exile in Kirjath-jearim to the new sacred capital of the loved king. One sad incident alone, we are told, marred the glories of the day. Michal, his wife, as Stanley thinks, in the proud, almost conservative, spirit of the older dynasty, not without a thought of her father's fallen house, looked on contemptuously as King David danced before the Ark with the priests, his royal robes thrown aside; and later in the day seems to have poured out before the king her scornful feelings.

> "Preceding the blest vessel, onward came,
> With light dance leaping, girt in humble guise,
> Israel's sweet harper; in that hap he seemed
> Less and yet more kingly. Opposite,
> At a great palace, from the lattice forth
> Looked Michal, like a lady full of scorn
> And sorrow."—DANTE: *Purgatory*, x.

The sacred story goes on to say that Michal, as a childless wife in the royal palace of David, had time to mourn her fatal exhibition of pride. (See 2 Sam. vi. 12—23.)

XXVI.

(1—25) The Ziphites again Betray David to Saul—David surprises Saul asleep in his Camp, but once more Spares his Life, simply taking away the royal Spear and a Cruse of Water—Saul is again Moved by David's Nobleness.

(1) **The Ziphites came unto Saul.**—There is grave difficulty connected with the recital contained in this chapter. Is it another account of the incident told in chaps. xxiv., xxvi. by a different narrator? This is

ing, ^aDoth not David hide himself in the hill of Hachilah, *which is* before Jeshimon? ⁽²⁾ Then Saul arose, and went down to the wilderness of Ziph, having three thousand chosen men of Israel with him, to seek David in the wilderness of Ziph. ⁽³⁾ And Saul pitched in the hill of Hachilah, which *is* before Jeshimon, by the way. But David abode in the wilderness, and he saw that Saul came after him into the wilderness. ⁽⁴⁾ David therefore sent out spies, and understood that Saul was come in very deed.

⁽⁵⁾ And David arose, and came to the place where Saul had pitched: and David beheld the place where Saul lay, and ^bAbner the son of Ner, the captain of

a ch. 23. 19.

b ch. 14. 50 & 17. 55.

---

the opinion of some modern expositors of weight: for instance, Ewald and the Bishop of Bath and Wells in the *Speaker's Commentary*. The question at issue is as follows:—We have in this First Book of Samuel, in chaps. xxiii., xxiv. and xxvi., two recitals of David sparing his great adversary's life, at first sight under very similar circumstances. For instance: in both these occurrences (1) it is the same people, the Ziphites, who call Saul's attention to David's presence in their neighbourhood; (2) in both, Saul comes from Gibeah with the same number of men, 3,000; (3) *the general* bearing of the incident is identical in both—viz., the persuasions of David's followers to induce their leader to take Saul's life when in his power resisted by the noble-minded chieftain; the taking of something personal by David from the sleeping king, as a proof that the royal life had been in his hands; the sequel, which describes the heartfelt temporary repentance of Saul for the past. But here the resemblance ends. The circumstances of the night raid by David and his companions into *the camp* of the sleeping Saul are, when examined closely, so *entirely* different from the circumstances of the midday siesta of Saul in *the En-gedi cavern*, where David and his band were dwelling, that it is really impossible to assume that they are versions of one and the same incident. We conclude, therefore, with some certainty, that the accounts contained in chaps. xxiii., xxiv., and xxvi. refer to two distinct and separate events; and so Keil, Erdmann and Lange, Dean Payne Smith in the *Pulpit Commentary*, Wordsworth, &c. Bishop Hervey, in the *Speaker's Commentary*, is, however, supported in his hypothesis of the two accounts referring to only one incident by Ewald, De Wette, and others. In the course of this exposition, the more striking agreements and divergencies will be discussed.

There remains, however, a still graver question to be considered, the gravity and difficulty of which remains the same whether we assume, as we propose to do, that *twice* in the course of the outlaw life of David the king's life was in his power, or that only *once* David stood over the sleeping king, sword in hand, and that the two accounts refer to one and the same event—For *what purpose* did the compiler of the First Book of Samuel insert in his narrative this twenty-sixth chapter —where either the *old* story of chaps. xxiii. and xxiv. is repeated with certain variations, or else an incident of a similar nature to one which has been told before in careful detail is repeated at great length? To this important question no perfectly satisfactory reply can be given. The object of *one* such recital in an account of the early life of the great founder of Israelitic greatness is clear, but we may well ask why was a *second* narrative of an incident of like nature inserted in a book where conciseness is ever so carefully studied? All we can suggest is, that everything which conduced to the glory of the favourite hero of Israel was of the deepest interest to the people, and the surpassing nobility and generosity of the magnanimity of David to his deadly foe was deemed worthy of these detailed accounts even in the necessarily brief compilation of the inspired writer of the history of this time.

⁽²⁾ **Then Saul arose, and went down to the wilderness of Ziph.**—We assume, then, that after the marriage of David with Abigail he and his armed band returned again to his old neighbourhood in the south—in the desert of Judah—the district named after the Hill of Hachilah being, no doubt, in all respects well adapted for the permanent encampment of such a large band as David's now most certainly was. David, who had been forced on a previous occasion to leave it on account of the hot pursuit of Saul, aided by the Ziphites, who knew the country and its resources so well, probably now supposed, after the protestation of Saul at En-gedi, that he would now at least be left in peace. But he forgot with whom he had to do—forgot the state of mind of his determined foe, and how likely it was that the old mania would return with redoubled force. The Ziphites, however, who knew Saul, and the feeling respecting David which existed at the court of Saul, repeated their old tactics, and sent, as on a previous occasion, to suggest that with their help the obnoxious chieftain and his free lances could be destroyed. The temptation was too great to be resisted; so probably, with the advice of Abner, Saul took the field again. The 3,000 seem to have been the standing force which Saul kept round him in the Gibeah garrison. (See the first notice of this standing army in chap. xiii. 2.)

⁽³⁾ **But David abode in the wilderness.**—The former incident, when David spared Saul's life, happened long after the information of the Ziphites brought the king to the hill "Hachilah, on the south of Jeshimon." *Then* David, on hearing of the march of Saul and his army, retired into the wilderness of Maon. Saul pursued him, and David and his force were then only saved from destruction owing to the news of a formidable Philistine invasion. This intelligence called Saul's forces away from the pursuit of David. David, unmolested, drew off his band, and sought refuge at En-gedi (chap. xxiii.). After the Philistine invasion had been repulsed, Saul again commenced operations against David, and marched his force to En-gedi, in one of the caves of which took place the scene where David for the first time spared the king's life (chap. xxiv.). *Now*, after the information of the Ziphites had brought down Saul and his soldiers from Gibeah, David does not flee in haste to Maon, and thence to En-gedi, nor is Saul called away to any Philistine invasion; but David abides in the wilderness, and his scouts come and tell him that Saul *in very deed* (verse 4) was come after him in force.

⁽⁵⁾ **And David arose.**—Immediately after the scouts informed him of the purpose of Saul, and of the near proximity of the royal army David seems to

his host: and Saul lay in the ¹trench, and the people pitched round about him. ⁽⁶⁾ Then answered David and said to Ahimelech the Hittite, and to Abishai the son of Zeruiah, brother to Joab, saying, Who will go down with me to Saul to the camp? And Abishai said, I will go down with thee.

⁽⁷⁾ So David and Abishai came to the people by night: and, behold, Saul lay sleeping within the trench, and his spear stuck in the ground at his bolster: but Abner and the people lay round about him. ⁽⁸⁾ Then said Abishai to David, God hath ²delivered thine enemy into thine hand this day: now therefore let me smite him, I pray thee, with the spear even to the earth at once, and I will not *smite* him the second time. ⁽⁹⁾ And David said to Abishai, Destroy him not: for who can stretch forth his hand against the LORD's anointed, and be guiltless? ⁽¹⁰⁾ David said furthermore, *As* the LORD liveth, the LORD shall smite him; or his day shall come to die; or he shall descend into battle,

¹ Or, *midst of his carriages.*

² Heb., *shut up.*

---

have resolved upon that night adventure which resulted in the episode told in this twenty-sixth chapter.

In the trench.—The English Version (Margin) has, "in the midst of his carriages"; Keil renders, "by the wagon rampart"; The LXX. translate the Hebrew word by "covered chariots." The meaning is, no doubt, that the king lay down within the barricade or rampart formed by the baggage wagons.

⁽⁶⁾ **Ahimelech the Hittite.**—The Hittites were one of the old Canaanitish peoples; we hear of them round Hebron in the time of Abraham (Gen. xv. 20). The conquering Israelites subdued, but did not exterminate them; and gradually, in the days of the weakness and divisions which succeeded the first conquest, the Hittites, in common with many other of the old tribes, seem to have enjoyed the Land of Promise with the children of Israel in a kind of joint occupation. We find the Hittites ranking here among David's trusted faithful men; and later we hear of another Hittite, Uriah, the husband of Bathsheba, filling an important post in the royal army, and possessing a house and an establishment in the capital city of Jerusalem. We do not hear again of this Ahimelech in the sacred record.

Abishai the son of Zeruiah.—Zeruiah was David's sister. Abishai, later one of the famous generals of David, was brother to Joab, afterwards the captain of the royal host. Abishai was apparently nearly of the same age as David. There was a third younger brother also high in the favour of his kinsman David—Asahel, celebrated especially for his speed in running. Between these three sons of Zeruiah and Abner a blood feud seems to have existed. Abner, the near relative, and captain of the host of Saul throughout that monarch's reign, is closely associated with the fortunes of Saul. It has been supposed, and with some probability, that he was among the determined foes of David. Dreading the advent of the son of Jesse to the throne, he saw in his elevation the signal of the downfall of all Saul's family and friends. He, Abner, surely would no longer be captain of the host of Israel. The words of David to Abner in this chapter (verses 14—16) seem to point to the fierce hatred which existed between them. The bloody sequel to the feud between the great kinsman of Saul and the three brothers, the famous sons of David's sister, is strictly in accordance with what we should expect in these fierce, wild days. Some time after Saul's death Abner slew the young Asahel, who seems to have been passionately loved by his elder brother. Abner became reconciled to David, but the reconciliation saved not the friend of Saul and the slayer of Asahel from the vengeance of Joab and Abishai, who murdered the illustrious Abner in cold blood.

And Abishai said, I will go down with thee.—Ahimelech seems to have backed out of the perilous night enterprise, but Abishai, the son of Zeruiah, with the reckless gallantry and the intense devotion to David which, with all their pride and self-will, ever characterised these famous warrior kinsmen of the king, at once volunteered to go with his loved chief.

⁽⁷⁾ **Within the trench.**—As above, in verse 5, "within the barrier of the wagons."

His spear ... at his bolster.—"Bolster," literally, *the place where his head is,* better rendered *at his head;* and so in verses 11, 12, 16. The same Hebrew word occurs in the narration of Jacob's dream (Gen. xxviii. 11); it is there rendered in our English Version, "his pillows." It was the tall spear which ever seems to have been in Saul's hand, or placed close to him. We read of it in battle in his hand, and in the council chamber and at the state banquet it was within his reach, and now it was evidently reared upright beside the sleeping king. "I noticed at all the encampments which we passed that the shiek's tent was distinguished from the rest *by a tall spear* stuck upright in the ground in front of it; and it is the custom when a party set out on an excursion for robbery or for war, that when they halt to rest the spot where the chief reclines or rests is thus designated"—Thomson, *Land and the Book.*

⁽⁸⁾ **I will not smite him the second time.**—The meaning of the savage words of Abishai is accurately given in Lange's paraphrase, "I will pin him to the ground so thoroughly with one blow that it will not need another to kill him;" "*et secundo non opus erit,*" as the Vulg. well renders it.

⁽⁹⁾ **Against the Lord's anointed.**—David—taught, no doubt, by the prophet Samuel—looked upon the person of Saul as made sacred and inviolable by the royal anointing. Through the anointing Saul had become the possession of Jehovah; only Jehovah, then, could lawfully take away that sacred life. This he elaborates in the next verse. It is possible that these exalted sentiments respecting the Divine rights of kings were not uttered by David while standing in the dark night among Saul's soldiers by the sleeping king, but subsequently, when he and Abishai were talking the incident over together.

⁽¹⁰⁾ **David said furthermore.**—David suggests three possible cases in which the Divine arm might smite the "anointed of Jehovah." The first, the Lord "shall smite him" by some sudden death from disease —no doubt, the recent death of Nabal was in his mind;

and perish. (11) The LORD forbid that I should stretch forth mine hand against the LORD's anointed: but, I pray thee, take thou now the spear that *is* at his bolster, and the cruse of water, and let us go. (12) So David took the spear and the cruse of water from Saul's bolster; and they gat them away, and no man saw *it*, nor knew *it*, neither awaked: for they *were* all asleep; because a deep sleep from the LORD was fallen upon them.

(13) Then David went over to the other side, and stood on the top of an hill afar off; a great space *being* between them: (14) and David cried to the people, and to Abner the son of Ner, saying, Answerest thou not, Abner? Then Abner answered and said, Who *art* thou *that* criest to the king? (15) And David said to Abner, *Art* not thou a *valiant* man? and who *is* like to thee in Israel? wherefore then hast thou not kept thy lord the king? for there came one of the people in to destroy the king thy lord. (16) This thing *is* not good that thou hast done. As the LORD liveth, ye *are* ¹worthy to die, because ye have not kept your master, the LORD's anointed. And now see where the king's spear *is*, and the cruse of water that *was* at his bolster.

(17) And Saul knew David's voice, and said, *Is* this thy voice, my son David?

1 Heb., *the sons of death.*

---

the second by what is termed "natural death;" and the third by some blow received in battle. The idea of an arrow winged by some unseen hand was evidently here in the speaker's thoughts.

(11) **The spear.**—The spear was Saul's especial sign of royalty. "This taking away of the spear from Saul's head as he slept was an omen of the transfer of his royalty to David."—*Bishop Patrick*, quoted by Wordsworth.

And the cruse of water. — "A very ancient usage explains why the cruse of water is here brought into such special prominence. According to this custom, some high dignitary always had in keeping a costly ewer for the king's necessary ablutions, and it was specially his duty to take it with him, and present it to the king during campaigns or other journeys, so that its disappearance would involve almost as great a disgrace to the king as the loss of his sceptre" (Ewald, in reference to Ps. lx. 8, states his belief that this custom existed in the time of David).— Ewald, *History of Israel*, "David," ii. 3 (Note). The same scholar also writes that "there are many other instances of similar stories, in which the future conqueror and founder of a new dynasty is represented as having received at first some symbol of royalty from his predecessors by accident, as it were, or in sport. Thus Alexander at first takes the royal divining cup from Dârâ as if in sport: a story which in the Shâhnâmeh no longer appears in its original light; and in nothing was the belief in omens so strong as in the high affairs of state."—"David," ii. 3 (Note).

(12) **No man saw it, nor knew it, neither awaked.**—The Hebrew is more graphic: "And none saw, and none knew, and none awaked."

A deep sleep from the Lord.— The inference here, at first sight, certainly is that an unnatural, or rather, a supernatural drowsiness had fallen on the camp of Saul. Still, it is not absolutely necessary to suppose that a special miracle was wrought on this occasion. The memory of great carelessness and want of vigilance in the royal army was evidently in David's mind when he sarcastically reproves the royal general Abner, in verses 14—16. They were in a friendly district, and never dreamed of a surprise, and possibly the rough soldiers on duty had been carousing. David too and Abishai, owing to their long experience in camp life, often flying before their enemies, were practised scouts, and in the dark night did their perilous work speedily and noiselessly.

(13) **David went over to the other side.**— That is to say, after taking the royal spear and cruse of water from beside the sleeping king, David with Abishai left the camp of Saul, then, crossing the deep ravine, re-ascended the opposite hill or mountain—there was then a deep gorge between him and the camp—and uttered his shrill cry, which awoke the sleeping sentinel, who seems at once to have roused Abner. Keil calls attention here to the special notice in the text that the mountain whence David spoke was afar off, not, as we should say, "as the crow flies," but afar, because a deep steep ravine lay between the camp of Saul and the hill on which David and Abishai stood. "On the previous occasion when, in the cave of En-gedi, the son of Jesse cut off the skirt of the royal garment, David fearlessly cried to Saul when the king was still evidently quite close to the cave. Now, however, he seems to have reckoned far less upon any change in the state of Saul's mind than he had done before . . . in fact, he rather feared lest Saul should endeavour to get him into his power as soon as he woke from his sleep."

(14) **Who art thou that criest to the king?** —The Vulg. rightly interprets with "Who art thou that criest and disquietest the king?" that is, disturbs the king's rest with your shouting.

(15) **A valiant man.**—The English translators have rightly emphasised the Hebrew *ish* here by rendering a "valiant" man. *Ish* was used not unfrequently in this " nobler " sense ; so in Ps. xlix. 2, when the *b'ne adam*, as "the poor mean ones," were contrasted with the *b'ne ish*, "the noble ones." (See also Isaiah ii. 9: "mean men and great men.")

Wherefore then hast thou not kept?—The whole of this bitter sarcastic address seems to imply that a deadly feud existed between David and Saul's captain and kinsman, Abner. If this be the case, the royal generosity and nobility of David's character was well shown in his subsequent friendship with this Abner, and in his deep sorrow for the great captain's untimely death. (See 2 Sam. iii.)

(17) **And Saul knew David's voice.**—The account is most natural throughout. Verse 7 speaks of the enterprise being undertaken "by night," when the soldiers of Saul had fallen into "a deep sleep" (verse 12). When David on his return stood on the opposite ridge, it

And David said, It is my voice, my lord, O king. ⁽¹⁸⁾ And he said, Wherefore doth my lord thus pursue after his servant? for what have I done? or what evil *is* in mine hand? ⁽¹⁹⁾ Now therefore, I pray thee, let my lord the king hear the words of his servant. If the LORD have stirred thee up against me, let him [1]accept an offering: but if *they be* the children of men, cursed *be* they before the LORD; for they have driven me out this day from [2]abiding in the inheritance of the LORD, saying, Go, serve other gods. ⁽²⁰⁾ Now therefore, let not my blood fall to the earth before the face of the LORD: for the king of Israel is come out to seek a flea, as when one doth hunt a partridge in the mountains.

[1] Heb., *smell.*

[2] Heb., *cleaving.*

---

was still, no doubt, the dawn of early morning. So Saul speaks of hearing *that* voice of David so well known to him, and which once he so dearly loved; he could not as yet discern the figure of his former friend.

⁽¹⁸⁾ **What have I done?**—The whole address of David to Saul is intensely reverent, even loving. The conspicuous trophy of his late "night raid" was in his hand; we can imagine the first rays of the morning sun lighting up the glittering royal spear grasped by David. Saul could not help recognising that at least the son of Jesse sought not his life.

⁽¹⁹⁾ **Let him accept an offering.**—The words here are difficult ones in a theological point of view. If, however, we are content to interpret them with Bishop Wordsworth according to the Arabic Version of the Chaldee Targum, the difficulty vanishes: "If the Lord hath stirred thee up against me for any fault of mine, let me know mine offence, and I am ready to make an offering for it to the Lord, that I may be forgiven."—*Wordsworth.* But by far the greater number of scholars and expositors understand the words of David in what seems to be their plain literal sense, viz.: "If Jehovah has incited you to do this evil thing, let Him smell an offering." The word for offering in the Hebrew is *minchah*, the meat offering, which signifies "sanctification of life and devotion to the Lord." In other words, "If you think or feel that *God* stirs you up to take this course against me—the innocent one—pray to God that He may take the temptation—if it be a temptation — from thee." This conception that the movement comes from God runs through the Old Testament. It is apparently expressed in such passages as "the Lord hardened Pharaoh's heart," and in such sayings as we find here in this Book of Samuel of an evil spirit *from the* Lord haunting Saul. "Some have explained the conception by referring it to the intensity with which the Israelites had grasped the idea of the omnipresence of the Deity, and of His being the one power by whose energy all things exist and all acts are done; alike evil and good come from God, for He alone is the source of all . . . but it does not follow that everything to which His providence seems to lead is therefore right for man to do; on the contrary, all leadings of Providence are to be judged by God's immutable law."—*Dean Payne Smith.* These seeming leadings must be tested by prayer offered by an earnest heart: that is the meaning of the offering (*minchah*) here. The conception—strange as it may seem at first —is a true one, as in the case of Pharaoh, and also—though with some important modifications—of Saul. The Holy Spirit had pleaded long, and had pleaded in vain. It is possible, we know, for us to *weary*, or, as St. Paul puts it, quench that Spirit of God pleading within us; then at length, wearied or quenched, it wings its flight away from the wicked soul. This spreading its wings in flight may be said to be God's work. The sad and invariable result is, the deserted heart becomes *hardened*, as in the case of Pharaoh; the empty shrine becomes the swept and garnished home for the evil spirit, as in the case of Saul.

But if they be the children of men.—But David goes on to say, "If the cruel, unjust thoughts are the result of the envy and hatred of men who are my enemies, may God punish them as they deserve; for see what they have done for me: they have by their calumnies—whispered in your ears—driven me into exile; they have violently bidden me to go and serve other and strange gods." He means that, far away from the only country where Jehovah is loved and honoured, away from the influence of Jehovah's prophets and beloved priests, he and his would be tempted to serve other gods, and to share in the foul and impious practice of the heathen nations.

⁽²⁰⁾ **Before the face of the Lord.**—Better rendered, *far from the presence of the Lord.* The same thought dwelt upon in the last verse is here enlarged. "If this savage persecution continues," David goes on to say, "sooner or later I shall fall a victim to one or other of the countless perils to which one in my situation, as leader of a band of outlaws, is daily exposed. Let not such hard, cruel fate be mine—to die a violent death far away from the land which Jehovah loves." It was the same thought which inspires so touchingly this last prayer he made to Saul which, ever present in his heart, made the bringing up of the Ark to a permanent sanctuary, where the visible symbol of the Eternal Presence should dwell for ever, the dream of David's life. It was the same holy thought which induced him to spend so much time and to lay up such vast stores for the building of a glorious sanctuary. The passionate longing of the "man after God's own heart" to worship his Eternal Master in a fitting house devoted to His service, and in the company of men who loved and honoured the Name of names, is to be found in some of the most soul-searching of his psalms.

To seek a flea.—The same humiliating comparison he had made once before on a similar occasion again occurs to him. Such repetition is of ordinary occurrence, as we well know, both in speeches and writings. The LXX. here substitute for "a flea" "my soul," probably with the view of avoiding the repetition of the simile of a flea, which David had made use of on the previous occasion of his sparing the king's life at En-gedi.

A partridge in the mountains.—The LXX. needlessly alters "partridge" into "screech-owl," and changes the sense: "as the screech-owl hunts on the mountains." The meaning of the simile in the Hebrew original is well given by Erdmann, in *Lange*: "The isolated from God's people, far from all association, a fugitive from their plots on the mountain heights, thou seekest at all cost to destroy, as one hunts a single fugitive partridge on the mountain, only to kill it at all costs, while otherwise, from its insignificance, it would

(21) Then said Saul, I have sinned: return, my son David: for I will no more do thee harm, because my soul was precious in thine eyes this day: behold, I have played the fool, and have erred exceedingly. (22) And David answered and said, Behold the king's spear! and let one of the young men come over and fetch it. (23) The LORD render to every man his righteousness and his faithfulness: for the LORD delivered thee into my hand to-day, but I would not stretch forth mine hand against the LORD's anointed. (24) And, behold, as thy life was much set by this day in mine eyes, so let my life be much set by in the eyes of the LORD, and let him deliver me out of all tribulation. (25) Then Saul said to David, Blessed *be* thou, my son David: thou shalt both do great *things*, and also shalt still prevail. So David went on his way, and Saul returned to his place.

B.C. cir. 1058.

1 Heb., *be consumed.*

CHAPTER XXVII.—(1) And David said in his heart, I shall now [1] perish one day by the hand of Saul: *there is* nothing better for me than that I should speedily escape into the land of the Philistines; and Saul shall despair of me, to seek me any more in any coast of Israel: so shall I escape out of his hand. (2) And David arose, and he passed over with the six

---

not be hunted, since partridges are to be found in the field in coveys." Conder (*Tent Life in Palestine*) especially tells us that partridges still tenant these wilds; and speaking of the precipitous cliffs overhanging the Dead Sea, he says: "Among the rocks of the wild goats the bands of ibex may be seen still bounding, and the partridge is still chased on the mountains, as David was followed by the stealthy hunter Saul."

(21) **I have played the fool.**—There seems something more in these words of Saul than sorrow for the past. He seems to blame himself here, as the Dean of Canterbury well suggests, for putting himself again in David's power through overweening confidence in his own strength. He reproaches himself with the unguarded state of his camp, but he pledges himself to do no harm to David for the future. He even begs that he will return to his court. But in these words, and also in his blessing of David (verse 25), there is a ring of falseness; and this was evidently the impression made on the outlaw, for he not only silently declined the royal overtures, but almost immediately removed from the dominions of Saul altogether, feeling that for him and his there was no longer any hope of security in the land of Israel so long as his foe, King Saul, lived.

Here the two whom Samuel had anointed as kings—the king who has forfeited his crown, and the king of the golden future—parted for ever. They never looked on each other's faces again; not even when the great warrior Saul lay dead was his former friend able to take a farewell look at the face he once loved so well. The kindest services his faithful subjects of Jabesh Gilead could show to their king's dishonoured remains, for which they had risked their lives, was at once, with all solemnity and mourning, to burn the disfigured body, and to draw a veil of flame over the mutilated corpse of Saul.

(25) **Thou shalt both do great things.**—"Saul is here again 'among the prophets,' and foretells David's exaltation and victory. 'Vicisti Nazarene!' was the exclamation of Julian."—*Bishop Wordsworth.*

XXVII.

(1—12) David and his Band take Refuge with Achish, King of Gath, who Receives him Kindly, and gives him Ziklag as a Residence—Their Expeditions against the Nomad Tribes lying south of Canaan.

(1) **And David said in his heart.**—David's position seems to have grown more and more untenable during the latter days of Saul's reign. Probably the paroxysms of the king's fatal malady grew sharper and more frequent, and his chieftains and favourites, whom, as we have already seen (chap. xxvi.), he had chosen mostly out of the one small tribe of Benjamin, feared—and with good reason—the advent of David to the throne, which they saw was imminent in the event of Saul's dying or being permanently disqualified to rule. These men, whose bitter hostility to David is more than hinted at in several places, doubtless taking advantage of the king's state of mind, incited him against David. The words and persuasions of such men as Cush the Benjamite (see Ps. vii.), Doeg the Edomite, probably Abner the captain of the host, the men of Ziph, and others, quickly erased from the memory of Saul such scenes as we have witnessed in the En-gedi cave, and, still more recently, in the hill of Hachilah, and more than counterbalanced the devotion and powerful friendship of true warriors like Jonathan, who loved and admired David. In David's words, after he had taken the spear and cruse from the side of the sleeping Saul, we see something of what was passing in his mind—his constant fear of a violent death; his knowledge that powerful and wicked men were constantly plotting against him; and his determination to seek a home in another land, where, however, he expected to find a grave far away from the chosen race, among the idolators and enemies of Jehovah of Israel. He now realises a part of these sorrowful forebodings. But in this determination of the son of Jesse we never hear of prayer, or of consultation with prophet or with priest. A dull despair seems to have at this time deprived David at once of faith and hope.

Into the land of the Philistines.—David chose to seek a refuge among these warlike people, for he believed he would be in greater security there than among his friendly kinsfolk, the Moabites, where, in former days, he had found such a kindly welcome for his family in the first period of Saul's enmity. He probably doubted the power of Moab to protect him.

(2) **The six hundred men.**—This was the original number. They still formed the nucleus of the force, but the total number was now far larger. These "six hundred" had each their households, besides which, many a group of warriors, large and small, had already joined the now renowned standard of the future king.

hundred men that *were* with him unto Achish, the son of Maoch, king of Gath. ⁽³⁾ And David dwelt with Achish at Gath, he and his men, every man with his household, *even* David with his two wives, Ahinoam the Jezreelitess, and Abigail the Carmelitess, Nabal's wife. ⁽⁴⁾ And it was told Saul that David was fled to Gath: and he sought no more again for him.

⁽⁵⁾ And David said unto Achish, If I have now found grace in thine eyes, let them give me a place in some town in the country, that I may dwell there: for why should thy servant dwell in the royal city with thee? ⁽⁶⁾ Then Achish gave him Ziklag that day: wherefore Ziklag pertaineth unto the kings of Judah unto this day. ⁽⁷⁾ And ¹the time that David dwelt in the country of the Philistines was ²a full year and four months.

⁽⁸⁾ And David and his men went up, and invaded the Geshurites, and the ³Gezrites, and the Amalekites: for those *nations were* of old the inhabitants of

¹ Heb., *the number of days.*
² Heb., *a year of days.*
³ Or, *Gerzites.*

Achish, the son of Maoch, king of Gath.—The same, we believe, as that Achish to whom David fled before (see chap. xxi. 11), and identical with Achish, son of Maachah (1 Kings ii. 39). This would involve the necessity of ascribing a fifty years' reign to this prince. (Such a lengthy reign is quite possible.) The whole of Philistia subsequently fell under King David's rule. It seems, however, that he permitted, even after the conquest, Achish to remain in his old city of Gath, most likely as his tributary: thus, we may suppose, paying back the old debt of kindness to Achish.

⁽³⁾ **And David dwelt with Achish at Gath.** —His reception by the Philistines seems to have been most kindly. There was a wide difference between the circumstances of this and his former visit to Gath. *Then* he was a fugitive, almost unattended; *now* he was at the head of an army of trained and devoted soldiers. Such a guest might be of the greatest service to the Philistines in their perpetual wars with Saul, with whom David would now be considered to have finally broken off all relations, seeing he had sought a home and shelter among the most bitter of his foes.

⁽⁴⁾ **And it was told Saul.**—This short statement tells us plainly that up to the moment when Saul heard that David had crossed the frontier, he had not ceased to pursue after him and to seek his life. Ewald considers that it was during the residence at Gath that David exercised himself as a musician in the Gittite— *i.e.*, the Philistine—style, which he afterwards transferred from there to Judah and Jerusalem. (See titles of Pss. viii., lxxxi., and lxxxiv., "upon the Gittith.") Gittith is a feminine adjective derived from Gath; the words possibly signify, "after the Gittith manner: some peculiar measure of style of Philistine music, or else the reference may be to a Philistine musical instrument."

⁽⁵⁾ **Why should thy servant dwell in the royal city with thee?**—The real reason why David wished a separate residence was that he might conduct his forays and other affairs apart from the supervision of his Philistine friends. *They* had one purpose in welcoming him and his band, *he* had quite another. Achish trusted that through David's assistance powerful military demonstrations in the southern districts of Saul's kingdom might be made. At this time the Philistine nation were preparing for that grand national effort against Saul which culminated in the battle of Mount Gilboa. David, on the other hand, intended, from a comparatively secure centre of operations somewhere in Philistia, to harry those nomad foes of Israel whose home was in the deserts to the south of Canaan.

⁽⁶⁾ **Ziklag.**—In the days of Joshua this place fell to the lot of Simeon (Josh. xix. 5). It was afterwards captured by the Philistines, not long before the time of David, and Keil thinks was left without inhabitants in consequence of this conquest. Its exact situation has never been clearly ascertained; it certainly lay far south, near the Amalekite borders.

Wherefore Ziklag pertaineth unto the kings of Judah unto this day.—These words supply us with a double note of time in the question of the date of this First Book of Samuel. They tell us that it was cast in its present shape *after* the revolt of Jeroboam, and certainly *before* the days of the carrying away of Israel to Babylon.

⁽⁷⁾ **A full year and four months.**—Keil calls attention to the exact statement of time here as a proof of the historical character of the whole narrative. The Hebrew expression, translated "a year," is a singular one: *yamim*—literally, *days*—a collective term, used in Lev. xxv. 29, 1 Sam. i. 3, ii. 19, &c., to signify a term or period of days which amounted to a full year. This year and four months were among the darkest days of David's life. He was sorely tried, it is true; but he had adopted the very course his bitterest foes would have wished him to select. In open arms, apparently leagued with the deadliest foes of Israel, like an Italian condottiere or captain of free lances of the Middle Ages, he had taken service and accepted the wages of that very Philistine city whose champion he once had slain in the morning of his career. At last his enemies at the court of Saul had reason when they spoke of him as a traitor. From the curt recital in this chapter, which deals with the saddest portion of David's career, we shall see that while he apparently continued to make common cause with the enemies of his race, he still used his power to help, and not to injure, his countrymen; but the price he paid for his patriotism was a life of falsehood, stained, too, with deeds of fierce cruelty, shocking even in these rough, half-barbarous times.

⁽⁸⁾ **Went up.**—The expression is strictly accurate. The nomad tribes against whom his expeditions were directed dwelt on higher ground than David's home at Ziklag, apparently on the wide extent of the mountain plateau, that high table-land at the north-east of the desert of Paran.

The Geshurites, and the Gezerites, and the Amalekites.—These were all "Bedaween" tribes, the scourge of the Israelitish families dwelling on the south of Canaan. It is not easy to identify the first

the land, as thou goest to Shur, even unto the land of Egypt. ⁽⁹⁾ And David smote the land, and left neither man nor woman alive, and took away the sheep, and the oxen, and the asses, and the camels, and the apparel, and returned, and came to Achish. ⁽¹⁰⁾ And Achish said, ¹Whither have ye made a road to day? And David said, Against the south of Judah, and against the south of the Jerahmeelites, and against the south of the Kenites. ⁽¹¹⁾ And David saved neither man nor woman alive, to bring *tidings* to Gath, saying, Lest they should tell on us, saying, So did David, and so *will be* his manner all the while he dwelleth in the country of the Philistines. ⁽¹²⁾ And Achish believed David,

1 Or, *Did you not make a road*, &c.

---

two named of these nomades against whom David directed his operations. We hear of these Geshurites in the neighbourhood of Bashan (Deut. iii. 14), and of another tribe of them in Syria (2 Sam. xv. 8). They were a widely scattered race of nomad Arabs. The Gezerites, or Gizrites, it has been supposed, were the remains of a once powerful race dispossessed by the Amorites. The third named, the Amalekites, were the remnant of that once powerful tribe destroyed by Saul in his famous war, when his disobedience incurred the wrath of Samuel.

For those nations were of old the inhabitants of the land, as thou goest to Shur, even unto the land of Egypt.—The grammar and construction of this sentence is confused and difficult. On the whole, the rendering and explanation of Erdmann in *Lange* seems the most satisfactory: "David . . . invaded the . . . and the Amalekites (for these were inhabitants of the land, who inhabited it of old) as far as Shur and Egypt." Thus David's raids extended as far as the desert frontier of Egypt.

⁽⁹⁾ **And left neither man nor woman alive.**—These acts of ferocious barbarity are simply without excuse; the reason for them is told us in verse 11. No captive was to be left alive to tell the tale to King Achish, who was under the delusion that David's feats of arms were carried out at the expense of his own countrymen, whose lands he was harrying. At this the Philistine rejoiced when he heard David was thus burning his only bridge of retreat : by alienating by these cruelties the affection of the people of Israel, by means of which, at some future time, he might have been recalled to his native land. There were a few occasions in the history of the chosen race when a war of extermination was commended. Then Israel was simply the stern instrument of wrath, used—as a pestilence is at times—to carry out the will of the earth's Master; but David had no such charge. Was it not these acts of ruthless cruelty which left on this king's hands the stain of blood which rendered them unfit in after days to build the House of the Lord he longed so passionately to erect? (1 Chron. xxviii. 3).

And took away the sheep, and the oxen, and the asses, and the camels, and the apparel.—To fight under David's banner now promised to be a lucrative service as well as an adventurous and wild career. Here at Ziklag, and for some time previously, we hear of brave discontented spirits from all parts of Israel joining him. In 1 Chron. xii. we have a long and accurate list of heroes who formed that Ziklag band. Amongst these gallant soldiers who now, to use the chronicler's term, "day by day came to David to help him," were a troop of Benjamites who had joined him some time before: their leader Amasai, on being questioned as to their reason for joining him, answered, "We are on thy side, thou son of Jesse . . . for thy God helpeth thee" (1 Chron. xii. 18). The words of Amasai express the feeling which seems to have pervaded Israel at that time in reference to David. The people throughout the land were coming to feel that Jehovah had indeed chosen David. The chronicler even speaks of David's band at Ziklag, after the recruits from all parts of Israel had poured in, "as a great host, like the host of God" (1 Chron. xii. 22).

⁽¹⁰⁾ **And David said, Against the south of Judah.**—The answer of David to his sovereign lord, the King of Gath—for he was now, to all intents and purposes, a vassal prince of Achish—was simply a falsehood. He had been engaged in distant forays against the old Bedaween enemies of Israel, far away in the desert which stretched to the frontier of Egypt; and from these nomads—rich in cattle and in other property, which they had obtained by years of successful plunder—he seems to have gained much booty, a share of which he brought to his "suzerain," Achish. But David represents that the cattle and apparel had been captured from his own countrymen, whose territory he was harrying. "The Jerahmeelites were descendants of Jerahmeel, the firstborn of Hezron (1 Chron. ii. 9, 25, 26), and therefore one of the three large families of Judah who sprang from Hezron."—*Keil.* They dwelt, it is believed, on the southern frontier of the tribe of Judah. The Kenites were a race living in friendship with and under the protection of Judah.

⁽¹¹⁾ **And David saved neither man nor woman.**—This and the following (12th) verse gives the reason for these atrocious acts of murder. The wild and irresponsible Arab chief alone seemed represented in David in this dark portion of his career. This saddest of all the chapters in David's life follows close upon the death of Samuel. It appears that the holy man of God had exercised, all the time that he had lived, a great and beneficent influence over the son of Jesse; and when he passed away, other and less wise counsellors prevailed with David. Want of trust in God and a craven fear for his own life (see his words, chap. xxvi. 20, 24) drove him to leave the land of Israel, and to seek a refuge among his Philistine foes. One sin led on to another, when, in Philistia—to preserve that life of his—he commenced a course of duplicity, to carry out which he was driven to commit these terrible cruelties. "The prisoners taken would naturally have been part of the spoil; but David dared not bring them to Gath, lest his deceit should be discovered. Obviously these tribes (Geshurites, Gezerites, and Amalekites) were allies of the Philistines."

Saying, So did David, and so will be his manner.—The English Version of this passage is in accordance with the present punctuation in the Hebrew Bible, and represents these words as the saying of the slaughtered enemies. This is of itself most improbable. The Hebrew, too, will scarcely bear this interpretation; for the verb "to dwell" is a past, and cannot correctly be

saying, He hath made his people Israel ¹utterly to abhor him; therefore he shall be my servant for ever.

^{1 Heb., to stink.}

CHAPTER XXVIII.—⁽¹⁾ And it came to pass in those days, that the Philistines gathered their armies together for warfare, to fight with Israel. And Achish said unto David, Know thou assuredly,

^{a ch. 25. 1.}

that thou shalt go out with me to battle, thou and thy men. ⁽²⁾ And David said to Achish, Surely thou shalt know what thy servant can do. And Achish said to David, Therefore will I make thee keeper of mine head for ever.

⁽³⁾ Now ^aSamuel was dead, and all Israel had lamented him, and buried him in Ramah, even in his own city.

---

rendered "while he dwelleth." The Masoretic punctuation of the present Hebrew text is of comparatively recent date. It is better, then, in their place, with Maurer and Keil, the LXX., and Vulg. Versions, simply to put a stop after the words "so did David," and then begin a new sentence, which will read, "And so was his manner all the while he dwelt in the land of the Philistines;" understanding these words as a remark of the narrator of the history.

XXVIII.

(1—25) The Philistines Invade the Land with a great Force—Saul's Fear—His Secret Visit to the Witch of En-dor, to Consult the Shade of Samuel.

⁽¹⁾ **The Philistines gathered their armies together for warfare.**—This was evidently, as Josephus remarks, a great effort on the part of the Philistines. It was no ordinary raid or border incursion, such as seems to have been so frequent all through the reign of Saul. Since their defeat in the Valley of Elah, which followed the single combat between Goliath and David, no such Philistine army had been gathered together. We are struck at once with the presence of the enemy in the heart of the land, no longer choosing the well-known and often-contested "Marches," or border districts. The Philistines are now strong enough to strike a blow at the centre of the kingdom, and to challenge a battle on the plain of Jezreel, or Esdraelon, north of Ephraim and Issachar. They probably marched along the sea-border of Canaan, collecting their forces as they advanced from each of their well-known military centres, and then, turning eastward, invaded the land by the Valley of Jezreel, or Esdraelon. They marched still eastward, and took up a strong position on the slopes of one of the groups of mountains that enclosed the broad plain of Jezreel toward the east, near the town of Shunem. King Saul, quickly assembling the fighting men of Israel, marched in pursuit, and coming up with them in the Esdraelon plain, took up his position opposite the Philistines—only a few miles parting the two hosts—on the slopes of another group of mountains, known as Mount Gilboa, lying to the south of the Philistine frontier. (There is a map of the Plain of Esdraelon in Stanley's *Jewish Church*, vol. ii., Lecture xxi., illustrative of this closing scene in Saul's career, well worth consulting.)

And Achish said.—David soon found into what a grievous error he had fallen by taking refuge with the hereditary foes of his people. Want of faith and patience had urged him to take this unhappy step. The sixteen months he had spent in Philistia had been certainly successful, inasmuch as they had strengthened his position as a "free lance" captain, but nothing more. They had been stained by bloodshed and cruelty. His life, too, was a life of duplicity and falsehood. The results of his unhappy course of action were soon manifest. His nation sustained a crushing and most humiliating defeat, which he narrowly escaped being obliged to witness, if not to contribute to. His own general recognition as king was put off for nearly seven years, during which period a civil war hindered the development of national prosperity; besides which, during this time of internal divisions the seeds were too surely laid of the future disastrous separation of Judah and the south from the northern tribes—a division which eventually took place in his grandson's time, when his strong arm and Solomon's wisdom and power were things of the past.

The summons of Achish to his great military vassal was perfectly natural: indeed, Achish had no reason to suspect that such a campaign as the one the Philistines were about to undertake against King Saul would be in any way distasteful to the wronged and insulted David. Not improbably the presence of David and his trained force—including, as the wily Philistine well knew, some of the bravest souls in Israel—encouraged Achish and the other Philistine lords to this great and, as it turned out, supreme effort against Israel. The King of Gath and his colleagues in Philistia saw that, in the divided state of Israel, their chances of success were very great, and it is highly probable that they looked forward to establishing their friend and follower David on the throne of Saul as a Philistine vassal king.

⁽²⁾ **And David said to Achish.**—Sorely perplexed, David temporises. He dares not refuse; and yet, the idea of commanding a Philistine division in a war with Israel was to him a terrible alternative.

And Achish said to David, Therefore will I make thee keeper of mine head for ever.—The King of Gath, like so many others with whom the winning son of Jesse came in contact in his career, seems to have been completely won by his loveable, generous character, and would not see any ambiguity in David's reply, but at once offers him in the coming campaign a most distinguished appointment in the army of Gath—the command of the body-guard: for this is what Ewald understands the offer of King Achish to signify.

But, as we shall see, the blind confidence of the king was not fully shared in by the Philistine chieftains; jealousy of the distinguished stranger captain opened their eyes to David's real feelings. (See chap. xxix. 3, 11.) It is also quite conceivable, too, that whispers respecting David's expeditions during the past year were current in some Philistine quarters. The eyes of the king, thought these more far-seeing nobles, were blinded by his partiality for his military vassal. (See Note on chap. xxix. 3.)

⁽³⁾ **Now Samuel was dead.**—A statement here repeated to introduce the strange, sad story which follows. The LXX., followed by the Vulg. and Syriac Versions, omitted it, not understanding the reason for its repetition.

And Saul had put away those that had familiar spirits, and the wizards, out of the land. ⁽⁴⁾ And the Philistines gathered themselves together, and came and pitched in Shunem: and Saul gathered all Israel together, and they pitched in Gilboa. And when Saul saw the host of the Philistines, he was afraid, and his heart greatly trembled. ⁽⁶⁾ And when Saul enquired of the LORD, the LORD answered him not, neither by dreams, nor by Urim, nor by prophets. ⁽⁷⁾ Then said Saul unto his servants, Seek me a woman that hath a familiar spirit, that I may go to her, and enquire of her. And his servants said to him,

---

And Saul had put away those that had familiar spirits, and the wizards, out of the land.—This statement is also inserted explanatory of what follows. In other words, the compiler says: "Now Samuel, whom Saul was so anxious to see, was dead and buried, and the possessors of familiar spirits, whose aid Saul was about to invoke to carry out his purpose, had long since been put out, by his own order, from the land." "Those that had familiar spirits"—those that had at their command *ôboth*, rendered "familiar spirits," the plural form of *ôb*, a word which has never been explained with any certainty. Scholars think they can connect it with *ôb, to be hollow*, and *ôb* is then "the hollow thing," or "bag;" and so it came to signify, "one who speaks in a hollow voice." It hence appears to mean the distended belly of the *ventriloquist*, a word by which the LXX. always render *ôb*. It thus is used to designate the male or female ventriloquist, as in verses 3 and 9, and Deut. xviii. 11, &c., and also the spirit which was supposed to speak from the belly of the ventriloquist; in this sense it is so used in verses 8 and 9, and Isa. xxix. 4. This is the explanation given by Erdmann in *Lange*, and the Bishop of Bath and Wells in the *Speaker's Commentary*.

The wizards.—Literally, *the wise people*. These are ever connected with the *ôboth*, "those that had familiar spirits." The name seems to have been given in irony to these dealers in occult and forbidden arts. The Mosaic command respecting these people was clear and decisive: "Thou shalt not suffer a witch (or wizard) to live" (Exod. xxii. 18; Lev. xx. 27). Saul, in his early zeal, we read, had actively put in force these edicts of Moses, which apparently, in the lax state of things which had long prevailed in Israel, had been suffered to lie in abeyance.

⁽⁴⁾ **And pitched in Shunem.**—As has been already described in the Note on verse 1, the Philistine army had penetrated into the heart of Palestine, and, marching across the Valley of Jezreel, took up a strong position on the south-western slope of "Little Hermon," near to the village, or town, of Shunem, a little to the north of Jezreel. Shunem is known in Biblical history as the home of Abishag (1 Kings i. 3), and the dwelling-place of the woman who entertained Elisha, and whose dead son he raised to life (2 Kings iv.).

It has been identified by modern travellers. Conder speaks of it as being at present only a mud hamlet, with cactus hedges and a spring; but the view, he says, extends as far as Mount Carmel, fifteen miles away. It is now called Sutêm.

And Saul gathered all Israel together, and they pitched in Gilboa.—Saul's position was only a few miles distant from the camp of his enemies, on the slope of the hills opposite Shunem, but parted by the deep Valley of Jezreel. From the high ground by his camp Saul could plainly see the whole of the Philistine army. Mount Gilboa is the name given to a range of lofty hills, rising 1,500 feet above the sea, and consisting of white chalk.

⁽⁵⁾ **He was afraid.**—There is no doubt that Saul was discouraged when he viewed the enemy's ranks from the eminence of Gilboa. They were far more numerous than he had expected. But the real reason of his trembling must be looked for in the consciousness that God had forsaken him. Many of the well-known Israelite warriors had, during the late events, taken service with his dreaded rival, David, and David, he knew, was now the vassal of Achish, a Philistine king. We may imagine Saul, the forsaken of God, as he stood on the white chalk hill of Gilboa, gazing on the long lines of Philistine tents pitched on the opposite hill of Shunem, wondering if his old friend was there, with his mighty following, in the division of Gath.

⁽⁶⁾ **And when Saul enquired of the Lord.**—The question has been asked, How was the enquiry made? for since the massacre at Nob, the high priest, or, at least, the priest in possession of the sacred ephod and the breastplate, with the Urim and Thummim, was, we know, in the camp of David, and we shall soon hear of a solemn use being made of the sacred gems. (See chap. xxx. 7, 8.) It has been suggested by eminent Biblical scholars that after the murder of Ahimelech and the flight of Abiathar to David, Saul removed the national Sanctuary from desecrated Nob, and established it at Gibeon, where, during the first year of David's reign, we find the Tabernacle, with Zadok, son of Ahitub, of the house of Eleazar, acting as high priest—probably placed in that office by Saul. This would account for the frequent reference in the time of David to two high priests, Zadok and Abiathar: Zadok, the high priest appointed by Saul, for a considerable period alone in charge of the Tabernacle; and Abiathar, who fled from Nob with the ephod and the sacred Urim, acknowledged by David as high priest, when the kingdom was restored eventually under one head. These two seemed to have divided the honours and responsibilities of the high priesthood. (See 2 Sam. viii. 17, xv. 24, 29, 35; 1 Chron. xv. 11, xviii. 16.)

This Zadok, we may assume, "enquired" for Saul: some suppose by means of an ephod made in imitation of the ancient breastplate with the Urim in possession of Abiathar; but, as may be readily imagined, no response was received. It is also likely enough that some "prophets"—so called—trained, not improbably, in the school of Samuel, were present with Saul. These, too, of course, received no Divine message, either by voice or in dreams.

⁽⁷⁾ **Seek me a woman that hath a familiar spirit.**—He was left alone to himself, and now the last spark of life, the religious zeal which he had once shown even to excess, then also vanished; or, rather, as must always be the case when it has thus swerved from the moral principle which alone can guide it, was turned into a wild and desperate superstition.

Saul seeks out   I. SAMUEL, XXVIII.   *the Witch of En-dor.*

Behold, *there is* a woman that hath a familiar spirit at En-dor.

(8) And Saul disguised himself, and put on other raiment, and he went, and two men with him, and they came to the woman by night: and he said, I pray thee, divine unto me by the familiar spirit, and bring me *him* up, whom I shall name unto thee. (9) And the woman said unto him, Behold, thou knowest what Saul hath done, how he hath cut off those that have familiar spirits, and the wizards, out of the land: wherefore then layest thou a snare for my life, to cause me to die? (10) And Saul sware to her by the LORD, saying, *As* the LORD liveth, there shall no punishment happen to thee for this thing. (11) Then said the woman, Whom shall I bring up unto thee? And he said, Bring me up Samuel.

The wizards and familiar spirits, whom in a fit of righteous indignation he had put out of the land, now became his only resource—

    Flectere si nequeo superos, Acheronta movebo.
      STANLEY: *Jewish Church*, vol. ii., Lect. xxi.

Behold, there is a woman that hath a familiar spirit at En-dor.—One of these women, mistress or possessor of an *ôb*, or familiar spirit, who apparently was well known, dwelt at or was left at Endor. "East of Nain is a village of mud-huts, with hedges of prickly pear. This is En-dor, famous in connection with the tragic history of the death of Saul. The adventurous character of Saul's night journey is very striking, when we consider that for the king to get to En-dor he had to pass the hostile camp, and would probably creep round the eastern shoulder of the hill hidden by the undulations of the ground."—Conder: *Tent Life in Palestine.* The distance from the camp of Israel on Gilboa to En-dor was about ten miles further, owing perhaps to the circuit they would have to make round the camp of the Philistines. Jewish tradition speaks of the "two men" who accompanied Saul as Abner and Amasa, and further mentions that the witch of En-dor was the mother of the great Abner. If this be true, it would account for her having escaped the general pursuit after witches mentioned above in the early days of Saul.

(8) **And Saul disguised himself.**—The disguise and the time chosen for the expedition served a double purpose. The king would, he thought, be unknown in the darkness and disguise when he came to the witch's dwelling, and there was, too, a far greater probability of his escaping his Philistine foes, whose army lay between him and the village of En-dor.

Divine unto me by the familiar spirit.—Literally, *divine unto me by the ôb.* Keil's remark is interesting: "Prophesying by the *ôb* was probably performed by calling up a departed spirit from Sheol, and obtaining prophecies—*i.e.,* disclosures—concerning one's own fate through the medium of such a spirit." No other commentator touches on the *ôb* here, and Keil leaves it in doubt as to whether he considered the *ôb* was some special spirit devoted to the service of the mistress of the *ôb*, or the spirit or soul of one already dead, who, through some occult power, was to be brought back again for a season to this earth. As far as we can judge of these old mysteries, the sorcerer or sorceress possessed, or was supposed to possess, a "familiar." Through the aid of this "familiar," the departed spirit was compelled or induced to re-visit this world, and to submit to certain questioning. The Hebrew rendered "divine unto me" is of Syriac origin, like most of those words describing illicit vaticinations.—*Speaker's Commentary.* This miserable power, if it did exist, was one of the things the Israelites learned from the original inhabitants of Canaan. These "black" arts, as they have been called, have, in all ages, in every degree of civilisation, always had an extraordinary fascination for men. It is well known that even in our own "cultured age" similar pretensions are put forth, and the dead are still invoked, summoned, and questioned, as they were in the half-barbarous age when Saul and his companions, in their desperate strait, sought the witch of En-dor.

And bring me him up.—The popular idea has always been that Sheol, the place of departed spirits, is somewhere *beneath* the ground or earth on which we live, just as heaven, the abode of God and His holy angels, is in a region *above* the earth. St. Paul speaks in this popular language (Eph. iv. 9), where he refers to the lower parts of the earth as the abode of departed spirits. Hence we have here, "bring me him up." The Christian Church, Bishop Wordsworth reminds us, has adopted this language into her creeds, where she says that Christ in His human soul *descended* into hell (Hades). Keil well remarks on this human idea of what is "above" and "below": "With our modes of thought, which are so bound up with time and space, it is impossible to represent to ourselves in any other way the difference and contrast between blessedness with God and shade-life in death."

(9) **What Saul hath done . . .**—The law, re-enacted by Saul in earlier days, which made the practice of these dark arts a capital offence, was evidently still in force. Sorcerers and witches, like the woman of En-dor, had, no doubt, been often hunted down by means of informers. The woman possibly at first suspected that something of the kind was intended now. The old tradition, however, which represents the two companions of the king as Abner and Amasa, would preclude such a supposition. Still, in any event, the act of summoning the dead was a capital offence, and the woman would be on her guard, even in the presence of her near relatives, which the old tradition asserts Abner and Amasa to have been. She may, too, by enhancing the peril in which she stood, have thought a larger present would be extorted from the stranger who sought her aid.

(11) **Bring me up Samuel.**—A remarkable passage in the Babylonian Talmud evidently shows that, at all events in the Rabbinical Schools of a very early date, the bringing up of Samuel was looked upon as owing to the witch's power.

"A Sadducee once said to Rabbi Abhu, 'Ye say that the souls of the righteous are treasured up under the throne of glory; how then had the witch of En-dor power to bring up the prophet Samuel by necromancy?' The Rabbi replied, 'Because that occurred within twelve months after his death; for we are taught

(12) And when the woman saw Samuel, she cried with a loud voice: and the woman spake to Saul, saying, Why hast thou deceived me? for thou *art* Saul.

(13) And the king said unto her, Be not afraid: for what sawest thou? And the woman said unto Saul, I saw gods ascending out of the earth. (14) And he

that during twelve months after death the body is preserved, and the soul soars up and down, but that after twelve months the body is destroyed, and the soul goes up, never to return.'"—Treatise *Shabbath*, fol. 88, col. 2.

Another Rabbinical tradition, however, seems to limit this near presence of the departed spirit to the body to four days:—"It is a tradition of Ben Kaphra's. The very height of mourning is not till the third day. For three days the spirit wanders about the sepulchre, expecting if it may return into the body. But when it sees that the form or aspect of the face is changed [on the fourth day], then it hovers no more, but leaves the body to itself. After three days (it is said elsewhere), the countenance is changed."—From the *Bereshith R.*, p. 1143: quoted by Lightfoot, referred to by Canon Westcott in his commentary on St. John xi. 39.

Saul's state of mind on this, almost the eve of his last fatal fight at Gilboa, affords a curious study. He felt himself forsaken of God, and yet, in his deep despair, his mind turns to the friend and guide of his youth, from whom—long before that friend's death—he had been so hopelessly estranged. There must have been a terrible struggle in the proud king's heart before he could have brought himself to stoop to ask for assistance from one of that loathed and proscribed class of women who professed to have dealings with familiar spirits and demons. "There is," once wrote Archbishop Trench, "something unutterably pathetic in the yearning of the dis-anointed king, now in his utter desolation, to exchange words once more with the friend and counsellor of his youth; and if he must hear his doom, to hear it from no other lips but his."

(12) **And when the woman saw Samuel, she cried with a loud voice.**—Nothing is more clear from the narration than that the woman of En-dor saw *something* she never dreamed of seeing. Whatever *did* appear that night was different from anything she had seen before. Whether or not she was an impostor matters little to us. From the severe enactments in the Mosaic code respecting these practices, it would *seem* as though in the background there was something dark and sinister. At all events, on this memorable occasion, the witch was evidently amazed and appalled at the success of her enchantments. Ewald supposes that she burst into a loud cry on seeing Samuel's shade, because it ascended with such frightfully threatening gestures, as it could have used only against its deadly enemy, Saul; and she then saw that the questioner must be Saul. This can, however, only be taken as an ingenious surmise. There is a singular passage in the *Chaggigah* Treatise of the Babylonian Talmud (quoted below), which—contrary to the usual interpretation of the word rendered "gods" (verse 13)—assumes that a second form "came up" with Samuel; and one Jewish interpretation tells us that these were "judges"—so rendering the *Elohim* of verse 13—judges robed in their judicial mantles; and it was the sight of these awful ministers of justice which appalled the consciously guilty woman. Deeply interesting, however, as are these traditions and comments, handed down probably from a school of expositors which flourished before the Christian era, we hardly need anything more to account for the cry of terror which burst from the woman than this appearance of the venerable seer, evidently by her quite unlooked for.

And the woman spake to Saul.—At this juncture the woman recognised in the unknown stranger King Saul. For a moment remembering his stern, ruthless procedure in such cases of sorcery as the one in which she was then engaged, she thinks herself betrayed, and given over to a shameful death of agony; and she turns to the king beside her with a piteous expostulation, "Why hast thou deceived me?" The question now comes up, How did she come to recognise Saul in the unknown? Ewald's ingenious suggestion has been mentioned above. Keil suggests that the woman had fallen into a state of clairvoyance, in which she recognised persons who, like Saul in his disguise, were unknown to her by face. Josephus (vi. 14, 2), no doubt writing from traditional sources, asserts that Samuel had most likely revealed the presence of Saul to the witch. "Samuel saw through Saul's disguise, which had deceived her whom Saul came to consult, as he spoke to Saul as Saul. So Ahijah the prophet, though blind by age, saw through the disguise of the wife of Jeroboam (1 Kings xiv. 2, 6)."—*Bishop Wordsworth*.

On the whole, Josephus's explanation is probably the true one. It was some word—probably spoken by Samuel—not related here which betrayed the king's identity to the woman. There is one other possible supposition, but it, of course, belongs to the realms of fancy. We know it was night, and Saul was disguised; no doubt his face was partially covered. Is it not to be imagined that with the appearance of the blessed prophet, with or without a companion, a *light* filled the dark room of the En-dor house? This would fall upon the king's face, who, in the agitation of the moment, would likely enough have thrown off the cape or mantle which shrouded his features. Something of the awful supernatural "light" Tennyson describes when he writes of the Holy Grail:—

"A gentle sound, an awful light!
Three angels bear the Holy Grail:
With folded feet in stoles of white,
On sleeping wings they sail."—*Sir Galahad*.

(13) **I saw gods ascending out of the earth.**—The king at once calms the witch's fears for her life, and impatiently, as it would seem, asks what she saw which called forth the cry of fear and terror. "Gods" —this is the rendering of the Hebrew word *Elohim*. The English Version, however, follows the majority of the Versions here. The Chaldee translates the word by "angels." Corn. à Lapide and the best modern scholars, however, reasoning from Saul's words which immediately follow—"What is *his* form?"—suppose the *Elohim* to signify, not a plurality of appearances, but one God-like form: something majestic and august. The feeling, however, of antiquity seems to have been in favour of more than one supernatural form entering into the En-dor dwelling on that awful night. Besides the testimony of the Versions above referred to, the passage in the Babylonian Talmud treatise *Chaggigah*, quoted below, speaks of two positively spirit forms—Samuel and another.

(14) **An old man cometh up; and he is covered with a mantle.**—The "mantle;" Heb.,

Saul Interrogates the   I. SAMUEL, XXVIII.   *Shade of Samuel.*

said unto her, ¹What form *is* he of? And she said, An old man cometh up; and he *is* covered with a mantle. And Saul perceived that it *was* Samuel, and he stooped with *his* face to the ground, and bowed himself.

(15) And Samuel said to Saul, Why hast thou disquieted me, to bring me up? And Saul answered, I am sore dis-

¹ Heb., *What is his form?*

² Heb., *by the hand of prophets.*

tressed; for the Philistines make war against me, and God is departed from me, and answereth me no more, neither ²by prophets, nor by dreams: therefore I have called thee, that thou mayest make known unto me what I shall do.

(16) Then said Samuel, Wherefore then dost thou ask of me, seeing the LORD is departed from thee, and is become thine

---

m'il. The garment so named was not a peculiar one, and bore no official signification; still, its mention here in this place would seem as though the woman recognised *the* well-known *m'il* which the prophet used to wear in life.

But it has been asked, How could a spirit bear the semblance of an old man? and further, How could such a being be clothed? Rabbi Moses Maimonides of Cordova (twelfth century), surnamed the "Eagle of the Doctors," in his *Yad Hachazakah*, admirably replies to these queries when discussing certain similar expressions used with regard to the Holy One, who is a Spirit without a body or a frame. "We find," says Maimonides, "such expressions as 'under His feet,' written with the finger of God,' 'the eye of the Lord,' &c. Of Him one prophet says, 'That he saw the Holy One—blessed be He!—whose garment was white as snow' (Dan. vii. 9); whilst another saw Him 'like a warrior engaged in battle.' Compare the saying of the sages in the *Yad Joseph* on Exod. xv. 3:—'On the sea He was seen like a man-of-war, and upon Sinai like a reader of prayers, wrapped (in a surplice); and all this though he had neither similitude or form, but that these things were in an apparition of prophecy, and in a vision.'"—*Yad Hachazakah*, bk. I., ch. i. "God designed," says Bishop Wordsworth, "that the spirit of Samuel should be recognised by human eyes; and how could this have been done but by means of such objects as are visible to human sense? Our Lord speaks of the *tongue* of the disembodied spirit of Dives in order to give us an idea of his sufferings; and at the Transfiguration He presented the form of Moses in such a garb to the three disciples as might enable them to recognise him as Moses."

And he stooped . . . and bowed himself.—It seems probable that at this juncture the king *saw* the form before him when he did obeisance. It is, however, not clear, from the language here used, whether this strange act of reverent homage did not at once follow the description of the woman.

(15) **And Samuel said to Saul, Why hast thou disquieted me, to bring me up?**—Erdmann, in *Lange*, argues from this that the incantation of the witch of En-dor had brought about the result, viz., the calling up of the shade of Samuel, and that hence the appearance of the prophet was not due to the command of God. Keil, however, rightly concludes that these words by themselves do not decide the question as to *what* power called up the "spirit." They simply assert that Samuel had been disturbed from his rest by Saul, and ask the reason why. In the Babylonian Talmud there is a remarkable comment on these words of the shade of the departed prophet. "Rabbi Elazar said, when he read this Scripture text, 'Why hast thou disquieted me?' If Samuel the righteous was afraid of the Judgment (to which he thought he was summoned when thus called up), how much more ought we to be afraid of the Judgment? And whence do we infer that Samuel was afraid? Because it is written, 'And the woman said unto Saul, I saw mighty ones [or perhaps judges]—Elohim—ascending out of the earth:' *ōlim*, ascending (a *plural* form), implies at least two, and one of them was Samuel; *who*, then, was the other? Samuel went and brought Moses with him, and said unto him, 'Peradventure I am summoned to Judgment. God forbid! O stand thou by me; lo! there is not a thing which is written in thy Law that I have not fulfilled."—Treatise *Chaggigah*, fol. 4, *b.*

I am sore distressed.—"O, the wild wail of this dark misery! There is a deep pathos and a weird awesomeness in this despairing cry, but there is no confession of sin, no beseeching for mercy—nothing but the overmastering ambition to preserve himself."—Dr. W. M. Taylor, of New York: "David."

For the gallant warrior Saul thus to despair was indeed strange, but his gloomy foreboding before the fatal field of Gilboa, where he was to lose his crown and life, were sadly verified by the sequel. Shakespeare thus describes *Richard III.* heavy and spiritless, with an unknown dread, before the fatal Bosworth field:—

"I have not that alacrity of spirit
Nor cheer of mind that I was wont to have."
King Richard III.

So *Macbeth* is full of a restless, shapeless terror at Dunsinane before the battle:—

"There is no flying hence, no tarrying here;
I 'gin to be aweary of the sun."—*Macbeth.*

Neither by prophets, nor by dreams.—Why does Saul omit to mention here the silence of the "Urim," especially mentioned in verse 6, and which seems also in these days to have been the more usual way of enquiry after the will of the Eternal King of Israel? The Talmud, treatise *Berachoth*, xii. 2, gives the probable answer. Saul knew the Urim was no longer in his kingdom. It had been worn by one whom he had foully murdered—Ahimelech, the high priest. Deep shame at the thought of the massacre of Ahimelech, and afterwards of the priests at Nob, stayed him from uttering the word "Urim" before Samuel.

Therefore I have called thee.—The Hebrew word here is a very unusual form, which apparently was used to strengthen the original idea, "I have had thee called"; in other words, "Hence this pressing urgent call to thee from thy rest."

(16) **Seeing the Lord is departed from thee.**—In other words, *If Jehovah have left thee, why comest thou to consult me, His servant and prophet?* The Hebrew word here translated "enemy" is only found in Ps. cxxxix. 20, and has been assumed to be an Aramaic form—*ain* for *tsadde*. There are, however, no other Aramaic forms in this book, which is written in pure "classical" Hebrew. The letter *ain*, or the

enemy? ⁽¹⁷⁾ And the LORD hath done ¹to him, ᵃ as he spake by ²me: for the LORD hath rent the kingdom out of thine hand, and given it to thy neighbour, *even* to David: ⁽¹⁸⁾ because thou obeyedst not the voice of the LORD, nor executedst his fierce wrath upon Amalek, therefore hath the LORD done this thing unto thee this day. ⁽¹⁹⁾ Moreover the LORD will also deliver Israel with thee into the hand of the Philistines: and to morrow *shalt* thou and thy sons *be* with me: the LORD also shall deliver the host of Israel into the hand of the Philistines.

⁽²⁰⁾ Then Saul ³ fell straightway all along on the earth, and was sore

¹ Or, *for himself.*

ᵃ ch. 15. 28.

B.C. cir. 1056.

² Heb., *mine hand.*

³ Heb., *made haste, and fell with the fulness of his stature.*

afraid, because of the words of Samuel: and there was no strength in him; for he had eaten no bread all the day, nor all the night. ⁽²¹⁾ And the woman came unto Saul, and saw that he was sore troubled, and said unto him, Behold, thine handmaid hath obeyed thy voice, and I have put my life in my hand, and have hearkened unto thy words which thou spakest unto me. ⁽²²⁾ Now therefore, I pray thee, hearken thou also unto the voice of thine handmaid, and let me set a morsel of bread before thee; and eat, that thou mayest have strength, when thou goest on thy way. ⁽²³⁾ But he refused, and

---

first letter in the text here, through a very slight error of the copyist, could easily have been altered from *tsadde*, the first letter of the usual word for "enemy." The LXX. and Vulg. Versions apparently had another reading before them, for they translate the last clause of the verse, "and is with thy neighbours."

⁽¹⁷⁾ **And the Lord hath done to him.**—Render, as in margin of the English Version, *the Lord hath done or performed for Himself.* The LXX. and Vulg. here needlessly change the text into, "the Lord hath done *to thee.*"

And given it to thy neighbour . . . David.—An *evil* spirit personating Samuel would not have spoken thus; he would not have wished to help David, "the man after God's own heart," to the throne of Israel; nor would an evil spirit have spoken in such solemn terms of the punishment due to rebellion against God.—*Bishop Wordsworth*, who argues against the supposition that the shade of Samuel was an evil spirit.

⁽¹⁹⁾ **Moreover the Lord will also deliver Israel . . . into the hands of the Philistines.**—Three crushing judgments, which were to come directly upon Saul, are contained in the prophet's words related in this 19th verse. (*a*) The utter defeat of the army of Israel. (*b*) The violent death of Saul himself and his two sons in the course of the impending fight. (*c*) The sacking of the Israelitish camp, which was to follow the defeat, and which would terribly augment the horrors and disasters of the rout of the king's army.

"This overthrow of the people was to heighten Saul's misery, when he saw the people plunged with him into ruin through his sin."—*O. von Gerlach.*

To morrow shalt thou and thy sons be with me.—The Hebrew word here rendered "to morrow," *machar*, need not signify "the next day," but some near future time. In saying "thou shalt be with me," Samuel does not pronounce Saul's final condemnation, for he had no mission to do so, but rather draws him by his tenderness to a better mind. He uses a mild and charitable expression, applicable to all, good and bad, "Thou shalt be as I am: no longer among the living." In the vision of the world of spirits, revealed to us by our blessed Lord, the souls of Dives and Lazarus may be said to be together in the abode of the departed spirits, for Dives saw Lazarus, and conversed with Abraham, though there was a gulf fixed between them. "If Samuel had said to Saul, 'Thou shalt be among the damned,' he would have crushed him with

a weight of despair, and have hardened him in his impenitence; but by using this gentler expression, he mildly exhorted him to repentance. While there was life there was hope: the door was still open."—*Bishop Wordsworth.*

"Shalt thou be with me" does not refer to an equality in bliss, but to a like condition of death.—*St. Augustine.* Augustine here means that to-morrow Saul would be "a shade," like to what Samuel then was; he says, however, nothing respecting Saul's enjoying bliss like that which he (Samuel) was doubtless then enjoying.

The host.—"Host" here should be rendered *camp.* The meaning, then, of the whole verse would be: first, there would be a total defeat of the royal army; secondly, Saul and his sons would fall; thirdly, the rout would be followed by the sack of the camp of Israel, and its attendant horrors.

⁽²⁰⁾ **Then Saul fell straightway all along on the earth.**—Up to this period we must understand Saul listening to the prophet's words in that attitude of humble reverence which he assumed when he perceived that he was in the presence of Samuel (verse 14); but now, on hearing the words of awful judgment, crushed with terror and dismay, and previously weakened by a long fast and the fatigue of the rough night walk from Mount Gilboa to En-dor, he fell prostrate to the earth.

⁽²¹⁾ **And the woman.**—The story is completed in these few concluding verses (21—25) in a most natural and unaffected style. The witch, though a grievous sinner, is struck with a woman's pity for the stricken king, and with kind words and still kinder acts does her best to recover him from the death-like swoon into which the hapless Saul had fallen. Her whole behaviour contradicts the supposition that she was moved by a bitter hatred against Saul (see *Excursus* L. at end of this Book) to desire the appearance of Samuel, and to imitate his voice by means of ventriloquism. Firstly, she was herself terrified at the apparition; and secondly, she was saddened by the effect of the dead seer's words on the king, and did her poor best to restore him to composure and strength again. We read in the next verse how the woman, with Saul's servants, used even a gentle compulsion to induce the king to take the nourishment he was so sorely in need of.

⁽²³⁾ **And sat upon the bed**—That is, upon the divan, or cushioned seat, which usually runs round the walls of rooms in Eastern dwellings. There is nothing in

said, I will not eat. But his servants, together with the woman, compelled him; and he hearkened unto their voice. So he arose from the earth, and sat upon the bed. (24) And the woman had a fat calf in the house; and she hasted, and killed it, and took flour, and kneaded *it*, and did bake unleavened bread thereof: (25) and she brought *it* before Saul, and before his servants; and they did eat. Then they rose up, and went away that night.

CHAPTER XXIX.— (1) Now the Philistines gathered together all their armies to Aphek: and the Israelites pitched by a fountain which *is* in Jezreel. (2) And the lords of the Philistines passed on by hundreds, and by thousands: but David and his men passed on in the rereward with Achish. (3) Then said the princes of the Phil-

a 1 Chron. 12. 19.

b ch. 18. 7 & 21. 11.

istines, What *do* these Hebrews here? And Achish said unto the princes of the Philistines, *Is* not this David, the servant of Saul the king of Israel, which hath been with me these days, or these years, and I have found no fault in him since he fell *unto me* unto this day? (4) And the princes of the Philistines were wroth with him; and the princes of the Philistines said unto him, *a* Make this fellow return, that he may go again to his place which thou hast appointed him, and let him not go down with us to battle, lest in the battle he be an adversary to us: for wherewith should he reconcile himself unto his master? *should it not be* with the heads of these men? (5) *Is* not this David, of whom they sang one to another in dances, saying, *b* Saul slew his thousands, and David his ten thousands?

---

the narration to support the common idea, represented so often in painting, that the scene above related took place in a cave. The witch probably lived in a dwelling of her own at En-dor. There is nothing either in the narrative to indicate that she was living in a place of concealment.

(24) **Unleavened bread.**—There was no time to be lost; so she did not wait to leaven the dough, but at once baked it, and set it before the king.

(25) **Went away that night.**—The same night they retraced their steps, and returned to Gilboa. "Saul was too hardened in his sin to express any grief or pain, either on his own account or because of the predicted fate of his sons or his people. In stolid desperation he went to meet his destiny. This was the terrible end of one whom the Spirit of God had once taken possession of and turned into another man—of one who had been singularly endowed with Divine gifts to enable him to act as the leader of the people of God." —O. von Gerlach.

XXIX.

(1–11) David and his Band is looked upon by the Philistine Lords with Suspicion, and is obliged to withdraw; preserving still the Friendship of Achish.

(1) **Aphek.**—The name Aphek was a common one, and was given to several "places of arms" in Canaan. It signifies a fort or a strong place. This Aphek was most likely situated in the Plain of Jezreel. Eusebius places it in the neighbourhood of En-dor.

By a fountain which is in Jezreel.—"By a fountain." The LXX. wrongly adds "dor," supposing the spring or fountain to be the well-known En-dor—spring of Dor—but En-dor, we know, lay many miles away from the camp of Saul. This "fountain" has been identified by modern travellers as *Ain-Jalûd*, the Fountain of Goliath, because it was traditionally regarded as the scene of the old combat with the giant. It is a large spring which flows from under the cavern in the rock which forms the base of Gilboa. "There is

every reason to regard this as the ancient fountain of Jezreel, where Saul and Jonathan pitched before their last fatal battle, and where, too, in the days of the Crusades, Saladin and the Christians successively encamped."—Robinson, *Palestine*, iii. 167, 8.

(2) **And the lords of the Philistines passed on by hundreds, and by thousands.**—The orderly advance of this great military nation is thus described. The "lords," a different term to the expression "princes." There were apparently in the Philistine federation five sovereign princes, of whom Achish of Gath was one. Beneath these were other chieftains, who seemingly had great control over the sovereign princes.

David and his men.—David, in return for the lands round Ziklag given him by the King of Gath, seems to have owed a kind of military service to his suzerain Achish. The difference in the arms and equipments of the Israelitish warriors in the division of David, which was marching under the standard of Gath, no doubt excited questions. The general appearance of the Hebrews was, of course, well known to their hereditary Philistine foes.

(3) **These days, or these years.**—An indefinite expression of time. The versions have translated it in various ways. The English Version here is literal. The Syriac singularly renders, "this time, and time, and months." The LXX. is not very easy to understand here, but it apparently took the expression as signifying "two years." Maurer would translate, "who has been with me alway, for days, or rather, for years."

(4) **Go down.**—This is a technical military expression, used constantly, on account of the necessity of the troops descending from the *hill* country in which they were encamped to the plain in order to fight.

(5) **Of whom they sang.**—The folk-songs, which had originally excited Saul's jealousy of the young hero David, were current among the Philistines, who seem to have been a musical people. David's having apparently learned and practised Philistine music when

(6) Then Achish called David, and said unto him, Surely, *as* the LORD liveth, thou hast been upright, and thy going out and thy coming in with me in the host *is* good in my sight: for I have not found evil in thee since the day of thy coming unto me unto this day: nevertheless ¹ the lords favour thee not. (7) Wherefore now return, and go in peace, that thou ² displease not the lords of the Philistines. (8) And David said unto Achish, But what have I done? and what hast thou found in thy servant so long as I have been ³ with thee unto this day, that I may not go fight against the enemies of my lord the king? (9) And Achish answered and said to David, I know that thou *art* good in my sight, as an angel of God: notwithstanding the princes of the Philistines have said, He shall not go up with us to the battle. (10) Wherefore now rise up early in the morning with thy master's servants that are come with thee: and as soon as ye be up early in the morning, and have light, depart.

(11) So David and his men rose up early to depart in the morning, to return into the land of the Philistines. And the Philistines went up to Jezreel.

CHAPTER XXX.—(1) And it came to pass, when David and his men were come to Ziklag on the third day, that the Amalekites had invaded the south,

1 Heb., *thou art not good in the eyes of the lords.*

2 Heb., *do not evil in the eyes of the lords.*

3 Heb., *before thee.*

---

in Gath, which he subsequently introduced into Jerusalem, has been already noticed.

(6) **Surely, as the Lord liveth.**—This seems a strange oath for an idolatrous prince like the King of Gath to make use of—"By the life of Jehovah." It was probably the equivalent of the real oath of Achish, unless, as Keil supposes, the Philistine friend of David, in his oath, used the formula which he thought would be most acceptable to David, whom he looked upon as injured falsely by the suspicion of the Philistine leaders.

(8) **And David said unto Achish, But what have I done?**—David's words have a ring of falseness in them; he never contemplated fighting in the ranks against Israel, and yet he speaks thus. The generous confidence of the chivalrous Achish is here in painful contrast with the dissimulation of the Israelite chieftain, David.

It has been suggested that these suspicions of his loyalty on the part of the Philistine leaders had been aroused by David deliberately, in order to bring about his dismissal from the army in the field. This is possible, for the situation in which David now finds himself was most embarassing from every point of view.

(9) **As an angel of God.**—Again a simile, which Achish most likely borrowed from Hebrew thought, and made use of in his graceful courtesy as likely to be acceptable to David.

(10) **With thy master's servants.**—The words have perplexed expositors. It is hardly the expression we should expect Achish to use of David's followers. All Israelites were, of course, "subjects of Saul," but the term would hardly be used except by one hostile to David, as Nabal was; he once (chap. xxv. 10) made use of an insulting term of a like nature to David. Achish, we know, seemed ever kindly disposed to the outlawed son of Jesse. A probable suggestion has, however, been lately made, that the reference here is to those tribes of Manasseh (comp. 1 Chron. xii. 19—21) who had only lately come over to David. Was it not also possible that these very Manassites, who had only very recently deserted the king's cause for David's, were known to some of the Philistines as Saul's soldiers, and that their suspicions had been awakened in the first place by finding them marching under David's standard in the division of Gath?

(11) **To return into the land of the Philistines.**—No doubt David and his officers rejoiced at their escaping the terrible alternative of either turning traitors to the kindly man who had so hospitably received them in their distress, or of appearing in arms with the Philistines when they came into collision with the Israelites under Saul. But they little thought in how sore a danger their wives and children and homes were at this juncture. Their release from the Philistine army was not a moment too soon to save these.

XXX.

(1–31) Ziklag, David's City, is Sacked by the Amalekites—David, after Consulting the Urim, Pursues them—The Captives are Recovered—The Friendly Cities are Rewarded.

(1) **On the third day**—That is, on the third day after King Achish, in consequence of the remonstrances of the Philistine chieftains, had dismissed David and his contingent from the ranks of the Philistine army. This dismissal could hardly have taken place at Shunem, in the Esdraelon (Jezreel) Vale, for Shunem is some ninety miles distant from Ziklag. The division of Achish had marched from Gath with David; and somewhere in Philistia, after the whole force had been gathered into one, the scene which resulted in David's services being dispensed with took place.

The Amalekites had invaded the south.—This was partly in retaliation for the late raids of David in the Amalekite country, partly because Amalek had heard that, owing to the Philistine and Israelite armies having left the southern districts for the central part of Canaan, all the south country was left unguarded. "The south," that is, "the Negeb," or the dry land—all the southern part of Judea; it included also a part of the Arabian Desert.

And smitten Ziklag.—This was an act of vengeance, Ziklag being the city of that famous Israelite chieftain David, who had done so much damage to Amalek, and who had treated the captives with such cruelty. While other parts of the south were simply plundered, Ziklag was marked for utter destruction—was sacked and burned.

Ziklag Sacked by the Amalekites.   I. SAMUEL, XXX.   *David Consults the Ephod.*

and Ziklag, and smitten Ziklag, and burned it with fire; ⁽²⁾ and had taken the women captives, that *were* therein: they slew not any, either great or small, but carried *them* away, and went on their way. ⁽³⁾ So David and his men came to the city, and, behold, *it was* burned with fire; and their wives, and their sons, and their daughters, were taken captives. ⁽⁴⁾ Then David and the people that *were* with him lifted up their voice and wept, until they had no more power to weep. ⁽⁵⁾ And David's two wives were taken captives, Ahinoam the Jezreelitess, and Abigail the wife of Nabal the Carmelite. ⁽⁶⁾ And David was greatly distressed; for the people spake of stoning him, because the soul of all the people was [1] grieved, every man for his sons and for his daughters: but David encouraged himself in the LORD his God.

⁽⁷⁾ And David said to Abiathar the priest, Ahimelech's son, I pray thee, bring me hither the ephod. And Abiathar brought thither the ephod to David. ⁽⁸⁾ And David enquired at the LORD, saying, Shall I pursue after this troop? shall I overtake them? And he answered him, Pursue: for thou

[1] Heb., *bitter.*

⁽²⁾ **They slew not any.**—There was no one in the hapless city to resist the attack of the fierce sons of the desert. David—never dreaming of the sudden invasion—had marched with Achish, accompanied by his whole force. The Amalekites slew none of their captives; they were, we read, women and children. These possessed a marketable value, and were carried off to be sold into slavery, probably in Egypt, with which country the Amalekites, as neighbours, had constant dealings. We read a few verses on specially of an *Egyptian* slave in the army.

⁽³⁾ **And behold, it was burned with fire.**—A terrible reception for David and his free lances, on their return from their ill-omened expedition with the great Philistine army, to find only the charred and smoking ruins of their homes; not one of all their dear ones, whom they had left behind—as they thought in security—left to tell the story of the disaster. It was the Egyptian slave who had fallen sick, and, in consequence, had been deserted, and whom they came upon in the course of the pursuit, who gave them the details, and told them the story of the invasion, and described the route taken by the marauding force on their return to their country.

⁽⁴⁾ **Then David and the people.**—Verses 1—4 form one period, which is expanded by the introduction of several circumstantial clauses. The apodosis to "it came to pass when," &c., verse 1, does not follow till verse 4, "Then David and the people," &c.; but this is formally attached to verse 3. The statement, "So David and his men came," with which the protasis commenced in verse 1, is resumed in an altered form: "It came to pass, when David and his men were come to Ziklag . . . the Amalekites had invaded . . . and had taken away the women captive . . . and had gone their way . . . and David and his men came into the city, and behold, it was burned. . . . Then David and the people with him lifted up their voice."—*Keil.*

⁽⁶⁾ **For the people spake of stoning him.**—Probably the discontent and anger of the people had been previously aroused by David's close connection with Achish, which had entailed upon these valiant Israelites the bitter degradation of having had to march against their own countrymen under the banner of the Philistine King of Gath; and now, finding that David had neglected to provide against the Amalekite raid, their pent-up fury thus displayed itself. Then David, we shall see, threw himself, with all his old perfect trustfulness, upon the mercy of his God.

But David encouraged himself in the Lord his God.—He encouraged himself in prayer, thus casting himself and his fortunes on the God who, years before, had chosen him to be "His anointed." It was this *trust*, as we have before seen in his own case, in the case, too, of Jonathan, as it had been in old days with all the heroes of Israel—this perfect, childlike, implicit trust in the "Glorious Arm"—which had been the source of the marvellous success of the chosen people. When they forgot the invisible King, who for His own great purposes had chosen them, their fortunes at once declined; they fell to the level, and often below the level, of the surrounding nations. We have many conspicuous examples of this; for instance, in the lives of Samson and Saul, how, when with weeping and with mourning, they returned to their allegiance, and again leaned on the "Arm," success and victory returned to them. This is what happened now to David at Ziklag, while about the same time Saul, alone and distrustful, fought and fell on the bloody day of Gilboa. David, with the help of his God, on whose mercy he had thrown himself, obtained his brilliant success over Amalek, and restored his prestige not only among his own immediate followers, but through all the cities and villages of Southern Canaan.

⁽⁷⁾ **Abiathar.**—Abiathar had doubtless been with David, and he had joined him at Keilah. Through all his wanderings we hear, however, nothing of prayer and of consultation of the Urim. As regards the unfortunate Philistine sojourn, David seems to have determined upon that step entirely of himself; distrustful and despairing, he had fled the country, and taken refuge with the enemies of his people. One unbroken series of sin and calamity was the result he sees of his fatal error.

And Abiathar brought thither the ephod.—Modern commentators, as a rule, prefer to disbelieve in any response coming through the medium of the Urim in the ephod. They either pass over the whole transaction in silence, or assume that some Divine inspiration came to the high priest when vested with the sacred garment. The plain meaning, however, of the frequent references tells us in some way or other the Divine will was made known through the agency of the mysterious Urim and Thummim. See, for instance, in the case of Saul, where definitely it is stated that the Lord answered him not "by Urim" (chap. xxviii. 6), where this peculiar Divine response is carefully distinguished from the manifestation of the will of God in a dream or a vision, or through the Divine instrumentality

David is Guided in his Pursuit   I. SAMUEL, XXX.   *by an Egyptian Captive.*

shalt surely overtake *them*, and without fail recover *all*. ⁽⁹⁾ So David went, he and the six hundred men that *were* with him, and came to the brook Besor, where those that were left behind stayed. ⁽¹⁰⁾ But David pursued, he and four hundred men: for two hundred abode behind, which were so faint that they could not go over the brook Besor.

⁽¹¹⁾ And they found an Egyptian in the field, and brought him to David, and gave him bread, and he did eat; and they made him drink water; ⁽¹²⁾ and they gave him a piece of a cake of figs, and two clusters of raisins: and when he had eaten, his spirit came again to him: for he had eaten no bread, nor drunk *any* water, three days and three nights. ⁽¹³⁾ And David said unto him, To whom *belongest* thou? and whence *art* thou? And he said, I *am* a young man of Egypt, servant to an Amalekite; and my master left me, because three days agone I fell sick. ⁽¹⁴⁾ We made an invasion *upon* the south of the Cherethites and upon *the coast* which *belongeth* to Judah, and

---

of the prophet or seer. The ancient Hebrews had no hesitation in attributing to the sacred precious stones an occasional special power of declaring the oracles of God. The Talmudical traditions are clear and decisive here. Now, without attaching anything like an implicit credence to these most ancient Hebrew traditions—many of them fanciful and wild, many of them written in a cryptograph, or secret cypher, to which Christians in most cases do not possess the key—it does seem in the highest degree arbitrary to reject the ancient traditional belief of the Hebrew race contained in the Talmud with respect to this most mysterious ephod and its sacred gems, and to adopt another interpretation, which fits in very lamely with the plain text. The whole question respecting the traditions of the Urim and Thummim is discussed at some length in the short *Excursus* M on the Urim, at the end of this Commentary on the First Book of Samuel.

⁽⁹⁾ **So David went.**—Immediately on receiving the answer of the Urim, David started in rapid pursuit. The "six hundred" by no means represented his present force; but these were probably the old band of veteran soldiers, whose speed and endurance he could depend upon—men tried, no doubt, by many a weary night march, by many a rough, wild piece of work. A large contingent even of these veterans could not stand the forced march of their leader on this occasion.

In the words "for two hundred abode behind," the narrator anticipated what is told in verse 10. It is a proleptical expression, arising from the vivacious description of David's rapid march with four hundred men (*Lange*). The Vulg. paraphrases, or rather seeks to amend the text here: "and certain tired ones stayed." The Syriac changes the text into "David left two hundred men;" these men who had fallen out of the rapid march were gathered together, and kept the baggage and everything that could be left behind at the encampment at the brook Besor. It is to be supposed that owing to the hurried departure, but scanty provision for the forced march was made, hence the falling out through weariness in the course of the rapid advance. The brook Besor cannot be identified with certainty; and Raumer (*Palestine*) supposes it to be the Wady Shariah, which falls into the sea below Askelon.

⁽¹¹⁾ **An Egyptian.**—The Amalekites, as above stated, were a nomad race; their wanderings would have taken them to the frontiers of Egypt, hence the probability of their having Egyptian slaves in their tribe. The savage nature of these untamed sons of the desert has been already commented upon when the war of extermination with Amalek was discussed. They seem to have been a ruthless, cruel race, the scourge of the desert, and of the people dwelling near its borders. From the narrative, they had evidently many camels in their force (verse 17), so the abandonment of the sick slave, left, without food or water, to die of hunger, was a needless act of barbarity on their part.

⁽¹²⁾ **Three days and three nights.**—This was a note of time as to the amount of start the Amalekite leader with the plunder had. It may well be conceived there was no time to lose. The cruelty of the Amalekites to their slaves was the cause of their ultimate discomfiture, for with the very considerable start they already had, if David had not been quite certain, through the information of the Egyptian, of their route, the pursuit would have been utterly hopeless.

⁽¹⁴⁾ **We made an invasion . . . .**—The Egyptian, who apparently was a man of education, accurately describes to David the nature and scope of the Amalekite raid, which had closed with so signal a disaster to the inhabitants of his city of Ziklag. Taking advantage of the war between Israel and Philistia, and of the northerly march of the troops of both countries, Amalek made a swift and sudden descent upon the south country. The Cherethites were a Philistine people dwelling in the south, and along the sea-coast. Some have supposed that the name "Crēthites" which represents the Hebrew more accurately—came originally, as the name seems to indicate, from the island of Crete. Capthor, the home of the Philistines (Amos ix. 7), not improbably is identical with Crete. The whole question of the history of this singular Philistine people, who were certainly not indigenous to Canaan, but who were settlers in it at a comparatively recent date, and who gave their name "Palestine" to the whole land, is most obscure.

Before the arrival of Israel in Canaan the Philistines held a very strong position on the southern coast, and not long before Samson's time they had been strengthened by fresh arrivals from Crete and other western regions, and from this date rapidly gained power and influence, and at more than one period disputed the supremacy with the Hebrew race, whom they threatened to supplant altogether.

We hear subsequently of the Cherethites mentioned in the passage under the command of Benaiah, as a portion of King David's body-guard. This troop or regiment of Philistines was first, no doubt, enrolled during his residence at Ziklag. He retained this body of foreigners, of course continually recruited, about his

David Surprises　　　　　I. SAMUEL, XXX.　　　　　*the Amalekite Invaders.*

upon the south of Caleb; and we burned Ziklag with fire. ⁽¹⁵⁾ And David said to him, Canst thou bring me down to this company? And he said, Swear unto me by God, that thou wilt neither kill me, nor deliver me into the hands of my master, and I will bring thee down to this company.

⁽¹⁶⁾ And when he had brought him down, behold, *they were* spread abroad upon all the earth, eating and drinking, and dancing, because of all the great spoil that they had taken out of the land of the Philistines, and out of the land of Judah. ⁽¹⁷⁾ And David smote them from the twilight even unto the evening of ¹the next day: and there escaped not a man of them, save four hundred young men, which rode upon camels, and fled. ⁽¹⁸⁾ And David recovered all that the Amalekites had carried away: and David rescued his two wives. ⁽¹⁹⁾ And there was nothing lacking to them, neither small nor great, neither sons nor daughters, neither spoil, nor any *thing* that they had taken to them: David recovered all. ⁽²⁰⁾ And David took all the flocks and the herds, *which* they drave before those *other* cattle, and said, This *is* David's spoil.

⁽²¹⁾ And David came to the two hundred men, which were so faint that they could not follow David, whom they had made also to abide at the brook Besor: and they went forth to meet David, and to meet the people that *were* with him: and when David came near to

¹ Heb., *their morrow.*

---

person all through his reign. Such a body-guard, made up of foreigners, has always been a favourite practice among sovereigns. The Scottish archers and the corps of Swiss Guards, at different periods of the French monarchy, and, on a larger scale, the Varangian guard of the Greek emperors of Constantinople in the tenth century, are good examples of this preference for foreigners in the case of the body-guards of the sovereign.

And upon the coast which belongeth to Judah.—The eastern portion of the Negeb or south country, reaching from the Mediterranean to the Dead Sea.

And upon the south of Caleb.—One district of the Negeb or south country was given to Caleb, the companion of Joshua, as a reward for his faith and his courage. His portion, which was called Caleb after the famous chieftain, included all the country and villages round about Hebron, which became subsequently a city of the priests.

And we burned Ziklag with fire.—This act, which closed the reign of Amalek, was intended as a piece of stern revenge for the late incursion of David into their country, and for the cruelties practised on the captives.

⁽¹⁵⁾ **By God.**—The oath was to be by "Elohim," not by Jehovah, of whom the Egyptian knew nothing.

And I will bring thee down.—His accurate knowledge of the route taken by the Amalekites, and his clear account of the late raid, show that he was a person of no ordinary ability; he was probably an Egyptian merchant or wealthy trader captured in some border fray.

⁽¹⁶⁾ **Spread abroad upon all the earth, eating and drinking and dancing.**—We have here a vivid picture of the wild license which these barbarians allowed themselves, now that they were secure, as they thought, from all pursuit. When the picked warriors of David's troops looked on the scene of revelry and debauch, and thought *who* were among the captives in that disorderly encampment, and remembered what homes had been made desolate to provide much of that great spoil over which Amalek was rejoicing, we may well conceive with what strength and fury the little veteran force of Israelites fell upon these desert robbers, who evidently far out-numbered them.

⁽¹⁷⁾ **From twilight even unto the evening of the next day.**—Keil thinks the fighting went on from the evening twilight till the evening of the next day. Bishop Hervey, in the *Speaker's Commentary*, with greater probability, supposes that "the twilight is the morning twilight, as the contrast between twilight and evening rather suggests." David thus arrived at night, and finding his enemies eating and drinking, put off his attack until the morning dawn or twilight, when they would be still sleeping after their debauch. Although thus taken by surprise, their great numbers and their natural bravery enabled them to prolong the fierce struggle all through the day, and when the shades of evening were falling four hundred (we read) of the young men, a body of fugitives equal to David's own force, managed to get clear of the rout and escape. The number of slain on this occasion must have been very great.

⁽²⁰⁾ **The flocks and the herds, which they drave.**—In the English translation the word "which," inserted in italics, obscures the sense; the literal reading is, "And David took all the flocks and the herds; they drove them before their cattle, and said, this is David's spoil." David took, no doubt, by popular acclamation as *his* share of the plunder, all the flocks and herds belonging to the Amalekites, mostly acquired, no doubt, in the late raid; these were driven in front of "those cattle" thus particularising *the cattle of Ziklag* belonging to David's own people. Of course, this plunder went back to the original Israelitish owners. The drovers, as they marched behind the vast herds of Amalekite cattle, sung of the prowess of their leader in words long remembered, "See all this. This is David's spoil." It was "these herds"—numerically, probably very great—that David distributed among the friendly cities of the south. (See verses 26, 31.) All the other plunder of the camp—arms, accoutrements, ornaments, jewels, camels' cloths, &c.—was divided, as Bishop Hervey well suggests, among the little army. David's motive in choosing the sheep and oxen (for his warriors certainly the least desirable part of the Amalekite possession) is evident from verses 26—31. They were

the people, he ¹ saluted them. ⁽²²⁾ Then answered all the wicked men and *men* of Belial, of ² those that went with David, and said, Because they went not with us, we will not give them *ought* of the spoil that we have recovered, save to every man his wife and his children, that they may lead *them* away, and depart. ⁽²³⁾ Then said David, Ye shall not do so, my brethren, with that which the LORD hath given us, who hath preserved us, and delivered the company that came against us into our hand. ⁽²⁴⁾ For who will hearken unto you in this matter? but as his part *is* that goeth down to the battle, so *shall* his part *be* that tarrieth by the stuff: they shall part alike. ⁽²⁵⁾ And it was *so* from that day ³ forward, that he made it a statute and an ordinance for Israel unto this day.

⁽²⁶⁾ And when David came to Ziklag, he sent of the spoil unto the elders of Judah, *even* to his friends, saying, Behold a ⁴ present for you of the spoil of the enemies of the LORD; ⁽²⁷⁾ to *them* which *were* in Beth-el, and to *them* which *were* in south Ramoth, and to *them* which *were* in Jattir, ⁽²⁸⁾ and to *them* which *were* in Aroer, and to *them*

1 Or, *asked them how they did.*

2 Heb., *men.*

3 Heb., *and forward.*

4 Heb., *blessing.*

---

the most acceptable presents he could make to his friends in Judah.

⁽²²⁾ **Then answered all the wicked men and men of Belial.**—The scene here related chronicles an act of greed and of heartless covetousness—an act that has been many times repeated in the world's history. The wise compiler of the book chose it as part of the memoirs of David, which were to be preserved in the sacred volume, because it was another authoritative declaration on the part of the beloved king respecting a question which would crop up again and again on the conclusion of a campaign. The chronicler was justified in his selection, for this famous decision of David continued in force until the time of the Maccabees. (See 2 Macc. viii. 28—30.) A somewhat similar law was enacted by Moses. (See Num. xxxi. 27.) The dispute arose thus: The victorious troop with their enormous booty quickly returned to the brook Besor, where the 200 that had broken down on the rapid march had been left to guard the baggage. David salutes these with all kindly courtesy; but the harmony which prevailed in the little camp is speedily broken owing to the highhanded claims of the 400 who had actually taken part in the rescue. These refused to share the booty with their comrades who had been left behind, only proposing just to restore to them their wives and those things of their own which had been recovered from the Amalekites. David, however, refused to listen to these iniquitous claims, and decided that all the fighting part of the force, and those men who had stayed behind and guarded the baggage at the brook Besor. should share alike.

⁽²³⁾ **Ye shall not do so my brethren.**—Translate "Do not so my brethren with that which the Lord hath given us," that is, "in respect to that which the Lord," &c. Ewald prefers to render the phrase as an ejaculatory oath, "By that which the Lord," &c. Some commentators here quote a passage from Polybius, where a similar scene is depicted as having taken place after the capture of Nova Carthago, where Publius Scipio decided that the spoil then taken should be divided equally among the troops that had been actually engaged, and the reserves and the sick among the soldiery, and those in the army who had been detached from the main body on special service.

⁽²⁵⁾ **A statute and an ordinance for Israel.**—The decree that they, who for good reasons tarry with the stuff, shall share alike with those who go down to the battle, which became a received ordinance in Israel, is not without its meaning. In the *Heavenly Church of God*

> "His state
> Is kingly; thousands at his bidding speed,
> And post o'er land and ocean without rest:
> They also serve who only stand and wait."
> MILTON : *Sonnet* xix.

Moses praying on the hill contributed to the victory over Amalek even more than Joshua fighting in the plain (Exod. xvii. 11). "All Christians are not of equal strength, and some follow Christ to the conflict, others tarry with the stuff. Some fight the Lord's battles in the din of active life; others, aged men and women, the Simeons and Annas of the Church . . . . weak in body but strong in faith, fight with the peaceful arms of prayers and tears; Christ is omnipotent and merciful. He rewards those who tarry in patience with the stuff, as well as those who go forth in the march to fight valiantly in the battle."—Bishop Hall, in *Wordsworth*.

⁽²⁶⁾ **He sent of the spoil.**—To have made it worth while to have sent presents to all the places enumerated below, the spoil of the Amalekites captured on this occasion must have been enormous. One special circumstance connected with the history besides leads us to this conclusion. Although these desert Arabs were surprised and attacked at a terrible disadvantage after a debauch, they seem (so great evidently was their numbers) to have held their ground from early morning until evening, and then 400 managed to escape on their swiftest camels. It was not improbably the main division of the great tribe, and they had with them the bulk of their flocks and herds, besides what they had just captured in their raid in southern Canaan. No doubt the cities to whom rich gifts of cattle were sent were those places where, during his long wanderings, he and his followers had been kindly received and helped.

⁽²⁷⁾ **Bethel . . . South Ramoth . . . Yattir.**—Here follows an enumeration of the cities of Judah to whom David sent, most of which have been identified. Bethel—evidently not the well known place of that name, but Bethuel or Bethul in the tribe of Simeon. The LXX. read here Baithsour. South Ramoth, *i.e.*, Ramah of the South. Shimei, who was over David's vineyards, was most likely a native of this town (1 Chron. xxvii. 27). The place has not been identified. Yattir—the present *Attir* in the southern part of Judah. Its ruins are still visible.

⁽²⁸⁾ **Aroer . . . Siphmoth and . . . Eshtemoa.**—*Aroer*, a city, with colossal ruins of foundation walls,

David sends his Share   I. SAMUEL, XXXI.   *to the Cities of Judah.*

which *were* in Siphmoth, and to *them* which *were* in Eshtemoa, ⁽²⁹⁾ and to *them* which *were* in Rachal, and to *them* which *were* in the cities of the Jerahmeelites, and to *them* which *were* in the cities of the Kenites, ⁽³⁰⁾ and to *them* which *were* in Hormah, and to *them* which *were* in Chor-ashan, and to *them* which *were* in Athach, ⁽³¹⁾ and to *them* which *were* in Hebron, and to all the places where David himself and his men were wont to haunt.

CHAPTER XXXI.—⁽¹⁾ Now ^a the Philistines fought against Israel: and the men of Israel fled from before the Philistines, and fell down ¹ slain in mount Gilboa. ⁽²⁾ And the Philistines followed hard upon Saul and upon his sons; and the Philistines slew Jonathan,

a 1 Chr. 10. 1.

¹ Or, *wounded.*

---

south of Hebron. Of Siphmoth nothing is known. Zabdi, the Shiphmite (1 Chron. xxvii. 27), who was over King David's cellars, clearly comes from Siphmoth. Bishop Hervey well calls attention to a remarkable proof of the grateful nature of David and his fidelity to his early friendships, "that we find among those employed by David in offices of trust in the height of his power so many inhabitants of these obscure places, where he found friends in the days of his early difficulties. Ezri, the son of Shemei the Ramathite, Zabdi the Shiphmite, and many others, were among the friends of his youth." Eshtemoa, a priestly city, still survives, with ruins still visible, in the village of *Semua*.

⁽²⁹⁾ **Rachal.**—The name Rachal never occurs again, and is quite unknown. Here the LXX., instead of Rachal, have five different names—*Ged, Kimath, Saphek, Themath, Karmel*. No satisfactory explanation has been suggested for this strange addition; three of them are unknown, and the other two—Gad (Gath) and Carmel—places we should certainly not expect to meet in this catalogue.

The cities of the Jerahmeelites and Kenites.—These places were situated in the south of Judah; they cannot be traced.

⁽³⁰⁾ **Hormah . . . Chor-ashan . . . Athach.**—Hormah, called by the Canaanites Zephath, still exists in the modern village of Zep-ata. Chor-ashan is probably the same as Ashan (Josh. xv. 30): it has not been discovered in modern times. Athach is quite unknown.

⁽³¹⁾ **Hebron.**—Hebron is one of the most ancient known cities in the world. It is now called El-Khalil ("friend of God"), owing to Abraham's residence there. During the early years of David's rule, which followed the death of Saul, Hebron was the residence and royal city of David. Beneath the building of the present Mosque of Hebron is the famous Cave of Machpelah, where Abraham and Sarah and the patriarchs Isaac and Jacob, and his wife Leah, are buried.

XXXI.

^(1–13) Battle of Mount Gilboa—Death of Saul and his three Sons—Panic in Israel—The Philistines expose the King's Body on the Wall of Beth-shan—The Citizens of Jabesh-Gilead rescue the Royal Corpse.

⁽¹⁾ **Now the Philistines fought against Israel.**—The narrator here is very abrupt. No doubt a devoted patriot, it was very bitter for him to write the story of the fatal day of Gilboa. Yet there were certain things belonging to that fated day which were necessary for every child of Israel to know. It was right that the punishment of the rejected king should be known; right too that the people should be assured that the remains of the great first king lay in no unknown and unhonoured sepulchre. It was well too that coming generations should honour the devoted loyalty of the grateful men of Jabesh-Gilead. But the narrator hurries over his unwelcome task; very curtly he picks up the dropped threads of chaps. xxviii. 1—5, xxix. 2. The march of the Philistines northward into the valley of Jezreel has been told, and their gallant array—as under the many banners of their lords they passed on by hundreds and by thousands—has been glanced at. The assembling of the armies of Israel at Shunem, overlooking the Jezreel vale, has been narrated; and there the historian dwelt on the terror of King Saul, which led to the visit to the witch of En-dor. David's fortunes at this juncture then occupied the writer or compiler of the Book; but now he returns, with evident reluctance, to the battle which rapidly followed the En-dor visit of Saul.

He simply relates that the hosts joined battle. The locality of the fight is not mentioned, but it was most likely somewhere in that long vale which was spread out at the foot of the hills occupied by the hostile camps. Israel was defeated, and fled upwards, towards their old position on the slope of Gilboa.

⁽²⁾ **And the Philistines followed hard upon Saul and upon his sons.**—"The details of the battle are but seen in broken snatches, as in the short scene of a battle acted upon the stage, or beheld at remote glimpses by an accidental spectator. But amidst the showers of arrows from the Philistine archers, or pressed hard even on the mountain side by their charioteers, the figure of the king emerges from the darkness. His three sons have fallen before him; his armourbearer lies dead beside him."—Stanley: *Jewish Church*, Lect. xxi.

And the Philistines slew Jonathan, and Abinadab, and Melchi-shua, Saul's sons.—But while, in his own record of the national disaster, the compiler or historian, in his stern sorrow, expunges every detail, and represses every expression of feeling, he gives us in the next chapter (2 Sam. i. 1—27) the stately elegy, in the beautiful moving words which the successor to the throne wrote on the death of the first king and his heroic son. Without comment he copies into his record the hymn of David on Saul and Jonathan, just as he found it in the *Book of Jashar* (the collection of national odes celebrating the heroes of the Theocracy). "There David speaks of the Saul of earlier times—the mighty conqueror, the delight of his people, the father of his beloved and faithful friend—like him in life, united with him in death." (Stanley).

"Saul and Jonathan were lovely and pleasant in their lives,
And in their death they were not divided.
Than eagles they were swifter, than lions more strong."
(2 Sam. i. 23.) From the lost *Book of Jashar*.

Nothing is known of the two younger princes who fell fighting here by their father's side, sword in hand, against the enemies of their country.

| *The fatal Battle* | I. SAMUEL, XXXI. | *of Mount Gilboa.* |

and Abinadab, and Melchishua, Saul's sons. (3) And the battle went sore against Saul, and the ¹archers ²hit him; and he was sore wounded of the archers. (4) Then said Saul unto his armourbearer, Draw thy sword, and thrust me through therewith; lest these uncircumcised come and thrust me through, and ³abuse me. But his armourbearer would not; for he was sore afraid. Therefore Saul took a sword, and fell upon it. (5) And when his armourbearer saw that Saul was dead, he fell likewise upon his sword, and

¹ Heb., *shooters, men with bows.*
² Heb., *found him.*
³ Or, *mock me.*

The hero Jonathan and his two brave brothers, as far as we can gather from the scanty details of the battle after the army was routed in the valley of Jezreel, retreated (fighting all the while) to the hill of Gilboa. There, it seems, they made the last stand with the *fideles* of the royal house of Saul (verse 6), and there, no doubt defending the king to the last, they fell.

(3) **And the battle went sore against Saul.**—That is, after the death of Jonathan and his brothers. The great warrior king no doubt fought like a lion, but one by one his brave defenders fell in harness by his side; and the enemy seems to have directed their principal attention, at this period of the fight, to killing or capturing the famous Saul.

And the archers hit him.—It would seem as though, in that deadly combat, none could strike down that giant kingly form, so the archers—literally, as in the margin of our Version, *shooters, men with bows*, skilful shots—were told off, and these, aiming at the warrior towering above the other combatants, with the crown on his head (2 Sam. i. 10), hit him.

And he was sore wounded by the archers.—This is the usual rendering of the word, but the more accurate translation is, *He was sore afraid* (or was greatly alarmed at them): so Gesenius, Keil, Lange, &c. All seemed against him. His army was routed, his sons were dead, his faithful captains and companions were gone, and these bow-men were shooting at him from a distance where his strong arm could not reach them. Gradually weakened through loss of blood—perhaps with the words he had heard only a few hours before at En-dor from the dead prophet ringing in his ears, " To-morrow shalt thou and thy sons be with me "—the great undaunted courage at last failed him, and he turned to his armourbearer, who was still by his side.

(4) **His armourbearer.**—Jewish tradition tells us that this faithful armourbearer was Doeg, the Edomite, and that the sword which Saul took apparently from the hand of the armourbearer was the sword with which Doeg had massacred the priests at Gibeon and at Nob.

Lest these uncircumcised come and thrust me.—" Even in Saul's dying speech there is something of that religious formalism which marked his character after his fall from God, and which is a striking sign of spiritual blindness. He censures the Philistines as 'uncircumcised.' "—*Wordsworth.*

Saul had a strong consciousness of the sacredness of his person as the Lord's anointed; as it has been well said of him, no descendant of a long line of so-styled Christian or Catholic sovereigns has held a loftier claim of personal inviolability.

And abuse me.—He remembered how these same Philistines in former years had treated the hero Samson when he fell into their hands.

His armourbearer would not.—Love and devotion to his master we can well imagine stayed his hand from carrying out his fallen master's last terrible command. If the armourbearer—as the Jewish tradition above referred to asserts—was indeed Doeg the Edomite,

the two, the king and his confidential officer, had been fast friends for years. Some dread of the after consequences, too, may have weighed with the royal armourbearer, as he was to a certain extent responsible for the king's life. What possibly he dreaded actually came to pass in the case of the Amalekite who told David that he was the one who inflicted the fatal stroke when the king was dying; as a guerdon for his act, David had him at once put to death for having put forth his hand to destroy the Lord's anointed.

A sword.—It was a heavy weapon, a war sword, answering to the great *epée d'armes* of the Middle Ages. This he took from the reluctant hands of his faithful follower, and placing the hilt firmly on the ground, he threw the weight of his body on the point.

In 2 Sam. i. 6—10 we have another account of the death. There an Amalekite bearing the royal insignia of the late king, the crown royal and the well-known bracelet of Saul, comes to David at Ziklag after the fatal fight, and recounts how, finding the king leaning on his spear—possibly, as Bunsen supposes, "lying on the ground propping his weary head with the nervously-clutched spear," exhausted and seized with " cramp " (this is the Rabbinical translation of the word rendered " anguish "), at his urgent request, slew him. Most commentators — for instance, Kiel, Lange, Bishop Hervey, &c.—regard the Amalekite's story as an invention framed to extract a rich gift from David, who, the savage Arab thought, would be rejoiced to hear of his great enemy's fall. If this be so, then we must suppose that the Amalekite wandering over the field of battle strewn with the slain on the night which succeeded the battle, came upon the body of Saul, and, attracted by the glitter of the golden ornaments, stripped off the precious insignia, and hastened with his lying story to David. Ewald, however, sees no reason to doubt the trustworthiness of the Amalekite's story; in fact, the two accounts may well be harmonised. Stanley graphically paints the scene *after* he had fallen on his sword, and his faithful armourbearer had in despairing sorrow killed himself also. " His armourbearer lies dead beside him; on his head the royal crown, on his arm the royal bracelet; . . . the huge spear is still in his hand; he is leaning peacefully on it. He has received his death-blow either from the enemy (verse 3), or from his own sword (verse 4). The dizziness and darkness of death is upon him. At that moment a wild Amalekite, lured probably to the field by the hope of spoil, came up and finished the work which the arrows of the Philistines and the sword of Saul himself had all but accomplished."—*Jewish Church*, Lect. xxi. The words of the next verse (5) do not contradict this possible explanation. The armourbearer, seeing the king pierced with the arrows and then falling on his own sword, may well have imagined his master dead, and so put an end to his own life. But Saul, though mortally wounded, may have rallied again for a brief space; in that brief space the Amalekite may have come up and finished the bloody work; then, after the king was dead, he probably stripped the royal insignia from the lifeless corpse.

died with him. ⁽⁶⁾ So Saul died, and his three sons, and his **armourbearer**, and all his men, that same day together.

⁽⁷⁾ And when the men of Israel that *were* on the other side of the valley, and *they* that *were* on the other side Jordan, saw that the men of Israel fled, and that Saul and his sons were dead, they forsook the cities, and fled; and the Philistines came and dwelt in them.

⁽⁸⁾ And it came to pass on the morrow, when the Philistines came to strip the slain, that they found Saul and his three sons fallen in mount Gilboa.

So Saul died.—This is one of the very rare instances of self-destruction among the chosen people. It seems to have been almost unknown among the Israelites. Prior to Saul the only recorded example is that of Samson, and his was a noble act of self-devotion—the hero sacrificed his life in order to compass the destruction of a great crowd of men, powerful and influential foes of his dear country. His death in the great Dagon Temple at Gaza ranks, as it has been well said, with the heroism of one dying in battle rather than with cases of despairing suicide. There is another instance after the days of Saul—that of the wise privy councillor of King David, Ahithophel, who, in a paroxysm of bitter mortification, we read, went and hanged himself. There is another in the Gospel story familiar to us all. Theologians are divided in their judgment on King Saul. S. Bernard, for instance, thinks that Saul was lost for ever. Corn. à Lapide, followed by Bishop Wordsworth, has no kindly thought for the great first king. The Jewish historian Josephus, on the contrary, writes in warm and glowing terms of the patriotic devotion with which Saul went to meet his end. Many of the Rabbis sympathise with Josephus in his estimate of the unhappy monarch. Without in any way justifying the fatal act which closed the dark tragedy of his reign, we may well plead in extenuation the awful position in which the king found himself that evening after Gilboa had been fought and lost, and we may well remember the similar conduct of Brutus, Cassius, and the younger Cato, and call to our minds what posterity has said of these noble heathens, and how far they have judged them guilty of causeless self-murder.

Well would it be for men when they sit in judgment on Saul, and on other great ones who have failed, as they think, in the discharge of their duties to God as well as to man—well would it be for once to imitate what has been rightly called "the fearless human sympathy of the Biblical writers," and to remember how the "man after God's own heart," in strains never to be forgotten, wrote his touching lament over King Saul, dwelling only on the Saul, the mighty conqueror, the delight of his people, the father of his beloved and faithful friend, like him in life, united with him in death; and how with these words—gentle as they are lovely, inspired by the Holy Spirit—the Bible closes the record of the life, and leaves the first great king, the first anointed of the Lord, in the hands of his God.

⁽⁶⁾ **And all his men.**— We must not interpret this statement quite literally; 1 Chron. x. 6 explains it by "all his house." Ishbosheth, his son, for instance, and Abner, the captain of the host, we know were not among the slain on that fatal day. The meaning is that all his "*fideles*," his personal staff, as we should say, with his three sons fell fighting round him. The lines of the chivalrous Scottish ballad writer who with rare skill describes the devoted followers of King James V. falling round him at Flodden, well paints what took place on the stricken field of Gilboa round the hero king Saul:—

"No one failed him! He is keeping
Royal state and semblance still,
Knight and noble lie around him,
Cold, on Flodden's fatal hill.

"Of the brave and gallant-hearted
Whom you sent with prayers away,
Not a single man departed
From his monarch yesterday."—AYTOUN.

⁽⁷⁾ **On the other side of the valley.** — The words "on the other side of the valley" denote the country opposite to the battle-field in the valley of Jezreel, on which the writer supposes himself to be standing, the land occupied especially by the tribes of Issachar, Zabulon, and Napthali. The expression "on the other side of Jordan," is the usual phrase for the country east of the River Jordan. It is highly probable that the alarm caused by the great defeat of their king caused many of the dwellers in the smaller cities and villages to the east of Jordan hastily to abandon their houses rather than be exposed to the insolence and demands of the invading army. Still the Philistine army in this direction could not have penetrated very far, as shortly after Gilboa we hear of Abner rallying the friends of the house of Saul round the Prince Ishbosheth, whom he proclaimed king at Mahanaim, a town some twenty miles east of the river. The country to the south of the plain of Jezreel does not appear to have been overrun by the victorious army. The presence of David in that part no doubt insured its immunity from invasion.

⁽⁸⁾ **They found Saul and his three sons fallen in Mount Gilboa.**—It is expressly stated that the Philistines only found the royal corpses on the morrow of the great fight. So desperate had been the valour with which the king and his gallant sons had defended their last positions on the hill, that night had fallen ere the din of battle ceased. Nor were the enemy aware of the completeness of their success until the morning dawn revealed to the soldiers as they went over the scene, the great ones who were numbered among the slain. In the mean time the Amalekite had found and carried off the crown and royal bracelet. Only the bodies of Saul and the princes, and the armourbearer, are spoken of here. The crown royal, which would have formed so splendid a trophy, was already taken.

"O Saul,
How ghastly didst thou look, on thine own sword
Expiring in Gilboa, from that hour
Ne'er visited with rain from heaven, nor dew."
DANTE: *Purg.* xii.

The curse of barrenness alluded to by the great Italian poet was called down on the hill where the first anointed of the Lord fell, and where the body was stripped and dismembered by the triumphant foe (2 Sam. i. 21). Quickly the tidings were told, we learn, in the capital of Gath, and proclaimed through the streets of Askelon.

(9) And they cut off his head, and stripped off his armour, and sent into the land of the Philistines round about, to publish *it in* the house of their idols, and among the people. (10) And they put his armour in the house of Ashtaroth: and they fastened his body to the wall of Beth-shan. (11) And when the inhabitants of Jabesh-gilead heard [1] of that which the Philistines had done to Saul; (12) all the valiant men arose, and went all night, and took the body of Saul and the bodies of his sons from the wall of Beth-shan, and came to Jabesh, and *a* burnt them there. (13) And they took their bones, and *b* buried *them* under a tree at Jabesh, and fasted seven days.

[1] Or, *concerning him.*

a Jer. 34. 5.

b 2 Sam. 2. 4.

The historian with extreme brevity records the savage treatment of the royal remains, which, after all, was but a reprisal. The same generation had witnessed similar barbarous procedure in the case of Goliath, the great Philistine champion!

(9) **And they cut off his head, and stripped off his armour.**—Only *Saul's* head and armour is mentioned here, but on comparing verse 12, where the bodies of his sons are especially mentioned, it is clear that this act was not confined to the person of the king. The sense of the passage there is, the heads of the king and his three sons were cut off, and their armour stripped from their bodies. The heads and armour were sent as trophies round about the different towns and villages of Philistia, and the headless corpses were fastened to the wall of the city of Beth-shan.

(10) **The house of Ashtaroth.**—Literally, *of "the Ashtaroth."* The expression may signify that the pieces of armour belonging to the four men were divided between the different shrines of Astarte in the land, or placed together in the famous Astarte Temple, at Askelon, which Herodotus (i. 105) describes as the most ancient of the temples dedicated to the worship of the Syrian Venus. The latter supposition seems the more probable, as Askelon is specially mentioned by David in the funeral hymn of Saul and Jonathan (2 Sam. i. 20).

The wall of Beth-shan.—Beth-shan was in the tribe of Manasseh, some four miles west of the Jordan, and twelve miles south of the sea of Galilee. We are told in Judges i. 27, that the Canaanites, the original inhabitants of the city, were permitted by the conqueror to dwell still in the city. This Canaanitish element in the population was perhaps the reason why Beth-shan was chosen for the barbarous exhibition. The Canaanites would probably have welcomed the miserable spectacle which seemed to degrade their ancient enemies. The writer of the chronicle adds one more ghastly detail to this account: "They fastened the head (skull) of Saul in the Temple of Dagon."

(11) **The inhabitants of Jabesh-Gilead.**—The memory of the splendid feat of arms of their young king Saul, when he gallantly rescued their city (1 Sam. xi. 1—11) years before, when they were threatened with deadly peril by the Ammonites, was still fresh in the city of Jabesh-Gilead, and they burned to rescue the body of their hero from shame. It was singular how that first deed of splendid patriotism, done in the early fervour of his consecration, bore fruit after so many long years.

"Good deeds immortal are—they cannot die;
Unscathed by envious blight, or withering frost,
They live, and bud and bloom, and men partake
Still of their freshness, and are strong thereby."
AYTOUN.

Jabesh-Gilead, a city of Manasseh, on the further side of Jordan, on the road from Pella to Gerasa, perhaps about fourteen miles from Beth-shan (see Judges xxi. 8, and following). Its name still survives in the Wady Yabez, running down to the east bank of Jordan, near the head of which are still visible some ruins named El Deir, which Robinson has identified with Jabesh-Gilead.

(12) **And burnt them there.**—This "burning the corpse" was never the custom in Israel, and was restricted to criminals convicted of a crime of the deepest dye (Lev. xx. 14). The Jews in all cases buried their dead. The Chaldee therefore interpret the words relating this act of the men of Jabesh-Gilead, in the case of Saul and the princes, as referring to the solemn burning of spices, a ceremony which was afterwards performed at the burial of some of the kings of Judah. (See 2 Chron. xvi. 14, xxi. 19; Jeremiah xxxiv. 5.) But the language used in these cases is different; here it is expressly stated that "they burnt them." The reason for their thus acting is clear. The mutilated trunks had been exposed for some days to the air, and the flesh was no doubt in a state of putrefaction. The flesh here only was burned. The bones (see next verse) were reverently and lovingly preserved, and laid to rest beneath the friendly shade of the great tamarisk tree of Jabesh.

(13) **A tree in Jabesh.**—A tree, that is "the well-known" tamarisk (*éshel*). For Saul's love for trees see as an instance chap. xxii. 6. The men of Jabesh-Gilead well remembered this peculiar fancy of their dead king, and under the waving branches of their own beautiful and famous tamarisk they tenderly laid the remains of their dead hero and his princely sons.

Evidently King David, at a subsequent period, fetched away these royal remains, and had them reverently interred in the family sepulchre of Kish, the father of Saul, in Zelah of Benjamin (2 Sam. xxi. 12, 14).

And fasted seven days.—This was the period the sons of Israel mourned for Jacob at the threshing floor of Atad beyond Jordan (Gen. l. 10). The grateful men of Jabesh-Gilead thus paid the last honours to the fallen Saul.

It is probable that the Talmudic rule which enjoins strict mourning for seven days (fasting was mourning of the strictest kind) was originally based on these two historic periods of mourning recorded in the case of the great ancestor of the tribes, Jacob, and of the first King Saul, although the curious tradition preserved in the Babylonian Talmud gives a special reason for the period —seven days. Rav. Chisda said: The soul of the deceased mourns over him *the first seven days;* for it is said, Job xiv. 22, "and his soul shall mourn over him." Rav. Jehudah said: If there are no mourners to condole with, ten men sit down where the death took place. Such a case happened in the neighbourhood of Rav. Jehudah. *After the seven days of mourning*, the deceased appeared to Rav. Jehudah in a dream, and

I. SAMUEL, XXXI.

said "Mayest thou be comforted as thou hast comforted me."—Treatise *Shabbath*, fol. 152, col. 2.

To this day among the Jews ten men are hired to perform the usual daily prayers during *the seven days* of mourning at the house of the deceased.

On the reason for the number *seven* being fixed for the period of mourning, we read again in the *Seder Moed* of the Babylonian Talmud, "How is it proved that mourning should be kept up *seven days?*" It is written, Amos viii. 10: "I will turn your feasts into mourning," and these (usually) lasted seven days.—Treatise *Moed Katon*, fol. 20, col. 1.

"Again a long draught of my soul-wine! Look forth o'er the years!
Thou hast done now with eyes for the actual; begin with the seer's!
Is Saul dead? In the depth of the vale make his tomb, bid arise
A grey mountain of marble heaped four-square, till built to the skies.
Let it mark where the great First King slumbers; whose fame would ye know?
Up above see the rock's naked face, where the record shall go,
In great characters cut by the scribe. Such was Saul, so he did;
With the sages directing the work, by the populace chid—
For not half, they'll affirm, is comprised there! Which fault to amend,
In the grove with his kind grows the cedar, whereon they shall spend
(See, in tablets, it is level before them) their praise, and record,
With gold of the graver, Saul's story—the statesman's great word
Side by side with the poet's sweet comment. The rivers a-wave
With smooth paper-reeds grazing each other when prophet-winds rave:
So the pen gives unborn generations their due and their part
In thy being! Then, first of the mighty, thank God that thou art!"

BROWNING'S *Saul*.

EXCURSUS ON NOTES TO THE FIRST BOOK OF SAMUEL

EXCURSUS A: ON THE SONG OF HANNAH (chap. ii.).

The song of Hannah belongs to that group of inspired hymns of which examples have been preserved in most of the earlier books. Genesis, for instance, contains the prophetic song of the dying Jacob, Exodus the triumph hymn of Miriam, Numbers the glorious prophet song of Balaam, Deuteronomy the dying prayer and prophecy of Moses; Judges preserves for us the war song of Deborah.

The Book of the Psalms was a later collection of the favourite sacred hymns and songs of the people, written mostly in what may be termed the golden age of Israel, when David and Solomon had consolidated the monarchy.

Each of the greater songs embedded in the earlier books seems to have marked a new departure in the life of the chosen people.

This is especially noticeable in the prophetic song of Jacob, which heralded the period of the Egyptian slavery, and pointed to a glorious future lying beyond the days of bitter oppression. Miriam sung of the triumphs of the Lord; her impassioned words introduced the free desert life which succeeded the slavery days of Egypt. Moses' grand words were the preparation for the settlement of the tribes in Canaan.

Hannah was impelled by the Spirit of the Lord to make a strange announcement respecting her boy Samuel. She had learned by Divine revelation that he was to be God's chosen instrument in the future: first, as the restorer of the true life in Israel—which was then beginning to forget its God-Friend; and afterwards, as the founder of a new and kingly order of governors, who should unite the divided tribes, and weld into one great nation the scattered families of Israel.

It is probable that these "poems," which we find embedded in the oldest Hebrew records, were preserved in the nation, some as popular songs, sung and said among the people in their public and private gatherings as the best and noblest expression of their ideal national life; some as even forming part of the primitive liturgical service of those sacred gatherings of the chosen people which subsequently developed into the synagogue, the well-known sacred assemblies of Israel.

The various compilers or redactors of the several Old Testament Books, according to this theory, gathered these poems, hymns, and songs from the lips of the people as they repeated and chanted them in their sacred festal gatherings.

EXCURSUS B: ALLEGED DIFFICULTIES IN THE ASCRIPTION OF SONG TO HANNAH (chap. ii.).

The advocates of a later date for the song of Hannah, with some force allege two points in the composition, which they say forbids their ascribing the "song" to the mother of Samuel, or even to the period in which she lived. It will be well briefly to examine these. First, the "song," they say, is a triumph song, celebrating a victory over some foreign enemies. Such a theory, however, completely misinterprets the whole hymn. Nowhere is a *victory* spoken of, and the song contains only one allusion (verse 4: "The bows of the mighty men") which has anything to do with *war*; and this solitary passage contrasts the mighty bowmen with the stumbling or weak ones, and shows how, under the rule of God, the warrior is often confounded, and the weak unarmed one strengthened. It is, in fact, only one of several vivid pictures painting the marvellous vicissitudes which, under God's providence, so often happen to mortals. The strong often are proved weak, and the weak strong. The foes alluded to in the hymn of Hannah are not the enemies of Israel, but the unrighteous of the chosen people contrasted with the pious and devoted.

Secondly, the "song" in verse 10 assumes the existence of an earthly king in Israel, whereas when Hannah sung no king but Jehovah was acknowledged by any of the tribes. Erdmann, in Lange's Commentary, well observes, in explanation of this, that "at the period when Hannah gave birth to Samuel it was incontestable that in the consciousness of the people, and the noblest part of them too, the idea of a monarchy had then become a power which quickened more and more the hope of a realisation of the old promises that there should be a royal dominion in Israel, till it took shape in an express demand which the people made of Samuel. The Divine promise that this people should be a kingdom is given as early as the patriarchal period (Gen. xvii. 6, 16. See too Gen. xlix. 10; Num. xxiv. 17, 19; Deut. xvii. 14 to end of chapter). At the close of the period of the judges, when Hannah lived, the need of such a kingdom was felt the more strongly because the office which was entrusted with the duty of forming and guiding the theocratic life of the nation, namely, the high priestly office, was involved in the deepest degradation."

I. SAMUEL.

EXCURSUS C: THE HIGH PRIESTHOOD, AND THE FAMILY WHICH HELD IT (chap. ii.).

The supreme dignity in Israel was held by the family of Eleazar, the son of Aaron, until the death of the high priest Ozi. We are not in possession of the circumstances which led to the transference of the office to Eli, the descendant of Ithamar, the younger son of Aaron; probably the surviving son of the high priest Ozi, of the house of Eleazar, was an infant, or at all events very young, when his father died, and Eli — his kinsman, no doubt — had probably distinguished himself in some of the ceaseless wars in which the people during the stormy period of the judges were continually involved, and was in consequence chosen by the popular voice to the vacant dignity. After the death of Eli and his two sons, Hophni and Phinehas, the high priestly dignity never seems to have recovered its ancient power and dignity. The eyes of Israel were turned first to Samuel, and then to Saul and his royal successors, David and Solomon.

During the lifetime of Samuel, Saul, and David, though shorn of its old proportions and exposed to many vicissitudes, the high priesthood continued in the family of Eli, who was succeeded by his grandson, Ahitub, the son of Phinehas. In the days of Saul, Ahijah, or Ahimelech, the son of Ahitub, gave David the shewbread to eat at Nob, and was for this act murdered by King Saul, together with all the priests then doing duty at the national sanctuary. His son, Abiathar, escaped the massacre, and was allowed to assume his father's office. During the reign of David this Abiathar continued to be high priest, but was arbitrarily deposed by Solomon, who restored Zadok, of the old high priestly line of Eleazar. The descendants of Zadok continued to hold the office as long as the monarchy lasted.

The annexed table shows the double line of high priests to the reign of Solomon:—

	Aaron.	
Period of Joshua	Eleazar	Ithamar
Period of the Judges	Ozi	
		Eli—high priest, and judge of Israel.
		Phinehas — never high priest; he was slain in the battle of Aphek.
		Ahitub—reign of Saul.
		Ahimelech—reign of Saul.
		Abiathar—reign of David and Solomon.
Reign of Solomon	Zadok	

EXCURSUS D: ON THE ESTABLISHMENT OF THE MONARCHY IN ISRAEL (chap. viii.).

It is an error to see in the foundation of the Hebrew monarchy by Samuel in the person of King Saul merely a vain-glorious popular demand, merely a desire to emulate other nations in their pomp in circumstance of war, merely a wish to be free from the grave moral restraints of an austere Republican government, with an Invisible and Almighty Chief presiding over it.

Samuel, with all the passions of a father and prejudices of a Republican chieftain, at first resisted the popular request, but subsequently, influenced by nobler, more far-sighted considerations, yielded to it, and even furthered it with all his great power and the influence of his lofty character. The popular request—although many earthly feelings and passions influenced the people's prayer to their prophet-judge for an earthly king—was really suggested by the Spirit of the Eternal who had chosen Israel. Such an undivided and firmly established human authority within the chosen people was now indispensable to their progress. Roughly speaking, Israel, since it left Egypt and the degrading slavery to the Pharaohs, had gone through four phases: the *first*, the severe education under Moses in the Desert; the *second*, the period of the conquest and the age immediately succeeding it, when the people worshipped the Eternal, who had done such great things for them, with a fervour of enthusiastic gratitude; the *third*, the so-called age of the Judges, a period when the memory of the God-Friend was growing fainter and fainter, when the wish to live the life He loved was gradually dying out of Israel. They were becoming like the peoples who lived around them, and were gradually falling into subjection to the more warlike and stronger of their idol-worshipping neighbours. From this impending decay and ruin they were rescued by the splendid patriotism and the fervent religious zeal of Samuel, under whose wise rule Israel as a nation once more returned to the pure holy worship of the Eternal; this was the *fourth* phase of the national life. But in order to weld the once more faithful yet divided and ill-organised tribes into one great nation, the establishment of an earthly monarchy was indispensable. It was, indeed, no new thought; the great Hebrew lawgiver, who drew his wisdom direct from communing with the Most High, had spoken of it as of something which would in the coming ages be absolutely necessary for the progress and development of the nation. And now the time was ripe for it, and the same Being who watched over Israel with a Father's intense love put into the hearts of the elders of the people the desire for a king, and into their mouths the words with which they approached with their request His prophet and servant, Samuel the judge and seer.

We have seen how quickly that true patriot stamped down his first repugnance to a change which would alter the whole constitution of the people for whom he had done and suffered such great things, which would virtually set him aside as ruler and judge, and for ever destroy the natural hopes he had entertained of transmitting his nobly earned honours and power to his own house.

The seer laid the matter in prayer before his Master, and from Him received direct instructions how he should proceed. What entire trust must the Eternal have placed in this great prophet-judge to confide to him the momentous task of establishing a permanent monarchy in Israel, knowing that the first step in the establishment of such a monarchy must be Samuel's own voluntary abdication of rank and power! But the Master knew His servant.

The old man quietly accepted what must have been to him a painful, saddening mission. Acting under the Divine direction, he set out before the chiefs of the tribes a picture of the new burdens and duties which the sovereignty, if established, would require them to take upon themselves. As soon as he had received

I. SAMUEL.

their solemn acceptance of these new and altered conditions—in other words, as soon as he had received from the elders of the people an expression of their general willingness to exchange their old republican freedom for the comparative servitude which subjects of a powerful sovereign, especially in the East, must endure—he proceeded with all solemnity to the choice of a king for Israel. It has been well pointed out by Dean Payne Smith that the last three chapters of the Book of Judges, immediately preceding in the Hebrew the Books of Samuel (the insertion of the Book of Ruth in this place being a modern attempt at chronological arrangement), seems intended to point out the grave necessity of a king for the well-being of the Hebrew commonwealth. They relate the history of a fearful crime, punished with equally fearful cruelty, and, as the Dean observes, what makes it more remarkable is that it took place in the days of Phinehas, the grandson of Aaron. (See the chronological statement, Judges xx. 28, which shows that these awful scenes of national sin and vengeance probably took place within twenty years of the death of Joshua, that is, at a time when the public morality still stood high, and the religion of the Eternal still had a mighty influence over the people.) In the period of the later judges disorders were far more common in Israel than even in the days of Phinehas.

The lofty ideal which the teaching of Moses proposed to Israel and which, during its long chequered story, raised it high above all the other nations of the world, was that Israel should consider itself the peculiar kingdom of the Eternal King. And at first under men like Moses and Joshua, no earthly representative of the heavenly Sovereign was necessary. The people lived and worked as ever in the presence of the Most High; but in the very next generation, as we have seen, the invisible Sovereign began to be forgotten, and to each succeeding age the glorious Presence was still less of a reality. The people in the days of Samuel, led by the Spirit of God, demanded that to the theocracy the monarchy should be added, not in any way to subvert it, but, as Ewald happily phrases it, to share its task, and to supply the want which it could not satisfy. The earthly king was to be the *chosen* of the Eternal, the *anointed* of the invisible Friend. He was to be the visible image on earth, the vice-gerent of the invisible King of Israel, reigning in heaven. He was to be no absolute sovereign, reigning for his own pleasure and according to the dictates of his own will, like other monarchs of the world, but was to enter into the mind and spirit of the Eternal King, of whom he was the visible representative on earth. "We know with sufficient certainty that every king of Israel, immediately upon his accession, was pledged to the existing fundamental laws of the kingdom; in token of which he was required, when the crown was placed on his head to lay above it a written copy of the Law, and with these sacred emblems to show himself to the people before he could be anointed."

Nor were these noble hopes and lofty aspirations entirely disappointed. It is true that none of the anointed kings of Israel fulfilled the grand ideal of the people, yet there sat on that strange throne, hallowed by such awful memories of Divine glory, "men"—to quote the great historian Ewald's words—"in whom many forms of royal and manly excellence were exemplified, and whose like would be vainly sought among other nations in those early times. Here only in all antiquity was the true ideal of monarchy persistently aimed at." Indeed, all history might be searched in vain for sovereigns uniting so many splendid qualities as did David and Solomon, Jehoshaphat and Hezekiah.

Nor, again, was the change to human kings reigning as vice-gerents of the Eternal King, politically speaking, a disappointment. From the hour when the patriot-statesman Samuel poured the anointing oil on the head of the young king Saul, the nation gradually rose in importance.

In, comparatively speaking, a very few years from the time when it had to fight with doubtful success for very existence with those warlike Phoenician peoples who dwelt, "a long thin line," along the sea-washed coasts of Syria and Canaan, Israel, under the iron sceptre of David, and the golden sceptre of Solomon, rose to the position of one of the foremost nations of the East. It shared with Assyria and Egypt the chief place among Oriental nations; indeed, for a time, under the wise and splendid rule of David and his son Solomon, it even overshadowed those two historic powers. Though Israel declined from its great power and influence with strange, sad rapidity, it lasted sufficiently long to stamp its influence for ever on well-nigh all future religious worship, true and false, on the art and literature of the future leading peoples in the far Western, as well as in Eastern lands.

EXCURSUS E: ON THE CITY OF GILGAL (chap. xiii.).

On the south-west bank of the River Jordan, a little to the north-east of the old famous Canaanitish fortress-city of Jericho, was pitched the fortified camp of Joshua at the time of the Israelitish invasion. From this place of arms his armies went forth to the conquest of the cities of Ai and Jericho, in the immediate neighbourhood, the first important captures in the promised land.

Gilgal then seems to have been the first spot where the conquering Israelites established themselves. Out of the fortified camp of Gilgal grew the city bearing the same name. During the whole period of the conquest of the land under Joshua, it seems to have been the regular place of assembly for the chiefs of the tribes, and to have been a kind of head-quarters for the host of Israel. There, too, the festival and sacred meetings appear at first certainly to have been held. (Comp. Joshua v. 10, ix. 6, x. 6, 7, 9, 15, 43, xiv. 6; Judges ii. 1.)

Ewald considers that, from the notices preserved in the Books of Samuel, in the days of that famous judge-seer it was one of the most sacred places in Israel, and the town centre of the whole people, and that its importance dates from the days of the conquest under Joshua. Although after the establishment of the monarchy, and the permanent fixing the seat of government and the residence of the sovereign at Jerusalem, where was also erected the Temple, Gilgal declined in importance, still, centuries later, in the times of Amos and Hosea, it appears to have been a sacred place, held in high regard by the people. (See Amos v. 5; Hos. iv. 15, ix. 15.)

I. SAMUEL.

EXCURSUS F: ON THE SIN AND REJECTION OF KING SAUL (chap. xiii.).

The conduct of Samuel in the matter of his separation from Saul has been often called into question. The old prophet, in his dealings with the king, has been accused of harshness and precipitancy, and even Saul's punishment by the Most High has been looked upon as severe and disproportioned to the offence. Instead of conceding or denying these hasty conclusions, it will be well to consider what this offence was which alienated the prophet, and brought so terrible a judgment on the great first king of Israel and his royal house.

The existence of Israel, and their prosperity as a people, was based alone on the peculiar favour and protection of the Eternal God. Out of the peoples of the globe, He chose them for a special purpose. They were to keep burning the lamp of the knowledge of the Most High amid the darkness of the idolatry and sin of the world. As long as they were faithful the Lord sustained them against all their adversaries. He enabled them to win a beautiful land; He maintained them securely there; to use the language of their own records, they dwelt safe under the shadow of the Almighty wings. God would have led them higher, and ever higher, had they for their part remained true and loyal. In a great crisis of their history the Eternal chose out Saul from among them, and made him ruler and His own vice-gerent on earth of His chosen people.

Now, as we have said, the conditions of the existence and prosperity of Israel were the favour and help of the invisible King. *With* these they prospered, and went on from strength to strength; *without* these their power withered away at once; the moment the Glorious Arm was removed Israel at once sank to the level, or even below the level, of the other peoples of the earth.

King Saul possessed many rare and noble qualities. He was brave to a fault, simple, modest, even deeply religious. He was gifted, too, with prudence and moderation, and was undoubtedly a wise and able general, but when raised to the throne, and in possession of supreme power, he totally mistook the position of Israel. He thought it had won its own way to freedom, and the possession of the rich and fruitful land in which they dwelt, and that it could, by the exercise of prudence and valour, maintain itself in its conquests, and even rise to be one of the powerful monarchies of the world. In other words, without despising or making light of the true King who had in truth raised up Israel from slavery, and made it an independent nation, Saul considered that the people over whom he had been called to rule could, if necessary, do without this supernatural assistance.

Acting upon this false conception of the true position of Israel, he reserved to himself the right to act in certain emergencies without the advice of the Eternal, communicated through that great prophet, who in those days was the mouth-piece of the Most High, or if he judged it better for the interest of the people, even in direct opposition to this supernatural advice or even positive commands. In other words, when King Saul failed to see the wisdom or policy of the "word of the Lord," communicated to him by the accredited seer of the Eternal, he declined to follow its dictates.

The Inspired compiler of this book has chosen out of the records of the first king's reign two memorable instances of this strange and obstinate self-will on the part of the king: the first, the declining to wait for the prophet at Gilgal till the specified time for his coming had expired; the second, the refusal to destroy the Amalekite king and the rich plunder taken from him.

To the superficial reader the special acts of Saul which are cited in these books as the immediate occasion of the separation of the prophet and the king, and of the doom pronounced upon Saul and his house, may seem trivial—quite incommensurate with the fatal consequences; they were, no doubt, as the great German commentator Ewald suggests, *isolated cases*, which received their true significance from a long series of connected events—*instances* which were selected as perhaps the best known of Saul's permanent disposition towards the invisible Guardian of Israel. [May not such considerations, applied to other events chronicled in Holy Writ, assist us in understanding much that is now dark and difficult — for instance, the terrible woe which followed on the plucking and eating of the forbidden fruit in Eden? It is likely that, owing to their rebellious and self-willed spirit, the father and mother of our race were banished from a life for which their self-will rendered them utterly unfit. The sin, of which we possess such ample details in the early Genesis story, was probably a solitary instance of the self-will and disobedience of our first parents to a loving and generous Creator. Many difficulties in the Bible story are capable of explanation, if we adopt some such considerations as these which we have lightly sketched out here.]

King Saul was fully and fairly tested. No doubt, the want of faith and implicit trust—the *first* requisite for a true child of Israel—which led to the disobedience of Gilgal, had been manifested before, on other and less conspicuous occasions. *This* was in the face of the people, and the long-suffering of the Eternal could not pass over so glaring and public a manifestation of the king's intention to loosen the links which bound together in Israel the visible and the invisible. It was a fatal example, which might only too quickly have been followed by many. So the prophet and friend of Saul at once pronounced the doom; but even then, Saul might have repented, and, had he chosen, might again have won the old favour and love of the Eternal King; but we know he did not choose, alas for Saul! The heart grieves over the fatal blindness of the gallant and patriotic king. Gilgal taught him nothing. We feel that the alienation between Israel's visible and invisible Kings grew with each succeeding year, till again, in the matter of the Amalekite booty, a still more public manifestation of Saul's determination never to submit his will to God's will drove the reluctant Samuel to pronounce in still more fateful words the doom of the disobedient, and to close for ever his friendship with the unhappy sovereign. The words of the great seer—the friend of God—uttered under the influence of the Spirit of the Lord, when he finally determined to bid farewell to Saul, sum up the sin and its punishment. (See chap. xv. 22, 23.)

I. SAMUEL.

EXCURSUS G: ON THE CONDUCT OF AGAG, KING OF AMALEK, WHEN SAMUEL SLEW HIM BEFORE THE LORD (chap. xv.).

Although, on the whole, we prefer the usual interpretation of this scene, which the English Version clearly suggests—viz., that Agag, finding that the warrior-king had spared him, ceased to have any apprehensions any longer for his life, and that when summoned into the presence of the old prophet, came in a comparatively happy and joyous state of mind, imagining that he was only to be presented in a formal manner to the chief religious official in Israel—still, there is another and most interesting interpretation of this singular scene, which has the support of the distinguished scholar and expositor, Ewald. This interpretation of the original understands that the conquered Amalekite monarch was fully aware that the summons into the presence of the dread seer meant a summons to death, and that, conscious of his impending doom, he braced himself up as a warrior-king to meet his end heroically with a smile. Agag then met his fate "with delight" (this is the word rendered in English *delicately*), and cries out, moved by a lofty, fearless impulse, "Surely the bitterness of death is past." This willingness to die on the part of the royal captive was regarded by the people as a happy omen; and *possibly*, if we adopt this interpretation of the episode, this was one of the reasons which had preserved the circumstances of the incident with such exact detail, for there was a deeply rooted persuasion among the ancients that if the victims resisted when led to the altar, the incident was one of evil omen.

Compare the words which Æschylus, in the *Agamemnon*, puts into Cassandra's mouth before her death. If we understand the words of Agag in the sense suggested in this Excursus, the captive Trojan princess met her death in a similar spirit.

Cassandra. I will dare to die . . . I pray that I may receive a mortal blow—and without a struggle . . . that I close my eyes.
Chorus. . . . If thou really art acquainted with thy doom, how comes it that, like a divinely-guided heifer, thou advancest so courageously to the altar?—*Agamemnon*, 1261–1269

EXCURSUS H: ON THE SCHOOLS OF THE PROPHETS (chap. xix.).

"Long before Plato had gathered his disciples round him in the Olive Grove, or Zeno in the Portico, these institutions (schools of the prophets) had sprung up under Samuel in Judæa." (Stanley.)

Before the days of Samuel the name of "prophet" very rarely occurs; incidentally the title is once given to Abraham (Gen. xx. 7), and Moses is on many occasions so styled. (See especially the great passage in Deut. xviii. 15—18, where he is made the type of the old order.) Aaron, too (but in relation to Moses), was also called a prophet. At rare intervals we meet with the name: for instance, in the days of Gideon (Judges vi. 8); and most probably in the reign of the high priest Eli (1 Sam. ii. 27), in the person of the "man of God" who brought the stern message to Shiloh, we have another rare example. There is one solitary instance in those early days of a woman bearing the honoured name—Deborah, the judge and prophetess (Judges iv. 4).

Samuel, however, was the true founder of the prophetic order. Samuel, the Prophet and the Seer, was the title by which this great and loved man was known not only in his own, but in all succeeding generations. There is no doubt but that one of the great works of Samuel's life was to call into existence "unions," or, as they have been subsequently termed, "schools of the prophets." We must not, however, conclude that all, or that even a large proportion of the people trained in these schools of Samuel were prophets in the sense of being able to make predictions, or even to write or speak as inspired men. This Divine gift, we must remember, was a gift of God, which He bestowed on whom He would. He, in His omniscience, knew who among men were fitted for this grave and important office.

But the trained in Samuel's "Naioth," in that school of his by Ramah—those known in later days as "Sons of the Prophets"—were taught the study of the Law and the story of the Divine guidance of Israel; they were most carefully trained in music and singing; and in these quiet homes of learning and religious exercises, the records of the past, we may be certain, were examined and copied with extreme care, and the materials out of which the Divine records were in after days compiled were, no doubt, there arranged and classified.

In Samuel's schools by Ramah, we may assume, were trained, under their renowned master, David, Gad, Nathan, Heman, and others whose names as writers, prophets, and teachers subsequently became famous after the days of Samuel, during the reigns of David and Solomon, and of the earlier kings of Israel and Judah. After the separation, prophets are frequently mentioned—sometimes by name, as in the case of Gad and Nathan—sometimes we hear of a nameless prophet. We have to wait, however, until the days of Elijah and Elisha before we meet with a further allusion to these prophetic schools. Under the general name of "Sons of the Prophets," these seminaries, or schools, appear in the times of these great prophets in several localities. Their numbers evidently were considerable. It is an indisputable fact that during the later years of the independent existence of the people, and also in the Captivity, and for a time after the return, the prophets exercised an enormous influence over the tribes.

We may, then, fairly assume that the new impulse given to religious education by Samuel was never suffered to die out, and that from his days onward the schools of the prophets flourished among the chosen people. The company of prophets gathered round Samuel in the Naioth by Ramah—the "Sons of the Prophets"—who acknowledged men like Elijah and Elisha as their revered masters, were the direct ancestors of the scribes and rabbis of later days.

When Samuel first founded the new order, there was, it must be remembered, an utter want of lofty spiritual teaching. The sanctuary of Shiloh had been destroyed, the Ark removed, the priesthood dishonoured and disgraced. Later, it is noticeable that it was in the northern kingdom of the ten tribes, in the provinces of which there was no temple, no priests, no sacrifice, where we find those great schools of the Sons of the

I. SAMUEL.

Prophets, under the presidency of men like Elijah and Elisha. The prophetic order then, in the first place, owed its creation to a want of all spiritual guidance and influence, when Eli was dead and Shiloh desecrated; and further on, its development and rapid increase among the northern tribes is plainly attributable to the fact of there being no temple and no priestly order outside Jerusalem.

EXCURSUS I: ON THE SO-CALLED OUTLAW LIFE OF DAVID (chap. xxii.).

From the scattered notices we possess in this book, in 2 Sam., and in 1 Chron., it is clear that the career of David during the period of his life when he was declared by the reigning sovereign, Saul, to be a public enemy, was not the career of a vulgar freebooter, to whom he has been often wrongly likened. To his standard, as we shall see, quickly gathered a number of illustrious men, among whom were found many of high lineage, as well as men famous for their military achievements; distinguished representatives, too, of the priestly and prophetic orders were also to be found at this wandering Court of the future illustrious king. Among the principal reasons which induced so many and such distinguished persons to associate themselves with David may be enumerated growing discontent with Saul's rule; his frequent inability, owing to the recurring paroxysms of his distressing mental malady, to conduct the affairs of the kingdom; his growing distrust of his friends, especially of his gallant son; the unfortunate favouritism he displayed towards the tribe of Benjamin—his *own* tribe; his relentless and, at the same time, groundless animosity against his bravest and most successful captain, David. There were not wanting evidently in the border warfare—a warfare which greatly contributed to his popularity among the people, which David almost ceaselessly carried on with Philistia during this period—romantic incidents which show us the character of David's soldiers, and which well illustrate the spirit of devotion to his person with which this great man was able to inspire his followers. On one occasion, for instance, in the course of a border foray, the son of Jesse, exhausted and wearied, was heard to express a longing for a drink of water from his own home spring at Bethlehem, then occupied by a Philistine garrison. Three of his generous and devoted followers, determined to gratify the longing of their loved chief, with a reckless bravery broke through the enemy's line, and fetched the coveted water. But David, we read, touched to the heart by such reckless gallantry and love, refused to drink it, but poured it out—that water, won at such risk—as an offering to the Lord. (See 1 Chron. xi. 16—19.)

In this little army of heroes eleven men of great renown are in one passage positively mentioned by name, so distinguished were they—men of great military experience, from the distant tribe of Gad—in the graphic words of the writer of the Chronicles, "warriors equipped with shield and spear, like lions in aspect, and yet speeding over the mountains with the swift foot of the gazelle." Four hundred men-at-arms—of course this does not include the younger armour-bearers and the like accompanying these veteran soldiers—are mentioned as joining the armed camp of David. These four hundred seem soon to have increased to six hundred. Extraordinary weight and dignity were added to his counsels by the presence of men like Gad, the prophet of the Lord, trained in the school of Samuel, and endowed with the rare gifts of a seer of the living God; and Abiathar, the son and successor by direct descent of the murdered high priest Ahimelech, who brought with him to the exile's camp the precious Urim and Thummim, the greatest treasures of the sacred Tabernacle, by means of which the "outlaw" David was placed in direct communication with Jehovah, the covenant God of Israel.

In this school of fighting men were trained those generals and wise strategists who in the golden days of David's rule commanded his armies, and raised Israel from the obscurity of an "Arab" tribe, who with difficulty held their own among the ancient Canaanites, to the position of one of the great nations of the old Eastern world.

I cannot forbear transcribing from the Talmud a curious note on "the four hundred warriors of David." This ancient tradition evidently bestows on these "fighting men-at-arms" who rallied round David in his days of exile and poverty, the splendour which perhaps subsequently surrounded the great king's body-guard when he reigned as a mighty prince in Jerusalem over Canaan and the surrounding nations. "David had four hundred young men, handsome in appearance, and with their hair cut close upon their foreheads, but with long flowing curls behind, who used to ride in chariots of gold at the head of the army. These were men of power, the mighty men of the house of David, who went about to strike terror into the world."—Babylonian Talmud, Treatise *Kiddushin*, fol. 76, col. 2.

It is most probable that a corps of *élite*, in memory of the original "four hundred" of the days of the king's wanderings, was established when David possessed a powerful standing army.

EXCURSUS J: ON THE ESPECIAL VALUE OF THE EPISODE OF ABIGAIL AND NABAL (chap. xxv.).

We perhaps ask, What were the reasons which induced the inspired compiler of these records of the history of Israel, among the materials, no doubt, present in abundance to his hand, to relate the especial episode contained in this chapter in such detail of the life of David when chief of an outlaw band? The incidents seem at first sight trivial, scarcely worthy the important place they occupy in the Book of Samuel, and they certainly were not chosen with a view to exalt David's character.

In a singularly vivid way, however, they picture the future king's life during those days of temptation and anxiety, and show how well he used his position to win the affections of the people as chieftain of a powerful and somewhat reckless band. He seems to have acted as the protector and generous helper of all scattered dwellers in the southern part of Canaan. In a former chapter—in his rescue of the men of Keilah—it was *the corn growers*; in this section it is *a great sheep-master* whose herds and flocks he is represented

I. SAMUEL.

as having long protected. The people during the latter years of King Saul's reign were terribly exposed, not only to the Philistine encroachments, but also to the repeated and destructive forays of the powerful nomadic tribes bordering on the "Land of Promise." Another reason which seems to have induced the selection of this episode of Nabal and Abigail is supplied by the character of Abigail, who represents evidently a type of the Hebrew woman of the higher classes of that period. The influence of the schools of the prophets instituted by Samuel and of the prophetic order had already begun to be felt, and the result was that a loftier tone of morality and nobler and higher views of life began to be cultivated through the people. Abigail had doubtless learned her beautiful creed, her implicit trust in the Eternal Friend of Israel, her clear perception of truth and honour, from the Ramah schools of Samuel the seer.

But if we read carefully between the lines of the seemingly simple, almost childish, story, there is yet another reason for its having been selected by the Divinely helped compiler as a portion of the book which is to endure for ever. The question of the future life—*the life*, after death has dissolved the union between soul and body—is but little dwelt on in the earlier of the Divine records. God's revelation here was gradual. It is true that from the earliest chapters of Genesis the glorious hope of an endless life with God casts its bright light upon the present dark and shadowed existence; but still, comparatively little information seems to have been given even to the patriarchs on this subject. It was *there* certainly; a glorious hereafter lay in the far background of the present life, but no more seems to have been taught. In the words of Abigail to David there is, however, an indication that already a distinct advance had been made in Divine revelation on this subject. In the Notes on verse 29 of this chapter, the bearing of Abigail's words on the future of the human soul and on the question of the eternal life are discussed. It is more than strange how modern Christian commentators have missed the momentous teaching of the words in question. They would have done wisely had they searched a little among the great Hebrew commentators, who, as might be expected, in a passage where their eyes were not blinded by any false national prejudices, have caught the true meaning, and seen something of the extraordinary beauty of the teaching, scarcely veiled by the homeliness of the imagery. The presence of this passage (in verse 29) *especially*, I venture to think, influenced the compiler of the Books of Samuel to insert the Nabal and Abigail episode in his history.

EXCURSUS K: ON THE WORK OF SAMUEL (chap. xxv.).

After the death of Eli, the capture of the Ark, and the sack of Shiloh—the old religious capital of the land, and the residence for many years of the high priest and judge—the fortunes of Israel were at their lowest ebb. There was no Sanctuary, no religious life among the people. The Law of Moses was, save by a few scattered families, almost forgotten. Its precepts, as well as its moral ceremonies, were wholly ignored, and with the religious life the national life was quickly dying altogether out of Israel. It appeared to be the destiny of the people soon to be swallowed up among the Philistines and other native peoples. From this abyss of degradation Samuel raised the tribes. (1) He kept alive and fanned the dying spark of the old love of Israel for their God. (2) Instead of restoring the fallen Sanctuary and the elaborate system of ceremonial religion, he created the Prophetic Schools, whose work was to teach Israel who and what they really were—the chosen people—and for what high ends they had been so strangely favoured and assisted; and so he led the people back to God. (3) As the old religious life was slowly awakened out of its deadly torpor, the old national life seemed at the same time also to awaken. In Israel the latter was necessarily inseparable from the former. Then Samuel gave them a king to consolidate their national life, which had almost ceased to exist. The scattered tribes, as they awoke to the knowledge of that mighty God who loved them so well, were taught by the presence of a king that they were one nation, and that from Dan to Beersheba they had one common interest, one common work. The restoration of the Sanctuary and the ceremonial religion was also necessary, but it must be a later work, and one which could only follow the national and religious restoration of Samuel. This was accomplished by Samuel's pupil, David.

EXCURSUS L: ON WHAT HAPPENED AT EN-DOR? (chap. xxviii.).

In all times the question taken as the title of this Excursus has excited deep interest—*What happened at En-dor?* We will divide our general question into three parts.

(1) Did Samuel, the prophet of the Lord, really appear? and if so, what power brought him up from the realm of departed spirits?

(2) Granting that something did *appear* and *speak*, can we assume that the appearance was not Samuel, but a demon or evil spirit assuming Samuel's name?

(3) Is it possible that there was no appearance at all, and that the whole scene was a well-played piece of jugglery on the part of the woman? or, in other words, that the whole scene was merely a delusion produced by the woman, without any background at all.

On the *last* (No. 3), which assumes the whole scene at En-dor to have been a piece of jugglery on the part of the woman, we may observe that it is an hypothesis adopted by some great names, apparently by the illustrious Jewish commentator, Maimonides, who wrote in the twelfth century after Christ; by the majority of the less orthodox modern writers from the seventeenth century downwards, and even by such true divines and scholars as Dean Payne Smith It is, however, a purely *modern* hypothesis, and receives no support from the early Church writers. Dean Payne Smith admirably puts forth the best arguments employed by the defenders of this supposition in these words: "We cannot believe that the Bible would set before us an instance of witchcraft employed by the Divine sanction for holy purposes; but we can clearly

I. SAMUEL.

believe that the woman would gladly take a bitter revenge on the man who had cruelly put to death all persons reported to have such powers as those to which she laid claim . . . . She reproached him for these crimes, announced to him what now all were convinced of, that David was to be his successor, and foretold his defeat and death."—Dean Payne Smith, in *Pulpit Commentary* on 1 Sam. xxviii. 17—19. No. 2 assumes that there was an apparition, but that what appeared was not Samuel, but an evil spirit, which showed itself in the character of Samuel. Not a few of the fathers, with the great Protestant reformers, such as Luther and Calvin, have preferred this view. Ephrem Syrus explains the phenomenon by stating that "an apparent image of Samuel was presented to the eye of Saul through demoniacal arts." Luther plainly writes: "The raising of Samuel by a soothsayer, or witch, in 1 Sam. xxviii. 11, 12, was certainly merely a spectre of the devil . . . for who could believe that the souls of believers which are in the hand of God (Eccles. iii. 1), and in the bosom of Abraham (Luke xvi. 23), were under the power of the devil and of simple men?"—Luther, *Abuses of the Mass*, 1522. Calvin similarly tells us: "It is certain that it was not really Samuel, for God would never have allowed His prophets to be subject to such diabolical conjuring. For here is a sorceress calling up the dead from the grave."—Calvin, *Hom*. 100, in 1 Sam. No. 1 still remains. Did the spirit of Samuel the prophet himself really appear in the witch of En-dor's house to Saul? Now, without doubt, the ordinary reader would so understand the history. Everything *before* and *after* the incident is simple and natural. The woman herself is appalled at the sight, whatever it was, and describes it as resembling the dead seer. Whether or not Saul saw the spectre is uncertain, but he certainly heard the voice, which spoke a too true and mournful prophecy: nothing fierce or vindictive, as we have noticed in our comments on the scene—rather the contrary. The words, so simple and gentle, and yet unutterably sad, *were no mere words of a juggling old woman*; still less were they the utterances of an evil or malicious spirit.

We thus confess our full belief that the shade of Samuel was seen by the woman (perhaps by Saul; but this is uncertain from the narrative), and that his voice was certainly heard by King Saul; and this has been the common belief in all times. Bishop Wordsworth's note here is most learned and exhaustive, and he fully endorses this view (here styled No. 1). The bishop marshals an array of witnesses who support this, which I venture to call the plain, common sense interpretation of the history. He begins with the ancient Hebrew Church, and quotes Ecclus. xlvi. 20. The writer of that book evidently believed that Samuel himself appeared; and so did the LXX., who plainly express the belief in their addendum to the Hebrew text at 1 Chron. x. 13. Josephus affirms the same in *Antt*. vi., 14, 2. Among the early Christian fathers, Justin Martyr, *Trypho*, § 105; Origen, tom. II., 490—495; St. Ambrose *in Luc*, chap. i.; St. Basil, *Ep.* 80; St. Gregory Naz., *Orat*. III.; Theodoret, *Qu*. 63, hold the same belief that the shade of Samuel appeared at En-dor and spoke to Saul. Among the famous mediæval writers holding the same view, we may instance Cajetan, Lyra, and à Lapide; later, Waterland may be added to the list; in our own days, Bishop Hervey, in the *Speaker's Commentary*, and Bishop Wordsworth and the German writers, O. von Gerlach and Keil. Assuming, then, that the soul of Samuel did appear on earth that night at En-dor, we have still to deal with the question: By what power was he brought up from the realm of departed spirits? Here the narrative if carefully read, will supply us with the correct answer. Far from having herself, by any incantation she had used, brought Samuel back again to earth, the witch is represented as crying with a loud voice from very terror when the shade of the prophet appeared, so little apparently was she prepared for what she saw. We may, therefore, with Theodoret, dismiss the idea as unholy, and even impious, that the witch of En-dor, by any power or incantation of which she was mistress, conjured up the prophet Samuel; and we may affirm with considerable certainty that it was by the special command of God that he came that night to speak with King Saul at En-dor. Keil and Bishops Hervey and Wordsworth all agree in the main with this theory.

The above conclusions respecting the reality of the circumstance detailed in this remarkable episode in the history of Saul being, as we have seen, in strict harmony with the judgment of the ancient Hebrew Church (comp. the passage referred to above from Ecclus. xlvi. 20; the LXX. addition to 1 Chron. x. 13; Jos. *Antt*. vi. 14, § 2, besides the general sense of the more mysterious comments in the Talmud), are a most important contribution to our knowledge of the ancient Hebrew teaching concerning the state of the soul after death in the earliest Prophetic Schools, as early as the reigns of Saul, David, and Solomon.

We gather, then, that these old Hebrews held that *after death* the soul continued in a state of self-conscious existence; that it was capable of feeling and expressing grief and sorrow; that it retained the memory of transactions in which it had taken part when on earth; that it was—at least, in the case of a servant of God like Samuel—in a state of rest, from which it evidently had no wish to be summoned to share again in the fret and fever of this life—"Why hast thou disquieted me to bring me up?"

Of the *abode* of the souls of the departed we can gather but little from this passage. It was evidently not Heaven—the Heaven where is the throne of God, and where dwell the heavenly powers. The language used, though popular, and adapted to the ordinary conception of Sheol, or Hades, the unseen place or lodging of the disembodied souls of men, clearly distinguishes between the abode of souls like Samuel and the abode of the heavenly powers. Throughout the history the soul of Samuel is represented as *coming up*, instead of *coming down* or descending, which would be the popular language used of an angel of God.

The testimony which this history gives to the ancient Jewish belief in the existence of the soul after death fully accounts for the prominence which the compiler of the book has given to this episode. It is, besides, an important contribution to our knowledge of the complex character of the first great Hebrew monarch, so splendidly endowed by God, tried, and, alas! found wanting. The En-dor incident, besides, clearly and incisively gives us God's judgment on necromancy, and generally on all attempts to hold converse with the souls of the departed.

In every age these attempts have had an extraordinary fascination for men. In our own day necromancy, unfortunately, is not a lost art among ourselves. Men and women of education, as Dr. Fraser well observes in the *Pulpit Commentary*, are not ashamed or afraid

I. SAMUEL.

to practise arts and consult "mediums" that are referred to in the Old Testament as abhorrent to God, and utterly forbidden to His people.

> "How pure in heart and sound in head,
> With what Divine affection bold,
> Should be the man whose thought would hold,
> An hour's communion with the dead.

> "In vain shalt thou on any call
> The spirits from their golden day,
> Except, like them, thou too canst say,
> My spirit is at peace with all.

> "They haunt the silence of the breast,
> Imaginations calm and fair,
> The memory like a cloudless air,
> The conscience as a sea at rest."—TENNYSON.

EXCURSUS M: ON THE URIM AND THUMMIM (chap. xxx.).

We read in the description of the high priest's official vestments (Exod. xxviii. 2—32), that over the ephod there was to be a "breastplate of judgment," of gold, scarlet, purple, and fine linen, folded square and doubled, a span in length and width. In it were to be set four rows of precious stones, each stone with the name of a tribe of Israel engraved on it, that Aaron might "bear them upon his heart." Inside the breastplate were to be placed the Urim and Thummim (the Light and the Perfection), and they, too, were to be on Aaron's heart as he went in before the Lord.

What, now, were these mysterious gems? for that they were precious stones of some kind nearly all tradition seems agreed. Among the best supported traditional notices—quoted by Dean Plumptre in his learned article in Smith's *Dictionary of the Bible*—the following are the usually accepted ones.

(*a*) The Urim and Thummim "were identical with the twelve stones on which the names of the tribes of Israel were engraved, and the mode in which an oracle was given was by the illumination, simultaneous or successive, of the letters which were to make up the answer" (Jalkut Sifre, Zohar, *in Exod.*, f. 105; Maimonides, R. ben Nachman, *in Buxtorf, l.c.*). Josephus (*Antiq.* iii. 7, § 5) adopts another form of the same story, and, apparently identifying the Urim and Thummim with the sardonyxes on the shoulders of the ephod, says that they were bright before a victory or when the sacrifice was acceptable, dark when any disaster was impending. Epiphanius (*de xii. gemm.*) and the writer quoted by Suidas present the same thought in yet another form. A single diamond placed in the centre of the breastplate prognosticated peace when it was bright, war when it was red, death when it was dusky.

(*b*) In the middle of the ephod, or within its folds, there was a stone or plate of gold, on which was engraved the sacred name of Jehovah, the *Shem-hammephorash* of Jewish cabbalists; and by virtue of this, the High Priest, fixing his gaze on it, or reading an invocation which was also engraved with the name, or standing in his ephod before the mercy-seat, or, at least, before the veil of the Sanctuary, became capable of prophesying, hearing the Divine voice within, or listening to it as it proceeded, in articulated sounds, from the glory of the Shechinah (Buxtorf, *l.c.*, 7; Lightfoot, vi. 278; Braunius, *de Vestitu Hebr.*, ii.; Saalschütz, *Archäolog.*, ii 363).

That mighty storehouse of learning and tradition, the Babylonian Talmud, suggests, however, another and quite a different explanation of this mysterious and sacred possession of the Israelites in the earlier days of their existence as a people. (See note on verse 7 of chapter xxx.)

The Talmud begins by explaining why the oracle was called Urim and Thummim. It is called Urim because it gave explanatory light to its utterances; and it is called Thummim because it made perfect and complete its declarations.

How did the Urim and Thummim indicate or manifest its utterances? Rabbi Yochanan saith: *Boltoth* (by means of) *projection*. Resh Lakish saith: *Mitztaphoth* (by means of) *transposition*.

(1) *Boltoth* (by means of *projection*).—The several letters that were intended by the oracle to form the word or words in reply to an enquiry were raised from concave to convex (as the *engraved* letters on a seal were to become *raised* letters, as on a coin), and the priest, uniting these projected letters, thus ascertained the proper meaning of the intended answer, which he delivered to the enquirer. For instance: in the reply to David, *äleh*—"go;" the *ayin* in Simeon, the *lamedh* in Levi, and the *he* in Judah become *prominently raised*, and thus the answer was unmistakable.

(2) *Mitztaphoth* (by means of *transposition*).—The letters composing the names of the twelve tribes *transposed themselves into words*, which indicated the oracle's reply. But it is objected: How could the oracle express 1 Sam. xxx. 8 (*i.e.*, "Thou shalt without fail recover all"), since the letter *tsadde*, for instance, is not to be found in any of the names of the tribes? nor is the letter *teth* to be found there either. To this it is responded that Abraham, Isaac, and Jacob were engraved on the gems, as also the Hebrew words signifying "the tribes of Jeshurun."

Thus the Hebrew alphabet in the Urim and Thummim is made complete.—Treatise *Yoma*, fol. 73, cols. 1 and 2.

INTRODUCTION
TO
THE SECOND BOOK OF SAMUEL

The period embraced in this book may be roughly described as the forty years of the reign of David. The book opens immediately upon the death of Saul, a few days before David ascended the throne, and it closes while David was still living, though "old and stricken in years." It was an eventful period in Israel's history. David came to the throne immediately after the crushing defeat of Saul by the Philistines, and when almost the whole land was held in their grasp; and when the tribes of Israel were at variance with one another, and for seven and a half years refused to unite in the recognition of a common monarch. But at David's death the enemies of Israel had been subdued on every side, and he transmitted to Solomon an united empire, extending from "the river of Egypt" to the Euphrates, and from the Red Sea to Lebanon. The maritime nations of the Phœnicians alone appear not to have been conquered, but they were united to the Israelites in the closest bonds of friendship, and assisted both David and his successor in their works. The religious development of the people received a great impulse from the piety of the monarch and the influence of his sacred poetry. The outward observances of religion shone forth indeed with more splendour in the early part of the succeeding reign of Solomon; but at no period was there a more earnest effort to conduct the affairs of the nation on religious principles, or a truer devotion on the part of their ruler. Moreover, the services of the sanctuary were systematically arranged, and sacred song made prominent in them; the priesthood was had in honour; and abundant material and wealth were accumulated for the future building of the Temple.

David himself, the hero of the book, was a man to attract attention in any age of the world. Raised from the sheepfold of Bethlehem to a throne, tried by every vicissitude of great prosperity and great adversity, a man of noble presence and warlike prowess, of such physical power as to be able to wield the sword of Goliath, of such skill upon the harp as to be chosen to allay the paroxysms of Saul's insanity, of high literary culture and poetic inspiration, witnessed by the psalms of his composition, of such fervent piety as to be called of God "a man after my own heart," yet he was withal eminently "a man of affairs," a skilful general, a wise statesman, and possessed of that personal magnetism by which all who came under his influence were deeply and permanently attached to him. He was also a man of strong natural passions, which, although generally kept under control, yet led him at times to the commission of grievous sins from which both he and his people suffered severely. There was also a strain of weakness in his character. His domestic affections were indulged to the neglect of positive duties, and caused grave troubles and crimes in his household. The latter part of his reign was disturbed by formidable rebellions. He failed to deal with some of his powerful subjects as he knew that justice required. The period treated in this book is altogether a chequered one, presenting a history of earnest piety, of outrageous sin, and of deep repentance; of great prosperity and unusual blessings on the one hand, and of severe afflictions and punishments on the other. Nevertheless, it was, on the whole, a period of marked advance in both religious development and earthly prosperity, and it cannot fail to reward the most careful study.

The great prophet Samuel had now passed to his rest, but David's early intercourse with him must have remained vividly in his memory, and his life and government was doubtless largely influenced by the prophet's counsels. The "schools of the prophets," founded by him, were still flourishing, and it may have been in them that Gad and Nathan and Iddo were trained.

This is not the place to speak of the date and authorship of the book, since it is simply a continuation of the First Book of Samuel. Only it is not to be forgotten that the original documents from which it was compiled must have been somewhat later—in accordance with the events to which they relate. The literature in relation to the two books is essentially the same.

THE SECOND BOOK OF SAMUEL
OTHERWISE CALLED
THE SECOND BOOK OF THE KINGS

CHAPTER I.—⁽¹⁾ Now it came to pass after the death of Saul, when David was returned from ^athe slaughter of the Amalekites, and David had abode two days in Ziklag; ⁽²⁾ it came even to pass on the third day, that, behold, a man came out of the camp from Saul with his clothes rent, and earth upon his head: and so it was, when he came to David, that he fell to the earth, and did obeisance. ⁽³⁾ And David said unto him, From whence comest thou? And he said unto him, Out of the camp of Israel am I escaped. ⁽⁴⁾ And David said unto him, ¹How went the matter? I pray thee, tell me. And he answered, That the people are fled from the battle, and many of the people also are fallen and dead; and Saul and Jonathan his son are dead also. ⁽⁵⁾ And David said unto the young man that told him, How knowest thou that Saul and Jonathan his son be dead? ⁽⁶⁾ And the young man that told him said, As I happened by chance upon mount Gilboa, behold, Saul leaned upon his spear; and, lo, the chariots and horsemen followed hard after him. ⁽⁷⁾ And when he looked behind him, he saw me, and called unto me. And I answered, ²Here am I. ⁽⁸⁾ And he said unto me, Who *art* thou? And I answered him, I

B.C. cir. 1056.

a 1 Sam. 30. 17.

¹ Heb., *What was, &c.*

² Heb., *Behold me.*

At the moment when this book opens, the events narrated in 1 Sam. xxxi. were not known to David. At the time of the fatal battle between Saul and the Philistines, David had been engaged in his successful attack upon the Amalekites who had spoiled Ziklag (1 Sam. xxx.) and it was not until two days after his return (verse 2) that the news reached him.

⁽¹⁾ **After the death of Saul.**—These words are immediately connected with 1 Sam. xxxi., and the following words, "when David was returned," refer to 1 Sam. xxx. The two books really form one continuous narrative.

Two days in Ziklag.—The site of Ziklag has not been exactly identified, but it is mentioned in Josh. xix. 5 as one of the cities in the extreme south, at first assigned to Judah, but afterwards given to Simeon. It is also spoken of in connection with Beersheba and other places of the south as re-occupied by the Jews on their return from Babylon (Neh. xi. 28). Its most probable locality is some ten or twelve miles south of Beersheba, and nearly equidistant from the Mediterranean and the Dead Sea. It was thus quite four days' journey from Mount Gilboa, and the messenger who brought the news of the battle must have left the field before David's return to Ziklag.

⁽²⁾ **On the third day**—viz., after David's return, not the third day after Saul's death.

Did obeisance.—The following verses show that this was not merely an act of Oriental respect, but was intended as a recognition of David's rank as having now become king. The messenger, although an Amalekite (verses 8, 13), had earth upon his head and his clothes rent as marks of sorrow for the defeat of David's people, and the death of their king.

⁽³⁾ **Out of the camp of Israel.**—It has been questioned whether this Amalekite had actually been in the army of Israel, and the expression in verse 6, "As I happened by chance upon Mount Gilboa," has been cited to show that his presence there was merely accidental, but no one who is not concerned in the matter is likely to stray into the midst of a battle, and the expression "by chance" is better referred to his coming upon Saul when he was wounded. He certainly here claims to have been a part of the "camp of Israel." He tells David the general facts of the defeat, and the death of Saul and Jonathan, as they really occurred.

⁽⁶⁾ **Upon mount Gilboa.**—The battle appears to have been joined in the plain of Jezreel, but when the Israelites were routed they naturally fled up the mountain range of Gilboa, though apparently much scattered. It was in this straggling flight that the Amalekite happened upon that part of the mountain where Saul was. The true account of the death of Saul is given in 1 Sam. xxxi. 3—6. (See Note on verse 10.) It is uncertain whether the man saw Saul at all before his death, and it is extremely unlikely that he found him without warriors or armour-bearer, wounded and alone.

⁽⁸⁾ **An Amalekite.**—The Amalekites were hereditary foes of Israel, having attacked them on their first coming out of Egypt (Ex. xvii. 8—13), and at different times afterwards in the wilderness (Num. xix. 45; Deut. xxv. 18). During the period of the judges they had also repeatedly joined the foes of Israel (Judges iii. 13; vi. 3), but some years before this they had been terribly defeated by Saul (1 Sam. xv. 4—9), and it is possible that the present messenger may either have attached himself to the army of the conqueror, or have been compelled, according to ancient custom, to serve in its ranks. One of their bands had also just received

The Amalekite, who brought news   II. SAMUEL, I.   *of Saul's Death, is Slain.*

am an Amalekite. ⁽⁹⁾ He said unto me again, Stand, I pray thee, upon me, and slay me: for ¹anguish is come upon me, because my life *is* yet whole in me. ⁽¹⁰⁾ So I stood upon him, and slew him, because I was sure that he could not live after that he was fallen: and I took the crown that *was* upon his head, and the bracelet that *was* on his arm, and have brought them hither unto my lord. ⁽¹¹⁾ Then David took hold on his clothes, and *ª*rent them; and likewise all the men that *were* with him: ⁽¹²⁾ and they mourned, and wept, and fasted until even, for Saul, and for Jonathan his son, and for the people of the LORD, and for the house of Israel; because they were fallen by the sword.

⁽¹³⁾ And David said unto the young man that told him, Whence *art* thou? And he answered, I *am* the son of a stranger, an Amalekite. ⁽¹⁴⁾ And David said unto him, *ᵇ*How wast thou not afraid to stretch forth thine hand to destroy the LORD's anointed? ⁽¹⁵⁾ And David called one of the young men, and said, Go near, *and* fall upon him. And he smote him that he died. ⁽¹⁶⁾ And David said unto him, Thy blood *be* upon thy head; for thy mouth hath testified against thee, saying, I have slain the LORD's anointed.

⁽¹⁷⁾ And David lamented with this lamentation over Saul and over Jonathan his son: ⁽¹⁸⁾ (also he bade them teach the children of Judah *the use of*

1 Or, *my coat of mail, or, my embroidered coat hindereth me, that my; &c.*

a ch. 3. 31 & 13. 31.

b Ps. 105. 15.

---

a severe blow at the hands of David, but of this last attack the Amalekite could have known.

⁽⁹⁾ **Anguish is come upon me.**—The word for "anguish" occurs only here, and probably does not have either of the meanings given to it in the text and margin of our version. The Rabbis explain it of *cramp*, others of *giddiness*, and the ancient versions differ as to its sense. It indicates probably some effect of his wound which incapacitated him for further combat.

⁽¹⁰⁾ **Slew him.**—This story is inconsistent with that given in 1 Sam. xxxi. 4, 5, and was evidently invented by the Amalekite to gain favour with David. At the same time, he is careful not to carry the story too far, and asserts that Saul was only put to death at his own request, and after being mortally wounded. However, he must have been one of the first to find the body of Saul after his death, since he brought his crown and bracelet to David—a *primâ facie* evidence of the truth of his whole story. The offering of these emblems of royalty shows that the Amalekite recognised David as the future king, a recognition which most of the tribes of Israel were unwilling to make for a long time.

⁽¹²⁾ **They mourned.**—On hearing the tidings of the Amalekite, David and all his people showed the usual Oriental signs of sorrow by rending their clothes, weeping, and fasting. Although David thus heard of the death of his persistent and mortal enemy, and of his own consequent accession to the throne, yet there is not the slightest reason to doubt the reality and earnestness of his mourning. The whole narrative shows that David not only, as a patriotic Israelite, lamented the death of the king, but also felt a personal attachment to Saul, notwithstanding his long and unreasonable hostility. But Saul did not die alone; Jonathan, David's most cherished friend, fell with him. At the same time, the whole nation over which David was hereafter to reign received a crushing defeat from their foes, and large numbers of his countrymen were slain. It has been well remarked that the only deep mourning for Saul, with the exception of the men of Jabesh-gilead, came from the man whom he had hated and persecuted as long as he lived.

The people of the Lord.—Besides his personal grief, David had both a religious and a patriotic ground for sorrow. The men who had fallen were parts of that Church of God which he so earnestly loved and served, and were also members of the commonwealth of Israel, on whose behalf he ever laboured with patriotic devotion. The LXX., overlooking this distinction, has very unnecessarily changed "people of the Lord" into "people of Judah."

⁽¹⁴⁾ **How wast thou not afraid?**—David now turns to the Amalekite. It does not matter whether he fully believed his story or not, the man must be judged by his own account of himself. (See verse 16.) Regicide was not in David's eyes merely a political crime; he had showed on more than one occasion of great temptation (1 Sam. xxiv. 6; xxvi. 9, 11, 16) that he considered taking the life of "the Lord's anointed" as a religious offence of the greatest magnitude. It was an especially grievous thing for a foreigner and an Amalekite thus to smite him whom God had appointed as the monarch of Israel.

⁽¹⁵⁾ **Fall upon him.**—All question of David's authority to pronounce a capital sentence is here quite out of place. The Amalekite had just recognised him as king, and therefore acknowledged his authority. But, besides this, David and his band of 600 outlaws were accustomed to live by the sword, and to defend themselves against Philistines, Amalekites, and other foes as best they could; and here stood before them one, by his own confession, guilty of high treason.

⁽¹⁷⁾ **Lamented with this lamentation.**—This is the technical expression for a funeral dirge or elegy, such as David also composed on the death of Abner (chap. iii. 33, 34), and Jeremiah on the death of Josiah (2 Chron. xxxv. 25). It is the only instance preserved to us (except the few lines on the death of Abner) of David's secular poetry. "It is one of the finest odes of the Old Testament, full of lofty sentiment, and springing from deep and sanctified emotion, in which, without the slightest allusion to his own relation to the fallen king, David celebrates without envy the bravery and virtues of Saul and his son Jonathan, and bitterly laments their loss." (Keil.)

⁽¹⁸⁾ **The use of the bow.**—The words in italics, *the use of,* are not in the original, and should be omitted. David "bade them teach the children of Judah the bow": *i.e.,* the following dirge called "the bow," not merely from the allusion to Jonathan's bow in verse 22, but because it is a martial ode, and the bow

the bow: behold, *it is* written ᵃin the book ¹of Jasher.)

(19) The beauty of Israel is slain upon thy high places: how are the mighty fallen! (20) ᵇTell *it* not in Gath, publish *it* not in the streets of Askelon; lest the daughters of the Philistines rejoice, lest the daughters of the uncircumcised triumph. (21) Ye mountains of Gilboa, *let there be* no dew, neither *let there be* rain, upon you, nor fields of offerings: for there the shield of the mighty is vilely cast away, the shield of Saul, *as though he had* not *been* anointed with oil. (22) From the blood of the slain, from the fat of the mighty, the bow of Jonathan turned not back, and the sword of Saul returned not empty. (23) Saul and Jonathan were lovely and ²pleasant in their lives, and in their death they were not divided: they were swifter than eagles, they were stronger than lions. (24) Ye daughters of Israel, weep over Saul, who clothed you in scarlet, with *other* delights, who put on ornaments of gold upon your apparel. (25) How are the mighty fallen in the midst of the battle! O Jonathan, *thou wast* slain in thine high places. (26) I am distressed for thee, my brother Jonathan: very pleasant hast thou been unto me: thy love to me was wonderful, passing the love of women. (27) How are the mighty fallen, and the weapons of war perished!

ᵃ Josh. 10. 13.

¹ Or, *of the upright*.

ᵇ Mic. 1. 10.

² Or, *sweet*.

---

was one of the chief weapons of the time with which the Benjamites were particularly skilful (1 Chron. xii. 2; 2 Chron. xiv. 8; xvii. 17). The word is omitted in the Vatican LXX. He taught this song to "the children of Judah" rather than to all Israel, because for the following seven and a half years, while the memory of Saul was fresh, he reigned only over Judah and Benjamin.

In the book of Jasher.—This book is also referred to in Josh. x. 13, and nothing more is really known about it, although it has been the subject of endless discussion and speculation. It is supposed to have been a collection of songs relating to memorable events and men in the early history of Israel, and it appears that this elegy was included among them.

The song is in two parts, the first relating to both Saul and Jonathan (verses 19—24), the second to Jonathan alone (verses 25, 26), each having at the beginning the lament, "How are the mighty fallen!" and the whole closing with the same refrain (verse 27).

(19) **The beauty of Israel,** in the sense of the glory or ornament of Israel, referring to Saul and Jonathan. The rendering of the Syriac and some commentators, "the gazelle," as a poetic name for Jonathan, is uncalled for, both because the words are spoken of Saul and Jonathan together, and because there is no evidence elsewhere that Jonathan was so called, nor is there any allusion to him under this figure in the song.

Upon thy high places.—Comp. verses 21, 25. This line may be considered as the superscription of the whole song.

(20) **In Gath . . . in the streets of Askelon.**—Two chief cities of the Philistines, poetically put for the whole. In the former David had himself resided (1 Sam. xxi. 10; xxvii. 3, 4), and in the latter was a famous temple of Venus, which was doubtless "the house of Ashtaroth" (1 Sam. xxxi. 10), where the Philistines put the armour of Saul. "Tell it not in Gath" appears to have become a proverb. (See Micah i. 10.)

Lest the daughters of the Philistines.—It was customary for women to celebrate national deliverances and victories (Exod. xv. 21; 1 Sam. xviii. 6). The word *uncircumcised* might be applied to the heathen generally, but it so happens that, with the exception of Gen. xxxiv. 14, it is used in the historical books only of the Philistines (Judg. xiv. 3; xv. 18; 1 Sam. xiv. 6; xvii. 26, 36; xxxi. 4; 1 Chron. x. 4).

(21) **Nor fields of offerings.**—This somewhat obscure expression seems to mean, "Let there not be upon you those fruitful fields from which may be gathered the offerings of first-fruits." Of course, this malediction upon the mountains of Gilboa is to be understood as it was meant, only in a poetical sense.

Vilely cast away.—Another sense of this word is *defiled*. The ancient versions, as well as modern commentators, adopt some one, and some the other meaning, either of which is appropriate.

As though he had not been anointed.—This translation follows the Vulg., and makes a good sense = as though Saul had not been a king; but it is more than doubtful if the original can bear this construction. There is no pronoun in the Hebrew, and the word "anointed" refers to the shield, "the shield of Saul not anointed with oil." It was customary to oil metal shields, as well as those of wood and leather, for their preservation, and the idea here is that Saul's shield was thrown away uncared for.

(23) **Lovely and pleasant.**—This applies peculiarly to Jonathan, but also in a good degree to Saul in his earlier years and his better moments, which David chose at this moment to recall. It also applies truthfully to them both in their relations to each other.

(24) **Clothed you in scarlet.**—This refers to Saul's division among the people of the spoil of his conquered foes, and to the prosperity resulting from his many successful campaigns. Notwithstanding that his light at last went out under the cloud of a crushing defeat, he had been on the whole a successful warrior. The Philistines, the Ammonites, the Amalekites, and others, had felt the power of his arm, and the relations of Israel to the surrounding nations had been wonderfully changed for the better during his reign.

(26) **Passing the love of women.**—By this strong expression, comparing Jonathan's love for David to that of the faithful wife for her husband, David shows his appreciation of that wonderful affection which had existed between Jonathan and himself under the most untoward circumstances. It was such an affection as could only exist between noble natures and those united in the fear of God. In these last verses of the elegy, which relate to Jonathan alone, David has given expression to his own personal sorrow.

David made King.   **II. SAMUEL, II.**   *He commends the men of Jabesh-gilead.*

CHAPTER II.—⁽¹⁾ And it came to pass after this, that David enquired of the LORD, saying, Shall I go up into any of the cities of Judah? And the LORD said unto him, Go up. And David said, Whither shall I go up? And he said, Unto Hebron. ⁽²⁾ So David went up thither, and his two wives also, Ahinoam the Jezreelitess, and Abigail Nabal's wife the Carmelite. ⁽³⁾ And his men that *were* with him did David bring up, every man with his household: and they dwelt in the cities of Hebron. ⁽⁴⁾ *a* And the men of Judah came, and there they anointed David king over the house of Judah.

And they told David, saying, That

a 1 Mac. 2. 57.

b 1 Sam. 31. 13.

1 Heb., *be ye the sons of valour.*

B.C. cir. 1055.

2 Heb., *the host which was Saul's.*

b the men of Jabesh-gilead *were* they that buried Saul. ⁽⁵⁾ And David sent messengers unto the men of Jabesh-gilead, and said unto them, Blessed *be* ye of the LORD, that ye have shewed this kindness unto your lord, *even* unto Saul, and have buried him. ⁽⁶⁾ And now the LORD shew kindness and truth unto you: and I also will requite you this kindness, because ye have done this thing. ⁽⁷⁾ Therefore now let your hands be strengthened, and ¹ be ye valiant: for your master Saul is dead, and also the house of Judah have anointed me king over them.

⁽⁸⁾ But Abner the son of Ner, captain of ² Saul's host, took Ish-bosheth the

---

II.

By the death of Saul, David was now left as the anointed king of Israel. This chapter narrates the first steps he took towards securing the throne, and the opposition made to him by the adherents of the house of Saul. At first thought it may seem surprising that no invitation to assume the vacant throne should have come to David from his countrymen, by whom he had been formerly so greatly beloved and admired; but it must be remembered that for several years he had been secluded from their observation, living among their hereditary foes on friendly terms, and that the last news of him probably was his marching with the Philistines to the disastrous battle of Gilboa. As yet he had had no opportunity to place these things in their true light before his people.

⁽¹⁾ **Enquired of the Lord.**—At this important juncture of affairs, David's first care is to know the Divine will. His inquiry was, doubtless, made through the high priest Abiathar, as in 1 Sam. xxiii. 9, 10 (comp. chaps. xxii. 20; xxiii. 1, 4). The answer definitely directed him to go up to Hebron.

Hebron is one of the most ancient cities of the world (built "seven years before Zoan in Egypt," Num. xiii. 22), long the residence of Abraham (Gen. xiii. 18), and the place where he and Sarah, Isaac and Jacob, were buried. Its original name was Kirjath-arba (Gen. xxiii. 2; Josh. xiv. 15, &c.). It is situated in a valley among the hills of Southern Judea, at a height of nearly 3,000 feet above the Mediterranean. It is about twenty miles S.S.W. from Jerusalem, somewhat more than this N.E. of Beersheba, and about fifteen miles E.S.E. of the Philistine town of Gath. From Ziklag, where David had been living, it was distant about thirty-eight miles. It has always been famous for its vineyards, and its grapes are still considered the finest in Southern Palestine. The valley in which it is situated is probably the "valley of Eshcol," from which the spies brought the great "cluster of grapes" to Moses in the wilderness (Num. xiii. 23). It was a priestly city (Josh. xxi. 10, 11), and the most southerly of the cities of refuge (Josh. xx. 7). Here was the home and the throne of David for the next seven and a half years (verse 11; v. 5). The larger part of the land, since the recent defeat, was in the power of the Philistines; and Hebron, on account of its situation at the far south, and its strategical strength, as well as its sacred associations, was a peculiarly fitting place for the beginning of David's reign.

⁽²⁾ **His two wives.**—See 1 Sam. xxv. 42, 43.

⁽³⁾ **Dwelt in the cities of Hebron.**—David's whole force of 600 men, with their families, accompanied him, and made their permanent settlement in the towns of the district to which Hebron gave its name.

⁽⁴⁾ **They anointed David.**—The first private anointing of David (1 Sam. xvi.) had been in token of his Divine commission; this was a sign of his recognition as king by the tribe of Judah; and there was still a third subsequent anointing (chap. v. 4), when he was accepted by all Israel. Comp. Saul's anointing by Samuel privately (1 Sam. x. 1), and his subsequent double recognition as king by the people (1 Sam. x. 24; xi. 15). The "men of Judah" were not only of David's tribe, but were doubtless aware of his having been divinely selected for their future king, and, for the most part, had been on friendly terms with him during his long outlawry; they had also lately received presents from him in recognition of their kindness (1 Sam. xxx. 26—31).

The men of Jabesh-gilead.—This town had been destroyed in the civil war against the tribe of Benjamin (Judges xxi. 9—12), and its 400 virgins given in marriage to the surviving Benjamites. There was therefore a special connection between Saul, who was of the tribe of Benjamin, and this city. It is altogether probable also that the remnants of Saul's defeated army had sought refuge in Gilead.

⁽⁶⁾ **I also will requite you.**—David's message of kindness and blessing is quite in accordance with his whole bearing towards Saul and his house, and, at the same time, was one of wise policy. The literal rendering is, *I also show you this good,* the Hebrew not conveying directly the idea of future recompense, as in the English. The thought is that David, as now the rightful king of Israel, appreciates the act, and wishes to show publicly his favour to the men of Jabesh-gilead. He then, in the following verse, suggests the propriety of their now recognising him as the successor of their lost monarch and friend.

⁽⁸⁾ **But Abner the son of Ner.**—According to 1 Chron. ix. 36, Ner was the brother of Kish, Saul's father. Abner was therefore the cousin-german of

son of Saul, and brought him over to Mahanaim; (9) and made him king over Gilead, and over the Ashurites, and over Jezreel, and over Ephraim, and over Benjamin, and over all Israel. (10) Ish-bosheth Saul's son *was* forty years old when he began to reign over Israel, and reigned two years. But the house of Judah followed David. (11) And the ¹time that David was king in Hebron over the house of Judah was seven years and six months.

(12) And Abner the son of Ner, and the servants of Ish-bosheth the son of Saul,

1 Heb., *number of days.*

B.C. cir. 1053.

B.C. 1055.

2 Heb., *them together.*

went out from Mahanaim to Gibeon. (13) And Joab the son of Zeruiah, and the servants of David, went out, and met ²together by the pool of Gibeon: and they sat down, the one on the one side of the pool, and the other on the other side of the pool. (14) And Abner said to Joab, Let the young men now arise, and play before us. And Joab said, Let them arise. (15) Then there arose and went over by number twelve of Benjamin, which *pertained* to Ish-bosheth the son of Saul, and twelve of the servants of David. (16) And they

---

Saul, and had been made by him the commander-in-chief of his army (1 Sam. xiv. 51). He was thus, both by kindred and office, strongly attached to the house of Saul. He had been with Saul in his pursuit of David, and may have resented David's address to him on that occasion (1 Sam. xxvi. 14—16). There is no statement of the time that had elapsed after the death of Saul before Ish-bosheth was set up as king by Abner, but it was probably four or five years, for the following reasons: Ish-bosheth reigned only two years (verse 10), but David appears to have been acknowledged as king over all Israel soon after his death, and had then reigned over Judah alone seven and a half years. Again, at the death of Saul all the northern part of the country was under the control of the Philistines, and some time must have elapsed before the Israelites would have been in condition to make themselves a new king; and, finally, Ish-bosheth was the youngest of Saul's sons, born apparently some time after he came to the throne, and he was now forty years old (verse 10), Saul himself having reigned about forty years (Acts xiii. 21).

Ish-bosheth.—Called in 1 Chron. viii. 33; ix. 39, "Eshbaal" (*the fire of Baal*), just as his nephew, Mephibosheth (2 Sam. iv. 4), is called in the same places *Meribaal*, and Gideon's surname Jerubbaal (Judges vi. 32; viii. 35) is changed to Jerubbesheth (2 Sam. xi. 21). These names compounded with Baal may have been originally given, as certainly was the case with Jerubbaal, in consequence of the manful opposition to idolatry of those who bore them, and have been subsequently changed to a compound with "bosheth" (*shame*), in view of the sequel of their histories; or, on the other hand, in the case of Saul's family the compound with Baal may have been a later name, given in view of their opposition to the divinely appointed king, and to mark God's utter rejection of the house of Saul.

Mahanaim, famous in the story of Jacob (Gen. xxxii. 2), was on the east of the Jordan, and not far from the brook Jabbok. A Levitical city (Josh. xxi. 38), in comparative safety from the Philistines, was well chosen by Abner for the coronation and residence of his new king. Mahanaim afterwards became the place of refuge for David in his flight from Absalom (chap. xvii. 24). The expression "brought him over" refers to the crossing of the Jordan.

(9) **The Ashurites, and over Jezreel.**—This verse apparently expresses the gradual extension of Ish-bosheth's dominion as the country became freed from the Philistines. At first, his authority was established over Gilead—*i.e.*, the country on the east of the Jordan; then "over the Ashurites." No satisfactory explanation of this name as it stands has been found, but it is probably meant for *Asherites*, or the tribe of Asher, the reading of some MSS. and of the Chaldee Version; the name of this tribe standing for the whole region west of the Jordan, and north of the plain of Esdraelon; then southwards, "over Jezreel," the wide plain between the mountains of Gilboa and the little Hermon; then "over Ephraim," including the half-tribe of Manasseh; and, still southwards, "over Benjamin;" and finally, "over all Israel," excepting, of course, Judah.

(12) **To Gibeon.**—Gibeon, in the territory of Benjamin, had become noted in the original conquest of the land as the only city which succeeded, though by craft, in making a league with the conquerors (Josh. ix.). It was five and a half miles north-west from Jerusalem, and at a long distance both from Mahanaim and from Hebron. Here the generals of the rival monarchs met, possibly by design, but more likely each engaged in the effort to extend their respective masters' sway over the tribe of Benjamin.

(13) **Joab the son of Zeruiah.**—Zeruiah was David's sister (1 Chron. ii. 16), and Joab the most prominent of her three distinguished sons. Subsequently, by his successful leading of the forlorn hope in the siege of Jerusalem (1 Chron. xi. 6; comp. 2 Sam. v. 8), he became permanently established as commander-in-chief of David's army. He was undoubtedly among "the brethren of David" who came down to him at the cave of Adullam (1 Sam. xxii. 1), though he is not mentioned by name, like his brother Abishai (1 Sam. xxvi. 6—9), in the narrative of David's outlawry.

The pool of Gibeon is a large reservoir or tank, arranged to store the overflow from a subterranean reservoir fed by a spring in the rocky hill-side. Its ruins still remain, about 120 feet long by 100 broad. The hostile forces halted in full sight of each other on the opposite sides of the pool.

(14) **Let the young men.**—To avoid unnecessary bloodshed between the tribes of a common parentage, and also, perhaps, to prevent the weakening of the nation in the face of their common Philistine foe, Abner proposes that the struggle should be decided by a combat between a few champions chosen on either side, and Joab immediately accepts the proposal. Hervey (*Speaker's Commentary*) aptly compares this combat to that of the Horatii and Curiatii, under strikingly similar circumstances and with similar results, as described by Livy (I., c. x. 25).

(16) **Helkath-hazzurim** is interpreted in the margin "the field of strong men," but the etymology

caught every one his fellow by the head, and *thrust* his sword in his fellow's side; so they fell down together: wherefore that place was called ¹Helkath-hazzurim, which *is* in Gibeon. ⁽¹⁷⁾ And there was a very sore battle that day; and Abner was beaten, and the men of Israel, before the servants of David.

⁽¹⁸⁾ And there were three sons of Zeruiah there, Joab, and Abishai, and Asahel: and Asahel *was as* light ² of foot ³ as a wild roe. ⁽¹⁹⁾ And Asahel pursued after Abner; and in going he turned not to the right hand nor to the left from ⁴ following Abner. ⁽²⁰⁾ Then Abner looked behind him, and said, *Art thou* Asahel? And he answered, I *am*. ⁽²¹⁾ And Abner said to him, Turn thee aside to thy right hand or to thy left, and lay thee hold on one of the young men, and take thee his ⁵ armour. But Asahel would not turn aside from following of him. ⁽²²⁾ And Abner said again to Asahel, Turn thee aside from following me: wherefore should I smite thee to the ground? how then should I hold up my face to Joab thy brother? ⁽²³⁾ Howbeit he refused to turn aside: wherefore Abner with the hinder end of the spear smote him under the fifth *rib*,

¹ That is, *The field of strong men.*
² Heb., *of his feet.*
³ Heb., *as one of the roes that is in the field.*
⁴ Heb., *from after Abner.*
⁵ Or, *spoil.*
⁶ Heb., *from the morning.*
⁷ Or, *gone away.*

that the spear came out behind him; and he fell down there, and died in the same place: and it came to pass, *that* as many as came to the place where Asahel fell down and died stood still. ⁽²⁴⁾ Joab also and Abishai pursued after Abner: and the sun went down when they were come to the hill of Ammah, that *lieth* before Giah by the way of the wilderness of Gibeon.

⁽²⁵⁾ And the children of Benjamin gathered themselves together after Abner, and became one troop, and stood on the top of an hill. ⁽²⁶⁾ Then Abner called to Joab, and said, Shall the sword devour for ever? knowest thou not that it will be bitterness in the latter end? how long shall it be then, ere thou bid the people return from following their brethren? ⁽²⁷⁾ And Joab said, *As* God liveth, unless thou hadst spoken, surely then ⁶ in the morning the people had ⁷ gone up every one from following his brother. ⁽²⁸⁾ So Joab blew a trumpet, and all the people stood still, and pursued after Israel no more, neither fought they any more.

⁽²⁹⁾ And Abner and his men walked all that night through the plain, and passed over Jordan, and went through all Bith-

---

is very doubtful. Most modern expositors understand it as meaning "the field of sharp edges."

⁽¹⁷⁾ **A very sore battle.**—The combat of the twelve on each side having decided nothing, the two hosts joined battle. Abner and the Israelites were worsted. The numbers engaged were probably not large, as the whole number of the slain was nineteen on David's side, and 360 on that of Israel (verses 30, 31). It was, however, a turning-point in the struggle.

⁽¹⁹⁾ **Asahel pursued after Abner.**—Asahel, the youngest of the three nephews of David, took part in the battle with his elder brothers, and well knowing how completely the cause of Ish-bosheth depended upon Abner, pertinaciously sought him out in the pursuit. His great fleetness enabled him to overtake Abner and, coming behind him, endanger his life. Abner was unwilling to injure him, and only after remonstrating with him, and urging him to seek the spoil of some warrior more nearly his equal (verses 20—22), did he unwillingly slay him "with the hinder end of his spear." The spears were sharpened at the "hinder end" for the purpose of sticking them into the ground (1 Sam. xxvi. 7). Abner's reluctance to kill Asahel may have been partly on account of his extreme youth, but was chiefly through dread of the vengeance of Joab (verse 22). "The fifth rib" here, and wherever else it occurs (chaps. iii. 27; iv. 6; xx. 10), should be translated *abdomen.*

⁽²⁴⁾ **The hill of Ammah.**—No identification of either Ammah or Giah has yet been made, but as it was "by the way of the wilderness of Gibeon," it may be conjectured that it was not far from that town, and hence that the pursuit was not long.

⁽²⁵⁾ **The children of Benjamin.**—The rest of Abner's force appears to have been hopelessly scattered in the flight, but he succeeded in rallying the Benjamites, his own and Saul's kinsmen, in a strong position "on the top of an hill."

⁽²⁶⁾ **Abner called to Joab.**—It may be that Abner was already considering the expediency of transferring his allegiance to the house of David, or, at least, had had enough experience of Ish-bosheth to see that it would be impossible to unite the tribes under his sway. At all events, his sense of the disastrous effects of civil war was doubtless quickened by his own defeat and present danger.

⁽²⁷⁾ **Unless thou hadst spoken.**—Joab's reply to Abner admits of either of two interpretations: (1) Joab seeks to throw the whole blame of the conflict upon Abner, by saying that if he had not proposed the combat between the champions (verse 14) there would have been no battle, but "the people" of both sides would have separated peaceably at Gibeon; or (2), as the phrase is more generally and more probably understood, that Joab had intended to keep up the pursuit only until the following morning, but as Abner already sued for mercy, he was content, and would stop now.

⁽²⁸⁾ **Neither fought they any more**—*i.e.*, in this present campaign. In chap. iii. 1, it is said that "there was a long war between the house of Saul and the house of David."

⁽²⁹⁾ **Through the plain** (or the *Arabah*).—The wilderness of Gibeon lay to the east of the town, and

ron, and they came to Mahanaim. (30) And Joab returned from following Abner: and when he had gathered all the people together, there lacked of David's servants nineteen men and Asahel. (31) But the servants of David had smitten of Benjamin, and of Abner's men, *so that* three hundred and threescore men died. (32) And they took up Asahel, and buried him in the sepulchre of his father, which *was in* Beth-lehem. And Joab and his men went all night, and they came to Hebron at break of day.

CHAPTER III. — (1) Now there was long war between the house of Saul and the house of David: but David waxed stronger and stronger, and the house of Saul waxed weaker and weaker.

(2) And unto David were sons born in Hebron: and his firstborn was Amnon, of Ahinoam the Jezreelitess; (3) and his second, Chileab, of Abigail the wife of Nabal the Carmelite; and the third, Absalom the son of Maacah the daughter of Talmai king of Geshur; (4) and the fourth, Adonijah the son of Haggith; and the fifth, Shephatiah the son of Abital; (5) and the sixth, Ithream, by Eglah David's wife. These were born to David in Hebron.

Abner's flight had thus carried him towards the Jordan. He now passed up the valley of the Jordan (which the word here used generally designates), and, crossing at a ford, went "through all Bithron to Mahanaim." Bithron is evidently the name of a district on the east of the Jordan, but is not further known.

(30) **Joab returned.**—He cannot be supposed to have returned that day farther than to Gibeon, since it was already sunset (verse 24) before the pursuit ended. There, doubtless, he mustered his forces, and counted and buried the slain.

Nineteen men.—It is uncertain whether these numbers include the twelve champion combatants on each side. The great disparity of numbers slain on the two sides is to be accounted for partly by the advantage given by bow and spear, the chief weapons of ancient warfare, to the pursuer over the pursued, and partly by the fact that Joab's men had been long trained under David in hardship and deeds of valour, while Abner's men were the remnants of Saul's defeated army.

(32) **They took up Asahel.**—The bodies of the ordinary soldiers were probably buried on the spot, but on account of Asahel's position and near relationship to David, his body was carried to Bethlehem, for burial "in the sepulchre of his father." It thus appears that Zeruiah's husband (of whom there is no other mention) was also of Bethlehem. The burial must have taken place on the next day (see Note on verse 30), and, with the previous march of ten miles, would have filled up that day. It was, therefore, twenty-four hours after the close of the battle before they were ready to start from Bethlehem. The night may have been chosen for the march to avoid the heat; and the distance from Bethlehem to Hebron was about thirteen miles.

III.

(1) **There was long war.**—Not actual fighting of pitched battles, but a state of hostility, in which Ish-bosheth and David each claimed the allegiance of the whole nation, and this continued until the death of Ish-bosheth. During this time Ish-bosheth was too weak to carry on actual war, and David was content to abide the fulfilment of the promises of the Lord in His own good time.

Waxed stronger.—Time was working in David's favour, partly, doubtless, on account of Ish-bosheth's manifest incompetence, partly from a growing appreciation of the character and prowess of David, and a fuller realisation that he was the divinely appointed sovereign. In 1 Chron. xii. 19—22 there is an account of an important accession to David from the tribe of Manasseh on the eve of Saul's last battle, and a further mention of continued accessions to him "day by day." As the necessary result of this constant transference of strength to David, "the house of Saul waxed weaker and weaker."

(2—5) **And unto David.**—The list of David's sons born during his seven and a half years' reign in Hebron rather interrupts the continuity of the narrative, but is quite in accordance with the habit of the sacred historians to insert at the beginning or at some turning-point in each reign statistics about the house or family of the king. (See 1 Sam. xiv. 49—51; 2 Sam. v. 13; 1 Kings iii. 1; xiv. 21; xv. 2, 9, &c.)

Amnon.—Written "Aminon" in chap. xiii. 20. His great crime and miserable end are related in chap. xiii.

Chileab.—Called "Daniel" in 1 Chron iii. 1. None of the attempts to explain these as two forms of the same name have been successful. Either, therefore, "Chileab" is an error of the scribe (all but the first letter being the same as the first three letters of the following word), or, more probably, Chileab had a double name. Nothing further is known of him, and as he does not appear in the subsequent troubles, it is supposed that he died early. These two sons were born of the wives whom David had taken while an outlaw.

Absalom.—His history, rebellion, and death are narrated in chaps. xiii.—xviii. His mother was "the daughter of Talmai, king of Geshur," a petty province north-east of Bashan. How David was brought into connection with him, and whether this alliance had any political object or not, we are not told, but the fact that Absalom in his exile naturally sought refuge with his maternal grandmother (chap. xiii. 37) may have had a connection with David's subsequent campaigns in that region.

Adonijah.—After the death of his three elder brothers, Adonijah considered himself the rightful heir to the throne, and embittered the last days of his father by a rebellion (1 Kings i.). He was at last put to death by Solomon (1 Kings ii. 25).

Of the other two sons, Shephatiah and Ithream, and of the mothers of the last three, nothing is known, although there is an absurd Jewish tradition that "Eglah" was another name for "Michal."

(6) And it came to pass, while there was war between the house of Saul and the house of David, that Abner made himself strong for the house of Saul. (7) And Saul had a concubine, whose name *was* ᵃRizpah, the daughter of Aiah: and *Ish-bosheth* said to Abner, Wherefore hast thou gone in unto my father's concubine? (8) Then was Abner very wroth for the words of Ish-bosheth, and said, Am I a dog's head, which against Judah do show kindness this day unto the house of Saul thy father, to his brethren, and to his friends, and have not delivered thee into the hand of David, that thou chargest me to day with a fault concerning this woman? (9) So do God to Abner, and more also, except, as the LORD hath sworn to David, even so I do to him; (10) to translate the kingdom from the house of Saul, and to set up the throne of David over Israel and over Judah, from Dan even to Beer-sheba. (11) And he could not answer Abner a word again, because he feared him.

(12) And Abner sent messengers to David on his behalf, saying, Whose *is* the land? saying *also*, Make thy league with me, and, behold, my hand *shall be* with thee, to bring about all Israel unto thee. (13) And he said, Well; I will make a league with thee: but one thing I require of thee, ¹that is, Thou shalt not see my face, except thou first bring Michal Saul's daughter, when thou comest to see my face. (14) And David sent messengers to Ish-bosheth Saul's son, saying, Deliver *me* my wife Michal, which I espoused to me ᵇfor an hundred

a ch. 21. 10.

B.C. 1048

1 Heb., *saying.*

b 1 Sam. 18. 25, 27.

---

(6) **Abner made himself strong.**—It has already been noticed that the fortunes of the house of Saul depended entirely upon Abner, but the fact of Ish-bosheth's great obligation to him is again mentioned here in explanation of the following story.

(7) **Rizpah.**—The name of this woman is associated with her strong and tender grief over the loss of her sons, recorded in chap. xxi. 8—11.

Wherefore hast thou gone in?—The harem of an Eastern monarch was considered as the property of his successor, and therefore the taking of a woman belonging to it as the assertion of a claim to the throne. (See chaps. xii. 8; xvi. 21; 1 Kings ii. 22.) It is not probable that Abner had any such design, since he was exerting himself to maintain Ish-bosheth on the throne. But the king appears to have so regarded the act, as it is this implied charge of treachery that so greatly rouses the anger of Abner. The name of Ish-bosheth has dropped out of the Hebrew text, but appears in a few MSS., and is rightly restored in all the versions.

(8) **Am I a dog's head?**—The translation of this clause is taken from the Vulg., and is hardly possible; it should rather be, *Am I a dog's head belonging to Judah?*

(9) **So do God to Abner.**—The anger of Abner culminates in a solemn oath to transfer the kingdom to David, "as the Lord hath sworn to him." There is no record of a Divine oath to give the kingdom to David, but the prophetic declaration that God's choice of him was unalterable (1 Sam. xv. 29) may well have been considered to have the force of an oath. Abner does not propose to do this in order to fulfil the Divine will, for his words show that he had been acting hitherto in conscious opposition to that will, but to revenge himself for the insult now offered him. He had doubtless also become satisfied of his master's entire unfitness for the throne, and his power over Israel opened before him the prospect of high preferment from David.

(10) **To translate the kingdom.**—This sudden expression of Abner's resolve seems to imply that he had before had the matter under consideration, and shows that there was some ground for the reproach of Ish-bosheth. The following verse brings out clearly the utter weakness of Ish-bosheth.

(12) **Whose is the land?**—These words in themselves may be understood in either of two senses: (1) "Is not the land thine by promise?" or (2) "Who has the power to bring the land into subjection to whom he will except myself?" Since the question is put forward as the basis for making a league with Abner, the latter is evidently the sense intended, and it is quite in accordance with the pride and haughtiness of Abner's character. He proposes a league, that he may have a definite assurance of consideration for himself, and he makes this the price of exerting his influence on David's behalf. The repetition of the word "saying" has occasioned some difficulty to the commentators, but this disappears when it is remembered that the two clauses are separate parts of Abner's message. His messengers were charged first to represent the importance of Abner's influence, and then afterwards to say that he would exert it for David for a satisfactory consideration.

(13) **Except thou first bring Michal.**—David consents to negotiate with Abner only on condition of the previous restoration of his lawful wife. Besides the justice of this demand (Michal having been wrongfully taken from him by Saul), and besides all question of affection towards one who had loved him and saved his life (1 Sam. xviii. 20; xix. 11—17), there were political reasons of importance for the demand. The demand itself showed to all Israel that he bore no malice against the house of Saul, and the restoration would again constitute him Saul's son-in-law, and thus further his claims to the throne; while it also showed publicly that he was in a condition to enforce his rights as against the house of Saul.

(14) **To Ish-bosheth.**—The demand is made upon the *de facto* king that all may be done legally, and David may not appear to be reclaiming his wife by force. At the same time, Ish-bosheth is thus compelled to acknowledge the wrong done to David and his inability to refuse his demand. It appears from verse 16 that Abner was employed to execute the command, and, in fact, the whole matter was really determined by him, the king being merely the official and legal instrument.

An hundred foreskins—David had actually delivered to Saul as her dowry *two* hundred, but only one

foreskins of the Philistines. (15) And Ish-bosheth sent, and took her from *her* husband, *even* from ᵃ Phaltiel the son of Laish. (16) And her husband went with her ¹ along weeping behind her to Bahurim. Then said Abner unto him, Go, return. And he returned.

(17) And Abner had communication with the elders of Israel, saying, Ye sought for David ² in times past *to be* king over you: (18) now then do *it*: for the LORD hath spoken of David, saying, By the hand of my servant David I will save my people Israel out of the hand of the Philistines, and out of the hand of all their enemies. (19) And Abner also spake in the ears of Benjamin: and Abner went also to speak in the ears of David in Hebron all that seemed good to Israel, and that seemed good to the whole house of Benjamin. (20) So Abner came to David to Hebron, and twenty men with him. And David made Abner and the men that *were* with him a feast. (21) And Abner said unto David, I will arise and go, and will gather all Israel unto my lord the king, that they may make a league with thee, and that thou mayest reign over all that thine heart desireth. And David sent Abner away; and he went in peace.

(22) And, behold, the servants of David and Joab came from *pursuing* a troop, and brought in a great spoil with them: but Abner *was* not with David in Hebron; for he had sent him away, and he was gone in peace. (23) When Joab and all the host that *was* with him were come, they told Joab, saying, Abner the son of Ner came to the king, and he hath sent him away, and he is gone in peace. (24) Then Joab came to the king, and said, What hast thou done? behold, Abner came unto thee; why *is* it *that* thou hast sent him away, and he is quite gone? (25) Thou knowest Abner the son of Ner, that he came to deceive thee, and to know thy going out and thy coming in, and to know all that thou doest.

(26) And when Joab was come out from David, he sent messengers after Abner, which brought him again from the well of Sirah: but David knew *it* not.

ᵃ 1 Sam. 25. 44, Phalti.

¹ Heb., *going and weeping.*

² Heb., *both yesterday, and the third day.*

---

hundred had been required (1 Sam. xviii. 25, 27), and therefore only that number is mentioned.

(16) **Weeping behind her.**—Phaltiel appears to have been sincerely attached to Michal, and it may be supposed that his affection was reciprocated. But it is to be remembered that she was not rightfully his wife, and that David's claim was prior as well as better. According to 1 Sam. xxv. 44, Phaltiel was of Gallim, a place thought, from the connection in which it is mentioned in Isa. x. 30, to have been in Benjamin, and not far from Gibeah; but he had probably crossed the Jordan with the adherents of the house of Saul. Bahurim was on the road from the Mount of Olives to the Jordan valley, and hence on the way from Mahanaim to Hebron, and a long distance from the former. It was the residence of Shimei (chap. xvi. 5), and the place of concealment of David's messengers, Jonathan and Ahimaaz (chap. xvii. 18).

(17) **Ye sought for David.**—1 Sam. xviii. 5, 7, 16, 30; 1 Chron. xi. 1—3 (comp. verse 36), sufficiently testify to the great popularity of David throughout the nation, and its confidence in his prowess and wisdom. It was the influence and activity of Abner that had hitherto prevented his general recognition as king.

(18) **The Lord hath spoken.**—The promise here quoted is not contained in so many words in the records which have come down to us. It may have been either an unrecorded utterance of one of the prophets (Samuel, Gad, or Nathan), or simply a reasonable inference from what had been promised, and from the Divine support of David in his career hitherto.

(19) **Spake in the ears of Benjamin.**—Special and careful negotiations with the Benjamites were necessary, because they felt bound to their kinsmen of the house of Saul, and had hitherto enjoyed great advantages from their connection with their sovereign. Abner reported to David at Hebron the result of his negotiations both with Israel generally and with Benjamin in particular.

(20) **Twenty men.**—These were doubtless representative men, selected by Abner from Israel and Benjamin to accompany him and confirm his report. The feast which David made for them is not to be understood of mere conviviality, but of a solemn sacrificial feast, such as was customary in ancient times in connection with important negotiations. (See Gen. xxvi. 30; xxxi. 54; 1 Kings iii. 15.)

(22) **Joab came.**—He had been either on some expedition against the Philistines, the Amalekites, or other enemies of Judah, or else engaged in repelling some attack from them. In either case, he returned elated with victory, and bringing great spoil; but Abner had concluded his interview and gone away before his return.

(24) **What hast thou done?**—Joab's somewhat rough remonstrance with David may have been supported by an honest suspicion of Abner, for which there was some ground in Abner's long opposition to the known Divine will and his present revolt from Ish-bosheth; but there was also a personal enmity, due partly to the fear of being himself supplanted by an older and famous warrior, and partly to the desire to revenge the death of his brother Asahel. Joab seeks to poison David's mind against Abner, that he may better carry out his revenge.

(26) **Sent messengers after Abner.**—Whether this was done in his own or in David's name (though without his knowledge) does not appear, but in either case Abner would readily suppose that the coming of Joab had made further conference desirable. His

(27) And when Abner was returned to Hebron, ^a Joab took him aside in the gate to speak with him ¹quietly, and smote him there under the fifth *rib*, that he died, for the blood of ^b Asahel his brother.

(28) And afterward when David heard *it*, he said, I and my kingdom *are* guiltless before the LORD for ever from the ²blood of Abner the son of Ner: (29) let it rest on the head of Joab, and on all his father's house; and let there not ³fail from the house of Joab one that hath an issue, or that is a leper, or that leaneth on a staff, or that falleth on the sword, or that lacketh bread. (30) So Joab and Abishai his brother slew Abner, because he had slain their brother ^cAsahel at Gibeon in the battle.

(31) And David said to Joab, and to all the people that *were* with him, Rend your clothes, and gird you with sackcloth, and mourn before Abner. And king David *himself* followed the ⁴bier.

(32) And they buried Abner in Hebron: and the king lifted up his voice, and wept at the grave of Abner; and all the people wept. (33) And the king lamented over Abner, and said,

Died Abner as a fool dieth? (34) Thy hands *were* not bound, nor thy feet put into fetters: as a man falleth before ⁵wicked men, *so* fellest thou.

And all the people wept again over him. (35) And when all the people came to cause David to eat meat while it was yet day, David sware, saying, So do God to me, and more also, if I taste bread, or ought else, till the sun be down. (36) And all the people took notice *of it*, and it ⁶pleased them: as whatsoever the king did pleased all the people. (37) For all the people and all Israel understood that day that it was not of the king to slay Abner the son of Ner.

(38) And the king said unto his servants, Know ye not that there is a prince and a great man fallen this day in Israel?

a 1 Kings 2. 5.
1 Or, *peaceably.*
b ch. 2. 23.
2 Heb., *bloods.*
3 Heb., *be cut off.*
c ch. 2. 23.
4 Heb., *bed.*
5 Heb., *children of iniquity.*
6 Heb., *was good in their eyes.*

---

entire confidence in David is shown by his unsuspecting return.

The well of Sirah.—The only knowledge of this locality is from the testimony of Josephus (*Antt*. vii. 1, 5), that it was twenty stadia (two and a half miles) from Hebron; and there is still a spring and reservoir called *Ain Sareh*, rather more than a mile north of the town. If this is correct, Abner must have just left David when Joab arrived.

(27) **Aside in the gate.**—The gateway was a customary place of conference in the East, and Joab there awaited Abner's return; he then took him "aside" to some place of privacy, as the LXX. reads, "by the side of the gate." On the phrase "fifth rib," see Note on chap. ii. 23. The reason for this cold-blooded and treacherous murder on the part of Joab is expressly said to be "for the blood of Asahel his brother;" but no doubt his revenge was quickened by jealousy.

(28) **I and my kingdom are guiltless.**—This was true. Joab's act was entirely without David's knowledge, and was not only against his will on moral grounds, but was in danger of proving disastrous to him politically; hence he takes the strongest means of showing his abhorrence of the deed.

(29) **Let it rest on the head of Joab.**—The strong curse here pronounced by David shows that Joab's act could not be justified as that of the "Goel," or lawful avenger of his brother's blood, for Abner had slain Asahel in battle, unwillingly and in self-defence. It is also to be remembered that Hebron was a city of refuge (Josh. xxi. 13), and that here not even the "Goel" might slay the murderer without a trial (Num. xxxv. 22—25). The curse falls "on his father's house," since Abishai also (verse 30) had been concerned with him in the murder.

The phrase, "that leaneth on a staff," has been understood by many as "holding a distaff," *i.e.*, a person unfit for war. The word has the sense of "distaff" in Prov. xxxi. 19, and is so rendered here by the Vulgate; but the sense given by the English—which is also that of the LXX. and Targum—is better, and more in accordance with the other particulars.

For "on the sword" read "by the sword," there being no reference to the idea of suicide. On the violent end of Joab see 1 Kings ii. 31—34.

(30) **Slew . . . had slain.**—The words are different in Hebrew, the former denoting violence. Translate the latter *had put to death*. By this strong disapproval of Joab's act, David shows that it was done without his knowledge or consent. He still remains at fault, however, for continuing Joab in his high and responsible position; but this seems to have been the result of inability to inflict proper punishment upon so powerful a subject, an inability which David on his death-bed sought to remedy by his charge to Solomon. (See verse 39; 1 Kings ii. 5.)

(31) **Rend your clothes.**—David commands a public mourning with the usual signs of rent clothes and sackcloth, and lays this command especially upon Joab, who is thus required, as it were, to do public penance for his act. David himself followed the bier as chief mourner.

(32) **In Hebron.**—The family home, and therefore the natural burial-place, of Abner was at Gibeon (1 Chron. viii. 29, 33; ix. 33); but this may have been now under Ish-bosheth's control, and, at all events, a burial in the royal city of Hebron was more honourable and a more marked testimony to the grief of David.

(34) **Thy hands were not bound.**—The people were moved greatly by the sight of David's sorrow, but still more by this brief elegy over Abner. The whole circumstances are summed up in a few pregnant words: Abner, so valiant in war, with his hands free for defence, with his feet unfettered, unsuspicious of evil, fell by the treacherous act of a wicked man.

(35) **To eat meat.**—The fasting of David in his grief had already attracted attention, so that the people came to urge him to take food; but he utterly refused

Ish-bosheth Slain   II. SAMUEL, IV.   *by Baanah and Rechab.*

(39) And I *am* this day [1] weak, though anointed king; and these men the sons of Zeruiah *be* too hard for me: the LORD shall reward the doer of evil according to his wickedness.

CHAPTER IV.—(1) And when Saul's son heard that Abner was dead in Hebron, his hands were feeble, and all the Israelites were troubled. (2) And Saul's son had two men *that were* captains of bands: the name of the one *was* Baanah, and the name of the [2] other Rechab, the sons of Rimmon a Beerothite, of the children of Benjamin: (for Beeroth also was reckoned to Benjamin: (3) and the Beerothites fled to Gittaim, and were sojourners there until this day.)

(4) And Jonathan, Saul's son, had a son *that was* lame of *his* feet. He was five years old when the tidings came of Saul and Jonathan out of Jezreel, and his nurse took him up, and fled: and it came to pass, as she made haste to flee, that he fell, and became lame. And his name *was* Mephibosheth.

(5) And the sons of Rimmon the Beerothite, Rechab and Baanah, went, and came about the heat of the day to the house of Ish-bosheth, who lay on a bed at noon. (6) And they came thither into the midst of the house, *as though* they would have fetched wheat; and they smote him under the fifth *rib*: and Rechab and Baanah his brother escaped. (7) For when they came into the house, he lay on his bed in his bedchamber, and they smote him, and slew him, and beheaded him, and took his head, and gat them away through the plain all night. (8) And they brought the head of Ish-bosheth unto David to Hebron, and said to the king, Behold the head of Ish-bosheth the son of Saul thine enemy, which sought thy life; and the LORD hath avenged my lord the king this day of Saul, and of his seed.

B.C. cir. 1048.

1 Heb., *tender.*

2 Heb., *second.*

"till the sun be down," the usual time of ending a fast. David's conduct had a good effect upon the people, and, indeed, they were generally disposed to look favourably upon whatever the king did.

(39) **I am this day weak.**—David's high appreciation of the importance and value of Abner shows that Joab's jealousy was not without ground, and there is a tone of deep sadness in his words, "these men the sons of Zeruiah be too hard for me." He knew their ungoverned passions, their bold lawlessness, and at the same time their great power and popularity with the army, and he dared not punish them. He leaves their judgment to God.

IV.

(1) **All the Israelites were troubled.**— The death of Abner affected both Ish-bosheth and his people. For the former, "his hands were feeble," the whole support and strength of his throne being gone; the latter were "troubled" because they had been carrying on negotiations with David through Abner, and these were now thrown into confusion, and it became uncertain how they might result.

(2) **A Beerothite.**—Beeroth was one of the four cities of the Gibeonites (Josh. ix. 17), and was allotted with the others to the tribe of Benjamin (Josh. xviii. 25). It is identified with the modern *El-Bireh*, nine miles north of Jerusalem. It is mentioned here, in the past tense, that Beeroth "*was* reckoned to Benjamin," because in the time of the writer it was no longer inhabited. The fact that the murderers of Ish-bosheth were of his own tribe is made prominent.

(3) **Fled to Gittaim.**—Neither the cause of their flight, nor the place to which they fled, can be certainly determined. The Beerothites here appear as of the tribe of Benjamin, and it is probable that they fled from the incursions of the Philistines, and that Gittaim is the place mentioned in Neh. xi. 35 as occupied by the Benjamites returning from Babylon. The expression "until this day" makes it likely that the time of the writer was not very far removed from the events which he relates.

(4) **A son that was lame.**—The reason for the introduction here of this account of Mephibosheth, Jonathan's son, is to show that, he being physically incapacitated for the throne, the house of Saul became practically extinct with the death of Ish-bosheth. There were other descendants, but either illegitimate or of the female line (chap. xxi. 8, 9), and hence there was none other of his house to claim the throne.

(5) **Who lay on a bed at noon**—according to the custom in hot countries of taking a *siesta* at midday. Ish-bosheth's bed was, of course, in the coolest and most retired part of the house.

(6) **As though they would have fetched wheat.**—Literally, *fetching wheat.* The English version gives the sense, since the fetching wheat (probably for their soldiers) was a pretext to cover their purpose. The LXX. has here a curious addition: "And, behold, the portress of the house was cleansing wheat, and she slumbered and slept, and the brothers slipt through." On "the fifth rib" = abdomen, see Note on chap. ii. 23.

(7) **Took his head.**—There is no difficulty with the repetition in verse 7 of what has been already mentioned in verse 6, for it is common in the Scripture narratives to repeat statements when any additional fact (as here, the carrying off of the head) is to be mentioned. (See, *e.g.*, chap. iii. 22, 23, where Joab's arrival is twice mentioned, and chap. v. 1—3, where the mention of the assembly at Hebron is repeated.)

Through the plain.—As in chap. ii. 29, the *Arabah*, or valley of the Jordan, the natural way from Mahanaim to Hebron.

(8) **The Lord hath avenged.**—It is not to be supposed that the murderers pretended a Divine commission for their wicked deed; they only meant to say that, in the providence of God, David was thus avenged on the seed of his cruel persecutor. Yet they state the

Their Punishment. II. SAMUEL, V. *The Tribes of Israel come to David.*

(9) And David answered Rechab and Baanah his brother, the sons of Rimmon the Beerothite, and said unto them, As the LORD liveth, who hath redeemed my soul out of all adversity, (10) when ᵃ one told me, saying, Behold, Saul is dead, ¹ thinking to have brought good tidings, I took hold of him, and slew him in Ziklag, ² who *thought* that I would have given him a reward for his tidings: (11) how much more, when wicked men have slain a righteous person in his own house upon his bed? shall I not therefore now require his blood of your hand, and take you away from the earth? (12) And David commanded his young men, and they slew them, and cut off their hands and their feet, and hanged *them* up over the pool in Hebron. But they took the head of Ish-bosheth, and buried *it* in the ᵇ sepulchre of Abner in Hebron.

CHAPTER V.—(1) Then ᶜ came all the tribes of Israel to David unto Hebron, and spake, saying, Behold, we *are* thy bone and thy flesh. (2) Also in time past, when Saul was king over us, thou wast he that leddest out and broughtest in Israel: and the LORD said to thee, ᵈ Thou shalt feed my people Israel, and thou shalt be a captain over Israel. (3) So all the elders of Israel came to the king to Hebron; and king David made a league with them in Hebron before the LORD: and they anointed David king over Israel. (4) David *was* thirty years old when he began to reign, *and* he reigned forty years. (5) In Hebron he reigned over Judah ᵉ seven years and six

ᵃ ch. 1. 15.

¹ Heb., *he was in his own eyes as a bringer*, &c.

² Or, *which was the reward I gave him for his tidings.*

ᵇ ch. 3. 32.

ᶜ 1 Chron. 11. 1.

ᵈ Ps. 78. 71.

ᵉ ch. 2. 11.

---

fact in the way they thought best calculated to awaken the gratitude of David towards themselves.

(9) **Who hath redeemed.**—David's answer shows that he could trust in God to avenge him, and did not encourage or need the crimes of men to help him.

(10) **Who thought that I would have given him.**—The words *thought that I would* are not in the original, and the literal translation of the margin is better: "which was the reward I gave him." This shows very plainly David's view of the motive which prompted the Amalekite to his lie recorded in chap. i. 10.

(11) **A righteous person**—*i.e.*, righteous, not at fault, so far as the matter in hand and his relation to the assassins is concerned.

Take you away from the earth.—"Rather, *put you away out of the land*. The word is one specially used of removing evil or the guilt of evil from the land (Deut. xix. 13, 19, &c.). The guilt of murder defiled the land, until expiated by the execution of the murderer. (Num. xxxv. 33.)"—*Kirkpatrick.*

(12) **Over the pool in Hebron.**—The mutilation of the bodies of the criminals was itself a disgrace, and the hanging them up near the pool, to which all the people resorted, made this as public as possible and a terrible warning against the commission of such crimes by others. On the other hand, the head of Ish-bosheth was honourably buried in the sepulchre of his chief friend and supporter, Abner.

V.

Chapters v.—x. contain the account of the first half of David's reign over the whole nation. All the events mentioned in them occurred within this period, but are not arranged with a strict regard to chronology within themselves, it being the object of the historian to describe first the internal improvement of the kingdom, and then afterwards the external development of its power.

(1) **All the tribes.**—Not only as represented by their elders (verse 3), but by the large bodies of their warriors enumerated in 1 Chron. xii. 23—40. It is to be noticed, then, that the "children of Judah" (verse 24), over whom David was already king, joined in the assembly, and that there were 4,600 Levites with Jehoiada as the leader of the priestly family of Aaron, while Zadok appears only as a conspicuous member of that family (verses 27, 28).

Thy bone and thy flesh.—The Israelites, oppressed by the Philistines and their other enemies, and having seen the utter failure of the house of Saul and the death of their head, Abner, felt the necessity of union under a competent leader, and it is probable that this gathering to David, already prepared for by the negotiations of Abner, took place immediately after the death of Ish-bosheth. They assign three reasons for their action: (1) that they were of the same flesh and bone with David (comp. Gen. xxix. 14; Judges ix. 2; 2 Sam. xix. 12)—*i.e.*, were of such common descent that it was unfitting for them to constitute separate nations; (2) that David, even in Saul's reign, had been their military leader, and hence they knew him and had confidence in his prowess and sagacity; (3) that the Lord had chosen him for their king. The exact language of the Divine promise quoted is not found in the record, but is either (as in the case of Abner's words, chap. iii. 18) a summary of the communications made to David, or else some unrecorded language of one of the prophets.

(3) **Made a league with them.**—It would be an anachronism to understand this of the establishment of a constitutional monarchy, but the "league" may have had reference to certain special matters, such as leading them against their enemies, not destroying the remnant of the house of Saul or its late adherents, and not showing partiality (as Saul had done) to the members of his own tribe.

(4) **Thirty years old.**—This statement of the age and of the length of the reign of David (which is repeated in 1 Chron. xxix. 26, 27, at the end of the history of David's life) shows us approximately the length of time since the combat with Goliath as some ten or twelve years. It also proves that the greater part of Saul's reign is treated very briefly in 1 Samuel, and further shows that David was seventy years old at his death.

(5) **Seven years and six months.**—The six months is also mentioned in chap. ii. 11; 1 Chron. iii. 4,

months: and in Jerusalem he reigned thirty and three years over all Israel and Judah.

⁽⁶⁾ And the king and his men went to Jerusalem unto the Jebusites, the inhabitants of the land: which spake unto David, saying, Except thou take away the blind and the lame, thou shalt not come in hither: ¹thinking David cannot come in hither. ⁽⁷⁾ Nevertheless David took the strong hold of Zion: the same *is* the city of David. ⁽⁸⁾ And David said on that day, Whosoever getteth up to the gutter, and smiteth the Jebusites, and the lame and the blind, *that are* hated of David's soul, *ᵃhe shall be chief and captain.* ² Wherefore they said, The blind and the lame shall not come into the house.

⁽⁹⁾ So David dwelt in the fort, and called it the city of David. And David built round about from Millo and inward. ⁽¹⁰⁾ And David ³ went on, and grew great, and the LORD God of hosts *was* with him.

⁽¹¹⁾ And ᵇHiram king of Tyre sent messengers to David, and cedar trees, and

¹ Or, *saying, David shall not, &c.*
ᵃ 1 Chron. 11. 6.
² Or, *Because they had said, even the blind and the lame, He shall not come into the house.*
³ Heb., *went, going and growing.*
ᵇ 1 Chron. 14. 1.
B.C. cir. 1043.

---

but, as being only the fraction of a year, is generally omitted in the summary of the length of his reign, as in verse 4; 1 Chron. xxix. 27. It was the habit of the sacred historians either to omit such fractions or else to count them as whole years, thus introducing a certain element of indefiniteness into the chronology, which is very marked in the parallel narratives of the kings of Israel and of Judah.

⁽⁶⁾ **Went to Jerusalem.**—The king of Jerusalem had been defeated and slain by Joshua (Josh. x. 23—26; xii. 10), and the city had been subsequently taken and destroyed by Judah (Judges i. 7, 8). It was, however, only partially occupied by the tribes of Judah and Benjamin (Judges i. 21; xv. 63), and at a later time fell again entirely into the hands of the Jebusites (Judges xix. 11, 12). That Jebus and Jerusalem were two names of the same city is stated in 1 Chron. xi. 4. This expedition must have taken place immediately after the coronation, since the length of reign over all Israel and of the reign in Jerusalem are said in verse 5 to be the same. David doubtless saw the importance of at once uniting the tribes in common action as well as the advantages of Jerusalem for his capital (Hebron being much too far southward), and the necessity of dislodging this remnant of the old Canaanites from their strong position in the centre of the land.

Except thou take away.—A better translation is, *Thou shalt not come hither; but the blind and the lame shall keep thee off.* The Jebusites, confident in the natural strength of their fortress, boast that even the lame and the blind could defend it. Their citadel was upon Mount Zion, the highest of the hills of Jerusalem, south-west of the temple hill of Moriah, and surrounded on three sides by deep valleys.

⁽⁸⁾ **Getteth up to the gutter.**—The sense of this passage is obscure, partly from the difficulty of the Hebrew construction, partly from the uncertainty of the meaning of the word translated *gutter*. This word occurs elsewhere only in Ps. xlii. 7, where it is translated *waterspouts*. The ancient versions differ in their interpretations, but the most probable sense is *watercourses*, such as were connected with the precipices around Mount Zion. The two clauses also are unnecessarily transposed in our version, and the word *getteth*, by a very slight change in the Masoretic vowels, becomes *cast* or *hurl*. The whole clause will then read, "Whosoever smites the Jebusites, let him hurl into the watercourses (*i.e.*, down the precipice) the lame and the blind." David thus applies to all the Jebusites the expression they had just used of those who would suffice to resist his attack. The clause "that are hated of David's soul," shows that in this siege no quarter was to be given; the Jebusites were under the old ban resting upon all the Canaanites, and were to be destroyed. The English version inserts the clause, "he shall be chief and captain," which is not in the original, and is here obscure. In 1 Chron. xi. 6, however, the same statement is made more fully and is important. "David said, Whosoever smiteth the Jebusites first shall be chief and captain. So Joab the son of Zeruiah went first up and was chief." It thus appears that David promised the command of his army to the man who should successfully lead the forlorn hope; Joab did this, and won the place in the armies of all Israel which he had hitherto filled in that of Judah. This fact helps to explain the sense of obligation and restraint which David afterwards felt towards Joab.

Wherefore they said.—Rather, *they say*. This became a proverbial expression: no intercourse is to be had with such people as the Jebusites, here again called "the blind and the lame."

⁽⁹⁾ **The fort.**—The same word as *strong hold* in verse 7.

Millo.—A word always used in Hebrew with the definite article (except in Judges ix. 6, 20), *the Millo.* It is probably an old Canaanitish name for the fortification on the northern end of Mount Zion, "inward" from which the palace was situated. Subsequent kings, as Solomon (1 Kings xi. 27) and Hezekiah (2 Chron. xxxii. 5), saw its importance and added to its strength. On all other sides Zion was protected by precipitous ravines. There is, however, some difference of opinion about the topography of ancient Jerusalem.

⁽¹¹⁾ **Hiram king of Tyre.**—This is the same Hiram, variously spelt *Hirom* and *Huram*, who was afterwards the friend of Solomon (1 Kings v. 1; 2 Chron. ii. 3), and was still living in the twenty-fourth year of Solomon's reign (1 Kings ix. 10—14; comp. vi. 1, 38; vii. 1); either, therefore, he must have had a reign of some fifty-seven years, or else his embassy to David must have been some time after the capture of Jerusalem. It is not unlikely that several years may have elapsed between the two events, during which "David went on and grew great" (verse 10), thereby attracting the attention and regard of Hiram. But the statement quoted by Josephus from Menander (*c. Apion*, i. 18) cannot be correct, that Hiram reigned only thirty-four years; for David was already in his "house of cedar" (chap. vii. 2) when he formed the purpose of building the Temple, and this was before the birth of Solomon (chap. vii. 12; 1 Chron. xxii. 9). Huram's father, however, was also named Huram (2 Chron. ii. 13).

carpenters, and ¹masons: and they built David an house. ⁽¹²⁾ And David perceived that the LORD had established him king over Israel, and that he had exalted his kingdom for his people Israel's sake.

⁽¹³⁾ And ªDavid took *him* more concubines and wives out of Jerusalem, after he was come from Hebron: and there were yet sons and daughters born to David. ⁽¹⁴⁾ And ᵇthese *be* the names of those that were born unto him in Jerusalem; Shammuah, and Shobab, and Nathan, and Solomon, ⁽¹⁵⁾ Ibhar also, and Elishua, and Nepheg, and Japhia, ⁽¹⁶⁾ and Elishama, and Eliada, and Eliphalet.

⁽¹⁷⁾ ᶜBut when the Philistines heard that they had anointed David king over

1 Heb., *hewers of the stone of the wall.*
B.C. 1047.
a 1 Chron. 3. 9.
b 1 Chron. 3. 5.
c 1 Chron. 11. 16 & 14. 8.
d Isa. 28. 21.
2 That is, *The plain of breaches.*
e 1 Chron. 14. 12.
3 Or, *took them away.*

Israel, all the Philistines came up to seek David; and David heard *of it*, and went down to the hold. ⁽¹⁸⁾ The Philistines also came and spread themselves in the valley of Rephaim. ⁽¹⁹⁾ And David enquired of the LORD, saying, Shall I go up to the Philistines? wilt thou deliver them into mine hand? And the LORD said unto David, Go up: for I will doubtless deliver the Philistines into thine hand. ⁽²⁰⁾ And David came to ᵈBaal-perazim, and David smote them there, and said, The LORD hath broken forth upon mine enemies before me, as the breach of waters. Therefore he called the name of that place ²Baal-perazim. ⁽²¹⁾ And there they left their images, and David and his men ᵉ³burned them.

The Israelites evidently had little skill in architecture, since they relied on the Phœnicians for workmen both for this palace and for Solomon's, as well as for the Temple.

⁽¹²⁾ **For his people Israel's sake.**—David's prosperity had not blinded him to the fact that his blessings came to him as the head of the theocracy, and for the sake of God's chosen people.

⁽¹³⁾ **More concubines and wives.**—In Deut. xvii. 17, the law had been given for the future king, "Neither shall he multiply wives to himself." David certainly came perilously near a violation of this law, although he did not, like his son Solomon, take wives and concubines in enormous number for the sake of having a great harem—an important element in the Oriental ideas of regal magnificence. Any possible ambiguity in the phrase "*out of Jerusalem*" is removed by the expression in the parallel place (1 Chron. xiv. 3), "*at Jerusalem.*" Altogether, here and in Chronicles, the names of nineteen sons are mentioned; those of the daughters are not given, although one, Thamar, is mentioned in the story in chap. xiii.

⁽¹⁴⁾ **These be the names.**—The same list, with some variations, is given in 1 Chron. iii. 5—8; xiv. 5—7. According to 1 Chron. iii. 5, the first four were children of Bathsheba (Bath-shua), and were consequently not born until a later period of David's reign. Solomon and Nathan are the two sons through whom St. Matthew and St. Luke trace our Lord's genealogy. Although Solomon is placed last in all the lists, he appears, from chap. xii. 24, to have been the oldest of Bathsheba's sons, and could otherwise hardly have been old enough to take charge of the kingdom at his father's death. The variations in the names are chiefly mere differences of spelling. The first, *Elishama*, in 1 Chron. iii. 6, is evidently a copyist's mistake for *Elishua*, since Elishama occurs again in verse 8; and the names of Eliphalet and Nogah, given in both lists in Chronicles, are omitted here, probably because they died young, the name of the former being given again to the last son in all the lists. In 1 Chron. iii. 9, it is said that all these were sons of David's wives, besides those of his concubines.

⁽¹⁷⁾ **When the Philistines heard.**—After this general summary, the narrative goes back to take up detailed events in their order. First comes an attack of the Philistines. Their attention had naturally been hitherto occupied with Abner and Ish-bosheth, who ruled over the far greater part of the land; but when they heard that the old nation was united under their old foe, they saw that no time was to be lost in attacking him before his power should be consolidated. Yet their necessary consultations, and the mustering of their forces, allowed time for the conquest of Jerusalem, which David seems to have accomplished with the forces gathered at his coronation.

Went down to the hold.—As David went "down" to this place, and then "up" (verse 19) from it to the attack on the Philistines, it is not likely that "the hold" means the citadel of Zion. It must have been some stronghold near the Philistine army. It could not have been, as some have thought, the cave of Adullam. According to the monastic tradition, this was seven or eight miles S.E. of Bethlehem; according to the more ancient view, it was in the plain of Judah, west of the mountains; thus, in either case, quite remote from the scene of the battle.

⁽¹⁸⁾ **Rephaim.**—Translated in Josh. xv. 8, *the valley of the giants.* It was a fruitful valley, stretching some three miles S. and S.W. from Jerusalem, and only separated from the valley of Hinnom by a narrow ridge. It gave ample room for a large encampment, and its situation is an additional proof that the capture of Jerusalem had already been made, since the Philistines came here "to seek David." They had, however, encamped in the same place at earlier times also (see chap. xxiii. 13).

⁽²⁰⁾ **Baal - perazim** = *possessor* (or *lord*) *of breaches.* After David had inquired of the Lord and received a favourable answer (verse 19), he made a sudden attack, like a bursting forth of waters, and carried all before him. The victory was so signal as to give a new name to the locality, and to be remembered centuries afterwards as a memorable instance of Divine aid (Isa. xxviii. 21). The name has no reference to the heathen deity *Baal.*

⁽²¹⁾ **Their images.**—The Philistines took their idols with them to battle, as the Israelites had formerly taken the ark, and the suddenness and completeness of their defeat is shown by their leaving them on the

(22) And the Philistines came up yet again, and spread themselves in the valley of Rephaim. (23) And when David enquired of the LORD, he said, Thou shalt not go up; *but* fetch a compass behind them, and come upon them over against the mulberry trees. (24) And let it be, when thou hearest the sound of a going in the tops of the mulberry trees, that then thou shalt bestir thyself: for then shall the LORD go out before thee, to smite the host of the Philistines.

d 1 Chron. 13. 5, 6.

B.C. 1042.

1 Or, *at which the name, even the name of the LORD of hosts was called upon.*

(25) And David did so, as the LORD had commanded him; and smote the Philistines from Geba until thou come to Gazer.

CHAPTER VI.—(1) Again, David gathered together all *the* chosen *men* of Israel, thirty thousand. (2) And *a* David arose, and went with all the people that *were* with him from Baale of Judah, to bring up from thence the ark of God, ¹whose name is called by the name of

field. The statement that David "burned" them is taken from 1 Chron. xiv. 12, the Hebrew here being simply "took them away." (See Deut. vii. 5.)

(22) **Came up yet again.**—As David had not followed up his victory (probably because he was not yet in condition to do so) the Philistines repeated their attack in the same place.

(23) **Shall not go up.**—The enemy, on the same battle-ground, would have prepared for attack from the same direction as before; consequently David is directed to go round them and attack them unexpectedly from the opposite quarter.

(24) **The sound of a going.**—After David has gone to the rear of his enemies, he is to wait by "the mulberry trees," or, as now generally understood, *baca-shrubs*, a plant resembling the balsam. Here a Divine signal was to be given him in "the sound of a going," or, rather, of a march. The word is used of the march of the hosts of the Lord in Judg. v. 4; Ps. lxviii. 7. Then David was to "bestir himself," literally, *be sharp*; he was to act quickly and vigorously.

(25) **From Geba . . . to Gazer.**—In the parallel passage (1 Chron. xiv. 16) it is "from Gibeon to Gazer." One or the other is a slip of the scribe, and there can be little question that Gibeon is the true reading, since it lies about five and a half miles north-west of Jerusalem, while Geba (Gibeah) is about seven and a half miles north-east. The site of Gazer (or Gezer) has not been exactly identified, but it was certainly just on the edge of the Philistine plain. The distance of the pursuit from Gibeon was about twelve miles, and six miles more must already have been passed over before reaching Gibeon from the valley of Rephaim. The flight of the Philistines was determined in this north-westerly direction at first, from the fact that David had "fetched a compass," and attacked them from the south. In 1 Chron. xiv. 8—17, these battles are placed between the unsuccessful (chap. xiii. 5—14) and the successful (chap. xv.) attempts to bring up the ark to Jerusalem. It is impossible now to determine the exact details of the chronology.

VI.

This chapter contains a condensed narrative of the bringing up of the ark to Jerusalem, of which a much more full account is given in 1 Chron. xiii.—xvi. It was the impulse of David's piety to desire that the ark might be in the royal city, and the dictate of wise policy that his capital should become the centre of the national worship. The question may be asked, Why he did not at the same time bring up the Tabernacle? Two reasons may be suggested: (1) That by the force of circumstances there were now two high-priests, neither of whom could well be displaced—Abiathar,

the companion of David in his trials and outlawry, and the heir to the high-priesthood, as son of the murdered Ahimelech; and Zadok, the high-priest in the later years of Saul, whom David found in office when he came to the throne, and who had joined him at Hebron (1 Chron. xii. 28). It may have been wiser, therefore, for the present, to leave a necessity for high-priestly ministrations in different places. Zadok exercised his office at the Tabernacle at Gibeon (1 Chron. xvi. 39), and Abiathar was probably with the ark. (2) It might have been too great a change and shock to the people to concentrate everything at once in the new capital. The removal of the Tabernacle from Gibeon might have been resisted.

There is no sufficient reason to doubt that Ps. lxviii. was composed and chanted on this occasion, its martial tone being very natural in connection with the recent victories over the Philistines. Pss. ci. and xv. were probably sung at the removal of the ark from the house of Obed-edom (verses 12—16), while Ps. xxiv. was undoubtedly the triumphant chant with which the ark entered the city. All these should be studied in connection with this narrative. Ps. cxxxii. is also, more doubtfully, referred to this period.

(1) **Again, David gathered.**—The word "again" should be transposed: "David gathered together again"—referring to the former military musters. In 1 Chron. xiii. 1—4, mention is made of the consultations with the leaders of Israel which preceded this gathering, and the gathering itself is there (verse 5) said to be of "all Israel." But "all Israel" was evidently represented by the thirty thousand (the LXX. reads seventy thousand) of its more prominent men.

(2) **From Baale of Judah.**—There is either a textual error here, so that instead of *from* should be read *to*, or else the historian is so occupied with his main subject that he omits the mention of the journey to Baale. In Josh. xv. 9 and 1 Chron. xiii. 6, Baale is said to be another name for Kirjath-jearim. This was the place to which the ark was carried after its removal from Bethshemesh (1 Sam. vii. 2), and it had remained here ever since. It has been generally identified with *Kuryet-el-enab*, about eight miles a little north of west from Jerusalem. More recent opinion places it at *'Erma*, about eleven miles a little south of west from Jerusalem, and four miles east of Bethshemesh. In either case it was three or four hours' march from the capital.

Whose name is called.—Neither the text nor the margin of the English represents the original quite accurately. Translate, *which is called by the name, the name of Jehovah of hosts*. The ark is thus described

the LORD of hosts that dwelleth *between* the cherubims.

(3) And they ¹set the ark of God upon a new cart, and brought it out of the house of Abinadab that *was* in ²Gibeah: and Uzzah and Ahio, the sons of Abinadab, drave the new cart. (4) And they brought it out of ᵃthe house of Abinadab which *was* at Gibeah, ³accompanying the ark of God: and Ahio went before the ark. (5) And David and all the house of Israel played before the LORD on all manner of *instruments made of* fir wood, even on harps, and on psalteries, and on timbrels, and on cornets, and on cymbals.

(6) And ᵇwhen they came to Nachon's threshingfloor, Uzzah put forth *his hand* to the ark of God, and took hold of it; for the oxen ⁴shook *it*. (7) And the anger of the LORD was kindled against Uzzah; and God smote him there for *his* ⁵error; and there he died by the ark of God. (8) And David was displeased, because the LORD had ⁶made a breach upon Uzzah: and he called the name of the place ⁷Perez-uzzah to this day. (9) And David was afraid of the LORD that day, and said, How shall the ark of the LORD come to me? (10) So David would not remove the ark of the LORD unto him into the city of David: but David carried it aside into the house of

---

1 Heb., *made to ride.*
2 Or, *The hill.*
a 1 Sam. 7. 2.
3 Heb., *with.*
b 1 Chron. 13. 9.
4 Or, *stumbled.*
5 Or, *rashness.*
6 Heb., *broken.*
7 That is, *The breach of Uzzah.*

---

as being the visible symbol of God's presence and of His covenant with His people.

(3) **Upon a new cart.**—The *new* cart, one which had been used for no other purpose, was doubtless intended as a mark of respect (comp. 1 Sam. vi. 7); yet it was a violation of the law (Numb. vii. 9), requiring that the ark should be *borne* by the Levites. It is not necessary to suppose that David intended to violate the law; but the ark having been left neglected for more than two generations, the exact requirements in regard to it may easily have passed out of mind.

Abinadab that was in Gibeah.—Rather, *in the hill*, as the same word is translated in 1 Sam. vii. 1. Abinadab himself may have been long since dead, and Uzzah and Ahio may have been either his sons, now advanced in life, or his grandsons.

(4) **And they brought it.**—The text has undoubtedly suffered here through the repetition of a line by the scribes. The whole verse is omitted in the parallel passage in 1 Chron. xiii., and the first half of it (which is a repetition of verse 3) in the LXX.

(5) **Played.**—This word means dancing accompanied by music. (See 1 Sam. xviii. 7, xxi. 11, 1 Chron. xiii. 8, xv. 29, &c.)

On all manner of instruments made of fir wood.—Instead of this strange expression, the parallel passage in 1 Chron. xiii. 8 has "with all their might and with songs." The difference between the two is very slight in the Hebrew, and it is generally thought that the latter is the correct reading. The variation, however, must have been ancient, since the LXX. combines the two.

Cornets.—This word occurs only here, and is thought from its etymology to mean some kind of metal instrument with bells or rings, which gave forth its sound on being shaken. The Vulg. translates *sistra*. Instead of it Chronicles has "trumpets."

(6) **Nachon's threshingfloor.**—This place is entirely unknown. 1 Chron. xiii. 9 has "the threshingfloor of Chidon;" but it may be doubted whether the word is a proper name at all. The name, whatever it was, was now superseded by *Perez-uzzah* (verse 8). The turning aside of the oxen to snatch the scattered grain of the threshingfloor may have caused the trouble.

(7) **For his error.**—The original is here very obscure: 1 Chron. xiii. 10 has "because he put his hand to the ark." (Comp. 1 Sam. vi. 19.) Especial sacredness was by the law attached to the ark, and it was strictly commanded, that when it was to be moved it should be first covered by the priests, and then borne by the Levites by means of its staves; but until it was covered, the Levites might not look upon it, and might not touch it, upon pain of death (Numb. iv. 5, 15, 19, 20). Uzzah was probably a Levite, or, at any rate, had been so long in the house with the ark that he ought to have made himself familiar with the law in regard to it. What may seem, at first thought, an exceeding severe penalty for a well-meaning, though unlawful act, is seen on reflection to have been a very necessary manifestation of the Divine displeasure; for this act involved not only a violation of the letter of the law (of which David also was guilty), but a want of reverence for the majesty of God as symbolised by the ark, and showed a disposition to profane familiarity with sacred things. "Uzzah was a type of all who, with good intentions, humanly speaking, yet with unsanctified minds, interfere in the affairs of the kingdom of God, from the notion that they are in danger, and with the hope of saving them" (O. von Gerlach). Judgments of this kind were, however, temporal, and give in themselves no indication of the treatment of the offender beyond the grave.

(8) **Was displeased.**—More exactly, *was angry*. The cause of his vexation was the Divine judgment upon Uzzah; yet it does not follow that he was angry with God, but rather was simply vexed and disturbed at this most untoward interruption of his plans.

Made a breach.—Comp. Ex. xix. 22, where the same word is used of a sudden Divine visitation upon irreverence. The phrase "to this day" is extremely indefinite, and might have been used either ten years or centuries after the event.

(9) **David was afraid.**—The immediate effect of the judgment was to produce in David, and doubtless in all the people, that awe of the majesty of God in which they had shown themselves deficient. If this was at first excessive, it was soon moderated.

(10) **Obed-edom the Gittite.**—He was a Levite, but whether of the family of Kohath or of Merari is uncertain, since at this time the name appears in both these families (see for Merari, 1 Chron. xv. 17, 18, and for Kohath, *ib*. xxvi. 1, 4, 8, 13—15). The one here mentioned was a *Gittite, i.e.*, born at, or belonging to, Gath-rimmon, a Levitical city on the confines of Dan and Manasseh (Josh. xxi. 24, 25). One of these Levites is described as "the son of Jeduthun" (1 Chron. xvi. 38, where both are mentioned), and as Jeduthun probably belonged to the family of Merari, it is probable

Obed-edom the Gittite. ⁽¹¹⁾ And the ark of the LORD continued in the house of Obed-edom the Gittite three months: and the LORD blessed Obed-edom and all his household.

⁽¹²⁾ And it was told king David, saying, The LORD hath blessed the house of Obed-edom, and all that *pertaineth* unto him, because of the ark of God. ᵃ So David went and brought up the ark of God from the house of Obed-edom into the city of David with gladness. ⁽¹³⁾ And it was so, that when they that bare the ark of the LORD had gone six paces, he sacrificed oxen and fatlings. ⁽¹⁴⁾ And David danced before the LORD with all *his* might; and David *was* girded with a linen ephod. ⁽¹⁵⁾ So David and all the house of Israel brought up the ark of the LORD with shouting, and with the sound of the trumpet.

⁽¹⁶⁾ And as the ark of the LORD came into the city of David, Michal Saul's daughter looked through a window, and saw king David leaping and dancing before the LORD; and she despised him in her heart.

⁽¹⁷⁾ And they brought in the ark of the LORD, and set it in his place, in the midst of the tabernacle that David had ¹pitched for it: and David offered burnt offerings and peace offerings before the LORD. ⁽¹⁸⁾ And as soon as David had made an end of offering burnt offerings and peace

a 1 Chron. 15. 25.

1 Heb., *stretched.*

---

that the one here mentioned was called "the Gittite" for distinction's sake, and belonged to the family of Kohath, to which Gath-rimmon belonged (Josh. xxi. 20). Moreover, it is said of the Obed-edom of 1 Chron. xxvi. 4, 5, that "God blessed him," which seems to refer to this passage. The name, although a singular one (*servant of Edom*) was not uncommon, and was also borne by one having charge of the vessels of the sanctuary in the days of King Amaziah (2 Chron. xxv. 24). The Obed-edoms of David's time were porters of the Tabernacle, Levitical musicians, and took an active part in bringing the ark to Jerusalem, and afterwards in ministering before it (1 Chron. xv. 16, 18, 21, 24; xvi. 4, 5, 37, 38; xxvi. 1, 4, 13—15).

⁽¹²⁾ **Went and brought up.**—The immediate reason for David's action was the knowledge of the blessings which had come to Obed-edom through the presence of the ark, in contrast to the punishment of Uzzah; yet this implies neither jealousy nor a wish to deprive his subject of a blessing. It had been his original purpose to carry the ark to Jerusalem, and he had only desisted in a fit of vexation and then of fear. He now saw that such fear was groundless, and went on to the completion of his unfinished action. The word "with gladness" means with festal shouts and rejoicings.

⁽¹³⁾ **They that bare the ark.**—David no longer presumed to violate the law, but took care that the ark should be *borne* by the proper persons. In 1 Chron. xv. a detailed account is given of the sanctification of the priests and Levites for the purpose, and of the musical arrangements.

Had gone six paces.—As soon as the removal of the ark had been successfully begun, David offered sacrifices of thanksgiving and of prayer; and again, when the journey was completed, "they offered burnt sacrifices and peace offerings before God" (ver. 17, 1 Chron. xvi. 1). The work was begun and ended with solemn sacrifice. It is quite unnecessary to suppose that offerings were made at each six steps of the way, for although this might have been possible, it is not recorded. Of course, David offered these sacrifices, like ˣ "all Israel" in 1 Kings viii. 62, through the ministration of the priests whom he had called together.

⁽¹⁴⁾ **David danced.**—The religious dances on occasions of great national blessing were usually performed by women only (Ex. xv. 20, 21; Judg. xi. 34; 1 Sam. xviii. 6). The king, by now taking part in them himself, marked his strong sense of the importance of the occasion, and his readiness to do his utmost in God's honour.

Girded with a linen ephod.—This is usually spoken of as if David were arrayed in a distinctively priestly dress; but it is remarkable that the ephod was not prescribed as a part of the priestly dress—the ephod of the *high-priest* (Ex. xxv. 7, &c.) being quite a different thing—and was worn by others, as Samuel (1 Sam. ii. 18). The wearing of the ephod, however, is spoken of in 1 Sam. xxii. 18 as characteristic of the priests, and in Judg. viii. 27, xvii. 5, xviii. 14—20, it is connected with idolatrous worship. It is also to be noted that the high priest's ephod (Ex. xxviii. 6, 8; &c.) was made of *shesh*, while the garments of the ordinary priests, as well as the ephods of Samuel and David, were of *bad*. The explanation seems to be that the ephod of *bad* was simply a garment worn by any one engaged in a religious service, and it is used in 1 Sam. xxii. 18 to describe the priests, because such service constituted their ordinary life. It was not, therefore, a peculiarly priestly dress, though naturally more worn by them than by any one else.

⁽¹⁶⁾ **She despised him.**—The contrast is here strongly brought out between the spirit of Saul's house in which Michal had been brought up, and that of David. In Saul's time the ark had been neglected, and true religion was uncared for. Michal, therefore, who had fallen in love with David as a brave hero, could not understand the religious enthusiasm which led him to rank himself among the common people before the Lord.

⁽¹⁷⁾ **The tabernacle.**—Not the tabernacle made for it in the wilderness, and which seems to have been now at Gibeon, but a special tent which David, as is immediately added, had prepared for it.

⁽¹⁸⁾ **Peace offerings.**—While the "burnt offerings" were dedicatory, the peace offerings were eucharistic, and were also intended here, as in 1 Kings viii. 62—65, to supply the wants of the people by a religious feast of communion with God.

He blessed the people.—As Solomon did at the dedication of the temple (1 Kings viii. 14, 55), and in both cases this was eminently fitting; but such blessing is by no means to be mistaken for the peculiar priestly blessing for which the form was prescribed in Num. vi. 22—26.

offerings, ᵃhe blessed the people in the name of the LORD of hosts. ⁽¹⁹⁾ And he dealt among all the people, *even* among the whole multitude of Israel, as well to the women as men, to every one a cake of bread, and a good piece *of flesh*, and a flagon *of wine*. So all the people departed every one to his house.

⁽²⁰⁾ Then David returned to bless his household. And Michal the daughter of Saul came out to meet David, and said, How glorious was the king of Israel to day, who uncovered himself to day in the eyes of the handmaids of his servants, as one of the vain fellows ¹shamelessly uncovereth himself! ⁽²¹⁾ And David said unto Michal, *It was* before the LORD, which chose me before thy father, and before all his house, to appoint me ruler over the people of the LORD, over Israel: therefore will I play before the LORD. ⁽²²⁾ And I will yet be more vile than thus, and will be base in mine own sight: and ²of the maidservants which thou hast spoken of, of them shall I be had in honour. ⁽²³⁾ Therefore Michal the daughter of Saul had no child unto the day of her death.

CHAPTER VII.—⁽¹⁾ And it came to pass, ᵇwhen the king sat in his house, and the LORD had given him rest round about from all his enemies; ⁽²⁾ that the king said unto Nathan the prophet, See now, I dwell in an house of cedar, but the ark of God dwelleth within curtains. ⁽³⁾ And Nathan said to the king, Go, do all that *is* in thine heart; for the LORD *is* with thee.

⁽⁴⁾ And it came to pass that night, that the word of the LORD came unto

a 1 Chron. 16. 2.

1 Or, *openly*.

2 Or, *of the handmaids of my servants*.

b 1 Chron. 17. 2.

⁽¹⁹⁾ **A good piece of flesh.**—A peculiar word, used only here and in 1 Chron. xvi. 3, but the context shows that it is rightly interpreted in the English. The phrase "a flagon *of wine*" (used also in 1 Chron. xvi. 3; Cant. ii. 5; Hos. iii. 1) should be translated "a cluster of grapes or raisins."

⁽²⁰⁾ **Returned.**—Michal had seen David from the window as he passed by his house on his way with the ark to its tent. Now, having dismissed and blessed the people, he returns to bless those members of his household whom eastern custom had not allowed to take part in the ceremonies, and is met by Michal with her cutting irony. The account of this is omitted from the narrative in Chronicles.

⁽²¹⁾ **Therefore will I play.**—Rather, *have I danced*. (See verse 5.)

Before the Lord.—David first gives the true and sufficient reason of his conduct—what he had done was before the Lord, in honouring whom no man can be really humbled; and then he turns with a reproof to Michal, which should have shown her the utter unworthiness of her objections. God had set aside her father and his house for this very spirit of pride in which she was now indulging, and had chosen him instead.

⁽²²⁾ **Base in mine own sight.**—The LXX., not understanding this expression, has changed it to " in thine eyes." But the meaning is, that while Michal had charged him with making himself base in the eyes of the maidservants (who were no fit judges of such matters), he was ready to abase himself in his own eyes, to do anything, however humbling it might seem even to himself, which should be for the honour and glory of God.

⁽²³⁾ **Had no child.**—The severest privation to an Oriental woman. It is quite possible that during Michal's long separation from David, while he was an outlaw, and she was married to Phaltiel (who was deeply attached to her, chap. iii. 16), they had become somewhat alienated from each other; and when the totally different spirit by which they were animated was brought out on this occasion, David determined to have no further intercourse with her.

VII.

The parallel account to this chapter is in 1 Chron. xvii., and the differences are very slight.

⁽¹⁾ **Had given him rest.**—No intimation is given of how long this may have been after the events narrated in the last chapter; but it is evident that this narrative is placed here, not because it followed chronologically, but because it is closely related in subject, and the historian, after telling of the removal of the ark, wished to record in that connection David's further purposes in the same direction. It must have been after the successful close of David's principal foreign wars—" rest round about from all his enemies" —and the future in verse 10 does not necessarily imply that it was before the birth of Solomon; yet it is more likely to have been in a time of quiet prosperity, before the troubles of his latter years.

⁽²⁾ **Nathan.**—This is the first mention of him, but he was already a confidential counsellor of the king, and became prominent later in this reign and in the opening of that of Solomon (chap. xii.; 1 Kings i. 10, 12, 34, 38). Nathan "the prophet" and Gad "the seer" wrote parts of the history of this and the succeeding reign (1 Chron. xxix. 29; 2 Chron. ix. 29).

Within curtains.—This is the word used in Exod. xxvi. and xxxvi. for the covering of the tabernacle. The ark was not now within that, but in a similar temporary structure. David's heart is moved by a comparison of his own royal residence with the inferior provision for the ark. Compare the opposite state of things among the returned exiles in Haggai i. 10.

⁽³⁾ **Go, do all that is in thine heart.**—Nathan naturally considered that it must be right for David to execute his pious purpose; but he spoke only according to his own sense of right, and not by Divine direction.

⁽⁴⁾ **That night.**—The night following Nathan's conversation with David, when the prophet's mind would have been full of what he had heard, and thus prepared for the Divine communication. That communication is distinctly marked as coming from a

Nathan, saying, (5) Go and tell ¹my servant David, Thus saith the LORD, Shalt thou build me an house for me to dwell in? (6) Whereas I have not dwelt in *any* house since the time that I brought up the children of Israel out of Egypt, even to this day, but have walked in a tent and in a tabernacle. (7) In all *the places* wherein I have walked with all the children of Israel spake I a word with ²any of the tribes of Israel, whom I commanded to feed my people Israel, saying, Why build ye not me an house of cedar? (8) Now therefore so shalt thou say unto my servant David, Thus saith the LORD of hosts, *a* I took thee from the sheepcote, ³from following the sheep, to be ruler over my people, over Israel: (9) and I was with thee whithersoever thou wentest, and have cut off all thine enemies ⁴out of thy sight, and have made thee a great name, like unto the name of the great *men* that *are* in the earth. (10) Moreover I will appoint a place for my people Israel, and will plant them, that they may dwell in a place of their own, and move no more; neither shall the children of wickedness afflict them any more, as beforetime, (11) and as since the time that I commanded judges *to be* over my people Israel, and have caused thee to rest from all thine enemies. Also the LORD telleth thee that he will make thee an house. (12) And *b*when thy days be fulfilled, and thou shalt sleep with thy fathers, I will set up thy seed after thee, which shall proceed out of thy bowels, and I will establish his kingdom. (13) *c* He shall build an house for my name, and I will stablish the throne of his kingdom for ever. (14) *d* I will be his father, and he shall be my son. *e* If he commit iniquity, I will chasten him with the rod of men, and with the stripes of the children of men: (15) but my mercy shall not depart away from him, as I took *it* from

1 Heb., *to my servant, to David.*
2 1 Chron. 17. 6, *any of the judges.*
a 1 Sam. 16. 12; Ps. 78. 70.
3 Heb., *from after.*
4 Heb., *from thy face.*
b 1 Kings 8. 20.
c 1 Kings 5. 5 & 6. 12; 1 Chron. 22. 10.
d Heb. 1. 5.
e Ps. 89. 31, 32.

---

source external to the prophet himself, by its being in direct opposition to his own view already expressed.

(5) **Shalt thou build?**—The question implies the negative, as it is expressed in 1 Chron. xvii. 5, and as it is here translated in the LXX. and Syriac.

After David was told that he should not be allowed to build a temple for God as he desired, he is promised that God will make for him a sure house, and will accept the building of the temple from his son. David is called "my servant," an expression used only of those eminent and faithful in the service of God, as Moses and Joshua, thus showing—as in fact the whole message does—that the prohibition conveyed nothing of Divine displeasure; but no reason for it is here expressed.* But in, David's parting charge to Solomon (1 Chron. xxii. 8), and to the heads of the nation (*ib.* xxviii. 3), he says, "the word of the Lord came unto" him, giving as the reason, "because thou hast shed much blood on the earth," and "hast been a man of war." Those wars had been necessary, under the circumstances in which he was placed, and had never been disapproved of God; still the mere fact that he had been a man of blood unfitted him for this sacred office.

(7) **The tribes.**—In the parallel place, 1 Chron. xvii. 6, the word is "judges," the difference in Hebrew being only of a single similar letter. But a like use of "tribes" for the judges sprung from them may be found in Ps. lxxviii. 67, 68; 1 Chron. xxviii. 4.

(8) **Sheepcote.**—Better, *pasture.*

(10) **Will appoint . . . will plant.**—There is no change of tense in the original; read, *have appointed, . . . have planted.*

---

* Two reasons for the prohibition are found by nearly all commentators in this message itself. (1) That God must first build "a house" for David before he could properly build a temple for God; and (2) that the kingdom was not yet sufficiently established and peaceful for a temple to be built. But neither of these are assigned as reasons in the Divine word, and it is better to keep only to that which is assigned, however these other facts may convince us of the fitness and propriety of the postponement of David's purpose.

---

(11) **And as since the time.**—These words are connected with the last clause of the verse before. The Lord says that He had now given His people rest under David, not allowing "the children of wickedness to afflict them any more as before time," when they were in Egypt, nor as in the troubled period of the judges, "since the time that I commanded judges," &c.

(12) **Which shall proceed.**—The promise here given certainly has immediate reference to Solomon, and it is thought by many that the use of the future shows that he was not yet born. This may be the fact, and if so, the expression will give an important indication of the point in David's reign to which this passage belongs. But the same expression might have been used after Solomon's birth, the future tense being merely an assimilation to the futures of the whole passage, and the point of the promise being that David's son *shall* succeed to his throne.

(14) **If he commit iniquity.**—The promise has plainly in view a human successor or successors of David upon his throne; and yet it also promises the establishment of David's kingdom FOREVER by an emphatic threefold repetition (ver. 13, 16), which can only be fulfilled, and has always been understood as to be fulfilled, in the Messiah. There is a similar promise of a prophet, human and yet more than human, in Deut. xviii. 15—22, and the explanation in both cases is the same. The Divine word looks forward to a long succession of human prophets or heads of the theocracy who should for the time being, and as far as might be, fill the place of the true Prophet and King, all culminating at last in Him who should fully make known the Father's will and reign over His people, of "whose kingdom there shall be no end." (Luke i. 32, 33).

(15) **As I took it from Saul.**—He and his house were utterly and permanently set aside; David's descendants will be punished for their sins, yet shall never be forgotten, and shall ultimately issue in one who shall conquer sin and death for ever.

God's Promise to David. II. SAMUEL, VII. *David's Thanksgiving.*

Saul, whom I put away before thee. ⁽¹⁶⁾ And thine house and thy kingdom shall be established for ever before thee: thy throne shall be established for ever.

⁽¹⁷⁾ According to all these words, and according to all this vision, so did Nathan speak unto David.

⁽¹⁸⁾ Then went king David in, and sat before the LORD, and he said, Who *am* I, O Lord GOD? and what *is* my house, that thou hast brought me hitherto? ⁽¹⁹⁾ And this was yet a small thing in thy sight, O Lord GOD; but thou hast spoken also of thy servant's house for a great while to come. And *is* this the ¹ manner of man, O Lord GOD? ⁽²⁰⁾ And what can David say more unto thee? for thou, Lord GOD, knowest thy servant. ⁽²¹⁾ For thy word's sake, and according to thine own heart, hast thou done all these great things, to make thy servant know *them*. ⁽²²⁾ Wherefore thou art great, O LORD God: for *there is* none like thee, neither *is there any* God beside thee, according to all that we have heard with our ears. ⁽²³⁾ And *^a* what one nation in the earth *is* like thy people, *even* like Israel, whom God went to redeem for a people to himself, and to make him a name, and to do for you great things and terrible, for thy land, before thy people, which thou redeemedst to thee from Egypt, *from* the nations and their gods? ⁽²⁴⁾ For thou hast confirmed to thyself thy people Israel *to be* a people unto thee for ever: and thou, LORD, art become their God. ⁽²⁵⁾ And now, O LORD God, the word that thou hast spoken concerning thy servant, and concerning his house, establish *it*

1 Heb., *law*.

a Deut. 4. 7.

⁽¹⁶⁾ **Established.**—Two different Hebrew words are so translated in this verse. The first is the same word as that used in ver. 12, 13, while the second is translated *sure* in 1 Sam. ii. 35; Isa. lv. 3, and would be better rendered here also *made sure*.

Before thee.—The LXX. has unnecessarily changed this to *before me*. The thought is, that David is now made the head of the line in which shall be fulfilled the primeval promise "The seed of the woman shall bruise the serpent's head." This was originally given simply to the human race (Gen. iii. 15); then restricted to the nation descended from Abraham (Gen. xxii. 18, &c.); then limited to the tribe of Judah (Gen. xlix. 10, comp. Ezek. xxi. 27), and now its fulfilment is promised in the family of David.

⁽¹⁷⁾ **This vision.**—A word applied to any Divine communication, and not merely to that given in *vision* strictly so called. (See Isa. i. 1.)

⁽¹⁸⁾ **Then went king David in, and sat.**—As always at every important point in his life, David's first care is to take that which he has in his mind before the Lord. The place to which he went must be the tent he had pitched for the ark. Here he sat to meditate in God's presence upon the communication which had now been made to him, and then to offer his thanksgiving (ver. 18—21), praise (ver. 22—24), and prayer (ver. 25—29).

The Divine Name is here printed with the word GOD in small capitals. This is always done in the Authorised Version wherever it stands for JEHOVAH in the orginal. The same custom is also followed with the word LORD. Out of reverence for the name, Jehovah never has its own vowels in Hebrew, but is printed with those belonging to *Lord*, or in case this word also is used, then with those belonging to *God*.

⁽¹⁹⁾ **Is this the manner of man?**—This clause is very obscure in the original, and little help in determining its meaning can be had from the ancient versions. The word translated "manner" is a very common one, and never has this sense elsewhere; its well established meaning is *law*. Neither is there any reason to suppose that a question is intended. Translate, "And this is a law for man!" David expresses his surprise that so great a promise, even a decree of an eternal kingdom, should be given to such as himself and his posterity. The same thought is far less strikingly expressed in the parallel passage (1 Chron. xvii. 18), "Thou hast regarded me according to the estate of a man of high degree."

⁽²²⁾ **All that we have heard with our ears.**—Such expressions are common enough in all languages not only for that which has been communicated orally, but for all that has been made known in any way; the same word is used with reference to written records in Deut. iv. 6; 2 Kings xvii. 14, xviii. 12, xix. 16 (in Hezekiah's prayer in reference to Sennacherib's letter); Neh. ix. 29; probably Esth. ii. 8; and in many other places. (So also the corresponding Greek word, Rev. i. 3, &c.). It is therefore entirely unnecessary to suppose that David refers here only to oral tradition; he means the history of the Divine dealings with his people as recorded in their sacred books.

⁽²³⁾ **Whom God went to redeem.**—The word here used for God in this its usual plural form is always construed with a singular verb when it refers to the true God. Here the verb is plural, because the thought is, "What nation is there whom its gods went to redeem?"

For you.—These words, which can only refer to Israel, seem strange in a prayer to God. They are omitted by the LXX., and changed into *for them* by the Vulg. If they are retained as they are, it must be understood that David for the moment turns in thought to the people, instead of to God whom he is immediately addressing.

For thy land.—The LXX. and the parallel passage (1 Chron. xvii. 21), instead of this have, "by driving out." If the text here may be corrected in this way, there will be no occasion for inserting *from* before *the nations*, which is not in the Hebrew. This part of the verse will then read, *to do great things and terrible, by driving out before thy people, which thou redeemedst to thee from Egypt, nations and their gods.* The phrase, "great things and terrible," in reference to the Exodus, is taken from Deut. x. 21. The whole of this part of the prayer is evidently founded upon Deut. iv. 7, 32—34.

David's Prayer.   II. SAMUEL, VIII.   *He Smites the Philistines.*

for ever, and do as thou hast said. (26) And let thy name be magnified for ever, saying, The LORD of hosts *is* the God over Israel: and let the house of thy servant David be established before thee. (27) For thou, O LORD of hosts, God of Israel, hast ¹revealed to thy servant, saying, I will build thee an house: therefore hath thy servant found in his heart to pray this prayer unto thee. (28) And now, O Lord GOD, thou *art* that God, and *ᵃ*thy words be true, and thou hast promised this goodness unto thy servant: (29) therefore now ²let it please thee to bless the house of thy servant, that it may continue for ever before thee: for thou, O Lord GOD, hast spoken *it*: and with thy blessing let the house of thy servant be blessed for ever.

CHAPTER VIII.—(1) And *ᵇ*after this it came to pass, that David smote the Philistines, and subdued them: and David took ³ Metheg-ammah out of the hand of the Philistines.

(2) And he smote Moab, and measured them with a line, casting them down to the ground; even with two lines measured he to put to death, and with one full line to keep alive. And *so* the Moabites became David's servants, *and* brought gifts.

---

¹ Heb., *opened the ear.*

^a John 17. 17.

B.C. cir. 1040.

² Heb., *be thou pleased and bless.*

^b 1 Chron. 18. 1, &c.; Ps. 60. 2.

³ Or, *The bridle of Ammah.*

---

(26) **Let thy name be magnified.**—David here, in the true spirit of the Lord's prayer, puts in the forefront of his petition the "hallowed be thy name;" and this is the striking feature of all his life, into whatever sins he may at times have been betrayed, that his main object was to live to the glory of God.

(27) **Therefore hath thy servant.**—The ground of the believer's prayer must ever be the lovingkindness and promises of God.

(29) **Let it please thee.**—These words may be taken either in the optative, as in our Version, or better in the future, constituting a prophecy based upon the promise, "It will please thee." Compare a similar possibility in the translation of the last clause of the *Te Deum*, "Let me never," or "I shall never be confounded."

Several of the Psalms have been referred by various writers to this point in David's life; but while many of them take their key-note from the promise now made, and which was ever fresh in David's thought, none of them have notes of time definitely determining them to the present occasion, unless it be Ps. cx., which seems like an inspired interpretation of the promise of the perpetuity of his kingdom, and at the same time might have taken its "local colouring" from his recent successful wars.

VIII.

This chapter contains a general summary of David's successful wars, closing with the mention (verses 16—18) of the chief officers of his kingdom. The expression with which it opens, "after this it came to pass," is a formula of connection and transition, as we might say, "and besides this;" that it does not denote chronological sequence is plain from the fact that it is also used in chap. x. 1, of the beginning of the war with the Ammonites and Syrians, the conclusion of which is mentioned in this chapter, verses 5, 6, 11, 12.

The parallel passage is 1 Chron. xviii.

This chapter may be considered as the close of the direct narrative of David's reign, the rest of the book being occupied with more detailed accounts of particular incidents occurring at various periods during its course. Thus chap. ix. treats of his kindness to Mephibosheth in connection with his affection for his departed friend Jonathan; chaps. x.—xii. of the war with the Ammonites and Syrians in connection with the story of Bathsheba (this is the only one of David's wars treated of in detail, and this evidently for the reason just given); chaps. xiii.—xix. contain the story of Absalom's rebellion, and chap. xx. of that of Bichri; chap. xxi. is an account of the famine in punishment of Saul's sin—at what period is quite unknown—closing with incidents of several Philistine campaigns; chap. xxii. is a psalm of David; chap. xxiii., another psalm, followed by a more detailed account of the heroes during the whole reign; and the book closes with chap. xxiv., David's sin in numbering the people, and his consequent punishment, with no note of time to show in what period of his reign it occurred.

(1) **Subdued them.**—In its connection this implies not merely the victory of a single battle, but the reversal of the former relation of the Philistines to Israel, and their reduction to a condition of inferiority and tribute.

Took Metheg-ammah.—No place of this name is known. The first word means *bridle*, and the other is probably, although not certainly, a derivation from the word *mother*, and has the sense *metropolis*. The translation will then be, *took the bridle* (*i.e.*, the key) *of the metropolis*, and this seems sustained by the parallel phrase in 1 Chron. xviii. 1, "took Gath and her towns (*lit*. daughters)." Gath appears to have been already the principal among the five Philistine cities (1 Sam. xxvii. 2, xxix.), and with the rest of the country remained tributary to Solomon (1 Kings iv. 21, 24).

(2) **He smote Moab.** — David's former friendly relations with Moab (probably connected with his own descent from Ruth), are mentioned in 1 Sam. xxii. 3, 4. The cause of his entire change of bearing towards them is not certainly known, but according to Jewish tradition the Moabites had proved false to their trust, and had put to death David's father and mother. This is not unlikely, as his parents are never mentioned again after they were left in Moab. Others think that the Moabites had been guilty of some treachery towards David in his war with the Syrians and Ammonites. The two suppositions are quite consistent, and both may have been true. Many writers see in this conquest at least a partial fulfilment of the prophecy in Num. xxiv. 17.

With two lines.—This expression with the "one full line" of the next clause is equivalent to saying that David measured off the bodies of his prostrate enemies with a line divided into three equal parts. When they had been made to lie down upon the ground,

(3) David smote also Hadadezer, the son of Rehob, king of Zobah, as he went to recover his border at the river Euphrates. (4) And David took ¹from him a thousand ²*chariots*, and seven hundred horsemen, and twenty thousand footmen: and David houghed all the chariot *horses*, but reserved of them *for* an hundred chariots. (5) And when the Syrians of Damascus came to succour Hadadezer king of Zobah, David slew of the Syrians two and twenty thousand men. (6) Then David put garrisons in Syria of Damascus: and the Syrians became servants to David, *and* brought gifts. And the LORD preserved David whithersoever he went. (7) And David took the shields of gold that were on the servants of Hadadezer, and brought them to Jerusalem. (8) And from Betah, and from Berothai, cities of Hadadezer, king David took exceeding much brass.

(9) When Toi king of Hamath heard that David had smitten all the host of Hadadezer, (10) then Toi sent Joram his son unto king David, to ³salute him, and

¹ Or, *of his*.
² As 1 Chron. 18. 4.
³ Heb., *Ask him of peace*.

---

side by side, the line was stretched over them. Such as were found under the two first parts of it were put to death, those under the third part were spared, thus two-thirds of all the Moabite men perished. There is no mention of this in 1 Chron. xviii. 2.

Brought gifts.—A frequent euphemism for *paid tribute*. (Comp. verse 6.)

(3) **Hadadezer . . . king of Zobah.**—This name is sometimes (1 Chron. xviii. 3, 5, 7, &c.) spelt "Hadarezer," the letters *d* and *r* being much alike in Hebrew and easily confused; but the form given here is right, *Hadad* being the chief idol of the Syrians. Zobah (called in the title of Ps. lx. *Aram*-Zobah) was a kingdom, the position of which cannot be exactly determined, but lying north-east of Israel, and formerly governed by petty kings with whom Saul had wars (1 Sam. xiv. 47). When or by what means it had become united under a single sovereign is unknown, but from verse 4 with chap. x. 6, 16, it is plain that he was a monarch of considerable power, and controlled tribes beyond the Euphrates.

To recover his border.—Literally, *to cause his hand to return*, a phrase which in itself might mean either *to renew his attack*, or *to re-establish his power*. The latter is shown to be the sense here by the expression in 1 Chron. xviii. 3, "to establish his dominion," and is so translated in the LXX. What happened is more fully explained in chap. x. 13—19: the Ammonites had obtained the help of the Syrians when their combined armies were defeated by David; Hadadezer then attempted to summon to his aid the tribes "beyond the river" (*i.e.*, the Euphrates), but David cut short his plans by another crushing defeat, which reduced them all to subjection. Our Version inserts the word *Euphrates* on the authority of the margin of the Hebrew, several MSS., and all the ancient versions. *The river*, however, would in any case mean the Euphrates.

(4) **A thousand chariots.**—The word *chariots* has evidently dropped out of the text here, but is rightly inserted, following the LXX. and 1 Chron.; 700 horsemen should also be changed to 7,000, in accordance with 1 Chron., this being a more fitting proportion to 20,000 infantry in the plains of Syria, and the difference being only in two dots over the letter marking the numeral in Hebrew.

Houghed, *i.e.*, hamstrung, to render them incapable of use in war. (Comp. Josh. xi. 6, 9.) This is meant to apply not only to the chariot horses, but to all those of the cavalry. Whether David's reservation of the number needed for 100 chariots was wrong or not, is not said. David probably felt the need of these horses as a means of more rapid communication with the distant parts of his increasing empire; yet this act may have been the entering wedge for Solomon's direct violation of Deut. xvii. 16, by sending to Egypt to "multiply horses to himself."

(5) **Syrians of Damascus.**—So called from their capital, this being the most powerful branch of the Syrian race.

Two and twenty thousand men.—Josephus (*Ant.* vii. 5, § 2) quotes from the historian Nicolaus a mention of the defeat of Hadad at this place by David.

(6) **Garrisons.**—The primary meaning of this word in the original is something *placed*, and then *placed over*. Hence it comes to have the different derived meanings of *officer* in 1 Kings iv. 5, 19; 2 Chron. viii. 10, and *garrison* (1 Sam. x. 5, xiii. 3), which is probably its meaning here.

(7) **Shields of gold.**—Solomon also "made shields of gold" (1 Kings x. 17), which appear to have been a mark of oriental magnificence. Solomon's shields were ultimately carried off by Shishak (1 Kings xiv. 25—28). The LXX. has here a curious addition, saying that Shishak carried off the shields which David captured, a manifest error, since those were made by Solomon.

(8) **Betah and from Berothai.**—There is no satisfactory clue to the situation of these places. For Betah 1 Chron. xviii. 8 has *Tibhath* in the Hebrew, a mere transposition of the letters; and for Berothai, *Chun*. Berothah is mentioned in Ezek. xlvii. 16, as on the boundary of Palestine between Hamath and Sibraim. It is said in 1 Chron. xviii. 8, that "Solomon made the brazen sea, and the pillars, and the vessels of brass," of "the exceeding much brass" here captured. The LXX., and from it the Vulgate, has inserted the same notice here. It is very doubtful whether the metal intended was brass (copper and zinc) or simply copper, or, more probably, bronze (copper and tin). Some centuries earlier great quantities of copper were carried from Syria to Egypt.

(9) **Toi king of Hamath.**—The Vatican LXX. has the name, in accordance with Chron., *Tou*. Hamath, the capital of the kingdom of the same name, was situated on the Orontes. According to 1 Chron. xviii. 3, David's victory was on the borders of this kingdom. It was tributary to Solomon (1 Kings iv. 24, 2 Chron. viii. 3, 4), subsequently became independent, and was recovered by Jeroboam II. (2 Kings xiv. 28), and was finally captured by Assyria (2 Kings xix. 13). It is described as "the great" by Amos (vi. 2), and a considerable town still occupies its site.

(10) **Joram**=Hadoram, 1 Chron. xviii. 10. Joram is probably the Jewish form of the same name. An

The Spoils dedicated to God.　　　II. SAMUEL, VIII.　　　David's Officers.

to bless him, because he had fought against Hadadezer, and smitten him: for Hadadezer [1]had wars with Toi. And Joram [2]brought with him vessels of silver, and vessels of gold, and vessels of brass: (11) which also king David did dedicate unto the LORD, with the silver and gold that he had dedicated of all nations which he subdued; (12) of Syria, and of Moab, and of the children of Ammon, and of the Philistines, and of Amalek, and of the spoil of Hadadezer, son of Rehob, king of Zobah. (13) And David gat him a name when he returned from [3]smiting of the Syrians in the valley of salt, being eighteen thousand men. (14) And he put garrisons in Edom; throughout all Edom put he garrisons, and all they of Edom became David's servants. And the LORD preserved David whithersoever he went.

(15) And David reigned over all Israel; and David executed judgment and justice unto all his people. (16) And Joab the son of Zeruiah was over the host; and Jehoshaphat the son of Ahilud was [4]recorder; (17) and Zadok the son of Ahitub, and Ahimelech the son of Abia-

[1] Heb., was a man of wars with.
[2] Heb., in his hand were.
[3] Heb., his smiting.
[4] Or, remembrancer, or, writer of chronicles.

---

embassy headed by the king's son was an especially honourable one. The occasion was David's conquest of Toi's neighbour and constant enemy, and the large presents sent by him have something of the character of tribute. The phrase "to bless him," is simply equivalent to "congratulate him," by which the same word is translated in 1 Chron. xviii. 10.

(11) **Which also.**—The dedication of the gifts of Toi is especially mentioned, because these were not, like those of verses 7, 11, 12, the spoils of *conquered* nations. David, forbidden himself to build the temple, makes every provision possible for its erection.

(12) **Of Syria.**—1 Chron. xviii. 11 reads Edom. The two names differing in the original only by one very similar letter (the *d* and *r*, which are so often confused), it might be supposed that one was an error for the other, were it not that both were actually conquered and the spoils of both dedicated by David. Syria is spoken of here because Edom has not yet been mentioned, and the account of its conquest is given afterwards (verse 14; 1 Kings xi. 15—17); while Edom is given in Chron. because the booty from Syria had just before been spoken of particularly. It may be, however, that both names were originally in both places.

Amalek.—This is the only allusion to a war with Amalek after David came to the throne. They had been "utterly destroyed" by Saul (1 Sam. xv.); but they were a nation of many tribes, and Saul's victory can relate to only one branch, since David afterwards inflicted a severe blow upon them (1 Sam. xxx.), and there is no reason why still other branches of the nation may not have proved troublesome, and been defeated by him at other times.

(13) **When he returned from smiting of the Syrians.**—Possibly, from the similarity in the original between *Syria* and *Edom* (see verses 3 and 12), the words "he smote Edom" have dropped out of the text, but this supposition is not necessary. The course of affairs appears to have been as follows:—the war was originally undertaken against the Ammonites (chap. x. 1—12), who had obtained the aid of the Syrians. In the first campaign their combined armies were defeated (*ib.* 13, 14), and they sought aid from every quarter, from the tribes beyond the Euphrates, on the north (chap. x. 16), and from the Edomites on the south. David first inflicted a crushing defeat upon the allies near Hamath, and then "returned" to the south, where he again met them in "the valley of salt"—the *Arabah* south of the Dead Sea, this latter army being naturally chiefly composed of Edomites, and so called in 1 Chron. xviii. 12, and in the title of Ps. lx., but here spoken of as Syrians because the whole confederacy is called by the name of its most powerful member. David himself returned from the southern campaign; but what was done by his general, Abishai, under his orders, is naturally said to have been done by him. Meantime, when this first battle, attended with the slaughter of 18,000 men, had been won by Abishai, Joab, the general-in-chief, being set free by the victories in the north, gained another battle in the same locality, killing 12,000 (Ps. lx., title). The power of Edom was now completely broken, and the whole forces of Israel were mustered under Joab to overrun their country and destroy all its male inhabitants (1 Kings xi. 15, 16), certain of them, however, excepted (1 Kings xi. 17), and their descendants in after ages were relentless foes of Israel. (Comp. the prophecy of Isaac, Gen. xxvii. 40.)

In this summary of David's reign the historian here turns from his wars and victories over other nations to the internal affairs of his kingdom. Substantially the same list of officers is again given in chap. xx. 23—26.

(16) **Was recorder.**—This was a different office from that of "the scribe" (filled by Seraiah), and appears from 2 Kings xviii. 18—37; 2 Chron. xxxiv. 8, to have been one of considerable importance. (Comp. also Esther vi. 1.) His duty is supposed to have been something like that of the modern "chancellor," and he not only registered the king's decrees, but was his adviser. The same person continued to fill the office in the early years of Solomon's reign (1 Kings iv. 3).

(17) **Ahimelech, the son of Abiathar.**—So Ahimelech is also described in 1 Chron. xviii. 16; xxiv. 6; on the other hand, Abiathar is expressly said to be the son of Ahimelech in the narrative in 1 Sam. xxii. 20—23. This difficulty is increased by the further notices of the men bearing these names. Ahimelech was certainly the high priest who gave the shew-bread to David, and was slain in consequence by Saul (1 Sam. xxi., xxii.), and Abiathar, who fled to David, and afterwards became high priest, and was finally put out of the high-priesthood by Solomon (1 Kings i., ii.) was certainly his son; but, on the other hand, in 1 Chron. xxiv. 3, 6, 31 Ahimelech is said to have been the copriest with Zadok during the reign of David, and our Lord says that David ate the shew-bread "in the days of Abiathar, the high priest" (Mark ii. 26). These apparently conflicting facts have occasioned unnecessary perplexity. The simple solution of the difficulty seems to be that *both* names were borne alike by father and by son, so that both of them are spoken of sometimes under one name, sometimes under the other.

thar, were the priests; and Seraiah was the ¹scribe; ⁽¹⁸⁾ ᵃ and Benaiah the son of Jehoiada was over both the Cherethites and the Pelethites; and David's sons were ² chief rulers.

CHAPTER IX.—⁽¹⁾ And David said, Is there yet any that is left of the house of Saul, that I may shew him kindness for Jonathan's sake? ⁽²⁾ And there was of the house of Saul a servant whose name was Ziba. And when they had called him unto David, the king said unto him, Art thou Ziba? And he said, Thy servant is he. ⁽³⁾ And the king said, Is there not yet any of the house of Saul, that I may shew the kindness of God unto him? And Ziba said unto the king,

1 Or, *secretary*.

a 1 Chron. 18. 17.

2 Or, *princes*.

b ch. 4. 4.

Jonathan hath yet a son, which is ᵇlame on his feet. ⁽⁴⁾ And the king said unto him, Where is he? And Ziba said unto the king, Behold, he is in the house of Machir, the son of Ammiel, in Lo-debar. ⁽⁵⁾ Then king David sent, and fetched him out of the house of Machir, the son of Ammiel, from Lo-debar.

⁽⁶⁾ Now when Mephibosheth, the son of Jonathan, the son of Saul, was come unto David, he fell on his face, and did reverence. And David said, Mephibosheth. And he answered, Behold thy servant! ⁽⁷⁾ And David said unto him, Fear not: for I will surely shew thee kindness for Jonathan thy father's sake, and will restore thee all the land of Saul thy father; and thou shalt eat bread at

---

On the double high-priesthood of Zadok and Abiathar, see Note at the beginning of chap. vi.

⁽¹⁸⁾ **The Cherethites and the Pelethites.**—These bodies of men, here mentioned for the first time, afterwards appear frequently, constituting the most trusted part of the king's army, and forming his especial body-guard (chaps. xv. 18, xx. 7, 23; 1 Kings i. 38, 44; 1 Chron. xviii. 17). Benaiah, who commanded them, a hero from Kabzeel (chap. xxiii. 20), was afterwards promoted by Solomon to be general-in-chief (1 Kings ii. 35). But the meaning of the words, "the Cherethites and the Pelethites," has been much disputed. On the one hand it is urged that the form of the name indicates a tribal designation, and that there was a tribe of Cherethites living south of Philistia (1 Sam. xxx. 14), who are also mentioned in connection with the Philistines in Ezek. xxv. 16; Zeph. ii. 5. Besides, these names appear as those of bodies of troops only during the reign of David, and the objection that he would have been unlikely to employ foreign mercenaries may be met by the supposition that they had embraced the religion of Israel. On the other hand, the Chaldee ("archers and slingers") and Syriac ("nobles and rustics") understood them as appellatives, and it is said that they should properly be translated "executioners and runners," such offices falling to the chief troops in all Oriental armies; no tribe of "Pelethites" is known, and in chap. xx. 23 the expression translated "Cherethites and Pelethites" has another form for "Cherethites," which again occurs with "Pelethites" in 2 Kings xi. 4, 19, and is translated "the captains and the guard." The question does not seem to admit of positive determination.

Chief rulers.—So these words are rendered in all the ancient versions except the Vulg., and the same term is applied in 1 Kings iv. 5 to Zabud, with the explanation "the king's friend," and also in chap. xx. 26 to Ira, "a chief ruler about (literally, at the side of) David." The word, however (cohen), is the one generally used for "priest," and there seems here to be a reminiscence in the word of that early time when the chief civil and ecclesiastical offices were united in the head of the family or tribe. Such use of the word had become now almost obsolete, and quite so in the time when the Chronicles were written, since they substitute here (1 Chron. xviii. 17) "chief about (literally, at the hand of) the king." For this change in the use of the word, "exact analogies may be found in ecclesiastical words, as bishop, priest, deacon, minister, and many others."—*Speaker's Commentary*.

IX.

The account of David's kindness to the house of Saul (entirely omitted in Chronicles).

⁽¹⁾ **For Jonathan's sake.**—There is no note of time to show when this occurred, but, as Mephibosheth was only five years old at the time of his father's death (chap. iv. 4), and now had a young son (verse 12), it must have been several years after David began to reign in Jerusalem. His motive is sufficiently expressed—for the sake of his early and much-loved friend Jonathan.

⁽³⁾ **The kindness of God.**—Comp. 1 Sam. xx. 14, = kindness such as God shows, very great, and in the fear of God. The crippled Mephibosheth, the only surviving descendant of Saul in the male line, disheartened by the misfortunes of his house, and probably fearing the usual Oriental custom of cutting off all the heirs of a monarch of another line, was living in such obscurity that he was only found through the information of his servant Ziba, a man of considerable substance, and perhaps known to some of the court.

⁽⁴⁾ **Machir, the son of Ammiel, in Lo-debar.** —From chap. xvii. 27—29, the situation of Lo-debar must have been east of the Jordan, and near Mahanaim, and Machir appears as a man of wealth and position. Up to this time he was probably secretly an adherent to the house of Saul; but David's kindness to his master's son won his heart, and afterwards, in David's own great distress during his flight from Absalom, he proved a faithful friend. If this Ammiel is the same with the one mentioned in 1 Chron. iii. 5 (called Eliam in chap. xi. 3), Machir must have been the brother of Bath-sheba; but the name was not an uncommon one.

⁽⁶⁾ **Mephibosheth.**—Called Merib-baal in 1 Chron. viii. 34; ix. 40. (See Note on ii. 12.)

⁽⁷⁾ **Fear not.**—Mephibosheth could not have remembered the affection between David and his father Jonathan, and was naturally in fear. (See verse 3.) David at once reassures him, promises him all the real estate of his grandfather, which had either fallen to David or else to distant relations, and adds, "thou shalt

my table continually. (8) And he bowed himself, and said, What *is* thy servant, that thou shouldest look upon such a dead dog as I *am?*

(9) Then the king called to Ziba, Saul's servant, and said unto him, I have given unto thy master's son all that pertained to Saul and to all his house. (10) Thou therefore, and thy sons, and thy servants, shall till the land for him, and thou shalt bring in *the fruits,* that thy master's son may have food to eat: but Mephibosheth thy master's son shall eat bread alway at my table. Now Ziba had fifteen sons and twenty servants. (11) Then said Ziba unto the king, According to all that my lord the king hath commanded his servant, so shall thy servant do. As for Mephibosheth, *said the king,* he shall eat at my table, as one of the king's sons. (12) And Mephibosheth had a young son, whose name *was* Micha. And all that dwelt in the house of Ziba *were* servants unto Mephibosheth. (13) So Mephibosheth dwelt in Jerusalem: for he did eat continually at the king's table; and was lame on both his feet.

CHAPTER X.—(1) And it came to pass after this, that the *a* king of the children of Ammon died, and Hanun his son reigned in his stead. (2) Then said David, I will shew kindness unto Hanun the son of Nahash, as his father shewed kindness unto me. And David sent to comfort him by the hand of his servants for his father. And David's servants came into the land of the children of Ammon. (3) And the princes of the children of Ammon said unto Hanun their lord, ¹ Thinkest thou that David doth honour thy father, that he hath sent comforters unto thee? hath not David *rather* sent his servants unto thee, to search the city, and to spy it out,

B.C. cir. 1037.

a 1 Chron. 19.1.

1 Heb., *In thine eyes doth David.*

---

eat bread at my table continually,"—a mark of great honour in Oriental lands. (See chap. xix. 33; 1 Kings ii. 7; 2 Kings xxv. 29, &c.)

(8) **Such a dead dog.**—The most contemptible thing possible. (See chap. iii. 8, xvi. 9; 1 Sam. xxiv. 14.) Mephibosheth's humility is more than Oriental; it is abject, arising no doubt in part from his infirmity.

(10) **Thy sons, and thy servants.**—According to the latter part of the verse, and to chap. xix. 17, Ziba had fifteen sons and twenty servants, and was therefore able to take care of a large estate.

May have food to eat.—This is to be taken in the general sense of means for the support of his household as a royal prince.

(11) **He shall eat at my table.**—If these are taken as David's words, it is remarkable that he should have repeated them for the third time; but they are not likely to have been spoken, as some have suggested, by Ziba, either as a repetition, by way of assent, of David's words, nor as equivalent to saying, " but for this he should have eaten at my table." It is better to take them as a part of the narrative. In that case, David himself must have written this account, unless, with the LXX. and Syriac, we read, "at the table of David," instead of "my table."

(12) **Had a young son.**—As far as is recorded, this was his only child, but he had a numerous posterity (1 Chron. viii. 35—40; ix. 40—44).

(13) **Was lame.**—This fact is repeated here on account of its bearing upon the narrative in chap. xvi. 1—4; chap. xix. 24—30.

X.

Chapters x.—xii. give a detailed account of David's war with the Ammonites and their allies the Syrians, and of David's great sin, for which this war gave the occasion. The same war has already been briefly mentioned in chap. viii. 3—8, 13, 14, in the general summary of David's reign, but is here given with more detail in connection with his sin. The same account may be found in 1 Chron. xix.—xx. 3, but with no mention of the sin in regard to Bath-sheba and Uriah. Up to this point the reign has been one of exemplary piety and great prosperity; henceforward it is overclouded by sin and its consequent punishment. This turning point may be nearly fixed as about the middle of David's reign. It could not have been much later, since Solomon was born about two years after David's adultery, and had a son a year old when he came to the throne (1 Kings xi. 43, with xiv. 21); nor could it have been much earlier, since the whole narrative represents David's chief wars and conquests as already accomplished.

This war was altogether the greatest and most critical of David's reign, and it is not surprising that it should have been marked in song by the royal Psalmist. Ps. lx. is definitely assigned to this time by its title, which is fully confirmed by internal evidence. Ps. xliv. is also supposed by some writers to have been written during this period, but verses 9—16 speak of great calamities, of which we have no record at this time. Ps. lxviii. is also assigned by many to this period.

(1) **The king.**—His name is given in the next verse and in 1 Chron. xix. 1, as Nahash. He was probably a son or grandson of the Nahash whom Saul conquered (1 Sam. xi.), as more than fifty years must have passed away since that event. The kindness he had shown to David is not recorded, but may have been some friendly help during his wanderings, or merely a congratulatory embassy on his accession.

(3) **To search the city.** — The capital, and almost the only city of the Ammonites was Rabbah; it was strongly fortified, and a knowledge of its interior would be important to an enemy. The suspicions of the Ammonites may have been roused by David's growing power, and especially by his conquest of the neighbouring Moabites.

(4) Wherefore Hanun took David's servants, and shaved off the one half of their beards, and cut off their garments in the middle, *even* to their buttocks, and sent them away. (5) When they told *it* unto David, he sent to meet them, because the men were greatly ashamed: and the king said, Tarry at Jericho until your beards be grown, and *then* return.

(6) And when the children of Ammon saw that they stank before David, the children of Ammon sent and hired the Syrians of Beth-rehob, and the Syrians of Zoba, twenty thousand footmen, and of king Maacah a thousand men, and of Ish-tob twelve thousand men.

(7) And when David heard of *it*, he sent Joab, and all the host of the mighty men. (8) And the children of Ammon came out, and put the battle in array at the entering in of the gate: and the Syrians of Zoba, and of Rehob, and Ish-tob, and Maacah, *were* by themselves in the field. (9) When Joab saw that the front of the battle was against him before and behind, he chose of all the choice *men* of Israel, and put *them* in array against the Syrians: (10) and the rest of the people he delivered into the hand of Abishai his brother, that he might put *them* in array against the children of Ammon. (11) And he said, If the Syrians be too strong for me, then thou shalt help me: but if the children of Ammon be too strong for thee, then I will come and help thee. (12) Be of good courage, and let us play the men

---

(4) **Shaved off the one half of their beards.**—According to Oriental ideas, the extremest insult which could have been inflicted. "Cutting off a person's beard is regarded by the Arabs as an indignity quite equal to flogging and branding among ourselves. Many would rather die than have their beard shaved off" (Arvieux, quoted by Keil). It is remarkable that in none of David's wars does he appear as the aggressor.

(5) **Tarry at Jericho.**—In consideration for his mortified ambassadors, David directs them to remain at Jericho, which lay directly on their road. Jericho had been destroyed on the first entrance of the Israelites into Canaan, and a solemn curse pronounced upon whoever "riseth up and buildeth this city Jericho." This curse fell upon Hiel, more than a century after the time of David (1 Kings xvi. 34). But "buildeth" is here, as often, to be understood of "fortifying"; and Jericho, under the name of "the city of palm trees" (Judges i. 16; iii. 13), appears to have been all along an inhabited place.

(6) **Saw that they stank.**—The Hebrew, translated literally, shows that they were conscious that this was by their own fault—"that they had made themselves stink," and is so rendered in 1 Chron. xix. 6.

Hired.—Chronicles gives the amount of the subsidy, 1,000 talents of silver, a sum variously estimated at from £125,000 to twice that amount. It shows at once the wealth of Ammon, the importance of the auxiliaries, and the grave character of the war.

Syrians of Beth-rehob.—Called simply Rehob in verse 8. This has been understood of several different places. It can hardly have been the Rehob (or Beth-rehob) of Num. xiii. 21; Judges xviii. 28, since that was near Laish, and within the territory of the Israelites. Some identify it with "Ruhaibeh," twenty-five miles N.E. of Damascus; but it is more likely to have been "Rehoboth by the river" (*i.e.*, near the Euphrates) of Gen. xxxvi. 37, as this corresponds with "out of Mesopotamia' in the parallel passage 1 Chron. xix. 6, the situation of which is not more definitely known.

Zoba.—See Note on chap. viii. 3.

King Maacah.—Read, *King of Maacah*, as in Chronicles. For the situation of the country see Deut. iii. 14; Josh. xii. 5. It furnished only one thousand auxiliaries.

Ish-tob.—Translated, *men of Tob*, the first syllable not being a part of the proper name. Jephthah here found refuge when exiled by his countrymen (Judg. xi. 3, 5). It was probably just east of Gilead, between Syria and the land of Ammon; it is not mentioned in Chronicles.

The total number of auxiliaries mentioned in 1 Chron. xix. 7, thirty-two thousand, is the same as given here, Maacah being omitted from the number; but the composition of the force is different. Here only infantry are mentioned, there only chariots and cavalry. It is plain from the result of the battle (verse 18 in both places) that all three arms of the service were employed; either, therefore, some words have dropped out from both texts, or else the writer in each case did not care to go into details. Chronicles mentions that the allies mustered in Medeba, a place on a hill in the *Belka* plain, about four miles south-east of Heshbon, and well fitted strategically to repel an attack upon Rabbah. It had been originally assigned to the tribe of Reuben (Josh. xiii. 9).

(8) **At the entering in of the gate.**—The Ammonites and their allies formed separate armies, the former taking their stand immediately before the city, the latter "by themselves" at some distance, where the ground was more favourable for the manœuvres of their chariots.

(9) **When Joab saw.**—The keen eye of this experienced general at once took in both the advantages and the danger of this disposition of the enemy. He threw his whole force between their two divisions, organising his own army in two parts, one facing the Ammonites and the other the Syrians, but each capable of supporting the other in case of need. The enemy was thus cut in two, while the Israelites formed one compact body. He himself took command of the wing facing the Syrians with the choice troops of Israel, as having the stronger enemy to meet, while he gave the rest of the forces opposing the Ammonites into the hand of his brother Abishai.

(12) **Be of good courage, and let us play the men.**—Literally, *Be strong and let us strengthen ourselves.* The same phrase is translated in Chronicles,

Defeat of the Ammonites   II. SAMUEL, XI.   *and Syrians.*

for our people, and for the cities of our God: and the LORD do that which seemeth him good.

⁽¹³⁾ And Joab drew nigh, and the people that *were* with him, unto the battle against the Syrians: and they fled before him. ⁽¹⁴⁾ And when the children of Ammon saw that the Syrians were fled, then fled they also before Abishai, and entered into the city. So Joab returned from the children of Ammon, and came to Jerusalem.

⁽¹⁵⁾ And when the Syrians saw that they were smitten before Israel, they gathered themselves together. ⁽¹⁶⁾ And Hadarezer sent, and brought out the Syrians that *were* beyond the river: and they came to Helam; and Shobach the captain of the host of Hadarezer *went* before them. ⁽¹⁷⁾ And when it was told David, he gathered all Israel together, and passed over Jordan, and came to Helam. And the Syrians set themselves in array against David, and fought with him. ⁽¹⁸⁾ And the Syrians fled before Israel; and David slew *the men of* seven hundred chariots of the Syrians, and forty thousand horsemen, and smote Shobach the captain of their host, who died there. ⁽¹⁹⁾ And when all the kings *that were* servants to Hadarezer saw that they were smitten before Israel, they made peace with Israel, and served them. So the Syrians feared to help the children of Ammon any more.

CHAPTER XI.—⁽¹⁾ And it came to pass, ¹after the year was expired, at the time when kings go forth *to battle*, that *a* David sent Joab, and his servants with him, and all Israel; and they destroyed the children of Ammon, and besieged Rabbah. But David tarried still at Jerusalem.

¹ Heb., *at the return of the year.*

B.C. cir. 1036.

B.C. cir. 1035.

a 1 Chron. 20. 1.

"Be of good courage and let us behave ourselves valiantly." (Compare 1 Sam. iv. 9.) Joab felt that the battle was a critical one, and on it depended the welfare and even the safety of "our people" and "the cities of our God." The latter expression is in recognition of the fact that the whole land belonged to God, who allowed the use of it to His people.

The Lord do.—Rather, *The Lord will do*. Joab's courage rose here to that highest point which is marked by the full trust that whatever may be the result, it will be that which seems best to Infinite wisdom and love.

⁽¹³⁾ **Against the Syrians.**—The attack was begun, not against both parts of the foe at once, but Joab threw the weight of his forces against the stronger division of the enemy while Abishai watched and held in check the Ammonites. His tactics were completely successful. The Syrians fled, and the Ammonites, seeing that the whole army of Israel could now be thrown upon them, retired precipitately into the city.

⁽¹⁴⁾ **Came to Jerusalem.**—Why the victory was not at once followed up it is not said. Perhaps the army of Israel was too much exhausted by their victory; perhaps they were unprovided with the necessaries for a siege; and perhaps the season was already too far advanced. Whatever may have been the cause, the delay gave the allies opportunity to rally.

⁽¹⁶⁾ **Hadarezer.**—On the form of the name see Note on chap. viii. 3. He felt the importance of the defeat he had sustained, and now evidently made an effort to rally all his forces, even calling together vassal tribes from beyond the Euphrates.

They came to Helam.—The Hebrew word here is not necessarily a proper name, and might be translated *their host*; but as the name unquestionably occurs in verse 17, it is better taken as a proper name here also. It is entirely omitted in Chronicles. Its exact situation is unknown, but from chap. viii. 3; 1 Chron. xviii. 3, it is plain that it was in the general direction of the Euphrates and not very far from Hamath.

⁽¹⁷⁾ **He gathered . . . and passed.**—David, hearing of the great Syrian rally, now took the field in person. Joab may have been with him, but more probably was employed at the south in holding the Ammonites in check and preventing their forming a junction with their confederates.

⁽¹⁸⁾ **Seven hundred chariots.**—In this campaign David delivered a crushing blow upon his foes, from which they did not recover during the rest of his reign or that of his son. For the *seven hundred* here 1 Chron. xix. 18 has *seven thousand*, which is almost an incredible number of chariots, and the number here is evidently the more correct; but the same place has forty thousand *footmen*, while here it is forty thousand *horsemen*. Probably both statements are meant to include both infantry and cavalry, though only one of them is especially mentioned in each case. Comp. Note on verse 6.

⁽¹⁹⁾ **Servants to Hadarezer.**—The vassal kings, who had been tributary to Hadarezer, now transferred their allegiance to David; but it is not said that Hadarezer himself became a tributary, though it is plain from chapter viii. 3—7, that he was greatly weakened and suffered the loss of large booty. From 1 Kings xi. 23, 24, it is plain that an escaped dependent of Hadarezer maintained himself in the territory of Damascus as an enemy of Israel; it is also stated in 1 Kings iv. 21, that Solomon "reigned over all kingdoms" from the Euphrates to the border of Egypt. It is therefore probable that Hadarezer also acknowledged the suzerainty of David and Solomon.

XI.

⁽¹⁾ **After the year was expired.**—Literally, as in margin, *at the return of the year*. This refers back to chap. x. 14. Joab had spent the winter or rainy season at Jerusalem; now he returns to Ammon. David had evidently hurried his campaign against Hadarezer to prevent the junction of his foes, and Joab had probably been sent at first with only a small force to hold the Ammonites in check. With the speedy and successful close of David's own operations, he returned to Jerusalem, while the bulk of the army was sent to

(2) And it came to pass in an eveningtide, that David arose from off his bed, and walked upon the roof of the king's house: and from the roof he saw a woman washing herself; and the woman *was* very beautiful to look upon. (3) And David sent and enquired after the woman. And *one* said, *Is* not this Bathsheba, the daughter of Eliam, the wife of Uriah the Hittite? (4) And David sent messengers, and took her; and she came in unto him, and he lay with her;¹ for she was ᵃ purified from her uncleanness: and she returned unto her house. (5) And the woman conceived, and sent and told David, and said, I *am* with child.

(6) And David sent to Joab, *saying*, Send me Uriah the Hittite. And Joab sent Uriah to David. (7) And when Uriah was come unto him, David demanded *of him* ² how Joab did, and how the people did, and how the war prospered. (8) And David said to Uriah, Go down to thy house, and wash thy feet. And Uriah departed out of the king's house, and there ³ followed him a mess *of meat* from the king. (9) But Uriah slept at the door of the king's house with all the servants of his lord, and went not down to his house. (10) And when they had told David, saying, Uriah went not down unto his house, David said unto Uriah, Camest thou not from *thy* journey? why *then* didst thou not go down unto thine house? (11) And Uriah said unto David, The ark, and Israel, and Judah, abide in tents; and my lord Joab, and the servants of my lord, are encamped in the open fields; shall I then go into mine house, to eat and to drink, and to lie with my

¹ Or, *and when she had purified herself, &c., she returned.*

ᵃ Lev. 15. 19 & 18. 19.

² Heb., *of the peace of, &c.*

³ Heb., *went out after him.*

---

join Joab. By the curious insertion of a letter the Hebrew text reads "when angels (*or* messengers) go forth." It is corrected in the margin.

Destroyed the children.—1 Chron. xx. 1, explains "wasted the country of the children." After the custom of ancient warfare, while the army was besieging Rabbah, foraging parties were sent out to lay waste the country and cut off any stragglers. Comp. 1 Sam. xiii. 17, 18.

(2) **In an eveningtide.**—Late in the afternoon, when David had taken the *siesta* customary in Oriental countries, he rose from his couch and walked on the roof of his palace, which in the cool of the day was the pleasantest part of an eastern house. This palace was on the height of Mount Zion, and looked down upon the open courts of the houses in the lower city. In one of these he saw a beautiful woman bathing. In the courts of the houses it was common to have a basin of water, and the place was probably entirely concealed from every other point of observation than the roof of the palace, from which no harm was suspected.

David's grievous fall was consequent upon his long course of uninterrupted prosperity and power, which had somewhat intoxicated him and thrown him off his guard. It is no part of the plan of Scripture to cover up or excuse the sins of even its greatest heroes and saints. This sin was followed by the deepest repentance and by the Divine forgiveness; nevertheless its punishment overclouded all the remaining years of David's life. His fall, as St. Augustine has said, should put upon their guard those who have not fallen, and save from despair those who have.

(3) **Bath-sheba, the daughter of Eliam.**—Her name is spelt in Chronicles *Bath-shua*, and her father's name is said to be *Ammiel*. Ammiel and Eliam are the same name with its component parts transposed, as Scripture names are often varied: *God's people* and *the people of God*.

Wife of Uriah the Hittite.—His name appears (chap. xxiii. 39) in the list of David's thirty chief heroes, and the whole story represents him as a brave and noble-minded soldier. David had now given rein to his guilty passion so far that the knowledge of Bath-sheba's being a married woman, and the wife of one of his chief warriors, does not check him.

(4) **Sent messengers, and took her.**—This does not imply the use of violence. Bath-sheba, however beautiful, appears from the narrative of 1 Kings ii. 13—22, to have been a woman of little discretion, and now yielded to David's will without resistance, perhaps flattered by the approach of the king.

For she was.—Read, *and she was.* Under the Law she was unclean until the evening. She therefore remained in David's palace until that time, scrupulous in this detail while conscious of a capital crime and a high offence against God. David, nevertheless, was a far greater offender.

(5) **Sent and told David.**—Because her sin must now become known, and by the Law (Lev. xx. 10) adulterers must both be punished with death.

(6) **Send me Uriah.**—David proposed thus to cover up his crime. By calling for Uriah and treating him with marked consideration, he thought to establish a friendly feeling on his part, and then by sending him to his wife to have it supposed that the child, begotten in adultery, was Uriah's own.

(8) **A mess of meat.**—Lit. *a present.* The same word is used in Gen. xliii. 34, and no doubt refers to some choice dish sent by the king to the guest whom he wished to honour.

(9) **At the door of the king's house.**—Probably in the guard chamber at the entrance of the palace. (Comp. 1 Kings xiv. 27, 28.) It is quite unnecessary to suppose that Uriah had any suspicion of what had been done. His conduct and language is simply that of a brave, frank, generous-hearted soldier.

(11) **The ark, and Israel, and Judah.**—Notwithstanding the experience of the capture of the Ark by the Philistines in the days of Eli (1 Sam. iv. 11), it seems to have been still customary to carry it out in war as a symbol of God's presence and pledge of His favour. (Comp. 1 Sam. xiv. 18.) The separate mention of Israel and Judah gives no indication of a late date for this book, since these two parts of the nation had already been separated, and even hostile to each other in the early years of David's reign. This noble

wife? *as* thou livest, and *as* thy soul liveth, I will not do this thing. (12) And David said to Uriah, Tarry here to day also, and to morrow I will let thee depart. So Uriah abode in Jerusalem that day, and the morrow. (13) And when David had called him, he did eat and drink before him; and he made him drunk: and at even he went out to lie on his bed with the servants of his lord, but went not down to his house.

(14) And it came to pass in the morning, that David wrote a letter to Joab, and sent *it* by the hand of Uriah. (15) And he wrote in the letter, saying, Set ye Uriah in the forefront of the ¹hottest battle, and retire ye ²from him, that he may be smitten, and die.

(16) And it came to pass, when Joab observed the city, that he assigned Uriah unto a place where he knew that valiant men *were*. (17) And the men of the city went out, and fought with Joab: and there fell *some* of the people of the servants of David; and Uriah the Hittite died also.

(18) Then Joab sent and told David all the things concerning the war; (19) and charged the messenger, saying, When thou hast made an end of telling the matters of the war unto the king, (20) and if so be that the king's wrath arise, and he say unto thee, Wherefore approached ye so nigh unto the city when ye did fight? knew ye not that they would shoot from the wall? (21) Who smote *a* Abimelech the son of Jerubbesheth? did not a woman cast a piece of a millstone upon him from the wall, that he died in Thebez? why went ye nigh the wall? then say thou, Thy servant Uriah the Hittite is dead also.

(22) So the messenger went, and came and showed David all that Joab had sent him for. (23) And the messenger said unto David, Surely the men prevailed against us, and came out unto us into the field, and we were upon them even unto the entering of the gate. (24) And the shooters shot from off the wall upon thy servants; and *some* of the king's servants be dead, and thy servant Uriah the Hittite is dead also. (25) Then David said unto the messenger, Thus shalt thou say unto Joab, Let not this thing ³displease thee, for the sword devoureth ⁴one as well as another: make thy battle more strong against the city, and overthrow it: and encourage thou him.

(26) And when the wife of Uriah heard that Uriah her husband was dead, she

1 Heb., *strong*.
2 Heb., *from after him*.
a Judges 9. 53.
3 Heb., *be evil in thine eyes*.
4 Heb., *so and such*.

---

answer of Uriah should have stung David to the quick, but his conscience was so deadened by his sin that the only effect was to lead him to yet baser means of concealment.

(13) **He made him drunk.**—This fresh attempt of David to conceal his crime by attempting to send Uriah to his house while in a state of intoxication does not need comment, but Uriah's resolve was so strong that it still governed his conduct while in this almost irresponsible condition.

(14) **Sent it by the hand of Uriah.**—The brave soldier is made the bearer of his own death-warrant, and his well-known valour for his king is to be the means of accomplishing his destruction, to relieve that king of the consequences of his crime, which also involved a great wrong to himself. No reason is given to Joab for this order, but as a loyal and somewhat unscrupulous general he obeys without question.

(15) **Retire ye from him.**—This part of David's orders was not carried out. Perhaps Joab thought it would make the stratagem too evident, or perhaps it was impracticable. At all events, the consequence was that others were slain with Uriah, and thus a larger blood guiltiness fell upon David.

(16) **Observed the city.**—The word means *watched*, or *blockaded*. In the operations of the siege Joab so arranged some of his forces as to invite a sally from the city under circumstances in which it would be successful. It appears from verse 24 that Uriah's party had been sent so near as to come within reach of the archers on the wall.

(21) **Who smote Abimelech?**—See Judges ix. 53. Joab anticipated David's anger at his apparent rashness, and charged the messenger, when he should observe it, to mention's Uriah's death. This was not likely to awaken any suspicion in the messenger, as it would appear to him rather as an effort on Joab's part to throw the blame from himself upon Uriah as the leader of the assaulting party. The messenger appears to have told all in one breath, so that there was no opportunity for David to express displeasure. The reference to the case of Abimelech shows how familiar the Israelites were with the past history of their people.

(25) **One as well as another.**—While David's reply to Joab is ostensibly to encourage him, on the ground that the mishap was a mere accident of war, it is yet couched in such language as to imply a special regret for the loss of Uriah. "One as well as another," *i.e.*, "though Uriah was a brave hero whom we could ill spare, yet in the fortune of war we cannot choose who shall fall. Notwithstanding this loss, let Joab go on with a good heart."

(26) **Mourned for her husband.**—How long this mourning lasted we are not told. The usual period was seven days (Gen. l. 10; 1 Sam. xxxi. 13), and although that of a widow may well have been somewhat longer, it was doubtless, under the circumstances, made as short as was consistent with decency.

mourned for her husband. ⁽²⁷⁾ And when the mourning was past, David sent and fetched her to his house, and she became his wife, and bare him a son.

But the thing that David had done ¹displeased the LORD.

CHAPTER XII.—⁽¹⁾ And the LORD sent Nathan unto David. And he came unto him, and said unto him, There were two men in one city; the one rich, and the other poor. ⁽²⁾ The rich *man* had exceeding many flocks and herds: ⁽³⁾ but the poor *man* had nothing, save one little ewe lamb, which he had bought and nourished up: and it grew up together with him, and with his children; it did eat of his own ²meat, and drank of his own cup, and lay in his bosom, and was unto him as a daughter. ⁽⁴⁾ And there came a traveller unto the rich man, and he spared to take of his own flock and of his own herd, to dress for the wayfaring man that was come unto him; but took the poor man's lamb, and dressed it for the man that was come to him.

⁽⁵⁾ And David's anger was greatly kindled against the man; and he said to Nathan, As the LORD liveth, the man that hath done this *thing* ³shall surely die: ⁽⁶⁾ and he shall restore the lamb ᵃfourfold, because he did this thing, and because he had no pity.

⁽⁷⁾ And Nathan said to David, Thou *art* the man. Thus saith the LORD God of Israel, I ᵇanointed thee king over Israel, and I delivered thee out of the hand of Saul; ⁽⁸⁾ and I gave thee thy master's house, and thy master's wives into thy bosom, and gave thee the house of Israel and of Judah; and if *that had been* too little, I would moreover have given unto thee such and such things.

---

¹ Heb., *was evil in the eyes of.*

² Heb., *morsel.*

B.C. cir. 1034.

³ Or, *is worthy to die.*

ᵃ Ex. 22. 1.

ᵇ 1 Sam. 16. 13.

⁽²⁷⁾ **Bare him a son.**—Several months must have passed since the beginning of David's course of sin, and as yet his conscience had not brought him to a sense of what he had done, nor had the prophet Nathan been sent to him. It is to be remembered that during all this time David was not only the civil ruler of his people, but also the head of the theocracy, the great upholder of the worship and the service of God, and his psalms were used as the vehicle of the people's devotion. If it be asked why he should have been left so long without being brought to a conviction of his sin, one obvious reason is, that this sin might be openly fastened upon him beyond all possibility of denial by the birth of the child. But besides this, however hardened David may appear to have been in passing from one crime to another in the effort to conceal his guilt, yet it is scarcely possible that his conscience should not have been meantime at work and oppressing him with that sense of unconfessed and unforgiven sin which prepared him at last for the visit of Nathan.

XII.

We here pass from the story of David's great and aggravated crimes to that of his deep repentance. Beyond all question Ps. li. is the expression of his penitence after the visit of Nathan, and Ps. xxxii. the expression of his experience after the assurance of Divine forgiveness, set forth for the warning, instruction and comfort of others.

⁽¹⁾ **Sent Nathan.**—Nathan was already on intimate terms with David, and recognised by him as a prophet (chap. vii. 1—17).

⁽²⁾ **There were two men.**—The parable is designed to bring out David's indignation against the offender without being so clear as to awaken at first any suspicion of a personal application. It does not allude to the special crimes of David, but to the meanness and selfishness of the transaction—qualities which David was still in a condition to appreciate. For a similar use of parables see chap. xiv. 2—11; 1 Kings xx. 35—41.

⁽³⁾ **It grew up together.**—"All these circumstances are exquisitely contrived to heighten the pity of the hearer for the oppressed, and his indignation against the oppressor."—*Speaker's Commentary.*

⁽⁵⁾ **Was greatly kindled.**—David's generous impulses had not been extinguished by his sin, nor his warm sense of justice; his naturally quick temper (1 Sam. xxv. 13, 22, 33) at once roused his indignation to the utmost.

⁽⁶⁾ **Fourfold.**—In exact accordance with the Law (Exod. xxii. 1; comp. Luke xix. 8). The LXX. (in most copies "sevenfold," comp. Prov. vi. 31) and the Chaldee ("fortyfold") have expressed more of human indignation; but David knew the Law too well to change its terms.

⁽⁷⁾ **Thou art the man.**—The boldness and suddenness of this application bring a shock to David which at once aroused his slumbering conscience. This could not have been the case had David been essentially a bad man. He was a man whose main purpose in life was to do God's will, but he had yielded to temptation, had been entangled in further and greater guilt in the effort to conceal his sin, and all the while his conscience had been stupefied by the delirium of prosperity and power. Now what he had done is suddenly brought before him in its true light. For like prophetic rebukes of royal offenders see 1 Sam. xv. 21—23; 1 Kings xxi. 21—24; Isa. vii. 3—25; Matt. xiv. 3—5.

⁽⁸⁾ **Thy master's wives.**—In verses 7, 8 the prophet enumerates the chief favours and blessings shown to David, and these are so brought out as to show not only his base ingratitude, but also the unreasonableness of this particular sin. We are told of only one wife of Saul (1 Sam. xiv. 50) and of one concubine (chap. iii. 7) who was taken by Abner. If he had others, David certainly could not have taken them until more than seven and a half years after Saul's death. The prophet refers to the Oriental custom that the new king had a right to the harem of his predecessor

David's Confession and Pardon. **II. SAMUEL, XII.** *His Prayer and Fasting.*

(9) Wherefore hast thou despised the commandment of the LORD, to do evil in his sight? thou hast killed Uriah the Hittite with the sword, and hast taken his wife *to be* thy wife, and hast slain him with the sword of the children of Ammon. (10) Now therefore the sword shall never depart from thine house; because thou hast despised me, and hast taken the wife of Uriah the Hittite to be thy wife. (11) Thus saith the LORD, Behold I will raise up evil against thee out of thine own house, and I will *a* take thy wives before thine eyes, and give *them* unto thy neighbour, and he shall lie with thy wives in the sight of this sun. (12) For thou didst *it* secretly: but I will do this thing before all Israel, and before the sun.

(13) And David said unto Nathan, I have sinned against the LORD. And Nathan said unto David, *b* The LORD also hath put away thy sin; thou shalt not die. (14) Howbeit, because by this deed thou hast given great occasion to the enemies of the LORD to blaspheme, the child also *that is* born unto thee shall surely die. (15) And Nathan departed unto his house.

And the LORD struck the child that Uriah's wife bare unto David, and it was very sick. (16) David therefore besought God for the child; and David ¹fasted, and went in, and lay all night upon the earth. (17) And the elders of his house arose, *and went* to him, to raise him up from the earth: but he would not, neither did he eat bread with them. (18) And it came to pass on the seventh day, that the child died. And the servants of David feared to tell him that the child was dead: for they said, Behold, while the child was yet alive, we spake unto him, and he would not hearken unto our voice: how will he then ²vex himself, if we tell him that the child is dead? (19) But when David saw that his servants whispered, David perceived that the child was dead: therefore David said unto his servants, Is the child dead? And they said, He is dead. (20) Then David arose from the earth, and washed, and anointed *himself*, and changed his apparel, and came into the house of the LORD, and worshipped: then he came to his own house; and when he required, they set bread before him, and he did eat. (21) Then said his servants unto him, What thing *is* this that thou hast done?

a Deut. 28. 30; ch. 16. 22.

b Ecclus. 47. 11.

1 Heb., *fasted a fast.*

2 Heb., *do hurt.*

---

(9) **Hast slain him.**—This is a different and stronger word than "killed," in the first part of the verse, and might well be translated *murdered*. It was murder in the eyes of the Lord, although accomplished indirectly by the sword of the Ammonites.

(10) **Shall never depart.**—This word, in both its positive and negative forms, *for ever* and *never*, is constantly used to express the longest time possible in connection with the subject of which it is used. Here it must mean "as long as David lives;" and the punishment denounced found its realisation in a long succession of woes, from the murder of Amnon to the execution of Adonijah.

(13) **I have sinned.**—The same words were used by Saul (1 Sam. xv. 24, 30), but in a totally different spirit. Saul's confession was a concession to the prophet for the purpose of securing his support, and with no real penitence; David, in these few words, pours out before God the confession of a broken heart.

Thou shalt not die.—David had committed two crimes for which the Law imposed the penalty of death —adultery (Lev. xx. 10) and murder (Lev. xxiv. 17). As an absolute monarch he had no reason to fear that the sentence would be put in force by any human authority; and the Divine word is to him of far more importance as an assurance of forgiveness than as a warding off of any possible earthly danger. The phrase is thus parallel to, and explanatory of, the previous clause, "The Lord also hath put away thy sin."

(14) **Thou hast given great occasion.**—Although David was forgiven, yet since his sin had brought great scandal on the church, it was necessary that he should suffer publicly the consequences of that sin. We can see that this was especially important in David's case, both for the vindication of God's justice, and to destroy the hope that other sins also might go unpunished; yet it is not to be forgotten that the effect of sin generally is similar. The far greater part of David's sufferings were from what are called "the natural consequences" of his sin, *i.e.*, from consequences which flowed from it under the immutable laws of the world's moral government. These laws are always in force, and bring home the earthly consequences of sin, however the sinner may have repented and been forgiven.

The child also that is born.—The death of a little infant in the harem of a great Oriental monarch might seem of small significance, and but a light punishment; David, however, saw it in its true light— as an evidence of God's unalterable purpose, and a sign of the greater judgments that must come upon him. The people also, no doubt, saw and felt the appropriateness of this punishment.

(16) **Besought God for the child.**—It can hardly be necessary to say that this does not imply any want of submissiveness to God's will on David's part, nor an inordinate love for the child of his guilt. "In the case of a man whose penitence was so earnest and so deep, the prayer for the preservation of his child must have sprung from some other source than excessive love of any created object. His great desire was to avert the stroke as a sign of the wrath of God, in the hope that he might be able to discern, in the preservation of the child, a proof of Divine favour consequent upon the restoration of his fellowship with God. But when the

thou didst fast and weep for the child, while it was alive; but when the child was dead, thou didst rise and eat bread. (22) And he said, While the child was yet alive, I fasted and wept: for I said, Who can tell *whether* GOD will be gracious to me, that the child may live? (23) But now he is dead, wherefore should I fast? can I bring him back again? I shall go to him, but he shall not return to me.

(24) And David comforted Bath-sheba his wife, and went in unto her, and lay with her: and *a* she bare a son, and *b* he called his name Solomon: and the LORD loved him. (25) And he sent by the hand of Nathan the prophet; and he called his name ¹ Jedidiah, because of the LORD.

(26) And Joab fought against Rabbah of the children of Ammon, and took the royal city. (27) And Joab sent messengers to David, and said, I have fought against Rabbah, and have taken the city of waters. (28) Now therefore gather the rest of the people together, and encamp against the city, and take it: lest I take the city, and ² it be called after my name. (29) And David gathered all the people together, and went to Rabbah, and fought against it, and took it. (30) *c* And he took their king's crown from off his head, the weight whereof *was* a talent of gold with the precious stones: and it was *set* on David's head. And he brought forth the spoil of the city ³ in great abundance. (31) And he brought forth the people that *were* therein, and put *them* under saws, and under harrows of iron, and under axes of iron, and made them pass through the brick-kiln: and thus did he unto all the cities of the children of Ammon. So David and all the people returned unto Jerusalem.

a Matt. 1. 6.

b 1 Chron. 22. 9.

¹ That is, *Beloved of the Lord.*

B.C. cir. 1083.

² Heb., *my name be called upon it.*

c 1 Chron. 20. 2.

³ Heb., *very great.*

---

child was dead, he humbled himself under the mighty hand of God, and rested satisfied with His grace, without giving himself up to fruitless pain" (O. von Gerlach, quoted by Keil). Yet David's deep love for the child is not to be overlooked altogether.

(23) **I shall go to him.**—As far as the mere words themselves are concerned, this might be taken as the expression of a Stoic's comfort, "I shall go to the dead, but the dead will not come to me;" but David, in his whole nature and belief, was as far as possible from being a Stoic, and these words in his mouth can scarcely be anything else than an expression of confidence in a life of consciousness beyond the grave, and of the future recognition of those loved on earth.

(24) **Called his name Solomon.**—The birth of Solomon could hardly have taken place until after the events mentioned in verses 26—31, since it is not likely that the siege of Rabbah would have occupied two years. It is without doubt mentioned here (after the custom of Scripture narrative) to close the story of Bath-sheba in its proper connection. The birth of that son who should succeed to the kingdom, and through whom should pass the line to the Messiah, was too important to be overlooked.

(25) **Jedidiah.**—It does not appear that this name (*beloved of the Lord*) was intended to do more than express the Divine acceptance of Solomon; and it never came into use as a personal title.

(26) **Took the royal city.**—The parallel narrative is resumed at this point in 1 Chron. xx. 2. Rabbah was situated in the narrow valley of the upper Jabbok, on both sides of the stream, but with its citadel on the cliff on the northern side. The "royal city" of this verse, and "the city of waters" of the next, refer probably to the city proper, while the "city" of verses 28, 29 is no doubt the citadel, which was more strongly fortified.

(28) **The rest of the people.**—Joab proposes a general muster of the remaining forces of Israel, either because additional force was actually needed for the capture of the citadel, or simply to carry out the formal capturing of the city by David in person.

(30) **Their king's crown.**—The same Hebrew letters, translated *their king*, form the name of *Milcom*, the chief idol of the Ammonites, and hence some writers have quite unnecessarily supposed that the idol's crown is meant.

A talent of gold.—If this is according to the Hebrew weights, the amount is extraordinary, for the silver talent was above a hundred pounds, the gold talent twice as much. But there were various other Eastern talents, as the Babylonian and Persian, of much smaller weight, and it is not unlikely that a light talent may have been in use among the Ammonites. The weight, however, on any reasonable supposition, would have been too great to allow of this crown being commonly worn.

(31) **Put them under saws.**—The literal translation of the Hebrew (*put them with*, or *into, the saw*) does not give any good sense, and no doubt a single letter of the text should be changed, bringing it into agreement with 1 Chron. xx. 3, "cut them with saws." (Comp. Heb. xi. 37.)

Harrows of iron.—These are the heavy iron tools, often armed with sharp points on the lower side, which were used for the purposes of threshing the grain and breaking up the straw.

The brick-kiln.—This is the reading of the Hebrew text, and there is no sufficient reason to call it in question. The Hebrew margin, however, has "through Malchan;" and hence some have supposed that David made the Ammonites pass through the same fire by which they were accustomed to consecrate their children to Molech.

In the infliction of these cruelties on his enemies David acted in accordance with the customs and the knowledge of his time. Abhorrent as they may be to the spirit of Christianity, David and his contemporaries took them as matters of course, without a suspicion that they were not in accordance with God's will.

CHAPTER XIII.—⁽¹⁾ And it came to pass after this, that Absalom the son of David had a fair sister, whose name *was* Tamar; and Amnon the son of David loved her. ⁽²⁾ And Amnon was so vexed, that he fell sick for his sister Tamar; for she *was* a virgin; and ¹Amnon thought it hard for him to do any thing to her. ⁽³⁾ But Amnon had a friend, whose name *was* Jonadab, the son of Shimeah David's brother: and Jonadab *was* a very subtil man. ⁽⁴⁾ And he said unto him, Why *art* thou, *being* the king's son, ²lean ³from day to day? wilt thou not tell me? And Amnon said unto him, I love Tamar, my brother Absalom's sister. ⁽⁵⁾ And Jonadab said unto him, Lay thee down on thy bed, and make thyself sick: and when thy father cometh to see thee, say unto him, I pray thee, let my sister Tamar come, and give me meat, and dress the meat in my sight, that I may see *it*, and eat *it* at her hand.

⁽⁶⁾ So Amnon lay down, and made himself sick: and when the king was come to see him, Amnon said unto the king, I pray thee, let Tamar my sister come, and make me a couple of cakes in my sight, that I may eat at her hand. ⁽⁷⁾ Then David sent home to Tamar, saying, Go now to thy brother Amnon's house, and dress him meat. ⁽⁸⁾ So Tamar went to her brother Amnon's house; and he was laid down. And she took ⁴flour, and kneaded *it*, and made cakes in his sight, and did bake the cakes. ⁽⁹⁾ And she took a pan, and poured *them* out before him; but he refused to eat. And Amnon said, Have out all men from me. And they went out every man from him.

⁽¹⁰⁾ And Amnon said unto Tamar, Bring the meat into the chamber, that I may eat of thine hand. And Tamar took the cakes which she had made, and brought *them* into the chamber to Amnon her brother. ⁽¹¹⁾ And when she had brought *them* unto him to eat, he took hold of her, and said unto her, Come lie with me, my sister. ⁽¹²⁾ And she answered him, Nay, my brother, do not ⁵force me; for ᵃ⁶no such thing ought to be done in Israel: do not thou this folly. ⁽¹³⁾ And I, whither shall I cause my shame to go? and as for thee, thou

Marginal notes:
B.C. cir. 1032.
1 Heb., *it was marvellous*, or, *hidden in the eyes of Amnon.*
2 Heb., *thin.*
3 Heb., *morning by morning.*
4 Or, *paste.*
5 Heb., *humble me.*
a Lev. 18. 9.
6 Heb., *it ought not so to be done.*

XIII.

The series of narratives that follow, as far as chap. xxii., are chiefly accounts of the misfortunes that befel David and his household after his great sin. These are entirely omitted from the Chronicles, which also omit the account of that sin.

⁽¹⁾ **It came to pass after this.**—This formula applies to the narrative which follows as a whole: not, of course, to the fact immediately afterwards mentioned, that Absalom's sister was Tamar. This may illustrate the use of the same phrase in other places.

Absalom and Tamar were children of Maacah, daughter of Talmai, king of Geshur, and the former, at least, had been born during David's reign at Hebron (chap. iii. 3). It is probable that the events here narrated occurred soon after the war with the Ammonites and David's marriage with Bath-sheba.

Amnon was David's first-born son (iii. 2).

⁽²⁾ **Thought it hard.**—Rather, *it seemed impossible to Amnon.* The modest seclusion of Tamar in the harem of her mother seemed to leave him no opportunity to carry out his desires.

It appears from the narrative that the king's children lived in different households, and each grown-up son dwelt in his own house.

⁽³⁾ **Jonadab, the son of Shimeah.**—In 1 Sam. xvi. 9, Shimeah is called *Shammah*, and appears there as the third son of Jesse. He had another son, Jonathan, mentioned in chap. xxi. 21, as the conqueror of one of the giants. The word *subtil* is used simply to indicate sagacity and wisdom, whether rightly or wrongly exercised.

⁽⁵⁾ **Make thyself sick.**—Rather, *Feign thyself sick.* It has already been mentioned in verse 2 that Amnon "fell sick." That was the real pining of ungoverned and ungratified passion; this was a crafty feigning of sickness. Yet the miserable condition to which Amnon was brought by the former would give colour and plausibility to the latter.

⁽⁶⁾ **That I may eat at her hand.**—This request from an invalid seemed natural, and was readily granted.

⁽⁷⁾ **Sent home.**—Literally, *into the house;* i.e., to the private apartments of the women—the harem.

⁽⁹⁾ **He refused to eat.**—This also seemed natural enough in a whimsical invalid, and for the same reason his next requirement, "Have out all men from me," awakened no suspicion in the mind of Tamar.

⁽¹²⁾ **Do not thou this folly.**—Tamar, now left alone in the power of her half-brother, endeavours to escape by reasoning. She first speaks of the sinfulness in Israel of that which was allowed among surrounding heathen, quoting the very words of Gen. xxxiv. 7, as if by the traditions of their nation to recall the king's son to a sense of right. She then sets forth the personal consequences to themselves; if he had any love for her he could not wish that shame and contempt should meet her everywhere; and for himself, such an act would make him "as one of the fools in Israel," as one who had cast off the fear of God and the restraints of decency.

⁽¹³⁾ **Speak unto the king.**—The marriage of half-brothers and sisters was strictly forbidden in the Law (Lev. xviii. 9, 11, xx. 17), and it is not to be supposed that Tamar really thought David would violate its provisions for Amnon; but she made any and every

shalt be as one of the fools in Israel. Now therefore, I pray thee, speak unto the king; for he will not withhold me from thee. ⁽¹⁴⁾ Howbeit he would not hearken unto her voice: but, being stronger than she, forced her, and lay with her.

⁽¹⁵⁾ Then Amnon hated her ¹ exceedingly; so that the hatred wherewith he hated her *was* greater than the love wherewith he had loved her. And Amnon said unto her, Arise, be gone. ⁽¹⁶⁾ And she said unto him, *There is* no cause: this evil in sending me away *is* greater than the other that thou didst ² unto me. But he would not hearken unto her. ⁽¹⁷⁾ Then he called his servant that ministered unto him, and said, Put now this *woman* out from me, and bolt the door after her. ⁽¹⁸⁾ And *she had* a garment of divers colours upon her: for with such robes were the king's daughters *that were* virgins apparelled. Then his servant brought her out, and bolted the door after her.

⁽¹⁹⁾ And Tamar put ashes on her head, and rent her garment of divers colours that *was* on her, and laid her hand on her head, and went on crying. ⁽²⁰⁾ And Absalom her brother said unto her, Hath Amnon thy brother been with thee? but hold now thy peace, my sister: he *is* thy brother; ² regard not this thing. So Tamar remained ³ desolate in her brother Absalom's house.

⁽²¹⁾ But when king David heard of all these things he was very wroth. ⁽²²⁾ And Absalom spake unto his brother Amnon neither good nor bad: for Absalom hated Amnon, because he had forced his sister Tamar.

⁽²³⁾ And it came to pass after two full years, that Absalom had sheepshearers in Baal-hazor, which *is* beside Ephraim: and Absalom invited all the king's sons. ⁽²⁴⁾ And Absalom came to the king, and said, Behold now, thy servant hath sheepshearers; let the king, I beseech thee, and his servants go with thy servant. ⁽²⁵⁾ And the king said to Absalom, Nay, my son, let us not all now go, lest we be chargeable unto thee. And he pressed him: howbeit he would not go, but blessed him. ⁽²⁶⁾ Then said Absalom, If not, I pray thee, let my brother Amnon go with us. And the king said

---

1 Heb., *with great hatred greatly.*
2 Heb., *set not thine heart.*
3 Heb., *and desolate.*

---

suggestion to gain time and escape the pressing danger. Amnon, however, knew the Law too well to have any hope of a legitimate marriage with Tamar, and, therefore, persisted in his violence.

⁽¹⁵⁾ **Hated her exceedingly.**—"It is characteristic of human nature to hate one whom you have injured" (Tacitus, *quoted by* Kirkpatrick). This result shows that Amnon was governed, not by love, but by mere animal passion.

⁽¹⁶⁾ **There is no cause.**—The Hebrew is elliptical and difficult; various interpretations are suggested, among which that given in the Authorised Version expresses very well the sense, although not an accurate translation. Amnon was now doing her a greater wrong than at first, because he was now bound, in consequence of that, to protect and comfort her.

⁽¹⁷⁾ **Put now this woman out.**—Amnon doubtless intended to give the impression that Tamar had behaved shamefully towards him. The baseness of this insinuation is in keeping with his brutality.

⁽¹⁸⁾ **A garment of divers colours.**—The word is used only here and in connection with Joseph (Gen. xxxvii. 3, 23, 32), and is supposed to mean a tunic with long sleeves, in distinction from those with short sleeves commonly worn. The fact is mentioned to show that Tamar must have been recognised as a royal virgin by Amnon's servant, as well as by everyone else.

⁽¹⁹⁾ **Went on crying.**—Literally, *went going and cried;* i.e., as she went away she cried aloud. Tamar put on every external mark of the deep grief within; and this was not only fitting in itself, but was a proper means to obtain justice for her wrongs.

⁽²⁰⁾ **Hath Amnon.**—The Hebrew, by a clerical error, has here *Aminon*. Absalom at once sees how the case stands, comforts his sister, but counsels silence as necessary to the purpose of revenge he had at once formed, and takes his desolate sister to his own house.

⁽²¹⁾ **He was very wroth.**—The LXX. adds, "but he vexed not the spirit of Amnon his son, because he loved him, because he was his firstborn,"—which is doubtless in part the reason of David's guilty leniency. The remembrance of his own sin also tended to withhold his hand from the administration of justice. David's criminal weakness towards his children was the source of much trouble from this time to the end of his life.

⁽²³⁾ **Absalom had sheepshearers.** — Absalom had now silently nourished his revenge for "two full years." No doubt he chose also to give full opportunity for his father to punish Amnon's iniquity if he would; and by this long quiet waiting he so far disarmed suspicion that he was able to carry out his purpose. Sheepshearing always was, and still is, a time of feasting. (Comp. 1 Sam. xxv. 2.) The situation of Baalhazor and of Ephraim are quite unknown, but Absalom's property was probably not many miles from Jerusalem.

⁽²⁴⁾ **Came to the king.**—Absalom could hardly have expected the king to accept his invitation, but by pressing him to go he effectively disguised his real purpose, and secured David's blessing.

⁽²⁶⁾ **If not . . . let . . . Amnon.**—Absalom then asks that if the king himself will not come, Amnon, as his eldest son and heir-apparent, may represent him at the feast. David hesitates, but as he could not well refuse without acknowledging a suspicion which he was unwilling to express, he finally consents.

unto him, Why should he go with thee? ⁽²⁷⁾ But Absalom pressed him, that he let Amnon and all the king's sons go with him.

⁽²⁸⁾ Now Absalom ᵃhad commanded his servants, saying, Mark ye now when Amnon's heart is merry with wine, and when I say unto you, Smite Amnon; then kill him, fear not: ¹have not I commanded you? be courageous, and be ²valiant. ⁽²⁹⁾ And the servants of Absalom did unto Amnon as Absalom had commanded. Then all the king's sons arose, and every man ³gat him up upon his mule, and fled.

⁽³⁰⁾ And it came to pass, while they were in the way, that tidings came to David, saying, Absalom hath slain all the king's sons, and there is not one of them left. ⁽³¹⁾ Then the king arose, and tare his garments, and lay on the earth; and all his servants stood by with their clothes rent. ⁽³²⁾ And Jonadab, the son of Shimeah David's brother, answered and said, Let not my lord suppose that they have slain all the young men the king's sons; for Amnon only is dead: for by the ⁴appointment of Absalom this hath been ⁵determined from the day that he forced his sister Tamar. ⁽³³⁾ Now therefore let not my lord the king take the thing to his heart, to think that all the king's sons are dead: for Amnon only is dead. ⁽³⁴⁾ But Absalom fled.

And the young man that kept the watch lifted up his eyes, and looked, and, behold, there came much people by the way of the hill side behind him. ⁽³⁵⁾ And Jonadab said unto the king, Behold, the king's sons come: ⁶as thy servant said, so it is. ⁽³⁶⁾ And it came to pass, as soon as he had made an end of speaking, that, behold, the king's sons came, and lifted up their voice and wept: and the king also and all his servants wept ⁷very sore.

⁽³⁷⁾ But Absalom fled, and went to Talmai, the son of ⁸Ammihud, king of Geshur. And *David* mourned for his son every day. ⁽³⁸⁾ So Absalom fled, and went to Geshur, and was there three years. ⁽³⁹⁾ And *the soul of* king David ⁹longed to go forth unto Absalom: for

Marginal notes:
1 Or, *will you not, since I have commanded you?*
2 Heb., *sons of valour.*
3 Heb., *rode.*
4 Heb., *mouth.*
5 Or, *settled.*
6 Heb., *according to the word of thy servant.*
7 Heb., *with a great weeping greatly.*
B.C. 1030.
8 Or, *Ammihur.*
9 Or, *was consumed.*

⁽²⁷⁾ **He let Amnon go.**—The LXX. adds at the end of this verse an explanatory gloss, "And Absalom made a feast like the feast of a king."

⁽²⁹⁾ **As Absalom had commanded.**—It was quite customary for the servants of a prince to obey his orders without question, leaving the entire responsibility to rest with him. In this case, if Chileab (or Daniel) was already dead, as seems probable, Absalom stood next in the succession to Amnon, and, however it may have been with himself, his retainers may have looked upon this as a preparatory step towards the throne. The blow was too sudden and unexpected to allow of interference by the other princes.

Upon his mule.—Although David had reserved a number of horses from the spoil of his Syrian victories (chap. viii. 4), the mule was still ridden by persons of distinction (chap. xviii. 9; 1 Kings i. 33, 38). The breeding of mules was forbidden in the Law (Lev. xix. 19), but they were brought in by commerce (1 Kings x. 25).

⁽³⁰⁾ **There is not one of them left.**—The story of this exaggerated report, so true to the life, indicates contemporaneous authorship.

⁽³¹⁾ **Tare his garments.**—Rather, *rent his clothes*, the words being the same as in the last clause of the verse.

⁽³²⁾ **Jonadab.**—The same subtle counsellor who had led Amnon into his sin, now at once divined how the case really stood, and reassured the king.

By the appointment of Absalom this hath been determined.—Literally, *upon Absalom's mouth it hath been set*, an expression which has given rise to much variety of interpretation. The Authorised Version expresses the sense accurately.

⁽³⁴⁾ **Absalom fled.**—This is connected on one side with verse 29, and on the other with verse 37. Several things were happening at once. When the king's sons fled to the palace, Absalom, taking advantage of the confusion, escaped another way. The reason for mentioning the fact just here is that otherwise he would seem to be included among "the king's sons" of the two following verses.

Behind him—*i.e.*, from the west, the Oriental always being supposed to face the east in speaking of the points of the compass.

⁽³⁷⁾ **Went to Talmai.**—His maternal grandfather. (See Note on chap. iii. 2—5.) This verse may be considered parenthetical:—The king's sons came . . . and wept sore. ("Only Absalom fled and went to . . . Geshur.") In this case the omission of "David" in the latter clause of the verse is explained, as the nominative is easily supplied from verse 36.

For his son every day.—Amnon is certainly the son here meant, for whom David continually mourned until his grief was gradually assuaged by the lapse of time.

⁽³⁸⁾ **Was there three years.**—This is the third time the flight of Absalom has been mentioned; but, after the custom of Scripture narrative, each repetition has been for the purpose of introducing some additional fact. In verse 34 the simple fact of his flight is stated; in verse 37 it is added that he went to his grandfather, and here that he remained with him three years.

⁽³⁹⁾ **The soul of King David.**—The words, "the soul of," are not in the original, and the most opposite interpretations have been given of the rest of the sentence. The sense of the English is that of the Chaldee and of the Jewish commentators—that David, after his grief for Amnon had abated, longed after Absalom and pined for his return. But it may be he was comforted concerning Amnon, seeing he was dead.

CHAPTER XIV.—⁽¹⁾ Now Joab the son of Zeruiah perceived that the king's heart *was* toward Absalom. ⁽²⁾ And Joab sent to Tekoah, and fetched thence a wise woman, and said unto her, I pray thee, feign thyself to be a mourner, and put on now mourning apparel, and anoint not thyself with oil, but be as a woman that had a long time mourned for the dead: ⁽³⁾ and come to the king, and speak on this manner unto him. So Joab put the words in her mouth.

⁽⁴⁾ And when the woman of Tekoah spake to the king, she fell on her face to the ground, and did obeisance, and said, ¹Help, O king. ⁽⁵⁾ And the king said unto her, What aileth thee? And she answered, I *am* indeed a widow woman, and mine husband is dead. ⁽⁶⁾ And thy handmaid had two sons, and they two strove together in the field, and *there was* ²none to part them, but the one smote the other, and slew him. ⁽⁷⁾ And, behold, the whole family is risen against thine handmaid, and they said, Deliver him that smote his brother, that we may kill him, for the life of his brother whom he slew; and we will destroy the heir also: and so they shall quench my coal which is left, and shall not leave to my husband *neither* name nor remainder ³ upon the earth.

⁽⁸⁾ And the king said unto the woman, Go to thine house, and I will give charge concerning thee. ⁽⁹⁾ And the woman of Tekoah said unto the king, My lord, O king, the iniquity *be* on me, and on my father's house: and the king and his throne *be* guiltless. ⁽¹⁰⁾ And the king said, Whosoever saith *ought* unto thee, bring him to me, and he shall not touch thee any more. ⁽¹¹⁾ Then said she, I pray thee, let the king remember the LORD thy God, ⁴that thou wouldest not suffer the revengers of blood to destroy any more, lest they destroy my son. And he said, *As* the LORD liveth, there shall not one hair of thy son fall to the earth.

Marginal notes:
1 Heb., *Save*.
B.C. 1027.
2 Heb., *no deliverer between them*.
3 Heb., *upon the face of the earth*.
4 Heb., *that the revenger of blood do not multiply to destroy*.

---

objected to this view, (1) that there is no ground for supplying the ellipsis in this way; (2) that the verb (which is a common one) never has elsewhere the sense given to it; and (3) that the representation thus made is contrary to fact, since David could easily have recalled Absalom had he chosen to do so, and when he actually was brought back, through Joab's stratagem, the king refused to see him (chap. xiv. 24), and only after two years more (chap. xiv. 28), reluctantly admitted him to his presence. The other interpretation is better, which takes the verb impersonally, and gives the sense, *David desisted from going forth against Absalom*. He ought to have arrested and punished him for a murder, which was at once fratricide and high treason, as being the assassination of the heir-apparent; but the flight to Geshur made this difficult, and as time went by David "was comforted concerning Amnon," and gradually gave up the thought of punishing Absalom.

XIV.

⁽¹⁾ **Was toward Absalom.**—This, like the last verse of the previous chapter, may be understood in either of two opposite senses: either David's heart yearned for Absalom (as the Authorised Version, Vulg., LXX., Syr.), or it was hostile to him. The Hebrew preposition is used in both senses, though more frequently in the latter, and unquestionably expresses hostility in the only other place (Dan. xi. 28) in which this form of the phrase occurs. The verse would then be translated, "And Joab the son of Zeruiah knew that the king's heart was against Absalom." Hence his stratagem to obtain his recall, which would otherwise have been quite unnecessary.

⁽²⁾ **Tekoah.**—A village on a high hill five miles south of Bethlehem, the home of the prophet Amos. It was also the native place of Ira, one of David's thirty heroes (chap. xxiii. 26), and was near enough to Bethlehem, the home of Joab, for him to have had personal knowledge of this "wise woman." There is no ground whatever for suspecting her of being a "witch," or in any way disreputable.

The parable that follows was contrived by Joab, yet also required skill and address on the part of the woman. It is purposely made not too closely parallel to the case of Absalom, lest it should defeat its own object. In general it needs no comment.

⁽⁴⁾ **Spake to the king.**—Many MSS. and the LXX., Vulg., and Syriac have *came* to the king. The difference is immaterial.

⁽⁶⁾ **They two strove together.**—The woman represents the fratricide as unpremeditated and without malice. This really made the case essentially different from that of Absalom; but at this point of the story the object is to dispose the king favourably towards the culprit, while by the time the application is reached, this point will have passed out of mind.

⁽⁷⁾ **We will destroy the heir also.**—The woman puts this into the mouth of the family, because this would be the result of what they proposed. The effect of the parable is greatly heightened by this, and there is no doubt intended a covert allusion to Absalom as the heir of David.

⁽⁹⁾ **The iniquity be on me**—*i.e.*, if there be any wrong in thus condoning blood-guiltiness, let the responsibility rest on me. Although the king has granted her request, the woman seeks to prolong the interview that she may lead him to commit himself more completely.

⁽¹¹⁾ **Let the king remember the Lord.**—Having thus far succeeded, the crafty woman still further leads on the king to bind himself with the solemnity of an oath.

(12) Then the woman said, Let thine handmaid, I pray thee, speak *one* word unto my lord the king. And he said, Say on. (13) And the woman said, Wherefore then hast thou thought such a thing against the people of God? for the king doth speak this thing as one which is faulty, in that the king doth not fetch home again his banished. (14) For we must needs die, and *are* as water spilt on the ground, which cannot be gathered up again; ¹neither doth God respect *any* person: yet doth he devise means, that his banished be not expelled from him. (15) Now therefore that I am come to speak of this thing unto my lord the king, *it is* because the people have made me afraid: and thy handmaid said, I will now speak unto the king; it may be that the king will perform the request of his handmaid. (16) For the king will hear, to deliver his handmaid out of the hand of the man *that would* destroy me and my son together out of the inheritance of God. (17) Then thine handmaid said, The word of my lord the king shall now be ²comfortable: for as an angel of God, so *is* my lord the king ³to discern good and bad: therefore the LORD thy God be with thee. (18) Then the king answered and said unto the woman, Hide not from me, I pray thee, the thing that I shall ask thee. And the woman said, Let my lord the king now speak. (19) And the king said, *Is not* the hand of Joab with thee in all this? And the woman answered and said, *As* thy soul liveth, my lord the king, none can turn to the right hand or to the left from ought that my lord the king hath spoken: for thy servant Joab, he bade me, and he put all these words in the mouth of thine handmaid: (20) to fetch about this form of speech hath thy servant Joab done this thing: and my lord *is* wise, according to the wisdom of an angel of God, to know all *things* that *are* in the earth.

(21) And the king said unto Joab, Behold now, I have done this thing: go therefore, bring the young man Absalom again. (22) And Joab fell to the ground on his face, and bowed himself, and ⁴thanked the king: and Joab said, To day thy servant knoweth that I have found grace in thy sight, my lord, O king, in that the king hath fulfilled the request of ⁵his servant. (23) So Joab arose and went to Geshur, and brought

1 Or, *because God hath not taken away his life, he hath also devised means, &c.*
2 Heb., *for rest.*
3 Heb., *to hear.*
4 Heb., *blessed.*
5 Or, *thy.*

---

(13) **Against the people of God.**—This phrase, according to constant usage, can only mean *Israel.* The woman finds that the time has come when she must show the king that he stands condemned for his conduct towards Absalom by his own decision. She does this cautiously, and her language is therefore somewhat obscure; she rather hints at than plainly expresses what she wants to say. Her first point is that the king is in some way wronging the people, and then that he does this in opposition to the spirit of the decision he has just given, by leaving Absalom (whom she does not name) in banishment.

The king doth speak...—A more literal translation would be, *from the king's speaking this word he is as one guilty.*

(14) **We must needs die.**—The woman now goes on to a further argument from the uncertainty of life. Whether she would suggest the possibility of Absalom's dying in banishment (as some think), or of David's death before he has been reconciled to his son (as others hold) does not matter. She craftily withdraws attention from the real point—the question of right and justice—and, assuming that the thing ought to be done, suggests that delay is unsafe since life is uncertain. Still another explanation of her argument may be given: "Amnon is dead, and it is useless to grieve longer for him; God does not respect persons, Absalom too must die, and you yourself must die; improve the time and the blessings yet left while there is opportunity."

Neither doth God respect any person.—The Hebrew is difficult, but the English is certainly wrong. The literal translation is "And God doth not take away the soul, but thinketh thoughts that He may not banish the banished one;" and the meaning is that God in wrath remembers mercy, and does not press punishment to extremes.

(15) **Because the people have made me afraid.**—The woman here seeks to excuse her boldness in addressing the king by the pressure brought to bear upon her from without; but whether she means this in regard to what she has said of Absalom, or of her own affairs, is very doubtful. In the former case *the people* would mean the nation generally; in the latter, her own family connections. Certainly in the next verse she returns to her own affairs to keep up the pretence of reality; but here there seems to be an intentional and studied ambiguity.

(17) **An angel of God.**—Comp. ver. 20; chap. xix. 27; 1 Sam. xxix. 9.

(19) **The hand of Joab.**—The king at once penetrates the woman's disguise, and sees the stratagem. He knew Joab as "wily and politic and unscrupulous," but we do not know why he suspected him of this especial interest in Absalom. Perhaps it was only the prosperous courtier's interest in the heir-apparent, but probably Joab had made the same request before, so that the king recognised its source.

(21) **I have done.**—This is the Hebrew text; the margin has *thou hast done.* The former is simply a form of granting Joab's request; the latter would convey an implied censure on Joab's stratagem, although in the next clause there is a compliance with his wish.

Absalom's Beauty.   II. SAMUEL, XV.   *He Steals the Hearts of Israel*

Absalom to Jerusalem. (24) And the king said, Let him turn to his own house, and let him not see my face. So Absalom returned to his own house, and saw not the king's face.

(25) ¹ But in all Israel there was none to be so much praised as Absalom for his beauty: from the sole of his foot even to the crown of his head there was no blemish in him. (26) And when he polled his head, (for it was at every year's end that he polled *it*: because *the hair* was heavy on him, therefore he polled it:) he weighed the hair of his head at two hundred shekels after the king's weight. (27) And unto Absalom there were born three sons, and one daughter, whose name *was* Tamar: she was a woman of a fair countenance.

(28) So Absalom dwelt two full years in Jerusalem, and saw not the king's face. (29) Therefore Absalom sent for Joab, to have sent him to the king; but he would not come to him: and when he sent again the second time, he would not come. (30) Therefore he said unto his servants, See, Joab's field is ²near mine, and he hath barley there; go and set it on fire. And Absalom's servants set the field on fire. (31) Then Joab arose, and came to Absalom unto *his* house, and said unto him, Wherefore have thy servants set my field on fire? (32) And Absalom answered Joab, Behold, I sent unto thee, saying, Come hither, that I may send thee to the king, to say, Wherefore am I come from Geshur? *it had been* good for me *to have been* there still: now therefore let me see the king's face; and if there be *any* iniquity in me, let him kill me. (33) So Joab came to the king, and told him: and when he had called for Absalom, he came to the king, and bowed himself on his face to the ground before the king: and the king kissed Absalom.

CHAPTER XV.—(1) And it came to pass after this, that Absalom prepared him chariots and horses, and fifty men to run before him. (2) And Absalom rose up early, and stood beside the way of the gate: and it was *so*, that when any man that had a controversy ³ came to the king for judgment, then Absalom called unto him, and said, Of what city *art* thou? And he said, Thy servant *is* of one of the tribes of Israel. (3) And Absalom said unto him, See, thy matters are good and right; but ⁴ *there is* no man

---

¹ Heb., *And as Absalom there was not a beautiful man in all Israel to praise greatly.*

B.C. 1025.

² Heb., *near my place.*

³ Heb., *to come.*

⁴ Or, *none will hear thee from the king downward.*

---

(24) **Let him not see my face.**—David allowed Absalom's return, but forbade him his presence. The former had been done in weakness, the latter through a sense of justice. The effect of this half measure was unfortunate; Absalom was irritated, and yet placed in a favourable position to carry out his plots. It is probable that Absalom was confined to his own house.

(26) **Two hundred shekels.**—The value of the shekel "after the king's weight" is unknown. If it was the same with the shekel of the sanctuary, the weight mentioned would be about six pounds; if only half as much, the weight would still be very extraordinary. Some clerical error has probably arisen in copying the number in the MSS.

(27) **Three sons.**—Their names are not given, from which it might be supposed that they died in infancy, and this is made sure by chap. xviii. 18, where Absalom is reported as saying, "I have no son to keep my name in remembrance."

One daughter.—This daughter bore the name of Absalom's sister, Tamar, and shared her beauty. The LXX. here inserts the statement that she "became the wife of Roboam, the son of Solomon, and bore him a son, Abia." But this is evidently a confused gloss, founded upon 1 Kings xv. 2; 2 Chron. xi. 20—22. We are there told that Rehoboam's favourite wife was Maachah, the daughter of Absalom, and mother of Abijah; but this must mean that Maachah was his granddaughter through Tamar, since in 2 Chron. xiii. 2 Abijah is called the son of Michaiah, the daughter of Uriel. Tamar then married Uriel, and her daughter became the mother of a line of kings.

(29) **He would not come.**—Joab felt that he had already gone far enough in procuring Absalom's return, and, as he still continued under the displeasure of the king, he was not disposed to do anything more. Possibly also he thought Absalom should have shown some sign of penitence for his great crime.

(30) **Set it on fire.**—Absalom's stratagem for obtaining an interview with Joab was perfectly successful, but would only have been resorted to by a lawless and unscrupulous character.

(32) **If there be any iniquity.**—Absalom makes no acknowledgment of having done wrong, but simply says that this state of half-reconciliation is intolerable. He must either be punished or fully pardoned. Joab's intercession accomplishes its purpose; the king receives Absalom, and kisses him in token of complete reconciliation. In this David showed great weakness, for which he afterwards suffered severely.

XV.

(1) **Prepared him chariots and horses.**—As a preparation for his rebellion, it was necessary to impress the people with his wealth and splendour. (Comp. 1 Kings i. 5, where Adonijah does the same thing.) This was the first use in Israel of chariots and horses as a part of regal pomp.

(3) **There is no man deputed of the king.**—There is no official *hearer* appointed. It was impossible for the king to hear every case in detail; certain persons were therefore appointed to hear causes and report the facts to the king, who thereupon pronounced his judgment. Absalom uses the same arts which have

Absalom goes to Hebron. **II. SAMUEL, XV.** *His Conspiracy.*

deputed of the king to hear thee. (4) Absalom said moreover, Oh that I were made judge in the land, that every man which hath any suit or cause might come unto me, and I would do him justice! (5) And it was *so*, that when any man came nigh *to him* to do him obeisance, he put forth his hand, and took him, and kissed him. (6) And on this manner did Absalom to all Israel that came to the king for judgment : so Absalom stole the hearts of the men of Israel.

(7) And it came to pass after forty years, that Absalom said unto the king, I pray thee, let me go and pay my vow, which I have vowed unto the LORD, in Hebron. (8) For thy servant vowed a vow while I abode at Geshur in Syria, saying, If the LORD shall bring me again indeed to Jerusalem, then I will serve the LORD.

B.C. 1023.

(9) And the king said unto him, Go in peace. So he arose, and went to Hebron. (10) But Absalom sent spies throughout all the tribes of Israel, saying, As soon as ye hear the sound of the trumpet, then ye shall say, Absalom reigneth in Hebron. (11) And with Absalom went two hundred men out of Jerusalem, *that were* called; and they went in their simplicity, and they knew not any thing. (12) And Absalom sent for Ahithophel the Gilonite, David's counsellor, from his city, *even* from Giloh, while he offered sacrifices. And the conspiracy was strong; for the people increased continually with Absalom.

(13) And there came a messenger to David, saying, The hearts of the men of Israel are after Absalom. (14) And David said unto all his servants that *were* with

---

been used by the demagogue in all ages. He does not accuse the king himself of wrong, but insinuates that the system of government is defective, and expresses his own earnest wish to set things right.

(7) **After forty years.**—The reading is certainly incorrect. Absalom was born after David began his reign in Hebron, and his whole reign was only forty years. Absalom therefore was not yet forty at his death. The reading found in the Syriac and most MSS. of the Vulgate, and adopted by Josephus, *four* years, is probably correct. It remains uncertain from what point this four years is to be reckoned; probably it is from Absalom's return to Jerusalem.

Pay my vow . . . in Hebron.— We have no means of knowing whether this vow was real or fictitious; certainly Absalom now uses it as a pretext, and yet there is nothing improbable in his having actually made such a vow during his exile. Hebron was the place of his birth and childhood, as well as a holy city from very ancient times, and was thus a suitable place for the performance of his vow; it was also at a convenient distance from Jerusalem, and had been the royal city of David for the first seven years of his reign. It was thus well adapted to be the starting place of Absalom's rebellion, and it is not unlikely, moreover, that the men of Hebron may have resented the transfer of the capital to Jerusalem, and therefore have lent a willing ear to Absalom. Like many other culprits, Absalom veils his crime under the cloak of religion, pretending submission to his father, and receiving his blessing at the very moment when he is striking at his crown and also his life.

(10) **Sent spies.**—These were agents who were to sound the people in the various parts of the land, and doubtless to communicate the conspiracy only secretly, and to those whom they found favourably disposed. They started from Jerusalem, perhaps, at the same time with Absalom, or possibly had been sent out quietly, a few at a time, beforehand. The signal for rising was to be a messenger with a trumpet.

(11) **Went in their simplicity.**—The two hundred guests whom Absalom had invited to take part with him in his sacrifices, were doubtless prominent and influential citizens of Jerusalem. That they were entirely ignorant of Absalom's purposes shows the extreme secrecy with which the affair was managed. Absalom, no doubt, hoped when he once had them at Hebron, to secure them for his side, or, failing this, forcibly to prevent their opposition. In any case it would appear to the people that they were with him, and he would thus secure additional prestige.

(12) **Sent for Ahithophel.**—Giloh, the city of Ahithophel, was one of the groups of towns just south of Hebron (Josh. xv. 51), and Ahithophel may have gone there in readiness to be summoned by Absalom. Why he deserted David does not appear. It has been conjectured that he was aggrieved at David's treatment of Bath-sheba, who is supposed to have been his granddaughter. Bath-sheba's father was Eliam (chap. xi. 3), and Ahithophel had a son Eliam (chap. xxiii. 34), but there is no evidence that these were the same, and if they had been, Ahithophel probably would have felt honoured rather than aggrieved that his daughter should have been made queen. It is more likely that Ahithophel and many others of the tribe of Judah were alienated because, in the rapidly growing empire of David, their relative importance was of necessity constantly diminishing. It is noteworthy that the rebellion was cradled in Judah, and seems to have found there its chief strength.

There is a difference of opinion whether Ps. xli. was written on this occasion; but its ninth verse certainly applies very pointedly to Ahithophel; and his conduct, both in his treachery and his suicide, forms a striking parallel to that of Judas, to whom this verse is applied in John xiii. 18. Many writers also consider that Ps. lv. was composed with reference to Ahithophel.

While he offered sacrifices.—Absalom had arranged these, apparently with pomp and circumstance, to continue through several days. This gave time for the conspiracy to gain strength, and the accompanying feasting allowed Absalom an excellent opportunity for using his popular arts, and with such success that "the people increased continually with Absalom."

(14) **Let us flee.**—The sequel abundantly proved the wisdom of David's course. Ahithophel also (chap. xvii. 1, 2) and Hushai (chap. xvii. 7—13) recognised that delay would be fatal to Absalom's cause. His rebellion

him at Jerusalem, Arise, and let us flee; for we shall not *else* escape from Absalom: make speed to depart, lest he overtake us suddenly, and ¹bring evil upon us, and smite the city with the edge of the sword. ⁽¹⁵⁾ And the king's servants said unto the king, Behold, thy servants *are ready to do* whatsoever my lord the king shall ² appoint. ⁽¹⁶⁾ And the king went forth, and all his household ³after him. And the king left ten women, *which were* concubines, to keep the house. ⁽¹⁷⁾ And the king went forth, and all the people after him, and tarried in a place that was far off. ⁽¹⁸⁾ And all his servants passed on beside him; and all the Cherethites, and all the Pelethites, and all the Gittites, six hundred men which came after him from Gath, passed on before the king. ⁽¹⁹⁾ Then said the king to Ittai the Gittite, Wherefore goest thou also with us? return to thy place, and abide with the king: for thou *art* a stranger, and also an exile. ⁽²⁰⁾ Whereas thou camest *but* yesterday, should I this day ⁴make thee go up and down with us? seeing I go whither I may, return thou, and take back thy brethren: mercy and truth *be* with thee. ⁽²¹⁾ And Ittai answered the king, and said, *As* the LORD liveth, and *as* my lord the king liveth, surely in what place my lord the king shall be, whether in death or life, even there also will thy servant be. ⁽²²⁾ And David said to Ittai, Go and pass over. And Ittai the Gittite passed over, and all his men, and all the little ones that *were* with him. ⁽²³⁾ And all the country wept with a loud voice, and all the people passed over: the king also himself passed over the brook ⁵Kidron, and all the people passed over, toward the way of the wilderness.

⁽²⁴⁾ And lo Zadok also, and all the Levites *were* with him, bearing the ark of the covenant of God: and they set down the ark of God; and Abiathar went up, until all the people had done passing out of the city. ⁽²⁵⁾ And the king said unto Zadok, Carry back the ark of God into the city: if I shall find favour in the eyes of the LORD, he will bring me again, and shew me *both* it, and his habitation: ⁽²⁶⁾ but if he thus say, I have no delight in thee; behold, here am I, let him do to me as seemeth

---

¹ Heb., *thrust.*
² Heb., *choose.*
³ Heb., *at his feet.*
⁴ Heb., *make thee wander in going?*
⁵ Called, John 18. 1, *Cedron.*

---

was thoroughly unreasonable, and must lose ground with time given for reflection. By this course also much of the horror of civil war was averted, and Jerusalem saved from "the edge of the sword."

⁽¹⁷⁾ **Tarried in a place that was far off.**—Better, *halted at the far house, i.e.,* at a definite place known by this name, probably the last house on the outskirts of the city before the road crossed the Kidron. Here David mustered his forces and made the arrangements for his flight.

⁽¹⁸⁾ **Cherethites . . . Pelethites.**—See Note on chap. viii. 18.

Gittites.—This word in its form would naturally mean *men of Gath,* and it has therefore been understood by some commentators of a body of Philistines in David's service. But the term is distinctly explained here as meaning the "six hundred men which came after him from Gath," and called "Gittites" for that reason, a body of men with whom the previous history of David has made us very familiar. They had gathered to him during his outlawry (1 Sam. xxii. 1, 2), had been with him at Keilah (1 Sam. xxiii. 13), in the wilderness of Paran (1 Sam. xxv. 13), and at Gath (1 Sam. xxvii. 3), "came after him from Gath" to Ziklag, and shared with him in his life and exploits there (1 Sam. xxvii. 8, xxix. 2, xxx. 1—9), and went up with him to Hebron (2 Sam. ii. 3), and thence to Jerusalem (chap. v. 6). They are generally supposed to have afterwards constituted the body of "heroes" or "mighty men," to whom frequent reference is made (2 Sam. x. 7, xvi. 6, xx. 7; 1 Kings i. 8). The Vatican LXX. here, as often, adds considerably to the text.

⁽¹⁹⁾ **Ittai the Gittite.**—The patronymic must here be understood literally, since David calls him "a stranger and also an exile;" he had but comparatively recently (verse 20) attached himself to David's service, bringing with him his family and others of his countrymen. From the fact that David afterwards entrusted him with the command of a third of his forces, it is clear that he must have been an experienced general. It cannot be shown positively that he was a proselyte, although this is probable.

In the latter part of this verse the English has unnecessarily changed the order of the words. Read, "Return and abide with the king, for thou art a stranger and an exile at thy place," viz., at Jerusalem. David neither means to recognise Absalom as king, nor yet to speak of him ironically; he only means to tell Ittai that, as a foreigner, he need not concern himself in such a question, but is quite justified in serving the king *de facto*, whoever he may be. Ittai's answer may be compared with Ruth's (Ruth i. 16, 17).

⁽²³⁾ **The brook Kidron.**—A valley with a watercourse, filled in winter, lying immediately east of Jerusalem, between the city and the Mount of Olives.

⁽²⁴⁾ **Zadok also.**—Zadok appears here as in charge of the ark, and David (verse 27) addresses him exclusively, while Abiathar is merely mentioned. This gives no indication of the relations existing between the two, but merely shows how matters went on this day of hurry and confusion. The language is obscure, but probably means that Zadok and the Levites brought the ark out of the city, and set it down while the multitude were assembling; meantime Abiathar led the multitude forward up the Mount of Olives until they had all come out of the city.

⁽²⁶⁾ **Let him do to me as seemeth good.**—David recognises that he is suffering under the punish-

good unto him. (27) The king said also unto Zadok the priest, *Art not* thou a *⁎seer?* return into the city in peace, and your two sons with you, Ahimaaz thy son, and Jonathan the son of Abiathar. (28) See, I will tarry in the plain of the wilderness, until there come word from you to certify me. (29) Zadok therefore and Abiathar carried the ark of God again to Jerusalem: and they tarried there.

(30) And David went up by the ascent of *mount* Olivet, ¹and wept as he went up, and had his head covered, and he went barefoot: and all the people that *was* with him covered every man his head, and they went up, weeping as they went up. (31) And *one* told David, saying, Ahithophel *is* among the conspirators with Absalom. And David said, O LORD, I pray thee, turn the counsel of Ahithophel into foolishness.

(32) And it came to pass, that *when* David was come to the top *of the mount*, where he worshipped God, behold, Hushai the Archite came to meet him with his coat rent, and earth upon his head: (33) unto whom David said, If thou passest on with me, then thou shalt be a burden unto me: (34) but if thou return to the city, and say unto Absalom, I will be thy servant, O king; *as I have been* thy father's servant hitherto, so *will* I now also *be* thy servant: then mayest thou for me defeat the counsel of Ahithophel. (35) And *hast thou* not there with thee Zadok and Abiathar the priests? therefore it shall be, *that* what thing soever thou shalt hear out of the king's house, thou shalt tell *it* to Zadok and Abiathar the priests. (36) Behold, they *have* there with them their two sons, Ahimaaz Zadok's *son*, and Jonathan Abiathar's *son;* and by them ye shall send unto me every thing that ye can hear. (37) So Hushai David's friend came into the city, and Absalom came into Jerusalem.

CHAPTER XVI.— (1) And when David was a little past the top *of the hill*, behold, Ziba the servant of Mephi-

a 1 Sam. 9. 9.

¹ Heb., *going up and weeping.*

---

ment pronounced by Nathan for his sin, and he seeks to throw himself entirely into the hands of God, trusting in His mercy. (Comp. chap. xxiv. 14.) He is, therefore, unwilling to have the ark carried with him lest he should seem to undertake to compel the Divine presence and blessing. He feels sure that if God so will, he shall be brought again in peace; but if not, yet he will perfectly submit himself to God's ordering.

(27) **Art not thou a seer?**—The Hebrew is difficult, and must be translated either, *Art thou a seer?* or, with a very slight change in a vowel, as an address, *Thou seer.* Zadok is so called because he was now in some sort to fulfil the office of a prophet in guiding David's course, and also in making known to him the events taking place in Jerusalem which would show God's will concerning him. Nothing is said in any part of this narrative of Nathan and Gad, both of whom were certainly still living (chap. xxiv. 11, 13, 14; 1 Kings i. 11).

Your two sons with you.—Zadok only has been mentioned, and probably Abiathar was not present at the moment, but David shows by this way of speaking that he means to address them both.

(28) **The plain of the wilderness.**—This is the reading of the Hebrew margin here and at chap. xvii. 16, and is followed by the ancient versions. It is used for the wide valley of the Jordan in which Jericho is situated; but in both places the Hebrew text is better, *the fords*, both as a more definite place where messengers would find David, and also as a place of strategic importance where a retreat across the Jordan was open at any moment.

(31) **One told David.**—This is no doubt the meaning, but the preposition has dropped out of the Hebrew text, leaving it unintelligible, and reading literally, *and David told.*

(32) **Where he worshipped God.**—Rather, *where men worship.* The original indicates a customary act. David had taken the road over the crest of the Mount of Olives, and there, in all probability, was one of those "high places" which abounded in Israel.

Hushai the Archite.—His place is mentioned in Josh. xvi. 2 as on the border between Ephraim and Benjamin, and he may have been at his own home when the rebellion broke out. His coming appears as the beginning of the answer to David's prayer in verse 31.

(34) **Say unto Absalom.**— David here counsels fraud and treachery, and Hushai willingly accepts the part assigned to him, in order to thwart Ahithophel's counsel and weaken Absalom's rebellion. The narrative simply states the facts without justifying them. But while we cannot too strongly condemn such a stratagem, two things are to be remembered: first, that like frauds in time of war and rebellion have been practised in all ages, and still continue; and, secondly, that David and Hushai had but slender knowledge of the Divine revelation of truth and righteousness which enables us to condemn them, and, therefore, did with a clear conscience many things which we see to be wrong.

XVI.

(1) **Ziba . . . met him.**—It is evident from the sequel of the story (chap. xix. 24—30) that Ziba grossly slandered his master, doubtless for the purpose (as appears from verse 4) of personal gain. This story was, indeed, almost too improbable to be believed; for, quite independently of his obligations to David, Mephibosheth, a helpless cripple of the house of Saul, could hardly have hoped that Absalom's rebellion would bring the throne to him; yet David, apt to be hasty in his judgments, was in a state to believe in any story of

bosheth met him, with a couple of asses saddled, and upon them two hundred *loaves* of bread, and an hundred bunches of raisins, and an hundred of summer fruits, and a bottle of wine. (3) And the king said unto Ziba, What meanest thou by these? And Ziba said, The asses *be* for the king's household to ride on; and the bread and summer fruit for the young men to eat; and the wine, that such as be faint in the wilderness may drink. (3) And the king said, And where *is* thy master's son? And Ziba said unto the king, Behold, he abideth at Jerusalem: for he said, To day shall the house of Israel restore me the kingdom of my father. (4) Then said the king to Ziba, Behold, thine *are* all that *pertained* unto Mephibosheth. And Ziba said, ¹I humbly beseech thee *that* I may find grace in thy sight, my lord, O king.

(5) And when king David came to Bahurim, behold, thence came out a man of the family of the house of Saul, whose name *was* Shimei, the son of Gera: ²he came forth, and cursed still as he came. (6) And he cast stones at David, and at all the servants of king David: and all the people and all the mighty men *were* on his right hand and on his left. (7) And thus said Shimei when he cursed, Come out, come out, thou ³bloody man, and thou man of Belial: (8) the LORD hath returned upon thee all the blood of the house of Saul, in whose stead thou hast reigned; and the LORD hath delivered the kingdom into the hand of Absalom thy son: and, ⁴behold, thou *art taken* in thy mischief, because thou *art* a bloody man.

(9) Then said Abishai the son of Zeruiah unto the king, Why should this *a*dead dog curse my lord the king? let me go over, I pray thee, and take off his head. (10) And the king said, What have I to do with you, ye sons of Zeruiah? so let him curse, because the LORD hath said unto him, Curse David. Who shall then say, Wherefore hast thou done so? (11) And David said to Abishai, and to all his servants, Behold, my son, which came forth of my bowels, seeketh my life: how much more now *may this* Benjamite *do it?* let him alone, and let him curse; for the LORD hath bidden him. (12) It may be that the LORD will look on mine ⁵ ⁶affliction, and that the LORD will requite me good for his cursing this day. (13) And as David and his men went by the way, Shimei went along on the hill's side over against him, and cursed as he went, and threw stones at him, and ⁷ cast dust. (14) And the king, and all the people that *were* with him, came weary, and refreshed themselves there.

¹ Heb., *I do obeisance.*
² Or, *he still came forth and cursed.*
³ Heb., *man of blood.*
⁴ Heb., *behold thee in thy evil.*
a 1 Sam. 24. 14; ch. 3. 8.
⁵ Or, *tears.*
⁶ Heb., *eye.*
⁷ Heb., *dusted* him *with dust.*

---

ingratitude, and to be deeply affected by Ziba's large contribution to his necessities. Ziba shows entire want of principle, and could, therefore, have adhered to David's cause only because he had the shrewdness to foresee its ultimate success.

(4) **I humbly beseech thee that I may find grace.**—Literally, *I bow myself down; let me find favour.*

(5) **Bahurim.**—See Note on chap. iii. 16.

Of the family of the house of Saul.—That is, "of the family," in the larger sense of tribe. Many of the Benjamites naturally felt aggrieved when the royal house passed away from their tribe; and, although under restraint while David's government was strong, were ever ready to show their opposition and hatred when opportunity offered, as now with Shimei, and a little later with Sheba, the son of Bichri (chap. xx. 1, 2).

(6) **He cast stones.**—The road appears to have led along the side of a narrow ravine, on the opposite side of which (see verse 9, "let me go *over*") Shimei kept along with the fugitives, out of reach, and yet easily heard, and able to annoy them with stones.

(7) **Come out, come out.**—Rather, *Go out, go out.* It is doubtful whether by the words, "thou bloody man," Shimei meant anything more than that he considered David responsible for "the blood of the house of Saul" (verse 8), especially in the case of Ishbosheth and of Abner, and the execution of Saul's seven descendants at the demand of the Gibeonites (chap. xxi. 1—9). Yet he may have known of the crime in regard to Uriah, and have wished to point his curse with the charge of shedding that innocent blood.

(10) **So let him curse.**—This translation follows the margin of the Hebrew, as the LXX. and Vulg. also do. David, throughout, recognises that all his sufferings were from the Lord's hand, and he wishes to submit himself entirely to His will. He does not, of course, mean to justify Shimei's wrong; but only to say that, as far as his sin bears upon himself, it is of Divine appointment and he cannot resent it.

(11) **How much more now may this Benjamite.**—The "Benjamite" is in contrast to his own son, because he represents the adherent of another and rival dynasty. It is noticeable that David accuses Absalom not only of seeking his throne, but his life.

(12) **Look on mine affliction.**—The English here follows the LXX. and Vulg. The Hebrew margin has *mine eye,* but the text has *my iniquity,* which is probably the true sense. David expresses the hope that God will mercifully look upon his sin, of which he has repented, and for which he is now bearing punishment; a part of this punishment is the cursing of Shimei, and God may be well pleased that it should be patiently borne.

(14) **Came weary.**—The sentence seems to require the mention of some place, and the clause "refreshed themselves there" to imply that a place has already

(15) And Absalom, and all the people the men of Israel, came to Jerusalem, and Ahithophel with him. (16) And it came to pass, when Hushai the Archite, David's friend, was come unto Absalom, that Hushai said unto Absalom, ¹ God save the king, God save the king. (17) And Absalom said to Hushai, *Is* this thy kindness to thy friend? why wentest thou not with thy friend? (18) And Hushai said unto Absalom, Nay; but whom the LORD, and this people, and all the men of Israel, choose, his will I be, and with him will I abide. (19) And again, whom should I serve? *should I* not *serve* in the presence of his son? as I have served in thy father's presence, so will I be in thy presence.

(20) Then said Absalom to Ahithophel, Give counsel among you what we shall do. (21) And Ahithophel said unto Absalom, Go in unto thy father's concubines, which he hath left to keep the house; and all Israel shall hear that thou art abhorred of thy father: then shall the hands of all that *are* with thee be strong. (22) So they spread Absalom a tent upon the top of the house; and Absalom went in unto his father's concubines in the sight of all Israel. (23) And

¹ Heb., *Let the king live.*
² Heb., *word.*
³ Heb., *was right in the eyes of, &c.*
⁴ Heb., *what is in his mouth.*
⁵ Heb., *word.*
⁶ Heb., *counselled.*

the counsel of Ahithophel, which he counselled in those days, *was* as if a man had enquired at the ² oracle of God: so *was* all the counsel of Ahithophel both with David and with Absalom.

CHAPTER XVII.—(1) Moreover Ahithophel said unto Absalom, Let me now choose out twelve thousand men, and I will arise and pursue after David this night: (2) and I will come upon him while he *is* weary and weak handed, and will make him afraid: and all the people that *are* with him shall flee; and I will smite the king only: (3) and I will bring back all the people unto thee: the man whom thou seekest *is* as if all returned: *so* all the people shall be in peace. (4) And the saying ³ pleased Absalom well, and all the elders of Israel.

(5) Then said Absalom, Call now Hushai the Archite also, and let us hear likewise ⁴ what he saith. (6) And when Hushai was come to Absalom, Absalom spake unto him, saying, Ahithophel hath spoken after this manner: shall we do *after* his ⁵ saying? if not; speak thou. (7) And Hushai said unto Absalom, The counsel that Ahithophel hath ⁶ given *is* not good at this time. (8) For,

---

been mentioned. The word for *weary* is, therefore, generally taken as a proper name, *Ayephim*, which was probably a mere caravansary.

(16) **God save the king.**—In the original, wherever this phrase occurs, it is simply, *Let the king live.* This and the expression "God forbid" are exceptional instances in which modern phraseology refers more directly to God than the ancient. Absalom is surprised at Hushai's coming to him, and inclined to distrust one who has deserted his former friend and master. But Hushai succeeds in explaining his conduct as based upon the principle of loyalty to the government *de facto*; he urges that this has the Divine authority, and his faithfulness to the former king is a pledge of faithfulness to the present one.

(21) **And Ahithophel said.**—The counsel of Ahithophel was in effect that Absalom should make the breach between him and his father absolute and irreconcilable. His followers would thus be assured of the impossibility of his securing a pardon for himself while they were left to their fate. After adopting this course, he must necessarily persist to the end. The taking of the harem of his predecessor by the incoming monarch was an Oriental custom, to the enormity of which the mind was blunted by the practice of polygamy.

(22) **A tent upon the top of the house.**—Nathan had foretold that the nature of David's public punishment should correspond to the character of his secret crime. The fact that this punishment takes place on the very roof where David had first yielded to his guilty passion makes it particularly striking.

XVII.

(1) **Pursue after David this night.**—Ahithophel saw clearly that Absalom's success depended on striking an immediate blow. He felt confident, and perhaps with reason, that David in his distress and weariness was in no condition to resist a sudden onset. That he was wise in his counsel is made plain by the opposition of Hushai and the anxiety to send tidings to David with all speed. "This night" is generally taken to mean the night of the day on which David left Jerusalem; but from verse 16 and chap. xv. 28 it appears that he was already encamped by the fords of the Jordan, a greater distance than he could have accomplished in one day's march.

(2) **Will make him afraid.**—This translation is hardly strong enough. The thought is that Ahithophel will throw his band into a panic by a sudden night attack, and in the confusion will easily secure the person of the king.

(3) **Bring back all the people.**—This evil counsellor, with artful flattery, assumes that Absalom is the rightful king, and that the people who have gone off after David only need to be brought back to their allegiance.

(5) **Call now Hushai.**—The good sense of Absalom and all the people at once approved the counsel of Ahithophel; but, at a crisis so important, Absalom sought the advice also of the other famous counsellor of his father.

(7) **Not good at this time.**—The words, *at this time*, should be transposed. What Hushai says is

said Hushai, thou knowest thy father and his men, that they *be* mighty men, and they *be* ¹chafed in their minds, as a bear robbed of her whelps in the field: and thy father *is* a man of war, and will not lodge with the people. ⁽⁹⁾ Behold, he is hid now in some pit, or in some *other* place: and it will come to pass, when some of them be ²overthrown at the first, that whosoever heareth it will say, There is a slaughter among the people that follow Absalom. ⁽¹⁰⁾ And he also *that is* valiant, whose heart *is* as the heart of a lion, shall utterly melt: for all Israel knoweth that thy father *is* a mighty man, and *they* which *be* with him *are* valiant men. ⁽¹¹⁾ Therefore I counsel that all Israel be generally gathered unto thee, from Dan even to Beer-sheba, as the sand that *is* by the sea for multitude; and ³that thou go to battle in thine own person. ⁽¹²⁾ So shall we come upon him in some place where he shall be found, and we will light upon him as the dew falleth on the ground: and of him and of all the men that *are* with him there shall not be left so much as one. ⁽¹³⁾ Moreover, if he be gotten into a city, then shall all Israel bring ropes to that city, and we will draw it into the river, until there be not one small stone found there.

⁽¹⁴⁾ And Absalom and all the men of Israel said, The counsel of Hushai the Archite *is* better than the counsel of Ahithophel. For the LORD had ⁴appointed to defeat the good counsel of Ahithophel, to the intent that the LORD might bring evil upon Absalom.

⁽¹⁵⁾ Then said Hushai unto Zadok and to Abiathar the priests, Thus and thus did Ahithophel counsel Absalom and the elders of Israel; and thus and thus have I counselled. ⁽¹⁶⁾ Now therefore send quickly, and tell David, saying, Lodge not this night in the plains of the wilderness, but speedily pass over; lest the king be swallowed up, and all the people that *are* with him.

⁽¹⁷⁾ Now Jonathan and Ahimaaz stayed by En-rogel; for they might not be seen to come into the city: and a wench went and told them; and they went and told king David. ⁽¹⁸⁾ Nevertheless a lad saw them, and told Absalom: but they went both of them away quickly, and came to a man's house in Bahurim, which had a well in his court; whither they went down. ⁽¹⁹⁾ And the woman took and spread a covering over the well's mouth, and spread ground corn thereon; and the thing was not known. ⁽²⁰⁾ And when Absalom's servants came to the woman to the house, they said, Where *is* Ahimaaz and Jonathan? And the woman said unto them, They be gone over the brook of water. And when they had sought and could not

1 Heb., *bitter of soul.*
2 Heb., *fallen.*
3 Heb., *that thy face, or, presence go,* &c.
4 Heb., *commanded.*

"This time the counsel of Ahithophel is not good," implying that his previous advice (chap. xvi. 21) had been wise, thus assuming an appearance of candour.

⁽¹¹⁾ **I counsel that all Israel.**—Hushai had before him a difficult task. He had not only to "make the worse appear the better reason," but to do this in face of the counsel of a man very famous for his wisdom and devoted to the interests of Absalom, while his own fidelity had but just now been called in question. He accomplishes his task successfully by emphasising all the possible hazards and contingencies of the plan recommended by Ahithophel, and by proposing, on the other hand, a plan attended with no risk, on the supposition that the great mass of Israel already were, and would continue to be, on Absalom's side, a supposition which, with delicate flattery, he assumes as true.

⁽¹³⁾ **Bring ropes to that city.**—Hushai here makes use of hyperbole to show the irresistible power of all Israel united, and therefore the certain success of his plan. This was pleasing to the vanity and dazzling to the imagination of Absalom.

⁽¹⁶⁾ **Lodge not this night.**—Hushai's advice had been taken at the moment, but it might easily be exchanged for Ahithophel's. At all events there was instant danger for David, and Hushai urges him to place the Jordan without delay between himself and the rebels.

⁽¹⁷⁾ **En-rogel.**—A fountain just outside the city, on the boundary between the tribes of Benjamin and Judah (Josh. xv. 7; xviii. 16). There are two localities which claim to represent it, each of which has its earnest advocates: the "Fountain of the Virgin," on the western slope of the valley of the Kidron; and "Job's Well" just below the junction of the valleys of the Kidron and Hinnom. The latter answers much better to the description in Joshua, but either will suit the present passage. The loyalty of the high priests to David must have been well known, and it would have been quite unsafe for their sons to start from the city itself as bearers of tidings to David; even with all their care they were pursued. Their hiding-place, however, was well chosen, as women resorted to the fountains to draw water, so that communications could be had without attracting observation.

A wench.—*The maid-servant,* the definite article probably indicating some well-known maid of the high priest. The word *wench* is not found elsewhere in the English Bible.

⁽¹⁹⁾ **Ground Corn.**—This word occurs elsewhere only in Prov. xxvii. 22, and means wheat or barley beaten or ground so as to remove the hull; in this condition it was spread out to dry.

⁽²⁰⁾ **The brook of water.**—This peculiar word for *brook* occurs only here, and is thought by some writers

find *them*, they returned to Jerusalem. ⁽²¹⁾ And it came to pass, after they were departed, that they came up out of the well, and went and told king David, and said unto David, Arise, and pass quickly over the water: for thus hath Ahithophel counselled against you. ⁽²²⁾ Then David arose, and all the people that *were* with him, and they passed over Jordan: by the morning light there lacked not one of them that was not gone over Jordan.

⁽²³⁾ And when Ahithophel saw that his counsel was not ¹followed, he saddled *his* ass, and arose, and gat him home to his house, to his city, and ²put his household in order, and hanged himself, and died, and was buried in the sepulchre of his father.

⁽²⁴⁾ Then David came to Mahanaim. And Absalom passed over Jordan, he and all the men of Israel with him. ⁽²⁵⁾ And Absalom made Amasa captain of the host instead of Joab: which Amasa *was* a man's son, whose name *was* Ithra an Israelite, that went in to Abigail the daughter of Nahash, sister to Zeruiah Joab's mother. ⁽²⁶⁾ So Israel and Absalom pitched in the land of Gilead.

⁽²⁷⁾ And it came to pass, when David was come to Mahanaim, that Shobi the son of Nahash of Rabbah of the children of Ammon, and Machir the son of Ammiel of Lo-debar, and Barzillai the Gileadite of Rogelim, ⁽²⁸⁾ brought beds, and ³basons, and earthen vessels, and wheat, and barley, and flour, and parched *corn*, and beans, and lentiles, and parched *pulse*, ⁽²⁹⁾ and honey, and butter, and sheep, and cheese of kine, for David, and for the people that *were* with him, to eat: for they said, The people *is* hungry, and weary, and thirsty, in the wilderness.

CHAPTER XVIII.—⁽¹⁾ And David numbered the people that *were* with him, and set captains of thousands and captains of hundreds over them. ⁽²⁾ And David sent forth a third part of the people under the hand of Joab, and a

---

¹ Heb., *done*.

² Heb., *gave charge concerning his house*.

³ Or,

---

to be a proper name. A small brook bearing the same name, *Michal*, is said to exist now in this locality. On the deceit practised by the women, comp. Josh. ii. 4—7; 1 Sam. xix. 12—17. The historian simply records without comment what was done.

(23) **And hanged himself.**—Ahithophel was moved, not merely by chagrin at the rejection of his counsel, but was shrewd enough to see that, with this delay, Absalom's rebellion would inevitably fail, and he himself be likely to come to a traitor's death.

(24) **Mahanaim.**—See Note on chap. ii. 8. The same reasons which made it a favourable place for the capital of Ish-bosheth, recommended it also as a place of refuge to David and a rallying point for his adherents.

(25) **Amasa.**—Joab having adhered to David and gone away with him, Absalom chose his cousin to succeed him as commander-in-chief.

Ithra an Israelite.—Called in 1 Chron. ii. 17 *Jether the Ishmeelite*. *Jether* and *Ithra* are merely different forms of the same name; but *Israelite* is probably an error for *Ishmeelite*. The LXX. has, in the Alexandrian copy, Ishmaelite, and in the Vatican, Jezreelite,

Abigail the daughter of Nahash.—Since this Abigail is said to be "sister to Zeruiah," and in 1 Chron. ii. 16 both Abigail and Zeruiah are said to be the sisters of Jesse's sons, it follows, either that *sister* is used in the sense of half-sister, or else that Nahash, usually a man's name, was the name of Jesse's wife. It is impossible to decide certainly. The Jewish tradition that Nahash is another name for Jesse has no support.

(26) **Pitched in the land of Gilead.**—Gilead is the tract of country on the east of the Jordan, extending from the land of Moab on the south to Bashan on the north, the valley of the Hieromax forming probably its northern boundary. The site of Mahanaim has not been identified, but it was almost certainly within the territory of Gilead. Absalom, however, did not actually reach Mahanaim before he met and was defeated by the forces of David.

(27) **Shobi the son of Nahash.**—The narrative pauses in its course a moment to speak of the assistance sent to David during the time he was at Mahanaim and while Absalom had been gathering his forces. Among those whose friendly assistance was conspicuous was "Shobi the son of Nahash of Rabbah of the children of Ammon." Hanun, king of the Ammonites, was a son of Nahash, and was conquered by David at Rabbah (chap. x. 1; xii. 29—31). It is very possible that after dismantling the royal city David had left a brother of the late king as governor over the conquered territory, and that he now came forward to show his gratitude and faithfulness. It is also possible that Shobi was the son of some Israelite named Nahash, who lived in the conquered city of Rabbah.

Machir the son of Ammiel.—See note on chap. ix. 4. David now reaps a reward for his kindness to the crippled son of Jonathan.

(29) **Cheese of kine.**—A word occurring only here, and of uncertain meaning. The English follows the Chald., Syr., and Rabbinic interpretation; the Vulg. has "fat calves," and Theod. "sucking calves."

XVIII.

(1) **Numbered the people.**—The word means rather *mustered*. David was some time at Mahanaim, organising the forces which continually gathered to him there.

(2) **Ittai the Gittite.**—Comp. note on xv. 19. The arrangement of the army in three divisions was common both among the Israelites (Judg. vii. 16; xi. 43; 1 Sam. xi. 11) and their enemies (1 Sam. xiii. 17). Comp. also

third part under the hand of Abishai the son of Zeruiah, Joab's brother, and a third part under the hand of Ittai the Gittite. And the king said unto the people, I will surely go forth with you myself also. (3) But the people answered, Thou shalt not go forth: for if we flee away, they will not ¹care for us; neither if half of us die, will they care for us: but now *thou art* ² worth ten thousand of us: therefore now *it is* better that thou ³succour us out of the city. (4) And the king said unto them, What seemeth you best I will do. And the king stood by the gate side, and all the people came out by hundreds and by thousands.

(5) And the king commanded Joab and Abishai and Ittai, saying, *Deal* gently for my sake with the young man, *even* with Absalom. And all the people heard when the king gave all the captains charge concerning Absalom.

(6) So the people went out into the field against Israel: and the battle was in the wood of Ephraim; (7) where the people of Israel were slain before the servants of David, and there was there a great slaughter that day of twenty thousand *men*. (8) For the battle was there scattered over the face of all the country: and the wood ⁴devoured more people that day than the sword devoured.

(9) And Absalom met the servants of David. And Absalom rode upon a mule, and the mule went under the thick boughs of a great oak, and his head caught hold of the oak, and he was taken up between the heaven and the earth; and the mule that *was* under him went away. (10) And a certain man saw *it*, and told Joab, and said, Behold, I saw Absalom hanged in an oak. (11) And Joab said unto the man that told him, And, behold, thou sawest *him*, and why didst thou not smite him there to the ground? and I would have given thee ten *shekels* of silver, and a girdle. (12) And the man said unto Joab, Though I should ⁵receive a thousand *shekels* of silver in mine hand, *yet* would I not put forth mine hand against the king's son; for in our hearing the king charged thee and Abishai and Ittai, saying, ⁶Beware that none *touch* the young man Absalom. (13) Otherwise I should have wrought falsehood against mine own life: for there is no matter hid from the king,

¹ Heb., *set their heart on us.*
² Heb., *as ten thousand of us.*
³ Heb., *be to succour.*
⁴ Heb., *multiplied to devour.*
⁵ Heb., *weigh upon mine hand.*
⁶ Heb., *Beware whosoever ye be of, &c.*

---

2 Kings xi. 5, 6; David proposed to take the chief command in person.

(3) **Now thou art worth ten thousand of us.**—The Hebrew text reads *now*, but without *thou*, and as it stands must be translated, *now there are ten thousand like us*; but the change of a single letter alters the word *now* into *thou*, and this change should unquestionably be made in accordance with the LXX. and Vulg., followed by the English. The people urge truly that David is the very centre of their whole cause, and suggest that, even while avoiding unnecessary exposure, he may yet be equally helpful by keeping a reserve in the city to help them in case of need.

(4) **What seemeth you best.**—David was nothing loth to avoid the personal encounter with his son, and readily yielded. He, however, encouraged the troops by reviewing them as they passed out, and improved the opportunity to give his generals special and public charge concerning Absalom. He speaks of him tenderly as "the young man" (ver. 5; comp. ver. 29, 32), to imply that his sin was a youthful indiscretion.

(6) **The wood of Ephraim.**—No *wood of Ephraim* on the eastern side of the Jordan happens to be elsewhere mentioned in Scripture. Yet it is plain that the battle must have been on that side of the river for the following reasons: (1) both armies were on that side beforehand, and there is no mention of their crossing; (2) David remained in Mahanaim (ver. 3, 4) with the reserves, for the purpose of succouring the army in case of need; (3) he there received the news of Absalom's death (ver. 24—33); (4) the army returned thither after the battle (chap. xix. 3); and (5) David was obliged to cross the Jordan on his final return to Jerusalem, and was met at the crossing by the tribes (ver. 15, &c.). There is really no difficulty but such as arises from our ignorance of local names. The narrative clearly implies that there was a "wood of Ephraim," otherwise unknown, on the east of the Jordan.

(7) **Twenty Thousand.**—This number seems large, but we really know nothing of the size of the forces engaged on either side; and if the phrase "that day" be taken, as often, with sufficient latitude to include the whole campaign of which this battle was the culmination, there is nothing surprising in the destruction of 20,000 men. Of the human causes of the victory nothing is told. We may assume that the advantage of thorough military organisation and generalship was on David's side; but, in addition to this, was the vast power of the *right*, the prestige of law and authority.

(8) **The wood devoured more.**—The battle and the pursuit covered a wide range of country; more were slain in the pursuit through the wood, both by accident and by the sword, than in the actual battle itself.

(9) **His head caught hold of the oak.**—Absalom in his flight found himself among his enemies, and sought to escape into the denser parts of the forest. As he did so his head caught between the branches of a tree, his mule went from under him, and he hung there helpless. There is nothing said to support the common idea (which seems to have originated with Josephus), that he hung by his long hair, though this may doubtless have helped to entangle his head.

(13) **Against mine own life.**—The English, like the Vulg., here follows the margin of the Hebrew; the LXX., in most MSS., following the text, has *against*

and thou thyself wouldest have set thyself against *me*. ⁽¹⁴⁾ Then said Joab, I may not tarry thus ¹ with thee. And he took three darts in his hand, and thrust them through the heart of Absalom, while he *was* yet alive in the ² midst of the oak. ⁽¹⁵⁾ And ten young men that bare Joab's armour compassed about and smote Absalom, and slew him.

⁽¹⁶⁾ And Joab blew the trumpet, and the people returned from pursuing after Israel: for Joab held back the people. ⁽¹⁷⁾ And they took Absalom, and cast him into a great pit in the wood, and laid a very great heap of stones upon him: and all Israel fled every one to his tent.

⁽¹⁸⁾ Now Absalom in his lifetime had taken and reared up for himself a pillar, which *is* in *a* the king's dale: for he said, I have no son to keep my name in remembrance: and he called the pillar after his own name: and it is called unto this day, Absalom's place.

⁽¹⁹⁾ Then said Ahimaaz the son of Zadok, Let me now run, and bear the king tidings, how that the LORD hath ³ avenged him of his enemies. ⁽²⁰⁾ And Joab said unto him, Thou shalt not ⁴ bear tidings this day, but thou shalt bear tidings another day: but this day thou shalt bear no tidings, because the king's son is dead. ⁽²¹⁾ Then said Joab to Cushi, Go tell the king what thou hast seen. And Cushi bowed himself unto Joab, and ran. ⁽²²⁾ Then said Ahimaaz the son of Zadok yet again to Joab, But ⁵ howsoever, let me, I pray thee, also run after Cushi. And Joab said, Wherefore wilt thou run, my son, seeing that thou hast no tidings ⁶ ready? ⁽²³⁾ But howsoever, *said he*, let me run. And he said unto him, Run. Then Ahimaaz ran by the way of the plain, and overran Cushi.

⁽²⁴⁾ And David sat between the two gates: and the watchman went up to the roof over the gate unto the wall, and lifted up his eyes, and looked, and behold a man running alone. ⁽²⁵⁾ And the watchman cried, and told the king. And the king said, If he *be* alone, *there is* tidings in his mouth. And he came apace, and drew near. ⁽²⁶⁾ And the watchman saw another man running: and the watchman called unto the porter, and said, Behold *another* man running alone. And the king said, He also bringeth tidings. ⁽²⁷⁾ And the watchman said, ⁷ Me thinketh the running of the foremost is like the running of Ahimaaz the son of Zadok. And the king

---

1 Heb., *before thee.*

2 Heb., *heart.*

a Gen. 14. 17.

3 Heb., *judged him from the hand, &c.*

4 Heb., *be a man of tidings.*

5 Heb., *be what may.*

6 Or, *convenient.*

7 Heb., *I see the running.*

---

his life. Either makes a good sense, but the English is preferable. In this parley Joab thoroughly exposes his unscrupulous and self-willed character, and the man shows that he understood it.

(14) **I may not tarry thus.**—Joab evidently feels the home-thrusts made by the man in the argument, but, determined on his deed of violence, he sees that it is worse than useless to delay. His act was simply murder. In a lawless age it was defensible as the one act which terminated the rebellion and made a renewal of it impossible, and destroyed a traitor and would-be parricide who was likely otherwise to escape punishment; but it was a distinct disobedience of express orders, and Joab's taking the execution into his own hands was wilful and deliberate murder.

Three darts.—The word means a *rod* or *staff*. Also the word *heart* is the same as the following word *midst*, and is not therefore to be taken too literally. Joab seized such sticks as were at hand in the wood and thrust them into Absalom, giving him most painful and probably mortal wounds, but not instantly killing him. Then (ver. 15) the ten men who had Joab's armour and weapons came up and finally killed Absalom.

(16) **Blew the trumpet.**—Comp. ii. 28; xx. 22. With the death of Absalom the rebellion was at an end, and Joab would stop further slaughter.

(17) **Every one to his tent.**—An expression derived from the life in the wilderness, and meaning *every one to his home.* (Comp. Deut. xvi. 7; Josh. xxii. 4—8; 1 Sam. xiii. 2; chap. xix. 8, xx. 1, 22.)

(18) **The king's dale.**—Called also in Gen. xiv. 17 "the valley of Shaveh." Its site has not been identified, and writers differ as to whether it was near Jerusalem, in the valley of the Kidron, which seems probable, or was near the site of Sodom. On Absalom's statement that he had no son, see note on xiv. 27.

(20) **Thou shalt bear no tidings.**—Ahimaaz appears to have been in favour both with David (comp. ver. 27) and with Joab. Joab, therefore, well knowing how painful to David would be the news of the death of Absalom, refused to let Ahimaaz bear it. The word is used, with rare exceptions, of good tidings.

(21) **Cushi.**—Rather, the *Cushite*, probably an Ethiopian slave in Joab's service, for whose falling under the king's displeasure he had little care.

(22) **No tidings ready.**—The phrase is a difficult one, and is translated by the LXX. "no tidings leading to profit," and by the Vulg. "thou wilt not be a bearer of good tidings." The simplest and most probable sense is "no tidings sufficient" for a special messenger; the Cushite had already carried the news.

(23) **By the way of the plain.**—The word used here is generally applied to the valley of the Jordan, and hence it has been argued that the battle could not have been fought on the eastern side of the river, since, in that case, Ahimaaz could not have reached Mahanaim by the Jordan valley except by a long and tedious detour. But the word simply means *circuit*, or *surrounding country*, and is used in Neh. xii. 28 for the country about Jerusalem. Here it means that Ahimaaz ran

said, He *is* a good man, and cometh with good tidings. ⁽²⁸⁾ And Ahimaaz called, and said unto the king, ¹ ² All is well. And he fell down to the earth upon his face before the king, and said, Blessed *be* the LORD thy God, which hath ³ delivered up the men that lifted up their hand against my lord the king. ⁽²⁹⁾ And the king said, ⁴ Is the young man Absalom safe? And Ahimaaz answered, When Joab sent the king's servant, and *me* thy servant, I saw a great tumult, but I knew not what *it was*. ⁽³⁰⁾ And the king said *unto him*, Turn aside, *and* stand here. And he turned aside, and stood still. ⁽³¹⁾ And, behold, Cushi came; and Cushi said, ⁵ Tidings, my lord the king: for the LORD hath avenged thee this day of all them that rose up against thee. ⁽³²⁾ And the king said unto Cushi, *Is* the young man Absalom safe? And Cushi answered, The enemies of my lord the king, and all that rise against thee to do *thee* hurt, be as *that* young man *is*. ⁽³³⁾ And the king was much moved, and went up to the chamber over the gate, and wept: and as he went, thus he said, O my son Absalom, my son, my son Absalom! would God I had died for thee, O Absalom, my son, my son!

1 Or, *Peace be to thee.*
2 Heb., *Peace.*
3 Heb., *shut up.*
4 Heb., *Is there peace?*
5 Heb., *Tidings is brought.*
6 Heb., *salvation,* or, *deliverance.*
7 Heb., *by loving,* &c.
8 Heb., *that princes or servants are not to thee.*
9 Heb., *to the heart of thy servants.*

CHAPTER XIX.—⁽¹⁾ And it was told Joab, Behold, the king weepeth and mourneth for Absalom. ⁽²⁾ And the ⁶ victory that day was *turned* into mourning unto all the people: for the people heard say that day how the king was grieved for his son. ⁽³⁾ And the people gat them by stealth that day into the city, as people being ashamed steal away when they flee in battle. ⁽⁴⁾ But the king covered his face, and the king cried with a loud voice, O my son Absalom, O Absalom, my son, my son! ⁽⁵⁾ And Joab came into the house to the king, and said, Thou hast shamed this day the faces of all thy servants, which this day have saved thy life, and the lives of thy sons and of thy daughters, and the lives of thy wives, and the lives of thy concubines; ^{(6) 7} in that thou lovest thine enemies, and hatest thy friends. For thou hast declared this day, ⁸ that thou regardest neither princes nor servants: for this day I perceive, that if Absalom had lived, and all we had died this day, then it had pleased thee well. ⁽⁷⁾ Now therefore arise, go forth, and speak ⁹ comfortably unto thy servants: for I swear by the LORD, if thou go not forth, there will not tarry one with thee this night:

"by the way of the circuit," *i.e.*, in all probability, by a longer but smoother road than that taken by the Cushite, so that he was able to outrun him.

⁽²⁸⁾ **All is well.**—Literally, *Peace*, as in the margin. This is the cry with which Ahimaaz greets the king in his eager haste, as soon as he comes within hearing. He then approaches and falls down reverentially, with a distinct announcement of the victory.

⁽²⁹⁾ **Is . . . Absalom safe?**—The king's whole interest is centred in Absalom, and he cares for no other tidings. Ahimaaz skilfully, though untruthfully, evades the question. He had just been trained to untruthfulness in David's service.

The king's servant.—This can only refer to the Cushite; but by omitting the single letter which forms the conjunction in Hebrew, the phrase becomes "When Joab, the king's servant, sent thy servant," and so the Vulg. reads.

⁽³²⁾ **Absalom.**—To the Cushite's tidings David replies with the same question as before; but this messenger does not appreciate the state of the king's feelings, and answers with sufficient plainness, though in courteous phrase, that Absalom is dead.

⁽³³⁾ **Was much moved.**—David's grief was not merely that of a father for his first-born son, but for that son slain in the very act of outrageous sin. His sorrow, too, may have gained poignancy from the thought—which must often have come to him during **the progress of** this rebellion—that all this sin and wrong took its occasion from his own great sin. Yet David was criminally weak at this crisis in allowing the feelings of the father completely to outweigh the duties of the monarch.

XIX.

⁽⁵⁾ **And Joab came.**—This is a continuation of verse 1, the intervening verses being parenthetical. Joab's whole character appears strikingly in his conduct on this occasion. With his hand red with the blood of the beloved son, he goes, in the hardest and most unfeeling terms, to reproach the father for giving way to his grief; he treats the king with thorough insolence, and with the air of a superior; yet withal he counsels David for his own welfare and for that of the kingdom as a wise and loyal statesman. It may be doubted whether David yet knew of Joab's part in the death of Absalom.

The lives of thy sons.—Had Absalom succeeded he would no doubt not only have slain his father, but also, after the Oriental custom, have put out of the way all who might possibly have become rival claimants of the throne. (Comp. Judges ix. 5; 1 Kings xv. 29, xvi. 11; 2 Kings x. 6, 7, xi. 1.)

⁽⁷⁾ **I swear by the Lord.**—The statement which Joab emphasises with this solemn oath is not that he will lead the people into revolt—he does not seem to have conceived, far less to have expressed any such design—but it is simply an assurance of the extreme

and that will be worse unto thee than all the evil that befell thee from thy youth until now. ⁽⁸⁾ Then the king arose, and sat in the gate. And they told unto all the people, saying, Behold, the king doth sit in the gate. And all the people came before the king: for Israel had fled every man to his tent.

⁽⁹⁾ And all the people were at strife throughout all the tribes of Israel, saying, The king saved us out of the hand of our enemies, and he delivered us out of the hand of the Philistines; and now he is fled out of the land for Absalom. ⁽¹⁰⁾ And Absalom, whom we anointed over us, is dead in battle. Now therefore why ¹speak ye not a word of bringing the king back?

⁽¹¹⁾ And king David sent to Zadok and to Abiathar the priests, saying, Speak unto the elders of Judah, saying, Why are ye the last to bring the king back to his house? seeing the speech of all Israel is come to the king, *even* to his house. ⁽¹²⁾ Ye *are* my brethren, ye *are* my bones and my flesh: wherefore then are ye the last to bring back the king? ⁽¹³⁾ And say ye to Amasa, *Art* thou not of my bone, and of my flesh? God do so to me, and more also, if thou be not captain of the host before me continually in the room of Joab. ⁽¹⁴⁾ And he bowed the heart of all the men of Judah, even as *the heart of* one man; so that they sent *this word* unto the king, Return thou, and all thy servants. ⁽¹⁵⁾ So the king returned, and came to Jordan. And Judah came to Gilgal, to go to meet the king, to conduct the king over Jordan.

⁽¹⁶⁾ And *ᵃShimei the son of Gera, a Benjamite, which *was* of Bahurim, hasted and came down with the men of Judah to meet king David. ⁽¹⁷⁾ And *there were* a thousand men of Benjamin with him, and ᵇZiba the servant of the house of Saul, and his fifteen sons and his twenty

---

¹ Heb., *are ye silent.*

ᵃ 1 Kings 2. 8.

ᵇ ch. 16. 1.

---

danger of the course David was pursuing, put in such a strong and startling way as to rouse him from the selfishness of his sorrow.

⁽⁸⁾ **For Israel had fled.**—Translate, *but Israel fled*; "Israel" being used here, as throughout this narrative (see chaps. xvi. 15, 18, xvii. 5, 14, 15, 24, 26, xviii. 6, 7, 16, 17), for those who had espoused the cause of Absalom.

⁽⁹⁾ **The king saved us.**—With the collapse of the rebellion the accompanying infatuation passed away, and the people began to remember how much they owed to David. There seems to have been a general disposition among the people to return to their allegiance, yet the movement was without organisation or leadership.

⁽¹⁰⁾ **We anointed over us.**—There is no other mention of the anointing of Absalom, and it certainly would not have been performed by the high-priests. It may have been done by some prophet, or this may be a mere form of expression taken from the custom of anointing, and only mean "whom we appointed over us."

Why speak ye not?—There was evidently a hesitation and delay, arising probably from a mere want of organisation, but yet of dangerous tendency. It is under these circumstances that David shows that politic power which had so often before stood him in good stead. The LXX. very unnecessarily places at the end of this verse the clause which is found at the end of verse 11.

⁽¹¹⁾ **The elders of Judah.**—Judah was naturally particularly slow in returning to its allegiance. It had shown especial ingratitude to David, and had formed the cradle and centre of the rebellion, and even now Jerusalem probably had a garrison of Absalom's soldiers. They might naturally doubt how they would be received, and their military organisation in Absalom's interest threw especial obstacles in their way. The last words of the verse, "to his house," may be an accidental repetition from the previous clause.

⁽¹²⁾ **My bones and my flesh.**—More exactly, *bone*, as in verse 13 and chap. v. 1. Of course the tribe of Judah, from which David sprung, was more closely connected with him by blood than any other; but the point likely to influence them was that the king recognised this relationship.

⁽¹³⁾ **Say ye to Amasa.**—Amasa, like Joab, was David's nephew, although possibly his mother may have been only half-sister to David. In this offer of the command-in-chief to the rebel general, David adopted a bold, but a rash and unjust policy. Amasa should have been punished, not rewarded for his treason. He had given no evidence of loyalty, nor was there proof that he would be trustworthy. Moreover, this appointment would be sure to provoke the jealousy and hostility of Joab. But David had long been restless under the overbearing influence of Joab (see verse 22; chaps. xvi. 10, iii. 39), and now since he had murdered Absalom, was determined to be rid of him. He therefore took advantage of the opportunity by this means to win over to himself what remained of the military organisation of Absalom.

⁽¹⁵⁾ **Judah came to Gilgal.**—The two parties met at the Jordan, David coming from Mahanaim to the eastern side of the ford, near Jericho, and the representatives of the tribe of Judah to Gilgal on the opposite bank.

⁽¹⁶⁾ **Shimei the son of Gera.**—See Note on chap. xvi. 5. It is evident that Shimei was a man of influence and importance, and his accession to David at this juncture was of great value. At the same time, it is plain that Shimei himself was only a time-server, and that he was thoroughly disloyal in his heart, and only came now to David because he saw that his was "the winning cause."

⁽¹⁷⁾ **Before the king.**—Comp. the same phrase in chap. xx. 8. In both cases "before" is, literally, *before the face of*, and is equivalent to saying "they went over Jordan to meet the king." In their eagerness to prove their very doubtful allegiance, they dashed through the servants with him; and they went over Jordan before the king. (18) And there went over a ferry boat to carry over the king's household, and to do ¹what he thought good. And Shimei the son of Gera fell down before the king, as he was come over Jordan; (19) and said unto the king, Let not my lord impute iniquity unto me, neither do thou remember ᵃthat which thy servant did perversely the day that my lord the king went out of Jerusalem, that the king should take it to his heart. (20) For thy servant doth know that I have sinned: therefore, behold, I am come the first this day of all the house of Joseph to go down to meet my lord the king. (21) But Abishai the son of Zeruiah answered and said, Shall not Shimei be put to death for this, because he cursed the LORD's anointed? (22) And David said, What have I to do with you, ye sons of Zeruiah, that ye should this day be adversaries unto me? shall there any man be put to death this day in Israel? for do not I know that I *am* this day king over Israel? (23) Therefore the king said unto Shimei, Thou shalt not die. And the king sware unto him.

(24) And Mephibosheth the son of Saul came down to meet the king, and had neither dressed his feet, nor trimmed his beard, nor washed his clothes, from the day the king departed until the day he came *again* in peace. (25) And it came to pass, when he was come to Jerusalem to meet the king, that the king said unto him, Wherefore wentest not thou with me, Mephibosheth? (26) And he answered, My lord, O king, my servant deceived me: for thy servant said, I will saddle me an ass, that I may ride thereon, and go to the king; because thy servant *is* lame. (27) And ᵇhe hath slandered thy servant unto my lord the king; but my lord the king *is* as an angel of God: do therefore *what is* good in thine eyes. (28) For all *of* my father's house were but ²dead men before my lord the king: yet didst thou

¹ Heb., *the good in his eyes.*
ᵃ ch. 16. 5.
ᵇ ch. 16. 3.
² Heb., *men of death.*

---

waters of the ford, and met the king on the eastern side of the Jordan.

(18) **As he was come over.**—Rather, *as he was coming over, as he was about to cross.* Shimei and Ziba met the king on the east of Jordan, and his crossing is not spoken of until verses 31—40.

(20) **The house of Joseph.**—Shimei was not strictly of "the house of Joseph," but of Benjamin; and it is plain that Joseph, as the name of the most prominent member, stands for all the tribes outside of Judah. This usage is well recognised at a later time (see 1 Chron. v. 1, 2; Amos v. 15), and it has hence been argued that it indicates a late date for the composition of the book; but it is also found in Pss. lxxx. 1, 2, lxxxi. 5 (the date of which it would be rash to attempt to fix), in the reign of Solomon, 1 Kings xi. 28, and probably very early in Judges i. 35. There is no reason why the expression may not have been used at the earliest date when there began to be a certain separation and distinction between Judah and the other tribes, which was soon after the conquest of Canaan.

(22) **Adversaries.**—The word in the original here is *Satan.*

(23) **The king sware unto him.**—This oath of David assuring immunity to Shimei brings to mind his dying charge to Solomon concerning him (1 Kings ii. 8, 9): "His hoar head bring thou down to the grave with blood." The whole transaction is to be viewed from a political point. Shimei had been guilty of high treason in David's distress; at his return he had confessed his fault, and exerted himself to help on David's restoration to the throne. He had accordingly been pardoned, and David, somewhat rashly, had confirmed this pardon with an oath, in such a way that he was unable to punish any subsequent treasonable tendencies showing themselves in Shimei. From the character of the man, however, and from Solomon's address to him in 1 Kings ii. 44. it is plain that he remained thoroughly disloyal. David saw this, and hindered by his oath from treating him as he deserved, pointed out the case to Solomon. Solomon settled the matter by a compact (into which Shimei willingly entered), that his life should be forfeited whenever he should go out of Jerusalem. There he was under supervision; elsewhere he could not be trusted. After a few years he violated this condition, and was executed. David had made a rash oath, and observed it to the letter, but no farther, towards a thorough traitor.

(24) **Came down to meet.**—The obvious meaning of this is that Mephibosheth came down from the high land of Jerusalem to meet the king in the Jordan valley, and in this case the following verse should be translated, "And it came to pass when Jerusalem" (meaning its inhabitants, with Mephibosheth among them) "was come to meet the king." Some writers, however, prefer to keep verse 25 as it is, and to suppose that during the rebellion Mephibosheth had taken refuge on his ancestral estate near the heights of Gibeah, and that he came thence to Jerusalem to meet David. In either case the signs of deep mourning used by Mephibosheth "from the day the king departed" were an evidence of his loyalty. The word for *beard* is used only for the *moustache.*

(25) **Wentest not thou with me?**—David had heard and believed the story of Mephibosheth's ingratitude and treachery (chap. xvi. 3, 4), and his present remonstrance is so gentle and kindly as to show that Mephibosheth's appearance at once produced an impression, and suggested in David's mind a doubt of the truth of what Ziba had told him.

(26) **My servant deceived me.**—It now appears that the two asses laden with provisions which Ziba had brought to David in his flight (Chap. xvi. 1, 2) were those which he had been ordered to prepare for his master. When Ziba had stolen away with these, Mephibosheth was left helpless in his lameness. Most of the ancient versions read "said to him, Saddle," &c., but the sense is plain enough as the text stands.

set thy servant among them that did eat at thine own table. What right therefore have I yet to cry any more unto the king? ⁽²⁹⁾ And the king said unto him, Why speakest thou any more of thy matters? I have said, Thou and Ziba divide the land. ⁽³⁰⁾ And Mephibosheth said unto the king, Yea, let him take all, forasmuch as my lord the king is come again in peace unto his own house.

⁽³¹⁾ And Barzillai the Gileadite came down from Rogelim, and went over Jordan with the king, to conduct him over Jordan. ⁽³²⁾ Now Barzillai was a very aged man, *even* fourscore years old: and *ᵃ*he had provided the king of sustenance while he lay at Mahanaim; for he *was* a very great man. ⁽³³⁾ And the king said unto Barzillai, Come thou over with me, and I will feed thee with me in Jerusalem. ⁽³⁴⁾ And Barzillai said unto the king, ¹How long have I to live, that I should go up with the king unto Jerusalem? ⁽³⁵⁾ I *am* this day fourscore years old: *and* can I discern between good and evil? can thy servant taste what I eat or what I drink? can I hear any more the voice of singing men and singing women? wherefore then should thy servant be yet a burden unto my lord the king? ⁽³⁶⁾ Thy servant will go a little way over Jordan with the king: and why should the king recompense it me with such a reward? ⁽³⁷⁾ Let thy servant, I pray thee, turn back again, that I may die in mine own city, *and be buried* by the grave of my father and of my mother. But behold thy servant Chimham; let him go over with my lord the king; and do to him what shall seem good unto thee. ⁽³⁸⁾ And the king answered, Chimham shall go over with me, and I will do to him that which shall seem good unto thee: and whatsoever thou shalt ²require of me, *that* will I do for thee. ⁽³⁹⁾ And all the people went over Jordan. And when the king was come over, the king kissed Barzillai, and blessed him; and he returned unto his own place. ⁽⁴⁰⁾ Then the king went on to Gilgal, and Chimham went on with him: and all the people of Judah conducted the king, and also half the people of Israel.

⁽⁴¹⁾ And, behold, all the men of Israel came to the king, and said unto the king, Why have our brethren the men of Judah stolen thee away, and have brought the king, and his household, and all David's men with him, over Jordan? ⁽⁴²⁾ And all the men of Judah answered

ᵃ ch. 17. 27.

¹ Heb., *How many days are the years of my life?*

² Heb., *choose.*

⁽²⁹⁾ **Divide the land.**—When Ziba came to David with his false report about Mephibosheth, David had instantly transferred to him all his master's possessions (chap. xvi. 4); he now saw the injustice of his hasty action, and ought at least to have reversed it, if not to have punished Ziba besides. Either, however, because he had still some doubt of the real merits of the case, or more probably because he was unwilling for political reasons to offend Ziba, he resorts to that halfway and compromise course which was both weak and unjust. The circumstances of the case, the continued mourning of Mephibosheth, the silence of Ziba, concur with the physical infirmity of Mephibosheth to show the truth of his story.

⁽³²⁾ **Provided the king of sustenance.**—An old use of the preposition "of," meaning *with*. The word is the same here as that translated in the next verse "feed thee," and there is an especial fitness in the use of the same word in both cases which is lost in the English Version. It is translated "nourish" in Gen. xlv. 11, xlvii. 12, l. 21, &c., and "sustain" in 1 Kings xvii. 9, Neh. ix. 21, &c. The king proposes to return Barzillai's service in kind, but multiplied manifold.

⁽³⁷⁾ **Chimham.**—It appears from 1 Kings ii. 7, where David gives charge to Solomon to care for Barzillai's sons, that Chimham was his son. This might be supposed from the narrative here, but is not expressly stated. In Jer. xli. 17 mention is made of "the habitation of Chimham, which is by Bethlehem," from which it is supposed that David conveyed to Chimham a house upon his own paternal estate.

⁽³⁹⁾ **All the people.**—As "Israel" has been used throughout this narrative for Absalom's supporters, so "the people" is used for those faithful to David.

⁽⁴⁰⁾ **All the people.**—The tribe of Judah, deeply moved by the measures and words of David, had united generally in his restoration; the other tribes, who had first proposed to return to their allegiance (verses 9, 10), had not had time to join in the present movement, or had not generally known of it, and only Shimei with his one thousand Benjamites, and doubtless others living near, together with the tribes east of the Jordan, represented altogether as "half the people of Israel," were able to come together.

⁽⁴¹⁾ **All the men of Israel.**—When David had crossed the Jordan, he naturally made a halt at Gilgal, and then the representatives of the remaining tribes came to him, full of wrath at the apparent neglect of them. Jealousies between the tribes, and especially between Judah on the one side and the ten tribes on the other, had all along existed, the tribe of Ephraim being particularly sensitive (Judges viii. 1, xii. 1). By the successful wars of Saul these jealousies were held in check, but broke out in national separation on his death; after seven and a half years they were partially healed by David, and were kept in abeyance by the wise administration of Solomon, but at his death they broke out with fresh power, and dismembered the nation for ever.

⁽⁴²⁾ **Have we eaten.**—Judah justifies its course by its nearness of relationship to the king, and repels the idea of having received any especial favours from him. In this, then, may be a taunt to the Benjamites on

the men of Israel, Because the king *is* near of kin to us: wherefore then be ye angry for this matter? have we eaten at all of the king's *cost*? or hath he given us any gift? ⁽⁴³⁾ And the men of Israel answered the men of Judah, and said, We have ten parts in the king, and we have also more *right* in David than ye: why then did ye ¹despise us, that our advice should not be first had in bringing back our king? And the words of the men of Judah were fiercer than the words of the men of Israel.

CHAPTER XX.—⁽¹⁾ And there happened to be there a man of Belial, whose name *was* Sheba, the son of Bichri, a Benjamite: and he blew a trumpet, and said, We have no part in David, neither have we inheritance in the son of Jesse: every man to his tents, O Israel. ⁽²⁾ So every man of Israel went up from after David, *and* followed Sheba the son of Bichri: but the men of Judah clave unto their king, from Jordan even to Jerusalem.

⁽³⁾ And David came to his house at Jerusalem; and the king took the ten women *his* ᵃconcubines, whom he had left to keep the house, and put them in ²ward, and fed them, but went not in unto them. So they were ³shut up unto the day of their death, ⁴living in widowhood.

⁽⁴⁾ Then said the king to Amasa, ⁵Assemble me the men of Judah within three days, and be thou here present. ⁽⁵⁾ So Amasa went to assemble *the men of* Judah: but he tarried longer than the set time which he had appointed him. ⁽⁶⁾ And David said to Abishai, Now shall Sheba the son of Bichri do us more harm than *did* Absalom: take thou thy lord's servants, and pursue after him, lest he get him fenced cities, and ⁶escape us. ⁽⁷⁾ And there went out after him Joab's men, and the ᵇCherethites, and the Pelethites, and all the mighty

¹ Heb., *set us at light.*
ᵃ ch. 16. 22.
² Heb., *a house of ward.*
³ Heb., *bound.*
⁴ Heb., *in widowhood of life.*
B.C. cir. 1022.
⁵ Heb., *call.*
⁶ Heb., *deliver himself from our eyes*
ᵇ ch. 8. 18.

---

account of the partiality shown them by Saul. On the other hand, the Israelites urge their claim of numerical superiority. The whole dispute is a remarkable testimony to the fairness of David's government as between the tribes.

⁽⁴³⁾ **More right in David than ye.**—The LXX. adds "and I am the firstborn rather than thou,"—an unnecessary gloss, and certainly untrue as respects Benjamin, who was probably prominent in the discussion.

That our advice should not be first had.—Better, *was not our word the first for bringing back the king?* (Comp. verses 9, 10.)

XX.

The angry altercation between the tribes led, according to the proverb (Prov. xv. 1), to fresh troubles. These foreboded greater disasters than had yet occurred, but were happily arrested in the bud. Although suppressed, they must yet have intensified the tribal jealousies, and have sowed the seed of future dismemberment. So goes on the long catalogue of sorrows, following one after another from David's sin.

⁽¹⁾ **Sheba, the son of Bichri.**—The English follows the ancient versions in taking *Bichri* as a proper name. Most recent commentators consider it as a patronymic, *the Bichrite, i.e.,* of the family of Becher, the second son of Benjamin. He was, to this extent at least, of the same clan with Saul. He was *there,* at Gilgal, with the representatives of the ten tribes, and took advantage of the dispute just mentioned to renew the rebellion of Absalom.

Every man to his tents.—Comp. the cry of Jeroboam as he inaugurated his rebellion (1 Kings xii. 16). It was the signal of revolt.

⁽²⁾ **Men of Judah clave.**—David's negotiations with Judah had now resulted in an entire reversal of the position of the tribes towards him; Judah, among whom the rebellion originated, and who had been tardy in returning to their allegiance, were now fierce in their loyalty, while Israel, who had only joined the already organised rebellion, and afterwards had first proposed the return of David, had become alienated and rebellious.

⁽³⁾ **Living in widowhood.**—This was the necessary result, under the system of polygamy, of what had happened. The clause may be understood as "in widowhood of life," as in our version, or "in widowhood of the living," *i.e.,* while their husband was living, as in the Chaldee.

⁽⁴⁾ **To Amasa.**—Thus David begins the fulfilment of his promise of chap. xix. 13. It proved an act of very doubtful expediency at this crisis.

⁽⁵⁾ **He tarried longer.**—No cause is assigned for this, and various conjectures have been made. The simplest explanation may be drawn from the fact that, in verse 8, Amasa is met on his return at Gibeon. He had therefore gone quite out of the bounds of Judah into Benjamin, and had consumed more time in consequence of exceeding his instructions. The fact suggests great doubt of his fitness for the place David had promised him. Joab appears to insinuate (in verse 11) that Amasa was not really loyal.

⁽⁶⁾ **David said to Abishai.**—David is determined to pass over Joab, and, therefore, when Amasa fails in this crisis, requiring immediate action, he summons Abishai, and puts him in command of such forces as were at hand in Jerusalem, and gives him orders for the rapid pursuit of Sheba. The clause "escape us" is difficult, and doubtful in the original, and the English follows the Vulg. Others translate "pluck out our eye," *i.e.,* do us great harm; others as the LXX., "overshadow our eye," meaning either cause us anxiety, or hide where we cannot find him.

⁽⁷⁾ **Joab's men.**—The body of men who were usually under Joab's immediate command, and who would readily follow his brother, whom they had been

men: and they went out of Jerusalem, to pursue after Sheba, the son of Bichri. (8) When they *were* at the great stone which *is* in Gibeon, Amasa went before them. And Joab's garment that he had put on was girded unto him, and upon it a girdle *with* a sword fastened upon his loins in the sheath thereof; and as he went forth it fell out. (9) And Joab said to Amasa, Art thou in health, my brother? And Joab took Amasa by the beard with the right hand to kiss him. (10) But Amasa took no heed to the sword that *was* in Joab's hand: so he smote him therewith in the fifth *rib*, and shed out his bowels to the ground, and ¹struck him not again; and he died. So Joab and Abishai his brother pursued after Sheba the son of Bichri. (11) And one of Joab's men stood by him, and said, He that favoureth Joab, and he that *is* for David, *let him go* after Joab. (12) And Amasa wallowed in blood in the midst of the highway. And when the man saw that all the people stood still, he removed Amasa out of the highway into the field, and cast a cloth upon him, when he saw that every one that came by him stood still. (13) When he was removed out of the highway, all the people went on after Joab, to pursue after Sheba the son of Bichri.

(14) And he went through all the tribes of Israel unto Abel, and to Beth-maachah, and all the Berites: and they were gathered together, and went also after him. (15) And they came and besieged him in Abel of Beth-maachah, and they cast up a bank against the city, and ²it stood in the trench: and all the people that *were* with Joab ³battered the wall, to throw it down.

(16) Then cried a wise woman out of the city, Hear, hear; say, I pray you, unto Joab, Come near hither, that I may speak with thee. (17) And when he was come near unto her, the woman said, *Art* thou Joab? And he answered, I *am he*. Then she said unto him, Hear the words of thine handmaid. And he answered, I do hear. (18) Then she spake, saying, ⁴They were wont to

1 Heb., *doubled not his stroke.*
2 Or, *it stood against the outmost wall.*
3 Heb., *marred to throw down.*
4 Or, *They plainly spake in the beginning, saying, Surely they will ask of Abel, and so make an end.*

---

accustomed to see associated with him. On "the Cherethites and the Pelethites," see Note on chap. viii. 18. "The mighty men" (see chap. xxiii. 8) appear to have been an especial body of heroes, probably made up chiefly of those who had been with David in his life as an outlaw.

(8) **Went before.**—Translate, *met*. (Comp. Note on chap. xix. 6.)

As he went forth it fell out.—The object of this verse is to explain how Joab, in consequence of the arrangement of his dress, was able to stab Amasa without his purpose being suspected. He had a girdle bound round his military coat, and in this he had stuck a dagger so arranged that it might fall out as he advanced. He then picked this up naturally in his left hand, and stretching out his right hand to greet Amasa, his movements gave rise to no suspicion.

(10) **In the fifth rib**=*Abdomen*. (See Note on chap. ii. 23.)

So Joab and Abishai.—Joab here comes forward as the commander of the pursuit without previous mention. He may have accompanied Abishai from Jerusalem, or he may have joined him on the route; but, now, having murdered Amasa, he assumes his old place as commander-in-chief, doubtless with the connivance of his brother.

(11) **One of Joab's men.**—Comp. verse 7. Time was too precious for Joab himself to wait. He must put down the rebellion of Sheba by rapid action, and thereby render himself impregnable in the high office which had been his, and which he had now again usurped. He left one of his trusty men, however, by the body of Amasa, with a battle cry which should suggest that he had rightly been put to death for his doubtful loyalty, and that all who were attached to Joab and loyal to David should follow Joab. Joab's real motive for murdering Amasa, as for murdering Abner (chap. iii. 27), was personal jealousy and ambition.

(12) **The people stood still.**—These were probably the very people whom Amasa had just been gathering from Judah and Benjamin. Whoever they may have been, they were naturally overcome and paralysed for the moment at the sight of the great leader whom the king had just promoted wallowing in his blood. Joab's warrior, seeing the effect of their consternation, removed and concealed the body, and the pursuit then went on.

(14) **Unto Abel, and to Beth-maachah.**—Abel has been identified with the modern Christian village of Abil (called "Abil-el-Kamh," on account of the excellence of its wheat (north-west of Lake Huleh). It is called "Abel-Beth-maachah," in verse 15 (the "of" should be omitted), and is spoken of under that name in 1 Kings xv. 20 and 2 Kings xv. 29 in connection with Ijon and Dan, and in the same connection is called "Abel-maim" ("Abel of waters") in 2 Chron. xvi. 4, to distinguish it from other places of the same name. It was at the extreme north of the land.

All the Berites.—Apparently a family, or clan, in the north of Israel, otherwise entirely unknown. The LXX. and Vulg. here apparently follow a different text. The Bishop of Bath and Wells supposes the Hebrew word to be a form of the word for "fortresses," but no such form is known.

(15) **Abel of Beth-maachah.**—Omit the preposition "of." (See verse 14.)

Stood in the trench.—The "trench" is the space between the wall of the city and the lower outer wall. When the besiegers had succeeded in planting the mounds for their battering engines in this space they had already gained an important advantage.

(18) **Ask counsel at Abel.**—The simplest and most obvious explanation is here the true one, viz., that

speak in old time, saying, They shall surely ask *counsel* at Abel: and so they ended *the matter*. (19) I *am one of them that are* peaceable *and* faithful in Israel: thou seekest to destroy a city and a mother in Israel: why wilt thou swallow up the inheritance of the LORD? (20) And Joab answered and said, Far be it, far be it from me, that I should swallow up or destroy. (21) The matter is not so: but a man of mount Ephraim, Sheba the son of Bichri [1] by name, hath lifted up his hand against the king, *even* against David: deliver him only, and I will depart from the city. And the woman said unto Joab, Behold, his head shall be thrown to thee over the wall. (22) Then the woman went unto all the people in her wisdom. And they cut off the head of Sheba the son of Bichri, and cast *it* out to Joab. And he blew a trumpet, and they [2] retired from the city, every man to his tent. And Joab returned to Jerusalem unto the king.

(23) Now *a* Joab *was* over all the host of Israel: and Benaiah the son of Jehoiada *was* over the Cherethites and over the Pelethites: (24) and Adoram *was* over the tribute: and Jehoshaphat the son of Ahilud *was* [3] recorder: (25) and Sheva *was* scribe: and Zadok and Abiathar *were* the priests: (26) and Ira also the Jairite was [4] a chief ruler about David.

CHAPTER XXI.—(1) Then there was a famine in the days of David three years, year after year; and David [5] enquired of the LORD. And the LORD answered, *It is* for Saul, and for his

[1] Heb., *by his name.*
[2] Heb., *were scattered.*
[3] ch. 8. 16.
[a] Or, *remembrancer.*
[4] Or, *a prince.*
B.C. 1021.
[5] Heb., *sought the face,* &c.

Abel had become proverbial for its wisdom. An ancient Jewish interpretation, which has been incorporated into the Targum, is, however, of sufficient interest to be mentioned: "Remember now that which is written in the book of the Law to ask a city concerning peace at the first? Hast thou done so, to ask of Abel if they will make peace?" The reference is to Deut. xx. 10, &c.

(20) **Far be it from me.**—Joab strongly disclaims the idea of any further harm to any one than the necessary destruction of the rebel Sheba. Joab's character "is strongly brought out in the transaction. Politic, decided, bold, and unscrupulous, but never needlessly cruel or impulsive, or even revengeful. No life is safe that stands in his way, but from policy he never sacrifices the most insignificant life without a purpose."—*Speaker's Commentary.*

(21) **Mount Ephraim.**—The range of hills so called because much of it lay in the tribe of Ephraim, although extending south into Benjamin.

(22) **To his tent** = to his home. (Comp. verse 1, chap. xviii. 17; 1 Kings xii. 16, &c.)

(23) **Benaiah.**—In the four closing verses of this chapter there is again given a short summary of the chief men of David's reign, as if to form the conclusion of this account of his life. A similar summary has already been given in chap. viii. 16—18, and the changes introduced here mark a later period of the reign. It is noticeable that Joab still remains commander-in-chief. On Benaiah and the force which he commanded, see Note on chap. viii. 18. (See also chap. xxiii. 20—23.)

(24) **Adoram was over the tribute.**—The same office was held by *Adoniram* in Solomon's reign (1 Kings iv. 6, v. 14), and by *Adoram* at the beginning of the reign of his successor (1 Kings xii. 18). All those may have been the same person, or at least of the same family. "The tribute" should rather be *the levy*, the forced labour so largely employed by Solomon. It is remarkable that there is no trace of such an office in chap. viii. 16—18, nor in the parallel (1 Chron. xviii. 14—17). It was a feature of Oriental despotism only introduced towards the close of David's reign, and carried to much greater length under Solomon.

(25) **Sheva.**—This officer is called *Seraiah* in chap. viii. 17. Nearly all the officers mentioned here are the same as in chap. viii. 16—18, where see the Notes.

(26) **Ira also the Jairite.**—He is not mentioned in the other lists of the king's officers; *Ira, an Ithrite*, is found in the list of David's "thirty and seven" heroes in chap. xxiii. 38, but there is no ground for identifying the two persons. On the office of "chief ruler," or *cohen*, see Note on chap. viii. 18. Earlier in David's reign the office had been occupied by his own sons, but the murder of the eldest, the rebellion and death of Absalom, and other disorders in his household had led apparently to a change.

XXI.

(1) **Then there was.**—Read, *and there was*, there being no indication of time in the original. It is plain from verse 7 that the events here narrated occurred after David had come to know Mephibosheth; and if in chap. xvi. 7 there is (as many suppose) an allusion to the execution of Saul's sons, they must have happened before the rebellion of Absalom. There is no more definite clue to the time, and the expression "in the days of David" seems purposely indefinite. The narrative is omitted from the Book of Chronicles.

Three years.—A famine in Palestine was always a consequence of deficient winter rains, and was not very uncommon; but a famine enduring for three successive years was alarming enough to awaken attention and to suggest some especial cause.

Enquired of the Lord.—Literally, *sought the face of the Lord.* The phrase is a different one from that often used in Judges and Samuel, and agrees with other indications that this narrative may have been obtained by the compiler from some other records than those from which he drew the bulk of this book. David turned to the true Source for a knowledge of the meaning of this unusual affliction.

(2) **For his bloody house.**—Better, *for the blood-guilty house.* Saul's family and descendants are regarded, according to the universal ideas of the times, as sharers in his guilt. The story of the Gibeonites and of Joshua's league with them is told in Josh. ix., but Saul's attempt to destroy them is mentioned

bloody house, because he slew the Gibeonites. (2) And the king called the Gibeonites, and said unto them; (now the Gibeonites *were* not of the children of Israel, but *a* of the remnant of the Amorites; and the children of Israel had sworn unto them: and Saul sought to slay them in his zeal to the children of Israel and Judah). (3) Wherefore David said unto the Gibeonites, What shall I do for you? and wherewith shall I make the atonement, that ye may bless the inheritance of the LORD? (4) And the Gibeonites said unto him, ¹We will have no silver nor gold of Saul, nor of his house; neither for us shalt thou kill any man in Israel. And he said, What ye shall say, *that* will I do for you. (5) And they answered the king, The man that consumed us, and that ²devised against us *that* we should be destroyed from remaining in any of the coasts of Israel, (6) let seven men of his sons be delivered unto us, and we will hang them up unto the LORD in Gibeah of Saul, ³*whom* the LORD did choose. And the king said, I will give *them*.

(7) But the king spared Mephibosheth, the son of Jonathan the son of Saul, because of *b* the LORD's oath that *was* between them, between David and Jonathan the son of Saul. (8) But the king took the two sons of Rizpah the daughter of Aiah, whom she bare unto Saul, Armoni and Mephibosheth; and

a Josh. 9. 3, 16, 17.

¹ Or, *It is not silver nor gold that we have to do with Saul or his house, neither pertains it to us to kill, &c.*

² Or, *cut us off.*

³ Or, *chosen of the Lord.*

b 1 Sam. 18. 3 & 20. 8, 42.

---

only here. It is plain, from what is said of them in verse 8, that they had never become incorporated with the Israelites by circumcision, but remained a distinct people. Saul's sin consisted in the violation of the solemn oath, in the Lord's name, by which the nation of Israel was bound to the Gibeonites. "His zeal", in that case was of the same ungodly character with many other acts of his reign, in which pride, arrogance, and self-will were cloaked under a zeal for God's honour and His people's welfare.

The Amorites.—More precisely, the Gibeonites were *Hivites* (Josh. ix. 7); but they are called Amorites (= *mountaineers*) as a frequent general name for the old people of Palestine.

Two questions are often asked in connection with this narrative: (1) Why the punishment of Saul's sin should have been so long delayed? and (2) why it should at last have fallen upon David and his people, who had no share in the commission of the sin? The answer to both questions is in the fact that Israel both sinned and was punished *as a nation*. Saul slew the Gibeonites, not simply as the son of Kish, but as the king of Israel, and therefore involved all Israel with him in the violation of the national oath; and hence, until the evil should be put away by the execution of the immediate offender or his representatives, all Israel must suffer. The lesson of the continuity of the nation's life, and of its continued responsibility from age to age, was greatly enhanced by the delay. Besides this, there were so many other grievous sins for which Saul was to be punished, that it was hardly possible to bring out during his lifetime the special Divine displeasure at this one.

(3) **Make the atonement.**—This is the same technical word as is used throughout the Law in connection with the propitiatory sacrifices. It means literally, *to cover up*, and is here used in that literal sense. David asks what he can do to so *cover up* the sin of Saul as to remove it from the sight of those against whom it had been committed—the Gibeonites as the earthly sufferers from it, and God Himself as the one against whom he had chiefly offended. Then might God's blessing again return to His people.

(4) **No silver nor gold.**—Money compensations for sins of blood were extremely common among all ancient nations, but were expressly forbidden in the Law of Moses (Num. xxxv. 31), and in this respect the Gibeonites appear to have accepted the teaching of the law of Israel.

Kill any man in Israel.—Notwithstanding that the guilt of Saul's sin, until it should be expiated, rested upon all Israel, the Gibeonites recognise that it had been committed by him, and do not seek that, apart from their connection with him, any Israelite should suffer on their account. David appreciates the fairness of their view of the matter, and promises beforehand to do whatever they shall require.

(6) **Let seven men of his sons.**—The head of the house and his household were closely identified in all the ideas of antiquity. Saul being dead, his male descendants were considered as standing in his place, representing him, and responsible for his acts, just as is largely the case in legal affairs and matters of property at the present day. The number *seven* is, doubtless, fixed upon as being first, a considerable and sufficient number; and then, on account of its sacred associations, and as the representative of completeness.

We will hang them up.—The sons of Saul are only to be given up by David; their actual execution is to be by the Gibeonites, and the method is that of *hanging* or fastening to a stake, either by impaling or by crucifixion, the word being used for both methods of execution.

Unto the Lord—*i.e.*, publicly. (Comp. a similar expression in Numb. xxv. 4.) The sin had been outrageous; its punishment must be conspicuous. The place of execution is fitly chosen in the home of Saul. It seems strange that he should be here spoken of as "the Lord's chosen;" but this and the expression "unto the Lord" go together; what Saul had done he had done as the head of the theocracy, as God's chosen ruler, and now his family must be punished in the presence of Him against whom he had offended —"before the Lord." The idea of regarding the execution of these men as a propitiatory human sacrifice is utterly destitute of any shadow of support.

(8) **Took the two sons of Rizpah.**—The suggestion that David took advantage of this opportunity to strengthen himself further against the house of Saul is utterly set aside by two considerations: (1)

the five sons of ¹Michal the daughter of Saul, whom she ²brought up for Adriel the son of Barzillai the Meholathite: ⁽⁹⁾ And he delivered them into the hands of the Gibeonites, and they hanged them in the hill before the LORD: and they fell *all* seven together, and were put to death in the days of harvest, in the first *days*, in the beginning of barley harvest. ⁽¹⁰⁾ And ᵃRizpah the daughter of Aiah took sackcloth, and spread it for her upon the rock, from the beginning of harvest until water dropped upon them out of heaven, and suffered neither the birds of the air to rest on them by day, nor the beasts of the field by night. ⁽¹¹⁾ And it was told David what Rizpah the daughter of Aiah, the concubine of Saul, had done. ⁽¹²⁾ And David went and took the bones of Saul and the bones of Jonathan his son from the men of Jabesh-gilead, which had stolen them from the street of Beth-shan, where the ᵇPhilistines had hanged them, when the Philistines had slain Saul in Gilboa: ⁽¹³⁾ and he brought up from thence the bones of Saul and the bones of Jonathan his son; and they gathered the bones of them that were hanged. ⁽¹⁴⁾ And the bones of Saul and Jonathan his son buried they in the country of Benjamin in Zelah, in the sepulchre of Kish his father: and they performed all that the king commanded. And after that God was intreated for the land.

⁽¹⁵⁾ Moreover the Philistines had yet war again with Israel; and David went down, and his servants with him, and fought against the Philistines: and David waxed faint. ⁽¹⁶⁾ And Ishbi-benob, which *was* of the sons of ³the giant, the weight of whose ⁴spear *weighed* three hundred *shekels* of brass in weight,

¹ Or, *Michal's sister.*
B.C. 1019.
² Heb., *bare to Adriel.*
ᵃ ch. 3. 7.
ᵇ 1 Sam. 31. 10.
B.C. cir. 1018.
³ Or, *Rapha.*
⁴ Heb., *the staff*, or, *the head.*

David could not lawfully refuse the demand of the Gibeonites, since the Law absolutely required that blood-guiltiness should be expiated by the blood of the offender (Numb. xxxv. 33), which, in this case, became that of his representatives; and (2) David's choice of victims was directly opposed to such a supposition. He spared, for Jonathan's sake, the only descendants of Saul in the male line, who only could have advanced any claim to the throne and took (1) the two sons of Rizpah, a concubine of Saul, with whom Abner had committed adultery (chap. iii. 7), and (2) five sons of Saul's eldest daughter Merab, who had been promised in marriage to David himself, and then given to another (1 Sam. xviii. 17—19). The text has *Michal* instead of *Merab;* but this must be an error of the scribe, since it was Merab, not Michal, who was married to "Adriel the Meholathite" (1 Sam. xviii. 19), and Michal was childless (chap. vi. 23). The English phrase "brought up for" is taken from the Chaldee; the Hebrew, as noted in the margin, is *bare to.*

⁽⁹⁾ **The beginning of barley harvest.**—This was immediately after the Passover (Lev. xxiii. 10, 11), and therefore about the middle of April. The rains of autumn began in October, so that Rizpah's watch must have been about six months. She *spread* the *sackcloth* as a tent to form a rough shelter during the long watch. For *water dropped* read *water poured*, the word being used for *melting, flowing*, and hence for heavy rain. It was not until these rains began (which may probably have been somewhat earlier than usual) that the people were assured of the Divine forgiveness, and therefore the bodies of the executed were left unburied until then.

⁽¹²⁾ **Took the bones of Saul.**—Moved by the story of Rizpah's tender care, and wishing to show that he cherished no enmity against the house of Saul, David buried honourably the remains of Saul and of his descendants. In 1 Sam. xxxi. 10 it is said that the Philistines fastened the body of Saul "to the wall of Beth-shan;" here, that the men of Jabesh-gilead took them secretly from *the street.* The two statements are quite consistent, for the exact place where the Philistines hung up to public view the body of the slain and defeated monarch was the broad space or square, just inside the gate, where the people were wont to gather; and it was from the same place that they were taken. Most MSS. of the LXX. add to the previous verse: "And they were taken down, and Dan the son of Joa, of the descendants of the giant, took them down."

⁽¹⁴⁾ **In Zelah.**—According to Josh. xviii. 28 a town of Benjamin. It has not been identified, but was probably near Gibeah.

⁽¹⁵⁾ **Had yet war again.**—This, like the preceding narrative, bears no note of time except that it occurred after some other wars with the Philistines; but this is only to say that it was after David ascended the throne. From the latter part of verse 17 it is plain that it must have been after David had become king of all Israel, and probably after he had become somewhat advanced in years. In 1 Chron. xx. 4—8 much the same paragraph is placed immediately after the war with Ammon; but this seems to be a mere juxta-position rather than designed as a chronological sequence.

⁽¹⁶⁾ **Ishbi-benob.**—The name is a strange one, and it is generally thought that some error has crept into the text, but none of the suggested emendations are free from difficulty. Perhaps the most probable is that in the *Speaker's Commentary*, by which for *Ishbi* (the Hebrew margin) *they halted* is read, and *benob*, by a very slight change in one letter, becomes *at Gob;* then a clause is supplied, *there was a man*, so that the whole reads, "David waxed faint, and they halted at Gob. And there was a man which was of the sons," &c.; verse 18 (as well as verse 19) seems to imply a previous battle in Gob.

Three hundred shekels.—About eight pounds; just half the weight of Goliath's spear-head (1 Sam. xvii. 7).

Girded with a new sword.—The word *sword* is not in the original, and its omission, where intended, is unusual. Either it should be *girded with new*

he being girded with a new *sword*, thought to have slain David. (17) But Abishai the son of Zeruiah succoured him, and smote the Philistine, and killed him. Then the men of David sware unto him, saying, Thou shalt go no more out with us to battle, that thou quench not the ¹light of Israel.

(18) ᵃAnAnd it came to pass after this, that there was again a battle with the Philistines at Gob: then Sibbechai the Hushathite slew Saph, which *was* of the sons of ²the giant. (19) And there was again a battle in Gob with the Philistines, where Elhanan the son of Jaare-oregim, a Beth-lehemite, slew ᵇ*the brother of* Goliath the Gittite, the staff of whose spear *was* like a weaver's beam.

(20) And there was yet a battle in Gath, where was a man of *great* stature,

¹ Heb., *candle*, or, *lamp*.
ᵃ 1 Chron. 20. 4.
² Or, *Rapha*.
ᵇ ᶜec 1 Chron. 20. 5.
³ Or, *Rapha*.
⁴ Or, *reproached*.
ᶜ 1 Sam. 16. 9.
ᵈ Ps. 18. 2, &c.

that had on every hand six fingers, and on every foot six toes, four and twenty in number; and he also was born to ³the giant. (21) And when he ⁴defied Israel, Jonathan the son of ᶜShimeah the brother of David slew him.

(22) These four were born to the giant in Gath, and fell by the hand of David, and by the hand of his servants.

CHAPTER XXII. — (1) And David spake unto the LORD the words of this song in the day *that* the LORD had delivered him out of the hand of all his enemies, and out of the hand of Saul: (2) and he said,

ᵈThe LORD *is* my rock, and my fortress, and my deliverer; (3) the God of my rock; in him will I trust: *he is* my shield, and the horn of my salvation,

---

armour, or else the word for *new* is intended to denote some otherwise unknown weapon.

(17) **And smote.**—The original leaves it doubtful whether Abishai is the nominative to the verb, or whether it should be simply *he*, referring to David. Verse 22 seems to imply that one at least of the sons of the giant fell by David's own hand.

Sware unto him.—This was a solemn transaction, by which David should hereafter be restrained from personal exposure in battle. That he should be spoken of as "the light of Israel" implies that his government over all Israel had continued long enough already to make its immense benefits sensible.

(18) **At Gob.**—Comp. verse 19. The place is otherwise unknown. 1 Chron. xx. 4 reads "Gezer," and the LXX. substitutes "Gath." (Comp. verse 20.) It is not at all remarkable that the names of many small places should be lost after the lapse of three thousand years, nor that the locality of the hamlet should be marked in the later chronicles by the better known neighbouring town of Gezer.

Sibbechai the Hushathite.—Comp. 1 Chron. xx. 4. He is also mentioned in the list of heroes (1 Chron. xi. 29); but in chap. xxiii. 27 the name is changed into "Mebunnai the Hushathite by a slight alteration in the letters of the original. He was captain of the eighth division of the army (1 Chron. xxvi. 11). The giant whom he slew is called "Sippai" in the parallel place in Chronicles, and it is there said that the Philistines were subdued.

(19) **Jaare-oregim.**—The parallel place, 1 Chron. xx. 5, reads simply "Jair." It is generally supposed that "oregim (= *weavers*) has accidentally crept into the text from the line below, and "Jair" and "Jaare" are the same with a slight transposition of the letters. Another name for the same person must have been "Dodo," if this Elhanan, as seems altogether probable, is the same with "Elhanan the son of Dodo of Bethlehem," one of the thirty-seven heroes, in chap. xxiii. 24.

The brother of.—These words, not found in the Hebrew here, are taken from Chronicles, where also the name of the giant, "Lahmi," is given. It is quite possible, however, that the word "Beth-lemite," which is wanting in Chronicles, is a corruption of "Lahmi the brother of." There is a curious Jewish tradition that this Elhanan was David himself, and this has been preserved in the paraphrase of the Chaldee, "and David the son of Jesse, the weaver of veils for the sanctuary, who was of Bethlehem, slew Goliath the Gittite."

(21) **Jonathan the son of Shimeah.**—Hence he was the nephew of David (1 Chron. xx. 7), and was either the wily Jonadab mentioned in chap. xiii. 3, or, more probably, his brother. David's family connections seem to have constituted a clan of heroes.

(22) **Born to the giant.**—They were all descendants of Rapha, but not necessarily all the sons of one man.

XXII.

This chapter, with numerous slight variations, constitutes Ps. xviii., the first verse here serving as the title there, with only such differences as the nature of the Book of Psalms required. With this title may be compared the inscriptions of other historical psalms, as Exod. xv. 1; Deut. xxxi. 30.

No more definite time can be assigned for the composition of this hymn than that already given in its title. Verse 51 shows that it must have been after the visit of Nathan promising the perpetuity of David's kingdom.

As comment upon this psalm will naturally be expected in connection with the Book of Psalms, only the differences between these two copies will here be spoken of. On the whole, the form given in the Psalms seems to be the later, and to have been in some points intentionally altered—probably by David himself—to adapt it to the exigencies of liturgical worship; but it must also be remembered that minor differences inevitably grow up in the copying of manuscripts age after age, and that much of the lesser variation is undoubtedly due to this cause.

(2) **He said.**—The psalm here wants the opening line of Ps. xviii., "I will love thee, O Lord, my strength," forming a fitting introduction to the whole.

(3) **The God of my rock.**—In the psalm, "My God, my rock" (margin). The two expressions of the psalm are here united in one, and the recurrence of the

my high tower, and my refuge, my saviour; thou savest me from violence. ⁽⁴⁾ I will call on the LORD, *who is* worthy to be praised: so shall I be saved from mine enemies.

⁽⁵⁾ When the ¹ waves of death compassed me, the floods of ² ungodly men made me afraid; ⁽⁶⁾ the ³ sorrows of hell compassed me about; the snares of death prevented me; ⁽⁷⁾ in my distress I called upon the LORD, and cried to my God: and he did hear my voice out of his temple, and my cry *did enter* into his ears. ⁽⁸⁾ Then the earth shook and trembled; the foundations of heaven moved and shook, because he was wroth. ⁽⁹⁾ There went up a smoke ⁴ out of his nostrils, and fire out of his mouth devoured: coals were kindled by it. ⁽¹⁰⁾ He bowed the heavens also, and came down; and darkness *was* under his feet. ⁽¹¹⁾ And he rode upon a cherub, and did fly: and he was seen upon the wings of the wind. ⁽¹²⁾ And he made darkness pavilions round about him, ⁵ dark waters, *and* thick clouds of the skies. ⁽¹³⁾ Through the brightness before him were coals of fire kindled. ⁽¹⁴⁾ The LORD thundered from heaven, and the most High uttered his voice. ⁽¹⁵⁾ And he sent out arrows, and scattered them; lightning, and discomfited them. ⁽¹⁶⁾ And the channels of the sea appeared, the foundations of the world were discovered, at the rebuking of the LORD, at the blast of the breath of his nostrils.

⁽¹⁷⁾ He sent from above, he took me; he drew me out of ⁶ many waters; ⁽¹⁸⁾ he delivered me from my strong enemy, *and* from them that hated me: for they were too strong for me. ⁽¹⁹⁾ They prevented me in the day of my calamity: but the LORD was my stay. ⁽²⁰⁾ He brought me forth also into a large place: he delivered me, because he delighted in me. ⁽²¹⁾ The LORD rewarded me according to my righteousness: according to the cleanness of my hands hath he recompensed me. ⁽²²⁾ For I have kept the ways of the LORD, and have not wickedly departed from my God. ⁽²³⁾ For all his judgments *were* before me: and *as for* his statutes, I did not depart from them. ⁽²⁴⁾ I was also upright ⁷ before him, and have kept myself from mine iniquity. ⁽²⁵⁾ Therefore the LORD hath recompensed me according to my righteousness; according to my cleanness ⁸ in his eye sight.

⁽²⁶⁾ With the merciful thou wilt shew thyself merciful, *and* with the upright man thou wilt shew thyself upright. ⁽²⁷⁾ With the pure thou wilt shew thyself pure; and with the froward thou

1 Or, *pangs.*

2 Heb., *Belial.*

3 Or, *cords.*

4 Heb., *by.*

5 Heb., *binding of waters.*

6 Or, *great.*

7 Heb., *to him.*

8 Heb., *before his eyes.*

---

similar expression in verse 47 (but not in the psalm) indicates that this was intentional.

And my refuge, my saviour; thou savest me from violence.—These words are omitted from the psalm, being compensated in part by the opening line there.

⁽⁵⁾ **The waves of death.**—In Ps. xviii., "the sorrows of death," in the Authorised Version, but literally, *the bands of death*. The word is entirely different, and the variation can hardly have been accidental. The form here accords better with the parallelism of the next clause.

⁽⁷⁾ **Called ... cried.**—The original words are the same here, although differing in the parallel place in the psalm.

My cry did enter into his ears.—Literally, *my cry in his ears*, an elliptical expression which is filled out in the psalm, "my cry came before him, even into his ears."

⁽⁸⁾ **Of heaven.**—Ps. xviii., "of the hills." The thought is the same, but the strong poetic figure by which the mountains are spoken of as "the pillars of heaven" (comp. Job xxvi. 11) is softened in the psalm.

⁽¹¹⁾ **He was seen.**—Ps. xviii., "he did fly." The two words are exceedingly alike in the Hebrew, and either could easily be mistaken for the other. The form in the psalm is far more poetical.

⁽¹²⁾ **Made darkness pavilions.**—Ps. xviii., more fully, "He made darkness his secret place; his pavilion round about him *were* dark waters." A word appears to have dropped out here, and in the second clause the margin, "*binding* (or *gathering*) *of waters*" is a more exact translation, the word differing in one letter from that used in the psalm.

⁽¹³⁾ **Through the brightness.**—Rather, *Out of the brightness*. The psalm (with the same correction) is more full, and perhaps the more exact representation of the original: "Out of the brightness before him his thick clouds passed, hail *stones* and coals of fire."

⁽¹⁴⁾ **From heaven.**—Ps. xviii., "in the heavens," a difference found in the original; the two are otherwise alike in the Hebrew, except that the psalm adds the words, "hail *stones* and coals of fire."

⁽¹⁶⁾ **Of the sea.**—Ps. xviii., "of waters." There are several such slight differences between verses 15, 16, and the parallel verses in the psalm, which mark the two as distinctly different recensions. The most striking change is that of the last pronoun from "his" to "thy" in the psalm, as appropriate to its use in public worship.

⁽²³⁾ **His statutes, I did not depart from them.**—The psalm, by a very slight change in the original, has "I did not put away his statutes from me." The former is the more common form, the latter suits better the parallelism here.

⁽²⁵⁾ **To my cleanness.**—Ps. xviii., more poetically, "to the cleanness of my hands."

⁽²⁷⁾ **Unsavoury.**—Rather, *froward*, for although the form here is anomalous, it is the same word, and

wilt ¹shew thyself unsavoury. (28) And the afflicted people thou wilt save: but thine eyes *are* upon the haughty, *that* thou mayest bring *them* down. (29) For thou *art* my ²lamp, O LORD: and the LORD will lighten my darkness. (30) For by thee I have ³run through a troop: by my God have I leaped over a wall. (31) *As for* God, his way *is* perfect; the word of the LORD *is* ⁴tried: he *is* a buckler to all them that trust in him. (32) For who *is* God, save the LORD? and who *is* a rock, save our God? (33) God *is* my strength *and* power: and he ⁵maketh my way perfect. (34) He ⁶maketh my feet like hinds' *feet*: and setteth me upon my high places. (35) He teacheth my hands ⁷to war; so that a bow of steel is broken by mine arms. (36) Thou hast also given me the shield of thy salvation: and thy gentleness hath ⁸made me great. (37) Thou hast enlarged my steps under me; so that my ⁹feet did not slip. (38) I have pursued mine enemies, and destroyed them; and turned not again until I had consumed them. (39) And I have consumed them, and wounded them, that they could not arise: yea, they are fallen under my feet. (40) For thou hast girded me with strength to battle: them that rose up against me hast thou ¹⁰subdued under me. (41) Thou hast also given me the necks of mine enemies, that I might destroy them that hate me. (42) They looked, but *there was* none to save; *even* unto the LORD, but he answered them not. (43) Then did I beat them as small as the dust of the earth, I did stamp them as the mire of the street, *and* did spread them abroad. (44) Thou also hast delivered me from the strivings of my people, thou hast kept me *to be* head of the heathen: a people *which* I knew not shall serve me. (45) ¹¹Strangers shall ¹²¹³submit themselves unto me: as soon as they hear, they shall be obedient unto me. (46) Strangers shall fade away, and they shall be afraid out of their close places. (47) The LORD liveth; and blessed *be* my rock; and exalted be the God of the rock of my salvation. (48) It *is* God that ¹⁴avengeth me, and that bringeth down the people under me, (49) and that bringeth me forth from mine enemies: thou also hast lifted me up on high above them that rose up against me: thou hast delivered me from the violent man. (50) Therefore I will give thanks unto thee, O LORD, among ᵃthe heathen, and I will sing praises unto thy name. (51) *He is* the tower of salvation for his king: and sheweth mercy to his

---

1 Or, *wrestle*, Ps. 18. 26.
2 Or, *candle*.
3 Or, *broken a troop*.
4 Or, *refined*.
5 Heb., *riddeth*, or, *looseth*.
6 Heb., *equalleth*.
7 Heb., *for the war*.
8 Heb., *multiplied me*.
9 Heb., *ankles*.
10 Heb., *caused to bow*.
11 Heb., *Sons of the stranger*.
12 Or, *yield feigned obedience*.
13 Heb., *lie*.
14 Heb., *giveth avengement for me*.
ᵃ Rom. 15. 9.

---

has the same reference to the previous word as in the psalm.

(28) **Thine eyes are upon the haughty.**—More briefly, but in more common form, the psalm, "wilt bring down high looks."

(29) **Thou art my lamp.**—Comp. Ps. xxvii. 1. The psalm changes the figure, "thou wilt light my candle (*margin*, lamp)." With this comp. Ps. cxxxii. 17; 1 Kings xi. 36, xv. 4.

(33) **God is my strength and power.**—Better, *my strong fortress*. The psalm has quite a different thought, which is expressed in verse 40, "It is God that girdeth me with strength."

(36) **Thy gentleness.**—This is the translation of the word in Ps. xviii. 35. The word here, which differs very slightly, and is otherwise unknown, is undoubtedly meant for it; if taken as it stands it would, by its etymology, mean *thy answering*, viz., to the prayers offered. The psalm inserts between the two clauses of the verse, "and thy right hand hath holden me up."

(38) **Destroyed them.**—In the psalm, "overtaken them," an expression intended to suggest the same thing as the plain expression here. The second clauses are identical in the original.

(39) **I have consumed them, and wounded them.**—The former clause is wanting in the psalm, and the latter needs a stronger word—*crushed them*.

(42) **They looked.**—By the change of a letter this becomes in the psalm "They cried," and it is so translated here in the LXX., "they shall cry." One of the readings is doubtless a mere clerical error.

(43) **Dust of the earth.**—Ps. xviii. reads, "Dust before the wind," and in the second clause omits "did spread them abroad." The psalm thus combines in one compact figure what is here spread out in two clauses. The change is certainly designed, and heightens the poetic effect.

(44) **Thou hast kept me.**—The wording of the psalm, "Thou hast made me," involves only a slight difference in the original, and is a mere clerical variation.

(45) **As soon as they hear.**—This and the previous clause are transposed in the psalm, this clause there constituting verse 44.

(46) **Shall be afraid out of their close places.**—The English here follows Ps. xviii. 45, but the Hebrew verbs differ by the transposition of a letter. This is probably a mere clerical error, but if it be retained the sense will be a little changed. The psalm means, *came trembling from their fastnesses*, representing the conquered as submitting with fear; the text here, *came limping from their fastnesses*, suggesting that the remnant of the enemy had already been injured and wounded.

(51) **He is the tower of salvation.**—This translation follows the margin of the Hebrew. The text is found in the ancient versions and in Ps. xviii. 50. "Great deliverance giveth he." The difference in the

The Last Words II. SAMUEL, XXIII. *of David.*

anointed, unto David, and ᵃ to his seed for evermore.

CHAPTER XXIII.—⁽¹⁾ Now these be the last words of David. David the son of Jesse said, and the man *who was* raised up on high, the anointed of the God of Jacob, and the sweet psalmist of Israel, said, ⁽²⁾ The Spirit of the LORD spake by me, and his word *was* in my tongue. ⁽³⁾ The God of Israel said, the Rock of Israel spake to me, ¹He that ruleth over men *must be* just, ruling in the fear of God. ⁽⁴⁾ And *he shall be* as the light of the morning, *when* the sun riseth, *even* a morning without clouds; *as* the tender grass *springing* out of the earth by clear shining after rain. ⁽⁵⁾ Although my house *be* not so with God; yet he hath made with me an everlasting covenant, ordered in all *things*, and sure: for *this is* all my salvation, and all *my* desire, although he make *it* not to grow. ⁽⁶⁾ But *the sons* of Belial *shall be* all of them as thorns thrust away, because they cannot be

a ch. 7. 13.

¹ Or, *Be thou ruler*, &c.

---

original between the consonants of the two words is extremely slight.

This brief review of these two recensions of this magnificent hymn is instructive, as showing that Providence has dealt with the MSS. of the Old Testament as with those of the New, securing them during the long succession of ages from all substantial error, and yet not so destroying ordinary human action but that mere slips of the pen should sometimes creep in, and care and diligence be required to ascertain precisely what was originally written, and sometimes, perhaps, in the merest minutiæ, leaving the original form still uncertain.

The Psalm is a grand anthem of thanksgiving of David for the many mercies he had received—a full and confident expression of his trust in God under all circumstances, and of his well-assured hope in the fulfilment of the Divine promise of the perpetuity of his kingdom through the coming of Him "in whom all the families of the earth should be blessed."

XXIII.

This chapter consists of two entirely distinct parts. The first seven verses are "the last words of David," his last formal and inspired utterance; the rest of the chapter (verses 8–39) is an enumeration of the heroes of his life and reign. This prophecy has not been incorporated into the Book of Psalms, because it is not a hymn for public worship, although an unquestionable utterance of David, and laying especial claim to Divine inspiration.

⁽¹⁾ **The son of Jesse said.**—The description of the human author of the following prophecy is strikingly analogous to that of Balaam in Numb. xxiv. 3, 4, 15, 16. The word "said," used twice, is a peculiar form (used between two hundred and three hundred times) of direct Divine utterances, and applied to human sayings only here, in the places referred to in Numbers, and in Prov. xxx. 1, in all which special claim is made to inspiration.

The sweet psalmist of Israel.—Literally, *He that is pleasant in Israel's psalms,* i.e., by the composition and arrangement of Israel's liturgical songs he was entitled to be called "pleasant." David, with life now closing, fitly sends down this prophetic song to posterity with such description of its human writer as should secure to it authority.

⁽²⁾ **The Spirit of the Lord spake by me.**—In accordance with verse 1, there is here, and also in the next clause, most explicit assertion that this was spoken under the prompting and guidance of the Divine Spirit.

⁽³⁾ **The Rock of Israel.**—Comp. chap. xxii. 3. A frequent Scriptural comparison, appropriate here, to show the perfect reliability of what God declares.

He that ruleth.—The English gives the true sense, but the original is exceedingly elliptical, both here and in the following verse. The fundamental point of all just government has never been more perfectly set forth:—that it must be "in the fear of God."

⁽⁴⁾ **A morning without clouds.**—This description of the blessings of the ideally perfect government is closely connected with the Divine promise made through Nathan (chap. vii.). David recognises that the ruler of God's people must be just, and here, as in Ps. lxxii., the highest blessings are depicted as flowing from such a government. David knew far too much of the evil of his own heart and of the troubles in his household to suppose that his ideal could be perfectly realised in any other of his descendants than in Him who should "crush the serpent's head" and win the victory over the powers of evil. The sense of the verse will be made clearer by the following translation: "And as the light of the morning when the sun ariseth, a morning without clouds; *as* by means of sunlight and by means of rain the tender grass *grows* from the earth:—is not my house so with God?"

⁽⁵⁾ **Although my house.**—This verse is extremely difficult, and admits of two interpretations. That given in the English is found in the LXX., the Vulg., and the Syriac, and if adopted will mean that David recognises how far he and his house have failed to realise the ideal description set forth; yet since God's promise is sure, this must be realised in his posterity. Most modern commentators, however, prefer to take the clauses interrogatively: "Is not my house thus with God? for He hath made with me an everlasting covenant, ordered in all, and sure. For all my salvation and all my desire, shall He not cause it to spring forth?" The Hebrew admits either rendering, but that of the ancient versions gives a higher idea of David's spiritual discernment.

Ordered in all.—As a carefully drawn legal document, providing for all contingencies and leaving no room for misconstruction.

⁽⁶⁾ **The sons of Belial.**—According to the Masoretic punctuation, *Belial* is not here in the common form, but in the stronger abstract form = *worthlessness.* The coming in of Divine righteousness leads not only to the assimilation of that which is holy, but also to the rejection of that which is evil, by a law as necessary and immutable as that of action and reaction in the material world. The figures used are to show that, although the wicked injure whatever touches them,

A Catalogue   II. SAMUEL, XXIII.   *of David's*

taken with hands : (7) but the man *that* shall touch them must be ¹fenced with iron and the staff of a spear; and they shall be utterly burned with fire in the *same* place.

(8) These *be* the names of the mighty men whom David had : ²The Tachmonite that sat in the seat, chief among the captains ; the same *was* Adino the Eznite : ³ *he lift up his spear* against eight hundred, ⁴whom he slew at one time.

(9) And after him *was* ᵃ Eleazar the son of Dodo the Ahohite, *one* of the three mighty men with David, when they defied the Philistines *that* were there gathered together to battle, and the men of Israel were gone away : (10) he arose, and smote the Philistines until his hand was weary, and his hand clave unto the sword : and the LORD wrought a great victory that day ; and the people returned after him only to spoil.

(11) And after him *was* ᵇShammah the

1 Heb., *filled*.
2 Or, *Josheb-bassebet the Tachmonite, head of the three.*
3 See 1 Chron. 11. 11.
4 Heb., *slain*.
ᵃ 1 Chron. 11. 12.
ᵇ 1 Chron. 11. 27.

---

means will yet be found by which they may safely be put out of the way.

(7) **Fenced with iron.**—The thorns are to be handled with an iron hook on the end of a spear staff. The phrase, "in the same place," is used only here, and its meaning is quite uncertain. The Vulg. translates, *to nothing*, meaning to utter destruction ; the LXX. substitutes the word *shame*. The English rendering is as well sustained as any.

The Chaldee Targum upon these verses is very interesting, as giving the ancient Jewish interpretation of the prophecy. It is a much enlarged paraphrase, but gives a Messianic application to the whole. The following is a close translation of verses 1—3: " (1) These are the words of the prophecy of David, which he prophesied concerning the end of the age, concerning the days of consolation which are to come. David the son of Jesse said, and the man who was exalted to the kingdom said, the anointed by the word of the God of Jacob, and appointed that he might preside over the sweetness of the praises of Israel. (2) David said, In the spirit of prophecy of the Lord I speak these things, and the words of His holiness do I order in my mouth. (3) David said, The God of Israel spake concerning me, the Strong One of Israel who ruleth over the sons of men, the true Judge, said that He would appoint for me a king ; He is the Messiah, who shall arise and rule in the fear of the Lord."

(8) **These be the names.**—Here, in the summary at the close of David's reign, is very naturally given a list of his chief heroes. A duplicate of this list, with several variations, and with sixteen more names, is given in 1 Chron. xi. 10—47, which is useful in correcting such clerical errors as have arisen in both. The list in Chronicles is given in connection with David's becoming king over all Israel; but in both cases the list is not to be understood as belonging precisely to any definite time, but rather as a catalogue of the chief heroes who distinguished themselves at any time in the life of David.

The Tachmonite that sat in the seat.—The text of this verse has undergone several alterations, which may be corrected by the parallel passage in Chronicles. This clause should read, "Jashobeam the Hachmonite," as in 1 Chron. xi. 11. Jashobeam came to David at Ziklag (1 Chron. xii. 1, 6), and afterwards became the general of the first division of the army (1 Chron. xxvii. 2), being immediately followed by Dodo. One of the same family was tutor to David's sons (1 Chron. xxvii. 32).

The captains.—The word for *captain* and the word for *three* are much alike, and the text here and in Chronicles perpetually fluctuates between the two. Probably the sense here is that Jashobeam was the chief of the three who stood highest in rank among the heroes.

No mention is made in either list of Joab, because, as commander-in-chief, he stood in a rank by himself.

The same was Adino the Eznite.—It is difficult to attach any meaning to these words in their connection, and they are generally considered as a corruption of the words in 1 Chron. xi. 11, "he lifted up his spear," which are required and are inserted here in the English. For "eight hundred" Chronicles has "three hundred," as in verse 18. Variations in numbers are exceedingly common, but the probability is in favour of the correctness of the text here. This large number was slain by Jashobeam and the men under his command in one combat.

(9) **Dodo the Ahohite.**—So in the Hebrew margin here, and so also in 1 Chron. xi. 12; the text here has Dodai, as in 1 Chron. xxvii. 4, where he is mentioned as the general for the second month. The name is the same under slightly differing forms. "Ahohite" is a patronymic derived from Ahoah, son of Bela, Benjamin's son (1 Chron. viii. 4).

When they defied . . . there gathered.—The words "there gathered" require the mention of some place, and the construction of the word for "defied" is unusual. The parallel passage in Chronicles reads, "He was with David at Pas-dammim, and there the Philistines," &c. The difference between the two readings is not great in the original, and the latter is better. Pas-dammim is the Ephesdammim of 1 Sam. xvii. 1, where Goliath defied the armies of Israel, and was slain by David.

Were gone away—Rather, *were gathered* to battle. So it is translated in the LXX., Vulg., and Syriac, and so the Hebrew requires. The error is a curious one, and seems to have arisen in this way : In 1 Chron. xi. 13 the mention of the battle in which Shammah was engaged (verse 11) is altogether omitted, and the expression " the people fled from before the Philistines " therefore becomes connected with this battle. Josephus follows that text, and our translators were probably misled by him. Several lines have dropped out from the text in Chronicles.

(10) **Clave unto the sword.**—Instances are rare, but well authenticated, of a sort of cramp following excessive exertion, so that the hand could only be released from the sword by external appliances.

Returned after him.—Does not imply that they had at any time deserted him, but only that they turned wherever he went to gather the spoil of the men he slew.

(11) **Into a troop.**—Josephus, using different vowels, read "to Lehi," the scene of Samson's exploit (Judges xv. 9, 19); but as the same word recurs in

son of Agee the Hararite. And the Philistines were gathered together ¹into a troop, where was a piece of ground full of lentiles: and the people fled from the Philistines. ⁽¹²⁾ But he stood in the midst of the ground, and defended it, and slew the Philistines: and the LORD wrought a great victory.

⁽¹³⁾ And ²three of the thirty chief went down, and came to David in the harvest time unto the cave of Adullam: and the troop of the Philistines pitched in the valley of Rephaim. ⁽¹⁴⁾ And David *was* then in an hold, and the garrison of the Philistines *was* then *in* Beth-lehem. ⁽¹⁵⁾ And David longed, and said, Oh that one would give me drink of the water of the well of Bethlehem, which *is* by the gate! ⁽¹⁶⁾ And the three mighty men brake through the host of the Philistines, and drew water out of the well of Beth-lehem, that *was* by the gate, and took *it*, and

¹ Or, *for foraging*.
² Or, *the three captains over the thirty*.
a 1 Chron. 11. 20.
³ Heb., *slain*.
⁴ Heb., *great of acts*.
⁵ Heb., *lions of God*.
⁶ Heb., *a man of countenance*, or, *sight*: called, 1 Chron. 11. 23, *a man of great stature*.

brought *it* to David: nevertheless he would not drink thereof, but poured it out unto the LORD. ⁽¹⁷⁾ And he said, Be it far from me, O LORD, that I should do this: *is not this* the blood of the men that went in jeopardy of their lives? therefore he would not drink it. These things did these three mighty men.

⁽¹⁸⁾ And *a* Abishai, the brother of Joab, the son of Zeruiah, was chief among three. And he lifted up his spear against three hundred, ³*and* slew *them*, and had the name among three. ⁽¹⁹⁾ Was he not most honourable of three? therefore he was their captain: howbeit he attained not unto the *first* three.

⁽²⁰⁾ And Benaiah the son of Jehoiada, the son of a valiant man, of Kabzeel, ⁴who had done many acts, he slew two ⁵lionlike men of Moab: he went down also and slew a lion in the midst of a pit in time of snow: ⁽²¹⁾ And he slew an Egyptian, ⁶a goodly man: and the

---

verse 13, clearly in the sense of "troop," the English reading should be retained.

Lentiles.—Chronicles has "barley." The two words might easily be confounded in the Hebrew, and it is quite immaterial which is correct; the point is that the Philistines had made a foray to gather the ripe crops, the Israelites were terrified and fled, while Shammah, by his courage and valour, turned the tide of battle, and won a great victory.

⁽¹³⁾ **Three of the thirty.**—For "three" the Hebrew text reads "thirty" by a manifest error, which is corrected in the margin. These are not the same three (since there is no definite article) with those just mentioned, but were another three more eminent than the rest of the thirty, two of them being, no doubt, Abishai and Benaiah (verses 18, 23). "The thirty" seems to have been a common name for this band of heroes (comp. verses 23, 24, &c.), who were perhaps originally exactly thirty, but whose number varied from time to time, being here given (verse 39) as thirty-seven.

In the harvest time.—"The preposition does not mean *in*, and the reading in Chronicles xi. 15 'to the rock' is perhaps the true one" (*Kirkpatrick*). On "the valley of Rephaim," see Note on chap. v. 18.

⁽¹⁵⁾ **The well of Bethlehem.**—There are now no wells of living water at Bethlehem itself, the town being supplied by an aqueduct. Robinson could find none in the neighbourhood, and was assured that none existed (*Bib. R.* ii. 157—163); but Ritter (*Geog. of Pal.* iii. 340) says that a little north of the town "is" David's well, "with its deep shaft and its clear cool water."

⁽¹⁶⁾ **Poured it out unto the Lord.**—The brave act of the three heroes shows strikingly the personal power of David over his followers and the enthusiasm with which he inspired them. Yet, on the other hand, David would not suffer his own longing to be gratified by the hazard of men's lives. Taking the water, therefore, he "poured it out unto the Lord." The word is the technical term for the sacrificial libation, and David assimilated his act to a sacrifice by a solemn consecration of this dangerously won water to the Lord.

⁽¹⁷⁾ **Is not this the blood . . . ?**—The Hebrew here is simply an interrogative exclamation, "the blood of the men?" but in 1 Chron. xi. 19 the text reads, "Shall I drink the blood of these men?" &c., and so the LXX. and Vulg. translate here. To David the water gained only at the risk of life, "seemed the very blood in which the life resides" (Lev. xvii. 10, 11).

These three.—Rather, *the three.*

⁽¹⁸⁾ **Among three.**—The Hebrew margin has "the three," and so also the text in the following clause. "The three" are the triad of heroes just mentioned, of whom Abishai was first, Benaiah second, with an unnamed third. A somewhat similar feat of daring is told of Abishai in 1 Sam. xxvi. 6—12.

⁽²⁰⁾ **Benaiah.**—He was the general of the third division of the army (1 Chron. xxvii. 5, 6). This probably included the Cherethites and Pelethites, since he was also their commander (chaps. viii. 18, xx. 23). In consequence of his faithfulness to Solomon in the rebellion of Adonijah, he was finally made commander-in-chief (1 Kings i. 8, 26, 32; ii. 25, 29—35; iv. 4). His father Jehoiada is called "a chief priest" in 1 Chron. xxvii. 5, and in 1 Chron. xii. 27 mention is made of a "Jehoiada the leader of the Aaronites," who came to David at Hebron, and who may have been the same person.

Kabzeel.—A town on the extreme south of Judah, on the border of Edom (Josh. xv. 21).

Lion-like men.—Literally, *lion of God,* an expression used among Arabs and Persians of great warriors.

Slew a lion.—Comp. 1 Sam. xvii. 34—37. It is not said with what weapons he slew him, but the act was evidently a great feat of valour.

⁽²¹⁾ **A goodly man.**—The meaning is explained in the parallel place in Chronicles, where he is called "a man of stature," and it is added "five cubits high."

Egyptian had a spear in his hand; but he went down to him with a staff, and plucked the spear out of the Egyptian's hand, and slew him with his own spear. (22) These *things* did Benaiah the son of Jehoiada, and had the name among three mighty men. (23) He was ¹ more honourable than the thirty, but he attained not to the *first* three. And David set him over his ² ³ guard.

(24) *ᵃAsahel the brother of Joab *was* one of the thirty; Elhanan the son of Dodo of Beth-lehem, (25) Shammah the Harodite, Elika the Harodite, (26) Helez the *ᵇPaltite, Ira the son of Ikkesh the Tekoite, (27) Abiezer the Anethothite,

¹ Or, *honourable among the thirty.*
² Or, *council.*
³ Heb., *at his command.*
ᵃ ch. 2. 18.
ᵇ 1 Chron. 11. 27.
⁴ Or, *valleys.*

Mebunnai the Hushathite, (28) Zalmon the Ahohite, Maharai the Netophathite, (29) Heleb the son of Baanah, a Netophathite, Ittai the son of Ribai out of Gibeah of the children of Benjamin, (30) Benaiah the Pirathonite, Hiddai of the ⁴brooks of Gaash, (31) Abi-albon the Arbathite, Azmaveth the Barhumite, (32) Eliahba the Shaalbonite, of the sons of Jashen, Jonathan, (33) Shammah the Hararite, Ahiam the son of Sharar the Hararite, (34) Eliphelet the son of Ahasbai, the son of the Maachathite, Eliam the son of Ahithophel the Gilonite, (35) Hezrai the Carmelite, Paarai the Arbite, (36) Igal the son of Nathan of

Benaiah's exploit, therefore, consisted in coming, armed only with a staff, to this giant Egyptian, wresting his spear from him, and then slaying him with it.

(23) **Set him over his guard.**—The word translated *guard* means rather *private audience*. David either made him a member of, or set him over his council. If in 1 Chron. xxvii. 34 "Jehoiada son of Benaiah" is an error for "Benaiah son of Jehoiada," his holding of this office is also mentioned there.

(24) **Asahel.**—As he was killed by Abner while David reigned over Judah only, it is plain that this list is not restricted to any one definite time in David's reign. Leaving out Asahel, however, the names that follow are exactly "thirty." Of but few of them is anything further known.

(25) **Shammah the Harodite.**—In 1 Chron. xi. 27 *Shammoth the Harorite*. He may be the same with "Shamhuth the Izrahite," captain of the fifth division of the army (1 Chron. xxvii. 8). The next name is omitted in Chronicles.

(26) **Helez.**—"He was general of the seventh army division (1 Chron. xxvii. 10). There, and also in 1 Chron. xi. 27, he is called a *Pelonite*.

Ira was general for the sixth month (1 Chron. xxvii. 9). His home, Tekoah, was about six miles south of Bethlehem.

(27) **Abiezer.**—He was general for the ninth month (1 Chron. xxvii. 12). He was of Anathoth, a priestly city of Benjamin, the home of Jeremiah.

Mebunnai.—According to chap. xxi. 18 *Sibbechai*, and to 1 Chron. xi. 29 *Sibbecai*, these being the same in the Hebrew. The two names are much alike in the original and might be easily confused. He slew the giant Saph (chap. xxi. 18), and was the general for the eighth month (1 Chron. xxvii. 11).

(28) **Zalmon.**—In Chronicles *Ilai*.

Maharai.—He commanded the tenth division of the army (1 Chron. xxvii. 13).

(29) **Heleb.**—The name is variously written *Heled* (1 Chron. xi. 30) and *Heldai* (1 Chron. xxvii. 15). He was the general for the twelfth month.

Ittai, or *Ithai* (1 Chron. xi. 31), is to be distinguished from Ittai the Gittite, since this man was from Gibeah of Benjamin.

(30) **Benaiah the Pirathonite.**—He was general for the eleventh month (1 Chron. xxvii. 14). He is of course to be distinguished from Benaiah of verse 20.

Hiddai.—In 1 Chron. xi. 32, *Hurai*, owing to the frequent confusion of *d* and *r*.

(31) **Abi-albon.**—In 1 Chron. xi. 32 written *Abiel*, probably correctly, the *albon* having come in from *Sha-albon-ite* in the line below.

The Barhumite.—More correctly, *the Baharumite,* i.e., of the Bahurim mentioned in chap. iii. 16, xix. 16.

(32) **Of the sons of Jashen, Jonathan.**—The preposition *of* is not in the Hebrew, and should be omitted. For the rest 1 Chron. xi. 34 reads "the sons of Hashem the Gizonite. In both the words *the sons of* may be an accidental repetition of the last three letters of the preceding word; if not, they should be read as part of the proper name, *Jashen* (Chronicles *Hashem*), or *Bnejashen* (Chronicles *Bnehashem*) *the Gizonite*. Jonathan is then a separate name.

(33) **Shammah the Hararite.**—"Shammah the son of Agee the Hararite" has already been mentioned in verse 11, and here Chronicles reads "Jonathan the son of Shage the Hararite." As *Shage* is identical with *Agee* with a letter prefixed, we should probably read "Jonathan the son of Shammah the Hararite." Jonathan, one of "the thirty," was thus the son of one of "the first three."

Sharar is in Chronicles *Sacar*, and *Hararite* is spelt in the Hebrew here differently from the previous clause and from Chronicles.

(34) **Eliphelet the son of Ahasbai.**—The reading in Chronicles is quite different: "Eliphal the son of Ur, Hepher the Mecherathite," thus making two heroes instead of the one given here. So, also, instead of "Eliam the son of Ahithophel the Gilonite," Chronicles has *Ahijah the Pelonite*. In the latter case it seems likely that different persons are intended, one being mentioned in one list and the other in the other. It is interesting to know that a son of David's astute but treacherous counsellor was among his thirty heroes.

(35) **Hezrai.**—So the Hebrew margin; but the text has *Hezro*, as in Chronicles. He was of Carmel, seven miles S.S.E. of Hebron, famous in David's early history.

Paarai the Arbite.—In Chronicles "*Naarai* the son of *Ezbai*." It is impossible to decide whether *Paarai* or *Naarai* is the correct form, but *the son of Ezbai* is evidently a scribe's error for *the Arbite*, which it must resemble in the original.

(36) **Igal.**—Chronicles has *Joel*. The two names differ in Hebrew only in one letter, and that a very similar one; but he is described here as *the son of Nathan of Zobah*, in Chronicles as *the brother of Nathan*. Brother is in Hebrew *ahi*, and some MSS. in Chronicles read *the*

David forces Joab   II. SAMUEL, XXIV.   *to Number the People.*

Zobah, Bani the Gadite, ⁽³⁷⁾ Zelek the Ammonite, Nahari the Beerothite, armourbearer to Joab the son of Zeruiah, ⁽³⁸⁾ Ira an Ithrite, Gareb an Ithrite, ⁽³⁹⁾ Uriah the Hittite: thirty and seven in all.

CHAPTER XXIV.—⁽¹⁾ And again

¹ *Satan.* See Chron. 21, 1.

² Or, *Compass.*

B.C. 1017.

the anger of the LORD was kindled against Israel, and ¹he moved David against them to say, Go, number Israel and Judah. ⁽²⁾ For the king said to Joab the captain of the host, which *was* with him, ²Go now through all the tribes of Israel, from Dan even to Beersheba, and number ye the people, that

son of Ahinathan. If this be accepted, the only difference would be in the form of a name, *Nathan* or *Ahinathan*.

Bani the Gadite.—In Chronicles *Mibhar the son of Haggeri*. Entirely unlike as these readings appear, they are not so very different in the original. *Mibhar* is for Zobah of the previous clause, a word at present missing in Chronicles; *the son of* (*Ben*) is for Bani; and *the Gadite* (with the article) differs from *Haggeri* only by the change of the often confused letters *d* and *r*. The text here is the true one.

⁽³⁷⁾ **The Ammonite.**—A foreigner, like "Igal of Zobah" (a Syrian), and "Ittai the Gittite," and "Uriah the Hittite," who rose to distinction in David's service, and all of whom were probably proselytes.

Armourbearer.—It appears from chap. xviii. 15 that Joab had ten armourbearers. This one was probably their chief.

⁽³⁹⁾ **Thirty and seven in all.**—Only thirty-six names have been given, but either the third unnamed person in the second triad of heroes is counted, or else in verse 34 the names of the two given in Chronicles should be substituted for the one in the text here.

In 1 Chron. xi. 41—47 sixteen more names are given, either of men who took the place of these heroes as they died, or simply of other heroes thought worthy of record, though hardly reckoned with this especial body.

XXIV.

This chapter contains the account of David's sin in numbering the people, and the punishment in consequence. The same narrative is found in 1 Chron. xxi., but with such considerable variations as to show that neither can have been taken from the other, but both must have been drawn from the original documents, which were probably very full, quite independently of each other.

No definite note of time is given. The word *again* in verse 1 clearly refers to chap. xxi., and so places this after the three years' famine for the Gibeonites. The fact that Joab was engaged in the work nearly ten months (verse 8) shows that it must have been a time of profound peace. The story in Chronicles is immediately followed by the account of David's final preparations for the building of the Temple. All these considerations concur in placing it near the close of his reign.

The question of the nature of David's sin in this act has been much discussed. The mere taking of a census in itself could not have been wrong, since it was provided for in the Law (Exod. xxx. 12) and had been repeatedly carried out by Moses (Numb. i., xxvi.). Nor is it likely that it was for the reason given by Josephus, that David neglected to secure for the sanctuary, as required, a half shekel from each one numbered (Exod. xxx. 13), since there is no mention of this, and David was at this very time concentrating the whole wealth of the kingdom for the future sanctuary. Yet the sinfulness of the act is distinctly set forth in the narrative

(verse 1) and in the punishment inflicted (verses 15, 16), is recognised by David himself (verses 10, 17), and even forcibly impressed itself upon a person so little scrupulous as Joab (verse 3). It must, then, plainly be sought in the motive of David. The whole connection shows that it was a military census, and it was made, not through the priests and Levites, but through Joab and "the captains of the host." It would appear that prosperity and power, the natural generators of pride, had momentarily affected even David's humble dependence upon God, and led him to wish to organise his kingdom more perfectly as a worldly power among the nations of the earth. A first step in this direction must of course be the placing of his military forces upon a systematic footing. This same desire to turn aside Israel from being a simple theocracy, to become a great earthly power, was the constant sin of the nation. It had led at the first to the request for a king, and Solomon was so thoroughly possessed with it, and so ordered all his policy in view of it, as to draw down, at his death, the judgment of the breaking up of the unity of the nation; and it is not surprising that, after all his conquests, David, in a moment of weakness, should have given way to something of the same spirit. It was thus an act most absolutely at variance with that general character which made him "a man after God's own heart."

⁽¹⁾ **Kindled against Israel.**—This was not in consequence of the numbering of the people, but in consequence of that which ultimately led to that act. We are not told why the anger of the Lord was kindled, but doubtless because He saw both in king and people that rising spirit of earthly pride and reliance on earthly strength which led to the sin.

He moved.—The pronoun here stands for "the Lord," yet in 1 Chron. xxi. 1, the temptation is attributed to Satan, and Satan is clearly meant of the devil, and not simply of "an adversary." This is a striking instance of attributing directly to God whatever comes about under His permission. And yet it is more than that. God has established immutable spiritual as well as material laws, or rather those laws themselves are but the expression of His unchanging will. Whatever comes about under the operation of those laws is said to be His doing. Now David's numbering the people was the natural consequence of the condition of worldliness and pride into which he had allowed himself to fall. God then moved him, because He had from the first so ordered the laws of the spirit that such a sinful act should be the natural outcome of such a sinful state. Of other interpretations: that which makes the verb impersonal—"one moved"—is hardly tenable grammatically; and that which makes the nominative a sort of compound word—"the wrath of the Lord" (as in some of the ancient versions)—leads to substantially the same explanation as that given above.

The word "number" in this verse is a different one from that used in the rest of the chapter, and means

I may know the number of the people. ⁽³⁾ And Joab said unto the king, Now the LORD thy God add unto the people, how many soever they be, an hundredfold, and that the eyes of my lord the king may see *it*: but why doth my lord the king delight in this thing? ⁽⁴⁾ Notwithstanding the king's word prevailed against Joab, and against the captains of the host.

And Joab and the captains of the host went out from the presence of the king, to number the people of Israel. ⁽⁵⁾ And they passed over Jordan, and pitched in Aroer, on the right side of the city that *lieth* in the midst of the ¹river of Gad, and toward Jazer: ⁽⁶⁾ then they came to Gilead, and to the ²land of Tahtim-hodshi; and they came to Dan-jaan, and about to Zidon, ⁽⁷⁾ and came to the strong hold of Tyre, and to all the cities of the Hivites, and of the Canaanites: and they went out to the south of Judah, *even* to Beer-sheba. ⁽⁸⁾ So when they had gone through all the land, they came to Jerusalem at the end of nine months and twenty days. ⁽⁹⁾ And Joab gave up the sum of the number of the people unto the king: and there were in Israel eight hundred thousand valiant men that drew the sword; and the men of Judah *were* five hundred thousand men.

⁽¹⁰⁾ And David's heart smote him after that he had numbered the people. And David said unto the LORD, I have

¹ Or, *valley.*

² Or, *nether land newly inhabited.*

---

simply to *count*, while the other conveys the idea of a military muster.

(3) **Why doth my lord?**—Even in the eyes of the unscrupulous Joab David's act was abominable. Joab never gives evidence of being influenced by religious motives, but his natural shrewdness sufficed to show him that David's act was at variance with the fundamental principle of the national existence. Chronicles adds to Joab's words, "Why will he be a cause of trespass to Israel?" The strong objection of Joab shows that there was something obviously wrong in the action of David.

And against the captains.—Joab's objections were sustained by his subordinate officers, and David carried through his sinful act by sheer force of self-will.

(5) **Pitched in Aroer.**—The census began on the east of Jordan, at the extreme south, thence passed northwards through the eastern tribes, and crossing the Jordan, passed southwards through the western tribes. Aroer is the city described in Deut. ii. 36; Josh. xiii. 16 as on the river Arnon, at the extreme southern border of the trans-Jordanic territory.

Of Gad.—This follows the Masoretic reading. It is better to put a period after the word *river*, and for "of Gad" to read "towards Gad." Perhaps the words "and they came" (towards Gad) may have been lost from the text.

Jazer.—A boundary city of Gad (Josh. xiii. 25). Thence they went to Gilead.

(6) **Land of Tahtim-hodshi.**—This unknown and strange name, of which the ancient versions make nothing, is generally considered as a corruption. The most probable conjecture is that for "Tahtim" we should read "Hittites" (a change of only a single letter), and that "Hodshi" is the remnant of an expression designating the month of their arrival there.

Dan-jaan.—This is the only place in which the name "Dan" occurs with this addition. It seems certain that the same Dan must be meant as in verses 2, 15; and so the reading of the LXX. (Alex.) and Vulg. may be correct: "Dan-jaar = Dan in the forest."

Zidon.—This mother city of the Phœnicians was in the tribe of Asher nominally, but was never actually possessed by the Israelites. The same also is true of Tyre. Either the census-takers merely came to the confines of these cities, or, being on friendly terms, actually entered them to enumerate the Israelites living in them.

(7) **Of the Hivites, and of the Canaanites.**—The remnants of the original inhabitants appear still to have occupied distinct towns by themselves. The "Hivites" were chiefly in the northern part of the land, though Gibeon and its towns had belonged to them. "The Canaanites" is a general name for the remnants of all the other races.

(9) **In Israel eight hundred thousand.**—The numbers here differ greatly from those given in 1 Chron. xxi. 5, 6; but there is no reason to suppose any corruption of the text in either case. Joab undertook the work unwillingly, and performed it imperfectly. According to 1 Chron. xxi. 6 he refused altogether to number Levi and Benjamin; and according to 1 Chron. xxvii. 24 "he finished not," and no official record was made of the result; "neither was the number put in the account of the chronicles of king David." The numbers were, therefore, in part mere estimates. Here Israel is said to be 800,000, in Chronicles 1,100,000; but the latter probably includes an estimate of the omitted tribes of Benjamin and Levi, and perhaps of portions of other tribes. On the other hand, Judah is here 500,000 (a round number like all the rest), and in Chronicles 470,000. The difference is due perhaps to an estimate of the officiating priests and Levites reckoned to Judah. Another supposition is that the regular army of 288,000 (twelve divisions of 24,000 each) is included in Israel in one case and excluded in the other, and that in the same way in regard to Judah "the thirty" may have had command of a special body of 30,000. Possibly in one case the descendants of the old Canaanites were reckoned (since it appears from 2 Chron. ii. 17 that David "had numbered them"), and in the other were excluded. There is no reason to doubt the general reliability of the numbers, which would give a probable total population of five or six millions, or from 415 to 500 to a geographical square mile—a number not at all impossible in so fertile a country. (Robinson's estimate of the area of the country is about 12,000 geographical square miles.)

(10) **David's heart smote him.**—This time David's own conscience was awakened, without the necessity of being roused, as in the case of Uriah, by the visit of a prophet. He confesses his sin, and prays for

sinned greatly in that I have done: and now, I beseech thee, O LORD, take away the iniquity of thy servant; for I have done very foolishly. (11) For when David was up in the morning, the word of the LORD came unto the prophet Gad, David's seer, saying, (12) Go and say unto David, Thus saith the LORD, I offer thee three *things*; choose thee one of them, that I may *do it* unto thee. (13) So Gad came to David, and told him, and said unto him, Shall seven years of famine come unto thee in thy land? or wilt thou flee three months before thine enemies, while they pursue thee? or that there be three days' pestilence in thy land? now advise, and see what answer I shall return to him that sent me. (14) And David said unto Gad, I am in a great strait: let us fall now into the hand of the LORD; for his mercies *are* ¹great: and let me not fall into the hand of man.

(15) So the LORD sent a pestilence upon Israel from the morning even to the time appointed: and there died of the people from Dan even to Beer-sheba seventy thousand men. (16) And when the angel stretched out his hand upon Jerusalem to destroy it, the LORD repented him of the evil, and said to the angel that destroyed the people, It is enough: stay now thine hand. And the angel of the LORD was by the threshing-place of Araunah the Jebusite. (17) And David spake unto the LORD when he saw the angel that smote the people, and said, Lo, I have sinned, and I have done wickedly: but these sheep, what have they done? let thine hand, I pray thee, be against me, and against my father's house.

(18) And Gad came that day to David, and said unto him, Go up, rear an altar unto the LORD in the threshingfloor of Araunah the Jebusite. (19) And David, according to the saying of Gad, went up as the LORD commanded. (20) And Araunah looked, and saw the king and his servants coming on toward him:

1 Or, *many.*

a 1 Sam. 15. 11.

---

pardon. Still it must be remembered that ten months had passed (verse 8) before David saw his sin.

(11) **For when David.**—Read, *and when.* There is no suggestion in the original, as seems to be implied in the English, that David's repentance was in consequence of the visit of Gad; on the contrary, it was in consequence of his repentance and confession that the prophet was sent to him.

The prophet Gad.—This prophet has not been mentioned since his warning to David to return from the land of Moab (1 Sam. xxii. 5); but he had probably been all along one of David's counsellors. From 1 Chron. xxix. 29 it is not unlikely that this account was written by Gad.

(13) **Seven years.**—In Chronicles "three years," and so the LXX. reads here also. This would be more in accordance with the "three" months and "three" days.

(14) **Let us fall now into the hand of the Lord.**—Here the spirit of David in his earlier years reappears; he chooses that form of punishment which seems to him most directly and immediately dependent upon God Himself. He places himself in His hands rather than suffer those other punishments in which the will of man seemed to have a greater share. And it may be noticed also that he chooses that form of punishment from which his own royal position would afford him no immunity.

(15) **The time appointed.**—Much difficulty has been found with this expression; but, if the Hebrew can bear this meaning, it may be understood well enough of the time (somewhat less than three days, verse 16), which God in His good pleasure determined. The Hebrew, however, probably means "time of assembly," which is generally understood to signify the time of the evening sacrifice; so the Chaldee understand it, and so also St. Jerome. This would reduce the time of the pestilence to a single day.

When the angel.—The abruptness of the mention of "the angel" here is removed in 1 Chron. xxi. 15, "And God sent an angel unto Jerusalem to destroy it; and as he was destroying it, the Lord beheld, and he repented," &c.

Threshing-place.—Better, *threshing-floor,* as the same word is translated in verses 18, 21, 24.

Araunah the Jebusite.—The name is variously spelled, "Avarnah" (text), "Aranyah" (verse 18, text), and "Aravnah" (margin); in Chronicles it is uniformly "Ornan." The latter is thought to be the Hebrew, and the former the Jebusite name, slightly varied in expression in Hebrew. He was a Jebusite, *i.e.,* descended from the former possessors of Jerusalem; but we are not told whether he was now a proselyte.

When he saw the angel.—More fully (1 Chron. xxi. 16), "And David lifted up his eyes, and saw the angel of the Lord stand between the earth and the heaven, having a drawn sword in his hand stretched out over Jerusalem."

These sheep.—David seeks to take all blame to himself, and prays that punishment may fall only upon him and his father's house. But, without mooting the question as to how far the people actively shared in David's sin, his prayer was impossible to be granted. Such was the divinely ordained federal relation between the ruler and his people that they were necessarily involved in the guilt of their head.

(18) **Gad came.**—As appears from 1 Chron. xxi. 18, by direction of the angel. Daniel was still in Jerusalem proper, *i.e.,* the hill of Zion, and it was looking out from thence that he had seen the angel "by the threshing-floor of Araunah," *i.e.,* on the lower hill of Mount Moriah, which afterwards became the site of the Temple, and was included within the city. It was doubtless this event that determined the Temple-site.

(20) **Saw the king.**—Not *the angel,* as in Chronicles, the words in Hebrew being much alike.

and Araunah went out, and bowed himself before the king on his face upon the ground. ⁽²¹⁾ And Araunah said, Wherefore is my lord the king come to his servant? And David said, To buy the threshingfloor of thee, to build an altar unto the LORD, that the plague may be stayed from the people. ⁽²²⁾ And Araunah said unto David, Let my lord the king take and offer up what *seemeth* good unto him: behold, *here be* oxen for burnt sacrifice, and threshing instruments and *other* instruments of the oxen for wood. ⁽²³⁾ All these *things* did Araunah, *as a* king, give unto the king. And Araunah said unto the king, The LORD thy God accept thee. ⁽²⁴⁾ And the king said unto Araunah, Nay; but I will surely buy *it* of thee at a price: neither will I offer burnt offerings unto the LORD my God of that which doth cost me nothing.

So David bought the threshingfloor and the oxen for fifty shekels of silver ⁽²⁵⁾ And David built there an altar unto the LORD, and offered burnt offerings and peace offerings. So the LORD was intreated for the land, and the plague was stayed from Israel.

⁽²²⁾ **And Araunah said.**—Araunah, having heard David's errand, has not a moment's hesitation. That his threshing-floor is to be turned into the place of an altar, he at once considers as settled; but he would have preferred to make it a gift.

⁽²³⁾ **All these things did Araunah.** — This clause should be rendered as a part of Araunah's address to David: "The whole, O king, does Araunah give unto the king." (Comp. 1 Chron. xxi. 23.) Then, after a moment's pause, he added, "The LORD thy God accept thee." The first word *king*, however, is omitted in some MSS., and in the LXX., Vulg., and Syr. The word "give," of course, means only *offer*. David actually bought the threshing-floor and other things required.

⁽²⁴⁾ **Of that which cost me nothing.** — The principle on which David acted is that which essentially underlies all true sacrifice and all real giving to God.

For fifty shekels of silver.—This sum is expressly said to cover the cost both of the ground and of the oxen, and seems very small. In 1 Chron. xxi. 25, it reads "six hundred shekels of gold by weight." One of the most ingenious propositions for the reconciliation of the two statements is that our text speaks of fifty shekels, not of silver but of money, and that Chronicles means that these were of gold, in value equal to 600 shekels of silver. But the explanation is quite inconsistent with the text in both places. In one of them the statement of price must have been altered in transcription. In the entire uncertainty as to the extent of the purchase of Araunah (the whole hill of Moriah, or only a part), and of the value of land in the locality and at the time, it is impossible to decide between the two.

⁽²⁵⁾ **Built there an altar.**—The parallel place in Chronicles states that the tabernacle "and the altar of burnt offering were at that season in the high place at Gibeon," and that David was afraid to go before it "because of the sword of the angel," *i.e.*, the pestilence. It also mentions that when David "offered burnt offerings and peace offerings, and called upon the LORD," "He answered him from heaven by fire upon the altar of burnt offering." David then fixed upon this as "the house of the LORD God, and this is the altar of the burnt offering for Israel" (1 Chron. xxii. 1).

Thus, with David's repentance and reconciliation to God after his second great sin closes this narrative and this book. David's reign and life were now substantially ended—a witness to all time of the power of Divine Grace over human infirmity and sin, of God's faithfulness and mercy to those that trust in Him, and of the triumph of an earnest and humble faith notwithstanding some very great and grievous falls.

SUPPLEMENTARY NOTE ON THE TEXT OF II. SAMUEL.

It has been necessary from time to time to speak of errors of the scribes in copying the text, and of probable emendations suggested by the reading of the parallel passages in Chronicles. Such errors must necessarily arise in the often repeated copying of manuscripts during a succession of many centuries, unless it were prevented by a special and perpetual miracle. But we have not only no Scriptural or other reasonable ground for expecting such a miracle; we have positive proof against such a supposition. In the parallel case of the New Testament, where we have a large number of MSS., some of them very ancient, as well as versions made within a century of the original documents, and copious quotations in ancient writers, it is found that no single MS. contains a perfectly accurate text, and that the actual language of the original can only be determined in cases of doubt by a careful collation and weighing of all the evidence bearing upon the point. There is no ground to suppose that the text of the Old Testament has fared differently; but there do not exist the same means of testing and authenticating its readings. There are no MSS. of the Old Testament as ancient as several which have been preserved of the New; there are no translations at all as near the date of the original writings, and there are, of course, no quotations, outside of the sacred books themselves, for a long period after their publication. Yet a comparison of parallel accounts, such as have been occasionally noted above, and such as Ezra ii. with Neh. vii., shows conclusively that errors have been introduced into the text, especially in regard to numbers. Most of these appear to have been very ancient, before the oldest existing versions were made, and before the necessity was felt for such scrupulous care on the part of the scribes as was exercised in later times. For the correction of such errors we are necessarily compelled to rely mainly upon conjecture; but while conjecture is usually an uncertain guide, in the case of parallel accounts it often becomes possible to determine, by comparison, the original reading with a high degree of probability; and then, from the analogy of these corrections to determine slight changes in other passages also, where the text has apparently undergone alteration.

It is to be remembered, however, that all these errors and corrections are only in minutiæ, in proper names, in the bare statement of numbers, and such like matters. When all have been made that any sober criticism can suggest, the substance of the narrative remains unaffected, and the result of the most searching investigation is to place on an ever firmer basis the substantial accuracy of the copies of the Scriptures which have come down to us.

www.ingramcontent.com/pod-product-compliance
Lightning Source LLC
Chambersburg PA
CBHW081754300426
44116CB00014B/2113